THE **Building Christian English** SERIES

Building
Christian English

Preparing for Usefulness

Grade 8

Teacher's Manual

Rod and Staff Publishers, Inc.
Hwy. 172, Crockett, Kentucky 41413
Telephone: (606) 522-4348

Acknowledgments

We are indebted first and most of all to God, whose blessing made possible the writing and publishing of this book.

We express gratitude to each one who was involved in this work. The original edition was written by a group of writers, and the revision by Bruce Good. Marvin Eicher and Ernest Wine were the editors, H. Lynn Martin and various others were reviewers, and the artwork was done by Lester Miller. Jerry Nissley supplied the photograph on page 177. The West Virginia Department of Highways gave permission for the map on page 532. We are also indebted to the teachers who used the material on a laboratory basis in their classrooms, as well as to numerous people who assisted along the way by providing finances, by encouraging those directly involved in the work, and by interceding in prayer for the work.

Various reference books were consulted in accomplishing this task, such as English handbooks, other English textbooks, encyclopedias, and dictionaries. For these too we are grateful. We have chosen to favor the more conservative schools of thought that are considered authoritative in correct English usage.

—*The Publishers*

Copyright, 1997

First edition, copyright 1986

by

Rod and Staff Publishers, Inc.

Hwy. 172, Crockett, Kentucky 41413

Printed in U.S.A.

ISBN 978-07399-0533-3

Catalog no. 12898.3

8   9   10   —   21   20   19   18   17

Table of Contents

(Stars indicate Written Composition and Oral English lessons.)

Chapter 1   Sentence Elements
Writing Letters

Chapter 2   Sentence Structure
Writing Paragraphs

Chapter 3   Mechanics
Developing Paragraphs

Chapter 4   Nouns
Using Outlines

Chapter 5   Verbs
Preparing and Giving Reports

Chapter 6   Verb Usage
Writing Stories

Chapter 7   Pronouns
Writing Effective Sentences

Chapter 8   Adjectives
Studying Poetry

Chapter 9   Adverbs
Writing Persuasive Argument

Chapter 10   Prepositions, Conjunctions, and Interjections
Writing Directions and Descriptions

Chapter 11   Reference Sources
Giving Summaries and Book Reports

Worksheets

Tests

To the Teacher

This English course is designed for approximately 120 minutes of class time per week (four classes per week of 30 minutes each). The course includes a pupil's book, a teacher's guide, a worksheets booklet, and a test booklet. For a schedule with five classes per week, some lessons may be divided—especially the chapter reviews—or the worksheets may be used more often.

The Pupil's Book

The lesson text explains and illustrates the new concepts. The **Class Practice** exercises provide oral work to make the concepts of the lesson stick. If your schedule does not allow enough time for all the oral drill, try to cover at least several exercises in each section. You could also assign some of the Class Practice as written work.

The written work usually includes both **Written Exercises** (on the present lesson) and **Review Exercises** (on concepts taught previously). Depending on your students' abilities and other circumstances, you may not always be able to assign all of these exercises. Rather than omitting entire sections, you should consider assigning parts of each section.

A Chapter Review at the end of each chapter provides a review of the material taught in that chapter. The test booklet has a test for each chapter.

Note: This course intersperses lessons on oral and written composition throughout the textbook. This arrangement facilitates the teaching of a balance of grammar and composition throughout the year, rather than having the whole "composition load" in one large block. For simple reference, each of these composition lessons is marked with a string of pencils along the margin. Each chapter review and chapter test covers the composition material taught in that chapter.

A number of sentences used as illustrations or exercises are quotations from the Bible or other sources. All such quotations would normally be enclosed in quotation marks; but to avoid confusion, quotation marks are used only with Bible verses.

> **Examples:**
> "A friend loveth at all times." (Bible proverb)
> A friend in need is a friend indeed. (other proverb)

The Teacher's Guide

Each lesson in the teacher's guide begins by stating the **Purpose** of the lesson. A star indicates that the lesson introduces a new concept for this English series. If a concept was previously taught only to a certain degree, a note usually describes the extent of that previous experience.

Following the Purpose, some lessons have a part called **Teacher.** This is not a main part of the lesson but is rather for the teacher's information and awareness.

An **Oral Review** follows the Purpose. Use it to begin the class period. Generally, the first exercises deal with concepts from recent lessons to get the pupils' minds "in gear" for the new English lesson. The remaining exercises deal with less recent concepts (some from previous grades), usually to prepare the students for the written Review Exercises in the new lesson. If you wish, you may duplicate the Oral Review exercises and hand them to the students for personal study, especially if you have slow students or a tight schedule.

The **Lesson Introduction** suggests a way to introduce the lesson, and the **Lesson Outline** lists the specific points taught in the lesson. If a subpoint in the Lesson Outline is marked with a number or letter in double parentheses, such as (1) or (a), it matches the number or letter of a rule in the pupil's lesson.

Drill and Review

This course is designed to provide sufficient drill and review of all the English concepts taught. If the Class Practice, Written Exercises, and Review Exercises are used, the average pupil's mastery of the concepts should be satisfactory for this grade level.

For thorough mastery, however, overlearning the material by repeated drill and review is helpful (especially for slow students). This is the purpose of the Oral Reviews in the teacher's guide, and it is also one purpose of the Worksheets. If time allows, or if the pupils need further drill and review, the teacher is strongly encouraged to use these extra materials; however, they may be omitted if time is limited. **The Worksheets and the Oral Reviews are not required in order to teach this English course successfully.**

General Teaching Suggestions

Use the chalkboard frequently in demonstrating ideas. Keep a brisk pace, and do not waste precious class time to "major on minors." Students should follow along with open books during class discussion. Although thoroughly teaching the lesson may crowd the schedule, the time it will save over answering many student questions later is worthwhile.

Most of the written work, especially in grammar lessons, should be checked in class. Instruct students to use red ink pens for checking. Their checking should be done neatly, without unnecessary scribbling or doodling. If you read the answers clearly, and if you train your students to follow carefully, this should normally require only a few minutes.

Plan ahead so that you will complete the book. Make a schedule for the year, showing how many lessons you should cover each week and where you should be in the book at the end of each marking period. Then stick to your schedule as much as possible.

Develop a grading system that provides an accurate picture of the students' progress but does not bog you down with time-consuming work. Do not give full credit when students fail to follow directions.

It is also a good policy to grade on class participation. Students need to pay attention, follow along in their books, show interest in what is being said, and participate in answering questions during class discussion.

Check the class average periodically. If it is higher than a B, you may be moving too slowly through the book or grading too leniently. If it is much lower, you may be moving too fast or grading too strictly. This is only a general guide; every class has different abilities. Comparing your class records with those from previous years may prove helpful.

The **Worksheets** may be used for remedial practice or simply for extra drill on various concepts. They may be reproduced as needed in teaching this course.

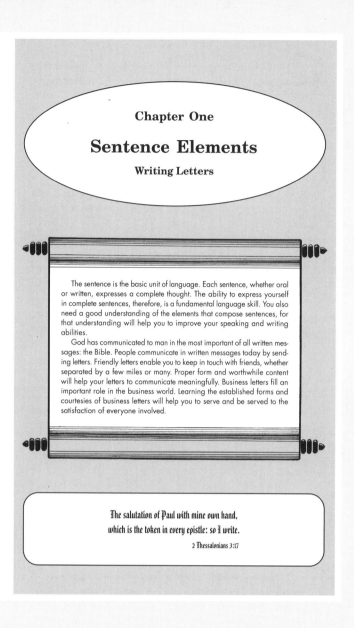

Chapter One

Sentence Elements

Writing Letters

The sentence is the basic unit of language. Each sentence, whether oral or written, expresses a complete thought. The ability to express yourself in complete sentences, therefore, is a fundamental language skill. You also need a good understanding of the elements that compose sentences, for that understanding will help you to improve your speaking and writing abilities.

God has communicated to man in the most important of all written messages: the Bible. People communicate in written messages today by sending letters. Friendly letters enable you to keep in touch with friends, whether separated by a few miles or many. Proper form and worthwhile content will help your letters to communicate meaningfully. Business letters fill an important role in the business world. Learning the established forms and courtesies of business letters will help you to serve and be served to the satisfaction of everyone involved.

The salutation of Paul with mine own hand,
which is the token in every epistle: so I write.

2 Thessalonians 3:17

1. The Gift of Language

Lesson Survey

- Man is the only earthly creature with the ability to communicate by complex language.
- Speaking and writing are skills that fill important roles in God's kingdom.
- English classes provide the opportunity to learn these skills better.

Imagine yourself standing near a forest pond on a warm summer evening as the twilight deepens around you. At the pond you can hear some frogs croaking. Suddenly a beaver's tail slaps a warning signal on the water. In the silence that follows, you hear some indistinct twitterings of birds settling down for the night. Then in a nearby tree an owl's screech makes you jump.

Were these creatures communicating? What were they saying? We know that animals do communicate, but they do so in a very limited way. Of all the earthly creatures God made, man is the only one with the ability to communicate by complex language. Only man can arrange words into complete sentences and paragraphs. He alone can express abstract ideas in words. He alone can communicate on a spiritual level with God.

Language includes four basic skills: speaking, listening, writing, and reading. In English class you will study speaking and writing primarily.

Speaking

Speaking fills an important place in God's kingdom. Consider a normal public worship service. The songs, prayers, Sunday school lessons, and sermons are meaningful to the whole congregation because words are spoken. Consider also God's intention for His people to spread the Gospel. "How then shall they call on him in whom they have not believed? and how shall they believe in him of whom they have not heard? and how shall they hear without a preacher?" (Romans 10:14). Preaching requires the effective use of language.

Nehemiah records the story of an outdoor worship service that must have involved a large multitude. Ezra and a number of other men made an important contribution to that occasion. "They read in the book in the law of God distinctly, and gave the sense, and caused them to understand the reading" (Nehemiah 8:8). Obviously these men had a good mastery of reading and speaking skills.

Now is your opportunity to learn to speak English well. Accept the challenge to develop proper speaking habits so that your speech will glorify God and not hinder the clear communication of the truth.

Lesson 1

Purpose: (1) To show the value of language as a special gift of God to man. (2) To encourage students to learn more effective communication for the glory of God.

Oral Review:

(Some Oral Review items deal with concepts taught in previous grades, to help prepare students for the written reviews.)

1. Name the sentence part described in each sentence.
   a. It tells *who* or *what* a sentence is about. (subject)
   b. It tells what the subject does or is. (predicate)
   c. It receives the action of a verb. (direct object)
   d. It names the person whom the speaker is addressing. (noun of direct address)
   e. It follows a linking verb and renames the subject. (predicate nominative)
   f. It comes between a verb and a direct object, and it tells *to whom or what* or *for whom or what* something is done. (indirect object)
   g. It follows a linking verb and describes the subject. (predicate adjective)
   h. It is a noun or pronoun that follows another noun or pronoun to identify or explain it. (appositive)
2. Name each group of words described below.
   a. It has one or more missing sentence parts and does not express a complete thought. (fragment)
   b. It occurs when two or more sentences are incorrectly written together. (run-on error)
   c. It expresses a complete thought. (sentence)

Strive to speak distinctly so that others can easily understand what you say. There are two essential ingredients in distinct speech: proper *pronunciation* and clear *enunciation.* Before you use a new word, make sure you know its correct pronunciation; that is, know the correct sounds and accents of the word. If you discover that you have been using a wrong pronunciation, learn to say the word correctly. Also, take care to enunciate your words clearly; that is, say each sound distinctly.

Good speaking habits also include using correct grammar. Especially as you study lessons on the correct usage of words, determine to correct any wrong speech habits you may have.

Writing

Writing also makes an important contribution to God's kingdom. Worthwhile stories illustrate truth in practical life. Friendly letters carry encouragement and neighborly warmth over many miles. Christian textbooks help us to study various fields of knowledge. Sunday school lessons and doctrinal books help us to understand the Bible. And of course, God has given us His Word in writing. "All scripture is given by inspiration of God." This eternal Word is the wellspring of all true knowledge.

Writing fills an important role in communication because it is the best way to preserve truth from generation to generation. God chose to have His message to man recorded in written form. Books, letters, and other documents help to preserve the doctrines of the church from one generation to the next. Such writings also help to keep alive the history of the church as well as the history of nations.

As in other books of this English series, this text will give you opportunities to write sentences, paragraphs, poems, stories, and other kinds of compositions. Apply the practical pointers that are given so that your writing skills improve. Use your knowledge of grammar to write clear, correct sentences. When you study the qualities of paragraphs and the methods of paragraph development, put these concepts to use in your writing. The same applies to poetry writing, story writing, and so forth; do not come to the lazy conclusion that you cannot write well. Do your best, and keep trying to improve your best.

Language is a gift of God. For God's glory and for your ability to serve Him most effectively, apply yourself to the study of the English language this school term.

Class Practice

Answer these questions.
1. How is man's communication more complex than that of animals?
2. How does Romans 10:14 illustrate the importance of speaking skills?

Lesson Introduction: Suppose you are a student in school, and you suddenly lose all ability to communicate by language. You can hear that your teacher is talking, but you cannot understand any of his words. The writing in your book and on the chalkboard becomes a jumble of meaningless symbols. When your fellow students close their books and put them into their desks, you look at the clock and see that it is time for recess. But playing softball is difficult with no way to understand the shouts of the other players. When the other students quit the game and head for the school building, you realize that recess is over. Imagine your relief at finding the gift of language restored to you again!

Lesson Outline:

1. Man is the only earthly creature with the ability to communicate by complex language.

Lesson 1 Answers

Class Practice

1. Man uses language, which involves arranging words into complete sentences and expressing abstract ideas in words. Man also communicates on a spiritual level with God.

2. The use of speaking skills is important in spreading the Gospel.

---

2. Language includes four basic skills: speaking, listening, writing, and reading. English class deals primarily with speaking and writing.

3. Speaking fills an important place in God's kingdom.

    a. Speaking is necessary in worship services and in spreading the Gospel.

    b. Ezra and the men with him are good examples of using speaking skills effectively.

4. Good speaking skills involve speaking distinctly.

    a. Pronounce your words correctly.

       1) Learn the correct pronunciations of new words.

3. Why were good speaking skills especially important on the occasion recorded in Nehemiah 8?

4. What are some ways in which writing is important to God's kingdom? Try to include some ways that are not mentioned in the lesson.

Written Exercises

A. Answer these questions.

1. What is the difference between pronunciation and enunciation?

2. Why is writing a valuable form of communication?

3. What are some things you can do to develop your speaking and writing skills?

B. Match the letters of the Scripture references to the statements below.

    a. 2 Chronicles 2:11   d. Daniel 9:2   f. 1 Corinthians 14:9, 19
    b. Revelation 14:13   e. Matthew 12:36, 37   g. Colossians 1:28
    c. Isaiah 30:8

1. One purpose of speaking is to present truth to others.
2. God will judge the way we use our speaking ability.
3. Words must be understandable if they are to be beneficial.
4. Writing is a valuable means of preserving records for a long time.
5. Writing can encourage believers with their future hope.
6. Studying books is an important way to gain knowledge.
7. One purpose of writing is to communicate with others.

Review Exercises

This exercise reviews things that you studied in previous grades. Use the index in the back of this book if you need help.

Write the abbreviation for the part of speech that matches each description.

    noun (n.)   adjective (adj.)   conjunction (conj.)
    pronoun (pron.) adverb (adv.)   interjection (interj.)
    verb (v.)   preposition (prep.)

1. It shows the relationship between its object and some other word in the sentence.
2. It names a person, place, thing, or idea.
3. It shows action or being.
4. It expresses strong feeling.
5. It connects words, phrases, or clauses.
6. It modifies a noun or pronoun.
7. It takes the place of a noun.
8. It modifies a verb, an adjective, an adverb, or a verbal.
9. It tells *how, when, where,* or *to what degree.*
10. It tells *which, whose, how many,* or *what kind of.*

---

    2) Learn to say correctly any word that you discover you have been mispronouncing.

  b. Enunciate words clearly; that is, say each sound distinctly.

5. Good speaking skills involve using correct grammar.

6. Writing makes an important contribution to God's kingdom.

    a. Writing is especially important because it is the best way to preserve truth from generation to generation.

    b. Apply the practical pointers for writing so that your writing skills improve.

3. Good speaking skills were important to having so many people understand what was said.

4. Stories illustrate truth in practical life. Friendly letters carry encouragement and neighborly warmth. Christian textbooks help us to study school subjects. Sunday school lessons and doctrinal books help us to understand the Bible. The Bible is the wellspring of all true knowledge.

    Ways not mentioned in the lesson: notes taken on sermons; tracts and Gospel signs; articles for church papers

Written Exercises

A. 1. Pronunciation relates to the correct sounds and accents of words. Enunciation pertains to saying each sound distinctly.

2. Written material can be preserved from generation to generation.

3. Learn the correct pronunciations of new words. Learn to say correctly any words that you may have been mispronouncing. Learn the correct grammar and usage of words. Use the knowledge of grammar to write clear, correct sentences. Put to use the concepts you learn about the qualities of paragraphs and the methods of paragraph development. Do your best in writing poetry, stories, and so forth.

B. 1. g   5. b
   2. e   6. d
   3. f   7. a
   4. c

Review Exercises

   1. prep.   6. adj.
   2. n.   7. pron.
   3. v.   8. adv.
   4. interj.   9. adv.
   5. conj.   10. adj.

2. Writing Friendly Letters

Lesson Survey

- A **friendly letter** should follow the proper form.
- A friendly letter should have meaningful content.
- A **social note** is a special kind of friendly letter.
- An envelope should include a return address and a mailing address.

"As cold waters to a thirsty soul, so is good news from a far country" (Proverbs 25:25). Good news, whether from a far country or a nearby friend, often travels in friendly letters.

Here is a sample of a *friendly letter* with good form and content. Refer to this example as you study the descriptions of the letter parts.

Heading

> 1156 Garber Rd.
> Chambersburg, PA 17201
> September 1, 20—

Greeting

> Dear Marjorie,

Body

> "Great is the Lord, and greatly to be praised." It's good to remember that God is with you in Guatemala as well as with us here in Pennsylvania. Are you adjusting to your new home and life on the mission field?
>
> On Sunday we visited Grandfather Lehman's. It seemed strange to have Uncle Mahlon and Aunt Edna in the other side of the farmhouse instead of your family. You know how Grandmother loves to sing. We took our *Zion's Praises* along and sang for half an hour. But we surely missed your family's voices.
>
> It's hard to believe that summer vacation is over and school starts tomorrow! I guess I'm silly, but I'm a little nervous. Going into eighth grade means moving over to the "big room," and this year we're having a new teacher. I've only seen Brother Leon once. Two weeks ago he was at church for prayer meeting.
>
> Do you remember that Nanny Sue had twin kids just before you left? They are running and jumping all over the place now. They especially like to play "king of the mountain" on the big rock pile out in the meadow. We named them Creamy and Freckles, and I'm sure you can easily guess which is which!
>
> Please write when you can. I'm eager to hear all about your trip and about Guatemala.

Closing
Signature

> With love and prayers,
> Martha Mae

Lesson 2

Purpose: (1) To study rules for writing friendly letters. (2) To encourage good communication by letter writing.

Oral Review:

(These exercises review concepts from previous grades.)

1. Name some methods of paragraph development. (adding details; giving steps; using examples; telling an incident; giving definitions)
2. What is meant by paragraph unity? (the quality of every sentence in the paragraph supporting the topic sentence)
3. What is meant by paragraph coherence? (the smooth flow of thought from one sentence to another)
4. How should this mailing address be corrected?

(*Teacher:* Write the following address on the board.)

> John D. Brown
> Route 1, Box 30
> Reinholds, Pa. 17569

(It should be written with all capital letters and no punctuation.)

Lesson Introduction: Have you ever watched eagerly for the mail to come because you were expecting a letter any day? Maybe you know the disappointment of waiting day after day, with no letter coming. And you probably know the pleasure of reading the long-awaited letter.

Exchanging letters with friends and relatives from near or far is a worthwhile privilege. In a matter of a few days or a few weeks, a letter you send can reach another person almost anywhere in the world. So

Friendly Letter Form

A friendly letter should follow the proper form. Each letter should have five parts: *heading, greeting, body, closing,* and *signature.* The heading is in the upper right-hand corner. Its first two lines show the writer's address, and the third line gives the date. Remember to follow the normal rules of capitalization and punctuation for these items.

The greeting addresses the person to whom the letter is written; it should be placed at the left margin. Capitalize the first word and all nouns in the greeting, and place a comma after it.

The body of the letter is the message, and it should be written in good paragraph form. The closing should be written below the last line of the body, with its left edge directly below the left edge of the heading. Capitalize only the first word of the closing, and place a comma after it.

Directly below the closing should be the signature. Even if you type the letter, you should write the signature by hand.

The general appearance of your letter should be neat and attractive. Use your best penmanship, and leave proper margins along the edges of the paper.

Friendly Letter Content

A friendly letter should have meaningful content. The following checklist may help you in writing your letters.

1. *Begin with a fitting Scripture verse, a few lines of poetry, or some other worthwhile quotation.*

2. *Move directly into the body of your letter.* Avoid the tendency to write sentences with little meaning, such as "Well, how are you?" or "I'm finally getting around to writing again."

3. *If any questions were directed to you in a previous letter, be sure to answer them.* If you cannot answer a question, explain why not.

4. *Share interesting and profitable information.* Think of things your friend will be interested in knowing. Has your family done anything special recently? Are you working on a particular project? Has anything of extra interest taken place at your church or school? Make a list of these things before you start writing, and then include them in your letter. Be sure to include enough details so that your descriptions are clear and meaningful.

5. *Show an interest in the person to whom you are writing.* Ask questions about his activities. Is he doing anything of special interest? Does he raise rabbits or have some other project that you would like to know about? What is happening at his school? Think of things you would ask your friend if you were talking to him, and ask those questions in your letter.

take the challenge to keep in touch by letter with friends that you are not able to visit very often.

Lesson Outline:

1. A friendly letter should follow the proper form.

    a. The heading consists of the writer's address and the date of the letter. It is written in the upper right-hand corner.

    b. The greeting addresses the person to whom the letter is written. It should be placed at the left margin.

       1) Capitalize the first word and all nouns.

       2) Place a comma after it.

    c. The body, or message of the letter, should be written in proper paragraph form.

    d. The closing should be written below the last line of the body.

       1) Place its left edge directly below that of the heading.

       2) Capitalize only the first word, and place a comma after the closing.

    e. The signature, always written by hand, should be directly below the closing.

    f. The general appearance of the letter should be neat and attractive, with good penmanship and proper margins.

2. A friendly letter should have meaningful content.

    (1) *Begin with a fitting Scripture verse, a few lines of poetry, or some other worthwhile quotation.*

    (2) *Move directly into the body of your letter.*

    (3) *If any questions were directed to you in a previous letter, be sure to answer them.*

6. *Use correct grammar.* A friendly letter may have an informal style, but it should not have slang or careless errors in English.

7. *End the letter by writing something worthwhile.* Avoid meaningless sentences like "I can't think of anything else to say, so good-bye." Much better would be "I hope to hear from you soon" or "I'm looking forward to your visit."

8. *Write an appropriate closing.* Here are some good closings for a friendly letter.

In Christian love,	Your friend,
Yours truly,	Your niece,
Sincerely,	Your loving daughter,
Sincerely yours,	With love and prayers,
Your cousin,	

Social Notes

A *social note* is a special kind of friendly letter. It is a short letter having one specific purpose, instead of discussing various topics as most friendly letters do. Social notes include thank-you notes, invitations, replies to invitations, and notes of apology. These social notes should contain the same five parts as other friendly letters.

A *thank-you note* should express sincere gratitude for a gift or for an expression of hospitality. Even if a gift is something that you do not especially like, you can express appreciation for the thoughtfulness of the giver. Always be completely honest, but take care that you do not hurt the feelings of the giver.

> 725 Talbot Street West
> Aylmer, ON N5H 2T9
> September 5, 20—
>
> Dear Uncle Lloyd,
> I enjoyed spending the past week at your farm to help you while Scott was away. Working with the produce was an interesting change from our beef-and-hog operation. Imagine my surprise when I unpacked my suitcase and found a book and a pocketknife tucked inside! Thank you very much.
>
> Your nephew,
> Frank

Invitations are often given by telephone; but for the times when you write them, you must be sure to include all the necessary information. A note of invitation should tell your friend exactly *what, when,* and *where* (the three W's of invitations). Include information about any special plans

(4) *Share interesting and profitable information.*

(5) *Show an interest in the person to whom you are writing.*

(6) *Use correct grammar.*

(7) *End the letter by writing something worthwhile.*

(8) *Write an appropriate closing.*

3. A social note is a special kind of friendly letter.

   a. A thank-you note should express sincere gratitude for a gift or for an expression of hospitality.

   b. A note of invitation should tell exactly *what, when,* and *where.* Include information about any special plans.

   c. A reply to an invitation should express appreciation for the invitation.

     1) To avoid any misunderstanding, repeat the details of the invitation.

     2) If you must decline, give a good reason.

   d. A note of apology should be a sincere expression of your regret for some wrong you have done to another person.

     1) Be specific about what you are apologizing for.

     2) Do not make excuses or blame other people or circumstances.

     3) Do what you can to pay for or otherwise make the wrong right.

4. An envelope should include a return address and a mailing address.

   a. The return address should be written in the upper left-hand corner with standard capitalization and punctuation.

that will affect the receiver's preparations.

2590 Yost Road
Waterloo, NY 13165
July 27, 20—

Dear Doris,

You mentioned in your last letter that your family plans to come to our all-day meeting on August 13. My parents and I wish to invite you to spend Monday and Tuesday with us. On Wednesday, Grandpa and Grandma Zehr are planning a special workday at their place. We could easily drop you off on our way there in the forenoon.

If you can come, bring a set of old work clothes along because on Tuesday we plan to clean out the goat pen. And that's a messy job! Hoping to see you soon.

Your friend,
Alma

A *reply to an invitation* should express appreciation for the invitation. To avoid any misunderstanding, it should also repeat the details of the invitation. If you must decline, give a good reason why you cannot accept the invitation.

Route 1, Box 135
Croghan, NY 13327
August 6, 20—

Dear Alma,

Thank you for inviting me to spend Monday and Tuesday (August 14 and 15) at your place. I'm very sorry that it won't suit this time. Jennie is scheduled for her monthly checkup with the bone specialist that Tuesday. Father and Mother must leave early in the morning and won't come home till late in the afternoon, so they decided I should stay and help with the chores.

I hope that something will work out another time. Anyway, I'm surely looking forward to seeing you at the all-day meeting!

Sincerely,
Doris

A *note of apology* should be a sincere expression of your regret for some wrong you have done to another person. Be specific about what you are apologizing for. Do not make excuses or blame other people or circumstances. Simply acknowledge the wrong and say you are sorry. If the wrong involved some damage that you can pay for or otherwise make right, be sure to do so.

  b. The mailing address should be placed about in the center, but a bit lower and farther to the right.

  c. Type or neatly print the mailing address with all capital letters and no punctuation so that the postal service can handle the letter most efficiently.

5. The letter should be folded and placed into the envelope correctly.

  a. For a large envelope, first fold the bottom third of the paper up, then fold the top third down.

  b. For a small envelope, first fold the lower half of the paper up, then fold it in thirds.

  c. Always place the letter in the envelope with the last fold line at the bottom.

7688 Possum Hollow Rd.
Shippensburg, PA 17257
September 12, 20—

Dear Rodney,

　　I'm sorry for breaking your pocketknife last week when we were at your place. I know I should have listened to you and not tried to pry that lid open with it. Please forgive me. Here is another knife to replace the one I broke. I want to be more careful in the future.

Sincerely,
Darwin

The Envelope

　　An envelope should include a return address and a mailing address. The return address should be written in the upper left-hand corner with standard capitalization and punctuation. The mailing address should be placed about in the center, but a bit lower and farther to the right. Type or neatly print the mailing address with all capital letters and no punctuation so that the postal service can handle the letter most efficiently.

Teacher: In the time since this book was originally published, the value of all capital letters and no punctuation in mailing addresses has diminished. Shift the emphasis to neatness and to printing each part precisely as the official source gave the address. This contributes the most toward efficient mailing service.

Darwin Schueler
7688 Possum Hollow Rd.
Shippensburg, PA 17257

RODNEY SIMMONS
ROUTE 2 BOX 622
ANNVILLE PA 17003

　　If you mail the letter in a large envelope, first fold the bottom third of the paper up, then fold the top third down. If you are using a small envelope, first fold the lower half of the paper up, then fold it in thirds. Always place the letter in the envelope with the last fold line at the bottom.

To use a large envelope:

fold paper in thirds

ready for large envelope

insert like this

To use a small envelope:

fold paper in half

fold in thirds

ready for small envelope

insert like this

Class Practice

A. Tell what is wrong with this friendly letter.

Thomas,

Well, I'm finely getting around to writing to you again. How's everybody at your house? We're all fine.

Last week we started bilding a new chicken house. It's going to be a big one. It was fun to watch the big bulldozers digging out for the foundation.

We had a heavy thunderstorm a couple days ago. It really pored, and the wind did some damage. Some people in the area had some hale damage too.

Nothing else intresting is happening around here, so I guess I'll close.

Your freind,

B. Tell what is wrong with this note of invitation.

Route 5, Box 335
Logan, OH 43138

Dear Charlotte,

Mother said that I could invite you to spend several days with us next month. You could come along with Aunt Geraldine when she comes to visit Grandpa Landis. I hope it suits you to come.

Your cousin,
Minerva

Written Exercises

A. Write a friendly letter to a friend, relative, or missionary. Address an envelope, and place your letter in it.

B. Write a thank-you note or a note of apology.

C. Write Harold's reply to the following note of invitation, either accepting or declining it. Use your home address and today's date.

Lesson 2 Answers

Class Practice

A. 1. There is no heading.
2. The greeting is not complete.
3. The letter does not begin in a worthwhile way.
4. Not enough details are given (about the chicken house and the storm).
5. The letter contains six wrong spellings (*finely, bilding, pored, hale, intresting, freind*).
6. The ending is not worthwhile.
7. The signature is missing.

B. 1. The date is missing in the heading.
2. It does not tell specifically when Charlotte is invited.
3. It does not say how Charlotte might return home.

Written Exercises

(All answers are individual work. You may wish to have envelopes available for Part A in case students forget to bring them from home.)

13222 Goudy Road
Dalton, OH 44618
August 15, 20—

Dear Harold,

I understand that your father is scheduled to have our school meeting topic on Friday evening, September 26. My parents have given me permission to invite you to spend Friday night, Saturday, and Saturday night at our place. My father is scheduled to teach Sunday school at Columbiana on Sunday morning, so we would bring you along then.

If the weather is suitable, we plan to hike back to the falls for a picnic lunch on Saturday.

Sincerely,
Marvin

---

3. Complete Sentences

Lesson Survey

- A **sentence** is a group of words that expresses a complete thought.
- A **fragment** is a group of words that does not express a complete thought.
- An **elliptical sentence** has one or more sentence parts missing, but it expresses a complete thought because the missing parts are understood.
- A **run-on error** occurs when two or more sentences are incorrectly written together.

The ability to put words together to form sentences is an important language skill. When you were a toddler, your parents likely waited eagerly for you to begin speaking in sentences. Those first sentences, however, were probably not complete sentences by the more mature standards that apply to an eighth grader.

A *sentence* is a group of words that expresses a complete thought. A sentence is usually understandable by itself, without the help of other sentences. It makes a specific statement or exclamation, gives a specific command, or raises a specific question.

Every sentence can be divided into two parts: the complete subject, which tells *who* or *what* the sentence is about, and the complete predicate, which tells what the subject does or is.

Lesson 3

Purpose: To study complete sentences, sentence fragments, *elliptical sentences, and run-on errors.

Oral Review:

1. Name the two basic language skills that you study in English classes. (speaking, writing)
2. Name and explain the two things that we must pay attention to in order to speak clearly and correctly. (pronunciation—using the correct sounds and accents of words; enunciation—saying each sound distinctly)
3. Why is writing especially valuable for preserving truth? (Writing makes it possible to preserve truth from generation to generation.)

Lesson Introduction: A rowboat that is missing one or both of its oars is not complete. You would find it difficult to make the boat go where you wanted it to go. Likewise, a group of words that is missing one or both of the basic sentence parts is not complete. It does not communicate clearly what the speaker or writer intended it to express. This lesson should help you in correctly using the "rowboats" of language—complete sentences.

Lesson Outline:

1. A sentence is a group of words that expresses a complete thought.

    a. It makes a specific statement or exclamation, gives a specific command, or raises a specific question.

    b. It has a complete subject and a complete predicate.

2. A fragment is a group of words that does not express a complete thought. It should be corrected either by joining it to another sentence or by adding words to make it a complete sentence.

| complete subject | complete predicate |
| The study of language should be an aid in good communication.

A *fragment* is a group of words that does not express a complete thought. It should be corrected either by joining it to another sentence or by adding words to make it a complete sentence.

Fragments:

The bear waded slowly into the creek. And waited for a fish to swim near.

Two hungry cubs on the bank, watching their mother.

The Churchill River flows through northern Manitoba. Then empties into the Hudson Bay.

Revisions:

The bear waded slowly into the creek and waited for a fish to swim near. (combined with previous sentence)

Two hungry cubs stood on the bank, watching their mother. (word added to make a complete sentence)

The Churchill River flows through northern Manitoba and then empties into the Hudson Bay. (combined with previous sentence)

The Churchill River flows through northern Manitoba. Then it empties into the Hudson Bay. (word added to make a complete sentence)

An *elliptical sentence* has one or more sentence parts missing, but it expresses a complete thought because the missing parts are understood. One example of an elliptical sentence is a command in which *you* is understood. Other elliptical sentences are understandable because of the context (surrounding sentences).

Elliptical sentences are rare in formal writing, such as reports and descriptions. But they are common in dialogue and some other places where informal language is used. The same group of words that would be a fragment by itself or in a formal composition may be a proper elliptical sentence in dialogue.

Read the following example of dialogue from the book *Evangelists in Chains.* It has two elliptical sentences, but the reader has no trouble understanding them. The understood words are in brackets.

They had come to another heavy door in the wall. Several men had already tried the latch, but it was locked.

"[I] Wonder where that leads?" Caspar asked.

"Likely [it leads] to another dungeon," one man suggested.

A *run-on error* occurs when two or more sentences are incorrectly written together. A run-on error can be corrected in several ways: (1) by adding

3. An elliptical sentence has one or more sentence parts missing, but it expresses a complete thought because the missing parts are understood.

    a. One example of an elliptical sentence is a command in which *you* is understood. Other elliptical sentences are understandable because of the context.

    b. Elliptical sentences are rare in formal writing, but common in dialogue and some other places where informal language is used.

    c. The same group of words that would be a fragment by itself or in a formal composition may be a proper elliptical sentence in dialogue.

4. A run-on error occurs when two or more sentences are incorrectly written together.

    a. Inserting only a comma between the two parts produces a comma splice.

    b. A run-on error can be corrected in several ways:

      1) by adding a comma and a coordinating conjunction between the two parts.

      2) by adding a semicolon.

      3) by changing one of the clauses to a dependent clause.

      4) by dividing it into two or more sentences.

a comma and a coordinating conjunction between the two parts (inserting only a comma produces a comma splice), (2) by adding a semicolon, (3) by changing one of the clauses to a dependent clause, or (4) by dividing it into two or more sentences.

Run-on error:
We had a heavy rain now the playground is all muddy.
Corrections:
We had a heavy rain, and now the playground is all muddy.
(comma and coordinating conjunction added)
We had a heavy rain; now the playground is all muddy.
(semicolon added)
Since we had a heavy rain, the playground is all muddy.
(one clause changed to dependent clause)
We had a heavy rain. Now the playground is all muddy.
(sentence divided)

Class Practice

A. Add words to these fragments to make them complete sentences.
1. When Jesus saw the moneychangers in the temple
2. And climbed into a sycamore tree
3. To answer the questions carefully
4. Watching Father plant corn
5. At a picnic table beside the highway

B. Tell which sentences in the following dialogue are elliptical. Read each elliptical sentence, filling in the understood words.
¹"Why didn't you finish the job?" Father asked.
²"I had homework," Sharon told him.
³"A lot?"
⁴"Three problems," she mumbled.
⁵"I see." ⁶Father frowned. ⁷"How long did it take to do them?"
⁸"About ten minutes." ⁹Sharon felt sick.

C. Tell how to correct each run-on error. Then read it with the correction.
1. Moses held his rod over the Red Sea, then God divided the waters.
2. The Egyptian army pursued the Israelites they were drowned when the water returned to its normal place.
3. The fire drill bell interrupted our class, soon we were standing in place out on the playground.
4. Brother Clarence briefly checked the building, then he called us in again.

Written Exercises

A. Rewrite these paragraphs, correcting the fragments and run-on errors. This is part of a formal composition and should not have elliptical sentences.

Lesson 3 Answers

Class Practice

A. (Sample answers; added words are underlined.)
1. When Jesus saw the moneychangers in the temple, He was filled with indignation.
2. Zacchaeus ran ahead and climbed into a sycamore tree.
3. The students worked hard to answer the questions carefully.
4. The little boys are watching Father plant corn.
5. We ate our lunch at a picnic table beside the highway.

B. (Elliptical sentences are shown with added words underlined.)
3. "Did you have a lot of homework?"
4. "I had three problems," she mumbled.
8. "It took about ten minutes."

C. (Sample corrections.)
1. Change the first part to a dependent clause: When Moses held his rod over the Red Sea, God divided the waters.
2. Add a comma and a conjunction: The Egyptian army pursued the Israelites, but they were drowned when the water returned to its normal place.
3. Add a semicolon: The fire drill bell interrupted our class; soon we were standing in place out on the playground.
4. Add a conjunction: Brother Clarence briefly checked the building, and then he called us in again.

God has given people the precious gift of communication. He intends man to use this gift to communicate with Himself. And to speak profitably with others. However, many use their tongues for evil. Instead of speaking things that glorify God.

James declares that "the tongue can no man tame; it is an unruly evil, full of deadly poison" (James 3:8). James is referring to men's words. When he speaks of the tongue. Is it really so bad as that, can it be that James is exaggerating? Indeed, this verse is no exaggeration. Men blaspheme God. The very Giver of their power to speak. They gossip, lie, and slander, they boast, complain, and quarrel.

B. Rewrite this dialogue, correcting the fragments and run-on errors. Add words only if necessary; do not change elliptical sentences.

"Would you like to walk down to the creek? That flows through our meadow?" asked Sharon.

"Sounds interesting," replied Myra. "The Red Clay Creek flows through our farm, sometimes we have picnics and go fishing there."

"Ours is just a small stream. Fed by a spring. See? Here we are."

"Look! A great blue heron!" exclaimed Myra. "We sometimes see a pair at our place, have you seen them often here?"

"Only a few times," answered Sharon. "I think they are among the most beautiful birds. That I have ever seen."

Review Exercises

These exercises review things that you studied in previous grades. Use the index in the back of this book if you need help.

A. Copy these sentences, and indicate the part of speech that each word is by writing the correct abbreviation above it.

noun (n.)	adjective (adj.)	conjunction (conj.)
pronoun (pron.)	adverb (adv.)	interjection (interj.)
verb (v.)	preposition (prep.)	

1. "Ah Lord God! behold, thou hast made the heaven and the earth by thy great power."
2. Nothing is too hard for the Lord.
3. Jeremiah certainly spoke truthfully when he said these words.

B. Write the correct verb form for each one that is underlined. If the verb is correct, write *correct*.
1. The disciples <u>seen</u> Christ's glory when He was transfigured.
2. Have you <u>chose</u> to develop godly fear in your life?
3. God has <u>wrote</u> in His Word all that we need to live right.
4. Satan has <u>drug</u> many into his snares a little at a time.
5. We rejoice that God has <u>did</u> wondrous things for us.

Written Exercises

A. (Corrections are underlined. Allow reasonable variation.)

God has given people the precious gift of communication. He intends man to use this gift to communicate with Himself <u>and</u> to speak profitably with others. However, many use their tongues for evil <u>i</u>nstead of speaking things that glorify God.

James declares that "the tongue can no man tame; it is an unruly evil, full of deadly poison" (James 3:8). James is referring to men's word<u>s w</u>hen he speaks of the tongue. Is it really so bad as that<u>? C</u>an it be that James is exaggerating? Indeed, these words are no exaggeration. Men blaspheme Go<u>d, t</u>he very Giver of their power to speak. They gossip, lie, and slander<u>;</u> they boast, complain, and quarrel.

B. (Corrections are underlined. Allow reasonable variation.)

"Would you like to walk down to the cree<u>k that</u> flows through our meadow?" asked Sharon.

"Sounds interesting," replied Myra. "The Red Clay Creek flows through our far<u>m. S</u>ometimes we have picnics and go fishing there."

"Ours is just a small strea<u>m fed</u> by a spring. See? Here we are."

"Look! A great blue heron!" exclaimed Myra. "We sometimes see a pair at our plac<u>e. H</u>ave you seen them often here?"

"Only a few times," answered Sharon. "I think they are among the most beautiful bird<u>s that</u> I have ever seen."

Review Exercises

A. 1. "<u>interj.</u> <u>n.</u> <u>n.</u> <u>interj.</u> <u>pron.</u> <u>v.</u> <u>v.</u> <u>adj.</u> Ah Lord God! behold, thou hast made the <u>n.</u> <u>conj.</u> <u>adj.</u> <u>n.</u> <u>prep.</u> <u>adj.</u> <u>adj.</u> <u>n.</u> heaven and the earth by thy great power."
2. <u>pron.</u> <u>v.</u> <u>adv.</u> <u>adj.</u> <u>prep.</u> <u>adj.</u> <u>n.</u> Nothing is too hard for the Lord.
3. <u>n.</u> <u>adv.</u> <u>v.</u> <u>adv.</u> <u>conj.</u> <u>pron.</u> Jeremiah certainly spoke truthfully when he <u>v.</u> <u>adj.</u> <u>n.</u> said these words.

B. 1. saw   4. dragged
   2. chosen   5. done
   3. written

6. Sinful living has always <u>cost</u> far too much to pursue.
7. We have <u>went</u> to Daley Nursing Home several times to visit Mrs. Hoffman.
8. The heifers have <u>ate</u> all their hay.
9. Two pumpkins rolled off the wagon and <u>busted</u> open.
10. Paul's model boat has <u>sank</u> in the pond.

6. correct
7. gone
8. eaten
9. burst
10. sunk

---

4. Subjects and Predicates

> **Lesson Survey**
> • Every sentence can be divided into two parts: the **complete subject** and the **complete predicate.**
> • The **sentence skeleton** consists of the **simple subject** and the **simple predicate.**

Every sentence can be divided into two parts: the complete subject and the complete predicate. Normally, the complete subject comes before the complete predicate. The *complete subject* tells *who* or *what* the sentence is about; it is literally the *subject* (topic) of the sentence. The *complete predicate* tells what the subject does or is.

| complete subject | complete predicate |
<u>The men on the ship</u> <u>rejoiced to see the land</u>.

The *sentence skeleton* consists of the simple subject and the simple predicate together. In the example above, the skeleton is *men rejoiced.*

The *simple subject* is the basic part of the complete subject. Usually it is a single noun or pronoun, but it may also be a compound noun (a two-word noun generally not capitalized) or a noun phrase (often a proper noun). In the following examples, the complete subjects are underlined, and the simple subjects are in italics.

Compound noun used as simple subject:
The *high priest* in Jesus' time was Caiaphas.

    high priest | was \ Caiaphas

Noun phrase used as simple subject:
West Virginia separated from Virginia during the Civil War.

    West Virginia | separated

Lesson 4

Purpose: To study complete subjects, complete predicates, simple subjects, simple predicates, and sentence skeletons.

Oral Review:

1. Give a brief definition of each term.
   a. sentence (a group of words that expresses a complete thought)
   b. run-on error (two or more sentences incorrectly written together)
   c. fragment (a group of words that does not express a complete thought)
   d. elliptical sentence (a group of words with one or more sentence parts missing, which expresses a complete thought because the missing parts are understood)
2. What are two ways to correct a fragment? (by joining it to another complete sentence; by adding words to make it a complete sentence)
3. Name several ways to correct a run-on error. (by adding a comma and a coordinating conjunction; by adding a semicolon; by changing one of the clauses to a dependent clause; by dividing it into two or more sentences)
4. In what kind of writing are elliptical sentences common? (dialogue)
5. Explain the difference between pronunciation and enunciation. (Pronunciation relates to using the correct sounds and accents of words; enunciation relates to saying each sound distinctly.)

Lesson Introduction: Look at the two main words in the lesson title. If the moderator of a meeting announces the subject, he names the topic or theme that the speaker is to talk about. As a verb, *predicate* means "to affirm or declare"; as a noun it can

If there is more than one simple subject in a sentence, the sentence has a *compound subject*. A compound subject names two or more persons or things that together serve as the subject. This is different from a compound noun or a noun phrase, which is simply a noun consisting of more than one word. Study the following example, in which a *compound noun* is part of a *compound subject*.

Compound subject:
A *pencil* and a *fountain pen* were lying on the desk.

The simple subject may be modified by single-word adjectives or adjective phrases. When identifying the simple subject, you must be careful not to include these modifiers. In the following examples, the complete subjects are underlined, and the simple subjects are in italics.

This *poem* was written by Mary Ellen.
"*The Owl in the Night*" was written by Mary Ellen.

A large *piece* of wood fell off the pickup.
Those *boys* stacking bales in the haymow are my brothers.

The *simple predicate* is the verb or verb phrase, which shows action or being. The complete predicate can include adverb modifiers or complements, but the simple predicate can consist only of verbs. In the following examples, the complete predicates are underlined, and the simple predicates are in italics.

The calf in the first hutch *was bawling* noisily.
Brother Friesen often *stresses* the importance of good work habits.
The students *have been* quietly *playing* in the play area.

If there is more than one verb or verb phrase, the sentence has a *compound predicate*. A compound subject or predicate is diagramed on a fork, with the conjunction placed on a broken line between the two words.

Both the gander and the goose protect the nest.

A gander watchfully guards the nest and viciously attacks any intruder.

mean "that which is affirmed." These definitions help us to understand the meanings of the two basic sentence parts. The subject is the topic of the sentence; the predicate declares something about the subject.

Lesson Outline:

1. Every sentence can be divided into two parts: the complete subject and the complete predicate.

    a. The complete subject tells *who* or *what* the sentence is about.

    b. The complete predicate tells what the subject does or is.

2. The sentence skeleton consists of the simple subject and the simple predicate.

    a. The simple subject is the basic part of the complete subject.

       1) Usually it is a single noun or pronoun.

       2) It may be a compound noun or a noun phrase.

       3) There may be more than one simple subject (a compound subject).

       4) The simple subject does not include the modifiers that may be a part of the complete subject.

    b. The simple predicate is the verb or verb phrase.

       1) It shows action or being.

       2) There may be more than one simple predicate (a compound predicate).

       3) The simple predicate does not include the modifiers or complements that may be a part of the complete predicate.

While the goslings are still young, the father and the mother may
shed their flight feathers and lose their ability to fly.

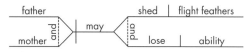

Class Practice

A. For each of these sentences, (1) identify the skeleton, (2) read the complete subject, and (3) read the complete predicate.
   1. God's people are called to be peacemakers.
   2. Men of the world often misunderstand Christians and call them cowards.
   3. A peacemaker actually must have a large measure of courage.
   4. The doctrine of nonresistance has often brought Christians into conflict with governments.
   5. Commitment to truth and a willingness to suffer are marks of true courage.
   6. Abigail Hursh, the girl at the door, is my first cousin.
   7. A move from one community to another requires much planning.
   8. Mr. Markey's love for children is known throughout our community.
   9. Several families from church sometimes gather in his home and sing for him.
   10. "Rock of Ages" is one of his favorite songs.

B. On the chalkboard, diagram the skeletons of these sentences.
   1. The bears are preparing for their long winter sleep.
   2. A mother and her two cubs are eating acorns under an oak tree.
   3. A pair of blue jays noisily scolds them from a nearby branch.
   4. Of course, the bears' sudden appearance alarmed the birds and interrupted their activities.
   5. Soon some starlings and sparrows joined the blue jays and made a tremendous racket.

Written Exercises

A. Copy each sentence, and draw one line under the simple subject and two lines under the simple predicate. Draw a vertical line to divide the subject from the predicate.
   1. Father and Nathan have almost finished their work in the corn patch.
   2. We need several hundred ears for today's orders.
   3. Our customer from town has already come and picked up his corn.
   4. He has been buying corn from us for three years.

Lesson 4 Answers

Class Practice

A. (Skeletons are underlined.)
   1. God's <u>people</u> | <u>are</u>|<u>called</u> to be peacemakers.
   2. <u>Men</u> of the world | often <u>misunderstand</u> Christians and <u>call</u> them cowards.
   3. A <u>peacemaker</u> | actually <u>must</u>|<u>have</u> a large measure of courage.
   4. The <u>doctrine</u> of nonresistance | <u>has</u> often <u>brought</u> Christians into conflict with governments.
   5. <u>Commitment</u> to truth and a <u>willingness</u> to suffer | <u>are</u> marks of true courage.
   6. <u>Abigail Hursh</u>, the girl at the door, | <u>is</u> my first cousin.
   7. A <u>move</u> from one community to another | <u>requires</u> much planning.
   8. Mr. Markey's <u>love</u> for children | <u>is</u>|<u>known</u> throughout our community.
   9. Several <u>families</u> from church | sometimes <u>gather</u> in his home and <u>sing</u> for him.
   10. "<u>Rock of Ages</u>" | <u>is</u> one of his favorite songs.

B. 1.
   bears | are preparing

   2.
   mother
   cubs (and)
   are eating

   3.
   pair | scolds

   4.
   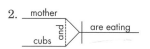
   appearance (and) alarmed / interrupted

   5.
   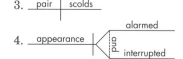
   starlings / sparrows (and) joined / made

Written Exercises

A. (Conjunctions in compound parts may also be underlined.)
   1. <u>Father</u> and <u>Nathan</u> | <u>have</u> almost <u>finished</u> their work in the corn patch.
   2. <u>We</u> | <u>need</u> several hundred ears for today's orders.
   3. Our <u>customer</u> from town | <u>has</u> already <u>come</u> and <u>picked</u> up his corn.
   4. <u>He</u> | <u>has</u>|<u>been</u>|<u>buying</u> corn from us for three years.

B. Diagram the skeletons of these sentences. Watch for noun phrases, verb phrases, and compound subjects or predicates.
1. No shortcut to happiness will bring satisfaction.
2. Paul and Simon Peter wrote about the promises of God.
3. God's promises have been established and will surely be fulfilled.
4. Faith in God's promises is a good antidote for worry.

C. Copy the simple subject and the simple predicate of each sentence in these paragraphs. Draw a vertical line between the two parts.

Dear Kenneth,

    [1]"The sleep of a labouring man is sweet." [2]Solomon surely spoke the truth there. [3]We have been very busy with our produce the last several weeks. [4]The Lord blessed us with plenty of rain and gave us a good harvest. [5]Both the market in town and our roadside stand had lots of business.

    [6]The job of tending the stand can be quite a task! [7]In general, most of our customers are pleasant people. [8]However, a few of them complain about the produce and pay only part of the price. [9]At such times I must pray for patience. [10]The unhappiness of such people is quite obvious.

Review Exercises

These exercises review things that you studied in previous grades. Use the index in the back of this book if you need help.

A. Name the three parts of a friendly letter that are *not* shown in Part C.

B. Write the correct verb for each sentence.
1. When Elijah was fleeing from Jezebel, he (laid, lay) under a juniper.
2. At the angel's word, Elijah (raised, rose) to eat and drink.
3. True faith (lets, leaves) God direct our lives.
4. He who kneels at the throne of grace and (sets, sits) at Jesus' feet can stand in the tests of life.
5. The Bible clearly says that we (can, may) not dabble in witchcraft.
6. I quickly (laid, lay) my book down and jumped to my feet.
7. Father (let, left) the stalled tractor in the field and went for help.
8. Grandpa (set, sat) in his rocking chair in the corner.
9. Lee would like to finish the job today if he (can, may).
10. The temperature has (raised, risen) over twenty degrees already!

B. 1.
shortcut | will bring

2. Paul (and) Simon Peter | wrote

3. promises | have been established (and) will be fulfilled

4. Faith | is

C. 1. sleep | is
2. Solomon | spoke
3. We | have been
4. Lord | blessed (and) gave
5. market (and) stand | had
6. job | can be
7. most | are
8. few | complain (and) pay
9. I | must pray
10. unhappiness | is

Review Exercises

A. heading, closing, signature

B. 1. lay   6. laid
2. rose   7. left
3. lets   8. sat
4. sits   9. can
5. may   10. risen

5. Subjective Complements

> ### Lesson Survey
> - A **subjective complement** completes the sentence skeleton by referring to the subject. Predicate nominatives and predicate adjectives are subjective complements.
> - A **predicate nominative** is a noun or pronoun that follows a linking verb and renames the subject.
> - A **predicate adjective** follows a linking verb and modifies the subject.

Every complete sentence is based on a sentence skeleton. Many sentences also have another basic part—a *complement*. The root word of *complement* is *complete,* and that is exactly what complements do: they complete the meaning of the sentence skeleton.

A *subjective complement* completes the sentence skeleton by referring to the subject. Only a linking verb can be followed by a subjective complement. Common linking verbs include the forms of *be* and verbs that can be replaced by them, such as *taste, look, grow, seem,* and *remain.*

Honey <u>tastes</u> sweet. (Honey *is* sweet. *Tastes* is a linking verb.)

There are two kinds of subjective complements: predicate nominatives and predicate adjectives.

Predicate Nominatives

A *predicate nominative* is a noun or pronoun that follows a linking verb and renames the subject. Usually a predicate nominative is a single noun or pronoun. In diagraming, remember to separate the verb from a subjective complement with a line that slants toward the subject.

The <u>Bible</u> is God's *message* to mankind.
Bible and *message* name the same thing.

| Bible | is \ message |

If a pronoun is used as a predicate *nominative,* it must be in the *nominative* case.

The only good <u>pitcher</u> on our team is *he.* (not *him*)

| pitcher | is \ he |

The <u>person</u> who called was *I.* (not *me*)

| person | was \ I |

Since the subject and the predicate nominative name the same person or object, these two words are often interchangeable. However, exchanging

---

Lesson 5

Purpose: (1) To study predicate nominatives and predicate adjectives. (2) To show their relationship to the sentence skeleton.

Oral Review:

1. Into what two parts can every complete sentence be divided? (complete subject, complete predicate)
2. What is the sentence skeleton? (the simple subject and the simple predicate)
3. What is an elliptical sentence? (a group of words with one or more sentence parts missing, which expresses a complete thought because the missing parts are understood)
4. In what kind of writing are elliptical sentences common? (dialogue)
5. What are two ways to correct a fragment? (by joining it to another complete sentence; by adding

words to make it a complete sentence)
6. Name several ways to correct a run-on error. (by adding a comma and a coordinating conjunction; by adding a semicolon; by changing one of the clauses to a dependent clause; by dividing it into two or more sentences)

Lesson Introduction: Write the following word groups on the board.

Manasseh was   Stanley's story sounded

Ask your students if these word groups are complete sentences. (no) They do have subjects and predicates, so why are they not complete sentences? (They need complements.) Have someone add a possible complement to each.

Lesson Outline:

1. A subjective complement completes the sentence skeleton by referring to the subject.

them may sound awkward if the verb is modified by a negative word or if the subject is specific and the predicate nominative is general. Also, if the verb is *become,* exchanging the two will usually make an untrue statement.

This <u>motto</u> will be my *gift* for Mother.
My <u>gift</u> for Mother will be this *motto.* (same meaning)

<u>Saul</u> was not a faithful *king.*
A faithful <u>king</u> was not *Saul.* (same meaning, but awkward)

<u>Houston</u> is a *city* in Texas.
A <u>city</u> in Texas is *Houston.* (same meaning, but awkward)

My <u>brother</u> has become our *teacher.*
Our <u>teacher</u> has become my *brother.* (different meaning; untrue)

Predicate Adjectives

A *predicate adjective* follows a linking verb and modifies the subject. Since the predicate adjective modifies the subject, it is usually sensible to say the adjective before the subject. But a pronoun subject may need to be replaced with its antecedent.

Lori's <u>idea</u> seems the most *practical.* (practical idea)
<u>She</u> sounded *enthusiastic* about her idea. (enthusiastic Lori)

Sometimes the same verbs that may be linking verbs are followed by sentence parts other than subjective complements, such as adverbs or direct objects. Before you decide that a sentence contains a subjective complement, be sure that the main verb expresses being rather than action and that the subjective complement does indeed rename or modify the subject.

The pancakes <u>turned</u> a golden brown in the pan.
   (The pancakes *were* brown. *Brown pancakes* is sensible. *Brown* is a predicate adjective.)
Mother <u>turned</u> them skillfully.
   (*Turned* expresses action, not being. Neither *them* nor *skillfully* renames or modifies *Mother. Them* is a direct object; *skillfully* is an adverb.)
The dog <u>was</u> still in her house.
   (*Was* expresses being. Neither *still* nor *in her house* renames or modifies *dog;* they are adverbs.)
Sheba <u>was</u> a friendly dog.
   (*Was* expresses being, and *dog* renames *Sheba. Dog* is a predicate nominative.)

Predicate nominatives and predicate adjectives are subjective complements.

2. A predicate nominative is a noun or pronoun that follows a linking verb and renames the subject.
   a. Usually a predicate nominative is a single noun or pronoun.
   b. If a pronoun is used as a predicate nominative, it must be in the nominative case.
   c. The subject and the predicate nominative are often interchangeable.

3. A predicate adjective follows a linking verb and modifies the subject.
   a. It is usually sensible to say the adjective before the subject.
   b. If the subject is a pronoun, it may need to be replaced with its antecedent.
   c. Predicate adjectives must not be confused with adverbs and direct objects in the predicate.

4. Predicate nominatives and predicate adjectives may be compound. A compound subjective complement is diagramed on a fork.

★ **EXTRA PRACTICE**
Worksheet 1 *(Subjective Complements)*

Both predicate nominatives and predicate adjectives may be compound. A compound subjective complement is diagramed on a fork.

Arnold was a hard worker and a kind friend.

The tiny seedling has grown tall and strong.

Wanda always seems kind, cheerful, and diligent.

Class Practice

A. Identify each subjective complement, and tell whether it is a *predicate nominative* or *predicate adjective*. Some sentences have more than one, and some have none.
1. "The Lord is my rock, and my fortress, and my deliverer."
2. "My soul shall be joyful in the Lord."
3. Moses has been on the mountain for many days.
4. The people have become guilty of idolatry.
5. I cautiously tasted the vinegar punch.
6. Surprisingly, it tasted rather good.
7. Vinegar punch is an effective thirst quencher.
8. The ice pack felt cool and soothing to my bruised forehead.
9. Everyone felt the difference between the two kinds of paper.
10. Our substitute teacher tomorrow will be my father.

B. On the chalkboard, diagram the skeletons and complements of the even-numbered sentences in Part A.

Written Exercises

A. Copy the subjective complements in these sentences. Write *PN* after each predicate nominative, and *PA* after each predicate adjective. If a sentence has no subjective complement, write *none*.
1. Two metals used in steel alloys are nickel and tungsten.

Lesson 5 Answers

Class Practice

A. 1. rock—predicate nominative;
       fortress—predicate nominative;
       deliverer—predicate nominative
   2. joyful—predicate adjective
   3. none
   4. guilty—predicate adjective
   5. none
   6. good—predicate adjective
   7. quencher—predicate nominative
   8. cool—predicate adjective;
       soothing—predicate adjective
   9. none
   10. father—predicate nominative

B.

Written Exercises

A. 1. nickel—PN; tungsten—PN

2. Mercury is a liquid metal at room temperature.
3. Aluminum is both light and tough.
4. Before the 1900s, aluminum had been too expensive for general use.
5. The pilot of the foundering ship sounded a distress signal.
6. The blast of the foghorn sounded faint through the roar of the storm.
7. Both martyrs appeared calm and trustful in the face of death.
8. The enemies of God became vicious in their persecution.
9. The truth of God's Word will remain unchanged.
10. Jesus Christ is our prophet, priest, and king.

B. Diagram the skeletons and the complements of these sentences.
1. Two prophets to the exiles were Jeremiah and Ezekiel.
2. Jeremiah was the object of severe persecution.
3. At times life may appear unfair and cruel.
4. We should never become discouraged at difficulties.
5. Rather we should grow strong in faith.

Review Exercises

These exercises review things that you studied in previous grades. Use the index in the back of this book if you need help.

A. Copy the correct pronoun for each sentence.
1. God gives you and (I, me) clear direction in His Word.
2. (We, Us) mortals should reverence and adore the Lord Almighty.
3. A young person (who, which) has learned to obey has learned one of life's most important lessons.
4. Several people (who, whom) Father has met in town have expressed interest in coming to church.
5. We boys fixed (ourself, ourselves) a quick lunch.
6. Laura and (I, myself) helped Aunt Rachel with her canning.
7. (Them, Those) are my favorite pies.
8. Either Judith or Kathryn should make (her, their) cookies now.
9. Uncle Levi taught us boys—Clair, Joel, and (I, me)—how to carve.
10. I see Brother Daryl's van, but I cannot find (ours, our's).

B. Copy the correct verb for each sentence.
1. Most of the apples (have, has) been picked.
2. Most of the applesauce (have, has) been canned.
3. Each of the children (is, are) working diligently.
4. Anyone from northern Ontario (know, knows) what cold temperatures are.
5. Few of the visitors from Pennsylvania (is, are) familiar with such cold.

2. metal—PN
3. light—PA; tough—PA
4. expensive—PA
5. none
6. faint—PA
7. calm—PA; trustful—PA
8. vicious—PA
9. unchanged—PA
10. prophet—PN; priest—PN; king—PN

B. 1.

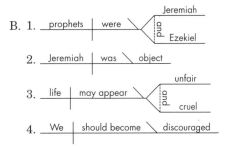

2.

3.

4.

5.

Review Exercises

A. 1. me   6. I
   2. We   7. Those
   3. who   8. her
   4. whom   9. me
   5. ourselves   10. ours

B. 1. have
   2. has
   3. is
   4. knows
   5. are

6. Writing Business Letters

Lesson Survey

- A **business letter** is written for a specific business purpose.
- The form of a business letter differs slightly from that of a friendly letter.
- The body of a business letter should be courteous, clear, and concise.
- A business letter should have a neat, formal appearance.

A *business letter* is written for a specific business purpose. You may wish to order something by mail or to inquire about an order. You may request information about products or services that a business offers. You may write to a government agency for information about points of interest to visit or about details of geography, population, and industry.

The following example illustrates a well-written business letter. Refer to this example as you study the lesson.

Heading	210 North Peartown Rd. Reinholds, PA 17569 Sept. 20, 20—
Inside Address	Dept. of Economic Development 1259 U.S. Rt. 20 Albany, NY 12245
Salutation	Dear Sirs:
Body	Please send me a copy of your booklet #57, titled "Weed Control Without Chemicals." I am enclosing a check for $1.50.
Closing	Very truly yours,
Signature	*Jean Sipes* Jean Sipes

A business letter has the same five parts that a friendly letter has: heading, greeting, body, closing, and signature. In addition, a business letter has an *inside address,* which shows the name and address of the person or business that receives the letter. The inside address is placed at the left-hand margin of the letter, between the heading and the greeting. A blank space should be left between each letter part and the next, so that every part stands out distinctly.

The greeting of a business letter is generally called a *salutation.* The matching birdhouse and bird feeder, you could likely use the same pattern for some parts of each. But of course, since the two have different purposes, you could not use identical patterns for all the parts. Friendly letters and business letters also have many similarities. But the two kinds of letters serve two different purposes, so they are not the same in every way.

Lesson 6

Purpose: To study rules for writing business letters.

Oral Review:

1. Name the five parts of a friendly letter. (heading, greeting, body, closing, signature)
2. What two things should be included in the heading? (the writer's address, the date)
3. For the greatest efficiency of the postal service, how should the mailing address on the envelope appear? (typed or neatly printed in all capital letters and without punctuation)
4. Name several kinds of social notes. (thank-you notes, invitations, replies to invitations, notes of apology)
5. How are these social notes similar to friendly letters? (They have the same five parts.)

Lesson Introduction: If you wanted to make a

Lesson Outline:

1. A business letter is written for a specific business purpose.

    a. Its purpose may be to order something by mail or to inquire about an order.

    b. It may be to request information about products or services that a business offers.

    c. It may be to request information about points of interest to visit or about details of geography, population, and industry.

salutation and the closing should be more formal than those in a friendly letter, and the salutation should be followed by a colon rather than a comma. Here are examples of appropriate salutations and closings for a business letter.

Business letter salutations:
Dear Sir: (Use this if the name of the businessman is not known.)
Dear Mr. Brown: (Use the name if it is known.)
Dear Sirs: *or* Gentlemen: (Use this when writing to a company.)
Dear Madam: (Use this when writing to a businesswoman.)

Business letter closings:
Very truly yours,   Yours truly,   Sincerely yours,
Cordially yours, (Use this for a business acquaintance.)
Respectfully yours, (Use this for very formal letters.)

The body of the letter should be courteous, clear, and concise (the three C's of business letter content). God's people especially should be courteous, even when pointing out a problem. Expressions like *please, I would appreciate,* and *at your convenience* should be used in business letters.

A business letter should clearly state exactly what the sender wants. If it is an order for merchandise, it should include specific information such as catalog number, size, color, and quantity for each item. A request for information should tell specifically what type of information is wanted. Since a businessman may need to read many letters every day, a business letter should not be cluttered with details not essential to the point of the letter.

A business letter should have a neat, formal appearance, with proper margins all around. If the letter is short, it should be centered on the paper. If it is written by hand, it should be done neatly with black or blue ink on lined white paper. But usually a business letter is typed on unlined white paper. The signature of a business letter should be written by hand and also typed or printed.

Many businesses put their letters on letterheads, which are pages with the business name and address printed at the top. Study the following sample.

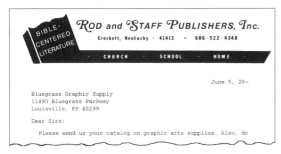

2. The form of a business letter differs slightly from that of a friendly letter.

a. A business letter has the same five parts as a friendly letter, plus an inside address.
b. The inside address shows the name and address of the receiver of the letter.
c. The greeting of a business letter is generally called a salutation. It should be followed by a colon.
d. The salutation and the closing should be more formal than those in a friendly letter.
e. The signature should be written by hand and also typed or printed.
f. A blank space should be left between each letter part and the next.

3. The body of a business letter should be courteous, clear, and concise.

a. Expressions like *please, I would appreciate,* and *at your convenience* give a courteous tone.
b. The letter should give specific information about the order, the request for information, or the problem.
c. A business letter should not be cluttered with unnecessary details.

4. A business letter should have a neat, formal appearance.

a. There should be proper margins all around.
b. If the letter is short, it should be centered on the paper.
c. The letter should be typed on unlined white paper or written neatly with black or blue ink on lined white paper.
d. Many businesses put their letters on letterheads.

Notice that no separate heading is needed in the sample above because the letterhead shows the company's name and address. The only part of the heading that the writer must add is the date.

Class Practice

Tell what is wrong with these business letters.

Letter A:

                                        September 27, 20—

Dear Sirs,

    In your recent catalog I saw a beautiful terrar-
ium advertised. I have had one at home for several
years and plan to set one up at my school, so I would
like you to send me one. Also send me two <u>Golden</u>
<u>Guides</u> on insects and on mushrooms.

                                Your friend,
                                Thomas Martin

Letter B:

                                Route 3 Box 120
                                Lowville NY 13367

13587 Worleytown Rd.
Greencastle, PA 17225
Gentlemen:

    You have mixed up my order. I sent for a terrar-
ium, not an aquarium. Also, I wanted two copies of
each of the <u>Golden Guides</u>. I'm sending the aquarium
back. Please send me the terrarium and the other books
immediately.

                            Sincerely,

                            Thomas Martin

                            Thomas Martin

Written Exercises

A. Write a business letter to order the following materials.

    One copy of *Mag 5 Star Atlas,* #14003, for $7.00; one *Small Solar
System Mobile,* #84621, for $6.50; and 3 copies of *Star and Planet Locator,*
#35100, for $2.00 each. The receiver's name and address is Nature's
Workshop, 22777 St. Rd. 119, Goshen, IN 46526. (Use your home address
and today's date in the heading.)

Lesson 6 Answers

Class Practice

Letter A:

1. The heading does not include the address.
2. The inside address is missing.
3. There are no spaces between the letter parts.
4. The salutation is followed by a comma instead of a colon.
5. The letter is not courteous; there is no *please* or *thank you.*
6. No specific information is given.
7. Unnecessary details are included.
8. The closing is not appropriate for a business letter.
9. The signature should be also handwritten.

Letter B:

1. Punctuation is missing in the heading.
2. The heading does not include the date.
3. The inside address does not include the business name.
4. The letter is very discourteous.
5. It does not include specific information.

Written Exercises

(All answers are individual work.)

B. Write a business letter, using one of the suggestions below.
  1. Write to a local business for information on a specific kind of product or service that it offers, for information about the history of the business, or for information about touring the business place. Perhaps you can write to a brother in the church who owns a business.
  2. Write for information about historical sites, state parks, or other points of interest in a certain state. (To get an address, find an encyclopedia article on that state and look under a heading such as "Places to Visit," or look in the *World Almanac and Book of Facts* under "States of the Union.")
  3. Write to a local place of interest. Ask about their visiting hours, special tours, and other information that would help you to plan a visit there.

---

7. Object Complements

> **Lesson Survey**
> - An **object complement** completes the sentence skeleton by receiving the action of a transitive verb. Direct and indirect objects are object complements.
> - A **direct object** is a noun or pronoun that receives the action of a transitive verb directly.
> - An **indirect object** is a noun or pronoun that receives the action of a transitive verb indirectly.

In Lesson 5 you saw that a linking verb needs a complement to complete the sentence skeleton. Many action verbs also have complements. Whereas a linking verb is followed by a subjective complement, an action verb is followed by an object complement.

An *object complement* is an object that completes the sentence skeleton by receiving the action of a transitive verb. (Remember that *transitive* means "passing over.") The action of transitive verbs may be passed to two kinds of object complements: direct objects and indirect objects.

Direct Objects

A *direct object* is a noun or pronoun that receives the action of a transitive verb *directly*. In a sentence with a direct object, the subject performs the action, the verb expresses the action, and the direct object receives the

Lesson 7

Purpose: (1) To study direct and indirect objects. (2) To show their relationship to the sentence skeleton.

Oral Review:
1. What are the two kinds of subjective complements? (predicate nominatives, predicate adjectives)
2. Subjective complements always follow what kind of verbs? (linking verbs)
3. What are the two parts of a sentence skeleton? (simple subject, simple predicate)
4. Give the correct term for each description.
   a. Two or more sentences incorrectly written together. (run-on error)
   b. A group of words that expresses a complete thought. (sentence)
   c. A group of words that has one or more sentence parts missing, but which expresses a complete thought because the missing parts are understood. (elliptical sentence)
   d. A group of words that does not express a complete thought. (fragment)

Lesson Introduction: Call attention to the title of the lesson and then to the second verse of the song, "Hark! Ten Thousand Harps and Voices."

> King of glory! reign forever—
>   Thine an everlasting crown;
> Nothing, from Thy love, shall sever
>   Those whom Thou hast made Thine own;
> Happy <u>objects</u> of Thy grace,
> Destined to behold Thy face.

What is an object of God's grace? (someone who receives God's grace) In a similar manner, an object

action. To find a direct object, say the sentence skeleton and ask *whom* or *what.* Like subjective complements, direct objects may be compound.

> God created the world in six days. (God created *what*? World.)
> He placed Adam and Eve in the Garden of Eden.
> (He placed *whom*? Adam and Eve; compound direct object.)

If two nouns receive the action of one verb, the sentence has a compound direct object. A sentence may also have a compound verb, with each part having a separate direct object. Compare the following examples.

> God placed <u>Adam</u> and <u>Eve</u> in the Garden of Eden.
> (one verb with a compound direct object)
> They heeded <u>Satan</u> and disobeyed <u>God</u>.
> (compound verb with separate direct objects)

A direct object is diagramed on the horizontal line after the skeleton. A vertical line separates the verb from its direct object. A compound direct object is diagramed on a fork.

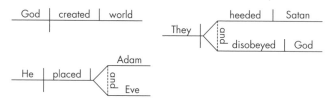

Indirect Objects

An *indirect object* is a noun or pronoun that receives the action of a transitive verb *indirectly.* An indirect object comes between a verb and its direct object. To find an indirect object, say the skeleton with the direct object, and then ask *to whom or what* or *for whom or what.*

Remember that many sentences with direct objects do not have indirect objects, but that no sentence can have an indirect object without a direct object. Like direct objects, indirect objects may be compound.

> My uncle told us an interesting story of his boyhood.
> (Uncle told *what*? story; *to whom*? us.)
> Nevin gave his calves some careful attention.
> (Nevin gave *what*? attention; *to what*? calves.)
> Mother packed Dorothy and me a delicious lunch.
> (Mother packed *what*? lunch; *for whom*? Dorothy and me.)

complement in English grammar receives the action of a verb.

Lesson Outline:

1. An object complement completes the sentence skeleton by receiving the action of a transitive verb. Transitive means "passing over."

2. A direct object is a noun or pronoun that receives the action of a transitive verb directly.

  a. To find a direct object, say the sentence skeleton and ask *whom* or *what.*

  b. Direct objects may be compound.

  c. A direct object is diagramed on the horizontal line after the skeleton.

    1) A vertical line separates the verb from its direct object.

    2) A compound direct object is diagramed on a fork.

3. An indirect object is a noun or pronoun that receives the action of a transitive verb indirectly.

  a. An indirect object comes between a verb and its direct object.

  b. To find an indirect object, say the skeleton with the direct object, and then ask *to whom or what* or *for whom or what.*

  c. Indirect objects may be compound.

  d. An indirect object is diagramed on a horizontal line beneath the skeleton.

    1) A slanted line connects it to the verb.

    2) Compound indirect objects are diagramed on a fork.

★ **EXTRA PRACTICE**

Worksheet 2 *(Object Complements)*

An indirect object is diagramed on a horizontal line beneath the skeleton, with a slanted line connecting it to the verb. Compound indirect objects are diagramed on a fork.

Class Practice

A. Read the direct objects in these sentences. If a sentence has no direct object, say *none*.
1. Your friends will influence your character.
2. Therefore, you should choose your friends with care.
3. You cannot easily break a habit.
4. A habit grows quickly into a powerful force.
5. A noble youth fears God and respects persons in authority.

B. Name and identify each object complement.
1. Even today scientists cannot give us a full explanation of magnetism.
2. Magnetism not only moves the tiny parts of an electric typewriter but also lifts huge loads.
3. A magnetic compass can show you the four directions.
4. Mother gave my paper a quick look and pointed out my mistake.
5. This morning Father showed Lowell and me the goose nest.

C. On the chalkboard, diagram the skeletons and complements of these sentences. Some sentences have subjective complements.
1. I wrote Grandfather and Grandmother a letter yesterday.
2. Grandmother has not felt well for several weeks.
3. An early frost damaged the tomatoes and peppers.
4. The cauliflower still looks fine and healthy.
5. Brother Snyder gave Lester and me some helpful directions.

Written Exercises

A. Copy each object complement, and label it *DO* for direct object or *IO* for indirect object. If a sentence has no object complement, write *none*.
1. Gaius practiced hospitality toward traveling ministers.
2. Diotrephes loved preeminence among the early believers.
3. Demetrius had a good report of all men.
4. John wrote Gaius a letter of encouragement.

Lesson 7 Answers

Class Practice

A. 1. character   4. none
   2. friends   5. God, persons
   3. habit

B. 1. us—indirect object; explanation—direct object
   2. parts—direct object; loads—direct object
   3. you—indirect object; directions—direct object
   4. paper—indirect object; look—direct object; mistake—direct object
   5. Lowell—indirect object; me—indirect object; nest—direct object

C.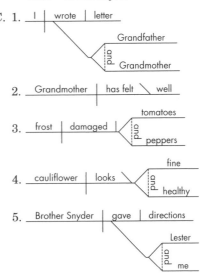

Written Exercises

A. 1. hospitality—DO
   2. preeminence—DO
   3. report—DO
   4. Gaius—IO; letter—DO

5. Perhaps John would soon visit with Gaius in person.
6. We gave the walls and ceiling a thorough cleaning.
7. A buildup of creosote had clogged the chimney and forced the smoke into the room.
8. Uncle Eugene enjoys his hobby of carving wood.
9. He carved Father a set of bookends and Mother a napkin holder.
10. We gave Spotty some basic lessons on obedience.
11. She has also learned some tricks.
12. The sun shone warmly upon the wet ground.
13. Father has already ordered the lumber.
14. We have never before planted a fall garden.

B. Diagram the skeletons and complements of these sentences. Some sentences contain subjective complements.
1. A grizzly bear eats both meat and plants.
2. One of its favorite foods is salmon.
3. Few animals can give the grizzly a tough fight.
4. Brother Reinford gave Leroy and Loren an unusual assignment.
5. Mother's fresh homemade bread tastes delicious.
6. This morning Diane baked a cake and cooked some pudding.

Review Exercises

These exercises review things that you studied in previous grades. Use the index in the back of this book if you need help.

A. Write the underlined part of each sentence, correcting the error in adjective usage.
1. Peter <u>wrote less epistles</u> than Paul did.
2. God can easily abase <u>the proud, conceited person</u>.
3. I enjoyed <u>singing that there song</u> which we learned today.
4. Do you know what <u>kind of a tractor</u> Uncle Bradley bought?
5. We <u>didn't have no rain</u> when Greenstown had a severe storm.
6. Yesterday Donna was sick, but today she is <u>feeling good</u> again.

B. Write the underlined part of each sentence, correcting the error in adverb usage.
1. We <u>should easy finish</u> this planting before supper.
2. These pretzels are <u>kind of salty</u> for me.
3. Has Merlin <u>connected up the hoses</u> yet?
4. Father <u>sure surprised</u> us today.

---

5. none
6. walls—IO; ceiling—IO; cleaning—DO
7. chimney—DO; smoke—DO
8. hobby—DO
9. Father—IO; set—DO; Mother—IO; (napkin) holder—DO
10. Spotty—IO; lessons—DO
11. tricks—DO
12. none
13. lumber—DO
14. garden—DO

B. 1.

2.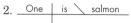

3.

4.

5.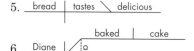

6.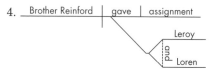

Review Exercises

A. 1. wrote fewer epistles
2. the proud person *or* the conceited person
3. singing that song
4. kind of tractor
5. didn't have any rain *or* had no rain
6. feeling well

B. 1. should easily finish
2. rather salty *or* somewhat salty
3. connected the hoses
4. surely surprised

8. Objective Complements

In Lessons 5 and 7 you reviewed the two classes of complements that you studied in previous years: subjective complements (predicate nominatives and predicate adjectives) and object complements (direct and indirect objects). There are three classes of complements altogether. This lesson introduces the third class: objective complements.

An *objective complement* is a noun or an adjective that follows and relates to a direct object. If it is a noun, it renames the direct object; and if it is an adjective, it describes the direct object. An objective complement is somewhat like a predicate nominative or a predicate adjective, but it relates to the direct object rather than to the subject.

Not every direct object can have an objective complement. Only the direct object of a verb that has the idea of "making" or "considering" can have one.

> The boys made the bottom step their <u>base</u>.
> (*Base* is a noun that names what they made the step to be.)
> Mr. Earl considered the stranger's idea quite <u>interesting</u>.
> (*Interesting* is an adjective that describes what he considered the idea to be.)

Look again at the two preceding examples. The verbs are *made* and *considered*, but they do not have their usual meanings. The boys did not *make* the step, and Mr. Earl did not simply *consider* the stranger's idea. The direct object must be associated with the objective complement for a proper understanding of the meaning.

Use the following steps to find an objective complement.

1. Identify the sentence skeleton and the direct object.
2. Determine whether the verb has the idea of "making" or "considering." If it does not, there can be no objective complement. If it does, go to step 3.
3. Determine whether the sentence has an indirect object. If it does, there can be no objective complement. If not, go to step 4.
4. Determine whether the direct object is followed by a noun that renames the direct object or by an adjective that modifies the direct object.

Lesson 8

Purpose: (1) To introduce *objective complements. (2) To show their relationship to basic sentence patterns.

Oral Review:

1. What does a complement do? (completes the sentence skeleton)
2. What kind of verb is followed by an object complement? (transitive)
3. How can you find the direct object in a sentence? (by saying the skeleton and asking *whom* or *what*)
4. How can you find an indirect object? (by saying the skeleton with the direct object and asking *to whom or what* or *for whom or what*)
5. Where is an indirect object normally located? (between the verb and the direct object)
6. What is an elliptical sentence? (a group of words that has one or more sentence parts missing, but which expresses a complete thought because the missing parts are understood)

Lesson Introduction: Call attention to the titles of Lessons 5, 7, and 8. These titles name the three classes of complements. Two of the terms end with the suffix *-ive,* which means "tending toward or relating to." A subjective complement is a word that completes by relating to the subject. An object complement is a word that completes, but it does not relate to the object. It *is* the object. An objective complement is a word that completes by relating to the object. However, no complement *is* a subject; so the term *subject complement* is not used.

Lesson Outline:

1. An objective complement is a noun or an adjective that follows a direct object and renames or describes the direct object.

Samuel anointed David king of Israel.
1. Skeleton and direct object: *Samuel anointed David.*
2. The verb *anointed* has the idea of "making."
3. There is no indirect object.
4. The noun *king* renames *David. King* is an objective complement.

At first, Samuel had thought Eliab ideal for the responsibility.
1. Skeleton and direct object: *Samuel had thought Eliab.*
2. The verb *had thought* has the idea of "considering."
3. There is no indirect object.
4. The adjective *ideal* modifies *Eliab. Ideal* is an objective complement.

I made Mother a recipe box in art class.
1. Skeleton and direct object: *I made box.*
2. The verb *made* has the idea of "making."
3. There is an indirect object, *Mother;* there can be no objective complement.

The box holds her large collection of recipes quite nicely.
1. Skeleton and direct object: *box holds collection.*
2. The verb *holds* does not have the idea of "making" or "considering." There can be no objective complement.

Do not confuse a direct object followed by an objective complement with an indirect object followed by a direct object. Find the direct object first by saying the skeleton and asking *whom* or *what.* Then remember that an indirect object *comes between* the verb and the direct object, and an objective complement *follows* the direct object. Also, an objective complement renames or modifies the direct object.

Virginia considers Elizabeth a close friend.
(Virginia considers *whom*? Elizabeth. *Friend* comes after *Elizabeth.* It renames *Elizabeth. Friend* is an objective complement.)
Virginia wrote Elizabeth a letter.
(Virginia wrote *what*? Letter. *Elizabeth* comes between *wrote* and *letter. Elizabeth* is an indirect object.)

You may feel confused by the words *objective complement* and *object complement*—in addition to *subjective complement.* It may help you to keep these terms clear if you remember that a subjective complement *refers* to the subject, and an objective complement *refers* to the direct object. But an object complement *is* an object—either a direct object or an indirect object. (There is no such thing as a subject complement.)

An objective complement is diagrammed on the horizontal line after

2. Only the direct object of a verb that has the idea of "making" or "considering" can have an objective complement. When there is an objective complement, it must be associated with the direct object for a proper understanding of the meaning of the verb.

3. The following steps can be used to find an objective complement.
(1) Identify the sentence skeleton and the direct object.
(2) Determine whether the verb has the idea of "making" or "considering." If it does not, there can be no objective complement. If it does, go to step 3.
(3) Determine whether the sentence has an indirect object. If it does, there can be no objective complement. If not, go to step 4.
(4) Determine whether the direct object is followed by a noun that renames the direct object or by an adjective that modifies the direct object.

4. Do not confuse a direct object followed by an objective complement with an indirect object followed by a direct object.
a. Be sure to find the direct object by saying the skeleton and asking *whom* or *what.*
b. An objective complement follows the direct object; an indirect object comes between the verb and the direct object.
c. An objective complement renames or modifies the direct object to which it refers. This is not true of direct objects and indirect objects.

the direct object, separated from it by a slanted line. Study the diagrams of the example sentences above.

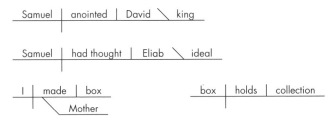

Class Practice

A. Read the skeleton and direct object in each sentence. Then give the objective complement.
  1. God created the universe perfect.
  2. In many ways, He made the earth fit for life.
  3. He considered man the crown of His creation.
  4. The sin of Adam made man a fallen creature.
  5. Before hearing Father's explanation, I thought the task very hard.
  6. This summer we painted our old barn white.

B. Find each complement, and tell whether it is a *direct object,* an *indirect object,* or an *objective complement.*
  1. David appointed Solomon the next king.
  2. The old men gave Rehoboam good advice.
  3. Rehoboam thought the young men's advice more suitable.
  4. Multitudes of Israelites considered the taxes too heavy.
  5. The rebellion under Jeroboam divided the kingdom.
  6. God gave Jeroboam the ten northern tribes.

C. On the chalkboard, diagram the skeletons and complements of all the sentences in Part B.

Written Exercises

A. Copy the objective complements in these sentences.
  1. God made His covenant with Abraham sure.
  2. Abraham saw obedience important in life.
  3. He would even offer his son a sacrifice to God.
  4. Father declared the bicycle too expensive.
  5. Nevin and Jay built their block tower high.
  6. Barbara has just washed these floors clean.

Lesson 8 Answers

Class Practice

A. 1. God created universe; perfect
   2. He made earth; fit
   3. He considered man; crown
   4. sin made man; creature
   5. I thought task; hard
   6. we painted barn; white

B. 1. Solomon—direct object;
      king—objective complement
   2. Rehoboam—indirect object;
      advice—direct object
   3. advice—direct object;
      suitable—objective complement
   4. taxes—direct object;
      heavy—objective complement
   5. kingdom—direct object
   6. Jeroboam—indirect object;
      tribes—direct object

C.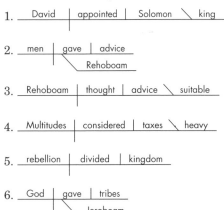

Written Exercises

A. 1. sure   4. expensive
   2. important   5. high
   3. sacrifice   6. clean

5. An objective complement is diagramed on the horizontal line after the direct object, separated from it by a slanted line.

★ **EXTRA PRACTICE**
   Worksheet 3 *(Objective Complements)*

7. Kenneth named his new puppy Freckles.
8. Historians consider the Phoenicians the inventors of the alphabet.

B. Copy each underlined complement, and label it *DO* for direct object, *IO* for indirect object, or *OC* for objective complement.
1. We must consider our <u>abilities</u> <u>gifts</u> from God.
2. He has given <u>us</u> these <u>gifts</u> for His glory.
3. He can make our <u>lives</u> <u>fruitful</u> in His service.
4. Arnold sanded the <u>wood</u> for the seats <u>smooth</u>.
5. He is making the <u>children</u> <u>swings</u> to put in the maple trees.
6. Father bought <u>James</u> a <u>car</u> from Mr. Johnson.
7. Mr. Johnson will paint the <u>car</u> <u>black</u>.
8. The heavy downpour has made our <u>creek</u> a raging <u>river</u>.

C. Diagram the skeletons and all the complements of these sentences.
1. We should consider the Christian school a priceless privilege.
2. Each privilege brings us added responsibilities.
3. God holds each person accountable for his opportunities in life.
4. Unthankfulness will certainly make a person an easy prey to the devil.
5. Jealousy often makes people cruel toward others.
6. Pride gives one a false sense of security.

Review Exercises

These exercises review things that you studied in previous grades. Use the index in the back of this book if you need help.

Write the underlined part of each sentence, correcting the error in preposition usage.
1. The Christian's values are quite <u>different than the</u> world's.
2. James and John wanted to <u>sit besides Jesus</u> in His kingdom.
3. The plain of Bashan lay <u>outside of the</u> boundaries of Canaan.
4. After Jesus entered Jerusalem, He went <u>in the temple</u>.
5. Uncle Joseph divided the work <u>between the five cousins</u>.
6. All the girls <u>accept Janice</u> and Linda were helping to clean.
7. Where did those two <u>go to</u>?
8. They are <u>in back of the house</u>, weeding the flower beds.

---

7. Freckles
8. inventors

B.
1. abilities—DO; gifts—OC
2. us—IO; gifts—DO
3. lives—DO; fruitful—OC
4. wood—DO; smooth—OC
5. children—IO; swings—DO
6. James—IO; car—DO
7. car—DO; black—OC
8. creek—DO; river—OC

C.
1.

| We | should consider | school | privilege |

2.

| privilege | brings | responsibilities |
us

3.

| God | holds | person | accountable |

4.

| Unthankfulness | will make | person | prey |

5.

| Jealousy | makes | people | cruel |

6.

| Pride | gives | sense |
one

Review Exercises
1. different from the
2. sit beside Jesus
3. outside the
4. into the temple
5. among the five cousins
6. except Janice
7. go
8. behind the house

9. Appositives and Independent Elements

Lesson Survey

- An **appositive** is a noun or pronoun used with another noun or pronoun to identify or explain it.
- A word that is not grammatically related to the rest of the sentence is called an **independent element.**

You expect a sentence to have a subject and a predicate, as well as other needed sentence parts. But many sentences have words (appositives and independent elements) that are not part of the basic sentence structure. That is, these parts do not function as a simple subject or predicate, a complement, or a modifier of a basic sentence part.

Appositives

An *appositive* is a noun or pronoun used with another noun or pronoun to further identify or explain it. A noun or pronoun in any part of the sentence may have an appositive. If the noun or pronoun is modified by one-word adjectives or adjective phrases, the whole unit is called an appositive.

> We <u>boys</u> raked all the leaves. (*Boys* identifies *We.*)
> Janet, <u>my older sister</u>, served lemonade.
>   (*My older sister* identifies *Janet.*)

Most appositives are *nonrestrictive appositives* and are set off with commas. Such an appositive simply gives additional information; it does not restrict the meaning of the noun or pronoun that it explains. The sentence means much the same with or without the nonrestrictive appositive. Note how this is true in the following sentences.

> Stephen was stoned outside Jerusalem.
> Stephen, <u>the first Christian martyr</u>, was stoned outside Jerusalem.

In the first example sentence, *Stephen* is clear without further explanation. The appositive is not needed to identify and restrict *Stephen* to a certain person. It simply gives additional information.

By contrast, a *restrictive appositive* does restrict the meaning of the noun or pronoun that it follows. A restrictive appositive contains information needed to make the sentence clear. Compare the meanings of the following sentences.

> The apostle <u>Paul</u> had been present at Stephen's death.
> The apostle had been present at Stephen's death.

Lesson 9

Purpose: To study *restrictive appositives, *nonrestrictive appositives, and *independent elements. (*Previous experience:* Concepts introduced, without use of the new terms.)

Oral Review:

1. What is an objective complement? (a noun or an adjective that follows a direct object and renames or modifies it)
2. An objective complement is found only after a verb that has the idea of —— or ——. ("making," "considering")
3. Name the two kinds of object complements, and tell what questions they answer. (direct objects, which tell *whom* or *what;* indirect objects, which tell *to whom or what* or *for whom or what*)
4. Name the two kinds of subjective complements. (predicate nominatives, predicate adjectives)
5. Describe four ways to correct a run-on error. (by adding a comma and a coordinating conjunction; by adding a semicolon; by changing one of the clauses to a dependent clause; by dividing it into two or more sentences)

Lesson Introduction: In this chapter you have studied subjects, predicates, subjective complements, object complements, and objective complements. These, along with their modifiers, make up the basic structure of sentences. However, many sentences include other words and expressions that are not basic to the sentence structure. In this last regular lesson of the chapter, you will study a number of such elements.

Lesson Outline:

1. An appositive is a noun or pronoun used with another noun or pronoun to identify or explain it.

Without the appositive, the sentence is not clear at all. Which apostle had been present at Stephen's death? The appositive restricts and clarifies the meaning of *apostle* by telling *which* apostle.

Since a restrictive appositive is essential to the meaning, it is not set off with commas. Also, most restrictive appositives consist of only one or two words, and there is no pause in reading them. This is another clue that an appositive is restrictive and should not be set off with commas.

The hymn "Safe in the Arms of Jesus" was written by Fanny Crosby.
My friend Carol has moved out of state.

An appositive is diagramed in parentheses after the word it identifies or explains. Adjective modifiers are placed below the appositive.

The apostle Paul visited Macedonia, a region of Europe.

Independent Elements

Words that are not grammatically related to the rest of the sentence are called *independent elements*. They are usually set off with commas or other punctuation, and are diagramed on separate lines to the left of the main diagram. You will study five kinds of independent elements.

1. *A noun of direct address* names the person or thing to whom one is speaking. Like an appositive, a noun of direct address may include adjective modifiers. Then the whole unit is considered a noun of direct address.

Peter, the calves are in the
yard!
"Ye that fear the Lord, bless the Lord."

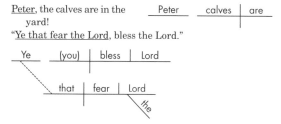

2. *An* expletive *introduces a sentence without adding to its meaning.* *There* and *it* are common expletives. However, these words are not expletives when they function as basic sentence parts. *There* can be an adverb telling *where*. *It* can be a normal pronoun that functions as a subject, direct object, or some other sentence part.

When these words are expletives, you can usually omit the expletive

---

a. If the noun or pronoun is modified by one-word adjectives or adjective phrases, the whole unit is called an appositive.

b. A nonrestrictive appositive simply gives additional information about the noun or pronoun that it follows, and it is set off with commas.

c. A restrictive appositive restricts the meaning of the noun or pronoun that it follows, and it is not set off with commas.

d. An appositive is diagramed in parentheses after the word it identifies or explains.

2. Words that are not grammatically related to the rest of the sentence are called independent elements. They are usually set off with commas or other punctuation, and are diagramed on separate lines to the left of the main diagram.

(1) *A noun of direct address* names the person or thing to whom one is speaking.

(2) *An* expletive *introduces a sentence without adding to its meaning.*

   a) *There* is a common expletive when not used as an adverb telling *where*.

   b) *It* is a common expletive when not used as a normal pronoun functioning as a subject, direct object, or other sentence part.

   c) When these words are expletives, you can usually omit the expletive without changing the meaning of the sentence.

(3) *An* exclamation *or* interjection *expresses strong feeling.*

   a) A few such terms are acceptable, but using them too freely can be a bad habit that mars our speech.

without changing the meaning of the sentence. Study the following examples to see the difference.

<u>There</u> is a surprise waiting for you on the porch.
(*There* merely introduces the sentence. The sentence can be reworded without *There:* A surprise is waiting for you on the porch.)

There	surprise	is waiting

<u>There</u> stood a new bicycle for me!
(*There* is an adverb telling *where.* The sentence cannot be reworded without *There.*)

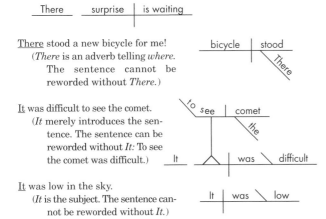

<u>It</u> was difficult to see the comet.
(*It* merely introduces the sentence. The sentence can be reworded without *It:* To see the comet was difficult.)

<u>It</u> was low in the sky.
(*It* is the subject. The sentence cannot be reworded without *It.*)

It	was	\ low

3. An exclamation *or* interjection *expresses strong feeling.* A few such terms are acceptable, but using them too freely can be a bad habit that mars our speech. A mild interjection is followed by a comma. An interjection said with strong feeling is followed by an exclamation point, and the next word is capitalized.

"<u>Lo</u>, this hath touched thy lips."

Lo	this	hath touched	lips

<u>The pigs</u>! They are ruining the garden!

pigs	They	are ruining	garden

4. A response *such as* yes *or* no *is sometimes used at the beginning of a sentence.*

<u>Yes</u>, this is the right book.

Yes	this	is	\ book

b) A mild interjection is followed by a comma. An interjection said with strong feeling is followed by an exclamation point, and the next word is capitalized.

(4) *A response* such as yes *or* no *is sometimes used at the beginning of a sentence.*

(5) Parenthetical expressions *include phrases such as* I think, for example, on the other hand, *and* we know.

★ *EXTRA PRACTICE*
Worksheet 4 *(Appositives and Independent Elements)*

5. Parenthetical expressions *include phrases such as* I think, for example, on the other hand, *and* we know. These are nonessential to the structure of a sentence.

God's people, <u>we know</u>, have often been despised by the world.

| we | know | people | have been despised |

For example, the early Christians suffered much persecution.

| for example | Christians | suffered | persecution |

Class Practice

A. Read each appositive, and tell whether it is *restrictive* or *nonrestrictive.* Tell where commas are needed.
  1. Noah a preacher of righteousness obeyed God's voice.
  2. He built the ark a large ship.
  3. Noah's son Japheth is the ancestor of the Europeans.
  4. My cousin Esther attends the Green Acres Christian School a small school in Wisconsin.
  5. Alaska the largest state of the Union is more than twice as big as Texas the second largest state.

B. Identify the independent elements. Tell where punctuation and capitalization are needed in these sentences.
  1. Jennifer have you seen the new bulletin board in the hall?
  2. Yes it is a lovely fall scene.
  3. There are several geese flying in the sky.
  4. The Vanderbilt girls I think made this one.
  5. Amazing they did the whole scene with colored chalk.

C. Tell whether each underlined word is an *expletive* or a *basic sentence part.*
  1. <u>There</u> comes to my heart one sweet strain.
  2. <u>It</u> is written in the Bible that the just shall live by faith.
  3. <u>There</u> the strange dog stood, looking at me.
  4. <u>It</u> wagged its tail and begged to come into the house.

D. On the chalkboard, diagram the skeletons and complements of sentences 1–3 in Part A and 1–5 in Part B. Include all the words that make up appositives and independent elements.

Written Exercises

A. Copy the appositives in these sentences. Label each one *R* for restrictive or *N* for nonrestrictive. Commas have been omitted.

Lesson 9 Answers

Class Practice

A. 1. a preacher of righteousness—nonrestrictive; Noah, righteousness,
  2. a large ship—nonrestrictive; ark,
  3. Japheth—restrictive (no commas)
  4. Esther—restrictive (no commas)
     a small school in Wisconsin—nonrestrictive; School,
  5. the largest state of the Union—nonrestrictive; Alaska, Union,
     the second largest state—nonrestrictive; Texas,

B. (Independent elements are underlined.)
  1. <u>Jennifer,</u>   4. girls, <u>I think,</u>
  2. <u>Yes,</u>   5. <u>Amazing!</u> They
  3. <u>There</u>

C. 1. expletive   3. basic sentence part
   2. expletive   4. basic sentence part

D. (Part A)

1.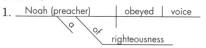

2.

3.

(Part B)

1. | Jennifer | you | have seen | bulletin board |

2. | Yes | it | is \ scene |

3. | There | geese | are flying |

4. | I | think | girls | made | one |

5. | Amazing | They | did | scene |

1. The Bible God's Holy Word tells us how to live.
2. Satan the archenemy of God strongly opposes God's Word.
3. When the scroll was burned by Jehoiakim the wicked king of Israel, God directed the prophet Jeremiah to write His words again.
4. My uncle Melvin plans to help Father build the produce shed a twenty-by-forty-foot block building.
5. Our new teacher Brother Elmer is boarding with my brother James and his family.

B. Copy these sentences, and underline the independent elements. Add any necessary punctuation and capitalization.
1. How nice there are some new books in the library Denise.
2. No I don't think that I have read any of them before.
3. Most of the other books on the other hand I have read several times.
4. It is good to have some new books again.
5. For example this one book I think looks like an interesting nature story.

C. Diagram the skeletons and complements of these sentences, as well as all the words that make up appositives and independent elements.
1. This tree, a large maple, gives us plenty of shade.
2. Yes, my grandfather planted it in his youth.
3. My dress! I tore my dress on that nail!
4. Harlan, you should hammer that nail into the board.
5. There are several jobs waiting for you.
6. For example, the lawn must be mowed this afternoon.

Review Exercises

A. Copy each underlined complement, and label it *PN* (predicate nominative), *PA* (predicate adjective), *DO* (direct object), *IO* (indirect object), or *OC* (objective complement). [5–8] (Turn to the lesson numbers in brackets if you need help.)
1. Dishonesty is a serious <u>menace</u> to noble character.
2. A gossiper does <u>himself</u> much <u>harm</u>.
3. We should make praiseworthy <u>thoughts</u> our constant <u>companion</u>.
4. Our thought life is <u>important</u>, for it largely determines our <u>choices</u>.

B. Diagram these sentences.
1. Mother made the hard workers a little treat.
2. The bars tasted rich and chocolaty.
3. Father tilled the garden and marked the rows.
4. Our produce venture has become a big success.
5. Some humus will make this soil more productive.

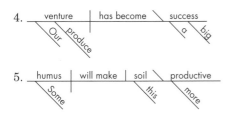

Written Exercises

A. 1. God's Holy Word—N
2. the archenemy of God—N
3. the wicked king of Israel—N; Jeremiah—R
4. Melvin—R;
   a twenty-by-forty-foot block building—N
5. Brother Elmer—N; James—R

B. (Corrections of punctuation and capitalization are marked with double underlining.)
1. How nice! There are some new books in the library, Denise.
2. No, I don't think that I have read any of them before.
3. Most of the other books, on the other hand, I have read several times.
4. It is good to have some new books again.
5. For example, this one book, I think, looks like an interesting nature story.

C.

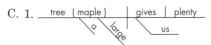

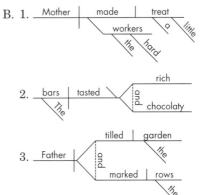

Review Exercises

A. 1. menace—PN
2. himself—IO; harm—DO
3. thoughts—DO; companion—OC
4. important—PA; choices—DO

10. Chapter 1 Review

Class Practice

A. Answer these questions about language.
1. In what ways is man's communication superior to that of the animals?
2. What is the difference between pronunciation and enunciation?
3. What advantage does writing have over speaking as a form of communication?

B. Tell whether each numbered item is a *complete sentence*, a *fragment*, an *elliptical sentence*, or a *run-on error*. Suggest ways to correct the fragments and run-on errors. Tell what words are understood in the elliptical sentences.

*¹*Yesterday we ate lunch outside. *²*Since it was a warm September day. *³*Across the road Brother Troyer was working in his field, a gentle breeze brought us the sweet scent of drying hay.

⁴"Smells good. *⁵*Wish I were on that tractor!" *⁶*Roy's comment revealed his farmer's heart.

⁷"And miss recess?" *⁸*Mark was incredulous.

⁹"Of course! *¹⁰*Even playing ball is not as much fun as raking hay," replied Roy.

C. Read each sentence skeleton. Then read the complete subject and the complete predicate.
1. A flock of sheep grazed contentedly in the lush pasture.
2. Conrad's daily job was to watch over these sheep.
3. Father and Gary are caulking some windows.
4. This old house obviously needs caulking.

D. Find each complement, and tell whether it is a *predicate nominative*, a *predicate adjective*, a *direct object*, an *indirect object*, or an *objective complement*.
1. Have you ever seen a spiny anteater?
2. The native home of this creature is Australia.
3. An echidna and a spiny anteater are the same animal.
4. This unusual creature is small and round.
5. God has given this animal short spines over most of its upper body.
6. The spiny anteater also has brown hairs among the spines.
7. You would consider these hairs quite coarse.
8. With its strong front claws, the spiny anteater can dig itself a hole in a very short time.
9. This ability is often a means of escape from enemies.
10. The spiny anteater can also make such a hole its home.

Lesson 10

Purpose: To review the concepts taught in Chapter 1.

Lesson 10 Answers

Class Practice

A. 1. Only man can arrange words into complete sentences and paragraphs. He alone can express abstract ideas in words. He alone can communicate on a spiritual level with God.
2. Pronunciation relates to the correct sounds and accents of words. Enunciation relates to saying each sound distinctly.
3. Writing makes it possible to preserve truth from generation to generation.

B. (Corrections and understood words are in parentheses.)
1. complete sentence
2. fragment (Join to the preceding sentence.)
3. run-on error (Divide into two sentences.)
4. elliptical sentence; (That hay) smells good.
5. elliptical sentence; (I) wish I were on that tractor!
6. complete sentence
7. elliptical sentence; And (you would be willing to) miss recess?
8. complete sentence
9. elliptical sentence; Of course (I would be willing to miss recess)!
10. complete sentence

C. (Vertical lines divide subjects and predicates. Skeletons are underlined.)
1. A <u>flock</u> of sheep | <u>grazed</u> contentedly in the lush pasture.
2. Conrad's daily <u>job</u> | <u>was</u> to watch over these sheep.
3. <u>Father</u> and <u>Gary</u> | <u>are</u>|<u>caulking</u> some windows.
4. This old <u>house</u> | obviously <u>needs</u> caulking.

D. 1. spiny anteater—direct object
2. Australia—predicate nominative
3. animal—predicate nominative
4. small—predicate adjective; round—predicate adjective
5. animal—indirect object; spines—direct object
6. hairs—direct object
7. hairs—direct object; coarse—objective complement
8. itself—indirect object; hole—direct object
9. means—predicate nominative
10. hole—direct object; home—objective complement

11. Sometimes it finds the ground too hard for digging.

12. Then the creature becomes a spiny ball.

E. Identify the independent elements, and tell where punctuation or capital letters are needed.

1. Kevin did you know that this creek disappears back in the pasture?

2. No I never knew that!

3. There is a big hole in the middle of a rock pile.

4. Strange the water disappears down a hole!

5. The water comes out again Mr. Bremen says on the neighboring farm.

6. It would be interesting to see the underground path of the stream.

F. Do these exercises on letter writing.

1. Name the five parts of a friendly letter.

2. What additional part does a business letter have, and where is it located?

3. What punctuation should follow the greeting of a friendly letter? of a business letter?

4. What is another term for the greeting of a business letter?

5. Tell whether each closing is appropriate for a *friendly* letter, a *business* letter, or *both*.

  a. Your friend,   d. With love and prayers,

  b. Sincerely yours,   e. Yours truly,

  c. Respectfully yours,   f. In Christian love,

6. What are the three W's of a note of invitation?

7. What are the three C's of business letter content?

8. How are social notes different from other friendly letters?

9. What are some ways in which the form of a business letter is different from that of a friendly letter?

10. Explain how to fold a letter for a small envelope and for a large envelope.

11. Describe the form of the mailing address on an envelope.

Written Exercises

A. Rewrite this dialogue, eliminating fragments and run-on errors. Add words only if needed; do not change elliptical sentences.

"Mother is spending the afternoon with Mrs. Gehr. Our neighbor who broke her leg. Let's surprise her. When she comes home." Suggested seventeen-year-old Mae as she met Fern at the door.

"Sounds good, what do you have in mind?" wondered thirteen-year-old Fern. Who had just come home from school.

"Have any homework?"

"No."

---

11. ground—direct object; hard—objective complement

12. ball—predicate nominative

E. (Punctuation and capital letters are shown where needed. Independent elements are underlined.)

1. <u>Kevin</u>,   4. <u>Strange</u>! The

2. <u>No</u>,   5. again, <u>Mr. Bremen says</u>,

3. <u>There</u>   6. <u>It</u>

F. 1. heading, greeting, body, closing, signature

2. inside address; at the left-hand margin, between the heading and the greeting

3. a comma; a colon

4. salutation

5. a. friendly   d. friendly

  b. both   e. both

  c. business   f. friendly

6. what, when, where

7. courteous, clear, concise

8. They are short, having one specific purpose instead of discussing various topics as most friendly letters do.

9. It has an inside address; the different parts should be separated by blank spaces; a colon follows the salutation.

10. *Small envelope:* Fold the lower half of the paper up, then fold it in thirds.

Large envelope: Fold the bottom third of the paper up, then fold the top third down.

11. typed or neatly printed with all capital letters and no punctuation

Written Exercises

A. (Corrections are underlined. Allow reasonable variation.)

"Mother is spending the afternoon with Mrs. Gehr<u>,</u> <u>o</u>ur neighbor who broke her leg. Let's surprise her <u>w</u>hen she comes home<u>,"</u> <u>s</u>uggested seventeen-year-old Mae as she met Fern at the door.

"Sounds good<u>!</u> <u>W</u>hat do you have in mind?" wondered thirteen-year-old Fern<u>,</u> <u>w</u>ho had just come home from school.

"Have any homework?"

"No."

"Good. I think we can finish the downstairs cleaning and the ironing, she plans to be home by 5:00," said Mae.

B. Copy the sentence skeletons.
1. "A man's pride shall bring him low."
2. The Bible clearly identifies Satan as the author of pride.
3. God hates pride and pronounces strong condemnation upon the proud.
4. Too much concern about one's appearance may be a sign of pride.
5. Boastful words and stubbornness also indicate a proud heart.

C. Copy the subjective complements, and label them *PN* (predicate nominative) or *PA* (predicate adjective).
1. Humility is an important virtue to cultivate.
2. The humble person is thoughtful of others and respectful toward those in authority.
3. Kind consideration for others is the motive of every humble person.
4. The humble are never insistent upon having their own way.
5. The reward of the humble is God's blessing on their lives.

D. Copy each complement, and label it *DO* (direct object), *IO* (indirect object), or *OC* (objective complement).
1. A large flock of blackbirds covered the schoolyard and made a tremendous racket.
2. The view of that yawning chasm made me dizzy.
3. The sturdy fence did give me a sense of security.
4. Everyone saw the eagle's nest through the telescope.
5. We thought the scenery especially beautiful from this lookout point.
6. Brother Lee gave Father and Mother a hearty invitation to his home.
7. After dinner we children played Scrabble and Probe.

E. Copy each appositive, and label it *R* for restrictive or *N* for nonrestrictive. (Commas have been omitted.)
1. Saul Israel's first king lost the kingdom because of his wickedness.
2. God raised up David a man after His own heart to be the next king.
3. The prophet Nathan served during David's reign.
4. My uncle Charles sings with a loud, clear bass.
5. Our new teacher Brother Sweigart can sing tenor or bass quite well.

F. Diagram the skeletons and complements of these sentences, as well as all the words that make up appositives and independent elements.
1. In Bible class we are studying the lives of the twelve disciples and the journeys of Paul.
2. There are interesting accounts of the disciples in *Martyrs Mirror*.
3. Faithful Christians have always considered obedience more important than life.

"Good. I think we can finish the downstairs cleaning and the ironing. She plans to be home by 5:00," said Mae.

B. 1. pride shall bring
   2. Bible identifies
   3. God hates (and) pronounces
   4. concern may be
   5. words (and) stubbornness indicate

C. 1. virtue—PN
   2. thoughtful—PA; respectful—PA
   3. motive—PN
   4. insistent—PA
   5. blessing—PN

D. 1. school yard—DO; racket—DO
   2. me—DO; dizzy—OC
   3. me—IO; sense—DO
   4. nest—DO
   5. scenery—DO; beautiful—OC
   6. Father—IO; Mother—IO; invitation—DO
   7. Scrabble—DO; Probe—DO

E. 1. Israel's first king—N
   2. a man after His own heart—N
   3. Nathan—R
   4. Charles—R
   5. Brother Sweigart—N

F. 1.

   2. There ___ accounts | are

   3. Christians | have considered | obedience \ important

4. Some people, on the other hand, denied the Lord and renounced the faith.
5. Many Anabaptists, our spiritual forefathers, became outcasts and even martyrs.
6. Gerald, you surely look cheerful.
7. Well, I enjoyed a pleasant visit with Grandfather.
8. I gave him the casserole and the pudding.

G. Write a thank-you note for the following situation. Use your own address and today's date.

You spent a week with Uncle Frank and Aunt Susan. You enjoyed helping them in their sweet corn field and at their produce stand, even though it was hard work. You especially enjoyed Saturday's picnic lunch in the woods.

H. Rewrite the following business letter, correcting the errors and improving the body.

```
                              December 2, 20—
                              Route 2 Box 4301
                              Amelia, VA 23002

Country Bookstore
14595 Williamsport pike
Greencastle, Pa 17225

Dear Sir;
    I hope you are better organized than when you sent
me a shipment last week. I have here two new copies of
the book The Church in History. I ordered two copies of
the book Mr. World and Miss Church Member from your used
book selection. Return my money, or send me the books
I ordered. What shall I do with these books I did not
order?
                              Clifton Wade
```

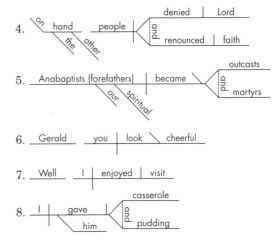

G. (Individual work.)

H. (The following corrections should be made.)
1. Move the date below the address in the heading.
2. Add a comma after *Route 2* in the heading.
3. Add a space between the heading and the inside address.
4. Capitalize *Pike* in the inside address.
5. In the inside address, change *Pa* to *PA*.
6. In the salutation, replace the semicolon with a colon.
7. Add a space between the salutation and the body.
8. Make the body of the letter more courteous.
9. Add a space after the body.
10. Add a closing.

Chapter Two

Sentence Structure

Writing Paragraphs

You already know how to express yourself in many different ways. For different purposes, you can write declarative, interrogative, imperative, or exclamatory sentences. For varying degrees of emphasis, you can employ different word orders (natural, inverted, or mixed) and different sentence styles (loose, periodic, or balanced). For clear relationships among ideas, you can utilize different sentence structures: simple, compound, complex, or compound-complex. Mastery of this variety will greatly enhance your skill in communication.

Paragraphs serve to divide compositions into manageable parts. An effective paragraph must have unity; that is, each sentence must develop the paragraph topic. An effective paragraph must also have coherence; that is, the sentences must build logically one upon another, and their ideas must flow smoothly from one sentence to another. The ability to write unified, coherent paragraphs is indispensable to good writing.

By Silvanus, a faithful brother unto you,
as I suppose, I have written briefly, exhorting, and testifying
that this is the true grace of God wherein ye stand.

1 Peter 5:12

11. Sentence Types and Word Order

> **Lesson Survey**
> - A **declarative sentence** makes a statement.
> - An **interrogative sentence** asks a question.
> - An **imperative sentence** gives a command or request.
> - An **exclamatory sentence** expresses strong feeling or emotion.
> - In **natural word order,** the complete subject precedes the complete predicate.
> - In **inverted word order,** the complete predicate precedes the complete subject.
> - In **mixed word order,** the complete subject comes between two parts of the complete predicate.
> - Varying sentence types and word order adds freshness and emphasis to your writing.

Sentence Types

There are four sentence types according to use: declarative, interrogative, imperative, and exclamatory. A *declarative sentence* makes a statement and ends with a period. Since a declarative sentence makes a statement, you can always logically ask the question, "Is this sentence true, or is it false?"

> God loves all men. (a true statement)
> All men love God. (a false statement)
> Love the Lord with all your heart. (A command cannot be true or false.)

An *interrogative sentence* asks a question and ends with a question mark. Often the subject of an interrogative sentence follows the verb or comes between two parts of the verb phrase.

> <u>Who</u> <u>is using</u> the thesaurus?
> <u>Is</u> <u>it</u> in your desk?
> <u>May</u> <u>I</u> <u>use</u> it for a little?

An *imperative sentence* gives a command or request. Most imperative sentences end with periods. The subject of every imperative sentence is *you*, even though the sentence may include a noun of direct address. However, the subject *you* is usually understood, not directly stated.

Be careful not to classify as an imperative sentence a declarative sentence that appears to be a command. Such a sentence may even express a

Lesson 11

Purpose: To study the four types of sentences according to use; and natural, inverted, and mixed word order.

Oral Review:

1. Name the complement described in each sentence.
   a. It follows an action verb and answers the question *whom* or *what*. (direct object)
   b. It follows a linking verb and renames the subject. (predicate nominative)
   c. It follows a direct object and renames or modifies it. (objective complement)
   d. It follows a linking verb and modifies the subject. (predicate adjective)
   e. It comes between an action verb and its direct object. (indirect object)
2. Give a brief definition of each term.
   a. elliptical sentence (a group of words with one or more sentence parts missing, which expresses a complete thought because the missing parts are understood)
   b. appositive (a noun or pronoun used with another noun or pronoun to identify or explain it)
   c. expletive (a word that introduces a sentence but does not add to its meaning)

Lesson Introduction: Have you recently entered a room after your mother rearranged the furniture? Perhaps you took special notice of a certain chair or a bookcase because it was somewhere other than its usual position. You can do something like that in your writing too. Using a different type of sentence or a sentence with its word order rearranged can be an effective way to help the reader notice a certain point. (*Teacher:* If you really want to emphasize this

request; but if it is written as a statement that is either true or false, it is declarative. The verb of such a sentence always includes a helping verb like *should* or *must*. In contrast, the verb in an imperative sentence never includes a helping verb.

Put your books neatly into your desks. (imperative; gives a command)

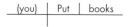

You should keep your papers orderly too. (declarative; a true statement)

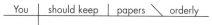

Mother, please pass the water. (imperative; gives a request)

An *exclamatory sentence* expresses strong feeling or emotion and ends with an exclamation point. Some exclamatory sentences have a unique word order. The skeleton may come at the end of the sentence so that an introductory word like *what* or *how* can come first. Other exclamatory sentences are constructed like a dependent clause that would be a fragment if it were not exclamatory.

How beautiful heaven must be!
    (skeleton last so that *How* can come first)
If only all men would serve the Lord!
    (dependent clause that would otherwise be a fragment)

In addition, any of the other three sentence types may be punctuated as an exclamation if it is expressed forcefully. Use exclamatory sentences sparingly so that when you do use them, they truly express strong feeling.

Grandfather has fallen down the steps!
    (declarative sentence expressed forcefully)
Where's Father! Call him quickly!
    (interrogative and imperative sentences expressed forcefully)

Word Order

Sentences may be written in natural, inverted, or mixed word order. The most common order is *natural word order,* in which the complete subject precedes the complete predicate. This is the way we naturally form our sentences when we speak.

The pup raced down the lane toward the barn. (natural order)

point, move your desk or a student's desk to a different spot in the room and point out to the students how they reacted when they entered the room!)

Lesson Outline:

  1. A declarative sentence makes a statement.
    a. It ends with a period.
    b. You can always logically ask the question, "Is this sentence true, or is it false?"

  2. An interrogative sentence asks a question.
    a. It ends with a question mark.
    b. The subject often follows the verb or comes between two parts of the verb phrase.

  3. An imperative sentence gives a command or request.
    a. Most imperative sentences end with periods.
    b. The subject is always *you,* and it is usually understood rather than directly stated.

    c. A sentence with a helping verb like *should* or *must* may appear to be imperative; and it may even communicate a command. However, the verb in an imperative sentence never includes a helping verb.

  4. An exclamatory sentence expresses strong feeling or emotion.
    a. It ends with an exclamation point.
    b. It may have a unique word order.
      1) The skeleton may come at the end of the sentence so that an introductory word like *what* or *how* can come first.
      2) It may be constructed like a dependent clause that would be a fragment if it were not exclamatory.
    c. Any of the other three sentence types may be punctuated as an exclamation if it is expressed forcefully.

The least common order is *inverted word order,* in which the complete predicate precedes the complete subject. Since inverted sentences are not used very frequently, a sentence in this order attracts attention and thus gives emphasis to the idea it expresses. A sentence with inverted word order should not have a comma between the complete predicate and the complete subject. It is also interesting to note that no sentence with an object complement can be written with inverted order.

Down the lane toward the barn raced the pup. (inverted order)

Many sentences are written in *mixed word order,* with the complete subject coming between two parts of the complete predicate. A sentence with mixed order often has a comma before the subject, especially if a long adverb phrase or an adverb clause begins the sentence. (Note that the entire adverb clause is considered part of the predicate.)

Down the lane to the barn, the pup raced.
(mixed order; long introductory adverb phrase; comma needed)
In his haste the pup almost fell over his own feet.
(mixed order; short introductory adverb phrase; no comma needed)
When Glen had called, the pup responded immediately.
(mixed order; introductory adverb clause; comma needed)

Look again at the sentence examples above. If the complete subject comes first, the sentence is in natural order. If the subject comes last, the order is inverted; and if it comes in the middle, the order is mixed. (The complete subject is generally not divided.) Thus, the position of the complete subject provides a quick way of telling whether a sentence has natural, inverted, or mixed word order.

Sentence Variety

Varying the sentence types and the word order in your writing adds freshness and emphasis. Although most of your sentences will be declarative, you should include a sprinkling of the other types. Of course, in dialogue there will likely be more variation of sentence types than in formal compositions. By contrast, a formal composition should have a greater variation of word order. Be careful not to overuse mixed and inverted word order, or your paragraphs will sound unnatural. As you read good literature, you will develop sentence sense to help you understand what makes good sentence variety.

Read the following paragraph, noting the variety of sentence types and word order.

Learning takes diligent effort. When you read informative books and when you listen to your teacher, knowledge comes to your mind.

d. Use exclamatory sentences sparingly so that when you do use them, they truly express strong feeling.

5. In natural word order, the complete subject precedes the complete predicate.

6. In inverted word order, the complete predicate precedes the complete subject.
a. A comma should not separate the complete predicate from the complete subject.
b. No sentence with an object complement can be written with inverted order.

7. In mixed word order, the complete subject comes between two parts of the complete predicate. A comma often comes before the subject, especially if a long adverb phrase or an adverb clause begins the sentence.

8. Varying sentence types and word order adds freshness and emphasis.
a. Although most of your sentences will be declarative, you should include a sprinkling of the other types.
b. In dialogue there will likely be more variation of sentence types than in formal compositions.
c. A formal composition should have a greater variation of word order.
d. Be careful not to overuse mixed and inverted word order, or your paragraphs will sound unnatural.
e. As you read good literature, you will develop sentence sense to help you understand what makes good sentence variety.

With each bit of knowledge comes a choice. Will you be like a person with his hands in his pockets? If you do not concentrate, that is what your mind is like. But God created your mind for a nobler purpose! Reach out, eager to learn and determined to keep what you learn.

Most of the sentences in the paragraph are declarative, but the other three types are also included. Some sentences are in natural word order; others are inverted or mixed. There is a good balance of short and long sentences. These things together produce a variety that helps to make the paragraph pleasant to read.

Class Practice

A. Tell which of the four sentence types and which of the three kinds of word order are used in each sentence. There is no end punctuation.
   1. Look up at the starry night sky
   2. When you see that splendor, how do you feel
   3. You should feel very small
   4. How very great is our God
   5. Certainly He deserves our praise and worship

B. Change the following sentences according to the directions in parentheses.
   1. Isaac and Rebekah sent Jacob to Padan-aram because they wanted him to get a wife from his mother's relatives. (Divide into two sentences, the first interrogative and the second declarative.)
   2. Twenty years later he returned to Canaan. He was afraid when Esau came to meet him with four hundred men. (Change one sentence to exclamatory.)
   3. This story has many important lessons for us. You should read it carefully. (Change one sentence to imperative.)

C. Change each sentence to the order specified in parentheses. Tell where any commas should be added.
   1. You should develop good study habits before you grow any older. (mixed)
   2. Many blessings of good study habits come to the diligent student. (inverted)
   3. As a faithful child of God, you will want to study the Bible. (natural)
   4. You may need to study technical manuals for your occupation. (mixed)
   5. A flock of white snow geese flew directly overhead. (inverted)
   6. A large flock of Canada geese overtook them swiftly and steadily. (mixed)
   7. As we watched, the Canada geese passed between us and the snow geese. (natural)
   8. Obviously the cold winter months are approaching. (natural)

Lesson 11 Answers

Class Practice

A. 1. imperative, natural
    2. interrogative, mixed
    3. declarative, natural
    4. exclamatory, inverted
    5. declarative, mixed

B. 1. Why did Isaac and Rebekah send Jacob to Padan-aram? They wanted him to get a wife from his mother's relatives.
    2. Twenty years later he returned to Canaan. How afraid he was when Esau came to meet him with four hundred men!
    3. This story has many important lessons for us. Read it carefully.

C. 1. Before you grow any older, you should develop good study habits.
    2. To the diligent student come many blessings of good study habits.
    3. You will want to study the Bible as a faithful child of God.
    4. For your occupation, you may need to study technical manuals.
    5. Directly overhead flew a flock of white snow geese.
    6. Swiftly and steadily, a large flock of Canada geese overtook them.
    7. The Canada geese passed between us and the snow geese as we watched.
    8. The cold winter months are obviously approaching.

Written Exercises

A. Label each sentence *dec.* (declarative), *int.* (interrogative), *imp.* (imperative), or *exc.* (exclamatory). There is no end punctuation.
1. If we want God's blessing, we must choose to do right
2. How easy it is sometimes to choose what is less than the best
3. The happiest people are always those who have a clear conscience
4. Have you found this to be true
5. Shun evil as you would shun a deadly poison

B. Write whether the word order of each sentence is natural (*N*), inverted (*I*), or mixed (*M*).
1. Into its hole scurried the little mouse.
2. As its tail disappeared, an owl's talons hit the dirt at the edge of the hole.
3. The hungry owl circled to a nearby tree and waited a long time.
4. Cautiously the mouse's nose tested the air.
5. Out into the night air inched the mouse.

C. Rewrite these sentences according to the directions in parentheses.
1. Delbert, your paper is too sloppy. You must use your eraser more faithfully. (Change one sentence to imperative.)
2. The three kings of Israel before the division were Saul, David, and Solomon. (Change to an interrogative sentence followed by a declarative sentence beginning with a pronoun.)
3. We found a hummingbird's nest in the lilac bush. It looked very tiny. (Reword one sentence to make it exclamatory.)

D. Change these sentences to natural word order.
1. Out of the brush ambled a skunk and her four babies.
2. As they came straight toward her, Ellen fled toward the house.
3. Soon Father had some live animal traps set for them.

E. Change some of these sentences to inverted word order and some to mixed word order. Add any needed commas. Write which order you used.
1. God has promised to hear when a person prays in true faith.
2. Many promises of answered prayers are in the Bible.
3. Strength for faithfulness is found through prayer.
4. God surely wants us to bring Him every trouble and care.
5. We should love the place of prayer.

Review Exercises

This exercise reviews things that you studied in previous grades. Use the index in the back of the book if you need help.

Copy each underlined word, and write the abbreviation for its part of speech.

Written Exercises

A. 1. dec.   4. int.
   2. exc.   5. imp.
   3. dec.

B. 1. I   4. M
   2. M   5. I
   3. N

C. (Sentences in parentheses do not need to be written.)
1. (Delbert, your paper is too sloppy.) Use your eraser more faithfully.
2. Who were the three kings of Israel before the division? They were Saul, David, and Solomon.
3. (We found a hummingbird's nest in the lilac bush.) How tiny it looked!

D. 1. A skunk and her four babies ambled out of the brush.
2. Ellen fled toward the house as they came straight toward her.
3. Father soon had some live animal traps set for them.

E. 1. When a person prays in true faith, God has promised to hear. mixed
2. In the Bible are many promises of answered prayers. inverted
3. Through prayer is found strength for faithfulness. inverted
   or Through prayer, strength for faithfulness is found. mixed
4. Surely God wants us to bring Him every trouble and care. mixed
5. The place of prayer we should love. mixed

1. God created <u>light</u> <u>before</u> He created the sun.
2. Jesus can <u>light</u> <u>each</u> man <u>that</u> comes into the world, <u>but</u> <u>some</u> reject Him.
3. The afflictions of <u>this</u> life are <u>light</u> when compared to eternal <u>glory</u>.
4. The <u>righteous</u> always <u>glory</u> in the Lord.
5. Everyone <u>but</u> Father left <u>early</u> <u>for</u> our new <u>farm</u>.
6. He came <u>later</u> with a load of <u>farm</u> equipment.
7. <u>Oh</u>, we had <u>some</u> help with the chores for a <u>few</u> days.
8. Father did not <u>farm</u> on his own <u>before</u> <u>this</u>.

---

12. Phrases and Clauses

> ### Lesson Survey
> - A **phrase** is a group of related words without a skeleton.
> - There are three kinds of phrases: prepositional phrases, verbal phrases, and phrases of a single part of speech.
> - A **clause** is a group of related words that contains a skeleton.
> - An **independent clause** expresses a complete thought and can stand alone as a sentence.
> - A **dependent clause** does not express a complete thought but must function within an independent clause.

When you first learned to read, you read haltingly, word by word. Now you read much more smoothly because your eyes take in several words at a time. Often those word groups are phrases or short clauses. For example, your eyes might take in the following sentence in groups as shown.

> The Lord Jesus Christ | has ascended | back to His heavenly glory | to reign forever.

Phrases

A *phrase* is a group of related words without a skeleton. There are three kinds of phrases: prepositional phrases, verbal phrases, and phrases of a single part of speech. A *prepositional phrase* begins with a preposition, ends with an object, and includes all the words in between. It may be used as an adjective or an adverb.

> An angel <u>of the Lord</u> appeared <u>unto Gideon</u>.
>   (*Of the Lord* is an adjective phrase that modifies *angel*. *Unto Gideon* is an adverb phrase that modifies *appeared*.)

Lesson 12

Purpose: To teach the definition and recognition of phrases and clauses.

Oral Review:

1. Give the definition and end punctuation for each of the four sentence types. (declarative—makes a statement and ends with a period; interrogative—asks a question and ends with a question mark; imperative—gives a command or request and ends with a period; exclamatory—expresses strong feeling or emotion and ends with an exclamation point)
2. Tell which kind of word order fits each description.
   a. The complete subject comes between two parts of the complete predicate. (mixed)
   b. The complete subject precedes the complete predicate. (natural)

Review Exercises

1. light—n.; before—conj.
2. light—v.; each—adj.; that—pron.; but—conj.; some—pron.
3. this—adj.; light—adj.; glory—n.
4. righteous—n.; glory—v.
5. but—prep.; early—adv.; for—prep.; farm—n.
6. later—adv.; farm—adj.
7. Oh—interj.; some—adj.; few—adj.
8. farm—v.; before—prep.; this—pron.

c. The least common word order. (inverted)
d. The complete predicate precedes the complete subject. (inverted)
e. The most common word order. (natural)
3. What two things must a speaker pay attention to in his speaking? (proper pronunciation, clear enunciation)
4. Why is writing especially valuable for preserving truth? (Writing makes it possible to preserve truth from generation to generation.)

Lesson Introduction: Read the following sentence in a halting, word-by-word manner. Then read it again by phrases and short clauses as shown.

> Paul Raymond Newswanger, | who lives next door, | has been helping | with our chores | while Father is gone.

Very little communication is done one word at a

A *verbal phrase* contains a verb form used as another part of speech. The verbal may be a gerund, a participle, or an infinitive. The verbal phrase includes the verbal and all its modifiers and complements.

1. *A gerund phrase contains an -ing form used as a noun.*

Comparing yourself with others is not wise.
(The underlined gerund phrase is the subject.)

2. *A participial phrase contains a past participle or an -ing form.* It is used as an adjective.

The coneys lying on the rocks seemed unaware of danger.
A jackal, hidden by the brush, crept closer and closer.
(The underlined participial phrases modify *coneys* and *jackal.*)

3. *An infinitive phrase contains a basic verb form preceded by* to. It is used as a noun or an adjective.

Everyone wanted to work quickly.
(The underlined infinitive phrase is the direct object.)
There was a large harvest to bring in.
(The underlined infinitive phrase modifies *harvest.*)

In a *phrase of a single part of speech,* several words work together as the same part of speech. Such a phrase is used as a noun or a verb.

Brother Linford is the minister at Alton Mennonite Church.
(The underlined parts are noun phrases.)
I have been working on this math problem for ten minutes.
(The underlined part is a verb phrase.)

The following examples show how various phrases are diagramed.

Prepositional phrases:
The stars in the sky bring glory to God. (adjective and adverb phrases)

Verbal phrases:
Working hard brings a reward. (gerund phrase)

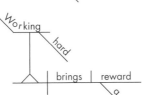

time. Rather, we express ourselves in groups of related words called phrases and clauses. These word groups are the topic of this lesson.

Lesson Outline:

1. A phrase is a group of related words without a skeleton.

2. There are three kinds of phrases: prepositional phrases, verbal phrases, and phrases of a single part of speech.

3. A clause is a group of related words that contains a skeleton.

4. An independent clause expresses a complete thought and can stand alone as a sentence.

5. A dependent clause does not express a complete thought but must function within an independent clause.

Paul wanted <u>to visit the believers in Rome</u>. (infinitive phrase)

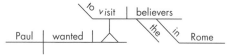

We watched the goats <u>frisking outside</u>. (participial phrase)

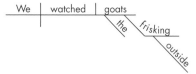

Phrases as single parts of speech:

<u>Uncle Ira</u> owns <u>Country Produce</u>. (noun phrases)

We <u>were building</u> a new shop. (verb phrase)

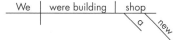

Clauses

A *clause* is a group of related words that contains a skeleton. An *independent clause* expresses a complete thought and can stand alone as a complete sentence. Every simple sentence is actually an independent clause, but this term is generally used only when a sentence has more than one clause. Study the following sentences, in which the independent clauses are italicized and the skeletons are underlined.

> *Ralph <u>sprained</u> his ankle.* (simple sentence: one independent clause)
> *Ralph <u>sprained</u> his ankle* when <u>he</u> <u>fell</u> on the ice.
> (second clause is a dependent adverb clause)
> *Ralph <u>sprained</u> his ankle,* and *<u>he</u> <u>is resting</u> on the couch.*
> (compound sentence: two independent clauses)

A *dependent clause* does not express a complete thought but must function within an independent clause. Like a phrase, a dependent clause functions as a single part of speech. It may be used as a noun, an adjective, or an adverb. The following examples show how clauses can express the same ideas as single words or phrases of these parts of speech.

Single-word noun:
Martha knew the right *answer.*

Adjective phrase:
The books *on this shelf* are old textbooks.

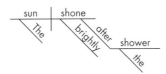

Adverb phrase:
The sun shone brightly *after the shower.*

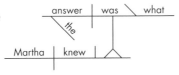

Noun clause:
Martha knew *what the answer was.*

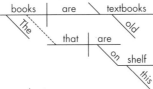

Adjective clause:
The books *that are on this shelf* are old textbooks.

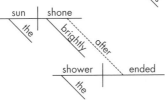

Adverb clause:
The sun shone brightly *after the shower ended.*

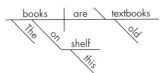

Class Practice

A. Tell whether each word group is a *phrase* or a *clause*.

1. after frost kills the plants
2. after the first hard frost
3. that work is finished now
4. standing beside the fence
5. to dig the rest of the potatoes
6. that we bought last year
7. because of the sudden storm
8. what we did not know

B. Tell whether each underlined phrase is a *prepositional phrase*, a *verbal phrase*, or a phrase of a *single part of speech*. Also give its function: *noun, verb, adjective,* or *adverb.*

1. The <u>Lord God</u> reigns <u>from His heavenly throne</u>.
2. The angels <u>of God</u>, <u>doing the Father's will</u>, encamp around the saints.
3. We <u>can claim</u> the promise <u>of God's protection</u>.
4. We <u>should seek</u> <u>to live under God's blessing</u>.

C. Tell whether the underlined clauses are *independent* or *dependent*.

1. This is the day <u>that the Lord has made</u>.
2. <u>Because God has so graciously blessed us</u>, we give Him our praise.
3. <u>Daily He loads us with benefits</u>, yet we often fail to thank Him.
4. The person <u>who cultivates a thankful attitude</u> brings praise to God.
5. Not only does this bring praise to God, but also <u>the thankful person brings joy to himself</u>.

D. Tell whether each underlined dependent clause functions as a *noun,* an *adjective,* or an *adverb.*

1. "Blessed is that man <u>that maketh the Lord his trust</u>."
2. "By this I know <u>that thou favourest me</u>."
3. "<u>As the hart panteth after the water brooks</u>, so panteth my soul after thee, O God."
4. "Our God . . . hath done <u>whatsoever he hath pleased</u>."
5. "I will sing praise to my God <u>while I have my being</u>."
6. "The stone <u>which the builders refused</u> is become the head stone of the corner."

Written Exercises

A. Label each word group *P* (phrase) or *C* (clause).

1. until the first day of April
2. until spring arrives
3. wherever we go
4. will have been started
5. under the stack of papers
6. Brother William has arrived
7. crackling in the fireplace
8. which Father had made
9. to mow Grandfather's lawn
10. asking meaningful questions

B. Copy the phrases indicated by the notes in parentheses. Label each one *n.* (noun), *v.* (verb), *adj.* (adjective), or *adv.* (adverb).

Lesson 12 Answers

Class Practice

A.
1. clause
2. phrase
3. clause
4. phrase
5. phrase
6. clause
7. phrase
8. clause

B.
1. single part of speech—noun; prepositional phrase—adverb
2. prepositional phrase—adjective; verbal phrase—adjective
3. single part of speech—verb; prepositional phrase—adjective
4. single part of speech—verb; verbal phrase—noun

C.
1. dependent
2. dependent
3. independent
4. dependent
5. independent

D.
1. adjective
2. noun
3. adverb
4. noun
5. adverb
6. adjective

Written Exercises

A.
1. P
2. C
3. C
4. P
5. P
6. C
7. P
8. C
9. P
10. P

1. In the Bahamas, summer temperatures rise high during the summer. (two prepositional phrases)
2. The sun's rays, striking the earth almost directly, are oppressive. (verbal phrase)
3. Therefore gardening must be done over the winter months. (phrase of a single part of speech)
4. We planted a grove of mango trees behind the house. (two prepositional phrases)
5. Driving in the left lane seems very strange at first. (verbal phrase)
6. When did Brother Heatwole arrive? (two phrases of a single part of speech)
7. We tried to ignore the swarms of mosquitoes. (verbal phrase)
8. By next month my parents will have been married for twenty years. (phrase of a single part of speech)

C. Copy the independent clause in each sentence.
1. Lazarus, who suffered much in this life, is now enjoying eternal life.
2. Because the rich man was proud and selfish, he is now suffering eternal death.
3. Since this is such a beautiful day, we plan to take a hike in Brother Yoder's woods.
4. We were pleasantly surprised when Brother Yoder met us at the edge of the woods.
5. Since he knows many things about plants, he made our hike especially interesting.

D. Copy each dependent clause, and label it *n.* (noun), *adj.* (adjective), or *adv.* (adverb).
1. Jesus taught that the way of true greatness is the way of humility.
2. Those who humble themselves will be exalted.
3. Whoever would follow the Lord must walk in humility.
4. If a person is truly humble, he is not overly concerned about himself.
5. We should pattern our lives after Jesus, who is the supreme example of humility.
6. The humble person's desire is always that he might serve others.
7. Although everyone enjoys the friendship of humble people, not everyone enjoys being humble.
8. This is true because humility is not native to our hearts.

Review Exercises

Copy each complement, and label it *PN* (predicate nominative), *PA* (predicate adjective), *DO* (direct object), *IO* (indirect object), or *OC* (objective complement). [5–8]

B. 1. In the Bahamas—adv.;
      during the summer—adv.
   2. striking the earth almost directly—adj.
   3. must be done—v.
   4. of mango trees—adj.; behind the house—adv.
   5. Driving in the left lane—n.
   6. Brother Heatwole—n.; did arrive—v.
   7. to ignore the swarms of mosquitoes—n.
   8. will have been married—v.

C. 1. Lazarus is now enjoying eternal life
   2. he is now suffering eternal death
   3. we plan to take a hike in Brother Yoder's woods
   4. We were pleasantly surprised
   5. he made our hike especially interesting

D. 1. that the way of true greatness is the way of humility—n.
   2. who humble themselves—adj.
   3. Whoever would follow the Lord—n.
   4. If a person is truly humble—adv.
   5. who is the supreme example of humility—adj.
   6. that he might serve others—n.
   7. Although everyone enjoys the friendship of humble people—adv.
   8. because humility is not native to our hearts—adv.

1. The sky has been overcast all afternoon.
2. A soaking rain will give the gardens a boost.
3. The showers have washed the earth clean.
4. The sun warmed the earth and brightened the day.
5. The flowers in this bed are marigolds and zinnias.
6. They look bright and cheerful in the morning sun.

13. Paragraph Unity and Topic Sentences

Lesson Survey

- A **paragraph** is an organized unit of thought.
- The main idea of a paragraph is usually stated in a **topic sentence.**
- A paragraph has **unity** when every sentence supports and develops the topic sentence.
- Paragraphs vary in length according to the number of words and sentences needed to develop the topic.

Can you imagine reading a story or an essay that has no paragraph divisions? Line after line and page after page would consist of an unbroken series of sentences. If you glanced away from the page, how would you find your place again? Worse yet, how would you follow the writer's train of thought as he progresses from one idea to another?

Of course, the stories and essays you read are divided into paragraphs. A *paragraph* is an organized unit of thought. In a properly written composition, each paragraph division shows where one thought ends and another begins. In this way a large composition is divided into manageable segments, and the reader can digest each unit of thought before moving on to the next paragraph.

Topic Sentences

The main idea of a paragraph is usually stated in a *topic sentence.* In most paragraphs the topic sentence is the very first sentence, but it may also be in the middle or at the end of the paragraph. The following paragraphs show topic sentences in various positions.

The grace of contentment is an effective antidote against many sins. When a person's heart is filled with contentment, the complaining

Review Exercises

1. overcast—PA
2. gardens—IO; boost—DO
3. earth—DO; clean—OC
4. earth—DO; day—DO
5. marigolds—PN; zinnias—PN
6. bright—PA; cheerful—PA

Lesson 13

Purpose: To study topic sentences and their use in unifying paragraphs.

Oral Review:

1. Name the five parts of a friendly letter. (heading, greeting, body, closing, signature)
2. What is another term for the greeting of a business letter? (salutation)
3. *(a)* What additional part does a business letter have? *(b)* Where is it placed? (*a.* inside address; *b.* at the left-hand margin, between the heading and the salutation)
4. What are the three C's of business letter content? (courteous, clear, concise)
5. When writing a note of invitation, what details should you state clearly? (what, when, where, any plans that call for special preparation)

Lesson Introduction: When you eat your lunch, you do not stuff the whole meal into your mouth at once. You would have a terrible time trying to chew and swallow your food; in fact, you would probably choke! Rather, you take a mouthful at a time, and thus you eat your meal decently.

A composition is much like a meal. It presents not food but ideas for the reader to chew and digest in his mind. To keep the reader from having to stuff the entire composition into his mind at one time, we divide it into bite-size parts. Paragraphs are the mouthfuls that enable a reader to take in the whole composition piece by piece.

Lesson Outline:

1. A paragraph is an organized unit of thought.

spirit cannot grow. Nor can covetousness spread its poison in the heart of one who nurtures the healthful influence of contentment. Can you imagine a contented person boasting, being jealous, or acting selfishly? Of course not! Contentment occupies a person's heart with gracious and noble attitudes.

What makes your hand jerk away so quickly when you touch a hot object? This is a reflex action produced by certain special nerve cells. The nerve cells in your eyes and ears pick up information about the world around you. Other nerve cells carry these bits of information to your brain, where still other nerve cells interpret them. <u>Obviously, God designed the nervous system to fill a vital role in our bodies.</u> Perhaps the greatest example of this is the brain itself, a complex of nerves that enables us to think and reason.

When Paul wrote, "Be careful for nothing," was he suggesting that we should be careless? No; the primary meaning of *careful* has shifted from "to be anxious about" to "taking care to avoid mistakes." Another word that has changed in meaning is *let*. Paul wrote to the Christians in Rome that he had often purposed to visit them, "but was let hitherto." According to modern English usage, this sounds as if Paul had been permitted to go; but he was actually saying that he had been prevented from going. <u>Many such changes in English word meanings have occurred since the King James Bible was translated.</u>

A topic sentence should be specific, without giving too many details. It should focus on exactly what the paragraph is to tell about. Even if the topic sentence comes at the end of the paragraph, you should write it down first. Otherwise the paragraph is likely to ramble aimlessly. On the other hand, the topic sentence should not give too many details, or the rest of the sentences become unnecessary. Look again at the example paragraph about the nervous system above. Can you see why the following sentences would not make good topic sentences?

Obviously, God has given the nervous system a complex design. (does not focus on what the paragraph is about)
God has given the nervous system the vital roles of producing reflex actions, picking up information through the senses, and enabling us to think and reason. (gives too many details)

Some paragraphs have no topic sentences. This is especially true of narrative paragraphs and paragraphs of dialogue. As you read the following paragraphs, you can easily understand the topic of each one even though it is not expressed in a topic sentence.

2. The main idea of a paragraph is usually stated in a topic sentence.
    a. The topic sentence is usually at the beginning, but it may also be in the middle or at the end.
    b. A topic sentence should be specific, without giving too many details.
    c. Some paragraphs, especially in narrative writing, have no topic sentences.

3. A paragraph has unity when every sentence supports and develops the topic sentence.
    a. Include only one main idea in a paragraph.
    b. Remove any sentence that does not directly support the topic sentence.

4. Paragraphs vary in length according to the number of words and sentences needed to develop the topic.
    a. A good average length is sixty to one hundred words.
    b. Longer paragraphs can probably be divided into two or more paragraphs.
    c. Too many short paragraphs make a choppy composition.

★ **EXTRA PRACTICE**
Worksheet 5 *(Paragraph Unity and Topic Sentences)*

"Now that should hold you over until you can eat one of Mother's *real* breakfasts," Father remarked.

"Thank you, Father," the boys replied in unison as the pickup headed again for Uncle Lewis's farm.

White wisps of fog lay in ghostly ribbons across the road. As they rounded the sharp corner near the narrow bridge that spanned Big Coon Creek, the truck was suddenly swallowed in a wall of whiteness. Father hit the brakes and the dimmer switch for the headlights at the same time. Visibility was zero.

"Father!" Carl exclaimed, while Jonathan gave a startled gasp.

Unity

A paragraph has *unity* when every sentence supports and develops the topic sentence. In order to achieve paragraph unity, you must remove any sentence that fails to do this. A sentence may fit well with the sentence just before it; but if it does not develop the topic of the whole paragraph, it does not belong. Each sentence *must* contribute to the topic of the whole paragraph.

Paragraph unity also depends on proper paragraph divisions. Every paragraph, whether short or long, must be a single unit of thought. If you follow a well-planned outline, this usually is not a problem. But you should still evaluate each paragraph to be certain that it contains only one main idea.

The following selection should be divided into two paragraphs. Read it carefully to decide where the second paragraph should begin. Also find the sentence that should be deleted because it does not directly support the topic sentence.

[1]When life seems to go wrong, Satan tempts us to react in various ways. [2]He may tempt us merely to tell other people, who really cannot help us, instead of casting our burdens on the Lord. [3]Another of his clever tricks is to make the swamp of self-pity look like an inviting place to wallow in. [4]Is not the tendency to complain also a common reaction? [5]How often we are tempted to blame others for our problems or to envy others' successes! [6]Satan may even get us to think we should sit down and do nothing at all until life gets better. [7]How then should we respond to life's difficult times? [8]First, we should cast all our cares on the Lord because He always cares for us. [9]We should remember to thank Him when life is going well for us. [10]We should also look at the bright side of life. [11]If some things are going wrong, surely others are going right. [12]Another good response is to get our minds off ourselves and take an interest in others and their needs. [13]This is one of the surest ways to make our own problems shrink. [14]Finally, we should remember that no earthly trouble lasts forever; this, too, will pass away.

You should see that sentences 1–6 develop the topic stated in sentence 1. The question of sentence 7 is the topic of the second paragraph. However, sentence 9 fails to develop that topic. It refers to life going well, not life going wrong. So this detail does not belong in this paragraph.

Paragraphs vary in length according to the number of words and sentences needed to develop the topic. A good average paragraph length for your compositions is sixty to one hundred words. You should divide most paragraphs that are longer than that into two or more paragraphs that are more easily understood. However, if too many paragraphs are much shorter than that, you will have a choppy composition.

Class Practice

A. Tell which sentence is the topic sentence of each paragraph. Also tell which sentences in numbers 1 and 2 should be deleted.

1.   There are various types of so-called movable joints. The jaw, knee, elbow, finger, and toe joints are the hinge type. The shoulders and hips have ball-and-socket joints. They allow much freedom of movement. The joints of the neck are pivotal joints. Immovable joints connect the bones of the skull. Gliding joints are found between the back vertebrae and in the ankles. These allow one bone to slide over another.

2.   Muscles can exert only the force of contraction. Therefore, muscles cannot push; they can only pull. Since bones need to move both ways, God has provided for two-way movement. He has arranged bones to form levers and has placed muscles in pairs to operate those levers. For example, the muscle called the biceps, on the front of the upper arm, causes the lower arm to bend inward. A muscle called the triceps, on the back of the upper arm, causes the lower arm to straighten again. The biceps is a much larger muscle than the triceps.

3.   Perhaps in studying the body part by part, we will miss noticing the unity of the body. The systems of the body are not only dependent upon each other but also interconnected with each other. For example, every system has blood vessels of the circulatory system running through it. Also the nervous system is connected to all other systems. Both the skeletal and the muscular system would be useless if they did not have each other.

4.   The digestive system needs the oxygen provided by the respiratory system; the respiratory system in turn needs the food prepared by the digestive system. Both systems must have their nitrogen wastes removed by the kidneys. The kidneys, in turn, need both food and oxygen. And so it is throughout the entire body. Each part unselfishly gives what it can to the body and in turn receives services from the other parts.

Lesson 13 Answers

Class Practice

A. 1. *Topic sentence:* There are various types of so-called movable joints.
      Sentence to delete: Immovable joints connect the bones of the skull.
   2. *Topic sentence:* Since bones need to move both ways, God has provided for two-way movement.
      Sentence to delete: The biceps is a much larger muscle than the triceps.
   3. *Topic sentence:* The systems of the body are not only dependent upon each other but also interconnected with each other.
   4. *Topic sentence:* Each part unselfishly gives what it can to the body and in turn receives services from the other parts.

B. Tell which sentence in each pair would make a good topic sentence. Also tell what is wrong with the other one.
1. a. The Bible mentions standing, kneeling, and lying prostrate as proper postures for prayer.
   b. The Bible mentions various postures for prayer.
2. a. The New Testament provides greater privileges than the Old.
   b. The New Testament is different from the Old in many ways.
3. a. The names of North American rivers are derived from many different sources.
   b. North American rivers have many different names.

C. Read the selection below, and do the following exercises.
1. Read the sentence that should begin the second paragraph.
2. Read the topic sentence of each paragraph.
3. Read the sentence that mars the unity of the first paragraph.
   A material that is transparent allows light to pass through in an orderly manner. Since the light passes straight through, you can see objects through it clearly. Air, water, glass, and some kinds of plastic are common transparent materials. However, many plastics are opaque. Not every material that allows light to pass through is transparent. When light passes through a translucent material, it is scattered. This scattering of light rays through a translucent material permits you to see light but not any clear images. Clouds, milk, frosted glass, and some kinds of plastics are translucent.

Written Exercises

A. Write the letter of the sentence in each pair that would make a good topic sentence.
1. a. The buildup of static electricity can be discouraged.
   b. High humidity, warm temperatures, and grounding can discourage the buildup of static electricity.
2. a. Concave and convex lenses are interesting to study.
   b. There are several important differences between concave and convex lenses.
3. a. The Bible teaches us many practical things.
   b. The Bible gives us practical direction on the use of the tongue.

B. Read the selection below, and do these exercises.
1. Copy the sentence that should begin the second paragraph.
2. Copy the topic sentence of each paragraph.
3. Copy the sentence that mars the unity of each paragraph.
   The octopus catches much of its food by stealth. Since it does most of its hunting by night, its large eyes are designed to see well in the dim

B. 1. b; *a* gives too many details
   2. a; *b* is too broad
   3. a; *b* is too broad

C. 1. Not every material that allows light to pass through is transparent.
   2. *Paragraph 1:* A material that is transparent allows light to pass through in an orderly manner.
   Paragraph 2: When light passes through a translucent material, it is scattered.
   3. However, many plastics are opaque.

Written Exercises

A. 1. a
   2. b
   3. b

B. 1. The octopus not only hunts for food but also is hunted as food by other creatures.
   2. *Paragraph 1:* The octopus catches much of its food by stealth.
   Paragraph 2: God has given the octopus various means of defense against these enemies.
   3. *Paragraph 1:* If a tentacle is cut off, the octopus can grow a new one.
   Paragraph 2: The nerve poison is also used to stun the prey it catches.

underwater world. Furthermore, the octopus can rapidly change color to blend in with its surroundings. As some unsuspecting prey passes by, the camouflaged octopus suddenly sweeps out a tentacle and drags the prey to its powerful jaws. If a tentacle is cut off, the octopus can grow a new one. The octopus not only hunts for food but also is hunted as food by other creatures. God has given the octopus various means of defense against these enemies. Its camouflaging ability makes it nearly invisible to both its predators and its prey. Two other powerful defenses are its strong tentacles and a nerve poison that it can secrete. The nerve poison is also used to stun the prey it catches. In addition, the octopus can shoot out a cloud of black ink to disorient its predators. This black cloud contains a secretion that dulls the attacker's sense of smell. Finally, the octopus can shoot out a jet of water and escape from predators in a great burst of speed.

C. The following paragraphs do not have topic sentences. Write a suitable topic sentence for each one.

1.   The Bible does not give the actual height of this giant, but Deuteronomy 3:11 tells us that his bedstead was 4 cubits wide and 9 cubits long. That comes to 6 feet by 13½ feet! Og was among the Amorites killed by the Israelites when they conquered the land east of the Jordan River.

2.   He read Ezekiel 35:6, which contains the following words: "Sith thou hast not hated blood, even blood shall pursue thee." The boy pointed this out to his father, who had told him that the Bible contains no errors. Of course his father told him that it was no mistake; *sith* is merely an old form of *since*. And even if it had been a printing error, the Bible itself will always be the perfect, eternal Word of God.

3.   The number of dollars and cents is still the same, but the money no longer buys as much as it did before. In some countries, inflation has been so severe that it took a bag full of money to buy a bag full of groceries! One cause of inflation is people's loss of confidence in the money that their government produces.

Review Exercises

A. Write a thank-you note. Use your home address and today's date in the heading.

B. Write a business letter to order the following materials. Use your home address and today's date in the heading.

    One copy of each of these books: *The Lim Family of Singapore,* #2308, for $9.25; *The Man in Bearskin,* #6295, for $4.35; and *More*

C. (Sample answers.)

1. Og must have been a huge man.
2. Once there was a boy who thought he had found a mistake in the Bible.
3. Inflation takes place when money becomes less valuable.

Review Exercises

A. (Individual work.)

B. (Sample business letter.)

[Student's address and date]

Rod and Staff Publishers, Inc.
P.O. Box 3
Crockett, KY 41413–0003

Dear Sirs:

    Please send me one copy of each of these books: *The Lim Family of Singapore,* #2308, for $9.25; *The Man in Bearskin,* #6295, for $4.35; and *More Than Gold,* #2565, for $8.00. I am enclosing a check for $21.60. Thank you.

Very truly yours,
[Student's signature]
[Student's printed name]

Than Gold, #2565, for $8.00. You are enclosing a check for $21.60 for your order. The receiver's name and address is Rod and Staff Publishers, Inc., P.O. Box 3, Crockett, Kentucky 41413–0003.

_____

14. Simple and Compound Sentences

> **Lesson Survey**
> - A **simple sentence** contains one independent clause.
> - A **compound sentence** contains two or more independent clauses.

Sentences are classified into four types according to their structure: simple, compound, complex, and compound-complex. In this lesson you will study simple and compound sentences. In Lesson 15 you will study complex sentences, and in Lesson 16 you will learn about compound-complex sentences.

Simple Sentences

A *simple sentence* contains one independent clause. It may have a compound subject or verb, or it may have any number of phrases that may appear to include a skeleton. But if it has only one skeleton, the sentence is simple. Notice how this is true in the following examples.

Noah believed God's warning of divine judgment.

(one obvious skeleton)

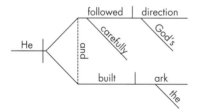

He carefully followed God's direction and built the ark.
(one skeleton with a compound verb)

Lesson 14

Purpose: To study simple and compound sentences.

Oral Review:

1. What is the main difference between a phrase and a clause? (A clause has a skeleton, but a phrase does not.)
2. What are the two classes of clauses, and what is the difference between them? (An independent clause expresses a complete thought and can stand alone as a complete sentence. A dependent clause is used as a single part of speech.)
3. Tell which kind of word order is used in each sentence.
   a. In his dream Jacob saw a ladder reaching to heaven. (mixed)
   b. Up and down this ladder went the angels of God. (inverted)
   c. God stood at the top of the ladder. (natural)

Lesson Introduction: Read the following paragraph to the class.

> One bold kitten stepped out of the nest. The other four cowered in the corner. The mother cat had caught a mouse. She was calling them all out.

Does this sound like an eighth grader's writing? Why not? (It is too choppy.) Does this sound better?

> One bold kitten stepped out of the nest, but the other four cowered in the corner. The mother cat had caught a mouse, and she was calling them all out.

Noah and his family obeyed God and found safety in Him.
(one skeleton with a compound subject and a compound verb)

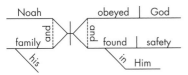

The whole world, completely ignoring God, perished in the Flood.
(one skeleton with a verbal phrase and a prepositional phrase)

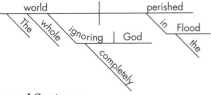

Compound Sentences

In contrast to a simple sentence, a *compound sentence* contains two or more independent clauses. These clauses are usually joined by a comma and a coordinating conjunction such as *and, but, or, for, nor, so,* or *yet.* But sometimes the clauses are very short and closely related, and the comma is omitted.

The two independent clauses may also be joined by a semicolon, without any conjunction. And occasionally they are joined by a semicolon and a conjunctive adverb such as *therefore, moreover,* or *nevertheless.* When this is done, a comma usually follows the conjunctive adverb.

Study the following sentences. The adverb *however* is included on the fourth diagram to show that it is primarily an adverb, not a conjunction.

Joined by a comma and a conjunction:
Jesus prayed in great agony, but the disciples slept.

Joined by a conjunction without a comma:
Jesus prayed but the disciples slept.

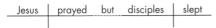

Joined by a semicolon:
Jesus prayed in great agony; the disciples slept.

The second paragraph uses compound sentences, which combine related ideas in a more readable arrangement.

Lesson Outline:

1. A simple sentence contains one independent clause. It may have compound parts or any number of phrases, but it has only one skeleton.

2. A compound sentence contains two or more independent clauses.

   a. The clauses may be joined by a comma and a coordinating conjunction, by only a coordinating conjunction (if the clauses are very short and closely related), by a semicolon, or by a semicolon and a conjunctive adverb.

   b. The clauses of a compound sentence must be related in a sensible way, and they must be worthy of equal emphasis.

Joined by a semicolon and a conjunctive adverb:
Jesus prayed in great agony; however, the disciples slept.

Three clauses joined by commas and a conjunction:
Ada took down the old display, Iva put up a new background, and May cut out new letters.

| Ada | took | display | Iva | put | background | and | May | cut | letters |

Of course, you cannot join every pair of independent clauses into a compound sentence. The clauses must be related in a sensible way, and they must be worthy of equal emphasis.

Weak: Clauses not well related
This morning we picked five bushels of beans, and it was the largest picking so far.
Improved: Unrelated clauses separated
This morning we picked five bushels of beans. It was the largest picking so far.
Weak: Clauses should not receive equal emphasis
A sudden storm came up, and we had to finish picking the tomatoes later.
Improved: One clause changed to an adverb clause
Because a sudden storm came up, we had to finish picking the tomatoes later.

Class Practice

A. Tell whether each sentence is *simple* or *compound.* Then on the chalkboard, diagram the skeletons, complements, and conjunctive adverbs.
1. Our actions and attitudes should express an interest in godliness.
2. "Rebellion is as the sin of witchcraft, and stubbornness is as iniquity and idolatry."
3. A rebellious person resists authority; indeed, he despises the thought of submission.
4. A submissive person understands the need for direction and respects the authority over him.
5. We watched the beautiful display of the northern lights, flashing their brilliant colors on the night sky.
6. Streaks of green and yellow blazed overhead, great balls of red

Lesson 14 Answers

Class Practice

A. 1. simple

2. compound

| Rebellion | is | and | stubbornness | is |

3. compound

4. simple

understands	need
person	
respects	authority

5. simple

| We | watched | display |

6. compound

| Streaks | blazed | balls | radiated | and | flashes | lit | s |

radiated from a point near the North Star, and flashes of various colors lit the sky.

7. The little brown rabbit peered out from the briers, twitched his nose nervously, and finally hopped out into the open.

8. Suddenly the rabbit hopped under cover again; in the same instant a hawk whizzed past the spot.

B. Tell how to correct these sentences. If a sentence is correct, say *correct*.

1. A trustworthy person earns the confidence of his parents and teachers; and he will be granted more privileges and responsibilities.

2. Parents and teachers cannot trust a careless person, rather they must constantly check on his work.

3. Uncorrected carelessness in a child becomes a habit, it often hinders his entire life.

4. Industriousness is essential to true success, so you should learn to apply yourself in the small tasks of life.

5. Paying careful attention to directions is important; sometimes people do not see a job through to its finish.

6. A maturing person learns the value of work. The quality of his work shows it.

Written Exercises

A. Match each sentence below to the proper description by writing the correct letter. Then diagram the skeletons and complements.

    a. simple sentence with no compound parts

    b. simple sentence with a compound subject

    c. simple sentence with a compound predicate

    d. simple sentence with a compound subject and compound predicate

    e. compound sentence with two clauses

    f. compound sentence with three clauses

1. Father has often invited Mr. Shiffler to church, yet he never seems interested.

2. Resisting the Lord, he boldly declares his own independence.

3. Someday he will recognize his need of God and bow his knee before Him.

4. God has been merciful to him, and we are still praying for his salvation.

5. The sun and moon not only give light but also mark divisions of time.

6. Jupiter and Saturn, with their huge sizes, have a powerful force of gravity.

7. The sun beamed cheerfully around us, a gentle breeze played among the trees, and a pair of mockingbirds filled the air with song.

8. This is a beautiful day to work in the garden or in the yard.

7. simple

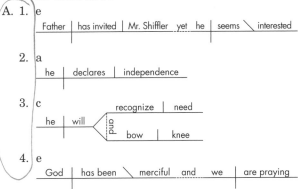

8. compound

| rabbit | hopped | | hawk | whizzed |

B. 1. teachers, and

2. person; rather,

3. habit; it *or* habit, and it

4. correct

5. important. Sometimes

6. work; the *or* work, and the

Written Exercises

A. 1. e

| Father | has invited | Mr. Shiffler | yet | he | seems \ interested |

2. a

| he | declares | independence |

3. c

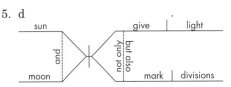

4. e

| God | has been \ merciful | and | we | are praying |

5. d

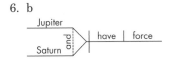

6. b

7. f

| sun | beamed | breeze | played | and | pair | filled | air |

8. a

| This | is \ day |

B. Join these choppy simple sentences into compound sentences according to the directions in parentheses.
   1. The days are becoming shorter. The leaves are taking on their brilliant autumn colors. (Use a coordinating conjunction.)
   2. The huge bear rolled the log. A feast of insects tried unsuccessfully to escape. (Use a semicolon.)
   3. We must cover the tomatoes tonight. A heavy frost may harm them. (Use a coordinating conjunction.)
   4. Everyone cooperated well. We had an enjoyable time together. (Use a semicolon and a conjunctive adverb.)

C. Find each error in these compound sentences, and write two or three words to show how the error should be corrected.
   1. A hungry cat crouched patiently at the hole, no mouse ventured forth.
   2. The sun moved out from behind the dark cloud and a beautiful rainbow arched across the sky.
   3. Sister Lena does much crocheting, indeed, she has made many lovely baby blankets.
   4. Without God we can do nothing; yet we often fail to recognize Him.
   5. God created human life, He sent His Son into the world and He daily provides for people everywhere.
   6. God has done many things for us let us continually praise His Name.

Review Exercises

A. Copy each appositive, and label it *R* for restrictive or *N* for nonrestrictive. Commas have been omitted. [9]
   1. The conscience an inner monitor of right and wrong is a gift from God the Creator.
   2. The apostle Paul had maintained a conscience void of offense.
   3. Brother Lee our Sunday school teacher read the words of the song "My Body Is God's Temple."
   4. My friend Jason plans to spend the weekend at our place.

B. Copy each independent element and the word before it, if there is one. Add any commas that are needed. [9]
   1. Behold how greatly God has loved mankind!
   2. This love we know is beyond man's comprehension.
   3. Yes our response should be to love Him.
   4. Did you know Father that the porch door is broken?
   5. It was pleasant to have Grandpa Hoover's spend the day with us.

B. (Allow reasonable variation.)
   1. The days are becoming shorter, and the leaves are taking on their brilliant autumn colors.
   2. The huge bear rolled the log; a feast of insects tried unsuccessfully to escape.
   3. We must cover the tomatoes tonight, or a heavy frost may harm them.
   4. Everyone cooperated well; indeed, we had an enjoyable time together.

C. (Allow reasonable variation.)
   1. hole; no *or* hole, but no
   2. cloud, and
   3. crocheting; indeed,
   4. nothing, yet
   5. world, and
   6. us; let

Review Exercises

A. 1. an inner monitor of right and wrong—N; the Creator—N
   2. Paul—R
   3. our Sunday school teacher—N; "My Body Is God's Temple"—R
   4. Jason—R

B. 1. Behold,
   2. love, we know,
   3. Yes,
   4. know, Father,
   5. It

15. Complex Sentences

> **Lesson Survey**
> - A **complex sentence** contains one independent clause and one or more dependent clauses.
> - The dependent clause in a complex sentence may function as an adjective, an adverb, or a noun within the independent clause.

A simple sentence expresses one main idea. A compound sentence expresses two or more related ideas and gives them equal emphasis. A complex sentence also expresses two or more related ideas, but it does not give them equal emphasis.

Because the ideas expressed in a complex sentence are not emphasized equally, such a sentence has two different kinds of clauses. The main idea in a complex sentence is expressed in an independent clause; the less important ideas are expressed in one or more dependent clauses. Thus a *complex sentence* contains one independent clause and one or more dependent clauses.

The independent clause (also called the main clause) forms the main part of a complex sentence. This clause can usually stand alone as a grammatically complete sentence. Study the following examples to see how this is true.

> <u>We love God</u> because He first loved us.
> (The main thought of this sentence is that we love God. The clause *because He first loved us* explains why.)
> <u>God sent His only begotten Son</u>, who willingly suffered for us.
> (The main thought of this sentence is that God sent His Son. The clause *who willingly suffered for us* describes *Son*.)

Notice how the two kinds of clauses are of unequal rank. A main clause can stand alone, but a dependent clause *depends* on a main clause for its meaning. The dependent clause in a complex sentence may function as an adjective, an adverb, or a noun within the independent clause.

Adjective Clauses

An adjective clause modifies a noun or pronoun in the independent clause. Usually an adjective clause begins with a *relative pronoun* (*who, whom, whose, which, that*).

> The minister <u>who preached yesterday</u> lives in Texas.
> (adjective clause telling *which* minister; *who* is a relative pronoun)

Lesson 15

Purpose: To identify and study complex sentences.

Oral Review:

1. Tell whether each of the following sentences is simple or compound.
   a. The old rooster stood on the fence post and crowed. (simple)
   b. A noisy truck rumbled up the road, and now the heifers are milling nervously around the barnyard. (compound)
   c. The three girls, each living in a different state, have not seen each other for a long time. (simple)
2. Tell which sentence type according to use each of the following is.
   a. Have you heard the meadowlark singing? (interrogative)
   b. What a beautiful song God has given this beautiful bird! (exclamatory)
   c. Marjorie, bring the binoculars here. (imperative)
   d. They are in Father's desk drawer. (declarative)
3. Tell whether each of the following items is a phrase or a clause.
   a. to follow the Lord at all times (phrase)
   b. because He understands our lives perfectly (clause)
   c. will have been studying (phrase)
   d. whose papers have been corrected (clause)

Lesson Introduction: What is complex about complex sentences? Are they hard to understand? Are they within the grasp of eighth graders, or can they be comprehended only by people of special intelligence?

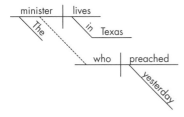

I did not know the man <u>whom he brought along</u>.
(adjective clause telling *which* man; *whom* is a relative pronoun)

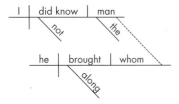

Adverb Clauses

An adverb clause usually modifies the verb of the main clause. Occasionally it modifies an adjective or adverb in the main clause. An adverb clause begins with a subordinating conjunction, which links the dependent clause to the independent clause. For a list of common subordinating conjunctions, see page 540.

I will praise my Maker <u>while I have any breath</u>.
(adverb clause telling *how long* about the verb *will praise; while* is a subordinating conjunction)

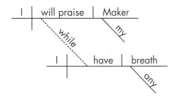

<u>When we are in heaven</u>, we shall praise God more perfectly <u>than we can do here</u>. (The first adverb clause tells *when* about the verb *shall praise; When* is a subordinating conjunction. The second adverb clause tells *to what degree* about the adverb *more*, which modifies *perfectly.*)

Simple and complex sentences do not always live up to their names. To illustrate, consider the following passage from the Bible.

> ¹Therefore leaving the principles of the doctrine of Christ, let us go on unto perfection; not laying again the foundation of repentance from dead works, and of faith toward God, ²of the doctrine of baptisms, and of laying on of hands, and of resurrection of the dead, and of eternal judgment. ³And this will we do, if God permit. (Hebrews 6:1–3)

Verses 1 and 2 are one long simple sentence. But verse 3 is a complex sentence! This shows clearly that a complex sentence is not necessarily long and hard to understand. It is merely a sentence with one independent clause and at least one dependent clause.

Lesson Outline:

1. A complex sentence contains one independent (main) clause and one or more dependent clauses. Dependent and independent clauses are of unequal rank.

2. The dependent clause in a complex sentence may function as an adjective within the independent clause.
   a. It modifies a noun or pronoun in the independent clause.
   b. It usually begins with a relative pronoun.

3. The dependent clause may function as an adverb within the independent clause.
   a. It usually modifies the verb of the main clause, but it may also modify an adjective or adverb.
   b. It begins with a subordinating conjunction.

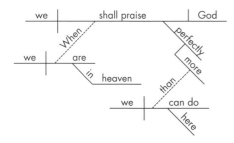

Noun Clauses

A noun clause can function as a subject, direct object, predicate nominative, or almost any other sentence part that a single-word noun can fill. A sentence with a noun clause is different from other complex sentences. Since the noun clause is an essential part of the independent clause, the independent clause is not a sensible sentence without the dependent clause.

Father said <u>that I may go along to town</u>.
   (noun clause used as direct object)

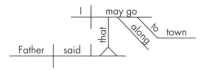

<u>Whatever made that loud noise</u> surely gave me a scare.
   (noun clause used as subject)

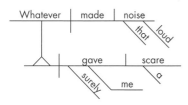

A complex sentence usually has only one adjective, adverb, or noun clause. However, it may have any combination of these clauses. As you can see, these sentences may become very complex. Then their name fits well!

4. The dependent clause may function as a noun within the independent clause.
   a. It may function as a subject, direct object, predicate nominative, or almost any other place where a single-word noun can be used.
   b. A sentence with a noun clause is unique because the noun clause is an essential part of the independent clause.

5. A complex sentence may have any combination of adjective, adverb, and noun clauses.

★ EXTRA PRACTICE
Worksheet 6 *(Complex Sentences)*

After the rain ended, the creek that flows through our meadow was flooded.

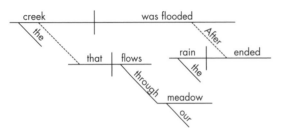

One thing that my mother often says is that forgetfulness is expensive.

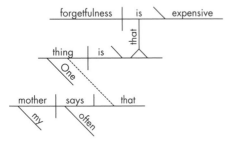

Class Practice

A. Read each adjective clause, and tell what word it modifies.
   1. The axhead that the man lost had been borrowed.
   2. God chose Joshua, whose faithfulness had been well proven, to lead Israel.
   3. Jesus, who was the rightful king of Israel, entered Jerusalem on a donkey that had never been ridden before.

B. Read each adverb clause, and tell what word it modifies.
   1. We could hardly wait until Grandfather Moyer came.
   2. Since the Martins have been serving as missionaries in Guatemala, we see them less often than we did formerly.
   3. Although I sat completely still, the little fawn never moved while I was there.

C. Read the noun clauses in these sentences, and tell what function each fills in the sentence.

Lesson 15 Answers

Class Practice

A. 1. that the man lost, axhead
   2. whose faithfulness had been well proven, Joshua
   3. who was the rightful king of Israel, Jesus; that had never been ridden before, donkey

B. 1. until Grandfather Moyer came, could wait
   2. Since the Martins have been serving as missionaries in Guatemala, see; than we did formerly, less
   3. Although I sat completely still, moved; while I was there, moved

1. Wherever God leads is where we should go.
2. Have you studied what the Bible teaches about the tongue?
3. God gives whoever truly seeks His aid the clear direction for whatever life brings.

D. On the chalkboard, diagram these sentences.
  1. When he had his tenth birthday, Grandfather Mast planted the maples that still shade the old farmhouse.
  2. His father had decided that the front lawn looked too empty.
  3. The answer that you gave was what I had expected.

Written Exercises

A. Copy the first and last word of each adjective or adverb clause, with ellipsis points in between. Label the clause *adj.* or *adv.*, and copy the word that it modifies.
  1. Although the common people heard Jesus gladly, many of the Jewish rulers hated Him.
  2. The Pharisees, who seemed intent on retaining their own power, were especially bitter against Him.
  3. The sufferings that Jesus endured were greater than we can fully comprehend.
  4. Because He loved us so greatly, He willingly endured the sufferings that evil men heaped upon Him.

B. Copy the first and last word of each noun clause, with ellipsis points in between. Label the function of the clause by writing *S* (subject), *PN* (predicate nominative), *DO* (direct object), or *OP* (object of a preposition).
  1. How we relate to the Bible determines much about our lives.
  2. We know that the Bible is God's eternal Word.
  3. Its precepts are what our lives should be guided by.
  4. The Bible supplies the answers to life's difficulties for whoever seeks its pages diligently.

C. Copy the first and last word of each dependent clause, with ellipsis points between, and write *adj.* (adjective), *adv.* (adverb), or *n.* (noun) to tell how it functions in the sentence.
  1. Although I cannot repay you, I greatly appreciate the kindness that you have shown.
  2. Have you discovered how kindness brings happiness to yourself?
  3. The joy of a person who is kind will exceed the happiness of a person who is selfish.
  4. Whoever seeks happiness from others finds discontentment instead.
  5. If you would be truly happy, you must think less about your own happiness and more about others' happiness.

C. 1. Wherever God leads—subject;
     where we should go—predicate nominative
  2. what the Bible teaches about the tongue—direct object
  3. whoever truly seeks His aid—indirect object;
     whatever life brings—object of a preposition

D. 1.

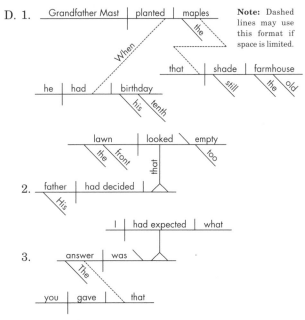

Note: Dashed lines may use this format if space is limited.

Written Exercises

A. 1. Although ... gladly—adv., hated
  2. who ... power—adj., Pharisees
  3. that ... endured—adj., sufferings;
     than ... comprehend—adv., greater
  4. Because ... greatly—adv., endured;
     that ... Him—adj., sufferings

B. 1. How ... Bible—S
  2. that ... Word—DO
  3. what ... by—PN
  4. whoever ... diligently—OP

C. 1. Although ... you—adv.; that ... shown—adj.
  2. how ... yourself—n.
  3. who ... kind—adj.; who ... selfish—adj.
  4. Whoever ... others—n.
  5. If ... happy—adv.

6. An important test of a person's character is how willing he is to help others.
7. The example of Jesus, who was always kind and helpful, is what we should follow.
8. When anyone in need appealed to Him, Jesus was ready to respond.

D. Diagram these complex sentences.
1. Although the sun was shining brightly, the breeze was chilly.
2. The geese that Grandfather has in the pasture chased the boys when they climbed over the fence.
3. As we toured the museum, we learned how people lived in pioneer days.
4. The man who takes this job must be someone who enjoys hard work.

Review Exercises

A. Write whether the word order of each sentence is natural (*N*), inverted (*I*), or mixed (*M*). [11]
1. If a man truly loves the Lord, he will obey His voice.
2. In faithful obedience is found true happiness.
3. Unfortunately, many claim to love God without obeying Him.
4. Their disobedience proves their claim to be false.

B. Rewrite each sentence in the word order named in parentheses. Add any needed commas. [11]
1. We shall likely have a frost tonight if the breeze stops blowing. (mixed)
2. The full moon appeared over the eastern horizon. (inverted)
3. By morning the ground was white with frost. (natural)
4. The smoke of a wood fire rose from the chimney. (inverted)

---

16. Compound-Complex Sentences

Lesson Survey
- A **compound-complex sentence** has two or more independent clauses and at least one dependent clause.
- The diagram of a compound-complex sentence resembles that of both a compound and a complex sentence.

When a writer wants to express one main idea in a sentence, he writes a simple sentence with one independent clause. If he wants to express two related ideas with equal emphasis, he writes a compound sentence. And if

Lesson 16

Purpose: To introduce and identify *compound-complex sentences.

Oral Review:

1. For each description, name the sentence type according to structure.
   a. It has two independent clauses. (compound)
   b. It has only one clause. (simple)
   c. It has one independent clause and at least one dependent clause. (complex)
2. For each description, name the sentence type according to use.
   a. It asks a question. (interrogative)
   b. It gives a command or request. (imperative)
   c. It makes a statement. (declarative)
   d. It expresses strong feeling or emotion. (exclamatory)

6. how ... others—n.
7. who ... helpful—adj.; what ... follow—n.
8. When ... Him—adv.

D. 1.

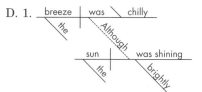

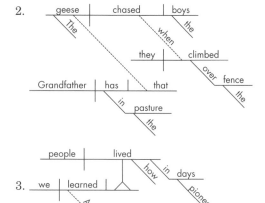

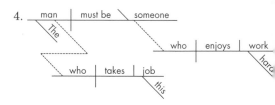

Review Exercises

A. 1. M   3. M
   2. I   4. N

B. 1. If the breeze stops blowing, we shall likely have a frost tonight.
   2. Over the eastern horizon appeared the full moon.
   3. The ground was white with frost by morning.
   4. From the chimney rose the smoke of a wood fire.

---

3. Tell which word order is described in each sentence.
   a. The complete subject comes between two parts of the complete predicate. (mixed)
   b. The complete subject comes before the complete predicate. (natural)

he wants to express two related ideas with unequal emphasis, he writes a complex sentence. You have studied these three sentence types in previous years and in the preceding two lessons.

A writer may also want to express two related ideas with equal emphasis, along with another idea of unequal emphasis. In that case he will write a *compound-complex sentence*. Such a sentence is not always as difficult as the name may suggest. It is simply a compound sentence in which at least one independent clause includes a dependent clause. The following sentences show the relationship between these four sentence types.

> **Simple:**
>> Elijah prayed earnestly. (one independent clause)
>
> **Compound:**
>> Elijah prayed earnestly, and God withheld rain for three and one-half years. (two independent clauses)
>
> **Complex:**
>> Elijah prayed earnestly that it would not rain. (one independent clause and one dependent clause)
>
> **Compound-complex:**
>> Elijah prayed earnestly that it would not rain, and God withheld rain for three and one-half years. (two independent clauses and one dependent clause)

Here are several more compound-complex sentences. The independent clauses are underlined, and the dependent clauses are in parentheses. Notice that each sentence has at least two independent clauses and at least one dependent clause.

> The presidents and princes tried to find fault with Daniel, (whom the king had promoted); but they could find nothing, for Daniel was faithful.
>
> (When God told Noah) (that the Flood was coming), Noah built an ark; and God spared him and his family.
>
> Noah earnestly warned the people, for he knew (that the Flood would surely come).

You should remember that the independent clauses of a compound sentence can be joined in three ways: by a comma and a conjunction, by a semicolon, and by a semicolon and a conjunctive adverb. This applies as well to a compound-complex sentence. However, a semicolon often replaces the comma after an independent clause if the sentence contains other commas.

> The heat, which had oppressed us all day, lessened slightly after the sun set; but no cooling breeze brought true relief.

c. The complete subject comes after the complete predicate. (inverted)

Lesson Introduction: Notice the compound word in the title of this lesson. A compound word is formed to combine the meanings of two words into one. Therefore, you should have concluded that a compound-complex sentence is like both a compound sentence and a complex sentence. This lesson describes how that is true.

Lesson Outline:

1. A compound-complex sentence has two or more independent clauses and at least one dependent clause.

   a. The independent clauses can be joined in the same three ways as the independent clauses of a compound sentence.

   b. The comma used with a coordinating conjunction is often replaced with a semicolon if the sentence contains other commas.

2. The diagram of a compound-complex sentence resembles that of both a compound and a complex sentence.

   a. Diagram the independent clauses first as you would do with any compound sentence.

   b. Diagram the dependent clause or clauses.

★ *EXTRA PRACTICE*
Worksheet 7 *(Compound-Complex Sentences)*

A compound-complex sentence is a combination of a compound sentence and a complex sentence. Therefore, the diagram of a compound-complex sentence resembles that of both a compound and a complex sentence. First diagram the independent clauses as you would do with any compound sentence. Then diagram the dependent clause or clauses.

> Since the days are getting shorter, the leaves are changing colors; soon we can expect a heavy frost.

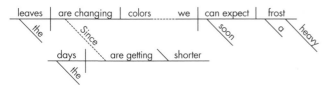

> Hidden Gap Road, which crosses Turkeyfoot Mountain, is quite narrow; but it is the main route that leads into Bear Valley.

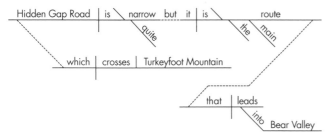

Class Practice

A. Read each clause, and tell whether it is *independent* or *dependent*.
  1. "He that is our God is the God of salvation; and unto God the Lord belong the issues from death."
  2. Even an adult still needs to submit to authority; indeed, no one ever grows so mature that he no longer needs to submit.
  3. Some people obey just enough to avoid punishment, but a submissive person obeys because he wants to please the Lord.
  4. "The Lord shall give that which is good; and our land shall yield her increase."

B. Tell whether each sentence in this paragraph is *simple, compound, complex,* or *compound-complex.* On the chalkboard, diagram the

Lesson 16 Answers

Class Practice

A. (Independent clauses are underlined; dependent clauses are in parentheses.)
  1. He (that is our God) is the God of salvation; and unto God the Lord belong the issues from death.
  2. Even an adult still needs to submit to authority; indeed, no one ever grows so mature (that he no longer needs to submit).
  3. Some people obey just enough to avoid punishment, but a submissive person obeys (because he wants to please the Lord).
  4. The Lord shall give that (which is good); and our land shall yield her increase.

B. 1. complex

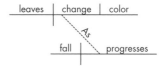

  2. simple

  3. complex

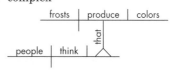

skeletons and complements of all the clauses.

¹As fall progresses, the leaves of many trees change color. ²What are the causes of these color changes? ³Some people think that frosts produce the colors. ⁴Cold weather does add some brilliance, but that is only part of the story. ⁵The main cause is the death of the cell layer between each leaf and its branch. ⁶Sap no longer flows into the leaves; the green chlorophyll breaks down; and the various colors, which were present ever since spring, become visible.

Written Exercises

A. Diagram the skeletons and complements of all the clauses in these compound-complex sentences.

1. Because God is glorious in majesty, He deserves the praise of all men; yet many people ignore Him.
2. Those who glorify God in this life enjoy His blessing, and they will share His eternal glory in heaven.
3. As we rise to each new day, we should praise God; and we should lift our hearts to Him again in the evening.
4. The sunlight that filtered through the thick leaves made interesting patterns on the trail, but it could not brighten the jungle very much.
5. A parrot squawked from a nearby tree, and a pair of monkeys capered among the branches as we watched.

B. Diagram the skeletons and complements of all the clauses in these sentences. There are two of each of the four kinds of sentences according to structure.

1. We should strive for improvement in our work; but if we are striving against another person, wrong attitudes have filled our minds.
2. Jealousy and pride are not good motives for diligence.
3. Those who compare themselves among themselves are not wise.
4. Competition then becomes the main goal, and the goal of personal improvement is pushed into the background.
5. Paul preached the Gospel at Philippi.
6. The Lord opened Lydia's heart, and she listened to the Word.
7. Her entire household was baptized when they received the Gospel.
8. Because she was grateful to the missionaries, Lydia constrained them to stay at her house; and they accepted her offer.

C. Match each sentence below to the proper description by writing the correct letter.
   a. simple sentence with no compound parts
   b. simple sentence with a compound predicate

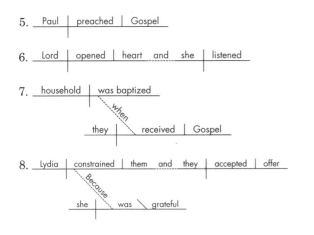

(Numbers 1–3 are on page 84.)

4. compound

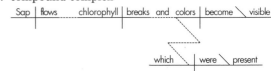

5. simple

6. compound-complex

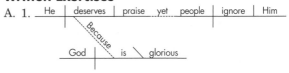

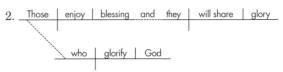

Written Exercises

A. 1.

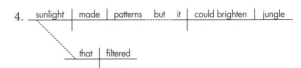

2.

3.

4.

5.

B. 1.

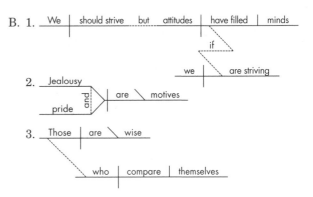

2.

3.

4.

c. compound sentence with two independent clauses
d. compound sentence with three independent clauses
e. complex sentence with one independent clause and one dependent clause
f. complex sentence with one independent clause and two dependent clauses
g. compound-complex sentence with two independent clauses and one dependent clause

1. God chose Saul to be the first king of Israel.
2. The Lord granted Saul victory when the Ammonites threatened Jabesh-gilead.
3. Because Saul obeyed the Lord, the Lord blessed him; and all went well for two years.
4. But later Saul lost faith in God and neglected His commandment.
5. Saul, who did not have the confidence of God's blessing, became quite fearful when the mighty Philistines camped at Michmash.
6. The men of Israel were afraid and hid themselves.
7. Saul wanted to fight, but he had been told to wait at Gilgal until Samuel came.
8. The morning of the seventh day arrived, but Samuel had not come.
9. The king foolishly offered the sacrifice, the prophet suddenly appeared on the scene, and Samuel pronounced judgment on the disobedient king.
10. Because the king had disobeyed God, his kingdom would be given to a man who was more worthy.

C.   1. a
     2. e
     3. g
     4. b
     5. f
     6. b
     7. g
     8. c
     9. d
    10. f

Review Exercises

A. Copy the topic sentence in Class Practice, Part B. [13]

B. Copy each complement, and label it *PN* (predicate nominative), *PA* (predicate adjective), *DO* (direct object), *IO* (indirect object), or *OC* (objective complement). [5–8]
   1. We prepared our visitors a quick meal.
   2. The bird on that rocky ledge is a ptarmigan.
   3. These late-blooming roses smell sweet.
   4. I can smell them from the front porch.
   5. Brother Lavern made the background of the bulletin board blue.
   6. Mother picked some flowers and made a beautiful bouquet.

Review Exercises

A. What are the causes of these color changes?

B. 1. visitors—IO; meal—DO
   2. ptarmigan—PN
   3. sweet—PA
   4. them—DO
   5. background—DO; blue—OC
   6. flowers—DO; bouquet—DO

17. Sentence Styles

Lesson Survey
- A **loose sentence** gives the main idea first and the details later.
- A **periodic sentence** gives the details first and saves the main idea until last.
- A **balanced sentence** has two well-matched clauses.

The English sentence is a remarkable structure. Already you have learned that the sentence can vary according to use, word order, and structure. This lesson will introduce you to the three sentence styles.

Loose Sentences

A *loose sentence* gives the main idea first and the details later. This is the style we use most naturally in speech. Often such a sentence could end at various points, and its main idea would still be complete. Study the following examples.

> We must obey God's Word if we hope to enter heaven.
>> (The main idea comes first. The sentence could end after *Word,* and the main idea would still be complete.)
> The Bible is our only safe guide in this world of darkness and confusion.
>> (The main idea comes first. The sentence could end after *guide, world,* or *darkness.*)

Loose sentences are the simplest kind to read and understand. Your mind can easily relate the details to the main idea because it comes first. Most of your sentences, therefore, should be of the loose variety.

Periodic Sentences

A *periodic sentence* gives the details first and saves the main idea until last. You must read all the way to the *period* in order to get the main idea. Because you must wait, your suspense builds up; and when you finally come to the main idea, it makes a stronger impression than if the sentence were of the loose type. This places emphasis on the main idea of the sentence.

> If we hope to enter heaven, we must obey God's Word.
>> (The main idea is emphasized.)
> "Finally, brethren, whatsoever things are true, whatsoever things are honest, whatsoever things are just, whatsoever things are pure, whatsoever things are lovely, whatsoever things are of good report; if there be any virtue, and if there be any praise,

Lesson 17

Purpose: To introduce *loose, *periodic, and *balanced sentences.

Oral Review:

1. Classify each sentence according to its structure.
   a. The heavy frost that blanketed the ground killed the last of the garden plants. (complex)
   b. Either the steers broke the fence, or someone failed to close the gate. (compound)
   c. The old barn, abandoned for many years, had almost fallen apart. (simple)
   d. After the floodwaters subsided, we had much cleanup to do. (complex)
   e. Most materials contract when they freeze, but water expands. (compound-complex)
2. Tell which word order is used in each of the following sentences.
   a. Faintly through the mist shone the morning sun. (inverted)
   b. Its great energy the fog could not resist. (mixed)
   c. Eventually the fog completely disappeared. (mixed)
   d. We enjoyed a beautiful fall day. (natural)
3. Name the complement described in each sentence.
   a. It comes between an action verb and its direct object. (indirect object)
   b. It follows a linking verb and modifies the subject. (predicate adjective)
   c. It follows an action verb and answers the question *whom* or *what.* (direct object)
   d. It follows a linking verb and renames the subject. (predicate nominative)
   e. It follows a direct object and renames or modifies it. (objective complement)

think on these things" (Philippians 4:8). ("Think on these things" is strongly emphasized. Contrast this wording: "Finally, brethren, think on whatsoever things are true, whatsoever things are honest, . . .")

A paragraph will sound unnatural if it has too many periodic sentences. Used occasionally, however, the periodic sentence is one of the best ways to give strong emphasis to a key idea.

Balanced Sentences

A *balanced sentence* has two well-matched clauses. In one kind of balanced sentence, the two clauses begin with words like "the more . . . the more," "the more . . . the less," or "the sooner . . . the better."

"The more they afflicted them, the more they multiplied and grew."
The closer we got to home, the more we longed for home.

In another kind of balanced sentence, a slight change of wording is used to produce a notable or unexpected contrast. The change is made by using different words or by rearranging the words.

You may hope for the best if you are prepared for the worst.
There may be a wrong way to do right, but there is no right way to do wrong.

Note the exchanging of *wrong* and *right* in the last sentence. This is an example of rearranging the words to produce a striking, memorable statement. Such a sentence stands out because of its unusual structure; not many expressions can be reworded in this way. Therefore, the balanced sentence is the least common of the three sentence styles.

Changing the *style* of a sentence may have the same result as changing the *word order* of the sentence. Study the following examples.

We could see farther as we went higher.
   (natural word order; loose sentence)
As we went higher, we could see farther.
   (mixed word order; periodic sentence)

Why is the change classified in two different ways? Word order deals mainly with the *mechanical arrangement* of words in sentences. Its primary concern is whether the subject comes at the beginning, in the middle, or at the end. Style has more to do with the "spirit" of a sentence. Its primary concern is how the *message* of a sentence is affected by different word arrangements. You will study sentence styles again in Chapter 7, where you will learn to use them for varying degrees of emphasis.

Lesson Introduction: Write the following sentences on the board.

We could see farther as we went higher.
As we went higher, we could see farther.
The higher we went, the farther we could see.

These are three different kinds of sentences. Are they three different kinds according to use? (No; all three are declarative.) Are they three different kinds according to structure? (No; the first two are complex and the third is compound.) Are they of three different word orders? (No; the first is natural, the second is mixed, and each clause in the third is mixed.) Then how are they all different from each other?

These sentences are of different *styles,* which is the subject of this lesson. The first sentence is loose, the second is periodic, and the third is balanced.

Lesson Outline:

1. A loose sentence gives the main idea first and the details later.

   a. This is the style we use most naturally in speech.

   b. Often such a sentence could end at various points, and its main idea would still be complete.

   c. Since loose sentences are the simplest kind to read and understand, most of your sentences should be of the loose variety.

2. A periodic sentence gives the details first and saves the main idea until last.

   a. Because you must wait for the main idea, your suspense builds up, and the main idea receives special emphasis.

   b. Too many periodic sentences will make a paragraph sound unnatural, but an occasional one gives strong emphasis to a key idea.

Class Practice

A. Tell whether each sentence is *loose, periodic,* or *balanced.*
1. When God speaks, men should listen.
2. The Bible has answers to every perplexity of man.
3. God's people have true contentment because they trust the Lord.
4. The more we use the uplook, the less we are discouraged by the outlook.
5. In the dedication of godly youth, God has a powerful witness.
6. Reputation is what men think you are; character is what God knows you are.

B. Change these loose sentences to periodic sentences.
1. Jezebel was furious when she learned that the prophets of Baal had been slain.
2. She threatened God's prophet, using bold and harsh language.
3. Elijah fled from the angry queen even though he had earlier faced hundreds of false prophets.
4. God encouraged the prophet in a still, small voice.

C. Complete or reword each sentence to make a balanced sentence.
1. If you see God's hand in everything, you can leave everything . . .
2. It is good to find a true friend; . . . to be a true friend.
3. Christ must be valued above all, or . . . at all.
4. As a man receives more truth, he is more responsible.

Written Exercises

A. Write whether each sentence is *loose, periodic,* or *balanced.*
1. The Bible will keep you from sin, and sin will keep you from the Bible.
2. We can be strong in the power of God.
3. We may tremble on the Rock, but the Rock never trembles under us.
4. After a long dry spell, the thunderstorms brought welcome rain.
5. With her right arm broken, Katrina can barely write.
6. Stanley has kept up with his work in spite of his long illness.
7. The sooner we start, the sooner we shall finish.
8. On a small ledge of the canyon wall stood a watchful mountain goat.

B. Rewrite these loose sentences as periodic sentences.
1. Lazarus was already dead when Jesus finally came to Bethany.
2. The boys found an old butter churn in a dark corner of the basement.
3. Grandmother Kurtz is amazingly spry even though she has turned ninety.
4. Many horses fled in panic at the sight of early automobiles.
5. We could see our farm far below in the valley.
6. A crop failure is likely unless it rains soon.

3. A balanced sentence has two well-matched clauses.
   a. It may be of the pattern "the more . . . the more."
   b. It may be a striking, memorable statement produced by rearranging the words.
   c. Balanced sentences stand out because of their unusual structure. They are the least common of the three sentence styles.

4. Changing the style of a sentence may have the same result as changing the word order of the sentence.
   a. Word order deals mainly with the *mechanical arrangement* of words in sentences. Its primary concern is whether the subject comes at the beginning, in the middle, or at the end.

Lesson 17 Answers

Class Practice

A. 1. periodic   4. balanced
   2. loose   5. periodic
   3. loose   6. balanced

B. 1. When she learned that the prophets of Baal had been slain, Jezebel was furious.
   2. Using bold and harsh language, she threatened God's prophet.
   3. Even though he had earlier faced hundreds of false prophets, Elijah fled from the angry queen.
   4. In a still, small voice, God encouraged the prophet.

C. 1. If you see God's hand in everything, you can leave everything in God's hand.
   2. It is good to find a true friend; it is better to be a true friend.
   3. Christ must be valued above all, or He is not valued at all.
   4. The more truth a man receives, the more responsible he is.

Written Exercises

A. 1. balanced   5. periodic
   2. loose   6. loose
   3. balanced   7. balanced
   4. periodic   8. periodic

B. 1. When Jesus finally came to Bethany, Lazarus was already dead.
   2. In a dark corner of the basement, the boys found an old butter churn.
   3. Even though she has turned ninety, Grandmother Kurtz is amazingly spry.
   4. At the sight of early automobiles, many horses fled in panic.
   5. Far below in the valley, we could see our farm.
   6. Unless it rains soon, a crop failure is likely.

   b. Style has more to do with the "spirit" of a sentence. Its primary concern is how the *message* of a sentence is affected by different word arrangements.

★ **EXTRA PRACTICE**
Worksheet 8 *(Loose, Periodic, and Balanced Sentences)*

C. Make a balanced sentence from each item. Write the complete sentences.
 1. The boy was not . . . ; he was hardly working.
 2. Little harm comes from deserving praise without receiving it, but great harm may come . . .
 3. Some speak because they have to say something; others speak because . . .
 4. As a man is more like God, he is less like the world.

Review Exercises

A. Write whether each sentence is *simple, compound, complex,* or *compound-complex.* [14–16]
 1. We can study effectively when we have a good attitude toward our work.
 2. The scholar who keeps his work area neat has a foundation for efficient study; moreover, he is likely to have a good attitude toward his work.
 3. Good posture is another essential for good study habits.
 4. Of course, a person can study either for selfish motives or for God's glory.
 5. Because good study habits demand diligence, some people ignore their value; but they are well worth every effort.
 6. This diligence brings the assurance of God's approval, and the habits themselves prepare one to be a good student of the Bible.

B. Write whether the word order of each sentence is natural (*N*), inverted (*I*), or mixed (*M*). [11]
 1. "The tongue can no man tame."
 2. "The harvest truly is great."
 3. "Great is thy faithfulness."
 4. "Out of the heart proceed evil thoughts."
 5. "When the Son of man cometh, shall he find faith on the earth?"

C. 1. The boy was not working hard; he was hardly working.
 2. Little harm comes from deserving praise without receiving it, but great harm may come from receiving praise without deserving it.
 3. Some speak because they have to say something; others speak because they have something to say.
 4. The more a man is like God, the less he is like the world.

Review Exercises

A. 1. complex
 2. compound-complex
 3. simple
 4. simple
 5. compound-complex
 6. compound

B. 1. M
 2. N
 3. I
 4. I
 5. M

18. Achieving Paragraph Coherence

Lesson Survey

- A paragraph has **coherence** when its thoughts are presented in a well-organized way.
- Good **sentence order** helps bring coherence to a paragraph.
- Smooth **sentence transitions** improve paragraph coherence.

Lesson 18

Purpose: To show methods of achieving coherence in paragraphs.

Oral Review:

1. What is a paragraph? (an organized unit of thought)
2. What is meant by paragraph unity? (every sentence supporting and developing the topic sentence)
3. In what two ways can you correct a paragraph that lacks unity? (Remove any sentence that does not develop the topic sentence. Divide the paragraph into two or more paragraphs.)
4. What are the three C's of business letter content? (courteous, clear, concise)
5. Name several ways in which a business letter is different from a friendly letter. (A business letter includes an inside address; the greeting is often called a salutation; the salutation is followed by a colon, not a comma; the salutation and the closing are more formal; a blank space should be left between each part.)

Lesson Introduction: For a literal illustration of coherence, you could give a demonstration on the cohesion of water molecules. Fill a glass level full with water, and then slowly add more until the water bulges above the rim of the glass. Explain that the molecules cohere, or stick together, and this keeps the water from spilling over. Then challenge the pupils to make their paragraphs stick together like that! Today's lesson will help them to develop this skill.

Lesson Outline:

1. A paragraph has coherence when its thoughts are presented in a well-organized way.

Unity is an essential quality of a good paragraph. Yet a paragraph may have excellent unity and still be a poorly written paragraph. A well-written paragraph must also have coherence.

A paragraph has *coherence* when its thoughts are presented in a well-organized way. The sentences progress from one idea to another in a clear, sensible order, and the ideas lead smoothly from one to the next.

Compare the following paragraphs. Although both have unity, the first one lacks coherence and is hard to follow.

Incoherent:

>   Fifteen-year-old Michael Metzler quickly pushed the lawn mower into the garage, then watched the downpour as he caught his breath. Only two strips of grass were left to mow when he glanced at the blackening sky. Thunder rolled, and raindrops pelted the freshly mowed lawn. With long strides he pushed the lawn mower over the remaining grass. His job completed, he raced toward the garage door.

Coherent:

>   Fifteen-year-old Michael Metzler quickly glanced at the blackening sky. With long strides he pushed the lawn mower over the remaining two strips of uncut grass. His job completed, he raced toward the garage door. Michael pushed the mower under the roof, then watched the downpour as he caught his breath. Thunder rolled, and raindrops pelted the freshly mowed lawn.

The first paragraph is hard to follow because the order of the actions is confusing. Both the first and the last sentence say that Michael went to the garage; did he finish the mowing in between? This paragraph is obviously not coherent.

Sentence Order

Good *sentence order* helps bring coherence to a paragraph. Three commonly used arrangements are chronological order, spatial order, and order of importance.

Chronological order. In a paragraph with this order, the details are presented in the order of time. A narrative paragraph (one that tells a story) is written in chronological order. This order is also used in writing directions or explanations. Imagine the difficulty in trying to make something if the directions were not written in chronological order! Look again at the above example that illustrates a coherent paragraph. Observe how this paragraph describes the action in clear chronological order.

Spatial order. A paragraph with spatial order presents details in a logical order of space (position). This is the order to use in describing an object

2. *Good sentence order helps bring coherence to a paragraph.*

    a. With chronological order, details are presented in the order of time. This order is used in narrative paragraphs and in paragraphs that give directions or explanations.

    b. With spatial order, details are presented in a logical order of space (position). This order is used in describing objects or scenes.

    c. With the order of importance, details are given in order from the least important to the most important, or vice versa. (The most effective arrangement generally is to build up to the most important detail.) This order is used for paragraphs of information or explanation.

3. *Smooth sentence transitions improve paragraph coherence.*

    a. Transitional words bring coherence to a paragraph because they show the relationships between sentences.

        1) Use the transitional words that state precisely the relationship you want to show.

        2) Use transitional words only when they definitely add to the smooth flow of the sentences.

    b. The repetition of key words emphasizes the main idea of a paragraph while it links the sentences.

        1) Repeat words that emphasize the main idea (not a secondary point).

        2) Use synonyms for some of the repetition.

    c. Pronoun reference can aid in coherence by referring to something mentioned earlier in the paragraph.

or a scene, and it can vary widely. You might present the details from left to right, from top to bottom, from near to distant, in a clockwise order, or in the order opposite from any of these. You could also begin by describing one outstanding item and presenting the rest of the details in relation to that item. Before you begin writing a paragraph of description, decide which order will enable the reader to best picture the scene.

The following paragraphs describe the floor plan of a new house that was to be built on the north side of the road. Can you picture the layout of the house?

> "All right," Father said as he drew a line in the dirt. "I'll show you what Mother and I are planning." He took a few more steps and drew another line. Measuring distances by counting his steps, Father drew more lines in the dirt. Then he explained. "In this southeast corner would be the boys' bedroom. The girls' bedroom would be next, and in this northeast corner would be Mother's and mine.
>
> "Against the north wall and our bedroom wall would be a small washroom. All along the wall facing west would be our kitchen and living area. We would put the cupboards against the wall facing the road, and the wood stove would be in the corner by the boys' bedroom."

Notice the spatial order of this example. Father's description begins in the southeast corner of the house, and it moves counterclockwise to the girls' bedroom, the parents' bedroom, the washroom, and the kitchen and living area. The description ends by giving the position of the cupboards and the wood stove.

Order of importance. With this arrangement, a paragraph gives details in order from the least important to the most important. The opposite order may also be used, but the most effective arrangement generally is to build up to the most important detail. Use this order when you write a paragraph of information or explanation.

Topic   <u>Respect for those in authority is an important quality.</u> The level
Reason 1   of your respect determines your usefulness in life. If you are respectful, you will inspire right attitudes in your brothers and sisters and in your friends. You will discover that your parents and teachers can trust you with responsibilities and privileges.
Reason 2   Your submission to authority also affects the development of your character. You can expect to grow in manly or womanly virtues only if your heart is not blighted with disrespect and bit-
Reason 3   terness. Above all, your honor for earthly authorities reflects your attitude toward God Himself. Only the person who respects all earthly authority—parents, teachers, ministers, and government leaders—can truly love and reverence God.

The paragraph above gives three ways that respect for authority is important. Note the progression from the least important to the most important: your usefulness in life; the development of your character; and finally, your attitude toward God Himself.

Sentence Transitions

Smooth *sentence transitions* improve paragraph coherence. In this lesson you will study three kinds of sentence transitions: transitional words, repetition of key words, and pronoun reference. These are three useful ways of making sentences in a paragraph flow smoothly.

Transitional words. The use of transitional words makes a paragraph coherent because these words show relationships between sentences. When you find a transitional word at the beginning of a sentence, it helps you to see how that sentence relates to the ones you have just read. You must choose transitional words carefully so that you state precisely the relationship you want to show. Read the following pairs of sentences, and notice how much difference the transitional words make.

> Heavy rain clouds obscured the rising sun. <u>Consequently</u>, Joan was excited.
>
> Heavy rain clouds obscured the rising sun. <u>Nevertheless</u>, Joan was excited.

The following chart shows some transitional words in various categories.

	Time	
first	next	eventually
second	after	at last
soon	meanwhile	finally

	Space	
near	ahead	to the right (left)
beyond	above	in the distance
around	inside	in the center
next	along	followed by

	Addition	
and	moreover	furthermore
too	likewise	again
besides	in addition	also

	Contrast	
but	however	nevertheless
yet	otherwise	on the other hand
still	although	on the contrary

Example or Illustration

| for example | to illustrate | specifically |
| for instance | in fact | in other words |

Result or Conclusion

| therefore | in summary | consequently |
| thus | in conclusion | as a result |

Use transitional words only when they definitely add to the smooth flow of the sentences in a paragraph. Not every sentence should have such an expression. Notice how the underlined transitional words contribute to the coherence of the following paragraph.

> Good posture—a person's manner of carrying himself when sitting or standing—is an important habit to cultivate. <u>For one thing</u>, good posture has a more pleasing appearance than poor posture. Consider how alert a person looks when he maintains an erect sitting position. <u>In contrast</u>, consider how careless and unconcerned a person appears when he slouches. <u>Furthermore</u>, a good carriage is healthier for the body than a poor carriage. When the lungs, intestines, and blood vessels are crowded, they cannot function as they should. A slouched posture <u>also</u> puts unnecessary strain on the muscles and bones. <u>Therefore</u>, out of respect for the way God made our bodies, we should practice good posture.

> *For one thing* means a reason will be given. *In contrast* shows that a contrast will follow. *Furthermore* and *also* indicate further explanation. *Therefore* signals a conclusion.

Repetition of key words. A kind of sentence transition that is less obvious but also very effective is the repetition of key words. These are words that refer directly to the topic of the paragraph. The key words in the following paragraph are underlined.

> Flying requires keen <u>eyesight</u>. And in some hawks, <u>vision</u> is eight to ten times more efficient than in humans. This does not mean that hawks have telescopic <u>vision</u>. But it does mean that their <u>eyes</u> have almost incredible resolving power. The most sensitive part of a hawk's <u>eye</u> contains up to 1.5 million cells that serve as <u>visual</u> receptors—in contrast to only 200,000 in that part of a man's <u>eye</u>.

Repetition of key words is an especially good way to achieve coherence because it emphasizes the main idea of the paragraph while it links the sentences. When you use this method, however, you must remember two important things: repeat words that emphasize the main idea (not a secondary point), and use synonyms for some of the repetition. In the sample above, the synonyms *vision* and *eyesight* are used along with the related words *visual* and *eyes*. These synonyms help to avoid the problem of tiresome repetition.

Pronoun reference. Pronouns can hold a paragraph together by referring to something mentioned earlier in the paragraph. The pronouns in the following paragraph all refer to the seven brethren mentioned in the first sentence.

> Back to prison the seven brethren were taken. There <u>they</u> remained for almost a year. Sometimes it seemed that the officers had forgotten all about <u>them</u>. But no, <u>they</u> had not been forgotten. All of <u>them</u> were sentenced to die.

Coherence is an essential ingredient of every well-written paragraph. As you proofread and revise your writing, test for good coherence by using the following questions.
1. Do the sentences follow a clear, logical order?
2. Do the ideas flow smoothly from one sentence to the next?
3. Have I made effective use of sentence transitions, such as transitional words, repetition of key words, and pronoun reference?

Class Practice

A. Tell which kind of sentence order is used in each paragraph.
1. Dark clouds floated above the bright, hilly landscape. The swaying tree branches still clung to a few yellow leaves. Among the trees stood black-and-white cows, sharply outlined in the late afternoon sunshine.
2. Air enters your body through the nose and passes through the moist nasal passages in the head. In these passages, the air is warmed and the dust is filtered out. From the throat, the air travels down your windpipe or trachea through an opening called the glottis. Above the glottis is a very wonderful trap door—the epiglottis. This flap covers the glottis whenever you swallow food. But when the food is past, the epiglottis opens and the flow of air continues. "I will praise thee; for I am fearfully and wonderfully made" (Psalm 139:14).
3. I am thankful that God created man with the gift of music. Do you not agree that singing is a pleasant way to express happiness? When I walk outside on a beautiful fall morning, my heart fills with joyful songs. When I am excited about some plans, it is easy to sing. Singing also is a good way to overcome temptations. If I am tempted to complain, a song of thanksgiving changes my attitude. If jealous thoughts fill my mind, a song of God's love chases them away. Above all, singing is a wonderful way to worship God. How much He deserves our praise! Let us sing and glorify His Name.

B. Answer these questions about the paragraphs in Part A.
1. What key word is repeated throughout number 2?

Lesson 18 Answers

Class Practice

A. 1. spatial
   2. chronological *or* spatial
   3. order of importance

B. 1. air

2. What transitional words are used in number 3?
3. What key words are repeated throughout number 3?
4. What pronouns in number 3 help to provide coherence?

Written Exercises

A. Rewrite this paragraph, using a logical sequence of spatial order. The progression should be from near to far and from right to left.

As we emerged from the trees on the brow of Eagle's Bluff, Grandfather's farm lay before us. To the right stood the old farmhouse, where the family of fourteen children had been raised. The hog barn and the chicken house extended away from the house to the left. At the foot of the bluff stood the even rows of Grandfather's apple orchard. Beyond the barns, the hayfields and cornfields stretched toward the left and into the distance. The orchard was hemmed in against the bluff by Eagle's Creek, which meandered across the valley. Beyond the creek lay the farm buildings. A long lane angled away from the house to Cheesetown Road, barely visible on the right.

B. Rewrite this paragraph, using clear chronological order. Also remove some transitional words and change others.

If you follow these directions, you can have soft potatoes in a few minutes. Put the potatoes and two cups of water into a pressure cooker. Cut the big ones in half so that they get done as fast as the small ones. Therefore, the potatoes should cook for eight to ten minutes. Put the lid on tightly, and then put the pressure control on. Subsequently, turn the heat on high. When the weight jiggles, turn the heat back to medium. When the weight starts jiggling again, then start timing the cooking. After the time is up, take the cooker off the burner. When the pressure is down, then cautiously lift the weight from the lid. Now you are ready to take off the lid, and afterwards check to see if the potatoes are soft. To get the pressure down, put the pressure cooker in the sink and run cold water over it. Naturally, if you cook the potatoes in the skins, scrub them first. Otherwise, if you do not, peel them.

C. Write a paragraph in the order of importance, using one of these topic sentences. Pay close attention to sentence transitions.
1. Keeping machinery lubricated is an important maintenance.
2. Fall (winter, spring, summer) is a beautiful time of the year.
3. Every teenager should learn the joy of making someone else happy.
4. I am glad to live on a farm.
5. Grandma is the most cheerful person I know. (Or choose another person and another good character trait.)

---

2. also, Above all
3. music, singing, songs, sing, song
4. I, my

Written Exercises

A. (Sample paragraph.)

As we emerged from the trees on the brow of Eagle's Bluff, Grandfather's farm lay before us. At the foot of the bluff stood the even rows of Grandfather's apple orchard. The orchard was hemmed in against the bluff by Eagle's Creek, which meandered across the valley. Beyond the creek lay the farm buildings. To the right stood the old farmhouse, where the family of fourteen children had been raised. A long lane angled away from the house to Cheesetown Road, barely visible on the right. The hog barn and the chicken house extended away from the house to the left. Beyond the barns, the hayfields and cornfields stretched toward the left and into the distance.

B. (Sample paragraph.)

If you follow these directions, you can have soft potatoes in a few minutes. Naturally, if you cook the potatoes in the skins, scrub them first. Otherwise, peel them. Cut the big ones in half so that they get done as fast as the small ones. Next, put the potatoes and two cups of water into a pressure cooker. Put the lid on tightly, and then put the pressure control on. Turn the heat on high. When the weight jiggles, turn the heat back to medium. When the weight starts jiggling again, start timing the cooking. The potatoes should cook for eight to ten minutes. After the time is up, take the cooker off the burner. To get the pressure down, put the pressure cooker in the sink and run cold water over it. When the pressure is down, cautiously lift the weight from the lid. Now you are ready to take off the lid and check to see if the potatoes are soft.

C. (Individual work.)

19. Transition Between Paragraphs

> **Lesson Survey**
> - Smooth transition between paragraphs is achieved when the thought of each paragraph leads logically to the thought of the next paragraph.
> - Transitional words show how the thought of one paragraph is related to the thought of the previous paragraph.
> - Repetition of key words can link paragraphs together.
> - Reference to an idea in the previous paragraph can provide good transition between paragraphs.

Coherence among the paragraphs of a composition is just as important as coherence within a paragraph. Therefore, a good writer pays attention to ways of providing smooth transition between paragraphs.

Smooth transition between paragraphs is achieved when the thought of each paragraph leads logically to the thought of the next paragraph. Some of the methods used to achieve coherence within paragraphs also aid coherence among paragraphs.

Here is a sample composition of five paragraphs. It illustrates the various ways of achieving transition between paragraphs.

1. The story is told of a **race** between a *colt* and a *pig*. The terms were that the *colt* must maintain a trot, with the starting place measured a half mile out from the *hog* farm and the finish line at the farm. The **race** was scheduled two weeks in advance.

2. Accordingly, the owner of the pig took the animal daily to the starting line and chased him home, where he was *rewarded* with a liberal supply of *corn*. Soon the pig was hurrying to get his *delicious meal.* When the time came for the **race,** the pig forgot all else but the *corn.* While the colt was <u>distracted</u> along the way, the pig was concentrating on reaching his *reward.*

3. Our life here on *earth* is something like a **race** to eternity. The devil would have us become <u>distracted</u> with this *world's* riches and pleasures. And just as the colt failed to win the **race,** so we shall fail to reach our heavenly reward if we become too involved in *earthly* pursuits.

4. The devil wants to <u>distract</u> us in this **race** of life with the *things* of time and sense. He would have us think that we should make the most of these *things* because life is so short. The one who lives for the *pleasures* of this world, however, will only experience sorrow and eternal destruction. At the end of life, he will have lived in vain, and

Lesson 19

Purpose: To show methods of *providing smooth transition between paragraphs.

Oral Review:

1. What is the meaning of coherence within a paragraph? (all the thoughts of the paragraph presented in a well-organized way)
2. Name the three types of sentence order in paragraphs, and tell in what kinds of paragraphs each is used. (chronological order—used in narratives, directions, and explanations; spatial order—used in descriptions; order of importance—used in paragraphs of information or explanation)
3. Suggest a good transitional word to link each pair of sentences.
   a. Gehazi should have known that he could not deceive God's prophet. He tried it. (nevertheless)
   b. Jesus suffered intense physical pain during His trial and crucifixion. He bore intense emotional pain. (furthermore, also, in addition)
   c. Jesus will return to this earth someday. He is preparing a place for His own. (meanwhile)
4. Should most sentences in a paragraph have transitional words? (no)
5. What two things should you remember in using repetition of key words? (Repeat words that emphasize the main idea. Use synonyms to avoid tiresome repetition.)

Lesson Introduction: Paragraphs can be likened to the stones in a wall. One stone by itself does not make the wall, but each stone is needed. Likewise, one paragraph alone does not make a composition, but each one contributes to the finished product.

But a pile of stones does not make a good wall. The stones need to be arranged, and they must be

he will be faced with a just God and the question, "What have you done for your soul?"

5.   Christ wants us to run the **race** of life for Him and come to a *triumphant* end. He has prepared the track before us by living *victoriously* here on earth. He is now in heaven and is willing to provide us the strength to begin and *successfully* finish the same **race.** He has set a goal at the end that cannot be improved or taken away. Therefore, "let us lay aside every weight, and the sin which doth so easily beset us, and let us run with patience the **race** that is set before us, looking unto Jesus"—who Himself has *successfully* run the **race** of life.

Transitional Words

Transitional words show how the thought of one paragraph is related to the thought of the previous paragraph. A transitional word does more than merely link two paragraphs. It also shows that the second paragraph adds a similar thought, presents a contrast, or is related in some other way. The chart in Lesson 18 has a list of good transitional words to show specific relationships.

Look at the first sentence of each sample paragraph. Do you see a transitional word in any of them? The word *Accordingly* at the beginning of paragraph 2 shows that this paragraph will tell what happened as a result of the action in paragraph 1. Transitional words are effective because as soon as you read them, you know what to expect in the coming paragraph.

Repetition of Key Words

Repetition of key words can link several paragraphs together. Remember that effective repetition emphasizes the main idea of a paragraph or a group of paragraphs. It should usually include synonyms so that the same words are not always repeated.

What key word is repeated throughout the sample composition above? It is the word *race,* which appears in boldface. No synonyms for *race* are used, but the repetition is not tiresome because the word is not repeated too close together. In addition, the words *starting place, finish line,* and *track* refer to a race without using the word itself.

Also notice the key words that are repeated within individual paragraphs. Some of them appear in italics in the sample composition.

Reference to Previous Idea

Reference to an idea in the previous paragraph can provide good transition between paragraphs. This is especially effective when a paragraph adds to or contrasts with an idea in the previous paragraph. In the sample composition, the idea of worldly distractions helps to link

held together with mortar. Likewise, the paragraphs of a composition need to be arranged logically. And they must be held together with the mortar of effective transitions between paragraphs.

Lesson Outline:

1. Smooth transition between paragraphs is achieved when the thought of each paragraph leads logically to the thought of the next paragraph.

2. Transitional words show how the thought of one paragraph is related to the thought of the previous paragraph.

3. Repetition of key words can link several paragraphs together.

4. Reference to an idea in the previous paragraph can provide good transition between paragraphs.

paragraphs 2, 3, and 4. (See the underlined words.) Paragraph 5 shows a contrast: completing the race victoriously instead of being distracted.

Well-written compositions do not just happen; they are built carefully. One of the essential ingredients is coherence—within paragraphs and among paragraphs. Use the tools discussed in these two lessons to write effective, well-linked paragraphs.

Class Practice

Read this essay, and answer the questions that follow.

The Importance of Study

We all have important things to do; eating, sleeping, working, and going to church are a few of them. Studying, however, is something that too many people neglect. And study is one of the most important activities that we should engage in.

The mind, like muscles, must be exercised if it is to be kept "in shape." We do not think much of a man who rarely uses his muscles enough to keep them strong, who puffs and sweats when he carries a fifty-pound box up a stairway. Minds that "lose their breath" after fifteen minutes of study are no better. The Bible says, "Neglect not the gift that is in thee" (1 Timothy 4:14). It is true that Paul was thinking of Timothy's spiritual gift, but it is also true that the mind is one of our most valuable gifts. God does not want us to neglect any of the gifts that He gives us.

Study makes a Christian stronger and more useful. We are assuming, of course, that he applies his study skills to the study of the Word as well as to other reading. As he does, he is daily reminded of what God has said. He is also better prepared to give a topic or teach a Sunday school class when he is asked. If he is requested to write an article, he will not have as much difficulty finding ideas as he would otherwise. Study will be a benefit to the person's own Christian life as well as to that of his brother.

1. What key word is used frequently to link the sentences and the paragraphs?
2. What transitional words are used within the first paragraph?
3. In the first sentence of the third paragraph, what idea provides a link to the second paragraph?
4. What two pronouns are used in the third paragraph as an effective link between sentences?

Written Exercises

The following essay has a number of weaknesses. Rewrite it more effectively, paying special attention to the following points.

1. A sequence of transitional words (such as *first* and *second*) should be used throughout the essay.

Lesson 19 Answers

Class Practice

1. study
2. however, And
3. It refers to a Christian's (spiritual) strength, whereas the previous paragraph described physical strength.
4. he, his

2. More transitional words are needed in paragraphs 1–3, as well as words like *this* and *these*.
3. Paragraph 4 has too many transitional words.
4. The key word *agent* or *agents* should be used at least once in each paragraph.
5. The following key words and ideas should occur at least one more time each.

    rock(s)   moving water   wind   God uses

The Formation of Soil

God uses a number of agents in breaking down rocks to form soil. One is temperature. Did you know that water trapped in a crack of a rock will expand by almost a tenth when it freezes? It will break things. Temperature changes cause rocks to expand and contract, resulting in cracking and splitting.

Another is moving water, which carries silt, sand, and small stones, wearing them on each other along the way. Did you know that the delta of the mighty Fraser River in British Columbia, Canada, is extending into the Pacific Ocean eight feet every year? Did you know that the lip of Niagara Falls is being worn back several feet every year?

Another is the wind, which is used mostly in desert regions to break down rocks. As fine particles of soil or rock are carried, they wear on each other and on any surface over which they travel. Many strange and interesting rock formations have been carved out.

Thus is soil formed by the three, along with other forces that God has designed. This is then an ongoing process, for new soil must continually be formed so that consequently plants can grow and produce the food needed by all living things.

————————————

Written Exercises

(*Teacher:* You may wish to photocopy the essay in the lesson and tell the pupils to improve it in five steps, one for each point listed. Then they should write the essay neatly by hand.)

(Improvements are marked. Allow reasonable variation.)

The Formation of Soil

God uses a number of agents in breaking down rocks to form soil. <u>The first of these</u> is temperature. Did you know that water trapped in a crack of a rock will expand by almost a tenth when it freezes? <u>This</u> will break <u>the rock</u>. Temperature changes <u>also</u> cause rocks to expand and contract, resulting in <u>more</u> cracking and splitting.

<u>A second agent</u> is moving water, which carries silt, sand, and small stones, wearing them on each other along the way. Did you know that the delta of the mighty Fraser River in British Columbia, Canada, is extending into the Pacific Ocean eight feet every year? <u>Or</u> that <u>moving water is wearing back</u> the lip of Niagara Falls several feet every year?

<u>A third agent</u> is the wind, which <u>God uses</u> mostly in desert regions to break down rocks. As <u>the wind carries</u> fine particles of soil or rock, they wear on each other and on any surface over which they travel. Many strange and interesting rock formations have been carved out <u>by this action of the wind</u>.

Thus is soil formed by <u>these</u> three <u>agents</u>, along with other forces that God has designed. This is ~~then~~ an ongoing process, for new soil must continually be formed so that ~~consequently~~ plants can grow and produce the food needed by all living things.

20. Chapter 2 Review
Class Practice

A. Give the correct term for each description.
1. A sentence that asks a question.
2. A sentence that gives a command or request.
3. A sentence that expresses strong feeling or emotion.
4. A sentence that makes a statement.
5. A group of related words that contains a skeleton.
6. A group of related words without a skeleton, which is used as a single part of speech.
7. Sentence word order in which the complete subject precedes the complete predicate.
8. Sentence word order in which the complete subject comes between two parts of the complete predicate.
9. Sentence word order in which the complete predicate precedes the complete subject.
10. A clause that cannot stand alone, but functions as a single part of speech.
11. A clause that can stand alone as a complete sentence.
12. A sentence with two or more independent clauses.
13. A sentence with only one independent clause.
14. A sentence with two independent clauses and at least one dependent clause.
15. A sentence with one independent clause and at least one dependent clause.
16. A sentence that gives the details first and saves the main idea until last.
17. A sentence that gives the main idea first and the details later.
18. A sentence that has two well-matched clauses.
19. The sentence that states the main idea of a paragraph.
20. The quality of thoughts within a paragraph being presented in a well-organized way.
21. The quality of all the sentences within a paragraph supporting and developing the topic sentence.

B. Tell whether each sentence is *declarative, interrogative, imperative,* or *exclamatory*. End punctuation has been omitted.
1. How exceedingly great is the majesty of our God
2. Above all earthly realms is this sovereign King
3. Trust Him in every experience of life
4. Do your actions reveal a simple trust in Him
5. If you truly trust Him, you will not worry and complain

Lesson 20 Answers

Class Practice

A. 1. interrogative sentence
2. imperative sentence
3. exclamatory sentence
4. declarative sentence
5. clause
6. phrase
7. natural order
8. mixed order
9. inverted order
10. dependent clause
11. independent clause
12. compound sentence
13. simple sentence
14. compound-complex sentence
15. complex sentence
16. periodic sentence
17. loose sentence
18. balanced sentence
19. topic sentence
20. coherence
21. unity

B. 1. exclamatory
2. declarative
3. imperative
4. interrogative
5. declarative

Lesson 20

Purpose: To review the concepts taught in Chapter 2.

C. Tell whether the word order of each sentence in Part B is *natural,
inverted,* or *mixed.*

D. Tell whether each underlined phrase is a *prepositional phrase,* a *verbal phrase,* or a phrase of a *single part of speech.* Also tell whether it functions as a *noun,* a *verb,* an *adjective,* or an *adverb.*
   1. As we drove <u>through Salmon Valley</u>, we saw several bald eagles <u>soaring high overhead</u>.
   2. A cold north wind <u>has been blowing</u> all afternoon.
   3. We had planned <u>to reach Grandfather Witmer's by evening</u>.
   4. <u>Brother Alvin Mast</u> preached <u>at our all-day meeting</u>.

E. Tell whether each underlined clause is *independent* or *dependent.* If it is dependent, also tell whether it functions as a *noun,* an *adjective,* or an *adverb.*
   1. <u>When a crocodile is hunting</u>, it can seize an animal <u>that comes to a river</u> and drag the victim underwater to be drowned.
   2. <u>A crocodile has powerful jaws for biting</u>, yet <u>a man can easily hold them shut</u>.
   3. <u>What we know about the crocodile</u> certainly shows the design of an all-wise Creator.

Written Exercises

A. Rewrite or complete each sentence, using the word order or sentence style named in parentheses.
   1. After Gideon died, Abimelech wanted to be king. (natural)
   2. Abimelech's support came from his mother's relatives. (inverted)
   3. God could not bless Abimelech's wicked ambitions. (mixed)
   4. Although he was Gideon's son, Abimelech was not humble like Gideon. (loose)
   5. His life came to a sudden end after a woman cast a piece of a millstone upon his head. (periodic)
   6. Whoever exalts himself will be humbled, but whoever humbles himself . . . (balanced)

B. Write whether each sentence is *simple, compound, complex,* or *compound-complex.*
   1. The morning was sunny, but the sky became cloudy after noon.
   2. Because rain was threatening, we worked especially hard in the garden.
   3. Just in time we finished the tomatoes and headed for the house.
   4. Although we had only a brief shower then, we had several more showers before dark; and that night we had a heavy rainfall.
   5. This rain was exactly what we needed.

C. 1. inverted
   2. inverted
   3. natural
   4. mixed
   5. mixed

D. 1. prepositional phrase, adverb;
      verbal phrase, adjective
   2. single part of speech, verb
   3. verbal phrase, noun
   4. single part of speech, noun;
      prepositional phrase, adverb

E. 1. dependent, adverb; dependent, adjective
   2. independent; independent
   3. dependent, noun

Written Exercises

A. 1. Abimelech wanted to be king after Gideon died.
   2. From his mother's relatives came Abimelech's support.
   3. Abimelech's wicked ambitions God could not bless.
   4. Abimelech was not humble like Gideon, although he was Gideon's son.
   5. After a woman cast a piece of a millstone upon his head, his life came to a sudden end.
   6. Whoever exalts himself will be humbled, but whoever humbles himself will be exalted.

B. 1. compound
   2. complex
   3. simple
   4. compound-complex
   5. complex

C. Diagram the skeletons and complements in all the clauses of these sentences.
1. A clear conscience is a valuable possession, but many people seemingly do not value it.
2. A wise person carefully trains his conscience and consistently obeys it.
3. A seared conscience is deceptive and dangerous.
4. The person who wants God's blessing must obey His Word.
5. The Bible reveals how God blesses His faithful servants.
6. If a person loves God, he will love God's Word.
7. A small red fox stepped into the clearing; but when it saw us, it dashed away.
8. Red foxes are plentiful here; though trappers have been catching many of them, their population remains at record levels.

D. Read the following paragraphs, and do the exercises that follow.

Poetry is easier to memorize than prose. For example, many people can readily quote the lines that tell how many days are in each month, but few could name the months in order and tell how many days each has. Poetry also is effective in saying much with few words. Try writing a good poem in prose, and see how many more words you need to use. Even more important, poetry fits well with worship. In fact, God has commanded that "psalms and hymns and spiritual songs" should be a part of our worship. Obviously, poetry is a valuable part of our language.

Since good poetry has such value, maybe you should accept the challenge of writing some. First of all, you should read plenty of good poetry, for that will give you the feel of what makes a poem effective. Then you must inspire yourself with a worthwhile message. Think of something beautiful or awe-inspiring in nature, or consider some theme from the Bible. Of course, you must eventually start writing down some thoughts, even if they do not seem to flow smoothly. Later you can improve the rhythm and rhyme and polish the expressive language.

1. Copy the topic sentence of each paragraph.
2. Write whether each paragraph is developed in chronological order, spatial order, or the order of importance.
3. What key words are repeated throughout both paragraphs?
4. Copy at least three transitional expressions from each paragraph.
5. Again read the first sentence of the second paragraph. What idea in this sentence provides a link between the two paragraphs?

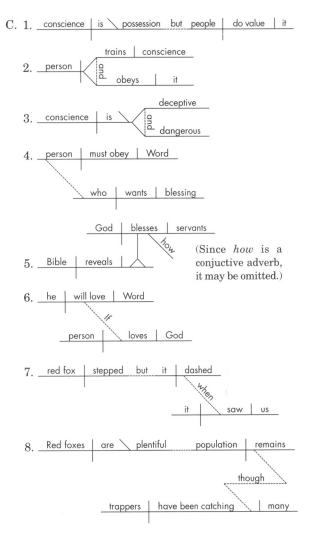

C. (Since *how* is a conjuctive adverb, it may be omitted.)

D. 1. *(1)* Obviously, poetry is a valuable part of our language.
   (2) Since good poetry has such value, maybe you should accept the challenge of writing some.
2. *(1)* order of importance
   (2) chronological order
3. poetry, poem
4. *(1)* For example; also; Even more important; In fact
   (2) First of all; Then; Later
5. the value of good poetry, which is the topic of the preceding paragraph

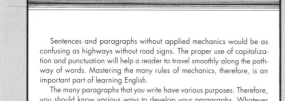

Chapter Three

Mechanics

Developing Paragraphs

Sentences and paragraphs without applied mechanics would be as confusing as highways without road signs. The proper use of capitalization and punctuation will help a reader to travel smoothly along the pathway of words. Mastering the many rules of mechanics, therefore, is an important part of learning English.

The many paragraphs that you write have various purposes. Therefore, you should know various ways to develop your paragraphs. Whatever method or combination of methods you use, remember that you develop paragraphs satisfactorily only as you include sufficient ideas to clarify and support the topic sentence. The ability to develop paragraphs well is an essential writing skill.

Then said [Jesus] unto them, Therefore every scribe
which is instructed unto the kingdom of heaven is like unto a man that is an householder,
which bringeth forth out of his treasure things new and old.

Matthew 13:52

21. Capitalization

Lesson Survey

- Capitalize the first word of every sentence, direct quotation, and line of poetry.
- Capitalize all proper nouns.
- Capitalize most modifiers derived from proper nouns.
- Capitalize the pronoun *I* and the interjection *O*.
- Capitalize the address, date, greeting, closing, and signature of a letter.
- Capitalize many abbreviations.

The main things involved in English mechanics are capitalization and punctuation. These things are like road signs along a highway: they tell the traveler (the reader) where the road of thought turns, pauses, or stops. The mechanics of English help a reader to understand what he is reading.

You should be quite familiar with most of the rules of capitalization summarized in this lesson. However, you may discover some new detail, or you may be reminded of a rule that you have trouble remembering. Pay special attention to such areas as you study the following rules of capitalization.

1. *Capitalize the first word of every sentence, direct quotation, and line of poetry.*

<u>T</u>he visitor said, "<u>Y</u>our pictures look beautiful."

<u>G</u>aze upon the stars so high—
<u>O</u>h, how small are you and I!
  <u>O</u>h, how great the God we love,
  <u>L</u>ord of heavenly realms above.

Sometimes explanatory words interrupt a direct quotation. When this happens, capitalize the first word of the second part only if it begins a new sentence.

"By next week," commented Father, "<u>w</u>e should be shelling corn."
  (Second part is a continuation of the sentence; no capital letter is needed.)
"The growing weather has been good this summer," said Father. "<u>W</u>e should have a bountiful harvest."
  (Second part begins a new sentence; a capital letter is needed.)

Lesson 21

Purpose: To study capitalization rules.

Oral Review:

1. Tell which kind of word order is used in each sentence.
   a. For three days Jesus' body lay in the tomb. (mixed)
   b. The grave could not hold Him when He rose from the dead. (natural)
   c. Out of the grave burst the Lord of life. (inverted)
2. Tell which sentence type according to structure fits each description.
   a. Two independent clauses. (compound)
   b. One independent clause. (simple)
   c. Two independent clauses and one dependent clause. (compound-complex)
   d. One independent clause and one dependent clause. (complex)
3. Name and identify the complements in these sentences. (Complements are underlined.)
   a. The Bible gives <u>us</u> true <u>knowledge</u>. (indirect object; direct object)
   b. God's people are <u>lights</u> in this dark world. (predicate nominative)
   c. They should make the <u>world</u> <u>brighter</u> by being here. (direct object; objective complement)
   d. At Jesus' words the waters became <u>peaceful</u>. (predicate adjective)

Lesson Introduction: What comes to your mind when you read the title of this chapter? You probably think of men with wrenches, screwdrivers, and other tools who work on cars to keep them running safely and smoothly. Auto mechanics are extremely important: our vehicles would often chug and sputter and

2. *Capitalize all proper nouns.* Study the following groups of proper nouns.

a. Names of specific persons, including initials and titles. Capitalize a title of respect (such as *doctor* and *king*) or a word that shows relationship (such as *brother* and *uncle*) only if it is used as part of a name or to replace a name. Always capitalize the word *president* when it refers to the current president of the United States.

> Mother and Father took Grandpa Beachy to see Dr. Roberts.
> My father asked the doctor if Grandpa was developing cataracts.
> The President receives thousands of letters every day.

b. Names of God and words referring to the Bible. Also capitalize personal pronouns that refer to God. However, do not capitalize words like *god* or *lord* when they refer to idols or people.

> The Lord wrote the Ten Commandments with His own finger.
> The principles of the Decalogue are expanded in the New Testament.
> The Philistine lords held an assembly to honor Dagon, their god.

c. Names of geographical features, such as countries, states, cities, rivers, lakes, and mountains. Capitalize words like *west* and *southeast* only when they name specific geographical regions, not when they name directions. When used as proper nouns, these words usually follow the word *the*.

> The Columbia River separates Oregon from Washington and flows into the Pacific Ocean.
> Many birds spend winter in the South and fly north in spring.

d. Titles of books, newspapers, magazines, stories, poems, and songs. Capitalize the first and last words and other important words. Articles, coordinating conjunctions, and prepositions of fewer than four letters should not be capitalized. (The subordinating conjunctions *as* and *if* should be capitalized.)

> We sang "How Calm and Beautiful the Morn" and "Fresh From the Throne of Glory."
> Have you read the book *The Lim Family of Singapore*?

e. Names of specific organizations, institutions, groups, races, and languages.

> The students of the Appleton Mennonite School sang at the Martinsville Nursing Home.
> The major ethnic groups in Belize are African, Mestizo, American Indian, and Creole.

even stop completely without their help.

Be assured that the *mechanics* of English are also quite important. They perform a valuable service in keeping our English sentences running "safely" and smoothly. Were there no English mechanics to help us, our sentences—which serve as vehicles to carry our thoughts—would often chug and sputter in their meaning and sometimes stop completely before they had expressed what we wanted to say. Be sure you treat these mechanics with the respect and appreciation they deserve.

This chapter does not deal with the usage of English words, but with mechanical aspects that affect the way we interpret words. These mechanics include capitalization, the various kinds of punctuation, and italics. Because there are established standards for these mechanics, written communication can be just as clear as oral communication.

Lesson Outline:

1. Capitalize the first word of every sentence, direct quotation, and line of poetry. If the second part of a divided quotation does not begin a new sentence, do not use a capital letter.

2. Capitalize all proper nouns.

(a) Names of specific persons, including initials and titles.

(b) Names of God and words referring to the Bible.

(c) Names of geographical features.

(d) Titles of books, newspapers, magazines, stories, poems, and songs.

(e) Names of specific organizations, institutions, groups, races, and languages.

(f) Names of specific ships, airplanes, trains, buildings, and monuments.

(g) Names of parks and historic sites, events, eras, and documents.

f. Names of specific ships, airplanes, trains, buildings, and monuments.

> The *Savannah,* a sailing ship with steam auxiliary, was the first ship to use steam in crossing an ocean.
>
> Someone has estimated that the Washington Monument would be the size of a pencil eraser if all the empty space in each atom were removed.

g. Names of parks and historic sites, events, eras, and documents. When used as proper nouns, these words usually follow the word *the.*

> The Revolutionary War had been in progress for over a year when the Declaration of Independence was signed.
>
> Many people deny that the Creation and the Flood are historical facts.

h. Brand names and registered trademarks. Do not capitalize any common noun that follows the brand name or trademark word.

> My uncle always buys Pilot pens and Ticonderoga pencils.
>
> Would you like Bufferin or Tylenol for your headache?

i. Names of school subjects derived from proper nouns or followed by numbers. The names of most school subjects are derived from common nouns and are not capitalized.

> Our afternoon classes include spelling, science, American history, and Typing I.

j. Calendar items, such as the names of months, days of the week, and holidays. Do not capitalize the names of the four seasons.

> This year winter begins on Saturday, December 21.
>
> We should thank God every day, not only on Thanksgiving Day.

3. *Capitalize most modifiers derived from proper nouns.* Most of these are proper adjectives, but occasionally such words become so common that they are no longer capitalized. Check a dictionary if you are not sure.

> Would you like some French dressing on your salad?
>
> I broke one of Mother's china serving dishes.

4. *Capitalize the pronoun* I *and the interjection* O. The word *O* is used mainly in poetry and in archaic English, such as that in the King James Bible. In modern prose, it is used to make a solemn appeal and is always followed by a noun of direct address. Do not confuse *O* with the interjection *oh,* which is capitalized only when it begins a sentence.

> "But I am poor and needy: make haste unto me, O God."
>
> To you, O people, I bring good tidings; oh, do not refuse this message.

(h) Brand names and registered trademarks.

(i) Names of school subjects derived from proper nouns or followed by numbers. The names of most school subjects are derived from common nouns and are not capitalized.

(j) Calendar items, such as the names of months, days of the week, and holidays (but not the names of the four seasons).

3. Capitalize most modifiers derived from proper nouns.

4. Capitalize the pronoun I and the interjection O.

5. Capitalize the address, date, greeting, closing, and signature of a letter.

6. Capitalize many abbreviations.

5. *Capitalize the address, date, greeting, closing, and signature of a letter.* You have just worked with this rule in the letters of Chapter 1.

6. *Capitalize many abbreviations.* Of course you must capitalize abbreviations of proper nouns and of titles used with proper nouns. Also capitalize the following miscellaneous abbreviations. Check a dictionary or an English handbook when you are not sure whether an abbreviation should be capitalized.

A.D.—*anno Domini* (in the year of the Lord)
A.M.—*ante meridiem* (before midday)
HP, H.P., hp, *or* h.p.—horsepower
P.M.—*post meridiem* (after midday)
T., tbs., *or* tbsp.—tablespoon
B.C.—before Christ   F *or* Fahr.—Fahrenheit
C—Celsius; centigrade   No. *or* no.—number

Class Practice
Tell which words or abbreviations have capitalization errors.
1. the holy scriptures reveal much to us about the lord god.
2. in the sermon on the mount, jesus gave specific teaching on how his people should live.
3. The true god showed his power over the Gods of egypt by sending great plagues.
4. What a mighty deliverance the israelite people experienced at the exodus!
5. My Grandfather, henry j. klassen, sr., was born in ukraine.
6. After world war II he moved his family to saskatchewan, a canadian province.
7. The un promotes pacifism, which is distinctly different from biblical nonresistance.
8. Historians generally agree that michael sattler wrote the schleitheim confession of faith in a.d. 1527.
9. Last Spring father bought an old farmall tractor from mr. lester gable, m.d.
10. The federal bureau of investigation (fbi) is part of the government branch that is headed by the president.
11. This quarter i must read *Where no one Stands Alone* and *Willie's acquaintance with Christ.*
12. Whereas grandpa Yoder's live in the south, grandpa Zimmerman's live just a few miles West of us.
13. "Make your sandwiches, children," mother directed. "you may choose from the lebanon bologna or the cold chicken meat."

Lesson 21 Answers

Class Practice
1. The, Holy Scriptures, Lord God
2. In, Sermon, Mount, Jesus, His
3. God, His, gods, Egypt
4. Israelite, Exodus
5. grandfather, Henry J. Klassen, Sr., Ukraine
6. World War, Saskatchewan, Canadian
7. UN, Biblical
8. Michael Sattler, Schleitheim, Confession, Faith, A.D.
9. spring, Father, Farmall, Mr. Lester Gable, M.D.
10. Federal, Bureau, Investigation, FBI, President
11. I, *No, One, Acquaintance, With*
12. Grandpa, South, Grandpa, west
13. Mother, You, Lebanon

14. The first macadam road was built by John L. McAdam, a scottish engineer.

Written Exercises

A. Each numbered line of this excerpt from a friendly letter has at least one capitalization error. Write correctly each word that has an error.

1.   route 1, box 693
2.   newmanstown, pa 17073
3.   october 25, 20—
4. dear freda,
5.   "our father's wondrous works we see
6.   in the earth and sea and sky;
7.   he rules o'er all in majesty,
8.   from his royal throne on high."
9.   Last friday we upper graders at Malvern Christian school took our
10. annual Fall hike. This year we went to brother Alvin Getz's farm near
11. texter mountain. His Dairy Farm includes several nice fields. His herd
12. of jersey and guernsey cows in the hilly pasture made a lovely scene.
13. He also owns seventy-five acres of woods on the South slope of the
14. Mountain. . . .
15.   your friend,
16.   velma

B. Write correctly each word or abbreviation that has a capitalization error.
1. "Hear my prayer, o lord."
2. because god is omniscient, man can never hide sin from his eyes.
3. "When you are tempted," father said, "Think of the song 'Yield not to temptation.'"
4. Both catholics and protestants persecuted the anabaptists in europe.
5. Do you want wheaties or kellogg's corn flakes?
6. "The high temperature on thursday," Marie reported, "Was 93°f."
7. Many States in the east are more heavily populated than those in the west.
8. This new Eureka Sweeper is quite an improvement over our old one.
9. Even before king Saul's death, David had been anointed as the next King.
10. The president lives in washington, d.c., in the white house.

C. Write a correct abbreviation for each word or phrase.
1. Alberta
2. miscellaneous
3. horsepower
4. quart
5. tablespoon
6. *post meridiem* (after midday)
7. rural free delivery
8. Mister
9. *anno Domini* (in the year of the Lord)
10. copyright

14. Scottish

Written Exercises

A. 1. Route, Box
    2. Newmanstown, PA
    3. October
    4. Dear, Freda
    5. Our, Father's
    6. In
    7. He
    8. From, His
    9. Friday, School
    10. fall, Brother
    11. Texter Mountain, dairy farm
    12. Jersey, Guernsey
    13. south
    14. mountain
    15. Your
    16. Velma

B. 1. O, Lord
    2. Because, God, His
    3. Father, think, Not, Temptation
    4. Catholics, Protestants, Anabaptists, Europe
    5. Wheaties, Kellogg's
    6. Thursday, was, F.
    7. states, East, West
    8. sweeper
    9. King, king
    10. President, Washington, D.C., White House

C. (Answers may vary according to reference sources used.)
    1. Alta.; AB   6. P.M.
    2. misc.   7. RFD; R.F.D.
    3. h.p.; HP   8. Mr.
    4. qt.   9. A.D.
    5. T.; tbsp.   10. c.; C.

Review Exercises

A. Name the five parts of a friendly letter. After each name, write the line number or numbers from Part A of Written Exercises which belong to that part. [2]

B. Copy each appositive, and label it *R* for restrictive or *N* for nonrestrictive. Commas have been omitted. [9]
   1. The prophet Nahum spoke concerning Nineveh the capital of Assyria.
   2. In 1 Corinthians 13 the Love Chapter the qualities of divine love are described.
   3. Paul the apostle to the Gentiles went many places with the Gospel the good news of salvation.
   4. Aquila and Priscilla instructed the eloquent teacher Apollos.

C. Diagram the skeletons and complements of these sentences, as well as all the words that make up appositives and independent elements. [7–9]
   1. My uncle Robert Kurtz has recently moved.
   2. There are four deer grazing in the field.
   3. My flowers! Somebody has ruined my flowers!
   4. Louise, have you finished the dishes?
   5. Brother Larry, an expert mechanic, fixed Grandfather's car.

---

22. End Punctuation

> ### Lesson Survey
> - Use a **period** after a declarative sentence, an indirect question, and an imperative sentence.
> - Use periods with initials and with many abbreviations.
> - Use **ellipsis points** to show an omission in a quoted passage.
> - Use a **question mark** after an interrogative sentence or a quotation.
> - Use a question mark within parentheses to indicate uncertainty about the preceding information.
> - Use an **exclamation point** after a strong interjection and after an exclamatory sentence or quotation.

The sentence is a basic unit of communication in the English language. In speaking, we indicate sentence divisions by pausing and by changing

Lesson 22

Purpose: To study the use of periods, question marks, exclamation points, and ellipsis points.

Oral Review:
1. Tell which words should be capitalized in these items. (Answers are underlined.)
   a. the <u>Lord</u> and <u>His</u> holy angels
   b. stories of the <u>Old</u> <u>Testament</u>
   c. an <u>English</u> walnut tree
   d. the first day of fall
   e. on <u>Monday</u>, <u>October</u> 10
   f. life in the <u>Northwest</u>
   g. the <u>Great</u> <u>War</u> in <u>European</u> history
   h. a set of <u>Craftsman</u> wrenches
   i. science and <u>Canadian</u> history
   j. traveling east on <u>Wayne</u> <u>Highway</u>
2. Each of these sentences contains a prepositional,

Review Exercises

A. heading, 1–3; greeting, 4; body, 5–14; closing, 15; signature, 16

B. 1. Nahum—R; the capital of Assyria—N
   2. the Love Chapter—N
   3. the apostle to the Gentiles—N; the good news of salvation—N
   4. Apollos—R

C. 1.

   2.

   3.

   4.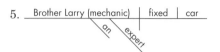

   5.

---

verbal, or single-part-of-speech phrase. Identify the phrase, tell what kind it is, and tell whether it functions as a noun, a verb, an adjective, or an adverb. (Phrases are underlined.)
   a. <u>Mr. Norman Taylor</u> owns this farm. (single part of speech; noun)
   b. The little boy, <u>whistling a merry tune</u>, brought the cows in. (verbal; adjective)
   c. Wilma made a beautiful motto and gave it <u>to Grandmother</u>. (prepositional; adverb)

Lesson Introduction: Write the following lines on the board.
   1. How great is the Lord
   2. You should at least try to fail in this assignment will be your disgrace

How would you punctuate number 1 if it was spoken by someone who does not know about God? (How

the pitch and volume of our voices. In writing, we use end punctuation and capitalization to show these divisions.

Periods

Use a *period* after a declarative sentence, an indirect question, and an imperative sentence. An indirect question is a question written as an indirect quotation. In such a sentence, the dependent clause expresses the question, but the independent clause (the main sentence) is declarative.

> The ability to withstand wrong influences is a mark of maturity. (declarative sentence)
> Father asked if we had finished the chores already. (indirect question)
> Follow the directions carefully. (imperative sentence)

Also use periods with initials and with many abbreviations. Among the most common exceptions are the two-letter abbreviations for states and provinces, and abbreviations for organizations and government agencies. If you are not sure whether to use a period, check a dictionary or an English handbook. Note that if an abbreviation that requires a period comes at the end of a sentence, only one period is used.

> Mr. G. O. Weaver has an appointment on October 22 at 10:15 A.M.
> You could ship this package either by USPS or by UPS.

> Multiply as shown to find the area of a square with sides 5 feet long.
> 5 ft. x 5 ft. = 25 sq. ft.

Remember that most abbreviations should not be used in formal writing, such as stories and reports. But they may be used where it is important to save time and space, as in taking notes or solving math problems. This is why *feet* is spelled out in the sentence before the math problem above, but is abbreviated in the math problem itself.

Ellipsis Points

Use three spaced periods, called *ellipsis points* (. . .), to show the omission of one or more words within a quotation, such as a Bible verse or a sentence copied from a reference source. The reason for such an omission is generally that the omitted words do not apply specifically to the subject under consideration. Look at these two examples.

> "In the beginning . . . the earth was without form, and void."
> "A big advantage of the diesel is the fact that it . . . may be as much as 10% more efficient than gasoline engines."

When you do omit part of a quotation, you must make sure that you do great is the Lord?) by a person who knows and honors God? (How great is the Lord!)

How can you punctuate number 2 to make a reasonable statement? (You should at least try. To fail in this assignment will be your disgrace.) to make an unreasonable statement? (You should at least try to fail. In this assignment will be your disgrace.)

End punctuation can make quite a difference!

Lesson Outline:

1. Use a period after a declarative sentence, an indirect question, and an imperative sentence.

2. Use periods with initials and with many abbreviations.

3. Use ellipsis points to show the omission of one or more words.

   a. The most common type of omission is one in which the middle part of a quotation is left out.

     1) Be sure not to change the meaning of the original statement by an omission.

     2) If the omission immediately follows a complete sentence, use the appropriate punctuation mark and then the ellipsis points.

   b. The omission may also be a sentence that trails off without a proper ending. In that case, use the ellipsis points without any other punctuation.

4. Use a question mark after an interrogative sentence or quotation.

   a. For emphasis, question marks may be used between items in a series within an interrogative sentence.

not change the meaning of the original statement. Look at the following example.

> **Original statement:**
> "Let him that stole steal no more: but rather let him labour, working with his hands the thing which is good."
> **Unacceptable quotation:**
> "Let him that stole steal no more . . . the thing which is good."

The sentence with the ellipsis completely changes the meaning of the original statement. Instead of forbidding all theft, it implies that some stealing may be all right. Such a quotation is totally unacceptable, especially since it changes a clear command in the Word of God.

The example above is extreme, of course, but it does show how greatly an omission can change the meaning of a quotation. Other improper omissions may not change the meaning so drastically and may not be detected as easily. In any case, you as a writer are responsible to use ellipsis points accurately.

If you quote more than one sentence and the first part makes a complete sentence, end the first part with the appropriate punctuation mark. Then use ellipsis points to show the omission, and continue with the quotation.

> period˥ ˏellipsis points
> "Ye shall know them by their fruits. ... Every tree that bringeth not forth good fruit is hewn down, and cast into the fire" (Matthew 7:16, 19).
> "And Moses said unto God, Who am I, that I should go unto Pharaoh? . . . And he said, Certainly I will be with thee" (Exodus 3:11, 12).

Ellipsis points are not used at the beginning or the end of a quotation. However, there are cases when a sentence trails off without a proper ending. Use ellipsis points without any other punctuation to show this kind of omission.

> We were wishing for a sunny day, but . . .

Question Marks

Use a *question mark* after an interrogative sentence or quotation. For emphasis, question marks may also be used between items in a series within an interrogative sentence.

> Do you have a purpose of heart as Daniel did?
> "Is everyone ready to go?" asked Father.
> Mother looked at me and asked, "Have you made your bed? combed your hair? brushed your teeth?"

Occasionally you may use a question mark within parentheses to indicate that you are not sure about the accuracy of the preceding information.

b. A question mark within parentheses may be used to indicate uncertainty about the accuracy of the preceding information.

5. Use an exclamation point after a strong interjection and after an exclamatory sentence or quotation. Avoid overusing the exclamation point.

Henry's grandfather was born in 1867(?), soon after the Civil War.
(The question mark means that the writer is not sure if 1867 is
the exact year in which Henry's grandfather was born.)

Exclamation Points

Use an *exclamation point* after a strong interjection and after an exclamatory sentence or quotation. Avoid overusing the exclamation point. Use it only when a word or sentence is truly exclamatory.

Indeed! I have no intention of doing that again.
If only I had listened to Father's advice!
"Lightning struck the barn!" shouted Melvin.

Class Practice

A. Tell how to divide this paragraph into sentences with proper capitalization and punctuation.

The electric eel is not a true eel, but it does have the ability to deliver a strong electric shock did you know that it generates the most powerful electric charge in the fish world it can produce a charge of more than six hundred volts actually, the electric eel is unusual in a number of ways it is a very sluggish creature, spending much of its time waiting for prey to swim near since the electric eel sometimes lives in water containing little oxygen, it may come to the surface and gulp in air even more strange, electric eels are so secretive that scientists still are not sure if they are born alive or are hatched from eggs.

B. Tell where end punctuation should be added.
1. The Lord hates dishonesty in any form
2. Hallelujah The Lord reigns from His heavenly throne
3. "Have you learned to be content, as the apostle Paul did" challenged Father
4. Well, I'm trying to learn, but
5. Length: 40 in; Width: 32 in
6. Is 3:00 PM your dismissal time
7. S J Weiler, Jr, is my uncle
8. What a surprise to see you
9. I wonder if you would help me with this project
10. Have you written a clear topic sentence kept the paragraph unified made smooth transitions

Written Exercises

A. Write the first and last words of each sentence, using ellipsis points to show omitted words between them. Use correct capitalization and punctuation.

If you can find the Big Dipper in the sky, you can also find the Little Dipper find the two stars at the lower end of the Big Dipper, which make

Lesson 22 Answers

Class Practice

A.   The electric eel is not a true eel, but it does have the ability to deliver a strong electric shock. Did you know that it generates the most powerful electric charge in the fish world? It can produce a charge of more than six hundred volts. Actually, the electric eel is unusual in a number of ways. It is a very sluggish creature, spending much of its time waiting for prey to swim near. Since the electric eel sometimes lives in water containing little oxygen, it may come to the surface and gulp in air. Even more strange, electric eels are so secretive that scientists still are not sure if they are born alive or are hatched from eggs.

B. 1. form.
2. Hallelujah! throne. *or* !
3. did?" Father.
4. but...
5. in.; in.
6. P.M. time?
7. S. J. Jr., uncle.
8. you!
9. project.
10. sentence? unified? transitions?

Written Exercises

A. If... Dipper. Find... bowl. Extend... star. This
... Dipper. From... Dipper.

the far side of the bowl extend a line from these two stars until it reaches a bright star this is Polaris, or the North Star, which is at the tip of the handle of the Little Dipper from Polaris, the Little Dipper curves back toward the Big Dipper.

B. Copy each item that should be followed by a punctuation mark, and add the correct punctuation.
1. "Have you seen Hannah's beautiful embroidery" asked Phoebe
2. What fine, even stitches she makes
3. I try to do a neat job too, but it seems
4. Do you remember Mrs A R Steckle
5. Do you know where we are going what time we plan to leave how long we shall be gone
6. Joshua asked why we had not started yet

C. Write a correct abbreviation for each word.
1. December
2. bushel
3. *anno Domini*
4. doctor of dental science
5. Vermont (two letters)
6. Central Standard Time
7. volume
8. teaspoon
9. avenue
10. miles per hour

D. Each of the following is a Bible quotation from which some words have been omitted. Copy the quotations, and use ellipsis points to show where the omissions are.
1. "Receive knowledge rather than choice gold" (Proverbs 8:10).
2. "Cast out the scorner, and strife and reproach shall cease" (Proverbs 22:10).
3. "A faithful messenger refresheth the soul of his masters" (Proverbs 25:13).

Review Exercises

A. Do these exercises with the paragraph in Class Practice, Part A. [13, 18]
1. Write the topic sentence.
2. Tell which kind of sentence order is used to develop the paragraph.
3. Copy one transitional word and one transitional phrase.
4. What key word is repeated several times?

B. Write whether the word order of each sentence is natural (*N*), inverted (*I*), or mixed (*M*). [11]
1. Because we are human, doing wrong is often easier than doing right.
2. From God's Word shines a message of good hope for the tempted.
3. God promises His aid to all who sincerely seek it.
4. The Bible contains both warning and encouragement.
5. By heeding His Word, we can keep ourselves free from evil.

B. 1. embroidery? Phoebe.
2. makes!
3. seems...
4. Mrs. A. R. Steckle?
5. going? leave? gone?
6. yet.

C. (Answers may vary according to reference sources used.)
1. Dec.
2. bu.
3. A.D.
4. D.D.S.
5. VT
6. CST *or* C.S.T.
7. vol.
8. t. *or* tsp.
9. ave. *or* Ave.
10. mph *or* m.p.h.

D. 1. "Receive... knowledge rather than choice gold" (Proverbs 8:10).
2. "Cast out the scorner, and... strife and reproach shall cease" (Proverbs 22:10).
3. "A faithful messenger... refresheth the soul of his masters" (Proverbs 25:13).

Review Exercises

A. 1. Actually, the electric eel is unusual in a number of ways.
2. order of importance
3. Actually, even more strange
4. electric eel

B. 1. M
2. I
3. N
4. N
5. M

C. Change these sentences to the word order or sentence style named in parentheses. Add any needed commas. [11, 17]
1. We saw some migrating geese when we went outside. (mixed)
2. As they winged their way south, they foretold the coming of winter. (loose)
3. A large flock of geese came down to our pond. (inverted)
4. They headed south again after several hours. (periodic)
5. Toward their winter homes flew these living testimonies of the Creator's wisdom. (natural)
6. As we study God's creation more, we see God's power more. (balanced)

C. 1. When we went outside, we saw some migrating geese.
2. They foretold the coming of winter as they winged their way south.
3. Down to our pond came a large flock of geese.
4. After several hours they headed south again.
5. These living testimonies of the Creator's wisdom flew toward their winter homes.
6. The more we study God's creation, the more we see God's power.

23. Commas

> ### Lesson Survey
> - Use a **comma** before a coordinating conjunction that joins the clauses of a compound sentence.
> - Use commas to separate items in a series.
> - Use a comma to set off certain introductory material.

Commas are used for four main purposes: to divide compound sentences, to separate items in a series, to set off introductory material, and to set off nonrestrictive and independent elements. In this lesson you will study the first three of these; and in Lesson 25 you will study the fourth, along with several miscellaneous uses of commas.

Compound Sentences

1. *Use a comma before a coordinating conjunction that joins the clauses of a compound sentence.* There are two exceptions to this rule. First, if the two clauses are very short and closely related, you may omit the comma. Second, if one or both of the clauses are longer and already contain one or more commas, the comma between the clauses may be changed to a semicolon. This helps to show the division between the two clauses more clearly.

Angels are spirits, but they can make themselves visible to men.
The ice cracked and I fell through.
The rain, which had fallen steadily for three days, stopped this morning; and by early afternoon the sun was shining brightly.

Lesson 23

Purpose: To study rules for using commas to divide compound sentences, to separate items in a series, and to set off certain introductory material.

Oral Review:
1. Tell what end punctuation should follow each sentence.
   a. When will the eclipse begin (question mark)
   b. How precisely God has made the world (exclamation point)
   c. I wonder if Richard will help with the hay again (period)
2. In addition to marking an interrogative sentence or quotation, what other use does the question mark have? (to show uncertainty about the accuracy of an item of information)

3. What is the function of ellipsis points? (to show the omission of one or more words)
4. What words in a title should *not* be capitalized? (articles, coordinating conjunctions, prepositions of fewer than four letters)

Lesson Introduction: Have you ever thought of how important it is to keep certain things separate? For example, if you do not keep your English papers separate from your math, science, and history papers, you will have considerable frustration when you try to find the right one. If some dogs are not kept apart, what a snarling and snapping and fighting there is! And if fire and gasoline vapors get together, it can cause a tremendous explosion. All these troubles can be avoided simply by keeping things properly separated.

In the same way, failing to keep certain words separated can cause confusion, frustration, and

Items in a Series

2. *Use commas to separate items in a series of words, phrases, or clauses, unless a pair within the series is joined by a conjunction.* Be sure to include the comma just before the final coordinating conjunction.

> Drawing, calligraphy, and woodworking are my favorite activities in art class.
> Tree branches were scattered in the garden, around the lawn, and across the road.
> The little boy was trying to carry his lunch box, his bat and ball, and his books.

To emphasize the number and variety of the things listed, a writer will sometimes connect all the items in a series with conjunctions. When this is done, no commas are used to separate the items.

> Men may dispute and revile and protest and rebel, but they will never change the truth of God's Word.

3. *Use commas to separate two or more descriptive adjectives that have equal rank.* In Grade 7 you studied three tests that help to determine whether adjectives in a series need commas between them.

(1) Do you pause between the adjectives as you read them?
(2) Does it sound right to use *and* between the adjectives?
(3) Does it sound right to change the order of the adjectives?

If the answer to all three of these questions is *yes,* the adjectives are of equal rank and should be separated by a comma. Consider how the adjectives in the following sentence pass all three tests and are therefore separated by commas.

> We ate our lunch beside the cool, clear, cascading stream.
> (three descriptive adjectives)

Now consider another sentence, in which the last two adjectives are not separated by commas.

> We hiked beside the clear, cascading mountain stream.

Why are *cascading* and *mountain* not separated by a comma? First, you should see that these words do not pass the three tests given above; they are not of equal rank. Further, the word *mountain* is closely related to *stream*—almost as closely as the two parts of a compound word. (Compare the compound words *mountaintop* and *mountain range.*) The sentence is describing a *mountain stream* that was *clear* and *cascading.* Watch carefully for adjectives that have such a close relationship to the words they modify. They should never be preceded by commas.

misunderstanding. That is why it is so important to use commas correctly. They keep words apart, and in this way they help to make writing clear, meaningful, and enjoyable.

Lesson Outline:

1. Use a comma before a coordinating conjunction that joins the clauses of a compound sentence.

  a. The comma may be omitted if the two clauses are very short and closely related.
  b. A semicolon may replace the comma if one or both clauses already contain one or more commas.

  (*Teacher:* Commas within clauses do not always mean that commas between clauses must be replaced by semicolons. For example, when a comma sets off an introductory word or a noun of direct address, the comma between two clauses is usually retained.

> Yes, Anna has swept the floor, and Ida has washed the windows.
> Lisa, if it starts raining, please bring in the laundry.)

2. Use commas to separate items in a series of words, phrases, or clauses, unless a pair within the series is joined by a conjunction. Sometimes a writer connects all the items in a series with conjunctions.

3. Use commas to separate two or more descriptive adjectives.

  a. If the answer to all three of the following tests is *yes,* you should use a comma.
    (1) Do you pause between the adjectives as you read them?
    (2) Does it sound right to use *and* between the adjectives?

Also remember that commas are used to separate only *descriptive* adjectives. Whenever any of the adjectives are *limiting,* no commas are used. Study this sentence.

> The four large boulders made a convenient bridge across the stream. (No comma is used between *The* and *four* because both are limiting. No comma is used between *four* and *large* because one is limiting and one is descriptive.)

Remember too that no comma should be used between the last adjective and the word that is modified.

> cool, clear stream—*not* cool, clear, stream

Introductory Material

4. *Use a comma to set off an introductory word.* This includes a response such as *yes* or *no,* or a mild interjection.

> No, we cannot see a person's heart as God does.
> Ah, but one's words and actions reveal what is in his heart.

5. *Use a comma to set off an introductory verbal phrase or a long introductory prepositional phrase.* After a short prepositional phrase, you may omit the comma unless it is needed to make the sentence clear. Also, no comma is needed if the sentence is written in inverted order.

> Whistling cheerfully, Nevin walked out to the barn. (verbal phrase)
> In the meadow across the brook, a herd of deer grazed contentedly. (long introductory phrase)
> In the meadow, grass grew luxuriantly. (Without the comma, the introductory phrase appears to be *In the meadow grass.*)
> In the meadow across the brook grazed a herd of deer. (No comma needed because the sentence has inverted word order.)

6. *Use a comma to set off an introductory adverb clause.*

> Although fall has officially arrived, the weather remains quite warm.

Class Practice

Tell where commas or semicolons are needed in these sentences.
1. Despising spiritual values Esau sold his birthright.
2. Abraham Isaac and Jacob were great patriarchs of faith.
3. Although Job was sorely tried he maintained a deep unwavering faith in God.
4. Naomi advised Ruth and Orpah to return to their homes but Ruth was determined to go with Naomi.
5. Naomi had moved with her family to the land of Moab and there she had lost Elimelech Mahlon and Chilion.

Lesson 23 Answers

Class Practice

1. values,
2. Abraham, Isaac,
3. tried, deep,
4. homes,
5. Moab; Elimelech, Mahlon,

   (3) Does it sound right to change the order of the adjectives?

   b. Do not place a comma before the final adjective if it is closely related to the noun it modifies.

   c. Do not use a comma between two limiting adjectives or between a limiting adjective and a descriptive adjective.

   d. Do not use a comma between the last adjective and the word that is modified.

4. Use a comma to set off an introductory word. This includes a response such as *yes* or *no,* or a mild interjection.

5. Use a comma to set off an introductory verbal phrase or a long introductory prepositional phrase.

   a. After a short prepositional phrase, you may omit the comma unless it is needed to make the sentence clear.

   b. No comma is needed if the sentence is written in inverted order.

6. Use a comma to set off an introductory adverb clause.

6. Inside the car wash the doors seats and dashboard.
7. No Kenneth will wash the car later.
8. Oh we worked hard but it rained before we could finish the baling.

Written Exercises

A. Write the number of the rule in this lesson that applies to the commas used in each sentence.
1. What a blessing to have a Christian environment at home, at school, and at church.
2. Yes, this certainly helps us to choose right.
3. Such blessings help us, but they do not guarantee a right response.
4. Even though a person does not have these blessings, he can choose right.
5. A warm, gentle breeze blew all afternoon.
6. Heavy clouds rolled in before evening, and rain began to fall.
7. In the center of the scrapbook page, Heidi drew a lovely picture.
8. Rachel, Priscilla, and Sarah planned this bulletin board.
9. After they had it planned, Brother Auker gave a few suggestions.
10. Indeed, it has a worthwhile theme in an attractive display.

B. Copy each word that should be followed by a comma or semicolon, and add the missing punctuation.
1. Many people thronged Jesus to hear His words to see His miracles and to eat the food He provided but few were willing to obey His teachings.
2. At the time of Jesus' trial the multitudes had rejected Him.
3. Yes Jesus' calm gracious forgiving manner testified of His character.
4. Because He loved sinful man Jesus was willing to endure rejection agony and death.
5. Lo His death provides redemption for mankind and His resurrection proves His power over death.
6. For the new school desks were purchased at a sale.
7. Three short gnarled apple trees guarded the lonely dilapidated cabin.
8. Several squirrels scampered across the clearing up a large tree and out of sight.
9. Before we stepped up to the cabin door a large blacksnake slithered across the threshold.
10. After that we girls would not go near the cabin but the boys did investigate it for a while.

Review Exercises

A. Write the letter of the correct description for each sentence below. [14–16]
   a. simple sentence with no compound parts
   b. simple sentence with a compound predicate
   c. compound sentence with two independent clauses

6. car,   doors,   seats,
7. No,
8. Oh,   hard, *or* ;

Written Exercises

A.   1. 2
     2. 4
     3. 1
     4. 6
     5. 3
     6. 1
     7. 5
     8. 2
     9. 6
     10. 4

B.   1. words,   miracles,   provided;
     2. trial,
     3. Yes, calm,   gracious,
     4. man,   rejection,   agony,
     5. Lo,   mankind, *or* ;
     6. school,
     7. short,   lonely,
     8. clearing,   tree,
     9. door,
     10. that,   cabin, *or* ;

d. compound sentence with three independent clauses
e. complex sentence with one independent clause and one dependent clause
f. complex sentence with one independent clause and two dependent clauses
g. compound-complex sentence with two independent clauses and one dependent clause

1. Before we eat breakfast, we gather for family worship.
2. With few exceptions, we sing several songs first.
3. We usually read from a Bible storybook, and we always read from the Bible.
4. After we have discussed the Bible passage, one of us children prays, and then Father prays.
5. Before cold weather set in, several families from church filled the woodshed for Brother Carl, who is old and feeble.
6. A number of sisters came along and cleaned house for Sister Ellen.
7. We children had plenty of work to do too.
8. The older boys helped stack the wood, the older girls helped clean the house, and some of us cleaned the yard.

B. Diagram the skeletons and complements of all the clauses in these sentences. [14–16]
1. We must follow the Lord and obey His voice.
2. If we humble ourselves, the Lord will exalt us, and we shall be blessed.
3. Paul suffered many things, but he had learned true contentment.
4. The youth who diligently avoids evil will be amply rewarded.

Review Exercises

A. 1. e   5. f
   2. a   6. b
   3. c   7. a
   4. g   8. d

B.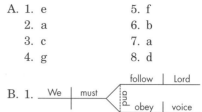
1.
2.

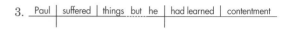
3.
4.

24. Types of Compositions

Lesson Survey

- An **exposition** is a composition that defines, clarifies, or explains.

- An **argument** is a composition that presents information or evidence in an attempt to persuade or move to action.

- A **narration** is a composition that tells a story.

- A **description** is a composition that paints word pictures.

In this English series so far, you have written three different kinds of paragraphs: paragraphs that explain, paragraphs that describe, and paragraphs that tell a story. This lesson introduces the specific name of each

Lesson 24

Purpose: To identify the *four types of writing: exposition, argument, narration, and description. (*Previous experience:* Expository, narrative, and descriptive writing without specifically categorizing them.)

Oral Review:

1. Give the correct term for each description.
   a. A sentence that states the main idea of a paragraph. (topic sentence)
   b. The quality of ideas flowing smoothly from one sentence to the next. (coherence)
   c. The quality of every sentence supporting and developing the topic sentence. (unity)
2. Name the kind of sentence order
   a. that gives details in the order of space. (spatial)
   b. that gives details in the order of time. (chronological)
   c. that gives the most important detail first or last. (order of importance)

Lesson Introduction: Imagine that your mother had one kettle that she used to prepare everything she ever made for the table. Whether she was frying eggs for breakfast or boiling potatoes for dinner, baking bread for the family or preparing meat loaf for visitors, mixing lemonade or baking cookies, she always used her one special kettle! Can you imagine that? Of course not. The different kinds of food call for different tools.

So it is with writing. No one single type of paragraph can fill the need for every kind of writing you must do. As a writer you need different "tools"—that is, different types of writing. This lesson summarizes the four basic types of paragraphs according to their paragraph type and shows how the different types compare with one another. It also introduces a fourth kind of paragraph.

All paragraphs fit into one of these four kinds. Understanding the difference between these paragraph types will help you to be more effective in your writing. The four basic paragraph types are exposition, argument, narration, and description.

Exposition

Exposition (also called expository writing) defines, clarifies, or explains. The root word of *exposition* is *expose;* the purpose of this writing is to expose facts or information. We are using exposition when we tell how something works or why something is the way it is. A builder is using exposition when he explains how to build with concrete blocks or how to put a roof on a house. Exodus 28:15–21, where God gave detailed instructions for fashioning the high priest's breastplate, is expository writing. All that you have read in this lesson thus far is exposition.

Exposition explains or instructs by using several different methods: comparison and contrast, definition, step-by-step directions, examples, reasons, or details. Generally the ideas given in expository writing are written in the order of importance or in chronological order. Consider the following paragraphs, both of which are exposition.

> A chemical change results in the formation of new substances; that is, the basic chemical elements in the original substances are separated and recombined to create new chemical compounds. A paraffin candle contains hydrogen and carbon combined in large hydrocarbon molecules. When the candle is burned, the hydrogen (H) and carbon (C) separate and then combine with oxygen (O) in the air to form carbon dioxide (CO_2) and water (H_2O).
>
> A simple demonstration will make this process visible. Hold a spoon in the flame of a candle. You will soon collect black carbon on the spoon. Ordinarily, this carbon burns and becomes a colorless gas, carbon dioxide. Now smother the flame inside a drinking glass. You should see water vapor forming on the inner surface of the glass.

Each of the sample paragraphs begins with a clear topic sentence. The first paragraph is developed by definition and example, and the second gives step-by-step directions.

Argument

Argument (also called argumentative, or persuasive, writing) is similar to exposition in that it, too, explains and clarifies. However, argument goes one step further. In addition to explaining, it presents information or

purposes. If you come to understand and use them well, you will be able to "cook up" many different kinds of "tasty" writing, just as your mother prepares various kinds of good, nourishing food.

Lesson Outline:

1. An exposition is a composition that defines, clarifies, or explains.

    a. The purpose is to expose facts or information.

    b. Exposition uses comparison and contrast, definition, step-by-step directions, examples, reasons, or details.

    c. Exposition is written in the order of importance or in chronological order.

2. An argument is a composition that presents information or evidence in an attempt to persuade or move to action.

    a. Argument is used when there is disagreement or when there seems to be conflicting evidence.

    b. The writer of argument selects and arranges evidence to support his opinion.

    c. The ideas should be presented in the order of importance.

    d. The writer of argument must use sound evidence and convincing facts, not merely emotional fervor.

    e. Argumentative writing will be unbalanced if it unfairly presents only one side of an issue.

3. A narration is a composition that tells a story.

    a. A story is written in chronological order.

    b. Narration presents truth and its practical

evidence in an attempt to persuade the reader or move him to action. Exposition seeks to have the reader say, "I understand"; argument tries to have him say, "I agree."

Obviously, argument is used when there is disagreement or when there seems to be conflicting evidence. The writer of argument selects and arranges evidence to support his opinion. The ideas given in argumentative writing should be presented in the order of importance. You will study more about writing arguments in Chapter 9.

Here is an example of argumentative writing.

> The farmer does not have an easy life. He puts much hard physical labor into farming his crops and caring for his livestock. The farmer is also much more dependent on favorable weather than most other people are. And the farmer must invest a large amount of money to start even a small farm.
>
> Nevertheless, farming is a good employment for the Christian. It enables him to work at home with his family, where he can teach his children and enjoy their company. The farmer avoids much association with the sinful world, for he does not need to work daily with those who swear, smoke, lie, cheat, or dress immodestly. The Christian farmer can observe the power of God at work among his crops and herds. He is not restricted in his work by laws and union rules about hours and holidays. Rather, he is able to arrange his work to allow time for church activities more easily than some others can do. Farming is an enterprise in which the Christian can use his abilities to support his family, employ his growing children, and honor his Creator.

In these paragraphs the writer is explaining the benefits of farming. But beyond that, he tries to convince the reader that these things truly are benefits to a Christian farmer.

Both the writer and the reader of argument should remember two important facts. First, emotional fervor alone does not determine whether something is right or wrong. Therefore, the writer of an argument must do more than make strong statements; he must use sound evidence and convincing facts. Second, argumentative writing will be unbalanced if it unfairly presents only one side of an issue. Of course, the writer of an argument will select those facts and evidences that support his opinion. But he must always be fair with the facts, even those that make his argument look weaker.

Narration

Narration (also called narrative writing) tells a story. A story, of course, is written in chronological order. This type of composition is important because it presents truth and its practical applications in a way that is

applications in a way that is interesting and easy to understand.

4. A description is a composition that paints word pictures.

    a. Vivid, concrete words help the reader to see what the writer has seen.

    b. Sometimes an entire essay is a description; but more often descriptive paragraphs are used in narratives, expositions, or arguments to provide a setting or to create a mood.

    c. The description of a person, a place, or an object should be written in spatial order.

    d. The description of an event should be written in chronological order.

5. A longer composition often includes several of these types of writing.

interesting and easy to understand. You have already studied narration in previous years, and you will study it again this year in Chapter 6.

Description

Description (or descriptive writing) uses carefully selected details to paint a picture in the reader's mind. The writer of a description uses vivid, concrete words to help the reader see what he has seen. Sometimes an entire essay is a description, but more often descriptive paragraphs are used in narratives, expositions, or arguments to provide a setting or to create a mood.

The details of a description must be arranged carefully. To describe a person, a place, or an object, you would arrange the details in spatial order; to describe an event, you would use chronological order. Without this order, even the most interesting and clearly described details would lose their effectiveness.

Notice the careful selection of words and the logical order used in the following description.

> The oat bins were in a roomy loft at one end of the woodshed. The loft was lighted by a large square window in the gable, arranged to swing back on hinges like a door. Besides three large oat bins, it contained a bin for barley, one for buckwheat, and one for bran. From the woodshed below, admittance to the loft was gained by a flight of open board stairs and a spacious trap door.

Longer compositions often include several of these types of writing. For example, 1 Corinthians 15 is primarily an argument, written to convince the Corinthians that a bodily resurrection is essential to Christianity. But the passage also includes a brief narrative of Christ's death, burial, resurrection, and post-resurrection appearances (verses 3–8), as well as some expository verses. For example, Paul used the different degrees of glory in earthly and heavenly bodies to illustrate the difference in glory between the believers' physical bodies and their glorified, resurrected bodies (verses 40–44).

The reason for the four types of writing is that writing is done for different purposes. With a clear understanding of these types and purposes, you can select and use the type of writing that best fulfills the purpose of your composition.

Class Practice

A. Tell what kind of composition is described in each statement.
1. It tells a story.
2. It is written to persuade or move to action.
3. It may be written to provide a setting or to create a mood.
4. It must not depend merely on emotional fervor.
5. It is written to explain, clarify, or inform.

Lesson 24 Answers

Class Practice

A. 1. narration
2. argument
3. description
4. argument
5. exposition

6. Most of this English book consists of this type of composition.
7. Vivid, concrete words are especially important.
8. It is written when there is disagreement or conflicting evidence.
9. It will be unbalanced if only one side of an issue is presented.
10. It paints word pictures.
11. It may be written in either chronological or spatial order.
12. It is written in chronological order.
13. It may be written in chronological order or in the order of importance.
14. It should be written in the order of importance.

B. Identify the kind of writing in each paragraph.
1.   "Now at the end of the days that the king had said he should bring them in, then the prince of the eunuchs brought them in before Nebuchadnezzar. And the king communed with them; and among them all was found none like Daniel, Hananiah, Mishael, and Azariah: therefore stood they before the king."
2.   "Thou, O king, sawest, and behold a great image. This great image, whose brightness was excellent, stood before thee; and the form thereof was terrible. This image's head was of fine gold, his breast and his arms of silver, his belly and his thighs of brass, his legs of iron, his feet part of iron and part of clay."
3.   "For as I passed by, and beheld your devotions, I found an altar with this inscription, TO THE UNKNOWN GOD. Whom therefore ye ignorantly worship, him declare I unto you. God that made the world and all things therein, seeing that he is Lord of heaven and earth, dwelleth not in temples made with hands; neither is worshipped with men's hands, as though he needed any thing, seeing he giveth to all life, and breath, and all things. . . . Forasmuch then as we are the offspring of God, we ought not to think that the Godhead is like unto gold, or silver, or stone, graven by art and man's device."
4.   "Beware of false prophets, which come to you in sheep's clothing, but inwardly they are ravening wolves. Ye shall know them by their fruits. Do men gather grapes of thorns, or figs of thistles? Even so every good tree bringeth forth good fruit; but a corrupt tree bringeth forth evil fruit. A good tree cannot bring forth evil fruit, neither can a corrupt tree bring forth good fruit. Every tree that bringeth not forth good fruit is hewn down, and cast into the fire. Wherefore by their fruits ye shall know them."

Written Exercises

A. Write which kind of composition each paragraph is.
1.   It seemed as though the kitchen was just calculated to make a boy feel cross. The table stood against the kitchen wall on its three legs, its tablecloth daubed with molasses and stained with gravy. A

6. exposition
7. description
8. argument
9. argument
10. description
11. description
12. narration
13. exposition
14. argument

B. 1. narration
2. description
3. argument
4. exposition

Written Exercises

A. 1. description

plate, with something in it that looked like melted lard, but which Tip's mother called butter, and a half loaf of bread were the only eatable articles as yet on the table. Around these the flies had gathered in such numbers that it seemed as though they might carry the loaf away entirely, if too many of them did not drown themselves in the butter. Over all, the July sun poured in its rays from the eastern window, the only one in the room.

2.   Find the dew point of the air in your schoolroom. Secure a metal cup or can with smooth metallic sides. A glass container will work also, but the condensation will be easier to detect on a metal surface. Fill the cup with cold water, ice, or ice and salt until the temperature of the can is low enough to cause moisture to condense on the outside of the cup. Use a thermometer to find the temperature of the inside of the can. The temperature at which moisture condenses out of the air is its dew point.

3.   Let us not be confused by the popular idea that wrong is one extreme and right is the other extreme, and that in between are a whole host of things that are neither right nor wrong. We must evaluate every idea, trend, and experience in the light of whether it will be a blessing or a curse to us.

4.   Kitty stood still in her astonishment and watched him while he took out the round, green sticks that she had put in, and laid in bits of dry paper and bits of sticks—laid them in such a careless, uneven way that it seemed to her they would never burn in the world. Only he speedily proved that they would, by setting fire to the whole. They crackled and snapped in a most determined manner, and finally roared outright.

2. exposition
3. argument
4. narration

B. Write a narrative or descriptive paragraph about one of the following topics. Label your paragraph to tell which kind it is.
1. a gathering storm
2. an automobile accident
3. pickle-canning day
4. shoveling out after a heavy snow
5. Mother's flowers
6. the cow stable

B. (Individual work.)

C. Write an argumentative paragraph about one of the following topics.
1. advantages of a large family
2. the need for more courtesy (or another virtue) in your school
3. benefits of living in the country
4. values of starting a worship service with singing

C. (Individual work.)

D. Write an expository paragraph about one of the following topics.
1. blessings of attending a Christian school
2. differences between a crocodile and an alligator
3. how snow is formed
4. how to make butter

D. (Individual work.)

Review Exercises

Read the selection below, and do the exercises that follow. [13, 18, 19]

[1]Have you ever listened to older people freely quoting Scripture verses? [2]Have you marveled at their ability to recall and recite these verses? [3]How did they develop such familiarity with the Scriptures? [4]Part of the answer lies in the simple fact that they love the Bible. [5]They read it, they think about it, they study it. [6]Some of the secret may also lie in their childhood training. [7]They may well have memorized Bible verses at home, in school, and in Sunday school. [8]And a great deal of the answer lies, no doubt, in their personal diligence. [9]Quality Bible memorization—the kind that results in long-lasting mastery—is hard work.

[10]Such familiarity with the Scriptures is a valuable aid in resisting temptation. [11]Jesus demonstrated this principle by quoting Scripture verses when the devil tempted Him in the wilderness. [12]Being able to quote Scripture verses is helpful, too, when you are talking with someone about the Bible but you do not have a Bible with you. [13]Furthermore, persecuted Christians have sometimes had to live for weeks or months without Bibles. [14]Imagine how precious the memorized Bible verses were then! [15]The songs they knew by memory also provided precious comfort. [16]Indeed there are numerous advantages to knowing many Scripture verses by memory.

1. Write the number of the topic sentence for each of the paragraphs.
2. Write the number of the sentence that should be deleted from the second paragraph.
3. Copy two transitional expressions from each paragraph.
4. What key words are repeated throughout these paragraphs?
5. How does the first sentence in the second paragraph provide a good transition between the two paragraphs?

Review Exercises

1. *paragraph 1:* 3
   paragraph 2: 16
2. 15
3. *paragraph 1:* also, And
   paragraph 2: too, Furthermore
4. Scripture, Scriptures, Bible
5. It mentions familiarity with the Scriptures, which is the theme of the first paragraph.

25. More Comma Rules

Lesson Survey

- Use commas to set off nonrestrictive and independent elements.

- Use commas in conventional situations such as in addresses and dates, in large numbers, after the greeting and the closing of a friendly letter, and with direct quotations.

- Use a comma anywhere it is needed to prevent misunderstanding.

Lesson 25

Purpose: To study the use of commas to set off non-restrictive words, independent elements, and various other items in sentences.

Oral Review:

1. What kind of sentence almost always needs a comma? (compound sentence)
2. Commas should separate words, phrases, or clauses that come in a ———. (series)
3. What three tests help to determine when commas should separate descriptive adjectives? (Do you pause between the adjectives as you read them? Does it sound right to use *and* between the adjectives? Does it sound right to change the order of the adjectives?)
4. What two types of introductory words should be set off with commas? (responses such as *yes* and *no;* mild interjections)
5. What kinds of introductory phrases should be set off with commas? (verbal phrases; long prepositional phrases)
6. What kind of introductory clause must be set off with a comma? (adverb clause)

Lesson Introduction: Commas are important. Sometimes they make a big difference in the meanings of sentences, and sometimes they simply make reading easier. Consider the following examples.

> Brother David rewarded all the students who had kept their desks neat.
> Brother David rewarded all the students, who had kept their desks neat.

What does the second sentence indicate that the first does not? (That all the students in the classroom had kept their desks neat.)

Commas again! Yes, commas are the most versatile and frequently used of all punctuation marks, for they indicate the numerous brief pauses that occur in speech. In Lesson 23 you studied the following six rules for using commas.

1. *Use a comma before a coordinating conjunction that joins the clauses of a compound sentence.*
2. *Use commas to separate items in a series of words, phrases, or clauses.*
3. *Use commas to separate two or more descriptive adjectives.*
4. *Use a comma to set off an introductory word.*
5. *Use a comma to set off an introductory verbal phrase or a long introductory prepositional phrase.*
6. *Use a comma to set off an introductory adverb clause.*

This lesson contains ten more rules for the use of commas.

Nonrestrictive and Independent Elements

7. *Use commas to set off nonrestrictive adjective clauses.* A restrictive clause restricts, or limits, the meaning of a noun or pronoun by telling *which*. But a nonrestrictive clause simply gives additional information about the word it modifies. In other words, a restrictive clause is needed to make the meaning of the sentence clear, but a nonrestrictive clause is not needed. Therefore, a nonrestrictive clause is set off with commas.

Note that when words are set off, two commas are needed if those words are in the middle of a sentence. Only one comma is needed to set off words at the beginning or end of a sentence.

> The Jordan River, <u>which flows through Palestine</u>, is a winding river. (The clause does not restrict *Jordan River* by telling which one; commas are needed.)
> I enjoyed meeting Lynette Heatwole, <u>who is living with my grand-mother</u>. (The clause does not restrict *Lynette Heatwole* by telling which one; commas are needed.)

Notice the difference in the following sentence, where the underlined clause is restrictive. Not all the cows must be chased into the meadow—just the ones in the neighbors' garden.

> The cows <u>that are ruining the neighbors' garden</u> must be chased into the meadow. (The clause restricts *cows* by telling which ones.)

8. *Use commas to set off nonrestrictive appositives.* A nonrestrictive appositive, like a nonrestrictive clause, simply gives additional information about the noun or pronoun it follows. This information is not needed to make the meaning of the sentence clear, so it is separated from the rest of the sentence by commas. Nearly all the appositives you studied in previous years are of this kind. In the following sentences,

Now write a large number on the board, without commas: 890129876194. Time how long it takes for any student to read the number. Then do the same for another large number, written with commas: 985,307,215,359. How much difference is there in the times?

These examples should help to impress the students with the importance of commas.

Lesson Outline:

(*Teacher:* Points 1–6 are a review of Lesson 23.)

1. Use a comma before a coordinating conjunction that joins the clauses of a compound sentence.

2. Use commas to separate items in a series of words, phrases, or clauses.

3. Use commas to separate two or more descriptive adjectives.

4. Use a comma to set off an introductory word.

5. Use a comma to set off an introductory verbal phrase or a long introductory prepositional phrase.

6. Use a comma to set off an introductory adverb clause.

7. Use commas to set off nonrestrictive adjective clauses.

   a. A restrictive clause limits the meaning of the word it modifies and is needed to make the meaning of the sentence clear.

   b. A nonrestrictive clause simply gives additional information about the word it modifies and is not needed to make the sentence clear.

8. Use commas to set off nonrestrictive appositives.

the nonrestrictive appositives are underlined.

> Dagon, <u>the god of the Philistines</u>, had fallen before the ark of the Lord.
>> (The appositive does not restrict *Dagon* by telling which one; commas are needed.)
>
> The best pitcher, <u>Melvin</u>, has sprained his arm.
>> (The appositive does not restrict *pitcher* by telling which one; commas are needed.)

A restrictive appositive is necessary to the meaning of a sentence because it restricts a noun or pronoun by telling *which*. Also, a restrictive appositive is often very short (one or two words), it is closely related to the noun or pronoun it follows, and there is no pause in reading it. For these reasons, restrictive appositives are not set off with commas.

> My cousin <u>Sheryl Weaver</u> likes to write stories.
>> (The appositive restricts *cousin* by telling which one; no commas are needed.)
>
> Father helped us <u>boys</u> to assemble the bicycle.
>> (The appositive restricts *us* by telling who is included; no commas are needed.)

9. *Use commas to set off titles of family relationship or professional rank that follow names.*

> Louise is under treatment by Dr. Carlton Walsh, M.D.
> Leonard R. Zimmerman, Jr., sold us this farm.

10. *Use commas to set off nouns of direct address.*

> Glenda, help Martha set the table.
> Have you considered, Lowell, how important your influence is?

11. *Use commas to set off parenthetical expressions.* Parenthetical expressions, like nonrestrictive clauses and appositives, are not essential to the meaning of the sentence. They are independent elements that may give an explanation, show a transition, or state a contrasting idea.

> The chapter on electricity, I'm sure, will be an interesting study.
> For example, we may get to make a simple electric motor.
> Science, not history or math, has always been my favorite subject.

Miscellaneous Uses

12. *Use commas to separate the parts of dates and addresses.*

> 3938 S. Park Ave.
> Tucson, AZ 85714
> October 9, 20—

a. A restrictive appositive is needed to limit the preceding noun.

b. A nonrestrictive appositive adds nonessential information.

9. Use commas to set off titles of family relationship or professional rank that follow names.

10. Use commas to set off nouns of direct address.

11. Use commas to set off parenthetical expressions.

a. They are not essential to the meaning of the sentence.

b. They may be used to give an explanation, to show a transition, or to state a contrasting idea.

12. Use commas to separate the parts of dates and addresses.

13. Use commas to separate large numbers into periods of thousands, millions, and so forth.

14. Use a comma after the greeting of a friendly letter and after the closing of any letter. (Use a colon after the greeting of a business letter.)

15. Use a comma to separate a direct quotation from the rest of the sentence unless some other punctuation is used.

16. Use a comma anywhere it is needed to prevent misunderstanding.

a. Commas not directly called for by one of the previous rules should be used only rarely.

b. Using too many commas is just as undesirable as omitting necessary commas.

★ **EXTRA PRACTICE**
Worksheet 9 (*Practice With Commas*)

The building of the Berlin Wall was begun on August 13, 1961, to prevent people from fleeing to freedom.

My uncle lives at Box 156, Emo, Ontario P0W 1E0.

13. *Use commas to separate large numbers into periods of thousands, millions, and so forth.*

$17,350   a population over 250,000,000

14. *Use a comma after the greeting of a friendly letter and after the closing of any letter.* (Use a colon, rather than a comma, after the greeting of a business letter.)

Dear Uncle Paul,   Sincerely,

15. *Use a comma to separate a direct quotation from the rest of the sentence unless some other punctuation is used.*

Brother Wilmer announced, "We are planning a school hike on October 17."

"Bring a sack lunch," he continued, "because we shall be going over lunch time."

"Where are we going?" questioned Jonathan.

(No comma is needed because a question mark separates the quotation from the explanatory words.)

Prevention of Misunderstanding

16. *Use a comma anywhere it is needed to prevent misunderstanding.* For the sake of clarity, you sometimes need to use a comma that is not directly called for by one of the previous rules. But be sure the comma you add is truly needed, for using too many commas is just as undesirable as omitting necessary commas. The following sentences definitely need commas to prevent misunderstanding.

Inside, the barn was damaged by the fire.

(comma needed to prevent reading *Inside the barn* as a phrase)

At the market, store these items in a cool place.

(comma needed to prevent reading *At the market store*)

Look at the following sentence. Which of the commas are unnecessary and should be removed?

In pioneer days, a person could often travel, by stagecoach, from one city, to another.

All of them should be removed! This sentence is perfectly clear without a single comma.

In pioneer days a person could often travel by stagecoach from one
city to another.

Class Practice

Tell where commas should be placed in these sentences. (The rules at
the beginning of the lesson also apply.)

1. "God's Word we know is eternally unchanging" Brother Alfred
   asserted.
2. "Because it will never change we can trust its promises" he continued "as well as its prophecies."
3. The full name of my cousin James is James Daniel Kauffman Jr.
4. The earth which is the only planet suited for life is 93000000 miles
   away from the sun.
5. We moved on July 6 1993 and our address is now Route 1 Box 295
   New Tripoli PA 18066.
6. Yes Jesus' many miracles demonstrated His power over human
   sickness over the elements of nature and over the powers of demons.
7. Besides the beans should be picked before it gets too warm Brian.
8. Sitting on the large front porch we enjoyed the soft cool breeze.
9. After a few days on the farm Glen Zwally a boy from the city could
   feed the calves by himself.
10. The place that he calls home is a rundown crowded apartment not
    a comfortable house as we have.

Written Exercises

Write the number of the rule that is followed for each comma used in
these sentences, including the rules at the beginning of the lesson. Each
letter applies to the commas used with the underlined words immediately following.

1. Even (a) Elijah, who boldly proclaimed the Lord's way, became
   (b) discouraged, and he fled at Jezebel's threats.
2. Although he was (a) discouraged, Elijah did listen to the (b) still,
   small voice of God.
3. The (a) earthquake, wind, and fire demonstrated God's (b) power,
   but they could not give direction to (c) Elijah, the discouraged prophet.
4. "God is still (a) faithful, we know, in speaking to those who are
   (b) discouraged," Father commented.
5. According to the World Almanac and Book of Facts for (a) 1992,
   (b) 450,000,000 people speak English and 885,000,000 people speak
   Mandarin Chinese.
6. (a) Well, four other major Chinese (b) languages, in addition, are
   spoken by several hundred million more people.

Lesson 25 Answers

Class Practice

1. Word, know, unchanging,"
2. change, promises," continued,
3. Kauffman,
4. earth, life, 93,000,000
5. 6, 1993, 1, 295, New Tripoli,
6. Yes, sickness, nature,
7. Besides, warm,
8. porch, soft,
9. farm, Zwally, city,
10. rundown, apartment,

Written Exercises

A. 1.	a. 7	b. 1	
2.	a. 6	b. 3	
3.	a. 2	b. 1	c. 8
4.	a. 11	b. 15	
5.	a. 5	b. 13	
6.	a. 4	b. 11	

7. (*a*) <u>Besides,</u> other languages and dialects are spoken in some areas of (*b*) <u>China, the most populous nation in the world.</u>
8. (*a*) <u>Glen,</u> I heard that on (*b*) <u>Saturday, January 10, 20—,</u> (*c*) <u>Milton Yoder, Jr.,</u> plans to leave for two years of service in Guatemala.

B. Copy each word or number that should be followed by a comma, and add the comma. If no comma is needed in a line, write *correct*.

1.   Route 1 Box 71
2.   Andreas PA 18211
3.   October 28 20—
4. Dear Nelson
5.   God who reigns over all is certainly worthy of our praise! Yes we
6. heard about the wind hail and lightning damage at your farm. At a
7. time like that it is wonderful to trust the Lord. Have you moved back
8. into your house or hasn't the damage been repaired well enough yet?
9. Many people I'm sure have been praying for you during this time.
10.   The reason I'm writing Nelson is to ask if it is true that your bicy-
11. cle was damaged beyond repair. If this is true our family would like
12. to replace it for you. Harvey Graybill Jr. one of my cousins repairs
13. old bicycles and sells them. When Father goes to town in two weeks
14. he could bring one to your place.
15.   Your friend
16.   Charles

C. Copy each word or number that should be followed by a comma, and add the comma. Write the large number correctly.

1. Lo God has answered our prayers and Father is getting better again.
2. "Come children" Mother directed "and we'll thank the Lord the true Healer of every disease."
3. Yes Dr. Harold Graham M.D. also had a part but we know that God deserves the glory.
4. Someday in the future time will cease.
5. Measuring approximately 3500000 square miles the Sahara is the largest desert in the world.
6. Although much of the dry barren desert is lifeless there are scattered oases that support plant animal and human life.

Review Exercises

Copy each complement, and label it *PN* (predicate nominative), *PA* (predicate adjective), *DO* (direct object), *IO* (indirect object), or *OC* (objective complement). [5–8]

1. Everyone is dependent both upon God and upon others for wisdom.
2. No one truly makes himself wise.

7. a. 16 *or* 4   b. 8
8. a. 10   b. 12   c. 9

B. 1. 1,   9. people, sure,
2. Andreas,   10. writing, Nelson,
3. 28,   11. true,
4. Nelson,   12. Graybill, Jr., cousins,
5. God, all, Yes,   13. weeks,
6. wind, hail,   14. correct
7. that,   15. friend,
8. house,   16. correct

C. 1. Lo, prayers,
2. Come, children," directed, Lord,
3. Yes, Graham, M.D., part,
4. future,
5. 3,500,000 miles,
6. dry, lifeless, plant, animal,

Review Exercises

1. dependent—PA
2. himself—DO; wise—OC

3. Therefore, the truly wise person gives God and others due credit.
4. Of course, diligence also remains a requirement for wisdom.
5. You must fear the Lord and seek true wisdom.

3. God—IO; others—IO; credit—DO
4. requirement—PN
5. Lord—DO; wisdom—DO

26. Quotation Marks

> ### Lesson Survey
> - A direct quotation is enclosed in **quotation marks.**
> - Quotation marks are used around the titles of minor works.
> - A quotation or a title within a quotation is enclosed in single quotation marks.
> - A comma or a period is placed inside the quotation marks.
> - A semicolon or a colon is placed outside the quotation marks.
> - When a quotation itself is a question or an exclamation, the question mark or exclamation point is placed inside the quotation marks.
> - When the whole sentence is a question or an exclamation but the quotation is not, the question mark or exclamation point is placed outside the quotation marks.

Stories are no doubt the place where you see the most quotation marks. And certainly the direct quotations in a story have an important part in making the story come alive. By having the characters say certain things, the writer can *show* their actions as well as their feelings (rather than merely telling them). A skillful writer makes careful use of quotation marks.

Double Quotation Marks

A direct quotation consists of the exact words of a speaker. It is enclosed in *quotation marks* and separated from the rest of the sentence by a comma or some other punctuation. An indirect quotation tells what a speaker said without repeating his exact words; it is written without quotation marks.

> Aunt Nancy said that she plans to bring some homemade bread along. (indirect quotation)
> Aunt Nancy said, "I plan to bring some homemade bread along." (direct quotation)
> "Have you ever tasted her bread before?" asked Mother.

Lesson 26

Purpose: To study the correct use of quotation marks.

Oral Review:

1. Most rules for comma usage fit into what four general categories? (to divide compound sentences; to separate items in a series; to set off introductory material; to set off nonrestrictive and independent elements)
2. What three tests help to determine when commas should separate descriptive adjectives? (Do you pause between the adjectives as you read them? Does it sound right to use *and* between the adjectives? Does it sound right to change the order of the adjectives?)
3. Name two kinds of nonrestrictive elements that need to be set off with commas. (nonrestrictive adjective clauses; nonrestrictive appositives)
4. Name some independent elements that need to be set off with commas. (titles that follow names; nouns of direct address; expressions like *I think* and *for example*)

Lesson Introduction: To highlight the value of quotation marks, point out how their absence in the King James Bible sometimes makes it hard to know where a quotation begins and ends. For example, have students turn to Acts 1:4, 5 and see if they can tell where Jesus' exact words begin. ("Saith he" was inserted by the translators, as indicated by the italics in many Bibles.) Then have them turn to Romans 3:10, which begins, "As it is written, There is none righteous..." Can the students tell where this quotation ends? (Verse 18 ends it.) It takes careful reading to determine this—and even then one does not always know for sure.

"It is simply delicious!" declared Martha.

When explanatory words divide a quotation, place quotation marks around each part of the speaker's actual words. Then decide whether the quoted words form one sentence or more than one. If the second part of the quotation is not a new sentence, place a comma after the explanatory words. If the second part is a new sentence, use a period and begin the second part of the quotation with a capital letter.

> "I believe the Bible account of Creation," Father stated, "rather than the unscriptural theory of evolution."
> "Godly fear is the foundation of true knowledge," he continued. "No one who rejects God can be truly wise."

When a quotation consists of more than one paragraph, quotation marks are used at the beginning of each paragraph. But they are not put at the end of each paragraph; only the last paragraph of the quotation ends with quotation marks.

> "This used to be my mother's bedroom suite," Aunt Josephine said pleasantly. "Probably you never had such hard furniture to dust before. Today's furniture is much smoother.
> "Did you remember to dust the grooves and the carvings in the headboard?"
> Janet shook her head. She had not even thought of that.

Quotation marks are also used around material quoted from a printed source. If the quotation is long, however, it may be printed in smaller type as an indented block. Quotation marks are unnecessary when a quotation is set off in this way.

> Menno Simons wrote to his persecuted brethren, "O soldiers of God, prepare yourselves and fear not! This winepress you must tread. This narrow way you must walk, and through this narrow gate you must enter into life."
>
> *   *   *   *   *
>
> Conrad Grebel, Felix Manz, and George Blaurock started the Anabaptist movement in Switzerland. The account of their rebaptism is described in the *Chronicle of the Hutterian Brethren* by Kaspar Braitmichel.
>
> > One day when they were meeting, fear came over them and struck their hearts. They fell on their knees before the almighty God in heaven and called upon him who knows all hearts. They prayed that God grant it to them to do his divine will and that he might have mercy on them. Neither flesh and blood nor human wisdom compelled them. They were well aware of what they would have to suffer for this.

Such an evaluation is no reflection against the King James Bible. It is simply a way of helping students to appreciate the advancement in mechanics that is brought by quotation marks.

Lesson Outline:

1. A direct quotation is enclosed in quotation marks.

    a. An indirect quotation should not be written with quotation marks.

    b. A comma or some other punctuation separates the quotation from the rest of the sentence.

    c. When both parts of a divided quotation form only one sentence, place a comma after the explanatory words.

    d. If the second part of a divided quotation is a new sentence, place a period after the explanatory words and begin the second part of the quotation with a capital letter.

    e. When a quotation consists of more than one paragraph, use quotation marks at the beginning of each paragraph, but after only the last one.

    f. Quotation marks are used around material quoted from a printed source. If the quotation is long, it may be printed in smaller type as an indented block, without quotation marks.

2. Quotation marks are used around the titles of minor works, such as short stories and poems, chapters of books, and songs. Short stories and poems are those that do not make up an entire book. Even a "long" poem of twenty-four or thirty-six stanzas is considered a minor work. I

> After the prayer, Georg Blaurock stood up and asked Conrad Grebel in the name of God to baptize him with true Christian baptism on his faith and recognition of the truth. With this request he knelt down, and Conrad baptized him, since at that time there was no appointed servant of the Word. Then the others turned to Georg in their turn, asking him to baptize them, which he did. And so, in great fear of God, together they surrendered themselves to the Lord. They confirmed one another for the service of the Gospel and began to teach the faith and to keep it. This was the beginning of separation from the world and its evil ways.

Quotation marks are also used around the titles of minor works. Minor works include short stories and poems (those less than book length), chapters of books, and songs. The titles of longer works are italicized, as you will see in Lesson 30. Generally, you should not place a comma before a title enclosed in quotation marks.

> Is the song "My God, How Endless Is Thy Love!" in the *Church Hymnal?* The boys especially enjoyed studying "Generating and Using Electricity" in *God's Orderly World, Science 9 & 10.*

Single Quotation Marks

When a quotation or a title lies within a quotation, it is enclosed in single quotation marks. This occurs when a speaker quotes someone else's words or states a title that must be enclosed in quotation marks. Begin this inner quotation with a capital letter. When a word like *said* or *asked* comes before the inner quotation, place a comma after that word, especially if there is a pause at that point.

> "Grandfather often said, 'No problem is too big or too little to pray about,'" Curtis said quietly.
> "'Someone to Thank' is what I'd like to sing," replied Abigail.
> "I think the proverb 'A soft answer turneth away wrath' is especially practical," Mother remarked. (No comma precedes the inner quotation because it is not introduced by a word like *said* or *asked,* and there is no pause at that point.)

Notice in each example that the inner quotation or title is enclosed in single quotation marks. The entire quotation, including the inner quotation or title, is enclosed in double quotation marks.

Punctuation With Quotation Marks

Four rules govern the use of punctuation with quotation marks. These rules apply to both single and double quotation marks.

1. *A comma or a period at the end of a quotation is placed inside the quotation marks.*

general, no comma is used before a title enclosed in quotation marks.

3. A quotation or a title within a quotation is enclosed in single quotation marks. Begin this inner quotation with a capital letter. When a word like *said* or *asked* comes before the inner quotation, place a comma after that word, especially if there is a pause at that point.

Note: Double and single quotation marks are alternated when there are several levels of quotations within quotations. The Bible contains a number of such "nested quotations." If quotation marks were used in the King James Version, 2 Kings 18:19–25 would be punctuated as shown below.

> 19. And Rabshakeh said unto them, "Speak ye now to Hezekiah, 'Thus saith the great king, the king of Assyria, "What confidence is this wherein thou trustest?
> 20. "Thou sayest, (but they are but vain words,) 'I have counsel and strength for the war.' Now on whom dost thou trust, that thou rebellest against me? . . .
> 22. "But if ye say unto me, 'We trust in the Lord our God': is not that he, whose high places and whose altars Hezekiah hath taken away, and hath said to Judah and Jerusalem, 'Ye shall worship before this altar in Jerusalem'? . . .
> 25. "Am I now come up without the Lord against this place to destroy it? The Lord said to me, 'Go up against this land, and destroy it.'"""

4. Four rules govern the use of punctuation with quotation marks.

"This incident shows only too well," Brother Isaac stated, "that 'Only by pride cometh contention.'"

An exception is made when a quotation from a written source is followed by a reference, such as the reference for a Bible verse. Then the reference is written in parentheses after the quotation marks, and the comma or period is placed after the parentheses.

"I hate vain thoughts: but thy law do I love" (Psalm 119:113).
It is true that "God is love" (1 John 4:8), but God never overlooks deliberate sin.

2. *A semicolon or a colon at the end of a quotation is placed outside the quotation marks.*

Father suggested, "You could start the service by leading 'Saviour, Like a Shepherd Lead Us'; and you could close it with 'The Old Rugged Cross.'"
I understand this from the proverb "It is as sport to a fool to do mischief": only a fool finds pleasure in wrongdoing.

3. *When a quotation itself is a question or an exclamation, the question mark or exclamation point is placed inside the quotation marks.*

"What does the Bible teach about cheerfulness?" asked William.
Ornan exclaimed, "If only we could teach more people about the Bible!"
Judith repeated, "Mother clearly asked, 'Are you ready to go?'"

4. *When the whole sentence is a question or an exclamation but the quotation is not, the question mark or exclamation point is placed outside the quotation marks.*

Did Reuben say, "The game is over"?
(The whole sentence is a question, but the quotation is not.)
What a blessing to say, "The Lord is my shepherd"!
(The whole sentence is an exclamation, but the quotation is not.)

This becomes more difficult to evaluate when the sentence contains a quotation within a quotation. Always put the question mark or exclamation point with the part of the sentence that is a question or an exclamation. Study these examples, which illustrate the correct placement of these punctuation marks in such sentences.

"Was it Job who said, 'I know that my redeemer liveth'?" asked Paula.
(The inner quotation is not a question, so the question mark is not inside the single quotation mark. But Paula's words are a question, so the question mark is inside the double quotation marks.)

(1) *A comma or a period at the end of a quotation is placed inside the quotation marks.* An exception is made when a quotation from a written source is followed by a reference, such as the reference for a Bible verse. Then the reference is written in parentheses after the quotation marks, and the comma or period is placed after the parentheses.

(2) *A semicolon or a colon at the end of a quotation is placed outside the quotation marks.*

(3) *When a quotation itself is a question or an exclamation, the question mark or exclamation point is placed inside the quotation marks.*

(4) *When the whole sentence is a question or an exclamation but the quotation is not, the question mark or exclamation point is placed outside the quotation marks.* The question mark or exclamation point always goes with the part of the sentence that is a question or an exclamation.

5. **Only one end punctuation mark is used after any sentence.** If both the quotation and the whole sentence are questions, only one question mark is used; and it is placed inside all the quotation marks.

(*Teacher:* You may also mention the following rule if you wish.

If one part of a sentence is a question and the other is an exclamation, use only the mark that belongs inside the *double quotation marks.*

How heartless it was of Cain to ask, "Am I my brother's keeper?"
Father commented, "How heartless it was to ask, 'Am I my brother's keeper'!")

★ *EXTRA PRACTICE*
Worksheet 10 *(Quotation Marks)*

"Father certainly did not say, 'You may have the whole afternoon off'!" exclaimed Mother.

(The inner quotation is not an exclamation, so the exclamation point is not inside the single quotation mark. But Mother's words are an exclamation, so the exclamation point is inside the double quotation marks.)

Only one end punctuation mark is used after any sentence. For example, if both the quotation and the whole sentence are questions, only one question mark is used. Such an end mark is placed inside all the quotation marks.

Incorrect: Roy asked, "Was it Pilate who said, 'What is truth?'?"
Correct: Roy asked, "Was it Pilate who said, 'What is truth?'"

Class Practice

A. Tell how to use correct punctuation and capitalization in these sentences.
1. Ivan answered that he had finished his chores.
2. Jesus clearly said my kingdom is not of this world; nevertheless, many people try to mix Christianity and worldly politics.
3. The following persons contributed to the hymn Jesus, Lover of My Soul: Charles Wesley, who wrote the words; Joseph P. Holbrook, who composed one tune; and Simeon B. Marsh, who composed another tune.
4. This hymn has been called the best-loved hymn in the language, commented Father.

B. These sentences give practice with single and double quotation marks. Tell how to use correct punctuation and capitalization in them.
1. Glen has already memorized A Psalm of Life! exclaimed Robert.
2. Who said, with God all things are possible? asked Rhoda.
3. Do you know who wrote I Owe the Lord a Morning Song? asked Gabriel.
4. I believe, answered Duane that Amos Herr wrote it.
5. We heard someone shout Help said Leona.
6. Here is a good reason to memorize the song Yield Not to Temptation: it is helpful to sing that song when you are tempted.

C. Tell what the mistakes are in these sentences.
1. Howard exclaimed, "Look at that beautiful sunset"!
2. Kathryn said that she wants to sing 'Twilight Is Stealing'.
3. "This makes me think of Grandfather's words, 'Every sunset reminds me that my life's sun must set soon," Darlene said.
4. "Forsake the foolish, and live; and go in the way of understanding." (Proverbs 9:6)

Lesson 26 Answers

Class Practice

A. 1. (contains an indirect quotation; correct)
2. Jesus clearly said, "My kingdom is not of this world"; nevertheless, many people try to mix Christianity and worldly politics.
3. The following persons contributed to the hymn "Jesus, Lover of My Soul": Charles Wesley, who wrote the words; Joseph P. Holbrook, who composed one tune; and Simeon B. Marsh, who composed another tune.
4. "This hymn has been called the best-loved hymn in the language," commented Father.

B. 1. "Glen has already memorized 'A Psalm of Life'!" exclaimed Robert.
2. "Who said, 'With God all things are possible'?" asked Rhoda.
3. "Do you know who wrote 'I Owe the Lord a Morning Song'?" asked Gabriel.
4. "I believe," answered Duane, "that Amos Herr wrote it."
5. "We heard someone shout, 'Help!'" said Leona. (The comma after *shout* is optional, since one does not necessarily pause at that point and the quotation is only one word.)
6. This is a good reason to memorize the song "Yield Not to Temptation": it is helpful to sing that song when you are tempted.

C. 1. sunset!"
2. "Twilight Is Stealing."
3. soon,'"
4. understanding" (Proverbs 9:6).

5. We cannot excuse unkind words by saying, "That was just a slip of the tongue;" indeed, the tongue does not say what the mind has not thought.

6. "John Burroughs said, 'A man can fail many times, but he isn't a failure until he begins to blame somebody else," stated Father.

7. "Did Mother say clean your bedrooms after the dishes are done?" asked Carolyn.

8. "Yes," Elizabeth answered, "That's what she said."

Written Exercises

A. Copy these sentences and supply the missing punctuation and capitalization. Treat a group of words as a direct quotation only when that is clearly indicated by explanatory words. (Sentences 3–5 give practice with single and double quotation marks.)

1. Who wrote the song All the Way My Saviour Leads Me

2. In what psalm did David say surely goodness and mercy shall follow me all the days of my life

3. Don't forget that Jesus said blessed are the peacemakers stated Father

4. By Friday morning announced Brother Jesse be ready to recite the poem God's Will for Us

5. James declared How relieved we were to hear the doctor say She has no broken bones

B. If the underlined part of the sentence is punctuated incorrectly, write it correctly. If it is correct, write *correct*.

1. "The prophet Isaiah wrote, 'But they that wait upon the Lord shall renew their <u>strength,"</u> said Brother Arthur.

2. God asked Job, "Canst thou bind the sweet influences of Pleiades, or loose the bands of <u>Orion"?</u>

3. God has promised, "I will never leave thee, nor forsake <u>thee;"</u> therefore, we can always trust His care for us.

4. "What a wonderful God we <u>serve!"</u> exclaimed Elsie.

5. Mrs. O'Brian <u>shouted, 'Your</u> house is burning!"

6. "How delighted we were when Brother Clayton said, 'You may have fifteen minutes of extra recess this <u>afternoon!'"</u> declared Kevin.

7. Clement of Alexandria, who lived in the third century A.D., wrote the words for "Shepherd of Tender <u>Youth".</u>

8. God commands us to give thanks "always for all <u>things:"</u> sickness and health, pain and pleasure, persecution and peace.

9. "<u>'I</u> want to finish this chapter' is not a proper response when your mother calls you," Father reprimanded.

10. "Have you read the story 'Cherry <u>Cobbler?'"</u> asked Benjamin.

5. tongue";

6. else,'"

7. say, 'Clean   done'?"

8. answered, "that's *or* answered. "That's

Written Exercises

A. (Corrections are underlined.)

1. Who wrote the song <u>"</u>All the Way My Saviour Leads Me<u>"?</u>

2. In what psalm did David say<u>,</u> <u>"</u>Surely goodness and mercy shall follow me all the days of my life<u>"?</u>

3. <u>"</u>Don't forget that Jesus said<u>,</u> <u>'</u>Blessed are the peacemakers<u>,'</u><u>"</u> stated Father<u>.</u>

4. <u>"</u>By Friday morning<u>,"</u> announced Brother Jesse<u>,</u> <u>"</u>be ready to recite the poem <u>'</u>God's Will for Us<u>.'"</u>

5. James declared<u>,</u> <u>"</u>How relieved we were to hear the doctor say<u>,</u> <u>'</u>She has no broken bones<u>'!"</u>

B. 1. strength,'"

2. Orion?"

3. thee";

4. correct

5. shouted, "Your

6. afternoon'!"

7. Youth."

8. things":

9. correct

10. Cobbler'?"

11. In his letter, Cousin Lee asks, "Have you had your first snow <u>yet"?</u>
12. "Thomas Edison <u>said everything</u> comes to him who hustles while he waits,'" said Uncle Eldon.

Review Exercises

Write correctly each word or abbreviation that has an error in capitalization. [21]

1. The flood of noah's day was the greatest disaster this World has known.
2. This account shows god's hatred for sin and his grace on the righteous.
3. At Apple View Mennonite school we have weekly Bible Memory assignments.
4. When constantine issued the edict of Milan in a.d. 313, christianity became a tolerated religion in the Roman empire.
5. On october 5, the temperature at Willow airport rose to 75°f.
6. Before recess we usually have English and Math classes.
7. My Grandfather is serving at a small Mission church in michigan.
8. Those who live in the north must make ample preparation for Winter.
9. "Did you know, Leroy," asked Nevin, "That father is buying a Ford Tractor?"
10. Usually i like french dressing on my salad.

11. yet?"
12. said, 'Everything

Review Exercises

1. Flood, Noah's, world
2. God's, His
3. School, memory
4. Constantine, Edict, A.D., Christianity, Empire
5. October, Airport, F.
6. math
7. grandfather, mission, Michigan
8. North, winter
9. that, Father, tractor
10. I, French

27. Colons and Semicolons

Lesson Survey

- Use a **colon** to separate the numbers in Scripture references and in expressions of time.
- Use a colon after the salutation of a business letter.
- Use a colon to introduce something that is to follow.
- Use a **semicolon** to join independent clauses when no conjunction is used or when a conjunctive adverb is used. A semicolon may also be used to join independent clauses when one or more of the clauses already contain commas.
- Use a semicolon to separate items in a series when the individual items contain commas.

Lesson 27

Purpose: To study the correct use of colons and semicolons.

Oral Review:

1. Name some examples of titles that should be enclosed in quotation marks. (short stories, short poems, chapters of books, songs)
2. What is the general purpose of single quotation marks? (to set off a quotation or title within a quotation)
3. Which two punctuation marks should always be placed inside the quotation marks? (comma, period)
4. Which two punctuation marks should always be placed outside the quotation marks? (colon, semicolon)
5. When should a question mark or an exclamation point be placed inside quotation marks? (when the quotation is a question or an exclamation)
6. When should a question mark or an exclamation point be placed outside quotation marks? (when the whole sentence is a question or an exclamation, but the quotation is not)

Lesson Introduction: Have your students turn to Proverbs 10. What is the first verse in this chapter that has no colon? (verse 18) What punctuation would we use in most of these verses instead of a colon? (comma) In modern English usage, the colon is not used nearly as much as it was in the past. Mechanics, like word usage, tend to change over a period of time.

Lesson Outline:

1. Use a colon to separate the numbers in Scripture references and in expressions of time.

2. Use a colon after the salutation of a business letter.

In most of your writing, you use many more commas than either colons or semicolons. But these less common marks also have important functions that will help you to express yourself clearly in writing.

Colons

1. *Use a colon to separate the numbers in Scripture references and in expressions of time.*

Genesis 1:26	3:00 P.M.
Ephesians 4:32	10:35 A.M.

2. *Use a colon after the salutation of a business letter.*

Dear Sir: Dear Mr. Jones: Gentlemen:

3. *Use a colon to introduce something that is to follow.* What follows may be a list, an explanation, a question, an appositive, or a formal quotation. The expression *as follows* or *the following* often precedes a colon used in this way.

This use of the colon can be likened to an arrow: it points to the information that follows, directing the reader's attention there. If a complete sentence follows a colon, it may begin with a capital letter, especially if the sentence is long.

> The boys' names are as follows: John Raymond, Dallas Paul, Jerry Lee, and Eli Henry. (introduces a list)
> Here is a serious question: Will (*or* will) your attitudes make you a better person or a worse person? (introduces a question)
> Only one Person knows the future perfectly: God.
>   (introduces *God,* which is an appositive to *Person*)

A formal quotation is a notable statement made by a respected or high-ranking person. Since it is a quotation, it must be written with quotation marks and proper capitalization.

> Concerning his many accomplishments, Dr. George Washington Carver made this statement: "Without God to draw aside the curtain, I would be helpless." (introduces a formal quotation)

The words before a colon must express a complete thought. Therefore, a colon should never separate a verb and its complements or a preposition and its objects.

Incorrect:	In later lessons we will write: reports, descriptions, poems, arguments, and stories.
Correct:	In later lessons we will write reports, descriptions, poems, arguments, and stories.
Correct:	In later lessons we will write various compositions: reports, descriptions, poems, arguments, and stories.

3. Use a colon to introduce something that is to follow. What follows may be a list, an explanation, a question, an appositive, or a formal quotation.

   a. The expression *as follows* or *the following* often precedes a colon used in this way.
   b. The colon points to the information that follows, directing the reader's attention there.
   c. If a complete sentence follows a colon, it may begin with a capital letter, especially if the sentence is long.
   d. A formal quotation is a notable statement made by a respected or high-ranking person.
   e. The words before a colon must express a complete thought. Therefore, a colon should never separate a verb and its complements or a preposition and its objects.

4. Use a semicolon to join independent clauses when no conjunction is used or when a conjunctive adverb is used. A semicolon may also be used to join independent clauses when one or more of the clauses already contain commas.

5. Use a semicolon to separate items in a series when the individual items contain commas.

Incorrect: The wagons were pulled by: horses, mules, and oxen.
Correct: The wagons were pulled by horses, mules, and oxen.
Correct: The wagons were pulled by several kinds of draft ani-
mals: horses, mules, and oxen.

Semicolons

4. *Use a semicolon to join independent clauses when no conjunction is used or when a conjunctive adverb is used. A semicolon may also be used to join independent clauses when one or more of the clauses already contain commas.* You should use a semicolon between clauses only if a period would also be correct.

Alta enjoys working inside; Melody prefers outside work.
(no conjunction used; period would also be correct)
Alta enjoys working inside; however, Melody prefers outside work.
(conjunctive adverb used; period would also be correct)
Alta enjoys inside work like cooking, cleaning, and sewing; but Melody prefers outside work like tending the garden, mowing the lawn, and feeding the calves.
(commas already used; period would also be correct)

5. *Use a semicolon to separate items in a series when the individual items contain commas.*

We are caring for our neighbors' pets while they are away: Boots, a Siamese cat; Bowser, a collie; and Frisky, a Toggenburg goat.

Class Practice

A. Tell where colons, semicolons, and capital letters are needed in these sentences.
1. In a short time Job lost almost everything most of his possessions, all his children, his health, and his wife's support.
2. Satan thought that Job served God only for material benefits, however, he did not understand Job's faith and commitment.
3. Job's friends, Eliphaz, Bildad, and Zophar, came to comfort him, but Job called them miserable comforters.
4. On our flight we stopped in several cities Denver, Colorado, Seattle, Washington, and Vancouver, British Columbia.
5. When we arrived at Prince George, British Columbia, Uncle Warren was waiting for us, and by 130 P.M. we left the airport.
6. The words of Proverbs 2131 came to my mind "safety is of the Lord."
7. My question is this what will be the long-term effects of our decision?

B. In this part of a business letter, tell how to correct each punctuation error in the numbered lines. If a line has no error, say *correct*.

Lesson 27 Answers

Class Practice

A. 1. everything:
2. benefits;
3. him;
4. cities: Colorado; Washington;
5. us; 1:30
6. 21:31   mind: "Safety
7. this: What *or* what

1. Dear Sirs,
2.   Please send me information about any of the following products that
3. you carry; garden netting, plastic mulch, and trays for starting seeds. I
4. am particularly interested in detailed descriptions of these items, in addi-
5. tion, I would like a complete catalog of your products.
6.   Sincerely,
7.   Henry Mast

B. 1. Sirs:
   2. correct
   3. carry:
   4. items;
   5. correct
   6. correct
   7. correct

Written Exercises

A. For each sentence, write *1, 2, 3, 4,* or *5* to tell which of the rules about colons and semicolons is illustrated.

1. At 8:30, Brother Sydney announced that this week's theme verse is Ecclesiastes 12:1.
2. Laurence Crider, who recently moved in from Pennsylvania, works at Shank's Dry Goods; his son Timothy teaches at our school.
3. The following students will plan the bulletin board this marking period: Mary Ellen, Jessica, and Cheryl.
4. The four teachers at our school are Sister Brenda Holdeman, grades 1 and 2; Sister Wendy Eberly, grades 3 and 4; Sister Joyce Siegrist, grades 5 and 6; and Brother Leon Hege, grades 7–10.
5. The way of righteousness brings true peace and joy; moreover, it promises eternal blessings.
6. The weather of the past week can be summarized in one word: sultry.

B. Copy the word or number just before each punctuation error. Add the correct punctuation mark, or omit any unnecessary mark.

1. Brother Jonathan began his devotional this morning with the following question, "Are you building on the rock or the sand?"
2. This morning we discussed attitudes that make a sandy foundation, tomorrow we shall look at attitudes that make a solid foundation.
3. These words from Isaiah 40 17 are written in large letters in the center of the bulletin board, "All nations before him are as nothing."
4. A world map, with most of the nations labeled, covers the top half of the display, and ten large cards, shaped like waterdrops, are scattered across the bottom.
5. Each card names one of the ten most populous nations in the world and gives these details; area, population, and population density.
6. To us these nations seem large and powerful, however, in God's sight they are "less than nothing, and vanity."
7. We sent cards to Sister Lucille, an elderly widow, Thomas Hartman, a man with heart trouble, and Willy Landis, a boy with two broken legs.

Written Exercises

A. 1. 1
   2. 4
   3. 3
   4. 5
   5. 4
   6. 3

B. 1. question:
   2. foundation;
   3. 40: board:
   4. display;
   5. details:
   6. powerful;
   7. widow; trouble;

8. The following mountains in North America are over 18,000 feet high, Mount McKinley, 20,320 feet, Mount Logan, 19,524 feet, Mount Citlaltépetl, 18,700 feet, and Mount St. Elias, 18,008 feet.

9. We found some information in: the science book, the encyclopedia, and two books on astronomy.

10. Whenever I think of Brother Eli, one quality stands out, thoughtfulness.

11. He sees the needs of others; and he helps them promptly and willingly.

12. Sister Edith makes and sells: pies, bread, rolls, and jellies.

Review Exercises

Diagram the skeletons and complements of all the clauses in these sentences. Also diagram all the words in the appositives and independent elements. [9, 14–16]

1. My friend, God loves a cheerful giver.
2. Since God sees our motives, we should guard our hearts carefully.
3. Submission to God, we know, is essential to true satisfaction.
4. Multitudes profess faith in God, yet few wholly obey His Word.
5. Temptation, an allurement to evil, tests our loyalty to God.
6. Those who fear the Lord will obey Him, and God will bless their lives.

---

28. Methods of Developing Paragraphs

> **Lesson Survey**
> - A narrative paragraph is developed by adding details.
> - An expository or argumentative paragraph is developed by adding facts.
> - An argumentative paragraph is developed by adding reasons.
> - A descriptive paragraph is developed by adding descriptions.

A paragraph, as you studied in Lesson 13, is an organized unit of thought. The paragraph has unity as all the sentences support and develop the theme stated in the topic sentence. It has coherence as the ideas flow smoothly from one sentence to another. Naturally, the fact that paragraphs have these qualities suggests that they need to be *developed;* with few exceptions, a topic sentence alone does not make a paragraph. Let us consider how this development is accomplished.

Lesson 28

Purpose: To study the development of paragraphs by adding details, facts, reasons, or descriptions.

Oral Review:

1. Name the four basic kinds of compositions. (exposition, argument, narration, description)
2. Tell which kind of composition fits each description.
   a. It tells a story. (narration)
   b. It defines or explains. (exposition)
   c. It paints a word picture. (description)
   d. It attempts to persuade or move to action. (argument)
3. What cautions should the writer of an argument remember? (Emotional fervor does not determine whether a matter is right or wrong. An argument will be unbalanced if it presents only one side of an issue.)

8. high: feet;   10. out:
   feet; feet;   11. others,
9. in   12. sells

Review Exercises

1.

2.

3.

4.

5.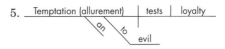

6.

4. In what two ways can you correct a paragraph that lacks unity? (Remove any sentence that does not develop the topic sentence. Divide the paragraph into two or more paragraphs.)
5. What are some methods for achieving coherence in paragraphs? (good sentence order; transitional words; repetition of key words; pronoun reference)

Lesson Introduction: Tell the class that you will try to draw a beautiful woodland scene on the chalkboard. Then make a simple sketch of a tree with a rock beside it (as a child might draw), and say, "Isn't that a beautiful scene?" Beautiful? Of course not. What is wrong? It doesn't show much? Oh, but it does! Look at the rock and the tree. A tree is beautiful, isn't it?

A good picture must have details—details and more details. If a woodland scene is to be beautiful,

Adding Details

One method of developing a paragraph is adding details. This method is especially suitable for narrative paragraphs. The topic sentence states or implies an incident, and the specific details expand and illustrate that idea.

To develop a paragraph by adding details, a writer must know his subject well. Otherwise he will not be able to add clear, specific details that make the paragraph both interesting and worthwhile. The following paragraph has unity and coherence, but it does not satisfy because it does not tell enough.

> When they had eaten, Tyndale seemed much better. He had been brought out of the dungeon, but what should his rescuers do next? It would soon be known that he had escaped, and his enemies would be looking everywhere for him.

As you read this, you may wonder, "What enemies would be looking for Tyndale? Where would they hope to find him?" The paragraph fails to tell you these things. The next paragraph gives details to answer these questions as well as questions you may not have thought to ask.

> When they had eaten, and Tyndale seemed already so much better, they faced the difficulties of the present and the immediate future. <u>Tyndale had been brought out of the dungeon, but what should the next step be?</u> It would soon be known that he had escaped, and the forest would be searched through and through, not only by Cochlaeus and the City Guard, but also by the robber lord who had lost a prize that was worth to him at least a thousand golden crowns.

The last paragraph above has a topic sentence (underlined), the same as most other paragraphs. But in many narrative paragraphs, the main idea is clear without being expressed in a topic sentence. The details of the paragraph make an organized unit of thought that is clearly understood by the reader. The following paragraphs have no topic sentences, but you clearly see the main idea of each as you read them.

> "You cooked a little for you, too, didn't you?" asked Tip in a saucy, good-natured tone. "Where's Father?"
>
> "Just where you have been all day so far—in bed and asleep," replied Mrs. Lewis. "Such folks as I've got! I'm sick of living."

Adding Facts

Adding facts is another method of developing paragraphs. Expository and argumentative paragraphs may be developed in this way. In such a paragraph, the topic sentence usually states a conclusion or general truth, and the other sentences give supporting evidence. Of course you must be

it must be filled in with dozens of intriguing and subtle details for the observer to admire.

The same is true of a paragraph. It may contain one obvious "rock" or "tree" (the main idea); but unless it is filled in with plenty of specific details, it can be as unsatisfactory as a crude sketch.

Lesson Outline:

1. A narrative paragraph is developed by adding details.

    a. The topic sentence states or implies an incident, and the specific details expand and illustrate that idea.

    b. The writer must know his subject well to make the paragraph both interesting and worthwhile.

    c. In many narrative paragraphs, the main idea is clear without being expressed in a topic sentence.

2. An expository or argumentative paragraph is developed by adding facts.

    a. The topic sentence usually states a conclusion or general truth, and the other sentences give supporting evidence.

    b. Facts (not merely opinions) must be added and their accuracy must be checked.

    c. The facts must be arranged in a logical sequence—either in the order of importance or in chronological order (as when giving steps in a process).

3. An argumentative paragraph is developed by adding reasons.

    a. The topic sentence states a belief or an opinion, and the other sentences give supporting reasons.

    b. The reasons must be based on solid principles and sound thinking.

sure that you are adding *facts,* not merely opinions. And you must be sure your facts are accurate. Use an encyclopedia, an almanac, a good textbook, or some other authoritative source to verify the points you write.

Furthermore, you must organize the facts in a logical sequence. Facts are most often listed in the order of importance, beginning with the least significant and leading up to the most convincing support of the topic sentence. The facts may also be listed in chronological order, as when they give steps in a process.

> The story of the birth of honeybees is quite interesting. Bees begin life as tiny oblong eggs that their mother, the queen, has stuck on end to the bottom of six-sided wax cells, one private chamber for each egg. The eggs hatch into white, wormlike curls called larvae. Adult bees put royal jelly and beebread into the cells to feed their tiny sisters. The bees grow until they fill their little chambers from the bottom to the top. At the appropriate time, the adults close the chambers with caps of wax. The young bees are now pupae, still white-bodied and pink-eyed, but they are taking on the shape of adult bees. Eventually they take on the black, brown, and yellow adult colors as well. Finally, they bite their way out through the caps of their cells.

Do you see the specific facts? The eggs are oblong, stuck on end. The cells are six-sided. Pick out some of the other facts. You can almost see what the author is talking about.

Adding Reasons

A paragraph may also be developed by adding reasons. Argumentative paragraphs, written to convince the reader, are often developed by this method. It is much the same as adding facts. The topic sentence states a belief or an opinion, and the other sentences give supporting reasons. However, be sure that your reasons are based on solid principles and sound thinking. To convince others, you must show that you have good reasons for the belief that you state in the topic sentence.

To produce this kind of paragraph, write your topic sentence and then give several reasons to show that it is true. Notice how the following example follows this pattern.

> We can be thankful that God has created the world with order. Without this order, the farmer could not grow crops to support life. Nor could an airplane pilot be sure that the laws of moving air currents would continue to hold up his plane. If the world were not orderly, you would not know in the evening when the sun would rise the next day—or if it would ever rise at all. Our very lives depend on the order that God has placed in His creation.

4. A descriptive paragraph is developed by adding descriptions.

    a. Often the topic sentence makes a general observation about one outstanding feature of a person, place, or thing.

    b. The supporting sentences then add specific descriptions to paint a clear picture in the reader's mind.

Adding Descriptions

Still another common method of developing a paragraph is adding descriptions. Obviously, this is how a descriptive paragraph is developed. In such a paragraph, the topic sentence often makes a general observation about one outstanding feature of a person, place, or thing. The supporting sentences then add specific descriptions to paint a clear picture in the reader's mind. In the following paragraph, notice the many descriptions that help the reader see the impressive fence along the roadway.

> The broad, straight road that led up to the royal hill, superb in itself, was made especially imposing by the tall fence of tiger grass enclosing it on either side. To build these fences, men drove posts ten or twelve feet in height into the ground at intervals of a few yards. In and out were then woven long, thick, horizontal ropes of reedlike grass stalks. Finally, to make the meshes closer, there were tied to the fence many vertical stalks of the same kind of grass. Fences such as this lined all the important roads in Uganda and were also used to enclose the private yards about the huts.

In a general sense, all paragraphs are developed by adding details of one kind or another. Whether these details are facts, reasons, or descriptions, they serve to explain and support the main topic of a paragraph. Try to fill all your paragraphs with clear, meaningful details.

Class Practice

Do these exercises on paragraph development.

1. You have learned that the four basic types of composition are exposition, argument, narration, and description. For each type, tell which method or methods a writer is likely to use in developing his paragraphs.
2. To develop a paragraph by adding details, why must the writer know his subject well?
3. Why should you check the accuracy of the points you write when adding facts to a paragraph?
4. When adding facts, you may use the order of ———— or ————.
5. When a paragraph is developed by adding reasons, why must the reasons be based on solid principles and sound thinking?
6. In a paragraph developed by adding descriptions, what does the topic sentence often do?

Written Exercises

A. Write a narrative paragraph by adding details. Use one of the following topic sentences or one of your own.

Lesson 28 Answers

Class Practice

1. exposition—adding facts; argument—adding facts or adding reasons; narration—adding details; description—adding descriptions
2. in order to add clear, specific details that make the paragraph both interesting and worthwhile
3. so that you are sure to add facts, not merely opinions, and so that you do not pass on inaccurate information
4. importance, time (chronological order)
5. so that the reasons are convincing
6. It makes a general observation about one outstanding feature of a person, place, or thing.

Written Exercises

(All paragraphs are individual work.)

1. The workday at Grandfather's house was tiring but enjoyable.
2. Giving Princess a bath was quite an experience!
3. Our last science demonstration was interesting.

B. Write an expository paragraph by adding facts to support one of these topic sentences or one of your own.
1. A desert is not as lifeless as one may think at first glance.
2. The earth was obviously created to be inhabited by man.
3. Lightning is a powerful display of energy.

C. Write an argumentative paragraph by adding reasons to support one of these topic sentences or one of your own.
1. We should appreciate the blessing of Christian schools.
2. Neat penmanship is a valuable skill.
3. Every student should use the dictionary regularly.

D. Write a descriptive paragraph by adding specific descriptions to one of these topic sentences or one of your own.
1. Grandmother's face radiates joy.
2. Our classroom has a cheery atmosphere.
3. This morning's sunrise was a breathtaking display of brilliant colors.

---

29. Dashes, Parentheses, and Brackets

Lesson Survey

- A **dash** is used to show a sudden interruption in thought, a parenthetical element that deserves special emphasis, or a sentence that is abruptly cut off.
- **Parentheses** are used to enclose a parenthetical element that is relatively unimportant, to enclose supplementary or illustrative matter, and to enclose figures used for enumeration within a sentence.
- **Brackets** are used to enclose a comment or correction within a quotation or as parentheses in material already enclosed by parentheses.
- Other punctuation marks are placed inside these marks if they relate to the enclosed matter, and outside if they relate to the whole sentence.

Dashes, parentheses, and brackets have two things in common. First, these marks are used less frequently than the other marks of punctuation. Second, they are all used to set off material within sentences.

Lesson 29

Purpose: To teach the proper use of *dashes, *parentheses, and *brackets.

Oral Review:

1. What is the general purpose of single quotation marks? (to set off a quotation or title within a quotation)
2. Tell what punctuation mark is used for each purpose.
   a. to indicate uncertainty about the accuracy of the preceding information (question mark)
   b. to separate the numbers in Scripture references and in expressions of time (colon)
   c. to set off nonrestrictive and independent elements (comma)
   d. to join independent clauses when no conjunction is used (semicolon)
   e. to separate items in a series (comma)
   f. to separate items in a series when the individual items contain commas (semicolon)
   g. to indicate the omission of one or more words (ellipsis points)
   h. to introduce a list, an explanation, or a formal quotation (colon)

Lesson Introduction: Write the following sentences on the board, punctuated in the three ways shown.

   a. Brother Harold, our substitute teacher, taught us a new song.
   b. Brother Harold (our substitute teacher) taught us a new song.
   c. Brother Harold—our substitute teacher—taught us a new song.

Can the students tell the difference in meaning conveyed by the three different kinds of punctuation? (Sentence *a* treats the added information as a

Dashes

A *dash* is two or three times longer than a hyphen. In typewritten work, two hyphens are used for a dash.

1. *A dash is used to show a sudden interruption in thought, a parenthetical element that deserves special emphasis, or a sentence that is abruptly cut off.* Because of the abruptness it indicates, a dash adds sharpness to writing. However, dashes must be used sparingly, or they lose their effectiveness. The following sentences illustrate the proper use of the dash.

> "The woods are beautiful with—oh, look at those deer!" exclaimed Susan.
>
> The car skidded off the road—a freezing rain was falling—and into a tree.
>
> Henry began to explain himself. "What really happened was—"
> "We know what happened," interrupted Michael. "What we'd like to know is how you did it."

The last example above shows an unfinished sentence. In Lesson 22 you learned that ellipsis points may also mark an unfinished sentence. However, ellipsis points suggest hesitancy or uncertainty, while a dash shows abruptness.

Parentheses

2. *Parentheses are used to enclose a parenthetical element that is relatively unimportant.*

> Mother served the cake (brought by Grandma) with fresh peaches.

Commas, dashes, and parentheses are all used to set off parenthetical elements. A writer must choose which to use according to the meaning he wants to convey. Consider these distinctions between the three.

a. Commas make the parenthetical material a part of the sentence. Of these three marks, commas are by far the most common in normal writing.

> We hiked on the Rock Ledge Trail, a three-mile trek one way.

b. Dashes sharply emphasize the parenthetical material. Sometimes they set off an exclamation.

> The Rock Ledge Trail—a rocky trail indeed!—is three miles long.

c. Parentheses minimize the importance of the parenthetical element. The material they enclose is somewhat beside the point of the sentence.

> Rock Ledge (an enormous flat rock near the peak of Bighorn Mountain) provides a beautiful view of Painted Creek Valley.

basic part of the sentence. Sentence *b* treats that information as having minor importance. Sentence *c* gives sharp emphasis to that information.) These differences should be fairly clear to the students after they work through this lesson.

Lesson Outline:

1. A dash is used to show a sudden interruption in thought, a parenthetical element that deserves special emphasis, or a sentence that is abruptly cut off.

    a. A dash is two or three times longer than a hyphen; in typewritten work, two hyphens are used for a dash.

    b. Both a dash and ellipsis points mark unfinished sentences. A dash shows abruptness, while ellipsis points indicate a sentence that trails away.

2. Parentheses are used to enclose a parenthetical element that is relatively unimportant. Commas, dashes, and parentheses all set off parenthetical elements. Consider the following distinctions.

    (a) Commas make the parenthetical material a part of the sentence (a nonrestrictive clause or appositive).

    (b) Dashes sharply emphasize the parenthetical material.

    (c) Parentheses minimize the importance of the parenthetical element.

3. Parentheses are used to enclose supplementary or illustrative matter, such as a Scripture reference or a short explanation.

4. Parentheses are used to enclose figures used for enumeration within a sentence.

3. *Parentheses are used to enclose supplementary or illustrative matter, such as a Scripture reference or a short explanation.*

"God is no respecter of persons" (Acts 10:34).
Because God is not a respecter of persons (someone who favors certain persons above others), His judgments are true and righteous.

4. *Parentheses are used to enclose figures used for enumeration within a sentence.*

At the beginning of class, Brother Snyder emphasized (1) that Christians take no active role in the government, (2) that the Bible does give definite principles related to governments, and (3) that God consistently honors those who honor Him.

Brackets

5. *Brackets are used to enclose a comment or correction within a quotation.*

"And, behold, there appeared unto them Moses and Elias [Elijah] talking with him" (Matthew 17:3).
Christians believe in "the plenary [complete] and verbal [word-by-word] inspiration of the Bible as the Word of God."

6. *Brackets are used as parentheses in material already enclosed by parentheses.*

The word *piedmont* (derived from the Latin words *pedis* [foot] and *montis* [mountain]) often refers to a region of foothills.

Relation to Other Punctuation

7. *Other punctuation marks are placed inside these marks if they relate to the enclosed matter, and outside if they relate to the whole sentence.* For example, if parentheses enclose a question or an exclamation, a question mark or an exclamation point is placed inside the parentheses because it applies to the enclosed matter. But if the whole sentence is interrogative or exclamatory and the enclosed matter is not, those end marks belong outside.

Last evening we sang for Mrs. Reilly—how friendly she is!—and several of her neighbors. (The parenthetical matter is an exclamation.)
Did she ask you to sing "Amazing Grace" (as she often does)?
(The sentence is a question, but the enclosed matter is not.)
We seek a better country (heaven); this earth is not our home.
(The semicolon relates to the whole sentence, not to the enclosed matter.)

5. Brackets are used to enclose a comment or correction within a quotation.

6. Brackets are used as parentheses in material already enclosed by parentheses.

7. Other punctuation marks are placed inside these marks if they relate to the enclosed matter, and outside if they relate to the whole sentence. If the parenthetical material is exclamatory or interrogative, it needs an exclamation point or a question mark.

★ *EXTRA PRACTICE*
Worksheet 11 *(Dashes, Parentheses, and Brackets)*

So many punctuation marks, and so many rules for using them! Were they invented just to make writing more difficult? No; they were developed so that writers can communicate exactly what they mean. As you gain experience with punctuation marks, you will probably learn to appreciate every one of these useful tools.

Class Practice

A. Tell where commas, dashes, and parentheses are needed in these sentences. Notes in parentheses tell what effect is to be produced.
   1. My uncle the tall man on the right will be teaching our class. (Treat the parenthetical phrase as being relatively unimportant.)
   2. Uncle Marvin's are coming tonight what a pleasant surprise! so we must hurry with the chores. (Emphasize the parenthetical material.)
   3. I remember Sister Carolyn she was my first grade teacher as being a good disciplinarian. (Treat the parenthetical clause first as being important and then as being unimportant.)
   4. We must even when it seems impossible give up our will to God if we want His blessing. (Emphasize the parenthetical material.)
   5. The five eighth graders who are all boys helped cut firewood for Brother Thomas. (Make the clause a basic part of the sentence.)

B. Tell how to correct the punctuation mistakes in these sentences.
   1. "The Lord is my shepherd; I shall not want (lack)" Psalm 23:1.
   2. Last week—or was it two weeks ago already—? Brother Kevin read Psalm 23 for devotions.
   3. Uncle Leo, he's my father's younger brother, helped us with the chores.
   4. Our assignments for this week included 1. writing a friendly letter, 2. completing three grammar lessons, and 3. writing a book report.
   5. "I think I heard it thunder. It's starting to, oh, Diane, all the wash is out on the lines!" Carol exclaimed.

Written Exercises

Copy these sentences, adding dashes, parentheses, and brackets where needed. Some sentences have notes to direct you.
   1. "Only let your conversation manner of life be as it becometh is worthy of the gospel of Christ" Philippians 1:27.
   2. A number of things your speech, your posture, your mannerisms soon give a stranger some definite clues about the kind of person you are. (Emphasize the parenthetical material.)
   3. In contrast to the state churches, the Anabaptists 1 believed in the final authority of the Bible, 2 embraced the doctrine of nonresistance, and 3 practiced nonconformity of life.

Lesson 29 Answers

Class Practice

A. 1. parentheses around *the tall man on the right*
   2. dashes before and after *what a pleasant surprise!*
   3. (treated as important) dashes before and after *she was my first grade teacher;*
      (treated as unimportant) parentheses around *she was my first grade teacher*
   4. dashes before and after *even when it seems impossible*
   5. commas before and after *who are all boys*

B. 1. [lack]" (Psalm 23:1).
   2. already?—
   3. (he's my father's younger brother)
      (Dashes may be used instead of parentheses.)
   4. (1) (2) (3)
   5. to—

Written Exercises

(Corrections are underlined.)
   1. "Only let your conversation [manner of life] be as it becometh [is worthy of] the gospel of Christ" (Philippians 1:27).
   2. A number of things—your speech, your posture, your mannerisms—soon give a stranger some definite clues about the kind of person you are.
   3. In contrast to the state churches, the Anabaptists (1) believed in the final authority of the Bible, (2) embraced the doctrine of nonresistance, and (3) practiced nonconformity of life.

Lesson 29   149

4. Kathy Zehr she's my cousin from New York is spending the weekend here. (Make the parenthetical element seem unimportant.)
5. "Mr. Henson, have you" began Vernon.
6. Hilda's question "Why did you take my paper?" came as quite a shock. (Show that the parenthetical element is just given as extra information.)
7. These marks of punctuation commas, dashes, parentheses, and brackets can all be used to set off sentence parts. (Call special attention to the parenthetical material.)
8. The Dakota Indians also called the *Sioux* pronounced like *sue* lived in the Dakotas and in Minnesota and Nebraska. (Use parentheses and brackets.)
9. "Mother, do you know when oh, here come Uncle Robert's now!" exclaimed Lily.
10. Johnny emptied the contents of his pocket three stones, two marbles, a dead grasshopper, and a short piece of string right out on the table. (Emphasize the things that were in his pocket.)
11. "Mother, look at" Johnny stopped abruptly when he saw Mother's face.
12. Anna Bussi do you remember when she lived next door? will turn ninety years old next week. (Show that the parenthetical element is unimportant.)
13. "Exhort servants to be obedient unto their own masters, . . . not answering again talking back" Titus 2:9.
14. The Golden Rule do to others as you would have them do to you would solve many of the problems in this world. (Give sharp emphasis to the parenthetical material.)
15. Joseph what an outstanding youth he was! did not allow hardships, allurements, or exaltation to weaken his commitment to God. (Treat the parenthetical element as being somewhat beside the point.)

Review Exercises

A. Write whether the word order of each sentence is natural (*N*), inverted (*I*), or mixed (*M*). [11]
1. God has richly blessed us with good things.
2. In true thanksgiving we praise His Name.
3. If we praise the Lord in word, we should also praise Him in deed.
4. From a heart of contentment comes joyful praise.
5. We shall praise God more perfectly when we get to heaven.

B. Change these sentences to the word order named in parentheses. Add any needed commas. [11]

4. Kathy Zehr (she's my cousin from New York) is spending the weekend here.
5. "Mr. Henson, have you—" began Vernon.
6. Hilda's question ("Why did you take my paper?") came as quite a shock.
7. These marks of punctuation—commas, dashes, parentheses, and brackets—can all be used to set off sentence parts.
8. The Dakota Indians (also called the *Sioux* [pronounced like *sue*]) lived in the Dakotas and in Minnesota and Nebraska.
9. "Mother, do you know when—oh, here come Uncle Robert's now!" exclaimed Lily.
10. Johnny emptied the contents of his pocket—three stones, two marbles, a dead grasshopper, and a short piece of string—right out on the table.
11. "Mother, look at—" Johnny stopped abruptly when he saw Mother's face.
12. Anna Bussi (do you remember when she lived next door?) will turn ninety years old next week.
13. "Exhort servants to be obedient unto their own masters, . . . not answering again [talking back]" (Titus 2:9).
14. The Golden Rule—do to others as you would have them do to you—would solve many of the problems in this world.
15. Joseph (what an outstanding youth he was!) did not allow hardships, allurements, or exaltation to weaken his commitment to God.

Review Exercises

A. 1. N   4. I
   2. M   5. N
   3. M

1. A doe rested in the shade of the trees. (inverted)
2. A little fawn was hiding nearby. (mixed)
3. A placid brook flows through the verdant meadow. (inverted)
4. Across the sky streaked a bolt of lightning. (natural)
5. A heavy roll of thunder shook the house after that streak. (mixed)

B. 1. In the shade of the trees rested a doe.
   2. Nearby a little fawn was hiding.
   3. Through the verdant meadow flows a placid brook.
   4. A bolt of lightning streaked across the sky.
   5. After that streak, a heavy roll of thunder shook the house.

30. Italics (Underlining) and Numbers

Lesson Survey

- **Italics** are used for the titles of major works; for the specific names of vehicles; for a word, letter, number, or symbol used as the subject of discussion; for foreign words that have not been adopted into the English language; and for special emphasis.

- **Number words** are spelled out if they can be expressed with one or two words.

- **Figures** are used for the following kinds of numbers: dates, time designations, and addresses; pages, book divisions, and Scripture references; decimals and percentages; scientific, mathematical, and technical statistics; and identification numbers.

This lesson does not deal with punctuation marks. But since the use of italics and the writing of numbers help us to communicate clearly, these matters are part of the mechanics of English just as capitalization and punctuation are.

Italics

Letters in *italics* are letters of a special style used in printed material. Italic letters slant to the right—*like this*. In handwritten or typewritten material, italics are indicated by underlining.

1. *Italics are used for the titles of major works.* Major works include books, newspapers, pamphlets, book-length poems, and periodicals such as magazines and newsletters. An article (*a, an, the*) is italicized and capitalized when it begins a book title, but not when it begins the title of a newspaper or periodical. Remember that the titles of minor works are enclosed in quotation marks (as you learned in Lesson 26).

> The story "Following As Geese Do" in the *Christian Pathway* teaches an important lesson. (The actual title of the periodical is *The Christian Pathway*.)

Lesson 30

Purpose: (1) To teach the proper use of italics. (2) To *teach when numbers should be spelled out and when they should be written as figures.

Oral Review:

1. With an unfinished sentence, when should you use ellipsis points and when should you use a dash? (Use ellipsis points to show hesitancy or uncertainty. Use a dash to show a sudden interruption.)
2. Tell whether you should use commas, dashes, or parentheses in each case.
   a. to minimize the importance of the parenthetical element (parentheses)
   b. to make the parenthetical material a part of the sentence (commas)
   c. to sharply emphasize the parenthetical material (dashes)

3. When should punctuation be placed within dashes or parentheses? (when it relates directly to the enclosed matter)
4. What are the two uses of brackets? (to enclose a comment or correction within a quotation; to serve as parentheses within parentheses)

Lesson Introduction: The mechanics of modern writing and printing are so well established today that we tend to take them for granted. But all the details of capitalization, punctuation, and italics had to be *invented* by someone; they did not develop automatically.

How did italic type receive its name? Regular roman type was first used around 1470 by a printer in Strasbourg, France (a German city at the time), and it was adopted and improved by printers in Italy. One of these was Aldus Manutius (1450–1515), who founded the famous Aldine Press and contributed

After reading *The Lim Family of Singapore,* I certainly appreciate a Christian home.

2. *Italics are used for the specific names of ships, airplanes, trains, and other vehicles.*

The *Titanic* was called unsinkable, but she sank on her maiden voyage.
In 1971, *Mariner 9* became the first spacecraft to orbit Mars.

3. *Italics are used for a word, letter, number, or symbol that is the subject of discussion.* That is, the item is not being used in its normal sense, but is referred to as a word or a letter.

The word *bookkeeper* has three pairs of double letters in a row: double *o*'s, double *k*'s, and double *e*'s.
This *b* looks like a *6*.
Do not use *&*'s in compositions; write out the word *and.*

4. *Italics are used for foreign words that have not been adopted into the English language.*

The words *E pluribus unum,* used on the Great Seal of the United States, mean "one out of many."
God created the world *ex nihilo* (out of nothing).

5. *Italics are used occasionally for special emphasis.* Such emphasis must be used sparingly, or it loses its effectiveness.

Be sure you repeat only *key* words, or your repetition will have little value.

Numbers

6. *Number words are spelled out if they can be expressed with one or two words.* A number at the beginning of a sentence is spelled out regardless of its length or use. However, you can often reword the sentence so that the number does not come first. If several numbers in a sentence are used to count things in the same category and one of them must be written as figures, use figures for all the numbers. Do not write some as words and others as figures.

The barn can hold over five hundred piglets.
Three hundred sixty-nine piglets died during the storm.
During the storm, 369 piglets died.

First Thessalonians 5:16 says, "Rejoice evermore."
In 1 Thessalonians 5:16 we read, "Rejoice evermore."

much to the development of modern punctuation. Manutius is said to have developed italic type from the beautiful handwriting of Petrarch, a famous Italian poet. This style was called italic to distinguish it from the roman style that was already in common use.

Lesson Outline:

1. Italics are used for the titles of major works. Major works include books, newspapers, pamphlets, book-length poems, and periodicals such as magazines and newsletters.

    a. An article *(a, an, the)* is italicized when it begins a book title, but not when it begins the title of a newspaper or periodical.

    b. Titles of minor works are enclosed in quotation marks (Lesson 26).

2. Italics are used for the specific names of ships, airplanes, trains, and other vehicles.

3. Italics are used for a word, letter, number, or symbol that is the subject of discussion. The item is not being used in its normal sense, but is referred to as a word or letter.

4. Italics are used for foreign words that have not been adopted into the English language. (*Teacher:* The foreign phrases in the pupil's text are pronounced as follows: *E pluribus unum* [ē plėr′•ə•bəs yü′•nəm]; *ex nihilo* [eks nē′•ə•lō].)

5. Italics are used occasionally for special emphasis.

6. Number words are spelled out if they can be expressed with one or two words.

    a. A number at the beginning of a sentence is spelled out regardless of its length. Otherwise, the sentence should be reworded so that the number does not come first.

The New Testament has 27 books, 260 chapters, and 7,957 verses. The longest verse of the Bible has 426 letters in ninety words, while the shortest verse has only 9 letters in two words.

7. *Figures are used to write dates, time designations, and addresses.*

At 5:35 P.M. on August 14, 1994, we arrived at our new home.
The store we want is at 127 West 82nd Street.

8. *Figures are used for pages, book divisions, and Scripture references.*

Unit 4 begins on page 125.
Can you quote Ephesians 4:32?

9. *Figures are used to write decimals and percentages.*

We had 2.5 inches of rain last night.
The salesman receives 12 percent of the sales as his commission.

10. *Figures are used in scientific or mathematical contexts and in giving technical specifications.* This includes the text of math and science books, as well as instructions for specific amounts of ingredients or medications.

Multiplying 12 by 25 is the same as multiplying 6 by 50.
Lead melts at 621° Fahrenheit.
Dosage: 5 cc penicillin 2 times daily

11. *Figures are used to write identification numbers.* Sometimes these identification numbers are Roman numerals.

We followed Interstate 70 to St. Louis.
The wicked reign of Jeroboam II is recorded in 2 Kings 14.

Class Practice

A. Tell where italics or quotation marks are needed.
1. The book Beyond the Trail begins with a chapter entitled Farewell.
2. The word pneumatic comes from the Greek word pneuma, which means "air."
3. As the travelers boarded the Arcadia, many wished them bon voyage.
4. The word shew, as used in the Bible, is pronounced the same as the modern word show.
5. According to Merriam Webster's Collegiate Dictionary, the i in respite is given the schwa sound by most speakers.
6. Have you read the story Lost and Found in the Christian Example?

B. Tell how the numbers in these sentences should be written.
1. The Nile River is over 4,000 miles long.
2. There are 150 psalms in the Book of Psalms.

b. If several numbers in a sentence are used to count things in the same category and one of them must be written as figures, use figures for all the numbers.

7. *Figures are used to write dates, time designations, and addresses.*

8. *Figures are used for pages, book divisions, and Scripture references.*

9. *Figures are used to write decimals and percentages.*

10. *Figures are used in scientific or mathematical contexts and in giving technical specifications.* This includes the text of math and science books, as well as instructions for specific amounts of ingredients or medications.

11. *Figures are used to write identification numbers.* Sometimes these are Roman numerals.

Lesson 30 Answers

Class Practice

A. 1. *Beyond the Trail*, "Farewell"
2. *pneumatic, pnuema*
3. *Arcadia, bon voyage*
4. *shew, show*
5. *Merriam Webster's Collegiate Dictionary, i, respite*
6. "Lost and Found", *Christian Example*

B. 1. four thousand
2. 150

3. Psalm 119, with 176 verses, is the longest psalm; but Numbers 7, with eighty-nine verses, is the longest chapter of prose in the Bible.
4. We traveled 200 miles on Tuesday, 325 miles on Wednesday, and 150 miles on Thursday.
5. Highway 16 is the only east–west route through central British Columbia.
6. 150 people can hardly fit into this auditorium.
7. By 10:30 A.M. the barometer had fallen to 29.85 inches, the temperature had risen to 85°, and the wind was blowing from the south.
8. The delivery man says he is looking for Winston Ketterman at 26 West Main Street.
9. The chart on page 76 summarizes the main points of Chapter Three.
10. For 3 days King Henry IV of Germany stood barefoot in the snow, begging forgiveness of Pope Gregory VII.

3. 119   176   7   89
4. 200   325   150
5. 16
6. One hundred fifty
    or This auditorium can hardly hold 150 people.
7. 10:30   29.85   85
8. 26
9. 76   3
10. three   IV   VII

Written Exercises

A. Copy the items that need italics or quotation marks, and add the underlining or the missing marks.
1. The first song in both the Church Hymnal and the Christian Hymnal is Come, Thou Almighty King.
2. We are studying the chapter Angels in the book Doctrines of the Bible.
3. The construction company took as its motto the following Latin phrase: Finis coronat opus ("The end crowns the work").
4. By the time the Bluebird had reached its destination, we were eager to get off the train.
5. The t in epistle and apostle is silent.
6. You have begun each sentence in this paragraph with He.
7. Write the title Bible Memory at the top of the chart.
8. The boys have fixed up the old sleigh and named it Queen of the Snow.

B. Find each incorrect number, and write it correctly. If a sentence has no error, write *correct*.
1. 2 Chronicles 1 says that Solomon offered 1,000 burnt offerings to the Lord.
2. When Solomon was preparing to build the temple, he appointed seventy thousand burden bearers, eighty thousand woodcutters, and 3,600 overseers.
3. Since the fire, the factory has been operating at only sixty percent of its previous capacity.
4. The damage to the building was estimated at 1.2 million dollars.
5. Grandfather Heatwole's farm is visible from Interstate 95, but they must drive 12 miles to get to the nearest exit.

Written Exercises

A. 1. Church Hymnal, Christian Hymnal, "Come, Thou Almighty King"
2. "Angels", Doctrines of the Bible
3. Finis coronat opus (*pronunciation:* fē·nəs kə·rō′·not ō′·pús)
4. Bluebird
5. t, epistle, apostle
6. He
7. "Bible Memory"
8. Queen of the Snow

B. 1. Second   one thousand
2. 70,000   80,000
3. 60
4. correct
5. twelve

6. Joanne, read the survey at the beginning of Unit Two; and Leonard, read the poem on page 110.
7. Our incubator holds 12 eggs and keeps them at 100° Fahrenheit.
8. 125 hogs were shipped to market today.
9. Grandfather was born on May 20, 1908, and he died when he was 79 years old.
10. A cubic foot of cork weighs 15 pounds.
11. 71 percent of the earth's surface is covered by oceans.
12. By the time the rain ended at 2:30 in the afternoon, we had received 4.2 inches of rain.

C. Three sentences in Part B begin with numbers written as figures. Rewrite those sentences so that the numbers do not come first.

Review Exercises

A. Label each sentence *S* (simple), *CD* (compound), *CX* (complex), or *CD-CX* (compound-complex). [14–16]
1. Men may try to destroy the Bible, but it is forever settled in heaven.
2. When men reject the Bible, they have no sure anchor.
3. The Bible has clear principles for every circumstance, but many reject them because they want their own way.
4. The way that seems right to man is often contrary to the Bible.
5. We should both study the Bible and apply it to our lives.
6. Our church is starting a new congregation; and Brother Andrew, who was recently ordained, plans to move there.
7. In our school, the upper graders study Spanish.
8. We could not play outside today, for it was raining too hard.

B. Copy these sentences, and indicate the part of speech that each word is by writing the correct abbreviation above it.

noun (n.)   adverb (adv.)
pronoun (pron.)   preposition (prep.)
verb (v.)   conjunction (conj.)
adjective (adj.)   interjection (interj.)

1. A man of true faith does not question a clear command of God.
2. If a person believes in God, he obeys willingly and cheerfully.
3. Alas, many people say they have faith, but they do not obey.

---

6. 2
7. twelve
8. One hundred twenty-five
9. seventy-nine
10. fifteen (Teacher: Accept *correct* also, since scientific information is given.)
11. Seventy-one
12. correct

C. (Sample sentences.)
1. In 2 Chronicles 1 we read that Solomon offered one thousand burnt offerings to the Lord.
8. Today 125 hogs were shipped to market.
11. Oceans cover 71 percent of the earth's surface.

Review Exercises

A. 1. CD   5. S
   2. CX   6. CD-CX
   3. CD-CX   7. S
   4. CX   8. CD

B. 1. A man of true faith does not question a clear command of God.
   adj. n. prep. adj. n. v. adv. v. adj. adj. n. prep. n.

2. If a person believes in God, he obeys willingly and cheerfully.
   conj. adj. n. v. prep. n. pron. v. adv. conj. adv.

3. Alas, many people say they have faith, but they do not obey.
   interj. adj. n. v. pron. v. n. conj. pron. v. adv. v.

31. Apostrophes and Hyphens

> ## Lesson Survey
>
> - An **apostrophe** is used to form the possessive case of a noun or an indefinite pronoun.
> - An apostrophe is used to show an omission in a contraction or other shortened form.
> - An apostrophe is used to form the plural of a letter, a figure, or an abbreviation followed by a period, and of a word used as the subject of discussion.
> - A **hyphen** is used to join some compound words.
> - When hyphenated adjective–noun combinations are used in a series, but the noun is included in only the last one, a hyphen follows each adjective.
> - A hyphen is used to divide a word between syllables at the end of a line.
> - A hyphen is used to show a series of connected verses in a Scripture reference.

Punctuation makes sentences easier to read. Some punctuation marks show where sentences end; others show various types of breaks within sentences. Apostrophes and hyphens are different in that they relate not to the structure of sentences but to the spelling of words.

Apostrophes

1. *An apostrophe is used to form the possessive case of a noun or an indefinite pronoun.* Three rules govern the formation of these possessive words.

    a. The possessive form of most singular nouns and of all indefinite pronouns is made by adding *'s*. When a singular noun contains two *s* or *z* sounds in the last syllable, add only an apostrophe. (Adding a third *s* or *z* sound makes the word awkward to pronounce.) For a compound noun, *'s* is added to the last word. Remember that personal pronouns have separate words for the possessive case.

my uncle's house	Moses' parents
Dennis's assignments	son-in-law's farm
Demetrius's concern	its nest
everybody's interest	either yours or hers

    b. The possessive form of plural nouns not ending with *-s* is made by adding *'s*. Again this applies to compound nouns, with the *'s* added only to the last word.

Lesson 31

Purpose: To study the uses of apostrophes and hyphens.

Oral Review:

1. What kinds of titles should be italicized? (titles of major works, such as books, newspapers, pamphlets, book-length poems, and periodicals)
2. Give some other uses of italics. (names of ships, airplanes, and other vehicles; a word, letter, number, or symbol that is the subject of discussion; foreign words that have not been adopted into the English language; special emphasis)
3. When should a number be spelled out? (when it can be expressed with one or two words; when it is the first word of a sentence)
4. Give some examples of numbers that should always be written in figures. (numbers in the same category, if one of them must be written as figures; dates, time designations, and addresses; pages, book divisions, and Scripture references; decimals and percentages; scientific, mathematical, and technical specifications; identification numbers)
5. In what three cases is a semicolon used to join the clauses of a compound sentence? (when no conjunction is used; when a conjunctive adverb is used; when commas are already used in one or more of the clauses)

Lesson Introduction: The word *apostrophe* comes from two Greek elements: *apo,* meaning "away," and *strephein,* meaning "to turn." One of the common uses of apostrophes is to indicate letters that have been "turned away," or omitted. The word *hyphen* also comes from two Greek elements: *hypo,* meaning "under" and *hen,* meaning "one." When compound

the brethren's help   larvae's destructiveness
the mice's squeaks   sisters-in-law's plans

c. The possessive form of plural nouns ending with -*s* is made by adding only an apostrophe. If a compound noun ends with -*s*, only an apostrophe is added to the last word.

the prophets' messages
the thieves' reactions
high priests' sacrifices
menservants' duties

2. *An apostrophe is used to show an omission in a contraction or other shortened form.* Contractions are acceptable for informal writing, such as friendly letters and the dialogue in stories. But in formal writing you should avoid most contractions.

They've been here since 8 o'clock.
We won't forget the blizzard of '93 for a long time.

3. *An apostrophe is used to form the plural of a letter, a figure, or an abbreviation followed by a period, and of a word used as the subject of discussion.* Remember also to italicize (underline) a word, letter, number, or symbol used as the subject of discussion; but do not italicize (underline) the '*s*.

Make sure your *e*'s do not look like undotted *i*'s.
Brother Henry preached about the *come*'s of the Bible.
Several M.D.'s examined the POWs that were released after the war.

For dates, the plural form is usually written without an apostrophe.

Many pioneers of the 1800s (*or* 1800's) endured severe hardships.

Hyphens

4. *A hyphen is used to join some compound words.* Pay special attention to the following groups of compound words.

a. Compound number words.

fifty-five   one hundred eighty-three

b. Fractions written in words. A hyphen is placed between the numerator and denominator unless either word already contains a hyphen.

three-fourths of the water
thirty-seven hundredths of an inch
four and one-half tons

words are hyphenated, one word is often "put under another"; that is, one part of the compound is subordinate to the other. Also, when a word is hyphenated at the end of a line, the second part of the word is "put under" the other.

These meanings should help students understand more fully the place filled by these punctuation marks.

Lesson Outline:

1. An apostrophe is used to form the possessive case of a noun or an indefinite pronoun.

(a) The possessive form of most singular nouns and of all indefinite pronouns is made by adding '*s*. When a singular noun contains two *s* or *z* sounds in the last syllable, add only an apostrophe.

(b) The possessive form of plural nouns not ending with -*s* is made by adding '*s*.

(c) The possessive form of plural nouns ending with -*s* is made by adding only an apostrophe.

2. An apostrophe is used to show an omission in a contraction or other shortened form. Avoid most contractions in formal writing.

3. An apostrophe is used to form the plural of a letter, a figure, or an abbreviation followed by a period, and of a word used as the subject of discussion. Remember to italicize a word, letter, number, or symbol used as the subject of discussion. For dates, the plural form is usually written without an apostrophe.

4. A hyphen is used to join some compound words.

(a) Compound number words.

(b) Fractions written in words.

c. Words ending with -in-law.

    brother-in-law   sisters-in-law

d. Compound words beginning with *great-* that refer to relatives.

    Great-uncle Eli   my great-great-grandfather

e. Compound words beginning with *self-*.

    self-controlled   self-reliant
    self-disciplined   self-righteous

f. Many compound words beginning with *all-*.

    the all-powerful Lord   an all-time record
    an all-day meeting   all-purpose flour

g. Many compound adjectives, when the two words form a unit that modifies a substantive.

    a three-dimensional picture
    iron-fisted rule
    snow-covered roads
    a three-bedroom house

Be careful, however, that you do not join an adverb to an adjective in this way. These words stand alone, not as a single unit of thought.

    rapidly rising water
    skillfully drawn picture

h. Proper nouns and adjectives with prefixes.

    a mid-December trip   non-Biblical history
    pre-Reformation times   un-American activities

While many compound words are hyphenated, others are written as one word or as two separate words. Always check a dictionary when you are not sure of the correct spelling.

5. *When hyphenated adjective–noun combinations are used in a series, but the noun is included in only the last one, a hyphen follows each adjective.*

This publisher offers one- and two-year courses in bookkeeping.
Father wanted six-, eight-, and ten-foot lengths of angle iron.

6. *A hyphen is used to divide a word between syllables at the end of a line.* Divide words only when necessary. When you must divide a word, be sure to divide only between syllables. Never leave a single letter at the

---

(c) Words ending with -in-law.

(d) Compound words beginning with *great-* that refer to relatives.

(e) Compound words beginning with *self-*.

(f) Many compound words beginning with *all-*.

(g) Many compound adjectives, when the two words form a unit that modifies a substantive.

(h) A proper noun or adjective with a prefix.

5. ***When hyphenated adjective–noun combinations are used in a series, but the noun is included in only the last one, a hyphen follows each adjective.***

6. ***A hyphen is used to divide a word between syllables at the end of a line.***
    a. Divide words only when necessary.
    b. Divide only between syllables.

    c. Never leave a single letter at the beginning or end of a line.
    d. Divide a hyphenated word only at the existing hyphen.

7. ***A hyphen is used to show a series of connected verses in a Scripture reference.*** (In printed material, an en dash is used instead of a hyphen.)

★ ***EXTRA PRACTICE***
Worksheet 12 *(Italics, Numbers, Apostrophes, and Hyphens)*

beginning or end of a line. Also, divide a hyphenated word only at the existing hyphen. The boldface entry word in a dictionary shows the permissible places to divide a word (except for a one-letter syllable at the beginning or end).

Incorrect:	**Correct:**
We can try to cross the stre-am up farther.	We can try to cross the stream up farther.
Uncle Wayne has a very ston-y garden.	Uncle Wayne has a very stony garden.
Do you know what causes an e-clipse?	Do you know what causes an eclipse?
The Bible says our self-right-eousness is as filthy rags.	The Bible says our self-righteousness is as filthy rags.

7. *A hyphen is used to show a series of connected verses in a Scripture reference.* In this use, the hyphen means "through." Use a comma to show a break in the series.

The most detailed account of Christ's birth is found in Luke 2:1–20.
The text of this Sunday school lesson is 2 Timothy 4:1–11, 14–18.

Class Practice

A. Tell how to make these words possessive. If no change is needed, say *none*.
   1. Doris
   2. zebra
   3. yours
   4. girls
   5. ladies
   6. anyone
   7. cacti
   8. firemen

B. Tell how to correct each error in the use of apostrophes or hyphens. Also tell what items need to be italicized. If there is no error, say *correct*.
   1. Korah, a self appointed leader of dissatisfied princes, rebelled a-gainst Moses's authority.
   2. When the rods were placed in the tabernacle, nobodys rod but Aarons budded.
   3. When you spell the word separate, make sure two as in the middle separate the two es.
   4. Many pagans concepts were largely anti God.
   5. Jesus earthly ministry didnt affect them as directly as later Christian's evangelism did.
   6. Do you know how to draw accurate three, six, and eight-sided figures?
   7. Six ands in one sentence are certainly too many!
   8. My brother's-in-law mower has a grass catcher; our's doesnt.

Lesson 31 Answers

Class Practice

A. 1. Doris's
    2. zebra's
    3. none
    4. girls'
    5. ladies'
    6. anyone's
    7. cacti's
    8. firemen's

B. 1. self-appointed, against, Moses'
    2. nobody's, Aaron's
    3. *separate*, *a*'s, *e*'s
    4. pagans', anti-God
    5. Jesus', didn't, Christians'
    6. three-, six-,
    7. *and*'s
    8. brother-in-law's, ours, doesn't

9. My grandfather, who was born in the 1920s, was one of the many COs in World War II.

10. In mid February of 52, he bought a farm of ninety two acres.

11. We cannot accept nonBiblical history with the same confidence as we accept the God inspired record of history.

12. No one is truly a self made man; everyones life is influenced by other's lives.

13. The nail tore a gash two and three fourths inches long in Galens' leg.

14. More than one half of the worlds population lives on the continent of Asia.

Written Exercises

A. Write these phrases, using hyphens correctly.

1. twenty four feet
2. his father in law
3. my great aunt
4. five eighths inch
5. non European settlers
6. self denying act
7. all inclusive statement
8. candy coated pill

B. Write these words, using hyphens to show each place where they may be divided at the end of a line.

1. abominable
2. crockery

C. Write correctly the items that have errors in the use of apostrophes or hyphens. If an item also needs to be italicized, show it by underlining.

1. Because of Pharaohs stubbornness, all the animals and people of Egypt suffered.

2. In several of the plagues, the Israelite's land was unaffected.

3. Even at eighty five years of age, Caleb wasnt ready to retire.

4. He was motivated by his faith in the all powerful Lord, not by self confidence.

5. This pink eyed, all white deer must be an albino.

6. Both of my parent's were born in the 1950 s.

7. We cant leave before 6 oclock, and this old 62 Mack wont climb those mountains very fast.

8. Great aunt Joyce greatly appreciated the three girls help.

9. The fleet footed cheetah was clocked at seventy miles per hour over a distance of about one fourth mile.

10. If your os look like as on your spelling test, I cant give you credit.

11. Jennifers ts look almost like +s.

12. In the preCommunist era, too many Russian Mennonites had lost the concept of true nonresistance.

13. Some Mennonites response even included the forming of self defense groups.

---

9. correct

10. mid-February, '52, ninety-two

11. non-Biblical, God-inspired

12. self-made, everyone's, others'

13. three-fourths, Galen's

14. one-half, world's

Written Exercises

A. 1. twenty-four feet

2. his father-in-law

3. my great-aunt

4. five-eighths inch

5. non-European settlers

6. self-denying act

7. all-inclusive statement

8. candy-coated pill

B. 1. abom-i-na-ble   2. crock-ery

C. 1. Pharaoh's, Egypt

2. Israelites'

3. eighty-five, wasn't

4. all-powerful, self-confidence

5. pink-eyed, all-white

6. parents, 1950s *or* 1950's

7. can't, o'clock, '62, won't

8. Great-aunt, girls'

9. fleet-footed, one-fourth

10. o's, a's, can't

11. Jennifer's, t's, ±'s

12. pre-Communist

13. Mennonites', self-defense

14. However, not everyones' faith had been lost; some did trust the Lords all sufficient grace.

14. everyone's, Lord's, all-sufficient

Review Exercises

Write the letter of the item that has correct capitalization. [21]

1. a. read the ten commandments
   b. read the Ten Commandments
2. a. on the Sea of Galilee
   b. on the sea of Galilee
3. a. the Egyptian ruler
   b. the egyptian ruler
4. a. with Uncle Paul and father
   b. with Uncle Paul and Father
5. a. "Now the Day Is Over"
   b. "Now the Day is Over"
6. a. the new School near Anson
   b. the new school near Anson
7. a. our Hoover sweeper
   b. our Hoover Sweeper
8. a. destroyed in a.d. 70
   b. destroyed in A.D. 70
9. a. algebra and Typing I
   b. algebra and typing I
10. a. the first day of Winter
    b. the first day of winter
11. a. my mother and Aunt Beth
    b. my Mother and Aunt Beth
12. a. when we lived in the East
    b. when we lived in the east
13. a. during the civil war
    b. during the Civil War
14. a. went south a few miles
    b. went South a few miles
15. a. made with italian seasoning
    b. made with Italian seasoning
16. a. Bible Memory and Science
    b. Bible memory and science
17. a. crackers and Swiss cheese
    b. crackers and swiss cheese
18. a. the events on palm Sunday
    b. the events on Palm Sunday
19. a. a large lake in Ontario
    b. a large Lake in Ontario
20. a. for Brother Ethan and him
    b. for brother Ethan and him

Review Exercises

1.	b	11.	a
2.	a	12.	a
3.	a	13.	b
4.	b	14.	a
5.	a	15.	b
6.	b	16.	b
7.	a	17.	a
8.	b	18.	b
9.	a	19.	a
10.	b	20.	a

32. More Methods of Developing Paragraphs

Lesson Survey

- A paragraph may be developed by using examples or an incident.
- A paragraph may be developed by giving a definition.
- A paragraph may be developed by using comparisons or contrasts.
- A paragraph is often developed by using more than one method.

In Lesson 28 you studied four specific methods of paragraph development and how they relate to the different types of compositions. But those are not all the possibilities. In this lesson you will study three more specific methods of developing paragraphs.

Lesson 32

Purpose: To study paragraph development by using examples or an incident, by giving a definition, and by using comparisons or contrasts.

Oral Review:

1. Tell whether the following methods of development are most likely to be used for narrative, expository, argumentative, or descriptive paragraphs.
   a. adding reasons (argumentative)
   b. adding facts (expository, argumentative)
   c. adding details (narrative)
   d. adding descriptions (descriptive)
2. What quality is lacking if a paragraph should be divided into two paragraphs? (unity)
3. What quality is lacking if the sentences of a paragraph do not flow smoothly? (coherence)
4. What quality is lacking if a sentence in a paragraph does not develop the topic sentence? (unity)

Lesson Introduction: A seedling is not a fully developed plant. Its leaves are tiny and not completely grown, and it has no flowers. You may look at the seedling and say, "What kind of plant is that?" But after a seedling develops into a mature plant with blossoms and fruit, you do not need to ask that question. You can clearly see what kind of plant it is.

So it is with writing. Each paragraph that you write needs to be developed so that instead of saying, "What does he mean?" the reader can say, "Oh yes, I know exactly what he means."

Further, not all seedlings develop in the same way. One may grow a single main stem, with a few leaves on its sides. Another may grow a bushy bundle of stems. Still others creep along the ground or up a wall. Not all paragraphs are developed in the

Using Examples or an Incident

Using examples or an incident is one good way to support or develop the topic sentence of a paragraph. Be sure to write only clear, specific examples that form a convincing picture in the reader's mind. You might use only two or three examples, with several details about each; or you might use more examples, with only a brief description of each. An incident is actually one example in the form of a brief story.

Developed by two examples well described:

Topic   God directs specific commands to the young person. For example, Solomon wrote these words: "Remember now thy Creator in

Example 1   the days of thy youth" (Ecclesiastes 12:1). We do this as we use our God-given abilities and moments of time to glorify the Creator. We also remember our Creator as we consciously seek His blessing and His will. Another example is found in the Decalogue:

Example 2   "Honour thy father and thy mother" (Exodus 20:12). Certainly this involves obeying our parents. But does it not also involve the way we obey? Grudging obedience does not honor them. Honoring our parents also involves doing what we know they want, even if they have not given a direct command.

Developed by four examples briefly described:

Topic   God directs specific commands to the young person. For example, the command to remember the Creator is especially given to

Example 1   youth. This addresses the young person's relationship to God Himself. The fifth commandment concerns the youth's relation-

Example 2   ship to his parents: "Honour thy father and thy mother." God also speaks to the young person's relationship to his own life and heart.

Example 3   In 2 Timothy 2:22 we read, "Flee also youthful lusts: but follow righteousness, faith, charity, peace, with them that call on the Lord out of a pure heart." Finally, God directs the youth's relationship

Example 4   to those who observe his life. "Let no man despise thy youth; but be thou an example of the believers" (1 Timothy 4:12).

Developed by one incident:

Topic   Today we benefit greatly from the work of men in the past. One of those men was Edward Jenner, who gave the first vac-

One   cination in 1796. Jenner had noticed that milkmaids, who often

Incident   contracted the rather harmless disease of cowpox, were not stricken with the dreaded smallpox. He suspected that having cowpox was making these girls immune to smallpox as well as cowpox. So he took a little material from cowpox sores and injected it into a healthy boy. Seven weeks later, Jenner exposed the boy to smallpox germs. As Jenner hoped, the boy did not

same way either. This lesson adds three more methods of paragraph development to the four that you studied in Lesson 28.

Lesson Outline:

1. A paragraph may be developed by using examples or an incident.

    a. Use clear, specific examples that form a convincing picture in the reader's mind.

    b. If you use only two or three examples, write several details about each. If you use more examples, write only a brief description of each.

    c. An incident is one example in the form of a brief story.

2. A paragraph may be developed by giving a definition.

    a. This is a good way to develop a paragraph that describes an abstract noun or a technical word in expository writing.

    b. The topic sentence often gives a brief definition, and the supporting sentences expand that definition by clarifying and illustrating it.

3. A paragraph may be developed by using comparisons or contrasts.

    a. A comparison points out similarities, and a contrast points out differences.

    b. Use something familiar as the basis for comparing or contrasting something less familiar.

    c. Comparisons and contrasts can be made only between items that have some obvious relationship.

4. A paragraph is often developed by using more than one method.

get sick; he had become immune to smallpox. Thus Jenner demonstrated the principle of vaccination, which is still considered the best weapon against contagious diseases.

Giving a Definition

Giving a definition is a good way to develop a paragraph that describes an abstract noun or a technical word in expository writing. In such a paragraph, the topic sentence often gives a brief definition of the word, and the supporting sentences expand that definition by clarifying and illustrating it.

> A rheostat is a device that regulates the flow of electricity in a circuit. You have operated a rheostat if you have pressed the foot pedal of a sewing machine to sew faster or slower, or have turned a knob to dim or brighten a light. The main part of a rheostat is a material that resists the flow of electricity, with a contact point that slides along this material. When the contact point is close to one end, the electricity travels only a short distance through the resistant material and the motor speeds up or the light shines more brightly. But when the contact point is moved farther from the end, the motor slows or the light becomes dimmer because the electricity must travel farther through the resistant material.

Using Comparisons or Contrasts

Comparison is one of the best ways to explain something new and unfamiliar. By showing a similarity between the new thing and something familiar, the speaker or writer provides a link to help his audience understand what he means. Jesus used this principle extensively in His ministry. He taught many truths new to His listeners by telling parables about a sower and his seed, a shepherd and his sheep, a father and his prodigal son, and numerous other things.

A contrast shows a difference between two things. Both comparison and contrast are valuable tools. It is inspiring to compare two outstanding Bible characters (such as Moses and Paul) to see how God worked in their lives. And it is enlightening to contrast two characters (like Peter and Judas) to see the outcome of the opposite courses they chose.

Comparisons or contrasts can be used to develop paragraphs. To write such a paragraph, you should generally use something familiar as the basis for comparing or contrasting something less familiar. Comparisons and contrasts can be made only between items that have some obvious relationship. You could hardly compare or contrast the ocean and a shoe, but you could compare or contrast the ocean and a river.

> Your eye resembles a camera in several ways. The eyelid is like the shutter, which admits or excludes light. To regulate the amount

of light admitted, the pupil becomes larger or smaller like the aperture of a camera. Behind the pupil, the lens focuses light to form an image on the retina, which is like the film in a camera. But the retina does not record images in permanent form as photographic film does. Rather, it has millions of light-sensitive cells that send electrical signals through the optic nerve to the brain.

Combining Methods

Most paragraphs are written with more than one method of development. In fact, very few paragraphs are developed strictly by one method. The example above illustrates paragraph development by using a comparison and then a contrast. But it also involves adding facts, which you studied in Lesson 28. While the specific method of development has some importance, the most important thing is to make sure the development is clear and effective.

Class Practice

A. Answer these questions about paragraph development.
 1. If a paragraph is developed by two examples, how should it be different from one developed by four or more examples?
 2. How is using an incident similar to using examples in paragraph development? How is it different?
 3. When might you develop a paragraph by giving a definition?
 4. In a paragraph developed by giving a definition, what does the topic sentence usually do?
 5. How are comparisons different from contrasts?
 6. Why could you not likely develop a paragraph by contrasting a mallard and a chipmunk?

B. Tell which of the seven methods in Lessons 28 and 32 could be used effectively to develop these topic sentences.
 1. Unusual situations have a way of making people friendly.
 2. Raising produce, we have learned, is quite different from tending an orchard.
 3. In the Bible, the word *hope* means more than it does in modern English.
 4. The construction of a Baltimore oriole's nest is worthy of close examination.
 5. As we first drove in the lane of the small farm Father had bought, we were struck with its rundown appearance.
 6. The proper care of your teeth is very important.
 7. Caring for your teeth is not a difficult procedure.
 8. I have learned that it is foolish to use the teeth as a pair of pliers.

Lesson 32 Answers

Class Practice

A. 1. If only two examples are used, each example should be described with several details. If four or more examples are used, each should be described more briefly.
 2. An incident is actually one example.
   It is different in that the incident is a brief story used as one example.
 3. when writing about an abstract noun or a technical word
 4. It usually gives a brief definition.
 5. Comparisons point out similarities; contrasts point out differences.
 6. The relationship is not close enough to make meaningful contrasts.

B. 1. using examples or an incident
 2. using examples or an incident; using comparisons or contrasts
 3. giving a definition
 4. adding facts; adding reasons; adding descriptions
 5. adding descriptions
 6. adding reasons
 7. adding facts
 8. using examples or an incident

Written Exercises

A. Write a paragraph using examples or an incident to develop one of the following topic sentences or one of your own.
 1. Daniel was a man of outstanding courage.
 2. Godly women often filled important roles in the history of God's people.
 3. Carelessness can have embarrassing results.

B. Write a paragraph of definition for one of these terms or for some other term that your teacher approves.
 1. mercantilism
 2. dew point
 3. maturity
 4. self-discipline

C. Write a paragraph developed by comparisons or contrasts, using one of the following topic sentences or one of your own.
 1. The Appalachian Mountains are different in many ways from the Rocky Mountains.
 2. The Earth is unique among the planets.
 3. The worship services of the early Christians were similar to those in the Jewish synagogue.

---

33. Chapter 3 Review

Class Practice

A. Tell how to correct the errors in capitalization, ellipsis points, and end marks.
 1. Jesus came to fulfill the old testament and establish one new body for both jews and gentiles
 2. can you imagine his sufferings in the garden of Gethsemane in Pilate's hall on mount Calvary
 3. what sufferings many Disciples of christ endured under the cruel reign of the emperor Nero
 4. did uncle James buy this minute maid orange juice at Shriver's groceries
 5. of course, i know oranges do not grow in the north, but
 6. a group of Doctors met with the president to discuss the proposed law.
 7. In the afternoon we study american history, science, and typing I.
 8. when mr l k smith describes african wildlife, you can tell that he has been there.

Lesson 33

Purpose: To review the concepts taught in Chapter 3.

Written Exercises

(All paragraphs are individual work.)

Lesson 33 Answers

Class Practice

A. 1. Old Testament, Jews, Gentiles.
 2. Can, His, Gethsemane? hall? Mount Calvary (*Garden* may be included.)
 3. What, disciples, Christ, Nero!
 4. Did, Uncle, Minute Maid, Groceries?
 5. Of, I, North, but...
 6. A, doctors, President
 7. American, Typing
 8. When, Mr. L. K. Smith, African

B. Tell where quotation marks and other punctuation should be added. Also tell which words need capital letters.
1. Father asked how did Peter answer Jesus' question
2. He said thou hast the words of eternal life responded Helen
3. Did you hear Grandpa say you can never develop too many good habits
4. In your youth he would often say is the time to develop good habits
5. Was it Grandpa who said a young person's habits greatly affect his later life asked Kristen
6. Grandpa quoted the words of Father, in My Life's Young Morning; then Father suggested that we sing it.

C. Tell where commas, colons, and semicolons should be added. Also tell which commas should be changed to colons or semicolons.
1. If we trust in the Lord we do not need to worry about the future.
2. Yes God knows the future and He cares tenderly for each of His own.
3. Charles Kettering made this interesting statement, "My interest is in the future because I am going to spend the rest of my life there."
4. Visitors at our church this morning included Gilbert Pellman's, a family from the community, Nevin Steiner, my uncle from Wisconsin, and Elsie Shank, an elderly widow.
5. Aunt Myra who lives in Ontario plans to spend a weekend with us.
6. Fred did you hear that Clair Stauffer Father's cousin is moving to our community on November 13 1998?

D. Tell how to correct the errors in the use of dashes, parentheses, brackets, apostrophes, and hyphens.
1. If we believe that the Lords all powerful hand is in control, we should never harbor self pity.
2. The devil hes always seeking to snare mens souls is clever at making people feel that life isnt fair.
3. When Goliath fell, the Philistine soldier's courage quickly melted.
4. "Be not deceived: evil communications associations corrupt good manners morals." 1 Corinthians 15:33
5. "Father, look at that long eared" Susie began.
6. These golden pumpkins John took good care of them will make many delicious pies.

E. Tell which words should be set off by italics or quotation marks.
1. We studied the chapter French-Canadian Settlements in The Story of Canada.
2. In a word like noticeable, the silent e is retained so that the c keeps the soft sound.

B. (Corrections are underlined.)
1. Father asked, "How did Peter answer Jesus' question?"
2. "He said, 'Thou hast the words of eternal life,'" responded Helen.
3. Did you hear Grandpa say, "You can never develop too many good habits"?
4. "In your youth," he would often say, "is the time to develop good habits."
5. "Was it Grandpa who said, 'A young person's habits greatly affect his later life'?" asked Kristen.
6. Grandpa quoted the words of "Father, in My Life's Young Morning"; then Father suggested that we sing it.

C. 1. Lord,
2. Yes, future,
3. statement:
4. community; Wisconsin;
5. Myra, Ontario,
6. Fred, Stauffer, cousin, 13,

D. 1. Lord's all-powerful should self-pity
2. devil—he's men's souls— isn't (Parentheses may be used.)
3. soldiers'
4. [associations] [morals]" (1 Corinthians 15:33).
5. long-eared—"
6. (John them) many (Dashes may be used.)

E. 1. "French-Canadian Settlements" *The Story of Canada*
2. *noticeable, e, c*

3. In English the a's can have a variety of sounds.

4. Uncle Douglas arrived on the Sky Rover, a private charter plane.

F. Tell how the numbers in these sentences should be written.

1. There are 45 students and 3 teachers at our school.

2. 750 gallons of milk were spilled on County Road 88, and the detour around the spill gave us 2.7 additional miles to school.

3. Lela's composition has about 650 words in 9 paragraphs.

4. For 12 consecutive days the temperature topped 100° Fahrenheit.

5. 1 Timothy 6 warns about the dangers of riches.

G. Tell which of the four types of compositions is associated with each of the following statements.

1. It is written to explain, clarify, or inform.

2. It may be written to provide a setting or create a mood.

3. A writer may tend to rely mainly on emotional fervor.

4. It is written when there are disagreements or conflicting evidence.

5. It paints word pictures.

6. It tells a story.

7. It is written to persuade or to move to action.

8. Vivid, concrete words are especially important.

Written Exercises

A. Copy correctly each item that has a capitalization error. Also copy each item that should be followed by an end mark, and add the punctuation.

1.   845 jersey ridge road

2.   zanesville, ohio 43701

3.   september 20, 20—

4. dear louise,

5. "my heart is fixed, o god, my heart is fixed: i will sing and give

6. praise" (psalm 57:7). For two mornings in devotions, brother leonard

7. discussed how the lord preserved the bible to our day In closing, he

8. challenged us by asking, "should we not have our hearts fixed on

9. God and his word"

10.   Last sunday we visited the boulder creek church. Since we took

11. uncle Jake's family along, we borrowed your grandfather's Ford Van.

12. Brother Henry Groff preached on "Serving God in all things."

13.   what beautiful scenery surrounds this church The leaves were in

14. the full glory of their Fall colors In front of the church, the waters of

15. boulder creek sang a merry tune Behind the church, the slope of

16. mount tea rose sharply.

17.   your cousin,

18.   miriam

---

3. *a*'s

4. *Sky Rover*

F. 1. forty-five   three

2. Seven hundred fifty   88   2.7

3. 650   nine

4. twelve   100

5. First   6

G. 1. exposition

2. description

3. argument

4. argument

5. description

6. narration

7. argument

8. description

Written Exercises

A. 1. Jersey Ridge Road

2. Zanesville, Ohio

3. September

4. Dear, Louise

5. My, O, God, I

6. Psalm, Brother Leonard

7. Lord, Bible, day.

8. Should

9. His, Word?"

10. Sunday, Boulder Creek Church

11. Uncle, van

12. All, Things

13. What, church!

14. fall, colors.

15. Boulder Creek, tune.

16. Mount Tea

17. Your

18. Miriam

B. Copy each word that should be followed by a comma, colon, or semicolon, and add the correct punctuation. You may need to change a comma to one of these marks.

1. Dwight Eisenhower who became an army general and the president of the United States disappointed his nonresistant River Brethren parents.

2. In 1988, over eighteen million acres of crops were harvested in the following states, Minnesota, 18,800,000, Illinois, 21,600,000, and Iowa, 23,100,000.

3. Pennsylvania is considered a farming state, however, it had only about 4200000 acres of crops that year.

4. Have you heard children that Lena Harnish our elderly neighbor broke her leg?

5. Well she was coming down the front steps and her knee buckled under her.

6. After we gave Mittens a bath her soft fluffy fur glistened.

7. In a barn fire can spread rapidly, the dry hay and straw burn hot and fast.

8. Fred L. Holtz Jr. on the other hand has moved to North Dakota.

C. Write correctly each underlined sentence part that has an error in the use of punctuation or capitalization. If it has no error, write *correct*.

1. What a comfort to know that God has <u>said, "I</u> will never leave <u>thee!"</u>

2. Why did Jesus ask Peter three <u>times, 'Simon,</u> son of Jonas, lovest thou <u>me?"</u>

B. 1. Eisenhower, States,

2. states: 18,800,000; 21,600,000;

3. state; 4,200,000

4. heard, children, Harnish, neighbor,

5. Well, steps,

6. bath, soft,

7. barn, rapidly;

8. Holtz, Jr., hand,

C. 1. correct thee"!

2. times, "Simon correct

3. It is easy for people to say, "Jesus is <u>Lord;" it</u> is harder for them to prove by their lives that they believe <u>it."</u>

3. Lord"; it   it.

4. Can you give the reference for these words of <u>Jesus: "If</u> ye love me, keep my <u>commandments?"</u>

4. correct   commandments"?

5. "I think it's John 14:15," replied <u>Sheila, "isn't</u> that <u>right"?</u>

5. Sheila. "Isn't   right?"

6. "Mother, did you hear Benny <u>say, My</u> head <u>hurts?"</u> asked Leah.

6. say, 'My   hurts'?"

D. Copy the items that should be enclosed in dashes, parentheses, or brackets, and add the correct marks. Some sentences have notes to direct you.

1. The wise men were there actually three of them came to worship Jesus. (Treat the parenthetical item as having minor importance.)

2. Herod jealous for his throne sought to kill the young King. (Emphasize the parenthetical item.)

3. John did not want to baptize Jesus he felt completely unworthy, but Jesus said it was the right thing to do. (Treat the parenthetical item as being somewhat beside the point.)

4. "And Jesus answering said unto him, Suffer allow it to be so now: for thus it becometh fits us to fulfil all righteousness" Matthew 3:15.

5. Before tomorrow morning, I must 1 finish my math assignment, 2 write a book report, and 3 study for a history test.

D. 1. (were there actually three of them?)

2. —jealous for his throne—

3. (he felt completely unworthy)

4. [allow] [fits]   (Matthew 3:15)

5. (1) (2) (3)

E. Copy each word that should be followed by a dash or by ellipsis points, and add the needed punctuation.

1. "Then Herod slew all the children that were in Bethlehem, and in all the coasts thereof, from two years old and under" (Matthew 2:16).

2. "Well, I just didn't" Mahlon started sheepishly.

3. "Do you know if oh, look at that beautiful bird!" exclaimed Priscilla.

E. 1. Herod . . .

2. didn't— *or* didn't . . .

3. if—

F. Copy the titles in these sentences, and show how they should be set off with quotation marks or underlining.

1. The poem God Is at the Anvil uses very descriptive language.

2. The chapter Fear and Despair in War-Torn Valley helps us appreciate modern medicines.

3. The song Praise Him! Praise Him! is number 29 in Songs of the Church.

F. 1. "God Is at the Anvil"

2. "Fear and Despair"
   <u>War-Torn Valley</u>

3. "Praise Him! Praise Him!"
   <u>Songs of the Church</u>

G. Write correctly all the words that should be italicized or that have errors in the use of apostrophes or hyphens.

1. In Jesus's response to the twelve disciple's arguments, He warned them against self exaltation.

2. Mans strongest efforts cant destroy Gods Word.

3. Be sure to spell Philippians with a single l and with two ps.

G. 1. Jesus', disciples', self-exaltation

2. Man's, can't, God's

3. <u>Philippians</u>, <u>l</u>, <u>p</u>'s

4. In spite of government mandated persecutions, the number of Anabaptist's often grew rapidly.
5. At the family gathering, the twelve, thirteen, and fourteen-year-old grandchildren took a walk in Grandfathers woods.
6. For many years Great uncle Abram Roth made and sold straw brooms.
7. Arizonas state motto—Ditat Deus—means "God enriches."
8. As the Breeze of Ohio steamed upriver, Fathers form faded from our sight.

4. government-mandated, Anabaptists
5. twelve-, thirteen-, Grandfather's
6. Great-uncle, brooms
7. Arizona's, <u>Ditat Deus</u>
8. <u>Breeze of Ohio</u>, Father's

H. Write one of the following terms for each description of paragraph development: *details, facts, reasons, description, examples, incident, definition, comparison, contrast.*
   1. Used to explain abstract nouns or technical words.
   2. Tells a brief story to illustrate or clarify a topic sentence.
   3. Used to convince a reader of an opinion or belief.
   4. Points out similarities between two things.
   5. Used to relate specific activities of story characters.
   6. Gives a word picture of a person, place, or thing.
   7. Used to give two or more points that form a clear idea in the reader's mind.
   8. Points out the differences between two things.
   9. Used to establish the validity of a general truth.
   10. Must be based on solid principles and sound reasoning.

H. 1. definition
    2. incident
    3. reasons
    4. comparison
    5. details
    6. description
    7. examples *or* facts
    8. contrast
    9. facts
    10. reasons

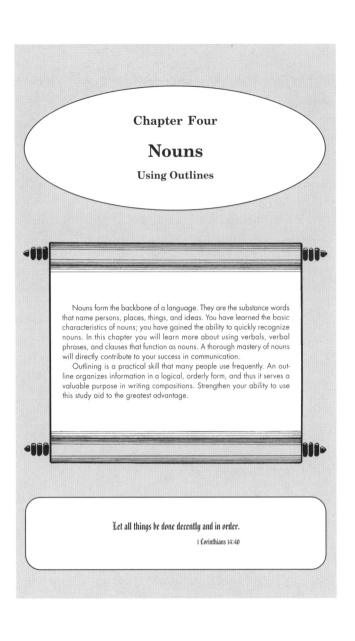

Chapter Four

Nouns

Using Outlines

Nouns form the backbone of a language. They are the substance words that name persons, places, things, and ideas. You have learned the basic characteristics of nouns; you have gained the ability to quickly recognize nouns. In this chapter you will learn more about using verbals, verbal phrases, and clauses that function as nouns. A thorough mastery of nouns will directly contribute to your success in communication.

Outlining is a practical skill that many people use frequently. An outline organizes information in a logical, orderly form, and thus it serves a valuable purpose in writing compositions. Strengthen your ability to use this study aid to the greatest advantage.

Let all things be done decently and in order.

1 Corinthians 14:40

34. Nouns and Substantives

Lesson Survey

- A **noun** names a person, place, thing, or idea.
- A **concrete noun** names a person, place, or thing that has definite, physical substance; an **abstract noun** names a condition, a quality, or an idea that does not have physical substance.
- A noun has gender: *masculine, feminine, neuter,* or *common.*
- A **common noun** is a general name for a person, place, or thing; a **proper noun** names a specific person, place, or thing.
- Many nouns can be identified by noun-forming suffixes.
- Some words are always nouns, some words are never nouns, and some words are sometimes nouns and sometimes other parts of speech.
- A **substantive** is any word or word group that functions as a noun.

In a normal school day, you probably hear, read, and say several thousand different words. Each of those words is one of the eight parts of speech: nouns, pronouns, verbs, adjectives, adverbs, prepositions, conjunctions, and interjections. Nouns, the subject of this chapter, are among the most important of these.

A *noun* names a person, place, thing, or idea. Many nouns name persons, places, and things that have definite, physical substance and can be perceived through the senses; they are *concrete nouns.* Other nouns name conditions, qualities, and ideas. Since they do not have physical substance and cannot be perceived through the senses, they are *abstract nouns.*

> **Concrete nouns:** students, Dorcas, city, Europe, mountain, cart
> **Abstract nouns:** faith, kindness, attitude, mischief, carefulness

All nouns have gender: masculine, feminine, neuter, or common. Masculine gender refers to persons or animals that are male. Feminine gender refers to persons or animals that are female. A noun of neuter gender names an object or idea that is neither male nor female. A noun of common gender names a person or an animal that is either male or female, or a group that may include any combination of genders.

In many cases, there are related words for masculine, feminine, and common gender. But there are no such related words for neuter gender. Study the following table.

Lesson 34

Purpose: To study nouns and substantives, including concrete and abstract nouns, the gender of nouns, and common and proper nouns.

Oral Review:

1. Name several kinds of compound words that should be hyphenated. (compound number words; fractions written in words; words ending with *-in-law;* compound adjectives used as a unit; words beginning with *great-* that refer to relatives; words beginning with *self-;* many that begin with *all-;* proper nouns and adjectives with prefixes)

2. Give some examples of the proper use of italics. (titles of major works; specific names of vehicles; a word or letter used as the subject of discussion; foreign words not adopted into the English language; words to be emphasized)

3. Commas, dashes, and parentheses are all used to set off parenthetical items. How are they used differently? (Commas make the item a part of the sentence; dashes sharply emphasize the item; parentheses minimize the importance of the item.)

4. Name and identify the complements in these sentences.
   a. School should be a place of learning. (place—predicate nominative)
   b. Dennis gave Father a useful gift. (Father—indirect object; gift—direct object)
   c. This new book is quite enjoyable. (enjoyable—predicate adjective)
   d. Abner made the letters on his motto black. (letters—direct object; black—objective complement)

5. On the chalkboard, diagram the skeletons and complements of the sentences in number 4.

Masculine	Feminine	Common	Neuter
ram	ewe	sheep	———
buck	doe	deer	———
brother	sister	sibling	———
host	hostess	———	
———	———	———	road
			mercy

A *common noun* is a general name for a person, place, or thing; a *proper noun* is the specific name of a person, place, or thing. Remember to capitalize all proper nouns. In Lesson 21 you studied ten groupings of proper nouns, including registered trademarks.

Band-Aid   Velcro   Dove soap   Stanley tools

In the last two examples, the trademarks are used as modifiers of common nouns. A noun used in this way is sometimes called an attributive noun. (It actually functions as an adjective.) Remember that a common noun used with a trademark is not capitalized.

Many nouns can be identified by noun-forming suffixes. This is especially true of abstract nouns. The following are common noun-forming suffixes: *-ment, -ion, -ation, -(i)ty, -ness, -dom, -ance, -ence, -ude, -al, -hood, -er, -or,* and *-ar.* Notice how these suffixes are used to form nouns in the following examples.

confuse—confusion	heathen—heathendom	approve—approval
lax—laxity	depend—dependence	mother—motherhood
clean—cleanness	quiet—quietude	school—scholar

By this time you should be able to look at a list of common words and recognize which ones are always nouns, which are never nouns, and which are sometimes nouns and sometimes other parts of speech. The following group contains two words of each kind. Can you identify them?

master	Noah	consider
faithfully	green	river

When used with their normal meanings, *Noah* and *river* are always nouns, while *faithfully* and *consider* are never nouns. *Master* and *green* are sometimes nouns and sometimes other parts of speech.

Of course, the use of a word in a sentence determines its part of speech. Therefore, the term *substantive* is used to mean any word or word group that functions as a noun. Substantives function in a number of different ways, such as subjects, direct and indirect objects, predicate nominatives, objects of prepositions, and objective complements. They include single-word nouns, compound nouns, noun phrases, noun clauses, and pronouns.

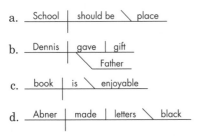

Lesson Introduction: Many of the first words that a child learns to say are names of people or things—nouns. Likewise a foreigner, completely unable to converse in the language of those around him, begins to learn a language by pointing to objects and learning the names of them. For Helen Keller, both blind and deaf, the door to language was opened when she discovered that everything has a name. Clearly, nouns are the foundation of a language.

Lesson Outline:

1. A noun names a person, place, thing, or idea.

2. A concrete noun names a person, place, or thing that has definite, physical substance. An abstract noun names a condition, a quality, or an idea that does not have physical substance.

3. All nouns have gender: masculine, feminine, neuter, or common.

    a. Masculine gender refers to persons or animals that are male.

    b. Feminine gender refers to persons or animals that are female.

    c. A noun of neuter gender names an object or idea that is neither male nor female.

    d. A noun of common gender names a person

In the following sentences, the substantives are underlined. Notice how each one names a person, place, thing, or idea, even though in a different sentence it might function otherwise.

    S   PN   OP   OP
Aaron was the first high priest for the nation of Israel.

    S   OP   DO
Yes, the *a* in *ravening* has the short sound.

    S   DO
King David wrote many inspirational psalms.

        S   DO
A good student wants to learn his lessons well.

    S   DO
We could not determine whose sweater had been left behind.

Class Practice

A. Read each noun in these sentences, tell whether it is *concrete* or *abstract*, and identify its gender.
1. In the reign of King David, the Israelites could follow a noble example.
2. Esther became the queen in Persia in a marvelous way.
3. With great courage, this queen risked her life for her people.
4. A person's thoughts definitely affect his character.

B. Read the proper nouns, including any that are used as modifiers. None of them are capitalized.
1. Did your aunt send you this hallmark stationery?
2. While uncle norman is in paraguay, philip lesher is helping father on the farm.
3. We bought some tylenol at carl's discount drugs.

C. Add a noun-forming suffix to each word.

1. loud	3. neighbor	5. magnify	7. humble
2. follow	4. express	6. important	8. able

D. Tell whether each word is *always, never,* or *sometimes* a noun when used with its normal meaning.

1. fear	4. purchase
2. every	5. rabbit
3. decision	6. finality

E. Read each substantive in these sentences. If a substantive is within a substantive phrase or clause, do not read it separately.
1. Clouds often cover part of Mount Robson.
2. Lying is always a serious wrong.
3. Sue Ellen drew a beautiful picture of a blue jay in a pine tree.
4. We shall seek to learn more about these strange snakes.
5. What Nelson just said was certainly a surprise!

or an animal that is either male or female, or a group that may include any combination of genders.
    e. In many cases, there are related words for masculine, feminine, and common gender; but there are no such related words for neuter gender.

4. A common noun is a general name for a person, place, or thing; a proper noun is the specific name of a person, place, or thing. Remember to capitalize proper nouns. (Review the groupings in Lesson 21.)

5. Many nouns can be identified by noun-forming suffixes.
    a. This is especially true of abstract nouns.
    b. The following are common noun-forming

Lesson 34 Answers

Class Practice

A. 1. reign—abstract, neuter;
King David—concrete, masculine;
Israelites—concrete, common;
example—abstract, neuter
2. Esther—concrete, feminine;
queen—concrete, feminine;
Persia—concrete, neuter;
way—abstract, neuter
3. courage—abstract, neuter;
queen—concrete, feminine;
life—abstract, neuter;
people—concrete, common
4. thoughts—abstract, neuter;
character—abstract, neuter

B. 1. Hallmark
2. Uncle Norman, Paraguay, Philip Lesher, Father
3. Tylenol, Carl's Discount Drugs

C. 1. loudness
2. follower
3. neighborhood
4. expression, expresser
5. magnitude, magnification, magnifier
6. importance
7. humility, humbleness
8. ability

D. 1. sometimes   4. sometimes
2. never   5. always
3. always   6. always

E. 1. Clouds, part, Mount Robson
2. Lying, wrong
3. Sue Ellen, picture, blue jay, (pine) tree
4. We, to learn more about these strange snakes
5. What Nelson just said, surprise

suffixes: *-ment, -ion, -ation, -(i)ty, -ness, -dom, -ance, -ence, -ude, -al, -hood, -er, -or,* and *-ar.*

6. Some words are always nouns, some words are never nouns, and some words are sometimes nouns and sometimes other parts of speech. The use of a word in a sentence determines its part of speech.

Written Exercises

A. Copy each noun, and label it *C* (concrete) or *A* (abstract).
1. A person's values are revealed by the clothes he wears and the places he goes.
2. Laziness and selfishness will greatly hinder one's usefulness.
3. With great difficulty the oxen pulled the wagon over the mountains.
4. We were impressed with the beauty of the neat rows of fruit.

B. Copy each noun, and identify its gender with the label *M, F, N,* or *C.*
1. Jezebel exerted an evil influence on her husband, Ahab.
2. Only Noah and his family were spared from destruction.
3. The cautious vixen watched over the pups playing in the sunshine.
4. The young child pointed with delight to the picture of the hart.

C. Use a noun-forming suffix to change each word in parentheses so that it fits in the sentence.
1. Joseph's (endure) through (afflict) reflects his (confide) in God.
2. In a Christian (brother), there is (loyal) to the Lord and warm (affect) for each other.
3. If you have an (apt) for writing, maybe you will be a (write) or an (edit) someday.

D. Write whether each word is *always, never,* or *sometimes* a noun when used with its normal meaning.
1. increase   4. shone   7. cities   9. answer
2. sweater   5. alike   8. brisk   10. invention
3. temperature   6. purchase

E. Copy each substantive in these sentences. If a substantive is within a substantive phrase or clause, do not list it separately.
1. The old horse slowed his pace as the steepness of the hill increased.
2. The Susquehanna River flows through eastern Pennsylvania into the Chesapeake Bay.
3. Mr. Grant felt great alarm as the fire spread through his barn.
4. A basic need of all men is to worship their Creator.
5. Mary Ann, please stop at the post office and pick up some stamps.
6. Writing can be hard work, but whoever perseveres gets the job done.

Review Exercises

Diagram the skeletons and complements of these sentences. Above each complement, write the correct label: *DO, IO, PN, PA,* or *OC.* [5–8]
1. Faith gives us an eternal outlook on life.
2. The fear of the Lord is essential for our lives.
3. The Christian obeys earthly authorities for conscience' sake.
4. A wise person considers the Bible worthy of his devotion.

Written Exercises

A. 1. values—A; clothes—C; places—C
   2. Laziness—A; selfishness—A; usefulness—A
   3. difficulty—A; oxen—C; wagon—C; mountains—C
   4. beauty—A; rows—C; fruit—C

B. 1. Jezebel—F; influence—N; husband—M; Ahab—M
   2. Noah—M; family—C; destruction—N
   3. vixen—F; pups—C; sunshine—N
   4. child—C; delight—N; picture—N; hart—M

C. 1. endurance, affliction(s), confidence
   2. brotherhood, loyalty, affection
   3. aptitude *or* aptness, writer, editor *(Note: Edit* is actually a back-formation from *editor,* and so is *beg* from *beggar.* A more recent back-formation is the word *burgle,* which describes the activity of a *burglar.)*

D. 1. sometimes   6. sometimes
   2. always   7. always
   3. always   8. never
   4. never   9. sometimes
   5. never   10. always

E. 1. horse, pace, steepness, hill
   2. Susquehanna River, Pennsylvania, Chesapeake Bay
   3. Mr. Grant, alarm, fire, barn
   4. need, men, to worship their Creator
   5. Mary Ann, post office, stamps
   6. Writing, work, whoever perseveres, job

Review Exercises

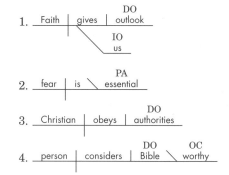

7. **A substantive is any word or word group that functions as a noun.**
   a. It may be a subject, a direct object, an indirect object, a predicate nominative, the object of a preposition, or an objective complement.
   b. It may be a single-word noun, a compound noun, a noun phrase, a noun clause, or a pronoun.

5. In God's Word is found true direction for life.
6. Every day we should read the Bible and seek God in prayer.
7. God's presence makes the darkest room a bright place.
8. Each decision of life is a stone in the structure of character.

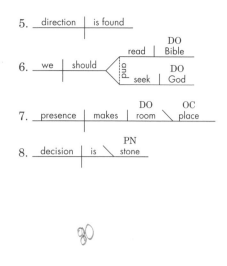

5. direction | is found

6. we | should [and] read | Bible (DO) ; seek | God (DO)

7. presence | makes | room \ place (DO ... OC)

8. decision | is \ stone (PN)

35. Outlining

Lesson Survey
- An **outline** is an orderly arrangement of the main points in a composition.
- An outline may consist of paragraphs, sentences, or topics.
- The form of an outline must follow a definite pattern.
- An outline should have a logical order, headings that do not overlap, and parallel structure.

An outline is a useful tool. It helps a speaker to organize his thoughts before he stands up to deliver a talk or sermon. It helps a writer to organize his thoughts before he begins to write. And it helps a listener or reader to comprehend the organization of the material he hears or reads. Sometimes a writer or speaker—especially an inexperienced one—feels that outlining is a waste of time. When that is the case, the finished product is often the waste that outlining may have prevented.

An *outline* is an orderly arrangement of the main points in a composition, showing the title, the main topics, and the subtopics. If necessary or desirable, an outline may be further divided into points, subpoints, and details. The following diagram shows this arrangement.

Title of Composition
I. Main topic
  A. Subtopic
  B. Subtopic
    1. Point
      a. Subpoint
        (1) Detail about subpoint *a*
        (2) Detail about subpoint *a*
          (a) Detail about detail *(2)*
          (b) Detail about detail *(2)*
      b. Subpoint
    2. Point

Lesson 35

Purpose: (1) To study the rudiments of outlining. (2) To teach the need for parallel points that do not overlap.

Oral Review:
1. How should a paragraph developed by two examples differ from one developed by four or more examples? (Each of the two examples should be more fully described.)
2. *(a)* Which of the following topics would be better for a paragraph developed by contrasts? *(b)* Why? *"The differences between grizzly bears and brown bears"* or *"The differences between grizzly bears and cougars"* (*a*. the first one; *b*. The two items are similar enough to make meaningful contrasts.)
3. What must a writer carefully avoid when developing a paragraph by adding reasons? (presenting opinions as facts; thinking that emotional fervor is as convincing as solid principles and sound reasoning)
4. Name the four basic types of composition. (exposition, argument, narration, description)
5. Name four methods of achieving coherence within paragraphs. (good sentence order; transitional words; repetition of key words; pronoun reference)
6. In addition to transitional words and repetition of key words, what method can be used for transition between paragraphs? (referring to an idea in the previous paragraph)

Lesson Introduction: Ask your students to name types of organization that God has built into the world. (Time is organized into days, weeks, months, seasons, and years; the planets are organized into specific orbits around the sun; the life cycles of plants and animals are organized into specific periods.) Now

II. Main Topic
   A. Subtopic
   B. Subtopic
      1. Point
      2. Point

An outline may consist of paragraphs, sentences, or topics. A paragraph outline is practical for an outline consisting only of main topics. In such an outline, each main topic is a brief summary. Paragraph outlines are not very common.

Most outlines are in sentence or topical form because they are usually more practical than paragraph outlines. A sentence outline has a complete sentence to express each idea. The advantage of this form is that a writer can copy many of the sentences for his composition directly from his outline. A topical outline has a word or brief phrase to express each idea. This form has several advantages. A speaker can see his ideas at a glance, and a writer can quickly put down a summary of the ideas he is planning to place in his composition.

Compare the following two outlines, which give the same information. The first is a topical outline, and the second is a sentence outline covering some of the same material.

Topical outline:

Clouds

I. Composed of moisture condensing out of saturated air
II. Formed as warm, moist air cools
   A. By nighttime cooling of earth
      1. Heat radiates from earth after sundown
      2. Air from warmer bodies of water moves over earth and cools
      3. Mist and fog may form
   B. By air rising and cooling
      1. Over mountains
         a. Frequent clouds above mountain peaks
         b. More rainfall on mountain slopes facing large bodies of water
      2. In convectional currents
         a. Over warm island in the ocean
         b. Over a plowed field
      3. At weather fronts
         a. Warm fronts
            (1) Warm, moist air collides with cooler air
            (2) Warmer air gradually forced upward
            (3) Long, steady rain may result

have them name several types of organization that we put into our lives. (home and school schedules, merchandise arranged on store shelves, books placed in a library)

As these examples show, people have learned that they must organize in order to make things operate smoothly and efficiently. Without such organization, life would be filled with confusion and tension. We must also organize our studying, speaking, and writing if we will be efficient and effective.

Lesson Outline:

1. An outline is an orderly arrangement of the main points in a composition.

2. An outline may consist of paragraphs, sentences, or topics.

   a. A paragraph outline has a paragraph for each main topic.

      1) This is practical for an outline consisting only of main topics.
      2) Each topic is a brief summary.
      3) This is not very common.

   b. A sentence outline has a complete sentence to express each idea. With this form, a writer can copy many sentences for his composition directly from his outline.

   c. A topical outline has a word or brief phrase to express each idea.

      1) A speaker can see his ideas at a glance.
      2) A writer can quickly put down a summary of the ideas in his composition.

3. The form of an outline must follow a definite pattern.

   (1) Center the title above the outline.
   (2) Begin each line with a capital letter.
   (3) Indent each level equally.

       b. Cold fronts
         (1) Cool air collides with warmer air
         (2) Warmer air forced upward abruptly
         (3) Brief, stormy weather may result

III. Classified into three main types
  A. Cumulus clouds
    1. Look like fluffy mounds of mashed potatoes
    2. Range from quite low to fairly high
    3. Mark fair weather, generally
    4. May develop into thunderheads
  B. Cirrus clouds
    1. Look like wispy gauze, mare's tails, or hazy curtains
    2. Are formed high in the sky
    3. Foretell coming precipitation
  C. Stratus clouds
    1. Form large layers, overcasting the sky
    2. Are generally low clouds
    3. May precede a long rainy spell

(4) Indent each level farther right than the previous level.

(5) Use a period or parentheses with each numeral or letter that marks an item.

(6) Have at least two parts when subordinate ideas come under an item. If there is only one subordinate point, include it with the item above it.

(7) Use either all paragraphs, all sentences, or all topics.

(8) Use proper end punctuation with paragraph and sentence outlines; omit end punctuation with topical outlines.

4. The content of an outline must also follow a definite pattern.

    a. Use a logical progression from the beginning to the end of the outline.

    b. Use headings that do not overlap in thought.

5. Keep the items of a topical outline as nearly parallel as possible. Begin each item in a set with the same part of speech, or use a similar structure for all of them.

Sentence outline: (partial)

Clouds

I. Clouds are composed of moisture condensing out of saturated air.

II. Clouds are formed as warm, moist air cools.
  A. The earth becomes cooler at night.
    1. Heat radiates from the earth after sundown.
    2. Air from warmer bodies of water cools when it moves over the earth.
    3. This may cause mist and fog to form.
  B. Air becomes cooler when it rises.
    1. Mountains force air to rise.
      a. Clouds frequently form above mountain peaks.
      b. Mountain slopes facing large bodies of water often have more rainfall.

The form of an outline must follow a definite pattern. Notice how the sample outlines above illustrate these rules.

1. Center the title above the outline.
2. Begin each line with a capital letter.
3. Indent each level equally.
4. Indent each level farther right than the previous level.
5. Use a period or parentheses with each numeral or letter that marks an item.
6. Have at least two parts when subordinate points come under an item. If there is only one subordinate point, include it with the item above it.
7. Use either all paragraphs, all sentences, or all topics.
8. Use proper end punctuation with paragraph and sentence outlines; omit end punctuation with topical outlines.

The content of an outline must also follow a definite pattern. Use a logical progression from the beginning to the end of the outline. Look at the sample outline again. Would the progression be just as good if items I and II were switched? No, it is more logical to consider first the composition of clouds and then their formation.

Use headings that do not overlap in thought. If they do overlap, either reword the headings or make the more specific ideas subordinate to the more general ones. Look at the following example.

Poor: Headings overlap

Early Church Leaders

I. Leaders of the first century

II. Apostles of Christ

III. Leaders at Jerusalem

These headings overlap because the twelve apostles all lived during the first century, and many of them were leaders at Jerusalem. Here are two different ways to improve the outline above.

Better: Headings restructured
Early Church Leaders
I. The apostles, who were taught by Jesus
II. Church leaders who were taught by the apostles

Better: Some headings subordinated
Early Church Leaders
I. First-century leaders
   A. The apostles, who were taught by Jesus
   B. Church leaders who were taught by the apostles
II. Second-century leaders

When you write a topical outline, keep the items of each level as nearly parallel as possible. All the items in a set should begin with the same part of speech or consist of a similar structure, such as a prepositional phrase, a clause, or a noun preceded by a modifier. Notice the parallel structure of the outlines titled "Early Church Leaders." The main topics on the first one (which are the same as the subtopics on the second) consist of a noun preceded by an adjective and followed by an adjective clause. Also, the main topics on the second outline have almost identical wording. Compare the following outline, which does not have parallel structure.

Not parallel:
Early Church Leaders
I. First-century leaders
   A. The apostles, taught by Jesus
   B. Church leaders who were taught by the apostles
II. Leaders of the second century

Class Practice

A. Tell how to correct this outline. A star marks each item that needs improvement.

Following the Example of Christ
Philippians 2
I. The pattern in Christ
  A. His condescension
    1. Had been part of the Godhead (v. 6)
  *2. emptied Himself of heavenly privileges and glory (v. 7)
    3. Accepted limitations of human life (v. 7)

Lesson 35 Answers

Class Practice

(Corrections are underlined. Refer to the rules in the lesson to make sure pupils understand the corrections.)

A.   **Following the Example of Christ**
     Philippians 2
  I. The pattern in Christ
   A. His condescension
     1. Had been part of the Godhead (v. 6)
     2. <u>Emptied</u> Himself of heavenly privileges and glory (v. 7)
     3. Accepted limitations of human life (v. 7)

*4. He took characteristic attributes of a servant (v. 7)
*5. Condemnation to a criminal's death (v. 8)
B. His consecration
*1. Compelled by a clear sense of purpose
*C. He was crowned (vv. 9–11)
II. The practice for Christians
A. Some important qualities
1. Unity (v. 2)
*2. Being humble (v. 3)
*3. interest in others (v. 4)
4. Contentment (v. 14)
*a. In all of life
*5. A blameless life (v. 15)
6. Consecration
*B. Some examples that are noble
1. Timothy (vv. 19–24)
a. Compassionate
*b. Unselfishness
*c. He was trustworthy
2. Epaphroditus (vv. 25–30)
*3. He was dedicated
*4. He was sympathetic

B. Tell how to improve this outline so that the headings do not overlap in thought.

Common Animals of the Bible
I. Clean Animals
II. Unclean Animals
III. Domestic Animals
IV. Wild Animals

Written Exercises
A. Copy this outline, following the rules for proper form. Each item that needs improvement is marked with a star.

Grizzly Bears
I. Their habitat
A. Live only in North America
*1. some in Mexico
2. Some in northwestern United States
*3. Most live in western Canada and Alaska
B. Prefer open meadows and valleys
*C. Sometimes living in woods or treeless wilderness

---

4. Took characteristic attributes of a servant (v. 7)
5. Was condemned to a criminal's death (v. 8)
B. His consecration—compelled by a clear sense of purpose
C. His coronation (vv. 9–11)
II. The practice for Christians
A. Some important qualities
1. Unity (v. 2)
2. Humility (v. 3)
3. Interest in others (v. 4)
4. Contentment in all of life (v. 14)
5. Blamelessness (v. 15)
6. Consecration
B. Some noble examples
1. Timothy (vv. 19–24)
a. Compassionate
b. Unselfish
c. Trustworthy
2. Epaphroditus (vv. 25–30)
a. Dedicated
b. Sympathetic

B. (Two possible improvements are shown.)

Common Animals of the Bible
I. Clean animals
A. Domestic
B. Wild
II. Unclean animals
A. Domestic
B. Wild

Common Animals of the Bible
I. Domestic animals
A. Clean
B. Unclean
II. Wild animals
A. Clean
B. Unclean

Written Exercises
A. (Corrections are underlined. Allow reasonable variation.)

Grizzly Bears
I. Their habitat
A. Live only in North America
1. Some in Mexico
2. Some in northwestern United States
3. Most in western Canada and Alaska
B. Prefer open meadows and valleys
C. Live in woods or treeless wilderness sometimes

*II. What they look like
   A. Size
     *1. may weigh up to 850 lb.
     *2. As much as 8 ft. long
   *B. Color
     *1. may range from creamy to almost black
     2. Have white-tipped hairs
       *a. this gives it the grizzled look
  *C. Their claws
     *1. Five on each foot
     2. Are dark in young bears but light in older bears
     3. Wear down during summer
       *a. grow back in winter

3. Here is the rest of the outline above. Copy it and add the missing details, choosing from the lists below.

III. Their diet
   A. Vegetation
     1.
     2.
     3.
   B. Meat
     1.
     2.
     3.

IV. Their behavior
   A. Moving about
     1.
     2.
     3.
   B. Preparing for winter
     1.
     2.
       a.
       b.
     3.
       a.
       b.
       c.

Points for III:
  Dig up small animals like mice and ground squirrels
  Dig various kinds of roots
  Eat grasses and other tender plants
  Enjoy berries especially
  Find insects under logs and rocks
  Hunt large animals like mountain sheep and moose

Points and subpoints for IV:
  Make a den
  Can run faster than a man
  A hollow log
  Can stand on hind legs

II. <u>Their appearance</u>
   A. Size
     1. <u>May</u> weigh up to 850 lb.
     2. <u>May reach</u> 8 ft. long
   B. <u>Color</u>
     1. <u>May</u> range from creamy to almost black
     2. Have white-tipped hairs <u>that give the grizzled look</u>
   C. <u>Claws</u>
     1. <u>Have</u> five on each foot
     2. Are dark in young bears but light in older bears
     3. Wear down during summer <u>but grow back in winter</u>

B. (Details already on the outline are underlined. Under main topic III, note the progression of <u>roots</u>, main <u>plants</u>, and <u>fruit</u> in subtopic A, and of the sizes of the animals in subtopic B. Under main topic IV, note the progression of standing, walking, and running in subtopic A. Other arrangements may also be acceptable.)

III. <u>Their diet</u>
   A. <u>Vegetation</u>
     1. Dig various kinds of roots
     2. Eat grasses and other tender plants
     3. Enjoy berries especially
   B. <u>Meat</u>
     1. Find insects under logs and rocks
     2. Dig up small animals like mice and ground squirrels
     3. Hunt large animals like mountain sheep and moose

IV. <u>Their behavior</u>
   A. <u>Moving about</u>
     1. Can stand on hind legs
     2. May look clumsy in walking
     3. Can run faster than a man
   B. <u>Preparing for winter</u>
     1. Eat much more
     2. Grow thick coat
       a. Short underfur for good insulation
       b. Long guard hairs for protection from rain and snow
     3. Make a den
       a. A cave
       b. A hollow log
       c. A hole in a steep hill

Eat much more
Grow thick coat
A hole in a steep hill
Long guard hairs for protection from rain and snow
May look clumsy in walking
Short underfur for good insulation
A cave

Review Exercises

Write whether each paragraph is developed by *facts, examples, reasons,* or *descriptions.* There is one of each kind. [28, 32]

1.   Mountains have a definite effect on our emotions. Poets and painters of all generations have been inspired by the mountains. Some of the noblest works of art and the finest passages in literature have been born of the heights. As we view the mountains, our thoughts are involuntarily drawn upward and thus to God, the Creator of their beauty. It is not strange that mountains remind us of God and stir feelings of awe and wonder. There they stand from ages past, strong, sure, and unmovable, seeming never to change.

2.   The mountains help to produce rain. If you live among the mountains, you probably have often noticed the clouds hanging over the peaks or floating along the ridges. As warm air moves across the earth, it is forced upward by the sudden ascent which forms a mountain. The rising air is cooled, its moisture forms clouds, and the clouds yield rain or snow.

3.   Why is it important to "abstain from all appearance of evil"? First, anything that appears evil can easily lead to sin, even if that thing is not evil in itself. Second, if another person sees us doing what appears evil, we may influence him to do something that actually is evil. Above all, doing things that appear evil is a dishonor to the God we claim to serve. We should be very careful to "give none occasion to the adversary to speak reproachfully" of the Lord or His people.

4.   Hannah Wright had just taken the last loaves from the oven. She dusted off some ashes from the wooden bread shovel before she replaced it in its corner. Bright spring sunlight streamed into the kitchen, warming the stone floor to a deep brown color and touching the mugs and platters on the dresser till they fairly winked back its brightness. A robin outside was whistling gaily, and a long branch of lilac buds peeped in at the open upper door.

Review Exercises

1. examples
2. facts
3. reasons
4. descriptions

36. Plural Nouns

> ### Lesson Survey
>
> - Form the plural of most nouns by adding -*s*. If a noun ends with *s*, *sh*, *ch*, *x*, or *z*, add -*es*.
> - Add -*s* to most nouns ending with *o* after a vowel. If the final *o* comes after a consonant, -*s* is added to some nouns and -*es* to others.
> - If a noun ends with *y* after a consonant, change the *y* to *i* and add -*es*. If it ends with *y* after a vowel, simply add -*s*.
> - For many nouns ending with *f* or *fe*, change the *f* to *v* and add -*s* or -*es*.
> - For most compound nouns, change the most important word to the plural form.
> - For some nouns, you must change the vowel.
> - A few plural nouns have an archaic -*en* ending.
> - A few nouns have the same form whether singular or plural.
> - A noun borrowed from another language may have a foreign plural ending.

In most cases, the form of a noun shows whether it is singular or plural in number. The following nine rules will help you to write the plural forms of nouns correctly.

1. *Form the plural of most nouns by adding* -s. *If a noun ends with* s, sh, ch, x, *or* z, *add* -es.

student—students	fox—foxes
bench—benches	quiz—quizzes

2. *Add* -s *to nouns ending with* o *after a vowel. If the final* o *comes after a consonant,* -s *is added to some nouns and* -es *to others.* Sometimes either way is correct. (Use a dictionary if you are not sure.) For musical terms ending with *o*, the plural is generally formed by adding -*s*.

studio—studios	tornado—tornadoes *or* tornados
folio—folios	alto—altos
echo—echoes	

3. *If a noun ends with* y *after a consonant, change the* y *to* i *and add* -es. *If it ends with* y *after a vowel, simply add* -s.

berry—berries	day—days
enemy—enemies	turkey—turkeys

Lesson 36

Purpose: To study rules for making plural forms of nouns.

Oral Review:

1. Explain the difference between concrete and abstract nouns. (Concrete nouns name things with physical substance, which can be perceived through the senses. Abstract nouns name ideas with no physical substance, which cannot be perceived through the senses.)
2. Add a noun-forming suffix to each word.
   a. national (nationality)
   b. banish (banishment)
   c. friendly (friendliness)
   d. confide (confidence)
   e. bury (burial)
   f. estimate (estimation)
3. Tell whether each word is always, sometimes, or never a noun when used with its normal meaning.
   a. share (sometimes)
   b. mystify (never)
   c. condescension (always)
   d. level (sometimes)
   e. statement (always)
   f. exemption (always)
4. Tell which words in these phrases need to be capitalized. (Answers are underlined.)
   a. <u>November</u>, autumn, <u>Wednesday</u>
   b. has become the <u>President</u> of the <u>United</u> <u>States</u>
   c. the president of <u>Valley</u> <u>Bakery</u>
   d. spelling, <u>American</u> history, <u>Typing</u> I
   e. your aunt <u>Louise</u>
   f. for <u>Aunt</u> <u>Louise</u>
   g. during the <u>Revolutionary</u> <u>War</u>
   h. a <u>Whirlpool</u> refrigerator
   i. <u>Swedish</u> rye bread with thick slices of <u>German</u> liverwurst
   j. the mountains across the <u>Poe</u> <u>River</u>

4. *For many nouns ending with* f *or* fe, *change the* f *to* v *and add* -s *or* -es. For others, simply add -s. A few words are spelled either way.

leaf—leaves   hoof—hoofs *or* hooves
knife—knives   scarf—scarfs *or* scarves
grief—griefs

If the last two letters are *ff,* the plural almost always ends with *-ffs.* Because of the many possibilities, always check a dictionary when you are in doubt.

cliff—cliffs   tariff—tariffs

5. *For most compound nouns, change the most important word to the plural form.* Nouns that end with *-ful* are an exception: add *-s* to the *-ful.* In a few other cases, each part of the compound word is made plural.

sister-in-law—sisters-in-law   pailful—pailfuls
bystander—bystanders   manservant—menservants

6. *For some nouns, you must change the vowel.* Only seven root words follow this pattern. Of course, any compound words formed with these roots also follow this pattern.

foot—feet   mouse—mice
tooth—teeth   man—men
goose—geese   woman—women
louse—lice

tenderfoot—tenderfeet   dormouse—dormice
eyetooth—eyeteeth   fireman—firemen

but mongoose—mongooses

7. *A few plural nouns have an archaic* -en *ending.*

child—children; ox—oxen (still used today)
brother—brethren (commonly used within the church)
hose—hosen (archaic; found once in the King James Bible)

8. *A few nouns have the same form whether singular or plural.* Most nouns in this category are names of animals.

(one) bison—(five) bison   (this) series—(these) series
(one) deer—(ten) deer   (a) species—(all) species
(one) sheep—(one hundred) sheep

9. *A noun borrowed from another language may have a foreign plural ending.* For many such nouns, the regular English pattern has also become acceptable. Study the following table.

5. Commas, dashes, and parentheses may be used to set off parenthetical elements.
   a. Which give sharp emphasis to the parenthetical element? (dashes)
   b. Which make the parenthetical element part of the sentence? (commas)
   c. How do parentheses affect the parenthetical element? (minimize its importance; make it somewhat beside the point of the sentence)

Lesson Introduction: Write the following words on the board, and ask your students if they can identify each one as singular or plural.

bacteria (plural)   vertebrae (plural)
species (either)   swine (either)
alumnus (singular)   analysis (singular)

This lesson reviews these and other forms of singular and plural nouns.

Lesson Outline:

1. Form the plural of most nouns by adding -s. If a noun ends with s, sh, ch, x, or z, add -es.

2. Add -s to nouns ending with o after a vowel. If the final o comes after a consonant, -s is added to some nouns and -es to others. Some plurals are formed either way. For musical terms ending with *o,* the plural is generally formed by adding *-s.*

3. If a noun ends with y after a consonant, change the y to i and add -es. If it ends with y after a vowel, simply add -s.

4. For many nouns ending with f or fe, change the f to v and add -s or -es. For others, simply add *-s.* A few words are spelled either way.
   a. If the last two letters are *ff,* the plural almost always ends with *-ffs.*
   b. Because of the many possibilities, always check a dictionary when you are in doubt.
   (*Teacher:* You could also warn that changing *f* to *v* may change the noun to a verb. *Examples:* belief—beliefs [*not* believes]; safe—safes [*not* saves]; strife—strifes [*not* strives]. Conversely, *not* changing the *f* to *v* may also result in a verb. *Examples:* loaf—loaves [*not* loafs]; wolf—wolves [*not* wolfs].)

Nouns With Foreign Plural Endings

Singular ending: -is
Plural ending: -es, pronounced (ēz)
Examples: axis—axes; diagnosis—diagnoses; oasis—oases

   (Most words in this group are not well suited to the regular English pattern because of the two *s* or *z* sounds in the last syllable. Adding a third *s* or *z* sound makes the word awkward to pronounce.)

Singular ending: -ex *or* -ix
Plural ending: -ices, pronounced (i·sēz)
Examples: index—indices *or* indexes; appendix—appendices *or* appendixes

Singular ending: -a
Plural ending: -ae, pronounced (ē)
Examples: alga—algae; formula—formulae *or* formulas

Singular ending: -us
Plural ending: -i, pronounced (ī)
Examples: cactus—cacti *or* cactuses; stimulus—stimuli

Singular ending: -on *or* -um
Plural ending: -a, pronounced (ə)
Examples: criterion—criteria *or* criterions; curriculum—curricula *or* curriculums; datum—data; memorandum—memoranda *or* memorandums

Class Practice

  Give the correct plural spellings of these nouns. Use the foreign spellings for numbers 13–18.

1. louse
2. fish
3. library
4. giraffe
5. volcano
6. soprano
7. brother (two forms)
8. latch
9. mail carrier
10. valley
11. hoof
12. nobleman
13. crisis
14. vertebra
15. bacterium
16. synopsis
17. radius
18. vortex

B. Tell whether the underlined words are *singular* or *plural*.
1. The Catholic Church faced a <u>crisis</u> when Luther wrote his Ninety-five <u>Theses</u> against indulgences.

5. For most compound nouns, change the most important word to the plural form.
    a. Nouns that end with *-ful* are an exception.
    b. In a few cases, each part is made plural.

6. For some nouns, you must change the vowel. Only seven root words, and any compound words formed with these roots, follow this pattern.

7. A few plural nouns have an archaic -en ending.

8. A few nouns have the same form whether singular or plural. Most nouns in this category are names of animals.

9. A noun borrowed from another language may have a foreign plural ending. For many such nouns, the regular English pattern has also become acceptable. (Examples given below are in addition to those in the pupil's text.)

Lesson 36 Answers

Class Practice

A.
1. lice
2. fish *or* fishes
3. libraries
4. giraffes
5. volcanoes *or* volcanos
6. sopranos
7. brothers, brethren
8. latches
9. mail carriers
10. valleys
11. hoofs *or* hooves
12. noblemen
13. crises
14. vertebrae
15. bacteria
16. synopses
17. radii
18. vortices

B. 1. singular, plural

---

a. For a noun ending with *-is,* the foreign plural ends with *-es,* pronounced (ēz).

    analysis—analyses
    basis—bases
    mantis—mantes *or* mantises
    thesis—theses

b. For a noun ending with *-ex* or *-ix,* the foreign plural ends with *-ices,* pronounced (i·sēz).

    cortex—cortices *or* cortexes
    vertex—vertices *or* vertexes
    matrix—matrices *or* matrixes

c. For a noun ending with *-a,* the foreign plural ends with *-ae,* pronounced (ē).

    larva—larvae *or* larvas
    vertebra—vertebrae *or* vertebras

2. The Bible contains the <u>criteria</u> by which to discern truth and error.
3. Sometimes scientists make erroneous <u>hypotheses</u> because they misinterpret the <u>data</u> they collect.
4. Topsoil is found in the upper <u>stratum</u> of the earth's crust.
5. I enjoy watching the <u>trout</u> as they flash through the water.

Written Exercises

A. Write the plural form of each singular noun and the singular form of each plural noun. If the form does not change, just copy the word. Use foreign plurals for numbers 21–30.

1. oxen	11. cargo	21. formulae
2. sheaves	12. mailman	22. index
3. tornado	13. waitress	23. bases
4. son-in-law	14. gaffe	24. phenomenon
5. goose	15. solo	25. appendices
6. adz	16. alloy	26. fungus
7. proof	17. sheep	27. memoranda
8. handful	18. lice	28. axis
9. groves	19. liberties	29. stimuli
10. curio	20. secretary-general	30. alga

B. Copy each underlined word, and label it *S* (singular) or *P* (plural).
1. Several <u>species</u> of <u>deer</u> live in North America.
2. The scientist finally isolated the <u>bacillus</u> causing the disease.
3. During the run of the <u>salmon</u>, bears and <u>Eskimo</u> came to the rivers.
4. Separate <u>analyses</u> of the problem were made by three experts.
5. God's people must limit their exposure to the news <u>media</u>.
6. This sheet lists the <u>errata</u> discovered after the book was printed.
7. Mother planted the <u>gladiolus</u> beside the front porch.
8. The sight of the <u>oasis</u> was a strong <u>stimulus</u> to the weary travelers.

Review Exercises

A. Write correctly each word that has a capitalization error. [21]
1. we studied the poem "The Pineapples And The Bee" in Reading class.
2. did uncle Edward buy the japanese car that he had talked about?
3. "Father," said Mother, "Would you please buy some tylenol when you stop at Taylor's pharmacy?"
4. During the civil war, the mennonites of the shenandoah valley suffered greatly.
5. In a.d. 1215, the english barons forced king John of england to sign the magna carta.
6. When alaska and hawaii became States, dwight d. eisenhower was president of the United States Of America.

2. plural
3. plural, plural
4. singular
5. plural

Written Exercises

A.
1. ox	16. alloys
2. sheaf	17. sheep
3. tornadoes *or* tornados	18. louse
4. sons-in-law	19. liberty
5. geese	20. secretaries-general
6. adzes	21. formula
7. proofs	22. indices
8. handfuls	23. basis
9. grove	24. phenomena
10. curios	25. appendix
11. cargoes *or* cargos	26. fungi
12. mailmen	27. memorandum
13. waitresses	28. axes
14. gaffes	29. stimulus
15. solos	30. algae

B. 1. species—P; deer—P
2. bacillus—S
3. salmon—P; Eskimo—P
4. analyses—P
5. media—P (*or* S)
6. errata—P
7. gladiolus—S *or* P
8. oasis—S; stimulus—S

Review Exercises

A. 1. We, and, the, reading
2. Did, Uncle, Japanese
3. would, Tylenol, Pharmacy
4. Civil War, Mennonites, Shenandoah Valley
5. A.D., English, King, England, Magna Carta
6. Alaska, Hawaii, states, Dwight D. Eisenhower, of

d. For a noun ending with *-us,* the foreign plural ends with *-i,* pronounced (ī).

radius—radii *or* radiuses
thesaurus—thesauri *or* thesauruses

e. For a noun ending with *-on* or *-um,* the plural form ends with *-a,* pronounced (ə).

phenomenon—phenomena
ganglion—ganglia *or* ganglions

bacterium—bacteria
stratum—strata *or* stratums

7. During the late Summer months, we are very busy at Hartman Valley produce market.
8. Give heed, o youth, to the counsels of the scriptures.

3. Copy these sentences, adding commas, dashes, or parentheses where needed. Some sentences have notes to direct you. [29]
   1. "For a day in thy courts is better than a thousand" Psalm 84:10.
   2. This year our tomatoes we raised two acres of them did quite well. (Treat the parenthetical element as being somewhat beside the point.)
   3. "A Thrilling Escape From Danger" a thrilling story indeed! is about a missionary's experience in Africa. (Give sharp emphasis to the parenthetical element.)
   4. "I certainly didn't expect" Anita stopped suddenly.
   5. Grandmother Risser who is eighty-six years old knitted this pillow top. (Make the parenthetical element a part of the sentence.)
   6. Grandmother Risser she turned eighty-six last week knitted this pillow top. (Treat the parenthetical element as being somewhat beside the point.)
   7. Grandmother Risser she is eighty-six years old already! knitted this pillow top. (Give sharp emphasis to the parenthetical element.)
   8. There are three good reasons to use neat penmanship: 1 it helps to develop preciseness, 2 it indicates the trait of carefulness, and 3 it shows thoughtfulness to others.

---

37. Possessive Nouns

Lesson Survey

- A **possessive noun** usually functions as an adjective.
- The possessive form of most singular nouns is made by adding *'s*.
- The possessive form of a plural noun not ending with *-s* is made by adding *'s*, and of a plural noun ending with *-s* by adding only an apostrophe.
- For a compound noun or noun phrase, only the last word is made possessive.
- Only nouns naming persons or animals are normally written in possessive forms.
- To show joint ownership, only the last noun is made possessive. To show separate ownership, each noun is made possessive.

Lesson 37

Purpose: To study the form and use of possessive nouns.

Oral Review:
1. Give the plural spellings of these words.
   a. baby (babies)
   b. chief (chiefs)
   c. solo (solos)
   d. valley (valleys)
   e. axis (axes)
   f. liberty (liberties)
   g. brother-in-law (brothers-in-law)
   h. staff (staffs, staves)
   i. fungus (fungi, funguses)
   j. hobo (hoboes, hobos)
2. Identify each noun in these sentences, and tell whether it is concrete or abstract. (Nouns are

---

7. summer, Produce Market
8. O, Scriptures

B. (Corrections are underlined.)
   1. "For a day in thy courts is better than a thousand" (Psalm 84:10).
   2. This year our tomatoes (we raised two acres of them) did quite well.
   3. "A Thrilling Escape From Danger"—a thrilling story indeed!—is about a missionary's experience in Africa.
   4. "I certainly didn't expect—" Anita stopped suddenly.
   5. Grandmother Risser, who is eighty-six years old, knitted this pillow top.
   6. Grandmother Risser (she turned eighty-six last week) knitted this pillow top.
   7. Grandmother Risser—she is eighty-six years old already!—knitted this pillow top.
   8. There are three good reasons to use neat penmanship: (1) it helps to develop preciseness, (2) it indicates the trait of carefulness, and (3) it shows thoughtfulness to others.

underlined; abbreviated labels are in parentheses.)
   a. The sun produces its own light, but the moon does not. (concrete; concrete; concrete)
   b. The courage of the Anabaptists was born of their commitment to the Lord. (abstract; concrete; abstract; concrete)
3. Tell whether each word is always, sometimes, or never a noun when used with its normal meaning.
   a. courage (always)   d. speak (never)
   b. snare (sometimes)   e. ability (always)
   c. officialdom (always) f. stand (sometimes)
4. What kinds of titles should be placed within quotation marks? (titles of minor works, such as short stories, short poems, chapters of books, and songs)
5. What kinds of titles should be italicized? (titles of major works, such as books, newspapers, pamphlets, and periodicals)

Not all languages have possessive forms of nouns. An English-speaking person may say, "John's book"; but a Spanish-speaking person must say, "El libro de Juan" (the book of John). The use of possessive nouns simplifies and smoothes our language.

Possessive nouns usually function as adjectives that show ownership or relationship. They always answer the question *whose.* If a possessive noun stands alone (without modifying another word), it functions as a noun.

> Joseph interpreted <u>Pharaoh's</u> dreams. (*Pharaoh's* tells whose dreams.)
> <u>Melanie's</u> motto has silver lettering, but <u>Sally's</u> has white lettering. (*Melanie's* is an adjective modifying *motto. Sally's,* meaning "Sally's motto," is the subject of the second clause.)

The possessive form of most singular nouns is made by adding *'s.*

the widow<u>'s</u> two mites	Charles<u>'s</u> books
Peter<u>'s</u> question	Doris<u>'s</u> coat
police<u>'s</u> duty	

When a singular noun contains two *s* or *z* sounds in the last syllable, add only an apostrophe. Adding a third *s* or *z* sound makes the word awkward to pronounce.

> Moses<u>'</u> faithfulness   Jesus<u>'</u> sacrifice   for conscience<u>'</u> sake

The possessive form of plural nouns not ending with *-s* is made by adding *'s,* and of plural nouns ending with *-s* by adding only an apostrophe.

the oxen's lowing	the elephants' loads
the bacteria's damage	the teachers' desks
the cattlemen's hard work	the angels' mission

Singular	Singular Possessive	Plural	Plural Possessive
student	student's	students	students'
ox	ox's	oxen	oxen's
wolf	wolf's	wolves	wolves'

For compound nouns or noun phrases, only the last word is made possessive. This is true even if the last word is not the most important word in the compound.

Singular	Plural
our brother-in-law's house	our brothers-in-law's houses
the mail carrier's route	the mail carriers' routes
the king of Israel's reign	the kings of Israel's reigns

Only nouns naming persons or animals are normally written in possessive

6. Give some other uses of italics. (specific names of vehicles; a word or letter that is the subject of discussion; foreign words that have not been adopted into the English language; special emphasis)

Lesson Introduction: Had you lived in England a thousand years ago, you would not have learned about using apostrophes to show the possessive case of nouns. Instead, you would have formed the different cases of nouns by using different endings. Write the following examples on the board to illustrate the difference between Old English and Modern English.

Old English	Modern English
cempa cyning	champion king
cempan cyning	champion's king
cempena cyning	champions' king

Do your students think they would prefer this system to what we use today? Use of apostrophes to make possessive forms can be confusing, but it is definitely simpler than using so many different word forms.

Lesson Outline:

1. A possessive noun usually functions as an adjective that shows ownership or relationship.
    a. It always answers the question *whose.*
    b. If a possessive noun stands alone (without modifying another word), it functions as a noun.

2. The possessive form of most singular nouns is made by adding 's. When a singular noun contains two *s* or *z* sounds in the last syllable, add only an apostrophe. Adding a third *s* or *z* sound makes the word awkward to pronounce.

3. The possessive form of a plural noun not ending with -s is made by adding 's, and of a

orms. For nouns that name inanimate objects, it is usually better to use a prepositional phrase. Exceptions are made for poetic or figurative language, or measures of time and money, and for a few other common expressions.

Correct: The cub's cry of distress brought its mother on the run.

Poor: This <u>book's</u> plastic cover is worn out. (inanimate object)
Better: The plastic cover <u>of this book</u> is worn out.

Correct: Swift to its close ebbs out <u>life's</u> little day;
<u>Earth's</u> joys grow dim, its glories pass away. (poetry)

Correct: an <u>hour's</u> work, a <u>month's</u> furlough, a <u>nickel's</u> worth, his <u>heart's</u> desire, a <u>stone's</u> throw, the <u>sun's</u> rays (measures of time and money, and other common expressions)

When two or more persons have joint ownership of something, only the last noun is made possessive. (The noun modified by the possessive words is usually singular.) When two or more persons have separate ownership, each noun is made possessive. (The noun modified by the possessive words is usually plural.)

Joint ownership:
Sister Elizabeth enjoyed Sharon and Elaine's visit.
    (one visit by two girls)
Nevin and Clarence's watermelons sold well.
    (one watermelon harvest owned jointly)
Separate ownership:
Sister Elizabeth enjoyed Sharon's and Elaine's visits.
    (two separate visits by two girls)
Nevin's and Clarence's watermelons sold well.
    (two watermelon harvests owned separately)

Class Practice

A. Tell how to spell each possessive form that is incorrect. If it has no error, say *correct*.
1. the brethren's help
2. the thieve's arrest
3. James's homework
4. Mr. Weaver's cows
5. Jesus's command
6. the two deers' flight
7. several prophet's warnings
8. my brother's-in-law's job
9. the two boys' responses
10. several ladie's pocketbooks

B. Give the singular possessive, plural, and plural possessive spellings of these nouns.
1. daughter
2. monkey
3. princess
4. fox
5. fireman
6. sister-in-law
7. secretary
8. fly
9. calf
10. disciple

plural noun ending with -s by adding only an apostrophe.

4. For a compound noun or noun phrase, only the last word is made possessive.

5. Only nouns naming persons or animals are normally written in possessive forms.
a. For nouns that name inanimate objects, use a prepositional phrase.
b. Exceptions are made for poetic or figurative language, for measures of time and money, and for a few other common expressions.

6. When two or more persons have joint ownership of something, only the last noun is made possessive. When two or more persons have separate ownership, each noun is made possessive.

Lesson 37 Answers

Class Practice
A. 1. correct
2. thieves'
3. correct
4. correct
5. Jesus'
6. deer's
7. prophets'
8. brother-in-law's
9. correct
10. ladies'

B. 1. daughter's, daughters, daughters'
2. monkey's, monkeys, monkeys'
3. princess's, (*Princess'* is also correct according to the rule in the lesson. However, that rule applies mainly to historical names such as Moses, Jesus, and Xerxes.) princesses, princesses'
4. fox's, foxes, foxes'
5. fireman's, firemen, firemen's
6. sister-in-law's, sisters-in-law, sisters-in-law's
7. secretary's, secretaries, secretaries'
8. fly's, flies, flies'
9. calf's, calves, calves'
10. disciple's, disciples, disciples'

C. Change each sentence to show separate ownership.
1. Susan and Sharon's garden is small but adequate.
2. Have you seen Arlin and Linford's homemade kite?
3. Freda and Heidi's letter has arrived today.

D. Change each sentence to show joint ownership.
1. Grandpa's and Grandma's suggestions were helpful.
2. Esther's and Alma's baskets are full already.
3. Here are Aaron's and David's melon patches.

Written Exercises

A. Write the possessive form of each noun.

1. angel	8. Dennis	15. wife
2. high priests	9. children	16. wives
3. apostles	10. leaders	17. larva
4. Jesus	11. mice	18. larvae
5. Israelites	12. fillies	19. prince
6. daughter-in-law	13. ostrich	20. princes
7. daughters-in-law	14. ostriches	

B. Rewrite each sentence to show joint ownership.
1. Jeffrey's and Loren's bedrooms have been cleaned thoroughly.
2. Noah Steiner's and Marcus Good's businesses are flourishing.
3. Has anyone found Anita's and Carol's kittens yet?
4. Have you learned what Aunt Rose's and Aunt Miriam's surprises were?

C. Rewrite each sentence to show separate ownership.
1. This is Leonard and Lamar's new bicycle.
2. Charlotte and Jessica's mother has brought a treat.
3. I enjoyed Peter and Jake's science demonstration.
4. Has anyone seen Lois and Lena's suitcase?

D. If the underlined part of the sentence needs improvement, write it correctly. If it has no error, write *correct*.
1. Moses's strong faith in God gave him courage and strength.
2. The traffic jam caused us an hour's delay.
3. My one sister's-in-laws talent for drawing faces is outstanding.
4. The three calve's pen is almost too crowded now.
5. The prophets' messages include many warnings against sinful living.
6. The table's legs are getting too wobbly.

Review Exercises

A. If the underlined part of the sentence is punctuated incorrectly, write it correctly. If it has no error, write *correct*. [26]
1. Do you know the reference for the words, "Yea, I have a goodly heritage?"

C. 1. Susan's and Sharon's gardens are small but adequate.
2. Have you seen Arlin's and Linford's homemade kites?
3. Freda's and Heidi's letters have arrived today.

D. 1. Grandpa and Grandma's suggestions were helpful.
  or Grandpa and Grandma's suggestion was helpful.
2. Esther and Alma's baskets are full already.
  or Esther and Alma's basket is full already.
3. Here are Aaron and David's melon patches.
  or Here is Aaron and David's melon patch.

Written Exercises

A.

1. angel's		11. mice's
2. high priests'		12. fillies'
3. apostles'		13. ostrich's
4. Jesus'		14. ostriches'
5. Israelites'		15. wife's
6. daughter-in-law's		16. wives'
7. daughters-in-law's		17. larva's
8. Dennis's		18. larvae's
9. children's		19. prince's
10. leaders'		20. princes'

B. 1. Jeffrey and Loren's bedroom has been cleaned thoroughly.
2. Noah Steiner and Marcus Good's business is flourishing.
3. Has anyone found Anita and Carol's kitten(s) yet?
4. Have you learned what Aunt Rose and Aunt Miriam's surprise was?
  or Have you learned what Aunt Rose and Aunt Miriam's surprises were?

C. 1. These are Leonard's and Lamar's new bicycles.
2. Charlotte's and Jessica's mothers have brought a treat (brought treats).
3. I enjoyed Peter's and Jake's science demonstrations.
4. Has anyone seen Lois's and Lena's suitcases?

D. 1. Moses' strong faith
2. correct
3. sister-in-law's talent
4. calves' pen
5. correct
6. legs of the table

Review Exercises

A. 1. heritage"?

2. Who wrote the song "Where Could I <u>Go?"</u>

3. "Grover Cleveland once expressed this worthy principle: 'Honor lies in honest <u>toil,"</u> remarked Brother Daniel.

4. Brother Noah gave us this paraphrase of the words, "He with earthly cares entwineth hope and comfort from <u>above:"</u> In the fabric of life, God weaves in hope and comfort along with the burdens and heartaches.

5. "Come into the house, girls," called <u>Mother, and</u> set the table."

6. <u>"The</u> sword of the Lord, and of Gideon' was the battle cry of Gideon's army," said Paul.

B. Copy the items that need italics or quotation marks, and add the underlining or the missing marks. [26, 30]

1. The hymn Teach Me the Measure of My Days is in both the Christian Hymnal and the Church Hymnal.

2. I have just finished the chapter Soldiers or Slaves? in the book Evangelists in Chains.

3. The plans for a church service sometimes include the abbreviation D.V., which stands for the Latin words Deo volente (God willing).

4. We went fishing in Uncle Howard's rowboat, The Silver Fish.

C. Write correctly the items that have errors in the use of apostrophes or hyphens. [31]

1. In the pre World War I era, my great grandfather Witmer served as a bishop.

2. My brother in law has turned twenty three.

3. I didnt want self rising flour; I wanted all purpose flour.

4. On this paper, I cant tell your *a*s from your *o*s.

---

2. correct

3. toil,'"

4. above":

5. Mother, "and

6. correct

B. 1. "Teach Me the Measure of My Days", <u>Christian Hymnal</u>, <u>Church Hymnal</u>

2. "Soldiers or Slaves?", <u>Evangelists in Chains</u>

3. D.V., <u>Deo volente</u>

4. <u>The Silver Fish</u>

C. 1. pre-World, great-grandfather

2. brother-in-law, twenty-three

3. didn't, self-rising, all-purpose

4. can't, <u>a</u>'s, <u>o</u>'s

---

38. Developing an Outline From a List of Notes

Lesson Survey

- When you write a composition, first make a list of notes that pertain to your subject.

- Look for related ideas that fit into general categories, which can be used as main topics.

- Arrange the facts into an outline.

Lesson 38

Purpose: To teach how to develop an outline from a disorganized list of notes.

Oral Review:

1. What is an outline in relation to a composition? (an orderly arrangement of the main points)

2. State a rule concerning each of these aspects of an outline.

   a. the title (Center the title above the outline.)

   b. indenting (Indent each level equally, and indent each level farther right than the previous level.)

   c. subordinate ideas (Have at least two parts when subordinate ideas come under an item. If there is only one subordinate point, include it with the item above it.)

   d. end punctuation (Use proper end punctuation with paragraph and sentence outlines. Omit end punctuation with topical outlines.)

3. When making headings for an outline, be sure they do not ——— in thought. (overlap)

4. As much as possible, the items of each level on a topical outline should be ———. (parallel in structure)

Lesson Introduction: Write the following words on the board.

beef	carrots	beets
cheese	butter	perch
pork	peas	custard

Have your students divide this list into three logical categories. You might point out that they could make three categories according to the first letters of the words (*b, c, p*). That would be logical—at least in one sense. What better division can they see?

We are glad for order. We appreciate the order of daytime and night-time, and the order of weeks, months, and years. Can you appreciate the order of the following words?

> Darkness had thrown its mantle over a vast place it occupied. They stand on one foot, storklike, through months and years that follow. I could have leaped for joy upon rich gold with keener emotions had been grasped at all. Before long he interrupted, and it brought a revelation to me as well. It became luminous that night.

Of course you cannot appreciate the order because the words are not in an order that gives you a clear, understandable message. They are only a confused jumble. In any composition, the words of each sentence, the sentences of each paragraph, and the paragraphs themselves must be properly organized before they will communicate to the reader. One important way to establish that organization is to develop an outline for the composition.

Generally, your first step in this process is to make a list of notes relating to the subject you have chosen. You should write these notes as they come to your mind or as you find them in research and reading. Do not worry that they have no organization. That will come later. The important thing is to write the ideas on paper so that they are not lost.

After you have a list of notes, you must consider them more carefully. Compare each item with the purpose of your writing, and cross out any that do not contribute. This will leave you with a list of notes that all relate closely to your subject. It will move you one step closer to an orderly composition.

Study the following list of notes for a composition about American white pelicans. Which of the items do not relate closely to the subject and should therefore be crossed out?

    five feet long
    enjoy shallow water
    white feathers with hidden black base
    brown pelicans also found in North America
    eat fish—catch them in pouch, squeeze out water, swallow them
    nest on inland lakes in Minnesota and northward
    brown pelicans nest on seacoast
    live in colonies
    fly in wedge formation with wings beating rhythmically and heads
        retracted
    spend winter on Gulf of Mexico
    are not disturbed by nearness of humans
    have distinctive bill—long and somewhat flattened with hooked tip
        and large pouch
    have short tail
    have large wings

(meats, milk products, vegetables) This lesson gives practice with seeing relationships among facts and organizing the facts into an outline.

Lesson Outline:

1. When you write a composition, first make a list of notes that pertain to your subject.

    a. Compare each item with the purpose of your writing.

    b. Cross out those that do not contribute.

2. Look for related ideas that fit into general categories.

    a. These general categories will serve as main topics for grouping the facts.

    b. Put the main topics in a logical order.

3. Arrange the facts into an outline.

The two notes about brown pelicans should be deleted. They do not relate directly to the subject of American white pelicans.

Having limited your list of notes, you must look for related ideas that fit into general categories. These general categories will serve as main topics for grouping the facts. In the example above, you may notice that the facts fit into three general categories: where pelicans live, how they act, and how they appear. These suggest three main topics: habitat, habits, and appearance.

Now put the main topics in a logical order. Which would be best to begin with? Which naturally follows it? Which would make the best conclusion? Give careful thought to this arrangement, for it will be the backbone of your composition.

For the example about American white pelicans, you could begin with either their habitat or their appearance. But their habits would definitely be most logical as the third point. Here is what the skeleton outline may look like.

American White Pelicans
    I. Habitat
    II. Appearance
    III. Habits

Now you are ready for the final step: filling in the skeleton outline with facts from your list of notes. Again, give thought to arranging the facts in a logical order. Place each of the more important ones as a subtopic under the main topic to which it relates. Place the less important ones as points under their corresponding subtopics.

This part of the process often calls for dividing or combining the details in your list of notes. Do not be afraid to do this. Shuffle the facts around in whatever way needed to have an orderly arrangement. The pattern of your composition does not have to resemble any that you have read before. In fact, it *should* not resemble the work of another writer, because this is your work. You are making a plan for your own original composition.

Compare the following outline with the list of notes about American white pelicans. Notice how the more important details are subtopics and the less important ones are points under them. Observe also how some notes have been divided. The notes about eating fish, about flying, and about the distinctive bill have each been divided into a subtopic with two or three points under it.

American White Pelicans
  I. Habitat
    A. Live in colonies
    B. Spend winter on the Gulf of Mexico
    C. Nest on inland lakes in Minnesota and northward
    D. Are not disturbed by nearness of humans

II. Appearance
  A. Five feet long
  B. White feathers with hidden black base
  C. Distinctive bill
    1. Long and somewhat flattened
    2. Hooked tip
    3. Large pouch
  D. Short tail
  E. Large wings
III. Habits
  A. Enjoy shallow water
  B. Eat fish
    1. Catch them in pouch
    2. Squeeze out water
    3. Swallow them
  C. Fly in wedge formation
    1. Wings beat rhythmically
    2. Heads are retracted

This example shows that by a careful, step-by-step procedure, an orderly outline can be developed from a disorganized list of notes. By using the same method, you too can gather facts from various sources and organize them into a logical, orderly plan for a composition.

Class Practice

Use the title and list of notes below for these exercises.
1. Tell which notes should be deleted because they do not apply directly to the subject.
2. Divide the remaining notes into three general categories. Which note does not fit into any of these categories and should therefore be deleted?
3. Form a skeleton outline of the three main topics, and arrange them in a logical order.
4. Fill in the skeleton outline with the remaining facts.

Volcanic Eruptions

Occur in West Indies
Occur in central Mediterranean Sea
Extinct volcanoes no longer erupting
Extreme heat deep in the earth
Volcanic eruptions have formed islands in the ocean
Heat also causes geysers, which are eruptions of steam
Force of eruption can destroy part of a mountain
Molten rock pushing toward surface rises through crack in earth's crust, expands as pressure decreases, and bursts forcefully into the air

Lesson 38 Answers

Class Practice

1. Extinct volcanoes no longer erupting
Heat also causes geysers, which are eruption of steam
Volcanic ash used as fine scouring material
2. (See number 3 for the first answer.)
Volcanic eruptions have formed islands in the ocean
3. I. Location of active volcanoes
  II. Cause of eruptions
  III. Damage from eruptions
4. (Sample outline.)

Volcanic Eruptions

 I. Location of active volcanoes
  A. West Indies
  B. Central Mediterranean Sea area
  C. Pacific Ocean rim
    1. Includes two-thirds of active volcanoes
    2. Is called the "ring of fire"
 II. Cause of eruptions
  A. Extreme heat deep in the earth
  B. Molten rock pushing toward surface
    1. Rises through crack in earth's crust
    2. Expands as pressure decreases
    3. Bursts forcefully into the air
 III. Damage from eruptions
  A. Force of eruption can destroy part of a mountain
  B. Flow of molten rock can do variety of damage
    1. Causes mud slides
    2. Destroys plant and animal life
    3. Buries whole towns
  C. Fall of rock and ash can bury towns

Fall of rock and ash can bury towns

Volcanic ash used as fine scouring material

Flow of molten rock can do variety of damage: causes mud slides, destroys plant and animal life, and buries whole towns

Pacific Ocean rim includes two-thirds of active volcanoes and is called the "ring of fire"

Written Exercises

A. Arrange these facts in logical sequence under the two main topics that are given. The starred items are points to be placed under one of the subtopics; all the others are subtopics.

Skeleton outline:

Fighting Against Germs

I. God has given the body natural defenses against germs.

II. We can help the body fight against germs.

List of notes:

A well-balanced diet provides the nutrition necessary for good health.

Antibodies destroy many germs that enter the bloodstream.

Cleanliness reduces the number of germs that threaten the body.

Hairlike cells in the nose filter out dust and germs.

*Harmless bacteria living on the skin fight off harmful bacteria.

Medications may kill germs or otherwise help the body to fight germs.

Mucous membranes trap and kill germs entering the nose and mouth.

*Natural acidity of skin destroys some bacteria.

Preventing the body from getting chilled enables the body to put its energy to fighting germs.

*Skin cells are tightly knit.

Stomach acids kill many germs that may be swallowed.

Tears contain a mild antiseptic that kills germs entering the eye.

The combination of rest and exercise helps to keep the body strong.

The skin prevents most germs from entering the body.

White blood cells engulf and destroy many germs that enter the bloodstream.

B. Organize these notes into an outline about the land of Portugal. First think of four main topics to use. Then arrange the facts as subtopics under your main topics. Divide each starred item into a subtopic with several points below it, as shown in the lesson.

List of notes:

Is slightly smaller than Indiana

Lies between 37° and 42° north latitude

*The northern region has rugged mountains, a temperate climate, and considerable rainfall

Written Exercises

A. (Sample outline.)

Fighting Against Germs

I. God has given the body natural defenses against germs.

A. The skin prevents most germs from entering the body.

1. Skin cells are tightly knit.

2. Harmless bacteria living on the skin fight off harmful bacteria.

3. Natural acidity of skin destroys some bacteria.

B. Tears contain a mild antiseptic that kills germs entering the eye.

C. Hairlike cells in the nose filter out dust and germs.

D. Mucous membranes trap and kill germs entering the nose and mouth.

E. Stomach acids kill many germs that may be swallowed.

F. White blood cells engulf and destroy many germs that enter the bloodstream.

G. Antibodies destroy many germs that enter the bloodstream.

II. We can help the body fight against germs.

A. A well-balanced diet provides the nutrition necessary for good health.

B. The combination of rest and exercise helps to keep the body strong.

C. Cleanliness reduces the number of germs that threaten the body.

D. Preventing the body from getting chilled enables the body to put its energy to fighting germs.

E. Medications may kill germs or otherwise help the body to fight germs.

B. (Sample outline.)

The Land of Portugal

I. Location

A. Occupies part of the Iberian Peninsula

B. Lies west of Spain

C. Lies between 37° and 42° north latitude

D. Lies between 8° and 10° west longitude

II. Size

A. Covers 35,553 square miles

B. Extends about 350 miles north to south and 125 miles east to west

C. Is slightly smaller than Indiana

*The northern region produces grapes, beans, and grains
Lies between 8° and 10° west longitude
*The southern region has rolling plains, a warm climate, and sparse rainfall
*The southern region produces olives and citrus fruits
Covers 35,553 square miles
Lies west of Spain
Occupies part of the Iberian Peninsula
Extends about 350 miles north to south and 125 miles east to west

---

39. Using an Outline to Write a Composition

> **Lesson Survey**
> - To write a composition from an outline, begin with a fresh, stimulating introduction.
> - Decide how the outline should be divided into paragraphs.
> - Develop each paragraph carefully.
> - Provide smooth transitions between paragraphs.
> - Write a good conclusion.

If you have prepared a good outline, much of your work in writing a composition is finished. You have already decided on a specific title and purpose. You have selected and organized your material. Now you must write a good introduction; you must follow the sequence of the outline, changing the details into sentences and paragraphs; and finally, you must write a good conclusion.

As you study this lesson, refer to the following outline and the composition written from it.

Outline:

Three Common Kinds of Storms

I. The thunderstorm
   A. Occurs more frequently than other storms
   B. Is caused by warm, moist updraft
   C. Can cause damage
     1. Heavy rain
     2. Hail

Lesson 39

Purpose: To teach how to use an outline to write a composition.

Oral Review:

1. What is an outline in relation to a composition? (an orderly arrangement of the main points)
2. What are the three basic steps in developing an outline? (Make a list of notes. Look for related ideas that fit into general categories. Arrange the facts into an outline.)
3. In what way should the items of each level on a topical outline be similar to each other? (They should be parallel in structure.)
4. What is wrong with the following skeleton outline? (*Teacher:* Write the following outline on the board.)

III. Physical features
   A. In the northern region
     1. Rugged mountains
     2. Temperate climate
     3. Considerable rainfall
   B. In the southern region
     1. Rolling plains
     2. Warm climate
     3. Sparse rainfall
IV. Agricultural products
   A. In the northern region
     1. Grapes
     2. Beans
     3. Grains
   B. In the southern region
     1. Olives
     2. Citrus fruits

   I. Grain crops
- II. Vegetable crops
  III. Corn crops
(The last two main topics overlap.)

Lesson Introduction: Probably no artist produces a finished picture by starting at one end of the paper and drawing everything in order as he works his way across to the other end. How would he ever keep things in proper proportion that way? No, he first sketches a light outline of the overall picture. Then he fills in the major details, followed by minor ones. Finally he adds the shading that makes a beautiful drawing.

The artist who works with words follows a similar process. First he forms an outline that summarizes the overall composition. Then he fills in the

3. High winds
4. Lightning
II. The hurricane
    A. Covers the largest area
    B. Begins over tropical water
    C. Is a whirling mass of air around a calm center
    D. Moves forward slowly
        1. West or northwest in lower latitudes
        2. North or northeast in higher latitudes
    E. Causes severe damage
        1. Winds up to 150 mph
        2. Flooding
III. The tornado
    A. Is the most violent
    B. Occurs in unstable atmosphere
    C. Whirls in funnel-like cloud at speeds up to 300 mph
    D. Covers a small area
        1. Usual width no greater than about 50 yards
        2. Usual length of path only 5 to 15 miles
    E. Causes almost total destruction because of its extremely high winds and low pressure

Composition:

Three Common Kinds of Storms

Introduction It was night. The wind was contrary. The waves were boisterous. And the disciples were in a tiny boat in the midst of the sea. They were seeing God's power displayed in a storm—the same power that we often face in storms today.

The thunderstorm is one such kind of storm. In fact, the thunderstorm occurs more frequently than any other storm. This storm is caused by an updraft of warm, moist air that condenses into high, billowy clouds. A thunderstorm can do much damage. Its heavy rains may cause erosion and even flash floods. Sometimes a thunderstorm produces hail, which can break windows, damage crops, and injure animals or people. High winds often uproot trees and damage roofs. Lightning may spark fires and bring severe injury and death.

Body A hurricane is another awesome storm. This storm, which may have a diameter of several hundred miles, covers the largest area of any storm. A hurricane begins over tropical water and becomes a whirling mass of air around a calm center, known as the eye of the hurricane. Although it whirls rapidly, its forward movement is quite slow. In lower latitudes

major details, followed by minor ones. Finally he adds the finishing touches that make an effective composition.

Lesson Outline:

1. To write a composition from an outline, begin with a fresh, stimulating introduction.
    a. The introduction should not be an apology or a complaint.
    b. A variety of beginnings is possible.
        1) Ask a question.
        2) Use an illustration.
        3) Give some interesting information.
        4) Begin with a direct statement.
    c. The length of an introduction may vary.
        1) It may be only a sentence or two.
        2) It is often a whole paragraph.

2. Decide how the outline should be divided into paragraphs.
    a. For an outline consisting mainly of main topics and subtopics, each main topic should be developed into one paragraph.
    b. For a more detailed outline, one paragraph may be written for each subtopic.

3. Develop each paragraph carefully.
    a. Start with the topic sentence.
        1) With a sentence outline, the topic sentences have already been written.
        2) With a topical outline, topic sentences must be formulated from the seed thoughts.
    b. Fill in the details from the appropriate headings of the outline.
    c. Be sure the paragraph has unity and coherence.

it moves west or northwest; and as it reaches higher latitudes, its movement becomes north or northeast. A hurricane causes severe damage with winds up to 150 miles per hour and heavy flooding.

The most violent storm is the tornado. It occurs when the atmosphere is very unstable. This storm is a funnel-shaped cloud, whirling at speeds up to 300 miles per hour. Although it is extremely violent, it affects a relatively small area. The width of a tornado is often no greater than about fifty yards, and its path is usually just five to fifteen miles long. However, a tornado causes almost total destruction of everything in its path because of its extremely high winds and low pressure.

Conclusion   After a severe storm, the sinner is sometimes softened and turns to God for mercy. And the Christian is humbled as he sees the mighty works of his all-powerful God. Truly "the Lord hath his way in the whirlwind and in the storm" (Nahum 1:3).

Now let us consider some specific pointers for writing compositions. We will look at each of the three basic parts in turn.

Introduction

Write a fresh, stimulating introduction to capture the reader's attention. After all, if you fail to get anyone's attention, you will be wasting your time. So give your best efforts to making an appealing introduction. Do not start by apologizing for your lack of knowledge about the subject or by telling how difficult the writing assignment is. You must start with something meaningful.

There is a variety of ways to begin. You may decide to ask a question or use an illustration. You may begin by giving some interesting information about your subject. Or you may begin with a direct statement that both introduces your subject and launches the reader immediately into the heart of your composition.

The introduction of a short composition may be only a sentence or two. Often, however, the introduction will be a paragraph that prepares the reader for the main body of the composition. Read the following sample introductions.

Question:
Have you ever seen God's power displayed in a severe storm? When lightning flashes across the sky and thunder crashes nearby, or when the wind begins blowing so hard that you fear the roof may be taken off, you get a small glimpse of the power of God. Many times He shows His power by the storms that come upon the earth.

4. Provide smooth transitions between paragraphs. Use transitional words and repeat key words when they fit well.

5. Write an appropriate conclusion.
    a. It should be convincing and satisfying.
    b. It should reinforce the main points of the composition.
    c. It should unite the entire composition into one harmonious whole.
    d. It should clinch the composition well and leave a final, meaningful thought with the reader.

Illustration:

It was night. The wind was contrary. The waves were boisterous. And the disciples were in a tiny boat in the midst of the sea. They were seeing God's power displayed in a storm—the same power that we often face in storms today.

Interesting information:

In 1925 one of the largest and fastest tornadoes on record roared through Missouri, Illinois, and Indiana at around 60 miles per hour. Nearly 700 people lost their lives in that storm. In 1969 Hurricane Camille killed more than 250 persons in seven states from Louisiana to Virginia and caused over $1 billion of damage. Truly God shows His power in the storms that come upon the earth.

Direct statement:

There are three common storm patterns: the thunderstorm, the hurricane, and the tornado. The one that occurs most frequently is the thunderstorm.

In the last example above, the introduction (underlined) is only one sentence. Since it is so short, it is not a paragraph by itself. Rather, it is part of the first paragraph in the body of the composition.

Body

The first step in developing an outline into the body of a composition actually involves no writing. Decide how the outline should be divided into paragraphs. For an outline consisting mostly of main topics and subtopics, each main topic should be developed into one paragraph. For a more detailed outline, in which most of the subtopics have points below them, one paragraph may be written for each subtopic. For the sample outline on storms, each main topic has been developed into a single paragraph.

Now you are ready for the main work in the writing process. Develop each paragraph carefully, starting with the topic sentence. Remember: The focal point of the paragraph is the topic sentence, regardless of where it is found. If you are working from a sentence outline, your topic sentences have already been written. Of course, you may rewrite some of them for the sake of variety or clarity. If you are working from a topical outline, you must take the seed thoughts on your outline and formulate topic sentences. Compare the main topics on the sample outline with the underlined topic sentences in the sample composition.

After you have written the topic sentence, fill in the details from the appropriate headings of the outline. Be sure that the paragraph is unified, with every sentence clearly supporting the topic sentence. Also provide good coherence by using transitional words, repetition of key words, and pronoun reference.

Look again at the sample composition. Do you see the transitional words *In fact* in the second paragraph and *However* in the fourth? You should see also that each paragraph of the body employs repetition of the key word *thunderstorm, hurricane,* or *tornado* as well as pronoun references to these terms.

You must also provide smooth transitions between the paragraphs in a composition. Remember to use transitional words and to repeat key words when they fit well. Again, the sample composition illustrates this. In the first sentence of the third paragraph, the word *another* provides a smooth transition from the discussion of the thunderstorm to that of the hurricane. The fifth paragraph begins with the phrase *After a severe storm,* which links this concluding paragraph to the discussions of the three kinds of storms. In addition, the key word *storm* occurs at least once in every paragraph.

Conclusion

The ending of a composition is worth as much thought and attention as any other part. You must not simply quit writing after you have presented all your ideas. You must add a positive conclusion. Make it convincing and satisfying. Use the conclusion to reinforce the main points of the composition and to unite the entire composition into one harmonious whole. An appropriate conclusion clinches the composition well and leaves a final, meaningful thought with the reader.

The sample composition begins by illustrating God's power as shown through storms. The body describes three common types of storms. And the conclusion points out how God accomplishes His purposes through the storms that come, once again emphasizing the mighty power of God.

Class Practice

Answer these questions about the lesson.
1. What are the three basic parts of a good composition?
2. What should the introduction of a composition do?
3. What are some effective ways to begin a composition?
4. What should you do before you begin writing the body of a composition?
5. What are some ways to provide smooth transitions between the paragraphs of a composition?
6. What are the purposes of the conclusion of a composition?

Written Exercises

Use the following outline to write a composition on God's miraculous care for Israel, based on information from the Bible verses given. Be sure to begin with a good introduction and end with a good conclusion.

Write only on every other line so that you have room to mark

Lesson 39 Answers

Class Practice

1. an introduction, a body, and a conclusion
2. capture the reader's attention
3. asking a question, using an illustration, giving some interesting information, or beginning with a direct statement
4. Decide how the outline should be divided into paragraphs.
5. using transitional words and repeating key words
6. It should reinforce the main points of the composition. It should unite the entire composition into one harmonious whole. It should clinch the composition well and leave a final meaningful thought with the reader.

Written Exercises

(Individual work.)

nprovements. Save this composition for a later lesson.

Divine Sustenance in a Wilderness

I. Manna from heaven
   A. When and how it was provided (Exodus 16:13–30)
   B. How it looked and tasted (Exodus 16:31; Numbers 11:7, 8)
   C. How it was eaten (Numbers 11:8)
   D. How long it was provided (Exodus 16:35; Joshua 5:10–12)

II. Water from a rock
   A. At Rephidim (Exodus 17:1–7)
      1. The need
      2. The provision
      3. The outcome
   B. At Kadesh (Numbers 20:1–13)
      1. The need
      2. The provision
      3. The outcome

III. Clothes and shoes that did not wear out (Deuteronomy 8:4; 29:5)

---

40. Verbals and Verbal Phrases Used as Nouns

> **Lesson Survey**
> - A **verbal** is a verb form used as another part of speech.
> - A **gerund** is the -*ing* form of a verb used as a noun.
> - An **infinitive** is the basic form of a verb preceded by *to*. It may be used as a noun.
> - Gerunds and infinitives may have complements and modifiers.
> - A noun or pronoun used as a modifier before a gerund must be in the possessive case.
> - A verbal or verbal phrase used as a noun is diagramed on a pedestal.

Verbals are interesting words that do double duty. As the root of *verbal* suggests, these words are verb forms. They have many characteristics of verbs, but they function as some other part of speech. Two kinds of verbals can be used as substantives: the gerund and the infinitive.

Lesson 40

Purpose: To study verbals and verbal phrases used as nouns.

Oral Review:

1. What is a substantive? (any word or word group that functions as a noun)
2. How is the possessive form of most singular nouns made? (by adding 's)
3. What are the two rules for forming plural possessives? (If the plural does not end with -*s*, add 's. If it ends with -*s*, add only an apostrophe.)
4. Change this sentence to show separate ownership: *Martha and Karen's mother has arrived.* (Martha's and Karen's mothers have arrived.)

Lesson Introduction: Children are sometimes so active that they seem to appear everywhere. Perhaps as you work in the kitchen, you see little Kevin peeking around a corner to watch. Later he is romping about in the playroom; and when you go outside, you see him running after his puppy. His activity helps to make things interesting and enjoyable.

Verbs are somewhat similar. They are so full of action that they seem to appear everywhere in writing—not only as verbs that express action, but also as verbals that name and describe things. Today's lesson is about two kinds of verbals that serve as nouns.

Lesson Outline:

1. A verbal is a verb form that is used as another part of speech.

2. A gerund is the -**ing** *form of a verb used as a noun.*

    a. Instead of expressing the action performed by a substantive, a gerund names an action.

Gerunds

A *gerund* is the *-ing* form of a verb used as a substantive. A verb expresses the action performed by a substantive, whereas a gerund *names* an action. Since a gerund is a substantive, its use in the sentence must be a noun function, such as subject, verb complement, or object of a preposition.

> Father has been <u>farming</u> this land for many years.
>> (*Farming* expresses the action of Father; it is a verb.)
> <u>Farming</u> is a worthy occupation.
>> (*Farming* names an action and is the subject; it is a gerund.)

> Laura was <u>reading</u> her new book.
>> (*Reading* expresses the action of Laura; it is a verb.)
> Laura enjoys <u>reading</u>.
>> (*Reading* names an action and is the direct object; it is a gerund.)

Not every verb form ending with *-ing* is a gerund; many are verbs. You can identify an *-ing* form that is a true verb because it is always part of a verb phrase with a form of *be* as a helping verb. A gerund, too, may follow a form of *be,* but it is clearly not part of the verb phrase. Instead it is a predicate nominative, renaming the subject with a word that refers to an action. Reading the skeleton should help you decide whether the *-ing* form is part of the verb phrase or is a gerund.

> Father is drawing a sketch of his boyhood farm.
>> **Think:** <u>Father</u> | <u>is drawing</u> is sensible.
>>> *Drawing* does not rename the subject; it is part of the verb.
> <u>One</u> of Father's talents <u>is</u> drawing.
>> **Think:** <u>One</u> | <u>is drawing</u> is not sensible.
>>> *Drawing* renames the subject; it is a gerund.

Infinitives

An *infinitive* is the basic form of a verb preceded by *to.* It may be used as a noun to name an action and fill a noun function in the sentence.

> A submissive person wants <u>to obey</u>.
>> (*To obey* names an action and is the direct object of *wants.*)
> Our goal in this work should be <u>to improve</u>.
>> (*To improve* names an action and is the predicate nominative.)

Do not confuse infinitives with prepositional phrases that begin with *to.* If *to* is used with the basic form of a verb, the combination is an infinitive. If *to* is followed by a noun or pronoun, the combination is a prepositional phrase.

> We were tired and decided <u>to rest</u>. (*to* + verb = infinitive)
> Yesterday we went <u>to church</u>. (*to* + noun = prepositional phrase)

b. Its use in the sentence must be a noun function, such as subject, verb complement, or object of a preposition.

c. Do not confuse a gerund with a verb ending with *-ing.*

3. An infinitive is the basic form of a verb preceded by to.

a. An infinitive may serve as a noun to name an action and fill a noun function in the sentence.

b. Do not confuse infinitives with prepositional phrases beginning with *to.*

1) If *to* is used with the basic form of a verb, the combination is an infinitive.

2) If *to* is followed by a noun or pronoun, the combination is a prepositional phrase.

4. Gerunds and infinitives may have complements and modifiers.

a. A verbal with its complements and modifiers is a verbal phrase.

b. The complete verbal phrase is a substantive because it fills a noun function in the sentence.

5. A noun or pronoun used as a modifier before a gerund must be in the possessive case.

6. A verbal or verbal phrase used as a substantive is diagrammed on a pedestal. Complements and adverb modifiers are diagrammed in relation to the verbal just as if it were a regular verb.

★ EXTRA PRACTICE

Worksheet 13 *(Verbals and Verbal Phrases Used as Nouns)*

Gerund and Infinitive Phrases

Gerunds and infinitives are not always used alone; they may have complements and modifiers. A verbal with its complements and modifiers is a verbal phrase. The complete verbal phrase is a substantive because it fills a noun function in the sentence. Notice how the simple verbals are expanded into verbal phrases in the following examples.

<u>Memorizing</u> is good mental discipline.
> (*Memorizing* is a simple gerund used as a subject.)

<u>Memorizing Scripture verses</u> is also good spiritual exercise.
> (*Memorizing Scripture verses* is a gerund phrase used as a subject; it consists of a gerund with a direct object.)

My little brother was trying <u>to help</u>.
> (*To help* is a simple infinitive used as a direct object.)

My little brother was trying <u>to help me in his childish way</u>.)
> (*To help me in his childish way* is an infinitive phrase used as a direct object; it consists of an infinitive with a direct object and an adverb phrase.)

Brother Clifford rebuked me for <u>daydreaming</u>.
> (*Daydreaming* is a simple gerund used as the object of a preposition.)

Brother Clifford rebuked me for <u>daydreaming during class</u>.
> (*Daydreaming during class* is a gerund phrase used as the object of a preposition; it consists of a gerund with an adverb phrase.)

If a verbal is a form of *be* or another linking verb, it may be followed by a predicate nominative or a predicate adjective.

<u>Being mature</u> calls for making many deliberate decisions.
> (*Mature* is a predicate adjective following the linking verbal *Being*.)

Do you expect <u>to become a teacher someday</u>?
> (*Teacher* is a predicate nominative following the linking verbal *to become*.)

One common error in the use of gerunds occurs when a noun or pronoun is used before a gerund. A noun or pronoun used as a modifier before a gerund must be in the possessive case. Look at these examples.

Incorrect: We eagerly anticipated <u>Uncle Ezra coming</u>.
Correct: We eagerly anticipated <u>Uncle Ezra's coming</u>.

Incorrect: We were pleased at <u>him offering some help for several days</u>.
Correct: We were pleased at <u>his offering some help for several days</u>.

A verbal or verbal phrase used as a substantive is diagramed on a pedestal. Complements and adverb modifiers are diagramed in relation to the verbal just as if it were a regular verb.

Trusting God continually gives security in life.

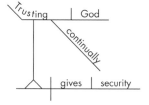

One evidence of pride is refusing help.

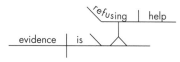

We should learn to speak clearly.

To fear the Lord means to obey Him.

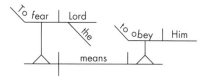

Being tenderhearted is noble for all.

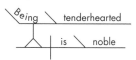

David expressed his praise to God by writing psalms.

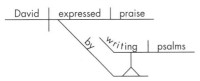

Class Practice

A. Read each verbal or verbal phrase, and tell whether it is a *gerund,* a *gerund phrase,* an *infinitive,* or an *infinitive phrase.* Also tell how it is used in the sentence.
  1. Disobeying always brings sad consequences.
  2. God's command to Moses was to speak to the rock.
  3. Moses dishonored God by speaking angrily to the Israelites.
  4. Striking the rock was also direct disobedience to God's command.
  5. God punished Moses by barring him from the Promised Land.
  6. Moses intensely desired to go, but his punishment was not changed.
  7. Father praised God for dealing graciously with us.
  8. The Christian's purpose in life is sharing the Gospel with others.

B. Tell which sentence in each pair is correct.
  1. a. We were surprised at his speaking out so forcefully.
     b. We were surprised at him speaking out so forcefully.
  2. a. John helping us made a big difference.
     b. John's helping us made a big difference.
  3. a. I surely appreciate Laura finding my papers.
     b. I surely appreciate Laura's finding my papers.

C. On the chalkboard, diagram the skeletons and complements of sentences 1–4 in Part A. Include the complete verbal phrases.

Written Exercises

A. Copy each verbal or verbal phrase, and write whether it is a gerund (*G*), a gerund phrase (*GP*), an infinitive (*I*), or an infinitive phrase (*IP*).
  1. Pursuing David consumed much of Saul's energy in his latter years.
  2. As Saul rejected God, the people began to lose respect for him.
  3. God had promised David the kingdom, and he continued to wait.
  4. To observe nature is to learn of God's greatness.
  5. Do you find satisfaction in identifying the songs of birds?
  6. Embroidering demands patience and accuracy.

Lesson 40 Answers

Class Practice

A. 1. Disobeying—gerund, subject
   2. to speak to the rock—infinitive phrase, predicate nominative
   3. speaking angrily to the Israelites—gerund phrase, object of a preposition
   4. Striking the rock—gerund phrase, subject
   5. barring him from the Promised Land—gerund phrase, object of a preposition
   6. to go—infinitive, direct object
   7. dealing graciously with us—gerund phrase, object of a preposition
   8. sharing the Gospel with others—gerund phrase, predicate nominative

B. 1. a   2. b   3. b

C.

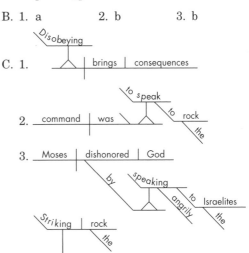

Written Exercises

A. 1. Pursuing David—GP
   2. to lose respect for him—IP
   3. to wait—I
   4. To observe nature—IP;
      to learn of God's greatness—IP
   5. identifying the songs of birds—GP
   6. Embroidering—G

B. Copy each verbal or verbal phrase, and write whether it is used as a subject (S), a direct object (DO), a predicate nominative (PN), or the object of a preposition (OP).
1. Drying wildflowers can be an interesting project.
2. Last summer our family decided to start a collection of dried wildflowers.
3. Our music assignment is researching the life of an Anabaptist hymn writer.
4. We found great inspiration in learning about these faithful Christians of the past.
5. One of my regular jobs is keeping the woodbox full.
6. Raising good watermelons in our area requires watering them regularly.

C. Diagram the skeletons and complements of these sentences. Include every word of the verbal phrases.
1. To please the Lord should be our supreme desire.
2. Playing with temptation is dangerous.
3. The devil cleverly seeks to ensnare the foolish.
4. His great desire is destroying God's work.
5. Have you learned to crochet?
6. Knitting is also an enjoyable pastime.
7. One of your goals should be to write neatly.
8. Following directions carefully prevents many problems.

Review Exercises

A. Copy the word just before each error in the use of colons or semicolons. Add the correct punctuation mark, or omit any unnecessary mark. [27]
1. I write letters regularly to friends in Duchess, Alberta, Crockett, Kentucky, Hagerstown, Maryland, and Vineland, New Jersey.
2. Scandinavia includes: Sweden, Denmark, and Norway, the Baltic States consist of Estonia, Latvia, and Lithuania, and the Low Countries are the Netherlands, Belgium, and Luxembourg.
3. The Bible states man's basic problem, he has a sinful nature.
4. The Jews despised publicans, indeed, they considered them criminals.
5. The most important tools will be: an ax, a shovel, and a pick.
6. In good books you keep coming across the same ideas, truth, honor, courage, wisdom, faith, and moral responsibility.

B. Copy these sentences, adding commas, dashes, or parentheses where needed. Some sentences have notes to direct you. [29]
1. "What a pleasant surprise to oh, look who else is here!" exclaimed Joy.
2. The Sadducees they didn't even believe in a resurrection! were

B. 1. "What a pleasant surprise to—oh, look who else is here!" exclaimed Joy.
2. The Sadducees—they didn't even believe in a resurrection!—were generally at odds with the Pharisees.

B. 1. Drying wildflowers—S
2. to start a collection of dried wildflowers—DO
3. researching the life of an Anabaptist hymn writer—PN
4. learning about these faithful Christians of the past—OP
5. keeping the woodbox full—PN
6. Raising good watermelons in our area—S; watering them regularly—DO

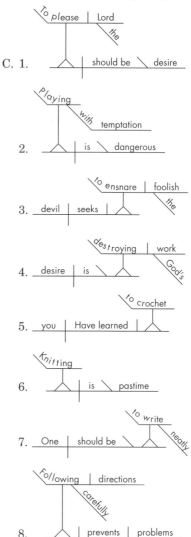

C. 1. – 8. (diagrams)

Review Exercises

A. 1. Alberta; Kentucky; Maryland;
2. includes Norway; Lithuania;
3. problem:
4. publicans;
5. be
6. ideas:

generally at odds with the Pharisees. (Emphasize the parenthetical material.)

3. The Sadducees they generally were upper-class Jews more readily accepted Greek and Roman ideas than did the Pharisees. (Treat the parenthetical element as relatively unimportant.)

4. The Sadducees who usually opposed the Pharisees actually joined hands with them to oppose Jesus. (Make the parenthetical element a part of the sentence.)

5. I want to faithfully follow Jehovah-nissi the Lord is my banner; indeed, He alone can give me victory over the enemy of my soul. (Treat the parenthetical element as relatively unimportant.)

3. The Sadducees (they generally were upper-class Jews) more readily accepted Greek and Roman ideas than did the Pharisees.

4. The Sadducees, who usually opposed the Pharisees, actually joined hands with them to oppose Jesus.

5. I want to faithfully follow Jehovah-nissi (the Lord is my banner); indeed, He alone can give me victory over the enemy of my soul.

---

41. Noun Clauses

> **Lesson Survey**
> - A **noun clause** is a dependent clause that functions as a substantive in a complex sentence.
> - A noun clause functioning as a subject, direct object, or predicate nominative serves as a basic part of the independent clause.
> - A noun clause functioning as the object of a preposition is not an essential part of the independent clause.
> - A noun clause is diagramed on a pedestal above the place where a one-word noun would normally go.

A noun names a person, place, thing, or idea. A noun is usually a single word, but it may also be a phrase or a clause. The following three sentences express similar ideas, but the subject is first a single word, then a phrase, and finally a clause.

<u>Submission</u> brings true inner peace.
<u>Submitting to the Lord</u> brings true inner peace.
<u>Whoever submits to the Lord</u> finds true inner peace.

Function of Noun Clauses

A *noun clause* is a dependent clause that functions as a substantive in a complex sentence. When a noun clause functions as a subject, direct object, or predicate nominative, it serves as a basic part of the independent clause. The independent clause would not be complete without the noun clause.

Lesson 41

Purpose: (1) To study dependent noun clauses. (2) To show their function as substantives in complex sentences.

Oral Review:

1. What is a substantive? (any word or word group that functions as a noun)
2. What is a verbal? (a verb form used as another part of speech)
3. Name and describe the two kinds of verbals that can be used as nouns. (gerund—the *-ing* form of a verb; infinitive—the basic form of a verb preceded by *to*)
4. Give the plural spellings of these words.
   a. motto (mottoes, mottos)
   b. bacterium (bacteria)
   c. key (keys)
   d. larva (larvae)
   e. leaf (leaves)
   f. secretary (secretaries)
   g. sister-in-law (sisters-in-law)
   h. index (indices, indexes)
   i. cactus (cacti, cactuses)
   j. salmon (salmon)

Lesson Introduction: Suppose that Mother and Elaine have picked several buckets of beans, and Mary is expected to come home in a few minutes. Mother needs to put the baby to sleep. As Mother leaves the kitchen, she tells Elaine that Mary is to help with the beans when she comes. Finish Elaine's statement when Mary arrives: "Mary, Mother said . . ." (that you are to help with the beans) The student, in completing the sentence, will give a noun clause—the subject of this lesson.

When a sentence contains a noun clause used as a direct object or a predicate nominative, the two clauses are generally quite obvious. Especially easy to find are the clauses that function as direct and indirect quotations; they are nearly always noun clauses used as direct objects. In the following sentences, the noun clauses are in brackets and the skeletons of both clauses are underlined.

> The <u>Bible</u> clearly <u>states</u> [that <u>God created</u> the world in six days].
>   (Bible states what? *That God created the world in six days* is the
>   direct object of the independent clause.)
> <u>Jesus said</u>, ["<u>Ye are</u> the light of the world."]
>   (Jesus said what? *Ye are the light of the world* is the direct object
>   of the independent clause.)
> Our <u>desire should be</u> [that our <u>lights are shining</u> clearly].
>   (Desire should be what? *That our lights are shining clearly* is the
>   predicate nominative in the independent clause.)

When a sentence contains a noun clause used as a subject, the two clauses may be less obvious. Since the subject of the independent clause is the entire noun clause, the skeleton of that independent clause may be difficult to detect. In the following sentences, the noun clauses are again in brackets. The skeletons of the noun clauses are underlined, and the verbs of the independent clauses are underlined.

> [Wherever <u>God leads</u>] <u>is</u> the best place to be.
>   (What is the best place to be? *Wherever God leads* is the subject
>   of the independent clause.)
> [Whoever <u>loves</u> the Lord] <u>will</u> surely <u>obey</u> His Word.
>   (Who will obey His Word? *Whoever loves the Lord* is the subject
>   of the independent clause.)

A noun clause functioning as the object of a preposition is not an essential part of the independent clause. Therefore, the two clauses should be easily recognized. The following sentences show the noun clauses in brackets, with the skeletons of both clauses underlined.

> The <u>truth can be known</u> by [<u>whoever</u> sincerely <u>seeks</u> it].
> <u>We should do</u> our best in [whatever <u>we are assigned</u>] .

Analyzing and Diagraming Noun Clauses

Before you are ready to diagram a noun clause, you must analyze its parts: the introductory word, the skeleton, and the complements and modifiers. The word that begins a noun clause often has a specific function within the clause; sometimes it is simply a conjunction that introduces the clause.

Lesson Outline:

1. A noun clause is a dependent clause that functions as a substantive in a complex sentence.

2. A noun clause functioning as a subject, direct object, or predicate nominative serves as a basic part of the independent clause.

a. In a sentence with a noun clause used as a direct object or a predicate nominative, the two clauses are generally obvious.

b. Direct and indirect quotations are nearly always noun clauses used as direct objects.

c. When a sentence contains a noun clause used as a subject, the two clauses may be less obvious.

> *(Teacher:* A quotation is sometimes a predicate nominative. Example: Jesus' <u>words were</u>, "Ye <u>are</u> the light of the world.")

3. A noun clause functioning as the object of a preposition is not an essential part of the independent clause.

4. Before a noun clause can be diagramed, its parts must be analyzed.

a. Determine the function of the introductory word.

1) The words *who, whoever, whom, whomever, what, whatever,* and *which* are pronouns that serve as subjects, complements, and objects of prepositions.

2) The words *whose* and *which* are adjectives that modify subjects or complements.

3) The words *how, why, where, wherever, when,* and *whenever* are adverbs that modify verbs.

4) The words *that, if,* and *whether* are conjunctions that introduce clauses. They serve no specific function within the clauses.

Analyze the underlined noun clauses in the following sentences. Find the introductory word, and then identify the skeleton, the complements, and the modifiers.

Man cannot fully explain <u>how a honeybee makes honey</u>.
>   **Think:** *How* is an adverb modifying the verb.
>   The skeleton is <u>honeybee</u> <u>makes</u>; *honey* is a direct object.

Peter declared <u>that he did not know Jesus</u>.
>   **Think:** *That* is simply a conjunction.
>   The skeleton is <u>he</u> <u>did</u> <u>know</u>; *Jesus* is a direct object.

<u>Whoever wrote this poem</u> had an excellent command of words.
>   **Think:** *Whoever* is a pronoun.
>   The skeleton is <u>Whoever</u> <u>wrote</u>; *poem* is a direct object.

None of us knew <u>who the strange man was</u>.
>   **Think:** *Who* is a pronoun.
>   The skeleton is <u>man</u> <u>was</u>; *who* is a predicate nominative.

Jonathan asked, "<u>Whose book do I have?</u>"
>   **Think:** *Whose* is an adjective modifying *book*.
>   The skeleton is <u>I</u> <u>do</u> <u>have</u>; *book* is a direct object.

Have your parents said <u>you may go with me</u>?
>   **Think:** There is no introductory word.
>   The skeleton is <u>you</u> <u>may</u> <u>go</u>; *with me* is a prepositional
>   phrase modifying *may go*.

Study the following table of words used to introduce noun clauses.

Introductory Words in Noun Clauses

Words	Part of Speech	Function in Clause
who, whoever, whom, whomever, what, whatever, which	pronoun	subject, complement, object of preposition
whose, which	adjective	modifier of subject or complement
how, why, where, wherever, when, whenever	adverb	modifier of verb
that, if, whether	conjunction	(no specific function)

    b. Identify the skeleton, the complements,
        and the modifiers.

 5. *A noun clause is diagramed on a pedestal
above the place where a one-word noun would
normally go.*
    a. The parts of the clause are diagramed on
        or below a horizontal line as with any other
        clause.
    b. If the first word is simply a conjunction, it
        is placed on the vertical line of the pedestal.

★ **EXTRA PRACTICE**
Worksheet 14 *(Noun Clauses)*

A noun clause is diagramed on a pedestal above the place where a one-word noun would normally go. The parts of the clause are diagramed on or below a horizontal line as with any other clause. If the first word is simply a conjunction, it is placed on the vertical line of the pedestal. The example sentences that you have just analyzed are diagramed below.

Man cannot fully explain how a honeybee makes honey.

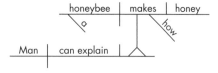

Peter declared that he did not know Jesus.

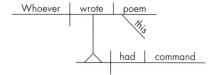

Whoever wrote this poem had an excellent command of words.

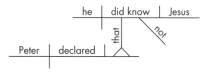

None of us knew who the strange man was.

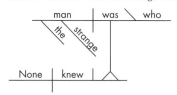

Jonathan asked, "Whose book do I have?"

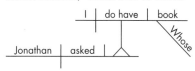

Have your parents said you may go with me?

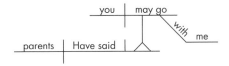

Here is the diagram of a sentence in which a noun clause is the object of a preposition.

Give this coat to whoever is the owner.

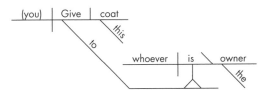

Class Practice

A. If the underlined clause is a noun clause, tell whether it is used as a *subject, direct object, predicate nominative,* or *object of a preposition.* If it is not a noun clause, say *not a noun clause.*
   1. Haman was furious <u>when he saw Mordecai sitting at the gate.</u>
   2. <u>That Mordecai would not bow</u> showed his loyalty to God.
   3. Mordecai faithfully honored God in <u>whatever he did.</u>
   4. Haman's pride was <u>what brought his downfall.</u>
   5. He decided <u>that he would seek the Jews' destruction.</u>
   6. <u>What Haman did not consider</u> was God's sovereignty and power.
   7. <u>Whoever rises against God's people</u> sets himself against God.
   8. God can certainly humble any man <u>who exalts himself.</u>

B. Read each noun clause. Then identify the skeleton, and tell what function the introductory word fills.
   1. Whoever is trustworthy will gain the trust of others.
   2. Every youth should determine that he will maintain a noble life.
   3. We should desire whatever God plans for us.
   4. Only God understands why some people must suffer great trials.
   5. No human can truthfully say, "I am perfect."

C. On the chalkboard, diagram the skeletons and complements of the main clauses and the complete noun clauses of the sentences in Part B.

Lesson 41 Answers

Class Practice

A. 1. not a noun clause
   2. subject
   3. object of a preposition
   4. predicate nominative
   5. direct object
   6. subject
   7. subject
   8. not a noun clause

B. 1. <u>Whoever is</u> trustworthy; subject
   2. that <u>he will|maintain</u> a noble life; conjunction
   3. whatever <u>God plans</u> for us; direct object
   4. why some <u>people must|suffer</u> great trials; adverb
   5. <u>I am</u> perfect; no introductory word

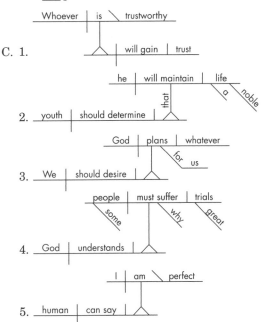

Written Exercises

A. If the underlined clause is a noun clause, identify its function by writing *subject, direct object, predicate nominative,* or *object of a preposition.* If it is not a noun clause, write *not a noun clause.*
  1. Did you ask <u>whether the new books have arrived</u>?
  2. Father did not know the man <u>who warned us about the bridge</u>.
  3. <u>How these groceries arrived on our porch</u> is a mystery to us.
  4. <u>That Grandmother Shank loves her Bible</u> is quite apparent.
  5. A good time to track wild animals is <u>when fresh snow covers the ground</u>.
  6. The rabbit hid in a thicket <u>where the fox could not go</u>.
  7. Sparky enjoys attention from <u>whoever will play with him</u>.
  8. I did not know <u>where I must have mislaid my paper</u>.
  9. <u>When the blizzard struck</u>, we were thankful for a warm house.
  10. The subject of Ellen's composition was <u>why salt kills plants</u>.

B. Copy each noun clause.
  1. Whether your life will be useful in God's kingdom depends largely upon your own choices.
  2. Our actions and words reveal what is in our hearts.
  3. We must obey whomever God places in authority over us.
  4. Our words should show gratitude for whatever God brings to us in life.
  5. The budding rod clearly showed which man God had chosen as high priest.
  6. Faithful Caleb said, "Give me this mountain."

C. Diagram the skeletons and complements of the main clauses and the complete noun clauses of these sentences.
  1. Brother Wenger announced that we would take a hike on Friday.
  2. Whether we go will depend on the weather.
  3. We have discovered what was making the strange noises.
  4. Whoever is ready may come along.
  5. A good place for our picnic is where the big tree shades the creek.

Review Exercises

A. Copy each word or number that should be followed by a comma, and add the comma. Also write each large numeral correctly. [23, 25]
  1. When Israel was numbered in the wilderness the number of men of war totaled 603550.
  2. The tribe of Levi was numbered separately and the total of the males over a month old was 22300.
  3. Yes God chose the Levites who had stood on the Lord's side as the priestly tribe in Israel.
  4. Father has an appointment with Dr. Lyle Bright M.D. in Akron Ohio.

Written Exercises

A. 1. direct object
   2. not a noun clause
   3. subject
   4. subject
   5. predicate nominative
   6. not a noun clause
   7. object of a preposition
   8. direct object
   9. not a noun clause
   10. predicate nominative

B. 1. Whether your life will be useful in God's kingdom
   2. what is in our hearts
   3. whomever God places in authority over us
   4. whatever God brings to us in life
   5. which man God had chosen as high priest
   6. "Give me this mountain."

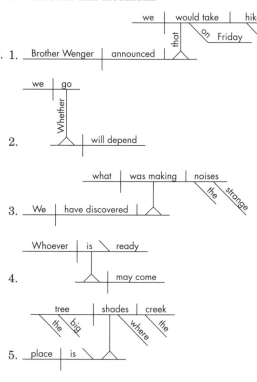

C. 1.
   2.
   3.
   4.
   5.

Review Exercises

A. 1. wilderness, 603,550
   2. separately, 22,300
   3. Yes, Levites, side,
   4. Bright, M.D., Akron,

5. Daryl you have heard I suppose that Uncle Dale's are coming tomorrow.
6. Above a gurgling stream cascaded down the mountain.
7. Beside the road stood a large majestic bull moose.
8. Suddenly seeing us the moose dashed across the road through a small meadow and into the forest.

3. Copy these sentences, adding the missing ellipsis points and brackets. [22, 29]
   1. "These things command and teach. Take heed unto thyself, and unto the doctrine" (1 Timothy 4:11, 16).
   2. "Let us therefore follow after things wherewith one may edify build up another" (Romans 14:19).
   3. Paul wrote that Philemon's slave (Onesimus which means "useful") was now profitable to Paul and to Philemon.
   4. "I had no idea" Margaret's voice trailed off miserably.

---

42. Proofreading Your Composition

Lesson Survey

- Careful proofreading takes time.
- Proofreading a composition includes the following points.
  1. Delete unnecessary material.
  2. Insert missing material that is needed to make the composition clear.
  3. Correct any transpositions.
  4. Check for mistakes in spelling, mechanics, grammar, and usage.
  5. Check for good paragraph development.
  6. Be sure the composition includes a good title and the three basic parts of a composition.
- Rewrite the composition, making the changes you marked when proofreading.

Just as binoculars need to be adjusted for a clear, distinct view of an object, so your writing needs to be adjusted in order for it to be easily read and clearly understood. You learn to do this adjusting by practice. Follow the instructions given in this lesson as they guide you in improving your compositions.

Careful proofreading takes time. After you have written the first draft, lay the composition aside for a time. Later you will be able to proofread it

Lesson 42

Purpose: (1) To teach the need for revising compositions. (2) To give practice with proofreading marks.

Oral Review:

1. What is an outline in relation to a composition? (an orderly arrangement of the main points)
2. Name the three parts of a composition. (introduction, body, conclusion)
3. What are some effective ways to introduce a composition? (ask a question; use an illustration; give some interesting information; make a direct statement)
4. What is the first step in developing a written composition from an outline? (Decide how the outline should be divided into paragraphs.)

Lesson Introduction: Revisions are a perfectly normal part of life. The weatherman revises his

5. Daryl,   heard,   suppose,
6. Above,
7. large,
8. us,   road,   meadow,

B. 1. "These things command and teach.... Take heed unto thyself, and unto the doctrine" (1 Timothy 4:11, 16).
   2. "Let us therefore follow after... things wherewith one may edify [build up] another" (Romans 14:19).
   3. Paul wrote that Philemon's slave (Onesimus [which means "useful"]) was now profitable to Paul and to Philemon.
   4. "I had no idea..." Margaret's voice trailed off miserably.

forecasts, and the businessman revises his sales figures. A mother may revise a recipe or a pattern, a father may revise his work plans, and a teacher may revise his daily classroom schedule. The artist revises his sketch, and the author revises his composition.

Do students really need to revise their compositions? Yes. Because we are human, we are imperfect; and because we are imperfect, we need to make revisions.

Lesson Outline:

1. **Careful proofreading takes time.**
   a. Lay the composition aside for a time, and proofread it later.
   b. Read through the composition several times, each time concentrating on only one or two areas.

more effectively. Take time to read through it several times, each time concentrating on only one or two areas.

Proofreading a composition includes the points discussed below.

1. *Delete unnecessary material.* Show a deletion by drawing a neat line through the material that you want to remove. Watch especially for the following kinds of unnecessary items.

a. *Padded writing.* This term refers to writing that is puffed up with extra, unnecessary words. These extra words are often adjectives and adverbs that are more distracting than meaningful. School students may be tempted to pad their writing when they are assigned to write a composition with a certain number of words. Notice how the following sentences are more forceful and just as clear without the padding.

> Four ~~tall,~~ stately, ~~magnificent,~~ ~~beautiful~~ pine trees
> lined the drive.
>
> The time passed quickly because we sang ~~merrily~~ while
> we worked ~~busily~~.

b. *Repetitious words and phrases.* Repetition may be the obvious repeating of synonymous expressions. Sometimes it is less obvious, as when a detail implied by other words is also stated directly. Notice that no meaning is lost when the repetitious words are removed from the following examples.

> With gratitude ~~and thanksgiving~~, we saw that no one
> was seriously hurt ~~or injured~~ in the crash.
> (*Gratitude* and *thanksgiving* are synonyms; *hurt* and *injured* are
> synonyms.)
>
> The ~~cold~~ ice cream tasted delicious to the ~~two~~ twins.
> (*Cold* is implied by *ice cream; two* is implied by *twins.*)

2. *Insert missing material that is needed to make the composition clear.* This may be a word, a letter, or a mark of punctuation. Or it may be an entire phrase, clause, or sentence. You are so familiar with your composition that you may omit some important detail without thinking about it. Try to read your composition as if you were unfamiliar with it. Use a caret (∧) as illustrated in this example to show where the material should be inserted.

> As each chick haᵗched we transferred it. ᵗᵒ ᵗʰᵉ ᵇʳᵒᵒᵈᵉʳ
> ∧   ∧   ∧

3. *Correct any transpositions.* A transposition occurs when two letters, words, phrases, or clauses are switched from their correct order. Often this results in awkward or absurd sentences. The following sentences illustrate

2. Proofreading a composition includes a number of points.

(1) *Delete unnecessary material.* Show a deletion by drawing a neat line through the material that you want to remove.

   a. Watch for padded writing, such as adjectives and adverbs that are more distracting than meaningful.

   b. Watch for repetitious words and phrases.

(2) *Insert missing material that is needed to make the composition clear.* Use a caret (∧) to show where the material should be inserted.

(3) *Correct any transpositions.* Use the transposition symbol to show the correction.

(4) *Check for mistakes in spelling, mechanics, grammar, and usage.* Use proofreading marks to cross out mistakes and to add corrections.

(5) *Check for good paragraph development.*

   a. Be sure that each paragraph is developed with sufficient material and in a logical manner.

   b. Keep the paragraph unified.

   c. Keep the paragraph coherent.

(6) *Be sure the composition includes a good title and the three basic parts of a composition.*

3. Rewrite the composition, making the changes you marked when proofreading.

   a. Use your neatest handwriting.

   b. Leave neat, even margins.

★ **EXTRA PRACTICE**

Worksheet 15 (*Proofreading Your Composition*)

the symbol for marking transpositions.

I do͡n't bel͡ei͡ve that I will be ab͡el͡ to help.

⌐Waddling across the road, I saw a family of ducks⌐.
(Or *was* the writer actually waddling across the road?)

4. *Check for mistakes in spelling, mechanics, grammar, and usage.* Double-check spellings like *ei* and *ie, ai* and *ia, ent* and *ant,* and so forth. Make sure you have the right choice of homonyms like *your—you're* and *here—hear.* Make sure you have correctly spelled technical terms and proper nouns. And pay close attention to words that you know you have difficulty spelling correctly. Mark corrections as shown in the following example.

Here̶in the mount͡ai͡ns, many pe͡ople seem quie͡t indepen-
dant.

Mechanics includes primarily what you studied in Chapter 3. Have you capitalized every proper noun and proper adjective? Have you avoided using capital letters where they do not belong? Look at each punctuation mark. Does it belong? Is it the right mark? Have you remembered the commas in a series? between coordinate adjectives? with nonrestrictive appositives and clauses? Study these corrections.

This ͡Indian corn was raised by ͡keith ͡mast my cousin
from ͡kentucky.

Grammar and usage relate to such things as writing complete sentences, having subject and verb agreement, and using the correct principal parts of verbs. If you know of particular areas where you commonly make mistakes, be sure to check for those errors. The errors in the following example are typical of those made by students of your age.

Either Helen or Julia a̶r̶e̶ baking bread . ͡For the picnic
we have planned.

5. *Check for good paragraph development.* Be sure each paragraph is developed with sufficient material and in a logical manner. Remember that a paragraph must be unified. Cross out any material that does not specifically develop the topic sentence. If a paragraph should be divided, use the symbol ¶ to show where the second paragraph should start. A paragraph also needs to be coherent. If necessary, add transitional words. Read carefully to see if the sentence order is clear.

Study the corrections and improvements in the following paragraph.

> But
> Solomon richly enjoyed God's blessing upon his life. ^
> Solomon failed miserably. ~~His father, David, although~~
> ~~he too sinned, never turned to idolatry.~~ There seem to
> be two primary causes for Solomon's failure. That he
> spent almost twice as long building his own house as
> he did building God's house may reveal a selfish love
> for luxury. The Bible clearly states that his heathen
> wives turned his heart away from God. This practice of
> marrying these heathen princesses proves that he failed
> to reckon with the power of influence.¶ One cannot turn
> away from God without suffering serious consequences.
> The Bible states that Solomon was punished for his
> wickedness. *First t* The righteous anger of the Lord came upon
> *Also t* him. The kingdom was taken from him and divided. *And* God
> raised adversaries to bring trouble to his once peace-
> ful reign.

6. *Be sure the composition includes a good title and the three basic parts of a composition.* Does the title relate clearly to the theme of the composition? Does it spark interest? Is the introduction fresh and stimulating? Does the body effectively develop the outline? Is the conclusion satisfying and convincing?

After you have carefully proofread your composition, your first draft probably has some proofreading marks on it. Rewrite the composition, making the changes you marked when proofreading. Use your neatest handwriting, and leave neat, even margins.

Class Practice

Proofread these paragraphs, going over the items discussed in this lesson one or two at a time.

> The tabernacel was a tent divided into too parts the
> holy place and the most holy place. Around the taberna-
> cle was an area enclosed by curtians, called the cort.

Lesson 42 Answers

Class Practice

(Allow reasonable variation. It would be good to make copies of the original paragraphs so that students can have actual practice with proofreading marks.)

> The tabernacell was a tent divided into *w* too parts
> the holy place and the most holy place. Around the
> tabernacle was an area enclosed by curtians, called

As the preist the court, he came to the alter of burnt offring. Hear the aminals were slain and offered. Next the priest comes to the laver, where he washes his hands and feet before going the holy place. The holy place contianed three items of furniture. To the left stood the golden candelstick. Which gave light to the room. This candlestick had nothing to do with candles as we think of them. It was actually a seven-branched oil lamp. Opposite stood the table of shewbread. Every sabbath, twelve laoves of bread to be eaten by the preists placed on the table. The altar of incense stands strait ahead. Hear sweat incense was burned every morning and evening.

The only item in the most holy place was the arc of the covenent which contained the tables of stone with the ten commandments. During the time of Eli, the ark was taken out of the tabernacle and captured by the Philistines. The lid of the ark was the mercy seat. On the lid were placed two cherubim, they faced each other with their wings touching. Here God wood meat with his peeple.

Written Exercises

A. Proofread the composition you wrote for Lesson 39.

B. Recopy your composition in your best handwriting.

---

43. Chapter 4 Review

Class Practice

A. Tell which words are nouns. Tell whether each noun is *concrete* or *abstract,* and identify its gender.
   1. A person must possess courage and commitment to the right if he will resist temptation.
   2. When Peter heard the cock crow, he was filled with remorse.

Lesson 43

Purpose: To review the concepts taught in Chapter 4.

---

the cort. As the preist *entered* the court, he came to the alter of burnt offring. Hear the aminals *animals* were slain and offered. Next the priest comes *came* to the laver, where he washes his hands and feet before going *into* the holy place. The holy place contianed three items of furniture. To the left stood the golden candelstick. Which *which* gave light to the room. This candlestick had nothing to do with candles as we think of them. It was actually a seven-branched oil lamp. Opposite stood the table of shewbread. Every sabbath, twelve laoves of bread to be eaten by the preists placed on the table. The altar of incense stands *stood* strait ahead. Hear *Here* sweat incense was burned every morning and evening.

The only item in the most holy place was the ark of the covenent which contained the tables of stone with the ten commandments. During the time of Eli, the ark was taken out of the tabernacle and captured by the Philistines. The lid of the ark was the mercy seat. On the lid were placed two cherubim, they faced each other with their wings touching. Here God wood meat with his peeple.

Written Exercises

(All answers are individual work.)

Lesson 43 Answers

Class Practice

A. 1. person—concrete, common; courage—abstract, neuter; commitment—abstract, neuter; right—abstract, neuter; temptation—abstract, neuter
   2. Peter—concrete, masculine; cock—concrete, masculine; remorse—abstract, neuter

3. I thought I saw two bucks; but when the deer came closer, I saw that one of them was a doe.

B. Tell whether each word is *always, never,* or *sometimes* a noun when used with its normal meaning.
1. tenderness
2. effectively
3. serfdom
4. treasure
5. ability
6. calm

C. Give the spellings of words to complete this chart. (Plural forms do not need to be given for numbers 7 and 8.)

Singular	Singular Possessive	Plural	Plural Possessive
1. ally	——	——	——
2. thief	——	——	——
3. monkey	——	——	——
4. cattleman	——	——	——
5. brother-in-law	——	——	——
6. fox	——	——	——
7. Moses	——		
8. Lois	——		

D. Change sentence 1 to show separate ownership and sentence 2 to show joint ownership.
1. Have you seen Hannah and Dorcas's project?
2. Timothy's and Daniel's assignments are not finished yet.

E. Read each verbal or verbal phrase, and tell whether it is a *gerund,* a *gerund phrase,* an *infinitive,* or an *infinitive phrase.* Then tell how it is used in the sentence.
1. Studying can be hard work.
2. To learn requires studying diligently and carefully.
3. One important goal of a good student is to recognize the main points of a lesson.
4. These students are applying themselves to learning some difficult science concepts.
5. Our desire should be to study to God's glory.

F. On the chalkboard, diagram the skeletons and complements of the main clauses and the complete noun clauses of these sentences.
1. Brother Amos announced when the history test was scheduled.
2. The stranger's first question was whether we believe the Bible.
3. Whoever washed these dishes must have been in a hurry.
4. We should be considerate in whatever we say.

3. bucks—concrete, masculine;
deer—concrete, common;
doe—concrete, feminine

B. 1. always
2. never
3. always
4. sometimes
5. always
6. sometimes

C. 1. ally's, allies, allies'
2. thief's, thieves, thieves'
3. monkey's, monkeys, monkeys'
4. cattleman's, cattlemen, cattlemen's
5. brother-in-law's, brothers-in-law, brothers-in-law's
6. fox's, foxes, foxes'
7. Moses'
8. Lois's

D. 1. Have you seen Hannah's and Dorcas's projects?
2. Timothy and Daniel's assignments are (or assignment is) not finished yet.

E. 1. Studying—gerund, subject
2. To learn—infinitive, subject;
studying diligently and carefully—gerund phrase, direct object
3. to recognize the main points of a lesson—infinitive phrase, predicate nominative
4. learning some difficult science concepts—gerund phrase, object of a preposition
5. to study to God's glory—infinitive phrase, predicate nominative

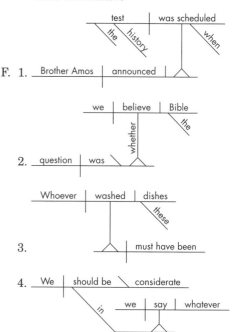

. Tell how to improve this outline.

Friends of Jesus Christ
John 15:14–21

I. The condition for this friendship
   A. Obedience (v. 14)
II. The privileges of this friendship
   A. closeness to God (v. 15)
      1. Placed above a servant
      2. Given understanding of God
   B. We are assured that God is directing us. (v. 16)
III. The results of this friendship
   A. fruitfulness (v. 16)
      1. By His enablement
      2. We must endure.
   B. We have power in prayer (v. 16)
   C. Love for each other (v. 17)
   D. enmity of the world (vv. 18–21)
      1. Their hatred for Jesus
      2. Being in disharmony with Jesus' friends
      3. They have rejected God.

Written Exercises

.. Copy each noun, and label it *concrete* or *abstract*. Also label its gender (*M, F, N,* or *C*).
   1. King David and his people bowed in thanksgiving and praise.
   2. The maid told Naaman's wife about God's prophet.
   3. God's power restored health to Naaman.

. Add a noun-forming suffix to each word.
1. deny	3. righteous	5. content
2. unite	4. cohere	6. separate

. Write the plural form of each word. Use the foreign plural spellings for numbers 8–12.
1. son-in-law	4. handful	7. country	10. vertex
2. sheep	5. trolley	8. basis	11. vertebra
3. potato	6. knife	9. curriculum	12. radius

). Write the possessive form of each word.
1. mouse	5. commander-in-chief
2. Doris	6. Jesus
3. oxen	7. teachers
4. babies	8. angels

G. (Improved lines are starred.)

Friends of Jesus Christ
John 15:14–21

*I. The condition for this friendship—obedience (v. 14)
II. The privileges of this friendship
   *A. Closeness to God (v. 15)
      1. Placed above a servant
      *2. Given understanding of God
   *B. Assurance of God's direction (v. 16)
III. The results of this friendship
   *A. Fruitfulness (v. 16)
      1. By His enablement
      *2. By our endurance
   *B. Power in prayer (v. 16)
   C. Love for each other (v. 17)
   *D. Enmity of the world (vv. 18–21)
      1. Their hatred for Jesus
      *2. Their disharmony with Jesus' friends
      *3. Their rejection of God

Written Exercises

A. 1. King David—concrete, M; people—concrete, C; thanksgiving—abstract, N; praise—abstract, N;
   2. maid—concrete, F; wife—concrete, F; prophet—concrete, M
   3. power—abstract, N; health—abstract, N; Naaman—concrete, M

B.
1. denial	4. coherence
2. unity, union	5. contentment
3. righteousness	6. separation, separateness

C.
1. sons-in-law	7. countries
2. sheep	8. bases
3. potatoes	9. curricula
4. handfuls	10. vertices
5. trolleys	11. vertebrae
6. knives	12. radii

D.
1. mouse's	5. commander-in-chief's
2. Doris's	6. Jesus'
3. oxen's	7. teachers'
4. babies'	8. angels'

E. Copy the verbal phrases and noun clauses. Label each one *gerund phrase, infinitive phrase,* or *noun clause.*
1. What this sentence says can hardly be deciphered.
2. Father has decided to paint the barn.
3. One reason for some people's success is that they work hard.
4. Meddling in other people's business destroys friendships.
5. My grandmother's favorite pastime is crocheting afghans.
6. To do good calligraphy requires a steady hand.

F. Diagram the skeletons and complements of all the clauses. Include the complete noun clauses and verbal phrases.
1. God has declared that His Word will never fail.
2. Serving the Lord brings true liberty.
3. A sure way to bondage is to please the flesh.
4. We must earnestly seek to be godly.
5. Whoever is pure will see God.

G. Organize this list into an outline with two main topics. (You will need to provide the main topics.) Follow the rules for good outlining.

Offering Thanksgiving
Always
For answered prayer
Before we eat
Deliverance from sin through Jesus Christ
In private worship
God is merciful
After an accomplishment
God's supply of our physical needs
In public worship
Victory over the power of death
For God's holiness

E. 1. What this sentence says—noun clause
2. to paint the barn—infinitive phrase
3. that they work hard—noun clause
4. Meddling in other people's business—gerund phrase
5. crocheting afghans—gerund phrase
6. To do good calligraphy—infinitive phrase

F.

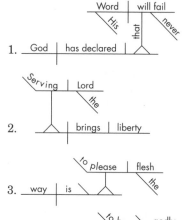

1.
2.
3.
4.
5.

G. (Allow reasonable variation.)

Offering Thanksgiving
I. Times to offer thanksgiving
   A. Before eating
   B. In private worship
   C. In public worship
   D. After an accomplishment
   E. At all times
II. Reasons to offer thanksgiving
   A. For God's holiness
   B. For God's mercy
   C. For answered prayer
   D. For God's supply of our physical needs
   E. For deliverance from sin through Jesus Christ
   F. For victory over the power of death

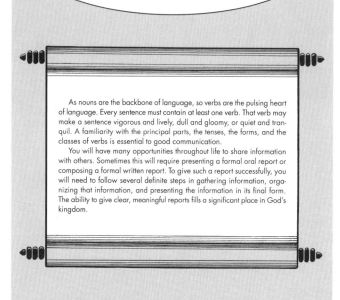

Chapter Five

Verbs

Preparing and Giving Reports

As nouns are the backbone of language, so verbs are the pulsing heart of language. Every sentence must contain at least one verb. That verb may make a sentence vigorous and lively, dull and gloomy, or quiet and tranquil. A familiarity with the principal parts, the tenses, the forms, and the classes of verbs is essential to good communication.

You will have many opportunities throughout life to share information with others. Sometimes this will require presenting a formal oral report or composing a formal written report. To give such a report successfully, you will need to follow several definite steps in gathering information, organizing that information, and presenting the information in its final form. The ability to give clear, meaningful reports fills a significant place in God's kingdom.

And when [Paul and Barnabas] were come, and had gathered the church together, they rehearsed all that God had done with them, and how he had opened the door of faith unto the Gentiles.

Acts 14:27

4. Gathering Information About a Topic

Lesson Survey

- To gather information about a topic, use the following steps.
  1. Choose a suitable topic.
  2. Use various reference sources to find information.
  3. Take notes from your reference sources.

In grade 6 you gathered information and organized notes for a written report, and in grade 7 you followed the same basic process for an oral report. In this chapter you will again follow the same basic process, first for an oral report and then for a written report.

Use the following steps to gather information about a topic.

Step 1: *Choose a suitable topic.* Sometimes your teacher may do the actual choosing for you. If not, be sure that you select a subject that you either know something about or are reasonably sure you can find information about. Your finished report will also be most effective if the topic holds a definite interest to you. As you choose a topic, you should think not only about yourself but also about your audience or readers. Will it be interesting and suitable for them? For your work in this chapter, plan to speak and write to your classmates.

An important part of choosing a suitable topic is limiting the scope of the topic. For example, the topic "Farming" is far too broad in scope. To touch briefly all the aspects of this topic, you would need to talk for hours or write a large book. The following sets of examples show how to limit broad subjects. The underlined topics would be suitable for brief reports like those you will be expected to prepare.

Farming
Changes in Farming in the Past Fifty Years
Changes in Dairy Farming in the Past Fifty Years
Farming Practices That Conserve the Soil

Canada
The Geography of Canada
The Climate of Canada
The Climate of Southern Ontario
The Geography of the Burns Lake District

The topic you choose at this point may be considered your *working title.* Perhaps you will keep it as your final title, or perhaps you will refine it later. Either way, your working title will give you the sense of direction you need in gathering information.

Lesson 44

Purpose: To teach students how to gather information about a topic.

Teacher: This lesson teaches the use of note cards in doing research for an oral report. While many adults do not use this method, they do follow the basic procedure taught in the lesson. They are able to omit some of the technical steps because they are organized in their minds—which is not true of most eighth grade students at this point. But as the students use note cards, they will be learning the steps of organization; and later they too may use a different method for gathering and organizing information.

Oral Review:
1. When is the best time to proofread a composition? (a while after you have finished the first draft)
2. (*Teacher:* Copy this quotation on the board, and have students demonstrate using proofreading marks:

    "For God so the world, that he gave [us] his begotten only Son.")

3. State two rules that relate to indenting on an outline. (Indent each level equally. Indent each level farther right than the previous level.)
4. On a topical outline, the items of each level should be ——— as much as possible. (parallel in structure)

Lesson Introduction: The twelve spies who were sent to search out the land of Canaan knew what it was to give a report. They reported to the other Israelites (who had not seen the land) what they had learned about Canaan.

The reports you write in school will be on subjects about which you have gathered information to share with the rest of the class. But report-writing

Step 2: *Use various reference sources to find information.* The most important source of information is the Bible, for it contains both specific information about many subjects and important principles relating to every subject. Other reference sources include Bible dictionaries, Bible handbooks, encyclopedias, and atlases. If possible, find a book on the subject; such a book usually has more details than you will find in an encyclopedia. However, do not spend time reading entire books. Instead, try to find information about your particular topic by checking the table of contents and the index. Scan through sections that look promising; read closely when you find information on your specific theme.

Using more than one source of information does three important things for your reports. First, it helps to make the report balanced. Having ideas from several sources will likely give a wider scope of details. Second, it requires you to express ideas in your own words, since you must blend together the ideas you find. Third, it enables you to verify facts. If two or three books say the same thing, you can be fairly sure that the information is correct.

Before you begin, decide what you will need to look for. Suppose your report is on the disease of leprosy in man. You could approach it in many ways: people who have had leprosy, lepers Jesus healed, the life of a leper, the symptoms of leprosy, and so forth. You would look for different material depending on the specific division of the subject you have chosen. Or you may decide to divide your report into three parts: conditions of the disease, victims of the disease, and the cure of the disease. Then as you search for material, you will choose only that which relates to these three areas.

Step 3: *Take notes from your reference sources.* Write careful notes, including only information that relates directly to your topic. Write only short phrases; do not copy whole sentences or paragraphs. Along with each note, indicate exactly where you found the information. This will be helpful later if you need to check the accuracy of your notes or add other details.

Write honest notes. It is not honest to copy another person's writing and pass it off as your own. This is a form of stealing known as plagiarism (plā′·jə·riz′·əm). Using *ideas* from other people is all right as long as you express those ideas in your own words. That is why your notes should consist of short phrases rather than whole sentences. It is acceptable to copy directly from a reference source if you want to include a short quotation in your report. But then you should clearly say that you are quoting someone else, and the quotation should be placed in quotation marks.

Write sufficient notes. To have a good report, you need a broad understanding of your subject. You should intend to have more notes than you will use, rather than barely enough. It is always easier to discard some notes than to go back through the reference books looking for more information.

days will probably not end for you when your school days are over. In future years you may need to make reports for committee meetings or for church business meetings. You may be asked to give reports to the home church about some special church project or about a foreign mission field where you have been working. Giving reports in school will prepare you to give effective oral and written reports later.

Lesson Outline:

1. To gather information about a topic, first choose a suitable topic.
  a. Choose a topic that you either know something about or are reasonably sure you can find information about.
  b. Choose a topic that is interesting and suitable for yourself and your audience or readers.
  c. Choose a topic that is limited enough for a brief report.

2. Use various reference sources to find information.
  a. The most important source of information is the Bible, for it contains both specific information about many subjects and important principles relating to every subject.
  b. Other reference sources include Bible dictionaries, Bible handbooks, encyclopedias, and atlases.
  c. A book on the subject usually has more details than you will find in an encyclopedia.
  d. Use more than one source of information.
    1) This will help to make your report balanced by giving a wider scope of details.
    2) It requires you to express ideas in your own words.
    3) It enables you to verify facts.
  e. Before you begin, decide what you will need to look for.

3. Take notes from your reference sources.
  a. Write careful notes.
    1) Include only information that relates directly to your topic.
    2) Write only short phrases; do not copy whole sentences or paragraphs.
    3) Along with each note, indicate exactly where you found the information. This will be helpful later if you need to check the accuracy of your notes or add other details.
  b. Write honest notes.
    1) It is plagiarism to copy another person's writing and pass it off as your own. (This can actually be a crime.)

Write orderly notes. One good way to do that is to use small note cards, such as three-by-five-inch index cards. Because the cards are small, you can easily write brief notes on them. Use one card for each specific idea. These cards will then be easy to shuffle when you are ready to organize the notes into an outline.

Certain types of information should appear on these cards. At the top of each card, write your topic and any subtopic heading (if you have already divided your topic into several categories). Give the source of the information, including the page number. If the source is an encyclopedia, be sure to specify which volume. If the information is from a periodical, include the date of the issue and the title of the article.

The first card from each source should have all this information written out in full, but on additional cards it may be abbreviated somewhat. You may abbreviate the title of the source, and you may omit the author's name. The important thing is that you can quickly identify where you found the information.

Completed note cards should follow the pattern shown below. Notice how the second note card abbreviates *New Unger's Bible Dictionary* as *NUBD*. For the book *Manners and Customs of Bible Lands,* the abbreviation *MCBL* could be used after the first card.

Houses of Bible Times	Houses of B. T.
Roofs	Roofs
New Unger's Bible Dictionary. p. 592	NUBD. p. 592
Unger. Merrill F.	Made of earth packed down on a foundation of branches or rafters
Generally flat, with no chimney and no overhang	

Class Practice

Answer these questions about gathering information for a topic.
1. What are some things you should consider when choosing a topic?
2. Name five reference sources that you could use to find material for a report.
3. State three reasons why you should use more than one source of information for your notes.
4. Give two reasons why using note cards is a good way to take notes.
5. What types of information should appear at the top of each note card?

For each broad subject, give several topics limited enough for a brief report.
1. The Tabernacle
2. Products of Guatemala
3. Wonders of Nature

Lesson 44 Answers

Class Practice

A. 1. Is it a topic you know something about or can find information about? Is the topic interesting and suitable for yourself and for your audience or readers? Is the topic limited enough?
2. the Bible, Bible dictionary, Bible handbook, encyclopedia, atlas, a book on the subject
3. It will help to make your report balanced, it will require you to express ideas in your own words, and it will enable you to verify facts.
4. You can easily write one specific idea on each card, and you can easily shuffle the cards when you are ready to organize the notes into an outline.
5. the topic, any subtopic heading (if you have already divided your topic into several categories), the source of the information, the page number, the volume number if the information is from an encyclopedia, the date of the issue and the title of the article if it is from a periodical

B. 1. The Plan of the Tabernacle; The Furniture of the Tabernacle
2. Agricultural Products of Guatemala; Mineral Products of Guatemala; Products of the Guatemalan Highlands
3. A Solar Eclipse; The Northern Lights; Microscopic Wonders in the Classroom

---

2) Your notes should consist of short phrases rather than whole sentences.
3) You may copy a short quotation from a reference source and use it in your report. But then you should clearly say that you are quoting someone else, and the quotation should be placed in quotation marks.
   c. Write sufficient notes.
1) You need a broad understanding of your subject.
2) You should intend to have more notes than you will use, rather than barely enough.
3) It is easier to discard some notes than to go back through the reference books looking for more information.

d. Write orderly notes.
1) Small note cards are good for this because you can easily write one specific idea on each card and you can easily shuffle them when you are ready to organize the notes into an outline.
2) Each card should have the following types of information at the top: the topic, any subtopic heading (if you have already divided your topic into several categories), the source of the information, the page number, the volume number if the information is from an encyclopedia, the date of the issue and the title of the article if it is from a periodical.

Written Exercises

A. The following information was gathered for the topic "Water—an Essential Substance." The division title is given in brackets. Write the notes properly on five index cards or in rectangles drawn on your paper.

1. From *Investigating God's Orderly World,* Book One [Importance to the earth]: covers 71% of earth's surface (p. 215); ocean currents affect climate of some areas of the world (p. 217)
2. From *Investigating God's Orderly World,* Book One [Importance to man]: body is about two-thirds water by weight (p. 364); is essential to digestion of food and removal of wastes (p. 364)
3. From *Biology: God's Living Creation* [Importance to man]: Promptly replace water lost in heavy sweating (p. 198)

B. Take notes from at least two sources on a topic suitable for both an oral report of four to six minutes and a written report. Choose one of the following or one of your own that is approved by your teacher. Save your notes for later lessons in this chapter.

1. The Geography of Jerusalem
2. The Synagogues of Jesus' Day
3. Common Waterfowl of North America
4. The Childhood of Abraham Lincoln
5. The Oregon Trail
6. The Organization of a Beehive

Review Exercises

A. Do these exercises on letter writing. [2, 6]
   1. Name in order the five parts of a friendly letter.

B. (Individual work.)

Review Exercises

A. 1. heading, greeting, body, closing, signature

Written Exercises

A. (Sample note cards.)

Water: An Essential Substance

Importance to the earth

Investigating God's Orderly World, Book One, p. 215

Covers 71% of earth's surface

Water: E. S.

Importance to the earth

IGOW, B1, p. 217

Ocean currents affect climate of some areas of the world

Water: E. S.

Importance to man

IGOW, B1, p. 364

Body is about two-thirds water by weight

Water: E. S.

Importance to man

IGOW, B1, p. 364

Water essential to digestion of food and removal of wastes

Water: E. S.

Importance to man

Biology: God's Living Creation, p. 198

Promptly replace water lost in heavy sweating

2. What additional part does a business letter have, and where is it placed?

3. What is another name for the greeting of a business letter?

4. What are some appropriate ways to begin a friendly letter?

5. How can you write an honest thank-you note for a gift you do not especially like?

6. How should the mailing address appear so that the postal service can handle a letter most efficiently?

7. How is the greeting of a business letter punctuated differently from that of a friendly letter?

8. What are the three C's of a business letter?

B. Do these exercises on paragraph unity and coherence. [13, 18]

1. When does a paragraph have unity?

2. What two things must sometimes be done if a composition lacks unity?

3. When does a paragraph have coherence?

4. Name and briefly describe the three types of sentence order that can be used in a paragraph.

5. Name three kinds of sentence transitions that improve coherence.

---

45. Identifying Verbs

Lesson Survey

- A **verb** expresses action or being to tell what the subject does or is.
- Every clause must have a verb, which is the **simple predicate.**
- A **verb phrase** consists of the main verb along with any helping verbs.
- Two or more verbs joined by a conjunction make a **compound verb.**

Nouns and verbs are the core of language. Nouns enable us to talk about objects and ideas. Verbs enable us to give many different kinds of information about those objects and ideas. Verbs make language flow and sparkle. Imagine trying to communicate without verbs!

A *verb* expresses action or being to tell what the subject does or is.

The shepherd <u>called</u> his sheep. (action)
The shepherd <u>is</u> watchful of his sheep. (being)

Lesson 45

Purpose: To study the definition and recognition of verbs.

Oral Review:

1. What is a substantive? (any word or word group that functions as a noun)

2. What is a verbal? (a verb form used as another part of speech)

3. Name and describe the two kinds of verbals that can be used as nouns. (gerund—the *-ing* form of a verb; infinitive—the basic form of a verb preceded by *to*)

4. What is an elliptical sentence? (a group of words with one or more sentence parts missing, but which expresses a complete thought because the missing parts are understood)

---

2. inside address; at the left-hand margin, between the heading and the greeting

3. salutation

4. with a Scripture verse, a few lines of poetry, or some other worthwhile quotation

5. express appreciation for the thoughtfulness of the giver

6. in all capital letters with no punctuation

7. The greeting of a business letter is followed by a colon instead of a comma.

8. courteous, clear, concise

B. 1. when every sentence supports and develops the topic sentence

2. Delete unrelated sentences; divide paragraphs properly.

3. when all the thoughts are presented in a well-organized way

4. chronological order—details presented in the order of time; spatial order—details presented in the order of space; order of importance—details presented from the least important to the most important

5. transitional words, repetition of key words, pronoun reference

---

5. Name and briefly describe the four types of sentences according to their structure. (simple—one independent clause; compound—two or more independent clauses; complex—one independent clause and one or more dependent clauses; compound-complex—two or more independent clauses and at least one dependent clause)

6. Tell which words should be capitalized in the following items. (Answers are underlined.)

a. "<u>There Is Life</u> for a <u>Look</u>"

b. the <u>Sermon</u> on the <u>Mount</u>

c. the <u>Lord</u> and <u>His Word</u>

d. lived in the <u>South</u>

e. the lords of the <u>Philistines</u>

f. a <u>Farmall</u> tractor

g. today, <u>O</u> people

h. <u>Cousin Ira</u> and my brother <u>David</u>

Every clause must have a verb, which is the *simple predicate.* If a clause is elliptical (with some words understood), the verb may not be stated. Each verb in the example sentences below is underlined. But notice that in the second sentence, which is an elliptical sentence, no verb is stated.

"The cows <u>are</u> on the road!" <u>shouted</u> Daryl.
"On the road! How <u>did</u> they <u>get</u> out?" <u>asked</u> Father as he <u>pulled</u> on his coat.

Many times the verb of a sentence consists of more than one word. A *verb phrase* consists of the main verb along with any helping verbs. In a verb phrase, the main verb always comes last. The following lists show all the verbs that may be used as helping verbs.

Words that may be helping verbs or main verbs:
am, is, are, was, were, be, been, being (forms of *be*)
have, has, had
do, does, did

Words that are used only as helping verbs:
may, might, must
can, could
shall, should
will, would

Other words often interrupt a verb phrase. Pay special attention to the following words: *not, never, hardly, always, ever, surely.* Although these words are closely associated with the verb phrase, they are never verbs; they are adverbs. The contraction *n't* is an adverb too, even though it is attached to the verb. Other adverbs may also interrupt a verb phrase. And in a question, the subject often comes between the helping verb and the main verb.

God's promises <u>can</u> never <u>fail</u>.

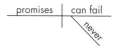

We <u>should</u> always <u>trust</u> Him.

Lesson Introduction: When a person must learn a foreign language with no interpreter, he probably learns some nouns first. He can point to objects and communicate with signs that he wants to know what they are. It is much harder to get a grasp of the verbs. Harder still is learning to know the different tenses of verbs. But no meaningful communication can take place without knowing the verbs in a language.

Lesson Outline:

1. A verb expresses action or being to tell what the subject does or is.

2. Every clause must have a verb, which is the simple predicate. If a clause is elliptical, the verb may not be stated.

3. A verb phrase consists of the main verb along with any helping verbs.

a. In a verb phrase, the main verb alway comes last.

b. The following words may be helping verb or main verbs: *am, is, are, was, were, be been, being; have, has, had; do, does, did.*

c. The following words are used only as helping verbs: *may, might, must; can, could shall, should; will, would.*

d. Other words often interrupt a verb phrase

4. Two or more verbs joined by a conjunction make a compound verb.

He <u>hasn't</u> <u>spoken</u> one word in vain.
(Note that *n't* is diagramed as the word *not.*)

Would a mere man <u>doubt</u> the promises of God?

Two or more verbs joined by a conjunction make a *compound verb*. The parts of a compound verb share the same subject. Sometimes the main verbs also share the same helping verb, which may be stated only before the first main verb.

Noah <u>built</u> the ark and <u>warned</u> the people.

God <u>was preserving</u> Noah's family but <u>destroying</u> the wicked world.

Noah <u>came</u> out of the ark, <u>built</u> an altar, and <u>worshiped</u> the Lord.

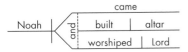

Class Practice

A. Give all the verbs that may be used as helping verbs or main verbs, and all those that are used only as helping verbs.

B. Read all the verbs and verb phrases in these sentences.
1. After they had eaten supper, Jesus and His disciples sang a hymn.
2. They crossed the Kidron and entered into Gethsemane.
3. Had the disciples slept while Jesus was praying?

Lesson 45 Answers

Class Practice

A. *May be used as helping verbs or main verbs:* am, is, are, was, were, be, been, being; have, has, had; do, does, did

Used only as helping verbs: may, might, must; can, could; shall, should; will, would

B. 1. had eaten; sang
2. crossed; entered
3. Had slept; was praying

4. They couldn't fully understand the struggle that Jesus was facing.
5. Jesus was willing to do the Father's will.
6. Although the forces of evil had been doing their worst, they could not overcome the Lord's purposes.

C. Tell whether each word is *always, sometimes,* or *never* a verb.
   1. plate   4. reason
   2. unify   5. dedicate
   3. absolute   6. paralyze

D. On the chalkboard, diagram the skeletons and complements of these sentences. Put any single-word adverbs on slanted lines beneath the verbs.
   1. We must surely follow noble examples.
   2. We can't do wrong and escape the consequences.
   3. Are you being a good example for others?
   4. Somebody is watching your life and following your example.

Written Exercises

A. List all the verbs and verb phrases in these sentences. Underline the main verb in each verb phrase.
   1. Tiger sharks live primarily in tropical waters but range into temperate zones during the summer.
   2. They may reach sixteen feet in length and may weigh over a ton.
   3. God gave these creatures several things that make them effective hunters.
   4. Their sensory system must surely rank among the keenest in nature.
   5. Even a trace of blood can't escape the notice of a shark in the area.
   6. The tiger shark has been created with sensitive electroreceptors.
   7. These receptors can even pick up faint muscle twitches.
   8. Have you ever seen a tiger shark's teeth?
   9. A tiger shark's powerful jaws are lined with large, notched teeth.
   10. If a tooth is broken, a new one will soon replace it.

B. Diagram the skeletons and complements of these sentences. Put any adverbs on slanted lines beneath the verbs.
   1. A fool will proudly deny his need of advice.
   2. Many fools have taken their own way and suffered serious consequences.
   3. Will a wise man accept the counsel of others?
   4. He does recognize his imperfection and actively seeks advice.
   5. A wise man will surely be rewarded.

4. could understand; was facing
5. was
6. had been doing; could overcome

C. 1. sometimes   4. sometimes
   2. always   5. always
   3. never   6. always

D.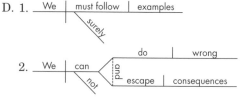
1. We | must follow | examples
   surely

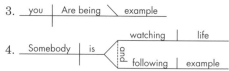
2. We | can | and [do | wrong] [not] [escape | consequences]

3. you | Are being \ example

4. Somebody | is | and [watching | life] [following | example]

Written Exercises

A. 1. live, range   6. has been <u>created</u>
   2. may <u>reach</u>, may <u>weigh</u>   7. can <u>pick</u>
   3. gave, make   8. Have <u>seen</u>
   4. must <u>rank</u>   9. are <u>lined</u>
   5. can <u>escape</u>   10. is <u>broken</u>, will <u>replace</u>

B.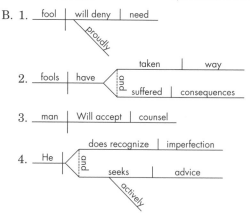
1. fool | will deny | need
   proudly

2. fools | have | and [taken | way] [suffered | consequences]

3. man | Will accept | counsel

4. He | and [does recognize | imperfection] [seeks | advice]
   actively

5. man | will be rewarded
   surely

eview Exercises

. For each numbered sentence below, write the letter of the correct description. [14–16]

    a. Simple sentence with no compound parts

    b. Simple sentence with a compound predicate

    c. Compound sentence with two independent clauses

    d. Compound sentence with three independent clauses

    e. Complex sentence with one independent clause and one dependent clause

    f. Complex sentence with one independent clause and two dependent clauses

    g. Compound-complex sentence with two independent clauses and one dependent clause

1. Dishonesty is an abomination to God and will defile a person's soul.
2. The notion that dishonesty can be a white lie is a trick of the devil.
3. The Bible declares that God will judge all liars; therefore, godly fear causes us to flee all forms of dishonesty.
4. Although many people profess faith in God, only those who obey His Word have true faith.
5. Faith in God does not mean merely an acceptance of His existence; it means a commitment of life to Him.
6. James writes that faith without works is dead.
7. Creation displays the invisible things of the Godhead, the Bible reveals much about His character and work, and the lives of faithful Christians portray His life.
8. Our response should be simple faith in God.

. Write correctly each word with a capitalization error. [21]

1. unchanged god's word fore'er shall stand,
   unchanged each precept, each command;
      unmoved, o lord, help me to stand.
2. "the lord jesus was willing to give his life," concluded brother enos, "so that we might have life."
3. At the close of the Service, we sang "There is Power in the Blood."
4. On the ship were italians, bulgarians, and romanians seeking a better life in north america.
5. My Brother Vernon lives in the midwest.
6. On saturday i went to Pineville general store and bought some hallmark stationery and a papermate pen.

Review Exercises

A. 1. b
  2. e
  3. g
  4. f
  5. c
  6. e
  7. d
  8. a

B. 1. Unchanged, God's Word, Unchanged, Unmoved, O, Lord
  2. The, Lord Jesus, His, Brother Enos
  3. service, Is
  4. Italians, Bulgarians, Romanians, North America
  5. brother, Midwest
  6. Saturday, I, General Store, Hallmark, Papermate

Principal Parts of Common Verbs

First (Present)	Second (Past)	Third (Past Participle)	First (Present)	Second (Past)	Third (Past Participle)
awake	awoke	(have) awoke	kneel	knelt	(have) knelt
	or awaked	(have) awaked		or kneeled	(have) kneeled
be (is)	was	(have) been	know	knew	(have) known
bear	bore	(have) borne	*lay	laid	(have) laid
begin	began	(have) begun	*leave	left	(have) left
bid	bade	(have) bidden	lend	lent	(have) lent
	or bid	(have) bid	*let	let	(have) let
blow	blew	(have) blown	*lie	lay	(have) lain
break	broke	(have) broken	put	put	(have) put
bring	brought	(have) brought	*raise	raised	(have) raised
*burst	burst	(have) burst	read	read	(have) read
buy	bought	(have) bought	ride	rode	(have) ridden
catch	caught	(have) caught	ring	rang	(have) rung
choose	chose	(have) chosen	*rise	rose	(have) risen
*come	came	(have) come	run	ran	(have) run
cost	cost	(have) cost	*see	saw	(have) seen
creep	crept	(have) crept	seek	sought	(have) sought
cut	cut	(have) cut	send	sent	(have) sent
dig	dug	(have) dug	*set	set	(have) set
*do	did	(have) done	shake	shook	(have) shaken
*drag	dragged	(have) dragged	shine	shone	(have) shone
draw	drew	(have) drawn		or shined	(have) shined
drink	drank	(have) drunk	shoot	shot	(have) shot
*drown	drowned	(have) drowned	shrink	shrank	(have) shrunk
eat	ate	(have) eaten		or shrunk	(have) shrunken
fall	fell	(have) fallen	shut	shut	(have) shut
fight	fought	(have) fought	sing	sang	(have) sung
find	found	(have) found	sink	sank	(have) sunk
fly	flew	(have) flown	*sit	sat	(have) sat
forbid	forbade	(have) forbidden	slay	slew	(have) slain
	or forbad	(have) forbid	sleep	slept	(have) slept
forget	forgot	(have) forgotten	speak	spoke	(have) spoken
freeze	froze	(have) frozen	steal	stole	(have) stolen
give	gave	(have) given	swim	swam	(have) swum
*go	went	(have) gone	*swing	swung	(have) swung
grow	grew	(have) grown	*tag	tagged	(have) tagged
hang	hung	(have) hung	take	took	(have) taken
	(suspend)		teach	taught	(have) taught
hang	hanged	(have) hanged	tear	tore	(have) torn
	(execute)		think	thought	(have) thought
hit	hit	(have) hit	throw	threw	(have) thrown
hold	held	(have) held	wear	wore	(have) worn
hurt	hurt	(have) hurt	weep	wept	(have) wept
keep	kept	(have) kept	wring	wrung	(have) wrung
			write	wrote	(have) written

NOTE: *Hanged* for "executed" is a formal usage. Informal usage allows *hung,* especially in a sentence like "He hung himself."

*These troublesome verbs are often used incorrectly.

46. Principal Parts of Verbs

Lesson Survey

- A verb has three **principal parts,** which are used to show tense. They are the present form, the past form, and the past participle.

- The second and third principal parts of most verbs are made by adding *-ed* to the first principal part.

- The second and third principal parts of some verbs are formed irregularly. The verb *be* is especially irregular.

- Most verbs also have two other forms:
  1. The **present participle,** which ends with *-ing*.
  2. The *-s* form, used for third person singular subjects in the present tense.

A verb has a number of different forms that show specific distinctions in the meanings of the verb. These changes are involved in forming the tenses and in showing progression and number. The most important forms are the *principal parts,* which are used to show tense. The following set of sentences will help you to remember the three principal parts of verbs.

Present: Today I <u>pray</u>.
Past: Yesterday I <u>prayed</u>.
Past participle: Every day I <u>have prayed</u>.

The second and third principal parts of most verbs are made by adding *-ed* to the first principal part. Other spelling changes may be necessary when adding *-ed*. If the verb ends with *e,* drop the *e*. If the verb ends with *y* after a consonant, change the *y* to *i*. If a one-syllable verb ends with a single consonant after a short vowel, double the final consonant. Remember that the past participle is never used as a verb alone; it is always the main verb in a verb phrase.

Today I <u>help</u>.
Yesterday I <u>helped</u>.
Every day I <u>have helped</u>.

Today I <u>study</u> hard.
Yesterday I <u>studied</u> hard.
Every day I <u>have studied</u> hard.

Today I <u>move</u> my sore leg.
Yesterday I <u>moved</u> my sore leg.
Every day I <u>have moved</u> my sore leg.

Today I <u>nap</u>.
Yesterday I <u>napped</u>.
Every day I <u>have napped</u>.

The second and third principal parts of some verbs are formed irregularly. Because they are irregular, these verb forms must be memorized. The chart before this lesson shows the principal parts of many irregular verbs. Refer to that chart as you consider the following types of irregular spellings.

Lesson 46

Purpose: To study the principal parts of verbs, and their uses.

Oral Review:

1. Name each verb or verb phrase in these sentences.
   a. We should never give up in the battle against temptations. (should give)
   b. Do you pray for God's help when you are facing a temptation? (Do pray; are facing)
   c. We can certainly look to God and depend fully upon Him. (can look [and] depend)

2. Tell whether each word is always, sometimes, or never a verb when used with its normal meaning.
   a. cover (sometimes)   c. faith (never)
   b. consider (always)   d. forget (always)

3. Name each noun clause in these sentences. (Noun clauses are underlined.)

   a. Father said, "<u>I think it might snow tonight</u>."
   b. Nobody knew <u>whose gloves were lying in the driveway</u>.
   c. <u>That Brownie would snap at anyone</u> is a surprise.

4. Name and briefly describe the three types of word order. (natural—the complete subject precedes the complete predicate; inverted—the complete predicate precedes the complete subject; mixed—the complete subject comes between two parts of the complete predicate)

5. Which two punctuation marks should always be placed inside the quotation marks? (comma, period)

6. Which two punctuation marks should always be placed outside the quotation marks? (colon, semicolon)

7. When should a question mark or an exclamation point be placed inside the quotation marks? (when the quotation is a question or an exclamation)

8. When should a question mark or an exclamation

Some irregular verbs have the same spelling for the second and third principal parts: *catch, caught, (have) caught; lay, laid, (have) laid.* Others have a different spelling for each principal part: *blow, blew, (have) blown; swim, swam, (have) swum.* Still others have the same spelling for all three principal parts: *cost, cost, (have) cost; hurt, hurt, (have) hurt.* And a few have the same spelling for the first and third principal parts: *come, came, (have) come; run, ran, (have) run.*

The verb *be* is especially irregular. It has four present forms: *be, am, is,* and *are. Be* is used as a main verb in imperative sentences and in a few clauses like *if it be possible.* The two past forms of *be* are *was* and *were.* There is only one past participle: *been.* Although these forms can be quite confusing to someone learning English, we use them so much that they generally give us little trouble.

Today I <u>am</u> joyful.	Today you <u>are</u> joyful.
Yesterday I <u>was</u> joyful.	Yesterday you <u>were</u> joyful.
Every day I <u>have been</u> joyful.	Every day you <u>have been</u> joyful.

In addition to the three principal parts, most verbs have two other forms. The *-ing* form of the first principal part, called the *present participle,* is used in progressive verb forms. (These forms are taught more thoroughly in Lesson 50.) The *-s* form of the first principal part is used with third person singular subjects in the present tense.

Satan <u>is working</u> hard against God.
He <u>works</u> against God's kingdom and everyone in it.

Whenever you are not sure about the correct form of a verb, use a dictionary or use the chart before this lesson. Most dictionaries show the second and third principal parts of irregular verbs. Many also give the *-ing* and *-s* forms. If no forms are shown, the verb is regular.

Class Practice

A. Give the three principal parts of each verb. Use *have* as a helping verb.
   1. bear   4. drink   7. kneel
   2. drag   5. set   8. do
   3. run   6. write   9. find

B. Use the *-ing* and *-s* forms of each verb in sentences of your own.
   1. catch   4. throw
   2. shake   5. shrink
   3. freeze

C. Give the correct form of each verb in parentheses. Use the third principal part only if there is a helping verb in the sentence.
   1. Moses (write) the first five books of the Bible.

---

point be placed outside the quotation marks? (when the whole sentence is a question or an exclamation, but the quotation is not)

Lesson Introduction: Spanish-speaking students do not study three principal parts of verbs. But rather than wish that English did not have them, you should be thankful for the simplicity they give to our verbs. In English the following six sentences in the simple present tense require only two forms of the verb *study.*

I study.	We study.
You study.	You study.
He (she, it) studies.	They study.

In Spanish, however, the same six sentences require four different forms of the verb *estudiar.*

Yo estudio.	Nosotros estudiamos.
Usted estudia.	Ustedes estudian.
Él estudia.	Ellos estudian.

Lesson 46 Answers

Class Practice

A. 1. bear, bore, (have) borne
   2. drag, dragged, (have) dragged
   3. run, ran, (have) run
   4. drink, drank, (have) drunk
   5. set, set, (have) set
   6. write, wrote, (have) written
   7. kneel, knelt *or* kneeled, (have) knelt *or* (have) kneeled
   8. do, did, (have) done
   9. find, found, (have) found

B. (Individual work.)

C. 1. wrote

Spanish verbs have several dozen other forms in addition to the four that are shown. By contrast, most English verbs have no more than four or five possible forms.

Lesson Outline:

1. A verb has three principal parts, which are used to show tense. They are the present form, the past form, and the past participle.

2. The second and third principal parts of most verbs are made by adding -ed to the first principal part.
   a. Other spelling changes may also be necessary.
      1) If the verb ends with *e,* drop the *e.*
      2) If the verb ends with *y* after a consonant, change the *y* to *i.*

2. The Egyptian army (drown) in the Red Sea.
3. Certainly God had (do) many things for Israel.
4. David has (slay) his ten thousands.
5. Today God (speak) to us through His Word.
6. We are constantly (choose) for good or for ill.

Written Exercises

. Write the correct form of each underlined verb. If the verb is correct, write *correct*.
1. Out on the Sea of Galilee, the wind <u>blowed</u> furiously.
2. The disciples feared that their boat would be <u>sank</u> in the waters.
3. Jesus calmly <u>slept</u> through the tempest.
4. The disciples <u>awoke</u> the Master.
5. Jesus <u>bidded</u> the wind and waves to be still.
6. During His ministry, Jesus <u>done</u> many miracles.
7. Have you <u>forgot</u> to thank the Lord for His goodness today?
8. If you have <u>spoke</u> the untruth, you should make it right.
9. Mother <u>wrung</u> the dishcloth and wiped the table.
10. Brother Harold <u>hanged</u> the mobiles from the ceiling.
11. The children <u>swung</u> for a while before dinner.
12. My drawing is not a masterpiece, but I <u>done</u> my best.
13. The pond has finally <u>froze</u> over.
14. The dog <u>shook</u> the rat vigorously.
15. We have often <u>sang</u> this song by memory.
16. The stationery that I wanted <u>costed</u> too much.
17. These kittens have <u>growed</u> up very fast.
18. I must have <u>ate</u> something that upset my stomach.
19. Grandmother has <u>borne</u> her blindness patiently these many years.
20. My sweater has <u>shrank</u> because it was washed in hot water.

. Write the correct form of each verb in parentheses. Use the past participle only if there is a helping verb in the sentence.
1. The sun has (rise) above Mount Dobson for another day.
2. The baby is still (sleep), so be quiet.
3. Whoever lifts himself up in pride (fall) the hardest.
4. He who has (break) others' confidence has a hard time regaining it.
5. If you have (run) with the foxes, you must fear the baying hounds.
6. Only those who have (fight) victoriously can wear the victor's crown.
7. He who has (kneel) the most humbly can rise the most nobly.
8. If you have (drink) deeply of the water of life, you will not wilt under the tests of life.
9. The man who savored the water most is the man who (dig) the well.
10. The early bird (catch) the worm.

3) If a one-syllable verb ends with a single consonant after a short vowel, double the final consonant.
b. The past participle is never used as a verb alone; it is always the main verb in a verb phrase.

3. The second and third principal parts of some verbs are formed irregularly.
a. They may have the same spelling for the second and third principal parts, but not the regular *-ed* ending.
b. They may have a different spelling for each principal part.
c. They may have the same spelling for all three principal parts.
d. They may have the same spelling for the first and third principal parts.

2. drowned
3. done
4. slain
5. speaks
6. choosing

Written Exercises

A. 1. blew   11. correct
    2. sunk   12. did
    3. correct   13. frozen
    4. correct   14. correct
    5. bade   15. sung
    6. did   16. cost
    7. forgotten 17. grown
    8. spoken   18. eaten
    9. correct   19. correct
   10. hung   20. shrunk *or* shrunken

B. 1. risen
    2. sleeping
    3. falls
    4. broken
    5. run
    6. fought
    7. knelt *or* kneeled
    8. drunk
    9. dug
   10. catches *or* caught

4. The verb be is especially irregular.
a. It has four present forms: *be, am, is,* and *are. Be* is used as a main verb in imperative sentences and in a few clauses like *if it be possible.*
b. The two past forms of *be* are *was* and *were.*
c. There is only one past participle: *been.*

5. In addition to the three principal parts, most verbs have two other forms.
a. The *-ing* form of the first principal part, called the *present participle,* is used in progressive verb forms.
b. The *-s* form of the first principal part is used for third person singular subjects in the present tense.

★ **EXTRA PRACTICE**
Worksheet 16 (*Principal Parts of Verbs*)

Review Exercises

A. Rewrite each sentence in the order specified in parentheses. [11]
   1. The boys dashed up the steps. (inverted)
   2. Mother certainly prepared a delicious lunch. (mixed)
   3. On these shelves are kept the reference books. (natural)
   4. The whole school gathered to sing after our last recess. (mixed)

B. Write *loose, periodic,* or *balanced* to identify the word order of each sentence. [17]
   1. Although it is small and fragile, the orchid is an especially beautiful flower.
   2. We saw a dazzling display of beauty in the western sky.
   3. Along the eastern horizon, a large full moon was slowly rising.
   4. It is right to be little; it is wrong to belittle.

C. If the underlined part of the sentence contains a mistake in the use of quotation marks, write it correctly. If it is correct, write *correct.* [26]
   1. Do you know the song "Jesus Has Died for <u>Me</u>"?
   2. "Was it Joshua who said, 'But as for me and my house, we will serve the <u>Lord?"</u> asked Glenda.
   3. "<u>You</u> never told me' is no excuse for something that you knew better than doing," Father stated firmly.
   4. Mother said, "Set the table after the wash is brought <u>in;</u>" then Ruth heard the door close.

Review Exercises

A. 1. Up the steps dashed the boys.
   2. Certainly Mother prepared a delicious lunch.
   3. The reference books are kept on these shelves.
   4. After our last recess, the whole school gathered to sing.

B. 1. periodic
   2. loose
   3. periodic
   4. balanced

C. 1. correct
   2. Lord'?"
   3. " 'You
   4. in";

---

47. Organizing Your Notes

> ### Lesson Survey
> - To organize notes for a report, sort them into groups of related main topics.
> - Organize the main topics and supporting points into an outline.

Almost all worthwhile activities depend on a good measure of organization. This is certainly true of producing an oral or a written report. Without organization, the report will be a rambling jumble of information that communicates hardly anything. With organization, the report can be a sensible sequence of information that communicates effectively.

The first step in organizing your notes is to sort them into groups of related main topics. Perhaps as you gathered the information, you already

Lesson 47

Purpose: To study organizing notes into an outline.

Oral Review:

1. Why should you take notes for a report from more than one reference source? (to have a balanced report; to require you to express ideas in your own words; to verify facts)
2. When may you copy the exact words of a reference source in your notes? (when you plan to quote those words in your report, and if you place those words in quotation marks)
3. What are the advantages of using small cards for taking notes? (You can easily write one specific idea on each card. You can easily shuffle the cards to organize your notes.)

Lesson Introduction: Has your mother ever made "Refrigerator Stew"? In the refrigerator she finds some leftover meat, a few beans and peas, and some other vegetables. By using a little of this and a little of that, she can make a delicious stew for dinner.

That is fine for a vegetable stew, but *not* for a report. Rather than a hodgepodge of ideas, a report should be a logical arrangement of information that communicates one main theme. This lesson will give some help in producing an organized basis for an effective report.

Lesson Outline:

1. To organize notes for a report, sort them into groups of related main topics.

2. Organize the main topics and supporting points into an outline.
   a. Arrange the main topics in a logical order.
   b. Fill in the rest of the outline with information from your cards.

ad decided on the main topics. If not, you must now carefully review your
notes, looking for general ideas to use as main topics.

Below is a set of ten cards with notes for a report on "Canals in
Pennsylvania." You will probably have many more notes when you prepare
to write your own report, but this example should be enough to show the
steps in organizing notes. Study these cards, and try to think of some general ideas that could be used as main topics. The cards are numbered for
simple reference.

Canals in Pennsylvania   #1

Pennsylvania: A Bicentennial History. p. 20

Soon-to-be completed Erie Canal
built in New York in mid-1820s.
threatened western trade by
bypassing Pa. cities

Canals in Pa.   #2

Pa. Bicen. Hist. p. 93

Before railroads. provided most comfortable and convenient means of
crossing the state. from 1830-1840
carried $14.5 million worth of
goods

Canals in Pa.   #3

Pennsylvania: Seed of a Nation.
p. 164

Penn himself considered linking
Susquehanna and Delaware R.
as important to economy: hauling heavy loads on turnpikes
was expensive

Canals in Pa.   #4

Pa.: Seed of a Nat. pp. 166-171

linked far-flung parts of state by
cheap transportation: helped introduce railroad

Canals in Pa.   #5

A History of Pennsylvania. p. 593

Pa. had total of 790 miles of canals

Canals in Pa.   #6

Hist. of Pa. p. 594

Canals helped to develop towns

Canals in Pa.   #7

The Pennsylvania Main Line
Canal. p. 89

On the main E-W link of Main
Line Canal. more than 2,600
boats came to Hollidaysburg per
year

Canals in Pa.   #8

Pa. M. L. C. p. 92

Only one canal was directly linked
to interstate canal traffic: the
Susquehanna & Tidewater Canal
to Maryland

Canals in Pa. #9	Canals in Pa. #10
Pa. M. L. C. pp. 152—168	United States History in Christian Perspective. p. 255
Canals failed to pay for themselves. State Assembly called for sale of Main Line Canal in 1844. Schuylkill Canal carried last canal freight in state. Load of 3,100 tons of coal refuse in 1931	Couldn't compete with advantages of railroads: speed, ease of building, and all-weather use

Do you recognize four general categories in the cards above? Cards 1 and 3 give some reasons for building canals. Cards 2, 5, and 7 give facts about how important they became. Cards 4 and 6 describe some benefits they produced, and cards 9 and 10 deal with reasons they went out of business. The information on card 8 does not fit in any of these categories, so it should be laid aside.

Now that you have four general categories, you must arrange them in a logical order. In this case, a logical order would be to look first at the reasons for building canals, second at the era of their prosperity, third at their closing, and fourth at the benefits they produced. Your basic plan might look like the following outline.

Canals in Pennsylvania

I. Why they were built

II. How important they became

III. Why they went out of business

IV. What benefits they produced

Now that you have your basic outline, you are ready to expand the outline with information from your cards. From cards 1 and 3, you might outline the motivation for building the canals as shown by the following example.

I. Why they were built

   A. William Penn's proposal for a canal linking Susquehanna and Delaware Rivers

   B. Expense of hauling heavy loads on turnpikes

   C. Threat of Erie Canal in New York taking trade away from Pennsylvania cities

Although the order of these points could vary, the sample outline gives them both in chronological order and in the order of importance. Penn made his proposal over one hundred years before the canal era, and the Erie Canal was built at the beginning of that era. Penn's proposal likely provided little direct motivation. Point B probably meant the most to the common people, but point C would have been the strongest motivation for the leaders in big business and the government officials most directly involved in building the canals.

After organizing the details for the first main topic, you must do the same thing for the rest of the main topics on the outline. Prepare your outline carefully, for it will be the basis of both the oral report and the written report that you will give later in this chapter.

Class Practice

A. Using cards 2, 5, and 7, organize the information for the second main point of the outline on "Canals in Pennsylvania."

B. Using cards 9 and 10, organize the information for the third main point of the outline on "Canals in Pennsylvania."

C. Using cards 4 and 6, organize the information for the fourth main point of the outline on "Canals in Pennsylvania."

Written Exercises

A. Using the information you gathered in Lesson 44, write a basic outline of three or four main points. Show this outline to your teacher before you do Part B.

B. Use additional information from your notes to make a more detailed outline.

---

48. Simple Verb Tenses

Lesson Survey

- Verbs have different forms to indicate tense.
- The **present tense** shows action or existence that occurs in the present.
- The **past tense** shows action or existence that occurred in the past.
- The **future tense** shows action or existence that will occur in the future.
- A **conjugation** is a table showing certain forms of a verb.

Man is very much bound by time. Home schedules, school schedules, airline schedules, and doctors' appointments all testify to the importance of time. With the exception of two miracles recorded in the Bible, time has been marching steadily forward since the dawn of Creation. And we are assured that time will continue its steady march until God declares that

Lesson 48

Purpose: To study the concept of tense and the formation of the three simple tenses.

Oral Review:

1. Give the second and third principal parts of these verbs.
   a. teach (taught, [have] taught)
   b. choose (chose, [have] chosen)
   c. burst (burst, [have] burst)
   d. swing (swung, [have] swung)
   e. bid (bade, [have] bidden)
   f. shake (shook, [have] shaken)
   g. drag (dragged, [have] dragged)
   h. tear (tore, [have] torn)

2. Give all the verbs that may be used as helping verbs or main verbs. (am, is, are, was, were, be, been, being; have, has, had; do, does, did)

Lesson 47 Answers

Class Practice

A–C. (Sample outline.)

 II. How important they became
  A. Had total of 790 miles of canals
  B. Carried $14.5 million worth of goods from 1836–1840
  C. Handled more than 3,600 boats per year at Hollidaysburg, a town on the main east–west link of the Pa. Main Line Canal
  D. Provided most comfortable and convenient means of crossing the state prior to railroad
 III. Why they went out of business
  A. Failure to pay for themselves
  B. Advantages of railroad
   1. Faster
   2. Easier to build anywhere
   3. Easier to use in all kinds of weather
 IV. What benefits they produced
  A. Linked far-flung parts of state by cheap transportation
  B. Helped develop towns
  C. Helped introduce the railroad

Written Exercises

(All answers are individual work.)

---

3. Give all the verbs that are used only as helping verbs. (may, might, must; can, could; shall, should; will, would)

4. For each purpose, tell whether a colon or a semicolon should be used.
   a. to join independent clauses when no conjunction is used (semicolon)
   b. to separate the numbers in a Scripture reference and in an expression of time (colon)
   c. to separate items in a series when the individual items contain commas (semicolon)
   d. to introduce a list, an explanation, or a formal quotation (colon)

5. What kinds of titles should be italicized? (titles of major works, such as books, newspapers, pamphlets, and periodicals)

6. Give some other uses of italics. (specific names of vehicles; a word or letter used as the subject of

there shall be "time no longer." We live always in the present. But since time is moving on, the present constantly changes to the past, and the future constantly changes to the present.

Verbs have different forms to indicate action or existence in the past, present, or future. English verbs have three simple tenses and three perfect tenses.

The *present tense* shows action or existence that occurs in the present. It is also used for statements of general truth. The first principal part (present form) is used for the present tense. The third person singular form of the present tense ends in -s.

Present action:
    We <u>do</u> our homework on notebook paper.
Present existence:
    Brother John <u>is</u> our substitute teacher today.
Statement of general truth:
    Magellan proved that the earth <u>is</u> round.

The *past tense* shows action or existence that occurred in the past. The second principal part (past form) is used for the past tense.

Jesus <u>performed</u> many miracles while He <u>lived</u> here on earth.

The *future tense* shows action or existence that will occur in the future. The first principal part (present form) is used with the helping verb *shall* or *will* for the future tense. In formal writing such as legal documents and business letters, *shall* is used for first person subjects and *will* is used for second and third person subjects. In general usage, *will* is used for all three. Use formal writing for English exercises, except for story dialogue and friendly letters where formal usage would sound unnatural.

First person: shall
    I <u>shall study</u> for my test before supper.
    We <u>shall sorrow</u> no more in heaven.
Second and third persons: will
    You <u>will attain</u> the goal only by God's grace.
    The faithful <u>will be rewarded</u>.

To show determination, compulsion, or promise, the normal pattern of *shall* and *will* is reversed in formal English. That is, *will* is used for first person subjects, and *shall* is used for second and third person subjects.

"Faith of our fathers! holy faith!
We <u>will</u> be true to thee till death!"

The greatest rebel <u>shall</u> someday bow before Christ the Lord.

discussion; foreign words not adopted into the English language; words to be emphasized)

7. What are some kinds of compound words that should be hyphenated? (compound number words; fractions written in words; words ending with *-in-law;* words beginning with *great-* that refer to relatives; words beginning with *self-;* many that begin with *all-;* compound adjectives used as a unit; proper nouns and adjectives with prefixes)

Lesson Introduction: God is infinite: in no way is He limited to time or by time. He created time solely for man's benefit, not for His own. Because time is so important to us, we need to master the tenses of verbs.

Lesson Outline:

1. Verbs have different forms to indicate tense.

2. The present tense shows action or existence that occurs in the present.

   a. It is also used for statements of general truth.

   b. The first principal part (present form) is used for the present tense.

   c. The third person singular form ends in -s.

3. The past tense shows action or existence that occurred in the past. The second principal part (past form) is used for the past tense.

4. The future tense shows action or existence that will occur in the future.

   a. The first principal part (present form) is used with the helping verb *shall* or *will* for the future tense.

   b. In formal writing, *shall* is used for first person subjects and *will* is used for second and third person subjects.

A *conjugation* is a table showing certain forms of a verb. Here are the conjugations of the verbs *be* and *go* in the simple tenses.

Be

Person	Singular	Plural

Present Tense

First:	I am.	We are.
Second:	You are.	You are.
Third:	He is.	They are.

Past Tense

First:	I was.	We were.
Second:	You were.	You were.
Third:	He was.	They were.

Future Tense

First:	I shall be.	We shall be.
Second:	You will be.	You will be.
Third:	He will be.	They will be.

Go

Person	Singular	Plural

Present Tense

First:	I go.	We go.
Second:	You go.	You go.
Third:	He goes.	They go.

Past Tense

First:	I went.	We went.
Second:	You went.	You went.
Third:	He went.	They went.

Future Tense

First:	I shall go.	We shall go.
Second:	You will go.	You will go.
Third:	He will go.	They will go.

Class Practice

Read each verb or verb phrase, and tell which tense it is.
1. A tiny ruby-throated hummingbird looks like a jewel in the sunshine.
2. We watched the little bird as it hovered among the flowers.
3. Soon it will thrust its long bill into a flower.
4. From the flower the bird sucks nectar for its food.
5. God created this unique bird for a definite purpose.
6. As it feeds, it carries pollen from one flower to the next.

Lesson 48 Answers

Class Practice

A. 1. looks—present
2. watched—past; hovered—past
3. will thrust—future
4. sucks—present
5. created—past
6. feeds—present; carries—present

c. In general usage, *will* is used for all three.
d. The normal pattern of *shall* and *will* is reversed in formal English for statements of determination, compulsion, or promise.

(*Teacher:* The pupil's text gives instruction to "use formal writing for English exercises." This refers mainly to exercises that focus on the various verb forms, especially conjugations. Elsewhere, *I shall* or *I will* is acceptable.)

5. A conjugation is a table showing certain forms of a verb.

7. A hummingbird is very small, but it will fearlessly attack a bird as large as a hawk.
8. We hung up a special feeder for them; perhaps next year we shall hang up several more.

B. Use each verb in three short sentences illustrating the three simple tenses. Begin the first sentence with *Today,* the second with *Yesterday,* and the third with *Tomorrow.*
1. catch   3. run
2. write   4. speak

C. Tell whether each underlined verb shows the *normal* pattern of future tense or the *reversed* pattern for determination, compulsion, or promise.
1. "The Lord my God <u>will enlighten</u> my darkness."
2. "The Lord is my shepherd; I <u>shall</u> not <u>want</u>."
3. "Surely goodness and mercy <u>shall follow</u> me all the days of my life: and I <u>will dwell</u> in the house of the Lord for ever."
4. "He <u>shall judge</u> the people righteously."

D. Conjugate the verb *choose* in the three simple tenses.

Written Exercises

A. Copy each verb or verb phrase, and write which tense it is.
1. Diligence will always produce better results than indifference.
2. Kindness is a key to good friendships.
3. Haman lifted himself up in pride, but God brought him low.
4. We develop true humility only as we see God properly.
5. Satan introduced pride and rebellion to man.
6. God will surely help us to be humble if we seek His help.
7. Earlier in the year we memorized part of Romans 12, and now we shall memorize part of Proverbs 4.
8. Because we recognize the importance of Bible memory, we will do our best.
9. A person keeps his conscience useful only if he heeds its warnings.
10. The person who ignores his conscience will soon ruin its usefulness.

B. Write the correct verb form for the tense shown in italics.
1. A good sport graciously (accept) a defeat in a game. *present*
2. The family reverently (sing) a hymn of praise. *past*
3. We (read) from 1 Samuel 17 this morning. *future*
4. Tomorrow the eighth graders (recite) their poem. *future*
5. Some water pipes (burst) in the barn last night. *past*

7. is—present; will attack—future
8. hung—past; shall hang—future

B. (Sample sentences.)
1. Today I catch fish.
   Yesterday I caught fish.
   Tomorrow I shall catch fish.
2. Today I write letters.
   Yesterday I wrote letters.
   Tomorrow I shall write letters.
3. Today I run.
   Yesterday I ran.
   Tomorrow I shall run.
4. Today I speak.
   Yesterday I spoke.
   Tomorrow I shall speak.

C. 1. normal   3. reversed; reversed
   2. normal   4. reversed

D.
Choose

Person	Singular	Plural
Present Tense		
First:	I choose.	We choose.
Second:	You choose.	You choose.
Third:	He chooses.	They choose.
Past Tense		
First:	I chose.	We chose.
Second:	You chose.	You chose.
Third:	He chose.	They chose.
Future Tense		
First:	I shall choose.	We shall choose.
Second:	You will choose.	You will choose.
Third:	He will choose.	They will choose.

Written Exercises

A. 1. will produce—future
   2. is—present
   3. lifted—past; brought—past
   4. develop—present; see—present
   5. introduced—past
   6. will help—future; seek—present
   7. memorized—past; shall memorize—future
   8. recognize—present; will do—future
   9. keeps—present; heeds—present
   10. ignores—present; will ruin—future

B. 1. accepts   4. will recite
   2. sang   5. burst
   3. shall read

6. The weatherman (predict) even colder temperatures for tonight.
   present

. Write six sentences: two in the present tense, two in the past tense, and two in the future tense. Use *shall* in one future tense sentence and *will* in the other one.

. Conjugate the verb *come* in the three simple tenses.

eview Exercises

. Copy the word or number before each error in the use of colons or semicolons. Add the correct punctuation, or omit any unnecessary mark. [27]
   1. Every good soldier of Jesus Christ needs: devotion, dedication, fortitude, and courage.
   2. The following quotation from Psalm 9012 graces the front wall of our classroom, "So teach us to number our days, that we may apply our hearts unto wisdom."
   3. Obviously, we cannot count the number of days we have to live, however, God wants us to direct our lives each day by His heavenly wisdom.
   4. Only one Book in the world is perfect and infallible, the Bible.
   5. The promises of the Bible inspire us to serve God; and the warnings motivate us to shun all evil.

. Copy the items that need italics, apostrophes, or hyphens. Add the underlining or the missing marks. [30, 31]
   1. We found some interesting information about the geography of Palestine in Baker's Bible Atlas.
   2. The Spanish word for hospital is spelled the same as the English word; however, its not pronounced the same.
   3. The t in apostle is silent.
   4. Because of the snow covered roads, we werent able to reach Grandfathers place until 9 oclock in the evening.
   5. My brother in law preached the morning message at our all day meeting.
   6. My two, seven, and ten year old brothers all have birthdays in mid July.

6. predicts

C. (Individual work.)

D.

Come

Person	Singular	Plural
Present Tense		
First:	I come.	We come.
Second:	You come.	You come.
Third:	He comes.	They come.
Past Tense		
First:	I came.	We came.
Second:	You came.	You came.
Third:	He came.	They came.
Future Tense		
First:	I shall come.	We shall come.
Second:	You will come.	You will come.
Third:	He will come.	They will come.

Review Exercises

A. 1. needs   4. infallible:
   2. 90: classroom: 5. God,
   3. live;

B. 1. <u>Baker's Bible Atlas</u>
   2. <u>hospital</u>, it's
   3. <u>t</u>, <u>apostle</u>
   4. snow-covered, weren't, Grandfather's, o'clock
   5. brother-in-law, all-day
   6. two-, seven-, ten-year-old, mid-July

49. Perfect Verb Tenses

> ### Lesson Survey
>
> - In the **perfect tenses,** the third principal part of the main verb is used with a form of *have* as a helping verb.
> - The **present perfect tense** indicates an action or a condition that began in the past and is completed as of the present time or continues into the present.
> - The **past perfect tense** indicates an action or a condition that was completed by a certain time in the past.
> - The **future perfect tense** indicates an action or a condition that will be completed by a certain time in the future.

In Lesson 48 you reviewed the three simple tenses. There are also three corresponding perfect tenses. In English grammar, the word *perfect* retains its archaic meaning of "mature; complete." The perfect tenses therefore express *completed* action or existence.

In the *perfect tenses,* the third principal part of the main verb is used with a form of *have* as a helping verb. Since the main verb is the same, the perfect tenses are distinguished by the helping verbs. The present forms *have* and *has* are used for present perfect, the past form *had* for past perfect, and the future forms *shall have* and *will have* for future perfect.

Present perfect tense: have finished *or* has finished
Past perfect tense: had finished
Future perfect tense: shall have finished *or* will have finished

The *present perfect tense* indicates an action or a condition that began in the past and is completed as of the present time or continues into the present.

Simeon <u>has mowed</u> the grass.
    (The action of mowing began in the past and is now completed.)
The weather <u>has been</u> warm for several days.
    (The condition of being warm began in the past and continues into the present.)

Both the simple past and the present perfect tenses refer to actions or conditions in the past. However, the simple past merely states that something happened at some time in the past—recently or long ago, of short or long duration. In contrast, the present perfect emphasizes that the action or condition *began* in the past, but it either is completed at the present moment or continues into the present time.

Lesson 49

Purpose: To study the formation of the perfect tenses and the time relationships they show.

Oral Review:

1. Name the three simple tenses, and tell which principal part of a verb is used for each one. (present tense—first principal part; past tense—second principal part; future tense—first principal part)
2. When should you use *shall* and when should you use *will* for the future tense in formal English? (*shall* for first person subjects; *will* for second and third person subjects)
3. For what purposes should you reverse this pattern? (to show determination, compulsion, or promise)
4. Give the second and third principal parts of these verbs.

a. hit (hit, [have] hit)
b. know (knew, [have] known)
c. creep (crept, [have] crept)
d. go (went, [have] gone)
e. tag (tagged, [have] tagged)
f. drown (drowned, [have] drowned)

5. Give the foreign plural spelling for each group o nouns.
a. ending with -*on* or -*um* (ending with -*a*)
b. ending with -*is* (ending with -*es*)
c. ending with -*a* (ending with -*ae*)
d. ending with -*ex* or -*ix* (ending with -*ices*)
e. ending with -*us* (ending with -*i*)

6. Name and describe the two kinds of verbals tha can be used as nouns. (gerund—the -*ing* form o a verb; infinitive—the basic form of a verb pre ceded by *to*)

Simple past:
> Dale <u>found</u> sixteen mushrooms in the woods.
>> (At some time in the past—today, last week, or last year—he found the mushrooms. He is not finding any at the present time.)

Present perfect:
> Dale <u>has found</u> sixteen mushrooms in the woods.
>> (He began finding them in the recent past and apparently just found the last one. Therefore this action is completed at the present time.)

Simple past:
> We <u>lived</u> in Missouri for five years.
>> (At some time in the past—a year ago or ten years ago—we lived there. Apparently we no longer live there.)

Present perfect:
> We <u>have lived</u> in Missouri for five years.
>> (We began living there five years ago and apparently still live there.)

The *past perfect tense* indicates an action or a condition that was completed by a certain time in the past. Whenever this tense is used, two past actions or conditions must be stated or implied. The action or condition that was completed first must be expressed in the past perfect tense.

Incomplete: Only one past action
> The boys <u>had finished</u> their chores.

Complete: Two past actions stated
> The boys <u>had finished</u> their chores before Father <u>returned</u>.

Complete: Two past actions, the second one implied
> The boys <u>had finished</u> their chores before Father's arrival.

The past perfect tense has two specific uses. First, it may be needed to clarify which of two past actions or conditions occurred first. Second, it may place special emphasis on the fact that one action or condition was completed at the time of the other one. Compare the differences in meaning and emphasis in the following sentences.

Not clear: Sounds as if the two actions occurred at the same time
> We <u>read</u> what the teacher <u>wrote</u>.

Clear: Clarifies that the writing came first
> We <u>read</u> what the teacher <u>had written</u>.

Completed action not emphasized: Both verbs in simple past tense
> Aunt Sue <u>arrived</u> before Father and Mother <u>left</u>.

Lesson Introduction: In the Book of Hebrews we read that "the law made nothing perfect." Does this mean that the Old Testament was a failure? No; it simply means that it was not complete. The Old Testament pointed forward to and prepared the way for the New Testament, and the New Testament completed the Old.

This meaning of *perfect* is important to understanding the perfect tenses. They emphasize that an action or a condition has been completed.

Lesson Outline:

1. In the perfect tenses, the third principal part of the main verb is used with a form of **have** *as a helping verb.*

    a. The perfect tenses are distinguished by the helping verbs.

    b. The present forms *have* and *has* are used for present perfect.

    c. The past form *had* is used for past perfect.

    d. The future forms *shall have* and *will have* are used for future perfect.

2. The present perfect tense indicates an action or a condition that began in the past and is completed as of the present time or continues into the present.

    a. The simple past tense merely states that something happened at some time in the past.

    b. The present perfect tense emphasizes that the action or condition *began* in the past, but it either is completed at the present moment or continues into the present time.

3. The past perfect tense indicates an action or a condition that was completed by a certain time in the past.

Completed action emphasized: First action in past perfect tense
Aunt Sue <u>had arrived</u> before Father and Mother <u>left</u>.

The *future perfect tense* indicates an action or a condition that will be completed by a certain time in the future. The future perfect must state or imply two actions or conditions. The action or condition that will be completed first must be expressed in the future perfect tense; the other action may be expressed in the simple future tense or the present tense.

Incomplete: Only one future action
Sister Mabel <u>will have lived</u> for ninety years.

Complete: Two future actions stated
Sister Mabel <u>will have lived</u> for ninety years when she has her next birthday.

Complete: Two future actions, the second one implied
Sister Mabel <u>will have lived</u> for ninety years by the time of her next birthday.

The future perfect tense can be used for the same two purposes as the past perfect tense. It may clarify which of two actions or conditions will be completed first, and it may emphasize that one action or condition will be completed by the time the other begins. Compare the differences in meaning and emphasis in the following sentences.

Not clear: Sounds as if Brother Ivan will teach *after* this term
When this school term <u>is</u> over, Brother Ivan <u>will teach</u> for ten years.

Clear: Clarifies that the teaching will be completed when the term ends
When this school term <u>is</u> over, Brother Ivan <u>will have taught</u> for ten years.

Completed action not emphasized: Both actions in simple tenses
Before you <u>finish</u> eighth grade, you <u>will write</u> many sentences.

Completed action emphasized: First action in future perfect tense
Before you <u>finish</u> eighth grade, you <u>will have written</u> many sentences.

Here are the conjugations of the verbs *be* and *go* in the perfect tenses.

Be

Person	Singular	Plural
	Present Perfect Tense	
First:	I have been.	We have been.
Second:	You have been.	You have been.
Third:	He has been.	They have been.

a. Two past actions or conditions must be stated or implied, and the action or condition that was completed first must be expressed in the past perfect tense.

b. The past perfect tense may be used to clarify which of two past actions or conditions occurred first.

c. The past perfect tense may be used to emphasize that one action or condition was completed at the time of the other one.

4. The future perfect tense indicates an action or a condition that will be completed by a certain time in the future.

a. Two actions or conditions must be stated or implied, and the action or condition that will be completed first must be expressed in the future perfect tense.

b. The future perfect tense may be used to clarify which of two actions or conditions will be completed first.

c. The future perfect tense may be used to emphasize that one action or condition will be completed by the time the other begins.

★ **EXTRA PRACTICE**
Worksheet 17 *(Perfect Verb Tenses)*

Past Perfect Tense

	Singular	Plural
First:	I had been.	We had been.
Second:	You had been.	You had been.
Third:	He had been.	They had been.

Future Perfect Tense

	Singular	Plural
First:	I shall have been.	We shall have been.
Second:	You will have been.	You will have been.
Third:	He will have been.	They will have been.

Go

Person	Singular	Plural

Present Perfect Tense

	Singular	Plural
First:	I have gone.	We have gone.
Second:	You have gone.	You have gone.
Third:	He has gone.	They have gone.

Past Perfect Tense

	Singular	Plural
First:	I had gone.	We had gone.
Second:	You had gone.	You had gone.
Third:	He had gone.	They had gone.

Future Perfect Tense

	Singular	Plural
First:	I shall have gone.	We shall have gone.
Second:	You will have gone.	You will have gone.
Third:	He will have gone.	They will have gone.

Class Practice

A. Read each verb or verb phrase, and tell which of the six tenses it is.
1. The largest desert in the world has been named *Sahara,* which means "desert."
2. It extends across northern Africa and is nearly as large as the United States.
3. Strangely enough, frosts will sometimes occur there in winter.
4. The only places where you will see crops are at the oases.
5. You will not find many animals in such a dry place.
6. Long before modern times, nomadic tribes had occupied the oases of this land.
7. In the course of a lifetime, many of these nomads will have traveled over vast areas of the desert.
8. Despite dangers that threaten, many camel caravans have crossed this desert.
9. Before anyone crosses the Sahara, he will have made careful preparations for the long, dangerous journey.
10. Travelers can expect to see mirages along the way.

Lesson 49 Answers

Class Practice

A. 1. has been named—present perfect; means—present
2. extends—present; is—present
3. will occur—future
4. will see—future; are—present
5. will find—future
6. had occupied—past perfect
7. will have traveled—future perfect
8. threaten—present; have crossed—present perfect
9. crosses—present; will have made—future perfect
10. can expect—present

B. Read each sentence, using the tense shown in italics for the verb in parentheses.
   1. By the time of the spelling test, I (review) these words many times. *future perfect*
   2. So far I never (make) a perfect score on a spelling test. *present perfect*
   3. But if my sister makes a perfect score, she (do) so for the sixth week in a row. *future perfect*
   4. Although I forgot about it this morning, Father (tell) me to clean out the van. *past perfect*
   5. The cheery canary (bring) some pleasure to old Mrs. Harding. *present perfect*

C. Read each sentence, changing one verb to a perfect tense so that the meaning is clear.
   1. A person who learned contentment will be satisfied with little in life.
   2. God delivered Lot out of Sodom because Abraham interceded for him.
   3. When the Red Sea swept over the Egyptians, the Israelites crossed safely over.
   4. We shall observe many wonders of nature by the time this hike is over.
   5. When a plane from Cleveland arrives in Seattle, it will fly two thousand miles.

D. Conjugate the verb *choose* in the three perfect tenses.

Written Exercises

A. Copy each verb or verb phrase, and write which of the six tenses it is.
   1. No man makes himself holy by his own power.
   2. A person will find overcoming power only as he depends on the Lord.
   3. Although Jesus had known the full glory of the Godhead, He willingly became a man.
   4. Jesus has brought eternal salvation through His death on Calvary.
   5. Before the saints enter heaven, Jesus will have prepared a place for them.
   6. By the time the snowstorm ended, we had received ten inches of snow.
   7. Since a strong wind had blown during the storm, there were many deep drifts.
   8. We shall fix the fence this morning since the steers broke through it.
   9. Grandfather Williams has lived with us since he had a stroke.
   10. If it rains tomorrow, we shall have had rain every day this week.

B. Write the correct verb form for the tense shown in italics.
   1. My mother (have) several poems published. *present perfect*
   2. She (write) her first poem before she turned ten. *past perfect*
   3. By tomorrow evening, I (do) Uncle Harvey's chores for two weeks. *future perfect*

B. 1. shall have reviewed   4. had told
   2. have made   5. has brought
   3. will have done

C. (Corrections are underlined.)
   1. A person who <u>has learned</u> contentment will be satisfied with little in life.
   2. God delivered Lot out of Sodom because Abraham <u>had interceded</u> for him.
   3. When the Red Sea swept over the Egyptians, the Israelites <u>had crossed</u> safely over.
   4. We <u>shall have observed</u> many wonders of nature by the time this hike is over.
   5. When a plane from Cleveland arrives in Seattle, it <u>will have flown</u> two thousand miles.

D.

Choose

Person	Singular	Plural

Present Perfect Tense

First:	I have chosen.	We have chosen.
Second:	You have chosen.	You have chosen.
Third:	He has chosen.	They have chosen.

Past Perfect Tense

First:	I had chosen.	We had chosen.
Second:	You had chosen.	You had chosen.
Third:	He had chosen.	They had chosen.

Future Perfect Tense

First:	I shall have chosen.	We shall have chosen.
Second:	You will have chosen.	You will have chosen.
Third:	He will have chosen.	They will have chosen.

Written Exercises

A. 1. makes—present
    2. will find—future; depends—present
    3. had known—past perfect; became—past
    4. has brought—present perfect
    5. enter—present;
       will have prepared—future perfect
    6. ended—past; had received—past perfect
    7. had blown—past perfect; were—past
    8. shall fix—future; broke—past
    9. has lived—present perfect; had—past
    10. rains—present;
        shall have had—future perfect

B. 1. has had   3. shall have done
   2. had written

4. The colored leaves (declare) the coming of fall. *present perfect*

5. Within a few days, the sheep (eat) all the grass in this pasture. *future perfect*

C. Write each of these sentences, using a perfect tense to express the action or condition that occurred first.

1. King Manasseh worshiped idols before, but now he served the Lord.

2. When Abraham left Egypt, he returned to Bethel.

3. Because Solomon sought the Lord earnestly, God richly blessed him.

4. Before the day is over, we shall drive into Illinois.

5. At this rate, the pigs will ruin the garden by the time we get them out.

D. Conjugate the verb *come* in the three perfect tenses.

Review Exercises

A. Write the correct plural spelling of each word. Use the foreign spellings for numbers 8–12. [36]

1. patio
2. loaf
3. quality
4. salmon
5. motto
6. proof
7. nobleman
8. memorandum
9. stimulus
10. analysis
11. formula
12. appendix

B. Write the correct possessive spelling of each word. [37]

1. eagle
2. eagles
3. Moses
4. geese
5. apostles
6. son-in-law
7. sons-in-law
8. filly
9. fillies
10. Lois

C. Write whether each underlined verbal phrase is a gerund phrase (*GP*) or an infinitive phrase (*IP*). Also write whether the phrase is a subject (*S*), a direct object (*DO*), a predicate nominative (*PN*), or the object of a preposition (*OP*). [40]

1. Our desire should be to serve the Lord with gladness.

2. Our gratitude to the Lord can be shown by surrendering to His will.

3. Obeying those in authority is an important part of obeying God.

4. God desires to bless our lives abundantly.

D. If the underlined clause is a noun clause, write whether it is a subject (*S*), a direct object (*DO*), a predicate nominative (*PN*), or an object of a preposition (*OP*). If it is not a noun clause, write *none*. [41]

1. Whoever prays to God in sincere faith can be assured of an answer.

2. God does not necessarily give whatever we wish for.

3. Whenever we pray, we must pray according to His will.

4. Our deepest desire should be that God's will is done.

5. God's purposes can be performed through whoever yields to His will.

---

4. have declared   5. will have eaten

C. 1. King Manasseh had worshiped idols before, but now he served the Lord.

2. When Abraham had left Egypt, he returned to Bethel.

3. Because Solomon had sought the Lord earnestly, God richly blessed him.

4. Before the day is over, we shall have driven into Illinois.

5. At this rate, the pigs will have ruined the garden by the time we get them out.

D.

Come

Person	Singular	Plural
	Present Perfect Tense	
First:	I have come.	We have come.
Second:	You have come.	You have come.
Third:	He has come.	They have come.
	Past Perfect Tense	
First:	I had come.	We had come.
Second:	You had come.	You had come.
Third:	He had come.	They had come.
	Future Perfect Tense	
First:	I shall have come.	We shall have come.
Second:	You will have come.	You will have come.
Third:	He will have come.	They will have come.

Review Exercises

A. 1. patios
2. loaves
3. qualities
4. salmon
5. mottoes *or* mottos
6. proofs
7. noblemen
8. memoranda
9. stimuli
10. analyses
11. formulae
12. appendices

B. 1. eagle's
2. eagles'
3. Moses'
4. geese's
5. apostles'
6. son-in-law's
7. sons-in-law's
8. filly's
9. fillies'
10. Lois's

C. 1. IP, PN
2. GP, OP
3. GP, S
4. IP, DO

D. 1. S
2. DO
3. none
4. PN
5. OP

50. Simple, Progressive, and Emphatic Forms of Verbs

Lesson Survey

- The **simple form** of a verb expresses an action or a condition as simply as possible.
- The **progressive form** uses the present participle and a form of *be* as a helping verb.
- The **emphatic form** uses the first principal part and a form of *do* as a helping verb.

As you have studied in Lessons 48 and 49, verbs have different forms to show tense. But a verb can have several different forms and still be in the same tense. Compare the following sentences. They are all in the present tense, and they all communicate the same basic idea. Yet three different forms are used.

We <u>serve</u> the Lord with reverence.
We <u>are serving</u> the Lord with reverence.
We <u>do serve</u> the Lord with reverence.

The three different forms in the sentences above are the simple form, the progressive form, and the emphatic form. The *simple form* of a verb expresses an action or a condition as simply as possible. No helping verb is used except *shall* or *will* in a future tense, or a form of *have* in a perfect tense. The simple form is the form that you immediately think of when you are asked to give a particular verb in any tense.

Simple form:
    Present: I <u>see</u> the woodchuck.
    Past: I <u>saw</u> the woodchuck yesterday.
    Future: I <u>shall see</u> the woodchuck again.
    Present perfect: I <u>have seen</u> the woodchuck often.
    Past perfect: I <u>had seen</u> the woodchuck many times before.
    Future perfect: I <u>shall have seen</u> the woodchuck every day
                   this week if I see it today.

The *progressive form* of a verb uses the present participle (*-ing* form) and a form of *be* as a helping verb. Unlike the simple form, the progressive form emphasizes that an action or a condition is in progress. All six tenses can be written in the progressive form. The perfect tenses must

Lesson 50

Purpose: To study the simple, progressive, and emphatic forms of verbs.

Oral Review:

1. What does *perfect* mean in English grammar? (completed)
2. Give the helping verbs used for each of the three perfect tenses. (*present perfect:* have *or* has; *past perfect:* had; *future perfect:* shall have *or* will have)
3. (*a*) How is the present perfect tense similar to the simple past tense? (*b*) How is it different? (*a.* Both refer to a happening in the past. *b.* The present perfect tense indicates an action or a condition that began in the past and is completed as of the present moment or continues into the present time, whereas the simple past merely states that something happened at some time in the past.)
4. What are the two uses for the past perfect tense (to clarify which of two past actions or conditions occurred first; to emphasize that one action or condition was completed at the time of the other one)
5. What are the two uses for the future perfect tense? (to clarify which of two actions or conditions will be completed first; to emphasize that one action or condition will be completed by the time the other begins)
6. Commas, dashes, and parentheses can be used to set off parenthetical elements. Tell how each kind of punctuation affects a parenthetical element. (Commas make it a part of the sentence; dashes sharply emphasize it; parentheses minimize its importance.)
7. If an omission within a quotation comes after a complete sentence, would you use three or four periods? (four)

nclude both a form of *be* and a form of *have* as helping verbs. Compare
he following sentences.

Simple form: General statement
 They <u>work</u> today.
 They <u>worked</u> yesterday.
 They <u>will work</u> tomorrow.
 They <u>have worked</u> all week.
 They <u>had worked</u> until we came.
 They <u>will have worked</u> two hours before we arrive.

Progressive form: Action in progress
 They <u>are working</u> today.
 They <u>were working</u> yesterday.
 They <u>will be working</u> tomorrow.
 They <u>have been working</u> all week.
 They <u>had been working</u> until we came.
 They <u>will have been working</u> two hours before we arrive.

The *emphatic form* of a verb uses the first principal part and a form of
do as a helping verb. As its name suggests, this form gives added emphasis, perhaps in response to a question or doubt. The emphatic form exists
only in the present and past tenses. Compare the following sentences.

Simple form: General statement   **Emphatic form:** Added emphasis
 We <u>believe</u> the Bible.   We <u>do believe</u> the Bible.
 I <u>finished</u> my lesson.   I <u>did finish</u> my lesson.

Not every verb phrase with a form of *do* is an emphatic form. *Do, does,*
and *did* also function as helping verbs in questions and negative statements. The verb in such a sentence is not emphatic.

<u>Did</u> Louella <u>bake</u> bread today? (question—not emphatic)
No, she <u>did</u> not <u>bake</u> bread yet. (negative statement—not emphatic)
She <u>does bake</u> bread nearly every Saturday. (emphatic statement)

Here are the conjugations of *see* in the simple, progressive, and emphatic
forms.

See

Person	Singular	Plural
	Present Tense, Simple Form	
First:	I see.	We see.
Second:	You see.	You see.
Third:	He sees.	They see.

8. What are two uses of brackets? (to enclose a com-
    ment or correction within a quotation; to serve as
    parentheses within parentheses)

Lesson Introduction: At the Zimmerman household, one of Mary Ellen's regular jobs is feeding the
calves. Aunt Lorraine, who has come to visit, is touring the farm with the children and asks who feeds
the calves. Using a form of the verb *feed,* tell what
answer the children would give. ("Mary Ellen feeds
the calves.") One morning, while Mary Ellen is in the
middle of the job, Father asks her sister where Mary
Ellen is. Again using a form of the verb *feed,* give her
sister's response. ("Mary Ellen is feeding the calves.")
Suppose her brother says that she does the job carelessly. Again using a form of the verb *feed,* give Mary
Ellen's answer that she does a careful job. ("I do feed
the calves carefully.") These responses illustrate the

need for varying forms of verbs in the same tense. In
this lesson we shall study the simple, progressive, and
emphatic forms of verbs.

Lesson Outline:

*1. The simple form of a verb expresses an ac-
tion or a condition as simply as possible.* No
helping verb is used except *shall* or *will* in a future
tense, or a form of *have* in a perfect tense.

*2. The progressive form of a verb uses the
present participle and a form of* be *as a helping verb.*

  a. This form emphasizes that an action or a
      condition is in progress.
  b. All six tenses can be written in the pro-
      gressive form.
  c. The perfect tenses must include both a form
      of *be* and a form of *have* as helping verbs.

Past Tense, Simple Form

First: I saw.   We saw.
Second: You saw.   You saw.
Third: He saw.   They saw.

Future Tense, Simple Form

First: I shall see.   We shall see.
Second: You will see.   You will see.
Third: He will see.   They will see.

Present Perfect Tense, Simple Form

First: I have seen.   We have seen.
Second: You have seen.   You have seen.
Third: He has seen.   They have seen.

Past Perfect Tense, Simple Form

First: I had seen.   We had seen.
Second: You had seen.   You had seen.
Third: He had seen.   They had seen.

Future Perfect Tense, Simple Form

First: I shall have seen.   We shall have seen.
Second: You will have seen.   You will have seen.
Third: He will have seen.   They will have seen.

Present Tense, Progressive Form

First: I am seeing.   We are seeing.
Second: You are seeing.   You are seeing.
Third: He is seeing.   They are seeing.

Past Tense, Progressive Form

First: I was seeing.   We were seeing.
Second: You were seeing.   You were seeing.
Third: He was seeing.   They were seeing.

Future Tense, Progressive Form

First: I shall be seeing.   We shall be seeing.
Second: You will be seeing.   You will be seeing.
Third: He will be seeing.   They will be seeing.

Present Perfect Tense, Progressive Form

First: I have been seeing.   We have been seeing.
Second: You have been seeing.   You have been seeing.
Third: He has been seeing.   They have been seeing.

Past Perfect Tense, Progressive Form

First: I had been seeing.   We had been seeing.
Second: You had been seeing.   You had been seeing.
Third: He had been seeing.   They had been seeing.

3. *The emphatic form of a verb uses the first principal part and a form of* do *as a helping verb.*

    a. This form gives added emphasis.

    b. This form exists only in the present and past tenses.

    c. The forms of *do* are also used in questions and negative statements. Such verbs are not emphatic forms.

Future Perfect Tense, Progressive Form
First: I shall have been seeing.   We shall have been seeing.
Second: You will have been seeing.   You will have been seeing.
Third: He will have been seeing.   They will have been seeing.

Present Tense, Emphatic Form
First: I do see.   We do see.
Second: You do see.   You do see.
Third: He does see.   They do see.

Past Tense, Emphatic Form
First: I did see.   We did see.
Second: You did see.   You did see.
Third: He did see.   They did see.

Class Practice

A. Tell whether each verb form is *simple, progressive,* or *emphatic.*
  1. Have you been guarding your attitudes carefully?
  2. Do you recognize the importance of wholesome thoughts?
  3. Our thoughts do reveal themselves in words and actions.
  4. We do not build good character by careless thoughts.
  5. God does have a keen interest in our thoughts.

B. Read each sentence, changing the verb to the progressive form. Do not change the tense of the verb.
  1. God's angels watch over the righteous.
  2. Ever since the Fall, the devil has tempted man.
  3. In the years before the Flood, Satan had succeeded almost entirely in his efforts.
  4. Only Noah and his family served the Lord faithfully.
  5. By the end of time, God's people will have resisted the devil for hundreds of years.
  6. Satan will war against God until his final defeat.

C. Read each sentence, changing the verb to the emphatic form. Do not change the tense of the verb.
  1. We began our chores at the regular time.
  2. Marie tries to be a peacemaker.
  3. They help us many times.

D. Make up short sentences for these descriptions, using pronouns and the correct verb forms.
  1. First person plural, past tense, progressive form of *think.*
  2. Second person, present tense, emphatic form of *need.*
  3. Third person singular, present perfect tense, progressive form of *speak.*

Lesson 50 Answers

Class Practice

A. 1. progressive   4. simple
   2. simple   5. emphatic
   3. emphatic

B. 1. God's angels are watching over the righteous.
   2. Ever since the Fall, the devil has been tempting man.
   3. In the years before the Flood, Satan had been succeeding almost entirely in his efforts.
   4. Only Noah and his family were serving the Lord faithfully.
   5. By the end of time, God's people will have been resisting the devil for hundreds of years.
   6. Satan will be warring against God until his final defeat.

C. 1. We did begin our chores at the regular time.
   2. Marie does try to be a peacemaker.
   3. They do help us many times.

D. 1. We were thinking.
   2. You do need.
   3. He (she, it) has been speaking.

Written Exercises

A. Label each underlined verb *simple, progressive,* or *emphatic.*
1. The rain <u>has been falling</u> steadily for several hours.
2. If it keeps falling this fast, by evening we <u>shall have gotten</u> several inches of rain.
3. For the last month we <u>have been having</u> dry weather.
4. We certainly <u>do thank</u> God for this beautiful rain.
5. Man <u>does</u> not <u>control</u> the weather.
6. If we <u>do trust</u> God, we will not complain about the weather.

B. Write the progressive form of the verb in each sentence. Do not change the tense.
1. For some time, Judas had sought an opportunity to betray Jesus.
2. During Jesus' agony in the Garden, the disciples slept.
3. Jesus' submission to the Father has served as an example to believers ever since.
4. No doubt before your thirtieth birthday, you will have found much inspiration from this account.
5. Now Jesus intercedes at the Father's right hand for us.
6. By God's grace, we will serve Him faithfully all the days of our lives.
7. Other faithful people inspire us to be faithful as well.
8. In the glorious future, God's people of all ages will enjoy eternal bliss.

C. Write the emphatic form of the verb in each sentence. Do not change the tense.
1. The Bible has the answers to all man's needs.
2. We believe its promises.
3. God miraculously preserved His Word through the centuries.
4. God speaks to us through His Word.

D. Write short sentences for these descriptions, using pronouns and the correct verb forms.
1. First person plural, past tense, emphatic form of *eat*
2. Third person singular, present tense, progressive form of *teach.*
3. Second person, present perfect tense, progressive form of *grow.*
4. Third person, plural, present tense, emphatic form of *draw.*
5. First person, singular, past tense, progressive form of *shake.*
6. Third person, singular, present tense, emphatic form of *forget.*
7. Second person, past tense, emphatic form of *bear.*
8. First person plural, present perfect tense, progressive form of *send.*

Review Exercises

A. Copy these sentences, adding commas, dashes, or parentheses where needed. Some sentences have notes to direct you. [29]

Written Exercises

A. 1. progressive
2. simple
3. progressive
4. emphatic
5. simple
6. emphatic

B. 1. had been seeking
2. were sleeping
3. has been serving
4. will have been finding
5. is interceding
6. will be serving
7. are inspiring
8. will be enjoying

C. 1. does have
2. do believe
3. did preserve
4. does speak

D. 1. We did eat.
2. He (she, it) is teaching.
3. You have been growing.
4. They do draw.
5. I was shaking.
6. He (she, it) does forget.
7. You did bear.
8. We have been sending.

1. King Solomon renowned for his great wisdom collected and wrote many proverbs. (Make the parenthetical element part of the sentence.)
2. King Solomon exceptionally wise yet extremely foolish fell into the very snares that he had warned about. (Give sharp emphasis to the parenthetical element.)
3. King Solomon he was the last king of Israel before the nation divided sowed many of the seeds of division. (Minimize the importance of the parenthetical element.)
4. "Is everyone ready to oh, who's coming in the lane?" asked Father.
5. Father wants the family to help with the following jobs: 1 clean out the garage, 2 dig potatoes, and 3 remove the stakes from the garden.

B. Copy these sentences, adding ellipsis points and brackets where needed. [22, 29]
1. "Rejoice evermore. In every thing give thanks" (1 Thessalonians 5:16, 18).
2. "For the grace of God hath appeared to all men" (Titus 2:11).
3. "I met Harry Swartz do you remember when he lived next door? in town today," Father said.
4. "I wonder if he remembers the time" Mother paused.

---

51. Giving an Oral Report

Lesson Survey

- In preparing for an **oral report,** use the following steps.
  1. Decide how you will describe and illustrate the points on your outline.
  2. Write the exact words of the introduction and the conclusion.
  3. Write your outline in a form that is easy to follow.
  4. Practice giving the report at home.
- In giving an oral report, remember the following points.
  1. Your appearance and speaking will be the most natural if you are relaxed.
  2. Eye contact with your audience will help you to communicate effectively.
  3. Use proper volume and enunciation so that you can be clearly understood.
  4. Avoid any appearance or habit that will distract from what you say.
  5. Do not forget to depend upon the Lord.

Lesson 51

Purpose: To present guidelines for giving an oral report.

Oral Review:

1. Give the two main steps in organizing the information that you gather on note cards. (Sort the cards into general categories. Organize them as main topics and supporting points.)
2. Why should you take notes for a report from more than one reference source? (to have a balanced report, to require you to express ideas in your own words, to verify facts)
3. Why is it good to find information in a book, if possible, rather than only in encyclopedia articles? (A book on the subject usually gives more details.)

Lesson Introduction: Does the idea of giving an oral report make you nervous? It should! If you

Review Exercises

A. 1. King Solomon, renowned for his great wisdom, collected and wrote many proverbs.
   2. King Solomon—exceptionally wise yet extremely foolish—fell into the very snares that he had warned about.
   3. King Solomon (he was the last king of Israel before the nation divided) sowed many of the seeds of division.
   4. "Is everyone ready to—oh, who's coming in the lane?" asked Father.
   5. Father wants the family to help with the following jobs: (1) clean out the garage, (2) dig potatoes, and (3) remove the stakes from the garden.

B. 1. "Rejoice evermore. . . . In every thing give thanks" (1 Thessalonians 5:16, 18).
   2. "For the grace of God . . . hath appeared to all men" (Titus 2:11).
   3. "I met Harry Swartz [do you remember when he lived next door?] in town today," Father said.
   4. "I wonder if he remembers the time . . ." Mother paused.

approach the report with no feelings of nervousness, you are likely too proud of your abilities. And you are setting yourself up for a major, embarrassing failure!

However, you should not use your nervousness as an excuse not to try or to do less than your best. There are ways to overcome some of your nervousness, and this lesson will teach you some of those ways.

Lesson Outline:

1. To prepare for an oral report, first decide how you will describe and illustrate the points on your outline. Go through the outline point by point, trying to think of ideas that will make your report interesting.

2. Write the exact words of the introduction and the conclusion.

Preparing for an Oral Report

In Lesson 47 you learned how to organize notes into an outline. Here is the partial outline that you were given.

Canals in Pennsylvania

I. Why they were built
- A. William Penn's proposal for a canal linking Susquehanna and Delaware Rivers
- B. Expense of hauling heavy loads on turnpikes
- C. Threat of Erie Canal in New York taking trade away from Pennsylvania cities

Such an outline, however, is only the skeleton of a finished report. If you were to go to the front of the room with just this, your report would likely be a boring recital of bare facts.

> Why did the people of Pennsylvania build a vast system of canals in the middle 1800s? For one thing, William Penn had proposed a canal linking the Susquehanna River and the Delaware River. Another reason was the high expense of hauling heavy loads on the turnpikes. Finally, there was the threat of the Erie Canal in New York taking trade away from Pennsylvania cities.

What you need to do is think of ways to describe and illustrate these facts. As you look at point A, you might remember from your research that Penn considered such a canal to be an economic necessity. You might also note that the Union Canal, built in 1827, followed his proposed route, and that Penn died over one hundred years before that canal was built.

In presenting point B, you should comment on why it was very expensive to haul freight by wagon. Freight companies had to pay toll for using many of the roads and bridges. They also had to maintain their wagons, pay their drivers, and feed and care for six-horse teams for the entire round trip. For point C, you should research briefly the route of the Erie Canal and discover why it would threaten Pennsylvania's share of the western trade.

Do you see how these additional ideas would make your report much more interesting?

> Why did the people of Pennsylvania build a vast system of canals in the middle 1800s? For one thing, William Penn had proposed a canal linking the Susquehanna River and the Delaware River. In his mind, such a canal was necessary for the economic development of the colony. Interestingly enough, the Union Canal, built in 1827, did follow his proposed route. When you consider that Penn died over

    a. The introduction sets the tone for the report.
    b. An effective introduction could be an interesting observation, an illustration, a thought-provoking question, a familiar quotation, or a direct statement.
    c. The introduction should weave in the title of the report.
    d. The conclusion should briefly summarize the main points or give a call to some response or action.

    3. Write your outline in a form that is easy to follow.
    a. Recopy the outline if necessary.
    b. Write your outline on note cards.
      1) Cards are easier to handle without causing distractions than one large sheet of paper is.

      2) It is easier to keep your place in your outline when it is on cards.

4. Practice giving your report.
    a. Know how to pronounce any difficult words.
    b. Let others point out how you can improve your report.
    c. Have someone time you, and then increase or decrease the amount of material you cover.

5. In giving an oral report, remember that your appearance and speaking will be the most natural if you are relaxed.
    a. Being well prepared is perhaps the most important help for being relaxed.
    b. Before standing up, breathe deeply and evenly several times.
    c. Remember that even experienced speakers get nervous and that a little nervousness can help to motivate you to do your best.

one hundred years before this canal was finished, you will see that he had amazing foresight.

Another reason for building canals was the expense of hauling heavy loads on the turnpikes. Freight companies had to pay toll to use many roads and bridges, and the charge for heavy loads was often quite high. Also, heavy loads put much strain on wagons and added significantly to the cost of maintaining them. In addition to these expenses, freight companies had to pay their drivers as well as feed and care for six-horse teams during the entire round trip. . . .

When expanding your outline in this way, how much should you write? needs to be enough so that you will not forget the ideas you want to clude. Yet you should not write too much, or your report will be little ore than an oral reading exercise. Therefore, write just enough (in phrases brief sentences) to remind you of the points you want to cover. Then hen you give your report, you can use your outline as a guide and prent each point in your own words as you come to it.

Here is what the first part of the outline may look like when you are ady to give your report.

Canals in Pennsylvania

I. Why they were built
  A. William Penn's proposal for a canal linking Susquehanna and Delaware Rivers
    — considered necessary for economic development
    — Union Canal of 1827 followed his proposed route
    — Penn died over 100 years before that
  B. Expense of hauling heavy loads on turnpikes
    — tolls on many roads and bridges; high for heavy loads
    — heavy loads added to cost of maintaining wagons
    — pay drivers
    — feed and care for six-horse teams
  C. Threat of Erie Canal taking trade away from Pennsylvania cities
    — was entirely in state of New York
    — linked Hudson River at Albany to Lake Erie at Buffalo
    — western freight passed through Erie Canal to New York City, bypassing Pa. cities
    — soon NYC was more important seaport than Philadelphia

Another important part of your preparation is to write the exact words f the introduction and the conclusion. The introduction sets the tone for the eport: your opening remarks will either spark or extinguish your listeners' iterest. An effective introduction could be an interesting observation, an

6. Eye contact with your audience will help you to communicate effectively.
  a. Do not begin speaking before you have turned around to face your audience.
  b. Let your eyes meet those of the listeners.

7. Use proper volume and enunciation so that you can be clearly understood.
  a. Speak loudly enough so that your listeners need not strain to hear you, but not so loudly that they feel uncomfortable.
  b. Open your mouth well so that you do not mumble.
  c. Be sure that you have finished your last sentence before you start back to your seat.

8. Avoid any appearance or habit that will distract from what you say.
  a. Be neat and clean, and maintain good posture at all times.
  b. Filling your pauses with *uh*'s and *ah*'s or constantly clearing your throat will weaken the effect of your report.
  c. Frequently adjusting your glasses or your hair, putting your hands into and out of your pockets, changing your posture, or shuffling your note cards will distract your listeners.

9. Do not forget to depend upon the Lord.
  a. Pray that God will help you to communicate facts effectively.
  b. After giving the talk, resist the temptation to feel discouraged or proud.
  c. Thank God for helping you, and remember that God simply asks you to do your best for His glory.

illustration, a thought-provoking question, a familiar quotation, or even a direct statement. It should weave in the title of the report so that your audience will know exactly what you will be talking about. Look at these sample introductions for a report on "Canals in Pennsylvania."

Observation:

God has blessed Pennsylvania with three great river systems: the Delaware, the Susquehanna, and the Allegheny-Monongahela-Ohio. Each of these river systems was an important transportation route in the early days of Pennsylvania. Before 1827, however, there was no efficient way to carry loads from one river system to another. This report on canals in Pennsylvania will present a few facts about the canals that were built to help deal with this problem.

We shall first consider why these canals were built. . . .

Question:

Did you ever consider how the early settlers in Pennsylvania transported their goods east and west across the colony? There were numerous ranges of steep mountains blocking the way. Pennsylvania has three great river systems, but they run generally north to south. In this report on canals in Pennsylvania, we shall look at the canals used to help overcome this transportation problem in the 1800s.

We shall first consider why these canals were built. . . .

Quotation:

We sometimes hear the saying, "Necessity is the mother of invention." While the people of Pennsylvania did not invent canals, it was through a sense of necessity that they developed a great canal system during the first half of the 1800s. In this report on canals in Pennsylvania, we shall notice some facts about the canals of that era.

We shall first consider why these canals were built. . . .

Direct statement:

Between 1827 and 1860, the state of Pennsylvania constructed many miles of canals. As we think about these canals, we shall first consider why they were built. . . .

An effective conclusion is just as important as an effective introduction. Unless you have a carefully planned conclusion, you are likely to end your report either by stopping abruptly after your last point or by groping about for some suitable closing remarks. An effective conclusion is brief and either summarizes the main points of the report or gives a call to some response or action. Study these sample conclusions for a report on "Canals in Pennsylvania."

Summary:

We have considered why canals were built in Pennsylvania, what role they filled, why they were so soon discontinued, and what benefits they produced. Undoubtedly, canals filled an important place in the history of Pennsylvania.

Call to response:

As we consider the era of canals in Pennsylvania, we should be impressed with the way God has enabled man to overcome natural obstacles and to subdue the earth as God commissioned him. God deserves all the glory because He provides the understanding as well as the materials needed for all such accomplishments.

After you have expanded your outline with descriptions and illustrations and have written out your introduction and conclusion, you should make sure that the outline you use in giving your report is easy to follow. Recopy it if necessary. Putting your outline on several cards (4″ x 6″ or 5″ x 8″) is a good idea. These cards are easier to handle without causing distractions than one large sheet of paper is. Also, it is easier to keep your place in your outline when it is on note cards.

The final step in preparing for your report is to practice. Be sure you know how to pronounce any difficult words. If possible, practice before your parents or other people. Ask them to point out how you can improve your report. Also ask them to time you, and then increase or decrease the amount of material you cover so that your report is the proper length. But do not rely on this too much; for when you give your report at school, you may be more tense and speak faster than you do at home.

Giving an Oral Report

When the time comes to actually give your report, remember several important things. First, your appearance and speaking will be the most natural if you are relaxed. Perhaps the most important help for being relaxed is to prepare well beforehand. Plan to become so involved in your topic that you forget yourself and your nervousness.

To relieve tension before you stand up, breathe deeply and evenly several times. Even the most experienced speakers must sometimes make a special effort to relax before they stand up to speak. Do not worry if you still feel a bit tense; a little nervousness can help to motivate you to do your best.

Another important point is that eye contact with your audience will help you to communicate effectively. Do not begin speaking before you have turned around to face your audience. Let your eyes meet those of the listeners. Talk directly to them, not to your outline, to the floor, or to the walls.

Use proper volume and enunciation so that you can be clearly understood. Speak loudly enough so that your listeners need not strain to hear you, but not so loudly that they feel uncomfortable. Open your mouth well so that you do not mumble. Be sure that you have finished your last sentence before you start back to your seat.

Avoid any appearance or habit that will distract from what you say. Be neat and clean, and maintain good posture at all times. Do not fill your pauses with *uh*'s and *ah*'s, and avoid constantly clearing your throat; these things weaken the effect of your report. Likewise, frequently adjusting your glasses or your hair, putting your hands into and out of your pockets, changing your posture, or shuffling your note cards will distract your listeners.

In giving your oral report, as with any other task in life, do not forget to depend upon the Lord. Pray that God will help you to communicate facts effectively. After giving the talk, resist the temptation to feel discouraged or proud. Thank God for helping you, and remember that God simply asks you to do your best for His glory.

Here is an evaluation chart that summarizes many of the specific points you should remember. Your teacher will likely use this or a similar form to grade your oral report.

Evaluation of Oral Report

Points possible	Points earned	
5	____	**Introduction**
		No clear introduction (3 points)
		Introduction weak or poorly related to topic (4 points)
		Clear, interesting introduction (5 points)
5	____	**Content**
		Poor organization; weak development (3 points)
		Fairly good organization and development (4 points)
		Clear main points; effective development (5 points)
5	____	**Conclusion**
		No clear conclusion (3 points)
		Conclusion weak or poorly related to topic (4 points)
		Clear, effective conclusion (5 points)
5	____	**Eye contact**
		Looked constantly at outline (3 points)
		Looked up occasionally (4 points)
		Looked at audience frequently (5 points)
5	____	**Posture**
		Slouched; head down; feet askew (3 points)
		Had fairly good posture most of the time (4 points)
		Stood straight; head up; feet flat on floor (5 points)
5	____	**Volume and enunciation**
		Many words hard to understand (3 points)
		Occasional words hard to understand (4 points)
		Good volume and clear enunciation (5 points)
5	____	**Expression**
		Voice flat and droning (3 points)
		Good expression most of the time (4 points)
		Meaningful, enthusiastic expression (5 points)
5	____	**Preparation**
		Often fumbled for words; many awkward pauses (3 points)
		Occasionally hesitated for words (4 points)
		Spoke with little hesitation (5 points)
5	____	**Mannerisms**
		Distracting habits throughout report (3 points)
		Occasional distracting habits (4 points)
		No distracting habits (5 points)
5	____	**Time**
		Less than three minutes (3 points)
		From three to four minutes (4 points)
		From four to six minutes (5 points)
50	____	**Total points**

Class Practice

Suggest some interesting descriptions and illustrations to add to this partial outline from Lesson 35.

Clouds

I. Composed of moisture condensing out of saturated air
II. Formed as warm, moist air cools
   A. By nighttime cooling of earth
      1. Heat radiates from earth after sundown
      2. Air from warmer bodies of water moves over earth and cools
      3. Mist and fog may form
   B. By air rising and cooling
      1. Over mountains
         a. Frequent clouds above mountain peaks
         b. More rainfall on mountain slopes facing large bodies of water

Written Exercises

A. Go through your outline from Lesson 47, adding ideas for descriptions and illustrations. Have your teacher check your notes before you do Part B.

B. Give your oral report at your teacher's direction.

---

52. Transitive Verbs

> ### Lesson Survey
> - A **transitive verb** passes its action to a substantive in the sentence.
> - A transitive verb usually passes its action to a direct object.
> - A transitive verb with a direct object may also have an indirect object or an objective complement.
> - A transitive verb may pass its action to the subject.

You know that many action verbs are followed by direct and indirect objects (the object complements). Sentences with a pattern of subject-verb-direct object are among the most common in our English language. Such a sentence always has a transitive verb.

A *transitive verb* passes its action to a substantive in the sentence. The word *transitive* comes from a Latin word that means "passing over." Study

Lesson 52

Purpose: (1) To study transitive verbs. (2) To emphasize that they always pass action to another word in the sentence.

Oral Review:

1. In a progressive verb form, what form is used for the main verb and for the helping verb? *(main verb: present participle; helping verb: form of be)*

2. In an emphatic verb form, what form is used for the main verb and for the helping verb? *(main verb: first principal part; helping verb: form of do)*

3. Which tenses can be written *(a)* in the progressive form? *(b)* in the emphatic form? *(a.* all six tenses; *b.* present, past)

4. How is the present perfect tense different from the simple past tense? (The simple past tense

Lesson 51 Answers

Class Practice

(Added ideas are marked with dashes.)

Clouds

I. Composed of moisture condensing out of saturated air
   — *saturated* means "holding as much moisture as possible"
II. Formed as warm, moist air cools
   — like seeing breath on cold day
   A. By nighttime cooling of earth
      1. Heat radiates from earth after sundown
         — how quickly air cools off
      2. Air from warmer bodies of water moves over earth and cools
         — water holds heat longer than ground
      3. Mist and fog may form
   B. By air rising and cooling
      1. Over mountains
         a. Frequent clouds above mountain peaks
            — have you ever watched the clouds above Mount ———?
         b. More rainfall on mountain slopes facing large bodies of water
            — average annual precipitation between Pacific Ocean and Sierra Nevada is over 80 inches, compared with ——— inches in our area

Written Exercises

(All answers are individual work.)

---

merely states that something happened at some time in the past, whereas the present perfect tense indicates an action or a condition that began in the past and is completed as of the present moment or continues into the present time.)

5. What are the two uses for the past perfect tense? (to clarify which of two past actions or conditions occurred first; to emphasize that one action or condition was completed at the time of the other one)

6. What are the two uses for the future perfect tense? (to clarify which of two actions or conditions will be completed first; to emphasize that one action or condition will be completed by the time the other begins)

7. How can you tell whether an adjective clause or

he following sentences. The first sentence does not express a complete
ought, because it has a transitive verb but no word to receive the action.

> **Incomplete:** Jesus <u>bore</u> for us.
> **Complete:**   Jesus <u>bore</u> intense *suffering* for us.

There are two kinds of transitive verbs: those that pass their action to
direct object and those that pass their action to the subject.

ction Passed to a Direct Object

A transitive verb usually passes its action to a direct object. In a sen-
ence with a direct object, the subject performs the action and the direct
bject receives the action. To find a direct object, say the skeleton and ask
hom or *what* after it. Diagram the direct object on the horizontal line
fter the skeleton, separating it from the verb by a vertical line.

> A wise person makes careful choices in life.
>> (The subject *person* performs the action of making; the direct
>> object *choices* receives the action.)

A verb may pass its action to more than one substantive. In such a case,
iagram the compound direct object on a fork after the verb. If the subject
erforms more than one action and each verb passes its action to a direct
bject, diagram the compound verb on a fork with a direct object after each
erb.

> Wise choices produce true joy and peace.
>> (The subject *choices* performs the action of producing; the com-
>> pound direct object *joy* and *peace* receives the action.)

> True wisdom glorifies God and enriches godly people.
>> (The subject *wisdom* performs the actions of glorifying and enrich-
>> ing; the direct object *God* receives the action of glorifying, and
>> the direct object *people* receives the action of enriching.)

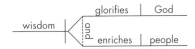

an appositive is restrictive or nonrestrictive? (It
is restrictive if it limits a substantive by telling
which. It is nonrestrictive if it simply gives additional information about a substantive.)

8. What three tests help to determine when commas should separate descriptive adjectives? (Do
you pause between the adjectives as you read
them? Does it sound right to use *and* between the
adjectives? Does it sound right to change the order of the adjectives?)

Lesson Introduction: Write the words *God blesses*
on the board. Ask the students if this is a complete
sentence. (No.) Why not? It has a subject and a verb.
(It does not express a complete thought.) Tell the students that the verb *blesses* is a transitive verb; as
this lesson teaches, it must pass its action to some
other word.

Lesson Outline:

> *1. A transitive verb passes its action to a sub-
> stantive in the sentence.*

> *2. A transitive verb usually passes its action
> to a direct object.*

>> a. In a sentence with a direct object, the sub-
>> ject performs the action and the direct ob-
>> ject receives the action.

>> b. To find a direct object, say the skeleton and
>> ask *whom* or *what* after it.

>> c. Diagram the direct object on the horizon-
>> tal line after the skeleton, separating it
>> from the verb by a vertical line.

>> d. A verb may pass its action to more than
>> one substantive. In such a case, diagram
>> the compound direct object on a fork after
>> the verb.

Since a verbal or a clause may be a substantive, it may also be a direct object.

> We should try to help those in need.
>> (The verbal phrase *to help those in need* receives the action of *should try*.)
>
> The Bible reveals what is truth.
>> (The clause *what is truth* receives the action of *reveals*.)

A transitive verb with a direct object may also have an indirect object. An indirect object comes between the verb and the direct object. To find an indirect object, say the skeleton and the direct object; then ask *to whom or what* or *for whom or what*.

> Nathan gave the chickens some fresh water.
>> (Ask: Nathan gave *what*? The direct object is *water*. Nathan gave water *to what*? The indirect object is *chickens*.)

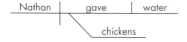

> Aunt Helen told Gladys and me an interesting story.
>> (Ask: Aunt Helen told *what*? The direct object is *story*. Aunt Helen told story *to whom*? The indirect object is *Gladys and me*.)

A direct object may be followed by an objective complement. This is a substantive or an adjective that follows a direct object and renames or modifies it. Remember that only verbs with the idea of "making" or "considering" can have objective complements.

> Everyone thought the story quite interesting.
>> (*Interesting* is an adjective that follows the direct object *story* and modifies it.)

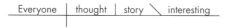

> Our proper response can make a difficulty a steppingstone.
>> (*Steppingstone* is a noun that follows the direct object *difficulty* and renames it.)

Action Passed to the Subject

A transitive verb may pass its action to the subject. Instead of the subject *performing* the action, it is *receiving* the action. Often some other

---

e. If the subject performs more than one action and each verb passes its action to a direct object, diagram the compound verb on a fork with a direct object after each verb.

f. The direct object may be a verbal or a clause.

3. A transitive verb with a direct object may also have an indirect object.

a. An indirect object comes between the verb and the direct object.

b. To find an indirect object, say the skeleton and the direct object; then ask *to whom or what* or *for whom or what*.

c. Diagram an indirect object on a horizontal line beneath the base line. A slanted line connects the indirect object to the verb.

4. A transitive verb with a direct object ma[y] also have an objective complement.

a. An objective complement is a substantiv[e] or an adjective that follows a direct objec[t] and renames or modifies it.

b. Only verbs with the idea of "making" o[r] "considering" can have objective comple[-] ments.

c. Diagram an objective complement on th[e] horizontal line after the direct object, sep[-] arating it from the direct object by a slante[d] line.

5. A transitive verb may pass its action t[o] the subject.

a. Instead of the subject *performing* the ac[-] tion, it is *receiving* the action.

b. Often some other substantive, found in [a]

substantive, found in a prepositional phrase at the end of the sentence, names the doer of the action. When the subject receives the action, the main verb must be a past participle, and a form of *be* must be used as a helping verb.

In each pair of sentences below, the same word receives the action of the same basic verb. But notice how the receiver shifts from the direct object to the subject.

Faithful ministers preach the Gospel.
The Gospel is preached by faithful ministers.
(In both sentences, *ministers* performs the action of preaching, and *Gospel* receives the action.)

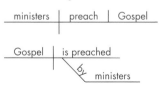

Princess killed this woodchuck.
This woodchuck was killed by Princess.
(In both sentences, *Princess* performed the action of killing, and *woodchuck* received the action.)

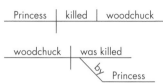

Class Practice

A. Read each transitive verb, and name the substantive that receives its action. Tell whether the receiver is the *subject* or the *direct object*. If the sentence does not have a transitive verb, say *not transitive*.
   1. John Bunyan boldly condemned the corruption in the Church of England and preached the Gospel.
   2. Because of this, he was imprisoned.
   3. Bunyan likely did not imagine that he would remain there for six years.
   4. During this imprisonment he wrote several poems and his autobiography.

Lesson 52 Answers

Class Practice

A. 1. condemned, corruption—direct object; preached, Gospel—direct object
   2. was imprisoned, he—subject
   3. did imagine, that he would remain there for six years—direct object
   4. wrote, poems—direct object, autobiography—direct object

prepositional phrase at the end of the sentence, names the doer of the action.

c. When the subject receives the action, the main verb must be a past participle, and a form of *be* must be used as a helping verb.

★ ***EXTRA PRACTICE***
Worksheet 18 *(Transitive Verbs)*

5. For less than one week, Bunyan enjoyed living in freedom.
6. On Sunday morning, Bunyan and several other worshipers were arrested.
7. Bunyan's most famous book, *The Pilgrim's Progress,* was penned during this prison stay.
8. Six years later, the Declaration of Indulgence granted freedom to hundreds of persecuted Christians.
9. This time Bunyan's freedom lasted for three years.
10. Bunyan wrote twenty-two books and many tracts.

B. Read each transitive verb, and name each complement. Identify each complement as a *direct object,* an *indirect object,* or an *objective complement.* If the sentence does not have a transitive verb, say *not transitive.*
1. Mother prepared the busy family a special treat.
2. We certainly considered the picnic lunch a wonderful idea.
3. We enjoyed watching the beautiful sunset.
4. Father made Judith and Rosanne a new doll cradle.
5. We listened carefully to Father's instructions.
6. The students told Brother Weaver their plans and asked his permission.
7. The abundance of rainfall has made this year's harvest very bountiful.
8. We know who controls the weather.

C. On the chalkboard, diagram the skeletons and complements of the sentences in Part B above.

Written Exercises

A. Copy each verb and the substantive that receives its action. Label the receiver *S* (subject) or *DO* (direct object). If the verb is not transitive, write *N* after it.
1. Our lives have been richly blessed by God.
2. We should love to praise His name.
3. When our actions praise Him, we point others to the truth.
4. Our lights should shine brightly in this dark world.
5. The eyes of many people are blinded by the devil.
6. We can demonstrate that the Bible guides our steps in life.
7. Divine grace is given by God for faithful living.
8. A faithful life will be rewarded in time and in eternity.

B. Copy the verbs and complements. Label the direct objects *DO,* the indirect objects *IO,* and the objective complements *OC.*
1. All insects have six legs and two antennae.
2. Their bodies include three distinct parts.
3. Insects help man by pollinating his crops.

Written Exercises

A. 1. have been blessed, lives—S
   2. should love, to praise His name—DO
   3. praise, Him—DO; point, others—DO
   4. should shine—N
   5. are blinded, eyes—S
   6. can demonstrate, that the Bible guides our steps in life—DO
   7. is given, grace—S
   8. will be rewarded, life—S

B. 1. have, legs—DO, antennae—DO
   2. include, parts—DO
   3. help, man—DO

5. enjoyed, living in freedom—direct object
6. were arrested, Bunyan—subject, worshipers—subject
7. was penned, book—subject
8. granted, freedom—direct object
9. not transitive
10. wrote, books—direct object, tracts—direct object

B. 1. prepared, family—indirect object, treat—direct object
   2. considered, lunch—direct object, idea—objective complement
   3. enjoyed, watching the beautiful sunset—direct object
   4. made, Judith—indirect object, Rosanne—indirect object, doll cradle—direct object
   5. not transitive
   6. told, Brother Weaver—indirect object, plans—direct object; asked, permission—direct object
   7. has made, harvest—direct object, bountiful—objective complement
   8. know, who controls the weather—direct object

C. 1.

2.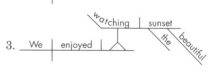

3.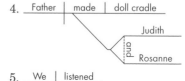

4.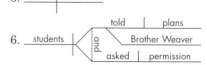

5. We | listened

6.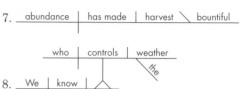

7. abundance | has made | harvest \ bountiful

8. We | know | who controls weather

4. Some insects even give man food.
5. Praying mantises and ladybugs help farmers and gardeners.
6. They eat many harmful insects.
7. Of course, we do not consider all insects welcome.
8. Some can bring our crops much destruction.
9. We do know that God created all things for a purpose.
10. God has made all things beautiful.

Diagram the skeletons and complements of these sentences.
1. The blue jay's cry gave the woodland creatures a warning of danger.
2. A panther's scream made the lone traveler anxious.
3. A beautiful buck raised his head and sniffed the air.
4. A plump rabbit was carried away by a red fox.
5. Two brown bears were overturning rocks and logs.
6. Several large trout provided the settler and his family a delicious meal.

Review Exercises

Copy each word that should be followed by a comma, and add the comma. [23, 25]
1. Yes the Lord is eternal He rules over all and He will destroy all evil.
2. Jesus Christ the Son of God defeated Satan at Calvary.
3. As we commit our lives to Him we share in His glorious eternal victory.
4. Inside the house was neat and clean and a homey atmosphere prevailed.
5. Many years ago Brenda your grandparents lived in this house.
6. In fact Great-uncle Clarence who was a carpenter built the house.

If the underlined verb is incorrect, write the correct principal part. If it is correct, write *correct*. [46]
1. The floodwaters have <u>creeped</u> up nearly to the house.
2. Myron has <u>tooken</u> more than his share of the pie.
3. Baby Helen <u>tore</u> a page out of my book.
4. This project has <u>costed</u> more than we had anticipated.
5. The dog <u>drug</u> a dead rabbit into the front yard.
6. Melanie <u>wrang</u> out the dishcloth vigorously.
7. In the sub-zero weather, some of our pipes <u>burst</u>.
8. I <u>lended</u> my pen to William.
9. Regina <u>done</u> the sweeping already.
10. Father has <u>went</u> to town for some parts.

4. give, man—IO, food—DO
5. help, farmers—DO, gardeners—DO
6. eat, insects—DO
7. do consider, insects—DO, welcome—OC
8. can bring, crops—IO, destruction—DO
9. do know, that God created all things for a purpose—DO
10. has made, things—DO, beautiful—OC

C. 1.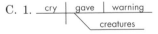

2.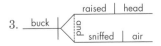

3.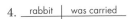

4.

5.

6.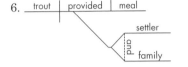

Review Exercises

A. 1. Yes, eternal, all,
2. Christ, God,
3. Him, glorious,
4. Inside, clean,
5. ago, Brenda,
6. fact, Clarence, carpenter,

B. 1. crept   6. wrung
2. taken   7. correct
3. correct   8. lent
4. cost   9. did
5. dragged   10. gone

53. Intransitive Complete Verbs

> **Lesson Survey**
> - An **intransitive complete verb** expresses action but does not pass the action to a receiver.
> - Some verbs may be either transitive or intransitive, depending on their use in a sentence.

In Lesson 52 you studied transitive verbs, which pass their action to a substantive in the sentence. But many action verbs do not have receivers for their action. Such verbs are *intransitive*. Since *transitive* means "passing over," you should recognize that *intransitive* means "not passing over."

An *intransitive complete verb* expresses action but does not pass the action to a receiver. The meaning of the verb is complete in itself; no complement is needed to finish the thought.

> **Transitive verb:** Incomplete without a direct object
> Jesus took . . .
>
> **Intransitive verb:** Complete without a direct object
> Jesus wept.

An intransitive complete verb may have adverb modifiers. However, these words simply modify the verb; they do not receive its action. Adverbs are diagrammed below the verb rather than after it.

Jesus spoke graciously to the blind man.
   (*Graciously* and *to the blind man* modify *spoke*.)

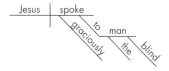

Jesus went where people needed help.
   (*Where people needed help* modifies *went*.)

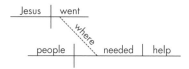

Lesson 53

Purpose: To study intransitive verbs whose meanings are complete without any complements.

Oral Review:
1. What does *transitive* mean? (passing action)
2. To what two sentence parts can a transitive verb pass its action? (subject, direct object)
3. Describe the main verb and the helping verb of a transitive verb that passes its action to the subject. (The main verb must be a past participle, and the helping verb must be a form of *be.*)
4. When is it correct to write *I will* in formal English? (when you want to make a determined statement or a promise)
5. Give the second and third principal parts of these verbs.
   a. bring (brought, [have] brought)
   b. wring (wrung, [have] wrung)
   c. come (came, [have] come)
   d. hit (hit, [have] hit)
   e. drag (dragged, [have] dragged)
   f. go (went, [have] gone)
6. (a) When are words like *god* and *lord* capitalized (b) When are they not? (a. when they refer to God b. when they refer to idols or people)
7. When is the word *president* capitalized? (when refers to the current president of the United State
8. When is the name of a school subject capitalized (when it is derived from a proper noun or followe by a number)

Lesson Introduction: Many times a farmer ca buy a complete feed for his animals. Nothing els needs to be added to give the animals the prope nourishment. Intransitive complete verbs are a b

Sometimes it almost seems that an intransitive complete verb passes its action to the subject. However, the structure of the sentence shows that the subject is really performing the action. You can tell that the subject does not receive the action because the verb is not a past participle with a form of *be* as a helping verb.

Intransitive complete verb: Subject performs the action
  The <u>snow</u> <u>melted</u> quickly under the warm sun.

Transitive verb: Subject receives the action
  The <u>snow</u> <u>was melted</u> by the warm sun.

Intransitive complete verb: Subject performs the action
  The <u>trees</u> <u>shook</u> violently during the hurricane.

Transitive verb: Subject receives the action
  The <u>trees</u> <u>were shaken</u> violently during the hurricane.

Some verbs may be either transitive or intransitive, depending on their use in a sentence. Most dictionaries tell whether a verb is transitive or intransitive. If the verb may be used either way, the dictionary will give definitions and examples for both uses.

Transitive verb: Action passed to direct object
  We <u>read</u> the Bible.

Intransitive complete verb: No action passed
  We <u>read</u> carefully.

Transitive verb: Action passed to subject
  The kite <u>was flown</u> by
    the two boys.

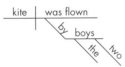

Intransitive complete verb: No action passed
  The kite <u>was flying</u> over
    the house.

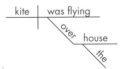

like that. No word needs to be added to the verb to complete its meaning. The sentence expresses a complete thought with just the subject and the verb.

Lesson Outline:

 1. An intransitive complete verb expresses action but does not pass the action to a receiver.

   a. An intransitive complete verb may have adverb modifiers.

   b. Sometimes it almost seems that an intransitive complete verb passes its action to the subject. But if the verb is not a past participle with a form of *be* as a helping verb, it does not pass its action to the subject. The subject is really performing the action, not receiving it.

 2. Some verbs may be either transitive or intransitive, depending on their use in a sentence.

Teacher: Intransitive complete verbs usually express action. But they may also express existence (with forms of *be*) and be complete in themselves.

  God *is*.

  The children *were* in school.

★ *EXTRA PRACTICE*
  Worksheet 19 *(Intransitive Complete Verbs)*

Class Practice

A. Read the verbs in these paragraphs, and tell if each is *transitive* or *intransitive complete*. If it is transitive, tell what word receives the action.

   ¹The waters of the river swirled musically beneath the overhanging spruce trees. ²In one of the quiet pools, a mink suddenly appeared, and in one fluid motion he slipped up onto the bank with a wriggling fish in his jaws. ³The mink found this a good place to fish, for it stood right at the head of the canyon. ⁴As the water dropped and leaped through the rocks in this narrow chasm, it created a mighty roar. ⁵This roar could be heard for miles.

   ⁶But for this noise, the mink would have heard another roar much sooner. ⁷Downstream a motorboat suddenly came into view around a bend. ⁸Startled, the mink dropped the fish and dived into the water.

B. Use each verb in two sentences. The verb should be transitive in the first sentence and intransitive complete in the second sentence.
   1. whistled   2. will turn   3. runs

C. On the chalkboard, diagram the skeletons, complements, and verb modifiers of these sentences.
   1. The windows rattled alarmingly during the hailstorm.
   2. The thunderstorm produced some dangerous winds.
   3. I must have dialed the wrong number.
   4. I shall dial carefully now.
   5. These books have been covered.
   6. Too many eggs are breaking in the hen house.

Written Exercises

A. Copy the verb in each sentence, and label it *T* for transitive or *IC* for intransitive complete. If it is transitive, write the word that receives the action.
   1. An African rock python may grow as long as thirty feet.
   2. A heavy snake, it may weigh up to three hundred pounds.
   3. Pythons can move swiftly on the ground, in a tree, or in the water.
   4. The python eats mainly small mammals.
   5. Its heat receptors can detect the body heat of a mammal over three feet away.
   6. In a year's time, a python requires about enough food to equal its own body weight.
   7. Therefore, a python's meal may last for several months.
   8. On at least one occasion, a leopard was found in a python's stomach.
   9. In cool weather, pythons will rest in the sun to absorb heat.
   10. In cold weather they will lie in a dormant state.

Lesson 53 Answers

Class Practice

A. 1. swirled—intransitive complete
   2. appeared—intransitive complete; slipped—intransitive complete
   3. found—transitive, this; stood—intransitive complete
   4. dropped—intransitive complete; leaped—intransitive complete; created—transitive, roar
   5. could be heard—transitive, roar
   6. would have heard—transitive, roar
   7. came—intransitive complete
   8. dropped—transitive, fish; dived—intransitive complete

B. (Individual work.)

C.
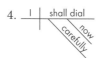
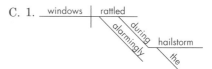
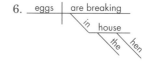

Written Exercises

A. 1. may grow—IC
   2. may weigh—IC
   3. can move—IC
   4. eats—T, mammals
   5. can detect—T, body heat
   6. requires—T, food
   7. may last—IC
   8. was found—T, leopard
   9. will rest—IC
   10. will lie—IC

3. Write two sentences for each verb. Use it as a transitive verb in the first sentence, and as an intransitive complete verb in the second.
1. study
2. sang
3. have grown
4. will move

7. Diagram the skeletons, complements, and verb modifiers of these sentences.
1. We should study diligently for the Lord's sake.
2. Every wise person studies the Bible.
3. The Lord must be honored by our actions.
4. The house shook in the fierce storm.
5. A robin sang sweetly in the tree.

Review Exercises

A. Write correctly each item with a capitalization error. [21]
1. In the ten commandments are found basic principles for god's people.
2. Yes, i am dependent upon thee, o lord.
3. When mr. Lloyd Stellar, jr., was President of the company, it prospered quite well.
4. Have you ever visited the washington monument in washington, d. c.?
5. Some of the special classes the ninth graders have are spanish, typing I, and biology.
6. During the middle ages, much of europe was bound by superstitions.
7. Yesterday father bought an echo chain saw from uncle Daniel.
8. Of course, thanksgiving day in the united states is always the last thursday in november.

B. Write which of the six tenses each underlined verb is, and whether its form is *simple, progressive,* or *emphatic.* [48–50]
1. While building the ark, Noah <u>was preaching</u> to the people.
2. The people <u>had rejected</u> God so completely that they paid Noah no heed.
3. No doubt, when the floodwaters rose, many <u>did beg</u> for mercy.
4. Before the end of the world, many of the conditions in Noah's day <u>will have been duplicated</u>.
5. We <u>have been studying</u> about the stars in science class.
6. <u>Do</u> you <u>enjoy</u> science class?
7. I <u>shall work</u> to earn an A on the test.
8. Brother Aden <u>does teach</u> very effectively.

B. (Individual work.)

C. 1.

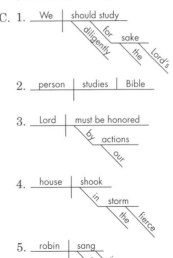

2. person | studies | Bible

3. Lord | must be honored \by actions \our

4. house | shook \in storm \the \fierce

5. robin | sang \sweetly \in tree \the

Review Exercises

A. 1. Ten Commandments, God's
2. I, Thee, O, Lord
3. Mr., Jr., president
4. Washington Monument, Washington, D. C.
5. Spanish, Typing
6. Middle Ages, Europe
7. Father, Echo, Uncle
8. Thanksgiving Day, United States, Thursday, November

B. 1. past, progressive
2. past perfect, simple
3. past, emphatic
4. future perfect, simple
5. present perfect, progressive
6. present, simple
7. future, simple
8. present, emphatic

54. Writing a Report From Your Notes

> **Lesson Survey**
> - The steps for gathering and organizing information for a **written report** are the same as those for an oral report.
> - Write a stimulating introduction for your report.
> - Write the body of your report, based on your outline and notes.
> - Write a positive, satisfying conclusion to your report.

In previous lessons you studied the procedures for giving an oral report. Now the focus will shift to written communication. The steps for gathering and organizing information for a *written report* are the same as those for an oral report. Therefore, you will use the same outline and notes that you used in Lesson 51.

For the first draft of your report, write only on every other line of the paper. You will need the blank lines for marking improvements later.

Like other kinds of compositions, a written report should have three parts: an introduction, a body, and a conclusion. The report should begin with a stimulating introduction. Lesson 51 lists the following as good introductions: an interesting observation, an illustration, a thought-provoking question, a familiar quotation, or a direct statement.

The introduction of an oral report should weave in the title, but this is not necessary for a written report; the title is written at the top of the paper. Since your report in this lesson will be longer than the composition you wrote in Chapter 4, the introduction should consist of a short paragraph, not merely a sentence or two.

The body of the report contains the information you are presenting, organized according to your outline. Express each important point on your outline in a clear topic sentence. Then develop each paragraph carefully with the facts, descriptions, and illustrations that you used for your oral report. Round out your report with other suitable details from your research. Remember, the outline is only the basic skeleton.

If you have suitable material, provide some variety by using several of the methods of paragraph development that you studied in Chapter 3.

A composition also needs a positive, satisfying conclusion. As with an oral report, the conclusion of a written report may summarize the main points of the report or give a call to some response or action.

When the first draft is completed, lay it aside for a while. You will revise and rewrite your report at a later time.

Lesson 54

Purpose: To present guidelines for writing the first draft of a report.

Oral Review:

1. Before giving an oral report, you should go through your outline point by point for what purpose? (to decide how you will describe and illustrate each point)

2. What are some good ways to introduce your report? (with an interesting observation, an illustration, a thought-provoking question, a familiar quotation, or a direct statement)

3. What are two good ways to conclude your report? (with a summary of the main points; with a call to some response or action)

4. When may you copy the exact words of a reference source in your notes? (when you plan to quote those words in your report, and if you place those words in quotation marks)

5. What are the advantages of using small cards for taking notes? (You can easily write one specific idea on each card. You can easily shuffle the cards to organize your notes.)

Lesson Introduction: There are two basic kinds of communication: oral and written. Both are important in the spreading of information and in the learning process. Preparing for the two types of communication is the same in many ways, but there are some differences. This lesson will give you direction in writing a report.

Lesson Outline:

1. The steps for gathering and organizing information for a written report are the same as those for an oral report.

Here is a written report based on the sample notes and outline given
n the lessons on oral reports. This report contains about 880 words.

Canals in Pennsylvania

1   Did you ever consider how the early settlers in Pennsylvania transported their goods east and west across the colony? There were
numerous ranges of steep mountains blocking the way. Pennsylvania
has three great river systems, but they run generally north to south.
Canals were one method used to help overcome this transportation
problem in the early and middle 1800s.

2   There are several main reasons why these canals were built. For
one thing, William Penn had proposed a canal linking the Susquehanna
River and the Delaware River. In his mind, such a canal was necessary for the economic development of the colony. Interestingly enough,
the Union Canal, built in 1827, did follow his proposed route. When
you consider that Penn died over one hundred years before this canal
was finished, you will see that he had amazing foresight.

3   Another reason for building canals was the expense of hauling
heavy loads on the turnpikes. Freight companies had to pay toll to
use many roads and bridges, and the charge for heavy loads was
often quite high. Also, heavy loads put much strain on wagons and
added significantly to the cost of maintaining them. In addition to
these expenses, freight companies had to pay their drivers as well as
feed and care for six-horse teams during the entire round trip.

4   The building of the Erie Canal in New York was a third reason for
the canal fever in Pennsylvania. Completed in 1825, the Erie Canal
linked the Hudson River to Lake Erie. It provided cheap water transportation between New York City and the entire Great Lakes region.
Thus, western trade threatened to completely bypass Pennsylvania
cities such as Philadelphia and Pittsburgh. In fact, the Erie Canal did
begin the process of making New York City, rather than Philadelphia,
the main seaport on the East Coast.

5   As canals were built in Pennsylvania, they quickly assumed an
important role. By the time the last canal was finished, the total length
of Pennsylvania canals was 790 miles. Some of the main ones connected into the Susquehanna River and the Allegheny River. Longest
of all was the Pennsylvania Main Line Canal, which extended from
Philadelphia to Pittsburgh—a distance of over three hundred miles.
Actually, part of this route was an inclined-plane railroad that carried boats over the Allegheny Mountains.

6   The high volume of traffic on these canals further indicates how
important they were. In just the five years from 1836 through 1840,

**2. Write a stimulating introduction for your
report.**

    a. As in an oral report, the introduction may
be an interesting observation, an illustration, a thought-provoking question, a familiar quotation, or a direct statement.

    b. In contrast to the introduction of an oral
report, the introduction of a written report
does not need to weave in the title.

    c. The introduction of a report should consist
of a short paragraph.

**3. Write the body of your report, based on
your outline and notes.**

    a. Express each important point on your out-
line in a clear topic sentence.

    b. Develop each paragraph carefully, filling
in the facts, descriptions, and illustrations
that you used for your oral report.

    c. Round out your report with other suitable
details from your research.

**4. Write a positive, satisfying conclusion to
your report.** This may be a summary of the main
points or a call to some response or action.

$14.5 million worth of goods traveled over Pennsylvania's state-owned canals. During the peak years, more than 3,600 boats per year passed through Hollidaysburg, an important station on the Main Line Canal.

7   In addition, Pennsylvania's canals were important because they provided the most comfortable and convenient means of crossing the state before railroads were common. Roads were generally quite rough, they twisted over and around hills and other obstructions, and in wet weather they were often impassable. By contrast, canals were much more level, much smoother, and much straighter.

8   In spite of such obvious importance, the canal system was relatively short-lived. The first Pennsylvania canal to be built was the Union Canal in 1827. In 1931 the Schuylkill Canal carried the last canal freight in the state: a load of 3,108 tons of coal refuse.

9   Two main reasons explain why the canals went out of business. First, they failed to pay for themselves. This was not true of all canals. The Erie Canal in New York, for instance, was a great economic success. But Pennsylvania's canals never produced long-term profits. Therefore, the Pennsylvania State Assembly called for the sale of the Main Line Canal in 1844.

10   The second reason is that railroads quickly made canals obsolete. Train locomotives could travel much faster than canal mules. Canals were possible only where water could be made to flow, but railroads could be built almost anywhere. And railroads were better suited for use in all kinds of weather. Freezing weather, floods, and prolonged droughts sometimes forced canals to close. An occasional flood would wash away a railroad bridge, and snow or ice would sometimes make the tracks impassable. But otherwise, rail transportation was rarely shut down because of the weather.

11   Even though the canal system was short-lived, it did produce several important benefits. Perhaps the most immediate benefit was the linking of far-flung parts of the state by cheap transportation. This helped to lower and hold down the prices of goods. It was also an advantage to travelers, who could more readily afford to visit family and friends in distant areas.

12   Another benefit that naturally followed the building of canals was the developing of towns. A number of small towns that held little promise of growth in 1800 began to boom when a canal brought steady traffic their way.

13   The most important benefit, no doubt, was the introducing of the railroad. The first railroads were actually part of the canal system. The Pennsylvania Main Line Canal, for example, used an inclined-plane railroad to cross the Allegheny Mountains. Soon it became

obvious that rail transportation was better overall than canal transportation, and railroads were built independent of canals.

14   As we consider why canals were built in Pennsylvania, what role they filled, why they were so soon discontinued, and what benefits they produced, we should see that canals filled an important place in the history of Pennsylvania.

Written Exercises

Write the first draft of your report based on the outline and notes you used for your oral report in Lesson 51. Write on every other line to allow room for changes.

---

55. Intransitive Linking Verbs

> **Lesson Survey**
> - An **intransitive linking verb** expresses a condition or state of being.
> - An intransitive linking verb may link the subject to a predicate nominative or a predicate adjective.
> - A linking verb followed by an adjective must not be confused with an action verb followed by a direct object or an adverb.

Both transitive and intransitive complete verbs are action verbs. There is also a small group of verbs that do not express action. These are the intransitive linking verbs. Such verbs have little actual meaning of their own; they serve mainly to link the subject to a subjective complement.

An *intransitive linking verb* expresses a condition or state of being. The most common linking verbs are the forms of *be: am, is, are, was, were, be, been, being.* The following sentences illustrate the difference between action verbs and intransitive linking verbs.

> **Action verb:** Verb shows something happening
>   The Lord <u>rules</u> in the kingdoms of men.
> **Linking verb:** Verb shows a state of being
>   The Lord <u>is</u> sovereign over all.

An intransitive linking verb may link the subject to a predicate nominative. Since the predicate nominative is a substantive that renames the subject, the linking verb can be considered an equal sign. On a diagram,

Lesson 55

Purpose: To study linking verbs, predicate nominatives, and predicate adjectives.

Oral Review:

1. In what way is an intransitive complete verb *complete*? (No complement is needed to finish the thought.)

2. Describe the main verb and the helping verb of a transitive verb that passes its action to the subject. (The main verb must be a past participle, and the helping verb must be a form of *be.*)

3. In the following sentences, the verb is a form of *answer.* Tell whether the verb is transitive or intransitive complete in each sentence. If it is transitive, tell what word receives the action.
   a. My question was answered satisfactorily. (transitive, question)

Lesson 54 Answers

Written Exercises
(Individual work.)

---

   b. He always answers clearly and carefully. (intransitive complete)
   c. We could not answer the stranger. (transitive, stranger)

4. Read this basic sentence in the six tenses, using a form of *sit* each time. *(Teacher:* Write the following form sentence on the board: *We —— beside the creek.)*
   a. present (We *sit* beside the creek.)
   b. past (We *sat* beside the creek.)
   c. future (We *shall sit* beside the creek.)
   d. present perfect (We *have sat* beside the creek.)
   e. past perfect (We *had sat* beside the creek.)
   f. future perfect (We *shall have sat* beside the creek.)

5. Tell which kind of sentence according to structure fits each description.

the subjective complement is placed on the horizontal line, separated from the verb by a slanted line.

> This dense <u>forest</u> <u>must be</u> the <u>home</u> of many deer.
> (*Home* renames *forest; forest = home.*)

> The <u>dishwashers</u> this evening <u>will be</u> <u>Marian</u> and <u>I</u>.
> (*Marian* and *I* rename *dishwashers; dishwashers = Marian and I.*)

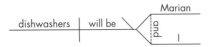

An intransitive linking verb may also link the subject to a predicate adjective. Since the predicate adjective modifies the subject, you can usually make a sensible phrase by placing it before the subject. Predicate adjectives may follow not only the forms of *be* but also verbs of sense (*taste, feel, smell, sound, look, appear*) and other linking verbs (*grow, seem, stay, become, remain, turn, prove*).

> The <u>wolves</u> <u>were</u> <u>hungry</u> and <u>vicious</u>.
> (*Hungry* and *vicious* modify *wolves: hungry, vicious wolves.*)

> James's <u>voice</u> <u>has</u> <u>been</u> <u>sounding</u> <u>hoarse</u> today.
> (*Hoarse* modifies *voice: hoarse voice.*)

> The veterinarian's <u>efforts</u> at treating the cow <u>proved</u> <u>successful</u>.
> (*Successful* modifies *efforts: successful efforts.*)

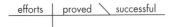

A linking verb followed by an adjective must not be confused with an action verb followed by a direct object or an adverb. So you must evaluate

a. Has two or more independent clauses and no dependent clause (compound)
b. Has only one independent clause (simple)
c. Has two or more independent clauses and at least one dependent clause (compound-complex)
d. Has one independent clause and one or more dependent clauses (complex)

Lesson Introduction: In most of the sentences that we speak and write, we use action verbs to describe things that happen.

> Thick clouds *have covered* the sky. Thousands of snowflakes *are swirling* through the air. A strong east wind *is blowing* them into huge drifts. Soon the snow *will have shut* all the roads.

However, sometimes we also need to express an idea that has no action. Rather, we are expressing merely the way something *is, was,* or *will be.*

> Likely this snowfall *will be* a record for ou[r] area.

Such sentences have intransitive linking verbs. They are *intransitive* because they have no action t[o] pass; they are *linking* because they join two senten[ce] parts together.

Lesson Outline:

1. An intransitive linking verb expresses [a] condition or state of being. The most common link[ng] verbs are the forms of *be: am, is, are, was, were,* be, been, being.

2. An intransitive linking verb may link th[e] subject to a predicate nominative.

a. Since the predicate nominative is a su[b]stantive that renames the subject, the link[ing] verb can be considered an equal sign.
b. On a diagram, the subjective complemen[t] is placed on the horizontal line, separate[d] from the verb by a slanted line.

hese verbs carefully. Does the verb express a condition or state of being
ather than an action? Can you replace the verb with a form of *be* without
hanging the meaning of the sentence? If the answers to these questions are
es, the verb is linking.

Transitive verb:
    The farmer <u>grew</u> wheat.
        (*Grew* expresses action, not condition. *The farmer was the
            wheat* is not sensible.)

Intransitive complete verb:
    The trees <u>grew</u> slowly.
        (*Grew* expresses action, not condition. *The trees were slowly*
            is not sensible.)

Intransitive linking verb:
    The weather <u>grew</u> cold.
        (*Grew* expresses condition, not action. *The weather was cold*
            is sensible.)

Class Practice

A. Read each linking verb, and tell what words it links together.
    1. Human reasoning may sound quite attractive.
    2. But sin is deceptive and deadly.
    3. The Bible remains the authority on right and wrong.
    4. God's help surely will be sufficient for us.
    5. In fact, the only true source of help is He.

B. Read each verb, and tell whether it is *transitive, intransitive complete,*
or *intransitive linking.*
    1. The sky remained black and stormy.
    2. The shoppers remained in the stores.
    3. A tornado appeared south of town.
    4. Brother Ralph appeared calm in the face of danger.
    5. Job's trust in God was proved beyond a doubt.
    6. He proved faithful even in severe trials.
    7. The girls looked in several cookbooks for the recipe.
    8. Samuel was turning the crank of the ice cream freezer.
    9. The wheel was turning slowly in midair.
    10. The bread was rapidly turning dark in the toaster.

C. On the chalkboard, diagram the skeletons and complements of these
sentences.
    1. The tomato soup smelled delicious.
    2. Naomi is Susan's cousin and close friend.

**3. An intransitive linking verb may link the
subject to a predicate adjective.**
        a. Since the predicate adjective modifies the
            subject, you can usually make a sensible
            phrase by placing it before the subject.
        b. Predicate adjectives may follow not only
            the forms of *be* but also verbs of sense *(taste,
            feel, smell, sound, look, appear)* and other
            linking verbs *(grow, seem, stay, become, re-
            main, turn, prove).*

**4. A linking verb followed by an adjective
must not be confused with an action verb followed by a direct object or an adverb.** A verb is
linking only if the answers to the following questions
are *yes.*
        a. Does the verb express a condition or state
            of being rather than an action?

Lesson 55 Answers

Class Practice

A. 1. may sound; reasoning—attractive
    2. is; sin—deceptive (and) deadly
    3. remains; Bible—authority
    4. will be; help—sufficient
    5. is; source—He

B. 1. remained—intransitive linking
    2. remained—intransitive complete
    3. appeared—intransitive complete
    4. appeared—intransitive linking
    5. was proved—transitive
    6. proved—intransitive linking
    7. looked—intransitive complete
    8. was turning—transitive
    9. was turning—intransitive complete
    10. was turning—intransitive linking

C. 1.

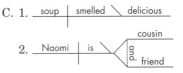

    b. Can you replace the verb with a form of *be*
        without changing the meaning of the sen-
        tence?

NOTE: It has been some time since the students diagramed indirect objects and objective complements.
To prepare them for the Written Exercises, diagram
at least sentences 4 and 5 of Class Practice Part C
together in class.

★ **EXTRA PRACTICE**
    Worksheet 20 *(Intransitive Linking Verbs)*

3. The mean billy goat suddenly appeared around the corner.
4. He gave us a bad scare.
5. Father has made the fence strong.
6. This milk has turned sour.

Written Exercises

A. Write each linking verb and the words it links together.
1. "The thoughts of the righteous are right."
2. "Ye shall be holy unto me."
3. In the last days the love of many will become cold.
4. At times Jesus' disciples appeared faithless and ignorant.
5. Jesus consistently remained loyal to the Father's will.
6. God's people have always been the object of Satan's wrath.
7. Many of men's theories have proven false.
8. Bible truth will never become outdated.

B. Write each verb, and label it *T* (transitive), *IC* (intransitive complete), or *IL* (intransitive linking).
1. This morning Benjamin was feeling ill.
2. The prisoner was feeling around in the dark corners of his cell.
3. Mother was feeling the different kinds of material.
4. Marlene's cookies will taste delicious.
5. I shall gladly taste one for her.
6. Both dogs seemed quite friendly.
7. The mockingbird's medley sounds beautiful.
8. At every crossing, the train whistle is sounded.
9. Uncle Alvin had been the cook at Bible school.
10. A dark cloud appeared on the horizon.

C. Diagram the skeletons and complements of these sentences.
1. The deer have been a nuisance.
2. They made our garden a mess.
3. Barry's mistake seems quite apparent now.
4. The corn has grown rapidly with plenty of moisture.
5. Today will be cool and damp.
6. We should give Mother a birthday gift.

Review Exercises

A. On the chalkboard, diagram the skeletons and complements of all the clauses in these sentences. There is at least one of each sentence type according to structure. [14–16]
1. God loves all men, but not all men love God.
2. Because God is love, He sent Jesus into the world.
3. Jesus taught the people and performed many miracles.

Written Exercises

A. 1. are; thoughts—right
2. shall be; Ye—holy
3. will become; love—cold
4. appeared; disciples—faithless (and) ignorant
5. remained; Jesus—loyal
6. have been; people—object
7. have proven; Many—false
8. will become; truth—outdated

B. 1. was feeling—IL
2. was feeling—IC
3. was feeling—T
4. will taste—IL
5. shall taste—T
6. seemed—IL
7. sounds—IL
8. is sounded—T
9. had been—IL
10. appeared—IC

C.

Review Exercises

4. The words that Jesus spoke to the people were given in authority.
5. Jesus taught the disciples whom He had chosen, and they continued His work after His death.

Write whether the word order of each sentence is *natural, inverted,* or *mixed.* [11]

1. In the quiet water of a pond, a frog may lay several thousand eggs at one time.
2. Out of the eggs come scores of little tadpoles.
3. The tadpoles eat the algae growing in the pond.
4. A tadpole has gills like those of a fish.
5. In a few months, the tiny tadpole becomes a young frog.
6. Many of the eggs and tadpoles are eaten by predators.

4.

```
        words  |  were given
      _ _ _ _ _|_____
Jesus | spoke |  \  that
```

5.

```
Jesus | taught | disciples | and | they | continued | work
                                _ _ _ _ _ _
He | had chosen | whom  \
```

B. 1. mixed   4. natural
    2. inverted   5. mixed
    3. natural   6. natural

---

56. Proofreading and Rewriting a Report

Lesson Survey
- Proofread the first draft of your report. Then write the report in its final form.

After you have written the first draft of your report, you must proofread it. Check the report specifically for organization and content by using the following questions. Some of them refer to the sample report "Canals in Pennsylvania," which is found in Lesson 54.

1. Are the main points given in logical sequence? They should be, of course, if you followed a good outline. However, do not hesitate to make any improvements that may be needed. The sample report follows the order that is given in Lesson 47.
2. Does the report include the three basic parts of a composition? In the sample report, paragraph 1 is the introduction, paragraphs 2–13 are the body, and paragraph 14 is the conclusion.
3. Are the paragraphs developed with specific facts and details? Again, if the outlining was done carefully, there should be no major problem here. But it is always good to check for it once more.
4. Does every paragraph have unity and coherence? Does every sentence develop the topic sentence? Is the sentence order clear? Are transitional words, repetition of key words, and pronoun reference used effectively? Look at paragraph 3 in the sample report. Do you

Lesson 56

Purpose: To present guidelines for writing the second draft of a report.

Oral Review:

1. How is planning a written report much like planning an oral report? (The steps for gathering and organizing the information are the same.)
2. What are the three parts of a report? (introduction, body, conclusion)
3. Should the title of a report always be woven into the introduction? Explain. (No; it should be woven into the introduction of an oral report, but it is not necessary for a written report.)
4. Where can you get the material you need to write well-rounded paragraphs in the body of your report? (from your research materials)

5. What are two good ways to conclude your report? (with a summary of the main points or a call to some response or action)

Lesson Introduction: Often when you give an oral report, you afterward see areas where you could have done better. Perhaps you could not always think of exactly the right words to use. Or maybe you forgot an interesting detail that you had wanted to make sure you included. But it is too late; the report has been given, and there is no way to improve it now.

A written report is different. You *can* go back and make improvements after the first writing. You can use more suitable words, and you can add whole sentences or paragraphs that you had forgotten in the first draft. This is the purpose of proofreading and rewriting: to examine the first draft for weaknesses and to make improvements so that the finished report will be as good as you can make it.

Lesson Outline:

1. Proofread your report for organization and content.

a. Are the main points given in logical sequence?
b. Does the report include the three basic parts of a composition?
c. Are the paragraphs developed with specific facts and details?
d. Does every paragraph have unity and coherence?
e. Does the thought flow smoothly from one paragraph to the next?

2. Proofread your report for errors in grammar and usage.

a. Read the first draft aloud to yourself or to someone else.

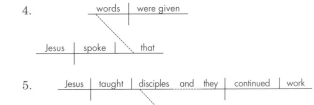

see the transitional words *Also, In addition,* and *as well as*? Note also the repeated use of key words: *expense* and *expenses,* along with *pay, toll, charge,* and *cost.*

5. Does the thought flow smoothly from one paragraph to the next? Look at the first sentences of paragraphs 2–13 in the sample. The following transitional words are used: *Another, a third reason, further, In addition, In spite of, Even though,* and *The most important.* Moreover, several paragraphs begin with a reference to an idea developed in a previous paragraph. In paragraph 2, the first sentence speaks of "these canals" (mentioned in paragraph 1). In paragraphs 6, 7, and 8, the first sentence refers to the importance of the canals (discussed in paragraph 5).

In addition to checking for organization and content, you should check your report for errors in grammar and usage. Read the first draft aloud to yourself or, better yet, to someone else. Look for any fragments or run-on errors. Be sure that all verbs agree with their subjects and that all pronouns agree with their antecedents. Check for awkward constructions, such as misplaced modifiers or unclear wording. Proofread for incorrect spelling, punctuation, and capitalization.

When you are satisfied that the report is as good as you can make it, recopy it on a clean sheet of paper. Write on every line this time, and use your best handwriting.

Remember that proofreading and rewriting are important steps to a good finished product. You may well need to revise your report several times before you have produced the best that you can.

Written Exercises

Carefully proofread and revise your first draft from Lesson 54. Then write your report in its final form.

---

57. Chapter 5 Review

Class Practice

A. Answer these questions about verbs.
1. Which principal part must be used with *have, has,* or *had* as a helping verb?
2. What helping verbs are used with each of the three perfect tenses?
3. How is the present perfect tense different from the simple past tense?

b. Look for fragments or run-on errors.
c. Be sure that all verbs agree with their subjects and that all pronouns agree with their antecedents.
d. Check for awkward constructions, such as misplaced modifiers or unclear wording.
e. Proofread for incorrect spelling, punctuation, and capitalization.

Lesson 56 Answers

Written Exercises
(Individual work.)

Lesson 57 Answers

Class Practice

A. 1. the third principal part (past participle)
   2. *present perfect:* have *or* has
      past perfect: had
      future perfect: shall have *or* will have
   3. The simple past merely states that something happened at some time in the past. The present perfect tense indicates an action or a condition that began in the past and is completed as of the present moment or continues into the present time.

Lesson 57

Purpose: To review the concepts taught in Chapter 5.

4. What are the two uses for (*a*) the past perfect tense? (*b*) the future perfect tense?
5. What do all transitive verbs do?
6. If a transitive verb passes its action to the subject, what helping verb will it have?
7. If an action verb does not pass its action to a receiver, what is it called?
8. In addition to the forms of *be,* what are some common intransitive linking verbs?

B. Give the answers.
1. When you take notes for a report, why should you use more than one reference source?
2. When may you copy the exact words of a reference source in your notes?
3. How should you show that you have copied words directly?
4. Name some good ways to introduce a report.
5. Name two good ways to conclude a report.

C. Give the second and third principal parts of these verbs. Use *have* with the past participle.
1. go
2. freeze
3. tag
4. wear
5. shrink
6. burst
7. drown
8. swim

D. Read each verb or verb phrase, and tell what tense it is. Also tell whether the verb form is *simple, progressive,* or *emphatic.*
1. Before his conversion, Saul had been persecuting the Christians.
2. However, he did not continue in that course of life.
3. We certainly do benefit greatly from his life as a Christian.
4. We have been studying his life in Bible class.
5. By the end of this month, we shall have completed this study.
6. We shall always appreciate the challenges of his life.

E. Tell whether the underlined verb is *transitive, intransitive complete,* or *intransitive linking.* If it is transitive, tell which word receives the action. If it is linking, tell what words are linked.
1. Conrad is plowing the garden.
2. Over the years, this garden soil has become fine and mellow.
3. This year's crops grew quite well.
4. The fresh watermelons tasted especially good.
5. The corn was damaged by a severe hailstorm.
6. Our whole family often works together in the garden.

4. *a.* to clarify which of two past actions or conditions occurred first; to emphasize that one action or condition was completed at the time of the other one. *b.* to clarify which of two actions or conditions will be completed first; to emphasize that one action or condition will be completed by the time the other begins
5. pass action to a substantive in the sentence
6. a form of *be*
7. intransitive complete
8. *verbs of sense:* taste, feel, smell, sound, look, appear
   other linking verbs: grow, seem, stay, become, remain, turn, prove

B. 1. to have a balanced report, to require you to express ideas in your own words, to verify facts
2. when you plan to quote those words in your report
3. put the words in quotation marks
4. with an interesting observation, an illustration, a thought-provoking question, a familiar quotation, or a direct statement
5. with a summary of the main points or a call to some response or action

C. 1. went, (have) gone
2. froze, (have) frozen
3. tagged, (have) tagged
4. wore, (have) worn
5. shrank *or* shrunk, (have) shrunk *or* (have) shrunken
6. burst, (have) burst
7. drowned, (have) drowned
8. swam, (have) swum

D. 1. had been persecuting—past perfect, progressive
2. did continue—past, simple
3. do benefit—present, emphatic
4. have been studying—present perfect, progressive
5. shall have completed—future perfect, simple
6. shall appreciate—future, simple

E. 1. transitive, garden
2. intransitive linking, soil—fine (and) mellow
3. intransitive complete
4. intransitive linking, watermelons—good
5. transitive, corn
6. intransitive complete

F. On the chalkboard, diagram the skeletons and complements of the sentences in Part E.

Written Exercises

A. Write the correct form of each underlined verb, without changing the tense. If it is correct, write *correct*.
1. Sin always has costed so much that playing with temptation is dangerous.
2. Through the deceptiveness of sin, Satan has stolen the hearts of many.
3. This man seen our Gospel sign and stopped in to talk.
4. The sun finally sunk below the horizon.
5. Benny has fell on the stones.
6. Everyone has took a doughnut from the bowl.
7. I tore my shirtsleeve on this nail.
8. After we had ate supper, we visited for a while.
9. We drug the branches into a pile to burn.
10. Several deer swum across the large lake.

B. Copy each verb or verb phrase, and write which tense it is. Also label each one *simple, progressive,* or *emphatic.*
1. Did you pray for God's blessing today?
2. God will answer every sincere prayer.
3. Indeed, we do need God's blessing every hour.
4. By the end of the day, you will have faced many choices and challenges.
5. We are facing a determined and deceptive enemy.
6. Long before our lifetime, he had been warring against the souls of men.
7. By His death and resurrection, Jesus has overcome the devil.
8. He will give us the power to overcome too.

C. In each sentence, one of the verbs should be changed to a perfect tense for a clearer or more emphatic relationship. Write that verb in the correct perfect tense.
1. When the flat tire was changed, we drove on again.
2. Before we return home, we shall drive many miles.
3. Our parents will teach us many things by the time we leave home.
4. Father questioned us about where we went.

D. Label each underlined verb *T* (transitive), *IC* (intransitive complete), or *IL* (intransitive linking). If the verb is transitive, write the word that receives the action. If it is intransitive linking, write the words that are linked.

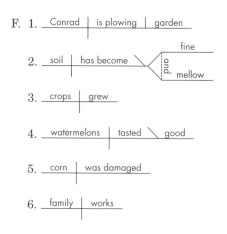

F. 1. Conrad | is plowing | garden

2. soil | has become \ fine *and* mellow

3. crops | grew

4. watermelons | tasted \ good

5. corn | was damaged

6. family | works

Written Exercises

A.
1. has cost
2. correct
3. saw
4. sank
5. has fallen
6. has taken
7. correct
8. had eaten
9. dragged
10. swam

B.
1. Did pray—past, simple
2. will answer—future, simple
3. do need—present, emphatic
4. will have faced—future perfect, simple
5. are facing—present, progressive
6. had been warring—past perfect, progressive
7. has overcome—present perfect, simple
8. will give—future, simple

C.
1. had been changed
2. shall have driven
3. will have taught
4. had gone

1. The stars <u>are shining</u> brightly tonight.
2. Oscar <u>was shining</u> his flashlight around in the large cave.
3. The flood warning <u>was sounded</u> through the valley.
4. The horse's hoofs <u>sounded</u> faintly in the distance.
5. The messenger's tone <u>sounded</u> very urgent.
6. That eagle <u>has been soaring</u> high in the sky for several hours.
7. The children <u>are working</u> in the garden.
8. They <u>will be</u> busy for another hour.
9. We <u>shall turn</u> to the right at the next crossing.
10. The leaves <u>will turn</u> colorful in a few weeks.

C. Diagram the skeletons and complements of these sentences.
1. A tree with deep roots remains strong in the stormy wind.
2. We must grow strong roots of faith.
3. The Bible gives us much encouragement to faithfulness.
4. A faithful person will stand solidly for the truth.
5. The lives of the faithful bring glory and praise to God.
6. Their own lives are richly rewarded by God.

F. Draw rectangles to represent three note cards for the following information on the topic "Water Supplies in Palestine." Fill in the cards properly.
— Cisterns more common than wells (*Manners and Customs of Bible Lands,* page 282)
— Because of hot climate and large numbers of sheep and cattle, good wells were valuable (*The New Unger's Bible Dictionary,* page 1363)
— Cisterns often covered to keep them hidden (*The New Unger's Bible Dictionary,* page 239)

D. 1. IC
   2. T, flashlight
   3. T, warning
   4. IC
   5. IL, tone—urgent

   6. IC
   7. IC
   8. IL, they—busy
   9. IC
   10. IL, leaves—colorful

E. 1. tree | remains \ strong

   2. We | must grow | roots

   3. Bible | gives | encouragement
      \ us

   4. person | will stand

   5. lives | bring | glory _and_ praise

   6. lives | are rewarded

F. (Sample note cards.)

Water Supplies in Palestine
Manners and Customs of Bible Lands. p. 282
Cisterns more common than wells

Water in P.
The New Unger's Bible Dictionary. p. 1363
Because of hot climate and large numbers of sheep and cattle, good wells were valuable

Water in P.
TNUBD. p. 239
Cisterns often covered to keep them hidden

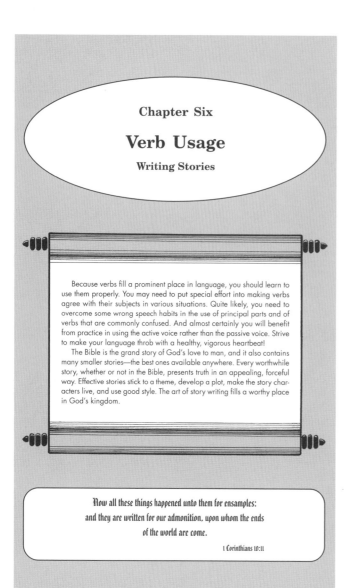

Chapter Six

Verb Usage

Writing Stories

Because verbs fill a prominent place in language, you should learn to use them properly. You may need to put special effort into making verbs agree with their subjects in various situations. Quite likely, you need to overcome some wrong speech habits in the use of principal parts and of verbs that are commonly confused. And almost certainly you will benefit from practice in using the active voice rather than the passive voice. Strive to make your language throb with a healthy, vigorous heartbeat!

The Bible is the grand story of God's love to man, and it also contains many smaller stories—the best ones available anywhere. Every worthwhile story, whether or not in the Bible, presents truth in an appealing, forceful way. Effective stories stick to a theme, develop a plot, make the story characters live, and use good style. The art of story writing fills a worthy place in God's kingdom.

Now all these things happened unto them for ensamples:
and they are written for our admonition, upon whom the ends
of the world are come.

1 Corinthians 10:11

58. The Theme of a Story

Lesson Survey

- The **theme** of a story is the lesson that the author seeks to impress on his audience.
- A good short story has one basic theme.
- The traits of the story characters should be consistent with the theme.
- The setting of the story should contribute to the theme.
- The conflict of the story should portray the theme clearly.
- The conclusion of the story should clinch the theme.

The writer of a good story should seek to do more than merely entertain his readers. Although he does try to capture the readers' attention, his main purpose is to communicate some inspiring truth or persuade his readers to follow a certain course of action. A good story does double duty: it holds our interest, and it gives us something worthwhile to think about.

Read the following sample story. You will be referring to it again in the story-writing lessons of this chapter.

The Trouble With George

The upper grade students chattered excitedly as they headed for the steep hill behind the Piney Mountain Mennonite School. "These Pennsylvania hills certainly beat southern Maryland for sledding," commented fourteen-year-old Titus. "Before we moved here, I hardly did any sledding at all."

"Huh!" snorted George, swinging his large frame to face Titus. "Don't need to tell us that. Nobody from here was ever as scared of this hill as you were. Course none of us is as short as you either."

"No, I guess southern Maryland doesn't have as good growing weather as western Pennsylvania," laughed Titus good-naturedly. "Anyway, I want to be satisfied whether I'm short or tall."

With a whoop, the boys sprinted up the last few yards to the top of the hill. Titus forgot George's words in the thrill of speeding over the snow, but later they came back to trouble him.

This was not the first time George had made remarks like that. Other scenes from the past several weeks flashed through his mind—scenes in which George had said and done things that clearly showed his dislike for Titus. "Wonder what he has against me," Titus mused. "I surely can't think of any wrong I've ever done to him."

Lesson 58

Purpose: (1) To teach the importance of a good story theme. (2) To show how it can be conveyed indirectly.

Oral Review:

1. Why would "Making Candles" not be a good title for a report in school? (It is too broad.)
2. How could you limit that subject to something suitable? ("Making Dipped Candles in Colonial America"; "Making Candles in Art Class")
3. When you gather information for a report, why should you take notes from more than one reference source? (to have a balanced report; to require you to express ideas in your own words; to verify facts)
4. When you are doing research, why is a book on the subject a better source of information than an encyclopedia? (A book usually gives more details.)

Lesson Introduction: Have you ever felt like giving up in a struggle against a certain temptation or bad habit? Then you read a story about a character who faced a similar struggle and overcame. Have you ever read a story, only to sheepishly admit to yourself that you had been too much like that character? The lesson in the story then helped you to improve your attitudes and actions. If these things have happened to you, those stories filled their intended purpose. They apparently had a clear, central theme. This lesson introduces you to this important ingredient in good story writing.

Lesson Outline:

1. The theme of a story is the lesson that the author seeks to impress on his audience.

2. A good short story has one basic theme.

Titus's problem was still on his mind as he helped with the milking that evening. "Father, . . ." he began hesitantly, but then he stopped. Nervously he scuffed his boot on the concrete floor.

"Yes?" Father glanced up from the milker he was adjusting on a cow. Seeing the troubled look on his oldest son's face, he continued, "Is there something I can help you with?"

"Oh, Father, it seems that ever since we moved here, George Weber has given me a hard time. He often makes fun of me for being so short. Sometimes he even calls me Shorty."

"I see." Father stroked his chin thoughtfully. "You're sure you haven't done anything to cause his ill will?"

"I've tried hard to think of something. But I don't have any idea why he should dislike me."

"Is Brother Wayne aware of what's happening?"

"I don't think so. George is careful not to say or do anything when Brother Wayne is close by."

"Well, I'll try to make a point of speaking to Brother Wayne sometime in the next few days. Meanwhile, remember that the Bible way is always the best way. Return good for evil, and you may be surprised at the results."

"Thanks, Father. Just talking about it helps me to feel better." Titus went back to his work with a lighter heart.

The next day at dismissal time, it happened again. "I'd better take this English and history along home," sighed Titus. "Hope I can get everything done this evening. I don't like to start a new day with unfinished assignments."

"Oh, so you haven't finished all your assignments either," commented Timothy. "Writing that composition is taking longer for me too than I had expected."

"Ho, ho! Homework tonight?" laughed George. With a quick glance, he saw that Brother Wayne was nowhere in sight. "Work hard, Shorty, but get out of my way!" Giving a well-aimed bump with his elbow, George barged past Titus and hurried out of the room. The neat stack of books and papers in Titus's hands scattered across the floor.

"That George. I wish—" Titus stopped abruptly as he remembered what Father had told him. It was not right to return evil for evil or even to think evil of George.

The next morning dawned clear and cold. As Titus entered his classroom, the first person he saw was George sitting there, one ankle wrapped in a heavy bandage. "Well! What's this?" asked Titus. "Whatever happened to you?"

"Slipped on the ice. Sprained my ankle," George replied curtly.

   a. Every incident, every conversation, and every description in your story should contribute to that theme.

   b. Do not try to weave in additional themes.

3. The traits of the story characters should be consistent with the theme. The next lesson teaches more about portraying the traits of characters in the story.

4. The setting of the story should contribute to the theme.

   a. The setting includes details about the time and place of the story.

   b. In many short stories, very little is directly stated about the setting.

5. The conflict of the story should portray the theme clearly.

   a. The conflict is the struggle or problem th[e] main character faces.

   b. This conflict may be between the main char[a]cter and another person, between the mai[n] character and his circumstances, or be[t]ween the main character and his own sel[f.]

   c. The story conflict should build up in in[-]tensity as the story develops until it finall[y] reaches the climax.

6. The conclusion of the story should clinc[h] the theme.

   a. Since the conflict is over and the reader['s] curiosity is satisfied, the conclusion shoul[d] be short and to the point.

   b. The conclusion should show rather than di[-]rectly state the theme.

"I'm sorry to hear that. I'd surely hate to miss all this good sledding!" Titus said sincerely. George just shrugged and turned his face away.

That morning before classes began, Brother Wayne remarked, "It looks as if George is a bit disabled today. Do we have a volunteer to stay inside with him at recess?"

Several of the boys glanced toward the hill visible from their classroom. How could anyone stand to miss such perfect sledding! No one offered.

"Think about it until first recess," Brother Wayne said. "Maybe someone will decide to volunteer by then. Otherwise, I'll need to appoint someone; perhaps a few of you can take turns."

Titus's mind was in a whirl. With sledding as ideal as it was, it would be hard enough to stay with George if Brother Wayne requested it. But to volunteer! Besides, if Titus did offer, how would George respond? What would he do if the two of them were together alone for a whole recess?

Titus still had not made up his mind by the time Brother Wayne announced recess. But when the teacher again asked for a volunteer to stay inside with George, Titus resolutely raised his hand. "Thank you, Titus," said Brother Wayne with a warm smile. "You may choose one of the games in the closet. Row 1 is dismissed."

An awkward silence hung over the room as the two boys set up the Scrabble game. Titus tried several times to make conversation, but with little success.

Suddenly George looked at him. "Uh, why did—did you offer—uh—to stay in with me?" he stammered self-consciously.

"Because I wanted to prove that I hold no ill feelings toward you. I really do want to be your friend," replied Titus quietly.

George did not speak for several moments. Finally he said, "I'm sorry. I—I know I've been plenty mean to you. I guess I was jealous. You see, when you started coming here, it seemed that everyone liked you right away. And—and I guess I couldn't stand that. We moved here over a year ago, and I had a hard time being accepted, no matter what I did. It didn't seem fair."

"Really?" asked Titus. "I don't know what that would be like. Are you sure there was actually a big difference?"

"I don't know; maybe it was just me. But anyway—I guess it wasn't your fault if things were that way; and I—I'd like to be your friend too. I also want to tell Brother Wayne and the others that—I'm sorry for the way I've treated you."

"I gladly forgive you," Titus warmly assured George. "Now let's see if we can use a few more of our letters before recess is over. I think it's your turn."

The *theme* of a story is the lesson that the author seeks to impress on his audience. In the story of the Good Samaritan, Jesus emphasized that anyone in need is the neighbor we are to love. Think of other stories you have read. What lessons have they taught? The following list mentions a few of the many possible themes for good stories.

> Honesty is always right.
> Confessing a wrong brings a clear conscience.
> A cheerful attitude makes work easier.
> We must be good stewards of our possessions.
> God is pleased when children respect those in authority.
> Taking responsibility is an important part of growing up.

Developing the Theme

A good short story has one basic theme. Every incident, every conversation, and every description in your story should contribute to that theme. Do not try to weave in additional themes. The author of the sample story emphasized only one theme: Kindness overcomes ill will. The author did not try to bring in other themes, such as "Children need to show respect for authority" or "We should show consideration to a person who is suffering."

By the character traits. The traits of the story characters should be consistent with the theme of the story. Consider the sample story again. The following details about Titus show consistency of character.

> He was good-natured.
> He shared his problems with his father.
> He was conscientious about finishing his homework.
> His books and papers were stacked neatly.
> He showed sincere interest in George's injury.

In the next lesson you will learn more about portraying these character traits in the story.

When you write a story, you should choose and arrange details carefully to develop your theme. The following paragraphs explain how to do this.

In the setting. The setting, which includes details about the time and place of the story, should contribute to the theme. In many short stories, very little is directly stated about the setting. In the sample story, the following details about the setting do contribute to the theme. You will learn more about the setting in Lesson 64.

> The story obviously occurs in the winter. (This gives George something to laugh at, since Titus has not sledded often before.)
> Titus's family moved from southern Maryland (where it is too flat and too warm to do much sledding) to western Pennsylvania (where it is both hilly and snowy enough to sled often).

In the conflict. The conflict of the story should portray the theme clearly. This conflict—the struggle or problem that the main character faces—may be between the main character and another person, between the main character and his circumstances, or between the main character and his own self. Here are some examples of the different kinds of conflict.

Main character versus another person:
Forgiving someone.
Struggling to appreciate someone else.
Resisting the wrong influence of another.

Main character versus his circumstances:
Accepting a change in plans.
Accepting a handicap or hardship.

Main character versus his own self:
Overcoming temptation or a bad habit.
Clearing the conscience by confessing a wrongdoing, apologizing to someone, or making restitution.

In "The Trouble With George," the conflict is obviously between the main character (Titus) and another person (George).

The story conflict should build up in intensity as the story develops until it finally reaches the climax. Except in very short stories, the main character generally faces his conflict at least two times before it is settled. This reoccurrence of the conflict, along with the fact that each incident involves stronger emotion, heightens the reader's suspense as the story unfolds. The climax is actually the most intense incident in the conflict. As the main character faces this point of the conflict, his response brings either victory or defeat.

In the sample story, Titus faces his conflict three times: first when George makes fun of him as the students are going up the steep sledding hill, second when George knocks the books from his hand, and third when he offers to stay in with George. Obviously, the second occasion involves greater intensity than the first. George both says and does something unkind, and Titus struggles briefly with thoughts of retaliation. In the third occasion, which is also the climax, the conflict is a bit different because of Titus's positive action. The greater intensity comes from the way in which George stammers out his confession and apology.

In the conclusion. The conclusion of the story should clinch the theme. Since the conflict is over and the reader's curiosity is satisfied, the conclusion should be short and to the point. However, the conclusion should show rather than directly state the theme. The impact of the theme is much more forceful if the outcome of the story leads the reader to the theme rather than directly stating it. In the sample story, Titus assures George that he is forgiven, and then he suggests going on with the game. This indicates that Titus's problem is solved: his kindness did overcome ill will, and he is ready to move on.

Class Practice

A. Read each story excerpt, and tell what theme the story might follow.

1.   A half hour later, Dean found himself in the garden pulling weeds, something he considered one of the worst jobs. As he reached the end of the first bean row, he slowly stood and stretched his aching back. "I still have two more rows. When will I ever get done?"

   Like a thunderclap, a wonderful idea struck him. "Sure, why not?" he wondered. "I could go fishing when I've finished this job. That is, if Mother lets me. I'm going to pull only the big weeds so I can get done faster."

2.   One evening, when Husky had grown much bigger, the Millers returned home late from a visit and hurried to do the chores. Daniel called softly as he entered the shed to feed his calf. But there was no response. Not a sound. No Husky!

   Daniel checked the fence but found no damage to the pen, and the door was latched. He was stunned. The calf was almost ready to sell. Daniel knew this meant no bicycle soon, and he also felt sick about losing his pet.

   "Father, Husky isn't here," Daniel called, after controlling the tears that wanted to come.

   "Oh, he must be somewhere around," Father answered. But after carefully searching, they realized Husky indeed was gone. There were tire tracks and footprints that clearly indicated he had been carried away.

3.   "Yes, Rhoda, you and Doreen may go ahead," Mother replied. "The rest of us will be over at the school shortly. Sister Martin said she would use her key to open the school so we can show our visitors around a little."

   "Come, Doreen, let's go!" Rhoda grabbed her blue sweater and scarf.

   Doreen reached for her coat, and together they skipped out the door. "School!" exclaimed Doreen. "I have enough of that five days a week!" She laughed.

   Rhoda looked up, stunned.

B. Tell which kind of conflict is shown in each excerpt in Part A.

C. Tell which of the two story endings better clinches a story theme.

1. a.   "I'm impressed again this morning," Brother Kenneth stated, "with the beauty of the snow, and the greatness of our God who made it. Did you know that no two snowflakes have been found that are alike? Surely it takes a great God to do that."

Lesson 58 Answers

Class Practice

A. (Sample answers; underlines indicate the them of the original story.)

1. <u>Shirking responsibility in order to play bring grief.</u> Work half-done is never satisfactory.

2. <u>God may use mysterious means to teach u not to overvalue material possessions.</u> God people need to take joyfully the spoiling of the goods. We must be ready to forgive those wh wrong us.

3. <u>We must stand for what is right regardless others.</u> We must carefully guard our attitude We need to appreciate the privileges we hav

B. 1. main character versus his own self
   2. main character versus his circumstances
   3. main character versus another person

C. (In both of the better endings, the lesson is im plied rather than being directly stated.)
   1. b

Dorcas smiled. Father was right. She should not complain about the cold; rather, she should thank God for the beauty of the snow.

b.   "I'm impressed again this morning," Brother Kenneth stated, "with the beauty of the snow, and the greatness of our God who made it. Did you know that no two snowflakes have been found that are alike? Surely it takes a great God to do that."

Dorcas smiled. She had one answer for Father already. Even if it was cold, she was glad for the rare beauty of the snow that God had sent for them to enjoy.

2. a.   Swinging his lunch pail, Timothy continued, "The other day Lloyd told me he really appreciates this school and how everybody accepts him. Then he added, 'To think I once had dreaded coming!'"

Brenda blushed in shame as she walked along the gravel road. "So Lloyd did dread coming at one time! It just proves that inside he really does have the same feelings as anyone else."

In Brenda's imagination, she could see the happy glow in Lloyd's brown eyes. Certainly he was not spoiling the fun at school as she had feared. Father was right; even though Lloyd was hand-icapped, he was on the same level as everyone else.

b.   Swinging his lunch pail, Timothy continued, "The other day Lloyd told me he really appreciates this school and how everybody accepts him. Then he added, 'To think I once had dreaded coming!'"

Brenda blushed in shame as she walked along the gravel road. "So Lloyd did dread coming at one time! It just proves that inside he really does have the same feelings as anyone else."

In Brenda's imagination, she could see the happy glow in Lloyd's brown eyes. Certainly he was not spoiling the fun at school as she had feared. Brenda had learned an important lesson. Whether handicapped or not, everyone is on the same level.

2. a

Written Exercises

A. Read this story, and do the exercises that follow.

Only Remembered

"Not there, Elizabeth," Margaret said sharply, her mouth set in a straight line and her face flushed in exasperation. "The corn cutters go in the third drawer. And hurry; the dish drainer is full."

Wearily Margaret turned back to the sticky pan she was scouring. "Whew, it feels like a furnace in the kitchen," she declared, wiping sweat from her forehead. "This corn mess seems endless!"

"Cheer up," soothed Mother, who was ready to take more corn to the basement freezer. "I know it's been a long, hard day, but just think how we'll enjoy eating corn this winter."

"Mother always looks on the bright side," Margaret thought a bit wistfully. "Doesn't she *ever* feel blue?"

Just then merry yells erupted at the doorway. A tousle-haired boy dashed through the kitchen with his brother in hot pursuit.

Suddenly an idea struck Margaret. She quickly stepped into the boys' path. "Listen, Andy," she spoke sternly, catching the second boy by the shoulder. "If you have that much energy, I'll put you to work. These buckets of corncobs must be carried—"

"Let me go," Andy whined. "Father said this is our time off." With a tug, he escaped Margaret's grip and raced out the door.

Tears of frustration pushed at Margaret's eyes. "Wish I could *make* those boys work," she fumed to Elizabeth. "All they think of is play, play, play."

Rrrring! It was the telephone.

"Oh, Mother's still downstairs. I guess I'll answer," Margaret muttered. Swiftly she dried her hands and lifted the receiver. "Hello."

"Is this Margaret?"

"Yes, Grandma," Margaret replied, recognizing the voice. "I answered because Mother's downstairs."

"That's all right." Grandma paused before continuing slowly. "We just received some sad news."

Margaret caught her breath. What now?

"Do you remember Anne Beachy, who stayed with us years ago?" Grandma asked.

Instantly a rush of memories flooded Margaret's mind—memories of Anne's kind eyes and warm smile. "Yes, I do."

"Well, she was killed in a car accident this afternoon," Grandma's voice trembled and then broke.

"No, not Anne!" Margaret thought wildly. She waited, speechless, till Grandma went on.

"I would surely think she was ready to go," Grandma said tenderly. "We'll always remember her thoughtful ways."

"Yes, we will," Margaret agreed quietly. After a few more words, they hung up.

Margaret turned to face the questioning eyes of Elizabeth and Mother. She told them the brief story.

Numbly Margaret resumed washing the dishes. Could it be true? Anne, her childhood heroine; Anne, who had read stories to her; Anne, who had pushed her on Grandpa's swing.

Then another thought struck her. "Suppose I had been suddenly taken? What would my family remember about *me*?" With shame, she recalled her irritable mood just minutes before.

"Anne's young life was a challenge to us." Mother put Margaret's thoughts into words. "We should live each day as though it were our last. Then we'll leave lots of pleasant memories behind."

Margaret took a deep breath. "I know I've been hard to live with sometimes," she admitted. "I wish I could always be kind and cheerful, but . . . it's so hard!"

"Don't give up," Mother encouraged. "I know it takes effort and perseverance to build a Christlike character. But God will help us if we trust in Him and really *want* to be like Him."

1. What is the one basic theme of this story?
2. Which of the three kinds of conflict does Margaret face?
3. The first incident in the conflict is when Margaret scolds Elizabeth. Describe the other two incidents of conflict, including the climax.
4. The climax shows greater intensity than the previous incidents in the conflict. Copy some supporting evidence of this fact from the story.
5. Does the climax show a response that brings victory or defeat?

3. Begin thinking about the theme and conflict of a story that you will write later in this chapter.

Review Exercises

A. Each line of this outline has one mistake. Write the outline correctly. [35]

David's Response to God's "No"
(2 Samuel 7)

I. David's Ambition (vv. 1–3)
   A. was centered on spiritual interests
     B. Was subject to scrutiny of God's prophet
II. The direction God gave (vv. 4–17)
   A. did not condemn his motives
   B. God did renew the assurance of His blessing.
   C. Is Always for the Best
III. David's Submission (vv. 18–29)
   A. yielded his will to God
     1. recognized God's perfect knowledge
     2. God's sovereignty
   B. He refused to dwell on shattered dreams.
     1. Trusted God's goodness
   C. Calmly committed himself to God

B. The following information was taken for the topic "Anthracite Coal Mining in Pennsylvania." Draw two rectangles to represent note cards, and copy the information correctly.

Written Exercises

A. 1. We must develop now the kind of character we want to be remembered by when we die.
2. conflict with her own self
3. Margaret impulsively tries to get Andy to do some work for her and becomes upset when he does not.
   Margaret learns that Anne Beachy has died and is forcefully reminded of her own unpleasant disposition in contrast to Anne's pleasant ways.
4. "No, not Anne!" Margaret thought wildly. Numbly Margaret resumed washing the dishes. With shame, she recalled her irritable mood just minutes before.
5. victory

B. (Individual work.)

Review Exercises

A. (Corrections are underlined.)

David's Response to God's "No"
(2 Samuel 7)

I. David's <u>a</u>mbition (vv. 1–3)
   A. <u>Was</u> centered on spiritual interests
   <u>B</u>. Was subject to scrutiny of God's prophet
II. <u>God's direction</u> (vv. 4–17)
   A. <u>Did</u> not condemn his motives
   B. <u>Did</u> renew the assurance of His blessing
   C. Is <u>a</u>lways for the <u>best</u>
III. David's <u>s</u>ubmission (vv. 18–29)
   A. <u>Y</u>ielded his will to God
     1. <u>Recognized</u> God's perfect knowledge
     2. <u>Recognized</u> God's sovereignty
   B. <u>Refused</u> to dwell on shattered dreams, <u>but trusted God's goodness</u>
   C. <u>Committed</u> himself calmly to God

— More than half the United States reserves of anthracite in Pennsylvania (*Encyclopedia International,* p. 526)

— Nearly 500 square miles of anthracite coalfields (*When Coal Was King,* p. 2)

---

59. Characterization in Story Writing

> ### Lesson Survey
> - **Characterization** is the process of portraying a story character.
> - Know the main character well before you begin to write.
> - The traits of a character are revealed by his actions, speech, thoughts, and appearance.
> - Secondary characters are characterized only as much as is necessary for the story.

Have you ever referred to a story without using the title? Perhaps you said something like this: "That reminds me of the story in our reader about Nancy flattering her sister." If you have done this, you have illustrated that characters are very important to most short stories.

Remember that the traits of story characters have a major part in developing the theme of a story. In particular, the traits of the main character should show that he needs the lesson expressed in the theme. For this reason, story characters must be portrayed in a way that shows their traits as clearly and effectively as possible.

Portraying the Main Character

Characterization is the process of portraying a story character. If the characterization is done skillfully, the character is realistic. Indeed, as you read the story, you feel that you are learning to know him.

Effective characterization does not happen automatically. If the main character in your story is to be realistic, you must know him well before you begin to write. Of course, if you write a real-life story about a person you know, this is simple. But then you will need to choose one or two specific traits that best support the story theme. Avoid mentioning traits that do not contribute.

If you make up a true-to-life story, you will need to put more conscious effort into knowing the main character. Picture in your mind the kind of person that will bring out your theme most effectively. List details about

Lesson 59

Purpose: (1) To study methods of showing character traits. (2) To emphasize consistency in characters. (3) To teach how to portray secondary characters. (*Previous experience:* Concept of characterization, without use of the term.)

Oral Review:

1. What is the theme of a story? (the lesson that the story teaches)
2. How many themes should a short story emphasize? (one)
3. What is the conflict in a story? (the struggle or problem the main character faces)
4. What are the three common kinds of conflict? (the main character in conflict with another person, with his circumstances, or with his own self)
5. How does a story conflict build up in intensity?

B. (Sample note cards.)

> Anthracite Coal Mining in Pennsylvania
>
> *Encyclopedia International,* p. 526
>
> More than half the United States reserves of anthracite in Pennsylvania

> Anthracite C. M. in Pa.
>
> *When Coal Was King,* p. 2
>
> Nearly 500 square miles of anthracite coalfields

(The main character generally faces his conflict more than once. Each successive incident in the conflict involves stronger emotion.)

Lesson Introduction: Have your students name several Bible stories that have long been among their favorites. Possibly they will name stories with titles like "David and Goliath," "Daniel in the Lions' Den," "Baby Moses in the Bulrushes," and "Jesus Feeds the Five Thousand." Whatever story they name, the title will likely include the name of a person. Can you imagine a story without a main character? This lesson gives pointers on making story characters seem real and alive.

Lesson Outline:

1. Characterization is the process of portraying a story character.

2. Know the main character well before you begin to write.

he person's appearance and character. Not all of these traits will neces-
arily be mentioned in the story, but you should have a well-rounded pic-
ure of the character in order to keep his behavior consistent throughout
he story.

Think back to the sample story in Lesson 58, "The Trouble With George."
The following lists could have been written for this story. Notice how only
he traits that contribute to the theme are woven into the story.

Appearance:
  Black hair and brown eyes (not important to story)
  Small for his age (part of the reason George made fun of him)
Character:
  Conscientious (right attitude toward school assignments; tried
    hard to be a peacemaker)
  Hardworking (not important to story)
  Good-natured (laughed off George's sneering remarks)
  Sympathetic (expressed sincere interest in George's injury; offered
    to stay in with him)

Characterization is accomplished by using details that show a person's
ctions, speech, thoughts, and appearance. Note that you should *show* the
raits of character; this is more effective than directly stating them.

A person's *actions* reveal his character. In the sample story, Titus neatly
tacked his books and he stayed inside with George. These actions reveal
is conscientious and sympathetic nature.

A person's *speech* reveals his character. This includes both the actual
vords of the speaker and the explanatory words that tell how he spoke.
Titus humorously suggested that he was short because southern Maryland
might not have as good growing weather as does western Pennsylvania.
Can you see his good-naturedness? One clue that he is conscientious is his
omment about not liking to start a day with unfinished assignments.

A person's *thoughts* reveal his character. This method of characteriza-
ion is used much less than the previous two; in fact, it may not be used
t all. But whenever a character's thoughts are given or implied, they
hould contribute to the overall impression the story gives of that charac-
er. At least twice in the story, Titus's thoughts suggest that he is consci-
ntious. Near the beginning, he was sincerely trying to understand why
George did not like him. Later when he was tempted to wish evil on George,
e remembered what his father had said.

Finally, a person's *appearance* reveals his character. Of the various
vays to characterize a person, this one is used the least. In fact, many good
hort stories say little or nothing about the main character's appearance.
n the sample story, the only description of Titus is that he was short, which

a. If you write a real-life story about a person
   you know, choose one or two specific traits
   that best support the story theme.
b. If you make up a true-to-life story, picture
   the kind of person that will bring out your
   theme most effectively, and list details
   about the person's appearance and character.

**3. The traits of a character are revealed in
a number of ways.**
   a. By his actions.
   b. By his speech. This includes both the ac-
      tual words of the speaker and the ex-
      planatory words that tell how he spoke.
   c. By his thoughts. This method of charac-
      terization is used much less than the pre-
      vious two. In fact, it may not be used at all.

   d. By his appearance. This method is used the
      least. Many good short stories say little or
      nothing about the main character's ap-
      pearance.

**4. Secondary characters are characterized
only as much as is necessary for the story.**
   a. The less a character contributes to the con-
      flict and theme, the less detail needs to be
      given about him.
   b. Characters with a very minor part may not
      even be named.

relates directly to the conflict; and the indication that he was neat, which contributes to the overall picture of Titus as a conscientious boy.

Portraying Secondary Characters

Although a good short story revolves around one main character, other characters are usually a part of the story as well. These secondary characters are characterized only as much as is necessary for the story. The less a character contributes to the conflict and theme, the less detail needs to be given about him. Characters with a very minor part may not even be named.

In the story "The Trouble With George," four secondary characters are named: George, Father, Brother Wayne, and Timothy. Of these, more is said about George than about the others because he is more closely related to the theme and conflict. Father fills a fairly important role in helping Titus to deal rightly with his problem. Brother Wayne is mentioned several times because the conflict occurs at school. Timothy is mentioned only briefly because he is not directly involved in the theme or conflict of the story.

Class Practice

A. Do these exercises, which are based on the story "Only Remembered" in Lesson 58, Written Exercises, Part A.
 1. Who is the main character?
 2. Describe the character traits of this person.
 3. Tell how this person's character is shown by each of the four methods of characterization.
 4. Mother is a secondary character. In what ways is she characterized?

B. Tell how the actions, speech, thoughts, or appearance of each character can be adjusted to make the change described in parentheses.
 1. As Naomi bounced into the kitchen, she burst out, "Mother, may I bake a cake? Something different from the chocolate cake I always make." (Change Naomi from an impulsive girl to a careful, particular girl.)
 2. "Fifteen minutes till chore time," Curtis thought as he glanced at his watch. "I could start chores early and work on my birdhouse before supper." Slowly he rolled over on his back and stretched. (Change Curtis from a lazy boy into an industrious boy.)

Written Exercises

A. Read this story, and do the exercises that follow.

All for the Good

Joyce scoured the frying pan almost viciously as she bent over the kitchen sink. "Oh," moaned the thirteen-year-old, a trickle of sweat running down her face. "I don't know how we'll *ever* get all our work done.

Lesson 59 Answers

Class Practice

A. 1. Margaret
 2. Margaret tends to be irritable, impulsive, and thoughtless.
 3. (Sample answers.)
 Actions: She turned back to her sticky pan wearily. She impulsively grabbed Andy.
 Speech: She scolded Elizabeth sharply. She exaggerated about the heat. She fumed to Elizabeth about the boys.
 Thoughts: She thought wistfully about Mother's cheerfulness. She had the sudden idea of making the boys help with the work. She considered what her family would remember about her if she had suddenly been killed.
 Appearance: Her mouth was set in a straight line, and her face was flushed with exasperation.
 4. She spoke soothingly to Margaret. Margaret said that she always looked on the bright side of things. She encouraged Margaret to persevere and to trust God to help her.

B. (Sample changes.)
 1. As Naomi stepped into the kitchen, she asked, "Mother, may I bake a cake? Do you have any suggestions?"
 2. "Fifteen minutes till chore time," Curtis thought as he glanced at his watch. "I could start chores early and work on my birdhouse before supper." He jumped to his feet and headed for the barn.

There's some washing to do, the cleaning isn't finished, and those peaches must be canned yet today. Mother says they can't wait till Monday. And there must be a dozen or two other odd jobs to be done.

"Besides all that, Uncle Isaac's are coming for dinner. Visitors? On a Saturday—of all things! What will we do?" She yanked the plugs out of the drains in the sink and swished the water off the counter top.

Then she half ran for the clothes basket and emptied the dirty wash from the hamper into it. "It's good there isn't much. Probably can do it in two loads," Joyce told herself. Before long, the washer hummed busily as it laundered the first load of clothes.

Meanwhile, Mother and Joyce hurried about, dusting, sweeping, and tidying the house. But there seemed to be so many interruptions.

"Mother, get me a drink."

"Joyce, tie my shoe."

"Here, can you hold the baby? I can't keep her quiet."

On and on went the requests. First one person and then another. The hands on the clock spun around twice as fast as on other mornings—or so it seemed. Somehow, the wash was hung on the line and the cleaning nearly completed, but the peaches were not even begun.

Then the telephone rang. After a short conversation, Mother said good-bye and turned to Joyce. "That was Mrs. Cooper. She wants me to take her to town," she informed simply.

"Mother, not today!" Joyce gasped. "It's so close to dinnertime, and we're having company. How will I ever get ready by myself?"

"Well, I guess we'll just have to let them see things the way they are," Mother replied, swiftly slicing potatoes into a casserole. "Besides, it really doesn't look too bad around here."

"But the peaches! When will we do them?"

"I don't know; probably after they leave." Mother slipped the food into the oven and prepared to go. "Set the table, Joyce, and watch the dinner. Take care of the children, and don't worry about the work. I'll try to be back soon. Father is coming in now. I'm sure he'll lend you a hand."

Joyce had nearly finished setting the table when she heard a car drive in. "Oh, no! They're here!" she cried. "And Mother isn't even home yet." Glancing about the house, she thought, "Sure doesn't look like I wanted it to. Why did things have to work out like this today?"

"Don't worry," spoke Father calmly. "Uncle Isaac's won't mind." He went to the door to invite the visitors in.

And Joyce need not have worried. Uncle Isaac was his usual, friendly self, and cheery Aunt Susan and some of the girl cousins were soon bustling about, helping to prepare the meal. Dinner was nearly ready when Mother arrived, and soon everyone was seated around the table.

When the meal was over, a crew of women and girls attacked the stack of dirty dishes while the men and boys went outside. "I'll tell you what," said Aunt Susan. "Some of us will begin the peaches while the others do the dishes."

"Oh, no!" Mother protested. "I won't have my company canning peaches!"

"Oh, yes, you will!" Aunt Susan laughed merrily. "You let me see to this! We wouldn't just sit here and visit when you have peaches to do." Soon she had a knife and a dishpan and began peeling peaches. She talked and laughed as if she always helped with peaches when she went visiting.

When the dishes and peaches were done, Cousin Lena said to Joyce, "We might as well bring in the wash and fold it yet." It did not take long till that job was finished. Then everyone sat down to visit for a short while.

By the time the visitors left, it seemed the work was almost done. "How refreshing a group of cheerful, helpful visitors can be!" Joyce mused. "I doubt if they realize how much their kindness brightened our day. Usually, having company means more work, but this time they helped with it!"

"And, dear heavenly Father," she prayed, "forgive my impatience and worry. Help me to trust Thee to work everything together for the good."

1. Name the main character, and give a brief general description of the kind of person she was.
2. Give specific examples that characterize the main character, as indicated below.
   a. three examples of actions
      Sample: Joyce scoured the frying pan almost viciously.
           (Find three other examples.)
   b. two examples of speech, from two different paragraphs
   c. one example of a thought
   d. one example of appearance
3. Give specific examples that characterize the following secondary characters.
   a. Mother—one example each of action and speech
   b. Father—one example of speech
   c. Aunt Susan—one example each of action and speech
4. Give the names of three other secondary characters.
5. What secondary characters are referred to but not named?

B. Rewrite the actions, speech, thoughts, or appearance of each character to make the changes given in parentheses.
   1.   "Wish there weren't so many beans to pick," grumbled Caleb to his younger brother. A scowl darkened his face as he thought of the

Written Exercises

A. 1. Joyce is a fast worker, who wants things to look nice. But she is impatient and easily worried.

2. (Sample answers.)
   a. She yanked the drain plugs out. She swished the water off the counter top. She half ran for the clothes basket.
   b. *Paragraph 1:* "I don't know how we'll ever get all our work done."
      Paragraph 2: "Visitors? On a Saturday—of all things!"
      Paragraph 10: "Mother, not today!" Joyce gasped.
      Paragraph 14: "Oh, no! They're here!"
   c. "Sure doesn't look like I wanted it to. Why did things have to work out like this today?"
   d. A trickle of sweat ran down her face.

3. (Sample answers.)
   a. *Action:* She took Mrs. Cooper to town even when busy. She swiftly sliced potatoes into a casserole while she talked.
      Speech: "Well, I guess we'll just have to let them see things the way they are." "I won't have my company canning peaches!"
   b. "Don't worry," spoke Father calmly.
   c. *Action:* She helped prepare the dinner. She soon was ready to do peaches after dinner.
      Speech: "Oh, yes, you will!" Aunt Susan laughed merrily. "We wouldn't just sit here and visit when you have peaches to do."

4. Mrs. Cooper, Uncle Isaac, Cousin Lena
5. Joyce's younger brothers or sisters; Uncle Isaac's children

B. (Sample paragraphs.)
   1.   "With all these beans, we'd better get started," remarked Caleb to his younger brother. A smile brightened his face as he thought of the new bicycle sitting in the garage.

new bicycle sitting in the garage. (Change Caleb from grouchy to pleasant.)

2.   Marla whisked her dustcloth over a few of the larger items in the living room. "Hope Mother doesn't check this too carefully before Uncle Aaron's come," she thought as she yanked out the sweeper. Quickly Marla swept through the middle of the floor, then shoved the sweeper back into the closet. (Change Marla from a careless worker to a careful one.)

3.   "Here, Benny, you shouldn't play with the scissors. Give them to me, please," requested Nelson, holding out his hand. (Change Nelson from a patient to an impatient boy.)

2. List some details about the main character in the story that you will write later, and about any important secondary characters. Include details about physical appearance, likes and dislikes, attitudes toward those in authority, mannerisms, and so forth. Save this work for future lessons.

2.   Marla carefully dusted each item in the living room. "Mother won't have time to check this before Uncle Aaron's come, so I'll do the best I can," she thought as she took out the sweeper. Marla swept the floor carefully, then placed the sweeper back into the closet.

3.   "Benny, you naughty boy. You shouldn't play with the scissors. Give them here!" shouted Nelson, grabbing them from Benny.

C. (Individual work.)

---

60. Subject–Verb Agreement

Lesson Survey

- Be especially careful to make the verb agree with the subject in the following situations.
    1. When the verb precedes the subject.
    2. When it may seem logical to make the verb agree with a noun other than the subject.
    3. When the verb is part of a contraction.
    4. When two subjects are joined by *and*.
    5. When two singular subjects are joined by *or* or *nor*.
    6. When the subject is an indefinite pronoun.
    7. When the subject looks like a plural noun but is singular in meaning.
    8. When the subject is usually considered plural but names a single object.
    9. When the subject is a collective noun.
    10. When the subject includes a plural form used as a topic of discussion.

For the vast majority of sentences, the matter of subject–verb agreement poses little difficulty. However, there are a number of problem areas that deserve careful attention.

Lesson 60

Purpose: To teach rules for subject–verb agreement.

Oral Review:

1. Name the word that receives the action of the verb in each sentence. (Answers are underlined.)
    a. The <u>Bible</u> has been preserved until our time.
    b. The Bible still provides the only <u>answer</u> to man's needs.
    c. God faithfully guides His <u>people</u>.
2. Name the two words that are linked by the verb in each sentence. (Answers are underlined.)
    a. Our <u>watermelons</u> grew <u>enormous</u>.
    b. This <u>one</u> sounds <u>ripe</u> already.
3. How is the simple past tense different from the present perfect tense? (The present perfect tense indicates an action or a condition that began in the past and is completed as of the present moment or continues into the present time. The simple past merely states that something happened at some time in the past.)
4. Read this sentence, changing the verb to the progressive form and then to the emphatic form: *We went to the orchard for apples.* (We were going to the orchard for apples. We did go to the orchard for apples.)

Lesson Introduction: When two horses are hitched to a wagon, they need to work together. If one tries to back up when the other tries to go forward, or if one pulls to the left when the other pulls to the right, there is likely to be much confusion and little progress. The skeleton of a sentence is the team that pulls the sentence along in meaningful communication. Like a team of horses, the subject and the verb must work together. This lesson gives instruction in a number of areas relating to subject–verb agreement.

1. *When the verb precedes the subject, think ahead to the subject and make the verb agree with it.* The verb (or part of it) precedes the subject in many questions and in most sentences that begin with *there* or *here.*

> <u>Have</u> the <u>disciples</u> <u>understood</u> Jesus' teaching?
> What <u>does</u> the <u>multitude</u> <u>expect</u> from Him?
> There <u>is</u> much <u>opposition</u> to Him among the religious rulers.

2. *Make the verb agree with the subject, not with some other substantive.* When a prepositional phrase comes between the subject and the verb, you may tend to make the verb agree with the object of the preposition. You may make a similar mistake when a plural predicate nominative renames a singular subject or when a singular predicate nominative renames a plural subject. But remember that the verb must always agree with its subject.

> A <u>basket</u> of apples <u>has been dropped</u>. (*not* apples <u>have been dropped</u>)
> <u>Father</u>, along with Roy and Grandfather, <u>is loading</u> the corn.
> (*not* <u>Father, Roy, and Grandfather</u> <u>are loading</u>)
> One <u>benefit</u> of hard work <u>is</u> strong *muscles*. (*not* <u>are</u> *muscles*)
> Strong <u>muscles</u> <u>are</u> one *benefit* of hard work. (*not* <u>is</u> *benefit*)

3. *Use a contraction as you would use the words it represents.* Be especially alert to contractions such as *here's, there's, how's, what's,* and *doesn't.* To test your use of a contraction, think of the two words from which it is made.

Singular	**Plural**
Here's (Here <u>is</u>) the <u>puzzle</u>.	Here <u>are</u> the <u>puzzles</u>.
What's (What <u>is</u>) the <u>answer</u>?	What <u>are</u> the <u>answers</u>?
My <u>answer</u> doesn't (<u>does</u> not) work.	My <u>answers</u> don't (<u>do</u> not) work.

4. *Use a plural verb with a compound subject joined by* and. The conjunction *and* means that the verb expresses action or condition for all parts of the subject.

> <u>Math</u> and <u>science</u> <u>are</u> my favorite subjects.
> (<u>Both</u> <u>are</u> my favorite subjects.)
> <u>Esther</u>, <u>Abigail</u>, and <u>Dorcas</u> <u>were</u> godly women.
> (<u>These</u> <u>were</u> godly women.)
> The <u>teacher</u> and the <u>writer</u> <u>are</u> busy. (<u>Both</u> <u>are</u> busy.)

Sometimes a compound subject names only one person or thing, as when one person holds two positions or one dish is composed of two foods. In this case, the verb is singular and an article or a possessive pronoun is used only before the first noun. In contrast, if the compound subject names two different persons or objects, the verb is plural and an article or a possessive pronoun is used before each of the nouns.

Lesson Outline:

1. When the verb precedes the subject, think ahead to the subject and make the verb agree with it. The verb (or part of it) precedes the subject in many questions and in most sentences that begin with *there* or *here.*

2. Make the verb agree with the subject, not with some other substantive. One source of trouble is a prepositional phrase that comes between the subject and the verb. Another is a plural predicate nominative that renames a singular subject, or a singular predicate nominative that renames a plural subject.

3. Use a contraction as you would use the words it represents. Be especially alert to contractions such as *here's, there's, how's, what's,* and *doesn't.* To test your use of a contraction, think of the two words from which the contraction is made.

4. Use a plural verb with a compound subject joined by and.

  a. The conjunction *and* means that the verb expresses action or condition for all parts of the subject.

  b. A compound subject may name only one person or thing, as when one person holds two positions or one dish is composed of two foods. In this case, the verb is singular and an article or a possessive pronoun is used only before the first noun.

  c. If the compound subject names two different persons or objects, the verb is plural and an article or a possessive pronoun is used before each of the nouns.

  d. If the two parts of a compound subject name the same thing but are modified by different adjectives, only one subject may be

Singular: One object or person
>The chicken and rice was delicious. (one dish)
>The teacher and writer is busy. (one person)
>My uncle and neighbor has helped us. (one person)

Plural: Two objects or persons
>The chicken and the rice were delicious. (two foods)
>The teacher and the writer are busy. (two persons)
>My uncle and my neighbor have helped us. (two persons)

If the two parts of a compound subject name the same thing but are modified by different adjectives, only one subject may be stated. However, an article or a possessive pronoun will generally be used before each adjective to clarify that the subject is compound. In contrast, if a single subject is modified by two adjectives, an article or a possessive pronoun will be used only before the first adjective.

>The white and the gray building are new.
>   (two buildings, one white and one gray)
>The white and gray building is new.
>   (one building, partly white and partly gray)

5. *Use a singular verb with two singular subjects joined by* or *or* nor. The conjunction *or* means that the verb expresses action or condition for only one of the compound parts. The conjunction *nor* means that the verb expresses action or condition for neither one of the compound parts.

>Susan or Kay was washing the floor. (Just one was washing the floor.)
>Neither Earth nor Mars is nearly as large as Jupiter.
>   (Neither one is as large.)

Of course, if the compound subjects are both plural, use a plural verb. If one is singular and the other is plural, make the verb agree with the subject that is nearer to the verb.

>The woodchucks or the rabbits have been eating our beans.
>Has the woodchuck or the rabbits been eating our beans?

>Neither the cats nor the dog is in sight.
>Neither the dog nor the cats are in sight.

6. *Use singular verbs with singular indefinite pronouns.* These include *each, either, neither, one, another,* and any compound with *one* or *body.* Often such a pronoun is followed by a prepositional phrase. But remember that the verb must agree with the subject, not with the object of a preposition.

>Each of the answers expresses the idea well.
>   (Each one expresses the idea.)

stated. However, an article or a possessive pronoun will generally be used before each adjective to clarify that the subject is compound.

    e. If a single subject is modified by two adjectives, an article or a possessive pronoun will be used only before the first adjective.

5. Use a singular verb with two singular subjects joined by or or nor.

    a. The conjunction *or* means that the verb expresses action or condition for only one of the compound parts. The conjunction *nor* means that the verb expresses action or condition for neither one of the compound parts.

    b. If the compound subjects are both plural, use a plural verb.

    c. If one subject is singular and the other is plural, make the verb agree with the subject that is nearer to the verb.

6. Use singular verbs with singular indefinite pronouns. These include *each, either, neither, one, another,* and any compound with *one* or *body.*

7. A singular verb is used when a noun that looks like a plural noun is singular in meaning.

    a. Nouns like *news, gallows,* and *bellows*

    b. Names of diseases like *measles, mumps, rabies,* and *rickets*

    c. Words ending with -*ics* like *civics, mathematics, ethics, politics, physics,* and *economics*

8. Some nouns are usually considered plural when they name a single object. Usually plural verbs are used with them.

<u>Neither</u> of the books <u>is</u> in good condition.
(Neither <u>one</u> <u>is</u> in good condition.)
<u>Someone</u> <u>was making</u> a loud noise. (Some <u>one</u> <u>was making</u> a loud noise.)

7. *A singular verb is used when a noun that looks like a plural noun is singular in meaning.* In this category are nouns like *news, gallows,* and *bellows;* names of diseases like *measles, mumps, rabies,* and *rickets;* and words ending with *-ics* like *civics, mathematics, ethics, politics, physics,* and *economics.* These nouns are usually singular.

Haman's <u>gallows</u> <u>was used</u> for himself instead of for Mordecai.
<u>Measles</u> <u>is</u> not nearly as common as it had been years ago.
Christian <u>economics</u> <u>includes</u> the practice of sharing with others.

8. *Some nouns are usually considered plural when they name a single object. Usually plural verbs are used with them.* Nouns like *shears, scissors, trousers, pliers, glasses,* and *tongs* are in this category. Of course, if the subject is *pair* followed by one of these words in a prepositional phrase, the verb should be singular to agree with *pair.*

My <u>glasses</u> <u>are broken</u>.
My new <u>pair</u> of glasses <u>is broken</u>.

These <u>scissors</u> <u>are</u> not sharp.
This <u>pair</u> of scissors <u>is</u> not sharp.

9. *Use a singular verb with a collective noun that refers to a group acting as a unit, and a plural verb with a collective noun that refers to individual members acting separately.* A collective noun names a collection of individuals. Some common collective nouns are *group, family, congregation, herd, flock,* and *swarm.*

Singular: Group acting as a unit
The <u>class</u> <u>is reciting</u> Psalm 42 by memory.
The <u>flock</u> <u>is grazing</u> on the lush, green grass.

Plural: Individuals acting separately
The <u>class</u> <u>are writing</u> their memory assignments.
The scattered <u>flock</u> <u>were trying</u> to find their ways home.

10. *Use a singular verb with a title or word that is a topic of discussion, even if it includes a plural form.* In such a sentence, the subject is singular because it refers to one title, one word, or one group of words.

<u>"The Pineapples and the Bee"</u> <u>teaches</u> an interesting lesson about forbidden joys.
<u>Hosen</u> <u>is</u> an archaic plural form of *hose.*

a. Nouns like *shears, scissors, trousers, pliers, glasses,* and *tongs* are in this category.
b. If the subject is *pair* followed by one of these words in a prepositional phrase, the verb should be singular to agree with *pair.*

9. Use a singular verb with a collective noun that refers to a group acting as a unit, and a plural verb with a collective noun that refers to individual members acting separately.

10. Use a singular verb with a title or word that is a topic of discussion, even if it includes a plural form.

★ *EXTRA PRACTICE*
Worksheet 21 *(Subject–Verb Agreement)*

Class Practice

Read each sentence, using the correct form in parentheses.
1. Our Saviour and Lord (is, are) Jesus.
2. Neither Jeremiah nor Baruch (was, were) afraid to obey the Lord.
3. (There's, There are) many warnings against sin in the Book of Jeremiah.
4. (Is, Are) the message of truth appreciated by the world?
5. Each of the books of the Bible (have, has) a definite message for us.
6. "The Ways of a Bear" (is, are) in the eighth grade reader.
7. The boy's trousers (is, are) spattered with mud.
8. The politics of this world (provide, provides) no lasting answers to man's problems.
9. Frequent blizzards (is, are) one danger to life on the prairies.
10. The flock of geese (have, has) flown many miles today.

B. Read each sentence, changing the singular subjects and verbs to plural and the plural ones to singular.
1. The books don't give the necessary information.
2. There is a dish of ice cream on the table.
3. When's the storm going to end?
4. Our trees bear good, sweet apples.

C. Read each sentence, following the directions in parentheses. Change the verb as needed to agree with the subject, but do not change its tense.
1. The goats are in the pasture. (Change *The goats* to *Neither of the goats.*)
2. Flossy or Frisky is in the garden. (Change *or* to *and.*)
3. There's one billy goat on the road. (Change *one* to *two.*)
4. Either the manager or the clerks were mistaken. (Reverse the order of *manager* and *clerks.*)

Written Exercises

A. Copy the correct verbs in parentheses.
1. The promises of the Bible (is, are) a source of inspiration.
2. The Old and the New Testament (contain, contains) many promises.
3. Everyone who trusts in these promises (find, finds) strength to endure.
4. (There is, There are) many examples of saints who endured faithfully.
5. God (don't, doesn't) make any promise that He cannot keep.
6. Peter, as well as the other disciples, (was, were) afraid to stay with Jesus after His arrest.
7. Neither the high priest nor the other rulers (was, were) ready to acknowledge Jesus' authority.
8. Christian ethics (require, requires) obedience to the Golden Rule.

Lesson 60 Answers

Class Practice

A. 1. is
    2. was
    3. There are
    4. Is
    5. has
    6. is
    7. are
    8. provides
    9. are
   10. has

B. (Corrections are underlined.)
1. The <u>book doesn't</u> give the necessary information.
2. There <u>are dishes</u> of ice cream on the table.
3. When <u>are</u> the <u>storms</u> going to end?
4. Our <u>tree bears</u> good, sweet apples.

C. (Corrections are underlined.)
1. Neither of the goats <u>is</u> in the pasture.
2. Flossy and Frisky <u>are</u> in the garden.
3. There <u>are</u> two billy goats on the road.
4. Either the clerks or the manager <u>was</u> mistaken.

Written Exercises

A. 1. are
   2. contain
   3. finds
   4. There are
   5. doesn't
   6. was
   7. were
   8. requires

9. A Christian family (pray, prays) together regularly.
10. The caroling group (have, has) dressed in their warmest clothes.
11. The larvae of mosquitoes (live, lives) in water.
12. *Larvae* (is, are) the plural of *larva*.
13. The shears on the workbench (is, are) quite dull.
14. Athletics (become, becomes) an idol to many pleasure-seeking people.
15. "Beautiful Things" (emphasize, emphasizes) that true beauty is not found where the world looks for it.
16. The black and brown horse (is, are) very friendly.
17. (What's, What are) the news from Aunt Louise?
18. Neither the cousins nor Uncle Glen (have, has) called today.
19. My blue and my black pen (have, has) quit writing.
20. (Don't, Doesn't) anybody know where the compass is?
21. Mathematics (follow, follows) very orderly laws.
22. Neither Mother nor the girls (have, has) gone over to Grandmother yet.
23. The high wind, in addition to the heavy rains, (have, has) caused much damage.
24. The class (have, has) finished their various projects.
25. (Is, Are) the tweezers in the drawer?
26. Macaroni and cheese (was, were) served as the main dish.

B. Rewrite these sentences, changing the singular subjects and verbs to plural and the plural ones to singular. Do not change the tense.
1. The disciples of Jesus walk in the way of His Word.
2. The commandments of Jesus don't seem grievous to the loyal.
3. The saint isn't promised an easy road.
4. There's a rich blessing for the faithful.

C. Rewrite each sentence, following the directions in parentheses. Change the verb as needed to agree with the subject, but do not change the tense.
1. The oral reports have been quite interesting. (Change *The oral reports* to *Each of the oral reports*.)
2. Either the cats or the dog likes to play with us. (Reverse the order of *cats* and *dog*.)
3. The strangers don't understand us. (Change *The strangers* to *One of the strangers*.)
4. The man and his son tend the market. (Change *and* to *or*.)
5. This pair of trousers has a hole in the knee. (Change *This pair of trousers* to *These trousers*.)
6. The flock of geese are foraging in various fields. (Change *foraging in various fields* to *circling to land on the pond*.)

9. prays
10. have
11. live
12. is
13. are
14. becomes
15. emphasizes
16. is
17. What's
18. has
19. have
20. Doesn't
21. follows
22. have
23. has
24. have
25. Are
26. was

B. 1. The disciple of Jesus walks in the way of His Word.
2. The commandment of Jesus doesn't seem grievous to the loyal.
3. The saints aren't promised an easy road.
4. There are rich blessings for the faithful.

C. 1. Each of the oral reports has been quite interesting.
2. Either the dog or the cats like to play with us.
3. One of the strangers doesn't understand us.
4. The man or his son tends the market.
5. These trousers have a hole in the knee.
6. The flock of geese is circling to land on the pond.

J

Review Exercises

. Copy the complements in these sentences. Label each one *DO* (direct object), *IO* (indirect object), *PN* (predicate nominative), *PA* (predicate adjective), or *OC* (objective complement). [5–8]
1. Early spring is the time for spiders to hatch.
2. One cluster of eggs may produce several hundred spiderlings.
3. However, only a few of these will become adults.
4. The spiderlings leave the cluster and climb a tall plant.
5. The wind gives each spiderling a ride to a new place.
6. Another plant would be suitable for the spiderling's new home.
7. By instinct, the spiderling makes its web an example of geometric beauty.
8. Truly the Creator is both wise and wonderful.

. If the underlined part contains a mistake in the use of quotation marks and related punctuation or capitalization, write it correctly. If it is correct, write *correct*. [26]
1. The psalmist <u>wrote "The</u> Lord is my shepherd."
2. "Every good gift and every perfect gift," wrote <u>James, "Is</u> from above."
3. "Let's sing 'I Owe the Lord a Morning <u>Song," suggested</u> Gary.
4. "Did you hear Carol say, 'Your book is on the <u>floor'?" asked</u> Martha.
5. "How wonderful to hear Daryl say, 'I'm <u>all right!'"</u> exclaimed Nevin.

Review Exercises

A. 1. time—PN
   2. spiderlings—DO
   3. adults—PN
   4. cluster—DO; plant—DO
   5. spiderling—IO; ride—DO
   6. suitable—PA
   7. web—DO; example—OC
   8. wise—PA; wonderful—PA

B. 1. wrote, "The
   2. James, "is
   3. Song,'" suggested
   4. correct
   5. all right'!" exclaimed

---

61. Using Problem Verbs

> **Lesson Survey**
>
> - *Lay* is a transitive verb that means "to put or place (something)."
> - *Lie* is an intransitive verb that means "to rest, recline, or remain in a flat position."
> - *Set* is usually a transitive verb that means "to put or place (something)." As an intransitive verb, it may mean "to move below the horizon," "to keep eggs warm for hatching," or "to become firm."
> - *Sit* is an intransitive verb that means "to rest or be seated."
> - *Raise* is a transitive verb that means "to cause (something) to go up or grow up."
> - *Rise* is an intransitive verb that means "to get up or go up."
> - *Can* means "to be able to."
> - *May* means "to be permitted to."

Lesson 61

Purpose: To study the correct usage of some confusing verbs.

Oral Review:
1. Tell whether *is* or *are* fits in each sentence.
   a. There ——— many examples of faithfulness in the Bible. (are)
   b. Each of the persons mentioned in Hebrews 11 ——— an inspiration to us. (is)
   c. The proverbs of Solomon ——— filled with valuable lessons. (are)
   d. The Acts of the Apostles ——— an account of the early church. (is)
   e. The shears ——— too sharp for a child to play with. (are)
   f. The class ——— finishing their various projects. (are)

2. Give the second and third principal parts of these verbs.
   a. swing (swung, [have] swung)
   b. drown (drowned, [have] drowned)
   c. go (went, [have] gone)
   d. shine (shone *or* shined, [have] shone *or* [have] shined)
   e. hit (hit, [have] hit)

Lesson Introduction: If you became acquainted with a set of identical twins, how would you learn to tell them apart? Probably you would look for small differences in their appearance or manners. And you would keep trying. You should treat these problem verbs in like manner. Study carefully the differences between the two verbs in each pair, and keep trying to use them correctly.

In the English language, there are a number of verbs in pairs with similar meanings. Sometimes people confuse these sets of verbs in their speaking and writing. Study these verbs carefully so that you are able to use them correctly.

Lay—Lie

Lay is a transitive verb that means "to put or place (something)." Its principal parts are *lay, laid, (have) laid.* Since *lay* is transitive, it must pass its action either to the direct object or to the subject.

> You <u>must lay</u> the papers in neat stacks.
> > (You *must place* the papers. *Papers* receives the action of *must lay.*)
>
> These bricks <u>were laid</u> by a skilled mason.
> > (These bricks *were placed. Bricks* receives the action of *were laid.*)
>
> Mr. Winters <u>has laid</u> many bricks in his lifetime.
> > (Mr. Winters *has placed* many bricks. *Bricks* receives the action of *has laid.*)

Lie is an intransitive verb that means "to rest, recline, or remain in a flat position." Its principal parts are *lie, lay, (have) lain.* Since *lie* is intransitive, it never passes action to another word in the sentence.

> The sluggard <u>lies</u> in bed after he should get up.
> > (The sluggard *rests* in bed. No action is passed.)
>
> All morning, the book <u>lay</u> on the shelf.
> > (The book *rested* on the shelf. No action is passed.)
>
> The overripe pumpkins <u>have lain</u> on the porch too long.
> > (The pumpkins *have remained* too long. No action is passed.)

Since the form *lay* is used both as the first principal part of *lay* and the second principal part of *lie,* it can be especially confusing. Note, however, that *lay* is used as a transitive verb only in the present and future tenses, and as an intransitive verb only in the past tense.

> Every morning we <u>lay</u> the songbooks on the desks.
> > (transitive verb; present tense)
>
> Tomorrow we <u>shall lay</u> the songbooks on the desks.
> > (transitive verb; future tense)
>
> The extra songbook <u>lay</u> on the shelf. (intransitive verb; past tense)

Set—Sit

Set is usually a transitive verb that means "to put or place (something)." Its principal parts are *set, set, (have) set.* Since *set* is transitive, it must pass its action either to the direct object or to the subject.

Lesson Outline:

1. Lay *is a transitive verb that means "to put or place (something)."*

    a. Its principal parts are *lay, laid, (have) laid.*

    b. It must pass its action either to the direct object or to the subject.

2. Lie *is an intransitive verb that means "to rest, recline, or remain in a flat position."*

    a. Its principal parts are *lie, lay, (have) lain.*

    b. It never passes action to another word in the sentence.

3. Set *is usually a transitive verb that means "to put or place (something)."*

    a. Its principal parts are *set, set, (have) set.*

    b. It must pass its action either to the direct object or to the subject.

    c. *Set* also has several meanings as an

intransitive verb: "to move below the hor[izon," "to keep eggs warm for hatching," an[d] "to become firm."

4. Sit *is an intransitive verb that means "t[o] rest or be seated."*

    a. Its principal parts are *sit, sat, (have) sat.*

    b. It never passes action to another word i[n] the sentence.

5. Raise *is a transitive verb that means "t[o] cause (something) to go up or grow up."*

    a. Its principal parts are *raise, raised, (have[)] raised.*

    b. It must pass its action either to the dire[ct] object or to the subject.

6. Rise *is an intransitive verb that mean[s] "to get up or go up."*

    a. Its principal parts are *rise, rose, (have) risen[.]*

We <u>must set</u> no evil thing before our eyes.
>   (We *must put* no evil thing before our eyes. *Thing* receives the
>   action of *must set.*)

Abraham <u>set</u> his faith in the Lord.
>   (Abraham *placed* his faith in the Lord. *Faith* receives the action
>   of *set.*)

The jars <u>have been set</u> on the shelves.
>   (The jars *have been placed* on the shelves. *Jars* receives the action
>   of *have been set.*)

Set also has several definitions as an intransitive verb: "to move below
the horizon," "to keep eggs warm for hatching," and "to become firm." When
set is used with these meanings, it does not pass action to a receiver.

The moon <u>has set</u>, and now we can view the stars.
>   (The moon *has moved below the horizon.*)

Several of our hens <u>are setting</u>.
>   (Several of our hens *are keeping eggs warm for hatching.*)

The gelatin dessert <u>has set</u> already.
>   (The gelatin dessert *has become firm* already.)

Sit is an intransitive verb that means "to rest or be seated." Its principal parts are *sit, sat, (have) sat.* Since *sit* is intransitive, it never passes
action to another word in the sentence.

A horned owl often <u>sits</u> on that large post.
>   (A horned owl often *is seated* on that large post. No action is passed.)

Grandfather <u>sat</u> contentedly on his rocker.
>   (Grandfather *rested* contentedly on his rocker. No action is passed.)

We <u>had sat</u> on the porch until it rained.
>   (We *had been seated* on the porch. No action is passed.)

Raise—Rise

Raise is a transitive verb that means "to cause (something) to go up or
grow up." Its principal parts are *raise, raised, (have) raised.* Since *raise* is
transitive, it must pass its action either to the direct object or to the subject.

My uncle <u>raises</u> popcorn to sell.
>   (My uncle *causes* popcorn *to grow up. Popcorn* receives the action
>   of *raises.*)

The large beam <u>was raised</u> carefully into place.
>   (The large beam *was caused to go up* into place. *Beam* receives
>   the action of *was raised.*)

Rise is an intransitive verb that means "to get up or go up." Its principal parts are *rise, rose, (have) risen.* Since *rise* is intransitive, it never

>   b. It never passes action to another word in
>   the sentence.

7. The helping verb can *means "to be able to."*

**8. The helping verb may *means "to be per-
mitted to."*** *May* is also used to indicate possibility,
but there is seldom a usage problem when it has this
meaning.

★ *EXTRA PRACTICE*
Worksheet 22 *(Using Problem Verbs)*

passes action to another word in the sentence.

> The kites <u>should rise</u> well in this wind.
> (The kites *should go up* well. No action is passed.)
> The elderly man <u>rose</u> slowly from his chair.
> (The elderly man *got up* slowly. No action is passed.)
> Before morning, the temperature <u>had risen</u> above the freezing point.
> (The temperature *had gone up* above the freezing point.)

Can—May

The helping verb *can* means "to be able to." Use this verb to express ability rather than permission.

> "I <u>can</u> do all things through Christ which strengtheneth me."
> (I *am able to* do all things through Christ.)
> <u>Can</u> you speak German? (*Are* you *able to* speak German?)

The helping verb *may* means "to be permitted to." Use this verb to express permission rather than ability.

> The younger children <u>may</u> go first.
> (The younger children *are permitted to* go first.)
> <u>May</u> I get a drink, please? (*Am* I *permitted to* get a drink?)

Sometimes either of these two verbs would fit in a sentence, depending on the intended meaning.

> Raymond <u>can</u> drive this tractor. (Raymond *is able to* drive this tractor.)
> Raymond <u>may</u> drive this tractor.
> (Raymond *is permitted to* drive this tractor.)

May is also used to indicate possibility. For example, the sentence "Raymond may drive this tractor" could mean "It is possible that Raymond will drive this tractor." There is seldom a usage problem when *may* has this meaning.

Class Practice

A. Read each sentence, using the proper form of *lay* or *lie*. If you use a form of *lay*, tell which word receives the action.
  1. For three hundred ninety days, Ezekiel ——— on his left side.
  2. The foundation of the Word has been ——— by the Lord.
  3. Our hope ——— in the immutability of God's Word.
  4. The sick man has ——— in bed for several weeks.
  5. No man could ——— any true charge against Jesus.

B. Read each sentence, using the proper form of *set* or *sit*. If you use a form of *set*, tell which word receives the action, or give the special intransitive meaning of *set*.

Lesson 61 Answers

Class Practice

A. 1. lay
  2. laid, foundation
  3. lies
  4. lain
  5. lay, charge

1. We must ——— our affection on things above.
2. Jesus is ——— at the right hand of the throne on high.
3. Job's three friends ——— quietly for seven days.
4. This concrete has ——— quite well.
5. The students ——— at their desks and studied.
6. We finished the work just as the sun ———.

C. Read each sentence, using the proper form of *raise* or *rise*. If you use a form of *raise*, tell which word receives the action.
   1. Jesus ——— the widow's son to life.
   2. Many prayers of thanksgiving have ——— from our grateful hearts.
   3. God's people have always ——— their eyes to the eternal realities.
   4. The smoke of the Old Testament sacrifices ——— as a sweet smell to God.
   5. When the sweet smell of sacrifice ——— from our lives, God is pleased.

D. Read each sentence, using *can* or *may* correctly.
   1. No student ——— run in the halls of this school.
   2. No one over four feet tall ——— stand up straight in this crawl space.
   3. ——— I please pass the candy dish?
   4. You ——— ride your bicycle only if your chores are finished.
   5. Louella ——— go first this time.

E. Read each sentence correctly. If the sentence is correct, say *correct*.
   1. At Jesus' words, the man raised up and walked.
   2. Today Christians can travel to mission areas much more easily than they could in the past.
   3. Jesus set down at Jacob's well to rest.
   4. While the storm raged, Jonah laid in the bottom of the ship and slept.
   5. Within every normal man lies the awareness of the eternal Godhead.

Written Exercises

A. Write the proper form of *lay* or *lie*.
   1. A good soldier of Jesus must never ——— at ease in enemy territory.
   2. A true disciple willingly ——— down his life for his master.
   3. The slothful servant ——— his talent in a napkin and buried it.
   4. Have your abilities ——— idly under the surface too?
   5. Or are you ——— aside selfish and lazy interests for God's glory?
   6. True greatness ——— in being humble and submissive.
   7. The care of many churches ——— on Paul's heart.
   8. Stephen prayed, "——— not this sin to their charge."

B. Write the proper form of *set* or *sit*.
   1. Mary ——— at Jesus' feet and heard His words.
   2. Truly, she had ——— her affection on heavenly values.

B. 1. set, affection
   2. sitting
   3. sat
   4. set, to become firm
   5. sat
   6. set, to move below the horizon

C. 1. raised, son
   2. risen
   3. raised, eyes
   4. rose
   5. rises

D. 1. may
   2. can
   3. May
   4. may
   5. may

E. (Corrections are underlined.)
   1. At Jesus' words, the man <u>rose</u> up and walked.
   2. correct
   3. Jesus <u>sat</u> down at Jacob's well to rest.
   4. While the storm raged, Jonah <u>lay</u> in the bottom of the ship and slept.
   5. correct

Written Exercises

A. 1. lie
   2. lays *or* laid
   3. laid
   4. lain
   5. laying
   6. lies
   7. lay
   8. Lay

B. 1. sat
   2. set

3. Never should we ——— in the seat of the scornful.
4. After we had ——— for an hour in the traffic jam, we were glad to move again.
5. In this weather, the concrete will ——— quickly.
6. Princess often ——— on the front steps to welcome us home.
7. The children have ——— reverently during family worship.
8. In this valley, darkness falls quickly when the sun ———.

C. Write the proper form of *raise* or *rise*.
1. Today God still ——— up men to fill His sovereign purposes.
2. Jesus ——— from the dead in victory over Satan.
3. Through faith in Jesus, all men now can ——— to newness of life.
4. Even before the Hebrews' anguished cry had ——— to the Lord, He was preparing their deliverance.
5. God ——— up Moses to be their deliverer.
6. The dense fog had ——— shortly before we left home.
7. Uncle George's have ——— some beef for butchering.
8. Feed prices have been ——— faster than meat prices.

D. Write *can* or *may* for each sentence.
1. I ——— hardly lift this heavy box by myself.
2. Father said that we ——— not go to the creek this afternoon.
3. The students who have finished their assignments ——— work on their art projects.
4. ——— we girls plan the next bulletin board?
5. Man ——— count neither the stars in the heavens nor the grains of sand on the seashore.

E. If the underlined verb is incorrect, write the correct verb (without changing the tense). If the verb has no mistake, write *correct*.
1. Do not <u>set</u> around when there is so much work to do.
2. The cows <u>laid</u> in the cool shade.
3. Only one student at a time <u>can</u> go to the bookshelves.
4. Behind our house a high mountain <u>rises</u> sharply.
5. Sicily <u>lays</u> off the coast of Italy.
6. Sometimes molten rock <u>raises</u> slowly out of the ground through a volcano.
7. According to John 15:5, a Christian <u>may</u> do nothing without Christ.
8. We have been <u>sitting</u> the paint cans on this shelf.

Review Exercises

A. Copy these sentences. Indicate the part of speech that each word is according to its use by writing the correct abbreviation above it.

3. sit
4. sat
5. set
6. sits *or* sat
7. sat
8. sets

C. 1. raises
2. rose
3. rise
4. risen
5. raised
6. risen
7. raised
8. rising *or* raised

D. 1. can
2. may
3. may
4. May
5. can

E. 1. sit
2. lay
3. may
4. correct
5. lies
6. rises
7. can
8. setting

noun (n.)   adjective (adj.)   conjunction (conj.)
pronoun (pron.)   adverb (adv.)   interjection (interj.)
verb (v.)   preposition (prep.)

1. Oh, a skunk family is coming from the woods!
2. Suddenly our dog looked up and spotted them.
3. Rover headed for the barn with his tail between his legs.
4. Although he is not very old, he has had some experience with skunks.

. Rewrite each sentence in the order given in parentheses. [11]
1. The assignment seemed easy after Brother Clair explained the lesson. (mixed)
2. An empty raft floated down the stream. (inverted)
3. Across the stormy water sailed the small ship. (natural)
4. We quickly unloaded the last wagon. (mixed)

. Copy each word that should be followed by a colon or semicolon instead of a comma, and add the correct mark. [27]
1. The answers to man's deepest needs are found in one Book, the Bible.
2. Many people own a Bible, however, few of them obey its precepts.
3. The following books were written primarily as Hebrew poetry, Job, Psalms, Proverbs, the Song of Solomon, and Lamentations.
4. Our family pets include Bumper, a collie, Patches, a half-grown cat, and Frisky, a billy goat.

Review Exercises

A. 1. Oh, a skunk family is coming from the woods!
   interj. adj. adj. n. v. v. prep. adj. n.

   2. Suddenly our dog looked up and spotted them.
   adv. adj. n. v. adv. conj. v. pron.

   3. Rover headed for the barn with his tail between his legs.
   n. v. prep. adj. n. prep. adj. n. prep. adj. n.

   4. Although he is not very old, he has had some experience with skunks.
   conj. pron. v. adv. adv. adj. pron. v. v. adj. n. prep. n.

B. 1. After Brother Clair explained the lesson, the assignment seemed easy.
   2. Down the stream floated an empty raft.
   3. The small ship sailed across the stormy water.
   4. Quickly we unloaded the last wagon.

C. 1. Book: 3. poetry:
   2. Bible;   4. collie; cat;

---

2. More Problem Verbs

> **Lesson Survey**
>
> • *Let* means "to allow or permit."
>
> • *Leave* means "to depart, go away from, or allow to remain."
>
> • Learn to use correctly the following verbs and the words that resemble them: *accept—except; adapt—adopt; advise—advice; affect—effect; alter—altar; emigrate—immigrate; imply—infer; lose—loose; propose—purpose.*
>
> • Do not use *of* for the verb *have.*

More problem verbs? Yes, verbs fill a vital role in our language, and it is important that we learn to use them correctly.

Lesson 62

Purpose: To study the correct usage of some additional problem verbs.

Oral Review:

1. Give the definitions of the eight verbs you studied in Lesson 61.
   a. lay (to put or place [something])
   b. lie (to rest, recline, or remain in a flat position)
   c. set (to put or place [something]; *special meanings:* to move below the horizon, to keep eggs warm for hatching, to become firm)
   d. sit (to rest or be seated)
   e. raise (to cause [something] to go up or grow up)
   f. rise (to get up or go up)
   g. can (to be able to)
   h. may (to be permitted to)

2. Name the helping verbs for the three perfect tenses. (*present perfect:* have *or* has; *past perfect:* had; *future perfect:* shall have *or* will have)

3. Change the verb in this sentence to the progressive and emphatic forms: *Mother bakes apple pies.* (Mother is baking apple pies. Mother does bake apple pies.)

Lesson Introduction: Write the following sentences on the board.

   Let the cows in.   Leave the cows in.

Ask a student to explain the difference in the meaning of the two sentences. (*First:* Allow the cows to come in. *Second:* Allow the cows to remain in.) This lesson will give practice in using these problem verbs, as well as a number of others.

Let—Leave

Let means "to allow or permit." Its principal parts are *let, let, (have) let.* The verb *let* is always followed by another verb form that expresses what the subject is permitted to do or to be. In the following sentences, the verb form that follows the verb *let* is italicized. Notice that when the verb *let* is replaced by *allow* or *permit,* the second verb form becomes an infinitive.

<u>Shall</u> we <u>let</u> Glenda *be* the first one on the bicycle?
  (<u>Shall</u> we <u>allow</u> Glenda *to be* the first one on the bicycle?)
Brother Galen <u>let</u> us *choose* appropriate sayings for our mottoes.
  (Brother Galen <u>permitted</u> us *to choose* appropriate sayings for
    our mottoes.)
The polite young man <u>has let</u> the elderly man *sit* on the chair.
  (The polite young man <u>has allowed</u> the elderly man *to sit* on the
    chair.)

Sometimes the second verb form is understood, not expressed. However, you can usually add it to the sentence quite easily. Compare the following sets of sentences.

<u>Let</u> some fresh air in.	<u>Let</u> some fresh air *come* in.
Conrad <u>has let</u> the cows out.	Conrad <u>has let</u> the cows *go* out.
I wanted to help, so Father <u>let</u> me.	I wanted to help, so Father <u>let</u> me *help.*

Leave means "to depart, go away from, or allow to remain." Its principal parts are *leave, left, (have) left.* Unlike *let, leave* is not used with another verb form.

We <u>shall leave</u> for home tomorrow morning, the Lord willing.
  (We *shall depart* for home tomorrow morning, the Lord willing.)
We <u>left</u> several books for the invalid to read.
  (We *allowed* several books *to remain* for the invalid to read.)
We apparently <u>had left</u> the house shortly before you came.
  (We apparently *had gone away from* the house shortly before you
    came.)

Notice that the definitions for both *let* and *leave* include the idea of allowing. How can you know which verb to use? First of all, notice that with the verb *let,* the subject allows someone or something to do or to be a certain thing. In contrast, with the verb *leave,* the subject allows someone or something to remain in a particular position or condition. Second, remember that the verb *let* is always followed by another verb form, either understood or directly stated. In contrast, the verb *leave* is not followed by such a verb form.

Lesson Outline:

1. **Let** *means "to allow or permit."*
   a. Its principal parts are *let, let, (have) let.*
   b. The verb *let* is always followed by another verb form that expresses what the subject is permitted to do or to be.
   c. When the verb *let* is replaced by *allow* or *permit,* the second verb form becomes an infinitive.
   > (*Teacher:* This second verb form is actually an infinitive with *to* omitted. It is the direct object of *let.* The substantive that usually comes between *let* and the infinitive is the subject of the infinitive.)
   d. Sometimes the second verb form is understood, not expressed.
   > (*Teacher:* A phrase like "let me" must always be completed by another word, either a stated verb form ["let me go"], an understood verb form that is stated previously ["I wanted to go, and he let me"], or an adverb ["let me out"]. The second verb form may be omitted only in the last two cases given. For this reason, an expression like "I'll just let it" is not correct; it should be changed to something like "I'll just let it go" or "I'll just leave it.")

2. **Leave** *means "to depart, go away from, or allow to remain."* Its principal parts are *leave, left, (have) left.*

3. **Accept** *is a verb that means "to receive."* **Except** *is usually a preposition that means "not including."* When **except** *is used as a verb, it means "to leave out; exclude."*

4. **Adapt** *means "to change or make suitable."* **Adopt** *means "to take as one's own."*

Gladys <u>left</u> her shoes out in the rain.
    (She *allowed them to remain* out in the rain.)
Father <u>has let</u> us children sled for a while. (He *has allowed* us to sled.)
The torn screen is <u>letting</u> too many flies into the house.
    (It is *allowing them to come* into the house.)

Accept—Except

Accept is a verb that means "to receive." *Except* is usually a preposition that means "not including." When *except* is used as a verb, it means "to leave out; exclude." You will have little trouble with *accept* and *except* if you remember that the prefix *ex-* means "away, out from."

> Please <u>accept</u> my sincere apologies.
> Everyone was present <u>except</u> Mary Lou.
> Brother Daniel <u>excepted</u> no one from the cleaning chores.

Adapt—Adopt

Adapt means "to change or make suitable." *Adopt* means "to take as one's own."

> We <u>adapted</u> our schedule for the benefit of the visitors.
> We should never <u>adopt</u> the values of the world.

Advise—Advice

Advise is a verb that means "to give counsel." *Advice* is a noun that means "counsel; guidance." (Hint: *Advice* and *ice* are both nouns.)

> Brother Harold <u>advised</u> us to study the lesson carefully.
> Those who took his <u>advice</u> seriously did well on the quiz.

Affect—Effect

Affect is a verb that means "to influence." *Effect* is usually a noun that means "the result of some action." As a verb, *effect* means "to bring to pass; to accomplish."

> A person's choices certainly <u>affect</u> his course of life.
> The <u>effect</u> of good choices is a noble life and a blessed eternity.
> The grace of God <u>effected</u> a great change in Saul's life.

Alter—Altar

Alter is a verb that means "to change." *Altar* is a noun that means "a place to offer sacrifices." (Hint: Smoke <u>arises</u> from an *alt<u>ar</u>.*)

> No man can <u>alter</u> the unchanging Word of God.

> Now from the <u>altar</u> of my heart,
>   Let sweetest incense rise.

5. Advise *is a verb that means "to give counsel."* Advice *is a noun that means "counsel; guidance."*

6. Affect *is a verb that means "to influence."* Effect *is usually a noun that means "the result of some action." As a verb,* effect *means "to bring to pass; accomplish."*

7. Alter *is a verb that means "to change."* Altar *is a noun that means "a place to offer sacrifices."*

8. Emigrate *means "to leave one country and settle in another."* Immigrate *means "to enter a foreign country for residence."*
   a. To *<u>e</u>migrate* is to *<u>ex</u>it* a country, and to *<u>im</u>migrate* is to come *<u>into</u>* a country.
   b. The verb *emigrate* is usually followed by the preposition *from;* the verb *immigrate* is usually followed by the preposition *to* or *into.*

9. Imply *means "to express indirectly."* Infer *means "to decide by reasoning; conclude."* A person who is writing, speaking, or acting implies; a person who is reading, listening, or observing infers.

10. Lose *is a verb that means "to suffer loss."* Loose *is often an adjective that means "not firm or tight." As a verb,* loose *means "to release."*

11. Propose *is a verb that means "to suggest."* Purpose *is often a noun that means "aim or goal." As a verb,* purpose *means "to determine."*

12. *Do not use* of *for the helping verb* have. Also, do not use nonstandard contractions like *could've* and *would've* in writing.

★ EXTRA PRACTICE
Worksheet 23 *(More Problem Verbs)*

Emigrate—Immigrate

Emigrate means "to leave one country and settle in another." *Immigrate* means "to enter a foreign country for residence." Notice that to *emigrate* is to *exit* a country, and to *immigrate* is to come *into* a country. The verb *emigrate* is usually followed by the preposition *from;* the verb *immigrate* is usually followed by the preposition *to* or *into.*

> Many Mennonites <u>emigrated</u> from the Palatinate and <u>immigrated</u>
> to North America.

Imply—Infer

Imply means "to express indirectly." *Infer* means "to decide by reasoning; conclude." A person who is writing, speaking, or acting implies; a person who is reading, listening, or observing infers.

> We should never <u>imply</u> that our successes result from our own abilities alone.
> From the Genesis account, we <u>infer</u> that likely no rain fell before
> the Flood.

Lose—Loose

Lose is a verb that means "to suffer loss." *Loose* is often an adjective that means "not firm or tight," as in the phrase "loose tooth." As a verb, *loose* means "to release."

> Where did you <u>lose</u> your new pen?
> I fell on the <u>loose</u> stones.
> The disciples <u>loosed</u> the colt and brought it to Jesus.

Propose—Purpose

Propose is a verb that means "to suggest." *Purpose* is often a noun that means "aim or goal." As a verb, *purpose* means "to determine" and is often followed by *to.* This is seldom the case with the verb *propose.*

> Theresa <u>proposed</u> an excellent idea for the bulletin board.
> One <u>purpose</u> of music class is to inspire appreciation for good singing.
> "Daniel <u>purposed</u> in his heart."

Have—Of

When a phrase like *could have* or *would have* is spoken rapidly, it sounds like *could of* or *would of.* Because that is how it sounds, some people write it that way. But *of* is a preposition; it must never be used for the helping verb *have.* Neither is it proper to write *could've* or *would've,* for these are not standard contractions. You must always write *have* in such phrases.

Incorrect: I <u>might of</u> gone if I <u>could of</u> known what I <u>should of</u> known.

Correct: I <u>might have</u> gone if I <u>could have</u> known what I <u>should have</u> known.

Class Practice

A. Read each sentence, choosing the correct word in parentheses.

1. Since their herdsmen were fighting, Abraham (proposed, purposed) that he and Lot separate.
2. Abraham (let, left) Lot choose first.
3. As a result of his unwise choice, Lot would finally (lose, loose) his testimony, his possessions, and part of his family.
4. Although many Anabaptists (emigrated, immigrated) from their Swiss homeland, others remained.
5. The older men did (advise, advice) Rehoboam to treat the people kindly.
6. Rehoboam would not (accept, except) their advice.
7. His refusal (affected, effected) the division of Israel.
8. We can (imply, infer) several lessons from this account.
9. Man can never (alter, altar) the message of truth.
10. Mother can (adapt, adopt) this shirt to fit David.

B. Read each sentence correctly. If it is correct, say *correct*. (These exercises cover Lessons 61 and 62.)

1. He who does not endure to the end will loose his reward.
2. Your life effects the lives of others who observe you.
3. Absalom's words inferred that David was not a good king.
4. Solomon advised youth to pay careful attention to the counsels of their parents.
5. The Israelites were accepted from several of the plagues upon Egypt.
6. The people of Nazareth should of believed in Jesus; then He would of done more miracles there.
7. The mailman left a package for us.
8. The smoke from the chimney raised almost straight up.
9. Last evening the children lay on the damp ground.
10. Now they must set by the warm stove because of their bad colds.
11. Patches has adopted the motherless kittens.
12. Our neighbors emigrated to this country five years ago.
13. The salesman proposed that we try the equipment for a few days.
14. Brother Kenneth said that we can play softball if the weather is suitable.
15. From the tracks in the snow, we inferred that a rabbit escaped a fox by fleeing into the thicket.

Lesson 62 Answers

Class Practice

A.
1. proposed	6. accept
2. let	7. effected
3. lose	8. infer
4. emigrated	9. alter
5. advise	10. adapt

B. (Corrections are underlined.)

1. He who does not endure to the end will <u>lose</u> his reward.
2. Your life <u>affects</u> the lives of others who observe you.
3. Absalom's words <u>implied</u> that David was not a good king.
4. correct
5. The Israelites were <u>excepted</u> from several of the plagues upon Egypt.
6. The people of Nazareth should <u>have</u> believed in Jesus; then He would <u>have</u> done more miracles there.
7. correct
8. The smoke from the chimney <u>rose</u> almost straight up.
9. correct
10. Now they must <u>sit</u> by the warm stove because of their bad colds.
11. correct
12. Our neighbors <u>immigrated</u> to this country five years ago.
13. correct
14. Brother Kenneth said that we <u>may</u> play softball if the weather is suitable.
15. correct

Written Exercises

A. Choose the correct words in parentheses.

1. No human help could (alter, altar) Naaman's leprosy.
2. However, God's power (affected, effected) a complete healing.
3. Although Naaman was displeased with Elisha's words, his servants did (advise, advice) him wisely.
4. After his healing, Naaman (proposed, purposed) to serve the true God.
5. Elisha (accepted, excepted) no gift from Naaman.
6. Jesus' power could (lose, loose) the demoniac from Satan's power.
7. Jesus (let, left) the demons go into the herd of swine.
8. The story *Which of the Nine?* was (adapted, adopted) from the original.
9. A large number of Mennonites (emigrated, immigrated) from Russia during the 1870s.
10. These settlers (proposed, purposed) to find a place where they would be exempt from military service.
11. They were not (accepted, excepted) from the dangers and difficulties of pioneering.
12. Many newcomers in America did not (adapt, adopt) the English language for several generations.
13. After milking, we (let, leave) the cows out to pasture.
14. One sick cow has been (let, left) in the barn.
15. The veterinarian's words (imply, infer) that he is not sure he can help the cow.

B. If the underlined word is incorrect, write the correct word. If it is correct, write *correct*. (These exercises cover Lessons 61 and 62.)

1. A person's choices <u>effect</u> his character.
2. Our true treasures must <u>lay</u> in heaven, not on this earth.
3. Only those who <u>purpose</u> in their hearts to be undefiled will have the strength to overcome.
4. If you follow the <u>advise</u> of godly parents, you will avoid many pitfalls.
5. When someone <u>purposes</u> that you do wrong, stand firm in what is right.
6. We <u>adopted</u> the game of "tree tag" to be played inside.
7. Due to his illness, Linford must be <u>accepted</u> from some of his chores.
8. Wang Tzu <u>immigrated</u> from China while Mao Zedong was in power.
9. The great blue heron <u>raised</u> gracefully into the air.
10. We <u>set</u> on the bank of the creek and watched the waterfall.
11. We should <u>of</u> fixed that fence before.
12. We <u>inferred</u> from Mr. Watson's answer that he does not want us to cross his pasture.
13. Our new tractor <u>can</u> pull heavier loads than our old one could.
14. Father <u>left</u> us go sledding for a while last evening.

Written Exercises

A. 1. alter
2. effected
3. advise
4. purposed
5. accepted
6. loose
7. let
8. adapted
9. emigrated
10. purposed
11. excepted
12. adopt
13. let
14. left
15. imply

B. 1. affect
2. lie
3. correct
4. advice
5. proposes
6. adapted
7. excepted
8. emigrated
9. rose
10. sat
11. have
12. correct
13. correct
14. let

15. Men can <u>altar</u> the course of rivers to suit their purposes.
16. The passing of time has <u>effected</u> many changes on the old buildings.
17. Several Anabaptists had <u>laid</u> in prison for weeks.
18. The authorities said they would <u>lose</u> any prisoner who recanted.
19. We should <u>except</u> the challenge of doing our work well.
20. Someday God's people will <u>leave</u> all toils and temptations behind.

Review Exercises

A. Copy each verb or verb phrase, and write which of the six tenses it is. Also write *simple, progressive,* or *emphatic* to tell what form the verb is.
1. A normal youth has had many opportunities to develop patience.
2. You will be learning lessons in patience all your life.
3. Difficulties and changed plans do test our patience.
4. A thankful person counts his blessings, not his problems.
5. Even before our time, God had been preparing many blessings for us.
6. By the end of life, we shall have received innumerable blessings from God.
7. Have you thanked God today for His goodness to you?
8. Certainly God did hear our prayers of thanksgiving.

B. Label each underlined verb *T* (transitive), *IL* (intransitive linking), or *IC* (intransitive complete).
1. Mother's cornmeal mush <u>tastes</u> delicious.
2. The leftover mush <u>will be fried</u> for breakfast tomorrow.
3. This stew <u>was simmering</u> on the back of the wood stove all morning.
4. Mother <u>seasoned</u> this stew perfectly.

15. alter
16. correct
17. lain
18. loose
19. accept
20. correct

Review Exercises

A. 1. has had—present perfect, simple
2. will be learning—future, progressive
3. do test—present, emphatic
4. counts—present, simple
5. had been preparing—past perfect, progressive
6. shall have received—future perfect, simple
7. Have thanked—present perfect, simple
8. did hear—past, emphatic

B. 1. IL
2. T
3. IC
4. T

---

63. Effective Style in a Story

> **Lesson Survey**
> • Natural **dialogue** makes the story characters realistic.
> • Lively action verbs keep the story action flowing.
> • Exact, descriptive words paint clear word pictures.
> • **Imagery** paints vivid descriptions.

A story may have a worthwhile theme, an interesting conflict, and effective characterization, but it may still not be appealing to the reader. There

Lesson 63

Purpose: To study methods of improving the style of a story.

Oral Review:

1. What is characterization? (the process of portraying a story character)
2. Name four common methods of characterization. (showing actions, speech, thoughts, and appearance)
3. How much should secondary characters be characterized? (only as much as is necessary for the story)
4. Tell whether the following points relate to expository, argumentative, narrative, or descriptive writing.
   a. Paints a word picture of a person, place, or object. (descriptive)

   b. Written to persuade the reader of a certain point or to move him to action. (argumentative)
   c. Written to define, clarify, or explain. (expository)
   d. Tells a story. (narrative)

Lesson Introduction: Read these two versions of a story excerpt, and ask the questions that follow.

As the fire burned on, those hiding in the cellar became hotter and hotter. At one end the floor above them burned through, just a tiny spot in the darkness. Then it became larger.

Bumping against a barrel, Jacob Hochstetler had an idea. Quickly he seized upon it. As he tried to open the lid, he said, "Why do we not splash this on the fire? It might slow it down."

*   *   *   *   *

As the fire burned on, the searing heat engulfed them in the shallow cellar. At one end the floor

are a number of things that contribute to an interesting, readable style. In general, the pointers in this lesson will help you to *show* rather than merely *tell* your story. In this way the reader will feel as if the story is happening right before his eyes.

Natural Dialogue

Dialogue is a major ingredient that sets a story apart from a report or description. A story usually involves several people, and those people communicate with each other. If their dialogue (conversation) sounds natural, the story characters will seem alive and real. The following paragraphs describe several important elements of natural dialogue.

Informal tone. In real life, our conversations have an informal tone that is different from the tone of a report or description. We use *contractions* and *elliptical sentences* in our speech. Although these are not acceptable in formal writing, they do contribute to natural dialogue.

Some writers think that natural-sounding dialogue should include poor grammar and slang. While it is true that many people use nonstandard expressions, such language is not necessary to make conversations sound natural. It is beneath the dignity of Christian writing.

Frequent change of speakers. One speaker should seldom say more than a few sentences at a time. Long quotations stall the forward movement of a story.

Descriptive explanatory words. Do not be afraid to use *said* and *asked* when they are the best choice. But natural-sounding dialogue also includes plenty of words that describe exactly *how* the characters said or asked: *murmured, mumbled, shouted, called, whispered, demanded, prompted, inquired.*

Remember two more points about explanatory words. First, you do not need to include them in every paragraph of an extended conversation. Second, do not use explanatory words that cannot actually tell how a person *speaks.* For example, a character cannot *hum, whistle, pause,* or *point* his words.

Incorrect:
"What a surprise!" whistled Thomas.
(Can you *whistle* those words?)
"Put the towels in there," pointed Mary. (We cannot *point* words.)

Correct:
"What a surprise!" exclaimed Thomas with a whistle.
"Put the towels in there." Mary pointed.

Now compare these two story excerpts. The elements of natural-sounding dialogue make the example on the right much more realistic than the one on the left.

above burned through, just a tiny red eye glaring at them in the inky blackness. Then, like a glowing cancer, it spread and grew.

Stumbling against a large wooden barrel, Jacob Hochstetler was struck with an idea. With the desperation of a drowning man, he seized upon it. Fumbling with the tight-fitting cover, he exclaimed, "Why don't we splash this apple juice on the fire? It might slow it down."

Do the two versions give the same basic details? (yes) Which one is more interesting? (second) Why? (It shows the story, rather than merely telling it. It is more descriptive.)

This example illustrates the importance of writing style. In this lesson you will study some practical ways to improve your writing style.

Lesson Outline:

1. Natural dialogue makes the story characters realistic.

a. One element of natural dialogue is an informal tone.
1) Contractions and elliptical sentences contribute to natural dialogue.
2) Many people may use poor grammar and slang, but such language is not necessary to make conversations sound natural.

b. A second element of natural dialogue is the frequent change of speakers.

c. A third element of natural dialogue is descriptive explanatory words.
1) Words like *said* and *asked* are often the best to use. But natural-sounding dialogue includes plenty of words that

Father crossed the room and stopped beside Mark. Swaying Amy gently, he looked down at Mark's almost blank sheet of paper. Then he looked at Mark. "Well, how is it going, son?" he asked.

"It is not going so great," said Mark slowly.

"Why is it not going well?" asked Father. "Do you not understand the assignment?"

Father crossed the room and stopped beside Mark. Swaying Amy gently, he looked down at Mark's almost blank sheet of paper. Then he looked at Mark. "Well, how's it going, son?"

"Not so great," answered Mark slowly.

"Why?" questioned Father. "Don't you understand the assignment?"

Lively Action Verbs

Lively action verbs keep the story action flowing. This is especially true if the verbs are in the active voice—though verbs in the active voice can still be dull and weak if they are not expressive. Many verbs in the passive voice also express action, but they tend to weaken the force of the action. Linking verbs express no action; they tend to make characters seem motionless.

Compare the sets of examples below. Notice how those on the right communicate more clearly and forcefully than those on the left.

Dull active voice verbs:

"What are you <u>going</u> to do today?" Elaine asked Mother as she <u>closed</u> the last of the five lunch boxes.

"I need to <u>work</u> at the pile of mending that <u>has gotten</u> so big."

Lively action verbs:

"What are you <u>planning</u> to do today?" Elaine asked Mother as she <u>snapped</u> shut the last of the five lunch boxes.

"I need to <u>tackle</u> the pile of mending that <u>has been collecting</u>."

Weak passive voice verbs:

Brother Samuel's words <u>were</u> clearly <u>recalled</u> by Noah. "Pride <u>is shown</u> by your bragging," he had explained.

Lively action verbs:

Noah clearly <u>recalled</u> Brother Samuel's words. "Your bragging <u>shows</u> pride," he had explained.

Motionless linking verbs:

The October sun <u>was</u> bright. The rays coming through the windows of the Sharp Mountain Mennonite School <u>were</u> warm.

"I wonder what our art project <u>will be</u>," mused Donald. His hand <u>was</u> tilted to catch a sunbeam.

Lively action verbs:

The October sun <u>shone</u> brightly, <u>sending</u> warm rays through the windows of the Sharp Mountain Mennonite School.

"I wonder what we <u>will do</u> for art class," mused Donald as he <u>tilted</u> his hand to catch a sunbeam.

describe exactly *how* the characters said or asked.

2) Explanatory words need not be included in every paragraph of an extended conversation.

3) Words that cannot actually tell how a person speaks should not be used as explanatory words.

(*Teacher:* Occasionally a student seems to think, "If some dialogue is good, more is better"—to the point that he tries to use all dialogue in his story. Though it is more common not to have enough dialogue, the teacher should also be aware of the opposite extreme.)

2. *Lively action verbs keep the story action flowing.*

a. Most verbs should be in the active voice—though active voice verbs can still be dull and weak if they are not expressive.

b. Passive voice verbs tend to weaken the force of the action.

c. Linking verbs tend to make characters seem motionless.

3. *Exact, descriptive words paint clear word pictures.* They give the story a concrete image.

4. *Imagery paints vivid descriptions in a story.*

a. A simile makes a figurative comparison by using *like* or *as.*

b. A metaphor makes a figurative comparison without using *like* or *as.*

c. Personification pictures a quality or an inanimate object as having the characteristics of a person or an animal.

d. A hyperbole is a figurative exaggeration for the purpose of emphasis.

e. Onomatopoeia is the use of a word having an imitative sound.

Exact, Descriptive Words

Exact, descriptive words paint clear word pictures. They give the story a concrete image. In contrast, general words leave the reader with only a vague picture. Why write *house* if *cottage* or *cabin* would give the reader a more distinct picture? Why write *big cat* if *lynx* or *panther* would communicate better? As you compare the following set of examples, notice how the example on the right paints a more specific word picture than the one on the left.

Poor: Too general	**Better:** More exact
The <u>vehicle</u> was filled with the usual <u>sounds</u> as it <u>went</u> up the <u>road</u>. "Did you <u>do</u> your <u>lesson</u>?" Rosalyn asked Susan.	The <u>school van</u> was filled with the usual <u>lively chatter</u> as it <u>bounced</u> up the <u>gravel road</u>. "Did you <u>finish</u> your <u>math</u>?" Rosalyn asked Susan.

Imagery

Imagery paints vivid descriptions in a story. Imagery involves figures of speech (similes, metaphors, personification, hyperbole) and onomatopoeia. A *simile* makes a figurative comparison by using *like* or *as.*

No imagery:
   <u>Suddenly</u> an idea <u>came to</u> Roy.

Simile: (and metaphor)
   <u>Like a thunderclap</u> an idea <u>struck</u> Roy.

A *metaphor* makes a figurative comparison without using *like* or *as.* Many metaphors use a form of the verb *be* to say that one thing is another. Others say that something happens in a literal, physical way when it actually happens only in a figurative sense.

No imagery:
   Benny <u>looked cheerful</u> again.
   "Your kindness <u>has helped keep things happy</u> today, Linda," Mother commended warmly.

Metaphor:
   Benny's <u>face became a sunbeam</u> again.
   "Your kindness <u>has spread a lot of sunshine</u> today, Linda," Mother commended warmly.

In *personification,* a quality or an inanimate object is pictured as having the characteristics of a person or an animal. The quality or thing may be said to speak or act in a way that only a person can do, or something abstract may be described as having human features.

No imagery:
> The approaching thunderstorm <u>made the travelers anxious</u>.
> <u>Nevin became very frightened</u> as he saw the bull charging for Susan.

Personification:
> The dark clouds <u>muttered angry threats to the anxious travelers</u>.
> <u>Fear wrapped icy fingers around Nevin's heart</u> as he saw the bull charging for Susan.

A *hyperbole* (hī·pėr′·bə·lē) is a figurative exaggeration for the purpose of emphasis. The exaggeration of a true hyperbole is so great that it is obviously intended to be figurative.

No imagery:
> The stolen pocketknife <u>bothered Sam's conscience</u> as it lay in his pocket.

Hyperbole:
> The stolen pocketknife <u>weighed a ton</u> as it lay in Sam's pocket.

Onomatopoeia (ŏn′·ə·măt′·ə·pē′·ə) is the use of a word having an imitative sound. Expressions like the *hum* of an electric motor or the *rattle* of an empty wagon make use of onomatopoeia.

No imagery:
> We can hear the <u>noise</u> of the brook from our house.
> The <u>sound</u> of escaping steam caught the watchman's attention.

Onomatopoeia:
> We can hear the <u>murmur</u> of the brook from our house.
> The <u>hiss</u> of escaping steam caught the watchman's attention.

Class Practice

A. Tell how to change this dialogue so that it sounds more natural.

"Was that not an interesting demonstration in science class?" asked Thelma.

"Yes, it was an interesting demonstration," said Kendra. "I did not know air pressure was that strong!"

"Were you surprised at how flat the can was?" asked Thelma.

"I surely was surprised at how flat the can was," said Kendra. "Were you surprised?"

B. Change these sentences to include more lively action verbs.
1. The day was sunny and pleasantly warm.
2. Kevin was chased out of the woods by a swarm of angry bees.
3. The frightened deer ran across the field and went over the fence.

C. Change these sentences so that they use exact, descriptive words.
1. Some birds landed on the water.

Lesson 63 Answers

Class Practice

A. (Sample improved dialogue.)

"Wasn't that an interesting demonstration in science class?" asked Thelma.

"Yes," replied Kendra. "I didn't know air pressure was that strong!"

"Were you surprised at how flat the can was?" asked Thelma.

"I surely was," answered Kendra. "Were you?"

B. (Sample improvements.)
1. The sun shone brightly, and warm breezes blew gently.
2. A swarm of angry bees chased Kevin out of the woods.
3. The frightened deer dashed across the field and leaped over the fence.

C. (Sample improvements.)
1. Five geese landed on the pond.

2. As I went into the building, I could hear someone cutting wood.

3. Stanley took another bite of Mother's good dessert.

D. Change these sentences so that they include the type of imagery named in parentheses.

1. The boys dashed down the mountain trail. (simile)

2. William's curt reply hurt Roy's feelings. (metaphor)

3. My cap was knocked off as I rode under the low branches of the oak. (personification)

Written Exercises

The writing style of this story excerpt is weak. Rewrite all five paragraphs, following the directions after the story.

Dale *went* through the kitchen, as usual *a little* ahead of his older brother Leroy. As he *got* his jacket off the hook, he heard *something fall* to the floor in the kitchen. Without a backward *look*, he *pushed* open the door and *went* down the steps.

"Dale!" Mother's stern voice called him back to the house. "You do not need to *go* through the house <u>so fast and violently</u>. Come back and pick up the chair you *made fall* over. And where are your school clothes?" said Mother. "Are they hanging on their hooks, or are they scattered on the floor?"

"I am sorry, Mother," Dale said contritely. "I just can hardly wait to start mowing again. I do not know where my clothes are. They are probably on the floor."

"Go up and check. Then walk downstairs and through the kitchen more decently."

In the shop Dale quickly *got the new mower ready*. As he pulled the mower out, it bumped into Leroy's bicycle. "I guess I ought to pick it up," he said to himself. "But Leroy does not have to park his bike so close to the mower."

1. Change the italicized words in the first two paragraphs to more lively action verbs or more exact, descriptive words.

2. Make four paragraphs out of paragraphs 2 and 3, with both Mother and Dale each speaking twice.

3. Make all the dialogue more natural by using contractions, elliptical sentences, and more descriptive explanatory words.

4. Change the underlined expression in paragraph 2 to a figure of speech.

5. In the last paragraph, improve the italicized words by changing them to tell what he did to get the mower ready.

___

2. As I entered the shop, I could hear Father sawing the oak planks.

3. Stanley took another bite of Mother's delicious apple pie.

D. (Sample improvements.)

1. The boys dashed like frightened rabbits down the mountain trail.

2. William's curt reply was an arrow in Roy's heart.

3. The low branches of the oak reached out and grabbed my cap as I rode by.

Written Exercises

(Sample improvements are underlined. Accept reasonable variation.)

Dale <u>darted</u> through the kitchen, as usual <u>several minutes</u> ahead of his older brother Leroy. As he <u>grabbed</u> his jacket off the hook, he heard <u>a chair</u> <u>crash</u> to the floor in the kitchen. Without <u>a</u> backward <u>glance</u>, he <u>threw</u> open the door and <u>bounded</u> down the steps.

"Dale!" Mother's stern voice called him back to the house. "You <u>don't</u> need to <u>tear</u> through the house <u>like a windstorm</u>! Come back and pick up the chair you <u>knocked</u> over."

"<u>I'm</u> sorry, Mother," Dale <u>replied</u> contritely. "<u>I</u> just can hardly wait to start mowing again."

"And where are your school clothes, <u>Dale?</u>" <u>asked</u> Mother. "Are they hanging on their hooks, or are they scattered on the floor?"

"<u>I don't know</u>," replied Dale. "<u>Probably on the floor</u>."

"Go up and check. Then walk downstairs and through the kitchen more decently."

In the shop Dale quickly <u>filled the gas tank of the new lawn mower</u>. As he pulled the mower out, it bumped into Leroy's bicycle. "<u>Guess I ought to pick it up</u>," he <u>thought</u> to himself. "But Leroy <u>doesn't</u> have to park his bike so close to the mower."

64. The Opening of a Story

Lesson Survey

- A story may open with action, dialogue, or an unusual statement.
- The opening of a story should introduce the main character and establish the setting.
- The opening should hint at the theme and conflict of the story.
- The story should begin as near to the first scene of conflict as possible.
- An appealing title is an important part of a good story introduction.

Every good short story can be divided into three basic parts: opening, middle, and end. Each of these is important to the story. This lesson focuses primarily on the opening of the story.

Begin With Action, Dialogue, or an Unusual Statement

The opening sentences of a story are especially important. If they are dull, a reader may lay the story down without reading further. To attract a reader's interest, most short stories begin with action or dialogue. Read the following openings of stories that you have worked with earlier in this chapter, and notice how they make effective use of action and dialogue.

The Trouble With George

Action and dialogue

The upper grade students chattered excitedly as they headed for the steep hill behind the Piney Mountain Mennonite School. "These Pennsylvania hills certainly beat southern Maryland for sledding," commented fourteen-year-old Titus. "Before we moved here, I hardly did any sledding at all."

"Huh!" snorted George, swinging his large frame to face Titus. "Don't need to tell us that. Nobody from here was ever as scared of this hill as you were. Course none of us is as short as you either."

Only Remembered

Dialogue

"Not there, Elizabeth," Margaret said sharply, her mouth set in a straight line and her face flushed in exasperation. "The corn cutters go in the third drawer. And hurry; the dish drainer is full."

Another effective way to open a story is to make an unusual statement. Read the following story opening.

Lesson 64

Purpose: To teach characteristics of a good story opening.

Oral Review:

1. In general, effective style in a story means that a writer ——— the details of the story rather than ——— them. (shows, telling)
2. What two things help to make dialogue informal and natural? (contractions, elliptical sentences)
3. Name two other elements of natural dialogue. (frequent change of speakers, descriptive explanatory words)
4. What is the theme of a story? (the lesson that the story teaches)
5. What is the conflict in a story? (the struggle or problem the main character faces)

6. Name the three common kinds of conflict. (the main character in conflict with another person, with his circumstances, or with his own self)

Lesson Introduction: Have you ever scanned the titles of several stories in order to decide which one to read? What made you choose one and reject another? Perhaps a certain title caught your attention; but when you read the first several paragraphs of the story, you laid it aside for another. What made you do that? The opening of a story has the potential to either spark or extinguish interest in the story.

Lesson Outline:

1. A story may open with action, dialogue, or an unusual statement.

2. The opening of a story should introduce the main character.

Pouting Patsy Mae

One thing Joanna enjoyed was visiting old or sick people, but this visit was different. Very disappointedly, Joanna watched Patsy Mae closely and decided, "She is the most unhappy person I have ever seen."

Likely several questions immediately came to your mind as you read that paragraph. Why was this visit different? Why was Patsy Mae so unhappy? What was Joanna's response to her? If your story opening can raise questions in a reader's mind, he will most likely continue reading to find answers to his questions.

Introduce the Main Character

The opening of a story should introduce the main character. As you saw in Lesson 59, the main character is the central figure in the whole story. Therefore, the first person to speak, to do something, or to be described should be the main character. Read again the opening paragraphs in the examples above. Notice how the main character is introduced immediately.

Establish the Setting

The opening of a story should establish the setting; that is, the time and place of the story. This is generally not done with a lengthy description of those details. Instead, details of the setting are given as they are needed to make the story clear.

For example, the day of the week is not important in most stories. But if Albert's friend asks him to go fishing on Saturday afternoon and Albert has certain chores to do each Saturday, the day does become significant. Likewise, detailed information about the place is usually beside the point. In a story with its setting in Guatemala, you would not need to mention the mountainous terrain or the poverty of the people unless these details have a part in the conflict of the story.

Look again at the story openings above. What do you learn about the time and place? The first story occurs at school during winter. The second one opens in the kitchen of the main character's home. And the third one takes place on a visit to someone who is old or sick.

The setting also includes the emotional mood or atmosphere of the story. The story may open with the main character in a calm mood, or he may be tense, angry, excited, tired, or homesick. The emotional mood is especially significant in the second example above.

Hint at the Theme and Conflict

The opening should hint at the theme and conflict of the story. This hint is what holds the reader's interest and lures him on to read the rest of the story. A hint, of course, gives a mere suggestion, not a direct statement. To

    a. The main character is the central figure in the whole story.
    b. The first person to speak, to do something, or to be described should be the main character.

3. *The opening of a story should establish the setting.*
    a. The setting includes the time, place, and emotional mood or atmosphere of the story.
    b. A lengthy description of the setting is not necessary in a short story.

4. *The opening should hint at the theme and conflict of the story.*

5. *The story should begin as near to the first scene of conflict as possible.*
    a. Avoid a long, rambling introduction that gives background information but does not involve action and conflict.
    b. Important background information can be given later in a flashback.

6. *An appealing title is an important part of a good story introduction.*
    a. A good title does not give away the outcome of the story.
    b. A good title is short.
    c. A good title is fresh and original.
        1) It may have rhyming words or alliteration.
        2) It may make an unusual statement.
        3) It may raise a question.

e most effective, the full impact of the lesson being emphasized should
ome at the very end of the story. Do you see that hint in the unkind words
poken by George and Margaret?

Begin Near the First Scene of Conflict

The story should begin as near to the first scene of conflict as possible.
Avoid a long, rambling introduction that gives background information but
does not involve action and conflict. Important background information
can often be given later in a *flashback*—a sentence or paragraph that
flashes back to a previous scene.

In the opening of the story "The Trouble With George," a flashback
occurs in paragraph 5: "This was not the first time George had made
remarks like that. Other scenes from the past several weeks flashed through
his mind—scenes in which George had said and done things that clearly
showed his dislike for Titus."

The flashback in the following example is a whole paragraph. It is
underlined.

> "But I won't have time this evening," Ray groaned inwardly. "By
> the time I get those steers fed and bedded and fill the feed chute, it
> will be suppertime, and then I have to grease the rake. I'll never get
> back to that new sinkhole Father found."
>
> Ray kicked off his boots, sending them sliding over the edge of
> the porch. They just missed the tops of Mother's marigolds, whose
> orange blossoms bordered the walk.
>
> As he retrieved his boots, an idea came to him. "What is Lowell going
> to do all evening? Maybe he could grease the rake. If I don't get to that
> sinkhole before Lowell does, then very likely he'll be the one to name it."
>
> Since Ray's family had moved to this farm with its bountiful lime-
> stone rocks and several sinkholes, there had never been anything
> quite as exciting as a new sinkhole. The ground had simply sunk down
> five to fifteen feet lower than the ground around it. It was mysteri-
> ous. What caused it? Was there a stream under the farm that had
> dried up and let the ground collapse into it?

Begin With an Appealing Title

An appealing title is also an important part of a good story introduction.
Since readers often scan titles to decide what to read, your title must catch
the reader's attention and arouse his interest. Look at the following titles.

Fair:
    Kindness Overcomes Ill Will
    Margaret Determines to Be Sweet
    Meekness Demands Courage

Freda's Problem
Mark Learns to Accept Responsibility
Linda's Deception Is Discovered

Better:
The Trouble With George
Only Remembered
Weak or Meek?
Freda's Fault
Too Many Responsibilities?
Caught by a Dead Mouse

What makes the titles in the second list better than the ones in the first? For one thing, a good title does not give away the outcome of the story; rather, it makes you wonder what the outcome will be. In contrast, most of the titles in the first list tell you quite plainly what the outcome of the story will be.

Another quality of a good title is its shortness. A good title rarely contains more than five words, and those words are usually short. In the first list above, most of the titles have four or five words, and some of the words are long. The titles in the second list have from two to five words, mostly short ones.

A good title is also fresh and original. Rhyming words, alliteration, unusual statements, and questions help to make titles fresh and catchy. Find examples of these in the second list above.

When you write a title, remember to capitalize the first and last words and all other words except articles, coordinating conjunctions, and prepositions of fewer than four letters. A title may have internal punctuation, such as commas after items in a series. But no end punctuation should follow a title unless it is a question or an exclamation.

The story opening, of course, is just the beginning; it merely hints at what is to follow. The middle of the story brings the conflict into sharp focus, often with a series of events that lead to the climax. In the story ending, the conflict is over and the theme of the story is made clear.

Class Practice

Read each pair of story openings, and tell why the second one is better than the first.

1.   **Joe's Honesty Pays**

Mother needed two gallons of milk. She took her last twenty dollars, gave it to Joe, and sent him down to the store.

Tired from running, Joe slowed to a walk. He walked even more slowly as he neared the hardware store. He stopped completely to have a quick peek through the dark window.

Lesson 64 Answers

Class Practice

1. The title does not give away the outcome as much. The title is more appealing with its alliteration. The main character is introduced first. It begins with dialogue. The second paragraph gives a hint of the conflict.

Truth Triumphs

"Here, Joe. Now don't lose this; it's our last twenty dollars. Bring two gallons of milk. And hurry back," reminded Mother as Joe raced out, placing his cap over his eyes as usual.

Tired from running, Joe slowed to a walk. He walked even more slowly as he neared the hardware store. His thoughts went back over the ball game yesterday—of how he had missed the balls and how some of the boys had laughed and others had been upset. He stopped completely to have a quick peek through the dark window at that much-wanted glove.

2.

The Importance of Good Manners

Father and the boys had been working hard in the fields all day on that warm Wednesday in June. Dwight was fourteen years old, Darrel was thirteen, and Elaine was eleven. The chores were finished, and the family had sat down to a delicious supper.

Dwight was eating hungrily. Each loaded spoonful was a miniature of the fluffy mountain of mashed potatoes on his plate.

Elaine observed that he was eating like Rover. He was chomping his food as if he were half starved.

Better Start Now

To see Dwight shoveling mashed potatoes into his mouth, you would have thought he had eaten nothing all day. Each loaded spoonful was a miniature of the fluffy mountain of mashed potatoes on his plate.

"Dwight eats like Rover," Elaine observed. "Kind of half-starved-like, and he chomps on his food."

Written Exercises

A. Rewrite this story beginning by following the directions after it. You do not need to supply a title. The main character is Charles.

Evan and Charles were eighth graders at the Sunny View Christian School. They had been good friends ever since Evan moved into the community two years before. One day at recess the students played prisoner's base, and Charles and Evan were on the losing team. They were not happy when recess was over. Charles had a problem with becoming peevish and disrespectful at times like this.

Charles and Evan went slowly toward the school. It was a warm, humid day. Charles said that the teams were not one bit fair, and the teacher did not even care.

Evan agreed with an unkind look toward Brother Stauffer. He said that the teacher always ruled in favor of the other team.

1. Use an opening sentence that contains dialogue and introduces the main character at the same time.

2. The title does not give away the outcome. The title is more appealing. The main character is introduced first. It begins with an unusual statement. The setting does not include unnecessary information.

Written Exercises

A. (Sample improvement.)

"Those teams weren't one bit fair," muttered eighth grader Charles as he headed slowly toward the school. "And the teacher didn't even care!" Charles pulled out a handkerchief and wiped the sweat from his forehead.

"That's for sure!" his friend Evan agreed with a dark look in Brother Stauffer's direction. "He always ruled in favor of the other team. No wonder we lost!"

2. Give a mere hint of the theme and conflict, rather than stating it directly.

3. Show the setting in a more natural and incidental way. Leave out details that do not contribute to the theme.

4. Use exact, descriptive words instead of vague, general words.

B. Write a good opening for the story described below. (You do not need to write the whole story.)

Walter has a habit of doing other things when he knows he should do his chores or schoolwork. After receiving a stern warning (from a teacher or parent), he determines to overcome the habit.

C. Write the letter of the better title in each pair. Be ready to tell why you chose as you did.

1. a. Thorns of Regret
    b. Elsie Regrets Her Choice
2. a. Being an Example of Honesty
    b. An Honest Example
3. a. Respect for Hunting Laws
    b. Deer Dilemma
4. a. Picked On?
    b. Martha's Self-pity
5. a. A Temptation Overcome
    b. The Forbidden Fruit
6. a. A Duck or a Sponge?
    b. Heedless or Receptive?

B. (Individual work.)

C. (Reasons in parentheses are to be given orally.)
1. a (shorter; more picturesque; *b* gives outcome away)
2. b (shorter)
3. b (shorter; has alliteration; *a* tells too much)
4. a (a question; *b* tells too much)
5. b (*a* gives away the outcome)
6. a (more picturesque)

65. Writing a Story

> **Lesson Survey**
> - To begin writing a story, make a careful plan.
> - Write the first draft of the story.

You have studied several lessons on story writing. Now it is time to use what you have learned, and write a story of your own. This lesson gives you direction on writing the first draft of a story, and a later lesson will help you to improve your story.

Writing a Plan

Very few worthwhile things are accomplished without careful planning, and this is certainly true of story writing. You have been thinking about writing a story for several days. This lesson will help you to make a definite plan for your story, and it will direct you in the actual writing.

A description of the pattern in a story is known as the *plot* of the story. This pattern can often be stated in just a sentence or two, like the one about

Lesson 65

Purpose: To study how to write the first draft of a story.

Oral Review:

1. What are three good ways to open a story? (with action, dialogue, or an unusual statement)
2. What three things are included in the setting of a story? (time, place, emotional mood of the story)
3. What is a flashback in a story? (a sentence or paragraph that provides important background information by describing a previous scene)
4. Name several things that contribute to natural dialogue. (an informal tone that includes contractions and elliptical sentences; frequent change of speakers; descriptive explanatory words)
5. Besides natural dialogue, what are some things that contribute to effective style in story writing? (lively action verbs; exact, descriptive words; imagery)
6. Name four common ways of portraying a story character. (showing actions, speech, thoughts, and appearance)
7. Name the three common kinds of conflict. (the main character in conflict with another person, with his circumstances, or with his own self)
8. To be most effective, the conclusion should —— rather than —— the theme of the story. (show, tell)

Lesson Introduction: Planning is a natural and important part of our lives. Someone plans the delicious meals you eat day after day. Have you ever tried to sew a dress or build a birdhouse without a plan? Of course not! The plan is essential to success. Likewise, you should not try to write a story without first making a plan.

Walter near the end of Lesson 64. To be useful in writing a story, however, your plan should be considerably more detailed. Here are some steps to follow in the planning process before you even write the first sentence.

1. *Write the theme your story will teach.* Choose one of the themes suggested on page 288, or one of your own that your teacher approves.

2. *Write a sentence describing the conflict.*

3. *List the incidents in the conflict, including the climax.*

4. *Write how the story will conclude.*

5. *Name the main character, and describe his primary traits.* Especially if the character is not a real person that you know, you must form a mental picture of him. Make a list of details about his most important characteristics and features.

Here is a sample plan for the story "The Trouble With George" in Lesson 58.

Theme: Kindness overcomes ill will.

Conflict: Titus struggles to overcome the ill will of George, who treats him unkindly.

Incident 1:
George makes fun of Titus for having been scared of sledding on a steep hill and for being short.

Incident 2:
George knocks books out of Titus's hands after school dismissal.

Incident 3: (climax)
George comes to school with a badly sprained ankle. Titus offers to stay in with him during recess.

Conclusion:
George apologizes for his meanness. Titus and George become friends.

Main character: Titus

Appearance:
Black hair and brown eyes (not important to story)
Small for his age (part of the reason George makes fun of him)

Character:
Conscientious (right attitude toward school assignments; tried hard to be a peacemaker)
Hardworking (not important to story)
Good-natured (laughed off George's sneering remarks)
Sympathetic (expressed sincere interest in George's injury; offered to stay in with him)

Lesson Outline:

1. To plan a story, first write the theme your story will teach.

2. Write a sentence describing the conflict.

3. List the incidents in the conflict, including the climax.

4. Write how the story will conclude.

5. Name the main character, and describe his primary traits.

6. To write the first draft, write a good beginning for the story.
   a. Start with action, dialogue, or an unusual statement.
   b. Introduce the main character and establish the setting very near the beginning.
   c. Hint at the theme and conflict.
   d. Start as near to the first scene of conflict as possible.

7. Write the middle part of the story.
   a. Develop the various incidents of the conflict.
   b. Increase the intensity of the conflict until the climax.

8. Write a brief conclusion to the story. Remember to *show* rather than tell the lesson of the story.

9. Write an interesting title for the story.
   a. Do not give away the outcome of the story.
   b. Keep the title short.
   c. Keep the title fresh and original.

Writing the First Draft

After you have planned the story, you are ready to write it. You should double-space this first copy of the story so that you can more easily proofread it in Lesson 67.

6. *Write a good beginning for the story.* Remember to start the story with action, dialogue, or an unusual statement. Be sure that you introduce the main character and establish the setting very near the beginning. Hint at the theme and conflict, and start as near to the first scene of conflict as possible.

7. *Write the middle part of the story.* Here you develop the various incidents of the conflict. Remember to increase the intensity of the conflict until you reach the climax.

8. *Write a brief conclusion to the story.* After the climax, the reader is satisfied. Bring the story to a prompt close. Remember, your entire story is to *show* a lesson to the reader. Do not try to tell the lesson at the end of the story.

9. *Write an interesting title for the story.* Think of a short, fresh title that does not give away the outcome of the story.

Written Exercises

A. Write your plan for a story, following steps 1–5 in the lesson.

B. Write the first draft of your story, following steps 6–9. Write on every other line to allow room for revising. Your story should have 400–800 words.

---

66. Active and Passive Voice

> ### Lesson Survey
> - A transitive verb in the **active voice** passes its action to a direct object.
> - A transitive verb in the **passive voice** passes its action to the subject.
> - The passive voice may be used in all six tenses.
> - The progressive form in the passive voice occurs mainly in the simple present and past tenses. The emphatic form does not occur at all in the passive voice.
> - A **retained object** is an object complement that is retained when a verb is changed from the active to the passive voice.

Lesson 66

Purpose: (1) To study the voice of transitive verbs. (2) To introduce *retained objects.

Oral Review:

1. Give the correct verb for each sentence. (Correct verbs are underlined.)
   a. Mr. Zelman (emigrated, <u>immigrated</u>) to this country.
   b. Mother has (laid, <u>lain</u>) down to rest.
   c. From your answer, a person can easily (imply, <u>infer</u>) that you are upset.
   d. As we mature, we must (<u>accept</u>, except) greater responsibilities.
2. Spell the plural form of each noun.
   a. library (libraries)   c. series (series)
   b. knife (knives)
3. Give the foreign plural spellings of these words.

Lesson 65 Answers

Written Exercises

(All answers are individual work.)

Teacher: Since Parts A and B in Written Exercises are both major assignments, you may want to assign them on two seperate days.

---

a. larva (larvae)   c. vertex (vertices)
b. datum (data)

4. Spell the possessive form of each noun.
   a. brothers (brothers')
   b. Jesus (Jesus')
   c. mice (mice's)
   d. calves (calves')
   e. sister-in-law (sister-in-law's)
   f. ox (ox's)
5. Tell whether each sentence shows separate or joint ownership.
   a. Larry's and Lester's chores are finished. (separate)
   b. Larry and Lester's work is finished. (joint)

Lesson Introduction: When you receive a vaccination for tetanus, a small amount of weakened tetanus bacteria is put into your bloodstream. These germs cause your body to produce antibodies that fight the

As you learned in Chapter 5, there are three general categories of verbs: transitive, intransitive complete, and intransitive linking. Of these, only the transitive verbs pass their action to another word in the sentence. Either the subject or the direct object may receive the action of a transitive verb.

Verbs in the Active Voice

A transitive verb in the *active voice* passes its action to a direct object. The subject is *active;* it is performing an action on a certain person or thing. Most transitive verbs are in the active voice.

> Moses <u>led</u> the *Israelites* out of Egypt.
> (*Moses* performs the action of *led; Israelites* receives the action.)

Moses	led	Israelites

Verbs in the Passive Voice

A transitive verb in the *passive voice* passes its action to the subject. The subject is *passive;* it receives the action rather than performing it. Often the doer of the action is named in a prepositional phrase near the end of the sentence. A verb in the passive voice is always a verb phrase, with a past participle as the main verb and a form of *be* as a helping verb.

> The <u>Israelites</u> <u>were led</u> out of Egypt by Moses.
> (*Israelites* receives the action of *were led; Moses* performs the action.)

Israelites	were led

Many sentences can be written with the verb in either active or passive voice. When a verb is changed from active to passive voice, the noun that names the doer may be placed in a prepositional phrase beginning with *by*. But this is not necessary; the sentence is complete without it.

> **Active voice:**
> Lucinda made these pies for Grandfather.
> **Passive voice:**
> These pies were made for Grandfather by Lucinda.
> These pies were made for Grandfather.

Tenses and Forms in the Passive Voice

The passive voice may be used in all six tenses. The main verb is always a past participle, and a form of *be* is always used as a helping verb. In addition, a form of *have* must be used in the perfect tenses.

disease. Because the vaccine causes your body to do something, the immunity that results is called *active immunity.* In contrast, when a flu epidemic threatens an area, people at risk may get a flu shot. This shot simply gives antibodies to a person; it does not cause his body to make antibodies. Therefore, the immunity that results is called *passive immunity.*

In this lesson you will study the active and passive voice of transitive verbs. In English as in medicine, something *active* is performing some action, whereas something *passive* has some action performed upon it.

Lesson Outline:

1. A transitive verb in the active voice passes its action to a direct object.

2. A transitive verb in the passive voice passes its action to the subject.

    a. Often the doer of the action is named in a prepositional phrase near the end of the sentence.

    b. The verb is always a verb phrase, with a past participle as the main verb and a form of *be* as a helping verb.

3. The passive voice may be used in all six tenses.

4. The progressive form in the passive voice occurs mainly in the simple present and past tenses. The emphatic form does not occur at all in the passive voice.

5. A retained object is an object complement that is retained when a verb is changed from the active to the passive voice.

    a. Only a verb in the passive voice can have a retained object.

Present: These heifers <u>are fed</u> plenty of hay.
Past: These heifers <u>were fed</u> plenty of hay.
Future: These heifers <u>will be fed</u> plenty of hay.
Present perfect: These heifers <u>have been fed</u> plenty of hay.
Past perfect: These heifers <u>had been fed</u> plenty of hay.
Future perfect: These heifers <u>will have been fed</u> plenty of hay.

Progressive forms in the passive voice follow the pattern *are being fed* (form of *be* + *being* + past participle). These progressive forms occur mainly in the simple present and past tenses. They are not common in the other tenses because those forms require clumsy repetition.

Present progressive: The heifers <u>are being fed</u> plenty of hay.
Past progressive: The heifers <u>were being fed</u> plenty of hay.

Seldom used because of clumsy repetition:
   Future progressive: The heifers <u>will be being fed</u>.
   Present perfect progressive: The heifers <u>have been being fed</u>.

Emphatic forms do not occur at all in the passive voice. Such forms would be especially strange and awkward.

Retained Objects

Compare the following sentences. In the first one, the verb is in the active voice and is followed by a direct object. In the second one, the verb is in the passive voice, and the receiver of the action (*coat*) is now the subject.

Hannah made a <u>coat</u>.
A <u>coat</u> was made by Hannah.

Here is the first sentence again, this time with an indirect object and a direct object. Now the action is passed to two objects—indirectly to *Samuel* and directly to *coat*.

Hannah made <u>Samuel</u> a <u>coat</u>.

Can this sentence still be rewritten so that the direct object becomes the subject? Yes, that can be done.

A <u>coat</u> was made <u>Samuel</u> by Hannah.

The rewritten sentence is in the passive voice, with the subject now receiving the action. But remember, there were *two* objects in the previous sentence. One has become the subject. What happened to the other? It is still there! The indirect object has been *retained* in the passive voice. *Samuel* is now a *retained indirect object.*

The same sentence can be rewritten so that the indirect object becomes

b. Only a sentence with a direct and an indirect object in the active voice can have a retained object in the passive voice.

c. Either a direct object or an indirect object may be retained.

★ *EXTRA PRACTICE*

Worksheet 24 *(Active and Passive Voice)*

he subject and the direct object is retained. The following sentence has a *retained direct object.*

Samuel was made a <u>coat</u> by Hannah.

These examples illustrate a peculiar fact about sentences with retained objects. The subject and the retained object can be exchanged, and the sentence means the same—as long as the verb is in the passive voice. Such an exchange cannot be made with any other kind of object.

A <u>coat</u> was made <u>Samuel</u>.   <u>Samuel</u> was made a <u>coat</u>.
A new <u>name</u> was given <u>Jacob</u>.   <u>Jacob</u> was given a new <u>name</u>.

Only a sentence with a direct and an indirect object in the active voice can have a retained object in the passive voice. Study the following diagrams of these related sentences.

Active voice:
Hannah made Samuel a coat.

Passive voice with retained indirect object:
A coat was made Samuel by Hannah.

Passive voice with retained direct object:
Samuel was made a coat by Hannah.

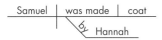

The following steps can be used to decide whether a sentence has a retained object.

1. See if the verb is in the passive voice, with a form like *is given* or *was made.* Remember, only passive verbs can have retained objects.
2. Find the substantives just before and after the passive verb, and exchange them to see how the meaning is affected. If it stays the same, the substantive after the verb is a retained object.
3. Determine what kind of object is retained by changing the verb to the active voice and identifying the direct and indirect objects. If the substantive after the verb is a direct object in the active voice, it is

a retained direct object in the passive voice. If that substantive is an indirect object in the active voice, it is a retained indirect object in the passive voice.

Problem: Matthew made Jesus a great feast.
   Think: (1) The verb *made* is not passive.
Solution: There is no retained object.

Problem: The students were taught calligraphy by Brother Neil.
   Think: (1) The verb *were taught* is passive.
       (2) Calligraphy was taught the students.
          The meaning is the same; *calligraphy* is a retained object.
       (3) Brother Neil taught the students calligraphy.
          Calligraphy is a direct object in the active voice.
Solution: *Calligraphy* is a retained direct object.

Problem: These rumors were spread by several thoughtless people.
   Think: (1) The verb *were spread* is passive.
       (2) There is no substantive just after the verb.
          (*People* is the object of a preposition; besides, "People were spread these rumors" is not sensible.)
Solution: There is no retained object.

Problem: This scrapbook was given Grandma by our family.
   Think: (1) The verb *was given* is passive.
       (2) Grandma was given this scrapbook.
          The meaning is the same; *Grandma* is a retained object.
       (3) Our family gave Grandma this scrapbook.
          Grandma is an indirect object in the active voice.
Solution: *Grandma* is a retained indirect object.

A sentence with a retained object has an unusual structure. It may even have an indirect object but no direct object! You may not be accustomed to this word order, but retained objects do provide another way to add variety to your speech and writing.

Class Practice

A. Read each verb, and tell whether it is in the *active* or *passive* voice. Tell what word receives the action of the verb.
1. The righteous seek the glory of God.
2. The righteous will always be blessed by God.
3. God's angels are sent as ministering spirits to the saints.
4. Angels have spoken God's message to men.
5. Lot and his family were urged by two angels to flee from Sodom.

Lesson 66 Answers

Class Practice

A. 1. seek—active, glory
   2. will be blessed—passive, righteous
   3. are sent—passive, angels
   4. have spoken—active, message
   5. were urged—passive, Lot (and) family

B. Change each sentence so that the verb is in the active voice.
1. Many wildflowers were identified by Uncle Harold.
2. This meal was furnished the workers by several local families.
3. A pleasant surprise has been planned by Father.
4. A short visit will be paid Sister Arlene by our class.

C. Change each sentence so that the verb is in the passive voice. In sentences 1 and 2, retain the direct object; in sentences 3 and 4, retain the indirect object.
1. Uncle Carl gave me this book.
2. The tour guide handed each person a set of papers.
3. Grandfather Mast often tells the children interesting stories.
4. Aunt Darlene sent the girls a long letter.

D. Find the retained objects in these sentences, and tell if each one is a *direct object* or an *indirect object*. If a sentence has no retained object, say *none*.
1. An honest worker gives each assignment his best efforts.
2. Others are offered the first choice by an unselfish person.
3. A peacemaker's ways are appreciated by others.
4. True glory is given the Lord by our faithful lives.
5. Many privileges are granted us by our government.

Written Exercises

A. Write whether each underlined verb is *active* or *passive*. Also write which of the six tenses it is, and label its form (*simple, progressive, emphatic*).
1. Our bulletin boards <u>have been put</u> up by several sisters from church.
2. Brother Levi <u>did teach</u> our music classes.
3. Brother Albert <u>has been giving</u> us quizzes in history and science.
4. Several book reports <u>will be given</u> today.
5. We <u>had been making</u> simple mottoes in art class.
6. The disobedient students <u>are being kept</u> in their seats.

B. Rewrite each sentence so that the verb is in the active voice.
1. The kitchen was swept by Glenda.
2. This collection of poems was gathered by Aunt Matilda.
3. A package was left us by the delivery man.
4. The sick girl was brought a sunshine box by Uncle Lloyd.

C. Copy each object complement, and label it *DO* (direct object) or *IO* (indirect object). Write *ret.* after the label if the object is retained.
1. The dog has snatched Jerry's hot dog.
2. The rabbit pens were given a thorough cleaning by the boys.

B. 1. Uncle Harold identified many wildflowers.
2. Several local families furnished the workers this meal.
3. Father has planned a pleasant surprise.
4. Our class will pay Sister Arlene a short visit.

C. 1. I was given this book by Uncle Carl.
2. Each person was handed a set of papers by the tour guide.
3. Interesting stories are often told the children by Grandfather Mast.
4. A long letter was sent the girls by Aunt Darlene.

D. 1. none
2. choice, direct object
3. none
4. Lord, indirect object
5. us, indirect object

Written Exercises

A. 1. passive, present perfect, simple
2. active, past, emphatic
3. active, present perfect, progressive
4. passive, future, simple
5. active, past perfect, progressive
6. passive, present, progressive

B. 1. Glenda swept the kitchen.
2. Aunt Matilda gathered this collection of poems.
3. The delivery man left us a package.
4. Uncle Lloyd brought the sick girl a sunshine box.

C. 1. hot dog—DO
2. cleaning—DO ret.

3. Frank offered Father his willing assistance.
4. Much trouble has been given us by these goats.
5. Father was provided clear directions by the police officer.
6. Brother Wilmer showed Angela her mistake.

D. Rewrite each sentence so that the verb is in the passive voice. Follow the directions in parentheses for retaining the objects.
1. The girls sent Mrs. Grayson a batch of cookies. (Retain the direct object.)
2. Her obvious gratitude afforded them ample payment. (Retain the indirect object.)
3. Uncle Galen sent us a letter describing the new mission. (Retain the indirect object.)
4. Brother Kurtz gave Marlin a stern warning. (Retain the direct object.)

Review Exercises

A. Copy each underlined word, and label it *S* (singular) or *P* (plural). [36]
1. The <u>bison</u> slowly made their way across the <u>plain</u>.
2. After we passed the <u>oasis</u>, we saw only a few <u>cacti</u>.
3. We noticed a <u>fungus</u> and some <u>algae</u> during our walk along the creek.
4. Our <u>speech</u> and actions are good <u>indices</u> to our thoughts.

B. If the underlined part of the sentence should be improved, write it correctly. If it is correct, write *correct*. [37]
1. This <u>chair's back</u> is too straight to be comfortable.
2. The <u>wolve's howls</u> frightened the lone traveler.
3. <u>Sherwin's and Wendell's bicycle</u> has been damaged.
4. <u>Uncle Moses's car</u> doesn't start.
5. <u>Mary's and Erma's dresses</u> have the same print.
6. My one <u>brother's-in-laws skill</u> at drawing faces is remarkable.

C. Label each underlined substantive *GP* (gerund phrase), *IP* (infinitive phrase), or *NC* (noun clause). [40, 41]
1. <u>Making others happy</u> brings happiness to one's own self.
2. Cindy's cheerfulness should encourage <u>whomever she meets</u>.
3. <u>That a cheerful smile can turn away anger</u> has often been shown.
4. Our goal should be <u>to brighten the world around us</u>.
5. We should be known for <u>having a joyful outlook on life</u>.

---

3. Father—IO; assistance—DO
4. us—IO ret.
5. directions—DO ret.
6. Angela—IO; mistake—DO

D. 1. Mrs. Grayson was sent a batch of cookies by the girls.
2. Ample payment was afforded them by her obvious gratitude.
3. A letter describing the new mission was sent us by Uncle Galen.
4. Marlin was given a stern warning by Brother Kurtz.

Review Exercises

A. 1. bison—P; plain—S
2. oasis—S; cacti—P
3. fungus—S; algae—P
4. speech—S; indices—P

B. 1. back of the chair
2. wolves' howls
3. Sherwin and Wendell's bicycle
4. Uncle Moses' car
5. correct
6. brother-in-law's skill

C. 1. GP
2. NC
3. NC
4. IP
5. GP

67. Proofreading and Rewriting a Story

Lesson Survey
- To finish writing a story, proofread the first draft.
- Write the final draft of the story.

You should never view proofreading and rewriting your work as unimportant. Even experienced writers must go through these steps. Sometimes they revise and rewrite a story many times before they are satisfied.

Proofreading

In Lesson 42 you studied the steps for proofreading a composition. You should use the same proofreading marks when you revise a story.

The upper grade students ⌐excitedly⌐ chattered⌐ as they headed ^for the steep hill behind the Piney Mountain Mennonite School. "These ~~here~~ Pennsylvania hills certainly beat southern Maryland for sleding." commented fourteen-year-old Titus. "Before ^we moved here, I hardly did any sledding at all."

First check the general content and structure of your story. As you proofread your story, ask yourself the following questions.

1. Does the story teach a worthwhile theme?
   a. Does the story *show* the lesson rather than *telling* it?
   b. Does every incident, conversation, and description in the story contribute to the theme?
2. Does the story open effectively with action, dialogue, or an unusual statement?
3. Does the story opening quickly introduce the main character, establish the setting, and hint at the theme and conflict? Does the story begin as near to the first scene of conflict as possible?
4. Is the conflict clear, and does it build up in intensity?
5. Is the climax the most intense incident of the conflict? Does it occur very near the end of the story?
6. Is the conclusion brief and satisfying?
7. Are the characters portrayed effectively and consistently?
8. Is the dialogue natural?
9. Have you used lively action verbs; exact, descriptive words; and colorful imagery?
10. Does the story have a fresh, original title that does not give away the outcome?

Lesson 67

Purpose: To study methods of evaluating and improving stories.

Oral Review:

1. Name five steps in making a plan for a story. (Write the theme your story will teach. Write a sentence describing the conflict. List the incidents in the conflict, including the climax. Write how the story will conclude. Name the main character, and describe his primary traits.)
2. Name four steps in writing the first draft of a story. (Write a good beginning for the story. Write the middle part of the story. Write a brief conclusion to the story. Write an interesting title.)
3. What are some qualities of a good title? (It does not give away the outcome of the story. It is short—rarely more than five words. It is fresh

and original—perhaps with rhyming words, alliteration, an unusual statement, or a question.)
4. What are some elements of effective style in a story? (natural dialogue; lively action verbs; exact, descriptive words; imagery)

Lesson Introduction: Are you satisfied with the story you wrote for Lesson 65? Have you carefully followed all the directions given in the story writing lessons of this chapter? Is your story the best that you can make it? Unless you are an exceptional writer, you certainly can find areas to improve your story. This lesson will help you to find those areas so that you can produce an interesting, well-written story.

Lesson Outline:

1. To finish writing a story, proofread the first draft. Use the proofreading marks that you studied earlier to mark corrections. Also ask the following questions.

(1) Does the story teach a worthwhile theme?
   (a) Does the story *show* the lesson rather than *telling* it?
   (b) Does every incident, conversation, and description in the story contribute to the theme?
(2) Does the story open effectively with action, dialogue, or an unusual statement?
(3) Does the story opening quickly introduce the main character, establish the setting, and hint at the theme and conflict? Does the story begin as near to the first scene of conflict as possible?
(4) Is the conflict clear, and does it build up in intensity?
(5) Is the climax forceful? Does it occur very near the end of the story?
(6) Is the conclusion brief and satisfying?
(7) Are the characters portrayed effectively and consistently?
(8) Is the dialogue natural?
(9) Have you used lively action verbs; exact, descriptive words; and colorful imagery?
(10) Does the story have a fresh, original title that does not give away the outcome?
(11) Are there any extra details that should be removed, or missing details that should be added to make the sentences clear?

When you are satisfied with the larger elements of your story, check for the smaller details of form and sentence structure. The following questions will help you with this kind of proofreading.

11. Are there any extra details that should be removed, or missing details that should be added to make the sentences clear?
12. Are there any awkward sentences that should be reworded?
13. Have you used correct spelling and punctuation?

Rewriting

For the final draft of your story, you should write on every line. Make the appearance of your paper as neat as possible by using your best penmanship. Also keep the left margin straight and the right margin as straight as possible.

> *The upper grade students chattered excitedly as they headed for the steep hill behind the Piney Mountain Mennonite School. "These Pennsylvania hills certainly beat southern Maryland for sledding," commented fourteen-year-old Titus. "Before we moved here, I hardly did any sledding at all."*

Written Exercises

A. Proofread the first draft of the story you wrote in Lesson 65. Use the proofreading marks you have learned, as well as the list of questions in this lesson.

B. Write the second draft of your story, making the improvements you marked. Use every line, write as neatly as you can, and keep neat margins.

---

68. Chapter 6 Review

Class Practice

A. Give the answers.
1. Tell which of the following verbs are usually transitive: *lay, lie, set, sit, raise, rise.*
2. Of the verbs *can* and *may,* which one is used (*a*) to ask permission? (*b*) to express ability?
3. Of the verbs *let* and *leave,* which one is usually followed by another verb form?
4. What is the theme of a story?
5. What are the three common kinds of conflict?

(12) Are there any awkward sentences that should be reworded?

(13) Have you used correct spelling and punctuation?

2. Write the final draft of your story.
   a. Write on every line.
   b. Have a neat paper, with good penmanship and proper margins.

Lesson 68

Purpose: To review the concepts taught in Chapter 6.

Lesson 67 Answers

Written Exercises

(All answers are individual work.)

Lesson 68 Answers

Class Practice

A. 1. lay, set, raise
   2. *a.* may; *b.* can
   3. let
   4. the lesson it teaches
   5. main character in conflict with another person with his circumstances, or with his own self

6. Where should the climax of a story occur?
7. Name four ways of portraying a story character.
8. Name several things that contribute to natural dialogue.
9. In addition to natural dialogue, what qualities contribute to effective style?
10. What are three good ways to open a story?
11. What three things are included in the setting of a story?
12. What makes an effective title?

B. Read each sentence, choosing the verb that agrees with the subject.
1. There (is, are) many illustrations of God's faithfulness in the Bible.
2. The encouragement of others, along with the promises of God's Word, (help, helps) us to be faithful.
3. The goal of all God's people (is, are) lives that honor God.
4. Neither Job's wife nor his three friends (was, were) much encouragement to him.
5. Anyone who trusts in the Lord (find, finds) His grace sufficient.
6. (Don't, Doesn't) the fear of the Lord produce a holy life?
7. Christ's teachings or His example (show, shows) us how to respond to every situation.
8. The family (have, has) started their various jobs for the morning.
9. The tweezers (is, are) not in the drawer.
10. "Ye Fair Green Hills of Galilee" (is, are) a beautiful song.

C. Read each sentence, choosing the verb with the correct meaning.
1. Joyful songs should (raise, rise) from our hearts every day.
2. Jesus (laid, lay) in the grave three days.
3. Believers in Christ can (set, sit) in heavenly places.
4. We must (accept, except) the help and advice of godly parents.
5. One who refuses godly advice (loses, looses) God's blessing.
6. Our elderly neighbors had (emigrated, immigrated) from their native Russia during World War II.
7. You (can, may) work on your bird feeder only if you have finished your regular chores.
8. We (adapted, adopted) the rules of the game to fit our situation.
9. Do not (let, leave) the door open in this cold weather.
10. Your answer (implies, infers) that you are not interested.

D. Tell what word receives the action of the verb, and tell whether the verb is in the *active* or the *passive* voice.
1. The milk cows have been let out to pasture.
2. Richard is feeding the dry cows.
3. Have the children finished their work with the calves?
4. Only the heifers must be fed yet.

6. very near the end of the story
7. through actions, speech, thoughts, and appearance
8. informal tone that uses contractions and elliptical sentences; frequent change of speakers; descriptive explanatory words
9. lively action verbs; exact, descriptive words; imagery
10. with action, dialogue, or an unusual statement
11. time, place, and emotional mood
12. not giving away the outcome of the story, short, fresh and original

B. 1. are
2. helps
3. is
4. were
5. finds
6. Doesn't
7. shows
8. have
9. are
10. is

C. 1. rise
2. lay
3. sit
4. accept
5. loses
6. emigrated
7. may
8. adapted
9. leave
10. implies

D. 1. cows, passive
2. cows, active
3. work, active
4. heifers, passive

E. Read each sentence, changing the voice of the verb from active to passive or from passive to active. Follow any directions in parentheses.
1. A cold front produced some severe thunderstorms.
2. The teacher gave us a helpful list of information. (Retain the indirect object.)
3. The wood was carefully stacked by the boys.
4. Patricia gave the teacher this bouquet of lilacs. (Retain the direct object.)

Written Exercises

A. Most of these sentences have mistakes in subject–verb agreement. Write the correct words, or write *correct*.
1. What's some reasons for the destruction of Jerusalem?
2. Each of the Ten Commandments express an important principle.
3. Noah, as well as his entire family, were spared from the Flood.
4. One person don't have all the gifts of the Spirit.
5. The carpenter crew have gone to their various jobs for today.
6. Rabies are not dreaded nearly as much since the development of vaccines.
7. Warren or his sisters is gathering the eggs this week.
8. There's five bushels of tomatoes to sort through.
9. Barry's trousers need to be lengthened.
10. The whole flock seem to be healthy again.
11. Bible ethics call for kindness and unselfishness.
12. A pink and white salmon were slowly circling in the pool.

B. Most of these sentences have mistakes in the use of problem verbs. Write the correct verb, or write *correct*.
1. God left Satan attack Job severely.
2. Many prayers raised on behalf of Peter in prison.
3. We should not set in judgment of others.
4. The handwriting on the wall affected a great change on Belshazzar's countenance.
5. Saul purposed that David wear his armor when he faced Goliath.
6. Father said that we can go sledding after chores.
7. Paul left David ride his bicycle.
8. David must have left the bicycle out in the rain.
9. This bread dough raised quite rapidly.
10. The plaster of Paris has not set sufficiently.
11. The little girls set on the couch and played with their dolls.
12. Fred laid on the couch until noon with a bad headache.
13. Your brother's actions do not necessarily infer wrong motives.
14. You must be careful, for you cannot see his heart.
15. That man works so diligently that he has raised to the rank of foreman.

E. 1. Some severe thunderstorms were produced by a cold front.
2. A helpful list of information was given us by the teacher.
3. The boys carefully stacked the wood.
4. The teacher was given this bouquet of lilacs by Patricia.

Written Exercises

A. 1. What are
2. expresses
3. was
4. doesn't
5. correct
6. is
7. are
8. There are
9. correct
10. seems
11. calls
12. was

B. 1. let
2. rose
3. sit
4. effected
5. proposed
6. may
7. let
8. correct
9. rose
10. correct
11. sat
12. lay
13. imply
14. correct
15. risen

B. Copy each object complement, and label it *DO* (direct object) or *IO* (indirect object). Write *ret.* after the label if the object is retained.
1. The two spies gave Rahab the assurance of protection.
2. The Bethlehemites were caused great suffering by King Herod.
3. Solomon wrote many wise proverbs.
4. Wise counsel was offered David by Abigail.

D. For each of these story plots, name which kind of conflict is involved.
1. Gary has a bad habit of daydreaming. After receiving a stern warning from the teacher, he realizes how strong the habit really is and determines to overcome it.
2. Sharon's family has opened their home to her cousin Marie for a few days. Sharon hardly knows how to respond when Marie begins to show disrespectful attitudes.
3. Andrew had eagerly anticipated spending several hours on Saturday fishing with Grandfather. When his father suddenly becomes ill, Andrew has to stay at home and help with the work.

E. For each theme below, write the number of the plot in Part D that best matches it.
1. A person of noble character stands up for what is right even when that is difficult.
2. True happiness is found in submission to God's will in our plans.
3. Victory is found through humble dependence on the Lord, coupled with personal determination.

F. Rewrite the following paragraphs to characterize Donald as a careful boy rather than a careless boy.

Donald quickly chopped down the biggest weeds between the corn rows. Fifteen minutes later he dashed into the shop and tossed his hoe into the corner. "Hope Father doesn't look at the corn too closely," he thought uneasily.

　　　*　　　*　　　*　　　*　　　*

"Oh, I never really check over my papers. Takes too much time and effort," replied Donald as he ran his hand through his tousled hair.

G. Rewrite this dialogue, making it sound more natural.

"It is always so peaceful here beside the lake," said Michelle. "Do you come here often?"

"Yes, we come here often. In fact, we have had several picnics here this summer," said Bernice.

"Does not this beauty make you think about God, the Creator?" said Michelle.

——————————

C. 1. Rahab—IO; assurance—DO
2. suffering—DO ret.
3. proverbs—DO
4. David—IO ret.

D. 1. main character in conflict with his own self
2. main character in conflict with another person
3. main character in conflict with circumstances

E. 1. 2
2. 3
3. 1

F. (Sample paragraphs; allow reasonable variation.)

Donald carefully hoed all the weeds in the corn rows. An hour later he stepped into the shop and hung up his hoe. "The corn patch looks much better now," he thought with satisfaction.

"Oh, I always check over my papers. It is well worth the time and effort," replied Donald as he smoothed his neatly combed hair.

G. (Sample improvement; allow reasonable variation.)

"It's always so peaceful here beside the lake," commented Michelle. "Do you come here often?"

"Yes. In fact, we've had several picnics here this summer," replied Bernice.

"Doesn't this beauty make you think about God, the Creator?" asked Michelle.

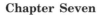

Chapter Seven

Pronouns

Writing Effective Sentences

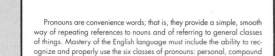

Pronouns are convenience words; that is, they provide a simple, smooth way of repeating references to nouns and of referring to general classes of things. Mastery of the English language must include the ability to recognize and properly use the six classes of pronouns: personal, compound personal, demonstrative, indefinite, interrogative, and relative.

You have learned to write grammatically correct sentences. You have also learned to write sentences with a variety of types, word orders, and structures. Grammatical correctness and broad variety, however, do not guarantee that the sentences in your paragraphs communicate well. Coherence, conciseness, parallelism, and other qualities must also characterize your sentences. Skill in producing sentences with these qualities will directly contribute to the clarity and appeal of your writing.

And the Lord answered me, and said,
Write the vision, and make it plain upon tables,
that he may run that readeth it.

Habakkuk 2:2

```
┌─────────────────────────────────────────────┐
│              Personal Pronouns                │
│              Nominative Case                  │
│                Singular          Plural       │
│  First person:   I               we           │
│  Second person:  you (thou)      you (ye)     │
│  Third person:   he, she, it     they         │
│                                               │
│              Objective Case                   │
│                Singular          Plural       │
│  First person:   me              us           │
│  Second person:  you (thee)      you          │
│  Third person:   him, her, it    them         │
│                                               │
│              Possessive Case                  │
│                Singular              Plural    │
│  First person:  my, mine            our, ours  │
│  Second person: your, yours (thy, thine)  your, yours │
│  Third person:  his, her, hers, its  their, theirs │
│                                               │
│    (Archaic pronouns are in parentheses.)     │
└─────────────────────────────────────────────┘
```

69. Personal Pronouns

Lesson Survey

- A **pronoun** is a word that takes the place of a noun. The noun for which a pronoun stands is its **antecedent.**

- **Personal pronouns** have different forms to show person, number, case, and gender.

- The **person** of a pronoun shows the relationship between the pronoun and the speaker.

- The **number** of a pronoun shows whether the pronoun is singular or plural.

- The **case** of a pronoun relates to its use in the sentence.

- The **gender** of a pronoun is *masculine, feminine, neuter,* or *common.*

- A pronoun must agree with its antecedent in person and number. A third person singular pronoun must also agree in gender.

Lesson 69

Purpose: To study the definition of pronouns and the characteristics of personal pronouns.

Oral Review:

1. Give a brief definition for each problem verb.
   a. raise (to cause [something] to go up or grow up)
   b. immigrate (to enter a foreign country for residence)
   c. infer (to decide by reasoning; conclude)
   d. imply (to express indirectly)
   e. lie (to rest, recline, or remain in a flat position)
   f. can (to be able to)
   g. effect (*noun*—the result of some action; *verb*—to bring to pass; accomplish)
   h. except (*preposition*—not including; *verb*—to leave out; exclude)

2. When should you capitalize a word like *doctor*? (when it is part of a name or used instead of a name)

3. When are words like *god* and *lord* not capitalized? (when they refer to idols or people)

4. What are the four main purposes of commas? (to divide compound sentences; to separate items in a series; to set off introductory material; to set off nonrestrictive and independent elements)

Lesson Introduction: How awkward our language would be without pronouns! Can you imagine needing to speak and write like this?

When David came into the Israelite camp, David immediately recognized that King Saul and King Saul's army were paralyzed with fear. David readily accepted Goliath's challenge, and soon David brought Goliath to Goliath's death.

You have learned that a substantive is any word or word group that names a person, place, thing, or idea. The most common substantives are single-word nouns and pronouns.

A *pronoun* is a word that takes the place of a noun. After identifying a thing or an idea with a noun, we frequently refer to it by using pronouns instead of repeating the *antecedent* (the noun that the pronoun replaces). In the following paragraph, the pronouns are underlined and the antecedents are italicized.

> *Jesus* was grieved when <u>He</u> came into the temple. With <u>their</u> animal market and business of money changing right within the *house* of God, the *Jews* were seriously abusing this holy place. In fact, Jesus said that <u>they</u> had made <u>it</u> a den of thieves.

Generally the antecedent precedes the pronoun, as with *Jesus* and *house* in the example. However, a pronoun may occasionally come first in an introductory phrase or clause, with the antecedent in the main part of the sentence. An example of this is *their* and *Jews* in the second sentence of the paragraph above.

Personal pronouns have different forms to show person, number, case, and gender. Each of these is explained below.

Person

The *person* of a pronoun shows the relationship between the pronoun and the speaker. When a speaker refers to himself, he uses the *first person pronouns: I, me, my, mine, we, us, our, ours.* When a speaker refers to the person to whom he is speaking, he uses the *second person pronouns: you, your, yours.* When a speaker refers to some other person or thing, he uses the *third person pronouns: he, him, his, she, her, hers, it, its, they, them, their, theirs.*

> God told the Israelites, "<u>I</u> will deliver the inhabitants of the land into <u>your</u> hand; and <u>thou</u> shalt drive <u>them</u> out before <u>thee</u>."
> (The first person pronoun, *I,* refers to God, who is speaking. The second person pronouns, *your, thou,* and *thee,* refer to Israel, to whom God is speaking. The third person pronoun, *them,* refers to the Canaanites, about whom God is speaking.)

Number

As with nouns, the *number* of a pronoun shows whether the pronoun is singular or plural. The pronouns *you, your,* and *yours* may be either singular or plural, depending on their antecedents.

> The *prophet* delivered <u>his</u> message boldly. (*Prophet* and *his* are singular.)
> The *prophets* delivered <u>their</u> messages boldly.
> (*Prophets* and *their* are plural.)

Certainly pronouns are important to our smooth communication. Learn to recognize and use them well.

Lesson Outline:

1. A pronoun is a word that takes the place of a noun. The noun that the pronoun replaces is its antecedent.

    a. Generally the antecedent precedes the pronoun.

    b. Occasionally a pronoun comes first in an introductory phrase or clause, and the antecedent follows in the main part of the sentence.

2. Personal pronouns have different forms to show person, number, case, and gender.

3. The person of a pronoun shows the relationship between the pronoun and the speaker.

    a. When a speaker refers to himself, he uses the first person pronouns: *I, me, my, mine, we, us, our, ours.*

    b. When a speaker refers to the person to whom he is speaking, he uses the second person pronouns: *you, your, yours.*

    c. When a speaker refers to some other person or thing, he uses the third person pronouns: *he, him, his, she, her, hers, it, its, they, them, their, theirs.*

4. The number of a pronoun shows whether the pronoun is singular or plural. The pronouns *you, your,* and *yours* may be either singular or plural, depending on their antecedents.

5. The case of a pronoun relates to its use in the sentence.

    a. A pronoun in the nominative case is used

Each of the visitors expressed <u>his</u> appreciation.
(*Each* and *his* are singular.)
Both of the visitors expressed <u>their</u> appreciation.
(*Both* and *their* are plural.)

Leon, have <u>you</u> finished <u>your</u> chores? (*Leon, you,* and *your* are singular.)
Boys, have <u>you</u> finished <u>your</u> chores? (*Boys, you,* and *your* are plural.)

Case

The *case* of a pronoun relates to its use in the sentence. There are three cases: nominative, objective, and possessive.

Nominative case. A pronoun in the nominative case is used as a subject, a predicate nominative, or an appositive to one of these. Be especially careful to use the nominative case for predicate nominatives, even though it may sound awkward.

The following pronouns are in the nominative case: *I, you, he, she, it, we, they;* archaic: *thou, ye.*

<u>We</u> are vessels in the Potter's hand.
(The nominative case *We* is the subject.)
The eighth grade boys, Daryl and <u>I</u>, both live on farms.
(The nominative case *I* is part of a compound appositive to the subject.)
The fastest runner in our school is <u>he</u>.
(The nominative case *he* is the predicate nominative.)
My oldest cousins are twins, Loretta and <u>she</u>.
(The nominative case *she* is part of a compound appositive to the predicate nominative.)

In the King James Bible, the archaic forms *thou* and *ye* are used as second person pronouns in the nominative case. *Thou* is singular and *ye* is plural.

"Lord, if <u>thou</u> wilt, <u>thou</u> canst make me clean."
(Antecedent of *thou* is the singular noun *Lord.*)
"And when Peter saw it, he answered unto the people, <u>Ye</u> men of Israel, why marvel <u>ye</u> at this?" (Antecedent of *Ye* is the plural noun *people.*)

Objective case. A pronoun in the objective case is used as an object complement, the object of a preposition, or an appositive to any of these. The following pronouns are in the objective case: *me, you, him, her, it, us, them;* archaic: *thee.*

Even if others despise <u>us</u>, we should determine to love <u>them</u>.
(The objective case *us* is the direct object of the verb *despise;* the objective case *them* is the direct object of the verbal *to love.*)

as a subject, a predicate nominative, or an appositive to one of these.
1) Be especially careful to use the nominative case for predicate nominatives, even though it may sound awkward.
2) The following pronouns are in the nominative case: *I, you, he, she, it, we, they;* archaic: *thou, ye.*
3) In the King James Bible, the archaic forms *thou* and *ye* are used as second person pronouns in the nominative case. *Thou* is singular and *ye* is plural.
b. A pronoun in the objective case is used as an object complement, the object of a preposition, or an appositive to any of these.
1) The following pronouns are in the objective case: *me, you, him, her, it, us, them;* archaic: *thee.*

2) The archaic form *thee* is used in the King James Bible as the second person singular pronoun in the objective case. The plural form is *you.*
3) The pronouns *you* and *it* can be either nominative or objective, depending on their use in a sentence.
c. A pronoun in the possessive case is used to show ownership.
1) Possessive pronouns are often used as adjectives to modify nouns. However, some can stand alone.
2) The following pronouns are in the possessive case: *my, mine, your, yours, his, her, hers, its, our, ours, their, theirs;* archaic: *thy, thine.*
3) The archaic forms *thy* and *thine* are used in the King James Bible as second

Melanie helped the little girls, Sharon and <u>her</u>, with their work.
> (The objective case *her* is part of a compound appositive to the direct object.)

Aunt Rosene told <u>me</u> an interesting story of her childhood.
> (The objective case *me* is an indirect object.)

We forgot to bring the book for <u>him</u>.
> (The objective case *him* is the object of a preposition.)

The archaic form *thee* is used in the King James Bible as the second person singular pronoun in the objective case. The plural form is *you*.

> "O righteous Father, the world hath not known <u>thee</u>."
> (Antecedent of *thee* is the singular noun *Father*.)
> "Then said Jesus unto his disciples, Verily I say unto <u>you</u>, That a rich man shall hardly enter into the kingdom of heaven."
> (Antecedent of *you* is the plural noun *disciples*.)

The pronouns *you* and *it* can be either nominative or objective, depending on their use in a sentence.

> Have <u>you</u> finished <u>it</u>? (*You*, the subject, is nominative; *it*, the direct object, is objective.)
> <u>It</u> has been a help to <u>you</u>. (*It*, the subject, is nominative; *you*, the object of a preposition, is objective.)

Possessive case. A pronoun in the possessive case is used to show ownership. Possessive pronouns are often used as adjectives to modify nouns. Some possessive pronouns can stand alone.

The following pronouns are in the possessive case: *my, mine, your, yours, his, her, hers, its, our, ours, their, theirs;* archaic: *thy, thine*.

> We were shocked to hear that <u>our</u> house was damaged by the storm.
> (*Our* modifies *house*.)
> These papers are <u>his</u>. (*His* stands alone as the predicate nominative.)
> <u>Your</u> story certainly excelled <u>mine</u>.
> (*Your* modifies *story; mine* stands alone as the direct object.)

The archaic forms *thy* and *thine* are used in the King James Bible as second person singular pronouns in the possessive case. *Thy* is used before consonant sounds, and *thine* is used before vowel sounds. In archaic usage, *my* is also used before consonant sounds, and *mine* is used before vowel sounds.

> "Be thou exalted, Lord, in <u>thine</u> own strength: so will we sing and praise <u>thy</u> power."
> "The Lord is the portion of <u>mine</u> inheritance and of <u>my</u> cup."

person singular pronouns in the possessive case. *Thy* is used before consonant sounds, and *thine* is used before vowel sounds. In archaic usage, *my* is also used before consonant sounds, and *mine* is used before vowel sounds.

6. The gender of a pronoun is masculine, feminine, neuter, or common.

(1) Masculine gender *refers to persons or animals that are male.*

(2) Feminine gender *refers to persons or animals that are female.*

(3) Neuter gender *refers to things or ideas that are neither male nor female.*

(4) Common gender *refers to persons, animals, or things that may be male, female, or neuter, or to a group that includes more than one gender.*

7. A pronoun must agree with its antecedent in person and number. Third person singular pronouns must also agree in gender.

★ **EXTRA PRACTICE**
Worksheet 25 (*Personal Pronouns*)

Gender

The *gender* of a pronoun is *masculine, feminine, neuter,* or *common.* In Lesson 34 you studied these four genders in relation to nouns.

1. Masculine gender *refers to persons or animals that are male.*

   he   him   his

2. Feminine gender *refers to persons or animals that are female.*

   she   her   hers

3. Neuter gender *refers to things or ideas that are neither male nor female.*

   it   its

4. Common gender *refers to persons, animals, or things that may be male, female, or neuter, or to a group that includes more than one gender.* The only pronouns with different forms according to gender are third person singular pronouns (like *he, she,* and *it*). All other pronouns are of common gender.

Pronoun–Antecedent Agreement

A pronoun must agree with its antecedent in person and number. Third person singular pronouns must also agree in gender. In the following sentences, the antecedents are italicized and the pronouns are underlined.

> Father said, "*Nevin,* you should be willing to help *Mr. Newman* with his work." (*You* is second person to agree with *Nevin. His* is third person, singular, masculine gender, to agree with *Mr. Newman.*)
> *Paula* gave the *puppies* some food; then she gave them fresh water. (*She* is third person, singular, feminine gender, to agree with *Paula. Them* is third person, plural, common gender, to agree with *puppies.*)

Class Practice

A. Name each personal pronoun, and tell its person and number.
   1. "My sheep hear my voice, and I know them, and they follow me."
   2. "Then took Mary . . . ointment . . . and anointed the feet of Jesus, and wiped his feet with her hair."
   3. "Mr. Gomez, come to our church, and you will hear the Gospel preached faithfully," assured Father.
   4. Boys, we are pleased with your progress.

B. Name each personal pronoun, and tell its case and gender.
   1. When Abigail came to him, David accepted her wise counsel.
   2. We know that God desires our praise.
   3. Moses threw down his rod, and it became a serpent.

Lesson 69 Answers

Class Practice

A. 1. My—first person, singular;
      my—first person, singular;
      I—first person, singular;
      them—third person, plural;
      they—third person, plural;
      me—first person, singular
   2. his—third person, singular;
      her—third person, singular
   3. our—first person, plural;
      you—second person, singular
   4. we—first person, plural;
      your—second person, plural

B. 1. him—objective, masculine;
      her—possessive, feminine
   2. We—nominative, common;
      our—possessive, common
   3. his—possessive, masculine;
      it—nominative, neuter

C. Tell whether the personal pronouns in each pair are different in *person, number, case,* or *gender.*
1. we, I
2. he, she
3. he, his
4. her, his
5. we, they
6. it, its

D. Choose the correct pronouns in parentheses.
1. The best person to ask right now would be (he, him).
2. Joseph is a good example for you and (I, me).
3. The last person to choose was (I, me).
4. Both of the song leaders knew (his, their) music well.
5. (They, Them) have planned to visit (we, us).

Written Exercises

A. Copy each personal pronoun. After it, write *1, 2,* or *3* to identify its person, and write *S* or *P* to identify its number.
1. My children, if you are content, your lives can be comfortable enough. (Plautus)
2. Every action of our lives touches some chord that will vibrate in eternity. (Edwin Chapin)
3. We give advice by the bucket, but take it by the grain. (William Alger)
4. My friend, you can't hold a man down without staying down with him. (Booker T. Washington)
5. Natural abilities are like natural plants; they need pruning by study. (Francis Bacon)

B. Copy each personal pronoun. After it, write *N, O,* or *P* to identify its case, and write *M, F, N,* or *C* to identify its gender.
1. Daniel purposed in his heart that he would not be defiled.
2. Queen Esther was willing to die for her people, but the king did hold out the golden scepter to her as she came to him.
3. Caleb and Joshua urged the people to trust in their God and enter the land that God had promised to them.
4. When the Israelites first saw the manna, they were puzzled by it.
5. King Saul offered David his armor, but David refused it because he had never proven it.

C. Write a personal pronoun to fit each description.
1. third person, singular, possessive case, neuter gender
2. first person, plural, nominative case
3. third person, singular, nominative case, feminine gender
4. second person, possessive case
5. first person, singular, objective case
6. third person, plural, nominative case

C. 1. number
2. gender
3. case
4. gender
5. person
6. case

D. 1. he
2. me
3. I
4. their
5. They, us

Written Exercises

A. 1. My—1, S; you—2, P; your—2, P
2. our—1, P
3. We—1, P; it—3, S
4. My—1, S; you—2, S; him—3, S
5. they—3, P

B. 1. his—P, M; he—N, M
2. her—P, F; her—O, F; she—N, F; him—O, M
3. their—P, C; them—O, C
4. they—N, C; it—O, N
5. his—P, M; it—O, N; he—N, M; it—O, N

C. 1. its
2. we
3. she
4. your *or* yours
5. me
6. they

7. first person, plural, objective case
8. third person, singular, possessive case, masculine gender

D. If there is an error in pronoun usage, write the correct pronoun. If the sentence is correct, write *correct*.
1. The man who rescued Joseph was him.
2. John and them were helping us clean up after the storm.
3. The last person to figure out the puzzle was I.
4. It was me who broke the window.
5. What a surprise to learn that our benefactors had been them!
6. The surprise visitor for dinner was her.
7. Several of the students have finished their work already.

Review Exercises

A. Write correctly each word that has a capitalization error. [21]
1. when elijah heard queen Jezebel's threats, he fled.
2. the Queen was upset that her God had been discredited and her Prophets slain.
3. Under the Juniper tree, Elijah prayed, "now, o lord, take away my life."
4. Later, on mount horeb, he told God, "I, even i only, am left."
5. God assured him that there remained seven thousand Faithful in israel.
6. Every Spring, Witmer's lawn and garden equipment becomes very busy.
7. Last march, father bought an ariens lawn mower from them.
8. Our Doctor claims to be a christian, but he does not believe that the sermon on the mount applies to our day.

B. Copy each word that should be followed by a comma, and add the comma. [23, 25]
1. Moving stealthily through the grass the lion stalked a zebra.
2. A lion is a huge powerful beast but it can stalk like a cat.
3. Yes Conrad a lion can often catch a zebra.
4. Brother Clyde moved on October 14 1994 and his new address is 171 Barber Road Peach Bottom PA 17563.
5. Centralia a small town in eastern Pennsylvania has become famous for its underground mine fire.
6. The boys who split and stacked Mr. Gordon's wood were motivated by Christian charity and they did not want any pay.
7. Outside the house was hardly damaged by fire smoke or water.
8. At the small clearing in the woods across the field I have for example often seen several red foxes at one time.

7. us
8. his

D. 1. he
2. they
3. correct
4. I
5. they
6. she
7. correct

Review Exercises

A. 1. When, Elijah, Queen
2. The, queen, god, prophets
3. juniper, Now, O, Lord
4. Mount Horeb, I
5. faithful, Israel
6. spring, Lawn, Garden, Equipment
7. March, Father, Ariens
8. doctor, Christian, Sermon, Mount

B. 1. grass,
2. huge, beast,
3. Yes, Conrad,
4. 14, 1994, Road, Bottom,
5. Centralia, Pennsylvania,
6. charity,
7. Outside, fire, smoke,
8. field, have, example,

70. Using Personal Pronouns Correctly

Lesson Survey

- Use the proper case when a pronoun is part of a compound.
- Use the proper case when an appositive follows a pronoun.
- Use the proper case when a pronoun follows *than* or *as*.
- Be sure the antecedent of a pronoun is clear.
- Be sure a pronoun agrees in number with its antecedent.
- Never use an apostrophe with a personal pronoun in the possessive case.
- When you speak about another person and yourself, refer to the other person first and yourself last.

In Lesson 69 you learned many details about the personal pronouns. Sometimes it is easier to identify and describe a pronoun than it is to use the correct one. In this lesson you will study several areas of pronoun usage in which people commonly make mistakes.

1. *Use the proper case when a pronoun is part of a compound.* Decide what sentence part the compound structure is. If it is a subject, a predicate nominative, or an appositive to one of these, use a nominative case pronoun. If it is an object complement, the object of a preposition, or an appositive to one of these, use an objective case pronoun. As a check, read the sentence with the pronoun alone.

> **Problem:** After David killed Goliath, Jonathan and (he, him) became close friends.
>
> *Think:* The pronoun is part of a compound subject. Use the nominative case.
>
> **Solution:** After David killed Goliath, Jonathan and <u>he</u> became close friends.
>
> *Check:* After David killed Goliath, <u>he</u> became a close friend of Jonathan.

> **Problem:** Mother taught us, Susan and (I, me), how to crochet.
>
> *Think:* The pronoun is part of a compound appositive to an indirect object. Use the objective case.
>
> **Solution:** Mother taught us, Susan and <u>me,</u> how to crochet.
>
> *Check:* Mother taught <u>me</u> how to crochet.

2. *Use the proper case when an appositive follows a pronoun.* As with a compound structure, you must first decide what part of the sentence

Lesson 70

Purpose: To study the proper use of personal pronouns.

Oral Review:

1. Give a personal pronoun for each description.
   a. third person, plural, objective case (them)
   b. first person, singular, possessive case (my, mine)
   c. third person, singular, nominative case, feminine gender (she)
   d. second person, possessive case (your, yours)
   e. third person, singular, objective case, masculine gender (him)
2. Tell whether each pair of pronouns is different in person, number, case, or gender.
   a. him, her (gender)   c. we, us (case)
   b. we, I (number)   d. them, us (person)

3. When is a semicolon used to join the clauses of a compound sentence? (when no conjunction is used; when a conjunctive adverb is used; when commas are already used in one or more of the clauses)
4. When should you use semicolons to separate items in a series? (when the individual items contain commas)
5. What punctuation mark is used to introduce something that is to follow? (colon)

Lesson Introduction: Can your students quickly identify the error in each of these sentences?

> Aunt Alice brought a gift for you and I. (you and me)
>
> Of course, us girls have a birthday tomorrow (we girls)
>
> Each of the horses had pricked up their ears (its ears)

the pronoun is. Check your choice by reading the sentence without the appositive.

Problem: (We, Us) eighth graders had a big math assignment today.
Think: The pronoun is the subject. Use the nominative case.
Solution: <u>We</u> eighth graders had a big math assignment today.
Check: <u>We</u> had a big math assignment today.

Problem: Brother Milton had a pleasant surprise for (we, us) students.
Think: The pronoun is the object of a preposition. Use the objective case.
Solution: Brother Milton had a pleasant surprise for <u>us</u> students.
Check: Brother Milton had a pleasant surprise for <u>us</u>.

3. *Use the proper case when a pronoun follows* than *or* as. In such sentences, the pronoun might be the subject or the direct object of an elliptical clause. Think what the completed construction of the clause would be, and then decide what sentence part the pronoun is.

Problem: Galen is older than (I, me).
Think: The completed clause would be *than I am old.*
Solution: Galen is older than <u>I</u>.

Problem: The alarm did not startle me as much as (he, him).
Think: The completed clause would be *as it startled him.*
Solution: The alarm did not startle me as much as <u>him</u>.

4. *Be sure the antecedent of a pronoun is clear.* Sometimes a pronoun comes after two nouns, either of which may logically be the antecedent. Such a sentence should be reworded so that the antecedent is clear.

Unclear: Pamela told Paula that her pet goat was in the garden.
(Whose goat was in the garden?)
Clear: Pamela said, "Paula, my pet goat is in the garden."
Clear: Pamela said, "Paula, your pet goat is in the garden."

Unclear: Michael called Father after he came back from Guatemala.
(Who came back from Guatemala?)
Clear: After Michael came back from Guatemala, he called Father.
Clear: After Father came back from Guatemala, Michael called him.

5. *Be sure a pronoun agrees in number with its antecedent.* Many of the rules for subject–verb agreement (Lesson 60) also apply to pronoun–antecedent agreement. A compound antecedent joined by *and* requires a plural pronoun if more than one item is clearly meant. If an article is used before only the first part of the compound, it refers to one individual and requires a singular pronoun.

This lesson addresses these and other common errors in pronoun usage.

Lesson Outline:

1. Use the proper case when a pronoun is part of a compound.
    a. Decide what sentence part the compound structure is.
    b. Use the correct pronoun for that sentence part.
    c. Check by reading the sentence with the pronoun alone.

2. Use the proper case when an appositive follows a pronoun. Follow the same steps as in point 1 above.

3. Use the proper case when a pronoun follows than *or* as.

    a. The pronoun might be the subject or the direct object of an elliptical clause.
    b. Think what the completed construction of the clause would be.
    c. Decide what sentence part the pronoun is.

4. Be sure the antecedent of a pronoun is clear. If necessary, reword the sentence so that the antecedent is clear.

5. Be sure a pronoun agrees in number with its antecedent.
    a. A compound antecedent joined by *and* requires a plural pronoun if more than one item is clearly meant.
    b. If an article is used before only the first part of the compound, it refers to one individual and requires a singular pronoun.

The poet and the painter have combined <u>their</u> talents in this motto.
(Two *persons,* the poet and the painter, have combined *their* talents.)

The poet and painter has finished <u>his</u> motto.
(One *person,* who is both a poet and a painter, has finished *his* motto.)

If a compound antecedent consisting of two singular nouns is joined by *or* or *nor,* it is singular and requires a singular pronoun.

Either Barbara or Lydia should say <u>her</u> poem next.
(Only one *girl* should say *her* poem next.)

If the antecedent is an indefinite pronoun followed by a prepositional phrase, be sure the pronoun agrees with the antecedent, not the object of the preposition.

Each of the boys has <u>his</u> boots. (*Each one* has *his* boots.)
Both of the boys have <u>their</u> boots. (*Both* have *their* boots.)

If the antecedent is a collective noun and it refers to the group acting as a unit, the pronoun should be singular. If it refers to the individual members of the group acting separately, the pronoun should be plural.

The swarm of bees is protecting <u>its</u> queen.
(singular: group acting as a unit)
The swarm of bees are performing <u>their</u> various jobs in the hive.
(plural: individuals acting separately)

There is no special pronoun for third person, singular, common gender. Therefore, a masculine pronoun (*he, him,* or *his*) is used for this purpose.

Each student faithfully did <u>his</u> part.
(*Each one* did *his* part, not *their* part.)

6. *Never use an apostrophe with a personal pronoun in the possessive case.* An apostrophe is used with the possessive form of a noun or some other classes of pronouns. However, an apostrophe is used with a personal pronoun only to form a contraction.

<u>Your</u> grades show that <u>you're</u> making good progress.
<u>It's</u> high time that dog learns <u>its</u> lesson.

7. *When you speak about another person and yourself, refer to the other person first and yourself last.* This is not only correct grammar but also good manners. The Bible principle is "In honour preferring one another."

Incorrect: Would you please help <u>me and Rhoda</u> for a while?
Correct: Would you please help <u>Rhoda and me</u> for a while?

---

c. If a compound antecedent consisting of two singular nouns is joined by *or* or *nor,* it is singular and requires a singular pronoun.

d. If the antecedent is an indefinite pronoun followed by a prepositional phrase, be sure the pronoun agrees with the antecedent, not the object of the preposition.

e. If the antecedent is a collective noun and it refers to the group acting as a unit, the pronoun should be singular. If it refers to the individual members of the group acting separately, the pronoun should be plural.

f. There is no special pronoun for third person, singular, common gender. Therefore, a masculine pronoun is used for this purpose.

6. Never use an apostrophe with a personal pronoun in the possessive case.

7. When you speak about another person and yourself, refer to the other person first and yourself last.

★ *EXTRA PRACTICE*
Worksheet 26 *(Using Personal Pronouns Correctly*

Class Practice

A. Read these sentences, using the correct words in parentheses.
1. God promises His sufficient grace for you and (I, me).
2. Paul and Silas sang praises to (his, their) Lord at midnight.
3. Jacob and (he, him) had opposite views of spiritual values.
4. Either Aaron or Eric left (his, their) bicycle out in the rain.
5. (We, Us) girls baked several dozen cookies this morning.
6. The electrician and plumber should finish (his job, their jobs) today.
7. The electrician and the plumber should finish (his job, their jobs) today.
8. The person in charge here must be (he, him).
9. That billy goat gave us, Harry and (I, me), quite a scare.
10. Eleanor helped both of us, but she helped me more often than (she, her).
11. The flock of sheep followed (its, their) shepherd faithfully.
12. I thought I had studied my lesson, but I surely hadn't learned it as thoroughly as (he, him).

B. Reword these sentences to make the pronouns clear and correct.
1. Janice told Karen that her lip was swollen.
2. Father is calling for me and you.
3. Either Noah or Alvin should say their memory selection in family worship this morning.
4. They're both memorizing Colossians 3 for they're instruction class.
5. Us children say our Sunday school memory verses in family worship.
6. I and Titus prayed in family worship yesterday morning.
7. Each of the farmers will be harvesting their corn.
8. Whenever we come home, our puppy wags it's tail in welcome for me and you.

Written Exercises

A. If the underlined word or phrase contains a mistake, write it correctly. If it is correct, write *correct*.
1. Neither Jeremiah nor Baruch would turn from <u>their</u> loyalty to God.
2. God protected these men, Jeremiah and <u>he</u>, in spite of much persecution.
3. Every person must guard <u>their hearts</u> diligently.
4. The only Bible that many people read is <u>we</u> who live the Bible.
5. Although we may be tempted to envy the people of the world, we have far greater blessings than <u>them</u>.
6. The butler and the baker told <u>their dreams</u> to Joseph.
7. Elijah called Ahab to Mount Carmel and there proved to Israel and <u>he</u> that the Lord is the true God.
8. Godly fear is an essential quality for you and <u>I</u>.
9. The worldly man's trust is in things of this world, but <u>our's</u> is in the almighty God.

Lesson 70 Answers

Class Practice

A.
1. me	7. their jobs
2. their	8. he
3. he	9. me
4. his	10. her
5. We	11. its
6. his job	12. he

B. (Corrections are underlined.)
1. Janice said, "Karen, <u>your</u> lip is swollen."
   or Janice said, "Karen, <u>my</u> lip is swollen."
2. Father is calling for <u>you and me</u>.
3. Either Noah or Alvin should say <u>his</u> memory selection in family worship this morning.
4. They're both memorizing Colossians 3 for <u>their</u> instruction class.
5. <u>We</u> children say our Sunday school memory verses in family worship.
6. <u>Titus and I</u> prayed in family worship yesterday morning.
7. Each of the farmers will be harvesting <u>his</u> corn.
8. Whenever we come home, our puppy wags <u>its</u> tail in welcome for <u>you and me</u>.

Written Exercises

A.
1. his	6. correct
2. him	7. him
3. his heart	8. me
4. correct	9. ours
5. they	

10. The king and poet wrote many of <u>his</u> psalms with picturesque language.
11. One of Jesus' disciples allowed Satan to enter <u>their</u> heart.
12. All of Jesus' disciples forsook <u>their</u> Master in the hour of crisis.
13. God hates religious hypocrisy; Jesus condemned no other group of sinners as sternly as <u>they</u>.
14. As older students, you and <u>me</u> should be noble examples to the younger.
15. It would be a pity if they should learn disrespect from you and <u>me</u>.
16. As we face life's challenges, <u>us youth</u> should recognize the seriousness of our choices.
17. If <u>you're</u> going to choose right in life, you must seek God's guidance.
18. Naomi advised both daughters-in-law, Orpah and <u>she</u>, to return to their people and gods; but Ruth stayed with her.
19. The congregation expressed <u>its</u> views about starting an outreach work near Mainsville.
20. The congregation supported <u>its</u> new deacon faithfully.

B. Rewrite these sentences to make the pronouns clear and correct.
   1. Kathryn learned to know Sarah when she visited Grandfather Stoltzfus.
   2. Anthony wants to go along with me and Lyndon.
   3. Father caught a glimpse of Uncle Ben just as he went out the door.
   4. Helen told Mary Ann that her apron was torn.

Review Exercises

A. Copy each word or number that should be followed by a colon or a semicolon, and add the correct mark. [27]
   1. In large letters across the front wall of our classroom is this familiar quotation, "Study to shew thyself approved unto God."
   2. These words are quite easy to memorize, however, they are much harder to obey consistently.
   3. My three trips to the dentist are scheduled for the following days, Thursday, September 8, Monday, October 17, and Monday, November 7.
   4. Because of the icy roads last evening, we could not visit Mrs. Zeigler, our elderly neighbor, but if the weather permits, we plan to go tomorrow evening.
   5. Mrs. Neil's cat can be described in one word, independent.

B. Write the correct verb for each sentence, using the tense and form given in italics. Include all the necessary helping verbs. [48–50]
   1. Someday we (see) the Lord as He is. *future tense, simple form*
   2. Wickedness (increase) as the end of time draws near. *present tense, progressive form*
   3. By the time Satan is cast into the lake of fire, he (deceive) multitudes of people. *future perfect tense, simple form*

10. correct
11. his
12. correct
13. them
14. I
15. correct
16. we youth
17. correct
18. her
19. their
20. correct

B. 1. When Kathryn visited Grandfather Stoltzfus, she learned to know Sarah.
      or When Sarah visited Grandfather Stoltzfus, Kathryn learned to know her.
   2. Anthony wants to go along with Lyndon and me.
   3. Just as Father went out the door, he caught glimpse of Uncle Ben.
      or Just as Uncle Ben went out the door, Father caught a glimpse of him.
   4. Helen said, "Mary Ann, your apron is torn."
      or Helen said, "Mary Ann, my apron is torn."

Review Exercises

A. 1. quotation:
   2. memorize;
   3. days: 8;   17;
   4. neighbor;
   5. word:

B. 1. shall see
   2. is increasing
   3. will have deceived

4. God (provide) for us richly through Jesus Christ. *present perfect tense, simple form*

5. Jesus (suffer) much for our sakes. *past tense, emphatic form*

6. Long before our birth, God (arrange) the circumstances that now affect our lives. *past perfect tense, progressive form*

?. Rewrite each sentence, using a perfect tense to express the action or condition that occurred first. [49]

1. Brother Eldon was a farmer before he became our schoolteacher.

2. By the time we arrive at Grandfather Kraybill's, we shall spend three days in travel.

3. When we shoveled open our driveway, we were tired.

4. has provided

5. did suffer

6. had been arranging

C. 1. Brother Eldon had been a farmer before he became our schoolteacher.

2. By the time we arrive at Grandfather Kraybill's, we shall have spent three days in travel.

3. When we had shoveled open our driveway, we were tired.

---

71. Writing Effective Sentences: Unity and Coherence

> ## Lesson Survey
> - An effective sentence has **unity** and **coherence.**
> - To have sentence unity, you must do the following things.
>   1. Avoid writing run-on errors.
>   2. Avoid joining poorly related ideas.
>   3. Avoid separating closely related ideas.
> - To have sentence coherence, you must do the following things.
>   1. Avoid unclear pronoun reference.
>   2. Avoid misplaced modifiers.
>   3. Avoid the careless separation of closely related sentence parts.

An effective sentence communicates clearly and directly to the reader. Two basic qualities of every effective sentence are unity and coherence.

Unity

You have already studied *unity* in paragraphs (Lesson 13). Sentences also need to be unified around one single thought. To write sentences with unity, observe the rules discussed in the following paragraphs.

1. *Avoid writing run-on errors.* You should not find it hard to identify a sentence with this kind of disunity. A run-on error is two or more sentences written together as one, with no punctuation or with only a comma

Lesson 71

Purpose: To encourage the writing of effective sentences, with special emphasis on unity and coherence.

Oral Review:

1. Name the three common kinds of conflict in a story. (main character in conflict with another person, with his circumstances, or with his own self)

2. Which of these kinds of conflict is in focus with each of these story ideas?

   a. Wilmer has been anticipating a weeklong stay at Uncle Myron's farm. A few days before leaving, Wilmer is asked to help with the neighbors' farm chores for several weeks because Mr. Brockman has broken his leg. (main character in conflict with his circumstances)

   b. Annette realizes that she spoke unkindly to Jessica yesterday, but she is ashamed to apologize. (main character in conflict with her own self)

   c. Charlotte is visiting with her cousin Sally, who begins talking disrespectfully about the ministers. Charlotte does not agree with her, but she is afraid to speak up. (main character in conflict with another person)

3. What are four common ways of portraying story characters? (through actions, speech, thoughts, and appearance)

Lesson Introduction: Once upon a time Mr. Careless wanted to build some brick walls for a front porch on his house at Heedless Acres. He had to make the bricks himself, so he made several forms to mold them. As his nature was, he found some odds and

between them. Correct the problem by dividing the clauses into separate sentences, by using proper coordination, or by making one of the clauses a dependent clause.

Lacks unity: Run-on error
> The Lord God formed Adam's body from the dust of the ground then He breathed into him the breath of life.

One unified compound sentence:
> The Lord God formed Adam's body from the dust of the ground; then He breathed into him the breath of life.

Lacks unity: Run-on error
> God made Eve from Adam's rib He brought her to Adam.

One unified complex sentence:
> After God made Eve from Adam's rib, He brought her to Adam.

2. *Avoid joining poorly related ideas.* A compound sentence lacks unity if the thoughts in the clauses are not closely related. This problem can be corrected in the same way as a run-on error: by dividing the clauses into separate sentences, by using proper coordination, or by making one of the clauses a dependent clause.

Lacks unity: Poorly related thoughts
> God created the world in six days, and the crown of creation was man.

Two unified sentences:
> God created the world in six days. The crown of creation was man.

A sentence also has poorly related ideas if there are confusing interruptions or details that detract from the main thought. Often you can simply remove these interruptions and distracting details. But if there is a good reason to include the information, you can set it off with dashes or parentheses.

Lacks unity: Distracting detail
> George Washington, <u>who married a widow</u>, was the first president of the United States.

Unified: Distracting detail removed
> George Washington was the first president of the United States.

Lacks unity: Distracting detail
> George Washington, <u>who felt that two terms as president were enough for one man</u>, was a notable statesman.

Unified: Distracting detail in parentheses
> George Washington (he felt that two terms as president were enough for one man) was a notable statesman.

ends of lumber, cut them to what looked like the right size for bricks, and nailed them together. When he had enough bricks, he started to build.

Of course the bricks did not fit together well, for the forms had not all been the same size. Still, Mr. Careless finally completed his walls. But the corners were not straight. The tops of the walls were not level. The whole thing looked—well, like something that belonged to Heedless Acres.

In English class you are also building. Instead of porches, you build various kinds of compositions. Instead of bricks, you use sentences. If you think, like Mr. Careless, that it is unnecessary to write each sentence with careful attention to detail, your finished work likewise will leave much to be desired. This lesson will help you to put into your sentences two of the most important ingredients: unity and coherence.

Lesson Outline:

1. Unity and coherence are two basic qualities of every effective sentence. A sentence has unity when it clearly communicates one single thought. It has coherence when its parts work together to express one thought smoothly and clearly.

2. Several things are required for unity in sentences.

(1) *Avoid writing run-on errors.* A run-on error can be corrected by dividing the clauses into separate sentences, by using proper coordination, or by making one of the clauses a dependent clause.

(2) *Avoid joining poorly related ideas.*

a) A compound sentence lacks unity if the thoughts in the clauses are not closely related. This problem can be corrected in the same way as a run-on error.

3. *Avoid separating closely related ideas.* This kind of disunity is the opposite of the kind just described. If two ideas are closely related, they should be combined in one compound or complex sentence to communicate most effectively.

Lacks unity: Related thoughts separated
Gehazi should have known that he could not deceive God's prophet. He secretly took gifts from Naaman and lied to Elisha.
One unified compound sentence:
Gehazi should have known that he could not deceive God's prophet, yet he secretly took gifts from Naaman and lied to Elisha.

Lacks unity: Related thoughts separated
Gehazi practiced this deception. He was afflicted with leprosy.
One unified complex sentence:
Because Gehazi practiced this deception, he was afflicted with leprosy.

Coherence

The quality of *coherence* is another essential to effective sentences. In Lesson 18 you learned that a paragraph has coherence when the ideas flow smoothly from one sentence to the next. Likewise, a sentence has coherence when its parts work together to express one thought smoothly and clearly. The following paragraphs describe several ways to provide sentence coherence.

1. *Avoid unclear pronoun reference.* Lesson 70 dealt with making the antecedent clear when two nouns precede a pronoun in a sentence. Another type of unclear pronoun reference occurs when a pronoun like *it* or *they* is used in an abstract way without any antecedent.

Unclear: Two possible antecedents
Joel visited Glen soon after <u>he</u> came back from the Bahamas.
Coherent:
When Joel returned from the Bahamas, he visited Glen.
When Glen returned from the Bahamas, Joel visited him.

Unclear: Abstract pronoun
In our reading story <u>it</u> tells about the Indian attack on the Jacob Hochstetler family.
Coherent:
Our reading story tells about the Indian attack on the Jacob Hochstetler family.

Unclear: Abstract pronoun
In some countries <u>they</u> eat mostly rice.
Coherent:
In some countries the people eat mostly rice.

b) A sentence also lacks unity if there are confusing interruptions or details that detract from the main thought. These distracting details should be removed or set off with dashes or parentheses.

(3) *Avoid separating closely related ideas.* If two ideas are closely related, they should be combined in one compound or complex sentence to communicate most effectively.

3. Several things are required for coherence in sentences.

(1) *Avoid unclear pronoun reference.*

a) Pronoun reference is unclear when two nouns precede a pronoun, either of which could logically be the antecedent.

b) Pronoun reference is also unclear when a pronoun like *it* or *they* is used in an abstract way without any antecedent.

(2) *Avoid misplaced modifiers.*

a) The position of modifiers like *almost, even, just, nearly,* and *only* can make a big difference in the meaning of a sentence.

b) Adjective phrases and clauses must be positioned carefully in order to modify the right words.

(3) *Avoid the careless separation of closely related sentence parts.*

a) A verb phrase should not be interrupted with a long modifier or parenthetical expression.

b) An infinitive should not be split unless that is the best way to express your idea clearly and smoothly.

2. *Avoid misplaced modifiers.* The position of modifiers like *almost, even, just, nearly,* and *only* can make a big difference in the meaning of a sentence. Also remember that adjective phrases and clauses must be positioned carefully in order to modify the right words.

Misplaced modifier:
　　The invalid could <u>only</u> move her arms and head.
　　　　(Could she not even think or breathe?)
Coherent:
　　The invalid could move only her arms and head.

Misplaced modifier:
　　<u>Having been injured</u>, the nurse gave first aid to the man.
　　　　(Was the nurse injured?)
Coherent:
　　The nurse gave first aid to the man who had been injured.
　　Having been injured, the man received first aid from the nurse.

3. *Avoid the careless separation of closely related sentence parts.* Try to avoid interrupting a verb phrase with a long modifier or parenthetical expression. Also avoid splitting an infinitive unless that is the best way to express your idea clearly and smoothly.

Divided verb phrase:
　　God's people <u>have</u>, even in the midst of severe hardship, <u>pointed</u> others to the truth.
Coherent:
　　Even in the midst of severe hardship, God's people <u>have pointed</u> others to the truth.

Split infinitive:
　　God commands us <u>to</u> carefully <u>guard</u> our hearts.
Coherent:
　　God commands us <u>to guard</u> our hearts carefully.

Acceptable split infinitive:
　　It is hard <u>to</u> always <u>know</u> the best thing to do.

In the last example above, it is hardly possible to communicate the same meaning without splitting the infinitive. The sentence could be reworded in the ways shown below, but none of them are as smooth and clear as the original.

　　It is hard always to know the best thing to do.
　　　　(*Always* could appear to modify *hard.*)
　　It is hard to know always the best thing to do.
　　　　(*Always* could appear to belong with *the best thing to do.*)

It is hard to know the best thing to do always.
(*Always* appears to modify *to do.*)

In comparison, "to guard our hearts carefully" is just as clear as "to carefully guard our hearts." So it is better not to split the infinitive in that phrase.

Class Practice

Read these sentences, improving the unity or coherence.
1. God will, according to His perfect wisdom, answer our prayers.
2. Our friends influence us greatly. We should choose them carefully.
3. In Old Testament times, they had to offer animal sacrifices.
4. Watching his father's sheep, many beautiful psalms were composed by David.
5. Rhinoceroses live in Asia and Africa, and the word *rhinoceros* means "horned nose."
6. Some rhinoceroses' horns almost grow to a length of four feet.
7. These horns are, unlike those of most animals, made of hairlike material.
8. Hard material cements these fibers together, and the horns grow out of the skin, not out of a bone.
9. Brother Enos told us to expressively read the poem.
10. He found this poem in an old book which describes a beautiful sunset.
11. My cousin Dean, who broke his leg in first grade, has a large stamp collection.
12. In upstate New York they have much colder weather than what we do here in Delaware.

Written Exercises

Rewrite these sentences, improving the unity or coherence.
1. An elephant can almost use its amazing trunk for anything.
2. An elephant's trunk is an extended nose and upper lip, at the very tip are its nostrils.
3. Very flexible and muscular, large or small objects can be picked up by these amazing trunks.
4. An elephant sometimes draws water into its trunk to, in a cooling shower, spray over its back.
5. An elephant gets thirsty. It fills its trunk with water and sprays the water into its mouth.
6. In a London zoo they often threw peanuts at an elephant.
7. The peanuts often fell between the two fences. They separated the elephant from the people.
8. The elephant would, using its trunk, blow the peanuts back to the people.

6. In a London zoo the people often threw peanuts at an elephant.
7. The peanuts often fell between the two fences that separated the elephant from the people.
8. Using its trunk, the elephant would blow the peanuts back to the people.

Lesson 71 Answers

Class Practice

(Sample answers.)
1. God will answer our prayers according to His perfect wisdom.
   or According to His perfect wisdom, God will answer our prayers.
2. Since our friends influence us greatly, we should choose them carefully.
3. In Old Testament times, people had to offer animal sacrifices.
4. Watching his father's sheep, David composed many beautiful psalms.
5. Rhinoceroses live in Asia and Africa. The word *rhinoceros* means "horned nose."
6. Some rhinoceroses' horns grow to a length of almost four feet.
7. Unlike those of most animals, these horns are made of hairlike material.
8. Hard material cements these fibers together. The horns grow out of the skin, not out of a bone.
   or These horns, consisting of fibers cemented together by hard material, grow out of the skin, not out of a bone. (Underlined phrase may be omitted.)
9. Brother Enos told us to read the poem expressively.
10. He found this poem, which describes a beautiful sunset, in an old book.
11. My cousin Dean has a large stamp collection.
12. The people in upstate New York have much colder weather than what we do here in Delaware.
   or In upstate New York the weather is much colder than what we have here in Delaware.

Written Exercises

(Sample answers. Allow reasonable variation.)
1. An elephant can use its amazing trunk for almost anything.
2. An elephant's trunk is an extended nose and upper lip. At the very tip are its nostrils.
3. Very flexible and muscular, these amazing trunks can pick up large or small objects.
4. An elephant sometimes draws water into its trunk to spray over its back in a cooling shower.
5. When an elephant gets thirsty, it fills its trunk with water and sprays the water into its mouth.

9. An itchy elephant cannot, you can well imagine, scratch itself with its feet.
10. Sometimes elephants use sticks to scratch themselves, which they pick up with their trunks.
11. The Harrisville Mennonite School, which is in a red brick building, has an enrollment of fifty-four.
12. Because of the snowy roads, they canceled school yesterday.
13. Kevin cut a sizable pile of firewood, and the supply of fuel was getting low.
14. Uncle Stephen's plan to visit Grandfather Beiler's while they are in Mexico.
15. James fell almost off the ladder while he was painting the ceiling.

Review Exercises

A. For each numbered selection, write whether the main character's traits are portrayed mostly by *actions, speech, thoughts,* or *appearance.* Also write what particular characteristic is portrayed. [59]

1. Janice smiled to herself. Of course she could help Sister Edith! "I know I'm not big for my twelve years," she thought. "But I might just surprise her!"

    Janice stood still until she heard Sister Edith close the bedroom door. "All she said I had to do this morning is to watch the children and do the washing, but I'm going to see what all else I can get done!" The three preschoolers were quietly playing at the toy box as Janice began washing the dishes.

2. Having found the paper he wanted, Elvin crawled backward across his bunk until his foot touched the top rung of the ladder. Then he quickly put the paper into his left hand, grabbed the light chain with his right hand, and jumped to the floor. "A quick way to turn off the light and get down at the same time," he decided.

    But he was a surprised boy when he landed with the chain still in his hand. Elvin looked up and saw that the light bulb was hanging crookedly from the ceiling. However, the light had gone off, so he threw the broken chain on the dresser top and ran for the stairs.

3. In the cloakroom, Rachel hung up her coat and carefully set her lunch pail on the shelf. Then she entered the classroom and set her books in a neat stack on her desk. Glancing at the clock, Rachel noted that the bell would ring in just seven minutes.

4. Brenda stared at her open history book, her shoulders sagging and her face wearing a dismal frown. They were reading about Francis Drake, but she found it hard to concentrate. What difference did it make whether Drake was knighted, killed by the Spaniards, or drowned by falling overboard?

---

9. An itchy elephant, you can well imagine, cannot scratch itself with its feet.
10. Sometimes elephants use sticks, which they pick up with their trunks, to scratch themselves.
11. The Harrisville Mennonite School has an enrollment of fifty-four.
12. Because of the snowy roads, school was canceled yesterday.
    or Because of the snowy roads, the school board canceled school yesterday.
13. Kevin cut a sizable pile of firewood, for the supply of fuel was getting low.
    or Kevin cut a sizable pile of firewood because the supply of fuel was getting low.
14. While Uncle Stephen's are in Mexico, they plan to visit Grandfather Beiler's.
    or While Grandfather Beiler's are in Mexico, Uncle Stephen's plan to visit them.
15. James almost fell off the ladder while he was painting the ceiling.

Review Exercises

A. (Sample characteristics. Allow reasonable variation.)

1. thoughts; diligence, willingness to work
2. actions; carelessness, hastiness
3. actions; carefulness, preciseness
4. appearance *or* thoughts; boredom, laziness, indifference

5.   "Oh, you have a new ball glove!" Charles exclaimed as soon as he saw Philip. "It looks like a really good one too. Where did you get it?"

"My uncle gave it to me," Philip explained with a happy smile.

"Well, that was surely nice of him," said Charles. "This glove is much better than that old one you used to have!"

B. Write whether each example shows conflict that the main character has with another *person*, with his *circumstances*, or with his own *self*. [58]

1.   Judith let out a deep sigh. It had happened again! James and Esther had received *95*, while she reluctantly wrote *90* at the top of her math paper.

"And to think that I had the most homework last evening." She sighed again, remembering the hours of studying. "How can they do it?" Judith's freckled face once more wilted as she bent over her math book.

After working a few problems, Judith's mind wandered back to her repeated disappointment. "I don't consider myself a slow learner, neither do I receive really low grades. But I seldom get as high a grade as my classmates, even though I study much more than they do. It doesn't seem fair."

2.   "What are you making, Carla?" asked eight-year-old Duane as he came bouncing into the kitchen.

"Just cookies," Carla replied as she poured in the flour and turned the mixer a little lower.

"May I help cut it into shapes, please?" Duane questioned eagerly.

Carla sighed. If only he would go out and play. It seemed he always was getting in her way. Now if he was going to help, it probably would take twice as long, and she would not have any time to read this afternoon.

3.   "But I can't believe a professional thief would have been in here and left without the camera, silverware, china, and typewriter. Your piggy bank can't be worth much to whoever took it. It had only about ten dollars in it, right?"

"Yes. But, Father, all my Canadian money was in it," said Faith Anne sorrowfully. The Canadian dollar bill and coins had been a souvenir of their trip to Canada the previous summer.

"That's too bad," sympathized Father. "I'm sure it was worth more to you than it will be to anyone else. I know it is a loss to you, but we have much to be thankful for tonight. First Thessalonians 5:18 says, 'In every thing give thanks.'"

5. speech; friendliness, unselfishness

B. 1. self
    2. person
    3. circumstances

72. Compound Personal Pronouns and Demonstrative Pronouns

Lesson Survey

- A **compound personal pronoun** ends with *-self* or *-selves*.
- A compound personal pronoun can be used intensively to add emphasis.
- A compound personal pronoun can also be used reflexively to show an action done by the subject to itself.
- Do not use a compound personal pronoun to replace a personal pronoun.
- The **demonstrative pronouns** (*this, that, these,* and *those*) are used to point out specific persons or things.
- Avoid the errors of using *them* as a demonstrative pronoun and of saying *this here* or *that there.*

In Lessons 69 and 70 you studied the most common class of pronouns: the personal pronouns. There are six classes of pronouns altogether. In the remaining grammar lessons of this chapter, you will be studying compound personal, demonstrative, indefinite, interrogative, and relative pronouns.

Compound Personal Pronouns

A *compound personal pronoun* ends with *-self* or *-selves*. The eight compound personal pronouns (and one archaic form) are shown in the following table.

Compound Personal Pronouns

	Singular	*Plural*
First person:	myself	ourselves
Second person:	yourself (thyself)	yourselves
Third person:	himself, herself, itself	themselves

Be sure to use the correct forms of compound personal pronouns. The following forms should be avoided: *ourself, themself, hisself, theirselves*.

A compound personal pronoun can be used *intensively* to add emphasis to some other substantive. Since it merely adds emphasis, the sentence is complete without the compound personal pronoun. Compare the following pairs of sentences.

Normal:
> We will pay for the damage.
> You must determine to improve.
> Uncle Earl painted the barn.

Lesson 72

Purpose: To study the usage of compound personal pronouns and demonstrative pronouns.

Oral Review:

1. Tell whether each pair of personal pronouns is different in person, number, case, or gender.
   a. she, he (gender)   c. us, them (person)
   b. he, they (number)   d. us, we (case)
2. Tell how to correct each sentence, or say *correct* if there is no mistake.
   a. Brother Burkholder gave us students an interesting assignment. (correct)
   b. Are these apples for you and I? (you and me)
   c. Mother is calling me and Lorraine. (Lorraine and me)
   d. Glen hoed more rows of corn than me. (than I)
3. Commas, dashes, and parentheses are all used to set off parenthetical items. How are they used differently? (Commas make the item a part of the sentence; dashes sharply emphasize the item; parentheses minimize the importance of the item.)
4. Name some things that should be italicized (or underlined). (titles of major works; specific names of vehicles; a word, letter, number, or symbol that is the subject of discussion; foreign words not adopted into the English language; words to be emphasized)
5. Name some uses of the apostrophe. (to form the possessive case of a noun or an indefinite pronoun; to show an omission in a contraction; to form the plural of a letter, a figure, or an abbreviation, and of a word used as the subject of discussion)
6. Name several kinds of compound words that should be hyphenated. (compound number words

Added emphasis:

We <u>ourselves</u> will pay for the damage.
You <u>yourself</u> must determine to improve.
Uncle Earl painted the barn <u>himself</u>.

A compound personal pronoun can also be used *reflexively* to show an action done by the subject to itself. In this usage the pronoun functions as the direct object, the indirect object, or the object of a preposition and *reflects* back to the subject.

I cut <u>myself</u> on a piece of glass.
(The direct object *myself* names the same person as the subject *I*.)
You made <u>yourself</u> some extra work.
(The indirect object *yourself* names the same person as the subject *You*.)
Some people always want the best for <u>themselves</u>.
(The object of the preposition *themselves* names the same person as the subject *people*.)

Do not use a compound personal pronoun to replace a personal pronoun. Compound personal pronouns should be used only to give added emphasis or to reflect back to the subject. Be especially careful not to misuse them in compound constructions.

Incorrect: If you need help, just call <u>myself</u>.
Did Stephen give <u>yourself</u> this book?
Edwin and <u>himself</u> came to visit.
Correct: If you need help, just call <u>me</u>.
Did Stephen give <u>you</u> this book?
Edwin and <u>he</u> came to visit.

Demonstrative Pronouns

The *demonstrative pronouns* (*this, that, these,* and *those*) are used to point out specific persons or things. *This* and *that* are singular; *these* and *those* are plural. *This* and *these* are used to point out nearby objects; *that* and *those* are used to point out distant objects.

<u>This</u> is a small town on top of a mountain. (singular, near)
<u>That</u> looks like a large city in the valley. (singular, distant)

<u>These</u> are just small foothills. (plural, near)
<u>Those</u> on the horizon include snowcapped peaks. (plural, distant)

These four words are pronouns only if they have a substantive function in the sentence. Many times they come right before nouns; then they are adjectives telling *which* rather than demonstrative pronouns. This is

fractions written in words; words ending with *-in-law;* words beginning with *great-* that refer to relatives; words beginning with *self-;* many that begin with *all-;* compound adjectives used as a unit; proper nouns and adjectives with prefixes)

Lesson Introduction: What instrument could you use to *intensify* sunlight so that it makes paper hot enough to burn? (a lens or magnifying glass) What instrument could you use to *reflect* sunlight and send coded messages? (a mirror)

A compound personal pronoun can act like a lens or a mirror. It can be used *intensively* to strengthen the emphasis of another noun or pronoun. It can also be used *reflexively* to reflect the action back to the subject. In this lesson we shall study compound personal pronouns and demonstrative pronouns.

Lesson Outline:

1. A compound personal pronoun ends with -self or -selves.

a. The following words are proper compound personal pronouns: *myself, yourself, himself, herself, itself, ourselves, yourselves, themselves;* archaic: *thyself.*

b. The following forms should be avoided: *ourself, themself, hisself, theirselves.*
(*Teacher:* Although the lesson indicates that *ourself* is an incorrect form, that word does have an accepted use in referring to the "editorial we"—that is, a writer's use of *we* to avoid using *I*. Example: "We [the writer] have never observed this ourself." But since *ourself* is incorrect in most everyday uses, students are told to avoid it.)

2. A compound personal pronoun can be used intensively to add emphasis.

different from a possessive personal pronoun like *our,* which is considered both a pronoun and an adjective.

> <u>This</u> is a well-known hymn. (pronoun used as subject)
> <u>This</u> hymn is well known. (adjective telling *which* about *hymn*)
>
> Apple pie is my favorite, but I like <u>those</u> too.
>   (pronoun used as direct object)
> Apple pie is my favorite, but I like <u>those</u> pies too.
>   (adjective telling *which* about *pies*)

There are two common errors to avoid in the usage of demonstrative pronouns. One is using the personal pronoun *them* instead of the demonstrative pronoun *those.* The other is using *this here* or *that there.*

Incorrect:	**Correct:**
<u>Them</u> are my rabbits.	<u>Those</u> are my rabbits.
Please give <u>this here</u> to Mother.	Please give <u>this</u> to Mother.
<u>That there</u> was an exciting game.	<u>That</u> was an exciting game.

Class Practice

A. Name each compound personal pronoun, and tell whether it is used *intensively* or *reflexively.*
1. Eugene himself admitted that he was wrong.
2. The drivers allowed themselves time to stop for gas.
3. Steven bought books for Norman and himself.
4. Elaine cut herself while paring apples.
5. We prepared the lunch ourselves.

B. Read each sentence correctly. If it is already correct, say *correct.*
1. The children of Israel prepared theirselves to cross the Jordan River.
2. If you will follow Him, God will lead yourself in the right way.
3. This here gives us confidence in life.
4. We should willingly commit ourself to God's hand.
5. Catherine and myself have finished our reports.
6. Father bought shoes for Jonathan and hisself.
7. Harold found himself a jacket among our outgrown ones.
8. Them are the neighbors' sheep.
9. I like the gourds on that far shelf, but these on the table are my favorites.
10. Aunt Mildred gave Nancy and myself two interesting books.

Written Exercises

A. Copy each compound personal pronoun and each demonstrative pronoun. Label the pronouns as follows: *CP-I* (compound personal, intensive);

3. A compound personal pronoun can also be used reflexively to show an action done by the subject to itself.

4. Do not use a compound personal pronoun to replace a personal pronoun.

5. The demonstrative pronouns (this, that, these, and those) *are used to point out specific persons or things.*
  a. *This* and *that* are singular; *these* and *those* are plural.
  b. *This* and *these* are used to point out nearby objects; *that* and *those* are used to point out distant objects.
  c. These four words are often used right before nouns; then they are adjectives telling *which.*

6. Avoid the errors of using them *as a*

Lesson 72 Answers

Class Practice

A. 1. himself—intensively
   2. themselves—reflexively
   3. himself—reflexively
   4. herself—reflexively
   5. ourselves—intensively

B. (Corrections are marked.)
   1. The children of Israel prepared <u>themselves</u> to cross the Jordan River.
   2. If you will follow Him, God will lead <u>you</u> in the right way.
   3. This ~~here~~ gives us confidence in life.
   4. We should willingly commit <u>ourselves</u> to God's hand.
   5. Catherine and <u>I</u> have finished our reports.
   6. Father bought shoes for Jonathan and <u>him-self</u>.
   7. correct
   8. <u>Those</u> are the neighbors' sheep.
   9. correct
   10. Aunt Mildred gave Nancy and <u>me</u> two interesting books.

demonstrative pronoun and of saying **this here** or **that there.**

★ *EXTRA PRACTICE*
Worksheet 27 (*Compound Personal Pronouns and Demonstrative Pronouns*)

CP-R (compound personal, reflexive); or D (demonstrative).

1. The apostle Paul besought the Lord three times for himself because of his thorn in the flesh.
2. If this would allow Christ to reveal His power, then Paul was content to bear it.
3. Those are outstanding words that we should read to encourage ourselves.
4. You yourself may be called upon to suffer like that.

B. If the underlined part of the sentence contains a mistake, rewrite it correctly. If it is correct, write *correct.*
   1. We must take to <u>ourself</u> the whole armor of God.
   2. Those who refuse God's armor open <u>theirselves</u> to Satan's attacks.
   3. No person is able by <u>himself</u> to resist the devil.
   4. God blesses <u>ourselves</u> far beyond what we deserve.
   5. <u>This</u> is a definite evidence of His love.
   6. Here are my papers; <u>those</u> must be Wayne's.
   7. Dale cut <u>hisself</u> a huge piece of cake.
   8. You should never let <u>yourself</u> become proud.
   9. Lynette and <u>myself</u> want to help you with your work.
   10. Heidi brought drinks for Sharon and <u>herself.</u>
   11. <u>This here</u> is quite a surprise!
   12. <u>Them</u> are the sweet potatoes that Alan dug this morning.
   13. Albert and <u>themselves</u> were busy for a while in the hog barn.
   14. We <u>ourselves</u> are planning to help Grandfather.
   15. Christa and <u>myself</u> want to make cookies for the Owen family.

C. Write a sentence with a compound personal pronoun used intensively. Then write a sentence with the same pronoun used reflexively.

Review Exercises

A. Write *commas, dashes,* or *parentheses* to tell which marks should be used to set off each underlined parenthetical element. Notes in parentheses tell what effects are to be produced. [29]
   1. This road <u>which goes right past Uncle Andrew's farm</u> is very bumpy. (The parenthetical element is a part of the sentence.)
   2. Did you meet Joseph <u>he is from Ohio</u> while he was living with Brother Eldon's? (The parenthetical element is of minor importance.)
   3. Yesterday <u>what a cold, damp day it was!</u> we cut firewood. (The parenthetical element is to be emphasized.)
   4. This book <u>Cousin Lena loaned it to me</u> is about a Russian Mennonite family after the Bolshevik Revolution. (The parenthetical element is of minor importance.)

Written Exercises

A. 1. himself—CP, R
   2. this—D
   3. Those—D; ourselves—CP, R
   4. yourself—CP, I; that—D

B. 1. ourselves   9. I
   2. themselves   10. correct
   3. correct   11. This
   4. us   12. Those
   5. correct   13. they
   6. correct   14. correct
   7. himself   15. I
   8. correct

C. (Individual work.)

Review Exercises

A. 1. commas
   2. parentheses
   3. dashes
   4. parentheses

B. Copy each item that should be italicized, and underline it. Also write correctly the items that need apostrophes or hyphens. [30, 31]

1. Some people pronounce sepulcher as if the l precedes the u.
2. Did you read the Christian Pathway that was among todays Sunday school papers?
3. Christopher Columbus was outfitted with three ships: the Santa Maria, the Niña, and the Pinta.
4. I dont think Ive ever committed such an embarrassing faux pas before.
5. I have had a low grade fever all day.
6. Having a self important attitude is not a well advised position.
7. We packaged oatmeal in five, ten, and fifty pound bags.
8. We counted twenty one cars on our walk home, a distance of one half mile.

B. 1. <u>sepulcher</u>, <u>l</u>, <u>u</u>
   2. <u>Christian Pathway</u>, today's
   3. <u>Santa Maria</u>, <u>Niña</u>, <u>Pinta</u>
   4. don't, I've, <u>faux pas</u>
   5. low-grade
   6. self-important, well-advised
   7. five-, ten-, fifty-pound
   8. twenty-one, one-half

73. Writing Effective Sentences: Conciseness and Parallelism

Lesson Survey

- An effective sentence has **conciseness** and **parallelism.**
- To have conciseness in a sentence, you must avoid deadwood, wordy expressions, and redundancy.
- To have parallelism in a sentence, you must do the following things.
  1. Use a coordinating conjunction to join only matching sentence parts.
  2. Avoid illogical shifts in areas such as person, number, tense, and voice.
  3. Be consistent in the use of articles before nouns in a series.
  4. Repeat introductory words before long phrases or clauses in a series.
  5. In a compound part, you may omit one of the words only if the parallel word would correctly fill its place.
  6. In defining a word, use another word of the same part of speech.

Lesson 71 emphasized unity and coherence, the two most important elements of effective sentences. Conciseness and parallelism are two more qualities that make sentences effective.

Conciseness

A *concise* sentence is one that expresses a thought clearly and directly, without the clutter of extra or repetitious words. To write sentences that are clear and concise, observe the rules discussed in the following paragraphs.

Lesson 73

Purpose: To encourage the writing of effective sentences, with special emphasis on conciseness and parallelism.

Oral Review:

1. What are two essential qualities of every effective sentence? (unity, coherence)
2. What three things mar sentence unity? (writing run-on errors; joining poorly related ideas; separating closely related ideas)
3. Name several ways to make sentences coherent. (avoiding unclear pronoun reference; avoiding misplaced modifiers; avoiding the careless separation of closely related sentence parts)
4. What is the theme of a story? (the lesson that the story teaches)

5. A good story ——— rather than ——— the theme. (shows, tells)
6. Why should you take notes for a report from more than one reference source? (to have a balanced report; to require you to express ideas in your own words; to verify facts)
7. When may you copy the exact words of a reference source in your notes? (when you plan to quote those words in your report, and if you place those words in quotation marks)

Lesson Introduction: No doubt Mr. Careless is still making bricks and building his brick walls. But so is Mr. Careful. This lesson will give you several more pointers on being a "Mr. Careful" in English, by helping you to write sentences with conciseness and parallelism.

1. *Avoid deadwood.* Deadwood is the use of words that add no meaning at all to a sentence. This is perhaps the simplest kind of clutter to identify and remove.

Sentences with deadwood:
> The <u>cold</u> ice chilled our hands.
> My <u>fellow</u> classmates agree <u>with the idea</u> that our school has a
> pleasant atmosphere.

Concise sentences:
> The ice chilled our hands.
> My classmates agree that our school has a pleasant atmosphere.

2. *Avoid wordy expressions.* A wordy expression uses more words than necessary to express an idea. A number of wordy expressions are listed below, along with shorter ways of saying the same things.

Wordy	Concise
ascend up	ascend
repeat again	repeat
meet up with	meet; encounter
large in size	large
tiny particle	particle
man who was kind	kind man
at this point in time	now
in the near future	soon
in the month of June	in June
man flying the plane	pilot

Whenever it is practical, reduce a sentence to a clause, a clause to a phrase, and a phrase to a word. Clauses fill an important place; but when an idea expressed in a clause can be expressed equally well in a phrase (which is shorter), the phrase will make the writing more concise and forceful. The same is true when the idea in a phrase can be expressed just as effectively with a single word.

Wordy:
> Jeremiah used the Rechabites as an object lesson to Judah. <u>He did
> this because they had remained faithful to their father Rechab.</u>

Concise: Sentence changed to clause
> Jeremiah used the Rechabites as an object lesson to Judah <u>because
> they had remained faithful to their father Rechab.</u>

Concise: Clause changed to phrase
> Jeremiah used the Rechabites as an object lesson to Judah <u>because
> of their faithfulness to their father Rechab.</u>

Lesson Outline:

1. An effective sentence has conciseness and parallelism. A concise sentence is free from the clutter of extra or repetitious words. In a sentence with parallelism, matching parts fit together properly.

2. Several things are required for conciseness in sentences.

   (1) *Avoid deadwood.* Deadwood is the use of words that add no meaning at all to a sentence.

   (2) *Avoid wordy expressions.* A wordy expression uses more words than necessary to express an idea. Whenever it is practical, reduce a sentence to a clause, a clause to a phrase, and a phrase to a word.

   (3) *Avoid redundancy.* Redundancy is the careless repetition of words or ideas.

3. Several things are required for parallelism in sentences.

   (1) *Use a coordinating conjunction to join only matching sentence parts.* Parallelism is marred by a construction such as a word joined to a phrase.

   (2) *Avoid illogical shifts in areas such as person, number, tense, and voice.*

   (3) *Be consistent in the use of articles before nouns in a series.* Parallelism suffers when articles are used with some of the nouns but not with others.

   (4) *Repeat introductory words before long phrases or clauses in a series.* The repeated words help to strengthen the parallelism.

   (5) *In a compound part, you may omit one of the words only if the parallel word would correctly fill its place.*

Wordy:

> As a usual rule, Grandma wears a sweater that is black in color.
> It is necessary for us to be aware of the fact that though worldly people may appear to be contented, they do not know true peace.

Concise:

> Usually Grandma wears a black sweater.
> We must realize that though worldly people may seem contented, they do not know true peace.

3. *Avoid redundancy.* Redundancy is the careless repetition of words or ideas. The repetition of key words can be an effective device for achieving paragraph coherence (as you saw in Lesson 18). But when words or ideas are thoughtlessly repeated within a sentence, the sentence becomes cluttered and ineffective.

Redundant:

> Shadrach, Meshach, and Abednego boldly and courageously declared their faith and trust in God.
> The Nile River is the longest river in the world.
> My uncle promised to give us any possible assistance that he could.

Concise:

> Shadrach, Meshach, and Abednego courageously declared their faith in God.
> The Nile is the longest river in the world.
> My uncle promised to give us any possible assistance.

A particular kind of redundancy to avoid is the repetition of a word when the two uses have different meanings. This can easily confuse the reader because it forces him to make a rapid shift from one meaning to the other. The reader will be distracted from the main thought in the sentence, with the result that communication is hindered.

Redundant:

> Your marks have shown marked improvement.
> The man who caused the fire was fired from his job.

Clear and concise:

> Your grades have shown marked improvement.
> The man who caused the fire was dismissed from his job.

Parallelism

A sentence has *parallelism* when matching parts fit together properly. Parallel constructions improve sentence effectiveness by making sentences smooth to read and easy to understand. The following paragraphs describe various ways to have parallelism in sentences.

(6) *In defining a word, use another word of the same part of speech.* A clause beginning with *when* or *where* seldom makes a good definition.

★ **EXTRA PRACTICE**

Worksheet 28 *(Unity, Coherence, Conciseness, and Parallelism in Sentences)*

1. *Use a coordinating conjunction to join only matching sentence parts.* For example, an adverb should be joined only to an adverb, an infinitive to an infinitive, and an adjective prepositional phrase to an adjective prepositional phrase.

Unparallel: Word joined to phrase
We should always speak <u>respectfully</u> and <u>with courtesy</u>.
Parallel:
We should always speak <u>respectfully</u> and <u>courteously</u>.

Unparallel: Phrase joined to clause
We read good books <u>for pleasure</u> and <u>because they encourage us to do right</u>.
Parallel:
We read good books <u>for pleasure</u> and <u>for encouragement to do right</u>.

2. *Avoid illogical shifts in areas such as person, number, tense, and voice.*

Unparallel: Illogical shift in tense
As I <u>stepped</u> out into the moonlight, I suddenly <u>see</u> a moose.
Parallel:
As I <u>stepped</u> out into the moonlight, I suddenly <u>saw</u> a moose.

Unparallel: Illogical shift in number
When <u>one</u> sees a moose, <u>they</u> are impressed with its majestic bearing.
Parallel:
When <u>one</u> sees a moose, <u>he</u> is impressed with its majestic bearing.

Unparallel: Illogical shift in voice
I <u>wondered</u> if other moose were nearby, but only that one <u>was seen</u>.
Parallel:
I <u>wondered</u> if other moose were nearby, but I <u>saw</u> only that one.

3. *Be consistent in the use of articles before nouns in a series.* Parallelism suffers when articles are used with some of the nouns but not with others.

Unparallel:
<u>A</u> car, bus, and <u>a</u> truck were involved in the accident.
Parallel:
<u>A</u> car, <u>a</u> bus, and <u>a</u> truck were involved in the accident.

4. *Repeat introductory words before long phrases or clauses in a series.* The repeated words help to strengthen the parallelism.

Weak parallelism:
God's people know <u>that</u> this world is not their friend, wickedness will abound more and more, and God will finally judge the world.

Strong parallelism:

God's people know <u>that</u> this world is not their friend, <u>that</u> wickedness will abound more and more, and <u>that</u> God will finally judge the world.

5. *In a compound part, you may omit one of the words only if the parallel word would correctly fill its place.* If the parallel word does not fit, you must state both words. For example, if one main verb is omitted, all the helping verbs must match the main verb that remains. If just *a* or *an* precedes two or more nouns, the article must match all the nouns. Study the following illustrations.

Unparallel:

God always <u>has</u> and always <u>will</u> <u>answer</u> the prayer of faith.

(*Will answer* is correct, but *has answer* is not.)

Parallel:

God always <u>has</u> <u>answered</u> and always <u>will</u> <u>answer</u> the prayer of faith.
God always <u>can</u> and always <u>will</u> <u>answer</u> the prayer of faith.

Unparallel:

We can learn important lessons from <u>a</u> <u>lion</u> or <u>eagle</u>.

(*A lion* is correct, but *a eagle* is not.)

Parallel:

We can learn important lessons from <u>a</u> <u>lion</u> or <u>an</u> <u>eagle</u>.
<u>A</u> <u>locust</u> or <u>spider</u> can also teach us valuable lessons.

6. *In defining a word, use another word of the same part of speech.* A clause beginning with *when* or *where* seldom makes a good definition.

Unparallel:

A Palestinian <u>wadi</u> is <u>where</u> a stream flows during the wet season but not during the dry season.

Parallel:

A Palestinian <u>wadi</u> is a <u>gully</u> or <u>valley</u> where a stream flows during the wet season but not during the dry season.

Unparallel:

<u>To sanctify</u> means <u>when</u> something is made holy or set apart for a sacred purpose.

Parallel:

<u>To sanctify</u> means <u>to make</u> something holy or <u>to set</u> something apart for a sacred purpose.

Class Practice

Read these sentences, improving the conciseness or parallelism.

1. The aye-aye, a strange mammal, is an animal that lives only in the bamboo forests of Madagascar.

Lesson 73 Answers

Class Practice

(Sample answers. Allow reasonable variation.)

1. The aye-aye, a strange mammal, lives only in the bamboo forests of Madagascar.

2. The tail, ears, and the claws make an aye-aye look strange.
3. The tail is big and bushy and looks as big as the rest of the body.
4. Its ears are large and covered with fur.
5. The finger that is in the middle of each hand is thin and quite long in length, and it ends with a claw that is sharp.
6. It is necessary that the aye-aye has these long, thin fingers so that it can perform the action of getting food.
7. If an aye-aye hears the sound of an insect boring into a tree, it opens the hole with its teeth, which are sharp, and it spears the insect with one of the sharp claws that it has.
8. My parents decided that we would take a trip to Uncle Floyd's this summer and to postpone the trip to the zoo.
9. Do you long for a long spell of snowy weather?
10. Jesus told His disciples that He would go up to Jerusalem, He would suffer and die, and He would rise again the third day.
11. When one thinks of Jesus' great suffering, you are overwhelmed with gratitude to Him.
12. Peter and John ran to the sepulcher, but Jesus was not seen by them at that time.

Written Exercises

Rewrite these sentences, improving the conciseness or parallelism.

1. To pray is when a person talks with God.
2. To read the Bible and praying are two important parts of our worship.
3. As Father explained the Bible passage in family worship, I think about our recent experiences.
4. Father and Charles cleaned the heifers' pen, and the goats' pen was cleaned by Sherwin and me.
5. The fleecy, fluffy clouds in the sky floated across the sun that was shining.
6. My neighbor knows how to fly an airplane or helicopter.
7. As a usual rule, you should finish to completion first those assignments that are due at the earliest time.
8. Beside the still waters and where the green pasture grows, the shepherd led his sheep.
9. Scientists classify the horse, zebra, and the donkey in the same genus.
10. Each and every tree that is found in this orchard has been planted by our family.
11. When one has seen the damage after a large hurricane, they are impressed with God's great power and might.
12. The man who was friendly appeared to be anxious to help us.

2. The tail, the ears, and the claws make an aye-aye look strange.
3. The big, bushy tail looks as big as the rest of the body.
4. Its ears are large and furry.
5. The middle finger of each hand is thin and quite long, and it ends with a sharp claw.
6. The aye-aye needs these long, thin fingers to get food.
7. If an aye-aye hears an insect boring into a tree, it opens the hole with its sharp teeth, and it spears the insect with one of its sharp claws.
8. My parents decided to take a trip to Uncle Floyd's this summer and to postpone the trip to the zoo.
9. Do you wish for a long spell of snowy weather?
10. Jesus told His disciples that He would go up to Jerusalem, that He would suffer and die, and that He would rise again the third day.
11. When one thinks of Jesus' great suffering, he is overwhelmed with gratitude to Him.
12. Peter and John ran to the sepulcher, but they did not see Jesus at that time.

Written Exercises

(Sample answers. Allow reasonable variation.)

1. To pray is to talk with God.
2. Reading the Bible and praying are two important parts of our worship.
3. As Father explained the Bible passage in family worship, I thought about our recent experiences.
4. Father and Charles cleaned the heifers' pen, and Sherwin and I cleaned the goats' pen.
5. The fluffy clouds floated across the sun.
6. My neighbor knows how to fly an airplane or a helicopter.
7. Usually you should finish first those assignments that are due first.
8. Beside the still waters and in the green pasture, the shepherd led his sheep.
9. Scientists classify the horse, the zebra, and the donkey in the same genus.
10. Every tree in this orchard has been planted by our family.
11. When one has seen the damage after a hurricane, he is impressed with God's great power.
12. The friendly man seemed anxious to help us.

13. Grandfather's hair has been white in color since a long time ago in the past.
14. Father has or soon will finish the doghouse.
15. Mother told us that Cousin Miriam had broken her leg, she would have her leg in traction for several weeks, and she surely would enjoy some letters and gifts.

Review Exercises

Write whether the verb in each sentence is active (*A*) or passive (*P*). Also copy the three retained objects, and label each one *DO* (direct object) or *IO* (indirect object). [66]

1. Jacob sent messengers to Esau.
2. Soon disturbing news was brought Jacob.
3. Esau was coming with four hundred men.
4. That night a strange man wrestled with Jacob.
5. Jacob's thigh was put out of joint.
6. He sought a blessing from the stranger.
7. Jacob was given a new name.
8. He called that place Peniel.
9. Esau was presented a generous gift.
10. The twin brothers parted in peace.

13. Grandfather's hair has been white for a long time.
14. Father has finished or soon will finish the doghouse.
15. Mother told us that Cousin Miriam had broken her leg, that she would have her leg in traction for several weeks, and that she surely would enjoy some letters and gifts.

Review Exercises

1. A	6. A
2. P; Jacob—IO	7. P; name—DO
3. A	8. A
4. A	9. P; gift—DO
5. P	10. A

74. Indefinite Pronouns

Lesson Survey

- An **indefinite pronoun** does not refer to a definite person, place, thing, or idea.

- The following indefinite pronouns are always singular: *each, either, neither, one, another, anybody, anyone, anything, everybody, everyone, everything, somebody, someone, something, nobody, no one, nothing.*

- The following indefinite pronouns are always plural: *both, few, many, others, several.*

- The following indefinite pronouns may be either singular or plural: *some, any, none, all, most.*

- The possessive form of an indefinite pronoun is made by adding *'s*.

- An indefinite pronoun is an adjective when it modifies a noun.

Lesson 74

Purpose: To study the correct uses of indefinite pronouns.

Oral Review:

1. Name several compound personal pronouns. (myself, yourself, himself, herself, itself, ourselves, yourselves, themselves)
2. In what two ways are compound personal pronouns used? (intensively, to add emphasis to another substantive; reflexively, to show an action done by the subject to itself)
3. Name the four demonstrative pronouns. (this, that, these, those)
4. What is the general purpose of single quotation marks? (to set off a quotation or title within a quotation)
5. What punctuation marks should always be placed

inside the quotation marks? (period, comma)
6. What punctuation marks should always be placed outside the quotation marks? (colon, semicolon)
7. *(a)* When should a question mark or an exclamation point be placed inside the quotation marks? *(b)* When should they be placed outside? (*a.* when the quotation is a question or an exclamation; *b.* when the whole sentence is a question or an exclamation, but the quotation is not)
8. Tell whether the nouns in this group are singular or plural: *civics, mathematics, chicken pox* (singular)
9. When the conjunction *or* or *nor* joins a singular and a plural subject, how can you tell whether to use a singular or a plural verb? (Make the verb agree with the subject that is nearer to the verb.)

The largest class of pronouns is the indefinite pronouns. Unlike most other kinds, these pronouns are often used without antecedents. As their name suggests, the *indefinite pronouns* do not refer to definite persons, places, things, or ideas.

Jesus taught <u>His</u> disciples about the heavenly kingdom.
>   (personal pronoun referring to a specific person; antecedent is *Jesus*)

<u>Everyone</u> who follows the Lord is part of this heavenly kingdom.
>   (indefinite pronoun not referring to specific persons; no antecedent)

The indefinite pronouns can be arranged in three groups: those that are always singular, those that are always plural, and those that may be either.

Singular Indefinite Pronouns

The following indefinite pronouns are always singular: *each, either, neither, one, another, anybody, anyone, anything, everybody, everyone, everything, somebody, someone, something, nobody, no one, nothing.* Notice that most of these have a singular word element: *other, one, thing,* or *body.*

When one of these singular pronouns is used as a subject, it is often followed by a prepositional phrase with a plural object. Be careful to make the verb agree with the indefinite pronoun, not with the object of the preposition. Also be sure that any personal pronoun referring to a singular indefinite pronoun is singular.

Incorrect:
>   <u>Each</u> of the Ten Commandments <u>contain</u> an important principle.
>   Only <u>one</u> of the healed lepers returned to express *their* thanks.
>   <u>Everybody</u> <u>are</u> responsible for *their* own choices.

Correct:
>   <u>Each</u> of the Ten Commandments <u>contains</u> an important principle.
>   Only <u>one</u> of the healed lepers returned to express *his* thanks.
>   <u>Everybody</u> <u>is</u> responsible for *his* own choices.

Plural Indefinite Pronouns

The following indefinite pronouns are always plural: *both, few, many, others, several.* Be sure to use plural verbs with these pronouns. Also be sure that any personal pronouns referring to them are plural.

>   <u>Many</u> <u>are</u> called, but <u>few</u> <u>are</u> chosen.
>   <u>Both</u> of the sons of Isaac wanted *their* father's blessing.

Singular or Plural Indefinite Pronouns

The following indefinite pronouns may be either singular or plural: *some, any, none, all, most.* When one of these words is used as a subject, you must decide whether it refers to a singular or a plural noun. That

Lesson Introduction: Many times we want to be specific and definite in our speech. If we know whom we brought along to church, we will not likely say, "We brought somebody along with us to church this morning." On the other hand, there are times when we do not want to be specific and definite. The sign at your church may well include the phrase, "Everyone welcome." The indefinite pronoun *Everyone* excludes *no one,* so it includes *anyone* who reads it. In this lesson you will review these and other indefinite pronouns.

Lesson Outline:

1. An indefinite pronoun does not refer to a definite person, place, thing, or idea.

2. The following indefinite pronouns are always singular: **each, either, neither, one, another, anybody, anyone, anything, everybody, everyone, everything, somebody, someone, something, nobody, no one, nothing.**

>   a. When one of these singular pronouns is used as a subject, make the verb agree with the pronoun, not with the object of the preposition that may follow the pronoun.
>   b. Any personal pronoun referring to a singular indefinite pronoun must be singular.

3. The following indefinite pronouns are always plural: **both, few, many, others, several.**

>   a. If a plural indefinite pronoun is used as a subject, the verb must be plural.
>   b. Any personal pronoun referring to a plural indefinite pronoun must be plural.

4. The following indefinite pronouns may be either singular or plural: **some, any, none, all, most.** The number of a pronoun in this group is determined by the noun it refers to.

noun is often found in a prepositional phrase right after the indefinite pronoun. If the noun is singular, the indefinite pronoun means a certain portion of that one thing and is singular. If the noun is plural, the indefinite pronoun means certain individual items in that set of things and is plural.

> <u>Some</u> of this *field* <u>has</u> been plowed.
>> *Some* refers to singular *field* and is singular.
> <u>Some</u> of this one thing <u>has</u> been plowed.
>
> <u>Some</u> of the *fields* <u>have</u> been plowed.
>> *Some* refers to plural *fields* and is plural.
> <u>Some</u> of these items <u>have</u> been plowed.
>
> <u>Most</u> of the *book* <u>was</u> written by Mr. Davis.
>> *Most* refers to singular *book* and is singular.
> <u>Most</u> of this one thing <u>was</u> written by Mr. Davis.
>
> <u>Most</u> of the *chapters* <u>were</u> written by Mr. Davis.
>> *Most* refers to plural *chapters* and is plural.
> <u>Most</u> of these items <u>were</u> written by Mr. Davis.

Possessive forms of indefinite pronouns are made by adding *'s*. This is different from the possessive forms of personal pronouns, which never have apostrophes.

> <u>Nobody's</u> answer was correct.
> A brief report was assigned, and <u>everyone's</u> was finished on time.

The words listed in this lesson are pronouns only if they have a substantive function in a sentence. Like demonstrative pronouns, these words are adjectives when they modify nouns.

> <u>Some</u> of the popcorn has been eaten. (pronoun used as the subject)
> <u>Some</u> popcorn has been spilled. (adjective modifying the subject)

Class Practice

A. Choose the correct words in parentheses.
1. Everyone (choose, chooses) (his, their) responses to life.
2. Some of the Beatitudes (is, are) written on posters that hang on the classroom wall.
3. Some of the Sermon on the Mount (was, were) committed to memory.
4. A few of the Jewish leaders (was, were) willing to identify with Jesus.
5. (Do, Does) everybody have (his, their) books with (him, them)?
6. Both of the families (is, are) coming for dinner.
7. Most of the wheat (have, has) been harvested.
8. Most of the trees (have, has) been planted.

Lesson 74 Answers

Class Practice

A. 1. chooses, his
   2. are
   3. was
   4. were
   5. Does, his, him
   6. are
   7. has
   8. have

a. If the noun is singular, the indefinite pronoun means a certain portion of that one thing; and it is singular.

b. If the noun is plural, the indefinite pronoun means certain individual items within that set of things; and it is plural.

5. The possessive form of an indefinite pronoun is made by adding 's. This is different from the possessive forms of personal pronouns, which never have apostrophes.

6. The words listed in this lesson are pronouns only if they have a substantive function in a sentence. Like demonstrative pronouns, these words are adjectives when they modify nouns.

★ **EXTRA PRACTICE**
Worksheet 29 (*Indefinite Pronouns*)

9. One of the boys (have, has) to redo (his, their) work.

10. Either of these quotations (illustrate, illustrates) my point.

B. Tell which word in each sentence needs an apostrophe.

1. Somebodys car skidded on the wet road and crashed into ours.

2. Theirs were lettered more neatly than anyones in our room.

3. Nobodys answer surprised the teacher as much as hers.

C. Name each pronoun, and tell whether it is *personal, compound personal, demonstrative,* or *indefinite.* (Do not include the pronouns *who* and *which.*)

1. These are perilous times in which we find ourselves.

2. No one except those people who truly obey the Lord are safe from evil.

3. All who truly love the Lord obey His Word.

4. Jesus Himself declared this to be true.

5. Somebody did a golden deed.

6. Was that you?

Written Exercises

A. If a pronoun or verb is used incorrectly, write the correct word. If the sentence is correct, write *correct.*

1. A few in our congregation lives more than thirty miles from church.

2. Everyone should devote their energies to the Lord's work.

3. Many have offered excuses for their failure to serve the Lord.

4. None of these excuses are ever acceptable to God.

5. Nobody living below the dam was expecting any danger to their life.

6. Some of this work have been scheduled for today.

7. Some of these jobs have been scheduled for today.

8. Either of these bicycles are a good buy.

9. One of my uncles raises several kinds of sheep on their farm.

10. Another has a herd of dairy goats.

11. Everybodys voice blended in songs of praise.

12. Most of the songbooks have been stacked neatly, but somebodys has been thrown carelessly on the bottom shelf.

13. Most of the time were spent in singing for the elderly neighbors.

14. Neither of these elderly ladies is able to leave their bed.

15. Someone has been giving his time to help Mr. Grover mow the lawn.

B. Copy each pronoun, and label it *P* (personal), *CP* (compound personal), *D* (demonstrative), or *ID* (indefinite).

1. Keep yourself in God's love, and He will surely bless your life.

2. This is the secret of a truly joyful life.

3. Many in this world try to find their joy in anything but God.

4. Everyone seeking joy in himself is sure to fail.

5. Another secret of joy is to forget yourself and find ways of helping others.

---

9. has, his

10. illustrates

B. 1. Somebody's

2. anyone's

3. Nobody's

C. 1. These—demonstrative; we—personal; ourselves—compound personal

2. No one—indefinite

3. All—indefinite; His—personal

4. Himself—compound personal; this—demonstrative

5. Somebody—indefinite

6. that—demonstrative; you—personal

Written Exercises

A. 1. live

2. his

3. correct

4. correct

5. his

6. has

7. correct

8. is

9. his

10. correct

11. Everybody's

12. somebody's

13. was

14. her

15. correct

B. 1. yourself—CP; He—P; your—P

2. This—D

3. Many—ID; their—P; anything—ID

4. Everyone—ID; himself—CP

5. yourself—CP; others—ID

6. Only those with a definite interest in other people find true joy.
7. Although God seeks to bless everybody, few actually surrender to Him.
8. Each of us has the potential to be someone useful in God's kingdom.

6. those—D
7. everybody—ID; few—ID; Him—P
8. Each—ID; us—P; someone—ID

Review Exercises

A. If the underlined part of the sentence is punctuated incorrectly, write it correctly. If it is correct, write *correct*. [26]

1. "What a notable statement of faith Job made," commented Brother Andrew, "when he said, 'Though he slay me, yet will I trust in him!'"
2. The Bible clearly says that we are to be "doers of the word, and not hearers only;" yet many professing Christians think God will overlook their disobedience.
3. "Rachel," Aunt Miriam asked, "did that sign say, 'Detour ahead?'"
4. "I distinctly remember," Joel added, "that Father asked, 'Did you close and latch the gate?'"
5. "Blessed are the peacemakers' is a good verse to remember when the neighbor boys try to get you upset," encouraged Father.

B. If the verb does not agree with its subject, write the correct verb. If it does agree, write *correct*. [60]

1. Where's the Beatitudes found?
2. Peter, along with the other disciples, were sure that they would not forsake Jesus.
3. Neither Paul nor Silas was ashamed to suffer for Christ.
4. The news of salvation have brought joy to people in many parts of the world.
5. A swarm of bees have begun a new colony.
6. A dish of pretzels was passed around.
7. Don't she like these hard pretzels?
8. Ham and eggs was served for breakfast.
9. Measles are a very uncomfortable disease.
10. Either the dog or the cats has been digging in Mother's flower beds.

Review Exercises

A. 1. him'!'"
   2. only";
   3. ahead'?"
   4. correct
   5. " 'Blessed

B. 1. are
   2. was
   3. correct
   4. has
   5. has
   6. correct
   7. Doesn't
   8. correct *or* were
   9. is
   10. have

---

75. Writing Effective Sentences: Action

Lesson Survey
- An effective sentence communicates in a lively, active manner.
  1. Make the subject perform the action of the verb in most sentences.
  2. Use more direct quotations than indirect quotations.

Lesson 75

Purpose: To teach how to write sentences that communicate in a lively, active manner.

Oral Review:

1. Name the four qualities, which you have studied in this chapter, that contribute to effective sentences. (unity, coherence, conciseness, parallelism)
2. What three things mar sentence unity? (writing run-on errors; joining poorly related ideas; separating closely related ideas)
3. Name several ways to make sentences coherent. (avoiding unclear pronoun reference; avoiding misplaced modifiers; avoiding the careless separation of closely related sentence parts)
4. Which of the following expressions contains deadwood: *the cold ice cream* or *the delicious ice cream*? (the cold ice cream)

5. Give six ways to have parallelism in sentences. (Use a coordinating conjunction to join only matching sentence parts. Avoid illogical shifts in areas such as person, number, tense, and voice. Be consistent in the use of articles before nouns in a series. Repeat introductory words before long phrases or clauses in a series. In a compound part, you may omit one of the words only if the parallel word would correctly fill its place. In defining a word, use another word of the same part of speech.)

Lesson Introduction: Did you ever step into a slow-moving game of prisoner's base? For some reason, few people were venturing off base. The dull game hardly made you feel like getting involved. Contrast that with stepping into a lively game. Many players from both teams are in the middle. Every player must stay alert and agile. The excitement pulls you right into the game.

When you hear about a man of action, what kind of man comes to your mind? You think of a man who works actively and energetically. He does every job with zeal and diligence. No one who is watching needs to ask, "Does he really expect to get something done?" The answer is obvious!

The same is true of an active sentence. It communicates in a lively, energetic manner. It does not make you wonder, "What is this sentence trying to accomplish?" The sentence is so clear and direct that there is no question about its purpose.

Sentences with action are obviously more interesting and meaningful than sentences without action. How can you write lively sentences? This lesson will give you some pointers.

Make the Subject Perform the Action

Read the following sentences. Can you tell what is wrong?

> That morning Mount Sinai was covered by a cloud. Thunder was heard. Lightning was seen. Smoke was produced. The whole mountain was shaken. Such a loud trumpet sound was heard that all the people were terrified.

This is obviously a notable scene—but what is taking place? Although we read of thunder, lightning, smoke, and a trumpet sound, everything seems to happen silently and automatically. No person or thing is acting. Even the terror of the people is caused by something that is not clearly identified.

What is the reason for this strange mental picture? All the verbs are in the passive voice! Compare the sentences below, noting that each verb expresses an action performed by a subject. Do you see the contrast?

> That morning a cloud covered Mount Sinai. Thunder rumbled. Lightning flashed. Smoke billowed upward. The whole mountain trembled. Such a loud trumpet sound blared forth that all the people shook with terror.

The passive voice is one of the greatest enemies of action in sentences. With passive verbs, things happen but nobody makes them happen. Sentence subjects let themselves be acted upon instead of taking part in the action. Therefore, take special pains to get rid of the passive voice in your writing. Do not allow your subjects to lie around in passive idleness; make them get up and do something!

The simplest way to eliminate the passive voice is to look for verbs with a *by* phrase after them. When you find such a sentence, see if you can rewrite it by changing the noun after *by* to the subject. But remember that the *by* phrase is not always present. Any verb consisting of *be* and a past participle is passive; see if you can change it to the active voice. In the following

These two games illustrate a contrast that is evident in writing. Some writing is dull. It lacks the power to hold a reader's attention. Other writing vibrates with energy. What makes the difference? This lesson provides two answers to that question.

Lesson Outline:

An effective sentence communicates in a lively, active manner.

    a. Make the subject perform the action of the verb in most sentences.

        1) The passive voice is one of the greatest enemies of action in sentences. (*Note:* It has been called the nobody voice because things happen, but nobody makes them happen.)

        2) To replace a passive verb with an active verb, do one of two things: supply a subject to perform the action of the verb, or change the verb so that it expresses an action that the subject can perform.

        3) The passive voice is suitable for a sentence that describes something unpleasant, like a tragedy or disaster. It may also be suitable when the doer of an action is unclear or unknown, or when there is a good reason not to name the doer of an action. But even then, it may be better to make the subject perform the action.

        4) Never be satisfied with a passive verb unless you have a specific reason for using it or you simply cannot improve on it.

        (*Teacher:* When a sentence with a passive verb is changed so that the subject

examples, notice how the change of voice makes the sentences more alive and active.

Passive: Lazarus was raised from the dead by Jesus.
Active: Jesus raised Lazarus from the dead.

Passive: Two songs were sung, and then a story was read.
Active: We sang two songs, and then Father read a story.

Passive: Suddenly a tremendous explosion was heard.
Active: Suddenly a tremendous explosion rent the air.

As the examples show, you will sometimes need to supply a subject (like *we* and *Father*) when you change to the active voice. If this does not work, change the verb so that it expresses an action that the subject can perform (like *rent* instead of *was heard*). Such changes take extra time and thought, but the improved action is well worth the effort.

If the active voice is so important, why does the passive voice even exist? The passive voice is suitable for a sentence that describes something unpleasant, like a tragedy or disaster. In such a sentence, a passive verb portrays the subject as a victim that usually cannot help himself. Notice how this is true in the following sentences.

Jonah was swallowed by a great fish.
The Jews were carried into captivity.
Stephen was stoned outside Jerusalem.

The passive voice may also be suitable in two other cases: (1) when the doer of an action is unclear or unknown, and (2) when there is a good reason not to name the doer of an action. But even in these cases, you should see if you can make the subject perform the action. Study the following examples.

The flight had been delayed.
> (If you do not know what caused the delay, the passive voice may be acceptable. But you could make the subject do something: The flight had come in late.)

The window was broken yesterday.
> (It is probably more kind not to name the person who broke the window. Note also that the window is a "victim.")

Verna was given that book for her birthday.
> (If you gave the gift, it is probably more humble not to say so. But with a different verb, you could use the active voice: Verna received that book for her birthday.)

In summary, you should try to make the subject perform the action of the verb in every sentence you write, unless you have a specific reason for

performs the action, the resulting verb is *active* [acting] but is not always in the *active voice*. It may be an intransitive complete verb, which does not have voice. [Compare "Bells were rung" with "Bells rang."] This technicality is of little significance here. The main emphasis is to *make the subject perform the action of the verb.)*

b. Use more direct quotations than indirect quotations. A direct quotation is more alive and active than an indirect quotation, and therefore it communicates more effectively.

using the passive voice or you simply cannot improve on it. Only then should you use a verb in the passive voice.

Use Direct Quotations

Direct quotations also help sentences to communicate effectively. They have more life and action than indirect quotations do. You take for granted that you will use direct quotations when you write stories. But will you use them in other writing too? Here are some examples.

Indirect: Alta called <u>for someone to help her chase the calves in</u>.
Direct: <u>"Help me!"</u> called Alta. <u>"Someone help me chase these calves in!"</u>

Indirect: After we let the air out of all four tires, the man asked in amazement <u>if we were sure our plan would work</u>.
Direct: After we let the air out of all four tires, the man asked in amazement, <u>"Are you sure your plan will work?"</u>

Indirect: In all the bustle and hurry, apparently no one stops and asks himself <u>what he is really trying to accomplish</u>.
Direct: In all the bustle and hurry, apparently no one stops and asks himself, <u>"What am I really trying to accomplish?"</u>

Do not let your writing be smothered by passive verbs and indirect quotations. Harness the energy of active subjects and direct quotations, and your writing will be fresh, lively, and truly interesting.

Class Practice

A. Try to improve each sentence by making the subject perform the action of the verb. (Supply a subject or use a different verb if necessary.) If the passive voice is more suitable, tell why.
1. Balak's riches were coveted by Balaam.
2. Jairus's daughter was raised to life.
3. The earth was divided in the days of Peleg.
4. Joseph was sold by his brothers.
5. Everything was coated with a thick layer of hoarfrost.
6. Our Gospel sign was broken down last night.
7. Our minister's family was given a surprise box of groceries.
8. Hurricanes are formed over tropical water.
9. Most of the town was leveled by the high winds.
10. Thunder could be heard in the distance.

B. Read each selection, changing the indirect quotation to a direct quotation.
1. We know that Jesus tenderly cares for His own. He declared plainly that He is the Good Shepherd.
2. Jesus told Zacchaeus to hurry and come down.

Lesson 75 Answers

Class Practice

A. 1. Balaam coveted Balak's riches.
   2. Jesus raised Jairus's daughter to life.
   3. (Passive voice is suitable because there is no clear doer of the action. "The earth divided in the days of Peleg" is not necessarily better.)
   4. (Passive voice is suitable because Joseph was a helpless victim.)
   5. A thick layer of hoarfrost coated everything.
      or Everything sparkled with a thick layer of hoarfrost.
   6. (Passive voice is suitable because the doer is likely unknown.)
   7. Our minister's family received a surprise box of groceries. (Passive voice may be considered suitable.)
   8. Hurricanes form over tropical water.
   9. The high winds leveled most of the town. (Passive voice may be considered suitable because of the disaster.)
   10. Thunder growled (rumbled, muttered) in the distance.

B. 1. We know that Jesus tenderly cares for His own. He declared plainly, "I am the Good Shepherd."
   2. Jesus called to Zacchaeus, "Hurry, and come down."

3. Material things can never truly satisfy. Even though Solomon gained an incredible store of wealth, he had to admit that all is vanity.

Written Exercises

A. Try to improve each sentence by making the subject perform the action of the verb. (Supply a subject or use a different verb if necessary.) If the passive voice is more suitable, explain why.
   1. The whole land of Canaan was viewed by Moses from Mount Pisgah.
   2. In Noah's time, the earth was destroyed by a flood.
   3. The ministry of John the Baptist was rejected by many of the Jews.
   4. The stone was rolled away from Jesus' grave.
   5. Linda's picture is shaded very attractively.
   6. Sulfur is used in the manufacturing of paper.
   7. Exposed flesh is frozen quickly in this extreme cold.
   8. High pressure is produced by forcing the water through a small opening.
   9. An interesting report on the mission in Paraguay was given by Brother Lloyd.
   10. Since Duane is away, the heifers have not yet been fed.

B. Rewrite this paragraph so that it contains no passive verbs and no indirect quotations.

   Of course, that little hole in the fence should not have been ignored by me on that Friday afternoon. But it was not reported to Father because I would probably be told to fix it. My mind was set on finishing my kite, and soon the matter was forgotten. Early on Sunday morning, I was suddenly awakened by a sharp rap on my door. In urgent tones, we boys were told by Father to hurry downstairs because the cornfield was being ruined by the cows. Right away that little hole was remembered. Grandfather Landis could almost be heard by me, saying that little things do not stay little very long.

Review Exercises

A. Rewrite these sentences, improving the unity or coherence. [71]
   1. One week Gerald visited his cousin Luke. Luke had moved to Virginia.
   2. Luke told Gerald that he had never climbed to the top of the mountain behind the house.
   3. That day the boys almost climbed to the peak.
   4. They would, as a matter of fact, have climbed all the way up, but they could not have returned before dark.
   5. They would try again someday, the next time they would start earlier.

B. Rewrite these sentences, improving the conciseness or parallelism. [73]
   1. The swifts, swallows, and the martins are common birds in Palestine.
   2. The Bible speaks of swallows flying, chattering, building nests, and that they migrate at the proper time.

B. (Allow reasonable variation.)
   1. The swifts, the swallows, and the martins are common birds in Palestine.
   2. The Bible speaks of swallows flying, chattering, building nests, and migrating at the proper time.

---

3. Material things can never truly satisfy. Even though Solomon gained an incredible store of wealth, he had to admit, "All is vanity."

Written Exercises

A. (Allow reasonable variation.)
   1. Moses viewed the whole land of Canaan from Mount Pisgah.
   2. In Noah's time, a flood destroyed the earth. (Passive voice may be considered suitable because of the disaster.)
   3. Many of the Jews rejected the ministry of John the Baptist.
   4. An angel rolled the stone away from Jesus' grave.
   5. Linda shaded her picture very attractively.
   6. (Passive voice is suitable because there is no clear doer.)
   7. Exposed flesh freezes quickly in this extreme cold.
   8. Forcing the water through a small opening produces high pressure. (Passive voice may be considered suitable because there is no clear doer.)
   9. Brother Lloyd gave an interesting report on the mission in Paraguay.
   10. Since Duane is away, no one has fed the heifers yet.

B. (Allow reasonable variation.)

   Of course, I should not have ignored that little hole in the fence on that Friday afternoon. But I did not report it to Father because he would probably tell me to fix it. I had set my mind on finishing my kite, and soon I forgot the matter. Early on Sunday morning, a sharp rap on my door suddenly awakened me. In urgent tones, Father said, "Boys, hurry downstairs. The cows are ruining the cornfield." Right away I remembered that little hole. I could almost hear Grandfather Landis saying, "Little things do not stay little very long."

Review Exercises

A. (Allow reasonable variation.)
   1. One week Gerald visited his cousin Luke, who had moved to Virginia.
   2. Luke said, "Gerald, I (or You) have never climbed to the top of the mountain behind the house."
   3. That day the boys climbed almost to the peak.
   4. As a matter of fact, they would have climbed all the way up; but they could not have returned before dark.
   5. They would try again someday, but the next time they would start earlier.

3. Swifts rarely perch on branches because of the fact that their feet are weak and small in size.
4. When you watch a chimney swift in flight, one gets the impression that its wings beat alternately.
5. Fast high-speed photography proves that the wings actually beat together in unison.

---

76. Writing Effective Sentences: Emphasis

> **Lesson Survey**
> • Effective sentences give proper emphasis to the ideas that they express.
>   1. Repeat key words for emphasis.
>   2. Write sentences of different styles for varying degrees of emphasis.

When you write, some of your sentences state main ideas, others give supporting ideas, and still others simply provide information for additional interest and meaning. Naturally, you want to emphasize some ideas more and other ideas less. How can you arrange words to show the proper emphasis clearly and naturally? This lesson will help you to write sentences in a way that best suits the purpose of each one.

Repetition of Key Words

Effective sentences emphasize the most important ideas. One way to emphasize ideas is by repeating key words. But you must do this carefully because thoughtless or clumsy repetition mars proper emphasis. Then you will detract from the very idea that you are trying to emphasize.

If repetition is to be effective, the repeated words must have the same meaning but serve in different settings. For example, if a noun or verb is repeated, it should have different modifiers each time. A repeated adjective should describe different nouns, and a repeated adverb should describe different verbs. The repetition must do more than merely repeat the same idea.

> **Unemphatic:** No repetition
>   <u>Beautiful</u> thoughts produce kind words and right actions.
> **Emphatic:** Proper repetition
>   <u>Beautiful</u> thoughts produce <u>beautiful</u> words and <u>beautiful</u> actions.
>   (*Beautiful* has the same meaning each time, and it describes three different nouns.)

Lesson 76

Purpose: To teach how to write effective sentences that have proper emphasis.

Oral Review:

1. Name the five qualities, which you have studied in this chapter, that contribute to effective sentences. (unity, coherence, conciseness, parallelism, action)
2. Which of the following expressions has better coherence: *to quietly listen* or *to listen quietly*? (to listen quietly)
3. State each of these expressions more concisely.
   a. sky that is blue in color (blue sky)
   b. a huge, enormous rock (a huge rock *or* an enormous rock)
   c. the man who was driving the green car (the driver of the green car)

---

3. Swifts rarely perch on branches because their feet are weak and small.
4. When you watch a chimney swift in flight, you get the impression that its wings beat alternately.
5. High-speed photography proves that the wings actually beat in unison.

---

4. State each of these expressions with improved parallelism.
   a. the ducks, geese, and the chickens (the ducks, the geese, and the chickens)
   b. diligently and with care (diligently and carefully)
5. What are two ways to have sentences with action? (Make the subject perform the action. Use direct quotations.)

Lesson Introduction: It is hard to explain why one piece of writing appeals to you while another piece does not. This is something like trying to explain why one song or picture is more beautiful than another. Yet beauty is not completely abstract and indefinable. Just as there are general rules for artists who compose songs or draw pictures, there are rules for artists who work with words. This lesson gives some guidelines for having effective emphasis in sentences.

Unemphatic: Poor repetition
> A <u>kind</u> person is careful about the <u>kind</u> of words he speaks. (*Kind* has two different meanings.)

Emphatic: Proper repetition
> A <u>kind</u> person is careful to speak <u>kind</u> words. (*Kind* has the same meaning each time, and it describes two different nouns.)

Unemphatic: Poor repetition
> A selfish person is <u>unkind</u> and <u>demanding</u> and often <u>demands</u> things <u>unkindly</u> from others. (The underlined words merely repeat the same idea.)

Emphatic: Proper repetition
> A <u>selfish</u> person thinks about <u>himself</u>, talks about <u>himself</u>, and demands many things for <u>himself</u>. (*Self* has the same meaning in each word, and it serves in four different settings.)

Loose, Periodic, and Balanced Sentences

In Lesson 17 you learned about the three sentence styles: loose, periodic, and balanced. As stated there, a loose sentence gives the main idea first and the details later. A periodic sentence gives the details first and saves the main idea until last. A balanced sentence has two well-matched clauses.

Most of your sentences should be of the loose variety, giving the main idea first and the details later. This places no special emphasis on the main idea of the sentence. But sometimes you do want to emphasize the main idea. Then you can write a periodic sentence, in which the reader does not come to the main idea until he reaches the end of the sentence. This builds up his suspense so that when he finally comes to the main idea, it makes a stronger impression.

Study the following periodic sentences, which all have the same main idea. Notice how the main idea is delayed longer and longer as more words are added to the first part. Do you see how this causes the suspense to build up?

Periodic sentences: Increasing emphasis on the main idea
> After several days of rainy weather, <u>the sun shone brightly again</u>.
> After several days of rainy weather, during which we were cooped up inside, <u>the sun shone brightly again</u>.
> After several days of rainy weather, during which we were cooped up inside for every recess and could get little exercise, <u>the sun shone brightly again</u>.

Loose sentence: No particular emphasis on the main idea
> <u>The sun shone brightly again</u> after several days of rainy weather, during which we were cooped up inside for every recess and could get little exercise.

Lesson Outline:

An effective sentence gives proper emphasis to the idea that it expresses.

    a. Repeat key words for emphasis. If repetition is to be effective, the repeated words must have the same meaning but serve in different settings. The repetition must do more than merely repeat the same idea.

    b. Write sentences of different styles for varying degrees of emphasis. A loose sentence gives the main idea first and the details later. A periodic sentence gives the details first and saves the main idea until last. A balanced sentence has two well-matched clauses.

        1) A loose sentence gives no special emphasis to its main idea. Most sentences should be of this style.

        2) A periodic sentence gives greater emphasis to its main idea.

        3) A balanced sentence can produce a striking emphasis because of its well-matched parts and its deft rewording.

        4) If a writer overuses periodic and balanced sentences, his writing will not only sound unnatural but will also lose its emphasis.

★ ***EXTRA PRACTICE***
Worksheet 30 (*Action and Emphasis in Sentences*)

Now read this paragraph from "The Rickshaw Puller of Calcutta." The last sentence is periodic. Notice how it effectively emphasizes a main idea.

> Rising, Hari strides purposefully toward his rickshaw. For him as well as for tens of thousands of others, pulling a rickshaw is the only possible way to earn his family's support. This makes him the envy of his less-fortunate neighbors. For the privilege, however, he must pay rent of five to ten rupees per day—usually about one-fourth of his earnings. <u>When the grueling strain finally breaks his health, other pullers will gladly take his place.</u>

For even stronger emphasis, write a balanced sentence sometimes. A sentence of the pattern "the more . . . the more" is more emphatic than a loose or periodic sentence. More striking still is a balanced sentence in which a slight change of wording produces a notable or unexpected contrast. The deft rewording often catches the reader by surprise and makes a pleasing and lasting impression on him. Such a sentence is emphatic by its very nature.

Loose sentence: No particular emphasis
We loaded the hay faster as the storm came nearer.

Balanced sentence: Strong emphasis
The nearer the storm came, the faster we loaded the hay.

Loose sentence: No particular emphasis
Happiness does not bring thankfulness; it comes from thankfulness.

Balanced sentence: Strong emphasis
It's not the happy people who are thankful; it's the thankful people who are happy.

Remember that you should write periodic and balanced sentences as a way to produce special emphasis. If you overuse them, your writing will not only sound unnatural but will also lose its emphasis.

Class Practice

A. Tell which sentence in each pair is more emphatic, and explain why.
1. a. Satan is mighty, but God is almighty.
   b. Satan has mighty power, but God is almighty, we know.
2. a. Today, as always since the Fall, the main problem in the world is sin.
   b. Today sin is the main problem in the world, as always since the Fall.
3. a. Joseph was a forgiving young man who forgave everyone that wronged him.
   b. Joseph is a model of forgiveness: he forgave his unjust master, forgave the negligent butler, and even forgave the brothers who had sold him.

Lesson 76 Answers

Class Practice

A. 1. a; a balanced sentence
   2. a; a periodic sentence (main idea at the end)
   3. b; has effective repetition

4. a. You can complain that roses have thorns, or you can be thankful that thorns have roses.
   b. You can complain that roses are thorny, or you can be thankful that thorn bushes have roses on them.
5. a. I have never done, never suggested, never even considered such a thing.
   b. I have not done such a thing, and I have never suggested it or even considered it.
6. a. Little Timmy sat at the edge of the flooded creek, playing innocently.
   b. At the edge of the creek, playing innocently, sat little Timmy.
7. a. Aunt Lucinda was faithful in her everyday tasks, faithful in her relationships with others, and faithful in her devotion to the Lord.
   b. Aunt Lucinda was faithful in her everyday tasks, in her relationships with others, and in her devotion to the Lord.
8. a. When she prayed more, God could bless her more.
   b. The more she prayed, the more God could bless her.

B. Tell how to make these sentences more emphatic.
1. Thomas Edison finally developed a practical electric light after many failures.
2. I was sick in just two days—in the stomach and in the head, and sick of the whole idea of traveling by sea.
3. John felt renewed courage after he discussed his problem with Father.
4. As we heed the Bible more, we become wiser.

C. Add words to make a balanced sentence from each item.
1. Duty is not beneficial because it is commanded, but it is . . .
2. Seek not to do what you like; seek . . .
3. Nothing is as strong as gentleness, and nothing . . .
4. Selfishness with much can do little, but love . . .

Written Exercises

A. Rewrite these sentences, improving the emphasis.
1. The frogs were everywhere—in the houses, in the bedrooms, in the ovens, and in the baking utensils.
2. Sincere Christians willingly follow their Master in spite of trials.
3. Getting Israel out of Egypt was hard, but it was harder to get Egypt out of Israel.
4. Balaam wanted to die the death of the righteous, but he did not want to live a godly life.

4. a; a balanced sentence
5. a; has effective repetition
6. b; a periodic sentence
7. a; has effective repetition
8. b; a balanced sentence

B. 1. After many failures, Thomas Edison finally developed a practical electric light.
2. I was sick in just two days—sick in the stomach, sick in the head, and sick of the whole idea of traveling by sea.
3. After he discussed his problem with Father, John felt renewed courage.
4. The more we heed the Bible, the wiser we become.

C. 1. Duty is not beneficial because it is commanded, but it is commanded because it is beneficial.
2. Seek not to do what you like; seek to like what you do.
3. Nothing is as strong as gentleness, and nothing is as gentle as true strength.
4. Selfishness with much can do little, but love with little can do much.

Written Exercises

A. (Allow reasonable variation.)
1. The frogs were everywhere—frogs in the houses, frogs in the bedrooms, frogs in the ovens, and frogs in the baking utensils.
2. In spite of trials, sincere Christians willingly follow their Master.
3. Getting Israel out of Egypt was hard, but getting Egypt out of Israel was harder.
4. Balaam wanted to die the death of the righteous, but he did not want to live the life of the righteous.

5. Sister Ludwig seems happy all the time—about the weather, with her neighbors, and about heaven.
6. A fierce hurricane pounded the island for several hours.
7. As a person learns more, he realizes his ignorance more.
8. The complete stillness was impressive—the water, the forest, the very atmosphere so still that the memory still lingers in my mind.

. Add words to make a balanced sentence from each item. Write the whole sentences.
1. You can give without loving, but you cannot . . .
2. Pray not for tasks equal to your strength; pray for . . .
3. Apply yourself to the Scriptures, and apply . . .
4. We often are afraid that God will not hear us, when we should be afraid . . .

Review Exercises

. Rewrite these sentences, making them more active. [75]
1. A strong commitment to right is needed by those who would overcome temptation.
2. Intense pressure to yield can be brought by unwholesome friends.
3. Grandfather often says that character is more important than reputation.
4. Every secret thought is known by our heavenly Father.

. Rewrite these sentences, improving the unity or coherence. [71]
1. Soaring majestically above the mountains, we watched the bald eagle.
2. We had several inches of rain last night, the Muddy Creek is flooded.
3. Baby Louella almost walked the whole way across the room.
4. Our goats have, now that the spring grass is growing, been eating no hay.

. Rewrite these sentences, improving the conciseness or parallelism. [73]
1. A big bird that was beautiful flew silently with hardly any noise toward the pond.
2. We sing in family worship and before we eat supper.
3. When one looks into the starry heavens, they are awed by God's greatness.
4. This donkey has always and still is refusing to pull a cart.

5. Sister Ludwig seems happy all the time—happy about the weather, happy with her neighbors, and happy about heaven.
6. For several hours a fierce hurricane pounded the island.
7. The more a person learns, the more he realizes his ignorance.
8. The complete stillness was impressive—the still water, the still forest, the very atmosphere so still that the memory lingers in my mind to this day.

B. 1. You can give without loving, but you cannot love without giving.
2. Pray not for tasks equal to your strength; pray for strength equal to your tasks.
3. Apply yourself to the Scriptures, and apply the Scriptures to yourself.
4. We often are afraid that God will not hear us, when we should be afraid that we will not hear God.

Review Exercises
(Allow reasonable variation.)
A. 1. Those who would overcome temptation need a strong commitment to right.
2. Unwholesome friends can bring intense pressure to yield.
3. Grandfather often says, "Character is more important than reputation."
4. Our heavenly Father knows every secret thought.

B. 1. We watched the bald eagle soaring majestically above the mountains.
2. We had several inches of rain last night, and the Muddy Creek is flooded.
3. Baby Louella walked almost the whole way across the room.
4. Now that the spring grass is growing, our goats have been eating no hay.

C. 1. A big, beautiful bird flew silently toward the pond.
2. We sing in family worship and before supper.
3. When one looks into the starry heavens, he is awed by God's greatness.
4. This donkey has always refused and still is refusing to pull a cart.

77. Interrogative and Relative Pronouns

Lesson Survey

- The words *who, whom, whose, which,* and *what* are **interrogative pronouns** when they introduce questions.

- The words *who, whom, whose, which,* and *that* are **relative pronouns** when they introduce adjective clauses.

- The relative pronouns *who* and *whom* refer only to people, *which* refers only to things, and *that* and *whose* refer to either people or things.

- *Who* is nominative case, *whom* is objective case, and *whose* is possessive case.

In the previous grammar lessons of this chapter, you have studied four classes of pronouns: personal, compound personal, demonstrative, and indefinite. The remaining two classes, interrogative and relative, consist of almost identical groups of pronouns. However, these pronouns are placed in different classes because they have different functions within a sentence.

Interrogative Pronouns

The words *who, whom, whose, which,* and *what* are *interrogative pronouns* when they introduce questions. Each of these pronouns also serves some function in the sentence.

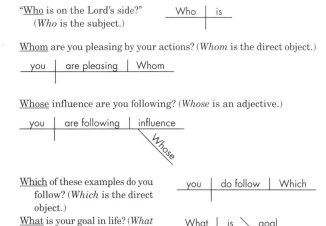

"Who is on the Lord's side?"   Who | is
    (*Who* is the subject.)

Whom are you pleasing by your actions? (*Whom* is the direct object.)

you | are pleasing | Whom

Whose influence are you following? (*Whose* is an adjective.)

you | are following | influence
                         Whose

Which of these examples do you   you | do follow | Which
    follow? (*Which* is the direct
    object.)
What is your goal in life? (*What*   What | is \ goal
    is the subject.)

Lesson 77

Purpose: To study the correct uses of interrogative and relative pronouns.

Oral Review:

1. Tell whether the indefinite pronouns in each group are always singular, always plural, or either singular or plural.
   a. few, both, several, many (always plural)
   b. all, any, most, none, some (either)
   c. another, anything, someone, either (always singular)
2. The pronouns *this, that, these,* and *those* are in which class? (demonstrative)
3. Name the compound personal pronouns in these sentences, and tell whether they are used intensively or reflexively. (Pronouns are underlined.)

a. John the Baptist felt <u>himself</u> unworthy to bap tize Jesus. (reflexively)
b. John the Baptist <u>himself</u> asked if Jesus wa the Christ. (intensively)
4. Give the second and third principal parts of thes verbs.
   a. fall (fell, [have] fallen)
   b. cut (cut, [have] cut)
   c. weep (wept, [have] wept)
   d. leave (left, [have] left)
   e. tag (tagged, [have] tagged)
   f. bring (brought, [have] brought)
   g. drown (drowned, [have] drowned)
   h. draw (drew, [have] drawn)
5. Tell whether the verb in each sentence is trans tive, intransitive complete, or intransitive linking
   a. Noah was a man of strong faith. (intransitiv linking)

Relative Pronouns

The words *who, whom, whose, which,* and *that* are *relative pronouns* when they introduce adjective clauses. A relative pronoun is so named because it relates the adjective clause to an antecedent in the main clause. Like an interrogative pronoun, a relative pronoun not only introduces an adjective clause but also serves some function in that clause.

The Lord God, *who* rules over all, is worthy of all glory. (*Who* relates the clause to the antecedent *Lord God.*)

Jesus, *whom* God sent into the world, has revealed the Father to man. (*Whom* relates the clause to the antecedent *Jesus.*)

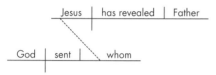

Satan, *whose* hatred against truth is intense, has deceived many. (*Whose* relates the clause to the antecedent *Satan.*)

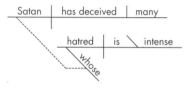

God's people seek the way *that* is right. (*That* relates the clause to the antecedent *way.*)

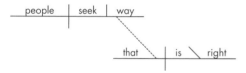

Be sure to use these pronouns correctly. The relative pronouns *who* and

b. In the midst of an evil society, he lived righteously. (intransitive complete)

c. He unflinchingly obeyed the voice of God. (transitive)

d. He and his family were marvelously preserved from the Flood. (transitive)

Lesson Introduction: Write the following sentence on the board: *Jesus raised the widow's son.* Have the students suggest questions for which this sentence could be an answer. (Who raised the widow's son? What did Jesus do? Whom did Jesus raise? Whose son did Jesus raise?) These questions, like many factual questions, begin with interrogative pronouns.

Lesson Outline:

1. The words who, whom, whose, which, *and* what *are interrogative pronouns when they*

introduce questions. Each of these pronouns also serves some function in the sentence.

2. The words who, whom, whose, which, *and* that *are relative pronouns when they introduce adjective clauses.*

a. A relative pronoun is so named because it relates the adjective clause to an antecedent in the main clause.

b. A relative pronoun not only introduces an adjective clause but also serves some function in that clause.

3. The relative pronouns who *and* whom *refer only to people,* which *refers only to things, and* that *and* whose *refer to either people or things.*

4. Who *is nominative case,* whom *is objective case, and* whose *is possessive case.*

★ **EXTRA PRACTICE**
Worksheet 31 (*Interrogative and Relative Pronouns*)

whom refer only to people, *which* refers only to things, and *that* and *whose* refer to either people or things. In the King James Bible, however, *which* is often used in referring to persons.

Incorrect:
A student <u>which</u> does his best is rewarded for his diligence.
Our pet lamb, <u>who</u> greatly enjoys attention, has become a nuisance.

Correct:
A student <u>who</u> does his best is rewarded for his diligence.
Our pet lamb, <u>which</u> greatly enjoys attention, has become a nuisance.
The preacher <u>that</u> had devotions told a story <u>that</u> I had heard before.
A boy <u>whose</u> clothes were ragged clung to a book <u>whose</u> covers were missing.
"The kingdom of heaven is likened unto a man <u>which</u> sowed good seed in his field" (Matthew 13:24).

The pronouns *who, whom,* and *whose* are actually three forms of the same word, used to show different case. *Who* is nominative case, *whom* is objective case, and *whose* is possessive case.

Uncle Bennet, <u>who</u> is a missionary in Mexico, has written a book.
(Subject of clause requires nominative *who.*)
Your teacher will be <u>who</u>?
(Predicate nominative of sentence requires nominative *who.*)
Lisa Gardner, <u>whom</u> I haven't met for years, plans to visit us soon.
(Direct object of clause requires objective *whom.*)
To <u>whom</u> are you writing this letter?
(Object of preposition requires objective *whom.*)
<u>Whose</u> bicycle do you want to ride? (Adjective must be possessive *whose.*)

Class Practice

A. Tell whether the underlined pronouns are *interrogative* or *relative.*
 1. A young person <u>who</u> honors his parents makes his own life easier.
 2. <u>Whose</u> advice do you seek?
 3. <u>Which</u> of the minor prophets was a gatherer of sycamore fruit?
 4. Why did Solomon, <u>whom</u> God had richly blessed, turn to idols?
 5. <u>What</u> does the Lord require of us?
 6. The man <u>whose</u> daughter had died was Jairus.

B. Read each adjective clause, and give the antecedent of the relative pronoun.
 1. The geese that Edna raised have been selling well.
 2. The neighbor whose cows got into our garden has offered to pay for the damage.

Lesson 77 Answers

Class Practice

A. 1. relative
   2. interrogative
   3. interrogative
   4. relative
   5. interrogative
   6. relative

B. 1. that Edna raised—geese
   2. whose cows got into our garden—neighbor

3. From a distance we watched the skunk family which ambled across the road.
4. Amy Kreider, who works for Burkholder's Dry Goods, boards with my grandparents.
5. Conrad Landis, whom you met before, will spend the weekend with us.

C. Read each sentence, using the correct pronoun in parentheses.
1. Adam named the animals (whom, which) God brought to him.
2. Samson, (who, whom) abused his great strength in various ways, apparently died in faith.
3. (Who, Whom) did the three Hebrew young men fear?
4. Many of the people (who, which) followed Jesus turned back when He set forth the conditions of discipleship.

D. Read each pronoun in these sentences, and identify it as *personal, compound personal, demonstrative, indefinite, interrogative,* or *relative.* Include the possessive pronouns used as adjectives.
1. King Herod beheaded John the Baptist, whose bold condemnation of sin earned him the hatred of many.
2. Actually Herod himself respected John, but Herodias hated him.
3. When the king promised to give Herodias's daughter anything she wanted, who would have imagined that the result would be someone's death?
4. Herodias's daughter herself did not think of this; her mother was responsible for the idea.
5. Anyone who would tell her daughter to ask for a man's head must have been filled with bitterness and rage.
6. This was a grief to King Herod, but many had heard his oath.

Written Exercises

A. Copy each interrogative or relative pronoun, and label it *I* or *R.* After each relative pronoun, also write its antecedent.
1. Who was the man who viewed the Promised Land?
2. What did Isaiah understand about himself when he saw the Lord, whose train filled the temple?
3. How did Nehemiah answer the enemies whom he was facing?
4. This is the day that the Lord has made.
5. Whom did Goliath challenge in those words which he flung across the valley?

B. Write the correct pronouns in parentheses.
1. (Who, Whom) did we see in town this morning?
2. Linda's cat, (who, which) mysteriously came to our house, is an excellent mouser.

3. which ambled across the road—family
4. who works for Burkholder's Dry Goods—Amy Kreider
5. whom you met before—Conrad Landis

C. (Corrections are underlined.)
1. Adam named the animals <u>which</u> God brought to him.
2. Samson, <u>who</u> abused his great strength in various ways, apparently died in faith.
3. <u>Whom</u> did the three Hebrew young men fear?
4. Many of the people <u>who</u> followed Jesus turned back when He set forth the conditions of discipleship.

D. 1. whose—relative; him—personal; many—indefinite
2. himself—compound personal; him—personal
3. anything—indefinite; she—personal; who—interrogative; someone's—indefinite (*That* introduces a noun clause.)
4. herself—compound personal; this—demonstrative; her—personal
5. Anyone—indefinite; who—relative; her—personal
6. This—demonstrative; many—indefinite; his—personal

Written Exercises

A. 1. Who—I; who—R, man
2. What—I; whose—R, Lord
3. whom—R, enemies
4. that—R, day
5. Whom—I; which—R, words

B. 1. Whom
2. which

3. Jonathan Groff, (who, whom) is staying with Uncle Laban, enjoys working with wood.
4. Father is talking to the feed salesman, (who, which) just arrived.
5. Randy asked, "The man out there is (who, whom)?"

C. Copy each pronoun, and write whether it is personal (P), compound personal (CP), demonstrative (D), indefinite (ID), interrogative (IR), or relative (R). Include the possessive pronouns used as adjectives.
1. What are the goals that you have for yourself?
2. One of these should be the goal of faithfulness to God and His Word.
3. Who is more worthy of our devotion than God Himself?
4. This has been an unusual experience, but we praise God, whose grace has been with us through everything.
5. Should anybody ever distrust God, whom we know can never fail?
6. Glen, who is a year older than I, is one of my best friends.
7. The flowers that somebody gave to Grandmother are blooming nicely.
8. Which of these do you want for yourself?

Review Exercises

A. Write the correct past form of each verb in parentheses. [46]
1. Have you (choose) your words carefully and thoughtfully?
2. If you have (speak) true and kind words, you can have peace of heart.
3. All day the children (do) helpful chores for their sick mother.
4. Father has (go) to Ohio for a special ministers' meeting.
5. Did someone (hurt) your feelings?
6. Have you gladly (forgive) him?
7. After the wicked servant (deny) forgiveness to his fellow servant, his master also refused to forgive him.
8. The faithful martyrs, who (see) life from an eternal perspective, were willing to suffer for Christ.

B. Write whether each verb is transitive (T), intransitive complete (IC), or intransitive linking (IL). [52–55]
1. Father is reading Psalm 46.
2. His voice sounds calm and pleasant.
3. The family is listening quietly to him.
4. Family worship is a time for reverence.
5. By our worship we are prepared to face the day's activities.
6. My parents' prayers go with me throughout the day.

3. who
4. who
5. who

C. 1. What—IR; that—R; you—P; yourself—CP
2. One—ID; these—D; His—P
3. Who—IR; our—P; Himself—CP
4. This—D; we—P; whose—R; us—P; everything—ID
5. anybody—ID; whom—R; we—P
6. who—R; I—P; one—ID; my—P
7. that—R; somebody—ID
8. Which—IR; these—D; you—P; yourself—CP

Review Exercises

A. 1. chosen
2. spoken
3. did
4. gone
5. hurt
6. forgiven
7. denied
8. saw

B. 1. T
2. IL
3. IC
4. IL
5. T
6. IC

78. Writing Effective Sentences: Variety

Lesson Survey
- An effective paragraph has good sentence variety.
- Good sentence variety includes varying the length, the word order, the beginnings, the type according to use, and the type according to structure.

When you write a paragraph, you should not sound as if you were giving a list of facts. The sentences should be varied in a way that is appealing and well balanced. Simply having variety is worthwhile, but variety that emphasizes the main points is especially valuable.

In this lesson you will study five kinds of sentence variety. Not every paragraph will have every one of these kinds of variety, but nearly every paragraph should have at least one or two of them. The different kinds of variety are illustrated with paragraphs adapted from the essay "Born to Fly."

1. *Write sentences of various lengths.* A paragraph of too many short sentences sounds choppy. On the other hand, a paragraph of too many long sentences is tiresome and may be hard to understand. Compare the following examples. The varied sentence lengths in the third paragraph make it much better than the other two.

Poor: Seven short, choppy sentences

> Birds' feathers are complex in structure and function. A pigeon's primary wing feather has more than a million parts. There are vanes and barbs and barbules. There are flanges and tiny hooks. These work together to form a natural zipper. The zipper comes open sometimes. It can be zipped up again by preening.

Poor: Two long, rambling sentences

> Birds' feathers are complex in structure and function; we are told that a pigeon's primary wing feather has more than a million parts, which include vanes and barbs and barbules and flanges and tiny hooks. These all work together to form a natural zipper; and when the zipper comes open, it can be zipped up again by preening.

Good: Four sentences of various lengths

> Birds' feathers are complex in structure and function. We are told that a pigeon's primary wing feather has more than a million parts. There are vanes and barbs and barbules and flanges and tiny hooks, and they all work together to form a natural zipper. When the zipper comes open, it can be zipped up again by preening.

Lesson 78

Purpose: To teach how to write effective sentences that have good variety.

Oral Review:

1. Name the six qualities, which you have studied in this chapter, that contribute to effective sentences. (unity, coherence, conciseness, parallelism, action, emphasis)
2. Tell which phrase has better parallelism: *(a) through the room and outside,* or *(b) through the room and out the door.* (phrase *b*)
3. What are two ways to make sentences active and lively? (Make the subject perform the action. Use direct quotations.)
4. What are two ways to achieve proper emphasis in sentences? (Repeat key words. Write loose, periodic, and balanced sentences.)

5. What three things mar sentence unity? (writing run-on errors; joining poorly related ideas; separating closely related ideas)
6. Name several ways to make sentences coherent. (avoiding unclear pronoun reference; avoiding misplaced modifiers; avoiding the careless separation of closely related sentence parts)

Lesson Introduction: God's vast creation demonstrates that He is a God of variety. Because of that variety, we have an endless array of different creatures to study and enjoy. In like manner, our writing should have variety.

Have you ever experimented with a sentence to see how many different ways it can be worded? For example, here is the third line from the famous "Elegy Written in a Country Churchyard," by Thomas Gray.

The plowman homeward plods his weary way.

Differing sentence lengths can be used not only for variety but also for emphasis. If a short, direct sentence comes after several longer sentences, the point of that sentence is sharply emphasized. This is especially effective at the end of a paragraph.

> The bones of a bird are extremely light. They are also hollow and full of warm, buoyant air. For instance, although a man-o'-war bird has a wingspan of about seven feet, its bones weigh only four or five ounces. Think of it—its feathers actually weigh more than its skeleton! <u>And feathers are light, you know.</u>

2. *Write sentences with a variety of word order.* Because natural word order is the simplest and most direct, it is used the most often. Mixed word order is also fairly common. Inverted word order, which is used quite sparingly, often is catchy and emphatic. Writing good sentences with inverted word order may take special effort.

In the following paragraph, the first sentence has inverted order and the second has mixed order. All the other sentences are in natural word order.

> There is even more. As a bird flies, every slight change in air flow is automatically compensated. The flight feathers of the wing tip act like the propeller of an airplane. They change pitch in response to the changing stresses that the air exerts upon them. The base part of the wing acts like the wing of an airplane. And the secondary and tertiary wing feathers function as flaps.

3. *Use a variety of sentence beginnings.* With mixed and inverted word order, your sentences will naturally begin in various ways. Here are some specific pointers for this kind of variety.

  a. *Begin with a single-word adverb, an adverb phrase, or an adverb clause.* This of course will result in a sentence with mixed word order.

  b. *Begin with a transitional expression.* This includes words like *and, but, therefore, in addition,* and *for example.*

  c. *Reverse the normal noun-appositive order.* If the subject of a sentence is followed by an appositive, write the appositive first for variety.

> Timothy, a sensible young man, soon figured out a way to fix the wagon. (subject first)
> A sensible young man, Timothy soon figured out a way to fix the wagon. (appositive first)

4. *Vary the sentence types according to use.* You should be well acquainted with these types: declarative, interrogative, imperative, and exclamatory.

It is said that these words can be rearranged in more than twenty different ways, all with much the same meaning. Five of them are shown below.

> The plowman plods his homeward weary way.
> The plowman plods his weary homeward way.
> His weary way the plowman homeward plods.
> His homeward weary way the plowman plods.
> Homeward the weary plowman plods his way.

With so many possibilities, there is little reason for sentences to follow the same monotonous pattern! The example above is unusual, of course; but if we put forth some effort, we can usually find one way or another to write sentences with appealing variety.

Lesson Outline:

1. To produce effective paragraphs, write sentences of various lengths. Differing sentence lengths can be used not only for variety but also for emphasis. If a short, direct sentence comes after several longer sentences, the point of that sentence is sharply emphasized.

2. Write sentences with a variety of word order.

  a. Natural word order, which is the simplest and most direct, should be used the most often.

  b. Mixed word order is also fairly common.

  c. Inverted word order, which is used quite sparingly, often is catchy and emphatic.

3. Use a variety of sentence beginnings. This happens naturally if sentences have mixed and inverted word order.

  (a) *Begin with a single-word adverb, an adverb phrase, or an adverb clause.*

lthough most of your sentences will be declarative, a sprinkling of the ther types adds variety. Notice how this is true in the following para- raphs, which include all four sentence types.

> But now listen. Embedded in the skin near the quill of each flight feather are nerve endings that actually convert the feathers into sensory receptors. They record the precise position of every feather. Then, by way of the spinal cord, they bring about continuous adjustment in the more than twelve thousand tiny muscles attached to the base of the feathers!
>
> That still is not everything. The precise body position of the bird is recorded by the semicircular canals of the inner ear. And the inner ear reports the changing conditions to the cerebellum of the bird's brain. What do you think of that?

Some beginning writers think many things are exclamatory! But an xclamation point is appropriate only if the sentence has something truly mphatic to say.

5. *Vary the sentence types according to structure.* In Chapter 2 you stud- ed these four types: simple, compound, complex, and compound-complex.)f course, most of your sentences will be simple. There should be a sprin- ;ling of compound and complex sentences. Compound-complex sentences hould be less common; many compositions have none. The "good" sample •aragraph under point 1 above has three of the four sentence types accord- ng to structure.

Variety is the spice of life; it is not the meat and potatoes. Therefore, lo not think that you must make every sentence different and catchy. Just •prinkle enough variety through your writing to make your compositions •ppealing and flavorful.

Class Practice

A. Change the word order or the beginning of each sentence.
1. Little Charles, a timid boy, feared thunderstorms.
2. He was playing at the creek one bright summer day.
3. The creek was shallow and excellent for wading at their place.
4. A horse and wagon came down a nearby country road.
5. A distant rumble sounded suddenly.
6. Charles ran home like a frightened rabbit.
7. Mother soon solved the riddle of the "thunder."
8. The wagon, making a rumble like thunder, had bumped across a wooden bridge.
9. Mother reminded Charles again not to be so fearful.
10. We should trust in God because He will surely watch over us.

(b) *Begin with a transitional expression.*
(c) *Reverse the normal noun-appositive order.* If the subject of a sentence is followed by an appositive, write the appositive first for variety.

4. Vary the sentence types according to use. Most of your sentences will be declarative, but a sprinkling of interrogative, imperative, and exclamatory sentences adds variety.

5. Vary the sentence types according to structure. Most of your sentences will be simple, some should be compound and complex, and a very few may be compound-complex.

Lesson 78 Answers

Class Practice

A. 1. A timid boy, little Charles feared thunderstorms.
2. One bright summer day he was playing at the creek.
3. At their place the creek was shallow and excellent for wading.
4. Down a nearby country road came a horse and wagon.
5. Suddenly a distant rumble sounded.
6. Like a frightened rabbit, Charles ran home. *or* Home ran Charles like a frightened rabbit.
7. Soon Mother solved the riddle of the "thunder."
8. Making a rumble like thunder, the wagon had bumped across a wooden bridge.
9. Again Mother reminded Charles not to be so fearful.
10. Because He will surely watch over us, we should trust in God.

B. Tell how to improve the sentence variety and emphasis by having a short sentence come after several longer ones.
   1. The lurking predator, which was a panther, was effectively concealed by the thick branches of the tree. Two furry ears and the crown of his head were all that could be seen of the beast.
   2. Louis developed the first practical system of reading and writing for blind people. The system could be applied to arithmetic and even to music. Thus an accident to a small boy started a chain of events that has enriched thousands of lives, for the boy's full name was Louis Braille.

C. Combine each pair into a compound or complex sentence.
   1. The Lord will hear us. We call upon Him.
   2. Martha went out to meet Jesus. Mary stayed in the house.
   3. Help your enemy. He is in trouble.
   4. The Lord was displeased with Israel. Achan had sinned.
   5. Jeremiah warned, "Repent and return to the Lord. You will go into captivity."

D. The following paragraph consists of only declarative sentences. Reword one sentence to make it interrogative and one to make it exclamatory.
   You may know how many lives were lost in World War II. About 55 million people were killed. If all these people could stand in a line, the line would reach (by land) from Anchorage, Alaska to Buenos Aires, Argentina, a distance of over ten thousand miles. This was a great waste of human lives.

Written Exercises

A. Rewrite these sentences so that a short sentence comes after several longer ones.
   1. After putting on his skates, Allen quickly moved out among the beginning skaters. He smiled as he glided easily in and out among them, and then down he went.
   2. Only one person can determine that you will always be honest. Only one person can decide that you will always do right no matter what the cost, and that person is you.

B. These paragraphs are lacking in sentence variety. Show how to improve them by rewriting sentences as indicated in the directions after each paragraph.
   1.   David wanted to fight the giant, so the other men brought him to Saul, but Saul thought he was too young to fight. David insisted that God would grant him victory over the giant, so Saul armed David with his own armor, but David could not use it. He took off the armor and

---

B. 1. The lurking predator was effectively conceale by the thick branches of the tree. Two furr ears and the crown of his head were all tha could be seen of the beast. It was a panther.
   2. Louis developed the first practical system o reading and writing for blind people. The sys tem could be applied to arithmetic and eve to music. Thus an accident to a small bo started a chain of events that has enriche thousands of lives. For the boy's full name wa Louis Braille.

C. 1. The Lord will hear us when we call upon Him
   2. Martha went out to meet Jesus, but Mar stayed in the house.
      or Though Martha went out to meet Jesus Mary stayed in the house.
   3. Help your enemy if he is in trouble.
      or Help your enemy when he is in trouble.
   4. The Lord was displeased with Israel, for Acha had sinned.
      or The Lord was displeased with Israel be cause Achan had sinned.
   5. Jeremiah warned, "Repent and return to th Lord, or you will go into captivity."

D. *Interrogative sentence:* Do you know how man lives were lost in World War II?
   Exclamatory sentence: What a great waste of hu man lives!

Written Exercises

A. 1. After putting on his skates, Allen quickl moved out among the beginning skaters. H smiled as he glided easily in and out among them. Then down he went.
   2. Only one person can determine that you wil always be honest. Only one person can decide that you will always do right no matter wha the cost. That person is you.

B. (Allow reasonable variation.)
   1. a. David wanted to fight the giant. The othe men brought him to Saul, but Saul con sidered him too young to fight.
         or David wanted to fight the giant, so the other men brought him to Saul. Bu Saul considered him too young to fight
      b. When David insisted that God would gran him victory over the giant, Saul armed him with his own armor. But David could no use it.

went out to meet the giant with only his sling and his staff, but Goliath mocked David when he saw him because David was only a youth.

  a. Change the first sentence to one simple sentence and one compound sentence.

  b. Change the second sentence to one simple sentence and one complex sentence.

  c. Change the third sentence to one simple sentence and one complex sentence with two adverb clauses. Begin the complex sentence with one of the adverb clauses.

2.   Simon was a Samaritan magician. You may wonder why the people honored him. They were amazed at the many great signs that he performed. The Samaritans turned away from magic after they believed the Gospel. They received the Holy Ghost when Peter and John laid hands on them. Simon envied such power. He offered money for it. Peter rebuked him soundly. "Pray for me," requested Simon, "that none of these things come upon me."

  a. Change one sentence to an interrogative sentence.

  b. Change one sentence so that the adverb clause comes first.

  c. Change one short sentence to mixed order.

  d. Join two short sentences into a compound sentence.

Review Exercises

A. If the underlined words are incorrect, write them correctly. If they contain no error, write *correct*. [70, 72]

1. Father assigned this job to <u>me and Gary</u>.
2. The ones in charge of the project are <u>Uncle John and he</u>.
3. He or Father will help us when <u>they</u> can.
4. <u>This here</u> is a new kind of work.
5. <u>We boys</u> have never done it before.
6. The men have had more experience than <u>us</u>.
7. Each of the workers has brought <u>their</u> own tools.
8. <u>Them</u> are the nails for the roof.
9. Is that hammer <u>your's</u>?
10. Father bought it for <u>myself</u> last summer.

B. Copy these sentences, and indicate the part of speech that each word is by writing the correct abbreviation above it. Label an infinitive as a single item.

    noun (n.)   adjective (adj.)   conjunction (conj.)

    pronoun (pron.)   adverb (adv.)   interjection (interj.)

    verb (v.)   preposition (prep.)

1. Living in holiness is vitally important for Christians.
2. "Who is he that will harm you, if ye be followers of that which is good?"

---

  c. He took off the armor and went out to meet the giant with only his sling and his staff. When Goliath saw David, he mocked him because David was only a youth.

2. a. Why did the people honor him?

    b. After they believed the Gospel, the Samaritans turned away from magic.

      or When Peter and John laid hands on them, they received the Holy Ghost.

    c. Such power Simon envied.

    d. He offered money for it, but Peter rebuked him soundly.

Review Exercises

A. 1. Gary and me
    2. correct
    3. he
    4. This
    5. correct
    6. we
    7. his
    8. Those
    9. yours
    10. me

B. 1.   n. prep.   n.   v.   adv.   adj.   prep.

      Living in holiness is vitally important for

      n.

      Christians.

    2.   pron. v. pron. pron.   v.   v.   pron. conj. pron. v. n.

      "Who is he that will harm you, if ye be fol-

          prep. pron. pron. v. adj.

      lowers of that which is good?"

3. To suffer for serving God is no disgrace.
4. "Behold, we count them happy which endure."

———————————

79. Chapter 7 Review

Class Practice

A. Name the class of pronouns represented by each list.
   1. this, that, these, those
   2. who, whom, whose, which, that
   3. anybody, everything, each, either
   4. hers, they, we, yours
   5. who, whom, whose, which, what
   6. himself, ourselves, themselves, myself

B. Give personal pronouns to fit these descriptions. Some have two answers, as shown by the numbers in parentheses.
   1. second person, possessive case (2)
   2. third person, singular, nominative case, feminine gender
   3. first person, plural, objective case
   4. third person, singular, possessive case, neuter gender
   5. first person, singular, possessive case (2)
   6. third person, plural, objective case

C. Choose the correct words in parentheses.
   1. Should Carol and (we, us) pick the tomatoes now?
   2. A courteous girl was (she, her).
   3. The farmer and feed salesman ran (his truck, their trucks) into a snowbank.
   4. Did (she, her) ever find the lost book?
   5. (We, Us) dairy farmers must get out of bed early in the morning.
   6. A privileged group of people are (we, us).

D. Reword these sentences, making the pronoun usage clear and correct.
   1. Me and Anthony plan to help Mrs. Lawrence with her mowing.
   2. Sister Edna visited Mrs. Gehr before she moved away. (two ways)
   3. Uncle Laban told Henry that his car had a flat tire. (two ways)

E. Read each sentence, filling in a compound personal pronoun. Tell whether the pronoun is used *intensively* or *reflexively*.
   1. The Israelites prepared ——— for the Passover.
   2. God ——— passed through the land of Egypt.
   3. We must deny ———, take up the cross, and follow Jesus.

Lesson 79

Purpose: To review the concepts taught in Chapter 7.

———————————

                    n.   prep.   n.   n. v. adj.   n.
3. To suffer for serving God is no disgrace.
          interj.   pron. v.   pron.   adj. pron.   v.
4. "Behold, we count them happy which endure."

———————————

Lesson 79 Answers

Class Practice

A. 1. demonstrative   4. personal
   2. relative   5. interrogative
   3. indefinite   6. compound personal

B. 1. your, yours
   2. she
   3. us
   4. its
   5. my, mine
   6. them

C. 1. we   4. she
   2. she   5. We
   3. his truck   6. we

D. 1. Anthony and I plan to help Mrs. Lawrence with her mowing.
   2. Before Sister Edna moved away, she visited Mrs. Gehr.
      or Before Mrs. Gehr moved away, Sister Edna visited her.
   3. Uncle Laban said, "Henry, your car has a flat tire."
      or Uncle Laban said, "Henry, my car has a flat tire."

E. 1. themselves—reflexively
   2. Himself—intensively
   3. ourselves—reflexively

F. Choose the correct words to agree with the indefinite pronouns.
1. All of God's people (have, has) needed to resist the devil.
2. Some of the world's persecution (have, has) resulted in severe suffering for Christians.
3. Each of God's promises (bring, brings) comfort and strength to us.
4. Both of these maps (show, shows) the country's borders.
5. (Do, Does) one of the calves need medicine?

G. Choose the correct interrogative or relative pronoun in each sentence.
1. (Who, Whom) shall we invite to come for dinner?
2. Do you know the family (who, whom) is coming for dinner?
3. The goats (whom, which) you saw in the pasture belong to our neighbor.
4. The girls (who, which) came for milk live down the road.

H. Read each adjective clause, and give the antecedent of the relative pronoun.
1. The high priest, who interceded to God for man, entered the most holy place once a year.
2. There he sprinkled blood on the mercy seat, which was actually the lid on the ark of the covenant.
3. In this way he made atonement for the sins of the people, whom he represented before God.

I. Give the answers.
1. What three things mar sentence unity?
2. Name several ways to make sentences coherent.
3. To have concise sentences, what three things should you avoid?
4. Name six ways to have parallelism in sentences.
5. Name two ways to improve the action in sentences.
6. In what three cases is it appropriate to use the passive voice?
7. Name two ways to achieve proper emphasis in sentences.
8. Name five ways to have variety in sentences.

J. Suggest why the passive voice is used in each sentence.
1. Most states of the United States are divided into counties.
2. My sincere apology was treated with scorn.
3. The family was trapped upstairs in their house as the floodwaters continued to rise.

Written Exercises

A. Write whether each pair is different in *person, number, case,* or *gender.*
1. I, we
2. hers, his
3. we, they
4. it, they
5. he, his
6. yours, theirs

F. 1. have
2. has
3. brings
4. show
5. Does

G. 1. Whom
2. who
3. which
4. who

H. 1. who interceded to God for man—high priest
2. which was actually the lid on the ark of the covenant—mercy seat
3. whom he represented before God—people

I. 1. writing run-on errors; joining poorly related ideas; separating closely related ideas
2. avoiding unclear pronoun reference; avoiding misplaced modifiers; avoiding the careless separation of closely related sentence parts
3. deadwood, wordy expressions, redundancy
4. Use a coordinating conjunction to join only matching sentence parts. Avoid illogical shifts in areas such as person, number, tense, and voice. Be consistent in the use of articles before nouns in a series. Repeat introductory words before long phrases or clauses in a series. In a compound part, you may omit one of the words only if the parallel word would correctly fill its place. In defining a word, use another word of the same part of speech.
5. Make the subject perform the action of the verb in most sentences. Use more direct quotations than indirect quotations.
6. when the sentence describes something unpleasant, like a tragedy or disaster; when the doer of the action is unclear or unknown; when there is a good reason (kindness, humility) not to name the doer
7. Repeat key words. Write loose, periodic, and balanced sentences.
8. by varying the length, the word order, the beginnings, the type according to use, and the type according to structure

J. 1. There is no clear doer of the action.
2. It is kinder not to name the doer.
3. The family was a helpless victim.

Written Exercises

A. 1. number
2. gender
3. person
4. number
5. case
6. person

B. If the underlined part of the sentence contains a mistake in the usage of a personal pronoun, rewrite it correctly. If it is correct, write *correct*.
1. The ones at fault were <u>us boys</u>.
2. Neither Marlin nor Neil finished <u>their chores</u> on time.
3. Uncle Silas offered to help <u>me and Alvin</u>.
4. My uncle and friend challenged me with <u>his</u> thoughtfulness.
5. Aunt Matilda gave <u>us girls</u> some beautifully embroidered dresser scarfs.
6. This job is for <u>you and I</u> to finish.

B. 1. we boys
2. his chores
3. Alvin and me
4. correct
5. correct
6. you and me

C. If the underlined part of the sentence contains a mistake in the usage of a compound personal pronoun or demonstrative pronoun, rewrite it correctly. If it is correct, write *correct*.
1. To please the Lord, we must dedicate <u>ourself</u> to His will.
2. The apostles gave <u>themselves</u> to the work of the Lord.
3. <u>These here bodies</u> of clay are subject to pain and death.
4. The sudden appearance of the deer surprised <u>Father and myself</u>.
5. <u>Them</u> are my favorite kinds of pies.

C. 1. ourselves
2. correct
3. These bodies
4. Father and me
5. Those

D. Write the correct words in parentheses.
1. Either of the hammers (is, are) good enough for me.
2. Some of these bananas (is, are) ripe enough to eat.
3. Each of us (is, are) making a scrapbook page.
4. (Was, Were) anybody watching the eclipse?
5. Most of the sugar (have, has) been used already.
6. This book is (somebodys, somebody's), but it isn't mine.

D. 1. is
2. are
3. is
4. Was
5. has
6. somebody's

E. Write the correct interrogative or relative pronouns in parentheses.
1. (Who, Whom) did you see at Bible school?
2. My cousin (who, which) lives in Georgia wrote me a letter.
3. Do you know the person (who, whom) wrote this story?
4. (Who, Whom) gave you that amaryllis?

E. 1. Whom
2. who
3. who
4. Who

F. Copy each pronoun, and write whether it is personal (*P*), compound personal (*CP*), demonstrative (*D*), indefinite (*ID*), interrogative (*IR*), or relative (*R*). Include the possessive pronouns used as adjectives.
1. He has some, but these are theirs.
2. We still have the long letter which he wrote.
3. What was that?
4. I heard nothing that sounded unusual.
5. How did Sarah cut herself with this?
6. Who damaged the motto that Carl was making for his grandfather?

F. 1. He—P; some—ID; these—D; theirs—P
2. We—P; which—R; he—P
3. What—IR; that—D
4. I—P; nothing—ID; that—R
5. herself—CP; this—D
6. Who—IR; that—R; his—P

G. Rewrite each sentence to make it more effective. The quality that is lacking is named after each sentence.

1. The authority of Moses was despised by Korah. (action)
2. He claimed to have a godly interest. He was rebellious at heart. (unity)
3. He told Moses that he took too much upon himself. (action)
4. His true and genuine desire was really to have a position of more authority for himself. (conciseness)
5. God judged this rebellion swiftly and with great force. (parallelism)
6. We must carefully guard the thoughts of our minds lest rebellious thoughts take hold and find root in our thoughts. (conciseness)
7. Tossed about dangerously on the waves, the storm threatened the ship. (coherence)
8. The severe storm buffeted the small ship, and the Christian passengers prayed earnestly to the Lord. (unity)
9. When one faces danger, they often think about God. (parallelism)
10. Of course, we should learn to at all times trust the Lord. (coherence)

H. In this paragraph, several verbs in the passive voice should be made active. Rewrite the sentences that should be made more effective.

> ¹A number of Thanksgiving boxes were packed by our congregation last evening. ²Brother Galen's family provided several bushels of apples, and a crate of oranges was brought by Brother Eli. ³Brother Marvin's family donated several turkeys for distribution to needy families. ⁴The names of needy people in the congregation and the community were listed by our deacon. ⁵Gospel literature was placed in the boxes for families in the community. ⁶The boxes were all distributed by eight o'clock.

I. The following are declarative sentences in natural word order. Rewrite each sentence or pair of sentences, changing it as indicated in parentheses.
1. The sparkling water splashed over the rocks. (word order)
2. The water was clear. (type according to use)
3. A deer drank from a quiet pool below the rapids. (word order)
4. The deer suddenly caught my scent. She jerked her head to attention. (type according to structure)
5. I wonder if you have ever had the privilege of seeing a deer in the wild. (type according to use)

G. (Allow reasonable variation.)
1. Korah despised the authority of Moses.
2. Although he claimed to have a godly interest, he was rebellious at heart.
   or He claimed to have a godly interest, but he was rebellious at heart.
3. He said, "Moses, you take too much upon yourself."
4. His true desire was to have more authority for himself.
5. God judged this rebellion swiftly and forcefully (forcibly).
6. We must carefully guard our minds lest rebellious thoughts find root there.
7. Tossed about dangerously on the waves, the ship was threatened by the storm.
8. While the severe storm buffeted the small ship, the Christian passengers prayed earnestly to the Lord.
   or The severe storm buffeted the small ship. The Christian passengers prayed earnestly to the Lord.
9. When one faces danger, he often thinks about God.
   or When people face danger, they often think about God.
10. Of course, we should learn to trust the Lord at all times.

H. 1. Our congregation packed a number of Thanksgiving boxes last evening.
2. Brother Galen's family provided several bushels of apples, and Brother Eli brought a crate of oranges.
4. Our deacon listed the names of needy people in the congregation and the community.

I. (Allow reasonable variation.)
1. Over the rocks splashed the sparkling water.
   or Over the rocks, the sparkling water splashed.
2. How clear the water was!
3. From a quiet pool below the rapids, a deer drank.
4. Suddenly the deer caught my scent, and she jerked her head to attention.
   or When the deer suddenly caught my scent, she jerked her head to attention.
5. Have you ever had the privilege of seeing a deer in the wild?

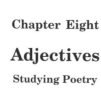

Chapter Eight

Adjectives

Studying Poetry

Adjectives fill a significant purpose in the beautifying of language. With limiting adjectives you make specific reference to substantives. With descriptive adjectives you add color and meaning to substantives. As you gain skill in using verbals, phrases, and clauses as adjectives, you will expand your ability to write specifically and descriptively.

Poetry is musical language. The poet usually expresses his noble thoughts in stanzas with rhythm and rhyme. He chooses words carefully to communicate exactly the right meaning and the right feeling. Often he embellishes his work with the special delights of alliteration, assonance, and onomatopoeia. Figurative language further enhances both the message and the music of poetry. God's people have richly benefited from poetry for many centuries.

Sing unto him, sing psalms unto him,
talk ye of all his wondrous works.

1 Chronicles 16:9

80. Recognizing Adjectives

Lesson Survey

- An **adjective** modifies a substantive by telling *which, whose, how many,* or *what kind of.*

- A **limiting adjective** limits a substantive by telling *which, whose,* or *how many.*

- A **descriptive adjective** describes a substantive by telling *what kind of.*

- Two or more descriptive adjectives may need to be separated by commas.

- An **attributive adjective** precedes the word it modifies.

- An **appositive adjective** immediately follows the word it modifies.

- A **predicate adjective** follows a linking verb and modifies the subject.

Adjectives are not as essential to language as are nouns and verbs. In comparing the following paragraphs, however, you will quickly see that adjectives are quite important.

Paragraph 1: Without adjectives
    And Jesse said to son David, "Take now for brothers ephah and loaves, and run to camp to brothers."

Paragraph 2: With adjectives
    "And Jesse said unto David <u>his</u> son, Take now for <u>thy</u> brethren <u>an</u> ephah <u>of this parched corn</u>, and <u>these ten</u> loaves, and run to <u>the</u> camp to <u>thy</u> brethren."

The use of adjectives in the second paragraph makes it possible to express the thoughts naturally and to describe things clearly.

Adjectives modify substantives by telling *which, whose, how many,* and *what kind of.* To modify is to change, and adjectives do exactly that. Notice how adjectives change the meanings of the following sentences.

Dogs were barking at boys.
<u>The friendly</u> dogs were barking at <u>the two laughing</u> boys.
<u>The vicious</u> dogs were barking at <u>the frightened</u> boys.

Classes of Adjectives

Adjectives are divided into two classes: limiting adjectives and descriptive adjectives. A *limiting adjective* limits a substantive by telling *which, whose,* or *how many.* Here are six groups of words that can be used as limiting adjectives.

Lesson 80

Purpose: To study the definition and recognition of adjectives.

Oral Review:

1. Tell whether each pair of pronouns is different in person, number, case, or gender.
   a. him, her (gender)   c. she, hers (case)
   b. we, they (person)   d. I, we (number)
2. The compound personal pronouns end with ——— or ———. (-self, -selves)
3. Tell whether the indefinite pronouns in each group are always singular, always plural, or either singular or plural.
   a. both, few, many, several (always plural)
   b. each, everything, somebody (always singular)
   c. none, most, any, some (either)
4. Give the singular possessive, plural, and plural possessive spellings of these nouns.
   a. family (family's, families, families')
   b. son-in-law (son-in-law's, sons-in-law, sons-in-law's)
   c. attorney (attorney's, attorneys, attorneys')
   d. princess (princess's, princesses, princesses')
5. Diagram the skeletons and complements of these sentences.
   a. The visitor was whom we had expected.

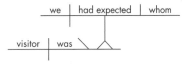

   b. Solving this problem took much hard work.

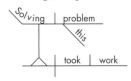

1. *The articles are always limiting adjectives.*
   a. *The* is a definite article; it indicates a specific noun.
   b. *A* and *an* are indefinite articles; they do not indicate specific nouns.

   > Please give me <u>a</u> book from the shelf. (no specific book indicated)
   > Please give me <u>the</u> book from the shelf. (indicates a specific book)

2. *Number words are often used as limiting adjectives.*
   a. Cardinal numbers (*one, two, three,* and so forth) tell *how many.*

   > <u>one</u> Lord   <u>twelve</u> disciples

   b. Ordinal numbers (*first, second, third,* and so forth) tell *which.*

   > <u>third</u> heaven   <u>fourteenth</u> get-well card

3. *Indefinite pronouns are sometimes used as limiting adjectives that tell* which *or* how many. You learned in Chapter 7 that these words are pronouns only when they stand alone and function as substantives. When they precede nouns, they are adjectives.

   > <u>each</u> command   <u>few</u> questions
   > <u>several</u> promises   <u>both</u> families

4. *Demonstrative pronouns are sometimes used as limiting adjectives that tell* which.

   > <u>that</u> parable   <u>these</u> students

5. *The interrogative pronouns* whose, which, *and* what *are sometimes used as limiting adjectives.*

   > <u>whose</u> pencil   <u>which</u> poem   <u>what</u> standard

6. *Possessive nouns and pronouns are often used as limiting adjectives that tell* whose. Remember to use apostrophes with nouns and indefinite pronouns, but not with personal pronouns.

   > <u>Gary's</u> eraser   <u>somebody's</u> coat
   > the <u>girls'</u> story   <u>her</u> pocketbook

A descriptive adjective describes a substantive by telling *what kind of.* How dull our language would be without descriptive adjectives! Read the following stanza, noticing the descriptive adjectives.

> The <u>breaking</u> waves dashed high
>   On a <u>stern</u> and <u>rock-bound</u> coast,
> And the woods against a <u>stormy</u> sky
>   Their <u>giant</u> branches tossed.

Lesson Introduction: Write the word *finger* on a large piece of paper and keep it hidden from the students. Tell them to get out a paper and a pencil, and be ready to write as many descriptive adjectives as they can about the noun that you will show them. Time them for one minute. Have them share at least a sampling of their adjectives to illustrate the variety and descriptiveness in adjectives.

Lesson Outline:

   1. An adjective modifies a substantive by telling **which, whose, how many,** *or* **what kind of.**

   2. A limiting adjective limits a substantive by telling **which, whose,** *or* **how many.**
      (1) *The articles are always limiting adjectives.*
         (a) *The* is a definite article; it indicates a specific noun.
         (b) *A* and *an* are indefinite articles; they do not indicate specific nouns.
      (2) *Number words are often used as limiting adjectives.*
         (a) Cardinal numbers (*one, two, three,* and so forth) tell *how many.*
         (b) Ordinal numbers (*first, second, third,* and so forth) tell *which.*
      (3) *Indefinite pronouns are sometimes used as limiting adjectives that tell* which *or* how many.
      (4) *Demonstrative pronouns are sometimes used as limiting adjectives that tell* which.
      (5) *The interrogative pronouns* whose, which, *and* what *are sometimes used as limiting adjectives.*
      (6) *Possessive nouns and pronouns are often used as limiting adjectives that tell* whose.

Descriptive adjectives can be classified according to their structure.

1. *Many descriptive adjectives are adjectives in their simplest form.*

<u>good</u> news   <u>dry</u> weather   <u>dark</u> clouds

2. *Some descriptive adjectives can be identified by adjective-forming suffixes.* The following list shows some of the most common of these.

-ish:	girlish, purplish	**-less:**	guiltless, treeless
-al:	Scriptural, optional	**-like:**	childlike, lifelike
-ic:	tragic, angelic	**-ous:**	wondrous, various
-ive:	excessive, massive	**-some:**	burdensome, lonesome
-y:	cloudy, stuffy, sunny	**-ant, -ent:**	tolerant, different
-ful:	peaceful, healthful	**-able, -ible:**	readable, sensible
-ary:	secondary, customary	**-an, -en:**	American, woolen

3. *Some descriptive adjectives are formed by changing the spellings of nouns, especially proper nouns.*

Switzerland—Swiss   Wales—Welsh

4. *Nouns are sometimes used as descriptive adjectives without any spelling change.* Such nouns may be called attributive nouns.

<u>Bible</u> teachings   <u>ship</u> travel
<u>dairy</u> farm   <u>farm</u> tractors

5. *Some descriptive adjectives are verbals.* Verbals used as adjectives usually end with *-ing, -ed,* or *-en.* You will study these adjectives more in Lesson 84.

<u>loving</u> Lord   <u>cooked</u> carrots
<u>singing</u> birds   <u>risen</u> Saviour

When two or more descriptive adjectives modify the same noun, they may need to be separated by commas. You have learned three tests to help determine whether a comma is needed between two descriptive adjectives.

Test 1: *Do you pause between the adjectives as you read them?*
Test 2: *Does it sound right to use* and *between the adjectives?*
Test 3: *Does it sound right to change the order of the adjectives?*

If the answer to all these questions is *yes,* the adjectives are of equal rank and should be separated by commas. Study these examples.

We have three frisky, friendly puppies.
 (No comma between *three* and *frisky* because *three* is a limiting adjective; comma between *frisky* and *friendly* because they are descriptive adjectives of equal rank.)

3. A descriptive adjective describes a substantive by telling what kind of.
 (1) *Many descriptive adjectives are adjectives in their simplest form.*
 (2) *Some descriptive adjectives can be identified by adjective-forming suffixes.*
 (3) *Some descriptive adjectives are formed by changing the spellings of nouns, especially proper nouns.*
 (4) *Nouns are sometimes used as descriptive adjectives without any spelling change.* Such nouns may be called attributive nouns.
 (5) *Some descriptive adjectives are verbals.*

4. When two or more descriptive adjectives modify the same noun, they may need to be separated by commas. Three tests are helpful in determining whether a comma is needed between two descriptive adjectives.

 (1) *Do you pause between the adjectives as you read them?*
 (2) *Does it sound right to use* and *between the adjectives?*
 (3) *Does it sound right to change the order of the adjectives?*

5. An attributive adjective precedes the word it modifies.

6. An appositive adjective immediately follows the word it modifies.
 a. This position tends to place greater emphasis on the adjectives.
 b. Appositive adjectives usually come in pairs, and they are set off by commas.
 c. Adjectives that refer to position are often used singly in the appositive position.

7. A predicate adjective follows a linking verb and modifies the subject.

They are playing on the wide, spacious front porch.

> (No comma between *the* and *wide* because *the* is a limiting adjective; comma between *wide* and *spacious* because they are descriptive adjectives of equal rank; no comma between *spacious* and *front* because they are not of equal rank: *front* is closely related to *porch*.)

Positions of Adjectives

An *attributive adjective* precedes the word it modifies. The adjective expresses a quality that is *attributed* (assigned) to the substantive that follows. This is the most common position of adjectives.

The *lovely, inspirational* psalm encouraged the *sad, lonely young* saint.

An *appositive adjective* immediately follows the word it modifies, just as an appositive noun follows another substantive. Using the appositive position adds variety, and it also tends to place greater emphasis on the adjectives.

Appositive adjectives usually come in pairs, and they are set off by commas. However, adjectives that refer to position are often used singly in the appositive position and are rarely set off by commas.

The psalm, <u>lovely</u> and <u>inspirational</u>, encouraged the young saint, <u>sad</u> and <u>lonely</u>.

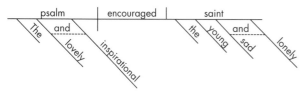

The rooms <u>upstairs</u> had been cleaned, but the rooms <u>downstairs</u> had not been touched.

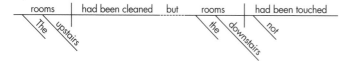

A *predicate adjective* follows a linking verb and modifies the subject.

The psalm was <u>lovely</u> and <u>inspirational</u>.

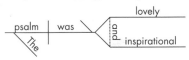

Class Practice

A. Identify all the adjectives in these sentences, and tell whether they are *limiting* or *descriptive*. Also tell whether they are *attributive, appositive,* or *predicate.*
1. A merciful person is considerate of others' faults.
2. Our friends, kind and sympathetic, helped us in many ways.
3. Two boys, singing and whistling, finished their difficult jobs quickly.
4. The stranger's decisive answer left no question about his wrath.
5. Soft, subdued responses often turn away wrathful expressions.
6. The only true God, faithful and just, rules from His throne in the realms above.

B. Read each sentence, supplying adjectives for the underlined nouns according to the directions in parentheses. Tell where commas should be used.
1. Grandmother's <u>cottage</u> was ———. (two descriptive adjectives in the predicate position)
2. The <u>bouquet</u> added a cheerful note to the classroom. (two descriptive adjectives in the appositive position)
3. <u>Trees</u> shaded our house from the sun. (one limiting and two descriptive adjectives in the attributive position)
4. We looked for the pen in the <u>grass</u>. (two descriptive adjectives in the attributive position and one in the appositive position)

C. Read each sentence, changing the word in parentheses to an adjective.
1. According to (Bible) principles, (God) people must demonstrate (nonresistance) love to all.
2. One (person) (faith) response is often an (effect) motivation to others.
3. We should remove the weeds of (self) desires from our hearts and plant the seeds of (whole) (Christ) desires.
4. Our (love) Shepherd is the only (depend) guide for our souls.

D. On the chalkboard, diagram these sentences.
1. The beautiful green trees withstood the stormy blasts.
2. Two timid deer leaped the old wooden fence.
3. The mountain stream, clear and cool, sang a cheerful song.
4. This Alpine valley is long and narrow.

D.

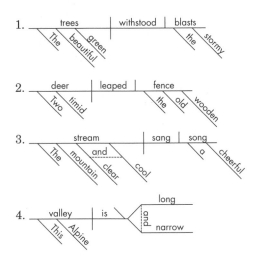

Lesson 80 Answers

Class Practice

A. 1. A—limiting, attributive;
      merciful—descriptive, attributive;
      considerate—descriptive, predicate;
      others'—limiting, attributive
   2. Our—limiting, attributive;
      kind—descriptive, appositive;
      sympathetic—descriptive, appositive;
      many—limiting, attributive
   3. Two—limiting, attributive;
      singing—descriptive, appositive;
      whistling—descriptive, appositive;
      their—limiting, attributive;
      difficult—descriptive, attributive
   4. The—limiting, attributive;
      stranger's—limiting, attributive;
      decisive—descriptive, attributive;
      no—limiting, attributive;
      his—limiting, attributive
   5. Soft—descriptive, attributive;
      subdued—descriptive, attributive;
      wrathful—descriptive, attributive
   6. The—limiting, attributive;
      only—limiting, attributive;
      true—descriptive, attributive;
      faithful—descriptive, appositive;
      just—descriptive, appositive;
      His—limiting, attributive;
      the—limiting, attributive;
      above—limiting *or* descriptive, appositive

B. (Sample answers.)
   1. Grandmother's cottage was <u>small but neat</u>.
   2. The bouquet<u>, fragrant and colorful,</u> added a cheerful note to the classroom.
   3. <u>Two large, spreading</u> (*or* <u>Two tall maple</u>) trees shaded our house from the sun.
   4. We looked for the pen in the <u>tall, green</u> grass <u>nearby</u>.

C. 1. According to <u>Biblical</u> principles, <u>God's</u> people must demonstrate <u>nonresistant</u> love to all.
   2. One <u>person's</u> <u>faithful</u> response is often an <u>effective</u> (*or* <u>effectual</u>) motivation to others.
   3. We should remove the weeds of <u>selfish</u> desires from our hearts and plant the seeds of <u>wholesome</u> <u>Christlike</u> (*or* <u>Christian</u>) desires.
   4. Our <u>loving</u> Shepherd is the only <u>dependable</u> guide for our souls.

Written Exercises

A. Copy each adjective. First label it *L* (limiting) or *D* (descriptive); then label it *AT* (attributive), *AP* (appositive), or *PR* (predicate).
  1. Hannah, godly and faithful, made her request in the Lord's house.
  2. God answered this earnest prayer of her burdened heart.
  3. A raging Mediterranean storm threatened the small ship.
  4. Paul's faith in his God remained unshaken.
  5. From the valley below we gazed up to the towering mountain peak.
  6. A high brick wall, crumbling and broken, surrounded the two ancient buildings.
  7. Each student in the eighth grade was assigned two book reports during these six weeks.
  8. Which girl left her blue Sunday sweater at our house?

B. Copy these sentences, replacing each word in parentheses with a descriptive adjective of the kind indicated. Use correct punctuation.
  1. Five (attributive) (attributive) apples stood in a (attributive) row on the (attributive) table.
  2. The (attributive) road (appositive) and (appositive) led across (attributive) streams, through (attributive) valleys, and over (attributive) hills.
  3. The panther's cry sounded (predicate) in the (attributive) night.

C. Write an adjective formed from each word in parentheses.
  1. With a (create) imagination and a little (artist) ability, one can make (beauty) and (inspiration) scrapbook pages.
  2. The (mass) head of the (charge) bull looked (frighten) indeed!
  3. With (consider) difficulty we finished setting the heavy (wood) posts.

D. Diagram these sentences.
  1. The white, fluffy snow reflected the sun's radiant brightness.
  2. Our school's assembly room is the large open area downstairs.
  3. These three bicycles are rusty and useless.
  4. The little stream, swollen and muddy, flooded our back lane.

Review Exercises

A. Write the singular possessive, plural, and plural possessive forms of these nouns. [36, 37]
  1. donkey   4. salesman   7. seamstress
  2. ox   5. calf   8. buffalo
  3. baby   6. brother-in-law

B. Diagram these sentences. [40, 41]
  1. Considering others' needs is important.
  2. We know that selfish people are unhappy.

  4. salesman's, salesmen, salesmen's
  5. calf's, calves, calves'
  6. brother-in-law's, brothers-in-law, brothers-in-law's
  7. seamstress's, seamstresses, seamstresses'
  8. buffalo's, buffalo(e)s, buffalo(e)s'
     or buffalo's, buffalo, buffalo's

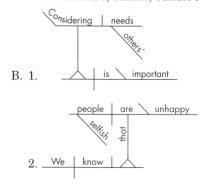

B. 1.

  2.

Written Exercises

A. 1. godly—D, AP; faithful—D, AP; her—L, AT; the—L, AT; Lord's—L, AT
  2. this—L, AT; earnest—D, AT; her—L, AT; burdened—D, AT
  3. A—L, AT; raging—D, AT; Mediterranean—D, AT; the—L, AT; small—D, AT
  4. Paul's—L, AT; his—L, AT; unshaken—D, PR
  5. the—L, AT; below—L *or* D, AP; the—L, AT; towering—D, AT; mountain—D, AT
  6. A—L, AT; high—D, AT; brick—D, AT; crumbling—D, AP; broken—D, AP; the—L, AT; two—L, AT; ancient—D, AT
  7. Each—L, AT; the—L, AT; eighth—L, AT; two—L, AT; book—D, AT; these—L, AT; six—L, AT
  8. Which—L, AT; her—L, AT; blue—D, AT; Sunday—L, AT; our—L, AT

B. (Sample answers underlined.)
  1. Five <u>large</u> <u>red</u> apples stood in a <u>neat</u> row on the <u>wooden</u> table.
  2. The <u>dirt</u> road, <u>rough</u> and <u>winding</u>, led across <u>rushing</u> streams, through <u>narrow</u> valleys, and over <u>steep</u> hills.
  3. The panther's cry sounded <u>eerie</u> in the <u>still</u> night.

C. 1. creative, artistic, beautiful, inspirational
  2. massive, charging, frightening
  3. considerable, wooden

D. 1.

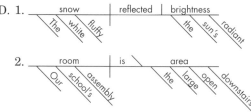

  2.

  (*Our* is diagramed under *room* even though it actually modifies *school's* [a possessive noun used as an adjective]. This technical distinction may be disregarded, especially since *Our* does modify *room* indirectly.)

  3.

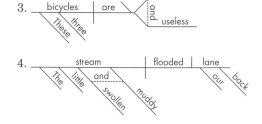

  4.

Review Exercises

A. 1. donkey's, donkeys, donkeys'
  2. ox's, oxen, oxen's
  3. baby's, babies, babies'

3. Our goal should be to serve the Lord.
4. Whose example we follow is our choice.

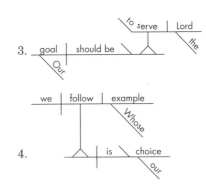

---

81. Rhyme in Poetry

> **Lesson Survey**
> - **Prose** is written in sentences and paragraphs; **poetry** is written in lines and stanzas.
> - The rhyming pattern of a poem can be shown by using small letters.
> - A **masculine rhyme** involves only one syllable; a **feminine rhyme** involves more than one syllable.
> - The intended rhyming words in poetry should be true rhymes.

The two main types of literature are prose and poetry. *Prose* is written in sentences and paragraphs. Compositions, reports, and stories are written in prose. *Poetry* is written in lines and stanzas, as in the following example.

> God's road is all uphill,
> But do not tire;
> Rejoice that we may still
> Keep climbing higher.
> —*Arthur Guiterman*

What makes this poetry different from prose? The first thing you might think of is rhyme: *still* rhymes with *uphill,* and *higher* with *tire.* Another thing easy to recognize is the rhythm. Reading the poem aloud, you can feel the regular beat of the words. Rhythm and rhyme are pleasing to the ear.

Good rhyme is one important thing that adds beauty to poetry. The rhyming pattern of a poem can be shown by using small letters; all the lines that rhyme with each other are marked with the same letter. Lines of poetry are generally indented to show that rhyming pattern.

> Lilies blooming in the garden,   a
>   Standing high beside the <u>wall</u>,   b
> Showing forth the Master's greatness—   c
>   God of beauty, God of <u>all</u>.   b
> —*Ruth R. Groff*

Lesson 81

Purpose: To study common rhyme patterns in poetry, and to introduce *masculine rhyme and *feminine rhyme.

Oral Review:

1. Name the five parts of a friendly letter. (heading, greeting, body, closing, signature)
2. What is another term for the greeting of a business letter? (salutation)
3. *(a)* What additional part does a business letter have? *(b)* Where is it placed? (*a.* inside address; *b.* at the left-hand margin, between the heading and the salutation)
4. What are the three C's of business letter content? (clear, courteous, concise)
5. Give the correct term for each description.
   a. A sentence that states the main idea of a paragraph. (topic sentence)
   b. The quality of thoughts within a paragraph being presented in a well-organized way. (coherence)
   c. The quality of all the sentences within a paragraph supporting and developing the topic sentence. (unity)
6. Name the sentence order described in each statement.
   a. It gives details in the order of space. (spatial)
   b. It gives details in the order of time. (chronological)
   c. It gives the most important detail first or last. (order of importance)

Lesson Introduction: Poetry is pleasing to the human ear. One evidence of this is seen in the way some parents name their children. You would expect a pair of twins to be named Ray and Jay, rather than Ray and Barry. Rhyme (as in *Ray* and *Jay*) is an important part of the beauty of poetry.

Spring is the morning of the <u>year</u>,　　　　a
　　And summer is the noontide *bright*;　　b
The autumn is the evening <u>clear</u>,　　　　a
　　That comes before the winter's *night*.　b
　　　　　　　　　—*Frank Dempster Sherman*

Softly now the light of <u>day</u>　　　　a
Fades upon my sight <u>away</u>;　　　　a
　　Free from care, from labor *free*,　　b
　　Lord, I would commune with *Thee*.　b
　　　　　　　　—*George W. Doane*

Sometimes you must read several stanzas or the entire poem to catch the full beauty of the rhyming pattern.

Space Travel

A journey into outer space　　　　　　a
Is one I do not care to face:　　　　　a
To give Orion merry chase,　　　　　　a
The orbit of the moon to trace;　　　　a
　　To view three sunsets in one day,　　b
　　While floating weightlessly away,　　b
　　　I do not yearn.　　　　　　　　　c

But let me see the stars that rise　　　　　d
In healthy, happy children's eyes;　　　　d
And this the weightlessness I prize—　　　d
A conscience pure, where no guilt lies.　　d
　　One day, transfigured, I shall climb　　e
　　Beyond all bounds of space or time　　e
　　　And not return.　　　　　　　　　c

In some poems, using these letters to indicate the rhyming pattern does not show the full beauty of the rhyme. Some of the lines may have *internal* rhyme; that is, rhyming words within the lines.

Though the cover is worn,
And the pages are torn,
　　And though <u>places</u> bear <u>traces</u> of tears,
Yet more precious than gold
Is the Book worn and old,
　　That can <u>shatter</u> and <u>scatter</u> my fears.

Masculine rhymes involve only one syllable. The rhyming words themselves may contain two or three syllables, but the rhyme is only in the last syllable. By far, most rhymes fall into this category.

Lesson Outline:

1. Prose is written in sentences and paragraphs; poetry is written in lines and stanzas.

2. The rhyming pattern of a poem can be shown by using small letters. All the lines that rhyme with each other are marked with the same letter.

　　a. Sometimes you must read several stanzas or the entire poem to catch the full beauty of the rhyming pattern.

　　b. Some poems have *internal* rhyme, which is not shown by writing the letters of the rhyming pattern.

3. A masculine rhyme involves only one syllable; a feminine rhyme involves more than one syllable.

　　a. Words with masculine rhyme may have two or three syllables, but the rhyme is only in the last syllable.

　　b. By far, most rhymes fall into this category.

　　c. Feminine rhymes add a special beauty to poetry.

4. The intended rhyming words in poetry should be true rhymes.

　　(1) *The vowel sounds of rhyming syllables must be the same.*

　　(2) *The final consonant sounds of rhyming syllables must be the same.*

　　(3) *The beginning consonant sounds of rhyming syllables must be different.*

　　(4) *The rhyming syllables must be accented.*

　　(5) *In a feminine rhyme, the accented syllables must rhyme, and the unaccented syllables that follow must be exactly alike.*

sun—done   restore—adore
vine—fine   attend—condescend

Feminine rhymes involve more than one syllable. The rhyming part of the word is not just the last syllable. Feminine rhymes add a special beauty to poetry.

salvation—oblation   entering—centering

The intended rhyming words in poetry should be true rhymes. The following five rules show what makes perfect rhymes.

1. *The vowel sounds of rhyming syllables must be the same.* Rhyme is a matter of sound, not spelling.

   <u>Bear</u> and <u>fair</u> rhyme; <u>bear</u> and <u>clear</u> do not.

2. *The final consonant sounds of rhyming syllables must be the same.*

   <u>Grade</u> and <u>shade</u> rhyme; <u>grade</u> and <u>great</u> do not.

3. *The beginning consonant sounds of rhyming syllables must be different.* If two different words sound exactly alike, they are homonyms, not rhymes.

   <u>Sight</u> and <u>bright</u> rhyme; <u>sight</u> and <u>site</u> do not.

4. *The rhyming syllables must be accented.* A final unaccented syllable is often pronounced with a schwa or some other unclear sound. Such a sound does not make a good rhyme.

   <u>Bestow</u> rhymes with <u>below</u> (be·stow′, be·low′).
   <u>Bestow</u> does not rhyme with <u>hallow</u> (be·stow′, hal′·low).

5. *In a feminine rhyme, the accented syllables must rhyme, and the unaccented syllables that follow must be exactly alike.*

   <u>Abating</u> rhymes with <u>awaiting</u> (a·<u>bat</u>′·ing, a·<u>wait</u>′·ing).
   <u>Abating</u> does not rhyme with <u>debating</u>, because the beginning consonant sounds of the accented syllables are alike (a·<u>bat</u>′·ing, de·<u>bat</u>′·ing).

   <u>Abounding</u> rhymes with <u>resounding</u> (a·<u>bound</u>′·ing, re·<u>sound</u>′·ing).
   <u>Abounding</u> does not rhyme with <u>resounded</u>, because the unaccented syllables that follow are not exactly alike (a·<u>bound</u>′·ing, re·<u>sound</u>′·ed).

Class Practice

A. Tell whether the words in each pair are a perfect rhyme. If they are not, tell which of the five rules is broken.

1. deter, alter
2. wearily, cheerily
3. sound, crown
4. touch, pouch
5. meant, sent
6. pleasure, fresher
7. wholly, holy
8. readily, steadily

Lesson 81 Answers

Class Practice

A. 1. 4
   2. perfect
   3. 2
   4. 1
   5. perfect
   6. 5 (2)
   7. 3
   8. perfect

B. Give the rhyming pattern of each selection.

1. Do you wish the world were better?
   Let me tell you what to do:
   Set a watch upon your actions,
   Keep them always straight and true.
   Rid your mind of selfish motives,
   Let your thoughts be clean and high;
   You can make a little Eden
   Of the sphere you occupy.

2. In days when He shall seem to hide His face,
   In trials when you need His richest grace,
   In moments when you're weary of the race,
   May God give strength.

   —Peter Van Wynen

3. Should you feel inclined to censure
   Faults you may in others view,
   Ask your own heart, ere you venture,
   If that has not failings too.

4. It is not raining rain to me,
   It's raining daffodils;
   In every dimpled drop I see
   Wild flowers on the hills.

   The clouds of gray engulf the day
   And overwhelm the town;
   It is not raining rain to me,
   It's raining roses down.

   —Robert Loveman

C. Give pairs of rhymes from the selections above.
1. A pair of feminine rhymes.
2. A pair of internal rhyming words.

D. Give words to complete these selections with perfect rhymes. You can tell by the indentations which lines are to rhyme.
1. O Lord, we come to Thee in ———;
   We ask Thy help, enlist Thy care.
      Upon our path may Thy light ———;
      O help us walk the path ———.

2. I am sailing o'er life's stormy ———;
      Fierce the winds, and the waves tossing high;
   Yet no fear, for my Lord pilots me;
      He will lead to that home in the ———.

B. 1. abcbdefe
   2. aaab
   3. abab
   4. ababcdad

C. 1. censure, venture (in selection 3; Some dictionaries indicate that this is an imperfect rhyme.)
   2. gray, day (in selection 4)

D. 1. prayer, shine, divine
   2. sea, sky

3. Now as the eastern sky's brightening,
  Lift I my soul in sweet ———,
  Trust I Thy heavenly ———,
  Find I great strengthening there!
  Jesus my pathway is ———.

Written Exercises

A. If the pair of words is a perfect rhyme, write *perfect*. If it is not, write the number of the rule that is broken.

 1. sword, word
 2. obey, way
 3. convict, restrict
 4. gleaming, cleaning
 5. saints, faint

 6. there, fear
 7. seen, scene
 8. place, disgrace
 9. alone, milestone
 10. crown, frown

B. Write the rhyming patterns for these stanzas. In number 5, be sure to write the pattern for the whole poem.

 1. All things bright and beautiful,
  All creatures great and small,
  All things wise and wonderful,
  The Lord God made them all.
    —*Cecil Frances Alexander*

 2. The bird that soars on highest wing
  Builds on the ground her lowly nest;
  And she that doth most sweetly sing
  Sings in the shade when all things rest.
  In lark and nightingale we see
  What honor hath humility.

 3. The year's at the spring
  And the day's at the morn;
  Morning's at seven;
  The hillside's dew-pearled;
  The lark's on the wing;
  The snail's on the thorn;
  God's in His heaven—
  All's right with the world!
    —*Robert Browning*

 4. Can you measure the treasure in Jesus you know
  Even though you must face
  Sorrow, pain, or disgrace?
  And 'tis weary and dreary, this path you must go?

---

3. prayer, care, lightening

Written Exercises

A.
 1. 1
 2. perfect
 3. perfect
 4. 5 (2)
 5. 2
 6. 1
 7. 3
 8. perfect
 9. 4
 10. perfect

B.
 1. abcb
 2. ababcc
 3. abcdabcd
 4. abba

5. **Stopping by Woods on a Snowy Evening**
   Whose woods these are I think I know.
   His house is in the village though;
   He will not see me stopping here
   To watch his woods fill up with snow.

   My little horse must think it queer
   To stop without a farmhouse near,
   Between the woods and frozen lake,
   The darkest evening of the year.

   He gives his harness bells a shake
   To ask if there is some mistake.
   The only other sound's the sweep
   Of easy wind and downy flake.

   The woods are lovely, dark, and deep.
   But I have promises to keep,
   And miles to go before I sleep,
   And miles to go before I sleep.
   — *Robert Frost*

C. Write pairs of rhymes from the selections above.
   1. A pair of feminine rhymes found at the ends of lines.
   2. Two pairs of internal rhyming words.

D. Write words to complete these selections with perfect rhymes. You can tell by the indentations which lines are to rhyme.
   1. Let's win the fight
          In Jesus' Name;
      Let's shun the blight
          Of sin and ———.
      Let's stand for ———!
   2. Jesus, help me to endure,
      Be a soldier brave and ———;
          Grant that I would never ———,
          Help me walk the Narrow ———.
   3. Hear the ocean's mighty ———
      As it breaks upon the ———;
          Think—a mightier voice is ———
          In God's everlasting ———.
   4. See the ocean's vast expanse
      As from side to side you ———;
          Think—what vastness we can't ———
          In the Lord's infinity.

5. aaba, bbcb, ccdc, dddd
(*Note:* The last two lines do not actually rhyme since they are identical.)

C. 1. dying, crying *or* seven, heaven
   2. measure, treasure; weary, dreary

D. (Other answers may be possible.)
   1. shame, right
   2. pure, stray, Way
   3. roar, shore, heard, Word
   4. glance, see

82. Rhythm in Poetry

Lesson Survey

- **Meter,** the pattern of accented and unaccented syllables, gives rhythm to a poem.
- A **poetic foot** contains one accented syllable and the unaccented syllable or syllables associated with it.
- The four common types of poetic feet are **iambic, trochaic, anapestic,** and **dactylic.**
- **Bible poetry** and **free verse** have no regular rhythm or rhyme.

We enjoy the rhythm of poetry because we ourselves are rhythmical. We walk with rhythm. We bounce a ball, shovel snow, stir tea, and even speak and write with a certain degree of rhythm.

Meter, the pattern of accented and unaccented syllables, gives rhythm to a poem. In poetry, words are so arranged that their natural accents produce a regular rhythm. It is easy to hear that the meters of the following lines are different.

ˇ   /   ˇ   /   ˇ   /   ˇ   /
It's like / the mu/sic of / a bell

/   ˇ   ˇ   /   ˇ   ˇ   /   ˇ   ˇ   /   /
In from the / highways and / byways of / sin

A *poetic foot* contains one accented syllable and the unaccented syllable or syllables associated with it. In the examples above, the poetic feet are marked off with slashes. Both examples have four poetic feet.

Marking off poetic feet as shown above is known as *scansion.* When poetic lines are *scanned* in this way, you can easily see the meter of the poetry.

The four common types of poetic feet are *iambic, trochaic, anapestic,* and *dactylic.* Each of these is explained and illustrated below. The number after each line of poetry shows the number of feet in that line.

1. *The* iambic (ī·am′·bik) *foot consists of one unaccented syllable followed by one accented syllable.* This is the most common pattern in English poetry. In fact, it is the closest to the rhythm of our ordinary speech. Page through any hymnal, and you will find more poems with this pattern than any other. Its light, cheerful rhythm is well suited to themes of praise, joy, and beauty.

In the following example, notice that the first and third lines end with an extra unaccented syllable. Such an extra syllable is disregarded when poetic feet are counted. The number of feet in a poetic line is always the number of accented syllables.

Lesson 82

Purpose: To study common rhythm patterns in poetry.

Oral Review:

1. Tell why each of these pairs of words is not a perfect rhyme.
   a. coast—lost (The vowel sounds are not the same.)
   b. stairs—stares (The beginning consonant sounds are not different.)
   c. cover—deter (The rhyming syllables are not accented.)
   d. friend—men (The final consonant sounds are not the same.)
2. What is a feminine rhyme? (a rhyme involving more than one syllable)
3. How is the rhyming pattern of a poem marked? (by using the same small letter for all the lines that rhyme with each other)
4. Name the four basic kinds of compositions. (exposition, argument, narration, description)
5. In what two ways can you correct a paragraph that lacks unity? (Remove any sentence that does not develop the topic sentence. Divide the paragraph into two or more paragraphs.)
6. What are some methods for achieving coherence in paragraphs? (good sentence order, transitional words, repetition of key words, pronoun reference)

Lesson Introduction: Copy the following poem on the chalkboard:

> Wherever He may guide me,
>   No want shall turn me back;
> My loving heavenly Father is beside me,
>   And not a thing can I lack.

Upon a simple canvas,   3
With colors sharp and clean,   3
God paints the flowers and rainbows— 3
A grand and gorgeous scene.   3

2. *The* trochaic (trō·kā′·ik) *foot consists of one accented syllable followed by one unaccented syllable.* This meter is the exact opposite of the iambic. Its heavier rhythm is well suited to sober, thoughtful themes.

In the example below, notice that the second and fourth lines end with an incomplete foot. (The unaccented syllable is missing.) Such a foot is still counted, for it contains an accented syllable. Remember, accented syllables are the most important ones; they determine the number of feet in a line.

Have you ever watched as children   4
Wrote their names upon the sand,   4
Using different things to write with, 4
Such as finger, toe, or hand?   4

3. *The* anapestic (an′·ə·pes′·tik) *foot consists of two unaccented syllables followed by one accented syllable.* This meter produces a flowing, almost galloping rhythm that is well suited to themes of hope, joy, and earnestness.

At the end of the way   2
When with Jesus we meet,   2
We shall know no more pain,   2
But have joy that's complete.   2

Lines written with anapestic rhythm often begin with an incomplete foot, like this example.

How firm a foundation, ye saints of the Lord,   4
Is laid for your faith in His excellent Word!   4
What more can He say than to you He hath said—   4
Who unto the Saviour for refuge have fled?   4

His wisdom ever waketh,
    His sight is never dim;
He understands all the way He taketh,
    And I will ever move forward with Him.

The first, second, fifth, and sixth lines are correct. Help the students shorten the other lines to make them conform to the rhythm pattern. The correct lines are given below.

Wherever He may guide me,
    No want shall turn me back;
My Shepherd is beside me,
    And nothing can I lack.

His wisdom ever waketh,
    His sight is never dim;
He knows the way He taketh,
    And I will walk with Him.
                    —A. L. Waring

Lesson Outline:

1. Meter, the pattern of accented and unaccented syllables, gives rhythm to a poem.

2. A poetic foot contains one accented syllable and the unaccented syllable or syllables associated with it. Marking off poetic feet in poetry is known as scansion.

3. The four common types of poetic feet are iambic, trochaic, anapestic, and dactylic.

(1) *The* iambic *foot consists of one unaccented syllable followed by one accented syllable.*

a) This is the most common pattern in English poetry.

b) It is the closest to the rhythm of our ordinary speech.

c) Its light, cheerful rhythm is well suited to themes of praise, joy, and beauty.

4. *The* dactylic (dak·til′·ik) *foot consists of one accented syllable followed by two unaccented syllables.* This meter is the exact opposite of the anapestic. Its flowing rhythm, like the anapestic, is well suited to themes of hope, joy, and earnestness. Because a dactylic foot ends with two unaccented syllables, you will rarely find a complete foot at the end of a line.

<pre>
  ′   ⌣   ⌣   ′   ⌣   ⌣   ′   ⌣   ⌣   ′
  O the unsearchable riches of Christ!   4
       ′   ⌣   ⌣   ′   ⌣   ⌣   ′
    Wealth that can never be told;   3
  ′   ⌣   ⌣   ′   ⌣   ⌣   ′   ⌣   ⌣   ′
  Riches exhaustless of mercy and grace,   4
    ′   ⌣   ⌣   ′   ⌣   ⌣   ′
    Precious, more precious than gold!   3
</pre>

Bible poetry and *free verse* have no regular rhythm or rhyme. Such poetry is divided into lines, or even stanzas, according to the thoughts. You will study free verse in this lesson and Bible poetry in Lesson 85. The following lines are from the beginning of a poem written in free verse.

The Giant Oak

Standing like a sentinel guarding the old farmhouse
Is the Giant Oak, with its dozen-odd arms stretched all around.
The balmy spring sun has awakened the flow of sap
    within its mighty chest;
The vitality of God-given life is once more pushing up
    to its topmost fingers;
The promise of rich foliage adorns each arm and each finger
    of the Giant Oak.

Although this example does not have rhythm or rhyme, it is poetry. The words are arranged in lines and stanzas. The whole poem is an example of personification. The language includes many colorful poetic expressions. Rhythm and rhyme do add to the appeal of poetry, but its primary beauty is found in vivid language that paints clear, colorful pictures in the reader's mind.

Class Practice

A. Copy and scan the first two lines of each stanza. Tell which kind of poetic foot is used, and how many feet are in each line.

1. This old Book is my guide,
   'Tis a friend by my side,
       It will lighten and brighten my way;
   And each promise I find
   Soothes and gladdens my mind
       As I read it and heed it each day.

> (*Note:* The word *iambic* is pronounced with iambic rhythm.)
>
> (2) *The* trochaic *foot consists of one accented syllable followed by one unaccented syllable.* Its heavier rhythm is well suited to sober, thoughtful themes.
>
> (3) *The* anapestic *foot consists of two unaccented syllables followed by one accented syllable.*
>   a) This meter produces a flowing, almost galloping rhythm that is well suited to themes of hope, joy, and earnestness.
>   b) Lines written with anapestic rhythm often begin with an incomplete foot.
>   (*Note:* The word *anapestic* is pronounced with anapestic rhythm.)
>
> (4) *The* dactylic *foot consists of one accented syllable followed by two unaccented syllables.*

Lesson 82 Answers

Class Practice

A. 1.
<pre>
   ⌣   ⌣   ′   ⌣   ⌣   ′
   This old Book / is my guide,
   ⌣   ⌣   ′   ⌣   ⌣   ′
   'Tis a friend / by my side,
</pre>
   anapestic; 2, 2, 3, 2, 2, 3

> a) Its flowing rhythm, like the anapestic, is well suited to themes of hope, joy, and earnestness.
> b) Because a dactylic foot ends with two unaccented syllables, you will rarely find a complete foot at the end of a line.
>   (*Note:* A dactyl is a finger. The dactylic foot, like a finger, has one "longer" part—the accented syllable—followed by two "shorter" parts—the unaccented syllables.)

4. Bible poetry and free verse have no regular rhythm or rhyme.

The rest of the sample poem illustrating free verse is given below, in case you want to share it with your students.

2. Do you wish the world were happy?
    Then remember, day by day,
Just to scatter seeds of kindness
    As you pass along the way;
For the pleasures of the many
    May be ofttimes traced to one,
As the hand that plants the acorn
    Shelters armies from the sun.

3. Oh, what a magic doors would hold
    If they could only tell
The tales of living they have seen
    Where happy families dwell.

                    —Elaine Gerber

4. Falling so softly from clouds low and gray,
    Millions of snowflakes, so dainty, so small;
Gazing in wonder upon this display,
    Millions of people are held in their thrall.

B. Choose the most suitable line to complete each stanza. Tell why the other choices do not fit as well.

"Come Ye Apart"

1. "Come ye apart!" It is the Lord who calls us,
    And oh, what tenderness is in His tone!
He bids us leave the busy world behind us
    _____

    a. And come and follow Him without a groan.
    b. And invites us to His blessed throne.
    c. And draw apart awhile with Him alone.

2. 'Mid restless crowds with all their noise and tumult,
    No rest, no leisure, find our spirits there;
Our vision fails, our sense of life's proportion,
    _____

    a. Unless we trust in our Master's good care.
    b. Unless we ask Him to our burdens bear.
    c. Unless we seek the quiet place of prayer.

3. He knoweth how for us to have compassion,
    _____

Shall we not go in answer to His bidding,
    "Come ye yourselves apart and rest awhile"?
    a. Whose strength is small and short as fleeting style;
    b. Whose feet have journeyed many a weary mile;
    c. Whose frail bodies have many a trial;

Summer's blazing sun is beaming down its blast of heat.
Richly adorned with a million large green leaves,
The Giant Oak spreads its arms of restful shade
    over the farmhouse and over the spacious front lawn.
Those arms also tenderly hold nests of precious eggs
    and helpless fledglings.
As the squirrels chase each other up one arm and down another,
    the Giant Oak almost seems to laugh.

With each passing day, the autumn sun is losing its strength
    and spending less time in the sky.
Richly adorned with a million leaves dyed in a pleasing mix
    of burnt orange and russet,
The Giant Oak stands as a monument to the artistic touch
    of the Creator.
Those arms also hold a rich treasure of acorns—
Food for the playful squirrels and others of God's creatures—
Parables of resurrection power.

        ˊ ˘ / ˊ ˘ / ˊ ˘ / ˊ ˘
2. Do you / wish the / world were / happy?
          ˊ ˘ / ˊ ˘ / ˊ ˘ / ˊ
    Then re/member, / day by / day,
trochaic; 4, 4, 4, 4, 4, 4, 4, 4

      ˘ ˊ / ˘ ˊ / ˘ ˊ / ˘ ˘ / ˊ
3. Oh, what / a mag/ic doors / would hold
      ˘ ˊ / ˘ ˊ/ ˘ ˊ
    If they / could on/ly tell
iambic; 4, 3, 4, 3

     ˊ ˘ ˘ / ˊ ˘ ˘ / ˊ ˘ ˘ / ˊ ˘ ˘ / ˊ
4. Falling so / softly from / clouds low and / gray,
       ˊ ˘ ˘ / ˊ ˘ ˘ / ˊ ˘ ˘ / ˊ
    Millions of / snowflakes, so / dainty, so / small;
dactylic; 4, 4, 4, 4

B. 1. a. *Groan* is poor word choice.
     b. poor rhythm
     c. (best choice)
  2. a. poor rhythm
     b. awkward wording
     c. (best choice)
  3. a. awkward and unclear
     b. (best choice)
     c. poor rhythm

In a hurried trip across the southern horizon,
    the winter sun makes a halfhearted effort to warm the earth.
Divested of its rich foliage yet clinging to a few keepsakes,
The Giant Oak stretches its arms to the sky
In silent tribute to the Creator who gave it life
    and now bids it rest through the long winter night.
No life now surges through its mighty chest—
Yet deep within, the miracle of life is still there—
Waiting for the touch of a springtime sun.

★ **EXTRA PRACTICE**
Worksheet 32 *(Rhythm and Rhyme in Poetry)*

4. And so He calls us into desert places

_____

  There to receive the fuller revelation
   He makes to those who wait with Him alone.
 a. Where human voices may not drown His own,
 b. Where He can speak to us in tender tones,
 c. Where we can make all our wishes known,

Written Exercises

A. Copy the first line of each stanza, and scan it by using accent marks
and slashes. Also write how many feet are in each line of the stanza,
and name the rhythm pattern: *iambic, trochaic, anapestic,* or *dactylic.*

1. No horse that is not harnessed
  Is ever worth a dime.
 No steam will ever function
  Until it is confined.
       —Fred D. Jarvis

2. Beautiful may be your life here,
  Like a perfect full-blown rose,
 If your character is molded
  Into beauty as it grows.
     —Mrs. Andrew N. Miller

3. Under His wings I am safely abiding;
  Though the night deepens and tempests are wild,
 Still I can trust Him, I know He will keep me;
  He has redeemed me, and I am His child.
      —William O. Cushing

4. I love thee when thy swelling buds appear
  And one by one their tender leaves unfold,
 As if they knew that warmer suns were near,
  Nor longer sought to hide from winter's cold.
      —Jones Very

5. There's a city of light 'mid the stars, we are told,
  Where they know not a sorrow or care;
 And the gates are of pearl and the streets are of gold,
  And the building exceedingly fair.
      —Aldine S. Kieffer

6. In Thy cleft, O Rock of Ages,
  Hide Thou me;
 When the fitful tempest rages,
  Hide Thou me;
   Where no mortal arm can sever
   From my heart Thy love forever,
 Hide me, O Thou Rock of Ages,
  Safe in Thee.
      —Fanny J. Crosby

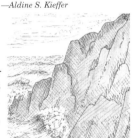

4. a. (best choice)
 b. imperfect rhyme; does not match the idea
  of "desert places"
 c. poor rhythm

Written Exercises

A. 1. No horse / that is / not har/nessed
   3, 3, 3, 3; iambic

 2. Beauti/ful may / be your / life here,
   4, 4, 4, 4; trochaic

 3. Under His / wings I am / safely a/biding;
   4, 4, 4, 4; dactylic

 4. I love / thee when / thy swell/ing buds / appear
   5, 5, 5, 5; iambic

 5. There's a cit/y of light / 'mid the stars, / we are told,
   4, 3, 4, 3; anapestic

 6. In Thy / cleft, O / Rock of / Ages,
   4, 2, 4, 2, 4, 4, 4, 2; trochaic

B. Write the letter of the line that best matches the thought, rhyme, and rhythm of the poem.

1. Character worthy of others' delight,
      Worthy of God's commendation,
   You must develop by facing the fight,

   _____

   a. That you meet in your daily temptation.
   b. Faced in the daily temptations.
   c. Standing against each temptation.

2. Compromise spreads like a cancerous curse,

   _____

   Starting a course that is hard to reverse—
      Character soon is benighted.
   a. Leaving the character blighted,
   b. Turning to God it is lighted,
   c. Leaving a person affrighted,

3. Faithfully stand for the noble and true,
      Even when others do wrongly;

   _____

      Battle in God's service strongly.
   a. By grace divine the prize hotly pursue,
   b. Daily the best and the holy pursue,
   c. Every day what is holy pursue,

C. Write a line of poetry to match the thought, rhythm, and rhyming pattern of each stanza. Your line should have the same number of feet as the line it rhymes with.

1. With help from God I will obey   a
      And serve with willing heart;   b
   I'll safely travel life's rough way: a
   _____   b

2. Drifting across the expanse of blue sky,   a
      Beautiful clouds of pure white   b
   _____   b
   Silently praising their Maker on high.   a

3. Over mountains rough, rugged, and cold,   a
      Into valleys of sweet, quiet rest;   b
   As I follow my Lord, I am bold,   a
   _____   b

B. (Notes in parentheses tell what is wrong with the other choices.)

1. c (Choice _a_ has incorrect rhythm. Choice _b_ has incorrect rhyme and poor repetition of _Faced_ after _facing._)

2. a (Choice _b_ is unclear. Choice _c_ does not fit the theme.)

3. b (Choice _a_ has poor rhythm, and _hotly_ is poor word choice. Choice _c_ has incorrect rhythm.)

C. (Sample lines.)

1. The Bible is my chart.

2. Shine in the sun's dazzling light,

3. For the way that He leads is the best.

83. Forms of Comparison for Adjectives

> **Lesson Survey**
>
> - The **positive degree** of an adjective is its simplest form. This form modifies without comparing.
> - The **comparative degree** is regularly formed by adding *-er* or using *more* or *less*. This form compares two items.
> - The **superlative degree** is regularly formed by adding *-est* or using *most* or *least*. This form compares more than two items.
> - Some common adjectives have irregular forms of comparison.
> - When you compare only two people or things, be especially careful to use the comparative degree.
> - Do not use *more* or *most* with an adjective that is already a form of comparison.
> - An adjective that expresses an absolute quality cannot logically have degrees of comparison.
> - When comparing one thing with a group of which it is part, do not omit the word *other* or *else*.

Many descriptive adjectives have three degrees of comparison: positive, comparative, and superlative. These three degrees are illustrated below.

Positive	Comparative	Superlative
dark	darker	darkest
hot	hotter	hottest
lazy	lazier	laziest
content	more content	most content
glorious	more glorious	most glorious

The *positive degree* of an adjective is its simplest form. This form modifies without comparing.

> These cookies seem quite <u>dark</u>.
> Flossie is a <u>lazy</u> donkey.
> Everyone should be <u>content</u> with his lot in life.

The *comparative degree* is regularly formed by adding *-er* or using *more* or *less*. This form compares two items. For most one-syllable and some two-syllable adjectives, the suffix *-er* is added. If necessary, double the final consonant or change a final *y* to *i* before adding the suffix. For most two-syllable words and for all longer words, *more* is used. The word

Lesson 83

Purpose: To study the three degrees of comparison for adjectives.

Oral Review:

1. What are the two classes of adjectives? (limiting, descriptive)
2. Which of these classes includes adjectives that tell *which, whose,* and *how many*? (limiting)
3. What do descriptive adjectives tell? (what kind of)
4. Name and describe the three positions of adjectives. (attributive—before the substantive; appositive—immediately after the substantive; predicate—after a linking verb and modifying the subject)
5. (*a*) What are ellipsis points? (*b*) What is their function? (*a.* three spaced periods; *b.* to show the omission of one or more words)

6. If an omission within a quotation immediately follows a complete sentence, would you use three periods or four? (four)
7. What are two uses of brackets? (to enclose a comment or correction within a quotation; to serve as parentheses within parentheses)

Lesson Introduction: Write the following on the board:

> We live in [state or province name].
>
> England   Turkey   China
>
> The distance to ——— is far.
> The distance to ——— is farther than to ———.
>
> The distance to ——— is the farthest of these three countries.

Have the students complete the sentences. Notice how the degree or extent of distance increases each time.

less is used for negative comparisons of all words.

> The first cookies we baked are <u>darker</u> than these.
> Brownie, our new donkey, is <u>lazier</u> than Flossie.
> Many times we are <u>less content</u> than we should be.

The *superlative degree* is regularly formed by adding *-est* or using *most* or *least*. This form compares more than two items. Follow the same guidelines for using the suffix or the words as for the comparative degree.

> Those are the <u>darkest</u> cookies of all the ones we baked.
> Brownie is the <u>laziest</u> donkey on our farm.
> Rich people are often the <u>least content</u> of all.

Some common adjectives have irregular forms of comparison.

Positive	Comparative	Superlative
good, well	better	best
bad, ill	worse	worst
far	farther	farthest
much, many	more	most
little	less	least

> Sharon's poem is <u>good</u>, but Beverly's is even <u>better</u>.
> Carl's injuries were <u>worse</u> than mine, but Leroy's were the <u>worst</u> of all.

The forms *less* and *least* are used when an amount is being described. For referring to size, the comparative and superlative degrees of *little* are *littler* and *littlest*.

> The <u>littlest</u> calves (size) ate the <u>least</u> grain (amount).

The most common mistake in using the forms of comparison is to use the superlative form when the comparative form should be used. When you compare only two people or things, be especially careful to use the comparative degree.

> **Incorrect:** Grandpa Weaver is the <u>oldest</u> of my grandfathers.
> Which of the twins picked up <u>the most</u> apples?
> **Correct:** Grandpa Weaver is the <u>older</u> of my grandfathers.
> Which of the twins picked up <u>more</u> apples?

Do not use *more* or *most* with an adjective that is already a form of comparison. The result is an improper double comparison.

> **Incorrect:** I chose the <u>more smaller</u> puppy for my pet.
> That was the <u>most warmest</u> day of the summer.
> **Correct:** I chose the <u>smaller</u> puppy for my pet.
> That was the <u>warmest</u> day of the summer.

Lesson Outline:

1. Many descriptive adjectives have three degrees of comparison: positive, comparative, and superlative.

2. The positive degree of an adjective is its simplest form. This form modifies without comparing.

3. The comparative degree is regularly formed by adding -er or using more *or* less. *This form compares two items.*

   a. Use *-er* for most one-syllable and some two-syllable adjectives.

   b. If necessary, double the final consonant or change a final *y* to *i* before adding the suffix.

   c. For most two-syllable words and for all longer words, use *more*.

   d. For negative comparisons of all words, use *less*.

4. The superlative degree is regularly formed by adding -est or using most *or* least. *This form compares more than two items.* Follow the same guidelines for using the suffix or the words as for the comparative degree.

5. Some common adjectives have irregular forms of comparison. These include *good, well, bad, ill, far, much, many,* and *little* (when referring to amount, not size).

6. When you compare only two people or things, be especially careful to use the comparative degree.

7. Do not use more *or* most *with an adjective that is already a form of comparison.* The result is an improper double comparison.

An adjective that expresses an absolute quality cannot logically have degrees of comparison. The following adjectives express absolute qualities: *square, straight, round, fatal, dead, perfect, true, unanimous.* One corner may be *more nearly square* than another, but it cannot be *more square.* One score may be *more nearly perfect* than another, but it cannot be *more perfect.*

Incorrect:
>The circle on your paper looks <u>rounder</u> than the one on mine.
>The boys were <u>more unanimous</u> in their opinions than the girls were.

Correct:
>The circle on your paper looks <u>more nearly round</u> than the one on mine.
>The boys were <u>more nearly unanimous</u> in their opinions than the girls were.

When comparing one thing with a group of which it is part, do not omit the word *other* or *else.* Without *other* or *else,* the sentence will be illogical or will not say what you intend.

Illogical:
>Charles is taller than any boy in his class.
>>(Obviously, Charles is in his own class. He cannot be taller than himself.)

Logical:
>Charles is taller than any <u>other</u> boy in his class.

Illogical:
>My brother Loren is taller than anyone in our family.
>>(Obviously, Loren is in our family. He cannot be taller than himself.)

Logical:
>My brother Loren is taller than anyone <u>else</u> in our family.

Now consider this sentence.

>Elvin is taller than anyone in eighth grade.

Is this sentence logical or illogical? It depends on whether Elvin is in eighth grade. If he is not an eighth grader, the sentence is logical; if he is an eighth grader, the sentence is saying that he is taller than himself.

Class Practice

A. Give the comparative and superlative degrees of these adjectives.

1. much	4. good	7. interesting
2. lonely	5. ill	8. little, in amount
3. flat	6. far	

8. An adjective that expresses an absolute quality cannot logically have degrees of comparison. Here are some adjectives that express absolute qualities: *square, straight, round, fatal, dead, perfect, true, unanimous.*

(*Teacher:* Many adjectives that express absolute qualities also have meanings that are not absolute, and then these adjectives may have forms of comparison. One example is *square* in the expression "a square meal." The form *squarest* is correct in the following sentence: *It was the squarest meal he had eaten in many days.*)

9. When comparing one thing with a group of which it is part, do not omit the word other **or** else.

Lesson 83 Answers

If an adjective has two syllables, and if *-er* and *-est* may be added, the answer key gives only those forms of comparison (such as *nobler* and *noblest*). Students may also make the forms of comparison by using *more* and *most* (such as *more noble* and *most noble*).

Class Practice

A. 1. more, most
   2. lonelier, loneliest
   3. flatter, flattest
   4. better, best
   5. worse, worst
   6. farther, farthest
   7. more interesting, most interesting
   8. less, least

B. Read each sentence correctly.
1. Although Lot recognized the God of Abraham, he was the least faithful of the two men.
2. Of Isaac's two sons, Jacob was the youngest.
3. A man of faith can be more calmer in adversity than an unbeliever.
4. Josiah was a gooder king than his grandfather Manasseh.
5. Samson had greater physical strength than any man.
6. The play area at the new school is more square than the one at the old school.
7. The longest of the two routes is the most scenic.
8. The Nile is longer than any river in the world.
9. Of Misty's five kittens, I prefer the one with the lighter fur.
10. Conrad thinks the black one is more prettier.

Written Exercises

A. Write correctly each adjective that is written in the wrong form. If a word is omitted, write it along with the words before and after it. If a word should be left out, copy it and draw a line through it. If the sentence contains no mistake, write *correct*.
1. Of Rachel's two sons, Benjamin was the youngest.
2. Saul was taller than any man in Israel.
3. Of all the tribes in Israel, the tribe of Judah was larger.
4. King Saul recognized that David was more nobler than he himself.
5. Brenda's aim with the bean bags is more perfect than mine.
6. Today many people have littler respect for God's Word than people had in years past.
7. Philip seems less healthier now than he was a month ago.
8. The brown coat is the most expensive of the three.
9. My cold became more worser after I was caught in the sudden rainstorm.
10. Little Bobby seemed more excited than anyone over the idea of a pet dog.
11. Larry's story was more true than we had thought.
12. Every day since we put out the feeder, the birds are becoming bolder.
13. The moon looks rounder tonight than it did last night.
14. This bouquet of flowers is the most loveliest of them all.
15. These puppies are littler than ours.

B. Write three sentences for each adjective, illustrating the three degrees of comparison. With the comparative and superlative degrees, be sure your sentences show comparisons clearly and correctly.
1. ill
2. godly
3. big
4. foolish

B. (Corrections are underlined.)
1. Although Lot recognized the God of Abraham, he was the <u>less</u> faithful of the two men.
2. Of Isaac's two sons, Jacob was the <u>younger</u>.
3. A man of faith can be <u>calmer</u> in adversity than an unbeliever.
4. Josiah was a <u>better</u> king than his grandfather Manasseh.
5. Samson had greater physical strength than any <u>other</u> man.
6. The play area at the new school is <u>more nearly</u> square than the one at the old school.
7. The <u>longer</u> of the two routes is the <u>more</u> scenic.
8. The Nile is longer than any <u>other</u> river in the world.
9. Of Misty's five kittens, I prefer the one with the <u>lightest</u> fur.
10. Conrad thinks the black one is <u>prettier</u> (o. <u>prettiest</u>).

Written Exercises

A.
1. younger
2. any other man
3. largest
4. nobler
5. more nearly perfect
6. less
7. less healthy
8. correct
9. worse
10. anyone else over
11. more nearly true
12. correct
13. more nearly round
14. loveliest
15. correct

B. (Individual work.)

Review Exercises

A. Rewrite each sentence in the order named in parentheses. [11]
1. Satan cannot defeat us when we trust in the Lord. (mixed)
2. Our confidence rests in the Almighty. (inverted)
3. God certainly loves to hear our prayers. (mixed)
4. Daily we should pray to the Lord. (natural)
5. Many earnest prayers rise from the hearts of the humble. (inverted)

B. If the sentence needs ellipsis points, write the word before the omitted part and add the ellipsis points. If the sentence needs brackets, copy the material that should be enclosed and add the brackets. [22, 29]
1. "And of his Jesus' fulness have all we received, and grace for grace" (John 1:16).
2. "He saith unto them, Come and see. One of the two which heard John speak, and followed him, was Andrew, Simon Peter's brother" (John 1:39, 40).
3. "The day following Jesus findeth Philip, and saith unto him, Follow me" (John 1:43).
4. The word *parable* (derived from the Greek words *para* beside and *ballein* to cast) refers to a story in which a natural incident is cast beside a spiritual truth.
5. The disciples declared that they understood everything Jesus had said, but

---

Review Exercises

A. 1. When we trust in the Lord, Satan cannot defeat us.
2. In the Almighty rests our confidence.
3. Certainly God loves to hear our prayers.
4. We should pray to the Lord daily. (*or* pray daily to the Lord)
5. From the hearts of the humble rise many earnest prayers.

B. 1. [Jesus']
2. see....
3. Jesus...
4. [beside] [to cast]
5. but...

---

84. Verbals and Phrases Used as Adjectives

Lesson Survey
- A **participle** is one verbal that can be used as an adjective.
- A **participial phrase** consists of a participle and its modifiers and complements.
- Like true verbs, participles can show tense.
- An **infinitive** is another verbal that can be used as an adjective.
- An **infinitive phrase** consists of an infinitive and its modifiers and complements.
- A prepositional phrase can be used as an adjective.

Lesson 84

Purpose: To study the correct uses of participles, infinitives, and phrases used as adjectives.

Oral Review:
1. Name the three degrees of comparison, and tell when each should be used. (positive—to modify without comparing; comparative—to compare two items; superlative—to compare more than two items)
2. Give the comparative and superlative degrees of these adjectives.
   a. comfortable (more comfortable, most comfortable)
   b. ill (worse, worst)
   c. many (more, most)
   d. good (better, best)
3. Give several adjectives that express absolute qualities and cannot logically have degrees of comparison. (square, straight, round, fatal, dead, perfect, true, unanimous)
4. Which class of adjectives tells *which, whose,* and *how many*? (limiting)
5. What do descriptive adjectives tell? (what kind of)
6. What is a retained direct object? (a direct object kept, or retained, in its original position when a verb is changed from the active to the passive voice)

Lesson Introduction: Turn with the students to Psalm 19, and read verse 7. Have the students name all the modifiers of *law. (The, of the Lord, perfect, converting the soul)* Only two of these modifiers are single-word adjectives. Can the students identify what the other two are? (prepositional phrase and participial phrase) You may want to do the same thing with the second half of the verse.

Do you remember that a verbal is a verb form used as another part of speech? In Chapter 4 you studied verbals used as nouns. Participles and infinitives are two kinds of verbals that can be used as adjectives.

Participles and Participial Phrases

In Lesson 46 you studied the three principal parts of verbs: present form, past form, and past participle. You also learned about the present participle, which ends with *-ing*. Several examples of these verb forms are listed here, with all the *participles* underlined.

> pray, prayed, have <u>prayed</u>; <u>praying</u>
> rise, rose, have <u>risen</u>; <u>rising</u>
> sing, sang, have <u>sung</u>; <u>singing</u>

A *participle* is one verbal that can be used as an adjective. When a participle is used in this way, it is not part of a verb phrase, and it does not express the action or being of the subject. Rather, it tells *what kind of* about a substantive. Remember to diagram a verbal across the angle of a slanting and a horizontal line, below the substantive it modifies.

Our <u>risen</u> Lord lives forevermore.
(past participle used as an adjective to modify *Lord*)

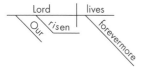

Peter's deliverance amazed the <u>praying</u> Christians.
(present participle used as an adjective to modify *Christians*)

The two apostles, <u>praying</u> and <u>singing</u>, were rejoicing in the Lord.
(present participles used as adjectives to modify *apostles*)

Although a verbal does not function as a verb, it does retain some

Lesson Outline:

1. A participle is one verbal that can be used as an adjective.
- a. When a participle is used as an adjective, it is not part of a verb phrase.
- b. A participle tells *what kind of* about a substantive.
- c. Diagram a verbal across the angle of a slanting and a horizontal line, below the substantive it modifies.

2. A participial phrase consists of a participle and its modifiers and complements. The participle is diagramed as described above; adverb modifiers are placed on slanting lines beneath the verbal; and complements are diagramed in the same way as with true verbs.

3. Like true verbs, participles can show tense.

- a. Use the present participle to express action or being that occurs at the same time as that of the main verb in the sentence.
- b. Use the present perfect form to express action or being that occurs before that of the main verb of the sentence. The present perfect form consists of the past participle preceded by *having*.

4. An infinitive is another verbal that can be used as an adjective.
- a. An infinitive consists of the word *to* used with the basic form of a verb.
- b. An infinitive used as an adjective immediately follows the substantive it modifies and usually answers the question *which* or *what kind of*.
- c. Like a participle, an infinitive is diagramed

characteristics of a verb. For example, it can have adverb modifiers and complements. A *participial phrase* consists of a participle and its modifiers and complements. The participle is diagramed as described above, adverb modifiers are placed on slanting lines beneath the verbal, and complements are diagramed in the same way as with true verbs.

Preaching the Gospel boldly, Peter proclaimed Jesus as the Messiah.
   (*Preaching the Gospel boldly* is a participial phrase modifying *Peter; Gospel* is the direct object of *Preaching; boldly* is an adverb that modifies *Preaching.*)

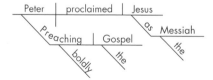

We watched the deer grazing peacefully.
   (*Grazing peacefully* is a participial phrase modifying *deer; peacefully* tells *how* about *grazing.*)

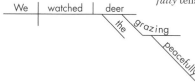

The large bear, being hungry, grew careless.
   (*Being hungry* is a participial phrase modifying *bear; hungry* is a predicate adjective.)

   In the last example above, the participle *being* acts like a linking verb that joins *bear* to the predicate adjective *hungry.* Of course, *being* is a verbal, not a true linking verb; and the "predicate adjective" is not actually an adjective in the predicate. These terms are used simply because verbals and their complements are so much like true verbs and their complements.
   Like true verbs, participles can show tense. Use the present participle to express action or being that occurs at the same time as that of the main verb in the sentence.

across the angle of a slanting and a horizontal line, below the word it modifies.

5. An infinitive phrase consists of an infinitive and its modifiers and complements. An infinitive phrase used as an adjective is diagramed like a participial phrase.

6. A prepositional phrase can be used as an adjective.
   a. A prepositional phrase consists of a preposition, the object of the preposition, and all the words between.
   b. A prepositional phrase used as an adjective always comes immediately after the substantive it modifies.

★ **EXTRA PRACTICE**
Worksheet 33 *(Verbals and Phrases Used as Adjectives)*

Seeing the idolatry in Athens, Paul was stirred in the spirit.
>   (Paul was stirred at the same time he saw the idolatry.)
We watched the bees *swarming* around the tree.
>   (We watched at the same time the bees were swarming.)
Being frightened, the mouse scurried into its hole.
>   (The mouse scurried into its hole at the same time it was frightened.)

Use the present perfect form to express action or being that occurs before that of the main verb in the sentence. The present perfect form consists of the past participle preceded by *having*.

Having seen the idolatry in Athens, Paul preached about the true God.
>   (Paul saw the idolatry before he preached.)
Having seen the bees, we called a local beekeeper.
>   (We saw the bees before we called the beekeeper.)
Having been frightened, the mouse stayed in its hole a long time.
>   (The mouse was frightened before it stayed in its hole.)

Infinitives and Infinitive Phrases

An *infinitive* is another verbal that can be used as an adjective. An infinitive consists of the word *to* used with the basic form of a verb. An infinitive used as an adjective immediately follows the substantive it modifies and usually answers the question *which* or *what kind of*. Like a participle, an infinitive is diagrammed across the angle of a slanting and a horizontal line, below the word it modifies.

The passage to memorize is written on the board.
>   (*To memorize* tells *which* about *passage.*)

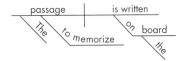

The Bible is a precious book to read and to study.
>   (*To read* and *to study* tell *what kind of* about *book.*)

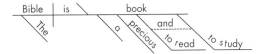

Like a participle, an infinitive can have adverb modifiers and complements. An *infinitive phrase* consists of an infinitive and its modifiers and
complements. An infinitive phrase used as an adjective is diagramed like
a participial phrase.

> Our purpose <u>to live faithfully</u> may be severely tested.
>> (*To live faithfully* is an infinitive phrase modifying *purpose; faith-
>> fully* tells *how* about *to live.*)

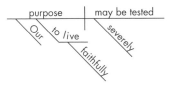

> The best time <u>to cultivate good habits</u> is today.
>> (*To cultivate good habits* is an infinitive phrase modifying *time;
>> habits* is the direct object of *to cultivate.*)

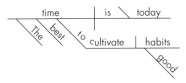

> The Bible reveals the way <u>to be an overcomer</u>.
>> (*To be an overcomer* is an infinitive phrase modifying *way; over-
>> comer* is a predicate nominative.)

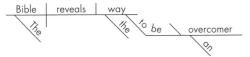

In the last example, *overcomer* is called a predicate nominative because
that is what it would be if the infinitive were a true verb. But what is the
predicate nominative renaming? The "subject" in this case is a generalized
substantive like *you* or *person,* which is understood rather than being
directly stated. Compare the following sentences.

> The Bible reveals the way for you to be an overcomer.
>> (*Overcomer* renames *you.*)

The Bible reveals the way for a person to be an overcomer.
(*Overcomer* renames *person.*)

Prepositional Phrases

A prepositional phrase can be used as an adjective. A prepositional phrase consists of a preposition, the object of the preposition, and all the words between. Like an infinitive phrase, a prepositional phrase used as an adjective always comes immediately after the substantive it modifies.

The plagues <u>upon Egypt</u> were directed against the gods <u>of Egypt</u>.

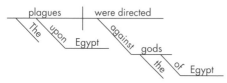

In the example above, *against the gods of Egypt* is an adverb phrase that modifies the verb. But *of Egypt* modifies *gods* by telling *which,* so it is an adjective phrase within the adverb phrase.

Class Practice

A. Read each participle or participial phrase, and tell which word it modifies.
   1. Groping in darkness, many people ignore God's revealed Word.
   2. God's people, hearing and obeying, are blessed by the Word.
   3. Jesus, turning around, saw the trembling woman.
   4. Having won a great victory on Mount Carmel, Elijah fled in fear from the threatening queen.

B. Read each sentence, choosing the correct words in parentheses.
   1. (Washing, Having washed) Jesus' feet with her tears, the sinful woman wiped them with her hair.
   2. (Watching, Having watched) her, the proud Pharisee found fault with Jesus.
   3. Jesus, (knowing, having known) the Pharisee's thoughts, told a story about two debtors.

C. Read each infinitive or infinitive phrase used as an adjective, and tell which word it modifies.
   1. On the sofa is some laundry to fold and to put away.
   2. Martha has some outside chores to do first.
   3. Gary needed some help to lift the heavy boxes.
   4. One problem to face squarely is the temptation to procrastinate.

Lesson 84 Answers

Class Practice

A. 1. Groping in darkness—people; revealed—Word
   2. hearing—people; obeying—people
   3. turning around—Jesus; trembling—woman
   4. Having won a great victory on Moun Carmel—Elijah; threatening—queen

B. 1. Having washed
   2. Watching
   3. knowing

C. 1. to fold—laundry; to put away—laundry
   2. to do first—chores
   3. to lift the heavy boxes—help
   4. to face squarely—problem;
      to procrastinate—temptation

D. Read each prepositional phrase used as an adjective, and tell which word it modifies.
1. A man from Virginia sold us the rabbits in these hutches.
2. The books in the boxes on the shelf were bought during the annual sale at the library.
3. The mountains in the distance remain snowcapped throughout every month of the year.
4. A pair of ducks is nesting near the pond behind our house.

E. On the chalkboard, diagram these sentences.
1. The peace of God is a wonderful blessing to cherish.
2. Many prophets, warning the people faithfully, were persecuted.
3. A person with a good conscience must reject any temptation to be dishonest.
4. Paul, having patiently tended the flock, could give much helpful counsel to the sheep in his care.

Written Exercises

A. Copy each verbal, verbal phrase, or prepositional phrase used as an adjective. Write the word each one modifies.
1. The people's failure to believe hindered Jesus' ability to work miracles.
2. The shepherds tending their flocks heard an angel proclaiming a wonderful message.
3. His message of joy comforted the startled shepherds.
4. No person in the Lord's work has any time to waste.
5. Disregarding the Lord, Saul disobeyed the command to utterly destroy the Amalekites.
6. The roads throughout early Rome joined the far regions of the empire.
7. The Appian Way was the first military highway to be built.
8. Handling large blocks, the army paved the surface of this road.
9. Close communication between the provinces strengthened the position of the rulers.
10. The remaining evidences of the grandeur of ancient Rome include the Colosseum.
11. Using a stethoscope, a doctor hears the heartbeat of his patient.
12. Several hundred branches along the Amazon's course feed the mighty river.

B. Choose the correct words in parentheses.
1. (Finishing, Having finished) his evening chores, Darwin worked on the bookshelves before bedtime.

D. 1. from Virginia—man;
    in these hutches—rabbits
2. in the boxes—books; on the shelf—boxes;
    at the library—sale
3. in the distance—mountains;
    of the year—month
4. of ducks—pair; behind our house—pond

E. 1.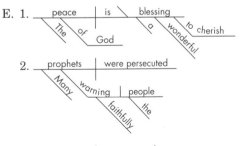

2.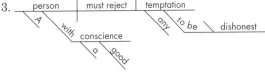

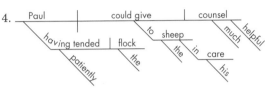

3.

4.

Written Exercises

A. 1. to believe—failure; to work miracles—ability
2. tending their flocks—shepherds;
   proclaiming a wonderful message—angel
3. of joy—message; startled—shepherds
4. in the Lord's work—person; to waste—time
5. Disregarding the Lord—Saul;
   to utterly destroy the Amalekites—command
6. throughout early Rome—roads;
   of the empire—regions
7. to be built—highway
8. Handling large blocks—army;
   of this road—surface
9. between the provinces—communication;
   of the rulers—position
10. remaining—evidences;
    of the grandeur—evidences;
    of ancient Rome—grandeur
11. Using a stethoscope—doctor;
    of his patient—heartbeat
12. along the Amazon's course—branches

B. 1. Having finished

2. (Stirring, Having stirred) the soup with one hand, Charlotte paged through the cookbook with the other.
3. (Hearing, Having heard) the crash, Mother came to the kitchen.
4. The cows, (being, having been) milked, were turned out to pasture.

C. Diagram these sentences.
1. The suffering Saviour won the victory over Satan.
2. His prayer of submission to the Father is a powerful example for us.
3. Honoring his God, Joseph entertained no desire to sin.
4. The children, pulling weeds, welcomed the refreshing breeze.
5. Whistling a cheerful tune, Raymond trimmed the bushes behind the house.
6. The trustees announced their plans to clean the church.

Review Exercises

A. Choose the correct verbs in parentheses. [61, 62]
1. Every morning our prayers should (raise, rise) to God.
2. The sheep of God's pasture can (lay, lie) down in safety.
3. Men must often (alter, altar) their ideas, but the Word of God never changes.
4. Did you (propose, purpose) to be respectful and thoughtful today?
5. I must have (let, left) my book at home.
6. Mabel's words (implied, inferred) her satisfaction.
7. The boys were (setting, sitting) on the bank of the creek.
8. (Can, May) I take some of these cookies over to Sister Minerva?
9. She gratefully (accepted, excepted) our token of thoughtfulness.
10. The severe flooding (affected, effected) quite a change in the landscape.

B. Rewrite each sentence, changing the verb to the passive voice. Retain the direct object in sentences 1 and 2, and the indirect object in sentences 3 and 4. [66]
1. The wise men offered Jesus rich gifts.
2. Paul's nephew gave the captain an important message.
3. Dorcas made the needy many garments.
4. Paul sent Titus an encouraging letter.

C. Try to improve each sentence by rewriting it to make the subject perform the action. If the passive voice is more suitable, explain why.
1. These chicks were hatched just yesterday.
2. My new softball was lost during first recess.
3. A worthy lesson is emphasized by this bulletin board display.
4. The small rabbit was caught by a large, hungry hawk.

---

2. Stirring   4. having been
3. Having heard

C. 1.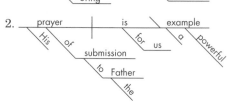

2.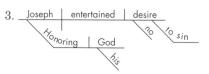

3.

4.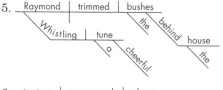

5.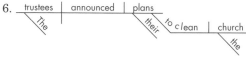

6.

Review Exercises

A. 1. rise   6. implied
2. lie   7. sitting
3. alter   8. May
4. purpose   9. accepted
5. left   10. effected

B. 1. Jesus was offered rich gifts by the wise men.
2. The captain was given an important message by Paul's nephew.
3. Many garments were made the needy by Dorcas.
4. An encouraging letter was sent Titus by Paul.

C. 1. These chicks hatched just yesterday.
2. (Passive voice is suitable because there is a good reason not to name the doer.)
3. This bulletin board display emphasizes a worthy lesson.
4. A large, hungry hawk caught the small rabbit. (Passive voice may be considered suitable because the rabbit was a victim.)

85. Repetition and Parallelism in Poetry

Lesson Survey

- **Alliteration** is the repetition of beginning consonant sounds.
- **Assonance** is the repetition of similar vowel sounds in accented syllables.
- **Parallelism** is the repetition of related ideas.

The two most obvious characteristics of poetry are rhythm and rhyme. These qualities provide much of the beauty in poetry. However, poets make use of other devices that make poetry enjoyable to hear and read.

Alliteration

Alliteration is the repetition of beginning consonant sounds. This is especially effective when the alliteration links words with related meanings, such as *cold* and *clear* or *sweet* and *sour.*

Alliteration can produce various effects. Repeating soft sounds like *s*, *f*, and *w* adds a tone of softness. Repeating harsh sounds like *b, d,* and *k* adds a tone of sharpness or harshness.

Study the alliteration in the following lines. The repetition of harsh sounds in the first stanza matches the thoughts of darkness and despondency. By contrast, the repetition of soft sounds enhances the thoughts of restfulness and submission in the second stanza. (*Laves* in the second stanza means "bathes.")

Submission

Dark the day, the dreary day—
    Clouds a crying canopy;
    Deep distress, despondency
Drag me down in dread dismay.

Hidden sun is shining still;
    Love of Jesus laves those skies!
    Sweetly now my spirit lies
In submission to God's will.

Assonance

Assonance is the repetition of similar vowel sounds in accented syllables, usually within one or two lines. The following lines contain assonance.

I've known the place where roses grow,
    And robins' notes are falling.

Lesson 85

Purpose: (1) To study alliteration and assonance. (2) To teach *synonymous, *antithetic, and *synthetic parallelism in Bible poetry. (*Previous experience:* Synonymous and antithetic parallelism, without use of the terms.)

Oral Review:

1. Finish these guidelines for good rhymes.
   a. The vowel sounds of rhyming syllables must be ———. (the same)
   b. The final consonant sounds of rhyming syllables must be ———. (the same)
   c. The beginning consonant sounds of rhyming syllables must be ———. (different)
   d. The rhyming syllables must be ———. (accented)
2. What is the difference between a masculine rhyme and a feminine rhyme? (A masculine rhyme involves only one syllable; a feminine rhyme involves more than one syllable.)
3. How is the rhyming pattern of a poem marked? (by using the same small letter for all the lines that rhyme with each other)
4. Name the type of meter illustrated in each of these lines.
   a. Falling so gently from frozen gray clouds (dactylic)
   b. God reigneth from His heavenly throne (iambic)
   c. In the cool, quiet evening (anapestic)
   d. Jesus spent the night in prayer (trochaic)
5. What is a poetic foot? (one accented syllable and the unaccented syllable or syllables associated with it)

Lesson Introduction: Write these two samples on the chalkboard.

    Softly from the silent sky
    Sifts the pure, white snow.

Oft upon the rock I tremble,
  Faint of heart and weak of knee.
But the solid "Rock of Ages"
  Never trembles under me.

Whereas alliteration tends to make us read poetry more rapidly, assonance tends to make us read more slowly. Assonance is more difficult to detect than alliteration, but they both add to the music of poetry.

Parallelism

Parallelism is the repetition of related ideas in similar grammatical structures. In Lesson 82 you were reminded that Bible poetry does not have rhythm and rhyme like most poetry. Instead, it has "rhythm and rhyme" in thought. There are three main kinds of parallelism: synonymous, antithetic, and synthetic.

1. Synonymous *parallelism occurs when parallel lines express similar thoughts.* (Remember the word *synonym*?) Synonymous thoughts run beside each other like two rails of a railroad track.

Search me, O God, and know my heart:
Try me, and know my thoughts. (Psalm 139:23)

Parallel lines do not come only in pairs. Sometimes several pairs occur together, all with similar thoughts, as when several sets of railroad tracks run parallel. The following example has two sets of lines with synonymous parallelism.

The heavens declare the glory of God;
And the firmament sheweth his handywork.

Day unto day uttereth speech,
And night unto night sheweth knowledge. (Psalm 19:1, 2)

2. Antithetic *parallelism occurs when parallel lines express opposite thoughts.* (Notice the prefix *anti-*.) Even though they express opposite thoughts, these lines are parallel because their ideas are related and their structure is similar. They are like trains traveling in opposite directions on parallel tracks.

They are brought down and fallen:
But we are risen, and stand upright. (Psalm 20:8)

A fool uttereth all his mind:
But a wise man keepeth it in till afterwards. (Proverbs 29:11)

3. Synthetic *parallelism occurs when parallel lines express thoughts that build one upon another.* (Synthesis is the combination of parts to

Gently from the quiet sky
Falls the pure, white snow.

In which of the two is the language more poetic? Why? Can your students hear the music of the alliteration? This lesson emphasizes three things that enhance the music of poetry.

Lesson Outline:

1. Alliteration is the repetition of beginning consonant sounds.

a. This is especially effective when the alliteration links words with related meanings.

b. Alliteration can produce various effects.

1) Repeating soft sounds like *s, f,* or *w* adds a tone of softness.

2) Repeating harsh sounds like *b, d,* or *k* adds a tone of sharpness or harshness.

2. Assonance is the repetition of similar vowel sounds in accented syllables.

a. Alliteration tends to make us read poetry more rapidly, but assonance tends to make us read more slowly.

b. Assonance is more difficult to detect than alliteration.

3. Parallelism is the repetition of related ideas in similar grammatical structures.

(1) Synonymous *parallelism occurs when parallel lines express similar thoughts.*

(2) Antithetic *parallelism occurs when parallel lines express opposite thoughts.*

(3) Synthetic *parallelism occurs when parallel lines express thoughts that build one upon another.*

produce a whole.) These lines are like the parallel rungs of a ladder, each line adding to the thought of the previous line.

> **Blessed is the man that walketh not in the counsel of the ungodly,**
>> **Nor standeth in the way of sinners,**
>> **Nor sitteth in the seat of the scornful. (Psalm 1:1)**

Do you see the progression in this familiar verse? It pictures two persons who are talking as they *walk* along. They get more involved in conversation and *stand* still to talk more freely. Finally they become so engrossed that they *sit* down to talk with each other.

Not all parallel lines of poetry are as perfectly matched as the examples in this lesson. But that does not detract from the beauty and majesty of the poems in the Bible.

Class Practice

A. For each selection, tell whether *alliteration* or *assonance* is used, and what sound is repeated.
  1. You may worry when you're weary,
       You may worry when you're well.
  2. O gracious Saviour, meet me
       Alone at break of day.
  3. Now the last light of amber day is dying
       Over the levels of this field in flower,
     And in my heart a voice of worship crying;
       O lovely, lovely is the earth, this hour.
  4. These evening clouds, that setting ray,
     And beauteous tints, serve to display
       Their great Creator's praise.

B. Add another line to each poetic line below, continuing the alliteration or assonance shown by the underlined letters. The lines need not rhyme, but they should be consistent in rhythm.
  1. The evening stillness falls, and sunlight slips away,
  2. Sunset, gleaming through the leaves,

C. Tell which kind of parallelism is found in each of these Bible verses.
  1. The hope of the righteous shall be gladness:
     But the expectation of the wicked shall perish. (Proverbs 10:28)
  2. Be not hasty in thy spirit to be angry:
     For anger resteth in the bosom of fools. (Ecclesiastes 7:9)
  3. He that loveth silver shall not be satisfied with silver;
     Nor he that loveth abundance with increase. (Ecclesiastes 5:10)

Lesson 85 Answers

Class Practice

A. 1. alliteration; *w*
   2. assonance; long *a*
   3. alliteration; *l, d, f*
   4. assonance; long *a*

B. (Sample answers.)
   1. The soothing silence steals across the countryside.
   2. Speaks to me of fleeting life.

C. 1. antithetic
   2. synthetic
   3. synonymous

4. Cast thy bread upon the waters:
   For thou shalt find it after many days. (Ecclesiastes 11:1)
5. In God will I praise his word:
   In the Lord will I praise his word. (Psalm 56:10)

Written Exercises

A. Read this poem, and do the exercises that follow.

A Prayer

Teach me, Father, how to go
Softly as the grasses grow;
    Hush my soul to meet the shock
    Of the wild world as a rock;
But my spirit, propt with power,
Make as simple as a flower.
    Let the dry heart fill its cup,
    Like a poppy looking up;
Let life lightly wear her crown,
Like a poppy looking down,
    When its heart is filled with dew,
    And its life begins anew.

Teach me, Father, how to be
Kind and patient as a tree.
    Joyfully the crickets croon
    Under shady oak at noon;
Beetle, on his mission bent,
Tarries in that cooling tent.
    Let me, also, cheer a spot,
    Hidden field or garden grot—
Place where passing souls can rest
On the way and be their best.
—Edwin Markham

1. From stanza 1, copy four sets of words with alliteration. One example should have more than two words.
2. From stanza 2, copy four sets of words with alliteration.
3. From stanza 1, copy two sets of words with assonance. (Rhyming words can be part of a set.)

B. From below, choose one poetic line that illustrates alliteration and one that illustrates assonance. Write another line for each one to continue that poetic music. Your lines do not need to rhyme with the ones given, but they should match in rhythm.
1. God feeds His sheep in fields of green,

4. synthetic
5. synonymous

Written Exercises

A. 1. (Any four of these; underlined set must be included.) grasses, grow; wild, world; propt, power; Like, looking; <u>Let, life, lightly</u>
   2. (Any four of these.) crickets, croon; Beetle, bent; Tarries, tent; garden, grot; Place, passing; be, best
   3. (Any two of these.) Father, how; as, grasses; shock, rock; propt, power; crown, poppy, down

B. (Sample answers.)
   1. And leads them by the quiet streams.

2. Beyond the blue, in realms of bliss,
3. Daily find a place to pray,
4. What are the words of the whispering wind,
5. Perched upon the primrose sprig,

2. Turn to the Book of Psalms. Write which of the three kinds of parallelism is used in each of these verses.
  1. 1:6   4. 6:9
  2. 3:4   5. 16:1
  3. 5:3   6. 18:27

---

2. A land of beauty beckons me.
3. Trusting God to make a way.
4. When through the willow trees warmly it blows.
5. Sings the pretty purple finch.

C. 1. antithetic   4. synonymous
   2. synthetic   5. synthetic
   3. synonymous   6. antithetic

86. Descriptive Language in Poetry

Lesson Survey
- Poetry often includes figures of speech, like **similes, metaphors, personification,** and **hyperboles.**
- Poetry sometimes includes **onomatopoeia,** the use of a word having an imitative sound.
- The words of poetry are carefully chosen for their **denotation** and **connotation.**

Good poets pack a wealth of meaning into a few words. They write descriptively, in a way that appeals to your imagination and stimulates your thinking. In this lesson you will study several methods that poets have long used in writing good poetry.

Figures of Speech

Poets often want to express ideas that cannot be conveyed well in plain language. To do this, they use imaginative comparisons and illustrations that are called figures of speech. Read the following poem, noting the figurative language. You will be referring to this poem for examples of figures of speech.

Morning Thoughts
I went outside this morning
  And touched the morning air;
Its fragrance spread around me
  Like flowers blooming fair.

Lesson 86

Purpose: (1) To teach the appreciation and use of figurative language and descriptive words in poetry. (2) To introduce *denotation and *connotation.

IMPORTANT: For Lesson 89, Class Practice, you will write a poem with your students. Plan ahead to make this a profitable activity.

Oral Review:
1. What words in these lines of poetry have assonance? (Answers are underlined.)

  But the Saviour will not fail you,
    He will write your name above,
  Break the power of sinful habits,
    Fill you with His peace and love.

2. What words in these lines of poetry have alliteration? (Answers are underlined.)

If you want life's truest treasures,
Do not build on sinking sand.

3. Name and describe the three common kinds of parallelism. (synonymous—lines with similar thoughts; antithetic—lines with opposite thoughts; synthetic—lines that build one thought upon another)
4. Tell what kind of rhythm is found in each line.
   a. Under the maple tree's cool, restful shade (dactylic)
   b. I know that my Redeemer lives (iambic)
   c. Softly falls the twilight curtain (trochaic)
   d. Trust each step to the One who the pathway can see (anapestic)
5. How do you count the number of feet in a line of poetry? (by counting the number of accented syllables)

Lesson Introduction: The students are probably familiar with many old figures of speech. See if

It gently rose about me,
    And sunlight sifted through;
I felt its arms surround me—
    It brought me life anew.

God's promises are with me,
    Just like the golden air.
I only need to grasp them
    In simple, fervent prayer.
                              —A. Amstutz

A *simile* makes a figurative comparison by using *like* or *as*. The poem above has two similes: *like flowers blooming fair* and *like the golden air*.

The simile in the first stanza compares the fresh smell of morning to the fragrance of blooming flowers. That is a good comparison, for flowers are often appreciated for their fragrance. The simile in the third stanza compares the presence of God's promises to the air. Of course, the air is always surrounding us, just as God's promises are always with us. Furthermore, God's promises are just as essential to our spiritual survival as the air is to our physical survival. Notice, too, that the poet says *golden air*. The air was golden from the sunrise colors. But gold also symbolizes God's glory and divinity.

A *metaphor* makes a figurative comparison without using *like* or *as*. Some metaphors contain a form of *be* and say that one thing *is* another thing. For example, in Genesis 49:9 Jacob said, "Judah is a lion's whelp." We know that Judah was not a young lion, but Jacob's description pictures well the strength that would reside in this kingly tribe.

Other metaphors use literal terms to describe something that happens only in a figurative sense. An example of this is found in Isaiah 59:5, where the prophet describes the sins of Israel with these words: "They hatch cockatrice' [vipers'] eggs, and weave the spider's web." Obviously, the Jews did not do these things literally, but the metaphor pictures well the deadliness and deceitfulness of their actions.

The last two lines of the poem above contain a metaphor. We cannot literally grasp in our hands God's promises, but the metaphor clearly pictures the need to have them firmly fixed in our minds.

In *personification,* a thing or quality is pictured as if it had the characteristics of a living creature. Here is an example in which wisdom and understanding are personified.

Doth not wisdom cry,
And understanding put forth her voice?
She standeth in the top of high places,
By the way in the places of the paths.
She crieth at the gates, at the entry of the city,
At the coming in at the doors. (Proverbs 8:1–3)

they can fill in the underlined words; these are all similes.

busy as a <u>bee</u>	white as a <u>sheet</u>
happy as a <u>lark</u>	clean as a <u>whistle</u>
red as a <u>beet</u>	neat as a <u>pin</u>
hungry as a <u>bear</u>	brave as a <u>lion</u>

Some common figures of speech are taken from the Bible. Who in the Bible said, "I am escaped with the skin of my teeth"? (Job in Job 19:20) Who described something small as being a drop of a bucket? (God in Isaiah 40:15) Figures of speech like these are important to the descriptive language of poetry, as this lesson teaches.

Lesson Outline:

1. Poetry often includes figures of speech, like similes, metaphors, personification, and hyperboles.

a. A *simile* makes a figurative comparison by using *like* or *as*.

b. A *metaphor* makes a figurative comparison without using *like* or *as*.

1) Some metaphors contain a form of *be* and say that one thing *is* another thing.

2) Other metaphors use literal terms to describe something that happens only in a figurative sense.

c. In *personification,* a thing or quality is pictured as if it had the characteristics of a living creature.

d. A *hyperbole* is what might be called an artistic exaggeration—something which everyone knows is not literally true but which makes a vivid picture in the mind. The hyperbole must not be confused with improper exaggeration.

Do you see the personification in the poem "Morning Thoughts"? The sunlight has no literal arms, but the poem says, "I felt its arms surround me."

A *hyperbole* is what might be called an artistic exaggeration—something which everyone knows is not literally true but which makes a vivid picture in the mind. Here is an example from the Book of Psalms.

> In my distress I called upon the Lord,
> And cried unto my God:
> He heard my voice out of his temple,
> And my cry came before him, even into his ears.
> Then the earth shook and trembled;
> The foundations also of the hills moved and were shaken,
> Because he was wroth.
> There went up a smoke out of his nostrils,
> And fire out of his mouth devoured:
> Coals were kindled by it. (Psalm 18:6–8)

In Class Practice of Lesson 81 is a poem with the following hyperbole.

> You can make a little Eden
> Of the sphere you occupy.

Our kindness certainly will make the world around us better and more enjoyable. But no place on this earth can literally be as glorious as the Garden of Eden was.

The hyperbole must not be confused with improper exaggeration. Such an exaggeration usually draws attention to the exaggerator himself, whereas a hyperbole paints a vivid mental picture that emphasizes an important fact and impresses people with truth.

Onomatopoeia

Poetry sometimes includes *onomatopoeia*, the use of a word having an imitative sound. Expressions like the *buzzing* of bees or the *pitter-patter* of rain are examples of onomatopoeia. Notice the onomatopoeia in the following poem.

Locomotives
Down at the station I like to see the trains
Sticking out their chests and coming down the lanes,
    <u>Dinging</u> and <u>a-hooing</u>, reaching out their light—
    How I wish that trains wouldn't cry at night.

Out in the country, <u>rushing</u> through the grass,
Trains seem happy, <u>purring</u> as they pass,
    Or across the highway, <u>clatter-banging</u> by—
    Why in the nighttime do the trains cry?

2. Poetry sometimes includes onomatopoeia, the use of a word having an imitative sound.

3. The words of poetry are carefully chosen for their denotation and connotation.

      a. Denotation is the strict, exact meaning of a word.

      b. Connotation is the "personality" of a word—the feeling it conveys in addition to its exact meaning.

Do you recognize another poetic device used in this poem? It speaks of trains sticking out their chests, reaching out with their lights, and crying at night. These and several other expressions are examples of personification.

Denotation and Connotation

The words of poetry are carefully chosen for their *denotation* and *connotation*. The poet who speaks of "the *sunshine* of God's love," for instance, means more by the word *sunshine* than "the direct rays of the sun." That would be the strict, exact meaning of the word—its denotation. The poet in this case wants the reader to feel that God's love is warm, cheery, and life-giving. Connotation is the "personality" of a word—the feeling it conveys in addition to its exact meaning.

Comparing the connotations of words can be intriguing after you catch on to it. Some dictionaries compare synonyms to give you the exact shades of meaning. For instance, under *shake* in the dictionary, you may find the following discussion.

> **Synonyms:** *tremble, quake, quiver, shiver*
> *Tremble* suggests a quick, slight shaking caused by an emotion like fear or anger. *Quake* refers to violent shaking caused by a physical or emotional shock. *Quiver* suggests a slight and tremulous shaking. *Shiver* indicates a rapid shaking like that of a person experiencing chill or fear.

A poet describing some tall, graceful trees might speak of their *slender* trunks because the word *slender* has just the right feel for this context. The poet might also use *slim* or *thin,* but he almost certainly would not use *skinny* if he wanted a word with a pleasant connotation. A good poet puts diligent effort into choosing exactly the right words.

Class Practice

A. Tell which of the four kinds of figurative language is found in each selection.
1. A tree that looks at God all day,
   And lifts her leafy arms to pray.
2. Thou hast given us a land
   That flows with milk and honey.
3. Thy calmness bends serene above,
   My restlessness to still.
4. Like a bird on the deep, far away from its nest,
   I had wandered, my Saviour, from Thee.
5. Encamped along the hills of light,
   Ye Christian soldiers, rise.

Lesson 86 Answers

Class Practice

A. 1. personification; *also* metaphor
   2. hyperbole *or* metaphor
   3. metaphor *or* personification
   4. simile
   5. metaphor

B. Suggest an original figure of speech to complete each line.
   1. The thunderclouds moved in like . . . (simile)
   2. The bushes on either side of the front door were . . . (metaphor)
   3. The deserted house . . . (personification)
   4. The remaining days before the trip . . . (hyperbole)

C. Describe the following situations with words that make use of onomatopoeia.
   1. A kettle lid falling on the floor.
   2. An airplane flying overhead.
   3. An empty wagon going across a wooden bridge.

D. Read each sentence, choosing the word with the best denotation and connotation.
   1. When our new neighbors moved in, we watched the activities (curiously, inquisitively, nosily).
   2. My little brother followed me around (curiously, inquisitively, nosily), asking questions about everything that caught his attention.
   3. Even though Grant knew he was wrong, he was too (steadfast, firm-willed, stubborn) to admit it.
   4. The apostle Paul was so (steadfast, firm-willed, stubborn) that he was not moved even by the threat of death.
   5. You should not be so (careful, cautious, fussy) that every hair must be in place.
   6. This answer shows evidence of (careful, cautious, fussy) thinking.

Written Exercises

A. Copy and finish the following sentences with original figures of speech.
   1. The flock of chickens from one end of the broiler house to the other looked like . . . (simile)
   2. The mountain road was . . . (metaphor)
   3. The . . . wind . . . (personification)
   4. Soon the guilt of those unkind words . . . (hyperbole)

B. Write which of the four kinds of figurative language is found in each selection.
   1. Like a rosebud, still unopened,
      Sparkling in the morning dew,
   2. Cast your all upon the Saviour,
      On the silent wings of prayer.
   3. And he knows the strength of the cruel sea
      When loosed in its angry might.
   4. Like a river glorious is God's perfect peace;
      Over all, victorious in its bright increase.

B. (Sample answers.)
   1. surging waves; a turbulent black sea
   2. fat green guards; flaming bonfires of color
   3. stared with empty windows across the weedy lawn
   4. stretched endlessly ahead of us

C. (Sample answers.)
   1. bang, clang, clatter, crash
   2. drone, whine, scream
   3. rattle, clatter, rumble

D. 1. curiously   4. steadfast
   2. inquisitively   5. fussy
   3. stubborn   6. careful

Written Exercises

A. (Sample answers are underlined.)
   1. The flock of chickens from one end of the broiler house to the other looked like <u>a white carpet (a field of white daisies)</u>.
   2. The mountain road was <u>a gray string threaded through the forest (a silver wire coiled across the hills)</u>.
   3. The <u>angry (laughing)</u> wind <u>tore at my clothes (wrestled with the birds)</u>.
   4. Soon the guilt of those unkind words <u>weighed a ton on my mind (was burning like hot coals inside me)</u>.

B. 1. simile
   2. metaphor
   3. personification
   4. simile

5. The waves beside them danced, but they
   Outdid the sparkling waves in glee.
6. Though a blizzard of troubles assailed me,
   Never once has my Saviour yet failed me.
7. This old Book is my guide,
   'Tis a friend by my side.
8. The juicy gossip morsels flew, within a day or two,
   Around the world at lightning speed, their havoc to pursue.

5. personification
6. hyperbole *or* metaphor
7. personification *or* metaphor
8. hyperbole

C. The following excerpts are from "The Leak in the Dike." In each set of lines, copy one word that makes use of onomatopoeia.
1. Then the goodwife turned to her labor,
      Humming a simple song,
   And thought of her husband, working hard
      At the sluices all day long;
2. With thoughts of his pleasant errand,
      He trudged along the way;
   And soon his joyous prattle
      Made glad a lonesome place—
3. He was stopping now to gather flowers,
      Now listening to the sound,
   As the angry waters dashed themselves
      Against their narrow bound.
4. But hark! Through the noise of waters
      Comes a low, clear trickling sound.
5. 'Tis many a year since then, but still,
      When the sea roars like a flood,
   Their boys are taught what a boy can do
      Who is brave and true and good.

C. 1. Humming
   2. prattle
   3. dashed
   4. trickling
   5. roars

D. Copy the word with the best denotation and connotation for each sentence.
1. The stampeding herd of buffalo (tripped, thundered, sped, tramped) across the prairie.
2. A frightened buck (tripped, thundered, sped, tramped) down the mountain trail.
3. The thirsty plant (hung, displayed, drooped, ran) its leaves sadly over the rim of the pot.
4. The morning glory boldly (hung, displayed, drooped, ran) its beautiful blossoms on the tree trunk.
5. We sat numb with disappointment. (Gloom, Dusk, Darkness, Twilight) hung over the kitchen table.

D. 1. thundered
   2. sped
   3. drooped
   4. displayed
   5. Gloom

6. We all had a good (giggle, laugh, guffaw, snicker).
7. Wilma wiped up the spilled water with an embarrassed (chuckle, giggle, guffaw, snicker).
8. We thought we were out of sight in the tree until we heard Grandpa's low (chuckle, giggle, guffaw, snicker).

E. Begin looking for a poem (not used in this chapter) that you will enjoy reading aloud to your classmates in Lesson 90. Get it approved by your teacher by the time you reach Lesson 89.

6. laugh
7. giggle
8. chuckle

E. (Individual work.)

---

87. Adjective Clauses

> ### Lesson Survey
> - An **adjective clause** is a dependent clause that modifies a substantive. It is introduced by a **relative pronoun** or a **relative adverb.**
> - A **restrictive adjective clause** is needed to make the meaning of a sentence clear.
> - A **nonrestrictive adjective clause** is not needed to clarify the meaning of a sentence.

In Chapter 2 you learned that a dependent clause is a group of words containing a skeleton and functioning as a specific part of a sentence. An independent clause expresses a complete thought, but a dependent clause does not.

An *adjective clause* is a dependent clause that modifies a substantive. The following sentences communicate the same basic idea. Notice how the underlined modifier of the italicized noun changes from a word to a phrase to a clause.

King Saul was a <u>tall</u> *man.*
King Saul was a *man* <u>of unusual height</u>.
King Saul was a *man* <u>who stood head and shoulders above others</u>.

An adjective clause is introduced by a *relative pronoun* or a *relative adverb*. In Chapter 7 you learned that the relative pronouns include *who, whom, whose, which,* and *that.* The relative adverbs are *when, where,* and *why.* These words are called *relative* pronouns and adverbs because they *relate* the adjective clause to the substantive that the clause modifies. For this reason, adjective clauses are sometimes called *relative clauses.*

Lesson 87

Purpose: To study the identification, recognition, and punctuation of restrictive and nonrestrictive adjective clauses, including those with *relative adverbs.

Oral Review:

1. Name three kinds of phrases used as adjectives. (participial, infinitive, prepositional)
2. Present participles always end with ———. *(-ing)*
3. Past participles usually end with ———. *(-ed)*
4. Name the three degrees of comparison, and tell when each should be used. (positive—to modify without comparing; comparative—to compare two items; superlative—to compare more than two items)
5. Give the comparative and superlative forms of these irregular adjectives.
   a. good (better, best)
   b. far (farther, farthest)
   c. much (more, most)
   d. little, in amount (less, least)
   e. ill (worse, worst)
   f. many (more, most)
   g. bad (worse, worst)
6. Tell what kind of complement the word *rich* is in these sentences.
   a. Abraham became quite rich. (predicate adjective)
   b. The Bible gives the rich many warnings. (indirect object)
   c. The poor often envy the rich. (direct object)
   d. The most contented are not necessarily the rich. (predicate nominative)
7. Name the direct object and the indirect object in this sentence: *Our family gave Grandmother Beiler a scrapbook. (direct object:* scrapbook; *indirect object:* Grandmother Beiler)

The Lord _whom we worship_ is the one _who created the universe_.
  (_Whom_ relates the clause _whom we worship_ to _Lord_. _Who_ relates
  the clause _who created the universe_ to _one_.)

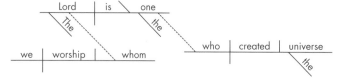

Jesus, _whose voice stilled the tempest_, is the Prince of Peace.
  (_Whose_ relates the clause _whose voice stilled the tempest_ to _Jesus_.)

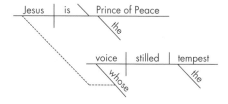

Bethel is the place _where Jacob saw a vision of angels_.
  (_Where_ relates the clause _where Jacob saw a vision of angels_ to
  place.)

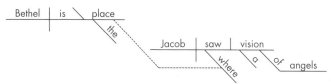

The word that introduces an adjective clause not only relates the clause to a substantive but also fills a specific function within the clause. The nominative case _who_ should be used for a subject or predicate nominative, and the objective case _whom_ should be used for an object. The possessive case _whose_ should be used when the relative pronoun modifies a substantive in the relative clause. If a relative adverb is used, it modifies the verb in the relative clause. Note the positions of the relative pronouns and the relative adverb in the diagrams above.

Sometimes the relative pronoun or relative adverb is omitted. Since its meaning is understood, it is placed in parentheses on a sentence diagram.

8. Change the sentence above to the passive voice, first with a retained direct object and then with a retained indirect object. (Grandmother Beiler was given a scrapbook by our family. A scrapbook was given Grandmother Beiler by our family.)

9. Tell which of the six classes of pronouns each group represents.
   a. himself, herself, themselves (compound personal)
   b. who, whom, whose, which, what (interrogative)
   c. this, that, these, those (demonstrative)
   d. anything, everybody, many, few (indefinite)
   e. who, whom, whose, which, that (relative)
   f. you, we, they, its (personal)

Lesson Introduction: Both of the following sentences are false. Can the students think of words to add that will make them true?

Everyone is foolish.
Nobody will enter heaven.

Adding the clause _who loves sin_ will make both sentences true because that clause restricts each subject to a specific group of people. This lesson is about adjective clauses, of which some are restrictive and some are nonrestrictive.

Lesson Outline:

   1. An adjective clause is a dependent clause that modifies a substantive.

   2. An adjective clause is introduced by a relative pronoun or a relative adverb.
   a. The relative pronouns include _who, whom, whose, which,_ and _that,_ and the relative adverbs are _when, where,_ and _why._
   b. Relative pronouns and relative adverbs fill specific functions within the clauses they introduce.

The man <u>they rescued</u> is my uncle.

A *restrictive adjective clause* is needed to make the meaning of a sentence clear. It does exactly what its name indicates: it restricts, or limits, the meaning of a substantive so that it identifies one specific person, thing, or group. Sometimes the sentence is not even true without the restrictive clause. A restrictive adjective clause should not be set off by commas.

> The heifers <u>that Father sold to Mr. Graybill</u> are in this pen.
> (The adjective clause clarifies the meaning by identifying specific heifers.)
> Everyone <u>who truly loves the Lord</u> obeys His Word.
> (The adjective clause clarifies the meaning by specifying certain people. The statement is not true without the adjective clause.)
> The students <u>whose Bible memory is not finished</u> must stay inside.
> (The adjective clause clarifies the meaning by identifying specific students.)

A *nonrestrictive adjective clause* is not needed to clarify the meaning of a sentence. It does not restrict the meaning of the substantive it modifies by identifying a specific person, thing, or group. Rather, a nonrestrictive adjective clause simply gives additional information about the word that it modifies. A nonrestrictive adjective clause must be set off by commas.

> Jesus Christ, <u>who gave His life on Calvary</u>, is the Saviour of the world.
> (The clause simply gives additional information about *Jesus Christ;* it is not needed to identify Jesus Christ.)
> Our house, <u>which was built one hundred years ago</u>, is still in good condition. (The clause simply gives additional information about *house;* it is not needed to identify a specific house.)

Class Practice

A. Read each adjective clause, and tell what word it modifies.
1. The prophets, who warned the sinful people, were not always appreciated.
2. The summer fruit God showed to Amos signified an end.
3. Jeremiah was the weeping prophet whose people had gone into captivity.
4. The ark which Noah had built rested upon the mountains of Ararat.

1) The nominative case *who* should be used for a subject or predicate nominative.
2) The objective case *whom* should be used for an object.
3) The possessive case *whose* should be used when the relative pronoun modifies a substantive in the relative clause.
4) A relative adverb modifies the verb in the relative clause.
c. Sometimes the relative pronoun or relative adverb is omitted. Since its meaning is understood, it is placed in parentheses on a sentence diagram.

3. A restrictive adjective clause is needed to make the meaning of a sentence clear.
   a. It restricts, or limits, the meaning of a substantive so that it identifies one specific person, thing, or group.

Lesson 87 Answers

Class Practice

A. 1. who warned the sinful people—prophets
   2. God showed to Amos—fruit
   3. whose people had gone into captivity—prophet
   4. which Noah had built—ark

---

   b. It should not be set off by commas.

4. A nonrestrictive adjective clause is not needed to clarify the meaning of a sentence.
   a. It does not restrict the meaning of the substantive it modifies by identifying a specific person, thing, or group. Rather, it simply gives additional information about that word.
   b. It must be set off by commas.

★ **EXTRA PRACTICE**
Worksheet 34 *(Adjective Clauses)*

5. Thornton Hills, where we stopped for lunch, is a small town.
6. Ferdinand Magellan commanded the first expedition that sailed around the world.
7. We saw the compass that had been used by this navigator.
8. We greatly enjoyed the days Aunt Pearl was here.

B. Tell whether each underlined adjective clause is *restrictive* or *nonrestrictive*. Also tell where commas should be added.
1. The Ten Commandments <u>which God gave to Moses on Mount Sinai</u> represent basic principles of righteousness.
2. The new commandment <u>that Jesus gave</u> was the commandment of love.
3. The ark <u>that Noah built</u> was designed by God Himself.
4. Noah <u>who found grace in the eyes of the Lord</u> preserved the faith in his generation.
5. God has not revealed to man the time <u>when the Lord will return</u>.
6. The location of the new church is Duck Mountain <u>where our congregation has done evangelistic work for several years</u>.
7. The boy <u>whose back was broken in a farm accident</u> is in the hospital.
8. My oldest brother <u>who turned nineteen last week</u> is giving a year of voluntary service to the mission in the Philippines.

C. On the chalkboard, diagram these sentences.
1. The dreams that God gave Joseph were fulfilled.
2. Deborah, whose faith encouraged Barak, was a true mother in Israel.
3. The tabernacle was the place where God would meet His people.
4. David married Abigail, from whom he had received wise counsel.
5. He was the new king God chose.

Written Exercises

A. Copy each adjective clause and the word it modifies.
1. I will praise the Lord, who has made everything beautiful.
2. "This is the day which the Lord hath made."
3. The crowd heard the man whom Peter had healed.
4. The man whose son was ill appealed to Jesus.
5. I cannot forget the summer I lived with Grandpa Stauffer's.
6. Soon we reached the place where Daniel had seen the deer.
7. The day when we began the trip was a rainy Tuesday.
8. The preacher who brought the first message is my uncle.
9. Those clouds that are gathering in the west look like thunderheads.
10. We plan to sing for Glenda Kurtz, who is my great-aunt.
11. The rabbit which Duke was chasing zigzagged across the meadow.
12. Then it darted into a brier patch that Duke could not penetrate.

9. that are gathering in the west—clouds
10. who is my great-aunt—Glenda Kurtz
11. which Duke was chasing—rabbit
12. that Duke could not penetrate—patch

5. where we stopped for lunch—Thornton Hills
6. that sailed around the world—expedition
7. that had been used by this navigator—compass
8. Aunt Pearl was here—days

B. 1. nonrestrictive; commas after *Commandment* and *Sinai*
2. restrictive; no commas
3. restrictive; no commas
4. nonrestrictive; commas after *Noah* and *Lord*
5. restrictive; no commas
6. nonrestrictive; comma after *Mountain*
7. restrictive; no commas
8. nonrestrictive; commas after *brother* and *week*

C. 1.

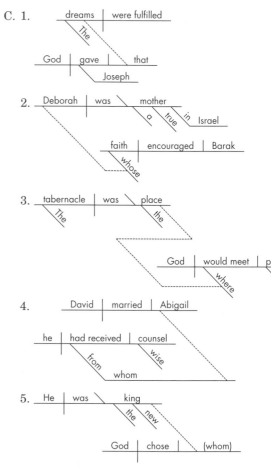

Written Exercises

A. 1. who has made everything beautiful—Lord
2. which the Lord hath made—day
3. whom Peter had healed—man
4. whose son was ill—man
5. I lived with Grandpa Stauffer's—summer
6. where Daniel had seen the deer—place
7. when we began the trip—day
8. who brought the first message—preacher

3. Write whether the underlined clause is restrictive (*R*) or nonrestrictive (*N*). Also write each word that should be followed by a comma, and add the comma.
  1. The disciple <u>who betrayed his Master</u> went and hanged himself.
  2. Judas <u>who betrayed his Master</u> went and hanged himself.
  3. We can understand the excitement of Rhoda <u>who failed to open the gate for Peter</u>.
  4. The girl <u>who failed to open the gate for Peter</u> must have been very excited.
  5. The cold front <u>that passed through today</u> brought stormy weather.
  6. A cold front <u>which occurs when a cold air mass pushes into a warm air mass</u> often brings cooler weather.
  7. The little building <u>where Grandfather went to school</u> has been converted into a house.
  8. That you are developing habits is one reason <u>why you should carefully consider your present conduct</u>.
  9. Those habits <u>that are developed in youth</u> often shape a person's adult life.
  10. Your habits <u>which are easier to form than to break</u> can be a strong force for good or for evil.

C. Diagram these sentences.
  1. Tomorrow is the day when the serviceman will check the furnace.
  2. The children who were selling the melons miscounted the money.
  3. The melons that we bought tasted delicious.
  4. The farmer whose steers ruined our garden will pay the damages.
  5. The man we helped had never heard the simple message of the Gospel.

Review Exercises

A. Copy each complement, and write whether it is a direct object (*DO*), an indirect object (*IO*), a predicate nominative (*PN*), a predicate adjective (*PA*), or an objective complement (*OC*). [5–8]
  1. The Lord called Moses to a great work.
  2. Fearlessly, Moses gave Pharaoh the Lord's message.
  3. Pharaoh remained stubborn and haughty.
  4. Because of Pharaoh's rebellion, God made his heart hard.
  5. In many ways, Pharaoh is a type of Satan.

B. Copy each object complement, and label it *DO* (direct object) or *IO* (indirect object). Write *ret.* after the label if the object is retained. [66]
  1. Even a large spider can be given a paralyzing sting by a wasp.
  2. A spider web may contain over sixty feet of silk.

B. 1. R
  2. N; Judas, Master,
  3. N; Rhoda,
  4. R
  5. R
  6. N; front, mass,
  7. R
  8. R
  9. R
  10. N; habits, break,

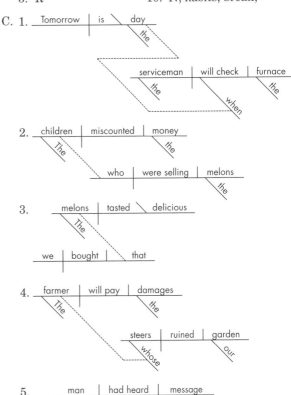

Review Exercises

A. 1. Moses—DO
  2. Pharaoh—IO; message—DO
  3. stubborn—PA; haughty—PA
  4. heart—DO; hard—OC
  5. type—PN

B. 1. sting—DO ret.
  2. feet—DO

3. The instinct for making a web is given the spider by God Himself.
4. The morning dew gives spider webs a silvery beauty.

C. Copy each pronoun, and label it *P* (personal), *CP* (compound personal), *D* (demonstrative), *ID* (indefinite), *IR* (interrogative), or *R* (relative). [69–77]
1. Whom are these for?
2. Have you told everyone about the visitor who came to school today?
3. Mr. Lorry himself helped us round up the steers that got out.
4. Some ran a mile down the road past his farm.
5. What would anybody do with that?

3. spider—IO ret.
4. spider webs—IO; beauty—DO

C. 1. Whom—IR; these—D
2. you—P; everyone—ID; who—R
3. himself—CP; us—P; that—R
4. Some—ID; his—P
5. What—IR; anybody—ID; that—D

---

88. Using Adjectives Correctly

> **Lesson Survey**
> - Use an adjective only when it makes a worthwhile contribution.
> - Use articles correctly in compound structures.
> - Do not use *a* or *an* after *kind of* or *sort of*.
> - Do not use *this (these) here, that (those) there*, or *them* as adjectives.
> - Capitalize most modifiers derived from proper nouns.
> - Place an adjective phrase or clause immediately before or after the word that it modifies.
> - Learn the correct usage of these adjectives: *awful, less—fewer, respectful—respectable—respective.*

The ability to recognize the various forms and functions of adjectives is important. But equally important is the ability to use them correctly. Here are some rules for the correct usage of adjectives.

1. *Use an adjective only when it makes a worthwhile contribution.* Can you see what is wrong with the underlined adjectives in the following expressions?

the <u>tall</u> giant   the <u>plush, luxurious</u> furnishings
the <u>dry</u> desert   the <u>saturated, drenched</u> clothes
the <u>damp</u> fog   <u>each and every</u> person

In the examples on the left, the meanings of the adjectives are already implied in the meanings of the nouns: all giants are tall, all deserts are

Lesson 88

Purpose: To study some additional rules for adjective usage.

Oral Review:
1. What are the two kinds of adjective clauses? (restrictive, nonrestrictive)
2. Which kind of adjective clause
   a. simply gives additional information? (nonrestrictive)
   b. identifies one specific person, thing, or group? (restrictive)
   c. must be set off with commas? (nonrestrictive)
3. Name three kinds of phrases used as adjectives. (participial, infinitive, prepositional)
4. Name the three degrees of comparison, and tell when each should be used. (positive—to modify without comparing; comparative—to compare two

items; superlative—to compare more than two items)
5. For each group, tell whether the substantives should be used with singular or plural verbs.
   a. measles, mathematics, gallows (singular)
   b. each, anyone, everybody (singular)
   c. trousers, scissors, pliers (plural)
6. When should a collective noun have (*a*) a singular verb? (*b*) a plural verb? (*a.* when it refers to the group acting as a unit; *b.* when it refers to the individual members of the group acting separately)
7. An apostrophe is used to make the possessive form of (a personal pronoun, <u>an indefinite pronoun</u>).
8. The relative pronoun (<u>who</u>, which) refers only to people, and (who, <u>which</u>) refers only to things.

Lesson Introduction: The way we use tools and equipment is important. We would not use a plow to cultivate between rows in the garden. Nor would we

dry, and all fog is damp. Therefore, these adjectives are redundant. In the examples on the right, the adjectives are synonyms. Only one of the two should be used: the plush furnishings or the luxurious furnishings; the saturated clothes or the drenched clothes; each person or every person.

Another problem, perhaps even more common among eighth graders, is the tendency to use worn-out and general adjectives. Use fresh, descriptive adjectives that paint clear mental pictures and say exactly what you mean.

> a <u>big</u> decision (important? momentous? difficult? major?)
> a <u>good</u> business (helpful? profitable? honorable?)
> a <u>real</u> help (actual? genuine? Or do you mean outstanding? impressive? satisfactory? valuable?)

Here are some more worn-out, general adjectives, with suggestions of fresher, more descriptive adjectives.

> **awful:** severe, serious, destructive, costly, terrifying, embarrassing, appalling, dire, dreadful, formidable
> **nice:** pleasant, admirable, fine, excellent, accurate, careful, considerate, well-mannered, gracious, polite
> **funny:** amusing, humorous, laughable, entertaining, witty
> (Do not use *funny* to mean "strange" or "unusual.")
> **great:** huge, strong, vast, important, serious, notable, famous, prominent, majestic, exalted, noble, admirable
> (Do not use *great* to mean "excellent.")

2. *Use articles correctly in compound structures.* If two adjectives or nouns refer to one individual, use only one article. If two adjectives or nouns refer to more than one individual, use an article for each individual.

> <u>The</u> white and <u>the</u> green house are newer than <u>the</u> gray and brown house. (three houses: one that is white, one that is green, and one that is gray and brown)

> <u>The</u> chairman and <u>the</u> vice-chairman met with <u>the</u> secretary and treasurer. (three people: one who was chairman, one who was vice-chairman, and one who was both secretary and treasurer)

3. *Do not use* a *or* an *after* kind of *or* sort of.

> **Incorrect:** Which <u>kind of a</u> cookie do you want?
> What <u>sort of a</u> bee is that?
> **Correct:** Which <u>kind of</u> cookie do you want?
> What <u>sort of</u> bee is that?

4. *Do not use* this (these) here, that (those) there, *or* them *as adjectives.*

attempt to put the plow ahead of the tractor. A plow just was not made to be used for such a purpose or in such a manner. Using words properly is important too. This lesson gives some rules and practice in using adjectives correctly.

Lesson Outline:

1. Use an adjective only when it makes a worthwhile contribution.

    a. Do not use an adjective to modify a noun if the noun includes the meaning of the adjective.

    b. Avoid the meaningless repetition of synonymous adjectives that modify one word.

    c. Use fresh, descriptive adjectives that say exactly what you mean.

2. Use articles correctly in compound structures.

    a. If two adjectives or nouns refer to one individual, use only one article.

    b. If two adjectives or nouns refer to more than one individual, use an article for each individual.

3. Do not use a or an after kind of or sort of.

4. Do not use this (these) here, that (those) there, or them as adjectives.

5. Capitalize most modifiers derived from proper nouns.

6. Place an adjective phrase or clause immediately before or after the word that it modifies.

    a. A misplaced modifier often makes an absurd statement.

    b. An introductory participle is assumed to modify the subject. If it does not logically do that, it is called a *dangling participle*.

Incorrect: <u>This here</u> book has been quite a challenge to my faith.
<u>Those there</u> Christians were ready to suffer for Jesus.
I want to be just as faithful as <u>them</u> saints were.

Correct: <u>This</u> book has been quite a challenge to my faith.
<u>Those</u> Christians were ready to suffer for Jesus.
I want to be just as faithful as <u>those</u> saints were.

5. *Capitalize most modifiers derived from proper nouns.* Most of these are proper adjectives, but such words occasionally become so commonplace that they are no longer capitalized. Check a dictionary when you are not sure.

Mother served <u>French</u> toast for breakfast.
The <u>Gregorian</u> calendar was adopted in the <u>American</u> colonies in 1752.
A <u>china</u> plate was broken.

6. *Place an adjective phrase or clause immediately before or after the word that it modifies.* A misplaced modifier often makes an absurd statement. If a participle begins a sentence, be especially careful to have it modify the subject. If it does not logically do that, it is called a *dangling participle.* In the second example below, the dangling participle does not logically modify *any* word in the sentence.

Incorrect:

We saw two deer <u>driving to town</u>.
<u>Walking down the hall</u>, the book fell out of my hand.
Give the man this bag of corn <u>with the wire-rimmed glasses</u>.
The man has learned to follow Christ's way of peace <u>who once fought in the army</u>.

Correct:

<u>Driving to town</u>, we saw two deer.
<u>Walking down the hall</u>, I dropped the book.
Give the man <u>with the wire-rimmed glasses</u> this bag of corn.
The man <u>who once fought in the army</u> has learned to follow Christ's way of peace.

Learn the correct usage of the following adjectives.

Awful

Use *awful* as an adjective meaning "inspiring awe or wonder" or "terrible." Do not use *awful* as an adjective meaning "disagreeable" or as an adverb meaning "very."

We approach the <u>awful</u> presence of God with reverence.
The tornado produced some <u>awful</u> damage in our area.

Poor: Cleaning out the basement was an <u>awful</u> job.
Better: Cleaning out the basement was a <u>disagreeable</u> job.

7. Learn the correct usage of the following adjectives.

a. Use *awful* as an adjective meaning "inspiring awe or wonder" or "terrible." Do not use *awful* as an adjective meaning "disagreeable" or as an adverb meaning "very."

b. Use *less* to indicate *how much* about a singular noun. Use *fewer* to indicate *how many* about a plural noun. Avoid the common error of using *less* with plural nouns.

c. *Respectful* means "showing courtesy or esteem." *Respectable* means "worthy of respect." *Respective* means "individual; particular."

Less—Fewer

Use *less* to indicate *how much* about a singular noun. Use *fewer* to indicate *how many* about a plural noun. Avoid the common error of using *less* with plural nouns.

Incorrect: Less students were absent today than yesterday.
Urban areas have less gravel roads than rural areas.
Correct: Fewer students were absent today than yesterday.
Urban areas have fewer gravel roads than rural areas.

Respectful—Respectable—Respective

Respectful means "showing courtesy or esteem." *Respectable* means "worthy of respect." *Respective* means "individual; particular."

The children maintained a respectful silence while the tour guide spoke.
You can earn the confidence of others by respectable behavior.
When the morning bell rings, the students gather in their respective classrooms.

Class Practice

A. Read these sentences, omitting the unnecessary or repetitious adjectives.
1. Daniel was a true and genuine godly saint.
2. A windy tempest swept across the small, little Sea of Galilee.
3. That tall skyscraper is more than nine hundred feet high.
4. The round full moon illuminated the worn, well-used path.

B. Tell which of the following adjectives could replace *clear* in each description: *comprehensible, indisputable, pure, sunny, transparent, unobstructed.*
1. a clear windshield
2. a clear answer
3. clear evidence
4. a clear conscience
5. a clear view
6. clear skies

C. Suggest several descriptive adjectives to replace each underlined adjective.
1. Brother Glen gave us a real test today.
2. We had a nice time visiting Uncle Fred's.
3. Alexander ruled a great empire.

D. Read each sentence correctly.
1. The king and queen ignored the prophet's message.
2. God told Noah to build an ark who had found grace in His eyes.
3. That there ship was three stories high.
4. What kind of a flower is in this pot?
5. Working busily, much nectar is brought to the hive every day.
6. Uncle Brian has less cows than we do.

Lesson 88 Answers

Class Practice

A. 1. Daniel was a true (*or* genuine) saint.
2. A tempest swept across the small (*or* little) Sea of Galilee.
3. That skyscraper is more than nine hundred feet high.
4. The full moon illuminated the worn (*or* well-used) path.

B. 1. transparent
2. comprehensible
3. indisputable
4. pure
5. unobstructed
6. sunny

C. 1. hard, difficult, demanding
2. pleasant, enjoyable, delightful
3. large, extensive, powerful

D. (Corrections are underlined.)
1. The king and the queen ignored the prophet's message.
2. God told Noah, who had found grace in His eyes, to build an ark.
3. That ship was three stories high.
4. What kind of flower is in this pot?
5. Working busily, bees bring much nectar to the hive every day.
6. Uncle Brian has fewer cows than we do.

7. Is your desk in respectful order?

8. We had an awful hard time getting the truck out of the deep mud.

Written Exercises

A. Copy each sentence, omitting the unnecessary or repetitious adjectives.

1. The mighty, powerful Roman Empire ruled the known world of Jesus' day.

2. A lame cripple was carried to Jesus.

3. Nobody appreciates a dishonest liar.

4. A herd of caribou foraged on the cold, frozen plain.

5. Wooded forestland can be the home of many numerous wild animals.

B. Write each expression, replacing the word *fine* with one of these adjectives: *delicate, keen, thin, pleasant, sound, pure.*

1. a fine day   3. fine lines   5. in fine health

2. fine gold   4. a fine knife edge   6. fine china

C. Write a descriptive adjective to replace each underlined adjective.

1. I made a <u>big</u> mistake on my art project.

2. After falling off the ladder, Paul had a <u>bad</u> bruise on his leg.

3. We watched a <u>pretty</u> sunset.

D. Find each error in these sentences, and write one to three words to show how it should be corrected. If there is a misplaced or dangling modifier, write the entire sentence correctly. If a sentence has no error, write *correct.*

1. Daniel gave Melzar a respectable answer.

2. The New Testament has less books than the Old Testament.

3. Returning from captivity, the Jews must have been eager to have their first glimpse of Jerusalem.

4. Not all the jewish captives were ready to return to Judah.

5. The tribes of Israel followed the ark of the covenant in their respective places.

6. What kind of an animal did Samson kill on his way to the Philistines?

7. The prophet and king met in the vineyard.

8. This vineyard was now possessed by the king that had belonged to Naboth.

9. That there innocent man had been falsely accused and put to death.

10. Queen Jezebel was an awful wicked person.

11. The children did a respectable amount of work this afternoon.

12. Walking through the woods, many signs of spring could be seen.

13. I had less trouble with my assignment than I had feared.

14. We anxiously watched the gathering storm working out in the hayfield.

15. The volcanic explosion wreaked awful destruction on surrounding areas.

7. Is your desk in <u>respectable</u> order?

8. We had <u>a very hard</u> time getting the truck out of the deep mud.

Written Exercises

A. 1. The mighty (*or* powerful) Roman Empire ruled the known world of Jesus' day.

2. A cripple was carried to Jesus.

3. Nobody appreciates a liar.

4. A herd of caribou foraged on the frozen plain.

5. Forestland can be the home of many (*or* numerous) wild animals.

B. 1. a pleasant day   4. a keen knife edge

2. pure gold   5. in sound health

3. thin lines   6. delicate china

C. (Sample answers.)

1. serious, disastrous, glaring

2. painful, serious, severe

3. beautiful, lovely, colorful

D. 1. respectful

2. fewer

3. correct

4. Jewish

5. correct

6. kind of animal

7. and the king

8. This vineyard that had belonged to Naboth was now possessed by the king.

9. That innocent

10. a very wicked

11. correct

12. Walking through the woods, I (we) could see many signs of spring.

13. correct

14. Working out in the hayfield, we anxiously watched the gathering storm.

15. correct

Review Exercises

A. Choose the correct words in parentheses. [60]

1. Anyone choosing to follow Christ (have, has) to be ready to pay the price of true discipleship.
2. Red-hot tongs (was, were) used to tear flesh from Michael Sattler's body as he was led to his execution.
3. (Don't, Doesn't) the stories of the martyrs stir your heart to be faithful unto death?
4. "Beautiful Things" (picture, pictures) the progression of life in poetic form.
5. Macaroni and cheese (include, includes) food from the bread and the milk group.
6. In the refrigerator (is, are) some leftovers to warm up for dinner.
7. Mathematics (is, are) used to predict eclipses many years in the future.
8. The family (is, are) doing their regular chores.

B. Choose the correct pronouns in parentheses. [70–77]

1. The eighth grade boys, Henry and (I, me), are working on a science project.
2. We want to finish it (ourself, ourselves).
3. Leroy is two inches taller than (he, him).
4. None of us recognized the man (who, which) stopped in at school.
5. (Somebodys, Somebody's) sweater is lying out in the rain.
6. Father was not sure (who, whom) he should ask for help.
7. Aunt Louise sent this letter for you and (I, me).
8. Each of the students is busy with (his, their) test.

Review Exercises

A. 1. has
   2. were
   3. Don't
   4. pictures
   5. includes
   6. are
   7. is
   8. are

B. 1. I
   2. ourselves
   3. he
   4. who
   5. Somebody's
   6. whom
   7. me
   8. his

89. Writing Poetry

> **Lesson Survey**
> - Before writing poetry, you need to be inspired with a message that you want to communicate.
> - The message of a poem is enhanced by good mechanics.

These lessons on poetry will not make a skillful poet out of every pupil who studies them. But they should disprove the idea that poets are geniuses whose poems flow effortlessly from their pens and that we ordinary people might as well not try. Probably most poets are no more intelligent than the rest of us, just as people who can ride a bicycle are not necessarily more

Lesson 89

Purpose: (1) To encourage interest in writing poetry. (2) To give specific guidelines on proper form and content.

Oral Review:

1. Which kind of figure of speech is represented in each of these lines?
   a. Upon the lonely pilgrims smiled the warming sun (personification)
   b. Like a cooling shower came those gracious words (simile)
   c. God's love is an ocean (metaphor)
   d. An exploding volcano of bitterest wrath (hyperbole)
2. What is onomatopoeia? (the use of a word having an imitative sound)
3. What is the difference between denotation and connotation? (*denotation:* the strict, exact meaning of a word; *connotation:* the feeling a word conveys in addition to its exact meaning)
4. What is alliteration? (the repetition of beginning consonant sounds)
5. What is assonance? (the repetition of similar vowel sounds in accented syllables)
6. Tell which kind of meter is in each of these lines.
   a. The king and all his mighty men (iambic)
   b. What a beautiful morning has dawned (anapestic)
   c. Come to the manger, ye shepherds, and see (dactylic)
   d. In the searching heart of youth (trochaic)

Lesson Introduction: Write the following poem on the board.

gifted than people who cannot. Rather, they became interested in bicycle riding, they began learning, and from then on it was a matter of practice.

Inspiration to Write Poetry

Writing poetry will go much better when you have a message, something you really want to say. But suppose you have nothing to say; what can you do to receive inspiration? One important starting point is the Bible. God's Word contains a vast store of thoughts and themes that can be expressed in poetry. Isaac Watts did that many times. For example, Psalm 139:5 says, "Thou hast beset me behind and before, and laid thine hand upon me." This passage gave Isaac Watts the inspiration for the following lines.

> Lord, Thou hast searched and seen me through:
> Thine eye commands, with piercing view,
>   My rising and my resting hours,
>   My heart and flesh with all their pow'rs.

Another good starting point is nature. The beauty of a sunset or a flower, the majesty of a mountain or the stars, the delicacy of a spider web—the possibilities are almost endless to anyone who beholds the beauty of God's creation.

> The hillsides are shouting God's glory;
>   It flames in each bush and tree,
> Like a giant signature written
>   In colors that all must see.

You can also find inspiration in everyday things—as you ride to school, talk to friends, play a game, or as you just sit and observe. Poets have been inspired by things that others have seen and heard dozens of times, but never considered worthy of special attention.

> I have found such joy in simple things:
>   A plain clean room, a nut-brown loaf of bread,
> A cup of milk, a kettle as it sings,
>   The shelter of a roof above my head,
> And in a leaf-laced square along the floor,
>   Where yellow sunlight glimmers through a door.

Mechanics of Writing Poetry

The message of a poem is its most important feature. A poem with no message is worthless, even if it has perfect rhythm and rhyme. However, a worthwhile theme can be greatly enhanced by good mechanics. Study the following points.

1. Capitalize the first letter in each line of poetry, and capitalize otherwise as you would in prose.

Our Saviour

> Our Saviour came from glory down
> To bear a cross and thorny crown.
>   He bled and died for you and me
>   Upon the cross of Calvary.
>
> Now He lives and reigns on high,
> Far above the lofty sky.
>   Soon He'll come to claim His own;
>   Then we'll gather round His throne.

How would the students grade the rhyme and rhythm of this poem—A, B, C, D, or E? The poem has good rhyme and smooth rhythm. It does switch from iambic to trochaic meter between stanzas, but this error does not seriously hurt the poem. It might deserve a B for rhyme and rhythm.

How would the students grade the content of the poem? Does it have a moving, inspirational message?

What the poem says is true, but it does not stimulate the mind. In fact, the poem was written in less than five minutes. The author put very little effort into it. It rates a D for content, if not an E.

Lest this discourage the students, tell them that their first efforts at poetry making will not be graded this harshly, since they would probably put more effort into a poem like this than the author did. But they should aim to write a poem with much more depth of meaning and beauty of expression than this one has.

Lesson Outline:

1. Before writing poetry, you need to be inspired with a message that you want to communicate. Such inspiration can be found in at least three places: the Bible, nature, and everyday things.

2. The message of a poem is enhanced by good mechanics.

   (1) Capitalize the first letter in each line of poetry, and capitalize otherwise as you would in prose.

   (2) In general, punctuate as you would in prose. Some lines may have no punctuation at the end, and some may have punctuation in the middle.

2. In general, punctuate as you would in prose. Some lines may have no punctuation at the end, and some may have punctuation in the middle.
3. Leave a space between each stanza and the next.
4. Indent according to the rhyming pattern. All the lines that rhyme should be indented unless the first line is a rhyming line. Then indent only the line or lines that do not rhyme.
5. Choose the kind of rhythm that matches the theme of the poem. Iambic meter is suitable for themes of praise, joy, and beauty. Trochaic meter is appropriate for sober, thoughtful subjects. Dactylic and anapestic meters are well suited for themes of hope, joy, and earnestness.
6. Use a simple rhyming pattern such as *abcb* for your first poems. Later you can try more difficult rhyming schemes. Also avoid imperfect rhymes until you have gained experience in writing poetry. Good poets use perfect rhymes as much as possible.
7. Arrange words in a smooth pattern. Avoid using awkward, unnatural word order to make the rhythm or rhyme come out.
8. Avoid words not used in common language, even if you did find them in a published poem.
9. Avoid overworked words. Be original.
10. Make sure figures of speech are appropriate. Some figures fit one poem but not another.
11. Choose words with the right connotation. If a word does not quite fit, keep looking for a better word or rewriting the line until you succeed.

Class Practice

Work together as a class to write four to eight lines of poetry about one of the following subjects.

School	Cats (*or* Dogs)	Perseverance
Home	The Bible	Heaven

Written Exercises

Begin writing a poem of three to five stanzas, with at least four lines in each stanza. Follow the rules for mechanics given in this lesson. Choose descriptive words. Include at least one figure of speech, one example of alliteration, one example of assonance, and one example of onomatopoeia. Your poem will be due at the end of this chapter.

A few suggested subjects are given below.

Description of something in nature, like a waterfall or thunderstorm
Description of one of the seasons
Description of a memorable experience

Lesson 89 Answers

Class Practice

(Activity to be done in class.)

Written Exercises

(Individual work.)

---

(3) Leave a space between each stanza and the next.
(4) Indent according to the rhyming pattern. All the lines that rhyme should be indented unless the first line is a rhyming line. Then indent only the line or lines that do not rhyme.
(5) Choose the kind of rhythm that matches the theme of the poem. Iambic meter is suitable for themes of praise, joy, and beauty. Trochaic meter is appropriate for sober, thoughtful subjects. Dactylic and anapestic meters are well suited for themes of hope, joy, and earnestness.
(6) Use a simple rhyming pattern such as *abcb* for your first poems. Later you can try more difficult rhyming schemes. Also avoid imperfect rhymes until you have gained

experience in writing poetry. Good poets use perfect rhymes as much as possible.
(7) Arrange words in a smooth pattern. Avoid using awkward, unnatural word order to make the rhyme or rhythm come out.
(8) Avoid words not used in common language, even if you did find them in a published poem.
(9) Avoid overworked words. Be original.
(10) Make sure figures of speech are appropriate. Some figures fit one poem but not another.
(11) Choose words with the right connotation. If a word does not quite fit, keep looking for a better word or rewriting the line until you succeed.

90. Appreciating Poetry

Lesson Survey

- To appreciate poetry, take time to understand its message.
- Read poetry aloud to better appreciate its music and its message.
- Read a poem by thoughts, not merely by lines.
- Learn to recognize figures of speech.
- Consider the poet's choice of words.

Good poetry is an artistic expression, inspired by noble feelings and composed to communicate those feelings. The reader who senses the beauty of the poem has his feelings touched as well. The pointers in this lesson should help you to see, hear, and feel the poems that you read.

Of course, some poems will mean less to you than other poems. However, if you have been speeding through poems the way you read children's stories, these suggestions should help you to get more out of them.

1. *Take time to understand the message of a poem.* Read a poem several times if necessary. A good poem has as much meaning as some complete stories. Read the following poem.

The Goldenrod

Spring is the morning of the year,
    And summer is the noontide bright;
The autumn is the evening clear
    That comes before the winter's night.

And in the evening, everywhere
    Along the roadside, up and down,
I see the golden torches flare
    Like lighted streetlamps in the town.

I think the butterfly and bee,
    From distant meadows coming back,
Are quite contented when they see
    These lamps along the homeward track.

But those who stay too late get lost;
    For when the darkness falls about,
Down every lighted street the Frost
    Will go and put the torches out!

               —*Frank Dempster Sherman*

Lesson 90

Purpose: To teach appreciation for good poetry.

Oral Review:

1. What are three good sources of inspiration for writing poetry? (the Bible, nature, everyday things)
2. Tell whether each line illustrates alliteration, assonance, or onomatopoeia.
   a. Shrieking and howling, a gale from the north (onomatopoeia)
   b. How pleasant to dwell in contentment together. (assonance)
   c. With gladness beholding the green grasses growing (alliteration)
3. Tell which kind of parallelism is found in each of these examples.
   a. A soft answer turneth away wrath:
   But grievous words stir up anger. (antithetic)
   b. It is a good thing to give thanks unto the Lord
   And to sing praises unto thy name, O most High. (synonymous)
   c. But I am poor and needy:
   Make haste unto me, O God. (synthetic)
4. What is meter? (the pattern of accented and unaccented syllables)
5. What is a poetic foot? (a unit of rhythm consisting of one accented syllable and the unaccented syllable or syllables associated with it)
6. Name the correct meter for each description.
   a. two unaccented syllables followed by one accented syllable (anapestic)
   b. one accented syllable followed by one unaccented syllable (trochaic)
   c. one accented syllable followed by two unaccented syllables (dactylic)
   d. one unaccented syllable followed by one accented syllable (iambic)

Did you catch all the meaning of this poem in one reading? The following questions may help you evaluate whether you did.

    a. What are the golden torches and lamps spoken of in stanzas 2, 3, and 4?

    b. Why are these torches flaring *in the evening*?

    c. What then is the falling of darkness?

    d. What is happening when the torches are being put out?

  2. *Read poetry aloud to better appreciate its music and its message.* The music of the rhythm and rhyme can be fully appreciated only when it is heard aloud. This is true even more of the music of alliteration, assonance, and onomatopoeia. Hearing that music will often impress the message of the poem more forcefully upon you than a silent reading will do.

  3. *Read a poem by thoughts, not merely by lines.* The following stanza illustrates the importance of this guideline. The second line does not make sense unless it is read in connection with the thought that begins in line 1.

> "Fear not," the flowers whisper. "Since thus He hath arrayed
> The buttercup and daisy, how canst thou be afraid?"
>   Then don't you trouble trouble till trouble troubles you;
>   You'll only double trouble, and trouble others too.
>   —*Mark Guy Pearse*

  4. *Learn to recognize figures of speech.* The figurative language of some poems is so veiled that, unless you stop and analyze it, you will not grasp the full meaning of the poem. How many times have you sung these words (from "Oh, Worship the King") without considering what they really mean?

> Oh, tell of His might and sing of His grace,
> Whose robe is the light, whose canopy space.

A *robe* is an outer garment that reveals the status or position of a person: God manifests His essential being in the glory and warmth of light. A *canopy* is a cover placed above a high-ranking official: God is so great that infinite space alone can cover Him.

  5. *Consider the poet's choice of words.* The author probably put great effort into finding words with exactly the right denotation and connotation for the poem. We should likewise put forth effort to understand it. Observe how the underlined words in the stanza below are more effective and appropriate than the words in parentheses.

> <u>Hidden</u> (Resting) in the hollow of His blessed hand,
> Never foe can follow, never traitor stand;
>   Not a <u>surge</u> (rush) of worry, not a <u>shade</u> (bit) of care,
>   Not a <u>blast</u> (thrust) of hurry, touch the spirit there.

Lesson Introduction: If you catch a butterfly to study it closely, you might hurt it. In fact, you might have to kill it to find out all you want to know about it.

Does it hurt a poem to study it? Or should you simply sit back and enjoy it? You probably do lose some enjoyment by working over a poem. On the other hand, if you lay the enjoyment aside for a bit and really dissect a few poems, you will find out things about poetry that will help you enjoy poems even more in the future.

Lesson Outline:

  1. **To appreciate poetry, take time to understand its message.** Read a poem several times if necessary.

  2. **Read poetry aloud to better appreciate its music and its message.**

    a. The music of the rhyme, rhythm, alliteration, assonance, and onomatopoeia can be fully appreciated only when it is heard aloud.

    b. Hearing that music will often impress the message of the poem more forcefully upon you than a silent reading will do.

  3. **Read a poem by thoughts, not merely by lines.**

  4. **Learn to recognize figures of speech.** The figurative language of some poems is so veiled that, unless you stop and analyze it, you will not grasp the full meaning of the poem. (Review the four kinds of figurative language in Lesson 86.)

  5. **Consider the poet's choice of words.** The author probably put great effort into finding words with exactly the right denotation and connotation for the poem. (Review denotation and connotation in Lesson 86.)

Class Practice

Read aloud the poem that you have selected to read to your classmates. Do your best to communicate the beauty of the poem and the inspiration that it gives you.

Written Exercises

A. Read this poem, and do the exercises below.

O Word of God Incarnate

O Word of God incarnate,
   O Wisdom from on high,
O Truth, unchanged, unchanging,
   O Light of our dark sky;
We praise Thee for the radiance
   That from the hallowed page,
A lantern to our footsteps,
   Shines on from age to age.

The Church from her dear Master
   Received the gift divine,
And still that light she lifteth
   O'er all the earth to shine.
It is the golden casket
   Where gems of truth are stored,
It is the heav'n-drawn picture
   Of Christ, the living Word.

It floateth like a banner
   Before God's host, unfurled;
It shineth like a beacon
   Above the darkling world;
It is the chart and compass
   That, o'er life's surging sea,
'Mid mists and rocks and quicksands,
   Still guides, O Christ, to Thee.

O make Thy Church, dear Saviour,
   A lamp of purest gold
To bear before the nations
   Thy true light as of old;
O teach Thy wand'ring pilgrims
   By this their path to trace,
Till, clouds and darkness ended,
   They see Thee face to face.
                —*William W. Howe*

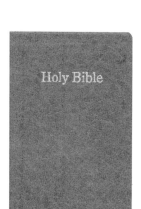

Lesson 90 Answers

Class Practice

(Oral exercise.)

1. In stanza 1, you must read (two, four, five) lines before you have a complete thought.
2. Copy the lines that express the same ideas as the following sentence: The church continues to hold forth the light of God's Word to the world.
3. Copy words for the following descriptions.
   a. one example of alliteration in stanza 2
   b. two examples of alliteration in stanza 3
   c. two examples of assonance in stanza 3
4. In stanzas 2 and 3, the poet uses four metaphors to describe the Bible. Name the four objects used for comparison in these metaphors.
5. Copy the two similes in stanza 3.
6. A banner (flag) was held up before a host (army) to show the soldiers where to go and to encourage them to keep fighting. How is the Bible like such a banner?
7. a. What is the purpose of a beacon or lighthouse in the dark?
   b. How is the Bible like such a beacon?
8. Both *radiance* and *brilliance* suggest a bright shining. Which of these two words has a connotation of warmth?

B. Continue working on the poem that you began in Lesson 89.

---

91. Chapter 8 Review

Class Practice

A. Give the term that fits each description.
   1. An adjective that modifies a substantive by telling *which, whose,* or *how many.*
   2. An adjective that modifies a substantive by telling *what kind of.*
   3. The position of an adjective that immediately follows the substantive it modifies.
   4. The position of an adjective that follows a linking verb and modifies the subject.
   5. The position of an adjective that comes just before the substantive it modifies.
   6. The form of an adjective used to compare more than two items.
   7. The form of an adjective used to modify without comparing.
   8. The form of an adjective used to compare two items.
   9. A verbal that can be used as an adjective, often ending with *-ing* or *-ed.*

Lesson 91

Purpose: To review the concepts taught in Chapter 8.

Written Exercises

A. 1. five
   2. And still that light she lifteth
      O'er all the earth to shine.
   3. a. light, lifteth
      b. (Any two.) banner, Before; surging, sea; 'Mid, mists
      c. (Any two.) Before, host; shineth, like; mists, quicksands; guides, Christ
   4. casket, picture, chart, compass
   5. like a banner, like a beacon
   6. The Bible teaches us how to fight against our enemy and encourages us to keep fighting.
   7. a. to show where danger is along a shore; to show where it is safe to sail a ship through a narrow channel
      b. The Bible shows us the evils we must avoid and teaches us the right way to go.
   8. radiance

B. (Individual work. Tell the students when they are to finish their poems. Check the poems for proper mechanics, descriptive words, figurative language, and poetic devices as mentioned in Lesson 89.)

Lesson 91 Answers

Class Practice

A.		
1. limiting adjective	6. superlative
2. descriptive adjective	7. positive
3. appositive	8. comparative
4. predicate	9. participle
5. attributive	

10. A verbal that can be used as an adjective, consisting of *to* and the basic form of a verb.
11. An adjective clause that simply gives additional information.
12. An adjective clause that limits the meaning of a substantive.
13. The pattern of rhythm.
14. An accented syllable and the unaccented syllable or syllables associated with it.
15. A rhyme involving more than one syllable.
16. The repetition of beginning consonant sounds.
17. The repetition of similar vowel sounds in accented syllables.
18. The use of a word having an imitative sound.
19. A figurative exaggeration for the purpose of emphasis.
20. A figurative comparison that uses *like* or *as.*
21. A figurative comparison that does not use *like* or *as.*
22. A figure of speech that pictures a thing or quality as having the characteristics of a living creature.

B. Identify the adjectives in these sentences, and tell whether each is *limiting* or *descriptive.* Also tell in which position it is.
   1. Jesus' twelve disciples became frightened.
   2. The Master, patient and loving, taught His disciples.
   3. From the rooftop above came some strange noises.

C. Give the comparative and superlative forms of these adjectives.
   1. precious   4. many
   2. good   5. tiny
   3. little, in amount   6. far

D. Read each adjective phrase, and tell whether it is a *participial, infinitive,* or *prepositional* phrase.
   1. The parakeet, chirping wildly, feared the cat on the floor.
   2. The note on the board gave us an incentive to work faster.
   3. The roosters crowing noisily outside tell me the time to get up.

E. Read each adjective clause, and tell whether it is *restrictive* or *nonrestrictive.* Also tell where commas are needed.
   1. The boy who is sitting beside me is writing an article for the school newspaper.
   2. Aunt Minerva whose leg was broken is in the hospital.
   3. Our only goat which Father bought last fall is hard to keep in a pen.
   4. The cats that we got from Grandfather's farm are better mouse catchers than these others.

F. Suggest several descriptive adjectives to replace each underlined adjective.

10. infinitive
11. nonrestrictive clause
12. restrictive clause
13. meter
14. foot
15. feminine rhyme
16. alliteration
17. assonance
18. onomatopoeia
19. hyperbole
20. simile
21. metaphor
22. personification

B. 1. Jesus'—limiting, attributive;
      twelve—limiting, attributive;
      frightened—descriptive, predicate
   2. The—limiting, attributive;
      patient—descriptive, appositive;
      loving—descriptive, appositive;
      His—limiting, attributive
   3. the—limiting, attributive;
      above—limiting *or* descriptive, appositive;
      some—limiting, attributive;
      strange—descriptive, attributive

C. 1. more precious, most precious
   2. better, best
   3. less, least
   4. more, most
   5. tinier, tiniest
   6. farther, farthest

D. 1. chirping wildly—participial;
      on the floor—prepositional
   2. on the board—prepositional;
      to work faster—infinitive
   3. crowing noisily outside—participial;
      to get up—infinitive

E. 1. who is sitting beside me—restrictive; no commas
   2. whose leg was broken—nonrestrictive; commas after *Minerva* and *broken*
   3. which Father bought last fall—nonrestrictive; commas after *goat* and *fall*
   4. that we got from Grandfather's farm—restrictive; no commas

1. Uncle Silas had a <u>big</u> responsibility at the children's home.
2. I just finished a very <u>good</u> book.
3. An <u>awful</u> storm swept through our county.

G. Read each sentence, omitting the unnecessary and repetitious adjectives.
   1. We were startled by a white albino deer.
   2. Uncle Benjamin's pleasant, congenial smile calmed our fearful apprehensions.
   3. The three triplets rested briefly for a few minutes in the shade.

H. Give the rhyme scheme of each stanza.
   1. Life is a paper whereon we may write
      Each one his message, and then comes the night.
         Write then with care, for although thou hast time
         But for a line or two—make it sublime.
   2. Christian, seek not yet repose,
         Cast thy dreams of ease away;
      Thou art in the midst of foes;
         Watch and pray.
   3. My life, my love I give to Thee,
      Thou Lamb of God, who died for me;
      Oh, may I ever faithful be,
         My Saviour and my God!
   4. Not a shadow can rise,
      Not a cloud in the skies,
         But His smile quickly drives it away;
      Not a doubt nor a fear,
      Not a sigh nor a tear,
         Can abide while we trust and obey.

I. On the chalkboard, copy and scan the first line of each stanza above. Tell how many feet are in each line of the stanza, and identify the rhythm pattern.

Written Exercises

A. Copy each adjective in these sentences, and write whether it is limiting (*L*) or descriptive (*D*). Also write whether its position is attributive (*AT*), appositive (*AP*), or predicate (*PR*).
   1. Christian poetry has good spiritual value.
   2. The pamphlets, clear and concise, describe a faithful, Scriptural lifestyle.
   3. Because of the brotherhood's consistent witness, several people became interested in the Gospel.

F. 1. heavy, weighty, demanding
   2. interesting, worthwhile
   3. destructive, severe

G. 1. We were startled by an albino deer.
   2. Uncle Benjamin's pleasant (congenial) smile calmed our apprehensions.
   3. The triplets rested briefly (for a few minutes) in the shade.

H. 1. aabb
   2. abab
   3. aaab
   4. aabccb

I. 1. Life is a / paper where/on we may / write
      4, 4, 4, 4; dactylic
   2. Christian, / seek not / yet re/pose,
      4, 4, 4, 2; trochaic
   3. My life, / my love / I give / to Thee,
      4, 4, 4, 3; iambic
   4. Not a shad/ow can rise,
      2, 2, 3, 2, 2, 3; anapestic

Written Exercises

A. 1. Christian—D, AT; good—D, AT; spiritual—D, AT
   2. The—L, AT; clear—D, AP; concise—D, AP; a—L, AT; faithful—D, AT; Scriptural—D, AT
   3. the—L, AT; brotherhood's—L, AT; consistent—D, AT; several—L, AT; interested—D, PR; the—L, AT

B. Copy each adjective phrase, and write whether it is participial (*part.*), infinitive (*inf.*), or prepositional (*prep.*).
1. The assignments to do each day are written on the board beside the teacher's desk.
2. Diving swiftly, the eagle attacked the hawk flying too near its nest.
3. The many interruptions to our schedule meant insufficient time to finish all the work.

C. Copy each adjective clause, and write whether it is restrictive (*R*) or nonrestrictive (*N*). Also write each word that should be followed by a comma, and add the comma.
1. Mrs. White whom we visit often is partially crippled with arthritis.
2. The elderly lady who lives across the road is Mrs. White.
3. The road that crosses Fox Mountain is narrow and rough.
4. Hidden Valley Road which crosses Fox Mountain is narrow and rough.
5. The students who are working on the bulletin board have planned a meaningful display.

D. Find each error in these sentences, and write one to three words to show how the error should be corrected. If there is a dangling or misplaced modifier, write the entire sentence correctly. If a sentence has no error, write *correct*.
1. A respectful reputation is rarely gained without effort.
2. Are you developing the right kind of a character?
3. People who live for self have far less contentment than those who live for God.
4. When we read these here promises in the Bible, we are encouraged to be faithful.
5. Our lives must be patterned after biblical ideals.
6. A person who learns to obey promptly when young usually has less problems in life than one who does not.
7. A person who truly fears God is respectable toward others.
8. Caring for the sheep, a burning bush was suddenly seen by Moses.
9. As Brother Harold read our names, we stood in our respectful places.
10. A little mouse frightened Mrs. Leister, scampering across the floor.

E. Diagram these sentences.
1. Sniffing the air, the black bear followed the scent of the delicious honey.
2. The hollow tree that contained the honey was huge.
3. The buzzing bees disputed his right to claim the honey.
4. The honey, sweet and delicious, repaid his strenuous efforts.

B. 1. to do each day—inf.;
      beside the teacher's desk—prep.
2. Diving swiftly—part.;
   flying too near its nest—part.
3. to our schedule—prep.;
   to finish all the work—inf.

C. 1. whom we visit often—N; White, often,
2. who lives across the road—R
3. that crosses Fox Mountain—R
4. which crosses Fox Mountain—N; Road, Mountain,
5. who are working on the bulletin board—R

D. 1. respectable
2. kind of character
3. correct
4. these promises
5. Biblical
6. fewer
7. respectful
8. Caring for the sheep, Moses suddenly saw a burning bush.
9. respective
10. Scampering across the floor, a little mouse frightened Mrs. Leister.
    or A little mouse, scampering across the floor, frightened Mrs. Leister.

E. 1.

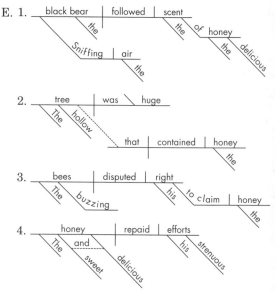

F. Read the following poem, and do the exercises that follow.

The Spacious Firmament on High
The spacious firmament on high,
With all the blue ethereal sky,
  And spangled heav'ns, a shining frame,
  Their great Original proclaim.
Th'unwearied sun, from day to day,
Does his Creator's pow'r display,
  And publishes to every land
  The work of an almighty hand.

Soon as the evening shades prevail,
The moon takes up the wondrous tale,
  And nightly to the list'ning earth
  Repeats the story of her birth;
Whilst all the stars that round her burn,
And all the planets in their turn,
  Confirm the tidings as they roll,
  And spread the truth from pole to pole.

What though in solemn silence all
Move round this dark terrestrial ball?
  What though no real voice nor sound
  Amidst their radiant orbs be found?
In reason's ear they all rejoice
And utter forth a glorious voice,
  Forever singing, as they shine,
  "The hand that made us is divine."
              —*Joseph Addison*

The
heavens
declare the
glory of God;
and the
firmament
sheweth
his handywork.
Psalm 19:1

1. Copy a line in stanza 3 that does not make sense until the next line is read.
2. Copy words from the poem to illustrate the following things.
   a. two examples of alliteration in stanza 3
   b. an example of assonance in stanza 1, including at least five words (Some of these may be rhyming words.)
   c. an example of assonance in stanza 3
3. Write how personification is used in stanzas 1 and 2 to describe each of these objects: the sun, the moon, and the stars.
4. Define the words *ethereal, spangled,* and *terrestrial.*
5. How is the connotation of *solemn* in stanza 3 more fitting than that of *deathly*?

_____

F. 1. What though in solemn silence all
      or What though no real voice nor sound
   2. a. solemn, silence; reason's, rejoice
      b. frame, great, proclaim, day, Creator's, display
      c. reason's, ear *or* forth, glorious
   3. The sun is unwearied; it publishes the work of God's hand.
      The moon tells the tale of her birth.
      The stars confirm the moon's story.
   4. *ethereal:* heavenly; related to the celestial spheres
      spangled: adorned with sparkling objects
      terrestrial: earthly
   5. *Solemn* fits well with the theme of reverence; *deathly* implies a sadness that does not match the theme.

Chapter Nine

Adverbs

Writing Persuasive Argument

Like adjectives, adverbs fill an important place in beautifying language. You use adverbs most often to make verbs more precise or more colorful. You also use them to beautify and intensify verbals, adjectives, and other adverbs. As you learn to use verbals, phrases, and clauses as adverbs, you will improve your powers of speaking and writing.

Throughout life you will have various opportunities to defend or promote certain ideas. A good understanding of the principles of persuasive argument will help you to uphold truth convincingly. To produce an effective persuasive argument, you must understand what makes a worthwhile proposition, how to organize the supporting points, and how to write the introduction, the body, and the conclusion of the argument. Learn to write persuasive arguments so that you will be able to convince others of eternal truths.

And [Paul] went into the synagogue,
and spake boldly for the space of three months, disputing and persuading
the things concerning the kingdom of God.

Acts 19:8

2. Recognizing Adverbs

Lesson Survey

- An adverb usually modifies a verb.
- An **adverb of degree** modifies an adjective or another adverb.
- An adverb can also modify a verbal.

Adverbs, like adjectives, are not as basic to language as nouns and verbs are. However, they are important because they add flesh to the skeletons, which helps to make sentences interesting and meaningful.

Adverbs That Modify Verbs

Adverbs usually modify verbs by telling *how, when,* and *where* things happened or existed. Many adverbs end with *-ly.*

We should <u>daily</u> look <u>heavenward</u>.
  (*Daily* tells *when* about *should look; heavenward* tells *where* about *should look.*)

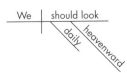

Softly and lovingly, Mother sang the lullaby.
  (*Softly* and *lovingly* tell *how* about *sang.*)

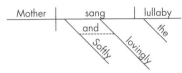

The words *not, never, ever, almost, always, hardly, scarcely,* and *seldom* are always adverbs. Often these words interrupt the verb phrases they modify. Sometimes the word *not* is compounded with the verb *can* in *cannot* or joined with a verb in a contraction ending with *n't.* In diagraming, the *not* or the *n't* must be separated from the verb and diagramed as the adverb *not.*

I have <u>almost</u> finished the assignment.

Lesson 92

Purpose: To study the definition and recognition of adverbs.

Oral Review:

1. What are the two classes of adjectives? (limiting, descriptive)
2. Name and describe the three positions of adjectives. (attributive—before the substantive; appositive—immediately after the substantive; predicate—after a linking verb and modifying the subject)
3. In which position are the adjectives usually in pairs and set off with commas? (appositive)
4. What two kinds of verbals are used as adjectives? (participles, infinitives)
5. Name three common uses of colons. (to separate the numbers in Scripture references and in expressions of time; to follow the salutation of a business letter; to introduce a list, an explanation, or a formal quotation)
6. When should a colon *not* be used to introduce a list? (when a list of complements follows a verb, or a list of objects follows a preposition)
7. When is a semicolon used to join independent clauses? (when no conjunction is used; when a conjunctive adverb is used; when commas are already used in one or more of the clauses)
8. When should a semicolon be used to separate items in a series? (when the individual items contain commas)

I haven't followed the instructions!

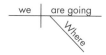

The words *how, when, where,* and *why* are also adverbs when they introduce interrogative sentences or adjective clauses.

<u>Where</u> are we going?

Adverbs That Modify Adjectives and Other Adverbs

Adverbs of degree modify adjectives and other adverbs. They tell *to what degree.* Almost without exception, adverbs of degree come immediately before the words they modify. The following words are commonly used as adverbs of degree.

completely	extremely	surely
dangerously	partly	surprisingly
definitely	quite	thoroughly
entirely	rather	too
especially	so	unusually
extraordinarily	somewhat	very

Samson's life is <u>rather</u> disappointing.
    (*Rather* tells *to what degree* about the predicate adjective *disappointing.*)

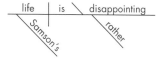

Suddenly an <u>extremely</u> bright light blinded Saul.
    (*Extremely* tells *to what degree* about the adjective *bright.*)

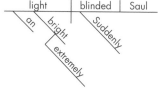

Lesson Introduction: Put the following on the board before class.

1. How?
2. When?
3. Where?

runs   reads

Ask pupils to suggest various adverbs that tell *how, when,* and *where* a person runs. Do the same for the verb *reads.*

Lesson Outline:
1. An adverb usually modifies a verb.

a. It tells *how, when,* or *where* something happened or existed.
b. Many adverbs end with *-ly.*
c. The words *not, never, ever, almost, always, hardly, scarcely,* and *seldom* are always adverbs.
    1) Often these words interrupt the verb phrases they modify.
    2) The *not* in *cannot* and the *n't* in a contraction must be separated from the verb and diagramed as the adverb *not.*
d. The words *how, when, where,* and *why* are also adverbs when they introduce interrogative sentences or adjective clauses.

2. An adverb of degree modifies an adjective or another adverb.

a. It tells *to what degree.*
b. It almost always comes immediately before the word it modifies.

Adverbs That Modify Verbals

Verbals can be used as substantives (gerunds and infinitives) and as adjectives (participles and infinitives). Because they come from verbs, verbals retain some characteristics of verbs, such as having adverb modifiers. Study these examples.

Speaking <u>kindly</u> often prevents troubles.

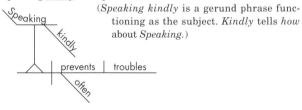

(*Speaking kindly* is a gerund phrase functioning as the subject. *Kindly* tells *how* about *Speaking*.)

Our desire should be to obey the Bible <u>always</u>.
(*To obey the Bible always* is an infinitive phrase functioning as the predicate nominative. *Always* tells *when* about *to obey*.)

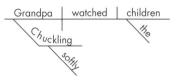

Chuckling <u>softly</u>, Grandpa watched the children.
(*Chuckling softly* is a participial phrase modifying *Grandpa*. *Softly* tells *how* about *Chuckling*.)

These are important truths to remember <u>always</u>.
(*To remember always* is an infinitive phrase modifying *truths*. *Always* tells *when* about *to remember*.)

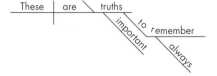

3. *An adverb can also modify a verbal.* Verbals can be used as substantives (gerunds and infinitives) and as adjectives (participles and infinitives).

Class Practice

A. Tell whether each underlined adverb modifies a *verb,* an *adjective,* an *adverb,* or a *verbal.*
1. Have you <u>thoroughly</u> searched the text for the answers?
2. Do <u>not</u> stop <u>too</u> quickly.
3. Taking notes <u>carefully</u> is a good way to listen <u>attentively</u> to a sermon.
4. The <u>dangerously</u> ill man stared <u>blankly</u> and talked <u>incoherently</u>.
5. The skies became <u>quite</u> clear, and the temperature rose <u>very</u> abruptly.

B. Identify each single-word adverb, and tell what word it modifies.
1. The thunder echoed loudly through the canyon.
2. We played the game very energetically at recess.
3. A turkey hen is somewhat smaller than a tom.
4. To see a wild turkey strutting stiffly and gobbling noisily in a forest glade is an extremely interesting experience.
5. Wild turkeys like to eat together under the trees.

C. On the chalkboard, diagram these sentences.
1. These plants must have been put out too soon.
2. An unusually heavy frost severely damaged them.
3. Quietly and respectfully, the students filed in.
4. Filling one's place diligently usually produces a relatively successful life.
5. This isn't a very nice trail to hike along.

Written Exercises

A. Copy each underlined adverb, and write whether it modifies a *verb,* an *adjective,* an *adverb,* or a *verbal.*
1. <u>Certainly</u> God can <u>never</u> fail.
2. To pray <u>earnestly</u> requires <u>very</u> diligent concentration.
3. People <u>often</u> think that another's lot in life is <u>much</u> easier than their own.
4. Thinking <u>so</u> <u>foolishly</u> invites discontentment.
5. My parents <u>never</u> learned to speak Spanish <u>fluently</u>.
6. Gliding <u>erratically</u> <u>down</u>, the disabled plane landed <u>safely</u>.
7. The stranger spoke <u>nervously</u> and <u>haltingly</u>.
8. These <u>deliciously</u> sweet apples <u>almost</u> <u>always</u> keep <u>well</u>.
9. The tractor, running <u>smoothly</u> <u>now</u>, <u>easily</u> pulled the <u>extremely</u> large load.
10. Father has <u>already</u> announced the time to go <u>home</u>.

B. Write each adverb and the word it modifies.
1. A swan's long neck curves more beautifully than a giraffe's.
2. Serenely floating around seems to be the swan's main occupation.

8. deliciously—adjective; almost—adverb; always—verb; well—verb
9. smoothly—verbal; now—verbal; easily—verb; extremely—adjective
10. already—verb; home—verbal

B. 1. more—beautifully; beautifully—curves
2. Serenely—floating; around—floating

Lesson 92 Answers

Class Practice

A. 1. verb
2. verb; adverb; verb
3. verbal; verbal
4. adjective; verb; verb
5. adjective; adverb; verb

B. 1. loudly—echoed
2. very—energetically; energetically—played
3. somewhat—smaller
4. stiffly—strutting; noisily—gobbling; extremely—interesting
5. together—to eat

C. 1.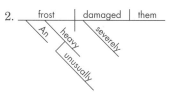

2.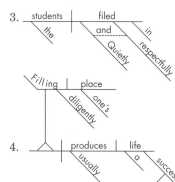

3.

4.

5.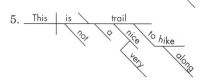

Written Exercises

A. 1. Certainly—verb; never—verb
2. earnestly—verbal; very—adjective
3. often—verb; much—adjective
4. so—adverb; foolishly—verbal
5. never—verb; fluently—verbal
6. erratically—verbal; down—verbal; safely—ver
7. nervously—verb; haltingly—verb

3. Having relatively short legs, a swan can never walk very gracefully.
4. The toucan's bill is quite long.
5. Since the toucan's bill is surprisingly light, its body is nicely balanced.
6. Yesterday the children eagerly dashed outside.
7. Aunt Alta, stepping quickly away, avoided a potentially serious accident.
8. Uncle Sidney finally made the decision to drive cautiously onward.

C. Diagram these sentences.
1. Using his small resources effectively, Shamgar mightily delivered Israel.
2. Man's heart is desperately wicked.
3. The Bible plainly teaches the only way to live righteously.
4. Those extremely destructive tornadoes moved amazingly fast.
5. Cleaning up afterward required especially strenuous efforts.

Review Exercises

A. Write correctly each underlined sentence part that contains an error in the use of a colon or semicolon. If it is correct, write *correct*. [27]
1. Father read from the <u>Bible, afterward</u> he asked Leroy to lead in prayer.
2. In our small garden we <u>planted: radishes</u>, carrots, lettuce, and sugar peas.
3. A writer once made this interesting <u>statement: "The</u> hardest tumble a man can make is to fall over his own bluff."
4. We have cottage meetings regularly for Mrs. Welch, an elderly <u>widow, for</u> Mr. Andrew, a paralyzed <u>man, and</u> for Stuart Goetz, a crippled youth.
5. After a heavy rain, these roads can be described in one <u>word, muddy</u>.

B. Copy these sentences, adding commas, dashes, and parentheses where needed. Some sentences have notes to direct you. [29]
1. Aunt Iva she's not really my aunt is a cheerful old lady. (Treat the parenthetical element as being relatively unimportant.)
2. "I just can't yes, now I remember her name!" exclaimed Janet.
3. John Bunyan wrote *The Pilgrim's Progress* what a delightful example of allegory! while he was in jail. (Give sharp emphasis to the parenthetical material.)
4. Our new school nestled at the foot of Tucker's Hill is quite attractive. (Make the parenthetical material a basic part of the sentence.)
5. "Wherefore let him that thinketh he standeth take heed lest he fall" 1 Corinthians 10:12.

---

4. Our new school, nestled at the foot of Tucker's Hill, is quite attractive.
5. "Wherefore let him that thinketh he standeth take heed lest he fall" (1 Corinthians 10:12).

3. relatively—short; never—can walk; very—gracefully; gracefully—can walk
4. quite—long
5. surprisingly—light; nicely—balanced
6. Yesterday—dashed; eagerly—dashed; outside—dashed
7. quickly—stepping; away—stepping; potentially—serious
8. finally—made; cautiously—to drive; onward—to drive

C.

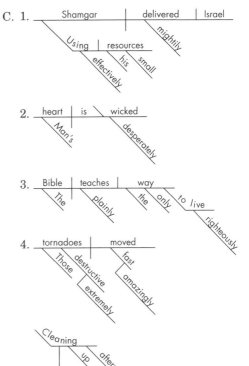

1.
2.
3.
4.
5.

Review Exercises

A. 1. Bible; afterward
   2. planted radishes
   3. correct
   4. widow; for man; and
   5. word: muddy

B. 1. Aunt Iva (she's not really my aunt) is a cheerful old lady.
   2. "I just can't—yes, now I remember her name!" exclaimed Janet.
   3. John Bunyan wrote *The Pilgrim's Progress*—what a delightful example of allegory!—while he was in jail.

93. Forms of Comparison for Adverbs

Lesson Survey

- The **positive degree** is the simplest form of an adverb. This form modifies without comparing.
- The **comparative degree** is regularly formed by adding -er or using *more* or *less*. This form compares two actions.
- The **superlative degree** is regularly formed by adding -est or using *most* or *least*. This form compares more than two actions.
- Some common adverbs have irregular forms of comparison.
- When you refer to only two people or actions, be especially careful to use the comparative degree.
- Do not make a double comparison by adding -er or -est and also using *more* or *most*.
- When comparing one member of a group with each of the other members individually or with the whole group as a unit, do not omit the word *else* or *other*.
- Do not change an adverb to an adjective in writing a comparative or superlative form.

Many adverbs have three degrees of comparison: positive, comparative, and superlative. These three degrees are illustrated on the chart below.

Positive	Comparative	Superlative
hard	harder	hardest
early	earlier	earliest
serenely	more serenely	most serenely

The *positive degree* is the simplest form of an adverb. This form modifies without comparing.

> William worked <u>hard</u> all afternoon.
> This morning we started chores <u>early</u>.
> Maria accepted the disappointment <u>serenely</u>.

The *comparative degree* is regularly formed by adding -er or using *more* or *less*. This form compares two actions. Use the suffix for the few one-syllable adverbs that do not end with -ly and for some two-syllable words. For most adverbs, use the word *more*. For negative comparisons of all words, use the word *less*.

Lesson 93

Purpose: To study the three degrees of comparison for adverbs.

Oral Review:

1. What common questions are answered by adverbs that modify verbs? (how, when, where)
2. What question is answered by adverbs that modify adjectives or other adverbs? (to what degree)
3. What are these other adverbs called? (adverbs of degree)
4. When are words like *father* and *aunt* capitalized? (when used as part of a name or to replace a name)
5. When are words like *north* and *west* capitalized? (when they name specific geographical regions)
6. When are names of school subjects capitalized? (when they are derived from proper nouns or are followed by numbers)
7. Name five uses of italics or underlining. (for the titles of major works; for the specific names of vehicles; for a word, letter, number, or symbol that is the subject of discussion; for foreign words that have not been adopted into the English language; and for special emphasis)
8. What kinds of plurals are formed by using apostrophes? (plurals of letters, figures, and abbreviations followed by periods, and of words used as subjects of discussion)
9. Name several groups of compound words that are hyphenated? (compound number words; fractions written in words; words ending with -in-law; compound words beginning with *great-* that refer to relatives; compound words beginning with *self-*; many compound words beginning with *all-*; many compound adjectives used as a unit; proper nouns and adjectives with prefixes)

Lesson Introduction: Read the following poem to the class.

The Comparative Degree

What weight of woe we owe to thee,
Accursed comparative degree!
   Thy paltry step can never give
   Access to the superlative;
For he who would the wisest be,
Strives to make others wise as he,
   And never yet was man judged best
   Who would be better than the rest.
So does comparison unkind
Dwarf and debase the haughty mind.

Make not a man your measuring rod
If you would span the way to God;
   Heed not our petty "worse" or "less,"
   But fix your eyes on perfectness.
Make for the loftiest point in view,
And draw your friends along with you.
         —Amos R. Wells

Glen worked <u>harder</u> today than he did yesterday.
Tomorrow we should start even <u>earlier</u>.
I received the disappointment <u>less serenely</u> than she did.

The *superlative degree* is regularly formed by adding *-est* or using *most* r *least*. This form compares more than two actions. Follow the same guide-ines for using the suffix or the words as given for the comparative degree.

Of all his afternoon chores, Samuel worked <u>hardest</u> at stacking wood.
Father started <u>earliest</u> of all of us.
Of all the children, I responded <u>least serenely</u> to the disappointment.

Some common adverbs have irregular forms of comparison.

Positive	Comparative	Superlative
well	better	best
badly (ill)	worse	worst
little	less	least
much	more	most
far	farther	farthest

Marvin lettered his motto <u>well</u>, but Charlotte did hers <u>better</u>.
I throw too <u>badly</u> to be the pitcher; no one pitches <u>worse</u> than I do.
Joseph's ball went <u>farther</u> than mine, but Allen's went <u>farthest</u>.

As with adjectives, the most common mistake in using the forms of com-parison is to use the superlative form when you should use the compara-ive form. When you are referring to only two people or actions, be especially careful to use the comparative degree.

Incorrect: Anita has made bread the <u>most</u> often of the two girls.
Eli ran fast, but Clarence ran <u>fastest</u>.
Correct: Anita has made bread the <u>more</u> often of the two girls.
Eli ran fast, but Clarence ran <u>faster</u>.

Do not make a double comparison by adding *-er* or *-est* and also using *more* or *most*.

Incorrect: The visitors came <u>more sooner</u> than we had expected.
Uncle James has traveled the <u>most farthest</u> of them all.
Correct: The visitors came <u>sooner</u> than we had expected.
Uncle James has traveled the <u>farthest</u> of them all.

Sometimes a sentence compares one member of a group with each of the other members individually, or with the whole group considered as a unit. Do not omit the word *else* or *other* in such a sentence, for then the sentence will be illogical or will not say what you intend.

Of course the comparative degree does have a proper use, but we fall into a dangerous trap if we use it to compare ourselves with others. "For we dare not make ourselves of the number, or compare ourselves with some that commend themselves: but they measuring themselves by themselves, and com-paring themselves among themselves, are not wise" (2 Corinthians 10:12). It is much better to compare ourselves with Jesus, whose perfect example always challenges us to better living.

Lesson Outline:

1. Many adverbs have three degrees of com-parison: positive, comparative, and superla-tive.

2. The positive degree is the simplest form of an adverb. This form modifies without com-paring.

3. The comparative degree is regularly formed by adding -er or using more or less. This form compares two actions.

    a. Use the suffix for the few one-syllable ad-verbs that do not end with *-ly* and for some two-syllable words.

    b. For most adverbs, use the word *more*.

    c. For negative comparisons of all words, use the word *less*.

4. The superlative degree is regularly formed by adding -est or using most or least. This form compares more than two actions. Follow the same guidelines for using the suffix or the words as given for the comparative degree.

5. Some common adverbs have irregular forms of comparison.

Illogical:

Elsie acted more calmly than anyone in her class. (Elsie is in her own class; she cannot act more calmly than herself.)

I arrived later than all the members in my family. (I am part of my own family; I cannot arrive later than myself.)

Logical:

Elsie acted more calmly than anyone <u>else</u> in her class.

I arrived later than all the <u>other</u> members in my family.

Do not change an adverb to an adjective in writing a comparative or superlative form. This error is rather common with adverbs that end with -*ly* in the positive form. Some writers and speakers tend to drop the -*ly* and add -*er* or -*est* to the *adjective* form of the word.

Incorrect: Arlene did her lettering <u>neater</u> than Sarah did hers.
Judy did her lettering the <u>neatest</u> of all the girls.

Correct: Arlene did her lettering <u>more neatly</u> than Sarah did hers.
Judy did her lettering the <u>most neatly</u> of all the girls.

Class Practice

A. Give the comparative and superlative degrees of these adverbs.
   1. well
   2. tightly
   3. fast
   4. simply
   5. urgently
   6. sleepily
   7. soon
   8. far

B. Read each sentence, using the correct form of the adverb in parentheses.
   1. Rachel was hurt (badly) in the accident than Susan was.
   2. Clifford is the (warmly) dressed of any of the students.
   3. Church leaders often were persecuted (severely) than other Christians.

C. Read each sentence correctly.
   1. Of Isaac's two sons, Jacob certainly lived most righteously.
   2. Jacob loved Joseph more than any of his sons.
   3. Israel went into apostasy more sooner than Judah did.
   4. The Samaritan acted kinder toward the wounded man than did the priest and the Levite.
   5. Manasseh reigned longer than anyone in Judah.
   6. David behaved himself wiser than King Saul.

D. Make up three sentences to illustrate the three degrees of comparison for these adverbs. For the comparative and superlative degrees, be sure your sentences show specific comparisons.
   1. softly   2. late

6. When you refer to only two people or actions, be especially careful to use the comparative degree.

7. Do not make a double comparison by adding -er or -est and also using more *or* most.

8. When comparing one member of a group with each of the other members individually or with the whole group as a unit, do not omit the word else *or* other.

9. Do not change an adverb to an adjective in writing a comparative or superlative form.

Lesson 93 Answers

Class Practice

A. 1. better, best
   2. more tightly, most tightly
   3. faster, fastest
   4. more simply, most simply
   5. more urgently, most urgently
   6. more sleepily, most sleepily
   7. sooner, soonest
   8. farther, farthest

B. (Corrections are underlined.)
   1. Rachel was hurt <u>worse</u> in the accident than Susan was.
   2. Clifford is the <u>most warmly</u> dressed of any of the students.
   3. Church leaders often were persecuted <u>more severely</u> than other Christians.

C. (Corrections are marked.)
   1. Of Isaac's two sons, Jacob certainly lived <u>more</u> righteously.
   2. Jacob loved Joseph more than any <u>other</u> of his sons.
   3. Israel went into apostasy ~~more~~ sooner than Judah did.
   4. The Samaritan acted <u>more kindly</u> toward the wounded man than did the priest and the Levite.
   5. Manasseh reigned longer than anyone <u>else</u> in Judah.
   6. David behaved himself <u>more wisely</u> than King Saul.

D. (Individual work.)

Written Exercises

A. Write the correct form of each adverb in parentheses.

1. No doubt, Daniel rested (peacefully) in the lions' den than King Darius did in the palace.
2. Of all those on the ship, the apostle Paul apparently behaved (calmly).
3. Of the two new mission workers, Janice learned Spanish (rapidly).
4. The blue jay comes to our feeder (often) than any other bird.
5. He also eats the (greedily) of them all.

B. Find the mistake in each sentence, and write one to three words to show how it should be corrected.

1. David acted more courageously than any man in Israel.
2. Of all the judges, Samson apparently helped littlest in promoting spiritual revival.
3. Apparently Samuel served as judge more longer than most of the other judges.
4. In studying the lives of Abraham and Isaac, we find that Abraham moved most often.
5. Baby Clyde is playing happier today than he did yesterday.
6. My brother Joshua built two doghouses, and the second certainly was the most sturdily built.
7. Brother Lemuel's arrived the most earliest of our guests.
8. Dennis can bat farther than anyone in his class.
9. Arlene folded the wash neater this time than she did before.
10. Of the two poems that Brenda wrote, the second one portrays spring the most descriptively.
11. Rose understood the lesson better this time because she listened more careful.
12. Which of the two boys did his work best?
13. Marlin can sing lower than anyone in his room at school.
14. Catherine explained the problem clearer than I could.
15. Alaskans live farther north than the people of any state in the United States.

C. Write three sentences to illustrate the three degrees of comparison for each adverb. For the comparative and superlative degrees, be sure your sentences show specific comparisons.

1. far   2. willingly   3. faithfully

Review Exercises

A. Write correctly each word with a capitalization error.

1. The lord is a loving father, and he tenderly cares for his people.
2. The new testament contains specific direction for christians.

Written Exercises

A. 1. more peacefully
2. most calmly
3. more rapidly
4. more often
5. most greedily

B. 1. any other man
2. least
3. judge longer
4. more often
5. more happily
6. more sturdily
7. the earliest
8. anyone else
9. more neatly
10. more descriptively
11. carefully
12. better
13. anyone else
14. more clearly
15. any other state

C. (Individual work.)

Review Exercises

A. 1. Lord, Father, He, His
2. New Testament, Christians

3. My Grandfather is living with uncle Roy and aunt Joyce.
4. Now that Spring is here, the geese are leaving their homes in the South and flying North again.
5. Did father buy shoregood hot dogs for our picnic at huckleberry valley?
6. After recess, we shall have Science and Typing I.
7. The statue of liberty welcomes newcomers to the united states.
8. This swiss cheese was on special at Myer's meat and cheese.

B. Write correctly the items with mistakes in the use of italics, apostrophes, or hyphens.
1. We are presently using the Church Hymnal for family worship.
2. Somebodys car has a flat tire, but its not ours.
3. When the shortage of a certain product is predicted, that prophecy is often self fulfilling.
4. We must package some two, five, and ten pound packages of rye flour.
5. If your ds look like cls, you wont receive credit.
6. We took a mid July trip to visit Great uncle Chester, who is ninety four years old.
7. Because of the twin babies fussiness, Mother wasnt able to attend every session of the all day meeting.
8. Brother Marvins answer was that either the second or the third syllable in Caribbean can receive the primary accent.

3. grandfather, Uncle, Aunt
4. spring, north
5. Father, Shoregood, Huckleberry Valley
6. science
7. Statue, Liberty, United States
8. Swiss, Meat, Cheese

B. 1. <u>Church Hymnal</u>
2. Somebody's, it's
3. self-fulfilling
4. two-, five-, ten-pound
5. <u>d</u>'s, <u>cl</u>'s, won't
6. mid-July, Great-uncle, ninety-four
7. babies', wasn't, all-day
8. Marvin's, <u>Caribbean</u>

94. Verbals and Phrases Used as Adverbs

Lesson Survey
- A prepositional phrase used as an adverb can modify a verb or verbal. It usually tells *how, when, where,* or *why.*
- A prepositional phrase used as an adverb can modify an adjective or an adverb by telling *to what degree, how,* or *how much.*
- Several prepositional phrases in succession may be all adverbs, each modifying the same word.
- A prepositional phrase used as an adverb may contain a prepositional phrase used as an adjective.
- An infinitive or infinitive phrase can be used as an adverb.

Lesson 94

Purpose: (1) To study the use of prepositional phrases as adverbs. (2) To teach the use of infinitives and infinitive phrases as adverbs.

Oral Review:
1. What four types of words do adverbs modify? (verbs, adjectives, adverbs, verbals)
2. What term is used for adverbs that modify adjectives and other adverbs? (adverbs of degree)
3. Give the comparative and superlative degrees of these adverbs.
   a. well (better, best)
   b. early (earlier, earliest)
   c. nearly (more nearly, most nearly)
   d. little (less, least)
   e. late (later, latest)
   f. proudly (more proudly, most proudly)
   g. badly (worse, worst)
   h. fairly (more fairly, most fairly)
4. Tell whether each sentence is simple, compound, complex, or compound-complex.
   a. The peace that Jesus gives is unmatched by anything of this world. (complex)
   b. In the truth of God's Word is found our stability. (simple)
   c. Because character is so important, we must guard our hearts diligently, and we must make our choices carefully. (compound-complex)
   d. Whenever we choose rightly, our character is strengthened. (complex)
   e. A good character is a priceless possession now, and it will bring eternal rewards. (compound)

Lesson Introduction: Write the following questions and partial answers on the board.

Single-word adverbs add to the descriptiveness of language as they modify verbs or verbals, adjectives, and other adverbs. Adverb phrases are likewise important to descriptive speaking and writing.

Prepositional Phrases

Remember that a prepositional phrase begins with a preposition and ends with a substantive that is the object of the preposition. A prepositional phrase used as an adverb can modify a verb or verbal. It usually tells *how, when, where,* or *why.*

God has blessed us <u>with many rich blessings</u>.
    (*With many rich blessings* tells *how* about the verb *has blessed.*)

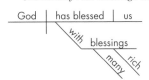

Nature's beauties, created <u>for God's own glory</u>, point man <u>to the Creator</u>.
    (*For God's own glory* tells *why* about the verbal *created. To the Creator* tells *where* about the verb *point.*)

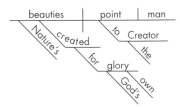

A prepositional phrase used as an adverb can modify an adjective or an adverb by telling *to what degree, how,* or *how much.* Such a phrase usually comes immediately after the adjective or adverb it modifies.

God's ear is always open <u>to our prayers</u>.
    (*To our prayers* tells *how* about the predicate adjective *open.*)

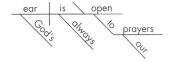

How long did God work in creating the world?
God created the world ———.

Why did God confound man's language at the Tower of Babel?
God confounded man's language to ———.

Point out that these questions cannot be answered with single-word adverbs only. Phrases must be used to give satisfactory answers. This lesson will help the students to understand adverb phrases.

Lesson Outline:

1. A prepositional phrase used as an adverb can modify a verb or verbal. It usually tells how, when, where, *or* why.

2. A prepositional phrase used as an adverb can modify an adjective or an adverb by telling to what degree, how, or how much. Such a phrase usually comes immediately after the adjective or adverb it modifies.

3. Several prepositional phrases in succession may be all adverbs, each modifying the same word. Each phrase modifies the same word independently of the others.

4. A prepositional phrase used as an adverb may contain a prepositional phrase used as an adjective. In this case, the whole string of prepositional phrases work together as one adverb.
    a. The first preposition introduces the entire adverb phrase, and the other prepositions introduce adjective phrases modifying the objects of previous prepositions.
    b. Each phrase in such a series must be tested to see which word it modifies. This is done by using it alone with different words that come before it.

Solomon ruled wisely <u>beyond comparison with any other king</u>.

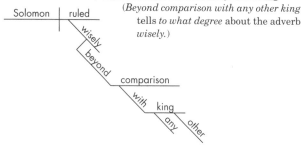

(*Beyond comparison with any other king* tells *to what degree* about the adverb *wisely.*)

Such a question is too difficult <u>for me</u>.
(*For me* tells *to what degree* about *too difficult.*)

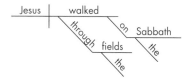

In the last example above, note that the prepositional phrase modifies *too difficult* (both words together). It is not logical to say that the phrase modifies only *too* or only *difficult,* for the two words work together as a unit.

A sentence may have several prepositional phrases in succession. Sometimes these phrases are all adverbs, each modifying the same word independently of the others.

Jesus walked <u>through the fields on the Sabbath</u>.
(*Through the fields* tells *where* about the verb *walked. On the Sabbath* tells *when* about the verb *walked.*)

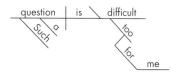

At other times, the first prepositional phrase is an adverb and the others are adjectives that modify the objects of previous prepositions. In this case, the whole string of prepositional phrases work together as one adverb. The first preposition introduces the entire adverb phrase, and the other

5. An infinitive or infinitive phrase can be used as an adverb.

    a. Such an infinitive or infinitive phrase almost always tells *why.*

    b. An infinitive or infinitive phrase that modifies an adjective tells *to what degree* or *how.* Usually it follows the adjective it modifies.

    c. An infinitive or infinitive phrase that modifies an adverb tells *to what degree* or *how.* Usually it follows the adverb it modifies.

★ *EXTRA PRACTICE*
Worksheet 35 *(Verbals and Phrases Used as Adverbs)*

prepositions introduce adjective phrases within the adverb phrase. These phrases do not modify the same word independently of each other.

Each phrase in such a series must be tested to see which word it modifies. This is done by using it alone with different words that come before it. Study the following example.

Jesus was displeased <u>with the activities in the court of the temple</u>.
> Was displeased *with the activities*? (yes; an adverb phrase)
> Was displeased *in the court*? (no; *in the court* modifies *activities*; an adjective phrase)
> Was displeased *of the temple*? (no; *of the temple* modifies *court*; an adjective phrase)
> *With the activities in the court of the temple* works together as one adverb phrase modifying the verb *was displeased*.

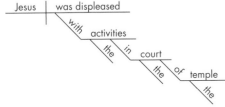

Infinitives and Infinitive Phrases

An infinitive is a verbal that consists of *to* and the basic form of a verb. An infinitive phrase consists of an infinitive and its complements and modifiers. You have already learned that infinitives and infinitive phrases can function as substantives or as adjectives. In this lesson you will see that they have one more function: they can act as adverbs.

An infinitive or infinitive phrase used as an adverb almost always tells *why*.

We have met <u>to worship</u>.
> (The infinitive *to worship* tells *why* about the verb *have met*.)

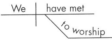

We study the Bible <u>to know the truth</u>.
> (The infinitive phrase *to know the truth* tells *why* about the verb *study*.)

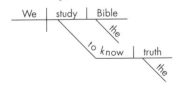

Like other adverbs, an infinitive or infinitive phrase can modify an adjective. Then it usually follows the adjective and tells *to what degree* or *how*.

Your question is difficult <u>to answer</u>.
(*To answer* tells *how* about the predicate adjective *difficult*.)

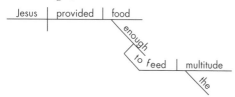

Jesus provided food enough <u>to feed the multitude</u>.
(*To feed the multitude* tells *to what degree* about the adjective *enough*.)

Jesus | provided | food

An infinitive or infinitive phrase can also modify an adverb. It follows that adverb and tells *to what degree* or *how*.

They arrived too late <u>to help</u>.
(*To help* tells *to what degree* about *too late*.)

In the last example, note again the unit (*too late*) that is modified. It is not logical to say that the infinitive modifies only *too* or only *late*.

Class Practice

A. Read each prepositional phrase used as an adverb, including any adjective phrase that may be in it. Tell what word the adverb phrase modifies. If it modifies a unit like *too late*, give both words.
1. David, fleeing from Saul's presence, hid in the wilderness.
2. David took his family to the safety of Moab.
3. On two occasions, David could have killed the king.
4. But David respected the Lord's anointed too greatly for such a deed.

Lesson 94 Answers

Class Practice

A. 1. from Saul's presence, fleeing;
   in the wilderness, hid
2. to the safety of Moab, took
3. On two occasions, could have killed
4. for such a deed, too greatly

5. Throughout these years of trial by persecution, David drew near to the Lord in prayer.
6. Nothing is too hard for our God.

B. Read each infinitive or infinitive phrase used as an adverb, and tell what word it modifies. If it modifies a unit like *too late,* give both words.
1. Jesus came to this world to die for mankind.
2. Jesus' yoke is easy to bear.
3. Some people are too proud to accept His yoke.
4. Many Europeans came to America to find religious freedom.
5. These people were not necessarily eager to leave their homelands.
6. But the opportunities of the New World beckoned too strongly to be ignored.

C. On the chalkboard, diagram these sentences.
1. We walked through the meadow to the creek.
2. In the afternoon we planted peas in the plot behind the house.
3. The children ran into the house to get drinks.
4. The rains fell too sparsely to water our garden sufficiently.
5. The roads have become clear of all ice.
6. Gossiping about others is a great evil.

Written Exercises

A. Copy each prepositional phrase used as an adverb, including any adjective phrase that may be in it. Write the word (or unit like *too late*) that the phrase modifies.
1. In His Word, God gives to the faithful many promises.
2. These promises are precious beyond our comprehension.
3. In the darkness of the world, the church shines as a light.
4. The holy angels encamp around God's people at all times for their protection.
5. When Esau sold his birthright, he acted foolishly in the extreme.
6. The mighty river flowed through the flooded valley too swiftly for the struggling pioneers.
7. The pioneers, too weary for such a challenge, gave up and returned to higher ground.
8. They decided to camp for the night.

B. Copy each infinitive or infinitive phrase used as an adverb. Write the word (or unit like *too late*) that it modifies.
1. Brother Neil has come to plow our garden.
2. During the prolonged drought, food became difficult to find.
3. We freeze many kinds of fruits to preserve them.
4. Facing the angry bear, Wesley was too scared to move.

---

5. Throughout these years of trial by persecution, drew;
to the Lord, near; in prayer, drew
6. for our God, too hard

B. 1. to die for mankind, came
2. to bear, easy
3. to accept His yoke, too proud
4. to find religious freedom, came
5. to leave their homelands, eager
6. to be ignored, too strongly

C.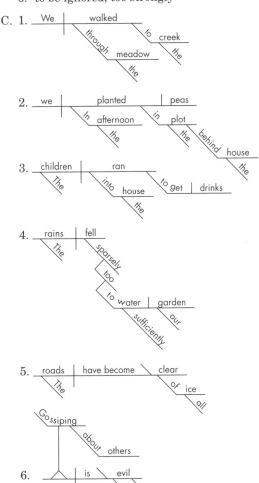

---

6. through the flooded valley, flowed;
for the struggling pioneers, too swiftly
7. for such a challenge, too weary;
to higher ground, returned
8. for the night, to camp

B. 1. to plow our garden, has come
2. to find, difficult
3. to preserve them, freeze
4. to move, too scared

Written Exercises

A. 1. In His Word, gives; to the faithful, gives
2. beyond our comprehension, precious
3. In the darkness of the world, shines;
as a light, shines
4. around God's people, encamp;
at all times, encamp;
for their protection, encamp
5. in the extreme, foolishly

5. Do you look into the night sky to see the constellations?
6. The box, too heavy to be lifted, remained on the pickup.
7. We go to church to worship the Lord.
8. We study God's Word to become more like Him.

C. Diagram these sentences.
  1. A tadpole changes gradually into a frog.
  2. These changes demonstrate a Creator's wisdom too forcefully to overlook.
  3. A young tadpole has gills to extract oxygen from the water.
  4. By the end of six weeks, it is growing hind legs.
  5. Its lungs, functional within ten weeks, replace its gills.
  6. Now the tadpole must come to the surface to get oxygen.
  7. The tail is absorbed into the tadpole's body during this time.
  8. Our God is wise beyond man's comprehension.

Review Exercises

A. Match each sentence below to the proper description by writing the correct letter. [14–16]
  a. simple sentence with no compound parts
  b. simple sentence with a compound predicate
  c. compound sentence with two independent clauses
  d. compound sentence with three independent clauses
  e. complex sentence with one independent clause and one dependent clause
  f. complex sentence with one independent clause and two dependent clauses
  g. compound-complex sentence with two independent clauses and one dependent clause
  1. This is our Father's world; in many ways it shows His greatness.
  2. The life of microscopic things shows His infinite skill as Creator.
  3. The vast expanses of outer space, which man cannot measure, speak of His infinite power.
  4. Although man can never comprehend God, he can believe Him; and he should surrender his life to Him.
  5. We can see God in the creation, we can hear Him in the Word, and we can feel His presence in our hearts.
  6. The Bible describes God's majesty and reveals His love to us.
  7. God has clearly revealed Himself to man, yet many ignore Him.
  8. Although multitudes rebel against Him, God reigns from His throne that can never be shaken.

B. Copy each word that should be followed by a comma, and add the missing comma. Each sentence needs at least two commas. [23, 25]

5. to see the constellations, Do look
6. to be lifted, too heavy
7. to worship the Lord, go
8. to become more like Him, study

C. 1.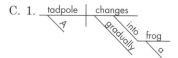

2.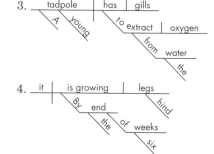

3.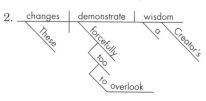

4.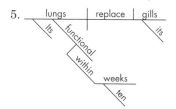

5.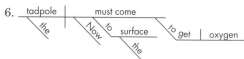

6.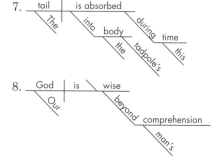

7.

8.

Review Exercises

A.
1. c
2. a
3. e
4. g
5. d
6. b
7. c
8. f

1. Stacked neatly on the shelves the boxes of ripe delicious strawberries attracted many customers.
2. Clyde O. Weaver Jr. raises strawberries corn and melons.
3. Yes the strawberries did quite well this year and the corn has a good start.
4. Although we had plenty of work at home we helped Lester Smith our next-door neighbor to repair his house roof.
5. Paula have you met Linda Gress who just started working at the children's home?
6. From the back porch steps lead all the way to a springhouse I think.

B. 1. shelves, ripe,
2. Weaver, Jr., strawberries, corn,
3. Yes, year,
4. home, Smith, neighbor,
5. Paula, Gress,
6. porch, springhouse,

95. Taking Notes From a Sermon

Lesson Survey
- Taking notes has value both during and after a sermon.
- Taking good notes requires good listening skills.
- Good notes should have a detailed heading and should consist of an orderly summary of the speaker's main points.

Preaching fills an important role in the New Testament church. God has chosen this as the primary method of indoctrinating believers and of spreading the Gospel to unbelievers. A faithful minister puts much time and effort into preparing the sermons he preaches. Faithful listeners are willing to put forth the effort needed to understand and remember these messages.

Values of Note-Taking

Taking notes is a valuable aid in better understanding a sermon. For one thing, the discipline of writing helps to keep you from daydreaming or falling asleep. In addition, the discipline of listening for the next point to write in your notes helps you to grasp the main points of the sermon better.

Notes also have value after the sermon. If you write things on paper, you will remember them better than if you only hear them. These notes can also be kept for future reference. Your notes can even benefit others. By reading your notes, someone who could not hear the sermon can gain some inspiration.

Listening Skills for Note-Taking

Taking good notes requires good listening skills. God commands us to listen. "He that hath ears to hear, let him hear." And again, "Keep thy foot

Lesson 95

Purpose: To study listening and note-taking skills.

Teacher: If you plan to do the Written Exercises in English class, you should prepare a presentation before class time. A sample outline is provided next to the Written Exercises.

Oral Review:
1. Briefly define these terms from your poetry study.
   a. feminine rhyme (a rhyme involving more than one syllable)
   b. meter (the pattern of accented and unaccented syllables)
   c. poetic foot (one accented syllable and the unaccented syllable or syllables associated with it)
   d. alliteration (the repetition of beginning consonant sounds)
   e. assonance (the repetition of similar vowel sounds in accented syllables)
   f. onomatopoeia (the use of a word having an imitative sound)
2. Briefly define these terms from your story-writing study.
   a. theme (the lesson that the story teaches)
   b. conflict (the struggle or problem the main character faces)
   c. climax (the final and most intense incident in the conflict)
   d. characterization (the process of portraying a story character)
   e. setting (the time and place of the story)
3. Why should you take notes for a report from more than one reference source? (to have a balanced report; to require you to express ideas in your own words; to verify facts)

when thou goest to the house of God, and be more ready to hear, than to give the sacrifice of fools."

One important listening skill is the ability to focus your whole attention on the speaker. You can think much faster than a person can speak. As a result, your mind runs beyond what the speaker is saying. Unless you purposely direct your thinking, sooner or later you will find yourself thinking about something completely unrelated to the message you are supposed to be hearing.

So what can you do to keep your mind from wandering to other things? Use your extra thinking time to review what the speaker has already said. Try to anticipate what he will likely say next. Consider how the different points of the message relate to each other. Using your extra thinking time in this way serves two purposes. First, it helps to keep your mind on the subject being addressed. Second, it helps you to better understand and remember the things you hear.

A listener with a wandering mind is bound to miss some important points of a message. Watching the speaker and noticing his expressions and gestures helps you to focus your attention on him.

A closely related skill is the ability to overcome distractions. There are some simple things that one can do to avoid distractions. Choosing a seat nearer to the front or farther from the windows can help. Establishing a reputation of refusing to misbehave is another big help. Of course, you will not always be able to remove all distractions. Then you must deliberately ignore them and ask God to help you to listen in spite of distractions.

Another important skill is to listen with interest. Sincerely appreciate the message even if the speaker is not as interesting as someone else. If you are listening with a mind open to truth, you will find it easy to concentrate.

Listening for main ideas is another basic listening skill. The many details and illustrations are important, but their value is primarily in establishing the main points of the message. Many speakers, in their introductory remarks, list the divisions of the subject they plan to address. Be aware that the inflections in the speaker's voice can tell you what is important. If he says something slowly and emphatically, or if he repeats it several times, it is probably a major point. The words "Now we will consider . . ." or "The next point is . . ." or "Moving on, . . ." indicate that another main point is coming.

Methods of Note-Taking

Good notes should have a detailed heading. Near the top of the paper, write the date, the speaker's name, and the place of the service. Of course, the most important part of the heading is the title of the sermon and, if the speaker gives a Scripture text, the reference of the text.

4. When may you copy the exact words of a reference source in your notes? (when you plan to quote those words in your report, and if you place those words in quotation marks)

5. What are some good ways to introduce your report? (with an interesting observation, an illustration, a thought-provoking question, a familiar quotation, or a direct statement)

6. What are two good ways to conclude your report? (with a summary of the main points; with a call to some response or action)

7. What are the three parts of a report? (introduction, body, conclusion)

Lesson Introduction: What was the theme of the sermon you heard last Sunday? What were the main points? Can you remember? No? Surely you understood the message clearly. You may even have discussed the sermon after the service or on the way home. And have you forgotten already? (Commend any students who do remember.) Taking notes on a sermon is one help in making the main points stick in your mind. This lesson will give you direction on the important skill of note-taking.

Lesson Outline:

1. Taking notes is a valuable aid in better understanding a sermon.

    a. The discipline of writing helps to keep you from daydreaming or falling asleep.

    b. The discipline of listening for the next point to write in your notes helps you to grasp the main points of the sermon better.

2. Notes have value after the sermon.

    a. If you write things on paper, you will remember them better than if you only hear them.

    b. These notes can also be kept for future reference.

Good notes consist of an orderly summary of the speaker's main points. Usually the most effective notes are in outline form. An outline shows the relationships among main points and subpoints.

However, a speaker's outline may be hard for you to follow. His own notes may not even be in outline form. In such cases, your notes may be written as a list of statements or ideas that have impressed you. Whether your notes are an outline or a list of ideas, you should include the Scripture references that the speaker gives with the points. And whatever the form of your notes, remember that they should summarize the speaker's main points.

Finally, notes should be written as neatly as possible. The original notes, which likely were written hurriedly, may need to be recopied. As you recopy them, write out any abbreviations that may be unclear, check for misspellings, fill in any missing words, and check Bible references for accuracy. Do these things as soon afterward as practical, while the sermon is still fresh in your mind.

Note-taking is a worthwhile skill. Through perseverance, practice, and positive attitude, you will increase your skill, and taking notes will become much easier. Do not be discouraged if you miss some points or if the sermon seems to be over your head. But do determine to develop this skill for the glory of God.

Here are two sets of notes taken from the same sermon. The first set is written in outline form—though the outline actually written by a listener is seldom as well organized as this one. The second set is a list of statements.

Sermon notes: Outline form

Jesus, an Exemplary Youth   February 26, 20—
Luke 2:40–52   Lester Shank
                                    Mount Smith Mennonite Church

I. In industry
  A. Responsible
    — Apparently took care of Mary after Joseph's death
  B. Productive
    — Later known as "the carpenter's son"
II. In study
  A. A teachable spirit (v. 46)
    1. Listened to others
    2. Asked questions
  B. A spiritual interest (vv. 46, 47)
III. In obedience (v. 51)
  A. Prompt
  B. Respectful

    c. Your notes can even benefit others. By reading your notes, someone who could not hear the sermon can gain some inspiration.

3. Taking good notes requires good listening skills.
    a. One important listening skill is the ability to focus your whole attention on the speaker.
    b. A closely related skill is the ability to overcome distractions.
    c. Another important skill is to listen with interest.
    d. Listening for main ideas is another basic listening skill.

4. Good notes should have a detailed heading.
    a. Near the top of the paper, write the date, the speaker's name, and the place of the service.

    b. The most important part of the heading is the title of the sermon and, if the speaker gives a Scripture text, the reference of the text.

5. Good notes should consist of an orderly summary of the speaker's main points.
    a. Usually the most effective notes are in outline form. An outline shows the relationships among main points and subpoints.
    b. Notes may also be written as a list of statements or ideas that have impressed you.
    c. Whether your notes are an outline or a list of ideas, you should include the Scripture references that the speaker gives with the points.
    d. Notes should be written as neatly as possible.

IV. In purpose
  A. Strength of character (v. 40)
  B. Commitment to God's purposes (v. 49)
V. In growth (v. 52)
  A. Physically: increased in stature
  B. Mentally: increased in wisdom
  C. Socially: in favor with man
  D. Spiritually: in favor with God

Sermon notes: List of statements

Jesus, an Exemplary Youth   February 26, 20—
Luke 2:40–52   Lester Shank
                                Mount Smith Mennonite Church

1. Jesus was responsible.
   — Apparently took care of Mary after Joseph's death
2. Jesus was productive.
   — Later known as "the carpenter's son"
3. Jesus had a teachable spirit (v. 46).
   — Listened to others and asked questions
4. Jesus showed a spiritual interest (vv. 46, 47).
5. Jesus obeyed promptly and respectfully (v. 51).
6. Jesus showed strength of character (v. 40).
7. Jesus was committed to God's purposes (v. 49).
8. Jesus was growing physically (increased in stature), mentally (increased in wisdom), socially (in favor with man), and spiritually (in favor with God).

Written Exercises

Take notes on one of the next sermons you hear or on a devotional in school. Recopy the notes with neat penmanship and good organization.

Review Exercises

Rewrite this partial outline correctly. Each starred line has a mistake. [35]

Lessons From the Life of Elisha

I. His call—1 Kings 19:16–21
  A. Fitness for the call
    *1. assurance of God's call (v. 16)
    2. Faithfulness in carrying out God's will (v. 17)
    *3. He worshiped faithfully (v. 18)
    *4. Diligent in fulfilling present responsibilities (v. 19)
    5. Honor for his parents (v. 20)
  B. Response to the call
    1. Acknowledged the source of the call promptly (v. 20)

Lesson 95 Answers

Written Exercises

(Individual work.)

(*Teacher:* The following outline is supplied f[ ] your use in giving practice with note-taking. Y[ ] could use it for a morning devotional or during clas[ ]

"And Be Ye Thankful"

I. Reasons for a thankful heart
  A. God understands and provides our eve[ ] need
    1. Physical needs (Phil. 4:19)
    2. Spiritual needs (2 Pet. 1:3)
  B. We are created with the capacity to worsh[ ] and praise
  C. Discontent always subtracts
    1. Achan—lost life because of covetou[ ] ness
    2. Gehazi—was smitten with leprosy
  D. It is commanded by God
    1. 1 Thess. 5:18
    2. Col. 3:15
II. Expressions of a thankful heart
  A. Gives verbal praise for gifts received
    1. To God (Eph. 5:20)
    2. To others
  B. Makes thrifty use of natural resources
    1. Doesn't throw food away
    2. Doesn't waste paper
  C. Remembers kindness received; forgets kin[ ] ness given
  D. Shares willingly with others
  E. Is content when needs are met (1 Tim. 6:[ ]
  F. Looks optimistically at every situation
III. Rewards for a thankful heart
  A. Escape from tensions of self-pity
  B. Inspiration to others
  C. Treasures laid up in heaven

Review Exercises

Lessons From the Life of Elisha

I. His call—1 Kings 19:16–21
  A. Fitness for the call
    1. Assurance of God's call (v. 16)
    2. Faithfulness in carrying out God's will (v. 1[ ]
    3. Faithfulness in worship (v. 18)
    4. Diligence in fulfilling present respons[ ] bilities (v. 19)
    5. Honor for his parents (v. 20)
  B. Response to the call
    1. Acknowledged the source of the c[ ] promptly (v. 20)

*2. He put first things first (v. 20)
*3. did not hide his mission (v. 21)
*4. Immediate service (v. 21)
  *a. In a lowly role
*II. He was constant—2 Kings 2:1–15
  A. Passed Elijah's threefold test
  *B. He kept the goal in view.
  *C. traveled on foot a great distance
    *1. Included much backtracking
  D. Was well rewarded for his efforts

2. Put first things first (v. 20)
3. Did not hide his mission (v. 21)
4. Served immediately in a lowly role (v. 21)
II. His constancy—2 Kings 2:1–15
  A. Passed Elijah's threefold test
  B. Kept the goal in view
  C. Traveled on foot a great distance, which included much backtracking
  D. Was well rewarded for his efforts

96. Adverb Clauses

Lesson Survey

- An **adverb clause** is a dependent clause that functions as an adverb and begins with a subordinating conjunction.

- If an adverb clause comes at the beginning or in the middle of a sentence, commas must separate it from the main clause.

- In an expression like *as soon as* or *so long that*, the first word is an adverb modifying the adjective or adverb in the middle, and the third word is a subordinating conjunction.

- When an adverb clause is introduced by *as . . . as* or by *than*, the clause is often elliptical.

A dependent clause is a word group containing a skeleton and functioning as a single sentence part. In Chapter 4 you studied noun clauses, and in Chapter 8 you studied adjective clauses. Now you are ready to study adverb clauses.

An *adverb clause* is a dependent clause that functions as an adverb. In the following sentences, notice how the underlined adverb modifier changes from a single word to a phrase to a clause.

Faithfully God leads us <u>onward</u>. (single word)
Faithfully God leads us <u>into new experiences</u>. (phrase)
Faithfully God leads us <u>where He can teach us new lessons</u>. (clause)

An adverb clause begins with a *subordinating conjunction*. The following list contains some of the most common subordinating conjunctions.

Lesson 96

Purpose: To study the use of adverb clauses.

Oral Review:

1. What four types of words do adverbs modify? (verbs, adjectives, adverbs, verbals)
2. An infinitive that modifies a verb usually answers what question? (why)
3. Infinitives that modify adjectives and adverbs usually answer what questions? (to what degree, how)
4. Give the helping verbs used for each of the perfect tenses. (*present perfect:* have or has; *past perfect:* had; *future perfect:* shall have or will have)
5. What helping verbs are used for the emphatic verb forms? (do, does, did)
6. Which tenses can be written in the emphatic form? (present, past)
7. Which tenses can be written in the progressive form? (all six tenses)
8. Tell whether the word *letter* is a retained direct object or a retained indirect object in each of these sentences.
   a. A few finishing touches were given the letter by Marsha. (retained indirect object)
   b. Grandmother Strite was given an interesting letter by Peter. (retained direct object)

Lesson Introduction: Write the following sentence on the board.

Sheep will prosper in a place <u>where they feel safe</u>.

Ask the students what the underlined part of the sentence is. (adjective clause) Challenge them to use the same clause as an adverb in a sentence. (A good shepherd leads his sheep <u>where they feel safe</u>.)

after	how	till
although	if	unless
as	in order that	until
as if	provided	when
as though	since	whenever
because	so that	where
before	than	wherever
even if	that	whether
even though	though	while

Just like single-word adverbs, adverb clauses can modify verbs, adjectives, adverbs, and verbals. Many adverb clauses answer the main adverb questions: *how, when,* and *where.* In addition, they can also answer these questions: *why, how long, how much, to what degree, in spite of what,* and *under what condition.*

When diagraming sentences with adverb clauses, remember to draw the broken line from the modified word in the main clause to the verb in the adverb clause. Study the following sentences, in which the adverb clauses are underlined.

Truth endures <u>*even though* many seek its destruction</u>.
(The adverb clause tells *in spite of what* about the verb *endures.*)

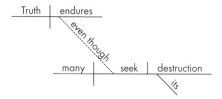

Our hearts, grateful <u>*because* God had answered our prayers</u>, rejoiced in His goodness. (The adverb clause tells *why* about the adjective *grateful.*)

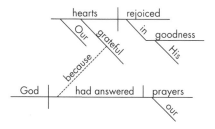

Although the words in the clause are the same, the two clauses fill different places in the sentences. In the sentence on the board, the clause modifies *place* by telling *which.* In the other sentence, it modifies *leads* by telling *where.*

Lesson Outline:

1. An adverb clause is a dependent clause that functions as an adverb and begins with a subordinating conjunction.

    a. Like single-word adverbs, adverb clauses can modify verbs, adjectives, adverbs, and verbals.

    b. Many adverb clauses answer the main adverb questions: *how, when,* and *where.*

    c. They can also answer these questions: *why, how long, how much, to what degree, in spite of what,* and *under what condition.*

    d. When diagraming sentences with adverb clauses, remember to draw the broken line from the modified word in the main clause to the verb in the adverb clause.

2. If an adverb clause comes at the beginning or in the middle of a sentence, one or two commas must separate it from the main clause.

3. In an expression like as soon as *or* so long that, *the first word is an adverb modifying the adjective or adverb in the middle, and the third word is a subordinating conjunction.* This conjunction introduces a clause that modifies the two-word unit.

4. When an adverb clause is introduced by as . . . as *or by* than, *the clause is often elliptical.*

★ **EXTRA PRACTICE**
Worksheet 36 *(Adverb Clauses)*

Grandfather hears better _than_ many older men do. (The adverb clause tells _to what degree_ about the adverb _better._)

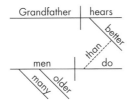

Father wanted to finish _before_ the sun went down.
(The adverb clause tells _when_ about the verbal _to finish._)

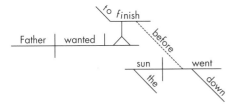

Unlike adjective clauses, which usually come right after the words they modify, adverb clauses can be placed at different locations in a sentence. If an adverb clause comes at the beginning of a sentence, a comma must separate it from the main clause. Two commas are used if the adverb clause comes in the middle. But if the clause comes at the end of the sentence, no comma is needed.

When Jesus called them, James and John followed Him at once.
James and John, _when Jesus called them,_ followed Him at once.
James and John followed Him at once _when Jesus called them._

In expressions like _as soon as_ and _so long that,_ the first word is an adverb modifying the adjective or adverb in the middle. The first two words work together as a unit; and the third word (a subordinating conjunction) introduces a clause that modifies the two-word unit.

A wise person seeks God's grace as soon _as temptation comes._ (The first _as_ tells _how_ soon. The second _as_ introduces a clause that tells _to what degree_ about _as soon._)

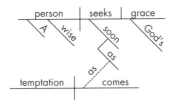

We should trust God so completely *that* <u>Satan cannot defeat us</u>.
   (*So* tells *how* completely. *That* introduces a clause that tells *to what degree* about *so* completely.)

When an adverb clause is introduced by *as . . . as* or by *than,* the clause is often elliptical. These elliptical clauses may be more difficult to recognize than adverb clauses that are complete.

My younger brother can throw a softball as far <u>as I</u>.
   (as far *as I can throw a softball*)

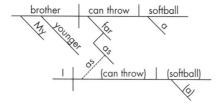

Beth has met Karen more often <u>than me</u>.
   (more often *than Beth has met me*)

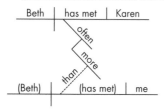

Class Practice

A. Tell which word (or unit) is modified by each underlined clause, and what question it answers.
   1. God rested <u>after He ended His work of creation</u>.

Lesson 96 Answers

Class Practice

A. 1. rested—when

2. Adam and Eve felt their guilt as soon <u>as they had taken of the forbidden fruit</u>.
3. <u>Although they had sinned grievously</u>, God was more gracious <u>than they deserved</u>.
4. <u>Because he had been with God</u>, Moses' face shone so much <u>that the people could not look at him</u>.
5. Gideon commanded his men to break their pitchers <u>when he blew the trumpet</u>.
6. Ahab pouted <u>as a spoiled child would</u>.

. Read the adverb clauses, and tell what words they modify. If a clause is elliptical, supply the omitted words.
1. Moses could not enter Canaan because he had disobeyed God.
2. Before the Flood began, God closed the door of the ark.
3. Although we may be tempted to think otherwise, God loves the heathen as much as us.
4. To compromise when others do wrong reveals grave weakness of character.
5. Is Kevin older than you?
6. Father wants to help Mr. Baldwin while he is sick.

. Tell where commas are needed in these sentences. If a sentence needs no commas, say *correct*.
1. Brother Dale before he dismissed the class made a few announcements.
2. Whenever Grandma Kurtz spends a week with us we bake a lot of pies.
3. The girls finished the cleaning while Mother rested.
4. Unless we soon have a good rain the garden crops will suffer.

. On the chalkboard, diagram these sentences.
1. Before the sun rose, we had crossed the Blue Mountains.
2. These horses must be stronger than I had imagined.
3. Brother Lester, cheerful even though he faces hardship, inspires our faith.
4. The birds sang so cheerily that nobody could remain sullen.
5. Rover obeys Father more readily than me.
6. To sleep because we have worked well is a blessing.

Written Exercises

. Copy the first and last words of each adverb clause, with ellipsis points between them. Write the word (or unit) that the clause modifies. Some sentences have more than one adverb clause.
1. If a man wants to please God, he must obey His Word.
2. Job, fearful that his sons had sinned in their hearts, offered sacrifices for them.
3. Although we may not understand God's purposes, we trust Him because He is God.

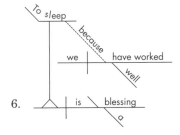

Written Exercises

A. 1. If... God, must obey
2. that... hearts, fearful
3. Although... purposes, trust;
   because... God, trust

2. as soon—to what degree
3. was—in spite of what;
   more gracious—to what degree
4. shone—why; so much—to what degree
5. to break—when
6. pouted—how

B. 1. because he had disobeyed God, could enter
2. Before the Flood began, closed
3. Although we may be tempted to think otherwise, loves;
   as (He loves) us, as much
4. when others do wrong, To compromise
5. than you (are old), older
6. while he is sick, to help

C. 1. Dale, class,   3. correct
   2. us,   4. rain,

D. 1.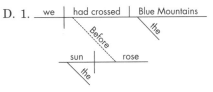

2.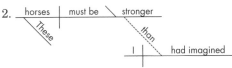

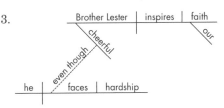

3.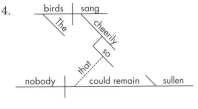

4.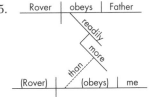

5.

4. Since He is God, He can direct our lives more perfectly than we ever could.
5. As long as we submit to Him, God can bless our lives.
6. To forgive even though a person never asks for forgiveness is a difficult challenge.
7. The rain is falling so heavily that we can hardly see the road.
8. Although heavy rains fell this morning, the skies have cleared earlier than the weatherman had predicted.
9. The nomadic tribes go wherever they can find pasture for their cattle.
10. After we started attending the new school, we learned to play the games as the students there normally played them.

B. Copy each word that should be followed by a comma, and add the missing comma. If no comma is needed, write *correct*.
1. An unselfish person waits until others have had a turn.
2. Because Satan knows the power of the mind he tries hard to corrupt our thoughts.
3. Your conscience when it is properly guided by the Bible is a valuable asset.
4. If you consistently follow the right God can bless your life.
5. The children of God because they live according to the Bible are often scorned by the world.

C. Diagram these sentences.
1. The skies cleared quickly after the cold front had passed.
2. The ground, wet because heavy rain fell yesterday, could not be plowed.
3. I passed the test more easily than I had expected.
4. Aunt Lois's pancakes were as good as I remembered them.
5. Until Grandmother's hip is healed, Cousin Grace is helping her.
6. Our desire is to help wherever we can.
7. The little girl spoke so longingly that we could not deny her request.
8. I cannot draw as neatly as she.

Review Exercises

A. Write which of the six tenses each underlined verb phrase is. Also write whether its form is simple (*S*), progressive (*P*), or emphatic (*E*). [48–50]
1. Sister Eileen <u>did leave</u> early in the morning.
2. <u>Did</u> Brother Leroy <u>speak</u> about the mission work in the Bahamas?
3. The boys <u>have been helping</u> with the dishes.
4. By tomorrow evening we <u>shall have finished</u> the last of the painting.
5. The children <u>had been stacking</u> the wood when Father came home.
6. Our neighbors <u>do</u> not <u>burn</u> wood in their fireplace.
7. I <u>have been studying</u> my Bible memory passage.
8. The Bible <u>does contain</u> many precious passages.

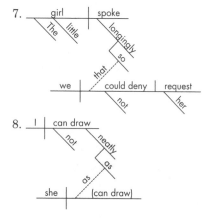

Review Exercises

A. 1. past, E
2. past, S
3. present perfect, P
4. future perfect, S
5. past perfect, P
6. present, S
7. present perfect, P
8. present, E

4. Since ... God, can direct;
than ... could, more perfectly
5. as ... Him, As long
6. even ... forgiveness, To forgive
7. that ... road, so heavily
8. Although ... morning, have cleared;
than ... predicted, earlier
9. wherever ... cattle, go
10. After ... school, learned; as ... them, to pla

B. 1. correct
2. mind,
3. conscience, Bible,
4. right,
5. God, Bible,

C. 1.

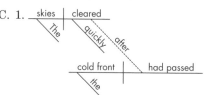

2.

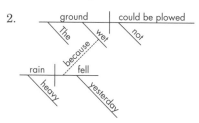

3.

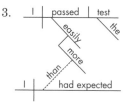

4.

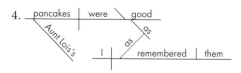

5.

6.

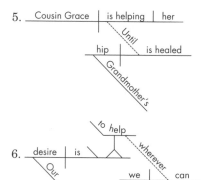

B. Rewrite each sentence according to the directions in parentheses. [66]
1. The Lord asked Job some searching questions. (Change to passive voice, retaining the direct object.)
2. Wise counsel was given David by Abigail. (Change to active voice.)
3. Brother Lynn handed the man a tract. (Change to passive voice, retaining the indirect object.)

C. Copy each object complement, and label it *DO* (direct object) or *IO* (indirect object). Write *ret.* after the label if the object is retained. [66]
1. Mother made a delicious casserole for supper.
2. Mrs. Barlow was given a scrapbook by our congregation.
3. Aunt Wilma brought us some treats.
4. A letter from Guatemala was sent us by Grandfather Yoder's.

B. 1. Job was asked some searching questions by the Lord.
2. Abigail gave David wise counsel.
3. A tract was handed the man by Brother Lynn.

C. 1. casserole—DO
2. scrapbook—DO ret.
3. us—IO; treats—DO
4. us—IO ret.

97. Distinguishing Between Adjectives and Adverbs

Lesson Survey
- Many adjectives and adverbs cannot be distinguished by their forms.
- Two tests are helpful in deciding whether a word is an adjective or an adverb.
  1. What part of speech does it modify?
  2. What question does it answer?
- To distinguish between adjective and adverb phrases and clauses, use the same two tests as well as a third test.
  3. Can the modifier be moved to a different place without changing the meaning of the sentence?

In Chapters 8 and 9 you have studied the two kinds of modifiers: adjectives and adverbs. Most words in these two classes can be distinguished easily because their forms are different. You should have no difficulty with identifying the part of speech of the underlined words in the following columns.

Adjectives:
the colorful leaves
the new books
the nervous lady

Adverbs:
flew swiftly
talked excitedly
arrived yesterday

Lesson 97

Purpose: To study distinguishing between adjectives and adverbs.

Oral Review:
1. What kind of word introduces an adverb clause? (subordinating conjunction)
2. Name several common subordinating conjunctions. (*Sample answers:* after, although, as, as if, as though, because, before, even if, even though, how, if, since, so that, than, that, though, till, unless, until, when, whenever, where, wherever, whether, while)
3. When must an adverb clause be separated from the main clause by commas? (when it comes at the beginning or in the middle of a sentence)
4. What two kinds of phrases can be used as adverbs? (prepositional, infinitive)

5. Tell which class of pronouns is represented by each group.
   a. who, whom, whose, which, what (interrogative)
   b. this, that, these, those (demonstrative)
   c. I, you, he, she, hers (personal)
   d. who, whom, whose, which, that (relative)
   e. somebody, anything, few, most (indefinite)
   f. themselves, myself, herself (compound personal)

Lesson Introduction: Your students have studied both adjectives and adverbs. Now challenge them to identify the underlined phrases in this sentence as adjectives or adverbs. If they can do this, they should have little trouble with the lesson.

Charles sat on the porch[1] beside a box on the porch[2] and talked to his friends on the porch.[3]
(1) adverb telling where Charles sat
(2) adjective telling which box

However, many adjectives and adverbs cannot be distinguished by their forms. Although the *-ly* suffix generally marks an adverb, some adverbs do not end with *-ly,* and some adjectives do.

Adjectives:	**Adverbs:**
in <u>lowly</u> service	has run <u>well</u>
gave a <u>costly</u> gift	to see <u>far</u>
an <u>elderly</u> man	did not fall <u>off</u>

The matter of distinguishing between adjectives and adverbs is further complicated by the fact that many words can be used as either part of speech. Compare the following pairs of sentences. The modifiers are underlined and the modified words are italicized.

Adjectives:	**Adverbs:**
A <u>kindly</u> *policeman* answered our questions.	The policeman <u>kindly</u> *answered* our questions.
That lightning *bolt* was <u>close</u>.	That lightning *struck* <u>close</u>.
We had an <u>early</u> *start* today.	Today we *started* <u>early</u>.

Since many adjectives and adverbs cannot be distinguished by their form, they must be distinguished by some other means. The following two questions are helpful tests in deciding whether a word is an adjective or an adverb.

Test 1: *What part of speech does it modify?*
   An adjective modifies a substantive (noun or pronoun).
   An adverb modifies a verb, an adjective, an adverb, or a verbal.

Test 2: *What question does it answer?*
   An adjective answers the question *which, whose, how many,* or *what kind of.*
   An adverb answers the question *how, when, where, why, how long, how much, to what degree, in spite of what,* or *under what condition.*

Now study the following sentences. Are the underlined modifiers adjectives or adverbs?

   This <u>shaggy</u> donkey has served its master <u>well</u>.
   Test 1: *Shaggy* modifies the noun *donkey.*
   Test 2: *Shaggy* tells *what kind of.*
       Shaggy is an adjective.

   Test 1: *Well* modifies the verb *has served.*
   Test 2: *Well* tells *how.*
       Well is an adverb.

   (3) adjective telling which friends, or adverb telling where Charles talked (either is acceptable)

This sentence illustrates that the same modifier may be either an adjective or an adverb. Distinguishing between these two parts of speech is not always easy.

Lesson Outline:

   1. Many adjectives and adverbs cannot be distinguished by their forms.
      a. The *-ly* suffix generally marks an adverb; however, some adverbs do not end with *-ly,* and some adjectives do.
      b. Many words can be used as either an adjective or an adverb.

   2. Two tests are helpful in deciding whether a word is an adjective or an adverb.

      a. What part of speech does it modify?
      b. What question does it answer?

   3. To distinguish between an adjective and an adverb phrase, use the same two tests as well as a third test: Can the modifier be moved to a different place without changing the meaning of the sentence? (*Note:* Many single-word adverbs also pass this test.)

   4. To distinguish between an adjective and an adverb clause, use the same three tests as those for distinguishing between an adjective and an adverb phrase. In addition, remember that an adjective clause usually begins with a relative pronoun (*who, whom, whose, which, that*) or a relative adverb (*when, where, why*). An adverb clause begins with a subordinating conjunction.

★ **EXTRA PRACTICE**
   Worksheet 37 (*Distinguishing Between Adjectives and Adverbs*)

These <u>past</u> days have seemed <u>lonely</u> because Mother has stayed with
    Grandma <u>quite</u> often.
    Test 1: *Past* modifies the noun *days.*
    Test 2: *Past* tells *which.*
        Past is an adjective.

    Test 1: *Lonely* modifies the noun *days.*
    Test 2: *Lonely* tells *what kind of.*
        Lonely is an adjective.

    Test 1: *Quite* modifies the adverb *often.*
    Test 2: *Quite* tells *to what degree.*
        Quite is an adverb.

Both prepositional phrases and infinitive phrases can be used as adjectives and as adverbs. Nothing in the structure or form of these phrases
indicates which part of speech they are. Indeed, the very same phrase
might be an adjective in one sentence and an adverb in another.

To distinguish between adjective and adverb phrases, use the same two
tests given above. In addition, a third test is often helpful.

    Test 3: *Can the modifier be moved to a different place without chang-*
            ing the meaning of the sentence?
        An adjective phrase usually comes right after the word it modifies.
        An adverb phrase usually can be moved to different places with-
            out changing the meaning of the sentence.

Abraham laid the animal <u>on the altar</u>.
    (*On the altar* modifies the verb *laid* by telling *where.* Also, the
        phrase could be moved to a different position. It is an adverb
        phrase.)
The sacrifice <u>on the altar</u> provided atonement for the faithful saint.
    (*On the altar* modifies the noun *sacrifice* by telling *which.* Also, the
        phrase must come right after *sacrifice.* It is an adjective phrase.)
The best place <u>to learn God's will</u> is the Bible.
    (*To learn God's will* modifies the noun *place* by telling *what kind
        of.* Also, the phrase must come right after *place.* It is an adjec-
        tive phrase.)
We study the Bible <u>to learn God's will</u>.
    (*To learn God's will* modifies the verb *study* by telling *why.* Also,
        the phrase could be moved to a different position. It is an
        adverb phrase.)

An adverb phrase may contain one or more other modifying phrases.
Each phrase must be tested carefully to see whether it is an adjective or

an adverb. If it modifies a noun in a previous phrase, it is an adjective. If it modifies a verbal, it is an adverb.

> The travelers hurried <u>to reach the town in the valley before dark</u>.
>> (*To reach the town in the valley before dark* modifies the verb *hurried* by telling *why*. It is an adverb phrase. *In the valley* modifies the noun *town* by telling *which*. It is an adjective phrase. *Before dark* modifies the verbal *to reach* by telling *when*. It is an adverb phrase.)

You must also distinguish between adjective and adverb clauses. Use the same three tests as those for distinguishing between adjective and adverb phrases. In addition, remember that an adjective clause usually begins with a relative pronoun (*who, whom, whose, which, that*) or a relative adverb (*when, where, why*). An adverb clause begins with a subordinating conjunction. (See the list on page 540.)

> The town, <u>which promised them rest</u>, beckoned them to hurry.
>> (*Which promised them rest* modifies the noun *town* by telling *what kind of*. The clause must come right after the noun it modifies. Also, it begins with the relative pronoun *which*. It is an adjective clause.)

> <u>Because they had traveled many miles</u>, they longed for rest.
>> (*Because they had traveled many miles* modifies the verb *longed* by telling *why*. The clause can be moved to a different location. Also, it begins with the subordinating conjunction *Because*. It is an adverb clause.)

Class Practice

A. Tell whether each underlined word is an *adjective* or an *adverb*.
 1. Leaving His <u>heavenly</u> glory, Jesus came as the <u>lowly</u> Son of Man.
 2. He <u>graciously</u> shed His <u>precious</u> blood.
 3. <u>Now</u> we can draw <u>near</u> to the <u>holy</u> presence of the Lord.
 4. God is <u>always</u> <u>near</u> to those who <u>humbly</u> bow <u>down</u> to Him.
 5. <u>Certainly</u> we should seek the Lord <u>early</u> in the morning.
 6. Our <u>early</u> prayers should include <u>earnest</u> petitions for God's blessing.

B. Tell whether each underlined phrase is an *adjective* or an *adverb*. A phrase that is part of another phrase is underlined twice and should be identified separately.
 1. The queen <u>of Sheba</u> came <u>to Jerusalem</u> <u>to visit King Solomon</u>.
 2. <u>In her own land</u>, she had heard many things <u>about the wealth of his kingdom</u>.
 3. The best way <u>to discover the truth of these reports</u> was to see <u>with her own eyes</u>.

Lesson 97 Answers

Class Practice

A. 1. heavenly—adjective; lowly—adjective
 2. graciously—adverb; precious—adjective
 3. Now—adverb; near—adverb; holy—adjective
 4. always—adverb; near—adverb; humbly—adverb; down—adverb
 5. Certainly—adverb; early—adverb
 6. early—adjective; earnest—adjective

B. 1. of Sheba—adjective; to Jerusalem—adverb; to visit King Solomon—adverb
 2. In her own land—adverb; about the wealth of his kingdom—adjective; of his kingdom—adjective
 3. to discover the truth of these reports—adjective; of these reports—adjective; with her own eyes—adverb

4. Father spoke <u>for a few minutes</u> <u>with the stranger</u> <u>from the city</u>.
5. Because it was nearly time <u>to leave for Grandpa's</u>, the children hurried <u>to do their chores</u>.
6. The oxen, weary <u>with long exertion</u>, could not pull the wagon full <u>of corn</u> <u>up the long hill</u>.

C. Tell whether each underlined clause is an *adjective* or an *adverb*.
1. <u>Because life is a serious responsibility</u>, we should carefully guard the attitudes <u>that we allow to develop in our minds</u>.
2. One reason <u>why this is not always easy</u> is the simple fact <u>that our hearts are deceitful</u>.
3. <u>Although we may want to please the Lord</u>, Satan, <u>who is the enemy of all righteousness</u>, can make wrong look attractive.
4. Therefore, we should diligently study the Bible, <u>where we can learn the truth about right and wrong</u>.
5. We must anchor our souls in the Word so thoroughly <u>that nothing can shake our faith</u>.

D. On the chalkboard, diagram these sentences.
1. The just Lord will judge rightly the motives of all people.
2. Because many do not love the Lord, they seek ways to contradict His Word.
3. The boy who had been sick is feeling well again.
4. Ellen learned the poem for this week quite well.
5. Mother was searching in the attic to find some dress material.
6. A large flock of geese landed on the pond behind the house.

Written Exercises

A. Write whether each underlined word is an adjective (*adj.*) or an adverb (*adv.*).
1. We worship the (*a*) <u>only</u> God, who has created all things (*b*) <u>well</u>.
2. The (*a*) <u>holy</u> angels of God will serve Him (*b*) <u>continually</u> (*c*) <u>forever</u>.
3. With (*a*) <u>fatherly</u> pity, God (*b*) <u>tenderly</u> watches from (*c*) <u>high</u> heaven over His (*d*) <u>earthly</u> creatures.
4. The (*a*) <u>outside</u> walls of the (*b*) <u>little</u> cottage are (*c*) <u>quite</u> (*d*) <u>attractive</u>.
5. The (*a*) <u>elderly</u> man welcomed us (*b*) <u>inside</u> for a (*c*) <u>friendly</u> visit.
6. (*a*) <u>Too</u> (*b*) <u>often</u> we are (*c*) <u>so</u> busy that we fail to listen (*d*) <u>politely</u> to others.
7. We agreed (*a*) <u>most</u> (*b*) <u>readily</u> to Father's suggestion that we visit Brother Lamar's (*c*) <u>tonight</u>.
8. (*a*) <u>Most</u> rivers in the Northern Hemisphere flow (*b*) <u>somewhat</u> (*c*) <u>southward</u>.

Written Exercises

A. 1. a. adj.   b. adv.
   2. a. adj.   b. adv.   c. adv.
   3. a. adj.   b. adv.   c. adj.   d. adj.
   4. a. adj.   b. adj.   c. adv.   d. adj.
   5. a. adj.   b. adv.   c. adj.
   6. a. adv.   b. adv.   c. adv.   d. adv.
   7. a. adv.   b. adv.   c. adv.
   8. a. adj.   b. adv.   c. adv.

4. for a few minutes—adverb;
   with the stranger from the city—adverb;
   from the city—adjective
5. to leave for Grandpa's—adjective;
   for Grandpa's—adverb;
   to do their chores—adverb
6. with long exertion—adverb; of corn—adverb;
   up the long hill—adverb

C. 1. Because life is a serious responsibility—adverb;
   that we allow to develop in our minds—adjective
2. why this is not always easy—adjective;
   that our hearts are deceitful—adjective
3. Although we may want to please the Lord—adverb; who is the enemy of all righteousness—adjective
4. where we can learn the truth about right and wrong—adjective
5. that nothing can shake our faith—adverb

D. 1.
2.
3.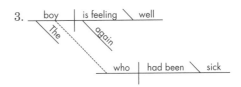
4.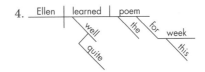
5.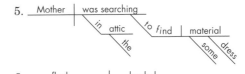
6.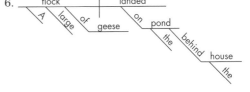

B. Write *adj.* or *adv.* for each underlined phrase. A phrase that is part of another phrase is underlined twice and should be labeled separately.
  1. (*a*) In our daily lives, we are to worship God (*b*) in spirit and truth.
  2. We learn many practical lessons (*a*) about temptation (*b*) from the account (*c*) of Jesus' temptation (*d*) in the wilderness.
  3. Mother has scrubbed hard (*a*) at my shirt (*b*) to remove the stain.
  4. (*a*) In the first period (*b*) of the afternoon, we had a quiz (*c*) to review our recent studies (*d*) about partial vacuums.
  5. We finally found the ball (*a*) under the back porch (*b*) after a fruitless search (*c*) of several minutes.
  6. (*a*) For several months our family has been making plans (*b*) to visit Uncle Mark's (*c*) in Manitoba.
  7. The boys' attempt (*a*) to finish the lawn work failed (*b*) because of a sudden shower.
  8. The horses trotted (*a*) down the road, (*b*) over the bridge, and (*c*) into the center (*d*) of the village.

C. Write *adj.* or *adv.* for each underlined clause.
  1. (*a*) When God speaks, men should listen (*b*) because His voice is authoritative.
  2. The Bible, (*a*) which is God's inspired Word, predicts a time (*b*) when the love of many will wax cold.
  3. (*a*) Although the sun shone all day, the wind was so cold (*b*) that we could not stay outside long.
  4. (*a*) If the weather is fit tomorrow, Father will help Brother Galen, (*b*) whose barn burned yesterday.
  5. The men (*a*) who investigated the fire have not determined the reason (*b*) why it started.
  6. The scenic area (*a*) that Uncle Ben described to us overlooks a place (*b*) where two rivers join into one.
  7. (*a*) Because the traffic is quite heavy, this part of the trip is taking longer (*b*) than Father had expected.
  8. Our neighbor, (*a*) whom we have learned to trust, is doing our chores (*b*) while we take this trip.

D. Diagram these sentences.
  1. The boys, who had been picking beans, looked weary.
  2. They looked wearily toward the end of the garden.
  3. Their eagerness to help Brother Marvin waned slightly when the sun became hot.
  4. Two lively dogs raced out the lane to welcome me.
  5. Early morning is the time when many birds are most active.
  6. We must rise early because we have many chores.

B. 1. a. adv.   b. adv.
   2. a. adj.   b. adv.   c. adj.   d. adj.
   3. a. adv.   b. adv.
   4. a. adv.   b. adj.   c. adv.   d. adj.
   5. a. adv.   b. adv.   c. adj.
   6. a. adv.   b. adj.   c. adv.
   7. a. adj.   b. adv.
   8. a. adv.   b. adv.   c. adv.   d. adj.

C. 1. a. adv.   b. adv.
   2. a. adj.   b. adj.
   3. a. adv.   b. adv.
   4. a. adv.   b. adj.
   5. a. adj.   b. adj.
   6. a. adj.   b. adj.
   7. a. adv.   b. adv.
   8. a. adj.   b. adv.

D. 1. [diagram: boys | looked \ weary; The; who | had been picking | beans]

2. [diagram: They | looked; wearily; toward; end; the; of garden; the]

3. [diagram: eagerness | waned; Their; to help | Brother Marvin; slightly; when; sun | became; the; hot]

4. [diagram: dogs | raced; Two lively; out lane; the; to welcome | me]

5. [diagram: morning | is \ time; Early; the; birds | are \ active; many; most; when]

6. [diagram: We | must rise; early; because; we | have | chores; many]

Review Exercises

A. Copy each pronoun, and write whether it is personal (*P*), compound personal (*CP*), demonstrative (*D*), indefinite (*ID*), interrogative (*IR*), or relative (*R*). [69–77]

1. God, whose Word can never fail, bids us trust in Him.
2. This is a privilege offered to all.
3. Who would not commit himself to this almighty Lord?
4. Everyone who truly trusts the Lord is willing to obey His Word.
5. Do not deceive yourself into believing the lie that one can have faith without obedience.

B. If the underlined part of the sentence contains an error, write it correctly. If it is correct, write *correct*. [70–77]

1. <u>Me and you</u> are supposed to clean the attic today.
2. Mother talked to <u>Janet and herself</u> last evening.
3. Clifford is a month older <u>than me</u>.
4. Brother Dale is going to help <u>us girls</u> in this game.
5. We are not able to finish this job <u>ourself</u>.
6. In "single base," everyone must choose <u>their</u> own base to start the game.
7. <u>Somebody's</u> sweater is lying on the floor.
8. Myron Coble, <u>which</u> bought the truck from Father, lives near Columbia.
9. Mr. Palski, <u>who</u> Father has often invited to church, plans to go with us this morning.
10. The carpenter and painter is planning to bring <u>his</u> equipment today.

Review Exercises

A.
1. whose—R; us—P; Him—P
2. This—D; all—ID
3. Who—IR; himself—CP
4. Everyone—ID; who—R; His—P
5. yourself—CP; that—R; one—ID

B.
1. You and I
2. Janet and her
3. than I
4. correct
5. ourselves
6. his
7. correct
8. who
9. whom
10. correct

---

98. Using Adverbs Correctly

Lesson Survey

- Use an adverb only when it makes a worthwhile contribution.
- Do not use an adverb repetitiously.
- Do not use two negative words to express one negative thought.
- Do not use *kind of* or *sort of* for *rather* or *somewhat*.
- Use *already* and *all ready* correctly.
- Do not use *alright* for *all right*.
- Use *farther* and *further* correctly.
- Do not use an adjective form as an adverb.

Lesson 98

Purpose: To teach some rules for adverb usage.

Oral Review:

1. Tell whether each statement describes an adjective or an adverb.
   a. It answers questions like *why, when,* and *to what degree.* (adverb)
   b. It modifies a noun or pronoun. (adjective)
   c. As a phrase or clause, it usually comes right after the word it modifies. (adjective)
   d. It answers questions like *whose, which,* and *what kind of.* (adjective)
   e. As a clause, it begins with a subordinating conjunction. (adverb)
   f. It modifies a verb, an adjective, an adverb, or a verbal. (adverb)
   g. As a clause, it begins with a relative pronoun or relative adverb. (adjective)

2. When must an adverb clause be separated from the main clause by commas? (when it comes at the beginning or in the middle of a sentence)

3. What two kinds of phrases can be used as adverbs? (prepositional, infinitive)

4. What is the general purpose of single quotation marks? (to set off a quotation or title within a quotation)

5. Are commas and periods placed inside or outside quotation marks? (inside)

6. Are colons and semicolons placed inside or outside quotation marks? (outside)

7. *(a)* When should a question mark or an exclamation point be placed inside quotation marks? *(b)* When should they be placed outside? (*a.* when the quotation is a question or an exclamation; *b.* when the whole sentence is a question or an exclamation, but the quotation is not)

The ability to recognize adverbs is important, but equally important is the ability to use them correctly. The eight rules of adverb usage in this lesson should help you.

1. *Use an adverb only when it makes a worthwhile contribution.* If an expressive verb conveys your idea clearly, do not use a general verb propped with an adverb. Likewise, if a descriptive adjective expresses your idea well, do not use a dull adjective propped with an adverb. Especially avoid overusing adverbs of degree, such as *very, really, surely,* and *extremely.*

> **Weak:** General verb with adverb
> The big rooster <u>walked proudly</u> around the barnyard.
> **Better:** Expressive verb
> The big rooster <u>strutted</u> around the barnyard.
>
> **Weak:** Dull adjective with adverb
> The boat capsized in the <u>very fast</u> current.
> **Better:** Descriptive adjective
> The boat capsized in the <u>swift</u> current.

Of course, this does not mean that you should weed out every adverb that you can. Adverbs do contribute to expressive, descriptive writing. In the examples above, adverbs can be used effectively with the more expressive verb and the more descriptive adjective.

> The big rooster <u>strutted haughtily</u> around the barnyard.
> The boat capsized in the <u>dangerously swift</u> current.

2. *Do not use an adverb repetitiously.* Be especially alert to adverbs like *after, again, back, ever, from, on,* and *up.* These words serve no useful purpose if they express an idea that is already present in the modified word. The underlined adverbs in the following expressions should be omitted.

seek <u>after</u>	leave <u>from</u>	connect <u>up</u>
repeat <u>again</u>	continue <u>on</u>	divide <u>up</u>
refer <u>back</u>	farther <u>on</u>	wash <u>up</u>
rarely <u>ever</u>		

Many people seek (*not* seek after) peace in wrong ways.
We referred (*not* referred back) to an earlier lesson.
Mother divided (*not* divided up) the pie among the children.

3. *Do not use two negative words to express one negative thought.* Here are some common negative words that mean "not" or "almost not."

no	never	nothing	barely
not	nobody	neither	hardly
none	no one	nowhere	scarcely

8. Give the second and third principal parts of these verbs.
   a. bring (brought, [have] brought)
   b. speak (spoke, [have] spoken)
   c. grow (grew, [have] grown)
   d. set (set, [have] set)
   e. drown (drowned, [have] drowned)
   f. drag (dragged, [have] dragged)
   g. go (went, [have] gone)
   h. wear (wore, [have] worn)

Lesson Introduction: When a young apprentice works in a garage, does the master mechanic teach him merely to identify a slip-joint pliers, the open end wrenches, and the electrical testers? Is he satisfied when the apprentice can name every tool in the toolbox? Of course not! What is the value of identifying the tools if the apprentice cannot use them properly?

Likewise, is the end goal of a schoolteacher merely to have his students identify single-word adverbs, adverb phrases, and adverb clauses? Is the teacher satisfied when his students can point out every adverb in a sentence? Of course not! What is the value of identifying adverbs if the student cannot use them correctly in his own sentences?

That is the theme of this lesson—using adverbs correctly.

Lesson Outline:
1. Use an adverb only when it makes a worthwhile contribution.
   a. If an expressive verb conveys your idea clearly, do not use a general verb propped with an adverb.
   b. If a descriptive adjective expresses your idea well, do not use a dull adjective propped with an adverb.

A sentence with a double negative often can be corrected in two ways, by removing either one of the negative words.

Incorrect: He doesn<u>'t</u> have <u>none</u> of his books along.
Correct: He doesn't have any of his books along.
              He has none of his books along.

Sometimes a person uses a double negative to make a positive statement, usually for a certain degree of emphasis. For most purposes, however, a simple positive statement is sufficient.

Father would <u>not</u> tell us to stay away from the pond for <u>no</u> reason at all.
      (Father has a good reason for telling us to stay away.)

4. *Do not use* kind of *or* sort of *for* rather *or* somewhat.

Incorrect:	**Correct:**
This road is <u>sort of</u> rough.	This road is <u>somewhat</u> rough.
The grass is <u>kind of</u> long.	The grass is <u>rather</u> long.

5. *Use* already *and* all ready *correctly. Already is an adverb that means* "by a certain time." *All ready is a phrase that means "completely prepared." It is also an expression indicating that everyone in a group is prepared.*

Incorrect: Uncle Paul's were <u>all ready</u> at Grandpa's when we arrived.
Correct: Uncle Paul's were <u>already</u> at Grandpa's when we arrived.
              I was <u>all ready</u> to go, but the others were not <u>all ready</u>.

6. *Do not use* alright *for* all right. *Words like* already, although, *and* altogether *are proper, but* alright *is never correct. Remember: You do not write* alwrong, *so you should not write* alright *either.*

This engine is old, but it runs <u>all right</u> (not *alright*).

7. *Use* farther *and* further *correctly. Farther means "a greater distance"; further means "in addition" or "to a greater degree." You can remember which word is which if you consider that farther contains the word far, which is used to describe distances. Although these two words are often used interchangeably, they should be distinguished in formal usage.*

Brother Lyle lives <u>farther</u> away from church than any of the others.
Father promised to consider the matter <u>further</u>.

8. *Do not use an adjective form as an adverb.*
   a. Avoid using the adjectives *real* and *sure* for the adverbs *really* and *surely.*

Incorrect: Dean did a <u>real</u> good job.
              Ada <u>sure</u> bakes good bread.

c. Especially avoid overusing adverbs of degree, such as *very, really, surely,* and *extremely.*

d. This does not mean that you should weed out every adverb, for adverbs do contribute to expressive, descriptive writing.

2. *Do not use an adverb repetitiously.* Be especially alert to adverbs like *after, again, back, ever, from, on,* and *up,* which serve no useful purpose if they express an idea that is already present in the modified word.

(*Teacher:* The "unnecessary" adverbs listed in the lesson are acceptable when they are part of idioms with meanings of their own. For example, *wash up* is proper when it is used without an object, to indicate washing one's hands, as in this sentence: *The men came inside and washed up for lunch.*)

3. *Do not use two negative words to express one negative thought.*

a. A sentence with a double negative often can be corrected in two ways, by removing either one of the negative words.

b. Sometimes a person uses a double negative to make a positive statement, usually for a certain degree of emphasis.

4. *Do not use* kind of *or* sort of *for* rather *or* somewhat.

5. *Use* already *and* all ready *correctly.*

6. *Do not use* alright *for* all right.

7. *Use* farther *and* further *correctly.*

8. *Do not use an adjective form as an adverb.*
   (a) Avoid using the adjectives *real* and *sure* for the adverbs *really* and *surely.*

Correct: Dean did a <u>really</u> good job.
Ada <u>surely</u> bakes good bread.

b. Avoid using the adjective *some* for the adverb *somewhat*.

Incorrect: I said my poem <u>some</u> better today.
Correct: I said my poem <u>somewhat</u> better today.

c. Avoid using the adjectives *good* and *bad* for the adverbs *well* and *badly*.

Incorrect: Today the boys worked <u>good</u>.
With his sore knee, Aaron is limping quite <u>bad</u>.
Correct: Today the boys worked <u>well</u>.
With his sore knee, Aaron is limping quite <u>badly</u>.

Class Practice

A. Read these sentences, replacing the underlined words with more expressive verbs or adjectives.
1. The north wind <u>blew noisily</u> around the corners.
2. The boys <u>talked loudly</u> to be heard above the wind.
3. As Father stacked the hay, his shirt became <u>very wet</u> with sweat.
4. The frightened fox <u>ran very fast</u> across the meadow.
5. Mother served a <u>really good</u> casserole for dinner.

B. Read these sentences correctly.
1. The battle between King Asa and the Ethiopians seemed kind of lopsided.
2. Jephthah didn't hardly expect his daughter to come out the door first.
3. God blesses those who seek after His kingdom.
4. David sure composed some beautiful psalms.
5. Apparently David, "the sweet psalmist of Israel," could sing good.
6. King Solomon did not continue on faithfully serving the Lord.
7. We often refer back to the Bible stories for our inspiration.
8. The sun has all ready been shining for an hour.
9. Because Mother was sick, we didn't go nowhere last evening.
10. We are glad that she is feeling some better this morning.
11. Did you make it through the storm alright?
12. In tomorrow's history class, we shall study farther about the Mennonites in Russia.
13. We should finish up this chapter next week.
14. We were sort of tired after the hard day of work.
15. This old mower runs rather bad now.

Written Exercises

A. Write a more expressive verb or adjective to replace the underlined words in each sentence.

Lesson 98 Answers

Class Practice

A. (Sample answers.)
1. howled, shrieked, wailed, screamed
2. shouted, yelled, hollered
3. drenched, soaked, saturated
4. dashed, streaked, bolted, raced, darted, spe
5. delicious, tasty, appetizing

B. (Corrections are marked.)
1. The battle between King Asa and th Ethiopians seemed <u>rather</u> (somewhat) lo sided.
2. Jephthah didn't ~~hardly~~ expect (Jephtha ~~didn't~~ hardly <u>expected</u>) his daughter to com out the door first.
3. God blesses those who seek ~~after~~ His king dom.
4. David <u>surely</u> composed some beautif psalms.
5. Apparently David, "the sweet psalmist Israel," could sing <u>well</u>.
6. King Solomon did not continue ~~on~~ faithfull serving the Lord.
7. We often refer ~~back~~ to the Bible stories fo our inspiration.
8. The sun has <u>already</u> been shining for an hou
9. Because Mother was sick, we didn't go <u>any</u> where (we ~~didn't~~ <u>went</u> nowhere) last evenin
10. We are glad that she is feeling <u>somewhat</u> be ter this morning.
11. Did you make it through the storm <u>all right</u>
12. In tomorrow's history class, we shall stud <u>further</u> about the Mennonites in Russia.
13. We should finish ~~up~~ this chapter next wee
14. We were <u>somewhat</u> (rather) tired after th hard day of work.
15. This old mower runs rather <u>badly</u> now.

(b) Avoid using the adjective *some* for the adverb *somewhat*.

(c) Avoid using the adjectives *good* and *bad* for the adverbs *well* and *badly*.

★ **EXTRA PRACTICE**
Worksheet 38 *(Using Adverbs Correctly)*

1. The sheep slowly <u>walked behind</u> the shepherd.
2. The soldiers <u>hit hard</u> on the door of the Anabaptist's house.
3. Kendra <u>walked quietly</u> to the couch and covered the sleeping child.
4. The <u>very high-pitched</u> noises hurt the dog's ears.
5. Our neighbor's children often seem to be <u>really unhappy</u>.
6. The refugees were <u>extremely hungry</u>.

B. If an unnecessary adverb is used, write the words before and after it, omitting the unnecessary adverb. If a wrong word is used, write the correct word.
  1. When the cloud of God's glory rose from the tabernacle, Israel knew it was time to leave from the wilderness of Sinai.
  2. At the first battle with Ai, the Israelites failed quite bad.
  3. After Achan's sin had been punished, victory was real simple.
  4. In spite of the people's frequent murmurings, Moses rarely ever grew impatient with them.
  5. God sure blessed the people beyond what they deserved.
  6. Like Balaam, many want to continue on in their own way and still have God's blessing.
  7. Balaam's death illustrates that such a course won't never work.
  8. Whenever you meet severe tests, remember that God has all ready tempered them for you.
  9. A noble person seeks after peaceable relationships with others.
  10. Everyone was real eager for Father's report.
  11. We are glad that things worked out alright for him.
  12. This irrigation pump worked bad last summer, but Brian has fixed it.
  13. Gerald couldn't barely endure the pain of his severe burns.
  14. We left from the airport at Prince George, British Columbia, around 8:00 A.M.
  15. Grandfather's old car still runs good.
  16. None of our neighbors knew nothing about the strange noises.
  17. Conrad can throw the ball a little further than Henry can.
  18. After I give the directions once, I shall not repeat them again for you.
  19. Yes, I do feel some excited about our planned trip.
  20. We hope our plans work out good.

Review Exercises

A. If the underlined part of the sentence has an error in the use of quotation marks, write it correctly. If it is correct, write *correct*. [26]
  1. "Jesus said, 'The things which are impossible with men are possible with <u>God,"</u> quoted Brother Leonard.
  2. Jesus asked His disciples, "Whom say ye that I <u>am"?</u>
  3. Jesus has promised, "Lo, I am with you <u>always;"</u> consequently, we can trust Him in every experience of life.

Written Exercises

A. (Sample answers.)
  1. followed, trailed
  2. pounded, thumped, hammered, beat
  3. tiptoed
  4. shrill, piercing
  5. miserable, sullen, forlorn, morose, gloomy, irritable
  6. famished, ravenous, starved

B. 1. leave the
  2. badly
  3. really
  4. rarely grew
  5. surely
  6. continue in
  7. will *or* ever *or* won't work
  8. already
  9. seeks peaceable
  10. really
  11. all right
  12. badly
  13. could
  14. left the
  15. well
  16. anything *or* Our *or* knew about
  17. farther
  18. them for
  19. somewhat
  20. well

Review Exercises

A. 1. God,'"
  2. am?"
  3. alway";

4. "How surprised Father was when little Helen lisped, 'I three!'" said Lisa.
5. Today we read the story "The Observing <u>Judge</u>".
6. "I especially enjoyed the story 'Which of the <u>Nine?</u>'" Lamar commented.

B. Write the correct form of each underlined verb that is incorrect. If the verb is correct, write *correct*. [46]
   1. The kitten <u>creeped</u> slowly toward the bird.
   2. Have Grandfather's <u>came</u> yet?
   3. Father <u>tagged</u> the trees he wanted to cut from the wood lot.
   4. The children <u>swang</u> on the tire swing for a while.
   5. Father has <u>went</u> to the barn already.
   6. You have not <u>shook</u> that can enough yet.
   7. I <u>wrung</u> the dishcloth as hard as I could.
   8. The puppies have <u>growed</u> enough to be sold now.
   9. These old horses have <u>borne</u> many heavy loads.
   10. Everyone <u>done</u> a good job, and the work was soon finished.

4. three'!"
5. Judge."
6. correct

B. 1. crept   6. shaken
   2. come   7. correct
   3. correct   8. grown
   4. swung   9. correct
   5. gone   10. did

---

99. Understanding Persuasive Argument

> **Lesson Survey**
> - A **persuasive argument** is an attempt to persuade or move to action.
> - A **fact** is a piece of information that can be known definitely; an **opinion** is a conclusion or a belief about something.
> - The **proposition** of an argument is usually an opinion that is not supported by everyone or a fact that is not universally accepted.
> - The points used to support a proposition must be facts.
> - Use proper caution when you read persuasive argument.

There are four basic types of composition: exposition, argument, narration, and description. In Chapters 4 and 5 you wrote expository compositions. In Chapter 6 you wrote a narrative composition (a story). In Chapter 10 you will write a descriptive composition. And here in Chapter 9 you will write a persuasive argument.

A *persuasive argument* is an attempt to persuade the reader of a certain point or to move him to a particular action. At or near the beginning of an argument, the writer usually states the idea that he is promoting. This statement is known as his *proposition*. An argument often includes

Lesson 99

Purpose: (1) To introduce *persuasive argument. (2) To teach its proper use.

Oral Review:

1. What are some advantages of taking notes from a sermon? (Taking notes helps to keep you from daydreaming or falling asleep, helps you to grasp the main points of the sermon better, and helps you to remember the sermon better. The notes can be kept for future reference and can benefit others who could not hear the sermon.)

2. What are some important listening skills for good note-taking? (the ability to focus your whole attention on the speaker; the ability to overcome distractions; the ability to listen with interest; the ability to listen for main ideas)

3. Why is an outline form usually the most effective

in note-taking? (An outline shows the relationships among main points and subpoints.)

4. Name the kind of meter that fits each description.
   a. one accented syllable followed by two unaccented syllables (dactylic)
   b. one accented syllable followed by one unaccented syllable (trochaic)
   c. one unaccented syllable followed by one accented syllable (iambic)
   d. two unaccented syllables followed by one accented syllable (anapestic)

5. Name the term for each of these descriptions.
   a. The repetition of similar vowel sounds in accented syllables (assonance)
   b. The repetition of beginning consonant sounds (alliteration)

6. Name the figure of speech that fits each description.

he elements of exposition: definitions, clarifications, and explanations. It
may well include description and even some narration. But the ultimate
goal of an argument is to have the reader say, "I agree" or "I need to take
some action."

Fact or Opinion?

In order to understand persuasive argument correctly, you must be able
to discern between facts and opinions. A *fact* is a piece of information that
can be known definitely. A statement is a fact if it expresses something
that has actually happened.

> Menno Simons joined the Anabaptists in 1536.

A statement is also a fact if it expresses a scientific, mathematical, or
statistical reality.

> Water expands when it freezes.
> A square has four angles of 90° each.
> In the United States, more people die in a year from bee stings than
>   from snakebites.

Of course, a statement is also a fact if it expresses a truth revealed by
God in His Word.

> God created the world in six days.
> Jesus died, rose again, and ascended to heaven.

No one can personally verify every fact that he hears or reads. But if
reliable sources give information that does not conflict with the Bible, we
can have reasonable confidence that the information is true. Since God
alone knows everything, His Word is the only source of information that
is absolutely reliable.

In contrast to a fact, an *opinion* is a conclusion or a belief about something. We form opinions as we evaluate facts in light of our own knowledge or experience. People have varied exposure to knowledge; they have
varying experiences; their lives are touched by varying influences. Therefore,
people's opinions vary.

Consider the following pairs of statements. In each one, which is a fact
and which is an opinion?

> Johann Gutenberg invented the movable-type printing press.
> The invention of the printing press was one of the most important
>   events of the fifteenth century.
>   (The first statement is a fact: it can be verified from reliable
>   sources. The second is an opinion: it is a conclusion based
>   upon historical facts.)

a. Gives a thing or quality the characteristics of
   a living creature. (personification)
b. Sometimes contains a form of *be,* saying that
   one thing is another thing. (metaphor)
c. Makes a figurative comparison by using *like*
   or *as.* (simile)

Lesson Introduction: Quite likely you never
thought that your English book would teach you how
to argue. Indeed, your parents and teachers have
been helping you to avoid arguments—for years! But
here it is, a lesson on "understanding persuasive argument."

Of course you know that *argument,* as used in
this lesson, is completely different from the arguments that are forbidden by your parents. Get a dictionary now and find the definition for *argument* that
fits what we shall study in this lesson. ("A reason
given as proof" or "a logical set of reasons.")

Lesson Outline:

*1. A persuasive argument is an attempt to
persuade or move to action.*

*2. A fact is a piece of information that can
be known definitely.*

   a. A statement is a fact if it expresses some-
      thing that has actually happened.
   b. A statement is a fact if it expresses a sci-
      entific, mathematical, or statistical reality.
   c. A statement is a fact if it expresses a truth
      revealed by God in His Word.

*3. An opinion is a conclusion or a belief
about something.*

   a. People form opinions as they evaluate
      facts in light of their own knowledge or
      experience.
   b. People's opinions vary.

The United States has a higher population than Canada.

The United States is a better place to live than Canada.

> (The first statement is a fact: it can be verified by comparing the census figures for each country. The second is an opinion: it is a conclusion based on a person's own knowledge or experience in relation to the two countries.)

The Proposition: Opinion

The *proposition* of an argument is usually an opinion that is not supported by everyone. It may also be a fact that is not universally accepted. This indicates that an argument generally deals with a controversial issue. But it must do more than merely describe the two sides of a controversy. A persuasive argument must have a proposition that states a realistic, worthwhile, and truly defensible stand in relation to the issue.

Consider the following statements. Which ones would make good propositions for persuasive arguments?

Bible memory is important in a Christian school.
> (Poor. No one acquainted with Christian schools would seriously question the validity of this opinion.)

Our school should require more Bible memory work of the students.
> (Good. No doubt some students would disagree with this opinion.)

Ford tractors are better than John Deere tractors.
> (Poor. This opinion will not make a worthwhile argument, nor is it truly defensible.)

God created the world in six twenty-four-hour days.
> (Good. This fact is not universally accepted.)

Boys should learn some basic housekeeping skills.
> (Good. No doubt some boys would disagree with this opinion.)

The cornerstone of an effective persuasive argument is a worthwhile proposition. When you have clearly defined your proposition, you are ready to look for material to develop your persuasive argument.

The Development: Facts

In order to be truly persuasive, an argument must support the proposition with convincing evidence in the form of concrete facts. Opinions are not enough, for the opinion of one person is often as valid as that of another. In fact, if the argument gives opinions that are shallow or illogical, it may persuade the reader to *disagree* with the writer!

Read the following argument, paying attention to the evidence in it.

4. The proposition of an argument is usually an opinion that is not supported by everyone or a fact that is not universally accepted. It must state a realistic, worthwhile, and truly defensible stand in relation to an issue.

5. The points used to support a proposition must be facts.

6. Use proper caution when you read persuasive argument.

>   a. Beware of propositions that are supported by misrepresented facts or faulty reasoning.
>
>   b. Remember that the validity of a proposition is not established by strong statements.
>
>   c. Avoid arguments that deal with unprofitable subjects.

Housework for Boys

In a family blessed with both boys and girls, a boy's chores are naturally not the same as a girl's. A boy is likely to do the heavier outside work, such as splitting wood, tilling the garden, and operating farm machinery. He may think all the cooking, cleaning, and laundering should be done by his mother and his sisters. However, a boy should also learn some basic housekeeping skills.

Of course, a boy expects to become a breadwinner, not a housekeeper. And boys who have plenty of outside chores may declare that they have no time for inside work. Nevertheless, by learning some housekeeping skills, a boy can show appreciation to his mother by occasionally volunteering to do some of her work. For example, mothers often remark that a woman's work is never done. Can you imagine how much it lifts a tired mother's spirits when her son offers to do the dishes or sweep the kitchen floor? *Showing* appreciation to Mother is worth much more than merely *saying,* "Thank you."

Furthermore, a boy who has learned some housekeeping skills is less likely to make extra work for Mother by his carelessness. If he has applied his muscles to scrubbing the kitchen floor, he will likely remember to wipe his shoes well before entering the house. If he has learned how much is involved in sorting dirty laundry, he will probably throw fewer inside-out shirts, trousers, and socks into the clothes hamper. Walking in another person's shoes is an excellent way to develop a sincere concern for that person.

Learning basic housekeeping skills also enables a boy to take responsibility if the housekeeping falls to his lot for a few days. His mother may become too ill to do her work. Someday he may even need to stay at home alone for several days. Then who will prepare the meals, wash the dishes, and launder the clothes? And what will the house look like when Mother is ready to take up her work again? These questions are not hard to answer if the boy has learned to do some of the basic work around the house.

A boy who does occasional housework knows an excellent way to show appreciation to his mother. His increased carefulness helps to lighten his mother's workload. And his ability to do some basic housekeeping means that he can take care of himself for a few days if that ever becomes necessary. Therefore, learning to do household chores does have value even for a busy farm boy.

Do you recognize the proposition? It is the last sentence in the first paragraph. The first paragraph is introductory, making some general statements on the subject and leading up to the proposition. Each of the next three paragraphs then develops one reason in support of the writer's opinion. The last paragraph concludes the argument by summarizing the three supporting facts and then restating the proposition.

Use With Caution

A reader needs to realize that argument can be used for wrong purposes. Therefore, you must use proper caution when you read persuasive argument. Beware of propositions that are supported by misrepresented facts or faulty reasoning. A skilled writer can present his argument so convincingly that his opinions seem like undeniable facts.

One good example is the letter that Sennacherib sent to King Hezekiah (2 Kings 19:10–13). His proposition was that Judah should surrender, and his main supporting statement was that no god had been able to deliver any other nation from the Assyrians. That statement was a fact, but it was a misrepresentation because the true God had often delivered Israel in the past. Moreover, Sennacherib's reasoning was not valid, for victory in the past did not guarantee victory in the future. Hezekiah recognized the error in the argument, and by faith in God he was not deceived.

Remember also that the validity of a proposition is not established by strong statements. A speaker who argues for a faulty proposition sometimes tries to make his points more emphatic by raising his voice. But the best argument does not necessarily come from the person with the loudest voice. Neither does it come from the writer who uses the most exclamation points and the strongest words (like *drastic, shocking,* and *foolhardy*). The merits of any argument finally depend, not on the intensity of the language, but on the quality of the supporting evidence.

Another important caution is to avoid arguments that deal with unprofitable subjects. "But foolish and unlearned questions avoid, knowing that they do gender strifes" (2 Timothy 2:23). Arguments about which teacher or minister you like best are often worse than worthless, for they promote ill will and improper attitudes. The only argument that is worthwhile is one that deals with a proposition truly worth defending.

Class Practice

A. Tell whether each statement expresses a *fact* or an *opinion.*
1. Spring is the most enjoyable season of the year.
2. Restitution is an important part of true repentance.
3. Gerbils make better pets than hamsters do.
4. Water is an especially valuable natural resource.
5. The geography of a land influences the lives of those who live there.

B. Tell whether each statement could be the proposition of a worthwhile argument.

Lesson 99 Answers

Class Practice

A. 1. opinion
2. fact
3. opinion
4. fact
5. fact

1. Every eighth grader should be required to read portions of *Martyrs Mirror*.
2. Sunday company meals should not be elaborate affairs.
3. Upstate New York is the best place to live.
4. The students in this school should be less wasteful.
5. Reading is an important skill for first graders to learn.

Written Exercises

A. Write whether each statement expresses a *fact* or an *opinion*.
   1. Aluminum is a versatile metal.
   2. Science is the most interesting subject in school.
   3. Raising hogs is more enjoyable than dairy farming.
   4. Jesus Christ is the divine Son of God.
   5. The New Testament clearly teaches the doctrine of nonresistance.
   6. A balanced diet is essential to good health.

B. Write *yes* or *no* to tell whether each statement could be the proposition of a worthwhile argument.
   1. Peer pressure can be a dangerous trap for young people.
   2. A good water supply is essential to successful gardening.
   3. Perseverance is more important than outstanding talents for success in life.
   4. Nature abounds with evidence of an all-wise Creator.
   5. Dogs make better pets than cats do.
   6. Keeping things organized is a time-saver.

Review Exercises

A. Name the kind of meter used in each of the following stanzas.
   1. Lonely I no longer roam
         Like the cloud, the wind, the wave;
      Where you dwell shall be my home,
         Where you die shall be my grave.
   2. "There shall be showers of blessing":
         This is the promise of love;
      There shall be seasons refreshing,
         Sent from the Saviour above.
   3. I am nearing the port, I will soon be at home,
         And the voyage of life will be o'er;
      And beneath the high arches of heaven's bright dome,
         I shall dwell with my friends gone before.
   4. The wild winds hushed; the angry deep
      Sank, like a little child, to sleep;
      The sullen billows ceased to leap,
         At Thy will.

B. 1. yes
   2. yes
   3. no (not truly defensible)
   4. yes
   5. no (no disagreement)

Written Exercises

A. 1. fact
   2. opinion
   3. opinion
   4. fact
   5. fact
   6. fact

B. 1. yes
   2. no (no disagreement)
   3. yes
   4. yes
   5. no (not worthwhile or truly defensible)
   6. yes

Review Exercises

A. 1. trochaic
   2. dactylic
   3. anapestic
   4. iambic

B. Do the following exercises with the stanzas above.
1. Write a simile from number 1 and from number 4.
2. What metaphor is used to describe life in number 3?
3. In what three ways is the sea personified in number 4?
4. Write one example of alliteration from each stanza.
5. Write an example of assonance from number 1.

C. Copy these sentences, and indicate the part of speech that each word is by writing the correct abbreviation above it. Label an infinitive as a single item.

noun (n.)	adjective (adj.)	conjunction (conj.)
pronoun (pron.)	adverb (adv.)	interjection (interj.)
verb (v.)	preposition (prep.)	

1. We have several boxes to fill with food and clothing.
2. Is that one large enough to hold this jar?
3. Well, putting that into it makes a bulging box.
4. The people to whom these things are given will surely appreciate receiving them.

---

100. Planning a Persuasive Argument

Lesson Survey
- To plan a persuasive argument, use the following steps.
  1. State your proposition in one sentence.
  2. Make a list of points that support your proposition.
  3. Arrange the points in logical order.
  4. Write out a plan for your argument.

In many ways, planning a persuasive argument is like planning other kinds of compositions. You must have a specific theme to develop, you must gather information, and you must organize your material. The following paragraphs describe four specific steps for planning a persuasive argument.

1. *State your proposition in one sentence.* Be sure that you indeed have a proposition—a worthwhile opinion that you can support. This proposition is the theme of your argument.

Examples: Farming is a good occupation for a Christian.
Every girl should learn to sew.

Lesson 100

Purpose: To teach *how to plan a persuasive argument.

Oral Review:
1. What is a persuasive argument? (an attempt to persuade or move to action)
2. What is the statement of the idea that the writer is promoting in an argument? (the proposition)
3. What is a fact? (something that has actually happened; something that expresses a scientific, mathematical, or statistical reality; or something that expresses a truth revealed by God in His Word)
4. What is an opinion? (a conclusion or belief about something, formed as a person evaluates facts in light of his own knowledge or experience)

B. 1. *(1)* Like the cloud, the wind, the wave;
   (4) like a little child
2. a sea voyage
3. It is called angry; it sinks to sleep; it is called sullen.
4. (Any one example for each stanza.)
   (1) Lonely, longer, Like; wind, wave
   (2) shall, showers; seasons, Sent, Saviour
   (3) high, heaven's
   (4) wild, winds; like, little; Sank, sleep, sullen ceased
5. Lonely, roam

C. 1. We have several boxes to fill with food and clothing.
(pron. v. adj. n. adj. prep. n. conj. n.)
2. Is that one large enough to hold this jar?
(v. adj. pron. adj. adv. adv. adj. n.)
3. Well, putting that into it makes a bulging box.
(interj. n. pron. prep. pron. v. adj. adj. n.)
4. The people to whom these things are given will surely appreciate receiving them.
(adj. n. prep. pron. adj. n. v. v. v. adv. v. n. pron.)

5. What are some important cautions to remember about persuasive arguments? (Beware of propositions that are supported by misrepresented facts or faulty reasoning. Remember that the validity of a proposition is not established by strong statements. Avoid arguments that deal with unprofitable subjects.)

Lesson Introduction: The kinds of arguments that your parents and teachers have taught against usually start and proceed with little or no forethought. A careless word, a thoughtless deed, or a misunderstanding causes an unholy reaction. If more than one person does not control his thoughts and his tongue, an argument starts.

An argument of the kind just described is seldom well-organized or logical. It almost never deserves to be called persuasive argument. In contrast, the

2. *Make a list of points that support your proposition.* Carefully consider why you hold the opinion you have, and list the reasons as they come to your mind. Do not try to put them in any particular order; the most important thing is to get your points on paper. Neither should you try to list all the possible reasons at one time. Lay your list aside for a while, and add points later as you think of them.

The following reasons could be listed for the proposition "Every girl should learn to sew."

1. can make her own clothes
2. can make plain, modest clothes
3. sewing is enjoyable
4. can help needy families
5. hand-sewn articles make useful gifts
6. can sew for others in the family
7. can choose her own fabrics and patterns
8. can make clothes that fit as they should
9. can help with the mending

After you have made your list, consider each point carefully. Have you listed solid facts that can be proven? Remember that facts are convincing to a thoughtful reader. Facts speak for themselves, but opinions do not. Which point in the list above is an opinion? Did you choose the one about sewing being enjoyable? You will probably agree that if a girl is not interested in sewing, the opinion that sewing is enjoyable will not help to convince her that she should learn to sew.

As you consider your list, also try to think of objections that the reader might raise. This will help you to evaluate your proposition more fairly and to think of ways to deal with those objections. Your argument will be stronger if you show that you have considered other opinions and still hold to the proposition you are defending. Here are several objections that a reader might raise to the proposition that every girl should learn to sew.

> takes patience to learn
> sewing machines are expensive
> more economical to buy clothes from a manufacturer

If you deal fairly with objections like these, your argument will be much more persuasive than if you present only the points in favor of your proposition.

3. *Arrange the points in logical order.* Do this by first looking for related points that you can group together. In the list above, the points can be put into three main groups. Numbers 1, 6, 8, and 9 tell how sewing can benefit a girl and her immediate family. Numbers 4 and 5 tell how sewing can

arguments that we are studying in this chapter require much careful planning; this helps to give them the persuasive power they need.

Lesson Outline:

1. To plan a persuasive argument, first state your proposition in one sentence. Be sure that you indeed have a proposition—a worthwhile opinion that you can support.

2. Make a list of points that support your proposition.
   a. Be sure to use solid facts that can be proven.
   b. Also think of objections that the reader might raise. Your argument will be stronger if you show that you have considered other opinions and still hold to the proposition you are defending.

3. Arrange the points in logical order.
   a. Group related points.
   b. List your reasons in the order of importance, saving the strongest and most important point for last.

4. Write out a plan for your argument.
   a. Write the proposition.
   b. List the objections that you will mention near the beginning of your argument.
   c. List the points that make up the supporting framework of your argument.

benefit people outside the family. And numbers 2 and 7 tell how sewing makes it simpler to have suitable clothes.

After putting your reasons in groups, arrange them in the order of importance. The strongest and most important point should come last; it should firmly clinch your argument.

4. *Write out a plan for your argument.* Your plan should consist of three parts. First comes the proposition. Spelling it out at the head of your plan will help you to keep every sentence focused on that proposition. Second should be a list of the objections that you will mention. They should usually be discussed near the beginning of your argument to show the reader from the start that you are trying to deal fairly with the issue. Third on your plan should be the points that make up the supporting framework of your argument. Study the following plan, which follows the pattern described.

The Privilege of Sewing

Proposition: Every girl should learn to sew.

Objections:
1. Takes patience
2. Is expensive to buy sewing machines
3. May be more economical to buy manufactured clothing

Supporting points:
1. Can make a profitable contribution to her family
   a. By sewing for herself
   b. By sewing for her sisters and brothers
   c. By making clothing that fits better than factory-made clothing
   d. By doing the mending
2. Can make useful items for others
   a. Gifts for her friends
   b. Clothes for baby nieces and nephews
   c. Clothes for needy families
3. Can make modest, plain clothes

If you develop a plan like this one, you will have a solid foundation on which to build. Your plan will help you to write a clear, well-ordered, and truly persuasive argument.

Written Exercises

A. Choose one of these propositions to defend, or choose one of your own that your teacher approves.
1. Brushing your teeth regularly is an important health practice.
2. It is better to finish your lunch with an apple than with a cookie.
3. You must be friendly if you want to win friends.

Lesson 100 Answers

Written Exercises

(All answers are individual work.)

4. Every student should develop neat handwriting.
5. History (geography, science) is an important school subject.
6. Every driver should be careful to obey speed limits (stop signs).
7. Getting to church on time is an important habit.
8. Visiting elderly people is well worth the effort it takes.
9. A dog (cat, rabbit) is a worthwhile pet to have.
10. Attending a Christian school is a valuable help in preparing for a useful life.

B. Write the plan for your persuasive argument.

---

101. Writing a Persuasive Argument

> **Lesson Survey**
> - To write a persuasive argument, use the following steps.
>   1. Write an introduction that leads to the proposition.
>   2. Write the body by developing each supporting point convincingly.
>   3. Write a conclusion that points back to the proposition.
>   4. Write an appealing title.
>   5. Revise and rewrite your persuasive argument.

Like any other composition, a persuasive argument should have three distinct parts: an introduction, a body, and a conclusion. This lesson describes how to write each of these three parts as they relate specifically to persuasive arguments.

Here is the argument developed from the plan shown in Lesson 100. You will be referring to it throughout this lesson.

The Privilege of Sewing

Sewing has long been one of the most time-consuming duties in a woman's life. Before the 1800s, every stitch in every garment had to be sewed by hand. Today sewing machines have changed things so much that a large amount of sewing can be done in a short time. In fact, sewing is a skill that every girl should learn.

True, learning to sew requires much patience. Sewing machines can be quite expensive, and buying manufactured clothes is sometimes more economical than making them at home. However, the girl who learns to sew can make a profitable contribution to her family. She will be able to sew dresses for herself as well as her younger sisters. She

---

Lesson 101

Purpose: To teach *how to write a persuasive argument.

Oral Review:

1. What is a persuasive argument? (an attempt to persuade or move to action)
2. What is the proposition of an argument? (the statement of the idea that the writer is promoting)
3. What is a fact? (something that has actually happened; something that expresses a scientific, mathematical, or statistical reality; or something that expresses a truth revealed by God in His Word)
4. What is an opinion? (a conclusion or belief about something, formed as a person evaluates facts in light of his own knowledge or experience)
5. What are some important cautions to remember about persuasive argument? (Beware of propositions that are supported by misrepresented facts or faulty reasoning. Remember that the validity of a proposition is not established by strong statements. Avoid arguments that deal with unprofitable subjects.)
6. What are the four steps in planning a persuasive argument? (State your proposition in one sentence. Make a list of points that support your proposition. Arrange the points in logical order. Write out a plan for your argument.)

Lesson Introduction: Persuasive argument is a specialized type of composition that we do not use as often as many other types. However, it does fill an important place. Doctrinal articles may include argument when they present an appeal to accept the simple teachings of the Bible and put them to practice. Tracts often include argument. Many are written to get readers to heed the message of salvation

can also make shirts and trousers for her brothers. As her skill increases, she will be able to sew clothes that fit better than factory-made clothes do. And a girl who can mend clothes is certainly a valuable asset to any busy mother.

Furthermore, a girl who has learned to sew can make many useful things for other people. She could make a homemade apron as a gift for a friend. She may especially enjoy making baby clothes for a little niece or nephew. Quite likely, she can think of some needy families who would appreciate good, serviceable clothing. A seamstress will have many joys as she uses her skill to serve other people.

Most important of all, the home seamstress can make modest, plain clothes. She can choose her own materials, picking suitable fabrics and patterns. Indeed, there is almost no other choice for a girl who wants to wear suitable dresses; for in many communities, acceptable ready-made dresses are not available. As long as a girl does not know how to sew, she must live with the handicap of depending on someone else to make her clothing.

A girl who can sew is a definite asset to her family. She can be a blessing to other people, and she can promote modesty and simplicity by the clothes she makes. Therefore, a girl from a Christian home has a great advantage if she learns to sew.

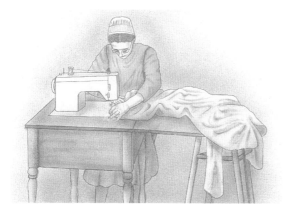

If a girl cannot sew, the argument above is designed to bring two responses from her: "I agree" and "It's time I start learning to sew." The following paragraphs explain the steps for writing the first draft of such

and discipleship. So as you write your persuasive argument for this lesson, remember that you are developing a skill that can be used for noble purposes to God's glory.

Lesson Outline:

1. To write a persuasive argument, first write an introduction that leads to the proposition.

    a. The first several sentences should catch the reader's attention by giving some appealing background information or making some interesting general statements about the subject.

    b. The introductory paragraph should end with the proposition.

2. Write the body by developing each supporting point convincingly.

    a. The first paragraph in the body may give two or three simple objections to your proposition and then move promptly to your first supporting point. If it discusses those objections in more detail, your first supporting point can be given in the next paragraph.

    b. Each succeeding paragraph of the body should be a well-rounded development of another point that supports your proposition. This development should consist of specific details, definitions, reasons, or illustrations.

    c. Keep analyzing your argument to be sure that you are using only concrete facts that are truly convincing.

3. Write a conclusion that points back to the proposition.

an argument. For the first draft, of course, you will write only on every other line so that you can mark improvements later.

1. *Write an introduction that leads to the proposition.* The introduction to a persuasive argument should be an entire paragraph. Its first several sentences are perhaps the most important; for if they fail to catch the reader's attention, he might lay your argument aside without even finishing it. Therefore, try to give some appealing background information or make some interesting general statements about your subject. These sentences should prepare the reader for your proposition, which should be the last sentence of the introductory paragraph.

Look again at the argument in Lesson 99 and the one above. Do you see this pattern in both? Notice that the argument in Lesson 99 begins by making some general statements about a boy's chores. The argument above begins by giving some background information about sewing.

2. *Write the body by developing each supporting point convincingly.* The first paragraph in the body may follow either of two patterns. If you deal with only two or three simple objections to your proposition, this paragraph should note them briefly and then move promptly to your first supporting point. If you wish to give more attention to the objections, you can devote the entire first paragraph to them. In that case, you would save your first supporting point for the next paragraph.

Each succeeding paragraph of the body should be a well-rounded development of another point that supports your proposition. Be sure to use specific details, definitions, reasons, or illustrations. As you write these paragraphs, keep analyzing your argument. Are you using only concrete facts that are truly convincing? Remember, mere opinions will hardly persuade anyone to change his mind.

3. *Write a conclusion that points back to the proposition.* The conclusion should generally be a short paragraph. Begin by summarizing the main supporting points, but do not merely repeat them in a first-second-third manner. Rather, write a sentence or two that restates the points in different words. End the paragraph with a restatement of the proposition—again, not by merely repeating it but by stating it in more conclusive terms than you used in the introduction. Often a transitional word like *then, therefore,* or *consequently* will help to give a conclusive tone to this last sentence.

4. *Write an appealing title.* Perhaps you already thought of a title in the planning and writing process. But more often, the best time to devise a suitable title is after the writing is finished. Your title should summarize the main idea of the argument in five words or less. Try to catch the reader's interest, but do not try to be clever or "cute." For example, when a reader sees the title "Housework for Boys," he is likely to think, "What?

   a. Begin by summarizing the main supporting points, but do not merely repeat them.
   b. End the paragraph with a restatement of the proposition—again, not by merely repeating it but by stating it in more conclusive terms than in the introduction. Often a transitional word like *then, therefore,* or *consequently* helps to give a conclusive tone.

4. Write an appealing title.
   a. The title should summarize the main idea of the argument in five words or less.
   b. Try to catch the reader's interest, but do not try to be clever or "cute."

5. Revise and rewrite your persuasive argument.

Isn't housework for girls?" When a girl sees "The Privilege of Sewing," she might think, "Sewing is hard work! How can it be a privilege?"

5. *Revise and rewrite your persuasive argument.* As usual, you should lay your first draft aside for a day or more and then proofread it. Check for sound reasoning and clear wording, and correct any mistakes in spelling, grammar, and punctuation. Then write the second draft, using your best penmanship and writing on every line.

Written Exercises

A. Write a persuasive argument based on the plan you made in Lesson 100. Lay it aside for a day or two before you do Part B.

B. Revise and rewrite your persuasive argument.

---

102. Chapter 9 Review

Class Practice

A. Identify each single-word adverb, and tell which word it modifies.
1. Even though he was very sorely tested, Job maintained his deeply committed faith and did not sin.
2. God always strictly limited Satan's liberty to test Job.
3. Job's three friends comforted him quite poorly.
4. They claimed to understand clearly the reasons for man's sufferings, but they proceeded to show quite definitely their ignorance.

B. Read each adverb phrase, and tell which word (or unit) it modifies.
1. "Rejoice in the Lord, O ye righteous: for praise is comely for the upright."
2. God's people sing to express their heartfelt praise.
3. The beauty of heaven is too glorious for words.
4. Because of the rain, Mother decided to postpone until tomorrow her washing.
5. Uncle Gerald's arrived too late to eat Grandma's dinner.

C. Read each adverb clause, and tell which word (or unit) it modifies. Also tell where any missing commas should be added.
1. If we truly seek God's praise we shall not be readily sidetracked when men flatter us.
2. Because the psalms are devotional in nature they are used for devotions more often than most other parts of the Bible.
3. God sustained the widow's oil and meal as long as the famine lasted.

Lesson 102

Purpose: To review the concepts taught in Chapter 9.

Lesson 101 Answers

Written Exercises

(All answers are individual work.)

Lesson 102 Answers

Class Practice

A. 1. very—sorely; sorely—was tested; deeply—committed; not—did sin
2. always—limited; strictly—limited
3. quite—poorly; poorly—comforted
4. clearly—to understand; quite—definitely; definitely—to show

B. 1. in the Lord—Rejoice; for the upright—comely
2. to express their heartfelt praise—sing
3. for words—too glorious
4. Because of the rain—decided; until tomorrow—to postpone
5. to eat Grandma's dinner—too late

C. 1. If we truly seek God's praise—shall be sidetracked; when men flatter us—shall be sidetracked; comma after *praise*
2. Because the psalms are devotional in nature—are used; than most other parts of the Bible—more often; comma after *nature*
3. as the famine lasted—as long
4. when we must suffer for Christ's sake—to rejoice

D. 1. From the place of his habitation—adverb; of his habitation—adjective; upon all the inhabitants of the earth—adverb; of the earth—adjective
2. earthly—adjective; past—adverb; quite—adverb; quickly—adverb

4. The Bible commands us to rejoice when we must suffer for Christ's sake.

D. Tell whether each underlined modifier is an *adverb* or an *adjective*. If a phrase is underlined twice, identify it separately.
1. "From the place of his habitation he looketh upon all the inhabitants of the earth."
2. The days of our earthly lives fly past quite quickly.
3. After he was a Christian, Paul said that his past achievements were worthless.
4. The day when Uncle Leo took me fishing was a day to be remembered.
5. The students of our school sang for the residents at the Oak Leaf Nursing Home.
6. Mother dashed outside to bring in the wash.

C. Read each sentence correctly.
1. The boys felt kind of foolish, but they couldn't blame no one else.
2. They thought sure they could finish up before lunch.
3. Of our two sets of grandparents, Grandpa Steiner's live closest to us.
4. How much further away do Grandpa Yoder's live?
5. I rarely ever do as good in math as in history.
6. Please see if the baby is sleeping alright.

F. Read these sentences, replacing the underlined words with an expressive verb or a descriptive adjective.
1. The injured deer walked painfully down to the stream.
2. We watched the very bright colors of the sunset fade into twilight.

G. On the chalkboard, diagram these sentences.
1. We slept well during the pleasantly cool nights.
2. The boxes on the porch should be stacked on the wagon.
3. The girls swept the floors as soon as the furniture was removed.
4. The travelers were hurrying to find shelter from the rain.
5. The children, thankful that Father was feeling better, worked with a will.

H. Answer these questions about note-taking.
1. What are some advantages of taking notes from a sermon?
2. What information should appear in the heading of sermon notes?
3. What are some important listening skills for good note-taking?

Written Exercises

A. Copy the single-word adverbs and the words they modify.
1. Heaven will always remain a perfectly holy place.
2. Certainly God expects us to obey fully His divinely inspired Word.

(Number 4 and Part D, numbers 1–2 are on page 512.)
3. After he was a Christian—adverb; past—adjective; worthless—adjective
4. when Uncle Leo took me fishing—adjective; to be remembered—adjective
5. of our school—adjective; at the Oak Leaf Nursing Home—adjective
6. outside—adverb; to bring in the wash—adverb

E. (Corrections are marked.)
1. The boys felt rather (somewhat) foolish, but they couldn't blame anyone else. (could blame no one else)
2. They thought surely they could finish ~~up~~ before lunch.
3. Of our two sets of grandparents, Grandpa Steiner's live closer to us.
4. How much farther away do Grandpa Yoder's live?
5. I rarely ~~ever~~ do as well in math as in history.
6. Please see if the baby is sleeping all right.

F. (Sample answers.)
1. limped, hobbled
2. brilliant, blazing

G. 1.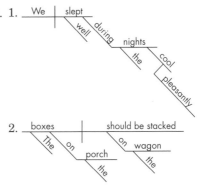

2.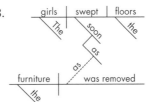

3.

4.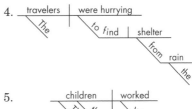

5.

H. 1. Taking notes helps to keep you from daydreaming or falling asleep, helps you to grasp the main points of the sermon better, and helps you to remember the sermon better. The notes can be kept for future reference and can benefit others who could not hear the sermon.
2. the date, the speaker's name, the place of the service, the title of the sermon, and the Scripture text
3. the ability to focus your whole attention on the speaker, the ability to overcome distractions, the ability to listen with interest, the ability to listen for main ideas

Written Exercises

A. 1. always—will remain; perfectly—holy
2. Certainly—expects; fully—to obey; divinely—inspired

3. The beauties of nature quite obviously speak of a divine Creator.
4. Have you ever stood outside on a starry night and reverently gazed up into that awesome vastness?
5. To completely comprehend that vastness is not possible for finite man.

B. Write each adverb phrase and the word (or unit) that the phrase modifies.
1. God's angels encamp around His people and minister to them.
2. We bow before the Lord to adore His holy Name.
3. The Lord is glorious beyond man's comprehension.
4. The Christian should stand too firmly to be led astray.
5. We must determine to stand firm until the end.

C. Copy the first and last words of each adverb clause, with ellipsis points between them. Also write the word (or unit) that the clause modifies.
1. Although hummingbirds eat some insects, their main food is nectar.
2. Because God has given the hummingbird a long bill, it can suck nectar out of flowers more easily than many other birds can.
3. These tiny birds pollinate flowers as they fly from one to another.
4. The hummingbird's plumage, brilliant when the sun shines on it, looks quite dull when it is in the shade.
5. The hummingbird is so agile that it can fly backward or upside down.

D. Write each underlined expression correctly.
1. You cannot expect to get nowhere in life without effort.
2. Hopefully you have all ready learned the value of diligence.
3. We refer back to history for many valuable lessons for today.
4. It is sort of sad to see how often people fail to learn from history.
5. Work that is done good shows a sense of respect toward others.
6. We must seek after God's will in every decision of life.
7. Of Isaac's two sons, Jacob was most interested in godliness and faith.
8. Esau sure stands as an example of one who ignores God in his life.
9. After Israel divided into two nations, the Northern Kingdom sank into apostasy the most quickly of the two.
10. Godly prophets were often treated quite bad in times of apostasy.
11. Most people were kind of relieved when the long, hard winter was over.
12. Have you thought farther about Father's question?
13. Mrs. Cobourn is feeling some better than she did last week.
14. We must wash up our hands for lunch.
15. We haven't scarcely begun the project yet.

E. Diagram these sentences.
1. While you are young, you should study the Bible to learn true values.
2. Our knowledge of the truth cannot be fully gained from other sources.

3. quite—obviously; obviously—speak
4. ever—Have stood; outside—Have stood; reverently—gazed; up—gazed
5. completely—To comprehend; not—is

B. 1. around His people—encamp; to them—minister
2. before the Lord—bow; to adore His holy Name—bow
3. beyond man's comprehension—glorious
4. to be led astray—too firmly
5. until the end—to stand

C. 1. Although . . . insects—is
2. Because . . . bill—can suck; than . . . can—more easily
3. as . . . another—pollinate
4. when . . . it—brilliant; when . . . shade—looks
5. that . . . down—so agile

D. 1. to get anywhere
2. have already learned
3. refer to history
4. rather (somewhat) sad
5. is done well
6. seek God's will
7. was more interested
8. surely stands
9. more quickly
10. treated quite badly
11. were rather (somewhat) relieved
12. thought further
13. feeling somewhat better
14. wash our hands
15. have scarcely

E. 1.

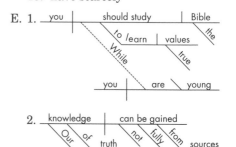

3. You should always speak kindly to everyone.

4. Before we move in, we shall remodel almost every room.

5. The little dog gave a surprisingly loud bark as soon as we stepped onto the porch.

F. Read the following argument, and answer the questions below.

Men of this world have learned volumes of information about the earth. They have recorded many details about the various kinds of energy that God has created. With that information, men have harnessed energy and developed amazing technology. Yet worldly men are surprisingly ignorant.

Many of the most learned men of today are woefully ignorant of God. To them, the marvels of the created world fail to speak convincingly of a Creator. Many are ignorant of the simple teachings of the Bible. That which is so plain that "the wayfaring men, though fools, shall not err therein" is obscured and made perplexing by worldly wisdom.

Moreover, the vast majority of men are almost totally ignorant of their own hearts. Although the truly enlightened mind understands that "the heart is deceitful above all things, and desperately wicked," the worldly wise thinks that man is inherently good. And what is clearly labeled sin by the enlightened is named a weakness or even a normal response by many. Indeed, how ignorant are men in their worldly wisdom!

1. What is the proposition?

2. Does the introductory paragraph give background information, or does it make general statements about the subject?

3. What are the two main points used to support the proposition? (State them briefly, using your own words as much as possible.)

4. Write the restated proposition in the conclusion.

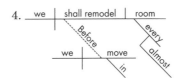

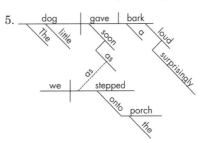

F. 1. Yet men are surprisingly ignorant.

2. gives background information

3. Many learned men are ignorant of God.
   Many are ignorant of their own hearts.

4. Indeed, how ignorant are men in their worldly wisdom!

Chapter Ten

Prepositions, Conjunctions, and Interjections

Writing Directions and Descriptions

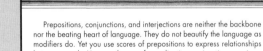

Prepositions, conjunctions, and interjections are neither the backbone nor the beating heart of language. They do not beautify the language as modifiers do. Yet you use scores of prepositions to express relationships between words. You use dozens of coordinating conjunctions, conjunctive adverbs, and subordinating conjunctions to join sentence parts. And you use an occasional interjection to express strong feeling. Learn to use these parts of speech properly for precise, clear communication.

A person who writes directions to a place usually tries to help a traveler reach a location that he has not visited before. A person who writes descriptions paints word pictures for others to enjoy. Instead of brush and paint, he uses exact nouns, expressive verbs, and colorful modifiers. He looks for ways to employ figures of speech and to include details that appeal to the reader's five senses. Develop skill in descriptive writing, and you will add color and appeal to all your compositions.

And he spake of trees, from the cedar tree that is in Lebanon even unto the hyssop that springeth out of the wall: he spake also of beasts, and of fowl, and of creeping things, and of fishes. And there came of all people to hear the wisdom of Solomon.

1 Kings 4:33, 34

103. Prepositions and Their Objects

> **Lesson Survey**
> - A **preposition** is a word that shows the relationship between its object and some other word in the sentence.
> - A **prepositional phrase** includes the preposition, its object, and any adjectives that modify the object.
> - A prepositional phrase can be used as an adjective, an adverb, or a noun.
> - A preposition must not be confused with an adverb.
> - A prepositional phrase beginning with *to* must not be confused with an infinitive.

Substantives and verbs constitute the core of our English language. Adjectives and adverbs fill an important role by modifying substantives and verbs. Prepositions and conjunctions, which you will study in this chapter, are connecting words that tie the other parts of speech together. Interjections are a small group of words used to express strong feeling or surprise.

A *preposition* is a word that shows the relationship between its object and some other word in the sentence. A difference in the preposition can completely change the meaning of a sentence. Compare the following sentences.

We walked <u>along</u> the trail.   We walked <u>off</u> the trail.
We walked <u>beside</u> the trail.   We walked <u>toward</u> the trail.

The following tables show the prepositions used most commonly. Study them so that you become thoroughly familiar with prepositions.

Common Prepositions

aboard	at	by	inside	outside	under
about	before	concerning	into	over	underneath
above	behind	despite	like	past	until
across	below	down	near	since	unto
after	beneath	during	of	through	up
against	beside	except	off	throughout	upon
along	besides	for	on	till	with
among	between	from	onto	to	within
around	beyond	in	out	toward	without
as	but				

Lesson 103

Purpose: To study common prepositions and their uses.

Oral Review:

1. Label the parts of speech for the words in these sentences. (*Teacher:* Write on the board and do together, or dictate for the students to do individually.)

   　　　adj.　　n.　　adv.　　v.　　n.
   a. Kindly smiles often bring joy.

   　　adj.　　n.　　v.　　adj.　　n.
   b. God's Word is revealed truth.

   　　pron. pron. adv.　　v.　　n.　 v.　adv.　 v.　pron.
   c. Those who truly believe God will also obey Him.

2. Tell whether the verb in each sentence is transitive, intransitive complete, or intransitive linking.

   a. We smelled smoke in the house. (transitive)

   b. The freshly baked bread smelled delicious. (intransitive linking)

   c. Each of the scented candles was smelled in turn. (transitive)

   d. A dog can smell better than a man can. (intransitive complete)

3. Choose the correct verb for each sentence. (Correct verbs are underlined.)

   a. There (is, <u>are</u>) many opportunities to show kindness to others.

   b. Clarence, along with the other boys, (have, <u>has</u>) worked hard.

   c. He (don't, <u>doesn't</u>) expect to finish before lunch.

   d. My uncle and close friend often (give, <u>gives</u>) me good advice.

   e. My uncle and my close friend (is, <u>are</u>) visiting our community.

Common Compound Prepositions

according to	by means of	in spite of	out of
along with	due to	instead of	owing to
aside from	in addition to	next to	prior to
as of	in front of	on account of	with regard to
because of	in place of		

A *prepositional phrase* includes the preposition, its object, and any adjectives that modify the object. The object of a preposition is the substantive that answers the question *whom* or *what* about the preposition. In the following sentence, the prepositional phrases are underlined.

The common people <u>of Israel</u> gladly heard Jesus <u>in spite of the leaders' hostility</u>.

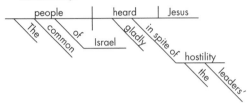

In the preceding example, *of* is a preposition. *Of whom or what? Of Israel* is a prepositional phrase, with *Israel* as the object of the preposition. *In spite of* is a preposition. In spite of *whom or what? Hostility* is the object of the preposition, making the complete phrase *in spite of the leaders' hostility.*

A preposition may have a compound object. As with other compound sentence parts, the compound object is diagramed on a fork. If an adjective modifies both parts, it is placed under the horizontal line before the fork. If it modifies only one part, it is placed under that word.

The doctrines of <u>outward nonconformity and complete nonresistance</u> are foundational <u>to Christian faith and practice</u>.

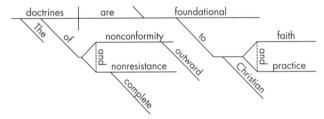

f. Joyce or Louise (have, <u>has</u>) already set the table.

g. Neither of the books (<u>is</u>, are) new anymore.

h. Smallpox (<u>is</u>, are) no longer a serious threat.

i. The congregation (is, <u>are</u>) returning to their various homes.

j. *Poems for Memorization* (<u>is</u>, are) a collection of poems.

Lesson Introduction: In many sentences, the relationship between two words is clear without any connecting word. In other sentences, a connecting word is needed to show the relationship. Consider the underlined words in the following sentences.

a. Paul's great zeal was to <u>know Christ</u>.

b. Paul's great zeal was to <u>know</u> about <u>Christ</u>.

The two sentences are identical except for the preposition *about*. Which sentence shows a close,

direct relationship between *know* and *Christ*? (sentence *a*) Which sentence shows a more distant relationship? (sentence *b*) Which sentence is a more accurate description of Paul's zeal? (sentence *a*)

Most prepositions are small words, but they can make a great difference in the meaning of a sentence.

Lesson Outline:

1. A preposition is a word that shows the relationship between its object and some other word in the sentence.

2. A prepositional phrase includes the preposition, its object, and any adjectives that modify the object.

a. The object of a preposition is the substantive that answers the question *whom* or *what* about the preposition.

b. A preposition may have a compound object.

A preposition normally comes before its object. But when the object is an interrogative or a relative pronoun, the preposition may come at the end of the sentence.

<u>Whom</u> did Joy sit <u>beside</u>? (beside whom)

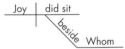
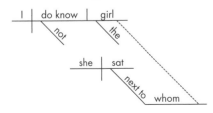

I do not know the girl <u>whom</u> she sat <u>next to</u>. (next to whom)

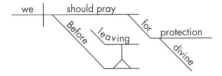

The object of a preposition is usually a noun or a pronoun, but it may also be a verbal, a verbal phrase, or a noun clause.

<u>Before leaving</u>, we should pray for divine protection.
(The object of the preposition *Before* is the verbal *leaving.*)

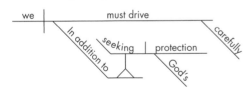

<u>In addition to seeking God's protection</u>, we must drive carefully.
(The object of the preposition *In addition to* is the verbal phrase *seeking God's protection.*)

c. A preposition normally comes before its object, except when the object is an interrogative or a relative pronoun.

d. The object of a preposition is usually a noun or a pronoun, but it may also be a verbal, a verbal phrase, or a noun clause.

3. A prepositional phrase can be used as an adjective, an adverb, or a noun.

a. A prepositional phrase used as an adjective usually comes right after the substantive it modifies.

b. A prepositional phrase used as an adverb modifies a verb, an adjective, an adverb, or a verbal.

1) An adverb phrase usually can be placed at different locations without changing the meaning of a sentence.

2) When several phrases are used in succession, you must decide if each phrase modifies the same word or if the second phrase modifies the object of the first preposition.

c. A prepositional phrase used as a noun names a place or a thing and is usually the subject of a sentence.

4. A preposition must not be confused with an adverb.

a. If a word is used alone to tell *when* or *where*, it is an adverb.

b. If it is followed by an object, it is a preposition.

5. A prepositional phrase beginning with to must not be confused with an infinitive.
Remember that if *to* is used with a verb form, the

We glorify God <u>in whatever is His will</u>.

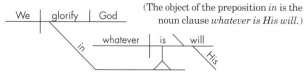

(The object of the preposition *in* is the noun clause *whatever is His will*.)

Prepositional phrases can be used as adjectives, adverbs, or nouns. A prepositional phrase used as an adjective modifies a noun or a pronoun. An adjective phrase usually comes right after the substantive it modifies.

The fence <u>along the road</u> needs a good paint job.
   (*Along the road* tells *which* about *fence*.)
Father bought a brown goat <u>with short, stubby horns</u>.
   (*With short, stubby horns* tells *what kind of* about *goat*.)

A prepositional phrase used as an adverb modifies a verb, an adjective, an adverb, or a verbal. An adverb phrase usually can be placed at different locations without changing the meaning of a sentence.

<u>Before lunch</u> we looked <u>at the globe</u> <u>for a few minutes</u>.
   (*Before lunch* tells *when* about the verb *looked; at the globe* tells
   where about *looked; for a few minutes* tells *how long* about *looked*.)

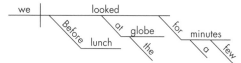

The floors, dirty <u>from the children's tracks</u>, have been washed too
   carelessly <u>for Mother's satisfaction</u>.
   (*From the children's tracks* modifies the adjective *dirty; for
   Mother's satisfaction* modifies the adverb unit *too carelessly*.)

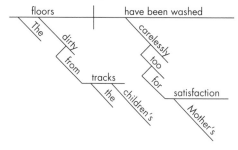

combination is an infinitive; if *to* is followed by a substantive, the combination is a prepositional phrase.

★ EXTRA PRACTICE

Worksheet 39 (*Prepositions and Their Objects*)

Keeping <u>on the slippery trail</u> was difficult.
    (*On the slippery trail* modifies the verbal *Keeping*.)

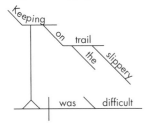

    When several phrases are used in succession, you must decide if each phrase modifies the same word or if the second phrase modifies the object of the first preposition.

We drove <u>along the river</u> <u>before sundown</u>.
    (*Along the river* tells *where* about the verb *drove*. *Before sundown*
      tells *when* about the verb *drove*.)

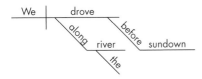

We ate our lunch <u>in a small park</u> <u>beside the river</u>.
    (The whole expression *in a small park beside the river* tells *where*
      about the verb *ate*. *Beside the river* tells *which* about *park*,
      the object of the first preposition.)

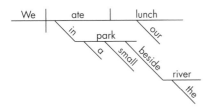

    On rare occasions a prepositional phrase can also be used as a noun. Such a phrase names a place or a thing and is usually the subject of a sentence.

<u>Through the forest</u> is the shortest way to our home.
> (*Through the forest* names the *way* that is the shortest; it is the subject of the sentence.)

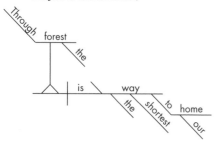

<u>Below zero</u> is cold!
> (*Below zero* names the *temperature* that is cold; it is the subject of the sentence.)

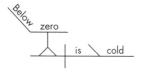

Prepositions must not be confused with adverbs. Many words can be used as either part of speech. If the word is used alone to tell *when* or *where,* it is an adverb. If it is followed by an object, it is a preposition.

Adverbs	**Prepositions**
We heard the owl <u>before</u>.	We heard the owl <u>before supper</u>.
We quickly stepped <u>outside</u>.	We quickly stepped <u>outside the door</u>.

Prepositional phrases beginning with *to* must not be confused with infinitives. Remember that if *to* is used with a verb form, the combination is an infinitive; if *to* is followed by a substantive, the combination is a prepositional phrase.

> We go <u>to church</u> to worship.
> (*To church* is a prepositional phrase; *to worship* is an infinitive.)

Class Practice

A. Read each prepositional phrase. If a phrase is part of a longer phrase, include it with the longer phrase and also read it separately. Tell whether each phrase is an *adjective,* an *adverb,* or a *noun.*

6.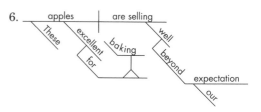

Written Exercises

A.   1. of you—adj.; of God—adv.
     2. to this world—adv.;
       by the renewing of your mind—adv.;
       of your mind—adj.

1. The words of the Master were attractive to many people because of their graciousness.
2. In spite of the intense hatred of the Jewish leaders, people from many places flocked to hear Him.
3. During His ministry Jesus often taught in parables.
4. No man like Jesus had ever lived on the earth.
5. On the cross was where Jesus atoned for man's sins.
6. Cormorants, birds with powerful, hooked bills, live along the seacoast.
7. On cliffs is where they usually rest.
8. These birds, with their long necks and flat heads, look like rows of bottles.
9. Asian people use cormorants in their fishing.
10. Having tied long cords to the birds, they place them on a perch over the water.
11. They also put metal rings around their necks to keep them from swallowing the fish.
12. From where they perch, cormorants can spot fish in the water.

B. Tell whether each underlined word is an *adverb* or a *preposition*.
1. The flock of geese suddenly soared <u>up</u> into the air and flew <u>off</u>.
2. Leroy jumped <u>off</u> the wagon and ran <u>inside</u>.
3. The mailman drove <u>past</u> without putting anything <u>inside</u> our box.
4. When we came to the small creek, we waded <u>across</u> and climbed <u>up</u> the steep bank on the other side.

C. On the chalkboard, diagram these sentences.
1. The weeds between the rows can be removed with the tiller.
2. Hoeing next to the beanstalks was a job for the older children.
3. By mulching the garden well, we keep many weeds out of it.
4. In the chicken pen is a good place for these rotten tomatoes.
5. According to what I remember, we have raised produce during the summer months for many years.
6. These apples, excellent for baking, are selling well beyond our expectation.

Written Exercises

A. Copy each prepositional phrase. If a phrase is part of a longer phrase, include it with the longer phrase and also copy it separately. Label each phrase *adj., adv.,* or *n.*
1. "If any of you lack wisdom, let him ask of God."
2. "And be not conformed to this world: but be ye transformed by the renewing of your mind."

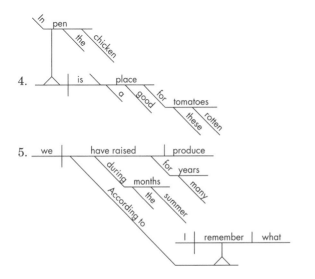

Lesson 103 Answers

Class Practice

A. 1. of the Master—adjective;
to many people—adverb;
because of their graciousness—adverb
2. In spite of the intense hatred of the Jewish leaders—adverb; of the Jewish leaders—adjective; from many places—adjective
3. During His ministry—adverb;
in parables—adverb
4. like Jesus—adjective; on the earth—adverb
5. On the cross—noun; for man's sins—adverb
6. with powerful, hooked bills—adjective;
along the seacoast—adverb
7. On cliffs—noun
8. with their long necks and flat heads—adjective; like rows of bottles—adverb; of bottles—adjective
9. in their fishing—adverb
10. to the birds—adverb; on a perch over the water—adverb; over the water—adjective
11. around their necks—adverb;
from swallowing the fish—adverb
12. From where they perch—adverb;
in the water—adverb

B. 1. up—adverb; off—adverb
2. off—preposition; inside—adverb
3. past—adverb; inside—preposition
4. across—adverb; up—preposition

C.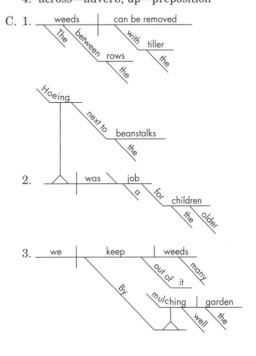

(The rest of this page's answers are on page 522.)

3. "Let us labour therefore to enter into that rest, lest any man fall after the same example of unbelief."
4. Vultures are birds of prey with slightly hooked bills.
5. Their heads are not feathered like those of other birds.
6. In the air is the only place where a vulture looks graceful.
7. In spite of their ugliness, they are useful in removing dead animals.
8. With their keen sense of sight and smell, they can locate dead animals from a distance.
9. In a cave is where the vulture may lay its eggs.
10. We should give thanks to the Creator for the vulture.

B. Copy each underlined word, and label it *adv.* or *prep.*
1. The cool spring water flowed <u>over</u> my feet and on <u>down</u> the valley.
2. Anita stepped <u>outside</u> and motioned for me to come <u>up</u> the steps.
3. Conrad wanted to go <u>along</u>, but he had to stay <u>behind</u> for this time.
4. After Charles climbed <u>down</u> from the tractor, we walked <u>along</u> the field lane looking for walnuts.
5. A large buck that had been hiding <u>behind</u> a stone wall jumped <u>up</u> and dashed away.

C. Diagram these sentences.
1. The influences of your present choices and habits will linger with you throughout the rest of your life.
2. Walking according to God's direction brings true blessing in life.
3. By studying the Bible, we are led in right paths.
4. In God's will is the only place of true satisfaction.
5. Sin, attractive to our natural hearts, can ruin the souls of its victims.
6. We can know little about God aside from what He has revealed.

Review Exercises

A. Write whether each underlined verb is transitive (*T*), intransitive complete (*IC*), or intransitive linking (*IL*). [52–55]
1. The Gospel message <u>has sounded</u> from shore to shore.
2. Many prophets <u>have sounded</u> clear warnings to the people.
3. This message <u>sounds</u> foolish to the worldly-wise.
4. Someday the Gospel message <u>will have been sounded</u> for the last time.
5. <u>Did</u> Paul actually <u>turn</u> the world upside down?
6. The bitterness of some <u>has turned</u> extremely fierce.
7. But God <u>can turn</u> persecution to the furtherance of the Gospel.
8. The believers <u>had turned</u> from idols to serve the living God.

B. Choose the correct words in parentheses. [60]
1. Jason or Galen (is, are) washing the van.
2. (Here's, Here are) the jars you wanted.

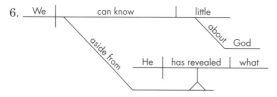

(About God may be diagramed under can know.)

Review Exercises

A. 1. IC   5. T
   2. T   6. IL
   3. IL   7. T
   4. T   8. IC

B. 1. is
   2. Here are

3. into that rest—adv.; after the same example of unbelief—adv.; of unbelief—adj.
4. of prey—adj.; with slightly hooked bills—adj.
5. like those of other birds—adv.; of other birds—adj.
6. In the air—n.
7. In spite of their ugliness—adv.; in removing dead animals—adv.
8. With their keen sense of sight and smell—adv.; of sight and smell—adj.; from a distance—adv.
9. In a cave—n.
10. to the Creator—adv.; for the vulture—adv.

B. 1. over—prep.; down—prep.
   2. outside—adv.; up—prep.
   3. along—adv.; behind—adv.
   4. down—adv.; along—prep.
   5. behind—prep.; up—adv.

C.

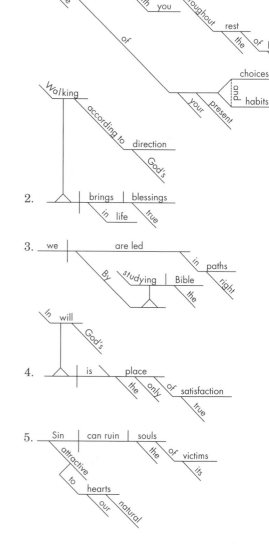

3. *Zion's Praises* (have, has) a large selection of songs.
4. Each of the calves (was, were) bawling loudly.
5. Karen and Alice (do, does) neat embroidery work.
6. The flock (is, are) going their various ways.
7. The shears (have, has) been found again.
8. (Have, Has) the bells been synchronized?
9. The kettle of stew (is, are) simmering on the wood stove.
10. The white and orange cat (is, are) sunning on the porch step.
11. Christian civics (include, includes) the paying of taxes.
12. The family (is, are) enjoying its time of worship.

3. has		8. Have	
4. was		9. is	
5. do		10. is	
6. are		11. includes	
7. have		12. is	

104. Using Prepositions Correctly

Lesson Survey

- Learn the correct usage of similar prepositions.
- Avoid nonstandard and informal uses of prepositions.
- Avoid unnecessary prepositions.
- If a compound sentence part requires different prepositions, be sure to include both prepositions.

Although most prepositions are simple words, they are important in showing specific relationships within sentences. Therefore, we must learn to use them correctly.

Similar Prepositions

Some prepositions are similar to other prepositions or to other words. Because of this similarity, these words are sometimes interchanged and used incorrectly. Study the following pairs of similar expressions.

1. In *refers mainly to location.* Into *refers to entrance or movement to a point of contact.* With a verb like *put* or *take,* either preposition may be correct, depending on whether entrance or location is being emphasized.

Incorrect:
Jesus went <u>in</u> the synagogue and taught.
Correct:
Jesus went <u>into</u> the synagogue and taught. (made an entrance)
Do you still live <u>in</u> Ohio? (live at this location)

Lesson 104

Purpose: To study the correct usage of prepositions.

Teacher: Because language constantly changes, the rules in this lesson are not absolute. A usage that is disapproved today may eventually be considered acceptable. In fact, some expressions labeled "incorrect" or "informal" in this course are already accepted as standard by some writers and editors. But this text favors the conservative schools of thought on English usage. All the rules in this lesson are supported by established usage or by current authorities on conservative usage.

Oral Review:

1. What is a preposition? (a word that shows the relationship between its object and some other word in the sentence)
2. A prepositional phrase can function as what three parts of speech? (adjective, adverb, noun)
3. In addition to a noun or pronoun, what may the object of a preposition be? (a verbal, a verbal phrase, a noun clause)
4. What are the four main purposes that commas are used for? (to divide compound sentences; to separate items in a series; to set off introductory material; to set off nonrestrictive and independent elements)
5. Tell how to correct the following expressions.
   a. what kind of a car (what kind of car)
   b. all them peaches (all those peaches)
   c. this here problem (this problem)
   d. further from school (farther from school)
   e. sort of sick (rather [*or* somewhat] sick)
   f. real loud (really loud)
   g. sure hurried (surely hurried)
6. When should you use *less,* and when should you

I ran <u>into</u> a brick wall. (moved to a point of contact)
Put this <u>into</u> your pocket. (entrance emphasized)
Put this <u>in</u> your pocket. (location emphasized)

2. Beside *means "by the side of."* Besides *means "other than or in addition to."*

Correct:

The fallen tree lay <u>beside</u> the road. (by the side of the road)
Nothing <u>besides</u> that tree was damaged.
     (nothing other than that tree)
<u>Besides</u> high wind, we had hail. (in addition to high wind)

3. Accept *is a verb that means "to receive."* Except *is usually a preposition that means "not including."* Except *can also be a verb that means "to exclude or leave out."*

Incorrect:

No one <u>accept</u> Father could lift the heavy bags.

Correct:

No one <u>except</u> Father could lift the heavy bags.
     (not including Father)
We should <u>accept</u> the advice of our parents.
     (should receive the advice)
Do not form a clique and <u>except</u> others from your friendship.
     (exclude others)

4. Between *refers to just two things.* Among *refers to more than two things.* (The second syllable of *between* means "two.")

Incorrect: The pie was divided <u>between</u> the three children.
Correct: The pie was divided <u>among</u> the three children.
                The pie was divided <u>between</u> the two children.

5. Differ from *is used when referring to things or ideas and means "to be unlike."* Differ with *is used when referring to people and means "to disagree with."*

Correct:

Christian ways <u>differ from</u> those of the world. (ways are unlike)
Politely but firmly, Father <u>differed with</u> the man who had come
     to the door. (people disagreed)

6. Wait on *means "to serve."* Wait for *means "to stay behind for" or "to anticipate."*

Incorrect: We <u>waited on</u> Larry until he arrived.
                How long must we <u>wait on</u> the surprise?

use *fewer*? (Use *less* to indicate *how much* about a singular noun. Use *fewer* to indicate *how many* about a plural noun.)

Lesson Introduction: Give your students a preview of some of the points they will be studying in this lesson. See if they can choose the correct words in these sentences.

As we sat in the living room visiting, little Sammy suddenly burst (in, into) the room. (into; We surely hope he didn't burst *in* the room!)

No one was on the bench (beside, besides) me. (either, depending on the intended meaning; *beside* if you mean by your side; *besides* if you mean in addition to you)

After we had waited (for, on) Leonard for an hour, we decided to go without him. (for; If

you waited *on* poor Leonard for a whole hour, he would probably be in no condition to go with you!)

Not all preposition errors are as obvious as these, but it is equally important that we learn to use all prepositions correctly.

Lesson Outline:

1. Learn the correct usage of similar prepositions.

(1) In *refers mainly to location.* Into *refers to entrance or movement to a point of contact.*

(2) Beside *means "by the side of."* Besides *means "other than or in addition to."*

(3) Accept *is a verb that means "to receive."* Except *is usually a preposition that means "not including."* Except *can also be a verb that means "to exclude or leave out."*

Correct: We <u>waited for</u> Larry until he arrived.
How long must we <u>wait for</u> the surprise?
The clerk who <u>waited on</u> us was friendly and helpful.

7. *Use* angry with *when referring to persons; use* angry at *when referring to things other than persons.*

Correct:
Mr. Watson became <u>angry with</u> Father for offering him a tract.
He becomes <u>angry at</u> any attempt to speak about his soul's need.

Nonstandard and Informal Uses of Prepositions

Prepositions are sometimes used in improper or informal ways. Such uses should be avoided in standard writing.

1. *Use* from, *not* than, *as a preposition after* different *or* differently.

Incorrect: This bread is <u>different than</u> Mother's bread.
This project turned out <u>differently than</u> my expectations.
Correct: This bread is <u>different from</u> Mother's bread.
This project turned out <u>differently from</u> my expectations.

Of course, if a clause follows *different* or *differently,* it may be introduced by the conjunction *than.*

This project turned out <u>differently than</u> I had expected.

2. *Do not use the wordy expression* in back of *for* behind.

Incorrect: <u>In back of</u> the storm clouds is the shining sun.
Correct: <u>Behind</u> the storm clouds is the shining sun.

The phrase *in the back of* is correct when it means "within, but at the back end of" something.

The library books are <u>in the back of</u> the classroom.
(within, but at the back end of the classroom)

3. *Do not use* by *for* at *or* to. When *by* is used with a verb like *come, go, or drive,* it implies continuous motion past a place.

Incorrect:
We shall drive <u>by</u> Grandpa's place and pick them up on our way.
(sounds as if we do not plan to stop)
Correct:
We shall drive <u>to</u> Grandpa's place and pick them up on our way.
On our way to Grandpa's, we drove <u>by</u> Uncle Leland's farm.
(drove past Uncle Leland's farm)

(4) Between *refers to just two things.* Among *refers to more than two things.*
(5) Differ from *is used when referring to things or ideas and means "to be unlike."* Differ with *is used when referring to people and means "to disagree with."*
(6) Wait on *means "to serve."* Wait for *means "to stay behind for" or "to anticipate."*
(7) *Use* angry with *when referring to persons; use* angry at *when referring to things other than persons.*

2. *Avoid nonstandard and informal uses of prepositions.*

(1) *Use* from, *not* than, *as a preposition after* different *or* differently. *Than* may be used if a clause follows.
(2) *Do not use the wordy expression* in back of *for* behind.

(3) *Do not use* by *for* at *or* to. When *by* is used with a verb like *come, go,* or *drive,* it implies continuous motion past a place.

3. *Avoid unnecessary prepositions.*

(1) *Do not use* of *with* off, inside, *or* outside.
(2) *Do not use* at *or* to *with* where.
(3) *Do not use* over *with* for *over.*
(4) *Do not use* in between *for the preposition* between.
   (*Note:* While *in between* must not be used as a preposition, this phrase is acceptable when it is used alone with the meaning "in an intermediate situation." Compare the following sentences.)

Incorrect:
Two criminals were crucified, with Jesus in between them.

Unnecessary Prepositions

A third type of usage error occurs when unnecessary prepositions are used. Study the following examples.

1. *Do not use* of *with* off, inside, *or* outside.

   Incorrect: I stepped <u>off of</u> the ladder.
   This calf does not stay <u>inside of</u> its hutch.
   Our cats must stay <u>outside of</u> the house.
   Correct: I stepped <u>off</u> the ladder.
   This calf does not stay <u>inside</u> its hutch.
   Our cats must stay <u>outside</u> the house.

2. *Do not use* at *or* to *with* where.

   Incorrect: Where is Father <u>at</u>?
   I don't know where he went <u>to</u>.
   Correct: Where is Father?
   I don't know where he went.

3. *Do not use* over with *for* over.

   Incorrect: After the work is <u>over with</u>, you may play.
   Correct: After the work is <u>over</u>, you may play.

4. *Do not use* in between *for the preposition* between.

   Incorrect: I found the book <u>in between</u> two boxes.
   Correct: I found the book <u>between</u> two boxes.

Prepositions in Compound Sentence Parts

If a compound sentence part requires different prepositions, be sure to include both prepositions. In the following sentences, the compound parts require the same preposition, so only one needs to be written.

   I have been writing and drawing <u>with</u> these new pencils.
   (writing *with* and drawing *with*)
   Brother Edwin gave a summary and an explanation <u>of</u> the passage.
   (summary *of* and explanation *of*)

Now look at the following pairs of sentences. Since the compound sentence parts require different prepositions, both prepositions must be stated.

   Incorrect:
   We marvel at both the <u>hatred</u> and the <u>courage of</u> the early Christians. (hatred of the Christians?)
   I have been <u>looking</u> and <u>asking about</u> my lost tablet.
   (looking about my tablet?)

   Correct:
   Two criminals were crucified, with Jesus between them.
   Correct:
   Two criminals were crucified, with Jesus in between.

   4. If a compound sentence part requires different prepositions, be sure to include both prepositions.

   ★ *EXTRA PRACTICE*
   Worksheet 40 *(Using Prepositions Correctly)*

Correct:

We marvel at both the <u>hatred against</u> and the <u>courage of</u> the early Christians.

I have been <u>looking for</u> and <u>asking about</u> my lost tablet.

Class Practice

Read these sentences correctly. Some are already correct.

1. All the saints accept Enoch and Elijah died before entering heaven.
2. Allow no idol to come in between you and the Lord.
3. God's hedge cannot protect one who steps outside of its bounds.
4. A Christian is a pilgrim and a testimony to the world.
5. As Jesus came in Jerusalem, many acclaimed Him as the Messiah.
6. Several rows of chairs can be set up in the back of the auditorium.
7. There was an open discussion in between the two messages.
8. As soon as breakfast is over with, we have our family worship.
9. One family's procedure for family worship may differ with another's.
10. The mountain goat jumped off of one narrow ledge and landed on another.
11. On a broader ledge, two mountain goats were standing besides each other.
12. Did you see where the first goat jumped to?
13. On our way to Wisconsin, we drove by Lake Michigan.
14. We have a stone incinerator in back of the garage.
15. Father built our greenhouse differently than the model he had inspected.
16. We should not become angry with the delays of life.
17. Besides my math lesson, I have science and history to finish.
18. Among the two of us, we should finish these chores in a few minutes.

Written Exercises

Write correctly each underlined expression that contains a mistake. If it has no error, write *correct*.

1. Jesus came <u>in this world</u> as an infant.
2. The Bible reveals nothing <u>accept a few glimpses</u> of Jesus' childhood.
3. We do know that He was <u>obedient and respectful of</u> His earthly parents.
4. After His parents left the temple, they did not know <u>where He was at</u>.
5. The people were <u>angry with</u> Jesus when He reminded them that God cares for the Gentiles.
6. For the Passover, many people <u>came by the temple</u>.
7. Dutifully but fretfully, Martha <u>waited on the Master</u>.
8. The publican's prayer was very <u>different than the Pharisee's</u>.
9. Several bales of hay have fallen <u>off of the wagon</u>.
10. The climate in New Mexico surely <u>differs from that</u> in Virginia.
11. Do you know <u>where we are going to</u> for our visit?

Lesson 104 Answers

Class Practice

(Corrections are underlined.)

1. All the saints <u>except</u> Enoch and Elijah died before entering heaven.
2. Allow no idol to come <u>between</u> you and the Lord.
3. God's hedge cannot protect one who steps <u>outside</u> its bounds.
4. A Christian is a pilgrim <u>in</u> and a testimony to the world.
5. As Jesus came <u>into</u> Jerusalem, many acclaimed Him as the Messiah.
6. (correct)
7. There was an open discussion <u>between</u> the two messages.
8. As soon as breakfast is <u>over</u>, we have our family worship.
9. One family's procedure for family worship may <u>differ from</u> another's.
10. The mountain goat jumped <u>off</u> one narrow ledge and landed on another.
11. On a broader ledge, two mountain goats were standing <u>beside</u> each other.
12. Did you see where the first goat <u>jumped</u>?
13. (correct)
14. We have a stone incinerator <u>behind</u> the garage.
15. Father built our greenhouse <u>differently from</u> the model he had inspected.
16. We should not become <u>angry at</u> the delays of life.
17. (correct)
18. <u>Between</u> the two of us, we should finish these chores in a few minutes.

Written Exercises

1. into this world
2. except a few glimpses
3. obedient to and respectful of
4. where He was
5. correct
6. came to the temple
7. correct
8. different from the Pharisee's
9. off the wagon
10. correct
11. where we are going

12. I admired the teacher's <u>understanding and solution to</u> my problem.
13. We had several minutes of <u>drill in between</u> the two math classes.
14. When we go to Grandpa Weaver's, we like to <u>drive by Bobcat Lake</u> because we often see wildlife there.
15. The results of my drawing often turn out quite <u>differently from my intentions</u>.
16. We <u>stopped by Uncle Lloyd's place</u> to get a box of supplies.
17. Father finally arrived, and our long wait <u>was over with</u>.
18. There are only two small pies to <u>divide between the ten children</u>.
19. I gasped in dismay when my book <u>fell in the mud puddle</u>.
20. <u>Beside the cake</u>, we had fruit and ice cream for dessert.
21. You can <u>differ with your friend</u> without feeling upset.
22. The speaker for the evening was caught in a traffic jam, and we <u>waited on him</u> for half an hour.

Review Exercises

A. Copy each word that should be followed by a comma, and add the comma. [23, 25]
1. Yes when we get to heaven every sacrifice for Christ will be well repaid.
2. God's infinite gracious love I realize cannot be fathomed by our finite minds.
3. Psalm 23 the Shepherd Psalm is a favorite of many people.
4. Dr. Joseph Kline M.D. wrote a prescription for Uncle Mark who is suffering from acute bursitis.
5. Writing as fast as I could I managed to note most of the main ideas.
6. I want you Darlene to dry the dishes sweep the kitchen and set the table.
7. Underneath the fern fronds have many clusters of spores.
8. At the end of the long weary day we thanked God for His blessing.

B. Write the correct words for these sentences. [83, 88, 93, 98]
1. We have (less, fewer) cows now than we did a year ago.
2. The younger children were (already, all ready) excited about the trip.
3. Tomorrow in history class, we shall study the Reformation (farther, further).
4. Of the Reformation and the Renaissance, the Reformation was (more, most) important in church history.
5. A window was broken, but everything else seemed (alright, all right).
6. Irene is feeling (some, somewhat) better today.
7. We were (rather, sort of) surprised at how well the work went.
8. Have you planted (them, those) bushes yet?
9. Arlen (can, can't) barely see without his glasses.
10. Of my two sisters, Sheryl can wash dishes (faster, fastest).

---

12. understanding of and solution to
13. drill between
14. correct
15. correct
16. stopped at Uncle Lloyd's place
17. was over
18. divide among the ten children
19. fell into the mud puddle
20. Besides the cake
21. correct
22. waited for him

Review Exercises

A. 1. Yes, heaven,
2. infinite, love, realize,
3. 23, Psalm,
4. Kline, M.D., Mark,
5. could,
6. you, Darlene, dishes, kitchen,
7. Underneath,
8. long, day,

B. 1. fewer
2. already
3. further
4. more
5. all right
6. somewhat
7. rather
8. those
9. can
10. faster

105. Writing Directions to a Place

> **Lesson Survey**
> - Use the following steps to write simple, clear directions.
>   1. First think through the whole route.
>   2. Begin with a main route close to the starting point.
>   3. Give special attention to each change in routes.
>   4. Give only helpful details.
>   5. Double-check your information.
>   6. Give the traveler a number to call in case he needs additional help.

Suppose a friend from another state has decided to visit you and wants written directions to your place, your church, or your school. Could you write a set of directions that would actually enable him to find you? What are the steps for writing simple, clear directions?

1. *First think through the whole route.* Find the approximate locations of your friend's place and of your place. Notice which highways and major roads connect the two areas.

Whenever practical, choose major highways. A shortcut on smaller roads is often more confusing than a longer route on a major highway. This is especially true for someone who is not familiar with the roads. The larger highways are generally well marked and easy to follow.

Decide how to direct your friend from the major highways to his destination. Choose a route that is easy to describe, even if it is not the shortest route.

Refer to the following set of directions as you study the points below.

> From your area near Front Royal, Virginia, follow U.S. Highway 522 north to Interstate 66 (I-66). Take I-66 west to Interstate 81, and turn north. Follow I-81 north through Maryland to Exit 1 in Pennsylvania. At the end of the ramp, turn right onto Route 163. Follow Route 163 west for about two miles until you come to a stop sign, and turn right onto Williamsport Pike. After about one mile, you will pass Coseytown Road, which turns off to the left. Our house is the third one on the left after Coseytown Road.

2. *Begin with a main route close to the starting point.* Your friend likely knows the best route from his place to this highway.

3. *Give special attention to each change in routes.* For a well-marked highway, give the number of the road and the direction of travel. The name of an important town or city is helpful in giving the travelers a sense of the distance they must travel to the next change in routes. If the new road is a small, hard-to-recognize country road, mention helpful landmarks such as a nearby business, a railroad, or a river, and give specific distances.

Lesson 105

Purpose: To give practice in writing clear, easy-to-follow directions to a place.

Teacher: For Written Exercises, Part A, choose a city from which a traveler must use about five different roads to reach your school.

Oral Review:

1. What is a persuasive argument? (an attempt to persuade or move to action)
2. What is the statement of the idea that the writer is promoting in an argument? (the proposition)
3. What is a fact? (something that has actually happened; something that expresses a scientific, mathematical, or statistical reality; or something that expresses a truth revealed by God in His Word)
4. What is an opinion? (a conclusion or belief about something, formed as a person evaluates facts in light of his own knowledge or experience)
5. What are some important cautions to remember about persuasive arguments? (Beware of propositions that are supported by misrepresented facts or faulty reasoning. Remember that the validity of a proposition is not established by strong statements. Avoid arguments that deal with unprofitable subjects.)
6. What is characterization? (the process of portraying a story character)
7. Name four ways of portraying a story character. (through actions, speech, thoughts, and appearance)
8. What are some elements of natural dialogue? (informal tone [contractions and elliptical sentences], frequent change of speakers, descriptive explanatory words)

Lesson Introduction: Read a set of directions telling how to get from your school to a well-known place in the area. But make the directions vague and inexact. For example, do not give distances or road names, and do not tell which way to turn. Can the students follow you and tell where you are taking them? You might close the introduction by saying, "There must be a better way to do this! Let's look at today's lesson."

Lesson Outline:

   1. To write simple, clear directions, first think through the whole route.
- a. Notice which highways and major roads connect the two areas.
- b. Whenever practical, choose major highways.
  1) A shortcut on smaller roads is often more confusing than a longer route on a major highway.
  2) The larger highways are generally well marked and easy to follow.
- c. Choose a route that is easy to describe, even if it is not the shortest route.

   2. Begin with a main route close to the starting point.

   3. Give special attention to each change in routes.

4. *Give only helpful details.* Too many details make the directions confusing and hard to follow. If there are points of interest that you think your friend would enjoy being alerted to, mention them separately.

5. *Double-check your information.* Make sure the steps are in the right order and are easy to understand. Be sure that each highway number and direction and each left or right turn is accurately stated.

6. *If possible, give the traveler a number to call in case he needs additional help.* Even though you double-check your directions, you may omit some essential information. Or perhaps your friend will encounter a detour because of road construction or an accident. In such a case, having a number to call will be much more convenient for him than needing to find his own way.

Class Practice

Do the following exercises with the map below.

1. Follow these directions, and tell what town you reach.

    From Markleysburg (lower right corner), go north on Route 281 to Route 40. Turn left and travel until you come to Route 381, which crosses Route 40. Turn right and follow Route 381 north until it ends at Route 711. Follow Route 711 north until it ends at Route 31. Turn left and travel about 16 miles.

2. Work together to write a set of directions for traveling from Graysville (lower left corner) to West Newton (top center, south of McKeesport).

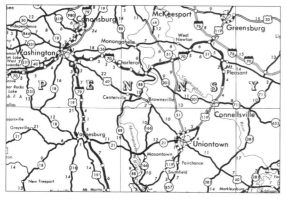

Written Exercises

A. Write directions to your school from a city that your teacher will specify.

B. Using the map in Class Practice, write directions for going from Uniontown to another town on the map. The trip should require traveling on

   a. For a well-marked highway, give the number of the road and the direction of travel.

   b. The name of an important town or city is helpful in giving the travelers a sense of the distance they must travel to the next change in routes.

   c. If the new road is a small, hard-to-recognize country road, mention helpful landmarks such as a nearby business, a railroad, or a river, and give specific distances.

4. *Give only helpful details.*

   a. Too many details make the directions confusing and hard to follow.

   b. If there are points of interest that you think your friend would enjoy being alerted to, mention them separately.

Lesson 105 Answers

Class Practice

1. Mt. Pleasant (*Teacher:* Mention that the small numbers along the roads indicate miles.)

2. Follow Route 21 east to Interstate 79. Travel on I-79 north to I-70, and turn east. Follow I-70 east to Route 31, and turn west. You will reach West Newton in about 5 miles.

Written Exercises

A. (Individual work. [*Teacher:* Choose a city from which a traveler must use about five different roads to reach your school.])

B. (Individual work. Have students read their directions to the class.)

_____

5. *Double-check your information.*

   a. Make sure the steps are in the right order and are easy to understand.

   b. Be sure that each highway number and direction and each left or right turn is accurately stated.

6. *If possible, give the traveler a number to call in case he needs additional help.*

   a. Even though you double-check your directions, you may omit some essential information.

   b. Perhaps there is a detour because of road construction or an accident.

four or five different roads. Be ready to read your directions in class, and see if your classmates can tell which town is the destination.

Review Exercises

A. For each selection, write whether the character's traits are revealed by *actions, speech, thoughts,* or *appearance.* Some selections involve more than one method of characterization. [59]

1. Melanie searched frantically for her sweater. Just as the school van drove in the lane, she found it on the floor of her closet. Dashing to the door, she tripped on her trailing shoelace.

2. "Here, let me help you with that," Ethan said to Timothy, who was struggling to open the dog food bag.

   "Thanks a lot," Timothy responded. "I just couldn't get the string to pull open."

   Ethan turned to finish his own chores, a cheerful smile lighting his face.

3. A cloud brooded over Esther Mae's usually sunny face. "Wonder how Mother is by now," she thought. "How long will she be in the hospital?" Then, as she hung up the last washcloth, she whispered, "Dear Lord, be with Mother in the hospital. Please make her well again if it is Thy will."

B. Rewrite this dialogue so that it sounds more natural.

   "Is all your homework finished?" said Stephen.

   "No, all my homework is not finished," said Nathan gloomily. "Is all your homework finished?"

   "Yes, and I am glad that it is finished. We are getting company tonight," said Stephen.

Review Exercises

A. 1. actions, appearance
   2. speech, appearance
   3. appearance, thoughts

B. (Allow reasonable variation.)

   "All your homework finished?" asked Stephen. "No," replied Nathan gloomily. "Is yours?"

   "Yes, and I'm glad. We're getting company tonight."

---

106. Coordinating Conjunctions

> **Lesson Survey**
> - A **coordinating conjunction** joins sentence parts of parallel structure and function.
> - **Correlative conjunctions** work in pairs to join sentence parts of parallel structure and function.
> - A **conjunctive adverb** can join and relate independent clauses.

The word *conjunction* comes from two Latin word elements meaning "to join together." That aptly describes the work of conjunctions: they join

Lesson 106

Purpose: To study the use of simple coordinating conjunctions, correlative conjunctions, and conjunctive adverbs.

Oral Review:

1. What is a preposition? (a word that shows the relationship between its object and some other word in the sentence)

2. A prepositional phrase can function as what three parts of speech? (adjective, adverb, noun)

3. In addition to a noun or pronoun, what may the object of a preposition be? (a verbal, a verbal phrase, a noun clause)

4. Tell how to correct these sentences.

   a. Several bales landed outside of the wagon. (outside the wagon)

   b. I sat besides Grandfather at the table. (beside Grandfather)

   c. This sweater is a little different than mine. (different from mine)

   d. Now where is that cat going to? (cat going)

   e. The car is parked in back of the house. (behind the house)

5. Commas, dashes, and parentheses can be used to set off parenthetical elements. Tell how each kind of punctuation affects a parenthetical element. (Commas make it a part of the sentence; dashes sharply emphasize it; parentheses minimize its importance.)

6. What is the function of ellipsis points? (to show the omission of one or more words)

7. If an omission within a quotation immediately follows a complete sentence, would you use three periods or four? (four)

words, phrases, or clauses in sentences. There are two main classes of conjunctions: coordinating and subordinating. This lesson covers three different types of coordinating conjunctions.

When two things are coordinated, they are arranged to work or fit together on an equal basis. So the work of *coordinating conjunctions* is to join sentence parts of parallel structure and function. *Parallel structure* means that the joined parts have the same structure: both are words, both are prepositional phrases, both are infinitive phrases, both are dependent clauses, and so forth. *Parallel function* means that the joined parts have the same function in the sentence: both are subjects, both are verbs, both are direct objects, and so forth.

Common Coordinating Conjunctions

The common coordinating conjunctions are *and, but, or, for, nor, yet,* and *so.* These words join sentence parts and show specific relationships between them. *And* shows addition or continuing thought; *but* and *yet* show contrast or unexpected outcome; *or* and *nor* show choice or option; and *for* and *so* show cause and effect.

> Shepherds of Bible times herded *sheep* <u>and</u> *goats.*
> (*And* joins single words; both are direct objects.)
> The puppies were not *under the porch* <u>or</u> *in the barn.*
> (*Or* joins prepositional phrases; both are adverbs.)
> *We had planned an early start,* <u>but</u> *the car battery was dead.*
> (*But* joins independent clauses.)

Sometimes writers or speakers use a coordinating conjunction to join a word to a phrase or a phrase to a clause. This is improper because the structure of the two parts is different. To correct such a mistake, either make the joined parts parallel or rewrite the sentence.

> **Incorrect:** Word joined to phrase
> The stream flowed *swiftly* <u>and</u> *with a merry sound* over the rocks.
> **Correct:** Joined parts made parallel
> The stream flowed *swiftly* <u>and</u> *merrily* over the rocks.
> **Correct:** Sentence rewritten
> With a merry sound, the mountain stream flowed swiftly over the rocks.
>
> **Incorrect:** Phrase joined to clause
> The pigs were rooting *in the rhubarb patch* <u>and</u> *where Mother had started a strawberry bed.*
> **Correct:** Joined parts made parallel
> The pigs were rooting *in the rhubarb patch* <u>and</u> *in Mother's new strawberry bed.*

8. What are two uses of brackets? (to enclose a comment or correction within a quotation; to serve as parentheses within parentheses)

Lesson Introduction: Before class, draw the following things on the board (or write the words): a road sign with the word *junction* and a local route number, a trailer hitch, a safety pin, a glue bottle, and a nail. Ask what these items have in common. (All are connectors.) A *junction* is the point where two roads connect. The hitch, safety pin, glue, and nail are the means of fastening two things together.

All of these illustrate the function of the conjunction. (Point out the *junction* in *conjunction*.) Conjunctions connect or fasten sentence parts together.

Lesson Outline:

1. A coordinating conjunction joins sentence parts of parallel structure and function.

a. *Parallel structure* means that the joined parts have the same structure: both are words, prepositional phrases, infinitive phrases, dependent clauses, and so forth.

b. *Parallel function* means that the joined parts have the same function in the sentence: both are subjects, verbs, direct objects, adjectives, and so forth.

c. A coordinating conjunction joins sentence parts and shows a specific relationship between them.

d. When a compound sentence is joined by a coordinating conjunction, a comma is usually placed before the conjunction. The comma may be omitted if the two clauses are very short and closely related.

2. Correlative conjunctions work in pairs to join sentence parts of parallel structure and function.

Remember that when a compound sentence is joined by a coordinating conjunction, a comma is usually placed before the conjunction. The comma may be omitted if the two clauses are very short and closely related.

Mother made some pies for supper, and Father bought some ice cream.
The bell rang and I jumped.

Correlative Conjunctions

Correlative conjunctions work in pairs to join sentence parts of parallel structure and function. The common correlative conjunctions are *both—and, either—or, neither—nor, not only—but also,* and *whether—or.*

Both the *Jew* and the *Gentile* can be saved through Jesus' blood.
(one-word subjects joined by *Both—and*)

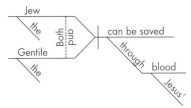

True Christians serve the Lord not only *in peaceful times* but also *in persecution.* (adverb prepositional phrases joined by *not only—but also*)

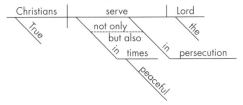

We can fully comprehend neither *how God made the world* nor *how He upholds all things today.* (noun clauses joined by *neither—nor*)

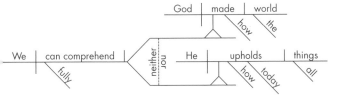

a. Be especially careful to place the correlative conjunctions just before the sentence parts that they join.

b. When using *not only—but also,* be careful not to omit the word *also.*

(Teacher: The combination "not only ... but" is correct in sentences like the following examples.

> I was not only tired but sick.
> Solomon was not only a wise king but a king wiser than any other.

In these sentences, the words after *but* serve to intensify the thought of the preceding noun or adjective, and they are heavily emphasized in speaking. *Not only* is not part of a correlative conjunction in such a construction; it is simply a combination of modifiers equal to *not just* or *not merely.*)

3. A conjunctive adverb can join and relate independent clauses. (*Note:* A conjunctive adverb acts as both a conjunction and an adverb. It is not a true conjunction, because it can be moved to different positions. In a sense, the two clauses are simply joined by a semicolon, with the conjunctive adverb modifying the verb of the second clause.)

a. A semicolon must precede a conjunctive adverb, and a comma often follows it. If the sentence reads smoothly without pausing after the conjunctive adverb, you may omit the comma.

b. Words used as conjunctive adverbs can also be used as simple adverbs.

★ **EXTRA PRACTICE**
Worksheet 41 (*Coordinating Conjunctions*)

Be especially careful to place the correlative conjunctions just before the sentence parts that they join. Otherwise, they will appear to join parts that are not parallel.

Incorrect:
> Ralph <u>either</u> *studied* his spelling words <u>or</u> his English *lesson.*

Correct:
> Ralph studied <u>either</u> his spelling *words* <u>or</u> his English *lesson.*

Incorrect: Harlan <u>not only</u> *forgot* his books <u>but also</u> his *lunch.*
Correct: Harlan forgot <u>not only</u> his *books* <u>but also</u> his *lunch.*

When using *not only—but also,* be careful not to omit the word *also.*

Incorrect: Harlan forgot <u>not only</u> his books <u>but</u> his lunch.
Correct: Harlan forgot <u>not only</u> his *books* <u>but also</u> his *lunch.*

Conjunctive Adverbs

Conjunctive adverbs join and relate independent clauses. The following words are often used as conjunctive adverbs.

accordingly	henceforth	namely
afterward	however	nevertheless
also	indeed	otherwise
anyway	instead	still
besides	likewise	then
consequently	meanwhile	therefore
furthermore	moreover	thus
hence		

Unlike the previous conjunctions, conjunctive adverbs cannot join words to words or phrases to phrases. They can join only independent clauses in a compound sentence. Notice that on a diagram the conjunctive adverb is not diagramed as a conjunction, because it is an adverb.

God is very gracious; <u>therefore</u>, we bring our needs to Him in prayer.

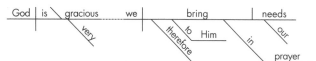

A semicolon must precede a conjunctive adverb, and a comma often follows it. If the sentence reads smoothly without pausing after the conjunctive adverb, you may omit the comma.

Incorrect:

I took aspirin for my headache, nevertheless the pain persisted.

Correct:

I took aspirin for my headache; nevertheless, the pain persisted.

The words listed above are not always conjunctive adverbs. When they are used as simple adverbs, no semicolon is needed. Only when they join independent clauses are they conjunctive adverbs.

Conjunctive adverb:

All morning we worked hard to get the hay in; then in the afternoon we had some free time.

Simple adverb:

We didn't know then that Father had planned a special treat for us.

Class Practice

A. Read the coordinating conjunctions and conjunctive adverbs. Tell whether each one is a *common coordinating conjunction,* a *conjunctive adverb,* or a *pair of correlative conjunctions.*
   1. Whales may look and act like fish in some ways; nevertheless, they really are mammals.
   2. Whales are warm-blooded, so they maintain a relatively high and constant body temperature.
   3. Fish, however, are cold-blooded; consequently, their body temperature changes with that of their environment.
   4. Whales do not have gills, but lungs.
   5. They must come up periodically for air, or they will drown.
   6. Unlike fish, whales both give birth to live offspring and nurse their young with milk.

B. Read each sentence correctly. Tell where semicolons or commas are needed.
   1. God both revealed His great love in the Old Testament and in the New.
   2. God provided for Israel faithfully and in many ways.
   3. A clear conscience is a priceless possession, therefore we should never attempt to hide wrongdoing.
   4. When our conscience smites us, either we will heed its warning or begin to harden our conscience.
   5. We must not only obey but honor our parents.

C. On the chalkboard, diagram these sentences.
   1. Both our successes and our failures should become steppingstones.
   2. We must learn from our failures; otherwise, they will not be a help.
   3. Our interests in life either build noble character or destroy it.
   4. Satan offers many allurements, yet he can provide no true satisfaction.

Lesson 106 Answers

Class Practice

A. 1. and—common coordinating conjunction; nevertheless—conjunctive adverb
   2. so—common coordinating conjunction; and—common coordinating conjunction
   3. consequently—conjunctive adverb
   4. but—common coordinating conjunction
   5. or—common coordinating conjunction
   6. both—and—pair of correlative conjunctions

B. (Improvements are underlined.)
   1. God revealed His great love both in the Old Testament and in the New.
   2. God faithfully provided for Israel in many ways.
   3. A clear conscience is a priceless possession; therefore, we should never attempt to hide wrongdoing.
   4. When our conscience smites us, we will either heed its warning or begin to harden our conscience.
   5. We must not only obey but also honor our parents.

C. 1.

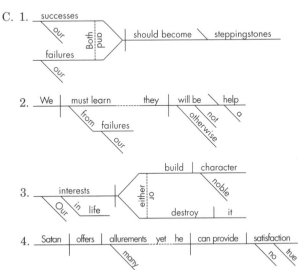

5. Righteousness provides true satisfaction not only in this life but also in the next life.

Written Exercises

A. Copy the common coordinating conjunctions (*CC*), correlative conjunctions (*Cor*), and conjunctive adverbs (*CA*); and identify them with the labels given. Some sentences have more than one conjunction.

1. Joseph eventually was made the chief ruler; however, he first suffered many things because of jealousy and false accusation.
2. His brothers had badly mistreated him, but he showed them no malice.
3. Neither he nor his family understood God's hand at work.
4. In prison Paul and Silas were chained in body; nevertheless, they were free in spirit.
5. The apostle Paul spent much time in prison, yet even there he became neither bitter nor discouraged.
6. His epistles have inspired not only our forefathers but also us.
7. Adverse circumstances are either a ladder or a stumbling block to us.
8. Fanny Crosby wrote, "To weep and sigh because I'm blind, I cannot and I won't."
9. She did not pity herself; consequently, she was happy and content.
10. Both rich and poor alike should learn contentment.

B. Write each sentence correctly.

1. Christ did not come to be served, instead He came to serve.
2. He not only taught His disciples but exemplified true service to them.
3. Neither during His years of ministry nor when He was crucified did the disciples fully understand Jesus' teachings.
4. Either Miriam scrubbed the woodwork or washed the windows.
5. Rhoda washed the dishes quickly but with care.
6. The elderly man walked down the steps slowly and with great difficulty.
7. The three girls sang at the rest home, then they visited Grandmother.
8. Mervin washed both the car and mowed the grass.

C. Diagram these sentences.

1. Wildlife not only provides useful products for us but also adds interest to our environment.
2. Our car was demolished, yet no one was badly injured.
3. I must have left my books either at home or in the car.
4. Mrs. Larson paid Mother a neighborly visit; moreover, she brought some freshly baked bread.
5. Both Henry and Jason must help in the garden.
6. Not only did Wilma bake some cookies, but also Laura made a pudding.

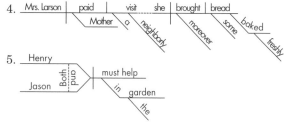

Written Exercises

5.

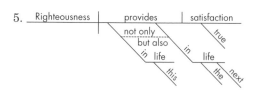

A.
1. however—CA; and—CC
2. but—CC
3. Neither—nor—Cor
4. and—CC; nevertheless—CA
5. yet—CC; neither—nor—Cor
6. not only—but also—Cor
7. either—or—Cor
8. and—CC; and—CC
9. consequently—CA; and—CC
10. Both—and—Cor

B. (Corrections are underlined. Some answers may vary slightly.)

1. Christ did not come to be served; instead, He came to serve.
2. He not only taught His disciples but <u>also</u> exemplified true service to them.
3. Neither during His years of ministry nor <u>at His crucifixion</u> did the disciples fully understand Jesus' teachings.
4. Miriam <u>either</u> scrubbed the woodwork or washed the windows.
5. Rhoda washed the dishes quickly but <u>carefully</u>.
6. <u>With great difficulty</u> the elderly man walked slowly down the steps.
7. The three girls sang at the rest home; then they visited Grandmother.
8. Mervin <u>both</u> washed the car and mowed the grass.

C. 1.

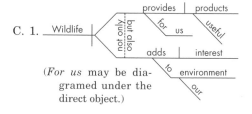

(*For us* may be diagramed under the direct object.)

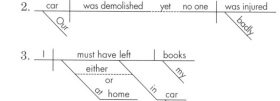

Review Exercises

A. Copy these sentences, adding commas, dashes, or parentheses where needed. Some sentences have notes to direct you. [29]

   1. Manasseh he was Hezekiah's son became deeply involved in idolatry. (Minimize the importance of the parenthetical element.)
   2. Manasseh one of Judah's most wicked kings humbled himself after the Assyrians captured him. (Make the parenthetical element part of the sentence.)
   3. Manasseh a changed man indeed removed his idols and worshiped the Lord. (Give sharp emphasis to the parenthetical element.)
   4. "The boys are watch your step, Leon!" called Father.

B. Copy these sentences, adding ellipsis points and brackets where needed. [22, 29]

   1. "The righteous also shall hold on his way, and shall be stronger and stronger" (Job 17:9).
   2. "Oh that I knew where I might find him! I would order my cause before him" (Job 23:3, 4).
   3. "The sword of him that layeth at him leviathan cannot hold: the spear, the dart, nor the habergeon coat of mail" (Job 41:26).
   4. "Do you think anyone" Michael's voice trailed away.

Review Exercises

A. 1. Manasseh (he was Hezekiah's son) became deeply involved in idolatry.
   2. Manasseh, one of Judah's most wicked kings, humbled himself after the Assyrians captured him.
   3. Manasseh—a changed man indeed—removed his idols and worshiped the Lord.
   4. "The boys are—watch your step, Leon!" called Father.

B. 1. "The righteous also shall hold on his way, and ... shall be stronger and stronger" (Job 17:9).
   2. "Oh that I knew where I might find him! ... I would order my cause before him" (Job 23:3, 4).
   3. "The sword of him that layeth at him [leviathan] cannot hold: the spear, the dart, nor the habergeon [coat of mail]" (Job 41:26).
   4. "Do you think anyone ..." Michael's voice trailed away.

107. Subordinating Conjunctions

Lesson Survey

- A **subordinating conjunction** joins a dependent adverb clause to the independent clause in a complex sentence.
- When an adverb clause introduces a sentence, it is separated from the main clause by a comma.
- When the conjunction *as* or *than* introduces an adverb clause of comparison, the clause may be elliptical.
- In formal English, the preposition *like* must not be used for the conjunction *as* or *as if*.

The two classes of conjunctions are coordinating conjunctions and subordinating conjunctions. Things that are coordinate work or fit together on an equal basis. In contrast, something that is subordinate works or fits on a lower level than another thing.

Lesson 107

Purpose: To study the use of subordinating conjunctions.

Oral Review:

1. What is a conjunction? (a word that joins words, phrases, or clauses)
2. The sentence parts joined by a coordinating conjunction must be parallel in ——— and ———. (structure, function)
3. What is meant *(a)* by "parallel structure"? *(b)* by "parallel function"? (*a.* The joined parts are both words, both prepositional phrases, and so forth. *b.* The joined parts are both subjects, both verbs, and so forth.)
4. Name the three classes of coordinating conjunctions, and give several examples of each. (common coordinating conjunctions: *and, but, or, for, nor, yet, so;* correlative conjunctions: *both—and, either—or, neither—nor, not only—but also, whether—or;* conjunctive adverbs: *accordingly, also, consequently, however, indeed, nevertheless, then, therefore*)
5. What is a preposition? (a word that shows the relationship between its object and some other word in the sentence)
6. In each sentence, identify the noun clause or the verbal phrase used as a noun, and give its function. (Noun clause and verbal phrase are underlined.)
   a. How a person studies certainly affects his actual learning experience. (subject)
   b. One goal of school life is to teach students proper methods of study. (predicate nominative)
7. Identify the verbals and verbal phrases used as adjectives or adverbs, and tell what words they

A *subordinating conjunction* joins a dependent adverb clause to the independent (main) clause in a complex sentence. The two clauses are not of equal rank. Rather, the dependent clause is subordinate to the main clause; it functions as an adverb modifying a word in the main clause.

> *Although* he was sorely tested, Job maintained his faith in God.
> (The underlined adverb clause modifies the verb *maintained* in the main clause. The subordinate clause, which has a lower rank than the main clause, is placed lower on the diagram.)

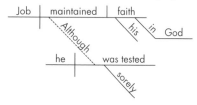

There are many subordinating conjunctions; the following list shows some common ones. A number of these words may also be used as adverbs or prepositions. They are subordinating conjunctions only when they introduce subordinate clauses.

after	even if	so that	when
although	even though	than	whenever
as	how	that	where
as if	if	though	wherever
as though	in order that	till	whether
because	provided	unless	while
before	since	until	

A subordinating conjunction shows a specific relationship between the dependent clause and the independent clause. These relationships include *when, where, how, why, under what condition, in spite of what,* and *to what degree.*

> *While* Moses held up his hands, Israel prevailed over Amalek.
> (*While* links the dependent clause to the independent clause by telling *when.*)

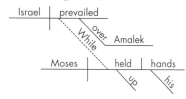

modify. (Verbals and verbal phrases are underlined; modified words are italicized.)

  a. The <u>startled</u> *birds* flew away quickly.

  b. In this book I found some *information* <u>to include in my report</u>.

  c. We *opened* the windows <u>to let in some fresh air</u>.

  d. Some people talk *too indistinctly* <u>to be understood clearly</u>.

Lesson Introduction: Tell your students to visualize a yoke of oxen pulling a wagon. (Or better yet, show them such a picture.) How is the yoke like a coordinating conjunction? (It joins two things that are equal.) Why is the hitch pin, which attaches the wagon to the yoke, not like a coordinating conjunction? (It does not join equal things.) The hitch pin is more like a subordinating conjunction. The wagon it joins to the oxen is very much dependent on the oxen that are pulling it.

Lesson Outline:

  1. A subordinating conjunction joins a dependent adverb clause to the independent (main) clause in a complex sentence. The two clauses are not of equal rank.

    a. The dependent clause is subordinate in that it functions as an adverb modifying a word in the main clause.

    b. There are many subordinating conjunctions. (Students should become familiar with those listed in the text.)

  2. A subordinating conjunction shows a specific relationship between the dependent clause and the independent clause.

    a. These relationships include *when, where, how, why, under what condition, in spite of what,* and *to what degree.*

Even though the way became hard, they should never have complained.
   (*Even though* links the dependent clause to the independent
   clause by telling *in spite of what.*)

We should not judge them more harshly *than* we judge ourselves.
   (*Than* links the dependent clause to the independent clause by
   telling *to what degree* about *more harshly.*)

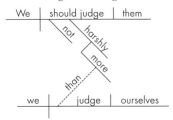

Because they show such specific relationships between clauses, subordinating conjunctions often join clauses more effectively than coordinating conjunctions do. Observe how this is true as you read the pairs of sentences below.

Compound sentence: Weak relationship
   We heard the bell, <u>and</u> we knew recess was over.
Complex sentence: Better relationship
   <u>When</u> we heard the bell, we knew recess was over.

Compound sentence: Weak relationship
   We have Bible school this week, <u>and</u> Brother Hoover has given
      smaller assignments.
Complex sentence: Better relationship
   <u>Because</u> we have Bible school this week, Brother Hoover has
      given smaller assignments.

In a complex sentence, be sure to use the main clause for the idea you want to emphasize. The other idea should be placed in the subordinate

   b. Because they show such specific relationships between clauses, subordinating conjunctions often join clauses more effectively than coordinating conjunctions do.
   c. Be sure to use the main clause for the idea you want to emphasize. This will communicate the relationship clearly and logically. (Putting the main idea in a subordinate clause is sometimes called "upside-down subordination.")

3. When an adverb clause introduces a sentence, it is separated from the main clause by a comma. Two commas are used if an adverb clause comes in the middle of a sentence.

4. When the conjunction as *or* than *introduces an adverb clause of comparison, the clause may be elliptical.* When you use a pronoun

in such an elliptical clause, be sure to choose the correct case.

5. In formal English, the preposition like *must not be used for the conjunction* as *or* as if.* In informal usage, *like* has become accepted as a conjunction.

clause. This will communicate the relationship clearly and logically.

Poor: Subordinate clause used for idea to be emphasized
When Jesus appeared to Saul, he was traveling toward Damascus.
The man was drawing his hand from his pocket when a $100 bill
dropped to the floor.
Better: Main clause used for idea to be emphasized
Jesus appeared to Saul when he was traveling toward Damascus.
As the man drew his hand from his pocket, a $100 bill dropped
to the floor.

When an adverb clause introduces a sentence, it is separated from the main clause by a comma. Two commas are used if an adverb clause comes in the middle of a sentence.

After Adam and Eve sinned, God drove them out of Eden.
Jesus, when He saw the multitudes, was moved with compassion.

When the conjunction *as* or *than* introduces an adverb clause of comparison, the clause may be elliptical. Because some words are omitted, the clause may appear to be a prepositional phrase.

The Amazon River is not as long as the Nile.
(as the Nile is long)
However, the Amazon River carries more water than the Nile.
(than the Nile carries)

When you use a pronoun in such an elliptical clause, be sure to choose the correct case. Mentally complete the clause, and decide whether the pronoun is a subject or an object. Then choose the correct pronoun.

I am not nearly as tall as he. (as he is tall)
The loud noise surprised me more than him. (than it surprised him)

In formal English, the preposition *like* must not be used for the conjunction *as* or *as if*. In informal usage, *like* has become accepted as a conjunction.

Formal: The car is running *as* it should.
Roy acted *as if* he knew a secret.
Informal: The car is running *like* it should.
Roy acted *like* he knew a secret.

Class Practice

A. Read each dependent clause, and identify the subordinating conjunction that introduces it.
1. Because Noah believed God, he built the ark as God had commanded him.

Lesson 107 Answers

Class Practice

A. (Subordinating conjunctions are underlined.)
1. Because Noah believed God;
as God had commanded him
2. While he was building the ark
3. even though Noah warned them
4. After God shut the door
5. until the waters had receded
6. than we can comprehend

2. While he was building the ark, Noah was a preacher of righteousness.
3. The people, wicked even though Noah warned them, probably mocked Noah.
4. After God shut the door, the rain began.
5. Noah's family stayed in the ark until the waters had receded.
6. Wickedness spread through the human family more rapidly than we can comprehend.

3. Read each sentence in correct, formal English. If a comma is missing, tell where it should be added. If the sentence is correct, say *correct*.
1. If we need wisdom we can seek it of God.
2. Godly wisdom enables us to view life like God views it.
3. This damp weather bothers Grandfather more than us.
4. Grandmother is limping like her arthritis causes her great pain.
5. Lucy has not swept the kitchen floor as often as me.

C. Make each sentence more effective either by changing it to a complex sentence with an adverb clause, or by rewording it so that the idea to be emphasized is in the main clause.
1. The Bible is God's Word, and we order our lives by its teachings.
2. Men slept while an enemy sowed tares in the field.
3. Although the mouse escaped, the trap snapped.
4. The bright colors flamed across the western sky, and we watched the sunset.

D. On the chalkboard, diagram the sentences in Part A.

Written Exercises

A. Copy each adverb clause, and underline the subordinating conjunction.
1. Since whales are powerful animals, early whaling was dangerous work.
2. When the lookout sighted a spout of shooting water, he called, "There she blows!"
3. The smaller boats were immediately lowered so that some of the crew could go closer to the whale.
4. The harpooner, standing with his harpoon ready as the boat neared the whale, waited until the boat almost touched the huge animal.
5. After the whale was harpooned, it usually dived or swam swiftly away.
6. If it dived too deeply, the men cut the line so that they would not be pulled underwater.
7. If a whale swam away, it often took the men on a fast "Nantucket sleigh ride" that lasted for hours.
8. Many whalers lost their lives because whales sometimes attacked their boats.

B. Copy the words that are wrong or informal, and write the correct words

Written Exercises

A. 1. <u>Since</u> whales are powerful animals
2. <u>When</u> the lookout sighted a spout of shooting water
3. <u>so that</u> some of the crew could go closer to the whale
4. <u>as</u> the boat neared the whale;
<u>until</u> the boat almost touched the huge animal
5. <u>After</u> the whale was harpooned
6. <u>If</u> it dived too deeply;
<u>so that</u> they would not be pulled underwater
7. <u>If</u> a whale swam away
8. <u>because</u> whales sometimes attacked their boats

(Numbers 2–6 are on page 542.)
B. 1. comma needed after *wisdom*
2. Godly wisdom enables us to view life <u>as</u> God views it.
3. correct
4. Grandmother is limping <u>as if</u> her arthritis causes her great pain.
5. Lucy has not swept the kitchen floor as often as <u>I</u>.

C. 1. Because the Bible is God's Word, we order our lives by its teaching.
2. While men slept, an enemy sowed tares in the field.
3. Although the trap snapped, the mouse escaped.
4. The bright colors flamed across the western sky as we watched the sunset.

D. 1.

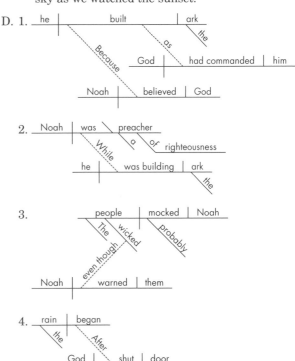

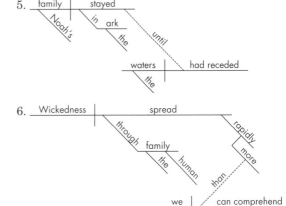

beside them. If a word should be followed by a comma, copy the word and add the comma. If the sentence has no error, write *correct*.

1. On one occasion, David acted like he was insane.
2. When the Philistine king saw his actions he wanted David to leave.
3. Martha certainly gets better grades in art than me.
4. These cookies do not look like I had expected them to look.
5. Fred worked in the garden longer than I.
6. Today we shall work until the sun sets.

C. Make each sentence more effective either by changing it to a complex sentence with an adverb clause, or by rewriting it so that the idea to be emphasized is in the main clause.

1. We prepared a downstairs bedroom, and Grandfather planned to spend a few months with us.
2. He was with us while we had the biggest snow in many years.
3. Father was plowing the back field, and the tractor broke down.
4. The cold front had passed, and the skies cleared quickly.
5. Although it was in surprisingly good condition, the book was quite old.

D. Diagram these sentences.

1. If we seek the Lord, He will bless our lives.
2. God's blessing, richer than we can measure, brings true contentment.
3. As we read the Bible, we should obey it because it is God's Word.
4. We should never live as if God's Word were unimportant.
5. The message of the Bible is presented so simply that all can understand it.

Review Exercises

A. Copy each verbal, verbal phrase, or clause used as a noun. Write what sentence part each one is: subject (*S*), direct object (*DO*), predicate nominative (*PN*), or object of a preposition (*OP*). [40, 41]

1. Memorizing Bible verses takes diligent effort.
2. Our deepest desire should be that God is glorified in our lives.
3. To forgive requires a right attitude toward God, others, and ourselves.
4. We want to be faithful to the Lord at all times.
5. By seeking advice from our parents, we safeguard our own lives.
6. Whoever lightly regards parental guidance is inviting spiritual disaster.

B. Copy each verbal or verbal phrase used as an adjective. Also copy the substantive that it modifies. [84]

1. Father posted a list of chores to be done today.
2. As we stepped inside, the aroma of fried potatoes greeted us.
3. The children, gathering for family worship, sat quietly in their seats.
4. The passage to read is found in 1 John 3.

Review Exercises

A. 1. Memorizing Bible verses—S
   2. that God is glorified in our lives—PN
   3. To forgive—S
   4. to be faithful to the Lord at all times—DO
   5. seeking advice from our parents—OP
   6. Whoever lightly regards parental guidance—S

B. 1. to be done today, chores
   2. fried, potatoes
   3. gathering for family worship, children
   4. to read, passage

B. 1. like, as if   4. like, as
   2. actions,   5. correct
   3. me, I   6. correct

C. (Allow reasonable variation.)

1. We prepared a downstairs bedroom because Grandfather planned to spend a few months with us.
2. While he was with us, we had the biggest snow in many years.
3. Father was plowing the back field when the tractor broke down.
   or While Father was plowing the back field, the tractor broke down.
4. When the cold front had passed, the skies cleared quickly.
5. Although the book was quite old, it was in surprisingly good condition.

D. 1.

2.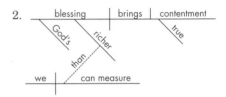

3.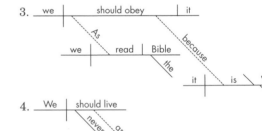

4.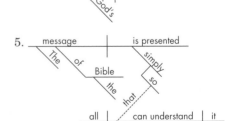

5.

C. Copy each infinitive or infinitive phrase used as an adverb. Also copy the word (or unit) it modifies. [94]
1. We should not pray to be seen of men.
2. Jesus went to a desert place to pray alone.
3. To welcome my uncle back from the Philippines, we had a family gathering.
4. Yesterday I felt too sick to get out of bed.

C. 1. to be seen of men, should pray
2. to pray alone, went
3. To welcome my uncle back from the Philippines, had
4. to get out of bed, too sick

---

108. Descriptive Writing

> **Lesson Survey**
> - Descriptive writing paints colorful word pictures of a scene or an event.
> - A good description uses vivid, concrete words.
> - A description often includes figurative language.
> - Descriptive writing appeals to the five senses.

An author may write a description for the sole purpose of describing something. More often, however, he weaves description into a larger piece of writing. For example, he may use description to help provide the setting or the mood in a story. Suppose he is writing about a visit to Grandma's house. By giving a short description of Grandma's cozy kitchen, with its aroma of popcorn and its old-fashioned cupboards full of goodies, he can set a pleasant, cheerful mood for the rest of the story. Descriptive writing definitely fills an important place in stories and other compositions.

Descriptive writing paints colorful word pictures of a scene or an event. A description of a scene portrays the outstanding details of a particular place such as a room or a landscape, usually in spatial order. It moves from left to right, from near to distant, from a main, central figure to less important details, or in any other progression that makes the description logical and meaningful.

A description of an event portrays in chronological order the outstanding details of a happening. Of course, such a description is actually a narrative. Its vivid, colorful expressions help to give the reader a clear mental picture of the action being described—almost as if it were taking place right before his eyes. Study the following examples.

Lesson 108

Purpose: To teach characteristics of good description.

IMPORTANT: Tell your pupils to choose a book, get it approved, and read it in preparation for giving an oral book report. (See Lesson 121.) They should read the entire book carefully, looking for information to include in the book report.

Oral Review:

1. When writing directions to a place, what information should you give about changing (a) to a large, well-marked highway? (b) to a small, hard-to-find road? (a. the route number and the direction of travel, a nearby town or city; b. helpful landmarks and specific distances)
2. Why is it important to give only helpful details? (to avoid confusion; to make directions easy to follow)

3. Define these terms.
   a. simile (figurative comparison using *like* or *as*)
   b. metaphor (figurative comparison without *like* or *as*)
   c. personification (describing a thing or quality as if it had the characteristics of a living creature)
   d. hyperbole (artistic exaggeration)
4. Which is generally more direct and forceful, the active voice or the passive voice? (active voice)

Lesson Introduction: Fanny Crosby became blind when but a few weeks old. Although she grew up without seeing the beautiful things in the world, she wrote many poems. How could she write the beautiful poetry that she did? The secret lay in her grandmother's patient, devoted efforts. Her grandmother, knowing that Fanny would never see, described everything about the surrounding world in

Description of a scene:

John Condon stood beside the clear, brawling stream in Madrone Canyon. Above the poplars and alders around him, the great cliff soared almost sheer, broken here and there by ledges and dotted with the dark green of sumac, juniper, and scrub oak. Along the crest almost a thousand feet above, he could see jutting black spires of pines and firs. He noted a lime-whitened ledge under a bulging overhang of rock, about a hundred feet from the top.

Description of an event:

Once more the falcon dived, and again the eagle rolled to receive him. Condon watched spellbound. That the falcon could avoid a death grip a third time appeared impossible. Then he executed a maneuver that left Condon gasping. Within five feet of those deadly claws and at lightning speed, the falcon flung himself to one side and instantly jibed back at the eagle's head, his hard-clenched talons striking with the force of a bullet.

The broad, powerful wings of the eagle threshed convulsively and then lay limp, and the great body plunged helplessly downward. Condon expelled his pent-up breath in a mighty sigh as the falcon circled out over the canyon, harshly screaming his victory.

The paragraphs above effectively paint colorful word pictures. What are the qualities that make them good descriptions?

Vivid, Concrete Words

A good description uses vivid, concrete words. For example, exact nouns help to paint clear, specific pictures. If possible, use a noun that names exactly what you mean, rather than a general noun modified by adjectives. In the first sample description, the author wrote "poplars and alders" rather than "slender trees." Find several other exact nouns that add to the descriptiveness of these paragraphs.

Does this mean that you should not use adjectives with exact nouns? Of course not. Colorful adjectives can further sharpen and describe exact nouns. The first example would be much less descriptive had the author merely written "stream" instead of "clear, brawling stream," "ledge" instead of "lime-whitened ledge," and "overhang" instead of "bulging overhang." Now look at the second example and pick out the colorful adjectives that sharpen the exact nouns.

Expressive verbs also contribute to the rich color of word pictures. Whenever practical, avoid linking verbs, weak action verbs modified by adverbs, and verbs in the passive voice. The examples above contain the expressive verbs *soared, dived, rolled, flung,* and a number of others. Compare the following expressions with the original wording.

order to train the little girl's imagination. These word pictures obviously bore fruit, for Fanny wrote over five thousand hymns during her ninety-five years of life.

Lesson Outline:

1. Descriptive writing paints colorful word pictures of a scene or an event.

    a. A description of a scene portrays the outstanding details of a particular place such as a room or a landscape, usually in spatial order.

    b. A description of an event portrays in chronological order the outstanding details of a happening. (It focuses on a scene rather than on a problem to be solved.)

2. A good description uses vivid, concrete words.

    a. Exact nouns help to paint clear, specific pictures.

    b. Colorful adjectives can further sharpen and describe exact nouns.

    c. Expressive verbs contribute to the rich color of word pictures. Whenever practical, avoid linking verbs, weak action verbs modified by adverbs, and verbs in the passive voice.

    d. Colorful adverbs can further sharpen and describe expressive verbs.

3. A description often includes figurative language.

4. Descriptive writing appeals to the five senses.

Linking verb:
> The great cliff <u>was</u> almost sheer.

Weak action verb and adverbs:
> Once more the falcon <u>flew</u> swiftly downward.

Verb in passive voice:
> Condon's pent-up breath <u>was expelled</u> in a mighty sigh.

Expressive verbs:
> The great cliff <u>soared</u> almost sheer.
> Once more the falcon <u>dived</u>.
> Condon <u>expelled</u> his pent-up breath in a mighty sigh.

This emphasis on expressive verbs does not mean that you should avoid all adverbs. As colorful adjectives sharpen exact nouns, so colorful adverbs sharpen expressive verbs. In the following sentence, all the descriptive adjectives and adverbs are underlined.

> The <u>broad</u>, <u>powerful</u> wings of the eagle threshed <u>convulsively</u> and then lay <u>limp</u>, and the <u>great</u> body plunged <u>helplessly</u> <u>downward</u>.

Figurative Language

Descriptions often include figurative language: similes, metaphors, personification, and hyperboles. By making effective comparisons, these figures of speech paint vivid word pictures. In the second sample description, "at lightning speed" is a hyperbole that describes the swiftness of the falcon's maneuver. The phrases "instantly jibed back" and "striking with the force of a bullet" are metaphors that further clarify the picture of the falcon's attack. *Jibe* in a literal sense means "to shift a sail from one side of a boat to the other when sailing before the wind."

Appeal to the Five Senses

Descriptive writing appeals to the five senses. An author of good description pays close attention to details that help the reader to form a clear mental image of the scene or event. He shares the things he sees, hears, feels, smells, or tastes so that the reader can experience them in his mind.

The sample paragraphs, like most descriptive writing, appeal primarily to the sense of sight. Can you see the steep cliff soaring upward, dotted with dark green shrubbery? Can you see the falcon's swift dive and the breathtaking maneuver by which he killed the eagle? Can you see the dead eagle plunging limp and helpless to the ground?

The sample description also contains a bit of appeal to your hearing. Can you hear Condon's mighty sigh as he expels his pent-up breath? Can you hear the falcon's harsh cry of victory?

A good description is based on personal observation. A writer who has learned to observe carefully for himself can describe things much more accurately than someone who depends on facts he has heard or read.

Class Practice

A. For each of these paragraphs, give examples of the following types of descriptive language: exact nouns, expressive verbs, colorful modifiers, figurative language.

1.   Hannah Wright had just taken the last loaves from the oven. She dusted off some ashes from the wooden bread shovel before she replaced it in its corner. Bright spring sunlight streamed into the kitchen, warming the stone floor to a deep brown color and touching the mugs and platters on the dresser till they fairly winked back its brightness. A robin outside was whistling gaily, and a long branch of lilac buds peeped in at the open upper door.

                                                   —From "Letitia's Plea"

2.   One side of the ravine was in darkness. Along the crest of the eastern slope was the rich foliage of many treetops—great pines and hemlocks of the ancient unviolated forest—revealed against the orange disk of a full moon just rising. The low rays slanting through the moveless tops lit strangely the upper portion of the opposite steep—the western wall of the ravine. It was barren, unlike its fellow, bossed with great rocky projections and harsh with stunted junipers. From the sluggish dark in the depths of the ravine came the brawl of a swollen, obstructed stream.

                                                   —From "The Cries in the Cabin"

3.   "It will soon be dark!" Herman exclaimed. The sky wore a troubled, grayish purple mask blotched with thick, dark clouds. The snow on the ground shifted uneasily in the teasing wind.

                                                —From "The One-Way Command"

4.   Under the deepening cover of darkness, the storm grew bolder. Faster and thicker fell the snowflakes. Wilder and fiercer wailed the wind. Snow on the ground whirled to join snow from above in one stinging, blinding mass. Sometimes Herman could see Mr. Wolfe cowering in the sleigh ahead, but often he was engulfed in the whirling whiteness.

                                                —From "The One-Way Command"

B. Write some descriptive sentences about the view from your classroom window or a picture in your classroom. Include exact nouns, expressive verbs, colorful modifiers, and figurative language.

Written Exercises

A. Write two descriptive sentences about each of these items. Include figurative language for at least two of the items.

Lesson 108 Answers

Class Practice

A. 1. *exact nouns:* loaves, oven, ashes, shovel, corner, sunlight, kitchen, mugs, platters, dresser, robin, buds

    expressive verbs: dusted, replaced, streamed, winked, whistling, peeped

    colorful modifiers: wooden, bread, Bright, spring, warming, stone, deep brown, touching, fairly, gaily, lilac, open, upper

    figurative language: winked back, lilac buds peeped in

2. *exact nouns:* ravine, crest, slope, foliage, pines, hemlocks, disk, rays, steep, projections, junipers, brawl, stream

    expressive verbs: lit

    colorful modifiers: eastern, rich, ancient, unviolated, revealed, orange, rising, low, slanting, moveless, strangely, upper, opposite, western, barren, bossed, rocky, harsh, stunted, sluggish, swollen, obstructed

    figurative language: the sluggish dark; the brawl of the stream

3. *exact nouns:* mask, clouds

    expressive verbs: exclaimed, wore, shifted

    colorful modifiers: troubled, grayish purple, blotched, thick, dark, uneasily, teasing

    figurative language: sky wore a mask, snow shifted uneasily, teasing wind

4. *exact nouns:* cover, storm, mass, sleigh, whiteness

    expressive verbs: fell, wailed, whirled, engulfed

    colorful modifiers: deepening, bolder, Faster, thicker, Wilder, fiercer, stinging, blinding, cowering, whirling (Participles make good adjectives for describing an event.)

    figurative language: storm grew bolder

B. (Individual work.)

1. A bookshelf in the classroom
2. The teacher's desk
3. The bulletin board display
4. A good friend

B. Write a descriptive paragraph about one of these subjects. Include exact nouns, expressive verbs, colorful modifiers, and figurative language.
   1. A thunderhead or thunderstorm
   2. A favorite spot
   3. Your front (or back) yard
   4. Your family gathering for a meal
   5. Your playground at recess

109. Interjections

> **Lesson Survey**
> - An **interjection** is a word that expresses strong feeling.
> - Use interjections cautiously and sparingly.
> - The use of a comma or an exclamation point depends upon the degree of emotion intended by the writer.
> - An interjection is diagramed on a line separate from the rest of the sentence.

Of the eight parts of speech, interjections are unique. An interjection never functions as part of a sentence; it always stands alone as an independent element. Therefore, an interjection can always be removed without changing the meaning of the sentence.

An *interjection* is a word that expresses strong feeling. The cry or exclamation of an interjection can express pleasure, admiration, adoration, surprise, pain, or any other feeling. The following list shows some common interjections.

ah	behold	ho	ouch	what
aha	good	hurrah	say	whew
alas	ha	lo	well	why
amen	hallelujah	oh		

<u>Hallelujah</u>! God has answered our prayers.
<u>Lo</u>, the presence of Jesus is ever with us.
<u>Ouch</u>! I hit my thumb.

In addition to the common interjections listed above, words that represent sounds are often used as interjections.

Written Exercises
(All answers are individual work.)

Lesson 109

Purpose: To study the definition, use, and punctuation of interjections.

Oral Review:
1. What is a subordinating conjunction? (a word that joins a dependent adverb clause to an independent clause)
2. The sentence parts joined by a coordinating conjunction must be parallel in —— and ——. (structure, function)
3. What is meant *(a)* by "parallel structure"? *(b)* by "parallel function"? (*a.* The joined parts are both words, both prepositional phrases, and so forth. *b.* The joined parts are both subjects, both verbs, and so forth.)
4. What three tests can you use in distinguishing between adjectives and adverbs? (What part of speech does it modify? What question does it answer? Can the modifier be moved to a different place without changing the meaning of the sentence?)

Lesson Introduction: The word *interjection* has three word elements: *inter,* meaning "between" or "among"; *ject,* from the Latin *jacere,* meaning "to throw"; and *ion,* meaning "action or condition of." So the etymological meaning of *interjection* is "the action of throwing something among other things." That describes interjections, doesn't it? They are forceful words used to express feelings, thrown among words used to express specific ideas.

Lesson Outline:
1. An interjection is a word that expresses strong feeling. (Students should become familiar with the common interjections listed in the lesson.)

Hiss! The escaping steam caught our attention.
Dong, dong! The town clock sounded out the time.
Moo! Bossie welcomed us to the stable.

In fact, almost any word used as an independent exclamation is an interjection. However, if a verb is used to give a one-word request or command, it is not considered an interjection.

Water! The thirsty travelers finally found water. (interjection)
Say, do you know what time it is? (interjection)
Beware! The enemy seeks your soul. (verb; a one-word command)

Do you see how the last two examples are different? In the sentence with *Say,* that word does not give a command. It is simply an introductory word, the same as an interjection like *oh* or *well*. The word *Beware* does give a command: (you) Beware!

Use interjections cautiously and sparingly. God's people must avoid many interjections used by the ungodly. The name of God or any alteration of it must never be used as an interjection, for that is a form of taking His Name in vain. It is sacrilegious to use interjections referring to characteristics of God (His goodness, graciousness, holiness, and so forth) or to parts of God's creation (such as heaven, earth, or the stars). Interjections that refer to hell, Satan, or any part of his kingdom are evil. Neither is it proper to use a common word like *boy, man,* or *rats* as an interjection that has nothing to do with its normal meaning.

Even interjections that are proper in themselves can be used in a wrong way. The Bible commands us to control our emotions and our words. It is wrong to use exclamations of anger or disgust. It is also wrong to use interjections too freely. Remember Jesus' words: "That every idle word that men shall speak, they shall give account thereof in the day of judgment" (Matthew 12:36).

The use of a comma or an exclamation point depends upon the degree of emotion intended by the writer. Mild interjections are followed by commas; more emphatic ones are marked with exclamation points. If an exclamation point is used, the next word must be capitalized. Strong interjections like *amen, hallelujah, hurrah, ouch, what,* and *whew* are usually followed by exclamation points, and so are many words that represent sounds. The other interjections are frequently punctuated either way. Consider the following examples as well as the ones used earlier in this lesson.

Well, the downstairs floors should be swept.
Well! We surely didn't expect this!

If the whole sentence shows strong feeling, a comma may be used after the interjection and an exclamation point at the end of the sentence.

a. Words that represent sounds are often interjections.

Note: An interjection is italicized when it "quotes" a sound but not when it simply names a sound. Compare the following examples.

Crash! The window shattered into many small pieces.
The window shattered with a loud crash.

b. Almost any word used as an independent exclamation is an interjection. However, if a verb is used to give a one-word request or command, it is not considered an interjection. (It is a complete sentence with *you* understood.)

2. Use interjections cautiously and sparingly.

a. Avoid using the following kinds of interjections.
1) The name of God or any alteration of it.
2) Words that refer to characteristics of God.
3) Words that refer to parts of God's creation.
4) Words that refer to hell, Satan, or any part of his kingdom.
5) Common words used as interjections that have nothing to do with their normal meanings.
b. Avoid using interjections in a wrong way.
1) Do not use exclamations of anger or disgust.
2) Do not use interjections too freely.

3. The use of a comma or an exclamation point depends upon the degree of emotion intended by the writer.

<u>Lo,</u> what peace Jesus gives!

Since an interjection has no direct relationship to the rest of the sentence, it is diagramed on a line separate from the rest of the sentence.

Good, you have returned your library book.

Alas! We waited too long.

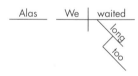

Class Practice

A. Identify each interjection, and tell whether it should be followed by a *comma* or an *exclamation point.* Say *yes* or *no* to tell whether the next word should be capitalized.
1. Behold the Lord is the sovereign King.
2. Hallelujah the grace of God is sufficient for every need.
3. Lo our God will make a way for His people.
4. *Snap* a breaking twig alerted the traveler to danger.
5. What nobody has seen a panther in these woods for several years.

B. Read these sentences, inserting a different appropriate interjection for each.
1. ——! That hurt!
2. ——, the wind in the trees is making that noise.
3. ——! Did you say it is snowing again?
4. ——, it was too late.

C. On the chalkboard, diagram the sentences in Part A.

Written Exercises

A. Copy the interjections used in these Bible verses. (Some verses have two.) Not every interjection is followed by a comma or an exclamation point.
1. Exodus 32:31   4. Ezekiel 26:2
2. Ruth 4:1   5. Daniel 3:25
3. 2 Kings 6:5   6. Revelation 19:4

B. Copy each interjection, and put a comma or an exclamation point after it. Also copy the word after it, using a capital letter if necessary.

    a. Mild interjections are followed by commas; more emphatic ones are marked with exclamation points.

    b. If an exclamation point is used, the next word must be capitalized.

    c. Strong interjections like *amen, hallelujah, hurrah, ouch, what,* and *whew* are usually followed by exclamation points, and so are many words that represent sounds.

    d. The other interjections are frequently punctuated either way.

    e. If the whole sentence shows strong feeling, a comma may be used after the interjection and an exclamation point at the end of the sentence.

    4. An interjection is diagramed on a line separate from the rest of the sentence.

Lesson 109 Answers
Class Practice
A. 1. Behold, no   4. *Snap!* yes
   2. Hallelujah! yes   5. What! yes
   3. Lo, no

B. 1. Ouch   3. What
   2. Oh (*or* ah, well)   4. Alas

C.

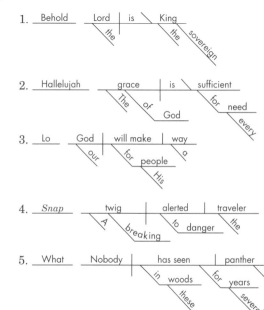

Written Exercises
A. 1. Oh   4. Aha
   2. behold, Ho   5. Lo
   3. Alas   6. Amen, Alleluia

1. Oh thank you for this delicious treat.
2. Hurrah this letter says Uncle Leland's plan to visit us next week.
3. Well you certainly were brave to try that!
4. Alas the car is out of gas.
5. Ouch that was a wasp!
6. Whew the air is muggy today.
7. Quick go call Father!
8. Plop my book fell onto the floor.
9. Ah this is just what I expected!
10. Cats we won't have cats in this house!

C. Diagram these sentences.
   1. Why, this is a pleasant surprise!
   2. Skunks! Do we have skunks under the back porch?
   3. Good, the mail has now arrived.
   4. Well, Aunt Louise did send us a lovely post card.
   5. Aha! Now I caught that runaway rabbit!

Review Exercises

A. Label each underlined item *adj.* or *adv.* [97]
   1. (a) In every distress, God bids us to look (b) up and trust His (c) fatherly care.
   2. God's love, (a) deep beyond our ability (b) to comprehend fully, inspires us to trust Him (c) even though life may seem perplexing.
   3. The experiences (a) that seem so perplexing can be steppingstones (b) to greater faith.
   4. A (a) godly person (b) daily turns (c) to the Lord (d) to seek His blessing.
   5. (a) If we truly love the Lord, we will seek His blessing so intently (b) that all else fades into the background.

B. Write correctly each underlined expression that contains a mistake. If it has no error, write *correct*. [104]
   1. As soon as I stepped in the kitchen, I smelled the pies.
   2. There should be plenty of pie to divide between the four boys.
   3. Have you heard where Mr. Shreeve is moving to?
   4. Rover sat beside the steps to welcome us home.
   5. Mr. Blake's idea of good recreation certainly differs with ours.
   6. Several people became angry at the brethren who were handing out tracts.
   7. My bicycle is parked in back of the house.
   8. Several times we had to wait on the younger ones to catch up.

B. (Allow reasonable variation.)

   1. Oh, thank   6. Whew! The
   2. Hurrah! This   7. Quick! Go
   3. Well, you   8. Plop! My
   4. Alas! The   9. Ah, this
   5. Ouch! That   10. Cats! We

C. 1.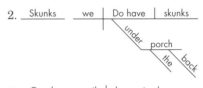

   2.

   3.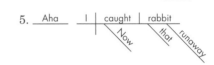

   4. Well   Aunt Louise | did send | post card
                            us   a   lovely

   5. Aha   I | caught | rabbit
              Now   that runaway

Review Exercises

A. 1. a. adv.   b. adv.   c. adj.
   2. a. adj.   b. adj.   c. adv.
   3. a. adj.   b. adj.
   4. a. adj.   b. adv.   c. adv.   d. adv.
   5. a. adv.   b. adv.

B. 1. stepped into the kitchen
   2. divide among
   3. is moving
   4. correct
   5. differs from ours
   6. angry with the brethren
   7. behind the house
   8. wait for the younger ones

110. Review of the Parts of Speech

Lesson Survey
- Know the definitions and abbreviations for all the eight parts of speech.
- The function of a word in a sentence determines what part of speech it is.

Generally you can look at a word and immediately recognize its part of speech. When you see the word *dictionary,* you know it is a noun. You recognize *silently* as an adverb and *or* as a conjunction. But what part of speech is *east*? It may be a noun, naming the general direction of the sunrise (in the *east*); an adjective, meaning "toward or from the east" (an *east* wind); or an adverb, meaning "toward the east" (traveled *east*).

As this example shows, the function of a word in a sentence determines what part of speech it is. The following paragraphs summarize the parts of speech and give some reminders that should be helpful for recognizing parts of speech in sentences.

1. *A noun (n.) names a person, place, thing, or idea.* Most nouns are simple to recognize, but others are more difficult. For example, an adjective is sometimes used as a noun, especially when it describes a particular characteristic of people (the *poor,* the *righteous*). Verbals can also be used as nouns (*walking, to walk*). All the nouns in the following sentences are labeled. Note that an infinitive is labeled as a single item.

> The <u>wise</u> follow the <u>way</u> of <u>truth</u>.
>
> <u>To distinguish</u> the <u>parts</u> of <u>speech</u> takes careful <u>thinking</u>.

2. *A pronoun (pron.) takes the place of a noun.* Sometimes a pronoun also modifies a noun (*his* shirt, *that* house, *which* book). When parts of speech are labeled, such a word should be considered an adjective. It should be labeled as a pronoun only when it stands alone.

> <u>That</u> is the man <u>whom</u> <u>I</u> met.
>
> Is that book the <u>one</u> <u>you</u> want? (*That* is an adjective.)

3. *A verb (v.) expresses action or being.* In general, there is only one verb or verb phrase in a clause, unless there is a compound verb. All other verb forms in a sentence are verbals.

> The girls <u>were</u> <u>baking</u> cakes and <u>cooking</u> pudding. (compound verb)

Lesson 110

Purpose: To study the eight parts of speech.

Oral Review:

1. What is an interjection? (a word that expresses strong feeling)
2. How is an interjection set off from the rest of a sentence? (a comma for a mild interjection; an exclamation point for a strong interjection)
3. Name the two general classes of conjunctions. (coordinating, subordinating)
4. Give several examples of each of the following words.
   a. common coordinating conjunctions (and, but, or, for, nor, yet, so)
   b. correlative conjunctions (both—and, either—or, neither—nor, not only—but also, whether—or)
   c. conjunctive adverbs (accordingly, also, consequently, however, indeed, moreover, nevertheless, then, therefore)
   d. subordinating conjunctions (after, although, because, even though, than, until, while)
5. Name the word order that fits each description.
   a. The complete predicate precedes the complete subject. (inverted)
   b. The complete subject comes between two parts of the complete predicate. (mixed)
   c. The complete subject precedes the complete predicate. (natural)
6. Which punctuation marks should always be placed inside quotation marks? (comma, period)
7. Which should always be placed outside quotation marks? (colon, semicolon)
8. (*a*) When should a question mark or an exclamation point be placed inside quotation marks? (*b*) When should they be placed outside? (*a.* when the quotation is a question or an exclamation; *b.* when the whole sentence is a question or an exclamation, but the quotation is not)

Lesson Introduction: Suppose a girl is baking a cake. The recipe calls for two cups of sugar, so she grabs a nearby canister. "I suppose this is sugar," she says to herself as she hastily scoops out two cups of the white granules. But sugar it is not! And the cake is—well, a disaster. Salt and sugar look quite similar. If only a little more care had been taken, think of the waste that could have been avoided.

Baking bread <u>is</u> a weekly chore at our house.
> (*Baking* is a verbal used as a noun.)

The baking bread <u>smelled</u> delicious.
> (*Baking* is a verbal used as an adjective.)

4. *An adjective (adj.) modifies a substantive by telling* which, whose, how many, *or* what kind of. Remember that nouns and verbals can be used as adjectives. If an infinitive is used in this way, it is labeled as a single item.

<u>That</u> <u>baking</u> <u>pumpkin</u> bread smells <u>delicious</u>.
We are <u>thankful</u> for <u>such</u> <u>good</u> things <u>to eat</u>.

5. *An adverb (adv.) modifies a verb, an adjective, another adverb, or a verbal by telling* how, when, where, *or* to what degree. Again, an infinitive is labeled as a single item if it is used in this way.

<u>Soon</u> the jet flew <u>too</u> <u>high</u> <u>to be</u> <u>easily</u> visible.

6. *A preposition (prep.) shows the relationship between its object and some other word in the sentence.* Remember that some words may be either prepositions or adverbs. They are prepositions only when they have objects.

Both <u>of</u> the children fell down as they ran <u>down</u> the path.
> (The first *down* is an adverb.)

7. *A conjunction (conj.) joins words, phrases, or clauses.*

We should love <u>and</u> serve the Lord, <u>for</u> He died for us.
> (The second *for* is a preposition.)

8. *An interjection (interj.) expresses strong feeling.* Remember that almost any word can be used as an interjection.

<u>Oh</u>, look! Aunt Sarah's flight has come in.
> (*Look* is a verb, not an interjection.)

<u>Home</u>! There is no place like home.

Class Practice

A. Name the part of speech for each underlined word.
1. We must <u>stand</u> <u>for</u> the <u>right</u> at <u>all</u> times.
2. A <u>mind</u> wholly <u>devoted</u> to <u>right</u> <u>values</u> is a <u>well</u> of righteousness.

Sometimes words are like sugar and salt. Adjectives may be hard to distinguish from adverbs, conjunctions from prepositions, and nouns from adjectives. But if we put some care into our work, we shall be better able to use the English language effectively for God's glory.

Lesson Outline:

1. Know the definitions and abbreviations for all the eight parts of speech.

2. The function of a word in a sentence determines what part of speech it is. The parts of speech are summarized below.

> (1) *A noun (n.) names a person, place, thing, or idea.* Adjectives and verbals can be used as nouns. If an infinitive is used as a noun (or some other part of speech), it is labeled as a single item.

Lesson 110 Answers

Class Practice

A. 1. stand—v.; for—prep.; right—n.; all—adj.
2. mind—n.; devoted—adj.; right—adj.; values—n.; well—n.

> (2) *A pronoun (pron.) takes the place of a noun.* If a pronoun also modifies a noun, it is considered an adjective rather than a pronoun.
>
> (3) *A verb (v.) expresses action or being.* In general, there is only one verb or verb phrase in a clause, unless there is a compound verb.
>
> (4) *An adjective (adj.) modifies a substantive by telling* which, whose, how many, *or* what kind of. Nouns and verbals can be used as adjectives.
>
> (5) *An adverb (adv.) modifies a verb, an adjective, another adverb, or a verbal by telling* how, when, where, *or* to what degree. Infinitives can be used as adverbs.

3. God's people have always <u>devoted</u> themselves to truth, <u>for</u> <u>that</u> is <u>right</u>.
4. You need <u>to right</u> the <u>plant</u> <u>stand</u> <u>that</u> you have knocked <u>over</u>.
5. <u>That</u> <u>plant</u> has <u>run</u> its <u>vines</u> <u>over</u> the <u>wall</u>.
6. <u>All</u> have finished their <u>work</u> <u>well</u>, and Brother Stephen <u>values</u> their efforts.

B. Name the part of speech for each word.
1. God promises to bless the faithful.
2. Lo, His presence continually surrounds us, although we do not see Him with our physical sight.
3. To deceive another person is never right.
4. The priest and the Levite ignored the injured man; however, the Samaritan showed a neighborly attitude to him.
5. The children's efforts to surprise their parents were well rewarded.
6. When we compared our pictures, most of us thought that his had the best shading.
7. In the morning Father will post the work to do for the day.
8. The broken fence post should be replaced before the cows push through the fence and get out.
9. The water of the mountain stream felt refreshingly cool to me.
10. Before evening, the creeks had become so flooded that many roads were nearly impassable.

Written Exercises

A. Write the abbreviations of the parts of speech for the underlined words.
1. "Blessed are the <u>pure</u> in heart."
2. A <u>pure</u> conscience is a wonderful blessing.
3. An important goal in life is <u>to please</u> God always.
4. One way <u>to please</u> Him is to please godly parents.
5. We obey the Bible <u>to please</u> the Lord.
6. The <u>humble</u> recognize their need of God.
7. "<u>Humble</u> yourselves in the sight of the Lord."
8. God will not despise a <u>humble</u> prayer.
9. God will not <u>clear</u> the unrepentant from their guilt.
10. Some people ignore the <u>clear</u> teachings of the Bible.
11. We stood <u>clear</u> of the carpenters as they built our new house.
12. The inspectors found everything in the <u>clear</u> at the butcher shop.
13. Father is <u>singing</u> as he plows.
14. <u>Singing</u> enthusiastically, Susan entered the house.
15. We must practice <u>singing</u> this song correctly.
16. <u>Before</u> recess was over, the rain had begun to fall.
17. The rain ended again <u>before</u> nightfall.
18. Mr. Bates hauled the oversize load, and a pilot car went <u>before</u>.

(6) *A preposition (prep.) shows the relationship between its object and some other word in the sentence.* Some prepositions can also be used as adverbs, but they are prepositions when they have objects.

(7) *A conjunction (conj.) joins words, phrases, or clauses.*

(8) *An interjection (interj.) expresses strong feeling.* Almost any word can be used as an interjection.

★ **EXTRA PRACTICE**
Worksheet 42 *(Review of the Parts of Speech)*

3. devoted—v.; for—conj.; that—pron.; right—adj.
4. to right—n.; plant—adj.; stand—n.; that—pron.; over—adv.
5. That—adj.; plant—n.; run—v.; vines—n.; over—prep.; wall—n.
6. All—pron.; work—n.; well—adv.; values—v.

B. 1. God promises to bless the faithful. (n. v. n. adj. n.)
2. Lo, His presence continually surrounds us, although we do not see Him with our physical sight. (interj. adj. n. adv. v. pron.; conj. pron. v. adv. v. pron. prep. adj. adj. n.)
3. To deceive another person is never right. (n. adj. n. v. adv. adj.)
4. The priest and the Levite ignored the injured man; however, the Samaritan showed a neighborly attitude to him. (adj. n. conj. adj. n. v. adj. adj.; n. adv. adj. n. v. adj. adj. n. prep. pron.)
5. The children's efforts to surprise their parents were well rewarded. (adj. adj. n. adj. adj. n. v. adv. v.)
6. When we compared our pictures, most of us thought that his had the best shading. (conj. pron. v. adj. n. pron. prep. pron. v. conj. pron. v. adj. adj. n.)
7. In the morning Father will post the work to do for the day. (prep. adj. n. n. v. v. adj. n. prep. adj. n.)
8. The broken fence post should be replaced before the cows push through the fence and get out. (adj. adj. adj. n. v. v. v.; conj. adj. n. v. prep. adj. n. conj. v. adv.)
9. The water of the mountain stream felt refreshingly cool to me. (adj. n. prep. adj. adj. n. v. adv.; adj. prep. pron.)
10. Before evening, the creeks had become so flooded that many roads were nearly impassable. (prep. n. adj. n. v. v. adv.; adj. conj. adj. n. v. adv. adj.)

Written Exercises

A. 1. n.   10. adj.
2. adj.   11. adv.
3. n.   12. n.
4. adj.   13. v.
5. adv.   14. adj.
6. n.   15. n.
7. v.   16. conj.
8. adj.   17. prep.
9. v.   18. adv.

19. <u>Before</u>! I thought you said after lunch.
20. We worked hard all morning, <u>but</u> the task still was not finished.
21. We did everything <u>but</u> the baking.
22. A description is a <u>word</u> picture of a scene or an event.
23. You should <u>word</u> this sentence more carefully.
24. Do you know the definition of this <u>word</u>?
25. Some apples are almost tasteless, but <u>these</u> are crisp and juicy.
26. <u>These</u>! I did not ask for these books.
27. Have you seen <u>these</u> pictures from my uncle's farm in Wisconsin?
28. The <u>cloud</u> formations look quite interesting this afternoon.
29. Do not <u>cloud</u> the issues of life with human reasoning.
30. A dark <u>cloud</u> is rising in the west.
31. Step <u>inside</u> out of the rain.
32. The <u>inside</u> of the van should be cleaned.
33. We peered <u>inside</u> the old cabin.
34. The walls <u>inside</u> were exposed logs.
35. We <u>behold</u> the starry heavens with awe.
36. <u>Behold</u>, how the starry heavens magnify God's glory!
37. One of Sharon's favorite jobs is <u>baking</u> bread.
38. We have been <u>baking</u> bread for our roadside market.
39. The smell of <u>baking</u> bread often fills our kitchen.
40. <u>Baking</u>! I would much rather be out in the garden.

B. Copy these sentences, and label the part of speech for each word.
1. Several neighbors are finding bacteria in their drinking water.
2. Well, we tested the water from our well, but it is still good to drink.
3. Several of these saplings are looking quite dry, so Curvin should water them well.
4. If we respond right, the most severe trials can produce much good.
5. A right view of life is essential to successful living.
6. Truly fearing the Lord is a powerful incentive to do right.
7. None but the righteous can view by faith the world to come.
8. Drinking of the living springs satisfies every soul need.

Review Exercises

A. Write whether the word order of each sentence is *natural, inverted,* or *mixed.* [11]
1. During the Civil War, the Mennonites in the Shenandoah Valley were sorely tested.
2. The Confederate Army, desperate for recruits, did not appreciate their nonresistant stand.
3. Through this fertile valley marched General Sheridan's army.

19. interj.
20. conj.
21. prep.
22. adj.
23. v.
24. n.
25. pron.
26. interj.
27. adj.
28. adj.
29. v.
30. n.
31. adv.
32. n.
33. prep.
34. adj.
35. v.
36. interj.
37. n.
38. v.
39. adj.
40. interj.

B. 1. Several neighbors are finding bacteria in thei
     (adj. n. v. v. n. prep. adj)
    drinking water.
    (adj. n.)
2. Well, we tested the water from our well, bu
    (interj. pron. v. adj. n. prep. adj. n. conj)
    it is still good to drink.
    (pron. v. adv. adj. adv.)
3. Several of these saplings are looking quite
    (pron. prep. adj. n. v. v. adv.)
    dry, so Curvin should water them well.
    (adj. conj. n. v. v. pron. adv.)
4. If we respond right, the most severe trials can
    (conj.pron. v. adv. adj. adv. adj. n. v.)
    produce much good.
    (v. adj. n.)
5. A right view of life is essential to successfu
    (adj. adj. n. prep. n. v. adj. prep. adj.)
    living.
    (n.)
6. Truly fearing the Lord is a powerful incen
    (adv. n. adj. n. v. adj. adj. n.)
    tive to do right.
    (adj. n.)
7. None but the righteous can view by faith the
    (pron. prep. adj. n. v. v. prep. n. adj)
    world to come.
    (n. adj.)
8. Drinking of the living springs satisfies every
    (n. prep.adj. adj. n. v. adj.)
    soul need.
    (adj. n.)

Review Exercises

A. 1. mixed   3. inverted
   2. natural

4. This army ruined many homes and farms because the Union leaders wanted to cripple the South.
5. Certainly the Lord was in full control of these events.

3. If the underlined part of the sentence contains a mistake, write it correctly. If it has no error, write *correct*. [26]
1. "When you organize these books," directed <u>Father, "Put</u> the larger ones on the bottom shelf."
2. At the end of the service, we sang "Can the Lord Depend on <u>You</u>"?
3. Today we finished the story "Letitia's <u>Plea";</u> tomorrow we shall begin the next story.
4. "I enjoyed the essay, 'How Did the Water Get Into the <u>Watermelon?'</u> declared Clifford.
5. "Did Mr. Grayson say, 'I surely appreciate all your <u>help?'</u>" asked Jay.

4. natural
5. mixed

B. 1. Father, "put
2. You?"
3. correct
4. Watermelon?' "
5. help'?"

111. Planning a Descriptive Composition

Lesson Survey
- To plan a descriptive composition, use the following steps.
  1. Choose a scene or an event to describe.
  2. Decide what outstanding impression you want to convey.
  3. Make a list of details that will paint the picture you want.
  4. Make an outline for organizing your details.

Descriptive writing is usually part of a longer composition or a story. Occasionally, however, you may write a descriptive composition to share your enjoyment of a particular scene or to relate an incident. The steps in the following paragraphs will help you to plan such a descriptive composition.

1. *Choose a scene or an event to describe.* This should be something very familiar that interests you. If you choose to describe a scene, you will be most effective if you can observe it in preparation for your writing.

2. *Decide what outstanding impression you want to convey.* In this respect, a description should be like a character sketch. Suppose you are describing a lake. Do you want to emphasize its peacefulness, its restless waves, or its great size? Suppose you describe a barn. Again, you must decide what impression you want to leave with the reader. You may want to capitalize on the neat simplicity of the barn. On the other hand, you might want to emphasize

Lesson 111

Purpose: To teach careful observation of an object or a scene, and the planning of a description that gives a specific impression about it.

Oral Review:
1. What kinds of vivid, concrete words should be used in descriptive writing? (exact nouns, expressive verbs, colorful adjectives and adverbs)
2. In addition to vivid, concrete words, what contributes to good descriptive writing? (figurative language, appeal to the five senses)
3. When writing directions to a place, what information should you give about changing (*a*) to a large, well-marked highway? (*b*) to a small, hard-to-find road? (*a.* the route number and the direction of travel, a nearby town or city; *b.* helpful landmarks and specific distances)

4. Why is it important to give only helpful details? (to avoid confusion; to make directions easy to follow)
5. What is a persuasive argument? (an attempt to persuade or move to action)
6. What is the statement of the idea that the writer is promoting in an argument? (the proposition)
7. What is a fact? (something that has actually happened; something that expresses a scientific, mathematical, or statistical reality; or something that expresses a truth revealed by God in His Word)
8. What is an opinion? (a conclusion or belief about something, formed as a person evaluates facts in light of his own knowledge or experience)
9. What are some important cautions to remember about persuasive arguments? (Beware of propositions that are supported by misrepresented facts or faulty reasoning. Remember that the validity of a proposition is not established by strong statements. Avoid arguments that deal with unprofitable subjects.)

how sturdy it is. Often a number of different impressions could be given, but your description should focus on only one of them.

3. *Make a list of details that will paint the picture you want.* Look for interesting, meaningful details that appeal to as many of your five senses as practical. The sense of sight will likely provide most of these, but you should put some effort into using your other senses as well. Are there any sounds that will contribute to your word picture? Do your senses of smell and taste pick up anything special? What do you feel? Perhaps the warm breeze or the cool rain will add to the effect of what you are describing.

A description of a scene should generally be a "photograph" taken from only one point of view. If you are describing an old barn, you will see only one or two sides of it at a time. It is acceptable to change the point of view, but this must be done very carefully so that the reader is not confused. For example, you might describe various details as you take the reader around the outside of the barn or as you explore the inside. But you will need to state exactly where you are going as you move from one scene to another.

The following list shows some details that may be written in preparing to describe a scene.

The Muskoka Lakes Region

Town of Hunter—very busy in fishing season; little activity now
Railroad trestle to the north
Long freight train whistling mournfully
Harbor and Georgian Bay to the west
Many islands in bay; several fishing boats
Smaller fishing craft in dry docks for winter
Wooded hills to the east and south
Many lakes among the hills

4. *Make an outline for organizing your details.* If you are describing a scene, use spatial order. A description of an event should follow chronological order.

Study the following outline for a descriptive composition about a scene.

The Muskoka Lakes Region

  I. Below—the town of Hunter
    A. Very busy in fishing season
    B. Little activity now
  II. To the west
    A. Harbor that opens into Georgian Bay
    B. Fishing craft in dry docks
    C. Bay reaching north and south
    D. Islands and fishing boats in bay

Lesson Introduction: Could you write a composition about the Victoria Falls in Africa? Yes, you could research its exact location, its size, and its discovery, and write a meaningful composition about it. Could you write a *descriptive* composition about the Victoria Falls? Now, that is a different matter! You could read how other people have described it and try to copy their descriptions. But your description would lack the definiteness and detail that comes from personal observation. To write a descriptive composition that is truly effective, you must be well familiar with the subject of your description.

Lesson Outline:

  1. To plan a descriptive composition, first choose a scene or an event to describe.
    a. This should be something very familiar that interests you.
    b. If you choose to describe a scene, you will be most effective if you can observe it in preparation for your writing.

  2. Decide what outstanding impression you want to convey. Often a number of different impressions could be given, but your description should focus on only one of them.

  3. Make a list of details that will paint the picture you want.
    a. Look for interesting, meaningful details that appeal to as many of your five senses as practical.
    b. A description of a scene should generally be from only one point of view. It is acceptable to change the point of view, but this must be done very carefully so that the reader is not confused.

  4. Make an outline for organizing your details.
    a. A description of a scene should follow spatial order.
    b. A description of an event should follow chronological order.

III. To the north
   A. Railroad trestle
   B. Freight train
IV. To the east and south
   A. Wooded hills
   B. Many lakes among the hills

Notice that the outline is not as descriptive as the list of details. For example, the detail "Long freight train whistling mournfully" is reduced to "Freight train" on the outline. This is as it should be, for the outline is mainly a plan for arranging the details in an orderly way. When the description is actually written, the writer can use the details in the list as well as additional details that he thinks of in the writing process.

Written Exercises

A. Choose a scene or an event to describe, and decide what impression you want to convey about it. Here are some suggestions.

| A farm sale | Housecleaning | School recess |
| Butchering day | A church service | A notable building |

B. Make a list of details about the scene or event you have chosen to describe, and make an outline to organize the details.

---

112. Writing a Descriptive Composition

> **Lesson Survey**
> - In writing a descriptive composition, follow your outline.
> - In each paragraph, describe one general section of a scene or one connected movement in an event.
> - Use descriptive language to show rather than tell the details you are portraying.
> - Revise and rewrite your descriptive composition.

Writing a descriptive composition is much like writing any other composition. You gather and organize information, you write a first draft, and then you revise it and write the second draft.

In writing a descriptive composition, follow your outline. This should keep your composition in proper spatial or chronological order. Also, it should help you to include all the details that you observed when taking notes.

Lesson 112

Purpose: To give practice in writing a descriptive composition.

Oral Review:

1. In what way should a descriptive composition be similar to a character sketch? (Both focus on one impression.)

2. What order of development should be used *(a)* for a description of a scene? *(b)* for a description of an event? (*a.* spatial; *b.* chronological)

3. What kinds of vivid, concrete words should be used in descriptive writing? (exact nouns, expressive verbs, colorful adjectives and adverbs)

4. In addition to vivid, concrete words, what contributes to good descriptive writing? (figurative language, appeal to the five senses)

Lesson 111 Answers

Written Exercises

(All answers are individual work.)

---

5. Name four kinds of figures of speech. (simile, metaphor, personification, hyperbole)

Lesson Introduction: Do you know an older person (perhaps one of your grandparents) who enjoys talking about his childhood? In the midst of those tales, have you ever floated in your imagination to those scenes and events of the long-ago past? Have you smelled the bacon frying and the coffee boiling, mingled with whiffs of wood smoke? Perhaps you smelled the sweet aroma of cooking apples and felt the sweat stinging your eyes and dripping from your chin as the apples were cooked down to make apple butter.

Now can you tell what made their descriptions so vivid? As much as possible, you must put into your written description those same qualities.

Lesson Outline:

1. In writing a descriptive composition, follow your outline.

In each paragraph, describe one general section of a scene or one connected movement in an event. Generally, this should correspond to the main points of your outline. Read the following composition, and compare it with the outline in Lesson 111. Notice how it describes the scene right at the viewers' feet in paragraph 1, the view toward the west in paragraph 2, the view toward the north in paragraph 3, and the view toward the east and south in paragraph 4.

The Muskoka Lakes Region

The crisp autumn air invigorates us as we slowly climb the fire tower at Hunter in the Muskoka Lakes region. Our eyes take in the ever-widening view as we ascend. Directly around our feet lies the town of Hunter. During the fishing season, it is a bustling beehive of activity. Now it is more like a woodchuck blinking sleepily before settling down for his long winter nap.

To the west of us is the harbor, which opens into Georgian Bay. Many of the smaller fishing craft have already been placed in dry docks for the winter. Beyond the harbor we see the china blue waters of the bay reaching north and south as far as the eye can see. We are almost blinded by the reflection of the late afternoon sun as it flashes from the rippling waters. Hundreds of islands of various sizes are scattered throughout the vast expanse of this bay, like flies stuck in a sea of blue paint. Accenting this scene of tranquillity are several boats bobbing peacefully on the surface. The occupants are doing some late-season fishing before the cold of winter locks the harbor in its icy grip.

North of us we see the giant spider web of a railroad trestle spanning a deep gorge. We hear the mournful whistle of a long freight train as it snakes its way along the tracks and then vanishes behind a wooded hill splashed with the fall colors of scarlet sumac and yellow maple. We savor the woodsy aroma as the soft breeze wafts it our way.

As our eyes wander around to the east and south, we marvel at the spectacle before us. Stretching to the far distant horizon is a land of wooded hills interspersed with innumerable lakes ranging in size from small ponds to lakes covering thousands of acres. Only the almighty God could have created something of such awesome beauty as the scene before us.

Use descriptive language to *show* rather than *tell* the details you are portraying. This is done very well in the composition above, as you should have noticed in reading it.

Remember the qualities of descriptive writing that you studied in Lesson 108. They are summarized below for your benefit in preparing to write a descriptive composition.

    a. This should keep your composition in proper spatial or chronological order.
    b. It should help you to include all the details that you observed when taking notes.

2. In each paragraph, describe one general section of a scene or one connected movement in an event.

3. Use descriptive language to show rather than tell the details you are portraying.

    a. Remember the qualities of descriptive writing that you studied in Lesson 108.
        1) Vivid, concrete words such as exact nouns, expressive verbs, and colorful adjectives and adverbs
        2) Figurative language
        3) Appeal to the five senses
    b. Avoid trite expressions and worn-out figures of speech.

4. Revise and rewrite your descriptive composition. The following questions should be helpful for doing this.

    (1) Does the description give a clear mental picture of the scene or event? (If possible, read your first draft to someone else for his comments.)
    (2) Does the description give details in a logical order?
    (3) Is the description full of colorful, specific words? Does it use fresh figures of speech?
    (4) Is the point of view consistent?
    (5) Are the paragraphs unified and coherent? Is there smooth transition between paragraphs?
    (6) Does it have correct grammar, punctuation, spelling, and capitalization?

1. Paint clear, vivid word pictures by using exact nouns, expressive verbs, and colorful adjectives and adverbs. Try to avoid linking verbs, weak action verbs modified by adverbs, and verbs in the passive voice.
2. Use figurative language: similes, metaphors, personification, and hyperboles.
3. Use words that appeal to the five senses. Your description may refer mostly to things that can be seen, but it should also involve the other four senses if possible.

In your quest for descriptive language, avoid trite expressions and worn-out figures of speech like *made a beeline, slow as molasses,* and *quiet as a mouse.* Mountains are often called majestic; try a fresher adjective like *imposing* or *awe-inspiring.* Better yet, describe the features that make the mountain majestic. Instead of saying a field is as flat as a pancake, try to think of a comparison of your own. Perhaps you could say it is as level as a quiet lake.

Proofread the first draft of your descriptive composition. Use the following questions for help in revising it, and then write the second draft.

1. Does the description give a clear mental picture of the scene or event? (If possible, read your first draft to someone else for his comments.)
2. Does the description give details in a logical order?
3. Is the description full of colorful, specific words? Does it use fresh figures of speech?
4. Is the point of view consistent?
5. Are the paragraphs unified and coherent? Is there smooth transition between paragraphs?
6. Does it have correct grammar, punctuation, spelling, and capitalization?

Class Practice

A. In the sample description, find exact nouns that are used instead of the following general phrases.
1. tall structure
2. protected body of water
3. places for ships out of the water
4. action of bouncing back
5. areas of land in water
6. persons inside
7. bridge of braced framework
8. steep, narrow valley
9. trees (two answers)
10. light wind

B. Find expressive verbs that tell the following things.
1. The autumn air has a certain effect on the writer.
2. The reflection off the water is very bright.
3. The sunlight is reflected from the rippling waters.
4. The train moves along the tracks.
5. The train goes behind a hill.
6. They appreciate the woodsy smell.

Lesson 112 Answers

Class Practice

A. 1. fire tower
2. harbor
3. dry docks
4. reflection
5. islands
6. occupants
7. trestle
8. gorge
9. sumac, maple
10. breeze

B. 1. invigorates
2. blinded
3. flashes
4. snakes
5. vanishes
6. savor

7. The breeze carries the woodsy smell to them.
8. The writer is deeply impressed by the scene.

C. Find colorful adjective and adverb modifiers of these words.
   1. air
   2. climb
   3. view
   4. waters (two answers)
   5. expanse
   6. bobbing
   7. fishing
   8. hill
   9. sumac
   10. maple
   11. aroma
   12. breeze
   13. horizon
   14. lakes
   15. beauty

D. Find examples of figurative language. Tell what kind of figure each one is.

Written Exercises

A. Write a description based on the outline you made for Lesson 111.

B. Revise and rewrite your description.

---

113. Chapter 10 Review

Class Practice

A. Give the correct term for each description.
   1. A word that joins words, phrases, or clauses.
   2. A word that shows the relationship between its object and some other word in the sentence.
   3. A word that expresses strong feeling.
   4. A conjunction that joins a dependent adverb clause to an independent clause.
   5. A conjunction that joins sentence parts of parallel structure and function.
   6. Conjunctions that work in pairs.
   7. An adverb that joins two independent clauses.

B. Read each prepositional phrase. Tell whether the phrase is an *adjective, adverb,* or *noun.*
   1. In our back yard is a strange place for a herd of deer.
   2. Under a large maple stood a buck with a large spread of antlers.
   3. Several deer, graceful in every movement of their bodies, are feeding in what we call our orchard.
   4. Down the back field lane is their normal path in coming to our place.

C. Read these sentences, correcting the errors in preposition usage. If a sentence has no error, say *correct.*
   1. No man beside Jesus could have paid the ransom for sin.

Lesson 113

Purpose: To review the concepts taught in Chapter 10.

7. wafts
8. marvel

C. 1. crisp, autumn
   2. slowly
   3. ever-widening
   4. china blue, rippling
   5. vast
   6. peacefully
   7. late-season
   8. wooded
   9. scarlet
   10. yellow
   11. woodsy
   12. soft
   13. far distant
   14. innumerable
   15. awesome

D. *Paragraph 1:* it is a bustling beehive of activity—metaphor;
      like a woodchuck blinking sleepily before se tling down for his long winter nap—simil
   Paragraph 2: like flies stuck in a sea of blu paint—simile;
      before the cold of winter locks the harbor i its icy grip—metaphor *or* personification
   Paragraph 3: the giant spider web—metaphor mournful whistle—personification

Written Exercises

(All answers are individual work.)

Lesson 113 Answers

Class Practice

A. 1. conjunction
   2. preposition
   3. interjection
   4. subordinating conjunction
   5. coordinating conjunction
   6. correlative conjunctions
   7. conjunctive adverb

B. 1. In our back yard—noun;
      for a herd of deer—adjective; of deer—adjectiv
   2. Under a large maple—adverb;
      with a large spread of antlers—adjective;
      of antlers—adjective
   3. in every movement of their bodies—adverb;
      of their bodies—adjective;
      in what we call our orchard—adverb
   4. Down the back field lane—noun;
      in coming to our place—adverb *or* adjective;
      to our place—adverb

C. (Corrections are underlined.)
   1. No man besides Jesus could have paid the ran som for sin.

2. A strong prayer life stands in back of every victorious Christian.
3. In many ways, the prayers of Christians differ from those of the heathen.
4. The Bible contains much teaching and encouragement to faithfulness.

D. Read the coordinating conjunctions and conjunctive adverbs. Tell whether each one is a *common coordinating conjunction,* a *conjunctive adverb,* or a *pair of correlative conjunctions.*
  1. Both the righteous and the unrighteous may suffer; however, only the righteous have the inner peace of God's presence.
  2. We trust the Lord, for we know that He does all things well.
  3. Whether through trials or through easy times, we must walk by faith and keep our eyes fixed on the Lord.
  4. Not only does God assure us of His presence now, but also He promises eternal blessings in heaven.

E. These sentences contain errors in relation to coordinating conjunctions. Tell how to correct each one.
  1. We not only sing at family worship but also before the evening meal.
  2. Family worship is a good opportunity to learn about the Bible, furthermore it knits a family together.
  3. We had planned to visit Grandpa this evening but Lloyd has a bad cold.
  4. Because of his severe arthritis, Grandpa walks slowly and with much pain.
  5. He is no longer able to work like he did several years ago.

F. Read each subordinating conjunction and the clause it introduces.
  1. Because Jesus is Lord of nature, He could walk on water as easily as He could walk on land.
  2. Peter too could walk on the water while he fixed his gaze upon Jesus.
  3. Even though Jesus was so near, Peter began to sink when he looked at the storm.

G. Make each sentence more effective by changing it either to a complex sentence or to a sentence in which the idea to be emphasized is in the main clause.
  1. Joseph reported his brothers' evildoing, and they hated him.
  2. Joseph came toward his brothers as those evil men were planning to get rid of him.

H. Identify each interjection, and tell whether it should be followed by a comma or an exclamation point. Also tell whether the next word should be capitalized.
  1. Alas the determined travelers would not take our warning.
  2. Ah these puppies surely are charming.
  3. Good we are very glad to have the planting done this week.

2. A strong prayer life stands <u>behind</u> every victorious Christian.
3. correct
4. The Bible contains much teaching <u>about</u> and encouragement to faithfulness.

D. 1. Both—and—pair of correlative conjunctions; however—conjunctive adverb
  2. for—common coordinating conjunction
  3. Whether—or—pair of correlative conjunctions; and—common coordinating conjunction
  4. Not only—but also—pair of correlative conjunctions

E. (Corrections are underlined.)
  1. We sing <u>not only</u> at family worship . . .
  2. . . . the Bible; furthermore, . . .
  3. . . . this evening, but . . .
  4. . . . walks slowly and <u>painfully</u>.
  5. . . . to work <u>as</u> he did . . .

F. (Subordinating conjunctions are underlined.)
  1. <u>Because</u> Jesus is Lord of nature;
     <u>as</u> He could walk on land
  2. <u>while</u> he fixed his gaze upon Jesus
  3. <u>Even though</u> Jesus was so near;
     <u>when</u> he looked at the storm

G. 1. Because Joseph reported his brothers' evildoing, they hated him.
  2. As Joseph came toward his brothers, those evil men were planning to get rid of him.

H. 1. Alas! The
  2. Ah, these
  3. Good! We *or* Good, we

I. Give the part of speech for each word.
   1. Well, God demonstrates His fatherly care in many ways.
   2. Those who seek the things above find lasting peace and satisfaction.
   3. If we care too much for the earthly, we shall never enter that life to come.
   4. To keep our sight focused above, we must daily think upon the Lord.

Written Exercises

A. Copy each prepositional phrase, and label it *adj., adv.,* or *n.*
   1. In the Father's hand is the place of our safety.
   2. Our lives, secure in Him, cannot be plucked out of God's hand by the enemy.
   3. Our willingness to remain within that safety is a key to our security.
   4. God faithfully provides a refuge for whoever trusts Him.

B. If the underlined part of the sentence contains a mistake, write it correctly. If it has no error, write *correct.*
   1. In what ways is a political map <u>different than a physical map</u>?
   2. We sat on folding chairs <u>in back of the last bench</u>.
   3. Mother has plenty of pie to divide <u>among the eight children</u>.
   4. Because Brother James's car had a flat tire, we had to <u>wait on him</u> fifteen minutes.
   5. By the time the tour was <u>over with</u>, my mind was full of new facts.
   6. Wherever you <u>are at</u>, God knows all about you.
   7. We can <u>differ with others</u> without becoming bitter toward them.
   8. I sat <u>besides Grandmother Fisher</u> and held the songbook for her.
   9. She knew all the songs <u>except the last one</u>.

C. Copy the common coordinating conjunctions (*CC*), correlative conjunctions (*Cor*), conjunctive adverbs (*CA*), and subordinating conjunctions (*SC*). Identify them with the labels given.
   1. Whenever we hear the Word preached, we should sit reverently; moreover, we should listen attentively.
   2. We should neither daydream nor whisper during a worship service.
   3. Turning to the Scripture references and taking notes are helps to good listening.
   4. Irreverence is not only a hindrance to ourselves and others but also a serious insult to the Lord.

D. Rewrite these sentences so that the correlative conjunctions are used correctly.
   1. The girls both baked bread and pies today.
   2. This clock either does not work, or the time has passed very swiftly!
   3. This year the peas were not only bushy but fruitful.

interj. n.   v.   adj. adj.   n. prep
I. 1. Well, God demonstrates His fatherly care i
       adj.   n.
       many ways.
       pron. pron. v.   adj.   n.   adj.   v.   adj.
   2. Those who seek the things above find lastin
       n.   conj.   n.
       peace and satisfaction.
       conj.pron. v.   adv.   adv. prep. adj.   n.   pron. v.
   3. If we care too much for the earthly, we shal
       adv.   v.   adj. n.   adj.
       never enter that life to come.
       adv.   adj. n.   adj.   adv. pron. v.   adv.
   4. To keep our sight focused above, we must dail
       v.   prep. adj.   n.
       think upon the Lord.

Written Exercises

A. 1. In the Father's hand—n.; of our safety—adj
   2. in Him—adv.; out of God's hand—adv.; by the enemy—adv.
   3. within that safety—adv.; to our security—adj
   4. for whoever trusts Him—adj. *or* adv.

B. 1. different from a physical map
   2. behind the last bench
   3. correct
   4. wait for him
   5. over
   6. are
   7. correct
   8. beside Grandmother Fisher
   9. correct

C. 1. Whenever—SC; moreover—CA
   2. neither—nor—Cor
   3. and—CC
   4. and—CC; not only—but also—Cor

D. (Corrections are underlined.)
   1. The girls baked <u>both</u> bread and pies today.
   2. <u>Either</u> this clock does not work, or the time has passed very swiftly!
   3. This year the peas were not only bushy but <u>also</u> fruitful.

E. Copy each word that should be followed by a comma or semicolon, and add the missing punctuation.
1. We have had several days of heavy rain consequently the rivers and creeks are flooded.
2. The chicken feed is nearly all gone so we should go to Greenmount Elevator tomorrow.
3. Either the gate is not shut or the fence is broken somewhere.

F. Copy these sentences, and above each word write the abbreviation for its part of speech.
1. When we rise to a new day, we should always stop to meditate upon God.
2. Many attempt to live without God's help; therefore, they see no value in daily prayers.
3. Alas, any attempt like that will result in spiritual ruin.
4. The elderly man, welcoming the visitors, stood up slowly and painfully.

G. Read this descriptive paragraph, and do the exercises that follow.

For the remaining hours of daylight, we derelicts huddled disconsolately on the roof. Now and then we were able to reach out a hand or pole and haul in somebody drifting by, until finally we numbered nineteen. Though we were in a backwash, many of the houses had been seriously damaged below the water line. Occasionally one would melt like a lump of sugar and vanish. We did not know whether our refuge had been undermined, but there was no way for us to escape to the surrounding hills which rose invitingly above the flood, so near and yet so impossible to reach. The cold rain was still driving down, and it was growing dark. We were so miserable that we decided to open the skylight and climb under cover.
—From *"Just Short of Eternity"*

1. Write exact nouns that are used instead of the following general phrases.
   a. helpless persons   c. deep waters
   b. place of safety   d. an opening in the roof
2. Write expressive verbs or verbals that tell the following things.
   a. They sat uncomfortably on the roof.
   b. They brought other victims onto the roof.
   c. Some houses around them disappeared. (two answers)
   d. The rain was coming down forcefully.
3. Copy the words that communicate this idea more expressively: at last there were nineteen.
4. Copy the descriptive adjectives and adverbs that modify these words.
   a. huddled   b. hills   c. rain   d. we
5. Copy one simile and one example of personification.

E. 1. rain; consequently,
   2. gone,
   3. shut,

<pre>
       conj. pron. v. prep.adj. adj. n. pron. v.   adv.
F. 1. When we rise to a new day, we should always
         v.   adv.   prep.   n.
      stop to meditate upon God.
        pron. v.   prep. adj. n.   adv.
   2. Many attempt to live without God's help; there-
       pron. v. adj.   n.   prep. adj.   n.
      fore, they see no value in daily prayers.
       interj. adj. n.   prep. pron. v.   v. prep.
   3. Alas, any attempt like that will result in
          adj.   n.
      spiritual ruin.
         adj.   adj.   n.   adj.   adj.   n.   v.
   4. The elderly man, welcoming the visitors, stood
       adv.   adv. conj.   adv.
      up slowly and painfully.
</pre>

G. 1. a. derelicts   c. flood
      b. refuge   d. skylight
   2. a. huddled   c. melt, vanish
      b. haul   d. driving
   3. finally we numbered nineteen
   4. a. disconsolately   c. cold
      b. surrounding   d. miserable
   5. *simile:* like a lump of sugar
      personification: rose invitingly

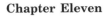

Chapter Eleven

Reference Sources

Giving Summaries and Book Reports

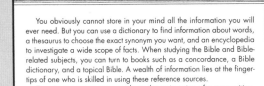

You obviously cannot store in your mind all the information you will ever need. But you can use a dictionary to find information about words, a thesaurus to choose the exact synonym you want, and an encyclopedia to investigate a wide scope of facts. When studying the Bible and Bible-related subjects, you can turn to books such as a concordance, a Bible dictionary, and a topical Bible. A wealth of information lies at the finger-tips of one who is skilled in using these reference sources.

To write a summary is to condense the main points of a composition. The ability to do this can be a valuable study aid. If you would write a good summary, you must study the original composition thoroughly, list the main points, and briefly present those points in your own words. A book report is a special kind of summary. It gives some of the main points found in a book, usually for the purpose of arousing other people's interest in reading the book for themselves.

In the first year of his reign I Daniel understood by books
the number of the years, whereof the word of the Lord came to Jeremiah the prophet,
that he would accomplish seventy years in the desolations of Jerusalem.

Daniel 9:2

114. Using a Dictionary

Lesson Survey

- Guide words help you to quickly find words in a dictionary.
- An entry word in a dictionary shows the correct spelling and syllable divisions of a word.
- Dictionary entries show pronunciations, parts of speech, inflections, definitions, usage labels, etymologies, derivatives, and synonyms and antonyms.

You have used the dictionary long enough that by this time it should be a familiar book to you. But are you sure you know about all the valuable features in your dictionary? Besides the entry words and their meanings, dictionaries contain many interesting sections that you may never have discovered.

For example, before the main dictionary section of *Funk and Wagnalls Standard College Dictionary,* you will find a brief history of the English language, a word pronunciation key of various regions in America, the dictionary plan, and a list of abbreviations that are used in the dictionary text. After the main dictionary part of *Webster's Seventh New Collegiate Dictionary,* you will find a biographical section about famous persons, a pronouncing gazetteer of more than ten thousand places in the world, and even a section of rhymes for your use in writing poetry.

You will find different types of information in other dictionaries. Therefore, you do well to become familiar with your dictionary from beginning to end so that you know about all the helps that are available to you in your study.

Guide Words

Guide words are printed at the top of dictionary pages to help you find words quickly. The first guide word shows the first word entered on that page, and the last guide word shows the last word entered. Any words that come alphabetically between these two words are found on that page.

Entry Words

Each word defined in a dictionary has an entry that begins with the entry word. An entry word shows two basic things about a word.

1. *Correct spelling.* Some words have two correct spellings that are close together in alphabetical order (such as *caliper,* which is also spelled *calliper*). For such a word, the two spellings are entered together, with the more common spelling as the main entry word. Other words have two spellings that are not close together (such as *caulk* and *calk*). Then each spelling is entered separately, and the entry for the less common spelling (*calk* in this case) refers to the more common spelling. In turn, the entry

Lesson 114

Purpose: To study the types of information found in dictionaries, including *derivatives.

IMPORTANT: Check your school's supply of the following reference books studied in Lessons 115, 117, and 118. If possible, it would be good to have a copy available for each student.

> thesaurus
> road atlas
> Strong's Exhaustive Concordance
> Bible dictionary
> Nave's Topical Bible

Oral Review:

1. Tell how a coordinating conjunction and a subordinating conjunction are different. (A coordinating conjunction joins words, phrases, or clauses that are parallel in structure and function. A subordinating conjunction joins a dependent adverb clause to an independent clause.)

2. Name three common uses of colons. (to separate the numbers in Scripture references and in expressions of time; to follow the salutation of a business letter; to introduce a list, an explanation, or a formal quotation)

3. Name two uses of semicolons. (to join independent clauses when no conjunction is used, when a conjunctive adverb is used, or when commas are already used in one or more of the clauses; to separate items in a series when the individual items contain commas)

4. What are dashes used for? (to show a sudden interruption in thought)

5. Name three uses of parentheses. (to enclose a parenthetical element that is relatively unimportant; to enclose supplementary or illustrative matter; to enclose figures or letters used for enumeration)

for the more common spelling (like *caulk*) shows the other as an alternate spelling. In many dictionaries, a spelling that follows the word *also* is definitely less common.

Closely related to correct spelling is correct capitalization. If a word is always capitalized, the entry word is shown that way. However, some words are capitalized only for certain definitions. In that case, some dictionaries list the word as two separate entries; others specify the definitions with which capitalization is required.

> **cal·i·per** or **cal·li·per** (kal′·ə·pər) *n.* An instrument having two legs used for measuring diameters and thicknesses.
> **calk** (kôk) See **caulk.**
> **caulk** (kôk) *v.* To make tight against leaks, as seams of a boat and cracks in a window frame. Also **calk.**
> **com·mun·ion** (kə·myün′·yən) *n.* 1. An intimate sharing of thoughts and feelings; close fellowship. 2. *cap.* The Christian ordinance in which the bread and the cup are shared together in memory of Christ's suffering and death; the Lord's Supper.

2. *Syllable division.* A space or a raised dot (·) shows where a word is divided into syllables. In some dictionaries, the entry words do not show the division for a beginning or ending syllable of only one letter, as in *a-dapt* and *cop-y*. This is because of the rule that a word must not be divided so that a single letter is left at the beginning or end of a line. So a word that actually has two syllables may appear to have only one. For such a word, you need to look at the pronunciation to see the two syllables.

Word Information

Information given after an entry word includes much more than the meaning of the word. Notice the many different kinds of information given.

1. *Correct pronunciation.* A complete pronunciation key is usually found in the front of the dictionary. Most dictionaries also print a short key at the bottom of each right-hand page. Since pronunciation keys vary considerably, you must become familiar with the key of the dictionary you are using.

Pronunciations vary even more often than spellings. Dictionaries treat these variations in different ways. Check the explanatory notes in the front of the dictionary to find whether the first option is preferred above the others. Sometimes a specific region is named where the variant pronunciation is used. If only part of the word has varied pronunciation, only those syllables with variations may be shown. As with variant spellings, any variant pronunciation following the word *also* is definitely less common.

> **a·pri·cot** (ap′·ri·kot, ā′·pri-)
> **been** (bin, *Brit.* bēn)
>   *Brit.* means that the second pronunciation is used in Great Britain.

6. Name two uses of brackets. (to enclose a comment or correction within a quotation; to serve as parentheses within parentheses)

Lesson Introduction: Write *fast* on the board and ask for as many definitions of the word as your students can think of. After they have exhausted their resources, read at least some of the additional definitions given in a dictionary. Point out that *fast* meaning "swift" and *fast* meaning "to abstain from food" have different histories, or etymologies. This lesson will give practice with using the dictionary, a common and valuable resource for information on words.

Lesson Outline:

1. Guide words help you to quickly find words in a dictionary. The first guide word shows the first entry word on that page, and the last guide word shows the last entry word on the page.

2. An entry word in a dictionary shows two basic things about a word.

  (1) *Correct spelling.*

    a) If a word has two correct spellings that are close together in alphabetical order, they are listed together, with the more common spelling as the main entry word.

    b) If the two spellings are not close together, each is listed as a separate entry word. The entry for the less common spelling refers to the more common spelling, and the entry for the more common spelling shows the other as an alternate spelling.

    c) In many dictionaries, a spelling that follows the word *also* is definitely less common.

2. *Part of speech and definitions.* The part of speech is shown by an abbreviation before the definition. If a word can be used as more than one part of speech, the definitions for each are listed in one grouping. Some dictionaries may list a word under separate, numbered entries for each part of speech. In addition, separate, numbered entries are used for words with the same spelling but different meanings and backgrounds.

Dictionary A:

   name (nām) *n.* 1. A word or phrase by which a person, thing, animal, or idea is distinctively known. 2. A usually derogatory term evaluating character or quality. 3. A reputation. 4. A famous or important person or thing. 5. Appearance as opposed to reality. —*v.* 1. To give a name to; call. 2. To mention or identify by name. 3. To decide upon. 4. To nominate; appoint. 5. To mention explicitly. —*adj.* Having or known by a name.

Dictionary B:

   *¹***name** (nām) *n.* 1. A word or phrase by which a person, thing, animal, or idea is distinctively known. 2. A usually derogatory term evaluating character or quality. 3. A reputation. 4. A famous or important person or thing. 5. Appearance as opposed to reality.
   *²***name** *v.* 1. To give a name to; call. 2. To mention or identify by name. 3. To decide upon. 4. To nominate; appoint. 5. To mention explicitly.
   *³***name** *adj.* Having or known by a name.

3. *Inflections.* Inflections are changes made in the forms of words to show things like number, tense, and degree of comparison. Most dictionaries show irregular plural forms of nouns, irregular principal parts of verbs, and irregular forms of comparison for adjectives and adverbs.

Irregular plural form:
   o•a•sis (ō·ā′·sis) *n. pl.* **o•a•ses** (-sēz)

Irregular principal parts:
   know (nō) *v.* **knew** (nü), **known** (nōn)

Irregular forms of comparison:
   heav•y (hev′·ē) *adj.* **heav•i•er, -est**
   well (wel) *adv.* **bet•ter** (bet′·ər), **best** (best)

4. *Usage labels.* Some labels alert you to words that you should completely avoid. You should never use words labeled *vulgar* because of their association with evil. Words labeled *nonstandard, substandard,* or *illiterate* also represent poor English and should be avoided.

Other labels limit the proper usage of words. *Slang* words were invented by people trying to say things in unique ways. Many slang expressions

   d) An entry word also shows correct capitalization.
      1) If a word is always capitalized, the entry word is shown that way.
      2) If a word is capitalized only for certain definitions, the dictionary will list the word as two separate entries or specify the definitions with which capitalization is required.
   (2) *Syllable division.* A space or a raised dot (·) shows where a word is divided into syllables.

3. Dictionaries show many other things about entry words.

   (1) *Correct pronunciation.*
      a) A complete pronunciation key is usually found in the front of the dictionary.
      b) Most dictionaries also print a short key at the bottom of each right-hand page.
      c) Variant pronunciations are shown in different ways, so check the explanatory notes in the front of the dictionary.
   (2) *Part of speech and definitions.*
      a) The part of speech is shown by an abbreviation before the definition.
      b) If a word can be used as more than one part of speech, the definitions for each are listed in one grouping. Some dictionaries may list a word under separate, numbered entries for each part of speech.
      c) Separate, numbered entries are used for words with the same spelling but different meanings and backgrounds.
   (3) *Inflections.* The following inflections are commonly shown.
      a) Irregular plural forms of nouns
      b) Irregular principal parts of verbs
      c) Irregular forms of comparison for adjectives and adverbs
   (4) *Usage labels.*
      a) The following labels alert you to words that you should completely avoid.
         1) You should never use words labeled *vulgar* because of their association with evil.
         2) Words labeled *nonstandard, substandard,* or *illiterate* also represent poor English and should be avoided.

come from the "street language" of immoral people. For this reason, godly people avoid the new, catchy expressions that are constantly showing up. The words *grub* and *turf* are perfectly acceptable when used with their normal meanings. But saying *grub* for "food" and *turf* for "territory" is not appropriate for people professing godliness.

Informal words are acceptable in everyday speaking or writing, such as in notes to yourself or in friendly letters. However, they are not suitable for formal speech (giving a topic or preaching a sermon) or formal writing (schoolwork, articles for publication, or legal papers). Informal words include *daddy* for "father," *chopper* for "helicopter," and *reckon* for "think" or "suppose."

Words labeled *regional* or *dialectal* are used in relatively small areas or by a limited group of people. Some dictionaries even specify regions where certain words are commonly used (as *Brit.* for the second pronunciation of *been* in one example above). The labels *archaic* and *obsolete* designate words that are no longer in general use. Some archaic words, like *canst* and *whereon,* are familiar to us because we use the King James Version of the Bible.

5. *Etymology.* Many dictionaries give an etymology, or brief history of a word. This information is usually given within brackets and is placed either before the definitions or at the end of the entry. The etymological information is helpful in comparing words with similar roots or affixes. Here is a typical etymology with an explanation of its meaning.

> **om•nip•o•tent** [< OF < L *omnipotens* < *omnis* all + *potens* < *posse*
> to be able]
> **Meaning:**
> > *Omnipotent* comes from an Old French word that came from the Latin word *omnipotens,* which is made of *omnis* (meaning "all") and *potens* (which comes from *posse,* meaning "to be able").

6. *Derivatives.* A *derivative* is a word that is derived from a simpler word by adding a prefix or suffix. Rather than being listed as separate entries, derivatives may be shown at the end of an entry.

> **leg•i•ble** (lej′•ə•bəl) *adj.* Capable of being read or deciphered.
> **—leg′•i•bil′•i•ty, leg′•i•ble•ness** *n.* **—leg′•i•bly** *adv.*

7. *Synonyms and antonyms.* Many of the advanced dictionaries list synonyms and antonyms for certain words. When these are given, they appear at the end of the entry. They help you to understand the meaning of the entry word more clearly as you compare it with words of similar or opposite meanings. The next lesson deals more specifically with synonyms and antonyms.

b) Other labels limit the proper usage of words.
  1) *Slang* words were invented by people trying to say things in unique ways. Godly people avoid the new, catchy expressions that are constantly showing up.
  2) *Informal* words are acceptable in everyday speaking or writing, but not in formal speech or formal writing.
  3) Words labeled *regional* or *dialectal* are used in relatively small areas or by a limited group of people.
  4) The labels *archaic* and *obsolete* designate words that are no longer in general use.
(5) *Etymology.* An etymology is a brief history of a word.

Written Exercises *(Continued)*

2. *Protestant:* A member of a Western Christian church whose faith and practice are founded on the principles of the Protestant Reformation, especially in the acceptance of the Bible as the sole source of revelation, in justification by faith alone, and in the universal priesthood of all the believers.
   protestant: One who makes a declaration or an avowal.

3. *Pilgrim:* One of the English Separatists who founded the colony of Plymouth in New England in 1620.
   pilgrim: A religious devotee who journeys to a shrine or sacred place. A traveler.

D. 1. elevator
   2. disease
   3. taken the bark off
   4. sailing ship used chiefly in coasting and fishing
   5. boundary
   6. forms a thread when poured from a spoon

a) This information is usually given within brackets and is placed either before the definitions or at the end of the entry.
b) The etymological information is helpful in comparing words with similar roots or affixes.
(6) *Derivatives.* A derivative is a word that is derived from a simpler word by adding a prefix or suffix. Rather than being listed as separate entries, derivatives may be shown at the end of an entry.
(7) *Synonyms and antonyms.*
  a) When these are given, they appear at the end of the entry.
  b) They help you to understand the meaning of the entry word more clearly as you compare it with words of similar or opposite meanings.

Class Practice

A. Tell where these words may be divided at the end of a line. Also give another correct spelling for each word.
1. chequer   2. hearken   3. honour

B. Pronounce these words correctly. If more than one pronunciation is given in the dictionary, say the word each way.
1. finance   3. ostrich   5. zoology
2. Slav   4. placate   6. manor

C. For each word, give one definition which would require that the word be capitalized and one definition which would not require capitalization.
1. confederate   2. lord

D. For each of these words, give as many separate definitions as you can find. In each case, tell the part of speech.
1. plain   2. flock

E. Give the inflections your dictionary lists for each word.
1. focus   2. purify   3. shiny

F. Tell what usage labels your dictionary gives for each of these words.
1. shew   2. glasshouse   3. gumption

G. Tell what you can find about the origins of these words.
1. local   2. draft   3. rife

Written Exercises

A. Write another spelling for each word.
1. gauntlet   3. licence   5. pedlar
2. quire   4. draught   6. neighbour

B. Copy all the pronunciations for each word except those that follow *also* or any label that limits the acceptability of a pronunciation.
1. program   2. scourge   3. vehemence

C. For each word, copy one definition which would require that the word be capitalized and one definition which would not require capitalization.
1. capitol   2. protestant   3. pilgrim

D. For each underlined word, copy a dictionary definition or a synonym that gives the correct meaning.
1. We used the <u>lift</u> to reach the top floor of the building.
2. Due to a strange <u>affection</u>, Brother Galen could not come.
3. The deer have <u>barked</u> the fruit trees quite badly.
4. A little <u>smack</u> came in with a load of fish.
5. Always stay within the <u>pale</u> of God's will.
6. Boil the mixture until it <u>threads</u>.

Written Exercises

A. 1. gantlet   4. draft
2. choir   5. peddler
3. license   6. neighbor

B. 1. (prō′·gram′, prō′·grəm)   3. (vē′·ə·məns)
2. (skẽrj)

C. (Sample answers.)
1. *Capitol:* The building in Washington, D.C., where the Congress of the United States meets.
capitol: A building or complex of buildings in which a state legislature meets.

(The rest of this page's answers are on page 570.)

Lesson 114 Answers

Teacher: Answers are based on *The American Heritage Dictionary, Third Edition.* Other dictionaries may vary considerably. Check your school's dictionaries in order to properly credit your students' work.

Class Practice

A. 1. cheq/uer; checker   3. hon/our; honor
2. hear/ken; harken

B. 1. (fə·nans′, fī·nans′, fī′·nans′)
2. (slov)
3. (os′·trich, ôs′·trich)
4. (plā′·kāt′, plak′·āt′)
5. (zō·ol′·ə·jē)
6. (man′·ər)

C. 1. *Confederate:* A supporter of the American Confederacy; of or having to do with the American Confederacy.
confederate: An ally; allied.
2. *Lord:* God; Jesus.
lord: A man of high rank in a feudal society.

D. 1. *n.* large area of level or rolling treeless country; something free from ornament or extras
adj. level; undecorated; pure; unobstructed; obvious; blunt; utter; common; not complicated; not patterned; not pretentious; having neither beauty nor ugliness
adv. clearly; simply
2. *n.* a group of birds or mammals; a group of people under the guidance of a leader; a large number; a tuft of wool or cotton fiber; woolen or cotton refuse used for stuffing furniture; inferior wool added to cloth for weight; very short fiber used to form a pattern on cloth, paper, or metal
v. to gather or move in a crowd; to fill or decorate with flock; to texture with flock

E. 1. *n.* focuses *or* foci; *v.* focused *or* focussed; focusing *or* focussing; focuses *or* focusses
2. purified, purifying, purifies
3. shinier, shiniest

F. 1. archaic   3. informal
2. chiefly British

G. 1. from Middle English, from Old French, from Late Latin *localis,* from Latin *locus,* place
2. from Middle English *draught,* act of drawing or pulling, from Old English *dreaht;* akin to *dragan,* to draw
3. from Middle English, from Old English *ryfe*

7. Father ordered a load of <u>deal</u> from Cleaver's Building Supply.
8. The pages of the old book were <u>fallow</u> and brittle.

E. Copy the inflections your dictionary gives for these words.

1. ferry   3. moody   5. slay
2. ill   4. podium   6. kneel

F. Copy any usage labels your dictionary gives for these words.

1. officious   2. list   3. pone   4. post

G. Write out the etymology of each word, using no abbreviations.

1. charter   2. twine   3. pentagon

Review Exercises

A. Copy the underlined part of each sentence, using colons, semicolons, dashes, parentheses, and brackets where they are needed. Some sentences have notes to help you. [27, 29]

1. The following books of the Bible are considered <u>poetical, Job</u>, Psalms, Proverbs, Ecclesiastes, and the Song of Solomon.
2. "The Lord is my shepherd; I shall not <u>want lack anything</u>" (Psalm 23:1).
3. The prophet had disobeyed <u>God, consequently</u>, he was slain by a lion.
4. All the Israelites who <u>disobeyed even Moses were</u> barred from Canaan. (The parenthetical element is to be emphasized.)
5. The Good Samaritan demonstrated one important <u>quality, compassion</u>.
6. Judas <u>Iscariot later he would betray Jesus was</u> appointed as the treasurer. (The parenthetical element is relatively unimportant.)

B. Write correctly each item that should be italicized (underlined), should be written out in words, or needs an apostrophe or a hyphen. [30, 31]

1. Be sure you dont pronounce gesture with a hard g sound.
2. We started 75 tomato plants on our sun warmed porch.
3. The missionarys new boat, The Roving Wind, was destroyed in the storm.
4. The cocoa was packaged in one, five, and ten pound bags.
5. Last winter we had a sudden mid January thaw that wasnt good for the fruit trees.
6. 25 people had arrived by 7 oclock in the morning.

C. Choose the correct verbs for these sentences. [61, 62]

1. The temperature has (raised, risen) above 90° for four days in a row.
2. You should (let, leave) others choose first.
3. We (implied, inferred) from Mr. Harmon's words that he appreciated our offer to help.
4. Father said that we (can, may) take a break after these rows are hoed.
5. Little Benny was sick and (laid, lay) in bed all day.
6. Did anyone (lose, loose) a pen on the playground this morning?

7. pine or fir wood
8. light yellowish brown

E. 1. *v.* ferried, ferrying, ferries; *n.* ferries
2. worse, worst
3. moodier, moodiest
4. podia *or* podiums
5. slew, slain, slaying, slays
6. knelt *or* kneeled, kneeling, kneels

F. 1. archaic
2. archaic; obsolete
3. chiefly southern U.S.
4. chiefly British; archaic; obsolete

G. 1. from Middle English *chartre,* from Old French, from Latin *chartula,* diminutive of *charta,* paper made from papyrus
2. from Middle English *twinen,* from *twin,* twine, from Old English *twin,* double thread
3. from Late Latin *pentagonum,* from Greek *pentagonon: penta-,* penta- + *-gonon,* -gon

Review Exercises

A. 1. poetical: Job
2. want [lack anything]"
3. God; consequently
4. disobeyed—even Moses—were
5. quality: compassion
6. Iscariot (later he would betray Jesus) was

B. 1. don't, <u>gesture</u>, g
2. seventy-five, sun-warmed
3. missionary's, <u>The Roving Wind</u>
4. one-, five-, ten-pound
5. mid-January, wasn't
6. Twenty-five, o'clock

C. 1. risen   4. may
2. let   5. lay
3. inferred   6. lose

7. Please (set, sit) the soap bottle back on the shelf.
8. When we moved to northern Ontario, we (adapted, adopted) some of our gardening practices to the different climate.
9. When did your grandparents (emigrate, immigrate) from Russia?
10. Failing to eat a balanced diet can (affect, effect) a person's health.

7. set
8. adapted
9. emigrate
10. affect

---

115. Using a Thesaurus

> **Lesson Survey**
> - A **thesaurus** is a special book of synonyms and antonyms.
> - To choose a good synonym from a thesaurus, consider carefully the denotation and connotation, the level of formality, and the range of application of the word.

History and Use of Thesauruses

The word *thesaurus* (thi·sôr′·əs) comes from the Greek word for "treasury." A thesaurus is indeed a treasury of related words. Each entry includes a list of words with similar meanings. At the end of this list of synonyms, the entry may include several antonyms along with a list of related entries for further study. A thesaurus is thus a help to expressive writing. It will remind you of words that might be suitable, and it will increase your vocabulary as you see new words related to words you already know.

The first known English thesaurus was developed by Peter Mark Roget (rō·zhā′), a British physician of the 1800s who enjoyed experimenting with words. Roget collected hundreds of words and placed them in groups according to their meanings. He numbered each group of words and made an index for the numbered groups. Then when he wanted a particular word to put into his writing, he could find exactly the right word.

In 1852, Roget published his *Thesaurus of English Words and Phrases* for the benefit of other writers. Many words have since been added to Roget's first collection, and many words that have outgrown their usefulness have been removed. Also, most modern thesauruses no longer use a system of numbered word groups keyed to an index; instead, all the entries appear in alphabetical order. But some thesauruses today still bear Roget's name.

How can you use a thesaurus to improve your writing? For an illustration, suppose you had written the following sentence in a story.

Father was concerned about Frank's indifference toward advice.

Lesson 115

Purpose: (1) To study the use of the thesaurus. (2) To encourage its use in selecting effective words.

Oral Review:

1. In what two ways are variant spellings shown in a dictionary? (If the spellings are close together in alphabetical order, they are listed together, with the more common spelling as the main entry word. If the two spellings are not close together, each is listed as a separate entry word. The entry for the less common spelling refers to the more common spelling, and the entry for the more common spelling shows the other as an alternate spelling.)
2. What three types of inflections are commonly shown in dictionary entries? (irregular plural forms of nouns, irregular principal parts of verbs, and irregular forms of comparison for adjectives and adverbs)
3. What are some usage labels that warn about words that we should avoid? (vulgar, nonstandard, substandard, illiterate, slang)
4. When is it acceptable to use words labeled *informal*? (in everyday speaking or writing, such as in notes to yourself or in friendly letters)
5. What do the labels *archaic* and *obsolete* indicate about words? (that they are no longer in general use)
6. Name the four main purposes for using commas. (to divide compound sentences; to separate items in a series; to set off introductory material; to set off nonrestrictive and independent elements)

Lesson Introduction: Somewhere in this classroom there is a valuable store of treasure! It is located in a space about [you supply the dimensions

But you are not satisfied with the word *indifference*. You want to express the idea of indifference with a bit more intensity. If you look up the word *indifference* in a thesaurus, you may find synonyms like *unconcern, apathy, coldness,* and *inattention*. None of these words says quite what you want, so you look at the related words at the end of the entry and find *dislike*. You turn to that entry, and there you find the words *distaste, disgust, antipathy, antagonism, aversion,* and *hatred*. These words communicate the more intense idea that you want. You decide to replace *indifference* with one of these synonyms.

Father was concerned about Frank's antagonism toward advice.

Choosing Effective Synonyms

When you find synonyms in a thesaurus, you must choose which one best fits your need. Very few English synonyms are interchangeable in every context. The following points will be helpful when you are choosing synonyms.

1. *Consider both the denotation and the connotation of the words.* The words *antique, old-fashioned, time-honored, decrepit,* and *out-of-date* are all synonyms of *old*. Here are definitions of these five synonyms.

> **antique**—1. Relating to ancient times or an earlier period. 2. Old-fashioned.
> **old-fashioned**—1. Relating to or characteristic of former times. 2. Favoring or adhering to customs of a past era.
> **time-honored**—Honored because of age or long use.
> **decrepit**—Weakened or worn-out by excessive age or use.
> **out-of-date**—Old-fashioned; outmoded; obsolete.

Although these words are synonyms, each word is different from the rest. Part of that distinction results from differences in the denotation—the strict, exact meanings of words. Notice especially that the basic meanings of *time-honored* and *decrepit* contrast sharply with each other and contain ideas not found in the other three definitions. In contrast, the basic meanings of *antique, old-fashioned,* and *out-of-date* are much more similar.

All words have denotation. In addition, each word has a distinct connotation—the "personality" of the word or the feeling it conveys. Consider the three synonyms above with similar denotations: *antique, old-fashioned,* and *out-of-date*. You could use any of these synonyms to describe a tractor. However, the connotation of *antique* makes you think of a tractor with high value because of its age. In contrast, *out-of-date* implies that the tractor is not as useful as modern tractors and may need to be replaced. The connotation of *old-fashioned* is more neutral. An old-fashioned tractor is not particularly valuable, but neither is it useless.

All this means that you need to be well familiar with the synonyms you consider using. If you choose a word whose usage is not familiar to you,

of a thesaurus in your classroom]. In fact, it is clearly labeled with a word that means *treasury*. Can you tell me where it is?

A thesaurus is a treasury indeed! This book, available at almost any bookstore for a few dollars, is a valuable aid to effective speaking and writing. Let's explore the treasure contained between the covers of this book.

Lesson Outline:

1. A thesaurus is a special book of synonyms and antonyms.

   a. Each entry includes a list of words with similar meanings.

   b. At the end of this list of synonyms, the entry may include several antonyms along with a list of related entries for further study.

   c. A thesaurus is a help to expressive writing because it reminds you of words that might be suitable, and it will increase your vocabulary as you see new words related to words you already know.

   d. Most modern thesauruses are arranged in alphabetical order.

    Note: In a thesaurus arranged according to Roget's original classification, the words are grouped according to related meanings with a number for each group. These numbers are keyed to an index to help you find the word you want.

2. When choosing a synonym, remember the following points.

   (1) *Consider both the denotation and the connotation of the words.*

you can easily write an absurd sentence. For example, suppose a writer wants a word to replace *break,* and he finds the following synonyms in a thesaurus: *smash, shatter, infringe, violate, transgress.* He chooses *violate* and writes the following sentence. Can you see what is wrong?

> Mother violated the eggs into the pan.

2. *Consider the level of formality of the words.* In the previous lesson, you learned that words labeled *informal* in a dictionary are acceptable only in everyday speaking and writing. Even some words that are not labeled *informal* may have a more informal tone than other words. *Fake* money could be called *counterfeit* or *phony,* but *counterfeit* is definitely more suitable for formal usage.

3. *Consider the range of application of the words.* Although *house, dwelling,* and *residence* are synonyms of *home,* each word has its own specific range of use. *House* and *dwelling* refer mainly to the building, while *home* suggests the warmth and security of family living. *Residence* is a more formal term; it is used in legal papers and in referring to the dwelling of a rich or high-ranking person. Use exact words when possible, but be sure their meaning fits your use.

> Love makes a <u>house</u> a <u>home</u>.
> The governor's <u>residence</u> stood in sharp contrast to the <u>dwellings</u> of the common people.

Use a thesaurus to make your writing more effective and interesting. The more precise and vivid your written words, the better the reader will understand and enjoy them. Instead of writing "He walked across the room," try "He sauntered," "He strolled," or "He paced across the room." Instead of "the light from the fireplace," write "the glow," "the gleam," "the radiance," or "the glare from the fireplace."

Do not be content with humdrum words when you have a treasury of words to choose from. Why write words that *exist,* when you can write words that *live?*

Class Practice

A. Use a thesaurus to find synonyms for these words.
   1. reject (verb)   2. obedience   3. healthy

B. Find a specific synonym, appropriate for formal writing, for each underlined word. Use a thesaurus and a dictionary as needed.

   The <u>captive</u> <u>fled</u> from the <u>lockup</u> where he had been <u>kept</u> in <u>lone</u> <u>constraint</u>.

Written Exercises

A. Using a thesaurus, write at least five synonyms for each of these words.
   1. frugal   2. add   3. absence

Lesson 115 Answers

Class Practice

A. (Sample answers.)
   1. refuse, repudiate, decline, deny, rebuff, repel
   2. observance, compliance, docility, tractability, deference, respect
   3. well, sound, hearty, hale, robust, vigorous

B. (Sample answers.)
   captive: prisoner, convict
   fled: escaped
   lockup: prison, jail, penitentiary
   kept: held, detained
   lone: solitary, isolated
   constraint: confinement, detention

Written Exercises

A. (Sample answers.)
   1. economical, careful, prudent, thrifty, temperate, moderate
   2. annex, affix, append, attach, join, total
   3. nonappearance, nonattendance, nonresidence, lack, need, want

a) The denotation of a word is its strict, exact meaning.
b) The connotation of a word is its "personality" or the feeling it conveys.
(2) *Consider the level of formality of the words.*
(3) *Consider the range of application of the words.*

B. For each underlined word, write a synonym appropriate for formal writing. Use a thesaurus to help you.
1. Roy has a special <u>talent</u> for woodworking.
2. The <u>pleasant</u> day would soon be over.
3. We finished our work before <u>night</u>.
4. The <u>noise</u> was unbearable.
5. I heard Doctor Sanders <u>suggest</u> that you stay in bed.
6. May's <u>despair</u> was sad to see.
7. The class had more <u>energy</u> than I had expected.
8. God's people should never be <u>stingy</u>.
9. Does he <u>often</u> go away?
10. We eagerly <u>expect</u> Grandfather Wenger's arrival.

C. Write the word that has the best connotation for its use in the sentence.
1. His sister is a (skinny, slender, gaunt) person.
2. The rescuers found the survivors (skinny, slender, gaunt) and dehydrated.
3. The rescue team had worked with great (confidence, courage, boldness) to free the trapped miners.
4. The disciples were often too (dull, feeble-minded, uneducated) to understand what Jesus was saying.
5. In many poor countries, large numbers of people are (dull, feebleminded, uneducated).
6. I sometimes make the (careless, foolish, reckless) mistake of writing *it's* for *its*.
7. The man who caused the accident was fined for (careless, foolish, reckless) driving.
8. Brother Charles (directed, commanded, ordered) the students to recite the poem together.
9. David felt (sad, sorry, heartbroken) after he cut off part of Saul's robe.
10. He was (sad, sorry, heartbroken) when he learned that Absalom was dead.

Review Exercises

A. Copy each word or number that should be followed by a comma, and add the missing mark. Some sentences need more than one comma. [23, 25]
1. You will need Bibles, pens and papers for this class.
2. We sang for Mr. Winslow but he declared that he would never come to church.
3. If you meet Sue tell her that we expect a visit from her.
4. They have lived at East King Street Lancaster since February 25 1956.
5. No Mother we have not seen Johnny since noon.
6. Nancy the twin with blond hair was hurt.
7. "Do the best job that you know how to do" the teacher encouraged.

B. (Sample answers. Check for connotation, formality, and range of application.)
1. ability, genius, knack, aptitude
2. enjoyable, delightful, fair, sunny
3. dark, darkness
4. clamor, din, clangor, uproar, racket
5. advise, recommend, propose, propound
6. dejection, depression, melancholy, despondency, gloom, hopelessness
7. vigor, stamina, zeal, spirit, ebullience, animation, vivacity, vitality (*Pep* is informal.)
8. miserly, ungenerous
9. repeatedly, regularly, frequently, habitually
10. anticipate, await, contemplate

C. 1. slender
2. gaunt
3. courage
4. dull
5. uneducated
6. careless
7. reckless
8. directed
9. sorry
10. heartbroken

Review Exercises

A. 1. pens,
2. Winslow,
3. Sue,
4. Street, Lancaster, 25,
5. No, Mother,
6. Nancy, hair,
7. do,

8. Brother Stauffer who is nearly blind preaches well without notes.
9. Grandfather's kind mellow voice I'm sure would convince anyone that he is a true friend.
10. The brethren who visited Louis Getz Sr. were happy to tell him the simple Gospel story.

B. If the underlined part of the sentence contains an error in preposition usage, write it correctly. If it has no error, write *correct*. [104]
1. God's answer to our prayers may be <u>different than our expectations</u>.
2. Although stormy trials beset us, we know that <u>in back of the clouds</u> shines God's great love.
3. God allows varied experiences <u>in our lives</u> to test our faith.
4. <u>Beside the clear teachings</u> of the Scriptures, many lessons from history can guide our steps.
5. Rather than becoming <u>angry at those</u> who mistreat us, we should love and forgive them.
6. If you step <u>outside of the boundaries</u>, you are automatically caught.
7. We are late because we had to <u>wait on a train</u> in Denver.
8. Everyone <u>except me</u> seemed to understand the puzzle.

8. Stauffer, blind,
9. kind, voice, sure,
10. Getz, Sr.,

B. 1. different from our expectations
2. behind the clouds
3. correct
4. Besides the clear teachings
5. angry with those
6. outside the boundaries
7. wait for a train
8. correct

---

116. Writing a Summary

Lesson Survey

- A **summary** is a condensed review of the main points in a composition.

- A summary promotes concentration, it is helpful for reviewing material quickly, and it is a benefit to those who may not have time to read the longer composition.

- Follow these steps in planning a summary.
  1. Skim the composition you plan to summarize.
  2. Read the composition carefully for thorough understanding.
  3. Write down the main points of the composition.

- Follow these steps in writing a summary.
  1. Write the title of the composition and the author's name (if it is given).
  2. Write the summary in your own words.
  3. Include the main points in their original order.
  4. Make the summary of an appropriate length.
  5. Check your summary for accuracy and clarity.

Lesson 116

Purpose: To show the purpose and method of writing a summary.

Oral Review:

1. In what way should a descriptive composition be similar to a character sketch? (Both focus on one impression.)
2. What kind of vivid, concrete words should be used in descriptive writing? (exact nouns, expressive verbs, colorful adjectives and adverbs)
3. In addition to vivid, concrete words, what contributes to good descriptive writing? (figurative language, appeal to the five senses)
4. What is a persuasive argument? (an attempt to persuade or move to action)
5. What is the proposition of an argument? (the statement of the idea that the writer is promoting)

6. What is a poetic foot? (one accented syllable and the unaccented syllable or syllables associated with it)
7. Name the correct meter for each description.
   a. one unaccented syllable followed by one accented syllable (iambic)
   b. one accented syllable followed by two unaccented syllables (dactylic)
   c. one accented syllable followed by one unaccented syllable (trochaic)
   d. two unaccented syllables followed by one accented syllable (anapestic)

Lesson Introduction: The sum of 2 + 2 + 2 is 6. The sum, one number, states the total of all the other numbers. We would not want to always say "the combination of numerals 2 + 2 + 2" whenever we needed the numeral 6. So summaries are a valuable aid, a concise way of giving information.

Even though you may not be able to tell another person how to summarize, you have been summarizing for years. Every time you tell someone else about a personal experience, you give a summary of the actual happening because you omit many of the details and tell only the highlights. A *summary* is a condensed review of the main points in a composition.

Importance of Summaries

Summaries have a number of advantages. First, the preparation for writing a summary promotes concentration. Unless you concentrate on what you are reading, you will not be able to identify the main points and put them into neat little packages of thought. Such concentration helps you to remember what you have read.

Second, summaries help you to review material quickly. Some textbooks place summaries at the end of lessons or chapters. The Lesson Survey before each lesson in this course is a kind of summary. The summaries you write when studying, whether in note form or paragraph form, provide convenient source material to review later when you prepare for a test. Sermon notes are really summaries of messages. They provide an excellent way to review what you have heard.

Third, summaries can benefit others. They can be read by those who may not have time to read the longer composition.

Planning a Summary

Before you can write a good summary, you need to be acquainted with the material to be summarized. Follow these steps in planning a summary.

1. *Skim the composition you plan to summarize.* If skimming is to be profitable, your mind cannot be lazy. You must be alert and observant—quick to sort out and evaluate what you are reading. As you scan through the composition, read any headings or subheadings in the text. Read the first sentence of each paragraph. Here and there read a sentence or two, or even a full paragraph occasionally. Watch for significant words and phrases in the composition.

2. *Read the composition carefully for thorough understanding.* Pay close attention to words in boldface or italics. Read the composition more than once if necessary to understand it fully.

3. *Write down the main points of the composition.*

Writing a Summary

Follow these steps in writing a summary.

1. *Write the title of the composition and the author's name (if it is given).* If you are summarizing an article from a periodical, include the name and date of the periodical.

You may have the students turn to Ecclesiastes 12:13, 14 and Hebrews 8:1, 2 for examples of summaries in the Bible.

Lesson Outline:

1. A summary is a condensed review of the main points in a composition.

2. The preparation for writing a summary promotes concentration.

    a. You must concentrate to identify the main points.

    b. Such concentration helps you to remember what you have read.

3. A summary is helpful for reviewing material quickly.

    a. Some textbooks place summaries at the end of lessons or chapters.

    b. You may write summaries in note form o[r] paragraph form when studying.

    c. Sermon notes are summaries of messages.

4. A summary can benefit those who may no[t] have time to read the longer composition.

5. Follow these steps in planning a summar[y]

    (1) *Skim the composition you plan to summa[-]rize.*

      a) You must be alert and observant—quic[k] to sort out and evaluate what you ar[e] reading.

      b) As you scan the composition, read an[y] headings or subheadings in the text.

      c) Read the first sentence of each paragrap[h] and even a full paragraph occasionall[y]

      d) Watch for significant words and phrase[s]

    (2) *Read the composition carefully for thoroug[h] understanding.*

2. *Write the summary in your own words.* Copy from the original composition only occasionally and only if you want to preserve the impact of the author's exact words. If you do quote the author's words, be sure to enclose them in quotation marks.

3. *Include the main points in their original order.* Avoid adding information not in the composition (such as your own thoughts and opinions). Do not include examples or illustrations unless they are essential to explaining a point. Include just enough material to make the summary clear.

4. *Make the summary of an appropriate length.* A summary may range from less than a hundred words to about one-third the length of the original composition. Its length is affected by how long the original composition is, how many main points there are, and how thorough the summary is. In this chapter, you will work with summaries having about 50 to 120 words.

5. *Check your summary for accuracy and clarity.* Does what you have written accurately convey the meaning of the original composition? Have you included all the main points? Are all quotations properly credited?

Read the following article. Then read the summary of the article.

Original article:

Strength in Weakness
By L. Birky

To be strong when we are weak is a Bible paradox contrary to man's reasoning. We discover this strength only as we realize our own weakness. We shall consider three expressions of weakness in which Christ's strength becomes available to us and we find true strength.

First is the weakness of weeping. "No sense in crying," the world would say. "Everybody does wrong occasionally. Forget it." But David, who knew and loved God's ways, mourned and would not forget his sin until it was forgiven. Also, as we weep for the sins of others and intercede for them, God convicts them of sin and some will repent. God has promised, "They that sow in tears shall reap in joy" (Psalm 126:5).

Next is the weakness of submission. The world would say, "Why do you think you must do what God says? Think for yourself. Be strong. Show that you have authority too." However valid this reasoning may sound, it can never make us strong, because man has no truly good ideas or authority of his own. We receive strength only by admitting our weakness and submitting to the God of all knowledge and authority, for we have knowledge and authority only in Him.

Third is the weakness of waiting. "Get busy, organize, and get things done. No time to be down on your knees," the world would say. But God can accomplish more through a weak saint on his knees

   a) Pay close attention to words in boldface or italics.
   b) Read the composition more than once if necessary to understand it fully.
 (3) *Write down the main points of the composition.*

6. Follow these steps in writing a summary.
 (1) *Write the title of the composition and the author's name (if it is given).* If you are summarizing an article from a periodical, include the name and date of the periodical.
 (2) *Write the summary in your own words.*
   a) Copy from the original composition only if you want to preserve the impact of the author's exact words.
   b) If you do quote the author's words, be sure to enclose them in quotation marks.

 (3) *Include the main points in their original order.*
   a) Avoid adding information not in the composition.
   b) Do not include examples or illustrations unless they are essential to explaining a point.
   c) Include just enough material to make the summary clear.
 (4) *Make the summary of an appropriate length.*
 (5) *Check your summary for accuracy and clarity.*

than what many strong men can accomplish by running here and there with airs of great importance. As we pray, obey, and wait, God will work for us. He is our strength as we wait in full obedience to Him.

True strength is the power of God in a powerless man.

A Summary of "Strength in Weakness"
By L. Birky

A strange Bible paradox is that the child of God finds strength in weakness. The world considers weeping a weakness. But weeping may be a sign of repentance or of concern for others' sins. The world considers submission a weakness. But we find strength, knowledge, and authority only by "submitting to the God of all knowledge and authority." The world considers waiting a weakness. But God can do more through one weak, praying saint than what many men can accomplish in their own strength. The writer concludes by saying, "True strength is the power of God in a powerless man."

The title and the author's name are given first. Then the main thought of each paragraph is stated briefly. The original composition is 291 words long. The summary is 100 words long—about one-third the length of the composition.

Class Practice

The following paragraph has 150 words. Following the steps in the lesson, work together on writing a summary that contains 40–50 words.

Stages of Parasitic Diseases

There are usually three stages to sickness from parasitic diseases. Before the symptoms appear is the first stage, called the *incubation period.* The patient may have been carrying the parasites in his body for several days while they grew and multiplied to a point where the body became ill from their effects. During the incubation period, while the parasites are growing and multiplying, the host may spread the disease to many more people. When the symptoms finally appear, the patient enters the second stage of the disease, called the *acute period.* The parasites are by this time causing the body much damage. During this period, a fierce battle rages between the body and the disease parasites. When the body wins the victory, the acute period ends and the recovery, or *convalescence period,* begins. During this period the body is repairing the damage caused by the parasites and regaining normal strength.

Written Exercises

A. Turn to the composition "Three Common Kinds of Storms" in Lesson 39. This essay contains about 350 words. Following the steps in this lesson, write a summary that contains 90–120 words.

Lesson 116 Answers

Class Practice

(Sample summary.)

A Summary of "Stages of Parasitic Diseases"

A sickness from parasitic diseases usually has three stages. During the incubation period, the parasites are making the body ill. During the acute period, the body is fighting to overcome the parasites. During the convalescence period, the body is repairing the damage caused by the parasites.

Written Exercises

A. (Sample summary.)

A Summary of "Three Common Kinds of Storms"

The most common storm is the thunderstorm, which is caused by warm, moist air condensing into billowy clouds. It can cause damage by heavy rains, hail, high winds, and lightning. The largest of storms is the hurricane, which begins over tropical water. This storm moves forward slowly, but it causes severe damage with its high winds and heavy rains. The most violent storm is the tornado, which is formed in an unstable atmosphere. Although it is relatively small, a tornado "causes almost total destruction of everything in its path because of its extremely high winds and low pressure."

3. Choose a composition and write a summary of it. Here are some suggestions to choose from. Get your teacher's approval if you choose a composition from a different source.

1. Genesis 12–14
2. Judges 6, 7
3. Acts 27, 28
4. A story in your reading textbook
5. A lesson in your science or history textbook

B. (Individual work.)

---

117. Using Encyclopedias and Atlases

Lesson Survey

- An **encyclopedia** contains articles on a wide range of subjects.
- An encyclopedia has a number of features that aid in research.
- You must use an encyclopedia with caution.
- An **atlas** is a book of maps.

Dictionaries and thesauruses are valuable tools for helping you to use words properly and effectively. Two valuable reference sources for other kinds of information are encyclopedias and atlases.

Encyclopedias

An *encyclopedia* contains articles on a wide range of subjects. These articles are arranged in alphabetical order and put into volumes with letters on the spine to show what subjects can be found in each one. For example, to find information on the library, look in the *L* volume of an encyclopedia.

The better acquainted you become with encyclopedias, the more uses you can find for them. They are important aids in preparing for reports or in finding how to make projects for history and art classes. They are full of biographical and geographical information to supplement your regular school studies.

Research aids. Encyclopedias have a number of features that aid in research. After some entries you may find cross-references that direct you to other entries, where you will find further related information. Some encyclopedias include bibliographies after many entries. These lists refer you to books that give more detailed information on the subject.

Another important research aid is the index, found in the last volume of the encyclopedia. Use it to find all the information that the encyclopedia gives on a particular subject. You may think all the other information can be found by using cross-references as mentioned above. But those cross-references

---

Lesson 117

Purpose: (1) To study the use of encyclopedias and atlases. (2) To teach the proper use of their indexes.

Oral Review:

1. In many dictionaries, a variant spelling that is definitely less common follows what word? *(also)*

2. What three kinds of inflections are commonly shown in dictionary entries? (irregular plural forms of nouns, irregular principal parts of verbs, irregular forms of comparison for adjectives and adverbs)

3. Name three things that you should consider when choosing a synonym from a thesaurus. (the denotation and connotation, the level of formality, the range of application)

4. Identify each sentence according to its structure.
   a. The Bible is our map to glory, and we can follow it with confidence. (compound)
   b. This is the day that the Lord has made, and we should rejoice in it. (compound-complex)
   c. When temptations allure us, we seek God's help. (complex)
   d. We should consider others and seek their best welfare. (simple)

Lesson Introduction: Write *encyclopedia* on the board. It comes from two Greek words: *enkyklios,* meaning "general," and *paideia,* meaning "education." Why is this an appropriate name? Do you know any one person who could write an encyclopedia? Why are there many writers? The encyclopedia is a handy reference for much of the knowledge that man possesses. Learn to use it effectively and discerningly.

Lesson Outline:

1. An encyclopedia contains articles on a wide range of subjects.

merely give the titles of related articles, whereas the index refers you to articles that may have only a few sentences dealing with your subject.

The following example shows what an index entry for *Bohemia* may look like.

> **Bohemia** [region, Czechoslovakia] **B:347** *with map*
>   Austria (The Hapsburgs) **A:909–910**
>   Czechoslovakia **Ci:966**; (The Rise of Bohemia) **Ci:972**
>   Moravia **M:657**

Furthermore, the index is useful in locating information about items for which there are no specific articles. For example, an encyclopedia will probably not have an article about the bark beetle. However, the index entry may look like this:

> **Bark beetle** [insect]
>   Dutch Elm Disease **D:316** *with picture*
>   Forestry (Diseases and Pests) **F:349**

Since new events are continually happening, encyclopedias cannot keep up to date. For this reason, some encyclopedias annually publish a yearbook, bringing the latest events and discoveries to you. If you need recent information that is not included in the encyclopedia, try the latest yearbook.

Important cautions. Although encyclopedias contain much useful knowledge and interesting information, you must use them with caution. Learn to detect the errors commonly found in encyclopedias. These books are written from a point of view that glorifies man and his achievements rather than honoring God and His eternal will. Furthermore, encyclopedias present as facts many ideas and theories, such as evolution, that are contrary to God's Word.

Compare all that you read with the standard of the Bible. Your parents and teachers will help you to recognize ideas that are merely the theories of men rather than the truth of God.

Do not assume that an article in the encyclopedia provides the ultimate information about a particular subject. Many writers miss the bountiful fruits of broad research by limiting their resource material to an encyclopedia article. You will find much more useful information by studying the book *The Hive and the Honeybee* than you will by merely reading the article "Bee" in an encyclopedia. An encyclopedia is an easily accessible source of general information. However, you must consult more detailed reference material for a thorough study of a certain subject.

Atlases

An *atlas* is a book of maps. World atlases have detailed maps of all the regions in the world, showing the world geographically and politically.

2. An encyclopedia has a number of features that aid in research.

a. After some entries you may find cross-references that direct you to other entries, where you will find further related information.

b. Some encyclopedias include bibliographies, which refer you to books that give more detailed information on the subject.

c. The last volume is an index that lists all the information that the encyclopedia gives on a particular subject.

d. An annual yearbook provides information about the latest events and discoveries.

3. You must use encyclopedias with caution.

a. Learn to detect the errors commonly found in encyclopedias.

1) They are written from a point of view that glorifies man and his achievements rather than honoring God and His eternal will.

2) They present as facts many ideas and theories that are contrary to God's Word.

b. Do not assume that an article in the encyclopedia provides the ultimate information about a particular subject.

4. An atlas is a book of maps.

a. World atlases have detailed maps of all the regions in the world, showing the world geographically and politically.

1) Geographical maps portray such things as topography, vegetation, land use, rainfall, climate patterns, and population density.

2) Political maps show the boundaries of nations, states, and provinces.

Geographical maps portray such things as topography, vegetation, land use, rainfall, climate patterns, and population density. Political maps show the boundaries of nations, states, and provinces. Since there are continual political changes and engineering improvements, the accuracy of these atlases often depends on how recently they were published.

A road atlas is a guide for traveling and an aid for learning many geographical facts. It contains maps showing roads, airports, national forests, and much more information useful to travelers. Besides the maps themselves, it may also have information about things like the topography and historical significance of places shown on the maps.

A Bible atlas has maps of Bible lands as they were at various periods of Bible history, such as Palestine in Abraham's time and in David's time. Besides maps, you will find many illustrations of things and places mentioned in the text. Fascinating accounts of archeological discoveries show what man has uncovered that corresponds exactly with Bible history. In addition, some larger Bible atlases (like *Baker's Bible Atlas* and *The Moody Atlas of Bible Lands*) contain information about the history and geography of an area, explaining how these affected the Bible characters who lived at the times and places being discussed.

An atlas usually has an index (sometimes called a gazetteer), which lists the names of places shown on the maps. Each index entry has numbers or letters indicating which maps show that place, along with a guide to find the place by latitude and longitude or by letters and numbers.

Class Practice

A. Answer these questions.
1. How is an encyclopedia similar to a dictionary?
2. How are these two reference sources quite different?
3. What dangers may you encounter when using an encyclopedia?
4. Of what special value is the index of an encyclopedia?
5. Why should a world atlas or a road atlas be of recent publication?
6. How is a Bible atlas similar to other atlases? How is it different?

B. Give the number of the encyclopedia volume in which you would find an article on each of the following subjects.
1. How rayon is manufactured
2. Chief exports of South Korea
3. Finger painting
4. How dew is formed
5. Subways
6. Tonsillitis

Written Exercises

A. Using the index, list all the volumes and page numbers where you could find information on the following subjects.
1. Mayflower Compact
2. Greenhouses
3. Strip mining
4. Peanut

3) Since there are continual political changes and engineering improvements, the accuracy of these atlases often depends on how recently they were published.

b. A road atlas is a guide for traveling and an aid for learning many geographical facts.
1) It contains maps showing roads, airports, national forests, and much more information useful to travelers.
2) It may also have information about things like the topography and historical significance of places shown on the maps.

c. A Bible atlas has maps of Bible lands as they were at various periods of Bible history.
1) It has many illustrations of things and places mentioned in the text.

Lesson 117 Answers

Class Practice

A. 1. Both are arranged alphabetically.
2. An encyclopedia gives much more extensive information.
3. the influence of looking at subjects from man's point of view rather than God's, and the idea that an encyclopedia article provides the ultimate information about a particular subject
4. The index tells where to find all the information that the encyclopedia contains about a particular subject.
5. because of continual political changes and engineering improvements
6. They all contain maps. A Bible atlas contains much historical as well as geographical information.

B. (Answers depend on the encyclopedia used.)

Written Exercises

A. (Answers depend on the encyclopedia used.)

---

2) Fascinating accounts of archeological discoveries show what man has uncovered that corresponds exactly with Bible history.
3) Some larger Bible atlases contain information about the history and geography of an area, explaining how these affected the Bible characters who lived at the times and places being discussed.

d. An atlas usually has an index that lists the names of places shown on the maps.

B. Use an encyclopedia to find and write answers to the following questions.
1. What kind of island is Krakatoa?
2. What is Henry Wadsworth Longfellow noted for? When did he live?
3. In what kind of soil does rice grow best?
4. Which states in the United States produce the most flaxseed?
5. Who were the first men to walk on the moon?
6. What is the largest lake in Utah?

C. Use an atlas index to find these places and answer these questions.
1. Which city is farther east: Bonn, Germany or Paris, France?
2. Which city is farther north: Montreal, Quebec or Caribou, Maine?
3. Which city is farther west: Pittsburgh, Pennsylvania or Miami, Florida?
4. Which city is farther south: Miami, Florida or Chihuahua, Mexico?
5. What interstate highway crosses Colorado from north to south?
6. What two United States highways intersect at Fremont, Nebraska?

Review Exercises

A. Match each sentence below to the proper description by writing the correct letter.
   a. simple sentence with no compound parts
   b. simple sentence with a compound predicate
   c. compound sentence with two independent clauses
   d. compound sentence with three independent clauses
   e. complex sentence with only one dependent clause
   f. complex sentence with two dependent clauses
   g. compound-complex sentence
1. Daily we kneel before the Lord and seek His guidance.
2. Those who love the Lord love to obey His Word.
3. A worldly person puts much emphasis on fun; but he can never have true joy, because he rejects the only source of joy.
4. In spite of unpleasant circumstances, the Christian rejoices in the Lord.
5. Seeds of thought become deeds, deeds become habits, and habits forge destinies.
6. If you would enjoy a full life, you must walk the path that brings joy.
7. Faithfulness in the little tests prepares us for the greater tests.
8. God's grace is always sufficient; however, sometimes men fail to trust His grace.

B. If the underlined part of the sentence has an error, write it correctly. If it is correct, write *correct*.
1. The man who helped us is he.
2. We hardly expected these heifers to be their's.
3. Brenda, Linda, and her will ride in our van.

B. 1. Krakatoa is a volcanic island.
2. Longfellow is famous for his poetry. He lived from 1807 to 1882.
3. Rice grows best in soil that holds water well.
4. North Dakota and South Dakota produce the most flaxseed.
5. The first men to walk on the moon were Neil A. Armstrong and Edwin E. Aldrin, Jr.
6. The Great Salt Lake is the largest lake in Utah.

C. 1. Bonn, Germany   4. Miami, Florida
   2. Caribou, Maine   5. Interstate 25
   3. Miami, Florida   6. Route 30 and Route 77

Review Exercises

A. 1. b
   2. e
   3. g
   4. a
   5. d
   6. f
   7. a
   8. c

B. 1. correct
   2. theirs
   3. she

4. Nevin picked more blackberries than <u>I</u>.
5. <u>Us eighth graders</u> have written several compositions this year.
6. Before you leave, please check with <u>myself</u>.
7. <u>Somebody's</u> paper has fallen to the floor.
8. The man <u>which</u> waved to us buys sweet corn at our stand.

4. correct
5. We eighth graders
6. me
7. correct
8. who

---

118. Using Concordances, Bible Dictionaries, and Topical Bibles

Lesson Survey

- A **concordance** lists Bible words alphabetically and gives references where the words are used.
- Some concordances give the original Hebrew and Greek words from which the English words in the Bible were translated.
- A **Bible dictionary** is a small encyclopedia of Bible knowledge.
- A **topical Bible** is an alphabetical arrangement of Bible topics.
- Use these reference books with discernment.

The previous lessons on reference sources have dealt primarily with the world of *secular* knowledge. But a far superior realm of knowledge is available to people who believe in God. This *spiritual* knowledge we find in the Holy Bible.

Possibly ever since you can remember, you have heard the Bible read every day, whether at home, at school, or at church. You have heard and read such words as *mantle* and *publican*. But what do these words really mean? Or you may occasionally think of a verse or verse fragment. Where can you find that verse? Where can you find Scripture verses that deal with a topic such as *honesty*? By using concordances, Bible dictionaries, and topical Bibles, you have the privilege of digging into God's Word and gaining a greater understanding of this Book of all books.

Concordances

A *concordance* lists Bible words alphabetically and gives references where the words are used. It is common for a Bible to have a small, limited concordance in the back. You can also find compact concordances that are more satisfactory than those found in most Bibles. However, a

---

Lesson 118

Purpose: To study the use of concordances, Bible dictionaries, and topical Bibles.

Oral Review:

1. Name four research aids found in many encyclopedias. (cross-references, bibliographies, index, yearbooks)
2. What are two important cautions to remember when using encyclopedias? (Learn to detect errors. Do not assume that an article in the encyclopedia provides the ultimate information about a particular subject.)
3. What is the difference between geographical and political maps? (Geographical maps portray such things as topography, vegetation, land use, rainfall, climate patterns, and population density. Political maps show the boundaries of nations, states, and provinces.)
4. Name three things that you should consider when choosing a synonym from a thesaurus. (the denotation and connotation, the level of formality, the range of application)

Lesson Introduction: How many students have heard or read the verse, "Weeping may endure for a night, but joy cometh in the morning"? How many can give the reference? (Psalm 30:5) The words *employer* and *employee* do not occur in the Bible. How could you find verses that deal with the subject of employment? (Use a topical Bible.)

All the work and intensive study involved in compiling concordances, Bible dictionaries, and topical Bibles is certainly worthy of our respect and appreciation. A part of showing this appreciation is to make practical use of these valuable tools.

complete concordance, like *Strong's Exhaustive Concordance of the Bible*, has the most value because it records every word found in the Bible. These words are arranged in alphabetical order as entries, with the references and a portion of each verse containing the listed word.

Some concordances give the original Hebrew and Greek words from which the English words in the Bible were translated. The main one that does this is *Strong's Exhaustive Concordance,* in which the entry word in each reference is keyed to a number. That number refers to a word in one of the dictionaries in the back of the concordance. Sometimes the same English word is used to translate two or more different Hebrew or Greek words. Then there are two or more different numbers in the entry.

Numbers for Old Testament words are shown in regular type, like this: 879; and numbers for New Testament words are shown in italics, like this: *1905.* The Old Testament was written in Hebrew (with a few portions in Chaldee); so the numbers for Old Testament words are found in the "Hebrew and Chaldee Dictionary" in the back of the concordance. The New Testament was written in Greek, so the numbers for New Testament words are found in the "Greek Dictionary of the New Testament."

Suppose you had read these words in Romans 12:11: "Not slothful in business; fervent in spirit." What is the connection between business and being fervent in spirit? Under *business* in *Strong's Concordance,* you will see "Ro 12:11 Not slothful in *b*; fervent in," followed by the number *4710.* Since this is a New Testament reference, find that number in the "Greek Dictionary of the New Testament." Entry number *4710* is shown here, with its various parts labeled.

```
         original   English   pronun-          root    related
      Greek word   spelling   ciation          word   English word
          ↓          ↓          ↓                ↓          ↓
4710. σπουδή  spŏudē, spoo-day'; from 4692; "speed",
i.e. (by impl.) despatch, eagerness, earnestness:—   ← meanings
business, (earnest) care (-fulness), diligence,     ← translations in KJV
forwardness, haste.
```

Notice the three main parts of the entry. First is the original word in Greek letters, followed by its spelling and pronunciation in English letters. Second is the meaning of the word in the original language. Third, after the colon and dash, the entry lists all the ways that the word is translated in the King James Version of the Bible.

This entry should give you a good understanding of the Greek word numbered *4710.* To broaden your understanding, you can look up the definition of word number *4692,* from which it was derived. (That word means "to speed.") You can also use the concordance to look up all the other English translations of the word (*care, carefulness, diligence, forwardness, haste*),

Lesson Outline:

1. A concordance lists Bible words alphabetically and gives references where the words are used.

2. Some concordances give the original Hebrew and Greek words from which the English words in the Bible were translated.
Strong's Exhaustive Concordance, the most common one of this kind, gives a number for the entry word in almost every reference.

    a. Numbers for Old Testament words are shown in regular type and refer to entries in the "Hebrew and Chaldee Dictionary."

    b. Numbers for New Testament words are shown in italics and refer to entries in the "Greek Dictionary of the New Testament."

    c. Each entry in these dictionaries consists of three main parts.

    1) It shows the original word in Hebrew or Greek letters, followed by its spelling and pronunciation in English letters.

    2) It explains the meaning of the word in the original language.

    3) After the colon and dash, it lists all the ways that the word is translated in the King James Version of the Bible.

3. A Bible dictionary is a small encyclopedia of Bible knowledge.

    a. Like an ordinary dictionary, it has entry words in alphabetical order, as well as guide words, pronunciations, and definitions.

    b. Illustrations are often included to clarify the definitions, as well as maps of Bible lands, reports on archaeological findings, biographies of Bible characters, and outlines of the books of the Bible.

and read the verses that are keyed to number *4710*. One is found in the expression "he that ruleth, with *diligence*," in Romans 12:8—just three verses earlier in the same chapter.

Bible Dictionaries

A *Bible dictionary* is a small encyclopedia of Bible knowledge. This book, like an ordinary dictionary, has entry words in alphabetical order, as well as guide words, pronunciations, and definitions. Illustrations are often included to clarify the definitions, as well as maps of Bible lands, reports on archaeological findings, biographies of Bible characters, and outlines of the books of the Bible. With this extensive information, many entries in a Bible dictionary resemble encyclopedia articles.

In reading the story of Elijah and the prophets of Baal, have you ever wondered just how big Mount Carmel was? A Bible dictionary indicates that it was a ridge more than twelve miles long, with an average height of 1,500 feet. In addition, you may learn that this mountain was considered sacred to Baal, which helps to explain why the contest between Elijah and the prophets of Baal took place there.

Topical Bibles

A *topical Bible* is an alphabetical arrangement of Bible topics. In contrast to a concordance, a topical Bible arranges verses according to themes. It includes verses that relate to a theme like holiness even if they do not contain the word *holiness*. This makes it simple for a Bible student to study a broad range of verses on any particular subject. Many of these topics are divided into subtopics for more detailed study.

In *Nave's Topical Bible*, the most complete one available, the entry "Temptation" includes the following subheadings: "A Test," "Leading Into," "Resistance to," and "Yielding to." There are also cross-references to topics such as "Demons," "Faith, Trial of," "Satan," and "Affliction, Design of."

The Works of Men: Use With Care

Although these reference books have much value, they are the works of men. Therefore, you must use them with discernment. Of the three reference books described in this lesson, concordances are the least affected by men's ideas. The original language dictionaries are produced by men, but they present factual information with only a minimum of man's interpretation. A topical Bible depends somewhat more on men's ideas because compilers arrange the verses according to their interpretation of Bible themes. But the articles in a Bible dictionary include information gathered from sources other than the Bible. This information is subject to error because man's observations and learning are not perfect.

4. A topical Bible is an alphabetical arrangement of Bible topics.

    a. This makes it simple for a Bible student to study a broad range of verses on any particular subject.

    b. Many of these topics are divided into subtopics for more detailed study.

5. Use these reference books with discernment.

    a. Concordances are the least affected by men's ideas. The original language dictionaries are produced by men, but they present factual information with only a minimum of man's interpretation.

    b. A topical Bible depends somewhat more on men's ideas because compilers arrange the verses according to their interpretation of Bible themes.

    c. Articles in a Bible dictionary include information gathered from sources other than the Bible. This information is subject to error because man's observations and learning are not perfect.

Class Practice

Answer these questions about the reference books discussed in this lesson.

1. a. In what two languages was the Old Testament originally written?
   b. In what language was the New Testament originally written?
2. What are the three main parts of each entry in the original language dictionaries of *Strong's Exhaustive Concordance*?
3. a. How is a Bible dictionary arranged like a regular dictionary?
   b. How is it more similar to an encyclopedia?
4. How would you benefit by looking up *humility* in a topical Bible rather than in a concordance?
5. How is a long entry in a topical Bible arranged so that it is simpler to find references for specific aspects of the topic?
6. Why must you use these reference books with care?

Written Exercises

A. Using a concordance, complete the following verses. Include the reference.
   1. "Rejoicing in hope; patient in tribulation; . . .
   2. "He which testifieth these things saith, . . .
   3. "The words of the Lord are pure words: as silver tried in a furnace . . .

B. Use *Strong's Exhaustive Concordance* to do these exercises.
   1. Look up the word *heaviness*.
      a. How many times does this word appear in the Old Testament?
      b. How many different Hebrew words were translated *heaviness*?
      c. Write the word from this list that could replace the word *heaviness* in each reference below.

      anxiety   feebleness   mourning
      fasting   grief   sickness
      (1) Ezra 9:5   (4) Proverbs 12:25
      (2) Psalm 69:20   (5) Isaiah 29:2
      (3) Proverbs 10:1   (6) Isaiah 61:3
   2. What is a bushel as mentioned in Matthew 5:15?
   3. What was the talent mentioned in Matthew 25:25?
   4. What is the meaning of *Belial* in the phrase "son of Belial" or "man of Belial"?
   5. What kind of people are the meek that are mentioned in Psalm 37:11?

C. Use a Bible dictionary to answer the following questions.
   1. What did the Jews use for tombs?
   2. The term *barbarian* was originally used by the Greeks in referring to whom?
   3. What was a sheepcote in Bible times?
   4. About how many acres did Jericho cover?

Lesson 118 Answers

Class Practice

1. a. Hebrew and Chaldee
   b. Greek
2. The word itself, the meaning of the word in the original language, and the various ways that the word is translated in the King James Version of the Bible.
3. a. It has entry words in alphabetical order as well as guide words, pronunciations, and definitions.
   b. It has long articles with extensive information.
4. A topical Bible would list all the references that deal with the theme of humility, even if the verses do not include the word *humility*.
5. It is divided into subtopics.
6. They are the works of men and subject to error.

Written Exercises

A. 1. continuing instant in prayer" (Romans 12:12).
   2. Surely I come quickly. Amen. Even so, come Lord Jesus" (Revelation 22:20).
   3. of earth, purified seven times" (Psalm 12:6).

B. 1. a. 9
      b. 7
      c. *(1)* fasting   *(4)* anxiety
         (2) sickness   *(5)* mourning
         (3) grief   *(6)* feebleness
   2. a certain dry measure
   3. a certain coin or sum of money
   4. without profit, worthlessness, destruction, wickedness
   5. gentle in mind, saintly

C. 1. caves
   2. people who spoke a language other than Greek
   3. a sheepfold or sheep pen
   4. 8½ acres

5. What is the meaning of *Azariah*? How many Bible characters had this name?

6. What kind of mirrors were used in Bible times?

D. Use a topical Bible to find verses about these subjects. For each one, copy two verses with their references from two different books of the Bible.

1. Perseverance   3. Fear of God, Guilty
2. Idleness   4. Righteousness, Fruits of

Review Exercises

A. Label each underlined item *adj.* or *adv.* [97]

1. A *(a)* <u>kindly</u> smile brightens the *(b)* <u>homeliest</u> face *(c)* <u>with its cheer</u>.
2. *(a)* <u>To cultivate contentment</u>, we should count our *(b)* <u>many</u> blessings.
3. God *(a)* <u>daily</u> loads us with blessings *(b)* <u>to use in His service</u>.
4. *(a)* <u>After the storm</u>, we saw a *(b)* <u>dazzling</u> rainbow, so beautiful *(c)* <u>that we gazed upon it in awe</u>.
5. The wind *(a)* <u>that accompanied the storm</u> flattened the corn in the *(b)* <u>far</u> end *(c)* <u>of the garden</u>.

B. Copy these sentences, and label the part of speech for each word. [110]

1. The righteous seek to please Jesus in all that they do.
2. A humble person willingly serves God and others.
3. Behold, God's grace is sufficient for every trying circumstance.

---

119. Using a Public Library

> **Lesson Survey**
> • A **public library** is a valuable source of information.
> • Use a library courteously and prudently.
> • Many libraries use the Dewey decimal system of classification, by which books are arranged according to subject.

Even though your home library may contain quite a large group of books, it is small in comparison to the number of books available for people to read. Public libraries give people access to a large number of books at a relatively small cost.

Values of the Library

A *public library* is a valuable source of information. In the library you will find numerous books of *fiction* (stories that are not factual) and of *nonfiction* (factual information). The library also contains other literary

---

Lesson 119

Purpose: (1) To teach the proper use of *the library as a reference source. (2) To introduce *the Dewey decimal system.

Oral Review:

1. In what languages were the Old and the New Testament written? (*Old Testament:* Hebrew and Chaldee; *New Testament:* Greek)
2. Name the three parts of each entry in the original language dictionaries in the back of *Strong's Exhaustive Concordance.* (the word itself, the meaning of the word in the original language, and the various ways that the word is translated in the King James Version of the Bible)
3. What advantage does a topical Bible have over a concordance? (It lists all the references that deal with a subject, even if the verses do not have a particular word.)

---

5. "helped by Jehovah" *or* "Jehovah has helped"; 22 or 23

6. mirrors made of polished metal

Review Exercises

A. 1. a. adj.   b. adj.   c. adv.
   2. a. adv.   b. adj.
   3. a. adv.   b. adj.
   4. a. adv.   b. adj.   c. adv.
   5. a. adj.   b. adj.   c. adj.

B. 1.
```
        adj.        n.      v.     n.        n.  prep.pron.pron.
```
The righteous seek to please Jesus in all that
```
   pron. v.
```
they do.

2.
```
   adj.    adj.       n.        adv.      v.    n.   conj.
```
A humble person willingly serves God and
```
   pron.
```
others.

3.
```
   interj.   adj.    n.   v.    adj.   prep. adj.   adj.
```
Behold, God's grace is sufficient for every trying
```
                n.
```
circumstance.

---

4. What are two important cautions to remember when using encyclopedias? (Learn to detect errors. Do not assume that an article in the encyclopedia provides the ultimate information about a particular subject.)

5. Tell how to diagram the following sentence parts.

a. an objective complement (after the direct object, separated by a slanted line)

b. verbals used as adjectives or adverbs (across the corner of a slanted and a horizontal line placed under the word modified)

c. verbals used as nouns (across the corner of a slanted and a horizontal line placed on a pedestal where a single-word noun would go)

materials such as magazines, newspapers, and language records. For a small fee, many libraries offer interlibrary services, whereby you can borrow books from other libraries. Furthermore, the librarians can help you locate hard-to-find information.

Courteous Use of the Library

A public library has rules for the benefit of everyone who uses it. You should show your appreciation for the library by obeying the rules courteously. One of these is the rule of quietness. Many people come to the library to read and study, and they need quietness for concentration. Respect this rule. Walk softly in the building, and talk quietly.

Another rule is carefulness. Handle the books gently, remembering that they do not belong to you. Turn pages without creasing or tearing them. Lay books down carefully instead of throwing them. As you handle a book, appreciate the thought and effort that went into making the book so that you can read it. When you take a book from its place on the shelves to examine it, remember where it was so that you can replace it correctly.

A third rule is punctuality. If you borrow some books, remember the return date and have them back to the library on time. If you discover that a book is overdue or that you have lost one, promptly make the payment that is required. Showing appreciation for the library by quietness, carefulness, and punctuality is a small fee to pay in return for all the privileges you have there.

Prudent Use of the Library

The great majority of books in a public library are written by unbelievers. Many of those books are unfit to read, especially the ones in the realm of fiction. Some works of fiction do show history or varied lifestyles in a way that helps us to understand people of other times and places. But often the evil so far outweighs the good that these books are still more harmful than helpful.

Even books of nonfiction present a danger. As you saw in Lesson 117, many reference books contain man's wrong theories. For these reasons, you should go to a public library only with your parents' supervision, and be sure you have your parents' approval before you read a book from a public library.

Only one thing will keep you from being harmed by finding untruth in books you read. That one thing is a full knowledge of God and His Word. God's Word is a library, too—a library of sixty-six books that cover all the subjects of life. As your mind is filled with the truth of the Bible, you will have a standard with which to compare all other books. Then you will know which books to reject as deception, and which to accept as providing helpful information.

Lesson Introduction: When a friend asks to borrow your book *Home Fires Beneath the Northern Lights,* what do you do? You probably go to your bookcase, find it, and gladly lend it to him. But if you have several bookcases filled with books arranged in no particular order, it would be much harder to find the one you want. The larger the group of books, the longer it takes to find one of them unless they are arranged in a particular order. That is why most public libraries use the Dewey decimal system. This lesson gives an introduction to using a public library.

Lesson Outline:

1. A public library is a valuable source of information.
- a. It has numerous books of fiction and of nonfiction.
- b. It also contains other literary materials such as magazines, newspapers, and language records.
- c. For a small fee, many libraries offer interlibrary services, whereby you can borrow books from other libraries.
- d. Librarians can help you locate hard-to-find information.

2. Use a library courteously.
- a. Be quiet so that others can read and study.
- b. Be careful to handle the books gently and to replace them correctly on the shelves in the right order.
- c. Be punctual in returning your books and in paying the amount required for overdue or lost books.

3. Use a library prudently. Go to a public library only with your parents' supervision, and be sure you have your parents' approval before you read a book from a public library.

The Dewey Decimal System

Many libraries use the Dewey decimal system of classification, by which books are arranged according to subject. Notice the careful arrangement of the Dewey decimal system below. The number and subject name of each classification are printed in boldface, followed by some of the subdivisions in that category.

000–099 General Works—encyclopedias, book lists, periodicals
100–199 Philosophy—nature of truth, superstition, logic
200–299 Religion—the Bible, church history, world religions, denominations
300–399 Social Sciences—government, law, education, societies, customs
400–499 Language—language study, composition writing, dictionaries
500–599 Pure Sciences—mathematics, astronomy, chemistry, biology
600–699 Applied Sciences—inventions, engineering, aviation, homemaking (cooking, sewing, improvements), business methods
700–799 Arts and Recreation—architecture, painting, music, sports
800–899 Literature—narratives, poetry, essays
900–999 Geography and History—atlases, national and world history, biographies

How does this reference system help you to find one book among the many on the shelves? A *call number* is written plainly on the spine of each book. This call number comes from the classification of the book according to the Dewey decimal system. A library database includes the correct call number with every book listed for the library. A computer is used to find a book by author name, by book title, or by subject keyword.

When you know the call number of the book you need, you can go straight to the shelves labeled with the appropriate range of numbers. For example, if your book is about stars, it will be on the shelves labeled 500–599. Then the numbers within that range of call numbers (502.52, 502.53, 503.01) enable you to move in the right direction along the shelves to the exact spot where your book is. Of course, even with the efficiency of the system, you will need practice in order to find books rapidly.

In the Dewey decimal system, the ten main classes are broken down into divisions and further into subdivisions. You have seen, for example, that the 200–299 class deals with *religion*. All the books listed under the 280's have to do with religious *denominations*. The 289's contain the subdivision of *other denominations* and *sects,* with the Mennonite bodies under 289.7. A particular book about the Mennonites might have the call number 289.724.

Class Practice

A. Answer these questions.
  1. What is the difference between fiction and nonfiction?

      a. The great majority of books in a public library are written by unbelievers.
        1) Many books of fiction are unfit to read.
        2) Many reference books contain man's wrong theories.
      b. Only a full knowledge of God and His Word will keep you from being harmed by finding untruth in books you read.

    4. Many libraries use the Dewey decimal system of classification, by which books are arranged according to subject.
      a. There are ten main classes of subjects in this system.
      b. Each class can be broken down into divisions and further into subdivisions.
      c. Each book in a library is given a specific call number, based on this system.

Lesson 119 Answers

Class Practice

A. 1. Books of fiction contain stories that are not factual. Books of nonfiction contain factual information.

2. In addition to the actual materials in a library, what services do libraries offer?

3. What are three ways to use a library courteously?

4. Why is it important to compare all books from a public library with the library of God's Word?

5. What is the call number of a book?

B. Tell whether these titles belong to the *fiction* or the *nonfiction* group.

1. *Caring for African Violets*
2. *The Life of Thomas Edison*
3. *Princess in Calico*
4. *Sunshine Country*
5. *Holy Bible*
6. *Traveling the Way*

C. Which number group of the Dewey decimal system would contain a book on these subjects?

1. a book that teaches Latin
2. a book on Canadian history
3. a cookbook
4. a book on trees
5. a Bible commentary
6. a book on the Anabaptists
7. a book on the life of Christ
8. a book about democracy in America
9. a book on beating time in music
10. a book on electrical work

D. What main class of the Dewey decimal system does each call number below fit into?

1. 533.2   2. 812.56   3. 945.7   4. 312.3

Written Exercises

A. Write *fiction* or *nonfiction* for each book title.

1. *Mennonites in Europe* (history of the Mennonite Church in Europe)
2. *Doctrines of the Bible* (summaries of major Bible doctrines)
3. *Pilgrim's Progress* (well-known allegory by John Bunyan)
4. *Timber: The Renewable Resource* (about forests and logging)
5. *Folk Tales From Norway* (traditional stories told in Norway)
6. *Sight Within: Helen Keller* (about a well-known woman who was blind and deaf)

B. For each call number in parentheses, write the subject name of the main class in the Dewey decimal system to which the book belongs (General Works, Philosophy, and so on.)

1. *Poems of Nature* (808.81)
2. *How to Read Faster and Better* (428.4)
3. *All the Women of the Bible* (220.92)
4. *Painting Landscapes* (758.1)
5. *Living Within Limits* (304.66)
6. *Presidents of the United States* (923.1)
7. *Storytelling: Art and Technique* (808.06)
8. *Conquering Shyness* (155.2)

2. For a small fee, many offer interlibrary services, whereby you can borrow books from other libraries. The librarians can help you locate hard-to-find information.

3. Be quiet. Be careful with the books. Be punctual in returning books or in paying for overdue or lost books.

4. to be able to detect falsehood in what we read

5. the number that a library assigns to a book, based on the Dewey decimal system

B. 1. nonfiction
2. nonfiction
3. fiction
4. fiction
5. nonfiction
6. fiction

C. 1. 400–499
2. 900–999
3. 600–699
4. 500–599
5. 200–299
6. 200–299
7. 200–299
8. 300–399
9. 700–799
10. 600–699

D. 1. Pure Sciences
2. Literature
3. Geography and History
4. Social Sciences

Written Exercises

A. 1. nonfiction
2. nonfiction
3. fiction
4. nonfiction
5. fiction
6. nonfiction

B. 1. Literature
2. Language
3. Religion
4. Arts and Recreation
5. Social Sciences
6. Geography and History
7. Literature
8. Philosophy

Teacher: In the time since this book was originally published, libraries have switched from card catalogs to computer databases. Since knowing about the card catalog may no longer be useful, you may want to omit most of Lesson 120. Discuss the Special Arrangements section on pages 596 and 597, and assign Part C of the Written Exercises and the Review Exercises. Also make the following changes.

Lesson 122: Omit numbers 4–6 in Part E on page 605. Also omit Parts E and F on pages 606 and 607.

Lesson 124: Omit numbers 5–7 in Part K on page 615.

Chapter 11 Test: Omit numbers 7–9.

9. *The Complete Book of Vitamins* (613.2)
10. *Halley's Comet* (523.6)

Review Exercises

A. Diagram these sentences.
1. In the Bible we find much advice to follow.
2. Because God loves us, He shows us the way of life.
3. Serving the Lord is man's highest duty.
4. We should consider the Bible a matchless treasure.
5. Jesus Christ, whom we love, deserves our loyalty and trust.
6. Father's answer was what we had expected.
7. Mother sliced some apples into a bowl after lunch to use them for pies.
8. At the edge of the clearing stood a small fox.

B. Write the letter of the item that is capitalized correctly. [21]
1. a. "Begin the Day with God"
   b. "Begin the Day With God"
2. a. in the Ten Commandments
   b. in the ten commandments
3. a. with Biblical principles
   b. with biblical principles
4. a. learned in Reading class
   b. learned in reading class
5. a. several days last winter
   b. several days last Winter
6. a. in the Revolutionary War
   b. in the revolutionary war
7. a. who live in the west
   b. who live in the West
8. a. over the Painted desert
   b. over the Painted Desert
9. a. for Brother Dale
   b. for brother Dale
10. a. Elkton Mennonite school
    b. Elkton Mennonite School

---

120. Using the Card Catalog

Lesson Survey

- The **card catalog** is an index of the books in a library.
- The card catalog contains title, author, and subject cards.
- Libraries often keep reference books, books of fiction, and biographies in separate locations.

One of the first things you will want to find as you enter a library is the card catalog. In most libraries it is found close to the librarian's desk. You can recognize it by its many small drawers, each one tagged with one or more letters. As you open the drawers, you will find them full of index cards.

Lesson 120

Purpose: To teach how to use *the card catalog to find books in a library.

Oral Review:

1. What are the three rules for courteous use of the library? (Be quiet; be careful; be punctual.)
2. Why must we use the library prudently? (Many books in a public library are not fit to read.)
3. What library can protect us from the untruths found in a public library? (the library of God's Word)
4. What is the name of the most commonly used classification system for library books? (Dewey decimal system)
5. Tell how to correct these sentences.
   a. Aaron has darker hair than anyone in his family. (anyone else)

9. Applied Sciences   10. Pure Sciences

Review Exercises

A. 1.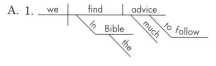

2.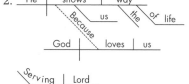

3.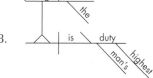

4.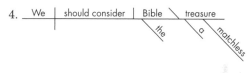

5.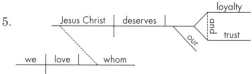

6.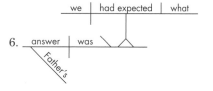

7.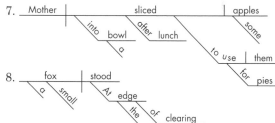

8.

B.
1. b	6. a
2. a	7. b
3. a	8. b
4. b	9. a
5. a	10. b

1 A–Am	6 D	11 I	16 N	21 S–Sl
2 An–Az	7 E	12 J–K	17 O	22 Sm–Sz
3 B	8 F	13 L	18 P–Pl	23 T
4 C–Cl	9 G	14 M–Mh	19 Pm–Pz	24 U–V
5 Cm–Cz	10 H	15 Mi–Mz	20 Q–R	25 W–Z

The Card Catalog

The *card catalog* is an index of the books in a library. Each book of non-fiction has three cards in the drawers to represent it: a title card, an author card, and a subject card. Each book of fiction has only two cards: a title card and an author card. Since these cards are all arranged in alphabetical order, you can easily find the card you are looking for. When you find the card, look for the call number in the upper left-hand corner. This call number tells you exactly where to find the book on the shelves.

In many modern libraries, books are found by using computers or microfilm instead of a card catalog with drawers and cards. These methods use more advanced technology, but they are still based on the concept of the card catalog and the Dewey decimal system.

The Cards

Title cards. Are you looking for a specific title? Then go by the first word of the title. But if the title begins with *A, An,* or *The,* go by the second word. The card for the book *The Bumble of the Bumblebee* would be found in the drawer labeled B of the pictured card catalog. The card may look like this:

Bumble of the Bumblebee, The

533.1
 Letle, Norman 1880–1962
  The Bumble of the Bumblebee
   Ransom Pub., Chicago, 1948
  164p. illus.

   A fascinating study of the bumblebee, showing many of its habits.

---

  b. Who put these here books on the couch? (these books)

  c. Room 2 has less students than Room 3. (fewer students)

  d. I just finished a real worthwhile book. (really worthwhile)

  e. This plant is an undesirable weed. (is a weed)

 6. Name the reference book that fits each description.

  a. An index of Bible verses containing specific words. (concordance)

  b. A book of maps. (atlas)

  c. A source of general information about many subjects. (encyclopedia)

  d. An encyclopedia of Bible knowledge. (Bible dictionary)

  e. A book that groups Bible verses according to topics. (topical Bible)

  f. A book that shows the spellings, pronunciations, meanings, and etymologies of words. (dictionary)

  g. A collection of synonyms. (thesaurus)

Lesson Introduction: When you go to a library for information, you may know exactly what book to look for. You may even know where to find it on the shelves. But more often you will be less sure of yourself. You may know the title of a book but not the author. Or you may have the name of an author but no titles. And perhaps you know only that you want information on a certain subject. Whatever your situation, you should go to the card catalog. It will help you to find books by titles, authors, or subjects.

Lesson Outline:

1. The card catalog is an index of the books in a library.

Notice the information that the card provides.
1. The title. Since this is a title card, the title is centered in the first line.
2. The call number. This is the Dewey decimal number, which tells you exactly where to find the book.
3. The author. The dates of his birth and death may be shown after his name.
4. The title, the publisher, and the place and date of publication.
5. Number of pages. If illustrations are included in the book, the card will tell you.
6. A brief description.

Any other information at the bottom of the card is for library personnel.

Author cards. Suppose you were looking for information about bees, and you know that Norman Letle has written on that subject. Then look for a card (an author card) with the name *Norman Letle* at the top. Since authors are listed by their last names, cards for books by Norman Letle will be found in the drawer labeled L. Every book written by Norman Letle will have an author card with the book title beneath his name. This card gives the same information as a title card, but the heading of the card is the author's name instead of the book title.

```
┌─────────────────────────────────────────────┐
│                                               │
│          Letle, Norman 1880–1962              │
│                                               │
│   533.1                                       │
│       The Bumble of the Bumblebee             │
│         Ransom Pub., Chicago, 1948            │
│       164p. illus.                            │
│                                               │
│         A fascinating study of the bumblebee, │
│   showing many of its habits.                 │
│                                               │
│                                               │
└─────────────────────────────────────────────┘
```

Subject cards. If you need information on bumblebees and have no particular title or author in mind, use the subject cards. You could try "bumblebees" for a heading. If there is no such heading, think of a similar heading such as "bees" or "insects." Or you may find a subject card that tells you to look under another subject for information.

The subject card is just like the title and author cards except that the heading of the card is the subject. Remember, there is no subject card for a book of fiction.

a. Each book of nonfiction is represented by three cards in the drawers: a title card, an author card, and a subject card.

b. Each book of fiction has only two cards: a title card and an author card.

c. These cards are all arranged in alphabetical order.

d. The call number of the book is written in the upper left-hand corner and tells you exactly where to find the book on the shelves.

2. The card catalog contains title, author, and subject cards.

a. A title card gives the following information.

1) The title. Since this is a title card, the title is centered in the first line.

2) The call number. This is the Dewey decimal number, which tells you exactly where to find the book.

3) The author. The dates of his birth and death may be shown after his name.

4) The publisher and the place and date of publication.

5) Number of pages. If illustrations are included in the book, the card will tell you.

6) A brief description.

b. An author card gives the same information, but the heading of the card is the author's name.

c. The subject card is just like the title and author cards except that the heading of the card is the subject. There is no subject card for a book of fiction.

3. Libraries often keep reference books, books of fiction, and biographies in separate locations.

a. Reference books are marked with an *R*, besides having a Dewey decimal number and

---

Bees

533.1
   Letle, Norman 1880–1962
      The Bumble of the Bumblebee
         Ransom Pub., Chicago, 1948
      164p. illus.

         A fascinating study of the bumblebee, showing
      many of its habits.

Special Arrangements

   All the books in a library are classified within the Dewey decimal system. But three groups of books—reference, fiction, and biography—are outstanding because they are so large. Therefore they are each kept in special places in the library, separate from the other books in the Dewey decimal system.

   Reference books. These are books that are not normally read from beginning to end, but are used for looking up facts. They are marked with an *R* for *reference,* besides having a Dewey decimal number. The third line has a Cutter number, which is a number that libraries assign to a particular author or compiler. The following illustration shows the spine tag that may be found on the book *The History of the United States,* by Theodore Smith.

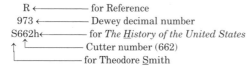

   Fiction. Books of fiction are part of the 800–899 group of the Dewey decimal system. They are marked with an *F,* which takes the place of the Dewey decimal number. They are arranged alphabetically by the last name of the author. *Struggling Upward,* by Horatio Alger, Jr., may have the spine tag shown below.

      F
   A395s (*A* stands for Alger; 395 is the Cutter number; *s* is the first
      letter in the title.)

   Biography. Books about the personal lives of individuals are found in the 920–929 classification. The spine tag may have a *B* for *biography* or

---

a Cutter number. (*Note:* Cutter numbers are named after their inventor, Charles A. Cutter, an American librarian of the late 1800s.)

  b. Books of fiction (in the 800–899 group) are marked with an *F,* which takes the place of the Dewey decimal number. They are arranged alphabetically by the last name of the author.

  c. Biographies (in the 920–929 group) may have a *B* for *biography* or the number 92 instead of a Dewey decimal number.

   1) They are arranged in alphabetical order according to the name of the person they are written about.

   2) Books about the same person are grouped together and arranged alphabetically by the authors' last names.

:he number 92 instead of a Dewey decimal number. Biographies are
arranged in alphabetical order according to the name of the person they
are written about. Books about the same person are grouped together and
arranged alphabetically by the authors' last names. A book written by
Benson about Daniel Webster may have the following spine tag.

> B
> W3781b (*W* stands for Webster; 3781 is the Cutter number; *b* stands
> for Benson, the author.)

Class Practice

A. Using the illustration of the card catalog in this lesson, tell the number of the drawer in which the following cards would be found.

1. Subject cards
   - a. Forestry
   - b. Oil painting
   - c. Mining
   - d. Flowers
2. Author cards
   - a. Faye Natilie
   - b. Ellen Zane
   - c. David Richards
   - d. Nevin Keen
3. Title cards
   - a. The Lively Art of Writing
   - b. Mountain Streams
   - c. Calling From Afar
   - d. The Long Way Home

B. Draw three rectangles on the board or on paper to represent index cards.
Make one each of the three kinds of cards for the following book.

Doctors Who Saved Lives; by Lynn and Gray Poole; Dodd, Mead &
Company, New York, 1966; illustrated; 148 pages; call number 926;
subject, Medical History. The stories of sixteen men of medicine and their
associates, who made significant contributions to medical advancement
from the 16*th* to the 20*th* century.

Written Exercises

A. Using the illustration of the card catalog in this lesson, write the number of the drawer in which the following cards would be found.

1. Subject cards
   - a. Typing
   - b. Pennsylvania history
   - c. Storytelling
   - d. Astronomy
   - e. Foods, preserving
   - f. Ospreys
   - g. Earthquakes
   - h. John Adams
2. Author cards
   - a. James Allen
   - b. W. Phillip Keller
   - c. Joan W. Blos
   - d. Shirley Graham
   - e. Patrick Moore
   - f. Peter Freuchen
   - g. Irwin T. Sanders
   - h. Frank B. Latham

Written Exercises

A. 1. a. 23   e. 8
      b. 18   f. 17
      c. 22   g. 7
      d. 2   h. 1
   2. a. 1   e. 15
      b. 12   f. 8
      c. 3   g. 21
      d. 9   h. 13

Lesson 120 Answers

Class Practice

A. 1. a. 8   b. 17   c. 15   d. 8
   2. a. 16   b. 25   c. 20   d. 12
   3. a. 13   b. 15   c. 4   d. 13

B. **Title card:**

Doctors Who Saved Lives
926
Poole, Lynn and Gray
Doctors Who Saved Lives;
Dodd, Mead & Company, New York, 1966
148p. illus.
The stories of sixteen men of medicine and their associates, who made significant contributions to medical advancement from the 16*th* to the 20*th* century.

Author card:

Poole, Lynn and Gray
926
Doctors Who Saved Lives;
Dodd, Mead & Company, New York, 1966
148p. illus.
The stories of sixteen men of medicine and their associates, who made significant contributions to medical advancement from the 16*th* to the 20*th* century.

Subject card:

History, Medical
926
Poole, Lynn and Gray
Doctors Who Saved Lives;
Dodd, Mead & Company, New York, 1966
148p. illus.
The stories of sixteen men of medicine and their associates, who made significant contributions to medical advancement from the 16*th* to the 20*th* century.

3. Title cards
   a. The Deep Earth
   b. Life in the Northwest Territory
   c. In the Hands of Senecas
   d. A Gathering of Days
   e. Traveling the Way
   f. Marketing of Farm Products
   g. The Story of Our Bible
   h. Doctrines of the Bible

B. Draw three rectangles on your paper to represent index cards. Make one each of the three kinds of cards for the following book.

   Exodusters; by Nell Irvin Painter; Alfred A. Knopf, Inc., New York, 1976; 288 pages; illustrated; call number 978.1; subject, Afro-American History; A vivid, well-documented account of the migration of thousands of recently freed Blacks from the South to Kansas.

C. Classify each item as *reference, fiction,* or *biography.*
   1. Imaginary stories.
   2. Books of general information.
   3. Belong to the 800–899 group of the Dewey decimal system.
   4. May have the number 92 instead of a Dewey decimal number.
   5. Stories about the personal lives of individuals.
   6. Books used for looking up facts.
   7. Belong to the 920–929 group of the Dewey decimal system.
   8. Books are arranged alphabetically by the last name of the author.
   9. Books are arranged alphabetically according to the name of the person written about.
   10. Books are arranged according to the Dewey decimal numbers.

Review Exercises

A. If the underlined part of the sentence contains an error in adjective or adverb usage, write it correctly. If it is correct, write *correct.* [83, 88, 93, 98]
   1. When Elijah told the people his plan, he <u>already knew</u> which God would answer by fire.
   2. <u>Them prophets</u> of Baal made quite a commotion.
   3. They <u>sure tried</u> hard to make Baal pay attention to them.
   4. Christians should lead <u>respectful lives</u> in society.
   5. Even though others may despise us, we must <u>continue on doing</u> right.
   6. Many have served the Lord with far <u>less freedoms</u> than we enjoy.
   7. These cows can feed on <u>lush, luxuriant pasture.</u>
   8. Nevin and Barry are the same age, but Nevin <u>is tallest</u> by six inches.

Review Exercises

A. 1. correct
   2. Those prophets
   3. surely tried
   4. respectable lives
   5. continue doing
   6. fewer freedoms
   7. lush (*or* luxuriant) pasture
   8. is taller

3. a. 6   e. 23
   b. 13   f. 14
   c. 11   g. 22
   d. 9   h. 6

B. **Title card:**

```
              Exodusters
978.1
    Painter, Nell Irvin
      Exodusters;
         Alfred A. Knopf, Inc., New York, 1976
    288p. illus.

      A vivid, well-documented account of the mi-
    gration of thousands of recently freed Negroes
    from the South to Kansas.
```

Author card:

```
            Painter, Nell Irvin
978.1
      Exodusters;
         Alfred A. Knopf, Inc., New York, 1976
    288p. illus.

      A vivid, well-documented account of the
    migration of thousands of recently freed
    Negroes from the South to Kansas.
```

Subject card:

```
           History, Afro-American
978.1
    Painter, Nell Irvin
      Exodusters;
         Alfred A. Knopf, Inc., New York, 1976
    288p. illus.

      A vivid, well-documented account of the mi-
    gration of thousands of recently freed Negroes
    from the South to Kansas.
```

C. 1. fiction   6. reference
   2. reference   7. biography
   3. fiction   8. fiction
   4. biography   9. biography
   5. biography   10. reference

9. In fact, Nevin is taller than <u>any student</u> in his class.
10. After I reread the lesson, the concepts seemed <u>some clearer</u>.

3. Write which reference book you would use to find each item of information. [117, 118]
 1. The distance between Bethlehem and Samaria.
 2. Scripture references for a study on fasting.
 3. A route from Columbia, South Carolina to Atmore, Alabama.
 4. New Testament verses that mention Balaam.
 5. Archaeological discoveries that show Bible incidents.
 6. How rubber is made.
 7. The latitude and longitude of Mardin, Turkey.
 8. Who wrote the books of 1 and 2 Chronicles.
 9. The meaning of the word translated *pulse* in Daniel 1:12.
 10. Which state produces the most cheese.

9. any other student
10. somewhat clearer

B. 1. Bible dictionary *or* Bible atlas
 2. topical Bible
 3. atlas
 4. concordance
 5. Bible dictionary *or* Bible atlas
 6. encyclopedia
 7. atlas
 8. Bible dictionary
 9. concordance
 10. encyclopedia

121. Giving an Oral Book Report

Lesson Survey

- A **book report** should include these kinds of information.
 1. Basic facts such as title, author, and publisher.
 2. The setting of the story.
 3. Brief descriptions of the main characters.
 4. The theme of the book.
 5. Lessons that the book teaches.
 6. Your evaluation of the book.
- Follow these steps in planning an oral book report.
 1. Read an approved book.
 2. List details for the six points given above.
 3. Write out your notes.
 4. Practice giving your book report.

Preparing and giving an oral book report has several advantages for yourself and for others. First, it compels you to read a book thoughtfully. If you just read it casually, you will not be prepared to describe the main characters, state the theme, and point out some lessons of the book. By reading thoughtfully, you are also clinching those main points in your own mind more strongly than a casual reading would do. Finally, if you give your report effectively, you are likely to inspire others to read the book.

Lesson 121

Purpose: To study the purpose and guidelines for giving oral book reports.

Oral Review:

1. What are some benefits in writing a summary? (promotes concentration; helps you to review material quickly; can be read by others)
2. In comparison with the original composition, a summary should be no more than (one-half, one-third, one-fourth) as long. (one-third)
3. What are the conflict and the climax of a story? (The conflict is the struggle or problem that the main character faces. The climax is the final and most intense incident in the conflict.)
4. Name some things that contribute to natural-sounding dialogue. (informal tone—contractions and elliptical sentences; frequent change of speakers; descriptive explanatory words)
5. What points should you remember when you give an oral report? (Be relaxed; maintain eye contact with your audience; use proper volume and enunciation; avoid distracting mannerisms.)

Lesson Introduction: The Bible declares, "Of making many books there is no end" (Ecclesiastes 12:12). Many books, of course, are not fit for godly people to read. Nevertheless, there are many worthwhile books that we can read for our benefit and enjoyment. Whether a book report is an informal description by one friend to another or a formal report given with more planning, it is one means of inspiring others to read one of these worthwhile books.

Lesson Outline:

1. A book report should include six kinds of information.

Contents of a Book Report

A *book report* should include six kinds of information. First, you must state the basic facts about the book. Name the title, the author, the publisher, and the copyright date. Tell where your listeners can find the book to read it for themselves.

Second, give some information about the setting (place and time) of the story. In some books the exact place and time are clearly stated; in others you may need to look for clues that suggest the setting.

Third, give brief descriptions of the main characters. Include details that will help your listeners to understand the theme of the story.

The greater part of your report should describe the theme of the story. Do more than merely *tell* what the theme is; *show* it by telling about a few incidents in the conflict. But be sure you do not tell the climax or the conclusion of the story. Leave your listeners in suspense so that they will want to read the story themselves. A good way to conclude this part of the report is to ask a few stimulating questions.

Since a good book is worthwhile, you should name several lessons that the book teaches. Does it inspire faith in God, respect for authority, love for others, or some other important quality? Does it help you to understand the lives of people in a setting different from yours? Think of at least two or three such benefits to mention in your report.

Finally, your report should include your own evaluation of the book. You might describe a part of the book that you especially enjoyed. Is the author's style especially appealing? Does he use figures of speech that are exceptionally fresh and descriptive? Give a few outstanding examples.

Planning a Book Report

Giving an oral book report is similar to giving any other oral report. You must follow definite steps in planning one. The first step is to read an approved book. Of course, you cannot give a meaningful book report unless you have read the entire book carefully and recently. When you are reading for a report, you must discipline your mind to find information for your report.

The second step is to list details for the six kinds of information that you should include in the report. Actually, this step may well overlap the first step. You may want to jot down ideas under the six headings as you read.

Now you are ready to write out your notes. Unlike the notes that you used for your oral report in Chapter 5, these notes may not be in outline form. You may simply follow the order of the six points in the first part of the lesson, organizing the details that you will give for each. Be sure to make your notes simple to follow. You can more easily handle several cards (4″ x 6″ or 5″ x 8″) without causing distractions, than one large sheet of paper.

a. Basic facts such as title, author, and publisher.
b. The setting of the story (the place and time).
c. Brief descriptions of the main characters.
d. The theme of the story.
   1) This should be the greater part of your report.
   2) Do more than merely *tell* what the theme is; *show* it by telling about a few incidents in the conflict.
   3) Do not tell the climax or the conclusion of the story, but leave your listeners in suspense so that they will want to read the story themselves.
   4) A good way to conclude this part of the report is to ask a few stimulating questions.
e. Lessons that the book teaches.
f. Your evaluation of the book.

2. *Several steps should be followed in planning an oral book report.*
   a. Read an approved book.
      1) You cannot give a meaningful book report unless you have read the entire book carefully and recently.
      2) Discipline your mind to find information for your report.
   b. List details for the six kinds of information that you should include in the report.
   c. Write out your notes.
      1) Instead of using an outline, you may simply follow the order of the six points in the first part of the lesson, organizing the details that you will give for each.
      2) You can more easily handle several cards without causing distractions, than one large sheet of paper.
   d. Practice giving your book report.

The final step in preparing for your oral book report is to practice. This will help you to know if you have sufficient, easy-to-follow notes. Practice before your parents or someone else. They may be able to tell whether or not your report covers the book well.

Sample notes for an oral book report:

1. <u>Where No One Stands Alone</u>, by Evelyn Hege
   Rod & Staff Publishers, copyright 1991
2. Setting: Koenigsberg, East Prussia; East Prussia is now divided between Poland and Russia.
   Spans about half a year, from the fall of 1874 to the spring of 1875
3. Main characters: Gerhard Barkman, a thirteen-year-old boy who lived with his grandmother; mother died when he was born; father disappeared soon afterward
   Muttickya, Gerhard's grandmother; was bitter against God and the church; moved away from the Mennonite church; didn't like to talk to Gerhard about the past
4. Main theme: Gerhard, so lonely and frustrated, came to know Jesus as his Friend and found that he did not need to face life alone.
   Near beginning of story, began attending Mennonite school; didn't want to go; enjoyed learning, but had hard time making friends; hated recess, so spent many recesses hiding in coal room
   Two older boys in coal room; teacher talked to him
   Letter from father; difficult decision
   What did he do? How did God work things out for both him and Muttickya?
5. Lessons taught:
   a. Understand Mennonite life in Prussia in late 1800s
   b. Appreciate Christian home
   c. Appreciate faithful church and Christian school
   d. Impressed with the way Jesus is our true Friend
6. Evaluation of the book:
   Author did very well at portraying the setting.
   Plenty of descriptive language: wrote of church bells that echoed "over the city that was still shrouded in the early morning mist"
   "John's expression was that of a thundercloud."
   "Even the playground was ghostly still."
   Spellbinding; had to keep reading

These notes, of course, are simply a guide to prompt you as you speak. The following paragraphs show what you might actually say in giving an oral report on the book *Where No One Stands Alone.*

Sample oral book report:

Where No One Stands Alone was written by Evelyn Hege and copyrighted in 1991 by Rod and Staff Publishers.

The book clearly states that the story took place in Koenigsberg, East Prussia, a country now divided between Poland and Russia. The story spans about half a year, from the fall of 1874 to the spring of 1875. It covers about the time of one school term.

The main character is Gerhard Barkman, a thirteen-year-old boy. Gerhard lived with his grandmother, who had raised him from his infancy. His mother died when he was born, and his father disappeared soon afterward, leaving him with his grandmother. Muttickya, as everyone called Gerhard's grandmother, had become bitter against God and the church. She felt that God had treated her unfairly and that the church people wanted nothing to do with her, so she moved to a different part of the city, away from the Mennonite church. She did not like to talk to Gerhard about the past.

The main theme of the story is how Gerhard, so lonely and frustrated, came to know Jesus as his Friend and found that he did not need to face life alone. Near the beginning of the story, he began attending the Mennonite school. He did not want to go, because he was afraid of the changes and uncertainties it would bring. He did enjoy learning, but he had a hard time making friends. He hated recess because he didn't know the games and couldn't play very well, so he spent many recesses hiding in the coal room. One day when he went to the coal room, he came upon two of the older boys looking at an evil magazine. Gerhard reported this to the teacher. Later the teacher talked to Gerhard to find out why he had been hiding in the coal room and why he was not enjoying school.

Then Gerhard received a letter from his father, who had become a Christian. He and his new wife would be coming any day, and they wanted to take Gerhard to their home. Gerhard would have to choose whether to go with his father or to stay with Muttickya. What did he do? How did God work things out for both him and Muttickya?

Where No One Stands Alone is certainly a worthwhile book. It helped me to understand Mennonite life in Prussia in the late 1800s. More important, it helped me to appreciate a Christian home. It also helped me to appreciate what a faithful church and a Christian school do for me. Above all, it impressed me with the way Jesus is our true Friend.

The author of this book did very well at portraying the setting of this faraway place. I felt almost as if I were right there. She used plenty of descriptive language. For example, she wrote of the church bells that echoed "over the city that was still shrouded in the early morning mist." When Gerhard reported the two boys' misdeed, the author wrote that "John's expression was that of a thundercloud." In the same event, she wrote that "even the playground was ghostly still."

This is a captivating book. I felt as if I had to keep reading to find out what would happen next. I'm sure you will also enjoy reading this absorbing and worthwhile book.

Class Practice

Answer these questions about oral book reports.
1. What six kinds of information should be included in a book report?
2. What two things does the setting of a story include?
3. Why should you not describe the climax and the conclusion of the book?
4. What four steps should you follow in planning an oral book report?

Written Exercises

A. Plan an oral report on an approved book that you have read recently.

B. Give your oral book report. Your report should take about three to five minutes.

Review Exercises

Rewrite each sentence, improving the quality named in parentheses. [71–75]
1. Our commitment to the truth is tested by various circumstances. (action)
2. We should pray both in times of peace and when we face trials. (parallelism)
3. It is necessary that we believe the fact that God exists. (conciseness)
4. Haman was a proud, conceited man who tried to destroy and eliminate the Jews. (conciseness)
5. God's Word encourages the believer, which is forever settled in heaven. (coherence)
6. True Christians always have and always will obey God's Word. (parallelism)
7. We should, as we read the Bible, seek for godly understanding. (coherence)
8. Before we left Sister Eva's home, Father read a chapter from the Bible and several songs were sung. (parallelism)
9. When one sings these songs of faith, we are inspired to trust God. (parallelism)
10. Sister Eva fervently declared that she deeply appreciated our visit. (action)

Lesson 121 Answers

Class Practice

1. (1) Basic facts such as title, author, and publisher; (2) the setting of the story; (3) brief descriptions of the main characters; (4) the theme of the book; (5) lessons that the book teaches; (6) your evaluation of the book.
2. the place and time of the story
3. Your report should leave the listeners in suspense so that they will want to read the book themselves.
4. (1) Read an approved book; (2) list details for the six kinds of information that you should include in the report; (3) write out your notes; (4) practice giving your book report.

Written Exercises

(Individual work.)

Review Exercises

(Allow reasonable variation.)
1. Various circumstances test our commitment to the truth.
2. We should pray both in times of peace and in times of trials.
3. We must believe that God exists.
4. Haman was a conceited man who tried to destroy the Jews.
5. God's Word, which is forever settled in heaven, encourages the believer.
6. True Christians always have obeyed and always will obey God's Word.
7. As we read the Bible, we should seek for godly understanding.
8. Before we left Sister Eva's home, Father read a chapter from the Bible and we sang several songs.
9. When we sing these songs of faith, we are inspired to trust God.
10. "I deeply appreciated your visit," Sister Eva declared fervently.

122. Chapter 11 Review

Class Practice

A. Define these terms.
1. inflections
2. etymology
3. denotation
4. connotation
5. nonfiction
6. fiction
7. biography
8. Dewey decimal system

B. Name the reference book that fits each description.
1. A book of information about Bible words, people, places, and so forth.
2. Volumes of information on a wide range of subjects.
3. A book of maps.
4. An index of Bible words and the references where they are used.
5. A special book of synonyms and sometimes of antonyms.
6. A book of Bible verses arranged by subjects.

C. Do these exercises on dictionary use.
1. Why does a word like *spike* have several numbered entries?
2. Name three types of inflections that most dictionaries show.
3. Give the usage labels that fit these descriptions. A number in parentheses indicates that more than one label fits.
   a. Words invented by people trying to say things in unique ways.
   b. Words used in relatively small areas or by a limited group of people. (2)
   c. Words acceptable only in everyday speaking and writing.
   d. Words to avoid because they represent poor English. (3)
   e. Words to avoid because of their association with evil.
   f. Words no longer in general use. (2)
4. Read this sample dictionary entry, and do the exercises that follow.
   mun•dane (mun′•dān′, mun′•dān′) *adj.* 1. Of, relating to, and characteristic of the world. 2. Characterized by the practical, transitory, and ordinary. [< ME *mondeyne* < MF *mondain* < LL *mundanus* < L *mundus* world] **mun•dane•ly** *adv.* **mun•dane•ness** *n.*
   a. Give the two pronunciations of the word.
   b. What part of speech is *mundane*?
   c. Read the etymology correctly.
   d. What derivatives of *mundane* are shown?
   e. Where could you divide *mundane* at the end of a line?

D. Do these exercises on using reference books.
1. Name three things that you should consider when choosing a synonym from a thesaurus.
2. Name four research aids found in many encyclopedias.

Lesson 122

Purpose: To review the concepts taught in Chapter 11.

Teacher: The Chapter 11 test is to be given after this lesson and before the two final review lessons.

Lesson 122 Answers

Class Practice

A. 1. Changes made in the forms of words to show things like number, tense, and degree of comparison.
2. A brief history of a word.
3. The strict, exact meaning of a word.
4. The "personality" of a word or the feeling it conveys.
5. Factual information.
6. A story that is not factual.
7. A book about the personal life of an individual.
8. A system of classification for arranging books in a library.

B. 1. Bible dictionary
2. encyclopedia
3. atlas
4. concordance
5. thesaurus
6. topical Bible

C. 1. Several words of different origins and meanings have the same spelling. In some dictionaries, a different entry is used for each part of speech that a word may be.
2. irregular plural forms of nouns, irregular principal parts of verbs, and irregular forms of comparison for adjectives and adverbs
3. a. slang
   b. regional, dialectal
   c. informal
   d. nonstandard, substandard, illiterate
   e. vulgar
   f. archaic, obsolete
4. a. mun′•dān′, mun′•dān′
   b. adjective
   c. From Middle English *mondeyne,* from Middle French *mondain,* from Latin *mundus,* meaning "world."
   d. mundanely, mundaneness
   e. between the *n* and the *d*

D. 1. the denotation and connotation, the level of formality, and the range of application
2. cross-references, bibliographies, index, yearbooks

3. What are two important cautions to remember when using encyclopedias?

4. What is the difference between a geographical and a political map?

5. In which original language dictionary of *Strong's Exhaustive Concordance* will you find words from the Old Testament? from the New Testament?

6. How are the numbers for these two dictionaries distinguished in the entries?

7. How would you benefit by looking up an entry like *perseverance* in a topical Bible rather than in a concordance?

8. a. How is a Bible dictionary arranged like a regular dictionary?
   b. How is it more similar to an encyclopedia?

9. Why must you use Bible dictionaries and topical Bibles with care?

E. Answer these questions about libraries.
1. What are the three important rules for using a library courteously?
2. Why must you be careful about selecting books from a public library?
3. What is the call number of a book?
4. What serves as an index to the books in a library?
5. What information is found on a title card?
6. What two other kinds of cards are found in a card catalog?
7. How are reference books arranged on the shelves?
8. What replaces the Dewey decimal number on books of fiction?
9. What replaces the Dewey decimal number on biographies?
10. How does a library arrange books of fiction? of biography?

F. Answer these questions about giving an oral book report.
1. What basic information should you give at the beginning of a book report?
2. What two things does the setting of a story include?
3. What should be described in the greater part of a book report?
4. What should you *not* tell in a book report?
5. How is reading for a book report different from your normal reading?

Written Exercises

A. Do these exercises on using a dictionary.
1. Find *date* in the dictionary.
   a. One word spelled *date* comes from the Greek word *daktulos.* This Greek word means (brave, time, give, finger).
   b. Another word spelled *date* comes from the Latin word *dare.* This Latin word means (brave, time, give, finger).
2. Write two phonetic spellings of *coyote.*
3. Write *creosote,* using hyphens to show the syllable divisions.
4. Write the inflections shown for these words.
   a. criterion   b. busy (verb)   c. busy (adjective)

Written Exercises

A. (Answers are based on *The American Heritage Dictionary, Third Edition.* Other dictionaries may vary.)
1. a. finger
   b. give
2. (kī·ō′·tē, kī′·ōt′)
3. cre-o-sote
4. a. criteria, criterions
   b. busied, busying, busies
   c. busier, busiest

3. Learn to detect errors. Do not assume that an article in the encyclopedia provides the ultimate information about a particular subject.

4. A geographical map shows such things as topography, vegetation, land use, rainfall, climate patterns, and population density. A political map shows the boundaries of nations, states, and provinces.

5. the Hebrew and Chaldee Dictionary; the Greek Dictionary of the New Testament

6. The numbers for the Hebrew and Chaldee dictionary are in regular type; those for the Greek dictionary are in italics.

7. The topical Bible would list all the references that deal with the subject, even if the word *perseverance* is not actually used.

8. a. The entry words are arranged in alphabetical order, and there are guide words, pronunciations, and definitions.
   b. Many entries have long articles with extensive information.

9. They are the works of men and subject to error.

E. 1. Be quiet; be careful; be punctual.
2. Many books in a public library are not fit to read.
3. the number that a library assigns to a book, based on the Dewey decimal system
4. the card catalog
5. the title, the call number, the author, the publisher, the place and date of publication, the number of pages, a brief description
6. author cards and subject cards
7. according to the Dewey decimal numbers
8. the letter *F*
9. the letter *B* or the number 92
10. Books of fiction are arranged in alphabetical order by the last name of the author. Biographies are arranged in alphabetical order according to the name of the person they are written about.

F. 1. title, author, publisher, copyright date
2. place and time
3. the theme of the story
4. the climax or the conclusion of the story
5. You must discipline your mind to find information for your report.

5. What usage labels are given in the entries for these words?
   a. boot   b. ain't   c. bushed

B. Do these exercises on using a thesaurus.
   1. Copy two synonyms that could replace the word *calm* in this sentence.
      The *calm* lake mirrored the snowcapped mountain.
   2. Write the word with the best connotation for each sentence.
      a. Paul proved from the Scriptures that Jesus is the Messiah, but many Jews (decisively, steadfastly, stubbornly) refused to believe in Him.
      b. The martyrs clung (decisively, steadfastly, stubbornly) to their faith regardless of the cost.
      c. The apostle John (celebrated, gloated, rejoiced) when he heard about those who were walking in truth.
      d. Haman (celebrated, gloated, rejoiced) over the fact that he alone had been invited to a banquet with the king and the queen.

C. Do these exercises on using encyclopedias.
   1. Using the index, list all the volumes and page numbers where you could find information on the following subjects.
      a. Komodo dragon   b. Pennsylvania Dutch
   2. Write answers to these questions.
      a. How large an area does the Amazon River drain?
      b. What are several principal crops raised in Alberta?
      c. What kind of government does Luxembourg have?
      d. Where did Leo Tolstoy live, and what was he famous for?

D. Do these exercises on using Bible reference books.
   1. In Proverbs 15:2, we read that "the mouth of fools poureth out foolishness."
      a. What are the original meanings of the word *poureth*?
      b. List the five different ways that this word is translated.
   2. The word *imaginations* is used twice in the New Testament.
      a. Copy the reference in which the original word means "discussion," "consideration," or "debate."
      b. What are the original meanings of the word in the other reference?
   3. From a topical Bible, list two Old Testament references and two New Testament references that speak about self-examination.
   4. Using a Bible dictionary, briefly describe the four kinds of ovens used in the East.

E. Using the illustration of the card catalog in Lesson 120, write the number of the drawer in which the following items would be found.
   1. title: *Gentle Ben*   4. author: Marie Killilea
   2. subject: magnetism   5. title: *All on a Mountain Day*
   3. author: Walt Morey   6. subject: Ceramics

5. a. chiefly British; slang; chiefly Southern U.S.; archaic
   b. non-standard
   c. informal

B. 1. (Sample answers.)
      quiet, tranquil, still, peaceful
   2. a. stubbornly   c. rejoiced
      b. steadfastly   d. gloated

C. 1. (Answers depend on the encyclopedia used.)
   2. a. 2.7 million square miles (7 million square kilometers)
      b. wheat, oats, barley, rye, hay, rapeseed
      c. constitutional monarchy
      d. Russia; famous for writing novels

D. 1. a. to *gush* forth; to *utter* (good or bad words); to *emit* (a foul odor)
      b. belch out, flowing, pour out, send forth, utter (abundantly)
   2. a. Romans 1:21
      b. computation; reasoning (conscience, conceit)
   3. (Answers will vary.)
   4. (1) A heated hollow in the sand, in which the dough was placed. (2) A hole in the earth, lined with pottery. (3) A large stone jar. (4) An iron plate over stones.

E. 1. 9   4. 12
   2. 14   5. 1
   3. 15   6. 4

F. Draw a rectangle to represent an index card. Make a title card for the following book.

    The Pioneers Go West, by George R. Stewart; published by Random House, Inc., New York; copyright 1987; 152 pages; call number: 978.02; Descriptions of overland journeys by covered wagon to California.

---

123. Final Review 1 (Chapters 1–6)

Class Practice

A. Give the term for each description below.

Sentence parts:

1. It consists of the simple subject and the simple predicate.
2. It follows a linking verb and renames the subject.
3. It completes a sentence skeleton by receiving the action of the verb directly.
4. It tells *who* or *what* the sentence is about.
5. It tells what the subject does or is.
6. It is a noun or an adjective that follows and relates to a direct object.
7. It is used with another noun or pronoun to identify or explain it.
8. It names the person or thing to whom one is speaking.
9. It helps to complete a sentence skeleton by telling *to whom or what* or *for whom or what* an action is performed.
10. It follows a linking verb and modifies the subject.
11. It introduces a sentence without adding to its meaning.

Groups of words:

12. It has a skeleton, but functions as a single part of speech.
13. It has no skeleton and functions as a single part of speech.
14. It has one or more sentence parts missing, but it expresses a complete thought because the missing parts are understood.
15. It does not express a complete thought.
16. It expresses a complete thought by making a statement or an exclamation, by giving a command, or by raising a question.
17. It occurs when two or more sentences are incorrectly written together.

B. Tell whether each sentence is *simple, compound, complex,* or *compound-complex.*

1. Many people hate dishonesty in others but overlook it in themselves.
2. If we jealously guard the virtue of honesty, it will grace our lives with true beauty; and God will bless us.

Lesson 123

Purpose: To review the concepts taught in Chapters 1–6.

F. (Sample card.)

```
┌──────────────────────────────────────────────┐
│         Pioneers Go West, The                 │
│  978.02                                        │
│      Stewart, George R.                        │
│        The Pioneers Go West;                   │
│          Random House, Inc., New York, 1987    │
│        152p.                                   │
│          Descriptions of overland journeys by  │
│      covered wagon to California.              │
└──────────────────────────────────────────────┘
```

Lesson 123 Answers

Class Practice

A. 1. skeleton
    2. predicate nominative
    3. direct object
    4. subject
    5. predicate
    6. objective complement
    7. appositive
    8. noun of direct address
    9. indirect object
  10. predicate adjective
  11. expletive
  12. clause
  13. phrase
  14. elliptical sentence
  15. fragment
  16. sentence
  17. run-on error

B. 1. simple
    2. compound-complex

3. Do you know a person who refuses to compromise with truth?
4. This person has true strength of character, and he will earn the confidence of others.

C. Tell where you should add end punctuation, commas, colons, and semicolons.
   1. When Jonah who did not want to preach to the Ninevites ran away God mercifully led him back
   2. Yes God prepared a whale to swallow the disobedient foolish prophet
   3. Have you memorized the following references Jesus' High Priestly Prayer John 17 the Love Chapter 1 Corinthians 13 the Resurrection Chapter 1 Corinthians 15 the Faith Chapter Hebrews 11 and the Discourse on the Tongue James 3
   4. The two greatest commandments have the same key word *love*
   5. What a pleasant surprise to see Grandfather Mast's drive in
   6. Nelson your help was greatly appreciated indeed we could not have finished in time without it
   7. Our neighbor Henry Watson is ninety years old but he still lives alone.
   8. Covering about 590000 square miles Alaska is more than double the size of Texas.
   9. Your penmanship for example has improved these papers look nice.
   10. On July 20 1993 we moved to 859 Martin's Church Road New Holland Pennsylvania 17557.

D. Read each substantive phrase or clause. Tell whether it is an *infinitive phrase, gerund phrase, prepositional phrase,* or *noun clause.*
   1. On the solid Rock is the only place of true security.
   2. No storms can ever harm whoever stands on that Rock.
   3. Trusting ourselves to God's care is a wonderful privilege.
   4. Satan's intent is to destroy that trust.

E. Say the second and third principal parts of these verbs. Use *have* with the third principal part.
   1. dig
   2. cost
   3. take
   4. tag
   5. go
   6. bring
   7. burst
   8. slay
   9. tread
   10. drown

F. Give the tense of each underlined verb or verb phrase. Tell whether its form is *simple, progressive,* or *emphatic.*
   1. Duane was staking the tomatoes.
   2. We have planted several rows of tomatoes already.
   3. The tomatoes do need to be staked this week.
   4. By the end of the week, Father will have staked most of them.

3. complex
4. compound

C. 1. Jonah, Ninevites, away, back.
   2. Yes, disobedient, prophet.
   3. references: Prayer, 17; Chapter, 13; Chapter, 15; Chapter, 11; Tongue, 3?
   4. word: *love.*
   5. in!
   6. Nelson, appreciated; indeed, it.
   7. neighbor, Watson, old, (*or* old;)
   8. 590,000 miles,
   9. penmanship, example, improved;
   10. 20, 1993, Road, Holland,

D. 1. On the solid Rock—prepositional phrase
   2. whoever stands on that Rock—noun clause
   3. Trusting ourselves to God's care—gerund phrase
   4. to destroy that trust—infinitive phrase

E. 1. dug, (have) dug
   2. cost, (have) cost
   3. took, (have) taken
   4. tagged, (have) tagged
   5. went, (have) gone
   6. brought, (have) brought
   7. burst, (have) burst
   8. slew, (have) slain
   9. trod, (have) trodden
   10. drowned, (have) drowned

F. 1. past, progressive
   2. present perfect, simple
   3. present, emphatic
   4. future perfect, simple

5. We <u>had been expecting</u> Uncle Mahlon to help, but he is sick.
6. We <u>shall try</u> to get someone else to help us.

G. Answer these questions about letter writing.
1. What are the five parts of a friendly letter?
2. What additional part does a business letter have?
3. How does the greeting of a business letter differ from that of a friendly letter?
4. What are the three C's of business letter content?
5. In what form should you write the mailing address on an envelope?

H. Answer these questions about paragraphs and paragraph development.
1. What does the topic sentence do for a paragraph?
2. What two things mar paragraph unity?
3. When does a paragraph have coherence?
4. What three common kinds of sentence order are used to develop paragraphs?
5. What are three types of sentence transitions that help build coherence?
6. What are some methods of developing paragraphs?

I. Answer these questions about reports.
1. Why should you take notes from more than one reference source?
2. When may you copy the exact words of a reference source in your notes?
3. What are the advantages of using small cards for taking notes?
4. What are the two main steps in organizing the information that you gather on note cards?
5. What are some good ways to introduce a report?
6. What are two good ways to conclude a report?

J. Answer these questions about story writing.
1. What is the theme of a story?
2. How many themes should a short story emphasize?
3. What is the conflict in a story?
4. What are the three common kinds of conflict?
5. How does a story conflict build up in intensity?
6. What is characterization?
7. What are four common methods of characterization?
8. How much should secondary characters be characterized?
9. What are some things that contribute to natural dialogue?
10. Besides natural dialogue, what are some things that contribute to effective style in story writing?
11. What are three good ways to open a story?
12. What three things are included in the setting of a story?
13. What is a flashback in a story?
14. What are some qualities of a good title?

8. only as much as is necessary for the story
9. informal tone (with use of contractions and elliptical sentences), frequent change of speakers, descriptive explanatory words
10. lively action verbs; exact, descriptive words; imagery
11. with action, dialogue, or an unusual statement
12. time, place, and emotional mood of the story
13. a sentence or paragraph that gives important background information by describing a previous scene
14. It does not give away the outcome of the story; it is short; it is fresh and original (perhaps with rhyming words, alliteration, an unusual statement, or a question).

5. past perfect, progressive
6. future, simple

G. 1. heading, greeting, body, closing, signature
2. inside address
3. It is more formal; a colon follows it, instead of a comma.
4. courteous, clear, concise
5. with all capital letters and no punctuation

H. 1. It states the main idea of the paragraph.
2. sentences that do not develop the main idea of the paragraph; two main ideas that should be divided into two paragraphs
3. when its thoughts are presented in a well-organized way
4. chronological order, spatial order, order of importance
5. transitional words, repetition of key words, pronoun reference
6. adding details, adding facts, adding reasons, adding descriptions, using examples or an incident, giving a definition, using comparisons or contrasts

I. 1. It helps to make the report balanced; it requires you to express your ideas in your own words; it enables you to verify facts.
2. when you plan to quote those words in your report, and if you place those words in quotation marks
3. You can easily write one specific idea on each card. You can easily shuffle the cards to organize your notes.
4. Sort the cards into general categories. Organize them as main topics and supporting points on an outline.
5. with an interesting observation, an illustration, a thought-provoking question, a familiar quotation, or a direct statement
6. with a summary of the main points or a call to some response or action

J. 1. the lesson that the story teaches
2. one
3. the struggle or problem that the main character faces
4. the main character in conflict with another person, with his circumstances, or with his own self
5. The main character generally faces the conflict more than once. Each successive incident in the conflict involves stronger emotion.
6. the process of portraying a story character
7. showing actions, speech, thoughts, and appearance

Written Exercises

A. Label each numbered word group *S* (complete sentence), *F* (fragment), *R* (run-on error), or *E* (elliptical sentence).

> ¹"My, this is a warm day," sighed Joel. ²As he wiped the sweat from his face.
>
> ³"I agree!" exclaimed Galen. ⁴"Hottest day of the summer."
>
> ⁵Just then Mother called from the porch she had a treat of lemonade and cookies for the boys.

B. Copy each underlined word, and write what sentence part it is. Use the following abbreviations.

S—subject	IO—indirect object
V—verb	OC—objective complement
PN—predicate nominative	AP—appositive
PA—predicate adjective	DA—noun of direct address
DO—direct object	

1. "Hear, ye <u>children</u>, the <u>instruction</u> of a father."
2. "I <u>give</u> <u>you</u> good doctrine."
3. "<u>Wisdom</u> is the principal <u>thing</u>."
4. The Bible, <u>God's Word</u>, makes the path of life <u>plain</u>.
5. Its <u>message</u> should be very <u>precious</u> to us.

C. Write whether each sentence is in *natural, inverted,* or *mixed* word order.
1. "Happy is the man that findeth wisdom."
2. "She is more precious than rubies."
3. "Then shalt thou walk in thy way safely."
4. "When thou liest down, thou shalt not be afraid."

D. Copy correctly each word with a capitalization error.
1. The Saints of the old Testament did not have the complete word of God as we do.
2. What influences caused king Solomon to worship the Gods of the heathen?
3. The story "Planting time is in the Spring" shows some experiences of the mennonites in soviet russia.
4. We had dark german bread and spicy italian chili for saturday dinner.
5. Yesterday father bought a ford pickup at hyke's auto sales.
6. In History class we learned about the hundred years' war that ravaged much of europe.

E. Copy the underlined part of each sentence, adding quotation marks correctly.
1. "Do you remember how Grandfather told you, 'Laziness is definitely a form of <u>selfishness? asked</u> Father.

Written Exercises

A. 1. S
  2. F
  3. S
  4. E
  5. R

B. 1. children—DA; instruction—DO
  2. give—V; you—IO
  3. Wisdom—S; thing—PN
  4. God's Word—AP; plain—OC
  5. message—S; precious—PA

C. 1. inverted
  2. natural
  3. mixed
  4. mixed

D. 1. saints, Old, Word
  2. King, gods
  3. Time, Is, Mennonites, Soviet Russia
  4. German, Italian, Saturday
  5. Father, Ford, Hyke's Auto Sales
  6. history, Hundred Years' War, Europe

E. 1. selfishness'?" asked

2. But my God shall supply all your need' is a promise we must claim by faith," Mother encouraged her hungry, shivering children.
3. We learn this from the words "Abstain from all appearance of evil: some things may become wrong because of their general influence.
4. We sang the song "What Will Your Answer Be?

F. Copy correctly each word or figure that should be italicized or that needs an apostrophe or a hyphen.
1. Ive certainly enjoyed reading The Demands of Love.
2. Today Great uncle Alvin Burkhart turns ninety three years old.
3. Mother doesnt usually buy self rising flour; she prefers the cheaper all purpose flour.
4. A single three legged stool stood before the rough hewn table in the old mans cabin.
5. To spell the word repetition, first repeat the es and then repeat the is.

G. Write the missing words for this chart. Use the foreign plurals for numbers 8–13.

Singular	Singular Possessive	Plural	Plural Possessive
1. wolf	——	——	——
2. child	——	——	——
3. lady	——	——	——
4. brother-in-law	——	——	——
5. hyrax	——	——	——
6. mouse	——	——	——
7. salmon	——	——	——
8. alumna	——	——	——
9. bacillus	——	——	——
10. paramecium	——	——	——
11. spadix		——	
12. prognosis		——	
13. phenomenon		——	
14. volcano		——	

H. Write numbers as shown to identify the patterns of these sentences. If the word is transitive, write the word that receives the action. If the verb is intransitive linking, write the words that are linked.
   Pattern 1: intransitive complete verb
   Pattern 2: transitive verb, active voice
   Pattern 3: transitive verb, passive voice
   Pattern 4: intransitive linking verb
1. The Levites lived in cities scattered throughout Israel.
2. God placed special significance on six of these.

2. " 'But
3. evil": some
4. Be?"

F. 1. I've, The Demands of Love
   2. Great-uncle, ninety-three
   3. doesn't, self-rising, all-purpose
   4. three-legged, rough-hewn, man's
   5. repetition, e's, i's

G. 1. wolf's, wolves, wolves'
   2. child's, children, children's
   3. lady's, ladies, ladies'
   4. brother-in-law's, brothers-in-law, brothers-in-law's
   5. hyrax's, hyraxes or hyraces, hyraxes' or hyraces'
   6. mouse's, mice, mice's
   7. salmon's, salmon, salmon's
   8. alumna's, alumnae, alumnae's
   9. bacillus's, bacilli, bacilli's
   10. paramecium's, paramecia, paramecia's
   11. spadices
   12. prognoses
   13. phenomena
   14. volcanoes or volcanos

H. 1. 1
   2. 2; significance

3. These six cities were places of special protection for an innocent manslayer.
4. However, the deliberate murderer could not be safe here.
5. The motives of an accused person were carefully judged in a trial.

I. Write the correct verb for each sentence.
   1. There (is, are) many expressions of praise in the Psalms.
   2. Praise and honor (belong, belongs) to our great God.
   3. He who would stand the test must (set, sit) daily at Jesus' feet.
   4. Everyone should (accept, except) the authority of God's Word.
   5. We must (let, leave) its precepts and warnings guide our steps.
   6. Both of these promises (assure, assures) us of God's care.
   7. Neither of these promises (leave, leaves) any room for doubt.
   8. In his conversation with Father, Mr. Kempel (implied, inferred) that he appreciated the *Star of Hope.*
   9. He said that we (can, may) plan a cottage meeting for his invalid wife.
   10. Mother's good scissors (have, has) a nick on the one blade.
   11. The open windows are (letting, leaving) too much cool air in.
   12. Sparky often (lays, lies) here on the front porch.
   13. The brown and white goat (is, are) our favorite pet.
   14. The cats or the dog (have, has) been digging in the flower bed.
   15. Linguistics (is, are) the scientific study of language.

J. Copy this outline correctly. Each starred line has one mistake.

The Word Made Flesh (John 1)
I. The divinity of Jesus
   *A. is equal with God (v. 1)
   *B. Is eternal in Existence (v. 2)
   *C. He is the creator of all things (v. 3)
   D. Is the source of life (v. 4)
*II. How Jesus was human
   A. Was made flesh (v. 14)
      *1. Dwelt among men
   *B. He was rejected of men (vv. 10, 11)
III. The activity of Jesus
   A. Has brought believers into sonship (v. 12)
   *B. God's glory has been revealed (vv. 14, 18)
   *C. has brought grace and truth (vv. 14, 17)
   *D. Spiritual fullness has been provided (v. 16)

---

3. 4; cities, places
4. 4; murderer, safe
5. 3; motives

I. 1. are
    2. belong
    3. sit
    4. accept
    5. let
    6. assure
    7. leaves
    8. implied
    9. may
   10. have
   11. letting
   12. lies
   13. is
   14. has
   15. is

J. (Corrections are underlined.)

The Word Made Flesh (John 1)
I. The divinity of Jesus
   A. <u>Is</u> equal with God (v. 1)
   B. Is eternal in <u>existence</u> (v. 2)
   C. <u>Is</u> the creator of all things (v. 3)
   D. Is the source of life (v. 4)
II. <u>The humanity of Jesus</u>
   A. Was made flesh <u>and dwelt among men</u> (v. 14)
   B. <u>Was</u> rejected of men (vv. 10, 11)
III. The activity of Jesus
   A. Has brought believers into sonship (v. 12)
   B. <u>Has revealed</u> God's glory (vv. 14, 18)
   C. <u>Has</u> brought grace and truth (vv. 14, 17)
   D. <u>Has provided</u> spiritual fullness (v. 16)

124. Final Review 2 (Chapters 7–11)

Class Practice

A. Identify the pronouns in each group as *personal, compound personal, demonstrative, indefinite, interrogative,* or *relative.*
 1. who, whom, whose, which, what
 2. this, that, these, those
 3. we, him, hers, them, it
 4. some, anyone, everybody, both, many
 5. itself, themselves, ourselves, herself
 6. who, whom, whose, which, that

B. Give the person, number, case, and gender of each underlined pronoun.
 1. Hannah gave <u>her</u> son to the Lord, and <u>he</u> did not disappoint <u>her</u>.
 2. Young people, are <u>you</u> faithful in doing <u>your</u> best for the Lord?
 3. <u>We</u> students have been memorizing Ecclesiastes 12; everyone has recited <u>it</u> already.

C. Identify each underlined adjective phrase as a *participial phrase,* an *infinitive phrase,* or a *prepositional phrase.*
 1. Every blessing <u>enriching our daily lives</u> is a gift <u>from our Father above</u>.
 2. The way <u>to enjoy God's blessing</u> is to daily seek His will.
 3. We must faithfully walk the path <u>of righteousness, outlined in the Bible</u>.

D. Tell whether each underlined clause is *restrictive* or *nonrestrictive.* Also tell where commas are needed.
 1. Jesus <u>whose gracious words attracted many</u> spoke with divine authority.
 2. The men <u>whom Jesus ordained</u> followed Him in His ministry.
 3. The twelve apostles <u>who had forsaken their businesses</u> followed Jesus.

E. Tell what words are modified by the underlined adverb phrases and clauses. Also tell whether the modified word is a *verb,* an *adjective,* an *adverb,* or a *verbal.*
 1. Abel presented <u>from his flocks</u> an offering acceptable <u>to the Lord</u>.
 2. <u>Because God did not accept his offering</u>, Cain became upset <u>to the point of wrath and bitterness</u>.
 3. <u>To stop Cain's downward course</u>, God spoke <u>to him</u>; but he had gone so far <u>that it did no good</u>.
 4. Having talked <u>to Abel</u>, Cain killed him <u>with his own hands</u>.
 5. Abel's blood, crying <u>to God</u> <u>from the ground</u>, could not be hidden.

F. Tell whether each underlined word or set of words is a *preposition,* a *common coordinating conjunction,* a *correlative conjunction,* a *conjunctive adverb,* or a *subordinating conjunction.*

Lesson 124

Purpose: To review the concepts taught in Chapters 7–11.

Lesson 124 Answers

Class Practice

A. 1. interrogative
 2. demonstrative
 3. personal
 4. indefinite
 5. compound personal
 6. relative

B. 1. her—third person, singular, possessive case, feminine gender
    he—third person, singular, nominative case, masculine gender
    her—third person, singular, objective case, feminine gender
 2. you—second person, plural, nominative case, common gender
    your—second person, plural, possessive case, common gender
 3. We—first person, plural, nominative case, common gender
    it—third person, singular, objective case, neuter gender

C. 1. participial phrase, prepositional phrase
 2. infinitive phrase
 3. prepositional phrase, participial phrase

D. 1. nonrestrictive; Jesus, many,
 2. restrictive
 3. nonrestrictive; apostles, businesses,

E. 1. presented—verb; acceptable—adjective
 2. became—verb; upset—adjective
 3. spoke—verb; spoke—verb; so far—adverb (unit)
 4. Having talked—verbal; killed—verb
 5. crying—verbal; crying—verbal

1. The earth is <u>not only</u> rotating on its axis <u>but also</u> revolving around the sun.
2. The gravitational pull of the moon is much less than that of the earth; <u>therefore</u>, on the moon you would weigh much less than you do on Earth.
3. <u>Because</u> Jupiter is much larger than Earth, its gravity is very great.
4. <u>Because of</u> its nearness to the sun, Venus cannot support human life.
5. The earth is placed at exactly the right distance from the sun, <u>for</u> God created it to be inhabited.

G. Answer these questions about note-taking and persuasive argument.
   1. What are some important listening skills for good note-taking?
   2. Why is an outline form usually the most effective in note-taking?
   3. What is a persuasive argument?
   4. What is the statement of the idea that the writer is promoting in an argument?
   5. What is the difference between a fact and an opinion?
   6. What are some important cautions to remember about persuasive argument?

H. Answer these questions about writing descriptions.
   1. What kinds of vivid, concrete words should be used in descriptive writing?
   2. In addition to vivid, concrete words, what are four common kinds of figurative language that can be used?
   3. In what way should a descriptive composition be similar to a character sketch?
   4. What order of development should be used for a description of a scene? for a description of an event?

I. Answer these questions about writing summaries and giving oral book reports.
   1. What is a summary?
   2. What are some benefits in writing a summary?
   3. How long should a summary be?
   4. What are some benefits in giving a book report?
   5. What six kinds of information should be included in a book report?

J. Name the reference book that matches each description.
   1. An index of Bible words and the references where they are used.
   2. A book of maps.
   3. A book of Bible verses arranged by subjects.
   4. A book of words, with various kinds of information about them.
   5. A special book of synonyms and sometimes of antonyms.
   6. Volumes of information on a wide range of subjects.
   7. A book of information about Bible words, people, customs, and places.

F. 1. correlative conjunction
   2. conjunctive adverb
   3. subordinating conjunction
   4. preposition
   5. common coordinating conjunction

G. 1. focusing one's whole attention on the speaker overcoming distractions, listening with interest, listening for main ideas
   2. An outline shows the relationship among the main points and between a main point and the subpoints under it.
   3. an attempt to persuade or move to action
   4. the proposition
   5. A fact is a piece of information that can be proven by evidence or that has been revealed by God in the Bible. An opinion is a conclusion or a belief about something, based on a person's evaluation of facts.
   6. Beware of propositions that are supported by misrepresented facts or faulty reasoning. Remember that the validity of a proposition is not established by strong statements. Avoid arguments that deal with unprofitable subjects.

H. 1. exact nouns, expressive verbs, colorful adjectives and adverbs
   2. simile, metaphor, personification, and hyperbole
   3. Both focus on one main impression.
   4. spatial order; chronological order

I. 1. a condensed review of the main points in a composition
   2. promotes concentration; helps you to review material quickly; can be read by others
   3. of an appropriate length
   4. compels you to read a book thoughtfully; clinches the main points in your mind; inspires others to read the book
   5. basic facts such as title, author, and publisher; setting; brief descriptions of the main characters; theme of the book; lessons that the book teaches; your evaluation of the book

J. 1. concordance
   2. atlas
   3. topical Bible
   4. dictionary
   5. thesaurus
   6. encyclopedia
   7. Bible dictionary

K. Answer these questions about libraries.
1. What is the difference between books of fiction and nonfiction?
2. What are the three rules for using a library courteously?
3. Why should you compare all books from a public library with the library of God's Word?
4. What is the call number of a library book?
5. What is the purpose of the card catalog?
6. What information is found on a title card?
7. What two other kinds of cards are found in a card catalog?

Written Exercises

A. Write whether each pair of pronouns differs in *person, number, case,* or *gender.*
1. she, her   3. he, she   5. we, they
2. us, me   4. your, you   6. its, theirs

B. Write the correct words for these sentences.
1. (We, Us) mortals should praise God by thought, word, and action.
2. God has a keen interest in you and (I, me).
3. The mother and writer is busy with (her, their) duties.
4. The mother and the writer are busy with (her, their) duties.
5. Each of these wagons carried (its, their) full capacity of hay.
6. Either Janet or Susan left (her, their) books on the table.
7. The bear looked even more startled than (I, me).
8. The family worked on (its, their) various Saturday chores.
9. The family took (its, their) turn at cleaning the church.
10. Our produce did not sell as quickly as (theirs, their's) did.
11. In the museum, each student must stay with (his, their) group.
12. Because Mark hurt his back last summer, Father did not help me as much as (he, him).
13. Grandfather helped Conrad and (I, me, myself) with our chores.
14. These are Jonathan apples, but (them, those) are Rome Beauty.
15. The man (who, whom, which) we visited receives the *Star of Hope.*

C. Copy each underlined adjective, and label it *L* (limiting) or *D* (descriptive). Also label each *AT* (attributive), *AP* (appositive), or *PR* (predicate).
1. The holy angels are ministering spirits to God's people.
2. God's name, holy and reverend, is worthy of our praise.
3. Many heavenly beings worship the one true God, who reigns from His throne above.

D. Write the comparative and superlative degrees of these adjectives and adverbs.
1. near   4. well   7. bad
2. lowly   5. little, in size   8. comfortable
3. humbly   6. little, in amount

K. 1. Books of fiction contain stories that are not factual. Books of nonfiction contain factual information.
2. Be quiet; be careful; be punctual.
3. Many books promote the false theories of men rather than the truth of God.
4. the number that a library assigns to a book, based on the Dewey decimal system
5. to give the call numbers of books in the library so that you can find them on the shelves
6. the title, the call number, the author, the publisher, the place and date of publication, the number of pages, and a brief description
7. author cards and subject cards

Written Exercises

A. 1. case   4. case
2. number   5. person
3. gender   6. number

B. 1. We   9. its
2. me   10. theirs
3. her   11. his
4. their   12. him
5. its   13. me
6. her   14. those
7. I   15. whom
8. their

C. 1. The—L, AT; holy—D, AT; ministering—D, AT; God's—L, AT
2. holy—D, AP; reverend—D, AP; worthy—D, PR; our—L, AT
3. Many—L, AT; heavenly—D, AT; one—L, AT; true—D, AT; His—L, AT; above—L *or* D, AP

D. 1. nearer, nearest
2. lowlier, lowliest
3. more humbly, most humbly
4. better, best
5. littler, littlest
6. less, least
7. worse, worst
8. more comfortable, most comfortable

E. If the underlined part of the sentence contains an error in adjective or adverb usage, write it correctly. If it is correct, write *correct*.
 1. The New Testament contains <u>less books</u> than the Old Testament does.
 2. When an older person speaks to you, give a <u>respectful answer</u>.
 3. A person's attitudes <u>sure affect</u> his ability to work.
 4. The worldling is often <u>sort of puzzled</u> by the Christian's faith.
 5. The fool says, "I don't see <u>no need</u> for God and religion."
 6. Uncle Mervin is always such <u>a cheerful optimist</u>.
 7. We moved the boundaries for prisoner's base <u>farther apart</u>.
 8. Brother Lester <u>divided up</u> the students into several small groups.
 9. The children worked <u>good</u> all morning.
 10. Did Lisa bake <u>them pies</u> all by herself?
 11. The <u>clear, transparent plastic</u> is almost as good as glass.
 12. Glenda is feeling <u>somewhat better</u> today.
 13. Do you know what <u>kind of a tree</u> this is?
 14. The <u>cat and dog</u> often nap together.
 15. Mother made apple pies and blueberry pies; I certainly like the apple pies <u>best</u>.

F. If the underlined part of the sentence contains an error in preposition or conjunction usage, write it correctly. If it is correct, write *correct*.
 1. Our interests must be <u>different from</u> those of the world.
 2. Making others <u>wait on</u> us is inconsiderate of their time.
 3. We can <u>differ with</u> others over certain ideas and still love them.
 4. After family worship was <u>over with</u>, we scattered to our various chores.
 5. Mr. Blake asked us to <u>drive by</u> his place and take him along to church.
 6. The refugee family was <u>both suffering from</u> malnutrition and exposure.
 7. Father built a grape arbor <u>in back of</u> the house.
 8. Expectantly <u>and with reverence</u>, the congregation waited for the service to begin.
 9. Since the small pie was <u>divided among</u> the eight of us, each had only a little piece.
 10. We have cottage meetings not only in nursing homes <u>but in</u> private homes.

G. Write whether each underlined phrase functions as an *adjective,* an *adverb,* or a *noun*. You may use abbreviations.
 1. The only safe place (a) <u>to anchor our souls</u> is (b) <u>in the solid Rock</u>.
 2. (a) <u>Mocking the poor</u> is actually a reproach (b) <u>against the Creator</u>.
 3. (a) <u>To produce greater fruitfulness</u>, God sometimes allows trials (b) <u>in the lives</u> (c) <u>of His children</u>.
 4. (a) <u>On the road</u> is no place for (b) <u>playing bicycle tricks</u>.

E. 1. fewer books
  2. correct
  3. surely affect
  4. rather (*or somewhat*) puzzled
  5. any need
  6. an optimist
  7. correct
  8. divided
  9. well
 10. those pies
 11. clear (*or transparent*) plastic
 12. correct
 13. kind of tree
 14. cat and the dog
 15. better

F. 1. correct
  2. wait for
  3. correct
  4. over
  5. drive to
  6. suffering from both
  7. behind
  8. and reverently
  9. correct
 10. but also in

G. 1. a. adj.   b. adv.
  2. a. n.   b. adj.
  3. a. adv.   b. adv.   c. adj.
  4. a. n.   b. n.

H. Write whether each underlined clause functions as an *adjective,* an *adverb,* or a *noun.* You may use abbreviations.
1. The knowledge (*a*) that God is on the throne encourages us (*b*) whenever life seems difficult.
2. (*a*) That we can share in His victory is assured (*b*) if we identify with Him.
3. In the Scriptures (*a*) which God gave to man, we learn (*b*) how we should live.

I. Copy each underlined word, and label it with the abbreviation for its part of speech. Label infinitives as one item.
1. We often marvel at the amazing evidence of design in the created world.
2. Today many people deny the fact that God created the universe.
3. Strange! They actually attribute the marvels of creation to chance!
4. Believing in evolution appeals to many, for they refuse to accept God's authority.
5. God's care for us exceeds our ability to comprehend fully.
6. With God's help, no temptation is too hard to overcome.
7. Although God dwells in heaven above, His presence is ever near.
8. Well, that fact should inspire us to look above ourselves and trust in Him.

J. Read the following stanzas, and do the exercises that follow.

Stanza A:
Thy Word, O Lord, like gentle dews,
Falls soft on hearts that pine;
Lord, to Thy garden ne'er refuse
This heav'nly balm of Thine.

Stanza B:
When I shall reach the more excellent glory,
And all my trials are past,
I shall behold Him, O wonderful story!
I shall be like Him at last.

1. What is the rhyme scheme of stanza A? of stanza B?
2. Copy the pair of words that is a feminine rhyme.
3. Name the meter and the number of feet in each line of stanza A.
4. Name the meter and the number of feet in each line of stanza B.
5. The first two lines of stanza A contain which kind of figure of speech?
6. The second two lines of stanza A contain which kind of figure of speech?

H. 1. a. adj.   b. adv.
2. a. n.   b. adv.
3. a. adj.   b. n.

I. 1. marvel—v.; amazing—adj.; design—n.; created—adj.
2. Today—adv.; many—adj.; that—conj.; created—v.
3. Strange—interj.; They—pron.; attribute—v.; marvels—n.
4. Believing—n.; appeals—v.; for—conj.; to accept—n.
5. care—n.; for—prep.; to comprehend—adj.; fully—adv.
6. help—n.; no—adj.; too—adv.; to overcome—adv.
7. Although—conj.; above—adj.; ever—adv.; near—adv.
8. Well—interj.; that—adj.; above—prep.; ourselves—pron.

J. 1. abab; abab
2. glory, story
3. iambic; 4, 3, 4, 3
4. dactylic; 4, 3, 4, 3
5. simile
6. metaphor

Name _____   *(Lesson 5)*

Worksheet 1
Subjective Complements

A. Underline each subjective complement. Write *PN* above each predicate nominative and *PA* above each predicate adjective.

    1. The angels are <u>superior</u> [PA] in many ways to man.

    2. Two angels named in the Bible are <u>Michael</u> [PN] and <u>Gabriel</u> [PN].

    3. (none) Angels have appeared in human form on various occasions.

    4. One role of the angels has been their <u>ministry</u> [PN] to the saints.

    5. A good student will be <u>diligent</u> [PA], <u>cooperative</u> [PA], and <u>respectful</u> [PA].

    6. Father's plan for a walk down to the woods sounded <u>interesting</u> [PA].

    7. (none) The captain of the sinking ship sounded an alarm.

    8. The early morning sky became a beautiful <u>display</u> [PN] of pink and red.

    9. (none) The sun appeared suddenly on the horizon.

    10. Melissa's contentment is a <u>key</u> [PN] to her happiness.

    11. To her, a wheelchair is not a <u>prison</u> [PN].

    12. Most of the time she remains <u>cheerful</u> [PA] and <u>pleasant</u> [PA].

    13. (none) Stepping into the house, I smelled Mother's freshly baked bread.

    14. All the food in the kitchen smelled <u>delicious</u> [PA].

    15. The loaves on the counter looked <u>neat</u> [PA] and <u>even</u> [PA].

    16. As you choose the right, your character will grow <u>strong</u> [PA] and <u>godly</u> [PA].

    17. Your life can be an <u>example</u> [PN] to others.

B. Diagram the skeletons and complements.
    1. To me, the best part of a warm summer day is the cool, fresh dawn.
    2. The Lord is a great King over all the earth.
    3. Even in the face of bitter foes, Jesus remained calm and kind.
    4. Stephen's final words were a prayer for his persecutors.
    5. The vision of Jesus must have been a comfort and an encouragement to the martyr.

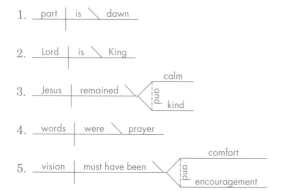

Name _____

Worksheet 2
Object Complements

A. Underline the object complements. Write *DO* above each direct object and *IO* above each indirect object.

  1. You must use your <u>muscles</u> and <u>bones</u> properly.
     (DO above muscles, DO above bones)

  2. In lifting heavy objects, do not bend your <u>back</u>.   (*Objects* may also be underlined and labeled DO.)
     (DO above back)

  3. Rather, you should bend your <u>knees</u> and use your leg <u>muscles</u>.
     (DO above knees, DO above muscles)

  4. Sitting gives each spinal <u>disk</u> more <u>pressure</u> than standing does.
     (IO above disk, DO above pressure)

  5. Therefore good posture in sitting is very important.
     (none)

  6. We took a <u>walk</u> to the meadow and saw the flooded <u>creek</u>.
     (DO above walk, DO above creek)

  7. The high water gave the <u>meadow</u> and the <u>woods</u> a strange <u>appearance</u>.
     (IO above meadow, IO above woods, DO above appearance)

  8. Father gave the <u>children</u> strict <u>orders</u> to stay away from the water.
     (IO above children, DO above orders)

  9. The water has washed a deep <u>gully</u> through a corner of the meadow.
     (DO above gully)

  10. Uncle Earl sent <u>Delbert</u> and <u>me</u> a <u>letter</u>.
      (IO above Delbert, IO above me, DO above letter)

  11. They have had mild <u>weather</u> and are making <u>hay</u> for the fourth time.
      (DO above weather, DO above hay)

  12. In your writing, you should avoid unnecessary <u>modifiers</u>.
      (DO above modifiers)

B. Underline the complements. Above each, write *PN, PA, DO,* or *IO* to tell which kind of complement it is.

  1. God gave <u>Moses</u> the <u>command</u> to speak to the rock.
     (IO above Moses, DO above command)

  2. This time Moses had become <u>upset</u> and <u>impatient</u> with the people.
     (PA above upset, PA above impatient)

  3. He angrily rebuked the <u>people</u> and struck the <u>rock</u>.
     (DO above people, DO above rock)

  4. Moses' punishment was the <u>loss</u> of his privilege to enter Canaan.
     (PN above loss)

  5. The guide at the museum gave the <u>students</u> and their <u>teachers</u> an educational <u>tour</u>.
     (IO above students, IO above teachers, DO above tour)

  6. He could be both <u>amusing</u> and quite <u>stern</u>.
     (PA above amusing, PA above stern)

  7. Did you see those fox <u>tracks</u> in the mud?
     (DO above tracks)

  8. Those are fresh coyote <u>tracks</u>.
     (PN above tracks)

  9. We were all enjoying the pleasant <u>sunshine</u>.
     (DO above sunshine)

C. Diagram the skeletons and complements.
  1. The watchman sounded a clear warning to the people.
  2. The message of the warning sounded clear and urgent.
  3. God assigned Ezekiel and Jeremiah a difficult task.
  4. They were unwelcome watchmen to a rebellious people.

Worksheet 3
Objective Complements

A. Underline each direct object or objective complement, and write *DO* or *OC* above it.
              DO OC   DO   OC
1. God called the light day and the darkness night.
              DO OC
2. Adam named his wife Eve.
               DO   OC
3. Lillian imagined her work finished before it was.
            DO   OC   DO   OC
4. Eli cut the boards straight and sanded them smooth.
                 DO OC
5. Clarence then painted each board white.
             DO   DO OC
6. Cheryl swept the walks and steps clean.
          DO   OC
7. She found the job quite pleasant in the cool evening.
                   DO   OC
8. We should esteem a Christian home invaluable.
                  DO   OC
9. We should also consider a Christian education a priceless privilege.
                    DO OC
10. With these blessings, we should make our lives fruitful for the Lord.

B. Underline the object complements and the objective complements. Above each, write *DO, IO,* or *OC*.
             IO   DO
1. Grandfather told us an interesting story.
                 DO
2. One night he rushed Barbara Jean to the hospital.
              DO   OC
3. He feared his old car too dilapidated to make the trip.
             IO   DO
4. But he told Grandmother the danger in any delay.
           DO OC
5. God made the car fit for this trip.
                        DO
6. Never again could Grandfather start the engine of that old car.
                   DO   OC
7. Haman apparently considered himself better than he really was.
          DO   OC   DO   OC
8. He wanted Mordecai dead and all of the Jews destroyed.
            IO   DO
9. God provided His people a marvelous deliverance.
          DO   OC
10. He made the Jews an honored people.

C. Diagram the skeletons and complements.
1. Charlotte found the assignment quite a challenge.
2. The pioneer must have built this cabin very sturdy.
3. The day's hard work made the horses weary.
4. We should consider heaven our home.
5. God has made heaven a perfect place for the redeemed.

1. Charlotte | found | assignment \ challenge

2. pioneer | must have built | cabin \ sturdy

3. work | made | horses \ weary

4. We | should consider | heaven \ home

5. God | has made | heaven \ place

Name _____

Worksheet 4
Appositives and Independent Elements

A. Underline the appositives in these sentences. If an appositive is nonrestrictive, add the missing commas.

1. The prophet Elijah performed many outstanding miracles.

2. The miracles of Elisha, another prophet of God, were usually of a more quiet nature.

3. The prophets had a school at Jericho, a city near the Jordan River.

4. My sister Phoebe just turned six years old.

5. My cousin Ruth spent the weekend at our place.

B. Underline each independent element. Add commas or exclamation points, and capitalize words as needed.

1. Hallelujah! ᴾpraise the Lord for His mercy!

2. Thou art worthy, eternal God, of all glory and honor.

3. There is no other God besides the Lord God.

4. Yes, He alone is the Creator and Sustainer of all things.

5. It is important that we give Him our praise.

6. Obedience, we know, is the best praise anyone can give to the Lord.

7. This encyclopedia, on the other hand, has detailed illustrations.

8. There are several books of poetry in our library.

9. Oh, I never knew that you had written so many poems.

10. We could have a heavy frost, I'm afraid, by morning.

11. Well, we have enjoyed a good harvest.

12. Before you come downstairs, Laura, be sure your bedroom is tidy.

13. Your bed, for example, should be made neatly.

14. You should be able, I'm sure, to tidy your room in a few minutes.

C. On other paper, diagram the skeletons and complements of these sentences. Include all the words that make up appositives and independent elements.
1. Well, we have finished that job once again.
2. Eric, you must sweep the barn floor this morning.
3. The flowers! Somebody crushed the flowers in my flower bed!
4. The eastern phoebe, a small flycatcher, eats many insects.
5. This bird's song, I think, sounds similar to the chickadee's song.
6. There are several species of flycatchers found in North America.

Name _____   *(Lesson 13)*

Worksheet 5
Paragraph Unity and Topic Sentences

A. In each pair, circle the letter of the topic sentence that is better.
   1. (a.) Joseph provides an outstanding example of a forgiving spirit.
      b. Joseph provides an outstanding example of noble character.
   2. a. The ancient Egyptians depended upon the Nile River for drinking water, for irrigation water, and for transportation.
      (b.) The ancient Egyptians depended much upon the Nile River.
   3. (a.) A healthy fear of God affects every aspect of our lives.
      b. A healthy fear of God affects our study habits, our likes and dislikes, our relationships with others, and our worship.

B. Underline the topic sentences. Cross out one sentence that mars the unity of paragraph 1.

   1. <u>Christopher Columbus did make several major contributions to the world in his day.</u> Although he was not the first to discover America, he does deserve the credit for uncovering America. ~~The honor of discovering America must go to Norwegian sailors several hundred years earlier.~~ Also, he proved the method of dead reckoning sailing, having only crude instruments and no landmarks to go by. From the Indians, he picked up the idea of hammocks and adapted it to life on board a ship. Finally, he proved his idea of sailing west on the trade winds and then tracking northward into the path of the westerlies to head home again.

   2. What do you do when you get a new book? Do you simply open it and start reading? <u>You should break in new books properly.</u> Use the same procedure for both clothbound and paperback books. Place the book spine down on a flat surface, and open the front and back covers while holding the pages vertical. Alternating between front and back, open a few pages at a time and gently press down from top to bottom near the spine. Continue working toward the middle of the book until all the pages are pressed out flat. Improper break-in results in damaged spines and misaligned sections of pages.

   3. Any marker thicker than heavy paper will place stress on the spine. This rules out using leather strips, strings of beads, rulers, pencils, and so forth. Placing an open book face down also can break the glue and loosen pages. Never fold down the corner of a page to mark your place. Dog-ears belong on our canine friends, not on books. <u>Always use a suitable bookmark.</u>

C. Divide this selection into three paragraphs, using the paragraph symbol (¶). Underline the topic sentences.

   <u>Learn to turn the pages of a book properly.</u> Lightly turn the next page from its upper corner. Grasping the bottom of the page near the spine results in wrinkled and torn pages. Never moisten your finger in your mouth for better traction in flipping pages.¶Handle your books only with clean hands unless you want them to look like mechanics' shop manuals. Keep them free of eraser particles, cookie crumbs, and doodle marks. Never use a good book as a fly swatter, Ping-Pong paddle, or booster seat. <u>These are important ways to keep your books clean.</u>¶<u>And finally, use common sense.</u> Inside the front cover of your book is a good place to keep your next assignment, but your book should not be used to store many papers. Avoid dropping books on the floor, jamming them into your desk, propping your elbows on open books, or folding both covers back against each other.

Name _____

Worksheet 6
Complex Sentences

A. Underline the adjective and adverb clauses. Identify each by writing *adj.* or *adv.* in the blank.

  adj.   1. Elijah, <u>who was a man like us</u>, is an example of powerful prayer.

  adv.   2. <u>When he prayed</u>, God heard and answered.

  adv.   3. We too can be assured of answered prayer <u>if we pray in true faith</u>.

  adv.   4. <u>Because the power of prayer comes from God</u>, only those

  adj.   <u>who are faithful to God</u> can claim the promise of answered prayers.

B. Underline the noun clauses. Identify each one by writing *S* (subject), *DO* (direct object), *PN* (predicate nominative), or *OP* (object of a preposition) above it.

                                        DO
  1. Nobody could comprehend <u>what the stranger was saying</u>.

        S   PN
  2. <u>That he had trouble with his car</u> was <u>what we finally understood</u>.

                             OP
  3. Father will try to deal with <u>whatever the problem is</u>.

         S
  4. <u>How handicapped we would be without language</u> became very apparent.

C. Underline the dependent clauses. Above each, write *adj.* (adjective), *adv.* (adverb), or *n.* (noun).

                          adj.
  1. Echidnas are strange animals <u>that live in Australia</u>.

                  n.
  2. Did you know <u>that these mammals lay eggs</u>?

         adv.   adv.
  3. <u>After a mother echidna lays an egg</u>, she places it in her pouch <u>where her body heat hatches it</u>.

         n.   adj.
  4. <u>What protects these strange-looking animals</u> is a covering of spines <u>that may be up to two inches long</u>.

        adv.   adj.
  5. <u>When an echidna is threatened</u>, it rolls into a tight, spiny ball <u>that few animals will attack</u>.

        adv.   adj.
  6. <u>Because echidnas eat ants and termites</u>, God gave them powerful claws <u>that can easily tear apart the hard nests of these insects</u>.

        adv.
  7. <u>Although their front claws are straight</u>, their back ones curve outward.

                   adv.
  8. They look <u>as if they are walking on the sides of their back feet</u>.

D. On other paper, diagram the skeletons and complements of these simple, compound, and complex sentences.
  1. While Father mowed the hay, we worked in the garden.
  2. Mother picked some beans, and the children hoed the potatoes.
  3. We have eaten fresh vegetables and have preserved some for winter.
  4. What I like best is vegetables that are fresh.
  5. Mother made an extra large breakfast because lunch will likely be late.
  6. The children whose chores are finished may go with Father when he fetches the lumber.

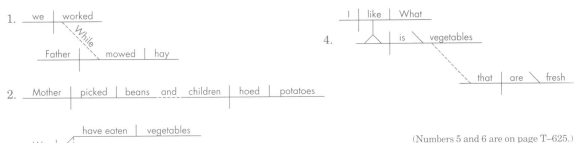

(Numbers 5 and 6 are on page T–625.)

Name _____   (Lesson 16)

Worksheet 7
Compound-Complex Sentences

A. Underline each independent clause, and put parentheses around each dependent clause in these compound-complex sentences.

1. (Although Job was severely tested,) he still trusted in God, and God could bless him.

2. Job's wife failed him; moreover, the men (who came to comfort him) actually added to his trials.

3. Men may fail us in time of need; God, (whose aid we seek above all,) never fails.

4. God does not always reward men (as He rewarded Job,) but the way of faith is always well rewarded.

B. Label each sentence S (simple), CD (compound), CX (complex), or CD-CX (compound-complex).

    __S__   1. Lightning is one of the marvels of God's world.

    __CD__   2. It is very beautiful, but it can also be destructive.

    __CX__   3. Lightning is a huge electric spark that passes from one cloud to another cloud or to the ground.

    __S__   4. One stroke of lightning may measure 100 million volts.

  __CD-CX__ 5. When lightning strikes, it heats the air in its path; and that air suddenly expands violently.

    __CX__   6. This sudden expansion creates a shock wave that is called thunder.

    __CD__   7. Lightning usually looks like streaks; sometimes it looks like balls.

    __CX__   8. Balls of lightning sometimes roll along the ground until they hit something and explode.

    __CX__   9. The Romans thought that lightning was a weapon of their god Jupiter.

  __CD-CX__ 10. We do not fear lightning as the Romans did because it is under God's control; rather, we trust His care for us.

C. Diagram the skeletons and complements of these compound-complex sentences.
1. Although you face unpleasant circumstances, you can trust God, and He will bless you.
2. No temptation that God allows is too great for the people of God; He always gives them His enabling grace.
3. We must carefully guard our hearts; if we think right thoughts, we shall be right in words and actions too.
4. Although no man can tame the tongue, God is able; but we must cooperate with Him.

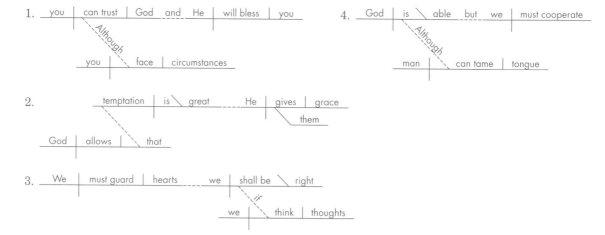

Name _____

Worksheet 8
Loose, Periodic, and Balanced Sentences

A. Write whether each sentence is loose (*L*), periodic (*P*), or balanced (*B*).

   L   1. The trees look beautiful with their coats of fall colors.

   P   2. After the thunderstorm, a brilliant, majestic rainbow appeared.

   B   3. The lower the sun is in the west, the higher a rainbow is in the east.

   L   4. The little children tracked right into Mother's clean kitchen with their muddy boots.

   L   5. The small stream splashed playfully over the rocks.

   P   6. Far out on the distant prairie, the settlers heard wolves howling.

   L   7. The wolves had killed fifteen sheep from the flocks.

   P   8. Although the settlers had tried various methods to kill or capture those wolves, they had not succeeded.

   P   9. Because the wolves were threatening the livestock, the settlers posted additional night watchmen.

   B 10. Wolves may dress in sheep's clothing, but sheep will not dress in wolves' clothing.

B. Rewrite each loose sentence as a periodic sentence, and each periodic sentence as a loose sentence.

  1. Jesus passed through Samaria on His way to Galilee. _____

     <u>On His way to Galilee, Jesus passed through Samaria.</u>

  2. Because He was weary from traveling, Jesus sat down at Jacob's well. _____

     <u>Jesus sat down at Jacob's well because He was weary from traveling.</u>

  3. The Samaritan woman was greatly surprised when Jesus spoke to her. _____

     <u>When Jesus spoke to her, the Samaritan woman was greatly surprised.</u>

  4. By talking about living water, Jesus tried to teach her a great truth. _____

     <u>Jesus tried to teach her a great truth by talking about living water.</u>

  5. Many Samaritans believed in Jesus when He stayed there two days. _____

     <u>When He stayed there two days, many Samaritans believed in Jesus.</u>

C. Add words to make a balanced sentence from each item.

  1. Many great men are in small places, and many   <u>small men are in great places.</u>

  2. Do not ask what others can do for you; ask   <u>what you can do for others.</u>

  3. Before you talk to men about God, be sure you   <u>talk to God about men.</u>

Worksheet 6, Part D *(Continued)*

5.

6.

Name _____

Worksheet 9
Practice With Commas

Add the missing commas.

1. My friend, if you appreciate others' kindness, you should show kindness.

2. Thoughtfulness, patience, and forbearance are traits of a loving heart.

3. Yes, the Golden Rule, which is found in Matthew 7:12, teaches that we should treat others as we would like to be treated.

4. Saul wanted to kill David, but Jonathan, Saul's son, showed great kindness to David.

5. He was willing, in fact, to risk his life for David's sake.

6. In his intense jealousy against David, Saul actually threw his javelin at Jonathan, who had spoken in defense of David.

7. Ah, that we would always follow Jonathan's noble, worthy example!

8. The reward for kindness, as Jonathan's life shows, does not always come in this life.

9. The owner is Victor Cari, Sr., who lives at 214 West Main Street, New Holland, Pennsylvania 17557.

10. "Little Sarah was born on July 24, 1997," stated Martha.

11. We searched through the shop, in the barn, and in the house for the missing tool.

12. The cold wind swept across the fields and blew the dry, fluffy snow into huge drifts.

13. In this book, reports of the early Christians' endurance are given.

14. Although the land of Palestine had no distinct boundaries, it is generally considered to be bounded by the Lebanon Mountains on the north, the Jordan River on the east, the Negev on the south, and the Mediterranean Sea on the west.

15. The area of Palestine, approximately 6000 square miles, is somewhat greater than that of Connecticut.

16. Palestine covers a small area, but its strategic location gave it an importance beyond its smallness.

17. No wonder God, the Sovereign of history, placed His people there!

18. "Esther, did you know," asked Naomi, "that the present nation of Israel covers approximately 8000 square miles?"

19. To surprise Sister Eleanor, we planned a card shower.

20. Since Fred's fever was quite high, we took him to Dr. John Carter, M.D.

Name _____

Worksheet 10
Quotation Marks

Add single and double quotation marks and related punctuation. Capitalize letters where needed. Use quotation marks to indicate direct quotations only when there are explanatory words.

1. John the Baptist plainly said,"I am not the Christ."

2. When he saw Jesus, he cried out,"^Bbehold the Lamb of God!"

3. Velma commented,"I am especially challenged by his words,'He must increase, but I must decrease.'"

4. "Will you please sing 'Rock of Ages'?"asked Mrs. Schaum.

5. "Even though you sing that song for me every time,"she continued,"it never grows tiresome to me,"

6. Did Mrs. Schaum say,"^Tthat song is my favorite"?

7. "What a blessing to know that God says, 'I will never leave thee, nor forsake thee'!" stated Brother Lamar.

8. "Is everyone ready to go?"Father asked. "^Iit's time to leave."

9. Paul reported how Jesus had said,"Saul, Saul, why persecutest thou me?"

10. "Only sincere love in the heart,"commented Ralph,"can motivate true nonresistance."

11. What a surprise ending awaits you in the story"The Old Maple Tree"!

12. The basis of nonresistance is found in Jesus' words,"But I say unto you, That ye resist not evil" (Matthew 5:39).

13. Barton asked,"Which prophet said, 'Then they that feared the Lord spake often one to another'?"

14. "It was Malachi,"answered Keith,"^Hhe was the last Old Testament prophet."

15. Conrad said,"I'm sorry"; however, Leon apparently did not hear him.

16. Have you ever read the poem"Drop a Pebble in the Water"?

17. "The Shepherd and the Sheep" is a descriptive poem.

18. Suddenly Norman shouted,"^Tthere's a rattlesnake!"

19. "Did you actually see a rattlesnake?"asked Father.

20. "If you saw no rattlesnake, you should certainly not have shouted "^Tthere's a rattlesnake!'"Father said firmly.

21. "Did Brother Edwin preach on 'Lot's Choices'?"asked Wanda.

22. Today's lesson is the poem"Where Are the Nine?"

23. "How much the Lord delights in thankful people!"declared Elizabeth.

24. "Do you enjoy watching clouds float across the sky?"asked Barbara.

25. "If you use your imagination,"she continued,"you can see many interesting shapes."

Name _____   *(Lesson 29)*

Worksheet 11
Dashes, Parentheses, and Brackets

A. Set off the parenthetical elements in these sentences with commas, dashes, or parentheses, as indicated by the notes. If there is not enough room in the sentence, use a caret (∧) and place the mark above the sentence.

1. At the time of Jesus' death, Pilate—what a weak character he had!—was governor of Judea. (Emphasize the parenthetical element.)

2. His wife (having suffered many things in a dream) warned him to have nothing to do with Jesus. (Treat the parenthetical element as having minor importance.)

3. The people—a mob spirit was clearly in control—demanded Jesus' death. (Give sharp emphasis to the parenthetical element.)

4. Jesus' disciples, without exception, failed their Master at this time. (Make the parenthetical element a part of the sentence.)

5. Peter (who had declared his loyalty only a few hours before) actually denied his Lord with cursings. (Show that the parenthetical element is just given as extra information.)

B. Add the missing brackets, dashes, and parentheses; some sentences have notes to direct you. If there is not enough room in the sentence, use a caret (∧) and place the mark above the sentence.

1. People moved to America because (1) they wanted to make a better living, (2) they wanted greater freedom from government control, and (3) they wanted greater freedom of religion.

2. Nevin Gerber (he's the boy with the black hair) is my cousin. (The parenthetical element should seem unimportant.)

3. "And having food and raiment [the basic necessities] let us be therewith content. But they that will be rich [have their hearts set on being rich] fall into temptation and a snare" (1 Timothy 6:8, 9).

4. "I'm so ashamed of the many times I've complained and—oh, I do want to be thankful!" exclaimed Helen.

5. Our watermelons produced well—Melvin watered them regularly—but the cantaloupe harvest was poor. (The parenthetical element is important.)

6. Two of the tenth grade boys (there are three of them altogether) are singing bass quite well. (The parenthetical element is of minor importance.)

7. I stumbled—how embarrassing!—on the way up front to recite the poem. (The parenthetical element deserves sharp emphasis.)

8. A good concordance (a necessity for every Bible student) can be obtained at a reasonable price. (The parenthetical element is just given as extra information.)

9. George lowered his voice and said, "We're planning a⁓" He stopped abruptly as the door opened.

10. We're planning a surprise (Brother Weaver's birthday is coming up) for next week. (The parenthetical element is a simple explanation.)

Name _____

Worksheet 12
Italics, Numbers, Apostrophes, and Hyphens

A. Add underlining or quotation marks to the titles in these sentences.

1. We are studying "Life on the Earth" in *God's Orderly World, Science 7.*

2. In <u>The World Book Encyclopedia</u>, check the article "Switzerland."

3. For our opening song, we sang "Lord, in the Morning."

4. Brother Yoder clipped an article from the <u>Morning News</u>.

B. Draw vertical lines to show each place where these words may be divided at the end of a line.

1. a b u n|d a n t|l y

2. t o t|t e r y

3. i t i n|e r|a r y

4. e v a n|g e l|i|c a l

C. Cross out any numbers that should be written with words, and write the words in the blanks.

1. Mr. Morris has ~~54~~ peach trees and ~~96~~ apple trees. <u>fifty-four, ninety-six</u>

2. The 1990 population of Vermont was 562,758, with a population density of 60.8 people per square mile.

   <u>(no change)</u>

3. ~~180~~ days is the standard length of school in many states. <u>One hundred eighty</u>

4. Father bought ~~45~~ 4′ x 8′ sheets of ¼″ plywood. <u>forty-five</u>

D. Add apostrophes, hyphens, and underlining. Cross out any incorrect punctuation. Correct any end-of-line errors.

1. Jesus' life is the supreme example of self-sacrificing love.

2. Every Christian's all-consuming desire is to follow that example.

3. The word <u>mere</u> rhymes with <u>here</u>, not <u>there</u>.

4. The *'s on your paper mark places where your paragraph's are not developed well enough.

5. I don't understand the science book's explanation about the generation of current e\ lectricity.

6. Great-grandma Neuenschwander is ninety-three years old, and her mind is cle\ ar.

7. In mid-January of '93, the snow-covered roads were quite slippery.

8. Somebody's self-discipline must have been lacking; was it your's?

9. Yes, we'll package this self-rising flour for you in five, ten, or fifty-pound bags.

10. My brother-in-law's long-haired dog is friendly.

Name _____   (Lesson 40)

Worksheet 13
Verbals and Verbal Phrases Used as Nouns

A. Identify each underlined verbal phrase by writing *I* (infinitive) or *G* (gerund) in the blank.

   G   1. We stand in awe at God's power in <u>creating the world</u>.

   I   2. Our minds fail <u>to comprehend many details in the creation</u>.

   G   3. <u>Studying these wonders</u> should increase our reverence for the Creator.

   I   4. Certainly our response should be <u>to praise our great God</u>.

   G   5. <u>Studying the stars</u> can deepen our awareness of God's greatness.

B. Underline each verbal or verbal phrase. Tell how it is used in the sentence by writing *S* (subject), *DO* (direct object), *PN* (predicate nominative), or *OP* (object of a preposition) in the blank.

   S   1. <u>Loading the calves</u> took longer than we had expected.

  DO   2. Miriam will help <u>to mix the batter for the cakes</u>.

   S   3. <u>To make these cookies</u> will take more flour than we have.

  OP   4. The children were commended for <u>doing some extra work</u>.

  PN   5. Our plans are <u>to split wood on Saturday</u>.

   S   6. <u>To interrupt</u> shows a serious disregard for others.

   S   7. <u>Excluding others from our friendship</u> is also impolite and unkind.

  DO   8. A noble person is seeking <u>to make others happy</u>.

  PN   9. One of the surest recipes for happiness is <u>to make someone else happy</u>.

  DO 10. If you are unhappy, try <u>smiling</u>.

   S   11. <u>Wearing a smile</u> puts sunshine in the heart.

  OP 12. We can lift our spirits by <u>singing hymns of praise</u>.

C. Underline the correct words in parentheses.

1. The (deer, <u>deer's</u>) browsing has destroyed many of the saplings.

2. Grandmother Lutz expressed her gratitude for (<u>our</u>, us) helping with her cleaning.

3. Have you heard about Uncle (Leroy, <u>Leroy's</u>) moving off the farm?

D. On other paper, diagram the skeletons and complements of these sentences, including the entire verbal phrases.
1. Receiving the top scores is not the most important thing.
2. A more noble goal is to do our best.
3. We should also determine to have good attitudes.
4. Being noble of heart should be our great interest.
5. We must seek to build consistently a godly character.

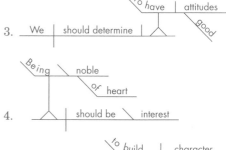

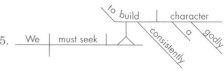

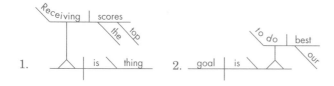

Name _____

Worksheet 14
Noun Clauses

A. Underline the noun clauses in these sentences.

1. The sheep know <u>which voice belongs to their shepherd</u>.

2. The call of their own shepherd is <u>what they will follow</u>.

3. <u>Wherever the shepherd goes</u> is a place of comfort to the sheep.

4. The Good Shepherd welcomes <u>whoever will be a part of His fold</u>.

5. <u>That He provides the best possible care</u> is obvious.

6. That is <u>why we willingly submit to His rod and staff</u>.

B. In each blank, write *S* (subject), *DO* (direct object), *PN* (predicate nominative), *OP* (object of a preposition), or *none* (not a noun) to tell what part the underlined clause fills in the independent clause.

DO   1. King Asa knew <u>that God can save even the few and weak</u>.

none   2. <u>When the powerful Ethiopian army came</u>, he trusted in the Lord.

S   3. <u>Whatever represented idol worship</u> was removed at Asa's command.

PN   4. The early part of Asa's reign was <u>when he followed the Lord</u>.

DO   5. The revival in Judah attracted <u>whoever was seeking the Lord in Israel</u>.

OP   6. King Baasha was much disturbed by <u>what he saw</u>.

C. In each italicized noun clause, underline the subject once and the verb twice. In the blank, label the function of the introductory word in the clause by writing *S* (subject), *DO* (direct object), *PN* (predicate nominative), *adv.* (adverb), *adj.* (adjective), or *conj.* (conjunction).

adj.   1. We finally discovered *whose <u>sweater</u> <u>was left</u> at our house*.

S   2. *<u>Whatever</u> <u>makes</u> such a loud noise* must be a large animal!

PN   3. The archaeologists have not decided *what these <u>ruins</u> <u>had been</u>*.

conj.   4. The agent said *that the <u>buses</u> <u>are running</u> on schedule*.

adv.   5. Do you remember *where the <u>title</u> <u>belongs</u>*?

DO   6. *Whatever that <u>dog</u> <u>smells</u>* has surely gotten him excited.

D. On other paper, diagram the skeletons and complements of the independent clauses and the entire noun clauses of these sentences.

1. Mother reported that Grandfather had become sick.
2. I know whose dog is chasing those cattle.
3. Whatever you saw must have escaped my eye.
4. Father has decided what his answer will be.
5. Whether this storm will hit us will soon be known.
6. The best time will be whenever it suits Aunt Pearl.

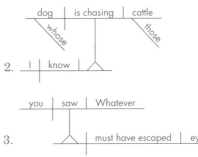

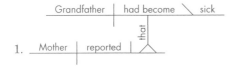

(Numbers 4–6 are on page T–632.)

Name _____   *(Lesson 42)*

Worksheet 15
Proofreading Your Composition

Proofread this composition, using the proper proofreading marks to show the corrections. Numbers in parentheses show how many errors are to be found in each paragraph. (Sentence joining or dividing counts as one item, and each comma or pair of commas counts as one item.)

What Is Africa Like?

Africa is a vast land of extreme variations, therefore, many people have wrong ideas about African life, climate, and culture. Many think of Africa as a land of small vilages. This *is* partailly true, but huge cities can be found on this continent with skyscrapers and heavy traffic. Niether is the climate all desertlike. True, the worlds largest dessert is ~~hear~~ *here*, but much of Africa is a tropical rain forest, Where it ~~reins~~ *rains* heavily almost evry day. ~~South America also has a large tropical forest, but no desert as large as the Sahara.~~ Also ~~their~~ *there* are several large lakes and ~~grate~~ *great* rivers. (18)

These differences in water supply, cause great *differences* in the way various Africans live. In the tropical rain forest, many eke out a living, *by* hunting and collecting food from the forest around them. The people, who live in the ~~planes~~ *plains* and grasslands of Africa, are generally the richest of the ~~trible~~ *tribal* communit~~ys~~ *ies*. Because ~~they're~~ *there* is plenty of good grazing, these Africans *own* many cattle. These cattle are ~~there~~ *their* money and ~~cymbals~~ *symbols* of wealth. In the desert regions, of course, life centers on the ~~ocassional~~ *occasional* ~~oasises~~ *oases*. Which are homes to the nomads. (16)

Besides the great variety in land and climate, the people of Africa also vary widely. ~~Their~~ *There* are ~~too~~ *two* predominant ethnic groups. One group is the black people, who constitute most of the population throughout the continent, the second group is the lighter-skinned Arabs, who live in countries along the Northern coast. The religoins of Africa vary as well. In many countries, most of the people adhere to native pagan religions. The Islam religion is almost exclusive in the arab countries. But a few countries (such as Ethiopia, Uganda, and Zaire) have a large number of nominal Christains. (8)

Worksheet 14, Part D *(Continued)*

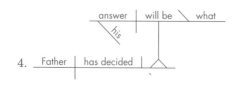

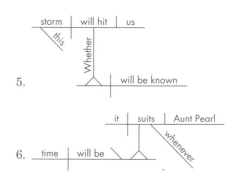

Name _____

Worksheet 16
Principal Parts of Verbs

A. Write the missing principal parts. Include *have* with the past participle.

First (Present)	Second (Past)	Third (Past Participle)
1. scurry	scurried	(have) scurried
2. drag	dragged	(have) dragged
3. come	came	(have) come
4. freeze	froze	(have) frozen
5. wring	wrung	(have) wrung
6. hurt	hurt	(have) hurt
7. begin	began	(have) begun
8. go	went	(have) gone
9. sink	sank	(have) sunk
10. buy	bought	(have) bought

B. Write the correct form of the verb before each sentence.

cost   1. Our forgetfulness has _____cost_____ us some lost time.

bear   2. The young children __bore *or* bear__ the pain very bravely.

sing   3. After we had _____sung_____ a hymn, we stood for prayer.

teach   4. Every Wednesday Brother Wilbur _____teaches_____ our music class.
or taught

come   5. We shall _____come_____ to the waterfall soon.

choose 6. Everyone had _____chosen_____ their pictures before I arrived.

creep 7. Cautiously the cat _crept *or* creeps_ up to the mouse.

swing 8. The monkeys _swung *or* swing_ expertly from branch to branch.

speak 9. Have you _____spoken_____ to Linda about the plans yet?

fly   10. The baby birds have _____flown_____ from the nest already.

C. Write the correct form of each underlined verb. If the verb is correct, write *correct*.

_____gone_____ 1. Have you <u>went</u> for your eye examination yet?

_____drowned_____ 2. With all this rain, the lima bean plants have <u>drownded</u>.

_____threw_____ 3. We <u>throwed</u> the rags on a pile.

_____come_____ 4. Has the mailman <u>came</u> this morning?

_____correct_____ 5. The dog <u>dug</u> a hole to bury his bone.

_____correct_____ 6. The fish must have all <u>swum</u> to the other side.

_____saw_____ 7. We <u>seen</u> a red-tailed hawk land in that tree.

_____run_____ 8. The tractor has <u>ran</u> out of gasoline.

_____tagged_____ 9. Henry is sure that he had <u>tug</u> me.

_____written_____ 10. Have you <u>wrote</u> a letter to Uncle Thomas?

_____correct_____ 11. A fox <u>stole</u> the bait right out of my trap.

_____burst_____ 12. The engine is hot because a water hose has <u>bursted</u>.

Name _____

Worksheet 17
Perfect Verb Tenses

A. Label the tense of each underlined verb by writing the correct letter.

a. present   c. future   e. past perfect
b. past   d. present perfect f. future perfect

___d___ 1. God has provided a haven of freedom in North America for His people.

___e___ 2. Before settling in America, many Mennonites had lived in poverty.

___b___ 3. In the New World they found economic opportunity as well as freedom.

___a___ 4. Today we are benefiting in many ways from their faith.

___d___ 5. Of course, God has blessed us so that we can serve Him.

___a___ 6. If we use our opportunities selfishly, we are failing God.

___c___ 7. God will punish those who live selfishly and luxuriously.

___e___ 8. Before you could understand much, a number of your habits had been formed.

___f___ 9. By the time you are an adult, you will have formed many more habits.

___a___ 10. You do have some responsibility in forming those habits.

B. In each sentence, one verb should be changed to a perfect tense to clarify or emphasize a clear relationship. Cross out that verb, and write a suitable perfect tense verb above it.

1. Myron ~~tilled~~ *had tilled* his cantaloupes when he mowed the grass.   *or Myron tilled his cantaloupes when he* ~~mowed~~ *had mowed the grass.*

2. By the end of the month, he ~~will till~~ *will have tilled* them several times.

3. When Father ~~gave~~ *had given* thanks, the food was passed around the table.

4. We certainly enjoyed the meal that Mother ~~made~~ *had made* for us.

5. By the time the blizzard ended, several feet of snow ~~fell~~ *had fallen*.

6. I wrote a report about an interesting book that I ~~read~~ *had read*.

7. We made a bulletin board display with the flowers that we ~~dried~~ *had dried*.

8. The cows ~~broke~~ *have broken* down the fence, and we must chase them in.

C. Write the proper form of the verb in the blank according to the directions in parentheses.

1. The closing bell _____had rung_____ before I was ready. (past perfect of *ring*)

2. Aunt Sue _____has become_____ ill, and Mother is helping with her work. (present perfect of *become*)

3. After I finish this book, I _____shall have taken_____ notes from three different sources. (future perfect of *take*)

Name _____

Worksheet 18
Transitive Verbs

A. Underline the substantive that receives the action of the transitive verb.

1. Abraham built several <u>altars</u> to the Lord God.

2. God honored this man's deep <u>faith</u>.

3. A wonderful <u>promise</u> was given to Abraham and Sarah.

4. Through them, all <u>nations</u> of the earth would be blessed.

5. Abraham believed <u>that God would keep His promises</u>.

6. At a very young age, <u>Isaac</u> was mocked by Ishmael.

7. Abraham sent <u>Hagar</u> and <u>Ishmael</u> away.

8. The Philistines gave Isaac much <u>trouble</u>.

9. They filled up several <u>wells</u> with dirt.

10. Isaac refused <u>to fight with them</u>.

B. Underline the complements. Above each one, write *DO* (direct object), *IO* (indirect object), or *OC* (objective complement).

1. To a large extent, a person must earn his <u>success</u>. [DO]

2. Most successful people have learned the <u>secret</u> of perseverance. [DO]

3. Perseverance brings <u>one</u> [IO] the <u>satisfaction</u> [DO] of a job completed.

4. The truly successful person makes his present <u>work</u> [DO] his <u>interest</u> [OC].

5. His responsibilities do not merely bring <u>him</u> [IO] <u>drudgery</u> [DO].

6. He considers productive <u>labor</u> [DO] a definite <u>privilege</u> [OC].

7. The lack of perseverance has ruined the <u>usefulness</u> [DO] of many people.

8. Without God's blessing, however, no amount of perseverance will produce true <u>success</u> [DO].

9. Nor does perseverance always bring a <u>person</u> [IO] material <u>wealth</u> [DO].

10. The satisfaction of persevering constitutes a richer <u>reward</u> [DO] than material wealth.

C. Diagram the skeletons and complements of these sentences.
1. That squirrel gave me quite a scolding.
2. Duke chased the cat up the tree.
3. Then he tried to climb the tree.
4. The stubborn donkey considered the load too heavy.
5. The cows have been brought in from pasture.
6. Our neighbor raises hamsters and gerbils.

Name _____   *(Lesson 53)*

Worksheet 19
Intransitive Complete Verbs

A. In the first blank, write *T* or *I* to tell whether the verb is transitive or intransitive complete. If the verb is transitive, write the word that receives the action in the second blank.

__I__ _____	1.	John the Baptist preached boldly to the people.
__T__ __message__	2.	He preached the message of repentance.
__I__ _____	3.	He was baptizing in the Jordan River.
__T__ __people__	4.	He was baptizing people from many walks of life.
__T__ __trees__	5.	Huge trees were snapped off by the fury of the storm.
__I__ _____	6.	The wire snapped under the huge tree.
__T__ __lesson__	7.	Have you read today's science lesson?
__I__ _____	8.	I read slowly and thoughtfully.
__I__ _____	9.	The china dish shattered into tiny pieces.
__T__ __windshield__	10.	The windshield was shattered by a falling stone.
__T__ __shirt__	11.	Michael tore his shirt during the hike.
__I__ _____	12.	His shirt tore on a thorny bush.
__I__ _____	13.	The man spoke excitedly in a high-pitched voice.
__T__ __language__	14.	The man spoke a strange language.
__T__ __lemonade__	15.	Thankfully we drank the cold lemonade.
__T__ __lemonade__	16.	Very soon the lemonade was all drunk.
__I__ _____	17.	On the way down the steps, I stumbled over a book.
__T__ __book__	18.	A book should never be left on the steps.
__T__ __person__	19.	A fall down the steps could injure a person.
__I__ _____	20.	We should think about such possible dangers.

B. On other paper, write two sentences for each verb. The verb should be transitive in one sentence and intransitive complete in the other.   (Individual work.)
   1. follow   3. has cracked
   2. will write   4. pushed

C. On other paper, diagram the skeletons and complements of these sentences.
   1. Clyde often watches for the evening stars to appear.
   2. He can quickly identify many constellations.
   3. Many different birds are listed in his notebook of sightings.
   4. He knows the songs of most birds in our area.
   5. He rarely complains about his confinement to a wheelchair.
   6. His back had been injured in a fall.

1. Clyde | watches   3. birds | are listed   5. He | complains

2. He | can identify | constellations   4. He | knows | songs   6. back | had been injured

Name _____

Worksheet 20
Intransitive Linking Verbs

A. Underline the words that are linked by each intransitive linking verb.

1. <u>Timothy</u> was a young <u>man</u> of unfeigned faith.

2. His <u>examples</u> of faith were his <u>mother</u> and his <u>grandmother</u>.

3. <u>He</u> became an influential church <u>leader</u>.

4. The <u>Witmers</u> have been our <u>neighbors</u> and close <u>friends</u> for years.

5. The <u>cries</u> of the coyote sounded <u>mournful</u> in the night.

6. Many wild <u>animals</u> appear <u>unhappy</u> in captivity.

7. <u>Potatoes</u> have become a main <u>food</u> of Americans.

8. <u>Brother Arnold</u> will be our <u>companion</u> on this trip.

9. Lynn's <u>plans</u> did not prove <u>workable</u>.

10. The <u>air</u> has been feeling <u>warm</u> and <u>humid</u>.

B. In each blank, label the verb *T* (transitive), *IC* (intransitive complete), or *IL* (intransitive linking).

__IL__ 1. The Roman Forum was the center of government in Rome.

__IC__ 2. Many important and beautiful buildings were standing there.

__T__ 3. The events at this place often affected the whole world.

__IC__ 4. At this place, famous orators often spoke to crowds.

__T__ 5. Valuables from battles were brought there for display.

__IL__ 6. The area had been a swamp in earlier days.

__T__ 7. Then the marshes were drained.

__IL__ 8. The Colosseum is one of the most famous ruins in the world.

__T__ 9. Many tourists to the area photograph these impressive ruins.

__IC__ 10. It stands near the center of present-day Rome.

__IL__ 11. Flamingos, beautiful water birds, are timid.

__IC__ 12. They often live together in large colonies.

__IC__ 13. They sometimes rest by standing on one leg.

__IL__ 14. Flamingos have long been prey to hunters.

__T__ 15. In some areas they are protected by law.

C. On other paper, diagram the skeletons and complements of these sentences.
1. The Amazon is the chief river of South America.
2. It drains a huge area of tropical rain forest.
3. It flows through low, flat land.
4. Consequently, its current is extremely slow.
5. In many places the lands around the river remain unexplored and inaccessible.

5. lands | remain \< unexplored / and / inaccessible

1. Amazon | is \ river   2. It | drains | area   3. It | flows   4. current | is \ slow

Name _____   *(Lesson 60)*

Worksheet 21
Subject–Verb Agreement

A. Underline the correct verbs in parentheses.

1. A true disciple (don't, <u>doesn't</u>) expect to be loved by the world.

2. Our speech, as well as our actions, (show, <u>shows</u>) what is in our hearts.

3. Each of our choices (influence, <u>influences</u>) our character.

4. The priest and king of Salem (<u>was</u>, were) Melchizedek.

5. The priest and the king (was, <u>were</u>) serving the Lord.

6. (<u>Where's</u>, Where are) the Golden Rule found in Luke's Gospel?

7. The pliers (<u>have</u>, has) been misplaced.

8. "Micha's Thanks" (<u>is</u>, are) a story set in Russia.

9. Mathematics (have, <u>has</u>) always been one of my favorite subjects.

10. The pack of wolves (<u>is</u>, are) following a wounded caribou.

11. The pack of wolves (<u>have</u>, has) all been running from the hunters.

12. One problem in many cities (<u>is</u>, are) traffic jams.

13. Traffic jams (is, <u>are</u>) one problem in many cities.

14. Wilma, along with Dorothy and Grace, (<u>is</u>, are) working in the bakery.

15. An apple or a carrot (act, <u>acts</u>) as a natural toothbrush.

16. It (don't, <u>doesn't</u>) look as if it will rain today.

17. (Haven't, <u>Hasn't</u>) the mailman gone yet?

18. (There's, <u>There are</u>) several new books on the shelf now.

19. *Plateaus* or *plateaux* (<u>is</u>, are) a correct plural spelling of *plateau*.

20. Chicken pox (<u>is</u>, are) a common childhood disease.

B. Rewrite each sentence, following the directions in parentheses and changing the verb to agree with the subject if necessary.

1. The poems fit well on this scrapbook page. (Change *The poems* to *Either of the poems*.)

   <u>Either of the poems fits well on this scrapbook page.</u>

2. A short poem or several Bible verses are appropriate on a greeting card. (Change the subject to *Several Bible verses or a short poem*.)   <u>Several Bible verses or a short poem is appropriate on a greeting card.</u>

   _____

3. Darwin and Dean have gone to dig potatoes. (Change *and* to *or*.) _____

   <u>Darwin or Dean has gone to dig potatoes.</u>

4. The class is studying the lesson together. (Change the ending to *working on their separate assignments*.)

   <u>The class are working on their separate assignments.</u>

Name _____

Worksheet 22
Using Problem Verbs

A. Write the proper form of *lay* or *lie*.

lay	1. The young Christian —— peacefully in his cell for days.
lies	2. The foundation of truth —— in the Word of God.
lain	3. Mr. Lake's deep need has —— on our hearts for many years.
lies	4. The secret to victory over sin —— in a holy fear of God.
laid	5. John the Baptist —— the axe to the root.
lain	6. This old Bible must have —— in a chest for many years.
lie	7. Do not —— on the damp ground.

B. Write the proper form of *set* or *sit*.

set	1. Did you —— the table correctly?
sit	2. Please —— up straight in your seats.
set	3. Last night we —— our alarms for 4:00 A.M.
set	4. That hen has —— for two weeks now.
sat	5. Earlier this year, I —— in the back of the room.
set	6. In this warm weather, the concrete will —— rapidly.
sat	7. This old machinery has —— behind the barn for years.

C. Write the proper form of *raise* or *rise*.

raised *or* rising	1. Our hearts were —— in gratitude for God's graciousness.
risen	2. We trust that our prayers have —— to the Lord's throne.
rises *or* rose	3. Every day the sun —— to light God's world again.
raised	4. When Moses —— his hands, Israel prevailed over Amalek.
rose	5. A covey of quails suddenly —— into the air before us.
raise *or* raised	6. My brother and I —— rabbits and guinea pigs.
risen	7. The early morning fog has —— now.

D. Write *can* or *may* for each sentence.

can	1. Do you think you —— carry this heavy box to the attic?
may	2. Brother Leon said that we —— eat outside today.
may	3. Those who have finished their work —— be excused.
can	4. Nobody —— ever fool God.
May	5. —— we go down to the creek this afternoon?
can	6. We are thankful that God —— supply all our needs.
may	7. If Grandmother feels well, she —— be in church tomorrow.

Name _____

Worksheet 23
More Problem Verbs

A. Underline the correct words in parentheses.

1. We must turn away from all who (<u>advise</u>, advice) us to disobey the Bible.

2. We dare not (<u>accept</u>, except) the idea that some Bible doctrines are unimportant today.

3. The devil may (<u>propose</u>, purpose) an easier road, but we must resist him.

4. When God's people (<u>adapted</u>, adopted) to the world, they soon lost God's blessing.

5. Have you (proposed, <u>purposed</u>) to do your best in your studies?

6. Those who play with temptation (<u>lose</u>, loose) God's protection and grace.

7. Hold fast to the Bible; do not (adapt, <u>adopt</u>) the ways of the world.

8. When Jonathan stripped himself of his princely robe, he (<u>implied</u>, inferred) that he recognized David as the next king.

9. Satan's efforts cannot (<u>alter</u>, altar) the fact of God's sovereignty.

10. Many Christians (emigrated, <u>immigrated</u>) to the New World for religious freedom.

11. I (implied, <u>inferred</u>) from Carl's answer that he would welcome our help.

12. If I (lose, <u>loose</u>) the calf from the tether, can you get her on the truck?

13. Kindness certainly (<u>affects</u>, effects) the way others respond to you.

14. Lee (<u>accepted</u>, excepted) the teacher's rebuke humbly.

15. Konrad Pavlaski (<u>emigrated</u>, immigrated) from Poland twenty years ago.

16. We soon (<u>adapted</u>, adopted) to the cold weather of the North.

17. Our willingness to help Mr. Layton (affected, <u>effected</u>) a great change in his attitude toward us.

18. Your complaining (<u>implies</u>, infers) dissatisfaction with God.

19. Mother (<u>altered</u>, altared) Beth's pattern to make me a dress.

20. The Weaver family (adapted, <u>adopted</u>) a six-month-old orphan from Costa Rica.

B. If the underlined word is incorrect, write the correct word. If it is correct, write *correct*. These sentences cover Lessons 61 and 62.

<u>implied</u>	1. Satan's words to Eve <u>inferred</u> that God was not fair.	<u>correct</u>	7. Dennis has <u>proposed</u> the best idea so far.
<u>let</u>	2. Adam and Eve <u>left</u> the devil deceive them.	<u>emigrated</u>	8. Several groups of Christians soon <u>immigrated</u> from Russia.
<u>correct</u>	3. Their sin <u>effected</u> a terrible change in their lives.	<u>may</u>	9. Helen asked if she <u>can</u> bring a special treat tomorrow.
<u>adopted</u>	4. Abram apparently <u>adapted</u> his nephew Lot.	<u>lay</u>	10. The old dog <u>laid</u> by the cozy fire most of the morning.
<u>rose</u>	5. In the still morning air, the smoke <u>raised</u> straight up.	<u>correct</u>	11. Do your work more carefully, or you will <u>lose</u> your recess.
<u>sat</u>	6. These cut flowers have <u>set</u> on the table for several days.	<u>accepted</u>	12. We gratefully <u>excepted</u> the help of our friends.

Name _____

Worksheet 24
Active and Passive Voice

A. Identify the verb in each sentence as active (A) or passive (P).

___A___ 1. True love works no ill toward others.

___P___ 2. The welfare of others should be placed ahead of our own.

___A___ 3. By Christ's grace, we can love the unlovely.

___A___ 4. Many professing Christians have rejected the doctrine of nonresistance.

___P___ 5. This doctrine is clearly taught by Christ and the apostles.

___A___ 6. Brother Edgar will conduct our morning worship.

B. The active voice is more direct and forceful than the passive voice. Rewrite each sentence so that the verb is in the active voice.

1. God's name should be held in reverence by us.   _We should hold God's name in reverence._

2. A house was built upon a rock by the wise man.   _The wise man built a house upon a rock._

3. Zacchaeus was called down from the tree by Jesus.   _Jesus called Zacchaeus down from the tree._

4. My sister's pen was lost by me.   _I lost my sister's pen._

5. This quilt was made by Grandmother Huber.   _Grandmother Huber made this quilt._

6. Cows were milked without machines by Grandfather.   _Grandfather milked cows without machines._

7. This lovely picture was drawn by Ellen for an art project.
   Ellen drew this lovely picture for an art project.

8. I was helped with my chores by Mark.   _Mark helped me with my chores._

9. A bad case of measles was had by my cousin Lavern.   _My cousin Lavern had a bad case of measles._

10. The title Caesar was used by the emperors of ancient Rome.
   The emperors of ancient Rome used the title Caesar.

C. Underline each retained object, and write whether it is a direct object (DO) or an indirect object (IO).

___DO___ 1. Joseph was given a high <u>position</u> by Pharaoh.

___IO___ 2. Many Bible truths have been taught <u>us</u> by our parents.

___DO___ 3. The apostles were assigned a great <u>work</u> by Jesus.

___IO___ 4. Considerable freedom was granted <u>Paul</u> by the centurion.

Name _____   (Lesson 69)

Worksheet 25
Personal Pronouns

A. Label the person, number, case, and gender of each pronoun, using the numbers or letters shown. For the number of one pronoun, write both *S* and *P*.

	Person 1, 2, 3	Number S, P	Case N, O, P	Gender M, F, N, C
1. them	3	P	O	C
2. he	3	S	N	M
3. your	2	S and P	P	C
4. us	1	P	O	C
5. she	3	S	N	F
6. its	3	S	P	N
7. I	1	S	N	C
8. hers	3	S	P	F

B. Write a personal pronoun to fit each description.

   <u>them</u>   1. third person, plural, objective case

   <u>I</u>   2. first person, singular, nominative case

   <u>her *or* hers</u> 3. third person, singular, possessive case, feminine gender

   <u>you</u>   4. second person, nominative case

   <u>him</u>   5. third person, singular, objective case, masculine gender

C. Underline each personal pronoun, and put parentheses around its antecedent.

1. Three times a day, (Daniel) knelt before <u>his</u> window to pray.

2. The (presidents and princes) watched (Daniel) because <u>they</u> envied <u>him</u>.

3. (Darius) regretted making the (law,) but <u>he</u> was powerless to change <u>it</u>.

4. The (lions) could not hurt Daniel, for an angel had shut <u>their</u> mouths.

D. Cross out each incorrect pronoun, and write the correct pronoun in the blank. If a sentence has no errors, write C for correct.

   <u>she</u>   1. It was ~~her~~ who sewed these clothes for them.

   <u>They</u>   2. ~~Them~~ appreciated her kindness very much.

   <u>he</u>   3. The new superintendent is ~~him~~.

   <u>C</u>   4. I shall help them with their work.

   <u>his</u>   5. Everybody brought ~~their~~ lunch in a paper bag.

   <u>C *or* its</u> 6. The horse found ~~his~~ way home in the storm.

   <u>C</u>   7. The friendly helpers must have been they.

   <u>they</u>   8. Father said ~~them~~ had done a good job.

   <u>C</u>   9. If a person works diligently, he will finish the job sooner.

   <u>we</u>   10. The last ones to arrive were ~~us~~.

Name _____

Worksheet 26
Using Personal Pronouns Correctly

A. Underline the correct words in parentheses.

1. God told Manoah and (she, <u>her</u>) that they would have a son.

2. Peter, James, and (<u>he</u>, him) often were with Jesus.

3. (<u>We</u>, Us) students must recognize the value of a Christian education.

4. God does not ask you and (I, <u>me</u>) to learn as well as others but to do our best.

5. God has given (we, <u>us</u>) youth clear standards of right conduct.

6. The carpenter and painter gave (<u>his estimate</u>, their estimates) to Father.

7. The carpenter and the painter gave (his estimate, <u>their estimates</u>) to Father.

8. Either Lucille or Ruth should bring (<u>her</u>, their) electric roaster.

9. The teenagers in our family, Marcus and (<u>I</u>, me), eat a lot of food.

10. Aunt Lovina sent a birthday card to you and (I, <u>me</u>).

11. The team captains are the two eighth grade boys, Michael and (<u>I</u>, me).

12. The ones in the barn, Joel and (<u>he</u>, him), did not see the raccoon.

13. Harvey does better at batting than (<u>I</u>, me).

14. Their cows are Holsteins; (<u>ours</u>, our's) are Guernseys.

15. A flock of geese stopped at our pond on (<u>its way</u>, their ways) north.

16. The flock of geese busily prepared (its, <u>their</u>) nests.

17. (<u>We</u>, Us) cousins played hide-and-seek for a while.

18. Apparently Father's words excited me more than (he, <u>him</u>).

19. Grandmother knitted mittens for (we, <u>us</u>) grandchildren.

20. Our farm has eighty acres; (<u>theirs</u>, their's) is much bigger.

B. Rewrite these sentences to make the pronouns clear and correct.

1. Mother wants me and you to set the table for dinner. _____
   <u>Mother wants you and me to set the table for dinner.</u>

2. Leroy helped Chester before he became ill.   <u>Before Leroy became ill, he helped Chester.</u>
   <u>*or* Before Chester became ill, Leroy helped him.</u>

3. Laura asked Rebecca if her dress had a grass stain. _____
   <u>Laura asked, "Rebecca, does my (*or* your) dress have a grass stain?"</u>

4. Me and Elmer chased the cows back into the pasture. _____
   <u>Elmer and I chased the cows back into the pasture.</u>

5. Donald told Enos that his bicycle tire was flat.   <u>Donald said, "Enos, your (*or* my) bicycle tire is flat."</u>

_____

Name _____   *(Lesson 72)*

Worksheet 27
Compound Personal Pronouns and Demonstrative Pronouns

A. Underline each compound personal pronoun. In the blank, write *I* if it is used intensively or *R* if it is used reflexively.

   __R__ 1. God has revealed <u>Himself</u> to man in various ways.

   __I__ 2. Nature <u>itself</u> shows His existence.

   __R__ 3. Many people make fools of <u>themselves</u> by denying His existence.

   __I__ 4. We <u>ourselves</u> can deny Him by ignoring Him in our daily lives.

   __R__ 5. You should inspire <u>yourself</u> by reading God's Word.

B. Underline each demonstrative pronoun. Do not underline words used as adjectives.

  1. My brother gave <u>this</u> to me, and that book he gave to her.

  2. Should these old nails be thrown into the bucket with <u>those</u>?

  3. Those clouds are becoming darker; <u>that</u> surely looks like a thunderhead.

  4. <u>These</u> should last a long time.

  5. Are <u>those</u> your boots?

C. Cross out each wrong word. If another word should be used instead, write the correction above it.

  1. God daily loads ~~ourself~~ ^{us} with blessings.

  2. Too often we take these ~~here~~ blessings for granted.

  3. The righteous avail ~~theirselves~~ ^{themselves} of God's blessings.

  4. Myron helped ~~hisself~~ ^{himself} to a piece of cake.

  5. Sharon and ~~myself~~ ^I made this caramel popcorn.

  6. ~~Them~~ ^{Those} are beautiful flower arrangements.

  7. Aunt Marlene made those ~~there~~ napkin holders.

  8. Lloyd told Daryl and ~~myself~~ ^{me} about his trip.

  9. These apples are sorted already; ~~them~~ ^{those} are not.

  10. Carla and ~~herself~~ ^{she} have been busy sorting apples all morning.

  11. We busied ~~ourself~~ ^{ourselves} with sorting the rest of the apples.

  12. Harold ~~hisself~~ ^{himself} could not fix our car.

  13. ~~Them~~ ^{Those} are the Blue Mountains on the horizon.

  14. This ~~here~~ is the Cumberland Valley.

  15. The boys made ~~themself~~ ^{themselves} a toboggan.

Worksheet 34, Part C *(Continued)*

Name _____

Worksheet 28
Unity, Coherence, Conciseness, and Parallelism in Sentences

A. Rewrite these sentences to improve the unity or coherence.   (Allow reasonable variation.)

1. In the Book of Judges it tells the story of Gideon.   _The Book of Judges tells the story of Gideon._

   _____

2. Gideon cut down a grove, and it was not a group of trees.   _____
   The grove that Gideon cut down was not a group of trees.

3. The grove was one or more wooden pillars or images. They were objects of idol worship. _____
   The grove was one or more wooden pillars or images that were objects of idol worship.

4. Gideon was, when threatened by the people, defended by his father.   _____
   When threatened by the people, Gideon was defended by his father.

5. Gideon sent out messengers, thousands of Israelites came to help him.   _____
   Gideon sent out messengers, and thousands of Israelites came to help him.
   or After Gideon sent out messengers, thousands of Israelites came to help him.

6. Seven-tenths of the men almost were fearful and returned home.   _____
   Almost seven-tenths of the men were fearful and returned home.

7. With three hundred men, Gideon was able to utterly defeat the Midianites.   _____
   With three hundred men, Gideon was able to defeat the Midianites utterly.

B. Make these sentences more clear and concise by crossing out the unnecessary words in numbers 1–3 and
   rewriting numbers 4 and 5.
   1. Because of the ~~big~~ giants, the Israelites wanted to return ~~back~~ to Egypt.
   2. Dozens of sparks from the ~~burning~~ fire were ascending ~~up~~ into the sky.
   3. By ~~the month of~~ November, many birds have departed ~~away~~ for the winter.

   4. A raven is a bird that is large in size and black in color.   _A raven is a large black bird._

   _____

   5. This picture makes it plain that a steppe is a plain.   _____
   This picture makes it clear that a steppe is a plain.

C. Rewrite these sentences to improve the parallelism.

   1. The little girl spoke softly but in a clear voice.   _The little girl spoke softly but clearly._

   2. She told us her name and what her age was.   _She told us her name and her age._

   3. Was Abimelech a Philistine, Israelite, or Egyptian?   _____
   Was Abimelech a Philistine, an Israelite, or an Egyptian?

   4. If you research this, one will learn about five different Abimelechs.   _____
   If you research this, you will learn about five different Abimelechs.

   5. As an Egyptian king was called Pharaoh, so the Philistines called their king Abimelech. _____
   As the Egyptians called their king Pharaoh, so the Philistines called their king Abimelech.

Name _____   *(Lesson 74)*

Worksheet 29
Indefinite Pronouns

A. Underline the correct words in parentheses.

1. Several of the prophets (<u>give</u>, gives) exact details about Jesus' birth.

2. One of the prophets (name, <u>names</u>) the place where He was born.

3. (<u>Do</u>, Does) any of the girls need more yarn?

4. (Do, <u>Does</u>) one of the girls need more yarn?

5. (<u>Do</u>, Does) all the girls need more yarn?

6. Neither of the girls (need, <u>needs</u>) more yarn.

7. None of the girls (<u>need</u>, needs) more yarn.

8. Most of the girls (<u>need</u>, needs) more yarn.

9. Some of the grass (<u>is</u>, are) very tall.

10. All of the stanzas (was, <u>were</u>) sung.

11. None of the cake (<u>was</u>, were) left over after supper.

12. Some of the milk (<u>was</u>, were) used to make pudding.

13. Most of the grass (have, <u>has</u>) become brown during this dry weather.

14. Few of the questions on the test (was, <u>were</u>) easy.

15. Everyone in the group raised (<u>his hand</u>, their hands).

16. Many of the young trees (<u>have</u>, has) grown well.

17. Either of the boys may bake (<u>his favorite cake</u>, their favorite cakes).

18. Both of the boys may bake (his favorite cake, <u>their favorite cakes</u>).

19. None of the sandwiches (<u>have</u>, has) been eaten.

20. None of the cheese (have, <u>has</u>) been eaten.

21. Everything in these boxes (go, <u>goes</u>) along.

22. Nothing in this room (seem, <u>seems</u>) to be in (<u>its place</u>, their places).

23. Something in these containers (smell, <u>smells</u>) rotten.

24. Someone actually refused to give (<u>his</u>, their) help.

25. Each should do (<u>his</u>, their) best.

B. Add the missing apostrophes.

1. Yours should be on this stack where everyone's was put.

2. Surely someone's worked better than hers.

3. Theirs seemed to be the best, but no one's worked perfectly.

4. Anyone's should work better than ours.

Worksheet 30
Action and Emphasis in Sentences

A. Rewrite these sentences so that there are no passive verbs and no indirect quotations.

(Sentences may vary somewhat.)

1. The book could not be found by Carol. ___Carol could not find the book.___

2. Carol asked Marlene if she had been reading it. ___Carol asked Marlene, "Were you reading it?"___

3. Marlene replied that she had put it on Carol's shelf. ___Marlene replied, "I put it on your shelf."___

4. Every shelf and drawer in Carol's room was searched. _____
   Carol searched every shelf and drawer in her room.

5. Finally the book was found under Carol's bed. ___Finally Carol found the book under her bed.___

6. Mother said that Carol must be more careful to put her things away. _____
   Mother said, "Carol, you must be more careful to put your things away."

B. Write whether the repetition in each sentence is effective (*E*) or poor (*P*).

___E___ 1. There was sand on the floor, sand on the table, and sand in the dishes.

___P___ 2. I rocked the baby in the rocking chair until I had rocked her to sleep.

___P___ 3. We admired the many plants around the plant where Father works.

___E___ 4. We saw tall plants and short plants, young plants and older plants.

C. Write whether each sentence is loose (*L*), periodic (*P*), or balanced (*B*).

___B___ 1. Give thanks part of the time, and live thanks all of the time.

___L___ 2. An elderly woman came into President Lincoln's office one day.

___P___ 3. Knowing that Lincoln was fond of cookies, she had brought him some.

___L___ 4. Lincoln stood speechless with surprise at her thoughtfulness.

___P___ 5. Of all the people who had come to see him, everyone except this woman had asked a favor.

___L___ 6. Many people fail to be content with the favors that they receive freely from God every day.

___B___ 7. The more they get, the more they want.

D. Add words to make a balanced sentence from each item.

1. We die by living to ourselves; we live ___We die by living to ourselves; we live by dying to ourselves.___

2. God put the church into the world, but Satan tries to _____
   God put the church into the world, but Satan tries to put the world into the church.

3. The beginning of anxiety is the end of faith, and the beginning of _____
   The beginning of anxiety is the end of faith, and the beginning of faith is the end of anxiety.

Name _____   *(Lesson 77)*

Worksheet 31
Interrogative and Relative Pronouns

A. Write whether each underlined pronoun is an interrogative pronoun (*I*) or a relative pronoun (*R*).

    __R__   1. The words <u>which</u> Jesus spoke are spirit and life.

    __I__   2. <u>What</u> did many of the Jewish leaders say about Jesus?

    __R__   3. Why did they refuse to believe in Him <u>whom</u> God had sent?

    __I__   4. <u>Whose</u> glory were these blind leaders seeking?

    __R__   5. The Messiah, <u>whose</u> coming had been long awaited, was rejected.

B. Underline each relative pronoun, and put parentheses around its antecedent.

    1. David's (men,) <u>whose</u> hearts were faint, kept pressing on.

    2. We are all (people) <u>who</u> have wandered away from God.

    3. The priceless (gift) <u>that</u> God has given us is His Son.

    4. The (birthright,) <u>which</u> Esau despised, represented spiritual values as well as material blessings.

    5. (Hannah,) <u>whose</u> son helped Eli in the temple, was a godly mother.

    6. The (saint) <u>who</u> had sewed many garments was Dorcas.

C. Underline the correct pronouns in parentheses.

    1. One of the insects (who, <u>which</u>) Solomon observed was the ant.

    2. Anyone (<u>who</u>, which) tends to be lazy should take a lesson from the ant.

    3. Solomon, (who, <u>whom</u>) God had blessed in a special way, was very wise.

    4. Solomon, (<u>who</u>, whom) was very wise, turned to idols in his later life.

    5. Our puppy, (who, <u>which</u>) loves chasing cats, was chased by a tomcat today.

    6. Great-aunt Hetty, (who, <u>whom</u>) we visited yesterday, lives alone.

D. Underline each pronoun, including possessive personal pronouns used as adjectives. Label each one *P* (personal), *CP* (compound personal), *D* (demonstrative), *ID* (indefinite), *IR* (interrogative), or *R* (relative).

    1. The sugarhouse <u>that</u>(R) Grandfather Zehr operates was built by <u>his</u>(P) father.

    2. <u>This</u>(D) is a busy place while <u>we</u>(P) are making maple syrup.

    3. Are <u>these</u>(D) <u>your</u>(P) woods, or do <u>they</u>(P) belong to <u>someone</u>(ID) <u>whom</u>(R) <u>I</u>(P) do not know?

    4. Aunt Rose made <u>herself</u>(CP) a cup of tea and offered <u>us</u>(P) <u>some</u>(ID) too.

    5. <u>What</u>(IR) are <u>these</u>(D) doing on <u>her</u>(P) dresser?

    6. <u>My</u>(P) whistle was carved by Grandfather <u>himself</u>(CP).

    7. Did <u>something</u>(ID) injure <u>itself</u>(CP) in the barbed wire?

    8. <u>Whom</u>(IR) is <u>everyone</u>(ID) expecting to come?

Name _____

Worksheet 32
Rhythm and Rhyme in Poetry

A. Scan the first line of each stanza. Then write which kind of meter it has (in the long blank), and show the rhyming pattern (in the short blanks).

1. _____ trochaic _____

Heavenly Father, hear our prayer   a

When the dawn is breaking   b

And our souls are waking   b

To life's newborn day.   c

Heavenly Father, hear our prayer   a

When the noon is blazing   d

And our foe is raising   d

War along life's way.   c

Heavenly Father, hear our prayer   a

When the day is ending   e

And we're homeward wending: e

Rest beyond the fray.   c

2. _____ trochaic _____

Cling to Christ, the Rock of Ages,   a

Till the tempests cease to roll.   b

Grovel not in fears perplexing;   c

Rest in God, O troubled soul.   b

3. _____ iambic _____

When darkness seems to veil the sky   a

And motivates a moaning sigh,   a

There's One who watches from on high;   a

Take heart and know that He is God.   b

4. _____ anapestic _____

The Assyrian came down like the wolf on the fold,   a

And his cohorts were gleaming in purple and gold;   a

And the sheen of their spears was like stars on the sea,   b

When the blue wave rolls nightly on deep Galilee.   b

5. _____ dactylic _____

Winging and stinging from mountaintop cold   a

Roars the raw wind to the valley below,   b

Filling and stilling the whole with its bold   a

Blizzard of fast-falling, wind-drifted snow.   b

B. Copy three sets of feminine rhymes. __breaking, waking; blazing, raising; ending, wending__

C. Copy the two sets of internal rhymes. __Winging, stinging; Filling, stilling__

Name _____   *(Lesson 84)*

<h1 align="center">Worksheet 33</h1>
<h1 align="center">Verbals and Phrases Used as Adjectives</h1>

A. Underline each participle or participial phrase. Draw an arrow from it to the word it modifies.

1. Esau, <u>despising spiritual values</u>, sold his birthright.
2. The <u>lowing</u> cattle and <u>bleating</u> sheep revealed King Saul's disobedience.
3. The Egyptian army, <u>destroyed so easily</u>, posed no threat to God's power.
4. <u>Spanning the sky</u>, the rainbow speaks of God's <u>established</u> promise.

B. Underline each infinitive or infinitive phrase. Draw an arrow from it to the word it modifies.

1. Jesus' decision <u>to cross Samaria</u> speaks of His love to all.
2. Many parables <u>to ponder</u> were spoken by Jesus.
3. God richly blessed Paul's efforts <u>to evangelize the world</u>.
4. Our desire <u>to please the Lord</u> should produce a willingness <u>to serve others</u>.

C. Underline each prepositional phrase used as an adjective. Draw an arrow from it to the word it modifies.

1. The doors <u>of the old cabin</u> sagged on their hinges.
2. The cellar <u>below the kitchen of our old house</u> had a dirt floor.   *or* The cellar <u>below the kitchen of our old house</u> had a dirt floor.
3. We will take the first road <u>beyond this small town</u>.
4. The old trail <u>through the mountains</u> was used by pioneers <u>of old times</u>.

D. Underline the correct words in parentheses.

1. (Establishing, <u>Having established</u>) many churches, the apostle Paul visited them again.
2. (<u>Hanging</u>, Having hung) on the cross, Jesus prayed, "Father, forgive them."
3. (Ascending, <u>Having ascended</u>) on high, Jesus now intercedes for us.

E. Diagram these sentences.
1. The singing birds cheered my days of recovery.
2. The kettle on the back burner contains a vegetable stew for our supper.
3. Helping my little brother, I forgot the problems burdening my mind.
4. The creek behind our barn is a good place to catch trout.
5. The trees along the south side of the house provide good shade.

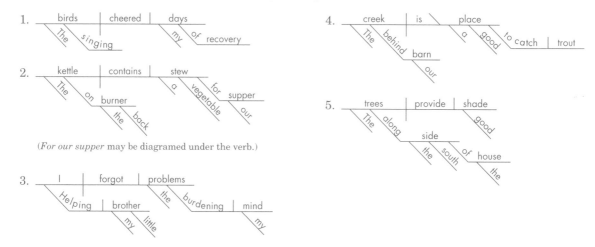

(*For our supper* may be diagramed under the verb.)

Name _____

Worksheet 34
Adjective Clauses

A. Underline each adjective clause, and draw an arrow from it to the item it modifies.

1. Molds, <u>which are very common fungi</u>, can be helpful or harmful to man.

2. People <u>who are not familiar with mushrooms</u> should never pick mushrooms to eat.

3. Edward Jenner, <u>whose work with vaccination stirred controversy</u>, felt sure that smallpox could be prevented.

4. The boy <u>whom he vaccinated</u> did not get smallpox.

5. Today the process <u>Jenner pioneered</u> saves thousands of lives every year.

6. The road <u>that runs past our farm</u> goes right into Summerville.

7. We could not find any place <u>where we could buy gasoline</u>.

8. The farmer <u>whose cows are on the road</u> is not home.

9. Easter commemorates the day <u>when Jesus arose from the dead</u>.

10. Do you know the reason <u>why many Jews rejected their Messiah</u>?

B. In each blank, write whether the underlined adjective clause is restrictive (R) or nonrestrictive (N). Add any commas that are needed.

__R__ 1. Mother could not find the recipe <u>that she wanted to use</u>.

__N__ 2. Aunt Lela, <u>who teaches school in Ohio</u>, will come home for the wedding.

__R__ 3. Mr. Lyle thanked the men <u>who cut and stacked the firewood for him</u>.

__R__ 4. All the students <u>whose names I read</u> will be on Team 1.

__N__ 5. My first grade teacher, <u>whom I have not seen for several years</u>, came to visit school today.

__N__ 6. The Appledale Mennonite School, <u>which was built two years ago</u>, has excellent facilities.

__R__ 7. Any car <u>that smokes that much</u> must have serious problems.

__N__ 8. Father took his car, <u>which was smoking badly</u>, to the garage.

__R__ 9. The poem <u>that Ellen read in class</u> was very descriptive.

__N__ 10. "Drop a Pebble in the Water," <u>which was written by James Foley</u>, is very descriptive.

C. On other paper, diagram these sentences.
1. I read an article that describes a volcanic explosion.
2. The mountains you see in the distance are the Rocky Mountains.
3. The students whose assignments were finished helped the teacher.
4. This old building is the place where my cousins attend school.
5. We visited Mrs. Bergy, who has been ill.

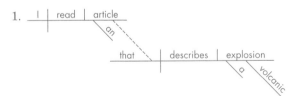

(Numbers 4 and 5 are on page T–644.)

Name _____

Worksheet 35
Verbals and Phrases Used as Adverbs

A. Underline each prepositional phrase used as an adverb, including any adjective phrase that may be in it. Draw an arrow from each underlined modifier to the item it modifies.

1. By God's grace, we can live faithfully in the midst of an evil world.
2. A song should ring in our hearts for God's goodness to us.
3. We can always be joyful in the Lord.
4. The ducks waddled down the lane, across the road, and into the meadow.
5. The children were chattering too noisily for Grandfather.
6. Hiking up the mountain proved too difficult for the boy with a lame leg.
7. During the night, a cold wind blew from the north with great force.
8. The bonfire was getting too large for safety.

B. Underline each infinitive or infinitive phrase used as an adverb. Then draw an arrow from each underlined modifier to the item it modifies.

1. Several brethren have gone to Pittsburgh to hand out tracts.
2. They spread the Gospel to bring others to Jesus.
3. We should never be too selfish to help others.
4. I sat at Father's desk to write my report.
5. The dog, eager to run, strained on his leash.
6. You were talking too softly to be heard.
7. The two men dashed to the pond to rescue the little boy.
8. Is it still too early to leave?

C. Diagram these sentences.
1. Father worked with the children in the greenhouse for several hours.
2. We found the answer in this book from Father's study.
3. A lion roars to frighten its prey.
4. The native spoke too rapidly for our comprehension.
5. We are eager to learn the language.
6. Mother, happy with our plans, gave us some helpful ideas.

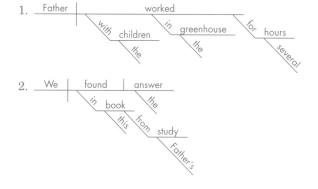

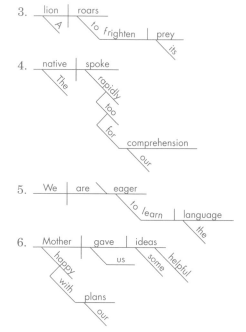

Name _____

Worksheet 36
Adverb Clauses

A. Underline each adverb clause, and put parentheses around the word (or unit) modified by each clause. Then draw an arrow from each underlined modifier to the item it modifies.

1. If we do not trust the Lord, we (will worry) when life seems difficult.

2. Whenever we make choices, we (should consider) God's viewpoint.

3. God called Isaiah (to preach) until the cities were wasted and the land was desolate.

4. We firmly (believe) the Bible even though multitudes are rejecting it.

5. When Gehazi saw Naaman's gifts, he (coveted) them (so much) that he lied.

6. Martha, (upset) because Mary was not helping her serve, complained to Jesus.

7. As the sun shone on the dewy spider webs, they (sparkled) (more beautifully) than I can describe.

8. This year the corn did not grow (as tall) as it did last year.

9. While we were waiting for Uncle Robert's to arrive, Mother (put) the finishing touches on the meal.

10. The trip took (longer) than Uncle Robert had realized.

11. (Making) hay while the sun shines is an important principle for life.

12. When we have thunderstorms, our dog (acts) as if he is afraid.

13. The waves, extra (high) while the storm raged, buffeted the small boat.

14. Most of the other students can run (faster) than I.

B. Add the missing commas in these sentences. Some sentences need none.

1. The boys, after Father had talked to them, realized their unkindness.
(no commas)
2. They had to do Sarah's chores because they had been so unkind.

3. When you are tempted to be unkind, you should remember the Golden Rule.

4. Although the song was difficult, we practiced until we had learned it.

5. Uncle Charles, since a heart attack has weakened him, can no longer hold a regular job.

C. Diagram these sentences on other paper.
1. Daniel suffered no harm because an angel shut the lions' mouths.
2. The king, restless while the night hours passed, hurried to the den.
3. When he heard Daniel's voice, Darius praised the Lord God.
4. Now the king honored Daniel more highly than he had done before.
5. The weather has turned warmer than it had been.
6. Studying while others are playing is quite difficult.
7. Diane can sing alto as well as Maria.

2.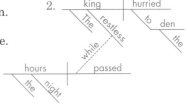

1.

3.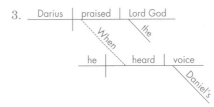

(Numbers 4–7 are on page T–660.)

Name _____   *(Lesson 97)*

Worksheet 37
Distinguishing Between Adjectives and Adverbs

A. Write *adj.* or *adv.* above each underlined word.
                         adj.   adj.
   1. David accepted the <u>blasphemous</u> challenge of the <u>mighty</u> giant.
     adv.   adj.   adj.
   2. <u>Boldly</u>, the <u>lowly</u> shepherd boy declared his <u>strong</u> faith in God.
                adv.   adj.   adv. adv.
   3. King Saul was <u>not</u> filling his <u>kingly</u> role <u>very</u> <u>well</u>.
               adj.   adj.   adv.
   4. The once <u>sickly</u> man has been <u>well</u> <u>recently</u>.
    adj.   adj.   adv.
   5. <u>This</u> <u>lonely</u> path leads <u>deep</u> into the forest.
                  adv. adj.   adj.   adj.   adj.
   6. Since the well is <u>much</u> <u>deeper</u>, it gives <u>good</u> water, <u>clear</u> and <u>fresh</u>.
       adj.   adj.   adv.   adj.
   7. The <u>kindly</u> young man escorted the <u>elderly</u> lady <u>right</u> to her <u>front</u> door.
    adj.   adv. adj.
   8. <u>Much</u> food has been given to the villagers, <u>too</u> <u>poor</u> to buy supplies.

B. Write *adj.* or *adv.* above each underlined phrase. If a phrase is underlined twice, write a separate label for it.
                  adj.   adv.   adv.
   1. Joseph, a youth <u>of strong principle</u>, was used <u>by God</u> <u>to preserve life</u>.
                       adv.   adv.   adj.
   2. Keep your vision <u>on heavenly things</u>, and you will better serve <u>in the things</u> <u>of this world</u>.
                     adj.   adv.
   3. A good rule <u>to remember in life</u> is that every choice affects eternity.
                      adj.   adj.
   4. Several families <u>from our congregation</u> visited the mission church <u>in Big Spring Valley</u>.
    adv.   adj.   adv.
   5. <u>To help people</u> <u>of the area</u>, two brethren employ them <u>in their businesses</u>.
           adj.   adv.   adj.   adj.
   6. The dog <u>in the yard</u> barked <u>at the men</u> <u>on horseback</u> <u>at the front gate</u>.

C. Above each underlined clause, write *adj.* or *adv.*
        adv.   adj.
   1. <u>Because we love the Lord</u>, we will do all <u>that He says</u>.
             adj.   adv.
   2. People <u>who are ashamed of Jesus</u> fear men more <u>than they fear God</u>.
                 adj.   adj.
   3. In the day <u>when God rewards the faithful</u>, the people <u>whose lives were devoted to the Lord</u> will not be ashamed.
                                   adv.
   4. We should love the Lord so deeply <u>that we will gladly suffer for Him</u>.
                                adv.
   5. A faithful disciple is prompt to obey <u>when God speaks</u>.
                             adj.
   6. An important place <u>where the Christian finds encouragement</u> is among God's people.

D. Diagram these sentences on other paper.
   1. We had an early breakfast so that we could drive to Grandfather Good's.
   2. The elderly man spoke wistfully about the years of his childhood.
   3. The men in the mow have worked hard to stack the bales neatly.
   4. This is a good book to read for your report.
   5. After the sun had set, we went outside to watch the stars.

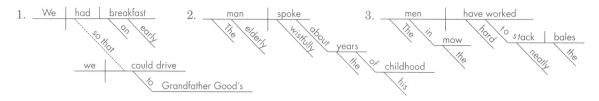

*(Numbers 4 and 5 are
on page T–660.)*

Name _____

Worksheet 38
Using Adverbs Correctly

A. In each blank, write an expressive verb or a descriptive adjective to replace the underlined expression.
(Sample answers.)

leaped, vaulted, bounded, sprang   1. The little frog <u>jumped high</u> into the air.

drifted, floated   2. The smoke <u>moved slowly</u> up from the chimney.

essential, necessary, vital, indispensable   3. A balanced diet gives our bodies <u>very important</u> nutrients.

tempestuous, stormy, turbulent   4. The <u>extremely rough</u> seas made difficult sailing.

B. Cross out each incorrect word, and write any correction above it.

1. No one who seeks ~~after~~ the Lord will be turned away.

2. The angels of God are ~~sure~~ surely interested in the welfare of the saints.

3. The depth of their interest may be ~~kind of~~ rather *or* somewhat hard for us to comprehend.

4. Nowhere in ~~neither~~ either of the Testaments does God overlook hypocrisy.

5. The New Testament ~~farther~~ further expands many of the Old Testament principles.

6. We refer ~~back~~ to the Old Testament for much of our knowledge about God.

7. Grandfather has been feeling ~~some~~ somewhat better the last few days.

8. I ~~couldn't~~ could hardly contain my excitement as the plane rose into the air.

9. Because the car was running so ~~bad~~ badly, we stopped at a garage.

10. Marie is washing ~~up~~ the dinner dishes.

11. Reuben has ~~all ready~~ already given his oral report.

12. Great-aunt Katrina has cataracts and ~~can't~~ can see nothing anymore.   *or* Great-aunt Katrina has cataracts and can't see ~~nothing~~ anything anymore.

13. Another family is planning to move into the house later ~~on~~ this month.

14. Father is ready to connect ~~up~~ the fans in the chicken house.

15. Our old dog acts ~~sort of~~ rather *or* somewhat lazy sometimes.

16. Brenda is trying ~~real~~ really hard to finish the dress this week.

17. The visitors left ~~from~~ our place early this morning.

18. I didn't see ~~nothing~~ anything wrong in the barn.

19. Father explained ~~farther~~ further what he wanted us to do.

20. If we work ~~good~~ well this morning, Father said we may go fishing later.

21. The grape arbor should be ~~some~~ somewhat stronger now.

22. We rarely ~~ever~~ have this many customers at one time.

23. Laura has told us scarcely ~~nothing~~ anything about her trip yet.

24. Never treat an animal so ~~bad~~ badly that it learns to distrust you.

25. We felt ~~kind of~~ rather *or* somewhat foolish when our project failed so miserably.

26. We ~~sure~~ surely thought we could make doughnuts without Mother's help.

27. We ~~couldn't~~ could blame nobody but ourselves for the mess we made.   *or* We couldn't blame ~~nobody~~ anybody but ourselves for the mess we made.

28. When we finished ~~up~~, however, we did have a few edible doughnuts.

29. The church is just a little ~~further~~ farther down this road.

Name _____   *(Lesson 103)*

Worksheet 39
Prepositions and Their Objects

A. Underline each prepositional phrase; and above it, write whether it is used as an adjective (*adj.*), an adverb (*adv.*), or a noun (*n.*). If the phrase is part of a longer phrase, underline it twice, and label it separately.

1.   The light <u>of God's people</u> shines <u>with increasing brightness</u> <u>in a darkening world</u>.
       adj.   adv.   adv.

2.   To compromise <u>with the darkness</u> is to fail <u>in being God's light</u>.

3.   Our lives, filled <u>with Christ's light</u>, should point others <u>to Him</u>.

4.   The seeds <u>of our words</u> lie <u>in what we think</u>.

5.   <u>In our thoughts</u> is also where our reactions are born.

6.   <u>Despite the arguments of some</u>, no wrong reactions can be excused <u>on the basis of being caught unguarded</u>.

7.   <u>According to the Bible</u>, wrong reactions always spring <u>out of wrong thoughts or unwholesome attitudes</u>.

8.   Today all the students <u>except Miriam</u> were <u>at school.</u>

9.   A large maple tree <u>in front of the house</u> keeps us cool <u>inside the house</u> <u>in spite of the hot sun</u>.

10.   <u>Under its shade</u> is our favorite place <u>for husking sweet corn</u>.

11.   <u>Aside from a few cuts and bruises</u>, no one was hurt when the car ran <u>off the road</u> <u>into the ditch</u>.

12.   <u>Around the table</u> sat the family as Father read <u>from the Bible</u> <u>for family worship</u>.

13.   My excitement, already intense <u>beyond description</u>, mounted as we climbed <u>aboard the huge jet</u>.

14.   <u>Throughout the flight</u> I was able to sit <u>beside a window</u>.

15.   <u>From where I was sitting</u>, I could see the city growing smaller <u>by the second</u>.

B. Diagram these sentences.
1. Since last evening the temperature has gone up by several degrees.
2. The girl next to Susan is my cousin from Virginia.
3. In this pen is the place for these calves.
4. These cookies, ready for Mr. Wentzel, should be put on the back seat of the car.
5. The horses trotted past the house and the barn.
6. To ask for help is no reason for shame.
7. We can learn many things of importance by asking questions.
8. We shall send the books with whoever is going to your area.

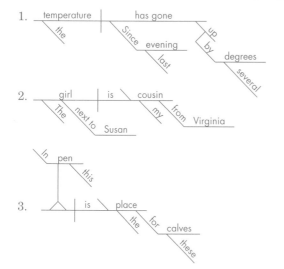

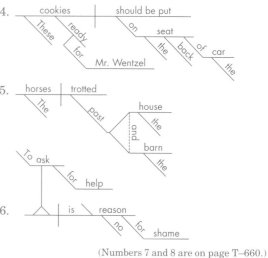

(Numbers 7 and 8 are on page T–660.)

Name _____

Worksheet 40
Using Prepositions Correctly

Cross out each wrong word. Mark any correction or insertion in the space above the error.

1. New Testament forms of worship differ ~~with~~ [from] Old Testament forms.

2. People journeyed to Jerusalem because that is where the temple was ~~at~~.

3. ~~Beside~~ [Besides] this, they had to offer many sacrifices.

4. Only the priests were allowed to go ~~in~~ [into] the temple itself.

5. In the Gospel age, God dwells [with] and relates to His people in a new way.

6. However, the believer does have greater provisions for living inside ~~of~~ the bounds of divine holiness.

7. Father wants to leave as soon as this game is over ~~with~~.

8. Mary Louise may sit ~~in~~ between Clara and Darlene at the table.

9. You may not bring that dog ~~in~~ [into] the house!

10. Have you been waiting ~~on~~ [for] us for a long time?

11. With the chores divided ~~between~~ [among] so many, the work was finished quickly.

12. Do not allow yourself to become angry ~~at~~ [with] another person.

13. Everyone ~~accept~~ [except] Eric is sitting at the table.

14. Thomas made the cabinet differently ~~than~~ [from] his first design for it.

15. If we trust the Lord, we need not become angry ~~with~~ [at] any circumstances.

16. Lawrence has finished mowing ~~in back of~~ [behind] the house.

17. Sometimes people put an extra *i* ~~in~~ between the *v* and the *o* of *grievous*.

18. Lilly dashed ~~in~~ [into] the house and called Mother.

19. I enjoyed the days I lived [with] and worked for Uncle Larry.

20. ~~Beside~~ [Besides] a dairy operation, he has a turkey house.

21. My time there was over ~~with~~ before I was ready.

22. None of us children ~~accept~~ [except] Susan, the baby, will be going along.

23. Do you know where the Sierra Blanca Peak is ~~at~~?

24. The money from this project will be divided ~~between~~ [among] the four children.

25. I could hardly get all the dirt washed off ~~of~~ the floor.

26. Your method of setting up these problems differs ~~with~~ [from] mine.

27. If others must wait ~~on~~ [for] you too much, practice being more prompt.

28. We plan to stop ~~by~~ [at] Mrs. Dunmire's place on the way to church.

29. Those two men seem to be very angry ~~at~~ [with] each other.

30. I found that I had been saying the word differently ~~than~~ [from] the pronunciation in the dictionary.

Name _____   *(Lesson 106)*

Worksheet 41
Coordinating Conjunctions

A. Underline the common coordinating conjunctions (*CC*), correlative conjunctions (*Cor*), and conjunctive adverbs (*CA*). Write the correct label above each underlined word.

    1. The Law came through Moses, <u>but</u> (CC) grace <u>and</u> (CC) truth came through Jesus.

    2. <u>Neither</u> (Cor) a smiling face <u>nor</u> (Cor) a cheerful song comes from an envious heart.

    3. God is <u>both</u> (Cor) omnipresent <u>and</u> (Cor) omniscient; <u>consequently</u> (CA), nothing can be hidden from Him.

    4. Paul wanted Christ magnified in his body, <u>whether</u> (Cor) in life <u>or</u> (Cor) by death.

    5. The Bible is authoritative <u>and</u> (CC) absolute; <u>accordingly</u> (CA), we order our lives by its principles.

B. Rewrite these sentences correctly.   (Corrections are underlined. Accept reasonable variation.)

    1. I either misunderstood the lesson or these directions.
I misunderstood <u>either</u> the lesson or these directions.

    2. We must water these plants for they are wilting in the hot sun.
We must water these plants, for they are wilting in the hot sun.

    3. The students worked diligently and for a long time on their reports.
The students <u>diligently</u> worked for a long time on their reports.

    4. I hurried down the steps and outside.
I hurried down the steps and <u>out the door</u>. (*or*... and went outside.)

    5. Glen worked in the field all morning, meanwhile Lucy cleaned and baked.
Glen worked in the field all morning; meanwhile, Lucy cleaned and baked.

    6. The work in the garden was finished quickly and in a satisfactory way.
The work in the garden was finished quickly and <u>satisfactorily</u>.

    7. Not only was the sun quite warm, but the humidity was very high.
Not only was the sun quite warm, but <u>also</u> the humidity was very high.

    8. Carla has both found the book and her paper.
Carla has found <u>both</u> the book and her paper.

    9. We enjoyed not only the hike but the picnic.   We enjoyed not only the hike but <u>also</u> the picnic.

    10. Michael neither washed his face nor his hands.   Michael washed <u>neither</u> his face nor his hands.

C. Diagram these sentences on other paper.
    1. Moses cut down a tree and cast it into the water.
    2. Neither Enoch nor Elijah experienced physical death.
    3. We must serve the Lord whether in peaceful times or under persecution.
    4. We threw down some extra bales, for tomorrow is Sunday.
    5. I must write more notes; otherwise, my report will be too short.

(Numbers 2–5 are on page T–660.)

Name _____

Worksheet 42
Review of the Parts of Speech

A. Write the name and abbreviation for the part of speech described by each sentence.

_____verb_____ __v.__ 1. It expresses action or being.

___adjective___ __adj.__ 2. It modifies a noun or pronoun by telling *which, whose, how many,* or *what kind of.*

__interjection__ _interj._ 3. It expresses strong feeling.

_____adverb_____ __adv.__ 4. It modifies a verb, an adjective, another adverb, or a verbal by telling *how, when, where,* or *to what degree.*

_____noun_____ __n.__ 5. It names a person, place, thing, or idea.

___preposition___ __prep.__ 6. It shows the relationship between its object and some other word in the sentence.

____pronoun____ __pron.__ 7. It takes the place of a noun.

___conjunction___ __conj.__ 8. It joins words, phrases, or clauses.

B. For each underlined word, identify the part of speech by writing its abbreviation in the blank.

a. __v.__ b. __n.__ 1. Jane's younger sister can (*a*) <u>cook</u> like an experienced (*b*) <u>cook</u>.

a. _interj._ b. __n.__ 2. (*a*) <u>Pudding</u>! I thought this (*b*) <u>pudding</u> was salad dressing.

a. __adv.__ b. __adj.__ 3. The king's wise men tried (*a*) <u>hard</u> to answer his (*b*) <u>hard</u> question.

a. __adj.__ b. _pron._ 4. Though (*a*) <u>many</u> people hope to reach heaven, (*b*) <u>many</u> will be disappointed.

a. _prep._ b. _conj._ 5. We must seek (*a*) <u>for</u> the heavenly city, (*b*) <u>for</u> all earthly cities will pass away.

C. Above each word, write the abbreviation for the part of speech that it is. Label each infinitive as a single item.

1.   n.   v.   adj. n.   prep. n.   pron.   v.   v.   n.   adj. n.
Alexander joined a group of men who were trying to ride a horse.

2. pron. prep. adj.   adj.   n.   v.   adv.   v.   adv.
Each of the other men was quickly thrown off.

3. conj.   adj.   n.   v.   pron. v.   adv.   prep. adj.   n.
When Alexander's turn came, he rode away with no trouble.

4. adv. pron.   v.   conj.   v.   adv. prep. adj.   adj.   n.
Soon he turned and rode back to the other men.

5. interj.   v.   pron. prep. pron.   adv.   v.   pron. v. pron.
"Well!" said one of them. "How did you do it?"

6. adj.   n.   v.   adj. prep. adj.   n.   v.
"The horse was afraid of his shadow," Alexander replied.

7. pron. v.   pron.   prep.   adj.   n.   conj. adv. pron. v. adv.   adv.   adj.
"I faced him toward the sun, and now he is no longer afraid."

8. interj. pron. v.   adv.   v.   v.   pron. adj.   n.   v.
Shadows! I could not have guessed what the problem was.

9. pron. pron.   v.   adj.   n.   v.   v.   n.   adj.   n.
Those who love the Lord will want to do His will.

10. v.   pron. interj. n.   adj.   n. prep. adj.   n.   conj. pron. v.   v. pron. prep. adj.   n.
"Teach me, O Lord, the way of thy statutes; and I shall keep it unto the end."

11. pron. v.   adj.   n.   adv.   adj.   n.   prep. n.
We study the Word to learn the way of truth.

12.   n.   conj.   n.   adj.   n.   v.   adj. conj.   n.   pron. v.   adv.   adj.
Reading and studying the Bible is good, but obeying it is most important.

Worksheet 36, Part C *(Continued)*

4.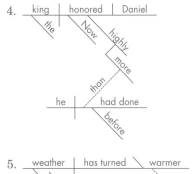

6.

7.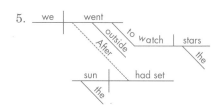

5.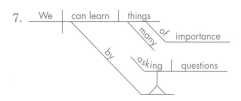

Worksheet 37, Part D *(Continued)*

4.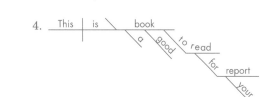

5.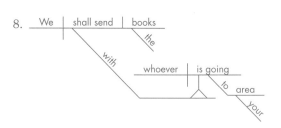

Worksheet 39, Part B *(Continued)*

7.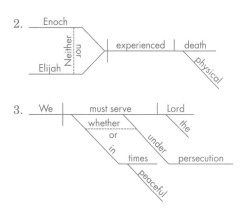

8.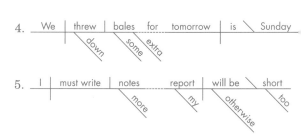

Worksheet 41, Part C *(Continued)*

Preparing for Usefulness

Chapter 1 Test   **Score** _____

Name _____ **Date** _____

A. Circle *T* if the statement is true or *F* if it is false.

(T) F   1. Elliptical sentences are more common in dialogue than in other kinds of writing.

(T) F   2. A subjective complement must follow a linking verb.

T (F)   3. An objective complement comes between the indirect object and the direct object.

(T) F   4. In a sentence with a predicate nominative, the subject and the predicate nominative are often interchangeable.

T (F)   5. Subjective complements include direct objects and objective complements.

(T) F   6. A nonrestrictive appositive should be set off with commas.

T (F)   7. An expletive is usually set off with commas.

(T) F   8. Social notes have the same parts that friendly letters do, but they are usually shorter.

(8 points)

B. Write *B* for business letter or *F* for friendly letter to tell what each sentence describes.

_B_   9. It includes a heading, inside address, salutation, body, closing, and signature.

_B_ 10. The following are suitable greetings or salutations.

      Dear Mr. Morrison: Dear Sir:

_F_ 11. The following are suitable closings.

      Sincerely yours,   With love and prayers,

_B_ 12. The different parts are separated by spaces.

_F_ 13. A note of apology is one type.

(5 points)

C. Write the letter of the correct term before each description.

    a. appositive
    b. elliptical sentence —
    c. expletive
    d. fragment —

    e. indirect object
    f. noun of direct address
    g. objective complement

_a_ 14. A word that is used with another noun or pronoun to identify or explain it.

_b_ 15. A group of words that has one or more missing parts but expresses a complete thought.

_g_ 16. A word that renames or modifies a direct object.

_f_   17. A word that names the person or thing to whom one is speaking.

_c_   18. A word that introduces a sentence but does not add to its meaning.

(5 points)

D. Label each numbered item *S* for complete sentence, *F* for fragment, *E* for elliptical sentence, or *R* for run-on error.

> ¹⁹Pamela dashed downstairs. ²⁰And into the kitchen. ²¹"Deborah, whatever did you do to make such a racket?"
> ²²There sat Deborah on the floor, plates and cups lay scattered about her. ²³"Slipped off the step stool. ²⁴I guess I wasn't being careful," she answered.

_S_ 19.	_S_ 21.	_E_ 23.
_F_ 20.	_R_ 22.	_S_ 24.

(6 points)

E. Draw a vertical line to show the division between the complete subject and the complete predicate. Underline each simple subject once and each simple predicate twice.

25. <u>God</u> | <u>blesses</u> His people and <u>makes</u> a way for them.

26. <u>Obedience</u> to His Word | <u>is</u> the key to that blessing.

27. <u>Daniel</u> and his <u>friends</u> | <u>knew</u> the wonderful power of God.

28. God's <u>presence</u> with these saints | <u>became</u> obvious to all.

(12 points)

F. Underline each complement, and write one of the following labels above it: *PN* (predicate nominative), *PA* (predicate adjective), *DO* (direct object), *IO* (indirect object), *OC* (objective complement).

29. Faith in God gives a <u>person</u> [IO] true <u>strength</u> [DO].

30. The godless man considers <u>life</u> [DO] an <u>end</u> [OC] in itself.

31. In reality, life is our <u>time</u> [PN] and <u>opportunity</u> [PN] to prepare for eternity.

32. The Bible teaches the eternal <u>existence</u> [DO] of man's soul.

33. This fact makes <u>life</u> [DO] <u>serious</u> [OC].

34. Disregard for eternal things is <u>foolish</u> [PA].

(10 points)

G. Underline the appositives and independent elements. Insert punctuation and capitalize words if necessary.

35. <u>There</u> are many ways of showing kindness to a younger brother or sister.

36. You will be rewarded, <u>for example</u>, if you give up some spare time to help them with a

project.

37. <u>Well</u>, doing good always brings its own rewards.

38. <u>Rewards!</u> W̌e shouldn't expect rewards for doing good.

39. I enjoy playing this game with Galen, <u>my youngest brother</u>.

40. <u>Father</u>, may we walk over to Mr. Stanley?

41. Mr. Stanley, <u>our nearest neighbor</u>, is confined to a wheelchair.

42. <u>It</u> is a pleasure to visit with a cheerful person like him.

(8 points)

H. Read the following note of invitation. In the numbered blanks below, list three mistakes that you see in the note.

August 19, 20—

Dear Ruth

Our family is planning to be at Mapleville for the Wednesday evening service. Father and Mother have said that I may invite you to come along back with us. Since your father is scheduled to lead a song service here Sunday evening, you could return home then. I have some special projects planned, so come prepared!

Christine

(Any three of these answers.)

43. <u>The heading is incomplete.</u>

<u>The greeting has no comma.</u>

44. <u>The letter is weak in detail, especially about the exact date and about how Ruth should prepare.</u>

45. <u>There is no closing.</u>

(3 points)

I. Read the following business letter. In the numbered blanks below, list three mistakes that you see in the letter.

Rt. 2, Box 98
Curtiss, WI 54422
September 4, 20—

Gentlemen;
Please send me one large embroidery hoop, three regular embroidery hoops, and the assorted pack of embroidery thread.

Your friend,

Jane Eberly

(Any three of these answers.)

46. <u>The inside address is missing.</u>

<u>The salutation has a semicolon instead of a colon.</u>

47. There is no space between the salutation and the body.

    The body is not specific enough.

48. The closing is not appropriate for a business letter.

    The signature should be also handwritten.

(3 points)

Total points: 60

Preparing for Usefulness

Chapter 2 Test   Score _____

Name _____ Date _____

A. Circle *T* if the statement is true or *F* if it is false.

(T) F   1. The subject of every imperative sentence is *you*.

T (F)   2. A comma is always used in a sentence with mixed word order.

T (F)   3. Phrases and independent clauses are similar in that both function as a single part of speech.

(T) F   4. If a conjunctive adverb is used to join the clauses of a compound sentence, a semicolon precedes the conjunctive adverb.

T (F)   5. A good topic sentence summarizes the details of a paragraph.

(5 points)

B. Label each sentence *dec.* (declarative), *int.* (interrogative), *imp.* (imperative), or *exc.* (exclamatory). Write the correct punctuation mark at the end.

int.   6. Does the calf barn need fresh bedding again?

dec.   7. Yes, Father said that we must do it this evening.

imp.   8. Galen, fetch the pitchforks.

exc.   9. How quickly the bedding gets wet in such weather!

imp. 10. Tell Father that the bedding straw is almost all gone.

(5 points)

C. Write whether the word order of each sentence is natural (*N*), inverted (*I*), or mixed (*M*). Then rewrite the sentence in a different word order. Watch the punctuation.

_N_ 11. The frightened deer crashed through the underbrush. __Through the underbrush crashed the
frightened deer.__   *or* Through the underbrush the frightened deer crashed.

_M_ 12. In the lush green meadow a herd of elk grazed contentedly. _____
A herd of elk grazed contentedly in the lush green meadow.

_N_ 13. We appreciated our blessings more after we spent a year in Guatemala. _____
After we spent a year in Guatemala, we appreciated our blessings more.

_I_ 14. In Guatemala live many poor people. _____
Many poor people live in Guatemala.

(8 points)

D. In the first blank, write *prep.* (prepositional), *vb.* (verbal), or *ps.* (single part of speech) to tell what kind of phrase is underlined. In the second blank, write *n., v., adj.,* or *adv.* to tell how the phrase functions.

prep. _adv._ 15. The sun is slowly sinking <u>from our sight</u>.

_ps._ _v._ 16. We <u>have committed</u> our lives to God for another night of rest.

prep. _adj._ 17. His tender care <u>for His people</u> is a source of comfort to us.

_vb._ _n._ 18. <u>To trust Him</u> is a wonderful privilege.

_vb._ _adj._ 19. God's people, <u>sheltered in God's arms</u>, are the happiest people.

(5 points)

E. Label each underlined clause *I* (independent clause), *D-adj.* (dependent adjective clause), *D-adv.* (dependent adverb clause), or *D-n.* (dependent noun clause).

_D-n._ 20. God alone knows <u>what the future holds for us</u>.

_I_ 21. He has a plan for us, but <u>we must choose to fit into that plan</u>.

D-adv. 22. <u>When we choose the noble and good</u>, we prepare ourselves to fulfill His plan for our lives.

_I_ 23. <u>We need to think carefully about the choices</u> that we make each day.

D-adj. 24. Then we can be one <u>who enjoys God's rich blessing</u>.

(5 points)

F. Label each sentence *S* (simple), *CD* (compound), *CX* (complex), or *CD-CX* (compound-complex).

_CX_ 25. The person who drew this picture has a good sense of perspective.

_S_ 26. This morning Mother cleaned the porch and mowed the lawn.

_CD-CX_ 27. A light snow was falling as we left, but it soon turned to rain.

_CD_ 28. At first the assignment looked hard; however, it was actually simple.

_CX_ 29. After you finish the test, check your answers carefully.

(5 points)

G. These sentences include one each of the four kinds of sentences: simple, compound, complex, and compound-complex. Diagram the skeletons and complements of all the clauses.

30. We should never despise politeness; rather, we should view it as a mark of true maturity.

| We | should despise | politeness | | we | should view | it |

31. A person who truly loves the Lord will be considerate of others.

32. Kindness in your heart produces courtesy in your actions.

| Kindness | produces | courtesy |

33. Because a humble person is unselfish, he freely shows thoughtfulness to others; but a proud person wants the best for himself.

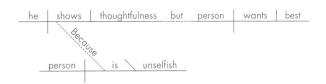

(24 points)

H. Write whether the style of each sentence is loose (*L*), periodic (*P*), or balanced (*B*).

  P 34. Though the Pharisees kept the letter of the Law, they completely missed its true spirit.

  L 35. They thought they were righteous because they kept many religious observances in strict detail.

  B 36. Knowledge puffs up, but love builds up.

  P 37. Even if we spend a lifetime in trying to be righteous, it is worthless without godly love.

(4 points)

I. Write whether each sentence refers to unity (*U*) or coherence (*C*) in a paragraph.

  C 38. The sentences fit together smoothly and logically.

  U 39. Every sentence supports and develops the topic sentence.

  U 40. If it is lacking, you may need to divide a paragraph into two.

  C 41. Repeating key words can be an effective aid.

  C 42. Transitional words can help produce it.

(5 points)

J. Read the paragraphs below, and do these exercises.

43. Identify the order of development by writing *C* (chronological), *S* (spatial), or *I* (importance) in each blank.

  C a. first paragraph

  I b. second paragraph

44. Write the numbers that identify these sentences.

    _1_ a. The topic sentence of the first paragraph.

    _8_ b. The topic sentence of the second paragraph.

    _9_ c. The sentence that mars the unity of the second paragraph.

45. Copy words that illustrate the following things.

    a. Repetition of a key word in both paragraphs. ___stars *or* constellations

    b. One transitional word from each paragraph. ___Then *or* Soon___   ___also, Second, *or* third___

46. What idea at the beginning of both paragraphs provides a link between the two?

    the idea of being acquainted with the stars

¹How can you become better acquainted with the stars that God created? ²Begin by identifying one prominent constellation both in the sky and on a star map. ³Then locate and name the surrounding constellations. ⁴It is best to become well acquainted with only four or five constellations each night. ⁵Soon the sky will seem very orderly, with Cassiopeia always next to Cepheus, and Pisces always below Andromeda. ⁶You will be surprised at how quickly you learn to find your way among the stars.

⁷Being acquainted with the constellations is interesting, but there is more to learn. ⁸You will also find it rewarding to identify some of the bright stars. ⁹Be careful not to confuse stars with planets. ¹⁰The brightest star of all is Sirius, the "Dog Star" in the constellation Canis Major. ¹¹Second brightest in the Northern Hemisphere is Arcturus in Boötes. ¹²The third brightest star is Vega in Lyra, and the fourth is Capella in Auriga. ¹³Rigel and Betelgeuse in the constellation Orion are two more of the brightest stars in the northern sky.

(9 points)

Total points: 75

Preparing for Usefulness

Chapter 3 Test   **Score** _____

Name _____ **Date** _____

A. Circle *T* if the statement is true or *F* if it is false.

  T (F) 1. Ellipsis points are used to show that a sentence is abruptly cut off.

  (T) F 2. A question mark in parentheses may indicate uncertainty about information.

  (T) F 3. If a comma separates two descriptive adjectives, it indicates that they are of equal rank.

  T (F) 4. Restrictive appositives should be set off with commas.

  T (F) 5. A colon or semicolon at the end of a quotation is always placed inside the quotation marks.

  (T) F 6. A question mark is placed outside the quotation marks if the whole sentence is a question but the quotation is not.

  T (F) 7. A colon may replace a comma in separating the clauses of a compound sentence if other commas are used within the clauses.

  (T) F 8. A parenthetical element is sharply emphasized when it is set off with dashes.

  T (F) 9. You can make an argumentative paragraph convincing by writing with strong emotional fervor.

  T (F) 10. Developing a paragraph by showing contrasts is most effective when the two items contrasted have no similarities.

  (10 points)

B. Cross out each error in capitalization, and write the correct letter above it.

  (Count 1 point for each compound noun.)

  11. We bring our praise, O Lord, to thy worthy Name.
       <small>O L   T</small>

  12. The principles of the Decalogue are repeated in the New Testament.
       <small>D   N T</small>

  13. Before David was King, he kept his Father's sheep at Bethlehem.
       <small>k   f   B</small>

  14. When Uncle Wesley came, he brought some Kraft Cheese and Ritz Crackers.
       <small>U   c   c</small>

  15. The Susquehanna River flows South into the Chesapeake Bay.
       <small>R   s   C   B</small>

  16. Many States in the East are densely populated.
       <small>s   E</small>

  17. Mr. H. Kratz is a German who moved here last Fall.   (Count 2 points for *H. Kratz.*)
       <small>H K   G   f</small>

  (20 points)

C. Add the missing commas, end marks, and ellipsis points.   (Count 1 point for each section set off by a bar.)

  18. Do you suppose, Duane, that Job knew about Satan's role in his | suffering?

  19. No, he probably knew nothing about | it, but God chose to reveal it to | us.

20. How would you respond if suddenly you lost nearly everything? if you were smitten with boils? if your friends turned against you?

21. What tremendous faith Job displayed!

22. Since the day was quite warm, the cool, clear water of the little stream was an inviting place to wade.

23. Father specifically said, on the other hand, that we shall not wade; so...

24. In a small shop at the edge of town, Eugene Mohler, whom my father has known for years, repairs electric motors.

25. Edwin Wade, Sr., a retired blacksmith, often tells stories of the past.

(18 points)

D. Add quotation marks and other related punctuation. Show any correction of capitalization as you did in Part B. Do not set off words with quotation marks unless a sentence has explanatory words.

(Count each pair of quotation marks [" " or ' '] as a single answer.)

26. "It is more important to do your best," stated Brother Sweigart, "than merely to get a good grade." (5 pt.)

27. Do you know which prophet said, "But the Lord is in his holy temple"? (4 pt.)

28. Bertha commented, "What a blessing to trust the Lord!" (4 pt.)

29. "Did you hear Father say, 'The straw must be baled today'?" asked Jerry. (5 pt.)

(18 points)

E. Add the missing colons and semicolons. For some corrections you will need to cross out a comma and write one of these marks above it.

30. The little boy quoted this verse perfectly: "We love him, because he first loved us."

31. Indeed, God loves us more than we can comprehend; therefore, we ought to love and serve Him.

32. Our visitors this week included Ivan Snyder, a teacher from another community; Peter Glick, the board chairman; and Vera Good, Susan's mother.

33. Anthracite, which burns cleaner than other coal, is found in only a few places; but bituminous, which is much softer, is more common.

34. The following dams are over seven hundred feet high: Oroville, Hoover, Dworshak, and Glen Canyon.

(5 points)

F. Add the missing dashes, parentheses, and brackets. If there is not enough space within the line, use a caret (∧) and place the correct mark above it. Use the following Scripture verse for help with number 38.

"For the word of God is quick, and powerful, and sharper than any twoedged sword."

35. Uncle Eli's garden tractor (he bought it used last week) works well.   (Dashes may be used.)

36. Father invited Harvey Petre's—what a pleasant surprise!—for dinner.

37. "Father, I don't want‾" Henry stopped when he saw Father's face.
        ∧

38. "For the word of God is quick [living, and powerful, and sharper than any twoedged
)   ∧
    sword" (Hebrews 4:12.
                      ∧

(5 points)

G. Add apostrophes, hyphens, underlining, and quotation marks.

39. Someone's dog is running around, but Mr. Smith said it isn't theirs.   (2 pt.)

40. The c in picture is not silent.   (2 pt.)

41. Most sweet cherry trees are not self-pollinating.   (1 pt.)

42. Be sure to include double c's and double m's when you spell accommodate.   (5 pt.)

43. When my great-grandfather Lutz was twenty-two years old, he moved from Switzerland to America.   (2 pt.)

44. The three boys' rowboat was named Brave Water.   (2 pt.)

45. According to the chapter "Debates and Early Persecution" in the book Bernese Anabaptists, the debates often helped the Anabaptists' cause.   (3 pt.)

46. The state church's anti-Biblical attitude was rejected by the Anabaptists, who viewed the Bible as the all-important guide in life.   (3 pt.)

(20 points)

H. Cross out the numbers that should be written with words, and write the words correctly in the blanks.

47. The ~~5~~ engines were pulling a string of 245 coal cars.   five

_____

48. ~~2,150~~ homes were destroyed by the series of tornadoes.   Two thousand one hundred fifty

_____

49. After driving ~~80~~ miles on Interstate 71, we went several miles on back roads to the church.

   eighty

(6 points)

I. In each blank, write *E* (exposition), *A* (argument), *N* (narration), or *D* (description).

  E 50. It is written to explain, clarify, or inform.

  A 51. It is written to persuade people or move them to action.

  D 52. It may be written to provide a setting or to create a mood.

  A 53. The writer may be tempted to state strong opinions rather than facts.

  N 54. It tells a story.

(5 points)

J. In each blank, write *DT* (details), *F* (facts), *R* (reasons), *DS* (description), *EI* (examples or incident), *DF* (definition), or *C* (comparison or contrast) to tell which method of paragraph development fits that description.

  EI 55. May be several points or one brief story illustrating a topic sentence.

  C 56. Points out the similarities or differences between two things.

  F 57. The sentences establish the validity of a general truth.

  DF 58. Used to explain abstract nouns or technical words.

  DT 59. Relates specific activities of story characters.

  R 60. Written to convince a reader of an opinion or belief.

  DS 61. Gives a word picture of a person, place, or thing.

  R 62. Must be based on solid principles.

(8 points)

Total points: 115

Preparing for Usefulness

Chapter 4 Test   Score _____

Name _____ **Date** _____

A. Circle *T* if the statement is true or *F* if it is false.

(T) F 1. Any word, phrase, or clause used as a noun is a substantive.

T (F) 2. Abstract nouns name persons, places, or things.

(T) F 3. The basic form of a verb preceded by *to* is an infinitive.

T (F) 4. The introductory word of a noun clause always serves as a pronoun or a modifier within the clause.

T (F) 5. The title of an outline should be indented the same amount as a main topic.

T (F) 6. If there is only one subtopic under a main topic, that idea must be deleted.

(T) F 7. It is better to proofread a composition some time after it has been written than immediately afterward.

(T) F 8. A short composition may have an introduction that is only a sentence or two.

(8 points)

B. In the first blank, write *C* or *A* to tell whether the noun is concrete or abstract. In the second blank, write *M, F, N,* or *C* to tell whether its gender is masculine, feminine, neuter, or common.

  _C_ _N_ 9. pencil   _A_ _N_ 13. happiness

  _A_ _N_ 10. humility   _C_ _C_ 14. student

  _C_ _F_ 11. maid   _C_ _F_ 15. mother

  _C_ _M_ 12. ram   _C_ _C_ 16. grandparents

(8 points)

C. Underline each word, phrase, or clause used as a substantive; do not mark separately the nouns within a substantive phrase or clause. Above each item you underline, write *N* (one-word noun), *P* (pronoun), *G* (gerund), *I* (infinitive), or *C* (clause).

          N   N   G
17. Our <u>job</u> on that <u>day</u> was <u>raking the leaves</u>.

   P   N   C
18. <u>We</u> will save this <u>material</u> for <u>whenever we make the quilt</u>.

          N   N   N
19. These three <u>sentences</u> in <u>succession</u> begin with <u>and</u>.

        P   I
20. Yesterday <u>I</u> failed <u>to write my memory passage perfectly</u>.

         C
21. <u>Whoever reaches into that nest</u> will likely be pecked.

(12 points)

D. Correct the capitalization errors by crossing out each incorrect letter and writing the correct letter above it.

(Words with errors are shown with corrections.)

22. When **G**randfather moved to **O**regon from the **E**ast, my father was a baby.

23. Although **M**r. **H**art claims to be a **C**hristian, he rejects the Bible account of the **C**reation.

24. We stopped at **J**ohnson's **D**rugstore for a tube of **C**olgate toothpaste, a bottle of **T**ylenol, and some **V**icks cough drops.

(10 points)

E. Write the plural form of each noun. For numbers 32–36, use the foreign spellings.

_____geese_____	25. goose	_____editors in chief_____	31. editor in chief
_____liberties_____	26. liberty	_____bacteria_____	32. bacterium
_____halves_____	27. half	_____larvae_____	33. larva
_____altos_____	28. alto	_____radii_____	34. radius
_____deer_____	29. deer	_____appendices_____	35. appendix
_____sheaves_____	30. sheaf	_____crises_____	36. crisis

(12 points)

F. Rewrite these expressions, using possessive forms. Show joint ownership for number 41 and separate ownership for number 42.

37. the words of Moses ___Moses' words___

38. the pens of the oxen ___the oxen's pens___

39. the sweater of the girl ___the girl's sweater___

40. the boots of the boys ___the boys' boots___

41. the turkeys of Glen and Leon ___Glen and Leon's turkeys___

42. the drawings of Louise and Doris ___Louise's and Doris's drawings___

(6 points)

G. Diagram the skeletons and complements of the independent clauses, including the complete verbal phrases and noun clauses.

43. Jesus said that the disciples' faith was weak.   (6 pt.)

44. Teaching the people was one job of the priest.   (5 pt.)

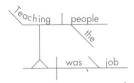

45. Jeremiah's mission was to warn the people.   (5 pt.)

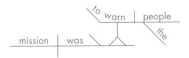

(16 points)

H. Organize this list into an outline with three main topics. (You will need to provide the main topics.) Be careful to follow the rules for good outlining.   (Allow reasonable variation.)

Observations on a Hike

A rushing waterfall
A quiet pond
Bellflowers
Buttercups
Day lilies
Four chipmunks

Seeing a gurgling stream
Some violets
Some deer—three does and five bucks
Ten squirrels
Watching a porcupine

Observations on a Hike

I. Water scenes

   A. A rushing waterfall

   B. A quiet pond

   C. A gurgling stream

II. Flowers

   A. Bellflowers

   B. Buttercups

   C. Day lilies

   D. Violets

III. Animals

   A. Four chipmunks

   B. Some deer

_____ 1. Three does

_____ 2. Five bucks

_____ C. Ten squirrels

_____ D. A porcupine

(16 points)

I. Proofread this selection, and mark fourteen corrections by using the proper proofreading marks. Note the following items.   (Corrections are marked. Check for the correct use of proofreading marks.)

   a. There are no mistakes in the spellings of proper nouns.
   b. There should be two paragraphs.
   c. Sentence combining or dividing counts as one correction.

The First Thanksgiving at Plymouth Colony

The first Thanksgiving Day in the Plymouth Colony was held in 1621. The previous year had been a difficult time. Poor and inadequate food, strenuous work, and changeable *whether* took their toll almost half the *colonists* died during that first winter. The outlook was dark indeed. Things went much better the following *Spring* one day an indian *walks* into the *little* village And introduced himself as Samoset. This man later brought Squanto, who taught the Pilgrims to catch fish and them use as fertilizer for planting corn, pumpkins and beans. Because of the bountiful harvest, the Pilgrims held a time of special thanksgiving sometime in the autumn of 1621. They invited *their* ~~they're~~ Indian freinds to join them in this thanksgiving.

(14 points)

Total points: 102

Preparing for Usefulness

Chapter 5 Test

Score _____

Name _____ Date _____

A. Circle *T* if the statement is true or *F* if it is false.

T (F) 1. In formal English, *I will* is correct to express simple future tense.

(T) F 2. A perfect tense emphasizes the completion of an action or a condition.

T (F) 3. The progressive form of a verb can be used only in the present and past tenses.

(T) F 4. *Transitive* means "passing over."

T (F) 5. An action verb cannot be intransitive complete.

(T) F 6. Intransitive linking verbs express a condition rather than an action.

T (F) 7. It is never proper to copy directly from a reference source to your notes.

T (F) 8. An encyclopedia usually gives more detailed information about a topic than other books do.

(8 points)

B. Write the missing principal parts. Use a helping verb with the third part.

First (Present)	Second (Past)	Third (Past Participle)
9. shake	shook	(have) shaken
10. know	knew	(have) known
11. come	came	(have) come
12. take	took	(have) taken
13. burst	burst	(have) burst
14. run	ran	(have) run

(12 points)

C. Underline each verb or verb phrase. In the blank, write the letter showing the tense of the verb.

   a. present   c. future   e. past perfect
   b. past   d. present perfect   f. future perfect

 d 15. "Master, we <u>have toiled</u> all the night."

 c 16. "Nevertheless at thy word I <u>will let</u> down the net."

 a 17. "Ye <u>call</u> me Master and Lord."

_f_ 18. By this time tomorrow, the Lord willing, we <u>shall have left</u> for Illinois.

_e_ 19. Before yesterday's hailstorm, we <u>had expected</u> a good crop.

_a_ 20. We <u>do trust</u> in the Lord's overruling hand.

_b_ 21. <u>Did</u> you <u>learn</u> your memory verse for tomorrow?

_b_ 22. The students <u>were studying</u> diligently.

(8 points)

D. Write the correct verb or verb phrase in each blank, as indicated in parentheses.

23. Aunt Lillian _____did bring_____ a surprise! (past tense, emphatic form of *bring*)

24. The boys _____have found_____ a huge blacksnake. (present perfect tense, simple form of *find*)

25. Next week, the Lord willing, we _____shall be helping_____ Grandfather Landis with his chores. (future tense, progressive form of *help*)

26. Until he went to Bible school, Cousin Leland _____had been doing_____ the chores. (past perfect tense, progressive form of *do*)

(4 points)

E. In each sentence, underline the word that receives the action of the verb.

27. The <u>plans</u> for the tabernacle were given in detail by God Himself.

28. Moses instructed the skilled <u>workmen</u>.

29. God had given special <u>wisdom</u> to these workmen.

30. The <u>tabernacle</u> was constructed as a type of Christ in many ways.

(4 points)

F. In each sentence, underline the words that are linked by the verb.

31. The <u>weather</u> has been quite <u>cold</u> lately.

32. My favorite <u>dessert</u> is vanilla <u>pie</u>.

33. <u>Mount McKinley</u> is the highest <u>peak</u> in North America.

34. The <u>song</u> of the meadowlark sounds <u>clear</u> and <u>sweet</u>.

(4 points)

G. Label the verb in each sentence *T* (transitive), *IC* (intransitive complete), or *IL* (intransitive linking).

_IL_ 35. A clear conscience is one of life's most valuable possessions.

_T_ 36. Dishonesty and disobedience can quickly damage the conscience.

__IL__ 37. A stifled conscience turns hard and worthless.

__IC__ 38. A tender conscience stands as a guard against a ruined life.

__T__ 39. The conscience must be taught according to Bible truth.

(5 points)

H. Diagram the skeletons and complements of these sentences.

40. The geese have flocked to the pond.   (2 pt.)

```
  geese  |  have flocked
```

41. They have made this spring-fed pond their home.   (4 pt.)

```
  They  |  have made  |  pond \ home
```

42. Much leftover corn is consumed by one flock of geese.   (2 pt.)

```
  corn  |  is consumed
```

43. They may provide us several meals of fresh meat.   (4 pt.)

```
  They  |  may provide  |  meals
            \ us
```

44. This roast goose is tender and savory.   (3 pt.)

```
                          tender
  goose  |  is  \ and <
                          savory
```

(15 points)

I. Write the following information on the note cards. The notes are taken for the topic "Mennonites in the French and Indian War."   (Sample note cards.)

— appealed to local authorities to respect their beliefs, but authorities said only the king of England could guarantee that (*Nonresistance in Colonial Pennsylvania*, page 11)

— Northkill congregation in Berks County completely died out (*Nonresistance in Colonial Pennsylvania*, page 12)

— since most Mennonites in the New World spoke German, they wanted the *Martyrs Mirror* translated from Dutch (*The Mennonite Church in America*, page 135)

```
Mennonites in the French and Indian War

Nonresistance in Colonial Pennsylvania, p. 11

Appealed to local authorities to respect
  their beliefs, but authorities said only
  the king of England could guarantee that
```

Mennonites in T—L W.

NCP. p. 12

Northkill congregation in Berks County completely died out

Mennonites in T—L W.

The Mennonite Church in America. p. 135

Since most Mennonites in the New World spoke German, they wanted the Martyrs Mirror translated from Dutch

(6 points)

Total points: 66

Preparing for Usefulness

Chapter 6 Test

Score _____

Name _____ Date _____

A. Circle *T* if the statement is true or *F* if it is false.

(T) F   1. Only a passive verb can be followed by a retained object.

(T) F   2. A good short story emphasizes one theme.

T (F)   3. The traits of most story characters are revealed mainly by their speech.

T (F)   4. The opening of a short story should give detailed information about the setting.

(T) F   5. The climax is the final incident of the conflict.

T (F)   6. The theme of a story should be stated clearly at the beginning.

(6 points)

B. Underline the correct words in parentheses.

7. King Saul, as well as his soldiers, (<u>was</u>, were) cowering in fear.

8. (Don't, <u>Doesn't</u>) anybody in the camp trust the Lord?

9. (How's, <u>How are</u>) the people to be brave when their leader is not?

10. One large branch or several smaller ones (<u>have</u>, has) fallen onto the roof.

11. A herd of goats (follow, <u>follows</u>) the goatherd up the mountain trail.

12. The large heavy-duty pliers (is, <u>are</u>) hanging above the workbench.

13. One pair of scissors (<u>was</u>, were) not put away.

14. The cleanup crew (<u>have</u>, has) gone to their various assignments.

15. *Thrilling Escapes by Night* (describe, <u>describes</u>) some of William Tyndale's life and work.

16. The bag of pretzels (<u>was</u>, were) placed on the table.

17. Civics (have, <u>has</u>) been debated by religious people for hundreds of years.

18. *Solos* (<u>is</u>, are) not spelled with -*es*.

(12 points)

C. Underline the correct verbs in parentheses.

19. A mature person willingly (<u>accepts</u>, excepts) advice.

20. It is irreverent to (set, <u>sit</u>) in a slouched position in church.

21. We must (<u>let</u>, leave) the light of God's Word shine on our pathway.

22. When Grandpa came into the room, I (raised, <u>rose</u>) and shook hands.

23. No one is (accepted, <u>excepted</u>) from God's watchful eyes.

24. Only the power of God could (affect, <u>effect</u>) the raising of Lazarus.

25. Even the king could not (<u>alter</u>, altar) the laws of the Medes and Persians.

26. Mother, (can, <u>may</u>) I bake cinnamon rolls for Sunday dinner?

27. Have you (let, <u>left</u>) your book at school again?

28. Our dog often (lays, <u>lies</u>) on the back porch.

29. Thelma has (<u>proposed</u>, purposed) an excellent idea for the bulletin board.

30. Gerald's words (<u>implied</u>, inferred) that he was working harder than the rest of us.

31. If you are so careless, you might (<u>lose</u>, loose) your pocketknife.

32. Did your ancestors (<u>emigrate</u>, immigrate) from Switzerland or from Germany?

33. Uncle Mark's (adapted, <u>adopted</u>) two children from Central America.

(15 points)

D. Write whether the voice of each verb is active (*A*) or passive (*P*).

   _P_ 34. This scrapbook sheet was made by Aunt Louise.

   _P_ 35. The upstairs floors must be swept tomorrow.

   _A_ 36. We visited Grandfather Boll's last evening.

   _A_ 37. Father and the boys are cleaning the goat pens.

   _P_ 38. One load of hay has already been put into the barn.

(5 points)

E. Label each underlined object *DO* (direct object) or *IO* (indirect object). Write *ret.* after the label if the object is retained.

   ___IO___ 39. Cousin Dennis sent <u>me</u> an interesting letter.

   ___DO___ 40. Mr. Getz usually delivers our <u>feed</u>.

   IO ret. 41. This motto was given <u>me</u> by Grandfather Heatwole.

   DO ret. 42. I was given an embroidered <u>handkerchief</u> by Sister Edna.

   ___DO___ 43. Duke chased the stray <u>cat</u> up a tree.

(5 points)

F. For each story plot, write whether the main character is in conflict with another person (*P*), with his circumstances (*C*), or with his own self (*S*).

  P   44. Curvin, a young Christian, is mocked and mistreated by Jay, a neighbor boy. Later, Curvin helps to save Jay's life.

  S   45. Marlene was reading instead of doing her schoolwork, and she lied to her parents about it. Now she feels guilty but tries to act as if nothing is wrong.

  C   46. Nathaniel had been anticipating a trip to Wisconsin for his brother's wedding. Now a case of rheumatic fever has him bedfast.

(3 points)

G. Improve each sentence so that the dialogue sounds more natural.

(Sample answers. Count 2 points for each sentence.)

47. "Have you heard where we are going on Sunday?" said Beth. _____

"Have you heard where we're going on Sunday?" asked Beth. _____

48. "No, I have not heard where we are going," said Arlene. "Where are we going?" _____

"No," answered Arlene. "Where?" _____

_____

49. "We are going to Grandfather Petre's for dinner," said Beth. _____

"To Grandfather Petre's for dinner," replied Beth. _____

(6 points)

H. Rewrite each sentence, improving it as indicated in parentheses.

(Sample answers. Count 2 points for each sentence.)

50. Diane <u>hastily wrote</u> a note and <u>put</u> it on the door. (Change the underlined words to lively action verbs.)

Diane scribbled a note and taped it on the door. _____

_____

51. Herbert climbed the <u>tree</u> behind the <u>big building</u> and viewed the <u>nice</u> scenery. (Change the underlined words to exact, descriptive words.) _____

Herbert climbed the oak behind the barn and viewed the beautiful scenery. _____

_____

52. The gentle breeze blew softly through the willow trees. (Rewrite this sentence to include imagery.)

The gentle breeze whispered softly to the willow trees. _____

_____

(6 points)

Total points: 58

Preparing for Usefulness

Chapter 7 Test   Score _____

Name _____ Date _____

A. Circle *T* if the statement is true or *F* if it is false.

    (T) F   1. The person of a pronoun shows the relationship between the pronoun and the speaker.

    T (F)   2. Apostrophes are used in spelling the possessive case of personal pronouns.

    T (F)   3. A compound personal pronoun is used reflexively when it follows a noun for emphasis.

    (T) F   4. An indefinite pronoun is often used without an antecedent.

    (T) F   5. Sentence unity can be improved by joining short sentences that have closely related ideas.

    T (F)   6. A sentence lacks conciseness if the verbs shift in tense.

    T (F)   7. The passive voice can be used to emphasize the doer of an action.

    (T) F   8. The active voice is generally more direct and forceful than the passive voice.

    T (F)   9. The main idea receives greatest emphasis if it is placed in the middle of the sentence.

    (T) F 10. Most sentences that you write should be simple declarative sentences.

(10 points)

B. Circle the number that identifies the person of the underlined pronoun, and the letter that identifies its number.

    (1) 2 3   S (P)   11. <u>We</u> are the sheep of God's pasture.

    1 2 (3)   S (P)   12. God loves His sheep and provides the best for <u>them</u>.

    1 2 (3)   (S) P   13. <u>His</u> voice guides the sheep in safety.

    1 (2) 3   (S) P   14. My friend, <u>you</u> should listen attentively to His voice.

(8 points)

C. Circle the letters that identify the case and gender of each underlined pronoun.

    N O (P)   M (F) N C   15. Dorcas was greatly appreciated for <u>her</u> deeds of kindness.

    (N) O P   M F N (C)   16. The believers suffered much, but <u>they</u> remained faithful.

    N (O) P   (M) F N C   17. When Jesus looked at <u>him</u>, Peter was moved to repentance.

    N (O) P   M F (N) C   18. Paul endured great persecution, but he endured <u>it</u> calmly.

    N O (P)   M F N (C)   19. Is <u>your</u> faith strong enough to stand your trials?

(10 points)

D. Underline the correct choices in parentheses.

20. Either Sheldon or Eldon left (<u>his book</u>, their books) here.

21. (<u>We</u>, Us) eighth graders made a map for our history class.

22. Father sent an important message to you and (I, <u>me</u>).

23. Katrina surely makes prettier quilt blocks than (<u>I</u>, me).

24. The ones most frightened by the explosion were (<u>we</u>, us) boys in the shop.

25. The craftsman and the baker sold (his, <u>their</u>) products at the market.

26. The craftsman and baker sold all the products that (<u>he</u>, they) had.

27. The flock is following (<u>its</u>, their) shepherd.

28. Mother commended the girls, Marla and (she, <u>her</u>), for their good work.

29. The boys, Raymond and (<u>he</u>, him), are pruning the apple trees.

(10 points)

E. Rewrite these sentences to make the pronouns clear and correct.

30. Elsie told Erma that she must have misunderstood. _____

    <u>Elsie said, "Erma, you (*or* I) must have misunderstood."</u>_____

31. Mother wants me and you to set the table. _____

    <u>Mother wants you and me to set the table.</u>_____

32. Conrad surprised Joel when he stepped into the room. __<u>When Conrad stepped into the room, he</u>

    <u>surprised Joel.</u>   *or* <u>When Joel stepped into the room, Conrad surprised him.</u>_____

(3 points)

F. Cross out the wrong word in each sentence. If another word should be used instead, write the correct word in the blank.

_____<u>Those</u>_____ 33. ~~Them~~ are the ones Melvin gathered.

_____<u>themselves</u>_____ 34. My parents ~~theirselves~~ suggested that we go along.

_____<u>me</u>_____ 35. Curvin surprised Larry and ~~myself~~ with his apology.

_____<u>ourselves</u>_____ 36. We should not consider ~~ourself~~ better than others.

_____ 37. Nobody picked this ~~here~~ book yet.

_____<u>himself</u>_____ 38. Allen made ~~hisself~~ an attractive bookshelf.

(6 points)

G. Underline the correct choices in parentheses.

39. Each person must determine in (<u>his heart</u>, their hearts) to serve God.

40. All of these proverbs (<u>give</u>, gives) practical advice for our lives.

41. All of this psalm (inspire, <u>inspires</u>) us to trust the Lord.

42. Somebody was willing to lend (<u>his</u>, their) influence in a good way.

43. Few people in the world (is, <u>are</u>) willing to surrender to the Lord.

(5 points)

H. Underline the relative pronoun in each sentence, and put parentheses around its antecedent.

44. This (farm,) <u>which</u> Father bought in 1970, has several acres of woodland.

45. The (man) <u>whose</u> leg is broken is my uncle.

46. Did you meet the (lady) <u>who</u> crochets these doll clothes?

(3 points)

I. Underline the correct choices in parentheses.

47. The elderly couple (who, <u>whom</u>) we visited seems quite contented.

48. This goat, (who, <u>which</u>) enjoys eating Mother's flowers, is too clever.

49. Herman, (<u>who</u>, which) is Uncle John's hired man, was born in Germany.

50. We sang for Mrs. Hartzler, (<u>who</u>, whom) is confined to a wheelchair.

(4 points)

J. Label the underlined pronouns *P* (personal), *CP* (compound personal), *D* (demonstrative), *ID* (indefinite), *IR* (interrogative), or *R* (relative).

 CP   51. We tell on <u>ourselves</u> by the friends we choose.

 D   52. <u>Those</u> who are wise will choose upright companions.

 R   53. A noble character, <u>which</u> is priceless, does not develop automatically.

 D   54. Only those who love the truth can have <u>this</u> for a possession.

 R   55. How can a man, <u>who</u> is a creature of dust, approach the Almighty?

 ID   56. <u>Nobody</u> can pray to the Father except in Jesus' Name.

 P   57. What a marvel that God hears <u>our</u> prayers!

 IR   58. <u>Who</u> can fathom such boundless love?

(8 points)

K. Write *X* before each sentence in which the passive voice is suitable.

   X   59. Linen is made from flax.

_____   60. A rare albino deer has been seen by several of our neighbors.

   X   61. Pompeii was buried under the lava when Mount Vesuvius erupted.

(3 points)

L. Rewrite each sentence more effectively by improving the quality named in parentheses.

(Allow reasonable variation.)

62. The ducks could not land on the pond, and it was frozen over. (unity) _____

The ducks could not land on the pond, for (*or* because) it was frozen over.

63. We tried baking a cake and to make pudding before the visitors came. (parallelism)

We tried to bake a cake and to make pudding before the visitors came.

or We tried baking a cake and making pudding . . .

64. Simmering in the kettle, I smelled Mother's stew. (coherence) _____

I smelled Mother's stew simmering in the kettle.

65. On the next day when it is sunny, Mother wants to wash and clean the windows. (conciseness)

On the next sunny day, Mother wants to wash the windows.

66. The broken wagon was welded by Arnold. (action) _____

Arnold welded the broken wagon.

67. When one visits various countries, they are impressed with North America's wealth. (parallelism)

When one visits various countries, he is impressed with North America's wealth.

68. We should desire to at all times live in humility. (coherence) _____

We should desire to live in humility at all times.

69. To lionize is when someone is treated as a person of great importance. (parallelism)

To lionize is to treat someone as a person of great importance.

(8 points)

M. The following paragraph consists of all declarative sentences. Follow the directions below to improve the sentence variety.   (Allow reasonable variation.)

God has given the frog powerful back legs. The frog uses them to escape from enemies. A frog can jump two feet or more if it is frightened. That is quite a leap for a small creature. A frog often jumps into the water. That is not very helpful in escaping from a snake. The snake comes right into the water.

70. Combine two sentences into a complex sentence. _____

God has given the frog powerful back legs, which it uses to escape from enemies.

_____

71. Combine two sentences into a compound sentence. _____

A frog often jumps into the water, but that is not very helpful in escaping from a snake.

_____

72. Begin one sentence with a clause modifier. _____

If it is frightened, a frog can jump two feet or more.

73. Change one sentence to an exclamatory sentence.   What a leap that is for a small creature!

or That is quite a leap for a small creature!

74. Change one sentence to inverted word order. _____

Right into the water comes the snake.

(5 points)

Total points: 83

Preparing for Usefulness

Chapter 8 Test   **Score** _____

Name _____   **Date** _____

A. Circle *T* if the statement is true or *F* if it is false.

   T (F) 1. A limiting adjective answers the question *what kind of*.

   (T) F 2. Appositive adjectives usually come in pairs and are set off with commas.

   T (F) 3. A nonrestrictive clause identifies a specific person, thing, or group.

   (T) F 4. Nonrestrictive clauses should be set off by commas.

   (T) F 5. A feminine rhyme involves more than one syllable.

   T (F) 6. Each meter in a poem consists of one accented syllable and the unaccented syllable or syllables
            associated with it.

   T (F) 7. The connotation of a word is its strict, exact meaning.

   (T) F 8. Bible poetry often makes use of parallelism.

                                                                          (8 points)

B. Underline the ten adjectives. Above each, write *L* for limiting or *D* for descriptive. Also write *AT* for attributive, *AP* for appositive, or *PR* for predicate.

         L, AT   L, AT   D, PR
   9. Doreen's first poem was inspirational.
           L, AT   L or D, AP   L, AT
   10. From His throne above, God observes life's circumstances.
         L, AT   D, AP   D, AP   L, AT
   11. God's Word, precious and authoritative, can direct our steps.

                                                                          (10 points)

C. Underline the five adjective phrases, and identify them by writing the correct letters in the blanks.

      a. participial   b. infinitive   c. prepositional

    _b_ _c_ 12. An important thing to consider daily is God's will for our lives.

    _a_ ___ 13. Finding our security there, we need not worry.

    _a_ _c_ 14. God's Word, settled eternally, is a source of great comfort.

                                                                          (5 points)

D. Underline each adjective clause, and write whether it is restrictive (*R*) or nonrestrictive (*N*). Add any missing commas.

    _N_ 15. My oldest sister, who is twenty-three, teaches school.

    _R_ 16. The man who just came in the door is Leonard Watson.

__R__   17. Flossie is the dog <u>that we bought from Uncle Lewis</u>.

(3 points)

E. Cross out each word that should not be used, and write any correction above it. If words are missing, use a caret (∧) to show where they belong, and write the words in the space above.

18. Conrad is older than anyone~~else~~ in his classroom.
    (else written above, caret after "anyone")

18. Conrad is older than anyone ∧ in his classroom.

19. Do you know what kind of ~~a~~ bird that is?

20. ~~Them~~ Those squirrels are busy gathering nuts for the winter.

21. I had ~~less~~ fewer mistakes on the quiz today than on the one last week.

22. You should greet your teacher with a ~~respectable~~ respectful "Good morning."

23. Miriam is the ~~tallest~~ taller of the twins.

24. The ~~cold~~ ice cream felt good to my sore throat.

25. Do you know where this ~~here~~ box belongs?

26. We hung our ~~wet,~~ drenched clothes on the rack to dry.   *or* We hung our wet, ~~drenched~~ clothes on the rack to dry.

(9 points)

F. Underline each misplaced adjective phrase or clause, and draw an arrow from it to the place where it belongs. For number 30, rewrite the sentence so that it does not have a dangling participle.

(Repositioned items are underlined.)

27. Our car is in the garage <u>which would not start this morning</u>.

28. For over an hour, the angry bull kept the children in the tree, <u>pawing the ground</u>.

29. Jerry's glove has been chewed up by Rover, <u>left out in the rain</u>.

30. Seeing the icy sidewalk, it was clearly understandable what had happened. _____

   <u>Seeing the icy sidewalk, I (*or* we) clearly understood what had happened.</u>

_____

(4 points)

G. Diagram these sentences.   (Count 5 points for each sentence.)

31. The psalms, which are beautiful Hebrew poems, have inspired many people.

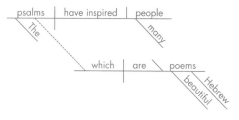

32. Proverbs, addressing many practical subjects, is a good book to study often.

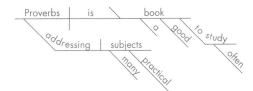

33. These proverbs, short and emphatic, give wholesome, dependable advice.

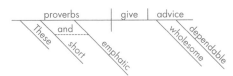

(15 points)

H. In the blank above each stanza, write which kind of rhythm the poem has. In the blanks after the lines, show the rhyming pattern.

34. _____ iambic _____

The little cares that fretted me,   __a__

I lost them yesterday,   __b__

Among the fields, above the sea,   __a__

Among the winds at play;   __b__

Among the lowing of the herds,   __c__

The rustling of the trees,   __d__

Among the singing of the birds,   __c__

The humming of the bees.   __d__

35. _____ trochaic _____

Like a beacon beaming   __a__

O'er the waters wild,   __b__

So Christ's light is streaming   __a__

O'er this world defiled.   __b__

36. _____anapestic_____

    Often weary and worn on the pathway below,   __a__

    When the burden is heavy, my heart throbs with woe;   __a__

    Oh, there comes a sweet whisper to quell ev'ry sigh,   __b__

    "Do not faint 'neath the load, there is rest by and by."   __b__

37. _____dactylic_____

    Cling to the Bible, though all else be taken;   __a__

    Lose not its promises, precious and sure;   __b__

    Souls that are sleeping its echoes awaken;   __a__

    Drink from the fountain, so peaceful, so pure.   __b__

(8 points)

I. Do these exercises.

38. Copy the three examples of onomatopoeia in number 34. _____

    lowing, rustling, humming

39. Copy the example of personification in number 34. _____

    winds at play

40. Write two pairs of words that show alliteration in number 35. _____

    beacon beaming; waters wild

41. Copy the simile in number 35. _____

    Like a beacon beaming o'er the waters wild

42. Number 37 uses a metaphor to describe the Bible. Write the word that names the object to which the

    Bible is compared. __fountain__

(8 points)

Total points: 70

Preparing for Usefulness

Chapter 9 Test   **Score** _____

Name _____   **Date** _____

A. Circle *T* if the statement is true or *F* if it is false.

Ⓣ F   1. An adverb clause at the beginning of a sentence should be separated from the main clause by a comma.

Ⓣ F   2. Most adverb phrases and clauses can be moved to different locations without changing the meaning of the sentences.

T Ⓕ   3. In an expression like *as soon as you can,* the first three words work together as a conjunction.

T Ⓕ   4. Sermon notes should always be taken in outline form.

T Ⓕ   5. In a persuasive argument, the points that support the writer's main idea are called propositions.

Ⓣ F   6. To have the strongest argument, the writer should use facts rather than opinions to support his main idea.

(6 points)

B. Underline the eight single-word adverbs, and draw an arrow from each one to the word it modifies.

7. Daily draw near to the Lord with a firmly anchored faith in Him.

8. Our daily prayers certainly help us to overcome temptation faithfully.

9. Too often, men forget to humbly seek the Lord.

(8 points)

C. Underline the eight adverb phrases, and draw an arrow from each one to the item it modifies.

10. By Noah's time, people were living wickedly to the extreme.

11. Because their wickedness was too great for God's toleration, He decided to destroy the earth with a great flood.

12. In this wicked society lived Noah, a man remarkable for his faith.

13. Noah preached to warn the people, but they were too unconcerned to heed his message.

(8 points)

D. Underline the six adverb clauses, and draw an arrow from each one to the item it modifies.

14. A beautiful rainbow, more brilliant than I had ever seen before, arched across the sky as the storm was passing.

15. Because Sister Mae cannot drive, several sisters have offered to take her to the hospital whenever she must go.

16. Aunt Kathryn told the story so interestingly <u>that we were spellbound</u>.

17. We must work as quickly <u>as we can</u>.

(6 points)

E. Label each underlined item by writing *adj.* or *adv.* above it.

           adj.   adv.
18. A <u>friendly</u> smile can be understood <u>in any language</u>.

                 adj.   adj. *or* adv.
19. The two families <u>from Virginia</u> visited their relatives <u>in Iowa</u>.

             adv.   adj.
20. Marvin <u>quickly</u> handed me the baskets <u>to fill with apples</u>.

           adj.   adv.
21. The <u>outside</u> walls sparkled so spotlessly <u>that we were shocked at the dirt inside</u>.

            adj.   adv.
22. The sheep <u>that belong in this pen</u> are running around <u>outside</u>.

(10 points)

F. Cross out each incorrect word, or use a caret (∧) to show where a word should be inserted. Write any correction in the blank.

_____surely_____ 23. Youth is ~~sure~~ an important time to establish good habits.

_____ 24. Early habits often become firmly rooted later ~~on~~ in life.

_____ 25. If you develop bad habits now, you are likely to continue ~~on~~ in them.

_____well_____ 26. Proper habits started in youth serve a person ~~good~~ in later years.

____already____ 27. Your habits are ~~all ready~~ influencing the future course of your life.

____further____ 28. To consider this fact ~~farther~~, study the Book of Proverbs.

_____better_____ 29. Of the two kinds, I like apple pie ~~best~~.

_____really_____ 30. The planting went ~~real~~ well today.

___somewhat___ 31. The work has gone ~~some~~ better today than it did earlier.

_____other_____ 32. The temperature dropped lower on New Year's Day than on any ∧ day in January.

_____ 33. Many of our forefathers left ~~from~~ Europe.

_____ 34. Most came to America seeking ~~after~~ religious freedom.

_____could_____ 35. Some were so poor that they ~~couldn't~~ hardly pay their way.

___somewhat___
or rather 36. It is ~~kind of~~ hard for us to imagine the difficulties they faced.

_____ 37. We rarely ~~ever~~ consider the many things we have received from our forefathers.

_____badly_____ 38. I enjoy history, but arithmetic goes rather ~~bad~~ for me.

   all right   39. However, I did ~~alright~~ on my last math quiz.

(17 points)

G. Diagram these sentences.   (Count 5 points for each sentence.)

40. An extremely old bus pulled up along the sidewalk.

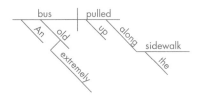

41. Father bought some glass to fix the window before the weekend.

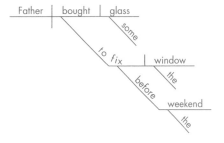

42. As the cold front approached, several showers passed through the area.

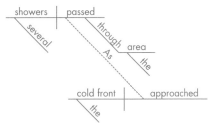

43. The wind blew so strongly that several trees were blown over.

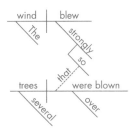

44. My new bicycle is somewhat bigger than my old one had been.

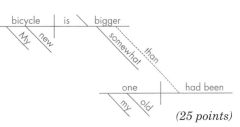

(25 points)

Total points: 80

Preparing for Usefulness

Chapter 10 Test

Score _____

Name _____ Date _____

A. Circle *T* if the statement is true or *F* if it is false.

   T (F) 1. The object of a preposition is always a noun or pronoun like *man* or *it*.

   T (F) 2. When giving directions to a place, you should include plenty of details about each landmark that you mention.

   (T) F 3. The same infinitive phrase may be used as two different parts of speech.

   (T) F 4. Subordinating conjunctions join clauses of unequal rank in a sentence.

   (T) F 5. An interjection does not function as part of a sentence.

(5 points)

B. Underline each prepositional phrase, and above it write whether it functions as an adjective (*adj.*), an adverb (*adv.*), or a noun (*n.*). If a phrase is part of a longer phrase, underline it twice and label both phrases clearly.

       adv.   adj.   adv.

   6. <u>Due to the deceptive nature <u>of sin</u></u>, it is foolish to play <u>with temptation</u>.

                                    adv.   adv.

   7. Unless youthful ambition is kept <u>under control</u>, it is useful <u>to no one</u>.

                 adj.   adj.

   8. Goals <u>for youth</u> should include a commitment <u>to whatever is right</u>.

             n.   adj.   adj.

   9. <u>On the pathway <u>of righteousness</u></u> is the best place <u>for every person</u>.

(10 points)

C. Underline the common coordinating conjunctions (*CC*), subordinating conjunctions (*SC*), correlative conjunctions (*Cor*), and conjunctive adverbs (*CA*); and write the correct label above each one. Be sure to include all parts of correlative conjunctions.

                                      CC   SC

   10. You should remember your Creator <u>and</u> serve Him <u>while</u> you are yet young.

          Cor   Cor

   11. You will <u>either</u> develop strength to resist evil <u>or</u> fall to its power.

                                  CA   SC

   12. The allurement of evil can be strong; <u>nevertheless</u>, God will richly enable you <u>if</u> you trust Him.

                 Cor   Cor

   13. You should look <u>not only</u> to God <u>but also</u> to Christian parents for guidance.

                                CC

   14. You should honor godly parents, <u>for</u> your welfare rests on their hearts.

                                CA

   15. Godly parents have had many experiences; <u>consequently</u>, they can offer much practical help.

(8 points)

D. Underline the interjections. Place a comma or an exclamation point after each one, and capitalize the next word if necessary.

          T

   16. <u>Cocoa</u>! that will be delicious for breakfast.

17. <u>Well</u>, my job was not so difficult after all.

18. <u>What</u> ̶ nobody fed the sheep?

        N

(6 points)

E. Cross out each mistake in preposition or conjunction usage. Write any corrections or insertions above it.

19. Aunt Esther's pancakes are different ~~than~~ Mother's.   *from*

20. We want to leave soon so that no one needs to wait ~~on~~ us.   *for*

21. The main character in this story acted ~~like~~ he never needed advice.   *as if*

22. Do not bring your boots ~~in~~ the house.   *into*

23. Sarah sat ~~in~~ between Norene and me.

24. We set up a croquet game ~~in back of~~ the house.   *behind*

25. We went ~~by~~ Widow Garber's house and visited with her for a while.   *to*

26. One large pumpkin fell off ~~of~~ the wagon.

27. That is where my uncle Harold's family lives ~~at~~.

28. It is not good to have a strong interest *in* and desire for riches.

(10 points)

F. Add the missing commas and semicolons to these sentences.

29. Undoubtedly, the *Titanic* was one of the safest ships on the ocean; however, she sank into the calm, icy waters of the Atlantic.

30. The threat of icebergs was reported to the captain, but he refused to slow down.

31. Not only was the captain determined to set a record maiden voyage for the *Titanic*, but also he wanted a distinguished end to his career.

(3 points)

G. Rewrite these sentences, correcting the mistakes in conjunction usage.

32. Aunt Laura looked cheerful and in good health. _____

    <u>Aunt Laura looked cheerful and healthy.</u> _____

33. Duane has neither swept the porch nor the walks. _____

    <u>Duane has swept neither the porch nor the walks.</u> _____

34. Not only was the milk spilled, but the jar was broken. _____

Not only was the milk spilled, but also the jar was broken. _____

(3 points)

H. Above each underlined word, write the abbreviation for the part of speech that it is.

(Count ½ point for each word.)

35. These milk cows look quite healthy.
     adj. adj.   adv. adj.

36. We must milk them by ourselves, for Father has gone to an early meeting.
     v.   prep.   conj.   adj.

37. The milk that was not put away has spoiled.
     n. pron.   adv.   v.

38. Milk! Did I forget to put it into the refrigerator after breakfast?
     interj.   n.   prep.   prep.

39. After the buck had dashed by, a pack of dogs came along.
     conj.   adv. n.   adv.

40. The trustees, meeting at the church, made plans to hold a cleanup day.
     adj.   n.   adj. adj.

41. Cleaning the church grounds takes time, so we should leave early.
     n.   adj.   conj.   adv.

(14 points)

I. Read the following descriptive paragraphs, and do the exercises that follow.

A few stray sunbeams (*a*) <u>came</u> through the bars of a (*b*) <u>tiny</u> window high in the tower wall. Reaching into the gloom below, they played dimly over a lanky figure sprawled on a heap of (*c*) <u>unclean</u> straw. Hans Hut, the prisoner, moaned softly as he painfully (*d*) <u>tried hard</u> to change his position.

       *   *   *   *   *

But the fire was too far advanced, and soon the whole straw pile was aflame. Choking and sputtering, Hans (*e*) <u>stumbled</u> to the door. He (*f*) <u>hit</u> on it with his fists and shouted for help. The thick smoke, having (*g*) <u>inadequate</u> place to escape, swirled around him, choking him.

(Sample replacements.)

42. Write a better word that could replace each underlined word or phrase that is not descriptive. If an underlined item is effective, write *effective* in the blank.

a. ___filtered, streaked___

b. ___effective___

c. ___filthy, dirty___

d. _struggled, endeavored_

e. ___effective___

f. ___pounded, beat___

g. ___effective___

43. a. Copy the example of figurative language in the first paragraph. (It includes a verbal and a verb.)

Reaching into the gloom below, they played _____

b. Which kind of figure of speech is this? _metaphor *or* personification_

(9 points)

Total points: 68

Preparing for Usefulness

Chapter 11 Test

Score _____

Name _____ Date _____

A. Circle *T* if the statement is true or *F* if it is false.

T (F) 1. The label *archaic* is used for a word that is poor English.

T (F) 2. Dictionaries usually show the plural forms of all nouns.

(T) F 3. Synonyms must be chosen carefully for the right connotation.

T (F) 4. The cross-references at the end of encyclopedia articles give more details on finding information than the index does.

(T) F 5. In *Strong's Exhaustive Concordance*, the original meanings of Old Testament words are found in the "Hebrew and Chaldee Dictionary."

T (F) 6. The numbers following Old Testament references in *Strong's* are in italics.

(T) F 7. Cards in a card catalog are arranged in alphabetical order.

T (F) 8. Every book in the library has a title, an author, and a subject card in the card catalog.

(T) F 9. The card catalog is an aid to finding the call numbers of books.

T (F) 10. A summary should be about half as long as the original article.

(T) F 11. The greater part of a book report should describe the theme of the story.

(T) F 12. In giving a book report, one should avoid describing the climax.

(12 points)

B. Write the letter of the correct term to match each description. Some letters may be used more than once, and some not at all.

<u>d</u> 13. A book of information about English words.

<u>a</u> 14. A book of maps.

<u>e</u> 15. Volumes of information on many subjects.

<u>f</u> 16. A book of synonyms.

<u>g</u> 17. A book showing verses on Bible subjects.

<u>c</u> 18. An index of Bible words and their references.

<u>b</u> 19. A book of information on Bible words, places, customs, and so forth.

<u>c</u> 20. A book that may have original language dictionaries.

a. atlas
b. Bible dictionary
c. concordance
d. dictionary
e. encyclopedia
f. thesaurus
g. topical Bible

<u>l</u>   21. A brief history of a word.

<u>i</u>   22. The "personality," or feeling, of a word.

<u>j</u>   23. The strict, exact meaning of a word.

<u>m</u>   24. The changes in a word to show number, tense, and so forth.

<u>n</u>   25. Words that are similar in meaning.

<u>k</u>   26. Words formed from root words by adding prefixes and suffixes.

h. antonyms
i. connotation
j. denotation
k. derivatives
l. etymology
m. inflections
n. synonyms

<u>o</u>   27. Stories about specific individuals.

<u>q</u>   28. Books used to look up information.

<u>p</u>   29. Imaginary stories.

<u>q</u>   30. Arranged by the Dewey decimal system.

<u>p</u>   31. Arranged alphabetically by authors.

<u>o</u>   32. May have the number 92 on the spine.

o. biographies
p. fiction
q. reference

(20 points)

C. Read these sample dictionary entries, and do the exercises that follow.

mail^1 (māl) *n.* 1. Letters, printed matter, and parcels sent through a postal system. 2. The postal system itself. 3. Postal matter collected or delivered at a specified time. —*v.* To send by mail; post. —*adj.* Pertaining to or used for handling mail. [< OF < OHG *malha* wallet] —**mail•a•ble** *adj.*

mail^2 (māl) *n.* 1. Flexible armor made of metal links or overlapping plates. 2. A defensive covering, as a turtle's shell. —*v.* To cover with or as with mail. [< OF < L *macula* spot, mesh of a net]

33. Why are there two numbered entries for *mail*? _____

    <u>There are two words from different origins.</u>_____

34. Write *1* or *2* to tell which entry fits each description.

    <u>2</u>   a. Comes from a Latin word.

    <u>1</u>   b. Can be used as a noun, adjective, or verb.

    <u>1</u>   c. Has a derivative.

(4 points)

D. For each number, write the letter of the correct choice.

_c_ 35. The words in each pair have similar denotations. In which pair do the words have different connotations?
 a. state, express
 b. argue, dispute
 c. converse, gossip

_b_ 36. Which statement is *not* a caution about using encyclopedias?
 a. Encyclopedia articles contain general information.
 b. Encyclopedia articles contain a wide range of information.
 c. Encyclopedia articles promote man's achievements and theories.

_a_ 37. Which of these statements is *not* true?
 a. You are less likely to find man's interpretations of the Bible in Bible dictionaries than in concordances and topical Bibles.
 b. A topical Bible can help you find a verse about a given subject even if that subject is not directly mentioned in the verse.
 c. In *Strong's Concordance,* the last part of an entry in the original language dictionaries lists all the ways a word is translated in the King James Version of the Bible.

_c_ 38. Which of these statements is *not* true?
 a. Many thesauruses are arranged in alphabetical order.
 b. A thesaurus can be used to find synonyms or antonyms.
 c. A thesaurus lists only synonyms that can be interchanged easily.

_b_ 39. Which of these is *not* a part of library courtesy?
 a. Walking and talking quietly.
 b. Politely explaining why you do not need to pay the fine for an overdue book.
 c. Handling books carefully.

(5 points)

Total points: 41

Preparing for Usefulness

Final Test   **Score** _____

Name _____   **Date** _____

A. Write abbreviations in the blanks to identify the parts of speech that are underlined.

(a) _adj._ (b) _v.__ 1. The (a) <u>early</u> morning should (b) <u>witness</u> our devotion.

(a) _n.__ (b) _v.__ 2. The (a) <u>witness</u> of Creation (b) <u>points</u> men to God.

(a) _n.__ (b) _conj._ 3. The (a) <u>wicked</u> despise truth, (b) <u>for</u> they hate God.

(a) _adj._ (b) _adv._ 4. (a) <u>These</u> bushes bloom (b) <u>early</u> in the spring.

(a) _interj._ (b) _pron._ 5. (a) <u>Ah</u>, (b) <u>these</u> are certainly beautiful!

(a) _n.__ (b) _prep._ 6. I want (a) <u>to cut</u> some lilacs (b) <u>for</u> Grandmother.

(a) _adj._ (b) _pron._ 7. (a) <u>Seeing</u> the fresh blossoms, (b) <u>she</u> beamed with joy.

(a) _pron._ (b) _adv._ 8. (a) <u>Someone</u> sent her a (b) <u>freshly</u> cut bouquet of flowers.

(16 points)

B. Use the abbreviations shown to identify the sentence parts that are underlined.

S—subject	PA—predicate adjective	OC—objective complement
V—verb	DO—direct object	AP—appositive
PN—predicate nominative	IO—indirect object	DA—noun of direct address

(a) _AP_ (b) _DO_   9. Jesus, the (a) <u>Good Shepherd</u>, nourishes His (b) <u>sheep</u>.

(a) _V_ (b) _IO_ 10. He (a) <u>supplies</u> (b) <u>them</u> living water and green pastures.

(a) _DA_ (b) _PA_ 11. Oh, (a) <u>Lord</u>, Thy wisdom is (b) <u>infinite</u>.

(a) _S_ (b) _OC_ 12. His (a) <u>grace</u> can make us (b) <u>strong</u>.

(a) _DA_ (b) _PN_ 13. My (a) <u>friend</u>, His grace is a basic (b) <u>source</u> of victory.

(10 points)

C. Label each sentence S (simple), CD (compound), CX (complex), or CD-CX (compound-complex).

__CX__ 14. The Indian python, which may grow to twenty feet long, preys mainly on warm-blooded animals.

__S__ 15. It locates its prey by its acute sense of smell and by its sensitive heat receptors.

__CD__ 16. A female Indian python makes a shallow nest, and there she lays as many as one hundred eggs at a time.

_CD-CX_ 17. If the temperature drops below 96.8°F, the mother contracts her muscles to raise her body temperature; then she wraps herself around her eggs.

__CX__ 18. Because a python's skin is richly patterned, it has been heavily hunted.

(5 points)

D. In the first blank, write *dec.* (declarative), *int.* (interrogative), *imp.* (imperative), or *exc.* (exclamatory) to identify the sentence structure. In the second blank, write *N* (natural), *I* (inverted), or *M* (mixed) to identify the word order. All punctuation is omitted.

  int.   M 19. Have you learned your Bible memory passage

  dec.   I 20. Across the yard dashed a red fox

  exc.   M 21. How well the gardens are growing this spring

  imp.   N 22. Thank the Lord for His goodness to us

(8 points)

E. Cross out each capitalization error, and write the letter correctly above it.

23. Jesus and **H**is disciples
24. the song "Great **I**s the Lord"
25. my **f**ather and his Dodge **v**an
26. a **c**hurch in the **s**outh
27. in **r**eading or English classes
28. some **S**wiss cocoa for a snack
29. buy **T**ylenol at Alton **D**rugstore
30. go **e**ast on Ridge Road
31. in Virginia during the **C**ivil **W**ar
32. the **t**en **c**ommandments in **E**xodus

(10 points)

F. Each of these sentences has two errors in punctuation or italics. Underline the word or words that should be italicized, and add the missing punctuation. Use a caret (∧) if necessary.

33. For victory in life's battles, we must develop a deep, genuine fear of God.

34. Many people practice self-restraint; however, only those who fear God can truly deny self.

35. Yes, many of the ills of mankind are caused by one basic problem: selfishness.

36. I've just finished reading a story about Thomas Edison, who invented many practical things.

37. The beautiful song "Teach Me to Pray" is in <u>Songs of the Church</u>.

38. You did not make your capital <u>C</u>'s large enough.

39. Which prophet wrote these words: "For I am the Lord, I change not"?

40. "Why is Princess barking so—oh, look! The cows are out!" shouted Leon.

41. The flood washed away the <u>Water Cruiser</u>, which the boys had tied to a tree.

42. "Do you remember Great-uncle Levi saying, 'A man should never be ashamed to be kind'?" asked Arlen.

43. "We had planned to work in the garden today, but with Father sick¨" Henry's voice
    trailed into silence.

44. You will need several two- and three-foot lengths of yarn.

(12 points)

G. Fill in the blanks of this chart. Use foreign plural spellings for starred words.

(Count ½ point for each word.)

Singular	Singular Possessive	Plural	Plural Possessive
45. nobleman	nobleman's	noblemen	noblemen's
46. editor in chief	editor in chief's	editors in chief	editors in chief's
47. wife	wife's	wives	wives'
48. salmon	salmon's	salmon	salmon's
49. enemy	enemy's	enemies	enemies'
50. goose	goose's	geese	geese's
51. child	child's	children	children's
*52. bacterium	bacterium's	bacteria	bacteria's
*53. octopus	octopus's	octopi	octopi's
*54. larva	larva's	larvae	larvae's
*55. basis		bases	
*56. vertex		vertices	

(16 points)

H. In the first blank, write *prep.* (prepositional), *ger.* (gerund), *inf.* (infinitive), or *part.* (participial) to tell what
   kind of phrase is underlined. In the second blank, write the abbreviation for *noun, adjective,* or *adverb* to
   tell how the phrase is used.

   inf. _n._ 57. Every youth's goal should be <u>to develop noble character</u>.

   prep. _adv._ 58. In every distress, we can turn <u>to the Lord</u>.

   ger. _n._ 59. <u>Serving the Lord</u> is a great privilege.

   part. _adj._ 60. Our God, <u>reigning in the heavens</u>, watches tenderly over His own.

   inf. _adv._ 61. We pray to the Lord <u>to receive divine strength</u>.

   prep. _adj._ 62. A Christian <u>on his knees</u> sees farther than a carnal man on his tiptoes.

(6 points)

I. In the first blank, write *D* or *I* to tell whether the underlined clause is dependent or independent. If the clause is dependent, write the abbreviation for *noun, adjective,* or *adverb* in the second blank.

   __D__ __adv.__ 63. Father wants to plant corn tomorrow <u>if the weather permits</u>.

   __I__ _____ 64. Jean baked a batch of cookies, but <u>they are all gone already</u>.

   __D__ __adj.__ 65. Uncle Kevin's, <u>whom we have not seen for years</u>, plan to visit.

   __D__ __n.__ 66. We hope <u>that they can stay over the weekend</u>.

   __D__ __adv.__ 67. The grass was so thick <u>that it choked the mower</u>.

(5 points)

J. Label the tense of the underlined verbs.

   _____present perfect_____ 68. Glen <u>has been working</u> carefully on this birdhouse.

   _____past_____ 69. Yesterday he <u>spent</u> most of the evening in the shop.

   _____present_____ 70. He certainly <u>does enjoy</u> working with wood.

   _____future perfect_____ 71. We hope he <u>will have finished</u> it before Ira's birthday.

   _____past perfect_____ 72. Before Father left, he <u>had checked</u> on Glen's progress.

   _____future_____ 73. We <u>shall check</u> the finished product carefully.

(6 points)

K. From Part J, copy the verbs that fit these descriptions.

   _____has been working_____ 74. a verb that is a progressive form

   _____does enjoy_____ 75. a verb that is an emphatic form

(2 points)

L. Use the numbers shown to identify the sentence patterns.

   __2__ 76. God will amply reward the faithful.

   __1__ 77. The faithful work diligently at their responsibilities.

   __4__ 78. A faithful person is a blessing to others.

   __3__ 79. Faithfulness should be developed at a young age.

Pattern 1: intransitive complete verb
Pattern 2: transitive verb, active voice
Pattern 3: transitive verb, passive voice
Pattern 4: intransitive linking verb

(4 points)

M. Underline the correct words.

80. (How's, <u>How are</u>) the beans growing by now?

81. The deer (<u>dragged</u>, drug) its injured leg painfully.

82. Father has (went, <u>gone</u>) to a meeting this evening.

83. Either Katrina or the boys (<u>have</u>, has) brought the milk.

84. Mother said that we (can, <u>may</u>) have some free time this afternoon.

85. How does temperature (<u>affect</u>, effect) the relative humidity of an air mass?

86. The Robert Higgs family (<u>emigrated</u>, immigrated) from England last year.

87. As you (set, <u>sit</u>) at your desk, do you maintain good posture?

88. In her letter, Viola (<u>implied</u>, inferred) that her arthritis is worse.

89. The cows (laid, <u>lay</u>) in the shade all afternoon.

90. The temperature has (raised, <u>risen</u>) considerably since morning.

91. One load of stones (<u>is</u>, are) not enough for this area.

92. Neil's glasses (was, <u>were</u>) broken.

93. Each of the students (have, <u>has</u>) finished the assignment.

94. Most of the corn (<u>was</u>, were) planted last week.

95. Most of the beans (was, <u>were</u>) planted last week.

96. Henry (let, <u>left</u>) his books at school.

97. Brother Roy (<u>advised</u>, adviced) us to listen respectfully to the tour guide.

98. Why were these books (<u>laid</u>, lain) on the table?

99. (<u>Let</u>, Leave) the younger children choose first.

(20 points)

N. Identify the person (*1, 2, 3*), number (*S, P*), case (*N, O, P*), and gender (*M, F, N, C*) of each underlined pronoun.

(Count ½ point for each answer.)

	Person	Number	Case	Gender
100. We have finished <u>our</u> work.	1	P	P	C
101. <u>She</u> has neat penmanship.	3	S	N	F
102. Mother called <u>him</u> for lunch.	3	S	O	M
103. When I dropped the dish, <u>it</u> broke.	3	S	N	N
104. Friends, have <u>you</u> prayed about it?	2	P	N	C

(10 points)

O. Underline the correct words.

105. This letter is for you and (I, <u>me</u>).

106. One of these buckets has a hole in (<u>its</u>, their) side.

107. (<u>We</u>, Us) boys wanted to play softball.

108. Uncle Jerry's garden is growing well, but (<u>ours</u>, our's) is too wet.

109. These are Karen's books; (<u>those</u>, them) are mine.

110. Nobody in our class can draw better than (<u>she</u>, her).

111. Do you know the man (<u>who</u>, which) came for eggs?

112. Aunt Lena asked if Hannah and (<u>I</u>, myself) could help her tomorrow.

113. She hardly knew (who, <u>whom</u>) she could find to help her.

114. Either Anthony or Mervin should start (<u>his</u>, their) chores early.

(10 points)

P. Write the comparative and superlative degrees of these adjectives and adverbs.

115. lovely _____lovelier_____ _____loveliest_____   118. hopeful __more hopeful__ __most hopeful__

116. ill _____worse_____ _____worst_____   119. good _____better_____ _____best_____

117. far _____farther_____ _____farthest_____   120. fast _____faster_____ _____fastest_____

(6 points)

Q. Cross out each adjective or adverb that should not be used, and write any correction above it. If a word is missing, use a caret (∧) to show where it belongs, and write the word in the space above.

121. We can ~~easy~~ easily see God's hand at work in history.

122. A ~~divine,~~ heavenly messenger spoke to Manoah and his wife.   *or* A divine, ~~heavenly~~ messenger spoke to Manoah and his wife.

123. God doesn't make ~~no~~ any mistakes.   *or* God ~~doesn't make~~ makes no mistakes.

124. The priest and ∧ Levite saw the injured man but did not help him. (the)

125. At Elijah's word, the Israelites killed ~~them~~ those prophets of Baal.

126. Since Brother Mark's moved, there are ~~less~~ fewer students in our classroom.

127. Mother divided ~~up~~ the leftover pie for us children.

128. Both Jean and Jane made cookies; I like Jean's buttermilk cookies ~~best~~ better.

129. Ray did his chores ~~good~~ well this time.

130. Grandmother is feeling ~~some~~ somewhat better today.

(10 points)

R. Cross out each preposition or conjunction that should not be used, and write any correction above it. If a word is missing, use a caret (∧) to show where it belongs, and write the word in the space above.

131. We have not waited ~~on~~ for you long, for we arrived just five minutes ago.

132. Since we changed seats, Joel Snyder sits ~~in back of~~ me.
 behind

133. This applesauce tastes quite different ~~than~~ ours.
 from

134. Modern farming methods differ ~~with~~ those of our forefathers.
 from

135. Father tried to divide the chores evenly ~~between~~ the three boys.
 among

136. The heifers are not only bawling but ^ milling around.
 also

(6 points)

S. Read this paragraph, and do the exercises that follow.

    ^aAs I stepped out into the fresh air, the bright sun foretold another beautiful April day. ^bI felt exhilarated as I took in the special beauty of the outdoors on a spring morning. ^cThe dewdrops on the grass sparkled like a thousand diamonds. ^dFrom his perch on the clothesline post, a mockingbird filled the air with a rich medley of notes. ^eThe air was sweetened by the mingled fragrance of lilacs and mock oranges drifting on the soft breeze. ^fEntering the barn, I was greeted by the sweet smell of the silage that Father was feeding.

  _b_   137. Write the letter of the topic sentence.

  _f_   138. Write the letter of the sentence that mars the unity.

  _d_   139. Write whether the paragraph is an example of (*a*) exposition, (*b*) argument, (*c*) narration, or (*d*) description.

(3 points)

T. For each paragraph, write whether the traits of the main character are shown mostly by *actions, speech, thoughts,* or *appearance.*

  appearance   140.   "Where's Father?" Merle asked as he stuck his tousled head in at the door. His trousers and boots were muddy, and there was even a streak of mud on his face.

  actions   141.   Roy quickly laid down his tools and dashed to the door. By the time Father arrived with his heavy box, Roy was holding the door open.

  speech   142.   "Oh, we were delighted to help you, Mrs. Stacey!" declared Gloria. "Just let us know when we can help again."

  thoughts   143.   "How will I ever get myself out of this fix?" Laurel groaned to herself as she considered the day's happenings.

(4 points)

U. Read the following lines of poetry, and do the exercises that follow.

> Contentment is a pearl
> Of value rich and rare.
> The closer saints will walk with God,
> His virtues they will share.
>
> Contentment is a jewel
> To hide within our heart;
> Then when our life is over,
> From God we'll not depart!

  iambic   144. Name the type of rhythm pattern used in this poem.

  abcbdefe   145. Write letters to show the rhyming pattern of the poem.

<u> metaphor </u>   146. What type of figure of speech is used in the first line?

<u> alliteration </u>   147. Name the special type of repetition found in these sets of words: *rich, rare* and *will walk with.*

<u> assonance </u>   148. Name the special type of repetition found in this set of words: *God, not, depart.*

(5 points)

V. Write the letter of the best choice in the blanks.

<u> d </u>   149. The first paragraph of a story should specifically introduce the (*a*) conflict and climax; (*b*) theme and conflict; (*c*) theme and main character; (*d*) main character and setting.

<u> b </u>   150. The conflict of a story (*a*) includes all the characters; (*b*) shows the main character's problem; (*c*) shows how the problem in the story is solved; (*d*) summarizes the lesson of the story.

<u> c </u>   151. The *least* effective way to begin a story is with (*a*) conversation; (*b*) an unusual statement; (*c*) a description of the setting; (*d*) action.

<u> c </u>   152. The part of a business letter that is *not* included in a friendly letter is the (*a*) salutation; (*b*) heading; (*c*) inside address; (*d*) signature; (*e*) body; (*f*) closing.

<u> b </u>   153. Which of the following is *least* related to paragraph coherence? (*a*) using logical sentence order; (*b*) dividing paragraphs properly; (*c*) repeating key words; (*d*) using transitional words

<u> b </u>   154. The proposition of an argument is most like (*a*) the climax of a story; (*b*) the topic sentence of a paragraph; (*c*) the title of an outline.

<u> c </u>   155. The use of a word having an imitative sound, like *purr* or *clatter,* is (*a*) parallelism; (*b*) alliteration; (*c*) onomatopoeia; (*d*) assonance.

<u> a </u>   156. The card catalog is to a library what (*a*) an index is to a book; (*b*) a table of contents is to a book; (*c*) an outline is to a composition.

<u> a </u>   157. The three kinds of cards found in the card catalog are (*a*) author, title, and subject cards; (*b*) biography, fiction, and reference cards; (*c*) title, index, and library cards.

<u> b </u>   158. The New Testament was originally written in (*a*) Hebrew; (*b*) Greek; (*c*) Latin; (*d*) Aramaic.

(10 points)

W. In each blank, write the letter of the reference book that names the best place to find the information described.

<u> f </u>   159. A synonym of *texture.*

<u> g </u>   160. Bible verses about consecration.

<u> a </u>   161. The location of Blue Rapids, Kansas.

<u> d </u>   162. The pronunciation and definition of *stratus.*

<u> b </u>   163. The length of a Sabbath Day's journey.

<u> c </u>   164. The reference of a Bible verse.

<u> e </u>   165. The method of processing chocolate.

<u> c </u>   166. The Hebrew meaning of a Bible word.

a. atlas
b. Bible dictionary
c. concordance
d. dictionary
e. encyclopedia
f. thesaurus
g. topical Bible

(8 points)

Total points: 192

Index

A